the ✗✗ MICHELIN guide
2016

THE MICHELIN GUIDE'S COMMITMENTS

EXPERIENCED IN QUALITY!

Whether they are in Japan, the USA, China or Europe, our inspectors apply the same criteria to judge the quality of each and every hotel and restaurant that they visit. The Michelin guide commands a worldwide reputation thanks to the commitments we make to our readers – and we reiterate these below:

Anonymous inspections

Our inspectors make regular and anonymous visits to hotels and restaurants to gauge the quality of products and services offered to an ordinary customer. They settle their own bill and may then introduce themselves and ask for more information about the establishment. Our readers' comments are also a valuable source of information, which we can follow up with a visit of our own.

Independence

To remain totally objective for our readers, the selection is made with complete independence. Entry into the guide is free. All decisions are discussed with the Editor and our highest awards are considered at a European level.

Selection and choice

The guide offers a selection of the best hotels and restaurants in every category of comfort and price. This is only possible because all the inspectors rigorously apply the same methods.

Annual updates

All the practical information, classifications and awards are revised and updated every year to give the most reliable information possible.

Consistency

The criteria for the classifications are the same in every country covered by the MICHELIN guide.

✿✿✿ THREE STARS MICHELIN
Exceptional cuisine, worth a special journey!

Our highest award is given for the superlative cooking of chefs at the peak of their profession. The ingredients are exemplary, the cooking is elevated to an art form and their dishes are often destined to become classics.

✿✿ TWO STARS MICHELIN
Excellent cooking, worth a detour!

The personality and talent of the chef and their team is evident in the expertly crafted dishes, which are refined, inspired and sometimes original.

✿ ONE STAR MICHELIN
High quality cooking, worth a stop!

Using top quality ingredients, dishes with distinct flavours are carefully prepared to a consistently high standard.

☺ BIB GOURMAND
Good quality, good value cooking

'Bibs' are awarded for simple yet skilful cooking for under £28 or €40.

The sole intention of Michelin is to make your travels safe and enjoyable.

Follow our anonymous inspectors:
@MichelinGuideUK

3

DEAR READER

We are delighted to present the 2016 edition of the Michelin guide to Great Britain and Ireland – a guide to the best places to eat and stay in England, Wales, Scotland, Northern Ireland and the Republic of Ireland.

The guide caters for every type of visitor, from business traveller to families on holiday, and lists the best establishments across all categories of comfort and price – from lively bistros and intimate townhouses to celebrated restaurants and luxurious hotels. So, whether you're visiting for work or pleasure, you'll find something that's right for you.

All of the establishments in the guide have been selected by our team of famous Michelin inspectors, who are the eyes and ears of our readers. They always pay their own bills and their anonymity is key to ensuring that they receive the same treatment as any other guest.

Each year, they search for new establishments to add – and only the best make it through! The 'best of the best' are then recognised with awards.

Our famous one ✿, two ✿✿ and three ✿✿✿ stars identify establishments serving the highest quality cuisine – taking into account the quality of ingredients, the mastery of techniques and flavours, the levels of creativity and, of course, consistency.

Stars are not our only awards; look out too for the Bib Gourmands ☺ and Bib Hotels ⌂, which highlight establishments offering good food and good value accommodation.

Michelin Travel Partner is committed to remaining at the forefront of the culinary world and to meeting the needs of our readers. Please don't hesitate to contact us – we'd love to hear your opinions on the establishments listed within these pages, as well as those you feel could be of interest for future editions.

We hope you enjoy your dining and hotel experiences – happy travelling with the 2016 edition of the Michelin guide!

CONTENTS

Introduction

As you flick through this year's Michelin guide you'll notice a new layout, with more colour and greater clarity: we wanted the 2016 edition to be more enjoyable to read and to make your search for establishments easier and faster!

The guide has been divided into sections – with London listed first. Each country is preceded by an introduction about the region and its food, along with a list of this year's Michelin Stars, Bib Gourmands and Top Picks.

This is because our commitment, for over a century, has been to help you make the best choices when it comes to your travels!

Hotels & restaurants 20

A CULINARY HISTORY

Britain hasn't always been known for its vibrant culinary scene – indeed, the food of the 'masses' started out dull and dreary, with meals driven by need rather than desire. So how did we get to where we are today? Well, it took quite a few centuries...

There's no place like Rome

The Romans kick-started things with their prolific road building, opening up the country and allowing goods to be transported more easily, country-wide. The Vikings brought with them new smoking and drying techniques for preserving fish, and the Saxons, who were excellent farmers, cultivated a wide variety of herbs – used not only for flavouring but to bulk-out stews. They also made butter, cheese and mead (a drink made from fermented honey); with the lack of sugar to sweeten things, honey was very important, and bees were kept in every village. The Normans introduced saffron, nutmeg, pepper, ginger and sugar – ingredients used in the likes of plum pudding, hot cross buns and Christmas cake. They also encouraged the drinking of wine. Meat was a luxury reserved for those with money, so the poor were left with bread, cheese and eggs as their staple diet.

Manchester House

The Middle Ages saw the wealthy eating beef, mutton, pork and venison, along with a great variety of birds, including blackbirds, greenfinches, herons and swans; and when the church decreed that meat couldn't be eaten on certain days, they turned to fish. Breakfast was eaten in private; lunch and dinner, in the great hall; and on special occasions they held huge feasts and banquets with lavish spectacles, musicians and entertainment. The poor, meanwhile, were stuck with their simple, monotonous fare: for lunch, cheese and coarse, dark bread made from barley or rye; and in the evening, pottage, a type of stew made by boiling grain, vegetables and, on occasion, some rabbit – if they could catch one.

Sugar and spice...

Things really began to take off in Tudor times, with spices being brought back from the Far East, and sugar from the Caribbean. Potatoes and turkeys were introduced from north America; the latter were bred almost exclusively in Norfolk, then driven to London in flocks of 500 or more and fattened up for several days before being sold. The poor baked bread, salted meat, preserved vegetables, made pickles and conserves, and even brewed their own beer. As the water was so dirty, the children drank milk, the adults drank ale, cider or perry, and the rich drank wine.

Little changed until the rise of the British Empire, when new drinks such as tea, coffee and chocolate appeared, and coffee houses started to spring up – places where professionals could meet to read the newspaper and 'talk shop'. More herbs and spices were brought back, this time from India, and exotic fruits such as bananas and pineapples came onto the scene. Despite improvements in farming, the poor continued to eat bread, butter, cheese, potatoes and bacon; butcher's meat remained a luxury.

Pierre Lapin/Cephas/Photononstop

Import – ant times

Advancements continued to pick up pace in Victorian times. The advent of the railways and steamships made it possible to import cheap grain from North America, and refrigeration units allowed meat to be brought in from Argentina and Australia. The first fish and chip shops opened in the 1860s and the first convenience food in tins and jars went on sale. The price of sugar also began to drop and sweets such as peanut brittle, liquorice allsorts and chocolate bars came into being.

In the early 20C, the cost of food fell dramatically: in 1914 it accounted for up to 60% of a working class family's income and by 1937, just 35%. Then, as things were beginning to look up, the war intervened and staple food items such as meat, sugar, butter, eggs and tea were rationed until long after the war had ended.

The late 20C saw a surge in technological and scientific advancements, and the creation of affordable fridges, freezers and microwave ovens meant that food could be stored for longer and cooked more easily. In an increasingly time-pressured world, convenience and time-saving became key, increasing the popularity of the 'ready meal' and takeaway outlets.

As immigration increased, so too did the number of restaurants serving cuisine from different nations. What started as a handful of Indian and Chinese restaurants, has now moved on in the 21C to cover everything from Thai to Turkish, Jamaican to Japanese.

Not only has the range of dining establishments increased but, with the opening up of European borders and the ease of travel and transport, many supermarkets have also started to stock a range of foreign products, from pierogi to paneer.

The British Aisles

Supermarkets may now offer an endless choice of products but at the same time, an increased interest in health and wellbeing has sparked a trend for using seasonal ingredients from small, local producers – with a focus on reducing food miles. With increasing concerns about the origins of produce and the methods used in mass-production, many people are now turning back to the traditional 'farmers' market' or opting for 'organic' alternatives, where the consumer can trace the product back to its source or be assured of a natural, ethical or sustainable production method.

This can be seen in a true British institution – the pub. Take the traditional Sunday roast, one of the country's favourite meals; some chewy meat and microwaved veg won't cut it anymore – consumers now want to see top quality seasonal ingredients on their plate, sourced from the nearby farmer or the local allotment, and freshly prepared in the kitchen. And chefs are rising to the challenge: exploring new ways of using British ingredients, and reviving and reinventing traditional regional recipes.

In the past Britain may have lagged behind its European neighbours, due, in part, to its having a largely industrial economy. But what is in no doubt today, is that it's certainly making up for lost time. It may not have such a clear culinary identity as say, France or Italy, but it now offers greater choice and diversity by providing chefs with the freedom and confidence to take inspiration from wherever they wish and bring together flavours from across the globe.

SEEK AND SELECT...
HOW TO USE THIS GUIDE

HOTELS

Hotels are classified by categories of comfort,
from 🏨🏨🏨 to 🏠.

Red: Our most delightful places.

🏠 🏠 Other accommodation (guesthouses,
farmhouses and private homes).

Within each category, establishments are
listed in order of preference.

Bib Hotel ─────────────

🏠 Good accommodation
at moderate prices.

RESTAURANTS

Restaurants are classified by categories of
comfort, from XXXXX to X.

Red: Our most delightful places.

Within each category, establishments are
listed in order of preference.

🍴 🍴 Pubs serving good food.

Stars ─────────────

❀❀❀ **Exceptional** cuisine,
worth a special journey!

❀❀ **Excellent** cooking, worth a detour!

❀ **High quality** cooking, worth a stop!

Bib Gourmand ─────────────

😊 Good quality, good value cooking.

Locating
the establishment ──────

Location and
coordinates on
the town plan,
with main sights.

Key words ─────────────

Each entry now comes with
two keywords, making it quick
and easy to identify the type
of establishment and/or the
food that it serves.

ENGLAND

BEAULIEU
Hampshire – Pop. 726 – Brockenhurst –
▶ London 55 mi – Coventry 88 mi – Ips

🏠🏠 **Manor of Roses**
ROMANTIC • STYLISH With its c
this charming 18C inn has a time
marry antique furniture with mo
lised. The wicker-furnished cons
18 rooms – ♦£62/ £120♦♦£6
Town plan: D1-a – *Palace Ln* ✉
🐾 Scott's –See restaurant listing

🏠🏠 **Wentworth**
🏠 FRIENDLY • COSY Ivy-clad Vict
the bedrooms; some are tradit
bright and modern. 19C restaura
28 rooms – ♦ £ 61/106♦♦£ 61,
Town plan: D1-c – *35 Charles S*
– www.wentworth.com – Close

XXX **Scott's**
❀ FRENCH • CLASSIC This elegan
18C inn; head to the terrace for
and efficient, and only top qualit
dishes. Cooking has a classical b
→Spiced scallops with cauliflo
Roast duck breast, smoked bac
soufflé with Sichuan spiced choc
Menu £30/50 (dinner only) – Car
Town plan: D1-a – *Palace Ln* ✉
essential) – www.Scotts.com –

XX **Sea Grill** 🆕
😊 MEATS AND GRILLS • BISTRO S
lage, this laid-back bar-restaura
classic. The eggs are from their
nearby farms.
Menu £28 (weekday dinner)
Town plan: D1-c – *12 Robert St*
www.seagrill.co.uk – Closed D

12

Facilities & services

🍇	Particularly interesting wine list
🍸	Notable cocktail list
🏠	Hotel with a restaurant
🛏	Restaurant or pub with bedrooms
🕊	Peaceful establishment
⪡	Great view
🛗 ♿	Lift (elevator) • Wheelchair access
AC	Air conditioning (in all or part of the establishment)
🍽	Outside dining available
☕ 🍱	Open for breakfast • Small plates
🥗	Restaurant offering vegetarian menus
🎭	Restaurant offering lower priced theatre menus
🧒	Special facilities for children
🚫	No dogs allowed
⊛	Wellness centre
♨ 🏋	Sauna • Exercise room
🏊 ⊠	Swimming pool: outdoor or indoor
🌳 🎾	Garden or park • Tennis court
🎣	Fishing available to hotel guests
🚩	Golf course
🏛	Conference room
⇔	Private dining room
P 🚗	Car park • Garage
⇎	Credit cards not accepted
⊖	Nearest Underground station (London)

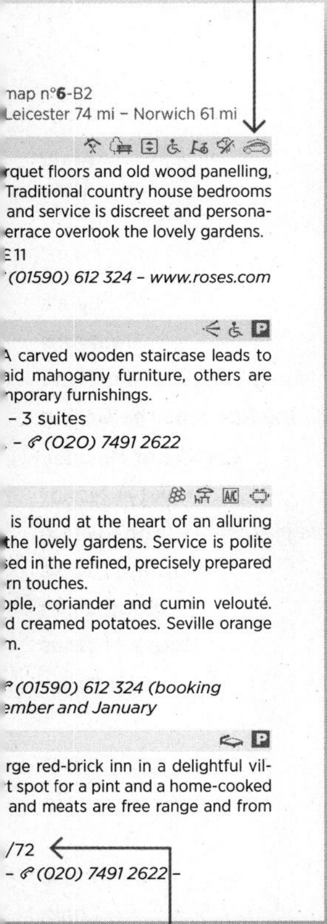

Prices

• Prices are given in £ sterling, and in € euros for the Republic of Ireland.

• All accommodation prices include both service and V.A.T. Restaurant prices include V.A.T. and service is also included when an **s** appears after the prices.

Restaurants		**Hotels**	
Menu £13/28	Fixed price menu. Lowest / highest price.	🛆 £50/90 🛆🛆 £100/120	Lowest / highest price for single and double room.
Carte £20/35	À la carte menu. Lowest / highest price.	⊊ 🛆🛆 £100/120	Bed & breakfast rate.
s	Service included.	⊊ £5	Breakfast price where not included in rate.

[left column partial text:]

map n°**6**-B2
Leicester 74 mi – Norwich 61 mi

🏠 🛏 🛗 ♿ 🏋 🚫 🚗

rquet floors and old wood panelling,
Traditional country house bedrooms
and service is discreet and persona-
errace overlook the lovely gardens.
£ 11
(01590) 612 324 – www.roses.com

⪡ ♿ P

A carved wooden staircase leads to
aid mahogany furniture, others are
nporary furnishings.
– 3 suites
– *(020) 7491 2622*

🍇 🍽 AC ⇔

is found at the heart of an alluring
the lovely gardens. Service is polite
sed in the refined, precisely prepared
rn touches.
pple, coriander and cumin velouté.
d creamed potatoes. Seville orange
m.

*(01590) 612 324 (booking
ember and January*

🛏 P

rge red-brick inn in a delightful vil-
t spot for a pint and a home-cooked
and meats are free range and from

/72
– *(020) 7491 2622 –*

13

2016...
THE NEWS!

STARS...

✿

✿✿

| London | Westminster/ Mayfair | **Araki** |
| | Westminster/ Mayfair | **Umu** |

✿

London	Hackney/ Shoreditch	**Lyle's**
	Westminster/ Mayfair	**Bonhams**
	Westminster/ Regent's Park and Marylebone	**Portland**
	Westminster/ Victoria	**Dining Room at The Goring**
England	Birmingham	**Carters of Moseley**
	East Grinstead	**Gravetye Manor**
	Leeds	**The Man Behind the Curtain**
	Loughborough	**John's House**
	Newbury	**Woodspeen**
	Newcastle upon Tyne	**House of Tides**
Scotland	Anstruther	**The Cellar**
Northern Ireland		
	Belfast	**Eipic**
	Belfast	**OX**
Republic of Ireland		
	Dublin	**Greenhouse**
	Galway	**Loam**

Clive Rowley

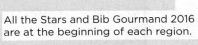
All the Stars and Bib Gourmand 2016
are at the beginning of each region.

... AND BIB GOURMAND

London

Hammersmith and Fulham/ Hammersmith	**L'Amorosa**
Hammersmith and Fulham/ Shepherd's Bush	**Shikumen**
Tower Hamlets/ Spitalfields	**Blixen**
	Taberna do Mercado
Westminster/ Soho	**Dehesa**

England

Ashendon	**The Hundred of Ashendon**
Borougbridge/ Lower Dunsforth	**The Dunsforth**
Bristol	**No Man's Grace**
Fence	**White Swan**
Hullbridge	**Anchor**
Ludlow	**Green Café**
Maltby	**Chadwicks Inn**
Marlow	**The Coach**
Oxford	**Oli's Thai**
Porthleven	**Square**
Stockport	**brassicagrill**
Tenterden	**Swan Wine Kitchen**
Isle of Wight/ Seaview	**Seaview**

Republic of Ireland

Adare	**1826**
Cashel	**Cafe Hans**
Dublin	**Delahunt**
Dublin/ Clontarf	**Pigeon House**
Fennor	**Copper Hen**
Killorglin	**Giovannelli**
Kinsale	**Bastion**

Starred establishments 2016

The colour corresponds to the establishment with the most stars in this location.

London	This location has at least one 3 star restaurant	✸✸✸
Dublin	This location has at least one 2 star restaurant	✸✸
Edinburgh	This location has at least one 1 star restaurant	✸

Lochinver

Sleat

Eriska

Dalry

NORTHERN
IRELAND

Belfast

Galway

Dublin

REPUBLIC
OF IRELAND

Kilkenny

Thomastown

Ardmore

GUERNSEY

JERSEY

La Pulente • St Helier

ISLES OF SCILLY

Port Isaac

Padstow

Sparkwell

Portscatho

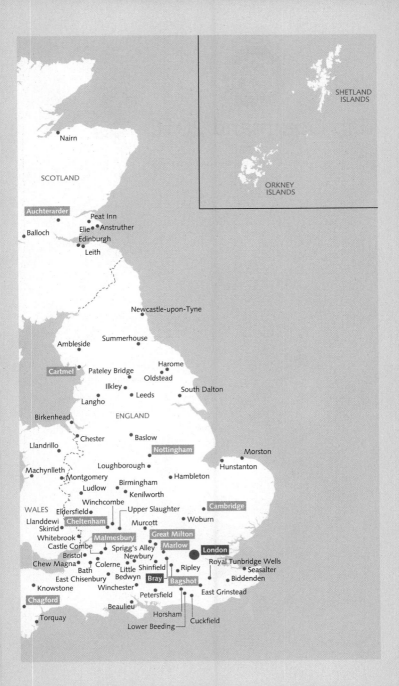

Bib Gourmand 2016

• Places with at least one Bib Gourmand establishment.

Kilberry

NORTHERN
IRELAND
•Holywood
Belfast •Lisbane

Carrickmacross

REPUBLIC
OF IRELAND
Dublin •Clontarf

Lisdoonvarna
Clonegall

Adare
Cashel
Dingle
Fennor• Duncannon
Killorglin
Kinsale

GUERNSEY

JERSEY

Beaumont

Padstow
Tavistock
Halsetown• St. Ives
Newlyn• Porthleven

GREAT BRITAIN

LONDON

London is one of the most cosmopolitan, dynamic, fashionable and cultured cities on earth, home not only to such iconic images as Big Ben, Tower Bridge and bear skinned guards, but also Bengali markets, speedboat rides through the Docklands and stunning views of the city atop the very best of 21C architecture. From Roman settlement to banking centre to capital of a 19C empire, the city's pulse has never missed a beat; it's no surprise that a dazzling array of theatres, restaurants, museums, markets and art galleries populate its streets.

The city is one of the food capitals of the world, where you can eat everything from Turkish to Thai and Polish to Peruvian; diners here are an eclectic, well-travelled bunch who gladly welcome all-comers and every style of cuisine. Visit one of the many food markets like Borough or Brixton to witness the capital's wonderfully varied produce, or pop into a pop-up to get a taste of the latest trends. If it's traditional British you're after, try one of the many pubs in the capital; this was, after all, where the gastropub movement began.

- Michelin Road map n° 504
- Michelin Green Guide: London

B. Stevens/Cultura Creative/ Photononstop

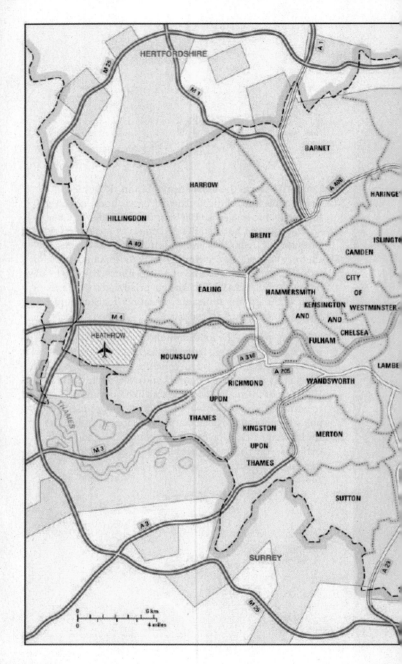

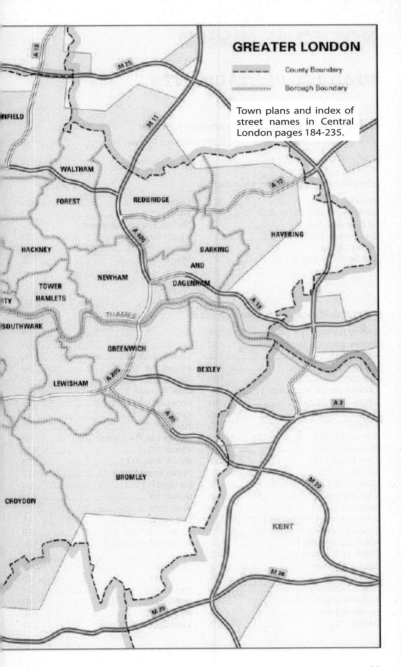

GREATER LONDON

County Boundary

Borough Boundary

Town plans and index of street names in Central London pages 184-235.

ENFIELD

WALTHAM

FOREST

REDBRIDGE

HAVERING

HACKNEY

BARKING

AND

NEWHAM

DAGENHAM

CITY

TOWER

HAMLETS

SOUTHWARK

THAMES

GREENWICH

BEXLEY

LEWISHAM

BROMLEY

CROYDON

KENT

NOT TO BE MISSED

STARRED RESTAURANTS

❀ ❀ ❀

Exceptional cuisine, worth a special journey!

❀ ❀

Excellent cooking, worth a detour!

❀

High quality cooking, worth a stop!

Wild Honey

BIB GOURMAND 😋

Good quality, good value cooking

ALPHABETICAL LIST OF HOTELS

PARTICULARLY PLEASANT HOTELS

🏨🏨🏨🏨

🏨🏨🏨

🏠🏠🏠

🏠🏠

ALPHABETICAL LIST OF RESTAURANTS

Pied a Terre

Gymkhana

Yauatcha

Pied a Terre

The Greenhouse

PARTICULARLY PLEASANT RESTAURANTS

RESTAURANTS CLASSIFIED ACCORDING TO TYPE

Michelin

Trishna

Japanese

Korean

Lebanese

Meats

Gymkhana

Pied a Terre

Moroccan

North-African

North-American

Peruvian

Polish

Portuguese

Spanish

Thai

Vietnamese

World cuisine

Restaurants with outside dining

Open late

Boroughs and areas

Greater London is divided, for administrative purposes, into 32 boroughs plus **the City:** these sub-divide naturally into minor areas, usually grouped around former villages or quarters, which often maintain a distinctive character.

BRENT
Church End

✗ Shayona

INDIAN · FAMILY Opposite the striking Swaminarayan Temple is this simple, sattvic restaurant: it's vegetarian and 'pure' so avoids onion or garlic. Expect curries from the north, dosas from the south and Mumbai street food. No alcohol so try a lassi.

Carte £15/22

Town plan: 2CU-a – *54-62 Meadow Garth* ✉ *NW10 8HD* – ⊖ *Stonebridge Park* – ✆ *(020) 8965 3365* – *www.shayonarestaurants.com* – *Closed 23-24 October, 11-12 November and 25 December*

Kensal Green

🍽 Paradise by way of Kensal Green

BRITISH MODERN · PUB Less a pub, more a veritable fun palace. Music, comedy and film nights happen upstairs; the bar and restaurant are wonderfully quirky; staff are contagiously enthusiastic and the European themed food is prepared with genuine care.

Menu £25 – Carte £26/39

Town plan: 10MZC-x – *19 Kilburn Ln* ✉ *W10 4AE* – ⊖ *Kensal Green.* – ✆ *(020) 8969 0098* – *www.theparadise.co.uk* – *dinner only and lunch Saturday and Sunday*

🍽 Parlour

BRITISH MODERN · INDIVIDUAL A fun, warmly run and slightly quirky neighbourhood hangout. The menu is a wonderfully unabashed mix of tradition, originality and reinvention. Don't miss the cow pie which even Dan, however Desperate, would struggle to finish.

Menu £10 (weekday lunch) – Carte £17/38

Town plan: 10MZC-r – *5 Regent St* ✉ *NW10 5LG* – ⊖ *Kensal Green* – ✆ *(020) 8969 2184* – *www.parlourkensal.com* – *Closed 1 week August and 10 days Christmas-New Year*

Queen's Park

✗ Ostuni

ITALIAN · NEIGHBOURHOOD The cuisine of Puglia, the red hot heel in Italy's boot, is celebrated at this rustic local restaurant. Don't miss the olives, creamy burrata, fava bean purée, the sausages and bombette, or the orecchiette – the ear-shaped pasta.

Menu £30/40 – Carte £15/39

Town plan: 10MZB-b – *43-45 Lonsdale Rd* ✉ *NW6 6RA* – ⊖ *Queen's Park* – ✆ *(020) 7624 8035* – *www.ostuniristorante.co.uk* – *Closed 25 December*

Willesden Green

✗ Sushi-Say

JAPANESE · INTIMATE Very popular with the locals, attracted by sweet service and an extensive selection of Japanese food. Sit at the counter to watch the skill of the owner as he prepares the sushi.

Carte £19/49

Town plan: 9LZB-a – *33B Walm Ln.* ✉ *NW2 5SH* – ⊖ *Willesden Green* – ✆ *(020) 8459 2971* – *dinner only and lunch Saturday-Sunday* – *Closed 2 weeks August, 25 December-2 January, Wednesday after bank holidays, Monday and Tuesday*

BROMLEY

Keston

XX Herbert's 🏠 AC

MODERN CUISINE · FASHIONABLE A neat, contemporary restaurant in shades of grey, occupying a pleasant spot overlooking the Common. The European cooking is modern but the combinations of ingredients are reassuringly familiar.

Carte £ 22/49

Town plan: 8HZ-x – 6 Commonside ⊠ BR2 6BP – ℰ (01689) 855 501 – www.thisisherberts.co.uk – Closed Sunday dinner and Monday

Farnborough

XxX Chapter One 🍷 AC ⇔ P

MODERN CUISINE · FRIENDLY Long-standing restaurant with many regulars, its stylish bar leading into an elegant, modern dining room. Wide-ranging menus offer keenly priced, carefully prepared modern European dishes; cooking is light and delicate, mixing classic and modern flavours. Assured service.

Menu £ 20/40

Town plan: 8HZ-a – Farnborough Common, Locksbottom ⊠ BR6 8NF – ℰ (01689) 854 848 – www.chapteronerestaurant.co.uk – Closed 2-4 January

Orpington

XX Xian AC

CHINESE · NEIGHBOURHOOD Stylish, modern dining room with banquette seating, bamboo matting on the walls and six super lithographs of the famous Terracotta Warriors of Xian. Appealing menu offers flavoursome, authentic Chinese dishes, with something for everyone.

Menu £ 10 (weekday lunch) – Carte £ 14/24

Town plan: 8JY-a – 324 High St. ⊠ BR6 0NG – ℰ (01689) 871 881 – Closed first 2 weeks April, 1 week October, 25-26 December, Sunday lunch and Monday

Petts Wood

XX Indian Essence ሤ AC

 INDIAN · NEIGHBOURHOOD Atul Kochhar of Benares is one of the owners of this smart and contemporary Indian restaurant. Everything is made in-house, from the masala paste to the kulfi; dishes are vibrant and flavoursome and the prices are good.

Menu £ 15/25 (weekdays) – Carte £ 24/35

Town plan: 8JY-e – 176-178 Petts Wood Rd ⊠ BR5 1LG – ℰ (01689) 838 700 – www.indianessence.co.uk – Closed Monday except bank holidays

Sundridge Park

XX Cinnamon Culture 🏠

INDIAN · NEIGHBOURHOOD Former Victorian pub transmogrified into a smart Indian restaurant where the cooking is undertaken with care. A plethora of menus include tasting and vegetarian options, as well as a monthly menu focusing on one region.

Carte £ 17/40

Town plan: 8HY-z – 46 Plaistow Ln ⊠ BR1 3PA – ℰ (020) 8289 0322 – www.cinnamonculture.com – Closed 26 December and Monday

© Michelin

CAMDEN

Belsize Park

XX XO   🍷 & AC ⇔

ASIAN · NEIGHBOURHOOD Busy bar behind which is a slick and stylish dining room. Vibrant atmosphere; popular with all the good-looking locals. Japanese, Korean, Thai and Chinese cooking; dishes are best shared.

Menu £18 (lunch) – Carte £20/44

Town plan: 11PZA-a – *29 Belsize Ln* ⊠ *NW3 5AS* – ⊖ *Belsize Park*
– 𝒞 (020) 7433 0888 – www.rickerrestaurants.com/xo
– Closed 25-26 December and 1 January

XX Hazara   🍴 AC

INDIAN · NEIGHBOURHOOD At this keenly run, modern Indian restaurant, the adventurous diner will find specialities from all regions. Game and fish stand out – the owner goes personally to Smithfield and Billingsgate to ensure the quality of the produce.

Carte £19/53

Town plan: 11PZA-n – *44 Belsize Ln* ⊠ *NW3 5AR* – ⊖ *Belsize Park* – 𝒞 (020) 7423 1147 – www.hazararestaurant.com – dinner only and lunch Saturday-Sunday*
– Closed 25-26 December and 1 January

X Retsina   AC

GREEK · RUSTIC Family-run restaurant whose unapologetically traditional menu offers all the Greek classics but the charcoal grill makes souvla, kebabs and cutlets the best choices. Simple, bright and airy room with a friendly atmosphere.

Menu £19/25

Town plan: 11PZA-n – *48-50 Belsize Ln* ⊠ *NW3 5AR* – ⊖ *Belsize Park*
– 𝒞 (020) 7431 5855 – www.retsina.squarespace.com – Closed 25-26 December, 1 January, Monday lunch and bank holidays

X Tandis   🍴 AC 🍽

WORLD CUISINE · NEIGHBOURHOOD Persian and Middle Eastern food whose appeal stretches way beyond the Iranian diaspora. The specialities are the substantial and invigorating khoresh stew and the succulent kababs; end with Persian sorbet with rosewater.

Carte £17/27

Town plan: 11QZB-x – *73 Haverstock Hill* ⊠ *NW3 4SL* – ⊖ *Chalk Farm*
– 𝒞 (020) 7586 8079 – www.tandisrestaurant.com – Closed 25 December

Bloomsbury

🏠 Covent Garden ☆ 🕭 ⊞ 🗚 ⅏ 🕍

LUXURY · STYLISH Popular with those of a theatrical bent. Boldly designed, stylish bedrooms, with technology discreetly concealed. Boasts a very comfortable first floor oak-panelled drawing room with its own honesty bar.

58 rooms – ♦£ 235/1175 ♦♦£ 235/1175 – ☲£ 20 – 1 suite

Town plan: **31ALU-x** – *10 Monmouth St* ✉ *WC2H 9HB* – ⊖ *Covent Garden* – ☎ *(020) 7806 1000* – *www.firmdalehotels.com*

Brasserie Max – See restaurant listing

🏠 Radisson Blu Edwardian Mercer Street ☆ 🕭 ⊞ 🗚 ⅏ 🕍

BUSINESS · MODERN Smart, modern group-owned hotel in an excellent central location. The best rooms are at the apex of the V-shaped building. Informal 1st floor restaurant offers British classics. Popular for afternoon tea.

137 rooms – ♦£ 180/450 ♦♦£ 195/675 – ☲£ 23

Town plan: **31ALU-r** – *20 Mercer St* ✉ *WC2H 9HD* – ⊖ *Covent Garden* – ☎ *(020) 7836 4300* – *www.radissonblu-edwardian.com*

🏠 Bloomsbury ☆ 🕭 ⊞ ♿ 🗚 ⅏ 🕍

BUSINESS · HISTORIC Neo-Georgian building by Edward Lutyens, built for the YWCA in 1929. Now boasts a smart, comfortable interior, from the lobby to the contemporary bedrooms. Restaurant with largely British menu and clubby bar.

153 rooms – ♦£ 185/450 ♦♦£ 185/450 – ☲£ 19

Town plan: **31AKT-n** – *16-22 Gt Russell St* ✉ *WC1B 3LR* – ⊖ *Tottenham Court Road* – ☎ *(020) 7347 1000* – *www.doylecollection.com/bloomsbury*

🏠 DoubleTree by Hilton London - West End ☆ 🕭 ⊞ ♿ 🗚 ⅏ 🕍

BUSINESS · CONTEMPORARY A modern, corporate hotel behind a traditional façade. The spacious ground floor includes an open-plan bar which flows into a restaurant offering a simple British menu. Rooms vary in size but all have a clean, branded feel.

216 rooms ☲ – ♦£ 130/230 ♦♦£ 150/270 – 8 suites

Town plan: **31ALT-x** – *92 Southampton Row* ✉ *WC1B 4BH* – ⊖ *Holborn* – ☎ *(020) 7242 2828* – *www.doubletree3.hilton.com*

✕✕✕ Pied à Terre 🕸 🗚 🕮 ⇆
❀

CREATIVE · ELEGANT For well over two decades David Moore's restaurant has stood apart in Charlotte Street, confident in its abilities and in the loyalty of its regulars. Subtle decorative changes keep it looking fresh and vibrant, while Marcus Eaves delivers elegant food with punchy flavours.

→ Roast breast, crispy leg and Kiev of quail, Douglas Fir purée and hazelnut vinaigrette. Monkfish with sea purslane, salsify and Morteau sausage broth. Caramel parfait with vanilla ice cream, toasted oats, whiskey crème anglaise and popcorn.

Menu £ 36/65

Town plan: **31AJT-f** – *34 Charlotte St* ✉ *W1T 2NH* – ⊖ *Goodge Street* – ☎ *(020) 7636 1178 (booking essential)* – *www.pied-a-terre.co.uk* – *Closed last week December-5 January, Saturday lunch, Sunday and bank holidays*

✕✕ Hakkasan Hanway Place 🕸 🍷 🗚 🕮
❀

CHINESE · TRENDY There are now Hakkasans all over the world but this was the original. It has the sensual looks, air of exclusivity and glamorous atmosphere synonymous with the 'brand'. The exquisite Cantonese dishes are prepared with care and consistency by the large kitchen team; lunch dim sum is a highlight.

→ Crispy duck salad with pomelo, pine nuts and shallots. Spicy prawn with lily bulb and almond. Coconut semifreddo.

Menu £ 35/128 – Carte £ 36/106

Town plan: **31AKT-c** – *8 Hanway Pl.* ✉ *W1T 1HD* – ⊖ *Tottenham Court Road* – ☎ *(020) 7927 7000* – *www.hakkasan.com* – *Closed 24-25 December*

XX Kitchen Table at Bubbledogs (James Knappett) [AC]

MODERN CUISINE · INDIVIDUAL Fight through the crowds enjoying a curious mix of hot dogs and champagne and head for the curtain – behind it is a counter for 19 diners. Chef-owner James prepares a no-choice menu of around 12 dishes. The produce is exemplary; the cooking has a clever creative edge; and the dishes have real depth.

→ Crispy chicken skin with rosemary mascarpone and bacon jam. Aged Dexter beef with yoghurt, wild garlic and caper sauce. Sorrel granité, custard cream and pear.

Menu £ 88 – set menu only

Town plan: 30AJT-g – 70 Charlotte St ⊠ W1T 4QG
– ⊖ Goodge Street – 𝒞 (020) 7637 7770 (booking essential)
– www.kitchentablelondon.co.uk – dinner only – Closed 1-14 January,
17 August-2 September, 23-27 December, Sunday and Monday

XX Mon Plaisir

FRENCH · FAMILY This proud French institution opened in the 1940s. Enjoy satisfyingly authentic classics in any of the four contrasting rooms, full of Gallic charm; apparently the bar was salvaged from a Lyonnais brothel.

Menu £ 14 (early dinner)
– Carte £ 28/43

Town plan: 31ALU-g – 19-21 Monmouth St. ⊠ WC2H 9DD
– ⊖ Covent Garden – 𝒞 (020) 7836 7243
– www.monplaisir.co.uk – Closed Christmas-New Year, Sunday and bank holidays

XX Roka

JAPANESE · FASHIONABLE Bright, atmospheric interior of teak and oak; bustling and trendy feel. Contemporary touches added to Japanese dishes; try specialities from the on-view Robata grill. Capable and chatty service.

Carte £ 16/109

Town plan: 31AJT-k – 37 Charlotte St ⊠ W1T 1RR
– ⊖ Goodge Street – 𝒞 (020) 7580 6464
– www.rokarestaurant.com – Closed 25 December

XX Brasserie Max

BRITISH MODERN · FASHIONABLE A boldly decorated and busy brasserie with an appealing and accessible menu of modern dishes with some Mediterranean influences. Very popular afternoon teas; cocktails at the large zinc bar and a weekend film club.

Menu £ 24 (lunch and early dinner) – Carte £ 29/72

Town plan: 31ALU-x – Covent Garden Hotel, 10 Monmouth St ⊠ WC2H 9HB
– ⊖ Covent Garden – 𝒞 (020) 7806 1007 (booking essential)
– www.firmdalehotels.com

X Dabbous (Ollie Dabbous)

MODERN CUISINE · DESIGN One of the hottest tickets in town – the kitchen adopts the 'less is more' approach; the food comes with elegantly restrained finesse and a bewitching purity. Most have the 7-course menu with its stimulating and sublime combinations of ingredients. The ersatz industrial room has a simple elegance.

→ Alliums in chilled pine broth. Braised halibut with lemon verbena. Barley sponge soaked in red tea with vanilla cream.

Menu £ 35/69 – set menu only

Town plan: 31AJT-r – 39 Whitfield St ⊠ W1T 2SF
– ⊖ Goodge Street – 𝒞 (020) 7323 1544 (booking essential)
– www.dabbous.co.uk – Closed 10 Christmas-New Year, Easter and Sunday

Kopapa

ASIAN · BISTRO Kopapa, a Maori word for a gathering, is Peter Gordon's just-drop-in-anytime place. It's busy but fun, with breakfast morphing into all-day dining. Go for the 'fusion'-inspired dishes - they'll give your taste buds the best workout.

Carte £ 29/49

Town plan: 31ALU-h – *32-34 Monmouth St* ✉ *WC2H 9HA* – ⊖ *Covent Garden*
– *𝒞 (020) 7240 6076 (booking advisable)* – *www.kopapa.co.uk*
– *Closed 25-26 December*

Gail's Kitchen

MEDITERRANEAN · BISTRO From the bakery people comes this engagingly run eatery that occupies a rather small space within the Myhotel. The enticing Mediterranean dishes are prepared with care and designed for sharing; the snacks are great too.

Menu £ 14/19 – Carte approx. £ 18

Town plan: 31AKT-s – *11-13 Bayley St* ✉ *WC1B 3HD* – ⊖ *Goodge Street*
– *𝒞 (020) 7323 9694* – *www.gailskitchen.co.uk*
– *Closed 25 December*

Drakes Tabanco

SPANISH · SIMPLE Taking advantage of our newfound fondness for fino is this simple tabanco, from the people behind nearby Barrica and Copita. The small, Andalusian-inspired tapas menu uses imported produce from Spain alongside British ingredients.

Menu £ 15/50 – Carte £ 14/30

Town plan: 31AJT-t – *3 Windmill St* ✉ *W1T 2HY* – ⊖ *Goodge Street*
– *𝒞 (020) 7637 9388* – *www.drakestabanco.com*
– *Closed Sunday and bank holidays*

Salt Yard

MEDITERRANEAN · TAPAS BAR Ground floor bar and buzzy basement restaurant specialising in good value plates of tasty Italian and Spanish dishes, ideal for sharing; charcuterie a speciality. Super wine list.

Carte £ 17/28

Town plan: 31AJT-d – *54 Goodge St.* ✉ *W1T 4NA* – ⊖ *Goodge Street*
– *𝒞 (020) 7637 0657* – *www.saltyard.co.uk*
– *Closed 25 and dinner 24 and 31 December, 1 January*

Honey & Co

WORLD CUISINE · SIMPLE The husband and wife team at this sweet little café were both Ottolenghi head chefs so expect cooking full of freshness and colour. Influences stretch beyond Israel to the wider Middle East. Open from 8am; packed at night.

Menu £ 16 (weekdays)/27 – Carte £ 24/31

Town plan: 18RZD-c – *25a Warren St* ✉ *W1T 5LZ* – ⊖ *Warren Street*
– *𝒞 (020) 7388 6175 (booking essential)* – *www.honeyandco.co.uk*
– *Closed 25-26 December and Sunday*

Barrica

SPANISH · TAPAS BAR All the staff at this lively little tapas bar are Spanish, so perhaps it's national pride that makes them run it with a passion lacking in many of their competitors. When it comes to the food authenticity is high on the agenda.

Menu £ 20/25 – Carte £ 19/48

Town plan: 31AJT-x – *62 Goodge St* ✉ *W1T 4NE* – ⊖ *Goodge Street*
– *𝒞 (020) 7436 9448 (booking essential)* – *www.barrica.co.uk*
– *Closed 25-26 December, 1 January, Sunday and bank holidays*

✗ Cigala

SPANISH · NEIGHBOURHOOD Longstanding Spanish restaurant, with a lively and convivial atmosphere, friendly and helpful service and an appealing and extensive menu of classics. The dried hams are a must and it's well worth waiting the 30 minutes for a paella.

Menu £18 (weekday lunch) – Carte £23/51

Town plan: 19TZD-a – *54 Lamb's Conduit St.* ✉ *WC1N 3LW* – ⊖ *Russell Square* – ℰ *(020) 7405 1717 (booking essential) – www.cigala.co.uk – Closed 25-26 December, 1 January, Easter Sunday and Easter Monday*

✗ Polpo at Ape & Bird

ITALIAN · RUSTIC Even experienced restaurateurs have to sometimes have a re-think. When Russell Norman found his Ape & Bird pub wasn't working, he simply turned it into another Polpo. Expect the same style of small plates, just in a bigger place with a couple of bars.

Carte £12/25

Town plan: 31AKU-q – *142 Shaftesbury Ave* ✉ *WC2H 8HJ* – ⊖ *Leicester Square* – ℰ *(020) 7836 3119 (bookings not accepted) – www.polpo.co.uk*

✗ Barnyard

BRITISH TRADITIONAL · RUSTIC Dude food prepared with integrity draws the crowds to this fun little place co-owned by Ollie Dabbous. The food arrives all at once on enamel plates, and dishes are full of rustic, artery-hardening goodness yet are prepared with precision and care. Just be ready to queue, as it seats fewer than 50.

Carte £17/33

Town plan: 31AJT-b – *18 Charlotte St* ✉ *W1T 2LZ* – ⊖ *Goodge Street* – ℰ *(020) 7580 3842 (bookings not accepted) – www.barnyard-london.com – Closed 25-26 December*

✗ Flesh & Buns

ASIAN · TRENDY A loud, fun basement next to the Donmar. There's plenty of Japanese dishes but star billing goes to the hirata bun – the soft Taiwanese-style steamed pillows of delight that sandwich your choice of meat or fish filling.

Menu £19 (lunch and early dinner)/40 – Carte £18/46

Town plan: 31ALU-q – *41 Earlham St* ✉ *WC2H 9LX* – ⊖ *Leicester Square* – ℰ *(020) 7632 9500 (booking advisable) – www.fleshandbuns.com – Closed 24-25 December*

🍴 Lady Ottoline

BRITISH TRADITIONAL · COSY A charming traditional feel and a palpable sense of history have always defined this classic Victorian pub. Stout British dishes are served in the ground floor bar and the more sedate upstairs dining room.

Carte £22/43

Town plan: 19TZD-c – *11a Northington St* ✉ *WC1N 2JF* – ⊖ *Chancery Lane.* – ℰ *(020) 7831 0008 – www.theladyottoline.com – Closed 25 December-2 January and bank holiday Mondays*

Camden Town

✗✗ York & Albany

MODERN CUISINE · INN This handsome 1820s John Nash coaching inn was rescued by Gordon Ramsay a few years ago after lying almost derelict. It's a moot point whether it's still an inn or more a restaurant; the food is sophisticated and the service is bright.

Menu £21 (weekdays)/24 – Carte £33/54

9 rooms – ♦£150/330 ♦♦£150/330 – ☲ £15

Town plan: 12RZB-s – *127-129 Parkway* ✉ *NW1 7PS* – ⊖ *Camden Town.* – ℰ *(020) 7592 1227 – www.gordonramsay.com/yorkandalbany*

✗ Market   AC ⟲

BRITISH MODERN · **NEIGHBOURHOOD** Market fresh produce used to create satisfying and refreshingly matter of fact British dishes, at excellent prices that entice plenty of passers-by. Appealing décor of exposed brick walls, old school chairs and zinc-topped tables.

Menu £ 10 (weekday lunch)/18 – Carte £ 28/46

Town plan: 12RZB-x – 43 Parkway ⊠ NW1 7PN – ⊖ Camden Town – 𝒞 (020) 7267 9700 (booking essential) – www.marketrestaurant.co.uk – Closed 25 December-2 January, Sunday dinner and bank holidays

✗ Made Bar & Kitchen   AC 🎐

WORLD CUISINE · **TRENDY** Attached to the Roundhouse is this large bar and dining room where the posters instil curiosity or nostalgia, depending on your age. What sets it apart is the food: small plates in vibrant, unusual and exciting combinations.

Carte £ 21/33

Town plan: 11QZB-a – Roundhouse, Chalk Farm Rd ⊠ NW1 8EH – ⊖ Chalk Farm – 𝒞 (020) 7424 8495 – www.roundhouse.org.uk/made – Closed 25 December, 1-2 January, Sunday dinner, Monday and bank holidays

Dartmouth Park

🍴 Bull & Last   ⛩

BRITISH TRADITIONAL · **NEIGHBOURHOOD** A busy Victorian pub with plenty of charm and character; the upstairs is a little quieter. Cooking is muscular, satisfying and reflects the time of year; charcuterie is a speciality.

Carte £ 23/42

Town plan: 12RZA-a – 168 Highgate Rd ⊠ NW5 1QS – ⊖ Tufnell Park. – 𝒞 (020) 7267 3641 (booking essential) – www.thebullandlast.co.uk – Closed 23-25 December

Hatton Garden

✗✗ Bleeding Heart   🐝 ⛩ ⟲

FRENCH · **ROMANTIC** A Dickensian yard plays host to this atmospheric, candlelit restaurant; popular with those from The City. Classic French cuisine is the draw, with service that's formal but has personality. Wines from owners' New Zealand estate.

Menu £ 21 (weekdays)/30 **s** – Carte £ 27/55 **s**

Town plan: 32ANT-e – Bleeding Heart Yard ⊠ EC1N 8SJ – off Greville St. – ⊖ Farringdon – 𝒞 (020) 7242 2056 (booking essential) – www.bleedingheart.co.uk – Closed 24 December-1 January, Saturday, Sunday and bank holidays

Holborn

🏨 Rosewood London   ☂ 🕙 🏔 ↳ 🈳 ⅃ ⅊ AC 🈹 P

HISTORIC · **ELEGANT** A beautiful Edwardian building that was once the HQ of Pearl Assurance. The styling is very British and the bedrooms are uncluttered and smart. Cartoonist Gerald Scarfe's work adorns the walls of his eponymous bar. A classic brasserie with a menu of British favourites occupies the former banking hall.

306 rooms – †£ 345 ††£ 365 – ☐ £ 25 – 44 suites

Town plan: 32AMT-x – 252 High Holborn ⊠ WC1V 7EN Holborn – ⊖ Holborn – 𝒞 (020) 7781 8888 – www.rosewoodhotels.com/london

🏨 The Hoxton 🆕   ☂ ⅃ ⅊ AC 🈹 🈹

TOWNHOUSE · **CONTEMPORARY** When the room categories are Shoebox, Snug, Cosy and Roomy, you know you're in a hip hotel. A great location and competitive rates plus a retro-style diner, a buzzy lobby and a 'Chicken Shop' in the basement.

174 rooms ☐ – †£ 69/299 ††£ 69/299

Town plan: 31ALT-h – 199 - 206 High Holborn ⊠ WC1V 7BD – ⊖ Holborn – 𝒞 (020) 7661 3000 – www.thehoxton.com

LONDON ENGLAND

✗✗ Moti Mahal   ⅋ 🅰🄲 🅉

INDIAN · DESIGN The menu follows the path of the 16C Grand Trunk Road, stretching from Bengal through northern India to the mountains of the northwest frontier. The tandoor features heavily but there are also plenty of unfamiliar dishes to try.

Menu £ 16 (weekday lunch) – Carte £ 39/54

Town plan: 31ALU-k – *45 Great Queen St.* ⊠ *WC2B 5AA* – ⊖ *Holborn* – 𝒞 *(020) 7240 9329* – *www.motimahal-uk.com* – *Closed 25-28 December, Saturday lunch, Sunday and bank holidays*

✗ Great Queen Street

🕭 BRITISH MODERN · RUSTIC The menu is a model of British understatement and is dictated by the seasons; the cooking, confident and satisfying with laudable prices and generous portions. Lively atmosphere and enthusiastic service.

Menu £ 18 (weekday lunch) – Carte £ 21/41

Town plan: 31ALT-d – *32 Great Queen St* ⊠ *WC2B 5AA* – ⊖ *Holborn* – 𝒞 *(020) 7242 0622 (booking essential)* – *www.greatqueenstreetrestaurant.co.uk* – *Closed Christmas-New Year, Sunday dinner and bank holidays*

✗ Asadal   🅰🄲 ⟷

KOREAN · FRIENDLY Sharing is the key in this busy basement, where you'll be oblivious to its unprepossessing location. Hotpots, dumplings and barbeques are the highlights from the easy-to-follow menu. Staff cope well with the evening rush.

Carte £ 20/30

Town plan: 31ALT-n – *227 High Holborn* ⊠ *WC1V 7DA* – ⊖ *Holborn* – 𝒞 *(020) 7430 9006* – *www.asadal.co.uk* – *Closed 25-26 December, 1 January and Sunday lunch*

Kentish Town

✗ Chicken Shop   ⅋ 🅰🄲

MEATS · RUSTIC Simply great chicken – marinated, steamed and finished over wood and charcoal – with a choice of sides and three desserts. It all happens in a noisy, mildly chaotic basement but it's great fun and good value. Be ready to queue.

Carte £ 16/21

Town plan: 12RZA-c – *79 Highgate Rd* ⊠ *NW5 1TL* – ⊖ *Kentish Town* – 𝒞 *(020) 3310 2020 (bookings not accepted)* – *www.chickenshop.com* – *dinner only and lunch Saturday-Sunday*

Primrose Hill

✗✗ Odette's   � 🅰🄲 🅉 ⟷

MODERN CUISINE · NEIGHBOURHOOD A long-standing local favourite. Warm and inviting interior, with chatty yet organised service. Robust and quite elaborate cooking, with owner passionate about his Welsh roots. Good value lunch menu.

Menu £ 15 (weekdays)/32 – Carte £ 29/47

Town plan: 11QZB-b – *130 Regent's Park Rd.* ⊠ *NW1 8XL* – ⊖ *Chalk Farm* – 𝒞 *(020) 7586 8569* – *www.odettesprimrosehill.com* – *Closed 25 December-7 January and Monday except December*

✗✗ Michael Nadra Primrose Hill   🍸 🌕 ⅋ 🅰🄲 🕭

MODERN CUISINE · INDIVIDUAL Michael Nadra went north for his second branch and took over this unusual, modern building. The menu resembles his Chiswick operation, which means flavours from the Med but also the odd Asian note. The bar offers over 20 martinis.

Menu £ 26/37

Town plan: 12RZB-m – *42 Gloucester Ave* ⊠ *NW1 8JD* – ⊖ *Camden Town* – 𝒞 *(020) 7722 2800* – *www.restaurant-michaelnadra.co.uk/primrose* – *Closed 24-28 December and 1 January*

✗ **L'Absinthe** 🏕 🅰🅒 🗔 ⇔

FRENCH · BISTRO A classic French bistro offering a great atmosphere, a roll-call of favourites from cassoulet to duck confit, and a terrific wine list where only corkage is charged on the retail price. Ask for a table on the ground floor.

Menu £10 (weekday lunch) – Carte £21/40

Town plan: 11QZB-s – 40 Chalcot Rd ⊠ NW1 8LS – ⊖ Chalk Farm – 𝒞 (020) 7483 4848 – www.labsinthe.co.uk – Closed 1 week Christmas and Monday dinner

Swiss Cottage

✗✗ **Bradley's** 🅰🅒 🗔

MODERN CUISINE · NEIGHBOURHOOD A stalwart of the local dining scene and ideal for visitors to the nearby Hampstead Theatre. The thoughtfully compiled and competitively priced set menus of mostly classical cooking draw in plenty of regulars.

Menu £21/28 – Carte £33/43

Town plan: 11PZB-e – 25 Winchester Rd. ⊠ NW3 3NR – ⊖ Swiss Cottage – 𝒞 (020) 7722 3457 – www.bradleysnw3.co.uk – Closed Sunday dinner

Tufnell Park

✗ **Shoe Shop** 🗔

FRENCH · NEIGHBOURHOOD From the former owners of Giaconda Dining Rooms comes this equally fun and modestly decorated neighbourhood spot. Go for the daily blackboard specials – the French-inspired dishes are hearty, satisfying and generously priced.

Carte £28/34

Town plan: 12RZA-t – 122a Fortess Rd ⊠ NW5 2HL – ⊖ Tufnell Park – 𝒞 (020) 7267 8444 (booking essential) – www.shoeshoplondon.com – Closed Sunday dinner and Monday

West Hampstead

✗ **One Sixty** 🌣 🅰🅒

NORTH-AMERICAN · SIMPLE A fun, stripped back bar and restaurant, based on an American smokehouse. Meats are smoked in-house to a temperature of 160°F – hence the name. Eat with your fingers and explore the list of over 50 craft beers from around the world.

Carte £23/40

Town plan: 10NZA-s – 291 West End Ln. ⊠ NW6 1RD – ⊖ West Hampstead – 𝒞 (020) 77949 786 – www.one-sixty.co.uk – dinner only and lunch Saturday-Sunday – Closed 24 December-2 January

© Angler

CITY OF LONDON

Hotels

Andaz Liverpool Street

BUSINESS · DESIGN A contemporary and stylish interior hides behind the classic Victorian façade. Bright and spacious bedrooms boast state-of-the-art facilities. Various dining options include a brasserie specialising in grilled meats, a compact Japanese restaurant and a traditional pub.

267 rooms – †£ 173/683 ††£ 189/699 – ☕£ 18 – 3 suites

Town plan: 34ART-t – *40 Liverpool St.* ✉ *EC2M 7QN* – ⊖ *Liverpool Street* – ✆ *(020) 7961 1234* – *www.andaz.com*

1901 – See restaurant listing

Threadneedles

BUSINESS · MODERN A converted bank, dating from 1856, with a smart, boutique feel and a stunning stained-glass cupola in the lounge. Bedrooms are very stylish and individual, featuring Egyptian cotton sheets, iPod docks and thoughtful extras. Spacious bar and restaurant; a striking backdrop to the classical menu.

74 rooms ☕ – †£ 199/499 ††£ 199/499

Town plan: 34ARU-y – *5 Threadneedle St.* ✉ *EC2R 8AY* – ⊖ *Bank* – ✆ *(020) 7657 8080* – *www.hotelthreadneedles.co.uk*

Apex Temple Court

BUSINESS · CONTEMPORARY Smart, corporate hotel fashioned out of former law firm offices and tucked away in a courtyard. Chambers is a well-kept brasserie with a Mediterranean menu. Four grades of bedroom, but all are bright, light and a good size.

184 rooms – †£ 120/500 ††£ 120/500 – ☕£ 21

Town plan: 32ANU-r – *1-2 Serjeant's Inn, Fleet St* ✉ *EC4Y 1LL* – ⊖ *Blackfriars* – ✆ *(020) 3004 4141* – *www.apexhotels.co.uk*

Montcalm London City at The Brewery

BUSINESS · STYLISH The majority of the contemporary rooms are in the original part of the Whitbread Brewery, built in 1714; ask for a quieter one overlooking the courtyard, or one of the 25 found in the 4 restored Georgian townhouses across the road.

235 rooms – †£ 168/350 ††£ 168/350 – ☕£ 25 – 7 suites

Town plan: 19VZD-r – *52 Chiswell St* ✉ *EC1Y 4SA* – ⊖ *Barbican* – ✆ *(020) 7614 0100* – *www.themontcalmlondoncity.co.uk*

Chiswell Street Dining Rooms – See restaurant listing

🏛 Hotel Indigo London - Tower Hill 🖵 🖨 ⚐ 🆔 ⚐

BUSINESS · MODERN Quieter than its city location would suggest, this business hotel comes with funky modern bedrooms equipped with iPod docks and coffee machines. Tower Bridge and Tower Hill suites have skyline views. Popular menu in Square Mile brasserie.

46 rooms – ♦£155/395 ♦♦£155/395 – ⌑ £9

Town plan: 34ASU-x – *142 Minories* ⊠ *EC3N 1LS* – ⊖ *Aldgate*
– *𝒞 (020) 7265 1014 – www.hotelindigo.com/lontowerhill*

Restaurants

𝕏𝕏𝕏 City Social ⚐ 🏆 ⪜ ⅙ 🆔 ⇔

⚒ **MODERN CUISINE · ELEGANT** Jason Atherton took over in 2014 and made the place bigger and better looking with a darker, moodier feel. The City views are as impressive as ever, especially from tables 10 & 15. The flexible menu is largely European and the cooking manages to be both refined and robust at the same time.

→ Yellow fin tuna tataki, cucumber salad, radish and avocado. Saddle and sausage of Lincolnshire rabbit with mustard mash and garlic. Pistachio soufflé with chocolate sorbet.

Carte £ 34/70

Town plan: 34ART-s – *Tower 42 (24th floor), 25 Old Broad St* ⊠ *EC2N 1HQ*
– ⊖ *Liverpool Street* – *𝒞 (020) 7877 7703 – www.citysociallondon.com*
– *Closed Sunday and bank holidays*

𝕏𝕏𝕏 Lutyens ⚐ 🆔 ⇔

MODERN CUISINE · FASHIONABLE The unmistakable hand of Sir Terence Conran: timeless and understated good looks mixed with functionality, and an appealing Anglo-French menu with plenty of classics such as fruits de mer and game in season.

Menu £ 24 (weekday lunch)/30 – Carte £ 28/62

Town plan: 32ANU-c – *85 Fleet St.* ⊠ *EC4Y 1AE* – ⊖ *Blackfriars*
– *𝒞 (020) 7583 8385 – www.lutyens-restaurant.com*
– *Closed 1 week Christmas-New Year, Saturday, Sunday and bank holidays*

𝕏𝕏𝕏 1901 🏆 ⅙ 🆔

BRITISH MODERN · ELEGANT The crisp white decoration and judicious lighting highlight the immense Doric columns, the cornicing and the beautiful cupola above. The menu champions British produce and the cooking is modern and quite ambitious in its reach.

Menu £ 26 – Carte £ 34/53

Town plan: 34ART-t – *Andaz Liverpool Street Hotel, Liverpool St.* ⊠ *EC2M 7QN*
– ⊖ *Liverpool Street* – *𝒞 (020) 7618 7000 – www.andaz.com*
– *Closed Christmas, Saturday lunch, Sunday and bank holidays*

𝕏𝕏 Club Gascon (Pascal Aussignac) ⚐ 🆔

⚒ **FRENCH · INTIMATE** The gastronomy of Gascony and France's southwest are the starting points but the assured and intensely flavoured cooking also pushes at the boundaries. Marble and huge floral displays create suitably atmospheric surroundings.

→ Pine-smoked foie gras with Génépi liqueur, croissant and hay ice cream. Squab pigeon with rhubarb, chicory and black garlic. Chocolate 'millionaire'.

Menu £ 29 (lunch)/65 – Carte £ 36/63

Town plan: 33APT-z – *57 West Smithfield* ⊠ *EC1A 9DS* – ⊖ *Barbican*
– *𝒞 (020) 7600 6144 (booking essential) – www.clubgascon.com*
– *Closed Christmas-New Year, Saturday lunch, Sunday and bank holidays*

XX Bread Street Kitchen

MODERN CUISINE · TRENDY Gordon Ramsay's take on NY loft-style dining comes with a large bar, thumping music, an open kitchen and enough zinc ducting to kit out a small industrial estate. For the food, think modern bistro dishes with an element of refinement.

Carte £ 27/65

Town plan: 33AQU-e – 10 Bread St ⊠ EC4M 9AJ – ⊖ St Paul's – ℰ (020) 3030 4050 (booking advisable) – www.breadstreetkitchen.com – Closed 25-26 December

XX New St Grill

MEATS · FRIENDLY D&D converted an 18C warehouse to satisfy our increasing appetite for red meat. They use Black Angus beef; grass-fed British and aged for 28 days, or corn-fed American, aged for 40 days. Start with a drink in the Old Bengal Bar.

Menu £ 27 (lunch and early dinner) – Carte £ 32/66

Town plan: 34ART-n – 16a New St ⊠ EC2M 4TR – ⊖ Liverpool Street – ℰ (020) 3503 0785 – www.newstreetgrill.com – Closed 23 December-7 January except dinner 31 December and Sunday dinner

XX Sauterelle

FRENCH · DESIGN Impressive location on the mezzanine floor of The Royal Exchange; ask for a table overlooking the Grand Café which was the original trading floor. A largely French-inspired contemporary menu makes good use of luxury ingredients.

Menu £ 29 – Carte £ 37/55

Town plan: 33AQU-a – The Royal Exchange ⊠ EC3V 3LR – ⊖ Bank – ℰ (020) 7618 2483 – www.royalexchange-grandcafe.co.uk – Closed Easter, Saturday, Sunday and bank holidays

XX Sushisamba

JAPANESE · TRENDY Stunning views, a great destination bar and a menu that blends Japanese, Peruvian and Brazilian influences – it may not come cheap but this US import is all about giving its young, fashionable fan base a fun night out.

Carte £ 30/66

Town plan: 34ART-d – Heron Tower (38th and 39th Floor), 110 Bishopsgate ⊠ EC2N 4AY – ⊖ Liverpool Street – ℰ (020) 3640 7330 (booking essential) – www.sushisamba.com

XX The Chancery

MODERN CUISINE · FORMAL An elegant restaurant that's so close to the law courts you'll assume your fellow diners are barristers, jurors or the recently acquitted. The menu is appealingly concise; dishes come with a classical backbone and bold flavours.

Menu £ 40/47

Town plan: 32ANT-a – 9 Cursitor St ⊠ EC4A 1LL – ⊖ Chancery Lane – ℰ (020) 7831 4000 – www.thechancery.co.uk – Closed 23 December-4 January, Saturday lunch, Sunday and bank holidays

XX Mint Leaf Lounge

INDIAN · DESIGN A bigger, shinier bar but a smaller dining room than the St James's original – well, this is the City, after all. The Indian food has a subtle southern bias and the tandoor oven, chargrill and tawa plate are all used extensively.

Menu £ 18 (weekday lunch) – Carte £ 29/50

Town plan: 33AQT-b – 12 Angel Ct, Lothbury ⊠ EC2R 7HB – ⊖ Bank – ℰ (020) 7600 0992 – www.mintleaflounge.com – Closed 25-26 December, 1 January, Saturday, Sunday and bank holidays

XX **Fenchurch** Ⓝ

MODERN CUISINE · DESIGN Arrive at the 'Walkie Talkie' early so you can first wander round the Sky Garden and take in the views. The smartly dressed restaurant is housed in a glass box within the atrium. Dishes are largely British; flavour combinations are complementary and ingredients top drawer.

Carte £ 41/63

Town plan: 34ARU-a – *Level 37, 20 Fenchurch St* ✉ *EC3M 3BY*
– ⊖ *Monument* – ℰ *(0333) 772 0020 (booking advisable)*
– *www.skygarden.london* – *Closed Sunday dinner*

XX **Vanilla Black**

CREATIVE · INTIMATE Proving that vegetarian food can be flavoursome, creative and satisfying, with a menu that is varied, imaginative and, at times, ambitious. This is a well-run, friendly restaurant with understated décor, run by a husband and wife.

Menu £ 25/42

Town plan: 32ANT-x – *17-18 Tooks Ct.* ✉ *EC4A 1LB*
– ⊖ *Chancery Lane* – ℰ *(020) 7242 2622* – *www.vanillablack.co.uk*
– *Closed 2 weeks Christmas and bank holidays*

XX **Yauatcha City** Ⓝ

CHINESE · FASHIONABLE A more corporate version of the stylish Soho original, with a couple of bars and a terrace at both ends. All the dim sum greatest hits are on the menu but the chefs have some work to match the high standard found in Broadwick Street.

Menu £ 40 – Carte £ 24/56

Town plan: 34 – *Broadgate Circle* ✉ *EC2M 2QS*
– ⊖ *Liverpool Street*
– ℰ *(020) 3817 9880* – *www.yauatcha.com*
– *Closed 25 December and Sunday*

XX **Cinnamon Kitchen**

INDIAN · TRENDY Sister to The Cinnamon Club. Contemporary Indian cooking, with punchy flavours and arresting presentation. Sprightly service in large, modern surroundings. Watch the action from the Tandoor Bar.

Menu £ 19 (lunch and early dinner) – Carte £ 26/50

Town plan: 34ART-e – *9 Devonshire Sq* ✉ *EC2M 4YL*
– ⊖ *Liverpool Street* – ℰ *(020) 7626 5000* – *www.cinnamon-kitchen.com*
– *Closed Saturday lunch, Sunday and bank holidays*

XX **Kenza**

LEBANESE · EXOTIC Exotic basement restaurant, with lamps, carvings, pumping music and nightly belly dancing. Lebanese and Moroccan cooking are the menu influences and the food is authentic and accurate.

Menu £ 30/50 – Carte £ 29/71

Town plan: 34ART-c – *10 Devonshire Sq.* ✉ *EC2M 4YP*
– ⊖ *Liverpool Street* – ℰ *(020) 7929 5533* – *www.kenza-restaurant.com*
– *Closed 24-25 December, Saturday lunch and bank holidays*

XX **Cigalon**

FRENCH · INTIMATE Pays homage to the food and wine of Provence, in an appropriately bright space that was a once an auction house. All the classics are here, from bouillabaisse to pieds et paquets. Busy bar in the cellar.

Menu £ 22 (weekdays)/33 – Carte £ 25/43

Town plan: 32ANU-x – *115 Chancery Ln* ✉ *WC2A 1PP*
– ⊖ *Chancery Lane* – ℰ *(020) 7242 8373* – *www.cigalon.co.uk*
– *Closed Christmas and New Year, Saturday, Sunday and bank holidays*

✗✗ The Mercer

BRITISH TRADITIONAL · BRASSERIE There's nothing like an old banking hall if you want a little grandeur and a feeling of space. The menu is from the John Bull wing of British cuisine: there are roasts and grills but the pies are the real favourites. Plenty of wines by the glass and some of the older Bordeaux vintages are well priced.

Carte £ 27/60

Town plan: 34ARU-x – *34 Threadneedle St* ✉ *EC2R 8AY* – ⊖ *Bank* – ℰ *(020) 7628 0001* – *www.themercer.co.uk* – *Closed 25-26 December, Saturday, Sunday and bank holidays*

✗✗ Boisdale of Bishopsgate

BRITISH TRADITIONAL · INTIMATE It's champagne and oysters on the ground floor and Scottish hospitality and live jazz in the clubby, unapologetically masculine vaulted restaurant below. Enjoy smoked salmon, roast haggis and dry-aged, grass-fed Aberdeenshire beef.

Carte £ 29/59

Town plan: 34ART-a – *Swedeland Crt, 202 Bishopsgate* ✉ *EC2M 4NR* – ⊖ *Liverpool Street* – ℰ *(020) 7283 1763* – *www.boisdale.co.uk* – *Closed Saturday lunch, Sunday and bank holidays*

✗✗ The White Swan

MODERN CUISINE · ELEGANT The classically educated kitchen uses British ingredients but also flavours from the Med. To reach this clubby, part-panelled first floor room – a haven of serenity – one must fight through the hordes of drinkers on the ground floor.

Menu £ 29 (lunch and early dinner) – Carte £ 27/48

Town plan: 32ANT-n – *108 Fetter Ln (1st floor)* ✉ *EC4A 1ES* – ⊖ *Chancery Lane* – ℰ *(020) 7242 9696* – *www.thewhiteswanlondon.com* – *Closed 25-26 December, Saturday, Sunday and bank holidays*

✗✗ Manicomio

ITALIAN · BRASSERIE They serve breakfast, cater for private parties, operate a café, provide takeaway, serve drinks and run a restaurant – all within this Norman Foster designed building. The regional Italian fare makes good use of quality ingredients.

Carte £ 28/51

Town plan: 33APT-s – *6 Gutter Ln* ✉ *EC2V 8AS* – ⊖ *St Paul's* – ℰ *(020) 7726 5010* – *www.manicomio.co.uk* – *Closed 1 week Christmas, Saturday, Sunday and bank holidays*

✗✗ Luc's Brasserie

FRENCH · BRASSERIE A classic French brasserie looking down on the Victorian splendour of Leadenhall Market and run with impressive efficiency. The menu has all the French favourites you'll ever need, along with steaks in all sizes and chops aplenty.

Menu £ 18 (lunch) – Carte £ 26/71

Town plan: 34ARU-v – *17-22 Leadenhall Mkt* ✉ *EC3V 1LR* – ⊖ *Bank* – ℰ *(020) 7621 0666 (booking essential)* – *www.lucsbrasserie.com* – *lunch only and dinner Tuesday-Thursday* – *Closed Christmas, New Year, Saturday, Sunday and bank holidays*

✗✗ Bevismarks

WORLD CUISINE · TRADITIONAL A kosher restaurant, licensed by the Sephardi Kashrut Authority & Beth Din (Glatt), and previously based at Bevis Marks Synagogue. Influences are Ashkenazi and Sephardi but there are also Asian touches and 'modern British' dishes.

Menu £ 19 (lunch) – Carte £ 33/47

Town plan: 34AST-b – *3 Middlesex St* ✉ *E1 7AA* – ⊖ *Aldgate* – ℰ *(020) 7247 5474* – *www.bevismarkstherestaurant.com* – *Closed Friday dinner-Sunday*

XX Barbecoa

MEATS · DESIGN Set up by Jamie Oliver, to show us what barbecuing is all about. The prime meats, butchered in-house, are just great; go for the pulled pork shoulder with cornbread on the side. By dessert you may be willing to share.

Menu £ 55/85 – Carte £ 32/64

Town plan: 33APU-v – *20 New Change Passage* ⊠ *EC4M 9AG* – ⊖ *St Paul's* – *ℰ (020) 3005 8555 (booking essential)* – *www.barbecoa.com* – *Closed 1 January, 31 August and 24-26 December*

XX Goodman City

MEATS · DESIGN Machismo reigns at this archetypal steakhouse with corn-fed, wet-aged USDA steaks and grass-fed, dry-aged Irish and Scottish steaks. All are perfectly cooked on the Josper grill, although starters and sides aren't quite as good.

Menu £ 22 (lunch) – Carte £ 43/66

Town plan: 33AQU-s – *11 Old Jewry* ⊠ *EC2R 8DU* – ⊖ *Bank* – *ℰ (020) 7600 8220* – *www.goodmanrestaurants.com* – *Closed Saturday, Sunday and bank holidays*

XX Chiswell Street Dining Rooms

BRITISH MODERN · INDIVIDUAL The Martin brothers used their Botanist restaurant as the model for this corner of the old Whitbread Brewery. The cocktail bar comes alive at night. Makes good use of British produce, especially fish from nearby Billingsgate.

Menu £ 27 – Carte £ 29/55

Town plan: 19VZD-r – *Montcalm London City, 56 Chiswell St* ⊠ *EC1Y 4SA* – ⊖ *Barbican* – *ℰ (020) 7614 0177* – *www.chiswellstreetdining.com* – *Closed 25-26 December, 1 January, Saturday and Sunday*

XX Duck & Waffle

MODERN CUISINE · TRENDY The UK's highest restaurant, on the 40th floor of Heron Tower, is a cheaper and less excitable alternative to Sushisamba one floor down. The menu is varied and offal is done well – try the crispy pig's ears. It's open 24 hours a day.

Carte £ 26/68

Town plan: 34ART-d – *Heron Tower (40th floor), 110 Bishopsgate* ⊠ *EC2N 4AY* – ⊖ *Liverpool Street* – *ℰ (020) 3640 7310 (booking essential)* – *www.duckandwaffle.com*

X Bird of Smithfield

BRITISH TRADITIONAL · DESIGN Feels like a private members' club but without the smugness. Five floors of fun include a cocktail bar, lounge, rooftop terrace and small, friendly restaurant. The appealing British menu makes good use of the country's larder.

Carte £ 28/46

Town plan: 33AOT-s – *26 Smithfield St* ⊠ *EC1A 9LB* – ⊖ *Farringdon* – *ℰ (020) 7559 5100 (booking essential)* – *www.birdofsmithfield.com* – *Closed Christmas, New Year, Sunday and bank holidays*

X Hawksmoor

MEATS · TRADITIONAL Fast and furious, busy and boisterous, this handsome room is the backdrop for another testosterone filled celebration of the serious business of beef eating. Nicely aged and rested Longhorn steaks take centre-stage.

Menu £ 27 (lunch and early dinner) – Carte £ 23/83

Town plan: 33AQT-a – *10-12 Basinghall St* ⊠ *EC2V 5BQ* – ⊖ *Bank* – *ℰ (020) 7397 8120 (booking essential)* – *www.thehawksmoor.com* – *Closed 24 December-2 January, Saturday, Sunday and bank holidays*

✗ José Pizarro ⑨ 🦐 ᚹ AK 🏮

SPANISH · TAPAS BAR The eponymous chef's third operation is a good fit here: it's well run, flexible and fairly priced – and that includes the wine list. The Spanish menu is nicely balanced, with the fish and seafood dishes being the standouts.

Carte £ 24/31

Town plan: 34ART-p – *36 Broadgate Circle* ✉ *EC2M 1QS*
– ⊖ *Liverpool Street* – ℰ *(020) 7256 5333* – *www.josepizarro.com*
– *Closed Sunday*

✗ Fish Market 🦐 ᚹ AK

FISH AND SEAFOOD · FRIENDLY How to get to the seaside from Liverpool Street? Simply step into this bright fish restaurant, in an old warehouse of the East India Company, and you'll almost hear the seagulls. The menu is lengthy and the cooking style classic.

Menu £ 20 – Carte £ 26/68

Town plan: 34ART-f – *16b New St* ✉ *EC2M 4TR* – ⊖ *Liverpool Street*
– ℰ *(020) 3503 0790 (booking advisable)* – *www.fishmarket-restaurant.co.uk*
– *Closed 25-26 December, 1 January, Sunday and bank holidays*

✗ Cellar Gascon 🍷 AK 🏮

FRENCH · TAPAS BAR It's not unlike a smart tapas bar and the monthly changing menu has plenty of treats: pâtés, rillettes, hams, cheeses and even some salads for the virtuous; but the Toulouse sausages and the Gascony pie stand out.

Menu £ 9 (weekday lunch) – Carte £ 12/26

Town plan: 33APT-c – *59 West Smithfield* ✉ *EC1A 9DS* – ⊖ *Barbican*
– ℰ *(020) 7600 7561 (booking essential at lunch)* – *www.cellargascon.com*
– *Closed Christmas-New Year, Saturday, Sunday and bank holidays*

✗ Vivat Bacchus 🍷 AK ⇄

MEATS · WINE BAR Wine is the star at this bustling City spot: from 4 cellars come 500 labels and 15,000 bottles. The menu complements the wine: steaks, charcuterie, sharing platters and South African specialities feature along with great cheese.

Carte £ 21/92

Town plan: 32ANT-c – *47 Farringdon St* ✉ *EC4A 4LL*
– ⊖ *Farringdon* – ℰ *(020) 7353 2648* – *www.vivatbacchus.co.uk*
– *Closed Christmas and New Year, Saturday, Sunday and bank holidays*

✗ Paternoster Chop House 🦐 AK

BRITISH TRADITIONAL · BRASSERIE Appropriately British menu in a restaurant lying in the shadow of St Paul's Cathedral. Large, open room with full-length windows; busy bar attached. Kitchen uses thoughtfully sourced produce.

Menu £ 20 (lunch and early dinner) – Carte £ 22/54

Town plan: 33APT-x – *Warwick Ct., Paternoster Sq.* ✉ *EC4M 7DX*
– ⊖ *St Paul's* – ℰ *(020) 7029 9400* – *www.paternosterchophouse.co.uk*
– *Closed Christmas and dinner Saturday and Sunday*

✗ 28°-50° Fetter Lane 🍷 AK ⇄

MODERN CUISINE · WINE BAR From the owners of Texture comes this cellar wine bar and informal restaurant. The terrific wine list is thoughtfully compiled and the grills, cheeses, charcuterie and European dishes are designed to allow the wines to shine.

Menu £ 20 (weekday lunch) – Carte £ 27/33

Town plan: 32ANU-s – *140 Fetter Ln* ✉ *EC4A 1BT*
– ⊖ *Temple* – ℰ *(020) 7242 8877* – *www.2850.co.uk*
– *Closed Saturday, Sunday and bank holidays*

X **Restaurant at St Paul's Cathedral** ✿

BRITISH MODERN · BISTRO Tucked away in a corner of the crypt of Sir Christopher Wren's 17C masterpiece, offering respite to tired tourists and weary worshippers. The monthly menu is reassuringly concise, seasonal and a celebration of all things British.

Menu £ 15/45 – Carte £ 23/36

Town plan: 33APU-s – *St Paul's Churchyard* ✉ *EC4M 8AD* – ⊖ *St Paul's*
– *☏ (020) 7248 1574 (booking advisable)* – *www.restaurantatstpauls.co.uk* – *lunch only* – *Closed 25 December and Good Friday*

🍴 **Jugged Hare** 🅐🅒 ▯ ▱ ✿

BRITISH TRADITIONAL · PUB Vegetarians may feel ill at ease – and not just because of the taxidermy. The atmospheric dining room, with its open kitchen down one side, specialises in stout British dishes, with meats from the rotisserie a highlight.

Menu £ 22 (early dinner) – Carte £ 29/59

Town plan: 19VZD-x – *42 Chiswell St* ✉ *EC1Y 4SA* – ⊖ *Barbican.*
– *☏ (020) 7614 0134 (booking advisable)* – *www.thejuggedhare.com*
– *Closed 25-26 December*

CROYDON

South Croydon

XX **Albert's Table** ♿ 🅐🅒

MODERN CUISINE · NEIGHBOURHOOD Named after the chef-owner's grandfather, this restaurant has a loyal local following. Gutsy, full-flavoured dishes use the best ingredients from Surrey, Sussex and Kent. Portions are generous and combinations rooted in the classics.

Menu £ 24 (lunch)/35

Town plan: 7FZ-x – *49b South End* ✉ *CR0 1BF* – *☏ (020) 8680 2010*
– *www.albertstable.co.uk* – *Closed Sunday dinner and Monday*

EALING

Acton Green

XX **Le Vacherin** 🅐🅒

FRENCH · BRASSERIE Authentic feel to this comfortable brasserie, with its brown leather banquette seating, mirrors and belle époque prints. French classics from snails to duck confit; beef is a speciality.

Menu £ 25 (lunch) – Carte £ 30/55

Town plan: 6CV-e – *76-77 South Par* ✉ *W4 5LF* – ⊖ *Chiswick Park*
– *☏ (020) 8742 2121* – *www.levacherin.com* – *Closed Monday lunch*

🍴 **Duke of Sussex** 🍽

MEDITERRANEAN · PUB Bustling Victorian pub, whose striking dining room was once a variety theatre complete with proscenium arch. Stick to the Spanish dishes; stews and cured meats are the specialities. BYO on Mondays.

Carte £ 23/36

Town plan: 6CV-e – *75 South Par* ✉ *W4 5LF* – ⊖ *Chiswick Park.*
– *☏ (020) 8742 8801* – *www.realpubs.co.uk*

Ealing

✗ Charlotte's Place

MODERN CUISINE · BISTRO Warmly run neighbourhood restaurant opposite the Common; divided between bright ground floor room and cosier downstairs. Menu is an appealing mix of British and Mediterranean influences.

Menu £ 20/35

Town plan: 2CV-c – *16 St Matthew's Rd* ✉ *W5 3JT* – ⊖ *Ealing Common* – ℰ *(020) 8567 7541* – *www.charlottes.co.uk* – *Closed 26 December and 1 January*

✗ Kiraku

JAPANESE · FRIENDLY The name of this cute little Japanese restaurant means 'relax and enjoy' - easy with such charming service. Extensive menu includes zen-sai, skewers, noodles, rice dishes and assorted sushi; ask if you want them in a particular order.

Menu £ 13 (lunch) – Carte £ 14/33

Town plan: 2CV-v – *8 Station Par, Uxbridge Rd.* ✉ *W5 3LD* – ⊖ *Ealing Common* – ℰ *(020) 8992 2848* – *www.kiraku.co.uk* – *Closed Christmas-New Year, Tuesday following bank holidays and Monday*

✗ Shikumen ⓝ

CHINESE · BRASSERIE Sister to the restaurant of the same name in Shepherd's Bush: this branch serves dim sum only – four choices are about right but if you're feeling hungry do order a rice bowl. Well-spaced tables and a dark, moody atmosphere.

Carte £ 18/28

Town plan: 5BV-s – *26-42 Bond St* ✉ *W5 5AA* – ⊖ *Ealing Broadway* – ℰ *(020) 8567 2770* – *www.shikumen.co.uk*

✗ Atari-ya

JAPANESE · SIMPLE Atari-ya are importers and suppliers of fish and assorted Japanese ingredients and so are well-placed to run a few accessibly-priced sushi bars around the capital. Go for nigiri to fully appreciate the texture and flavour of the fish.

Carte £ 15/30

Town plan: 2CV-v – *1 Station Par, Uxbridge Rd* ✉ *W5 3LD* – ⊖ *Ealing Common* – ℰ *(020) 8202 2789* – *www.atariya.co.uk* – *Closed bank holiday Mondays*

✗ Kerbisher & Malt

FISH AND CHIPS · SIMPLE The fish and chip shop reinvented... fresh, sustainably sourced fish is cooked to order in rapeseed oil; chips are made from British spuds and fried separately; and packaging is biodegradable. There's another branch in Hammersmith.

Carte £ 12/20

Town plan: 5BV-m – *53 New Broadway* ✉ *W5 5AH* – ⊖ *Ealing Broadway* – ℰ *(020) 8840 4418* – *www.kerbisher.co.uk*

South Ealing

Greater London – ✉ W5

🍴 Ealing Park Tavern ⓝ

BRITISH MODERN · TRENDY An impressive Arts and Crafts property, dating from 1886 and brought up to date thanks to a splendid refurbishment from the Martin Brothers. Cooking is robust yet with a refined edge. The pub also boasts its own brewery at the back.

Menu £ 19 (lunch and early dinner) – Carte £ 21/32

Town plan: 5BV-e – *222 South Ealing Rd* ✉ *W5 4RL Ealing* – ⊖ *South Ealing* – ℰ *(020) 8758 1879* – *www.ealingparktavern.com*

LONDON ENGLAND

✗✗ Inside   AC

MODERN CUISINE · NEIGHBOURHOOD Inside is tidy, comfortable and unclut-
tered, although it does take a few diners to generate an atmosphere. On offer is
a well-priced set menu, with quite elaborate, largely European cooking.
Menu £22 (weekday lunch)/26 – Carte £28/42
Town plan: 7GX-x – *19 Greenwich South St* ⊠ *SE10 8NW* – ⊖ *Greenwich
– 𝒞 (020) 8265 5060 – www.insiderestaurant.co.uk – Closed 25-26 December,
Sunday dinner and Monday*

✗ Craft London   ☕ & AC

BRITISH MODERN · BISTRO Chef Stevie Parle has created a striking space beside the O2 that includes a coffee shop, a cocktail bar, and a restaurant championing seasonal British produce. They do their own curing and smoking, and
roast their own coffee.
Menu £28/35 – Carte £29/45
Town plan: 8HV-e – *Peninsula Sq* ⊠ *SE10 0SQ* – ⊖ *North Greenwich* – *𝒞 (020)
8465 5910 – www.craft-london.co.uk – Closed Christmas-New Year, Sunday dinner
and lunch Monday and Tuesday*

✗ Rivington Grill   AC ⊡

BRITISH MODERN · SIMPLE Spread over two floors and part of the Picturehouse
complex. The extensive menu doubles as a placemat and is comfortingly familiar: there are pies, chops, plenty of things 'on toast' and assorted meats cooked
on the grill.
Carte £20/40
Town plan: 7GV-s – *178 Greenwich High Rd* ⊠ *SE10 8NN* – ⊖ *Greenwich (DLR)
– 𝒞 (020) 8293 9270 – www.rivingtongreenwich.co.uk – Closed 25-26 December*

© HKK London

HACKNEY

Dalston

✗ Rotorino
ITALIAN · SIMPLE You'll immediately warm to this stylish yet down to earth Italian. The staff are very welcoming and knowledgeable and the delicious Southern Italian specialities like caponata and gnudi are great value. Ask for one of the booths.

Menu £ 35 – Carte £ 19/39

Town plan: 14XZA-w – *434 Kingsland Rd* ⊠ *E8 4AA* – ⊖ *Dalston Junction* – ☎ *(020) 7249 9081* – *www.rotorino.com* – *dinner only and lunch Saturday-Sunday* – *Closed 23 December-2 January*

✗ The Richmond
FISH AND SEAFOOD · FASHIONABLE This was once a pub but where the bar was is now a counter where you're more likely to see someone shucking oysters, because seafood and excellent raw fish lie at the core of this operation. It's run by the team behind Elliot's.

Carte £ 25/43

Town plan: 14XZB-n – *316 Queensbridge Rd* ⊠ *E8 3NH* – ⊖ *Dalston Junction* – ☎ *(020) 7241 1638 (booking essential)* – *www.therichmondhackney.com* – *Closed 25-26 December*

✗ White Rabbit
MODERN CUISINE · SIMPLE Stripped down and sparse, with white walls, girders and bare concrete. Staff are a friendly bunch, the atmosphere is laid-back and the menu is all about small plates and sharing. Original cooking has Mediterranean and Asian influences.

Menu £ 18 (early dinner) – Carte £ 23/35

Town plan: 14XZB-r – *15-16 Bradbury St* ⊠ *N16 8JN* – ⊖ *Dalston Kingsland* – ☎ *(020) 7682 0163* – *www.whiterabbitdalston.com* – *dinner only and lunch Saturday-Sunday* – *Closed 25 December and 1 January*

Hoxton

🏨 M by Montcalm
BUSINESS · DESIGN Contemporary hotel within a striking modern building. Smart spa, relaxed restaurant and in the bedrooms – appropriately for a hotel in Tech City – you can control the lighting, music etc. from the bedside iPad.

269 rooms – 🛏£ 180/280 🛏🛏£ 180/500

Town plan: 13VZC-m – *151-157 City Rd* ⊠ *EC1V 1JH* – ⊖ *Old Street* – ☎ *(020) 3837 3000* – *www.mbymontcalm.co.uk*

🏠 The Hoxton   ⚡ 📶 🅰️ ⚒ 🔧

BUSINESS · STYLISH Industrial-styled urban lodge with a rakish, relaxed air; a youthful clientele and even younger staff. Bedrooms are compact but have some nice touches; choose a 'concept' room for something different. Open-plan restaurant with American menu and great cocktails.

210 rooms ⌷ – ♦£ 69/299 ♦♦£ 69/299

Town plan: 20XZD-x – *81 Great Eastern St.* ✉ *EC2A 3HU* – ⊖ *Old Street*
– ☎ *(020) 7550 1000* – *www.thehoxton.com*

✗ Fifteen London   🍷 ⚔ 🅰️ 🔲 🈁

MODERN CUISINE · NEIGHBOURHOOD Trainees at Jamie Oliver's charitable restaurant learn about cooking seasonal British food – dishes that have personality and are all about flavour. The same menu is served in the ground floor restaurant and the livelier cellar.

Menu £ 19 (lunch) – Carte £ 28/55

Town plan: 13VZC-c – *15 Westland Pl* ✉ *N1 7LP* – ⊖ *Old Street*
– ☎ *(020) 3375 1515 (booking essential)* – *www.fifteen.net*
– *Closed 25-26 December and 1 January*

✗ Beagle   🍷 🈁 ⚔

BRITISH TRADITIONAL · INDIVIDUAL Occupying three vast converted railway arches: one houses the bar; one the dining room; and the third is the kitchen. The British menu, with touches of Italian, changes twice a day and its contents are determined by the seasons.

Menu £ 15 (weekday lunch) – Carte £ 22/38

Town plan: 14XZB-e – *397-400 Geffrye St* ✉ *E2 8HZ* – ⊖ *Hoxton*
– ☎ *(020) 7613 2967 (booking essential)* – *www.beaglelondon.co.uk*
– *Closed Sunday dinner*

London Fields

✗ Lardo   🈁 ⚔ 🅰️ 🔲 🈁

ITALIAN · BISTRO Housed in the striking 1930s Arthaus building, this delightful Italian eatery may boast the ubiquitous faux industrial look but there's nothing bogus about the cooking – the small plates really hit the spot. Try the succulent home-cured meats and the terrific pizzas from the shiny wood-fired oven.

Carte £ 19/34

Town plan: 14YZB-h – *197-205 Richmond Rd* ✉ *E8 3NJ* – ⊖ *Hackney Central*
– ☎ *(020) 8985 2683* – *www.lardo.co.uk* – *Closed 21 December-2 January*

✗ Hill & Szrok ⓝ   🈁

MEATS AND GRILLS · INDIVIDUAL Butcher's shop by day; restaurant by night, with a central marble-topped table, counters around the edge and a friendly, lively feel. Daily blackboard menu of top quality meats, including steaks aged for a minimum of 60 days. No bookings.

Carte £ 19/50

Town plan: 14YZB-z – *60 Broadway Market* ✉ *E8 4QJ* – ⊖ *Bethnal Green*
– ☎ *(020) 7254 8805 (bookings not accepted)* – *www.hillandszrok.co.uk* – *dinner only and Sunday lunch* – *Closed 23 December-3 January*

✗ Market Cafe   🈁 🈁

MODERN CUISINE · NEIGHBOURHOOD This former pub by the canal appeals to local hipsters with its retro looks, youthful service team and Italian-influenced menu. Cooking is fresh and generous and uses some produce from the local market; homemade pasta a feature.

Carte £ 23/32

Town plan: 14YZB-m – *2 Broadway Mkt* ✉ *E8 4QG* – ⊖ *Bethnal Green*
– ☎ *(020) 7249 9070* – *www.market-cafe.co.uk*
– *Closed 25-26 December*

Shoreditch

Ace Hotel

BUSINESS • MINIMALIST The first Ace hotel in Europe and what better location for this achingly trendy hotel than hipster-central itself – Shoreditch. Locals are welcomed in, the lobby has a DJ, urban-chic rooms have day-beds if you want friends over and the minibars offer everything from Curly Wurlys to champagne.

258 rooms – †£ 155/600 ††£ 155/600 – ☐ £ 15 – 3 suites

Town plan: 20XZD-p – *100 Shoreditch High St ✉ E1 6JQ – ⊖ Shoreditch High Street – ✆ (020) 7613 9800 – www.acehotel.com*

Hoi Polloi – See restaurant listing

XXX Boundary

FRENCH • DESIGN Sir Terence Conran took a warehouse and created a 'caff' with a bakery and shop and this stylish, good-looking French restaurant serving plenty of cross-Channel classics. There's also a Mediterranean restaurant on the roof. Bedrooms are comfy and individual.

Menu £ 22/26 – Carte £ 31/62

17 rooms – †£ 190/240 ††£ 240/600 – ☐ £ 12 – 5 suites

Town plan: 20XZD-b – *2-4 Boundary St ✉ E2 7DD – ⊖ Shoreditch High Street – ✆ (020) 7729 1051 – www.theboundary.co.uk – dinner only and Sunday lunch – Closed Sunday dinner*

XXX L'Anima

ITALIAN • FASHIONABLE Very handsome room, with limestone and leather creating a sophisticated, glamorous environment. Appealing menu is a mix of Italian classics and less familiar dishes, with the emphasis firmly on flavour. Service is smooth and personable.

Carte £ 36/67

Town plan: 20XZD-a – *1 Snowden St, Broadgate West ✉ EC2A 2DQ – ⊖ Liverpool Street – ✆ (020) 7422 7000 (booking essential) – www.lanima.co.uk – Closed 25-26 December, Saturday lunch, Sunday and bank holidays*

XX HKK

✿

CHINESE • ELEGANT Cantonese has always been considered the finest of the Chinese cuisines and here at HKK it is given an extra degree of refinement. Expect classic flavour combinations yet delivered in a modern way. The room is elegant and graceful; the service smooth and assured.

➜ Cherry wood roasted Peking duck. King soy seared Wagyu beef with jasmine tea. Jasmine panna cotta with rhubarb sorbet.

Menu £ 35/98 – Carte lunch £ 24/65

Town plan: 20XZD-h – *88 Worship St ✉ EC2A 2BE – ⊖ Liverpool Street – ✆ (020) 3535 1888 – www.hkklondon.com – Closed 25 December and Sunday*

XX Merchants Tavern

BRITISH TRADITIONAL • BRASSERIE The 'pub' part – a Victorian warehouse – gives way to a large restaurant with the booths being the prized seats. The cooking is founded on the sublime pleasures of seasonal British cooking, in reassuringly familiar combinations.

Menu £ 25 (lunch) – Carte £ 30/52

Town plan: 20XZD-t – *36 Charlotte Rd ✉ EC2A 3PG – ⊖ Old Street – ✆ (020) 7060 5335 – www.merchantstavern.co.uk – Closed 25-26 December and 1 January*

XX Eyre Brothers

SPANISH • ELEGANT Sleek, confidently run and celebrating all things Iberian by drawing on the brothers' memories of their childhood in Mozambique. Delicious hams; terrific meats cooked over lumpwood charcoal. If a larger group, pre-order paella or suckling pig. Tapas served in the bar.

Carte £ 26/44

Town plan: 20XZD-k – *70 Leonard St ✉ EC2A 4QX – ⊖ Shoreditch High Street – ✆ (020) 7613 5346 – www.eyrebrothers.co.uk – Closed 24 December-4 January, Saturday lunch, Sunday and bank holidays*

«SEULEMENT LE MEILLEUR»

GEORGES H.MUMM

G.H.MUMM
CHAMPAGNE

PLEASE DRINK RESPONSIBLY

XX L'Anima Café **N**   &.   AC   ⇔

ITALIAN · BRASSERIE A baby sister to L'Anima around the corner but more than a mere café: this is big, bright restaurant with a busy bar and deli. The fairly priced menu includes plenty of pizza and pasta dishes. A DJ plays on Thursdays and Fridays.

Menu £ 35 (weekdays) – Carte £ 25/46

Town plan: 20XZD-h – 10 Appold St ⊠ EC2A 2AP – ⊖ Liverpool Street – ℰ (020) 7422 7080 – www.lanimacafe.co.uk – Closed Saturday lunch and Sunday

XX Hoi Polloi   &. AC ▫

BRITISH MODERN · BRASSERIE The boys from Bistrotheque are behind this hip, modern brasserie. It's open from early morning to the wee small hours offering everything from shakes first thing to midnight burgers and soundly prepared British dishes.

Carte £ 22/48

Town plan: 14XZD-p – Ace Hotel, 100 Shoreditch High St ⊠ E1 6JQ – ⊖ Shoreditch High Street – ℰ (020) 8880 6100 – www.hoi-polloi.co.uk

X Clove Club (Isaac McHale)   🍴 AC I○

⁂ MODERN CUISINE · TRENDY An unrelentingly sparse room at Shoreditch Town Hall is the chosen site for three friends who made their names in pop-ups. The set menu showcases expertly sourced produce in dishes that are full of originality, verve and flair – but where flavours are expertly judged and complementary.
→ Raw Orkney scallop, hazelnut, clementine, brown butter and Périgord truffle. Slow-cooked North Ronaldsay lamb with seaweed sauce and purple sprouting broccoli. Amalfi lemonade with Sarawak pepper ice cream.

Menu £ 35/65 – set menu only

Town plan: 20XZC-c – 380 Old St ⊠ EC1V 9LT – ⊖ Old Street – ℰ (020) 7729 6496 (bookings advisable at dinner) – www.thecloveclub.com – Closed 2 weeks Christmas-New Year, August bank holiday, Monday lunch and Sunday

X Lyle's (James Lowe)   AC

⁂ BRITISH MODERN · SIMPLE The young chef-owner is an acolyte of Fergus Henderson and delivers similarly unadulterated flavours from seasonal British produce, albeit from a set menu at dinner. This pared-down approach extends to a room that's high on functionality, but considerable warmth comes from the keen young service team.
→ Pumpkin, whey butter and hazelnut. Monkfish and seaweed. Pear, ginger loaf and caramel.

Menu £ 39 (dinner) – Carte lunch £ 23/31

Town plan: 20XZD-s – Tea Building, 56 Shoreditch High St ⊠ E1 6JJ – ⊖ Shoreditch High Street – ℰ (020) 3011 5911 – www.lyleslondon.com – Closed Sunday and bank holidays

X Andina   🍴 AC ▫ 🍽 I○ ⇔

PERUVIAN · SIMPLE Andina may be smaller and slightly more chaotic that its sister Ceviche, but this friendly picantería with live music is equally popular. The Peruvian specialities include great salads and skewers, and ceviche that packs a punch.

Carte £ 11/22

Town plan: 20XZD-w – 1 Redchurch St ⊠ E2 7DJ – ⊖ Shoreditch High Street – ℰ (020) 7920 6499 (booking essential) – www.andinalondon.com

X Rivington Grill   AC ▫

BRITISH TRADITIONAL · BISTRO Very appealing 'back to basics' British menu, with plenty of comforting classics including a section 'on toast'. This converted warehouse is popular with the local community of artists.

Carte £ 22/42

Town plan: 20XZD-e – 28-30 Rivington St ⊠ EC2A 3DZ – ⊖ Old Street – ℰ (020) 7729 7053 – www.rivingtonshoreditch.co.uk – Closed 25-26 December

✗ Tramshed   ﭏ 🅺 ⇧

MEATS · BRASSERIE Mark Hix's impressive brasserie – complete with Damien Hirst tank – is found within a 1905 Grade II warehouse. It's all about chicken and beef: Swainson House Farm chickens and Glenarm steaks are accurately cooked and delicious.

Carte £ 25/68

Town plan: 20XZD-v – *32 Rivington St* ⊠ *EC2A 3LX* – ⊖ *Old Street* – ℰ *(020) 7749 0478* – *www.chickenandsteak.co.uk* – *Closed 25-26 December*

✗ Viet Grill   🍽 🅺

VIETNAMESE · FRIENDLY Owned by the team behind Cây Tre which means that service is charming and helpful and the Vietnamese food is fresh and authentic. Larger parties should consider ordering one of their 'feast' menus, which require 48 hours' notice.

Menu £ 10/23 – Carte £ 16/32

Town plan: 14XZB-v – *58 Kingsland Rd* ⊠ *E2 8DP* – ⊖ *Hoxton* – ℰ *(020) 7739 6686 (booking essential)* – *www.vietgrill.co.uk*

🍴 Princess of Shoreditch   🍴 🍽

BRITISH TRADITIONAL · PUB There has been a pub on this corner site since 1742 but it is doubtful many of the previous incarnations were as busy or as pleasant as the Princess is today. The best dishes are those with a rustic edge, such as goose rillettes or chicken pie.

Carte £ 26/34

Town plan: 19VZD-a – *76-78 Paul St* ⊠ *EC2A 4NE* – ⊖ *Old Street* – ℰ *(020) 7729 9270 (booking essential)* – *www.theprincessofshoreditch.com* – *Closed 24-26 December*

South Hackney

🍴 Empress   🍽

MEDITERRANEAN · PUB Sourdough is from the local baker; the butcher and fishmonger are within walking distance. Dishes like pearl barley and feta risotto demonstrate the kitchen's confidence and ability; prices are good and Sunday lunch a languid affair.

Menu £ 20 (weekday dinner) – Carte £ 22/42

Town plan: 3GU-n – *130 Lauriston Rd, Victoria Park* ⊠ *E9 7LH* – ⊖ *Homerton.* – ℰ *(020) 8533 5123* – *www.empresse9.co.uk* – *Closed 25-26 December and Monday lunch except bank holidays*

Stoke Newington

✗ Foxlow 🆕   🍽 🅺

BRITISH TRADITIONAL · FAMILY Foxlow is the less bellicose brand from the people behind the Hawksmoor steakhouses. Here it's all about families and the local neighbourhood. The menu is safe and appealing but it would be churlish to avoid the steaks.

Carte £ 19/38

Town plan: 13VZA-s – *71-73 Church St* ⊠ *N16 OAS* – ⊖ *Canonbury* – ℰ *(020) 7481 6371* – *www.foxlow.co.uk* – *Closed 25 December*

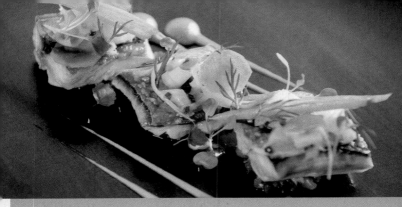

© Pied à Terre Central London restaurant

HAMMERSMITH and FULHAM

Fulham

✕✕ Blue Elephant 🛜 AC

THAI · **EXOTIC** Relocated from Fulham Road to these swankier and appropriately exotic premises, spread over two floors and with two great riverside terraces. The menu traverses Thailand; curries are a strength.

Carte £ 27/54

Town plan: 23PZH-x – *The Boulevard, Imperial Wharf* ✉ *SW6 2UB*
– ⊖ *Imperial Wharf* – ✆ *(020) 7751 3111 (booking advisable)*
– *www.blueelephant.com* – *dinner only and lunch Saturday and Sunday*
– *Closed 25-26 December and 1 January*

✕ Tendido Cuatro AC 🍽

SPANISH · **NEIGHBOURHOOD** Along with tapas, the speciality is paella. Designed for a hungry two, they vary from seafood to quail and chorizo; vegetarian to cuttlefish ink. Vivid colours used with abandon deck out the busy room.

Menu £ 35 (lunch and early dinner) – Carte £ 20/56

Town plan: 22NZH-x – *108-110 New Kings Rd* ✉ *SW6 4LY*
– ⊖ *Parsons Green* – ✆ *(020) 7371 5147* – *www.cambiodetercio.co.uk*
– *Closed 2 weeks Christmas*

✕ Koji AC 🍽

JAPANESE · **WINE BAR** After nearly 30 years, Mark Barnett retired his Mao Tai Chinese restaurant and in its place opened this fun, contemporary wine bar serving Japanese food. The menu mixes the modern with the classic, and the Nobu influences are obvious.

Carte £ 31/54

Town plan: 22NZH-e – *58 New King's Rd* ✉ *SW6 4LS* – ⊖ *Parsons Green*
– ✆ *(020) 7731 2520* – *www.koji.co.uk* – *Closed 24-26 December and Monday*

✕ Manuka Kitchen AC 🍽

MODERN CUISINE · **RUSTIC** The two young owners run their simple little restaurant with great enthusiasm and their prices are keen. Like the magical Manuka honey, the chef is from New Zealand; his menu is varied and his food is wholesome and full of flavour.

Carte £ 21/34

Town plan: 22NZG-k – *510 Fulham Rd* ✉ *SW6 5NJ* – ⊖ *Fulham Broadway*
– ✆ *(020) 7736 7588* – *www.manukakitchen.com* – *Closed 25-26 December, Sunday dinner and Monday*

X Claude's Kitchen

MODERN CUISINE · BISTRO Two operations in one converted pub: 'Amuse Bouche' is a well-priced champagne bar; upstairs is an intimate dining room with a weekly changing menu. The cooking is colourful and fresh, with the odd challenging flavour combination.

Carte £ 25/35

Town plan: 22NZH-c – 51 Parsons Green Ln ✉ SW6 4JA – ⊖ Parsons Green.
– ℰ (020) 7371 8517 (booking essential) – www.amusebouchelondon.com – dinner only – Closed Sunday

X Eelbrook

MEDITERRANEAN · DESIGN Fulham's version of a park café is a light, bright affair with an appealing terrace overlooking a small Common. The menu blends Mediterranean vitality with British stoutness; the modern, vibrant dishes display some clever touches.

Menu £ 16 (weekday lunch) – Carte £ 22/35

Town plan: 22NZG-e – Eel Brook Common, New King's Rd ✉ SW6 4SE
– ⊖ Fulham Broadway – ℰ (020) 3417 0287 – www.eelbrook.com – Closed Christmas

Harwood Arms

BRITISH MODERN · PUB Its reputation may have spread like wildfire but this remains a proper, down-to-earth pub that just happens to serve really good food. The cooking is very seasonal, proudly British, full of flavour and doesn't seem out of place in this environment. Service is suitably relaxed and friendly.

→ Berkshire game faggots with Jerusalem artichokes, pickled walnut and Muscat grapes. Roast and braised Herdwick lamb with artichoke, creamed spinach and black garlic. Warm heritage carrot cake with orange, lovage and stem ginger.

Menu £ 20 (weekday lunch)/40

Town plan: 22NZG-a – Walham Grove ✉ SW6 1QP – ⊖ Fulham Broadway.
– ℰ (020) 7386 1847 (booking essential) – www.harwoodarms.com
– Closed 24-27 December, 1 January and Monday lunch except Bank Holidays

Malt House

BRITISH MODERN · PUB A smart Fulham pub with a friendly atmosphere helped along by the charming young staff. The menu is all-encompassing enough to satisfy both the traditionalist and the more adventurous eater. Six elegant bedrooms upstairs.

Menu £ 17/35 – Carte £ 22/43

6 rooms ✇ – ♦£ 90/135 ♦♦£ 105/150

Town plan: 22NZG-m – 17 Vanston Pl ✉ SW6 1AY – ⊖ Fulham Broadway.
– ℰ (020) 7084 6888 – www.malthousefulham.co.uk – Closed 25 December

Sands End

BRITISH MODERN · PUB Cosy, warm and welcoming little corner pub, offering appealing bar snacks and a thoughtfully put-together menu with a British bias. Game is handled deftly and ingredients are well-sourced.

Menu £ 17 (weekday lunch) – Carte £ 29/41

Town plan: 22OZH-r – 135-137 Stephendale Rd ✉ SW6 2PR
– ⊖ Fulham Broadway. – ℰ (020) 7731 7823 (booking advisable)
– www.thesandsend.co.uk – Closed 25 December

Tommy Tucker

BRITISH TRADITIONAL · PUB The old Pelican pub was revamped by the owners of nearby Claude's Kitchen. It's bright and open plan, with an unstructured menu divided under headings of 'meat', 'fish' and 'fruit and veg'. The cooking is rustic and satisfying.

Menu £ 15 (weekday lunch) – Carte £ 21/36

Town plan: 22NZG-s – 22 Waterford Rd ✉ SW6 2DR – ⊖ Fulham Broadway
– ℰ (020) 7736 1023 – www.thetommytucker.com – Closed 25 December

Hammersmith

✕✕ **River Café** (Ruth Rogers) ⚭ 🏠 ♻

❀ ITALIAN · FASHIONABLE It's all about the natural Italian flavours of the superlative ingredients. The on-view kitchen with its wood-fired oven dominates the stylish riverside room; the contagiously effervescent atmosphere is helped along by very charming service.

→ Wood-roasted langoustines, chilli and oregano. Roast turbot tranche with an anchovy and rosemary sauce and broad beans. Chocolate Nemesis.

Carte £ 61/80

Town plan: 21LZG-v – *Thames Wharf, Rainville Rd* ✉ *W6 9HA*
– ↔ *Barons Court –* ☎ *(020) 7386 4200 (booking essential)*
– www.rivercafe.co.uk – Closed Christmas-New Year, Sunday dinner and bank holidays

✕✕ **Potli** 🏠 AC

INDIAN · NEIGHBOURHOOD Named after a sort of spiced bouquet garni – apt, since spicing plays a big part at this smart, warmly run Indian restaurant. Food markets across India provide the ideas, with smaller dishes like 'Chicken 65' inspired by street food.

Menu £ 10 (lunch) – Carte £ 19/28

Town plan: 21KZF-v – *319-321 King St* ✉ *W6 9NH –* ↔ *Ravenscourt Park*
– ☎ *(020) 8741 4328 – www.potli.co.uk*

✕✕ **Indian Zing** 🏠 AC 🍽

INDIAN · NEIGHBOURHOOD Chef-owner Manoj Vasaikar seeks inspiration from across India. His cooking balances the traditional with the more contemporary and delivers many layers of flavour – the lamb dishes and breads are particularly good. The restaurant is always busy yet service remains courteous and unhurried.

Menu £ 12/27 – Carte £ 20/43

Town plan: 21LZG-a – *236 King St.* ✉ *W6 0RF –* ↔ *Ravenscourt Park –* ☎ *(020) 8748 5959 – www.indianzing.co.uk*

✕ **Brackenbury** 🏠

MEDITERRANEAN · NEIGHBOURHOOD A much loved neighbourhood restaurant reopened by Ossie Gray of The River Café. The kitchen looks to Italy, France and the Med for inspiration and doesn't waste time on presentation; dishes feel instinctive and flavours marry well.

Menu £ 19 (weekday lunch) – Carte £ 24/40

Town plan: 15LZE-c – *129 - 131 Brackenbury Rd* ✉ *W6 0BQ*
– ↔ *Ravenscourt Park –* ☎ *(020) 8741 4928 – www.brackenburyrestaurant.co.uk*
– Closed Christmas and New Year and Easter

✕ **L'Amorosa** Ⓝ

☻ ITALIAN · NEIGHBOURHOOD Former Zafferano head chef Andy Needham has created a warm and sunny Italian restaurant – one that we'd all like to have in our high street. The quality of the produce shines through and homemade pasta dishes are a highlight.

Menu £ 16 (weekday lunch) – Carte £ 25/36

Town plan: 21KZG-s – *278 King St* ✉ *W6 0SP –* ↔ *Ravenscourt Park –* ☎ *(020) 8563 0300 – www.lamorosa.co.uk – Closed 1 week August, 1 week Christmas, Sunday dinner, Monday and bank holidays*

✕ **Azou** AC

☻ NORTH-AFRICAN · NEIGHBOURHOOD Silks, lanterns and rugs add to the atmosphere of this personally run, North African restaurant. Most come for the excellent tajines, with triple steamed couscous. Much is designed for sharing.

Carte £ 19/37

Town plan: 21KZG-u – *375 King St* ✉ *W6 9NJ –* ↔ *Stamford Brook –* ☎ *(020) 8563 7266 (booking essential) – www.azou.co.uk – dinner only – Closed 1 January and 25 December*

LONDON ENGLAND

🍴 Anglesea Arms   🛜

BRITISH MODERN · NEIGHBOURHOOD One of the daddies of the gastropub movement, reborn with new owners. The seasonal menu gives the impression it's written by a Brit who holidays on the Med – along with hardy dishes are some that display a pleasing lightness of touch.

Carte £ 24/35

Town plan: 15LZE-a – *35 Wingate Rd* ✉ *W6 0UR* – ⊖ *Ravenscourt Park*
– 𝒞 *(020) 8749 1291* – *www.angleseaarmspub.co.uk* – *Closed 24-26 December*

🍴 Havelock Tavern   🛜 AC

MEDITERRANEAN · PUB Warm, friendly and atmospheric pub with easy-going service and pleasantly mixed clientele. Blackboard menu offers robust, satisfying pub food. Arrive early if you don't want to wait for a table.

Carte £ 23/38 **s**

Town plan: 16MZE-e – *57 Masbro Rd, Brook Grn* ✉ *W14 0LS*
– ⊖ *Kensington Olympia.* – 𝒞 *(020) 7603 5374* – *www.havelocktavern.com*
– *Closed 25-26 December*

🍴 Crabtree   🛜 AC

MODERN CUISINE · PUB With a beer garden seating over 80 and a separate dining room terrace, this Victorian pub makes great use of its riverside location. Parfaits and terrines are highlights but Veggies are also considered. Service is unhurried.

Carte £ 20/33

Town plan: 21LZG-x – *4 Rainville Rd* ✉ *W6 9HA* – ⊖ *Barons Court.*
– 𝒞 *(020) 7385 3929* – *www.thecrabtreew6.co.uk*

Shepherd's Bush

XX Shikumen 🆕   ♿ AC 🎐

🏵 CHINESE · INTIMATE Impressive homemade dim sum at lunch and excellent Peking duck are the standouts at this unexpectedly sleek Cantonese restaurant in an otherwise undistinguished part of Shepherd's Bush.

Carte £ 19/46

58 Shepherd's Bush Grn ✉ *W12 8QE* – ⊖ *Shepherd's Bush* – 𝒞 *(020) 8749 9978*
– *www.shikumen.co.uk* – *Closed Christmas*

🍴 Princess Victoria   🎋 🛜 AC 🅿

BRITISH TRADITIONAL · PUB Magnificent Victorian gin palace, with original plasterwork. The kitchen knows its butchery; pork board, homemade sausages and terrines all feature. Excellent wine list, with over 350 bottles.

Carte £ 21/49

Town plan: 15KZE-a – *217 Uxbridge Rd* ✉ *W12 9DH* – ⊖ *Shepherd's Bush.*
– 𝒞 *(020) 8749 5886* – *www.princessvictoria.co.uk* – *Closed 24-27 December*

HARINGEY

Crouch End

X Bistro Aix   AC ⇆

FRENCH · BISTRO Dressers, cabinets and contemporary artwork lend an authentic Gallic edge to this bustling bistro, a favourite with many of the locals. Traditionally prepared French classics are the highlights of an extensive menu.

Menu £ 18 – Carte £ 25/45

Town plan: 3EU-v – *54 Topsfield Par, Tottenham Ln* ✉ *N8 8PT* – ⊖ *Crouch Hill*
– 𝒞 *(020) 8340 6346* – *www.bistroaix.co.uk* – *dinner only and lunch
Friday-Sunday* – *Closed 24 and 26 December*

HARROW

Harrow on the Hill

✕✕ Incanto   Aℭ

MODERN CUISINE · NEIGHBOURHOOD Within Grade II former post office; split-level restaurant to rear of well stocked deli. Well-paced service and modern, quite technical cooking from an ambitious kitchen. Notable wine list is predominantly Italian.

Menu £ 24 (weekday lunch) – Carte £ 32/40

Town plan: 1BU-z – *41 High St.* ⊠ *HA1 3HT* – ⊖ *Harrow on the Hill* – ℰ *(020) 8426 6767* – *www.incanto.co.uk* – *Closed 24-26 December, 1 January, Easter Sunday, Sunday dinner and Monday*

Pinner

✕✕ Friends   Aℭ

BRITISH TRADITIONAL · COSY This characterful, low-beamed restaurant has been proudly and personally run for over 20 years – and has a history stretching back over 500 more. Cooking is classical and carefully done, and the service is well-paced and friendly.

Menu £ 15 (weekday lunch)/35 – Carte £ 33/44

Town plan: 1BU-a – *11 High St* ⊠ *HA5 5PJ* – ⊖ *Pinner* – ℰ *(020) 8866 0286* – *www.friendsrestaurant.co.uk* – *Closed 25-26 December, 26-27 May, Sunday dinner, Monday and bank holidays*

HEATHROW AIRPORT

🏨 Sofitel   🖙 ⊕ 🍴 ⅄ 🔲 🔲 Aℭ ⅏ ⅏ 🚗

LUXURY · MODERN Smart and well-run contemporary hotel, designed around a series of atriums, with direct access to T5. Crisply decorated, comfortable bedrooms with luxurious bathrooms. Choice of restaurant: international or classic French cuisine.

605 rooms – ♦£ 150/289 ♦♦£ 150/289 – ☲ £ 20 – 27 suites

Town plan: 5AX-a – *Terminal 5, Heathrow Airport* ⊠ *TW6 2GD* – ⊖ *Heathrow Terminal 5* – ℰ *(020) 8757 7777* – *www.sofitelheathrow.com*

🏨 Hilton London Heathrow Airport Terminal 5 🖙 🖷 ⊕ 🍴

CHAIN HOTEL · FUNCTIONAL A feeling of light   ⅄ 🔲 🔲 Aℭ ⅏ ⅏ 🅿 and space pervades this modern, corporate hotel. Soundproofed rooms are fitted to a good standard; the spa offers wide-ranging treatments. Open-plan Gallery for British comfort food.

350 rooms – ♦£ 119/259 ♦♦£ 119/259 – ☲ £ 21 – 3 suites

Poyle Rd, Colnbrook ⊠ *SL3 OFF* – *West : 2.5 mi by A 3113* – ℰ *(01753) 686 860* – *www.hilton.com/heathrowt5*

Mr Todiwala's Kitchen – See restaurant listing

🏨 Hilton London Heathrow Airport 🖙 🔲 🍴 ⅄ 🔲 🔲 Aℭ ⅏ ⅏ 🅿

BUSINESS · CONTEMPORARY Group hotel with a striking modern exterior and linked to Terminal 4 by a covered walkway. Good-sized bedrooms, with contemporary styled suites. Casual dining in Aromi which occupies part of the vast atrium.

398 rooms – ♦£ 92/255 ♦♦£ 96/260 – ☲ £ 21 – 5 suites

Town plan: 5AX-n – *Terminal 4* ⊠ *TW6 3AF* – ⊖ *Heathrow Terminal 4* – ℰ *(020) 8759 7755* – *www.hilton.com/heathrow*

Zen Oriental – See restaurant listing

🏨 London Heathrow Marriott 🖙 🔲 🍴 ⅄ 🔲 🔲 Aℭ ⅏ ⅏ 🅿

CHAIN HOTEL · CONTEMPORARY Built at the end of 20C, this modern, comfortable hotel is centred around a large atrium, with comprehensive business facilities: there is an exclusive Executive floor. Italian cuisine in bright and convivial Tuscany. Grill favourites in Allie's.

393 rooms – ♦£ 125/209 ♦♦£ 125/209 – ☲ £ 18 – 2 suites

Town plan: 5AX-z – *Bath Rd, Hayes* ⊠ *UB3 5AN* – ⊖ *Heathrow Terminal 1,2,3* – ℰ *(020) 8990 1100* – *www.londonheathrowmarriott.co.uk*

XX Mr Todiwala's Kitchen

INDIAN • INDIVIDUAL Secreted within the Hilton is Cyrus Todiwala's appealingly stylish, fresh-looking restaurant. The choice ranges from street food to tandoor dishes, Goan classics to Parsee specialities; order the 'Kitchen menu' for the full experience.

Menu £ 45 – Carte £ 28/39

Hilton London Heathrow Airport Terminal 5 Hotel, Poyle Rd, Colnbrook ✉ SL3 OFF – West : 2.5 mi by A 3113 – ✆ (01753) 766 482 – www.hilton.com/heathrowterminal5 – dinner only and lunch Thursday-Saturday – Closed 19 December-2 January and Sunday

XX Zen Oriental

ASIAN • FASHIONABLE With its capable service and appealing menu of authentically executed classics, Zen Oriental has long been a favourite at the Hilton. Popular for business lunches; busy at dinner with hotel guests.

Carte £ 34/63

Town plan: 5AX-n – *Hilton London Heathrow Airport Hotel, Terminal 4 ✉ TW6 3AF – ⊖ Heathrow Terminal 4 – ✆ (020) 8759 7755 (booking essential at dinner) – www.hilton.com/heathrow – Closed 25-26 December*

HOUNSLOW

Brentford

Hilton London Syon Park

LUXURY • STYLISH A large, impressively decorated, purpose-built hotel in the grounds of Syon House – the London residence of the Duke of Northumberland. Most of the smart, stylish rooms have a terrace or balcony; ask for one overlooking the walled garden.

137 rooms – †£ 169/199 ††£ 169/199 – ☕ £ 18 – 1 suite

Town plan: 5BX-x – *Park Rd ✉ TW8 8JF – ✆ (020) 7870 7777 – www.londonsyonpark.com*

Chiswick

High Road House

TOWNHOUSE • MINIMALIST Cool, sleek hotel and club, the latter a slick place to lounge around or play games. Light, bright bedrooms with crisp linen. A carefully appointed, fairly-priced destination.

14 rooms – †£ 116/215 ††£ 116/215 – ☕ £ 22

Town plan: 21KZG-e – *162 Chiswick High Rd ✉ W4 1PR – ⊖ Turnham Green – ✆ (020) 8742 1717 – www.highroadhouse.co.uk*

High Road Brasserie – See restaurant listing

XX Hedone (Mikael Jonsson)

✿ MODERN CUISINE • DESIGN Mikael Jonsson, former lawyer turned chef, is not one for complacency so his restaurant continues to evolve. The content of his set menus is governed entirely by what ingredients are in their prime – and it is this passion for produce which underpins the superlative and very flavoursome cooking.

➜ Pertuis asparagus with pistachio, avocado, wild garlic and primrose. Roast breast and leg of squab pigeon, with offal sauce, smoked Jersey pearls, parsley and almond. Fresh raspberries with cinnamon and aromatic vinegar.

Menu £ 45/125 – set menu only

Town plan: 6CV-x – *301-303 Chiswick High Rd ✉ W4 4HH – ⊖ Chiswick Park – ✆ (020) 8747 0377 – www.hedonerestaurant.com – dinner only and lunch Thursday-Saturday – Closed two weeks summer, two weeks Christmas-New Year, Sunday and Monday*

✕✕ La Trompette

❀ **BRITISH MODERN · NEIGHBOURHOOD** Chez Bruce's sister is a delightful neighbourhood restaurant that's now a little roomier. The service is charming and the food terrific. Dishes at lunch are quite simple but great value; the cooking at dinner is a tad more elaborate.

→ Roast Isle of Orkney scallops with barley, buttermilk, miso and grilled cabbage. Shoulder of suckling pig, sprouting broccoli, white polenta and grapes. Rhubarb crumble soufflé with rhubarb ripple ice cream.

Menu £ 30 (lunch and early dinner)/48

Town plan: 21KZG-y – *5-7 Devonshire Rd* ✉ *W4 2EU* – ⊖ *Turnham Green – ℰ (020) 8747 1836 (booking essential) – www.latrompette.co.uk – Closed 24-26 December and 1 January*

✕✕ Michael Nadra

MODERN CUISINE · NEIGHBOURHOOD Hidden down a side street is this small, intimate place where the closely set tables add to the bonhomie. The cooking is influenced by the Mediterranean and the fish dishes stand out. Prices are fair and the service is warm.

Menu £ 21/37

Town plan: 21KZG-z – *6-8 Elliott Rd* ✉ *W4 1PE* – ⊖ *Turnham Green – ℰ (020) 8742 0766 – www.restaurant-michaelnadra.co.uk – Closed 24-26 December, 1 January and Sunday dinner*

✕✕ Charlotte's W4

MODERN CUISINE · NEIGHBOURHOOD A pleasant, unpretentious bistro; run by a friendly team, with a well-priced menu of flavoursome, well prepared dishes of largely European provenance. Little sister to Charlotte's Place in Ealing.

Carte £ 25/38

Town plan: 21KZG-a – *6 Turnham Green Terr* ✉ *W4 1QP* – ⊖ *Turnham Green – ℰ (020) 8742 3590 (booking advisable) – www.charlottes.co.uk – Closed 26 December and 1 January*

✕ Sam's Brasserie

MEDITERRANEAN · BRASSERIE A former Sanderson wallpaper mill, now a bustling, fun brasserie with Sir Peter Blake artwork adding to the hip feel. Appealing, modern menu; satisfying dishes deliver on flavour. Look out for regular Soul and Jazz evenings.

Menu £ 14 (lunch and early dinner) – Carte £ 22/45

Town plan: 2CV-a – *11 Barley Mow Passage* ✉ *W4 4PH* – ⊖ *Turnham Green – ℰ (020) 8987 0555 – www.samsbrasserie.co.uk – Closed 24-26 December*

✕ Vinoteca

MODERN CUISINE · NEIGHBOURHOOD Dinner bookings are a must at this 4th outpost of the group. A short menu has strong Italian roots, with dishes relying on quality ingredients for fresh flavours. Sunday is a traditional roast; Monday night, wine is at shop prices.

Menu £ 13 – Carte £ 26/38

Town plan: 21KZG-v – *18 Devonshire Rd* ✉ *W4 2HD* – ⊖ *Turnham Green – ℰ (020) 3701 8822 – www.vinoteca.co.uk – Closed 25 December*

✕ High Road Brasserie

FRENCH · FASHIONABLE Authentic brasserie, with mirrors, panelling and art deco lighting. Despite the high volume of customers, the classic dishes are prepared with care and staff cope well with being busy.

Carte £ 20/36

Town plan: 21KZG-e – *High Road House Hotel, 162 Chiswick High Rd.* ✉ *W4 1PR – ⊖ Turnham Green – ℰ (020) 8742 7474 (booking essential) – www.highroadhouse.co.uk*

Smokehouse

BRITISH TRADITIONAL · NEIGHBOURHOOD A sizeable pub with a delightful rear garden terrace is the site of the second Smokehouse. The Belted Galloway burgers with pulled pork fly out of the kitchen but the winning dish is the short rib Bourguignon with creamy mash.

Carte £ 26/36

Town plan: 6CV-s – *12 Sutton Ln North* ✉ *W4 4LD* – ⊖ *Chiswick Park*
– *⟨℘⟩ (020) 3819 6066* – *www.smokehousechiswick.co.uk*
– *Closed Monday-Thursday lunch*

© Wild Honey

ISLINGTON

Archway

✗ 500

ITALIAN · FRIENDLY Small, fun and well-priced Italian that's always busy. Good pastas and bread; the veal chop and rabbit are specialities. The passion of the ebullient owner and keen chef are evident.

Carte £ 24/31

Town plan: 12SZA-y – 782 Holloway Rd ⊠ N19 3JH – ⊖ Archway – 𝒞 (020) 7272 3406 (booking essential) – www.500restaurant.co.uk – dinner only and lunch Friday-Sunday – Closed 2 weeks summer and 2 weeks Christmas-New Year

ⅅ St John's Tavern

MODERN CUISINE · PUB Having undergone an English Heritage restoration, the pub is a beacon of hope on stubbornly unchanging Junction Road. Great bar snacks but head to the large, theatre-like dining room for robust English food with nods to the Med.

Carte £ 25/35

Town plan: 12RZA-s – 91 Junction Rd ⊠ N19 5QU – ⊖ Archway. – 𝒞 (020) 7272 1587 (booking advisable) – www.stjohnstavern.com – dinner only and lunch Friday-Sunday – Closed 25-26 December and 1 January

Barnsbury

✗✗ Roots at N1

INDIAN · NEIGHBOURHOOD A warm and welcoming Indian restaurant run with a palpable sense of pride by three friends who worked together at Benares. The menu is appealingly concise and combinations are original; tandoor cooked dishes are a highlight.

Carte £ 26/35

Town plan: 13UZB- d – 115 Hemingford Rd ⊠ N1 1BZ – ⊖ Caledonian Road – 𝒞 (020) 7697 4488 (booking essential) – www.rootsatn1.com – dinner only – Closed 25-26 December and Monday

 Prices quoted after the symbol 🛉 refer to the lowest rate for a single room in low season, followed by the highest rate in high season. The same principle applies to the symbol 🛉🛉 for a double room.

Canonbury

✗ Trullo

ITALIAN · NEIGHBOURHOOD While the ground floor has kept its well-worn, homely feel, the basement has a new, all-American look, with exposed brick, industrial ducting and red banquettes. Rustic, well-priced dishes include house specialities cooked on the charcoal grill and great pasta, hand-rolled before each service.

Carte £ 28/38

Town plan: 13UZB-t – *300-302 St Paul's Rd* ✉ *N1 2LH* – ⊖ *Highbury & Islington* – ℰ *(020) 7226 2733 (booking essential)* – *www.trullorestaurant.com* – *Closed Christmas-New Year and Sunday dinner*

✗ Canonbury Kitchen

ITALIAN · NEIGHBOURHOOD A bright, local Italian with seating for just 40; exposed brick walls and painted floorboards add to the fresh feel. The kitchen keeps things simple and the menu pricing is prudent.

Menu £ 12 – Carte £ 25/37

Town plan: 13UZB-c – *19 Canonbury Ln* ✉ *N1 2AS* – ⊖ *Highbury & Islington* – ℰ *(020) 7226 9791* – *www.canonburykitchen.com* – *dinner only and lunch Saturday-Sunday* – *Closed Sunday dinner*

✗ Primeur

MODERN CUISINE · SIMPLE Housed in a former garage, with huge concertina doors, communal and counter seating and a laid-back, quirky feel. The menu offers a mix of Mediterranean and classic British dishes, of which sharing is encouraged.

Carte £ 20/31

Town plan: 13VZA-p – *116 Petherton Rd* ✉ *N5 2RT* – ⊖ *Canonbury* – ℰ *(020) 7226 5271* – *www.primeurn5.co.uk* – *Closed Christmas, Monday, dinner Sunday and lunch Tuesday-Thursday*

⏍ Smokehouse

MODERN CUISINE · PUB You can smell the oak chips in the smoker as you approach this warm, modern pub. Meat is the mainstay – the peppered ox cheeks are a firm favourite – but whilst flavours are gutsy, the smoking and barbecuing is never overpowering.

Carte £ 26/37

Town plan: 13UZB-h – *63-69 Canonbury Rd* ✉ *N1 2DG* – ⊖ *Highbury & Islington.* – ℰ *(020) 7354 1144 (booking advisable)* – *www.smokehouseislington.co.uk* – *dinner only and lunch Saturday-Sunday* – *Closed 24-26 December*

Clerkenwell

⏍ Malmaison

TOWNHOUSE · MODERN Striking early 20C red-brick building overlooking pleasant square. Stylish, comfy public areas. Bedrooms in vivid, bold colours, with plenty of extra touches. Modern brasserie with international menu; grilled meats a highlight.

97 rooms – ♦£ 150/350 ♦♦£ 150/360 – ⧖ £ 15

Town plan: 19UZD-q – *18-21 Charterhouse Sq* ✉ *EC1M 6AH* – ⊖ *Barbican* – ℰ *(020) 7012 3700* – *www.malmaison.com*

⏍ The Rookery

TOWNHOUSE · PERSONALISED A row of charmingly restored 18C houses. Wood panelling, stone-flagged flooring, open fires and antique furniture. Highly individual bedrooms, with Victorian bathrooms.

33 rooms – ♦£ 228 ♦♦£ 294/672 – ⧖ £ 12

Town plan: 33AOT-p – *12 Peters Ln, Cowcross St* ✉ *EC1M 6DS* – ⊖ *Farringdon* – ℰ *(020) 7336 0931* – *www.rookeryhotel.com*

✗ St John

❀ BRITISH TRADITIONAL · MINIMALIST A glorious celebration of British fare and a champion of 'nose to tail eating'. Utilitarian surroundings and a refreshing lack of ceremony ensure the food is the focus; it's appealingly simple, full of flavour and very satisfying.

→ Roast bone marrow and parsley salad. Braised ox cheek, red wine and celeriac. Eccles cake and Lancashire cheese.

Carte £ 26/54

Town plan: 33APT-k – 26 St John St ✉ EC1M 4AY – ⊖ Farringdon
– ✆ (020) 7251 0848 (booking essential) – www.stjohnrestaurant.com
– Closed Christmas-New Year, Saturday lunch, Sunday dinner and bank holidays

✗ Comptoir Gascon

❀ FRENCH · BISTRO Buzzy restaurant; sister to Club Gascon. Rustic and satisfying specialities from the SW of France include wine, cheese, bread and plenty of duck, with cassoulet and duck rillettes perennial favourites – and the duck burger popular at lunch. Great value set 3 course menu. Produce on display to take home.

Menu £ 16 (weekday lunch) – Carte £ 23/44

Town plan: 33AOT-a – 61-63 Charterhouse St. ✉ EC1M 6HJ – ⊖ Farringdon
– ✆ (020) 7608 0851 (booking essential) – www.comptoirgascon.com
– Closed Christmas-New Year, Sunday, Monday and bank holidays

✗ Polpo Smithfield

❀ ITALIAN · FRIENDLY For his third Venetian-style bacaro, Russell Norman converted an old meat market storage facility; it has an elegantly battered feel. Head first for the Negroni bar downstairs; then over-order tasty, uncomplicated and very satisfying dishes to share. Bookings only taken up to 5.30pm.

Carte £ 12/26

Town plan: 33AOT-s – 3 Cowcross St ✉ EC1M 6DR – ⊖ Farringdon. – ✆ (020) 7250 0034 – www.polpo.co.uk – Closed Christmas, New Year and Sunday dinner

✗ Granger & Co Clerkenwell

MODERN CUISINE · FAMILY Aussie food writer and restaurateur Bill Granger's 2nd London branch is a stylish affair. His food is inspired by his travels, with the best dishes being those enlivened with the flavours of SE Asia; his breakfasts are also renowned.

Carte £ 28/30

Town plan: 19UZD-y – 50 Sekford Street ✉ EC1R 0HA – ⊖ Farringdon
– ✆ (020) 7251 9032 – www.grangerandco.com – Closed Sunday dinner

✗ Foxlow

MEATS · NEIGHBOURHOOD From the clever Hawksmoor people comes this fun and funky place where the staff ensure everyone's having a good time. There are steaks available but plenty of other choices with influences from Italy, Asia and the Middle East.

Carte £ 19/38

Town plan: 19UZD-a – 69-73 St John St ✉ EC1M 4AN – ⊖ Farringdon
– ✆ (020) 7014 8070 – www.foxlow.co.uk – Closed 24 December-1 January, Sunday dinner and bank holidays

✗ Hix Oyster and Chop House

BRITISH TRADITIONAL · BISTRO Appropriately utilitarian surroundings put the focus on seasonal and often underused British ingredients. Cooking is satisfying and unfussy, with plenty of oysters and aged beef served on the bone.

Carte £ 30/55

Town plan: 33AOT-e – 36-37 Greenhill Rents ✉ EC1M 6BN – ⊖ Farringdon
– ✆ (020) 7017 1930 – www.hixoysterandchophouse.co.uk – Closed 25-29 December, Saturday lunch and bank holidays

✗ Vinoteca   ⚗ 🅐🅒 ↔

MODERN CUISINE · BISTRO This cosy and enthusiastically run 'bar and wine shop' is always busy and full of life. The thrilling wine list is constantly evolving and the classic European dishes, cured meats and cheeses are ideal accompaniments.

Carte £ 20/33

Town plan: 33APT-a – *7 St John St.* ✉ *EC1M 4AA* – ⊖ *Farringdon* – ℰ *(020) 7253 8786* – *www.vinoteca.co.uk* – *Closed 25 December, 1 January, Sunday and bank holidays*

Finsbury

🏠 South Place   ⚗ 🛋 🝰 🅐🅒 🔌

BUSINESS · STYLISH Restaurant group D&D's first venture into the hotel business is a stylish affair; unsurprising as its interior was designed by Conran & Partners. Bedrooms are a treat for those with an eye for aesthetics and no detail has been forgotten. The ground floor hosts 3 South Place, a bustling bar and grill.

80 rooms – ♦£ 200/450 ♦♦£ 350/450 – ☑ £ 25 – 1 suite

Town plan: 34ART-v – *3 South Pl* ✉ *EC2M 2AF* – ⊖ *Moorgate* – ℰ *(020) 3503 0000* – *www.southplacehotel.com*

⚜ **Angler** – See restaurant listing

🏠 Zetter   ⚗ 🝰 🅐🅒 🔌 🐾 📷 🌡

TOWNHOUSE · MODERN A trendy and discreet converted 19C warehouse with well-equipped bedrooms that come with pleasant touches, such as Penguin paperbacks. The more idiosyncratic Zetter Townhouse across the square is used as an overflow.

59 rooms – ♦£ 186/270 ♦♦£ 186/270 – ☑ £ 14

Town plan: 19UZD-s – *St John's Sq, 86-88 Clerkenwell Rd.* ✉ *EC1M 5RJ* – ⊖ *Farringdon* – ℰ *(020) 7324 4444* – *www.thezetter.com*

✗✗ Angler   ⚗ 🍽 🝰 🅐🅒

⚜ **FISH AND SEAFOOD · ELEGANT** The rooftop restaurant of D&D's South Place hotel is a bright, light and very comfortable space; its adjoining bar and terrace the perfect spot for a pre-prandial cocktail. The menu champions the best of British seafood and the freshness of the ingredients really shines through.

→ Yellowfin tuna tartare, lime, chilli and avocado. Steamed wild sea bass, crab-crushed Pink Fir potatoes and sauce vierge. Chocolate fondant and pistachio ice cream.

Menu £ 35 (weekdays) – Carte £ 37/73

Town plan: 34ART-v – *South Place Hotel, 3 South Pl* ✉ *EC2M 2AF* – ⊖ *Moorgate* – ℰ *(020) 3215 1260 (booking advisable)* – *www.anglerrestaurant.com* – *Closed 26-30 December, Saturday lunch and Sunday*

✗ Quality Chop House   ⚗ 🅐🅒 ↔

BRITISH TRADITIONAL · CLASSIC Back in the hands of owners who respect its history, this 'progressive working class caterer' is once again championing gusty British grub. It also has a terrific, concise wine list with plenty of gems. The Grade II listed room, with its trademark booths, has been an eating house since 1869.

Menu £ 39 (weekday dinner) – Carte £ 22/62

Town plan: 19UZD-h – *92-94 Farringdon Rd* ✉ *EC1R 3EA* – ⊖ *Farringdon* – ℰ *(020) 7278 1452 (booking advisable)* – *www.thequalitychophouse.com* – *Closed Sunday dinner and bank holidays*

✗ Moro   ⚗ 🝰 🅐🅒

MEDITERRANEAN · FRIENDLY It's the stuff of dreams – pack up your worldly goods, drive through Spain, Portugal, Morocco and the Sahara and then back in London open a restaurant and share your love of Moorish cuisine. The wood-fired oven and chargrill fill the air with wonderful aromas and food is vibrant and colourful.

Carte £ 32/42

Town plan: 19UZD-m – *34-36 Exmouth Mkt* ✉ *EC1R 4QE* – ⊖ *Farringdon* – ℰ *(020) 7833 8336 (booking essential)* – *www.moro.co.uk* – *Closed dinner 24 December-2 January, Sunday dinner and bank holidays*

✗ Morito

SPANISH · INTIMATE From the owners of next door Moro comes this authentic and appealingly down to earth little tapas bar. Seven or eight dishes between two should suffice but over-ordering is easy and won't break the bank.

Carte £14/26

Town plan: 19UZD-b – *32 Exmouth Mkt ⊠ EC1R 4QE* – ⊖ *Farringdon*
– *𝒞 (020) 7278 7007* – *www.morito.co.uk*
– *Closed 24 December-2 January, Sunday dinner and bank holidays*

✗ The Modern Pantry

WORLD CUISINE · DESIGN Fusion cooking that uses complementary flavours to create vibrant, zesty dishes. The simple, crisp ground floor of this Georgian building has the buzz; upstairs is more intimate. Clued-up service.

Menu £23 (weekday lunch)/45 – Carte £26/39

Town plan: 19UZD-k – *47-48 St John's Sq. ⊠ EC1V 4JJ* – ⊖ *Farringdon*
– *𝒞 (020) 7553 9210 (booking advisable)* – *www.themodernpantry.co.uk*
– *Closed August bank holiday and 25-26 December*

✗ Caravan

WORLD CUISINE · TRENDY A discernible Antipodean vibe pervades this casual eatery, from the laid-back charm of the service to the kitchen's confident combining of unusual flavours. Cooking is influenced by owner's travels – hence the name.

Carte £19/45

Town plan: 19UZD-c – *11-13 Exmouth Market ⊠ EC1R 4QD* – ⊖ *Farringdon*
– *𝒞 (020) 7833 8115 (booking advisable)* – *www.caravanonexmouth.co.uk*

✗ Clerkenwell Kitchen

MODERN CUISINE · FRIENDLY The owner of this simple, friendly, tucked away eatery worked with Hugh Fearnley-Whittingstall and is committed to sustainability. Daily changing, well-sourced produce; fresh, flavoursome cooking.

Carte £15/26

Town plan: 19UZD-v – *27-31 Clerkenwell Cl ⊠ EC1R 0AT* – ⊖ *Farringdon*
– *𝒞 (020) 7101 9959 (booking advisable)* – *www.theclerkenwellkitchen.co.uk*
– *lunch only – Closed Christmas-New Year, Saturday, Sunday and bank holidays*

⅊ Well

BRITISH MODERN · PUB This well-supported local pub from the Martin Brothers comes with the sort of food that is reassuringly familiar yet done well, and service that instils confidence. Eat on the ground floor, rather than in the less welcoming basement.

Carte £23/41

Town plan: 19UZD-x – *180 St John St ⊠ EC1V 4JY* – ⊖ *Farringdon.*
– *𝒞 (020) 7251 9363* – *www.downthewell.com*
– *Closed 25-26 December*

Highbury

✗ Au Lac

VIETNAMESE · FRIENDLY Sweet, longstanding Vietnamese restaurant run by two brothers. New dishes are regularly added to the already lengthy but authentic and keenly priced menu, whose dishes exhibit plenty of fresh and lively flavours.

Carte £12/24

Town plan: 13UZA-b – *82 Highbury Park ⊠ N5 2XE* – ⊖ *Arsenal*
– *𝒞 (020) 7704 9187* – *www.aulac.co.uk* – *dinner only and lunch Thursday-Friday*
– *Closed 24-26 December, 1-2 January and 1 week early August*

Islington

XX Almeida

BRITISH MODERN • BRASSERIE Opposite the award-winning theatre of the same name is this smoothly run, sophisticated restaurant. The kitchen uses European and British influences to create confident and at times innovative dishes which allow the main ingredient to shine.

Menu £19 (lunch and early dinner) – Carte £33/54

Town plan: 13UZB-r – *30 Almeida St. ✉ N1 1AD – ⊖ Angel – ☎ (020) 7354 4777 – www.almeida-restaurant.com – Closed 26 December, 1 January, Sunday dinner and Monday lunch*

X Ottolenghi

MEDITERRANEAN • FASHIONABLE You've bought the book; now see how the dish is meant to taste at Yotam Ottolenghi's deli/restaurant. The freshness is palpable, with flavours from the Med, North Africa and Middle East. You'll never think of salad in the same way.

Carte £17/30

Town plan: 13UZB-k – *287 Upper St. ✉ N1 2TZ – ⊖ Highbury & Islington – ☎ (020) 7288 1454 (booking essential) – www.ottolenghi.co.uk – Closed 25-26 December, and dinner Sunday and bank holidays*

X Yipin China

CHINESE • SIMPLE The menu at this modest little place features Hunanese, Cantonese and Sichuanese specialities, but it is the spicy, chilli-based dishes from Hunan province which use techniques like smoking and curing that really stand out.

Carte £19/42

Town plan: 13UZB-b – *70-72 Liverpool Rd ✉ N1 0QD – ⊖ Angel – ☎ (020) 7354 3388 – www.yipinchina.co.uk – Closed 25 December*

X Vintage Salt

FISH AND CHIPS • RUSTIC Not exactly your average chippy – there are cocktails, weekend brunches and starters like crab on toast. Butties are fun for a quick snack but most come for Camden Hells battered fish. They do takeaway and more shops are planned.

Carte £15/35

Town plan: 13UZB-s – *189 Upper St ✉ N1 1RQ – ⊖ Highbury and Islington – ☎ (020) 3227 0979 (booking essential at dinner) – www.thefishandchipshop.uk.com – Closed 25 December*

Drapers Arms

BRITISH MODERN • NEIGHBOURHOOD Anyone unfamiliar with Britain's bounteous larder should get along to this down-to-earth Georgian pub to enjoy ingredients like lamb's tongues, smoked eel, blade steak and rabbit in dishes that are satisfying, gutsy and affordable.

Carte £20/34

Town plan: 13UZB-x – *44 Barnsbury St ✉ N1 1ER – ⊖ Highbury & Islington. – ☎ (020) 7619 0348 (bookings advisable at dinner) – www.thedrapersarms.com – Closed 25-26 December*

Pig and Butcher

BRITISH TRADITIONAL • PUB Dating from the mid-19C, when cattle drovers taking livestock to Smithfield Market would stop for a swift one, and now fully restored. There's a strong British element to the daily menu; meat is butchered and smoked in-house.

Carte £28/43

Town plan: 13UZB-e – *80 Liverpool Rd ✉ N1 0QD – ⊖ Angel. – ☎ (020) 7226 8304 (booking advisable) – www.thepigandbutcher.co.uk – dinner only and lunch Friday-Sunday – Closed 25-27 December*

© Michelin

KENSINGTON and CHELSEA
(ROYAL BOROUGH OF)
Chelsea

🏨 Jumeirah Carlton Tower

GRAND LUXURY · MODERN Imposing international hotel overlooking a leafy square and just yards from all the swanky boutiques. Well-equipped rooftop health club has great views. Generously proportioned bedrooms boast every conceivable facility.

216 rooms – 🛏£ 350/835 🛏£ 350/835 – ☕£ 32 – 50 suites
Town plan: 37AGX-r – *Cadogan Pl* ✉ *SW1X 9PY* – ⊖ *Knightsbridge* – ✆ *(020) 7235 1234* – *jumeirah.com/jct*
Rib Room – See restaurant listing

🏨 Chelsea Harbour

LUXURY · MODERN Formerly called Wyndham Grand. Modern hotel within an exclusive marina and retail development. Many of the large, well-appointed rooms have balconies for views across the Thames. Bright restaurant offers a wide-ranging menu.

157 rooms – 🛏£ 220/300 🛏£ 220/300 – ☕£ 24
Town plan: 23PZG-k – *Chelsea Harbour* ✉ *SW10 0XG* – ⊖ *Imperial Wharf* – ✆ *(020) 7823 3000* – *www.thechelseaharbourhotel.co.uk*

🏨 Park Tower Knightsbridge

LUXURY · MODERN Built in the 1970s in a unique cylindrical shape. The well-equipped bedrooms are all identical in size. Top floor executive rooms come with commanding views of Hyde Park and The City.

258 rooms – 🛏£ 279/759 🛏£ 279/759 – ☕£ 29 – 22 suites
Town plan: 37AGX-t – *101 Knightsbridge* ✉ *SW1X 7RN* – ⊖ *Knightsbridge* – ✆ *(020) 7235 8050* – *www.theparktowerknightsbridge.com*
One-O-One – See restaurant listing

🏨 The Capital

LUXURY · CLASSIC This fine, thoroughly British hotel has been under the same private ownership for over 40 years. Known for its discreet atmosphere, conscientious and attentive service and immaculately kept bedrooms courtesy of different designers.

49 rooms – 🛏£ 250/355 🛏£ 295/550 – ☕£ 17 – 1 suite
Town plan: 37AFX-a – *22-24 Basil St.* ✉ *SW3 1AT* – ⊖ *Knightsbridge* – ✆ *(020) 7589 5171* – *www.capitalhotel.co.uk*
❀ **Outlaw's at The Capital** – See restaurant listing

Draycott

TOWNHOUSE · STYLISH Charming 19C house with elegant sitting room overlooking tranquil garden for afternoon tea. Bedrooms are individually decorated in a country house style and are named after writers or actors.

35 rooms – **♦**£ 192/199 **♦♦**£ 378/558 – ☲ £ 22

Town plan: 37AGY-c – *26 Cadogan Gdns* ✉ *SW3 2RP* – ⊖ *Sloane Square*
– *℘ (020) 7730 6466* – *www.draycotthotel.com*

Egerton House

TOWNHOUSE · CLASSIC Compact but comfortable townhouse in a very good location, well-maintained throughout and owned by the Red Carnation group. High levels of personal service make the hotel stand out.

28 rooms – **♦**£ 295/425 **♦♦**£ 295/425 – ☲ £ 29

Town plan: 37AFY-e – *17-19 Egerton Terr* ✉ *SW3 2BX* – ⊖ *South Kensington*
– *℘ (020) 7589 2412* – *www.egertonhousehotel.com*

Knightsbridge

LUXURY · STYLISH Charming and attractively furnished townhouse in a Victorian terrace, with a very stylish, discreet feel. Every bedroom is immaculately appointed and has a style all of its own; fine detailing throughout.

44 rooms – **♦**£ 234/250 **♦♦**£ 264/475 – ☲ £ 18

Town plan: 37AFX-s – *10 Beaufort Gdns* ✉ *SW3 1PT* – ⊖ *Knightsbridge*
– *℘ (020) 7584 6300* – *www.knightsbridgehotel.com*

The Levin

TOWNHOUSE · CLASSIC A discreet townhouse and sister to The Capital next door. Impressive façade, contemporary interior and comfortable bedrooms in subtle art deco style, with marvellous champagne mini bars. Simple dishes served all day down at Le Metro.

12 rooms ☲ – **♦**£ 204/316 **♦♦**£ 204/316

Town plan: 37AFX-c – *28 Basil St.* ✉ *SW3 1AS* – ⊖ *Knightsbridge* – *℘ (020) 7589 6286* – *www.thelevinhotel.co.uk*

No.11 Cadogan Gardens

TOWNHOUSE · STYLISH Townhouse hotel fashioned out of four red-brick houses and exuberantly dressed in bold colours and furnishings. Theatrically decorated bedrooms vary in size from cosy to spacious. Intimate basement Italian restaurant with accomplished and ambitious cooking.

56 rooms – **♦**£ 270/450 **♦♦**£ 270/450 – ☲ £ 22 – 19 suites

Town plan: 37AGY-n – *11 Cadogan Gdns* ✉ *SW3 2RJ* – ⊖ *Sloane Square*
– *℘ (020) 7730 7000* – *www.no11cadogangardens.com*

Beaufort

TRADITIONAL · CLASSIC A vast collection of English floral watercolours adorn this 19C townhouse, set in a useful location. Modern and co-ordinated rooms. Tariff includes all drinks and afternoon tea.

29 rooms – **♦**£ 168/228 **♦♦**£ 228/312 – ☲ £ 16

Town plan: 37AFX-n – *33 Beaufort Gdns* ✉ *SW3 1PP* – ⊖ *Knightsbridge*
– *℘ (020) 7584 5252* – *www.thebeaufort.co.uk*

Sydney House

TOWNHOUSE · MODERN Stylish and compact Georgian townhouse made brighter through plenty of mirrors and light wood. Thoughtfully designed bedrooms; Room 43 has its own terrace. Part of the Abode group.

21 rooms – **♦**£ 125/355 **♦♦**£ 125/355 – ☲ £ 12

Town plan: 36ADY-s – *9-11 Sydney St.* ✉ *SW3 6PU* – ⊖ *South Kensington*
– *℘ (020) 7376 7711* – *www.sydneyhousechelsea.co.uk*
– *Closed 25-29 December*

🏠 The Sloane Square ✿ 🖨 🛗 AK ❄ 🛋

BUSINESS · MODERN Well-placed, red-brick hotel boasting bright, contemporary décor. Stylish, co-ordinated bedrooms, with laptops; library of DVDs and games available. Rooms at the back are slightly quieter.

102 rooms – ♦£ 150/250 ♦♦£ 170/295 – ⚏ £ 15

Town plan: 37AGY-k – *7-12 Sloane Sq.* ✉ *SW1W 8EG* – ⊖ *Sloane Square*
– *𝒞 (020) 7896 9988* – *www.sloanesquarehotel.co.uk*

XxxX Gordon Ramsay (Clare Smyth) 🕸 AK 🕥

❀❀❀ **FRENCH · FORMAL** Attention to detail ensures that Gordon Ramsay's flagship restaurant still provides the consummate dining experience. Composed, reassuring and discreet service adds to the calmness of the room; Clare Smyth's cooking is poised, elegant and a little more daring.

➔ Cornish crab with radish, kombu and sesame & oyster emulsion. Roast pigeon with fennel, foie gras, lavender, honey and orange. Poached Yorkshire rhubarb with Tahitian vanilla parfait, lemon balm and olive oil.

Menu £ 65/110

Town plan: 37AFZ-c – *68-69 Royal Hospital Rd.* ✉ *SW3 4HP*
– ⊖ *Sloane Square* – *𝒞 (020) 7352 4441 (booking essential)*
– *www.gordonramsay.com* – *Closed 21-28 December, Saturday and Sunday*

XxX Bibendum 🕸 AK 🕥

FRENCH · DESIGN Located on the 1st floor of a London landmark – Michelin's former HQ, dating from 1911. French food comes with a British accent and there's fresh seafood served in the oyster bar below. It's maintained a loyal following for over 20 years.

Menu £ 34 (weekdays) – Carte £ 27/63

Town plan: 37AEY-s – *Michelin House, 81 Fulham Rd.* ✉ *SW3 6RD*
– ⊖ *South Kensington* – *𝒞 (020) 7581 5817* – *www.bibendum.co.uk* – *Closed dinner 24 December, 25-26 December and 1 January*

XxX Rib Room ⇔ 🚗

MEATS · ELEGANT Rib of Aberdeen Angus, steaks and other classic British dishes attract a prosperous, international crowd; few of whom appear to have a beef with the prices at this swish veteran.

Menu £ 28 (weekday lunch) – Carte £ 50/120

Town plan: 37AGX-r – *Jumeirah Carlton Tower Hotel, Cadogan Pl* ✉ *SW1X 9PY*
– ⊖ *Knightsbridge* – *𝒞 (020) 7858 7250* – *www.theribroom.co.uk*

XxX Five Fields 🛗 AK ⇔

MODERN CUISINE · FORMAL Expect some rather daring combinations on the plate, along with bold flavours; desserts have a unique identity all of their own. This formally run restaurant may be comparatively small but it comes with a warm, intimate feel.

Menu £ 45/80

Town plan: 37AFY-s – *8-9 Blacklands Terr* ✉ *SW3 2SP* – ⊖ *Sloane Square*
– *𝒞 (020) 7838 1082* – *www.fivefieldsrestaurant.com* – *dinner only* – *Closed Christmas-mid January, first 2 weeks August, Sunday and Monday*

XxX One-O-One AK

FISH AND SEAFOOD · FORMAL Smart ground floor restaurant; it's lacking a little in atmosphere but the seafood is good. Much of the excellent produce is from Brittany and Norway; don't miss the King crab legs which are the stars of the show.

Menu £ 23 (lunch and early dinner) – Carte £ 47/107

Town plan: 37AGX-t – *Park Tower Knightsbridge Hotel, 101 Knightsbridge*
✉ *SW1X 7RN* – ⊖ *Knightsbridge* – *𝒞 (020) 7290 7101*
– *www.oneoonerestaurant.com*

XxX Toto's   🛋 AK

ITALIAN · ELEGANT A Chelsea institution returned in 2014, when new owners reopened this discreet Italian restaurant for grown-ups. The kitchen has made the food more contemporary without doing anything to alarm those with more traditional tastes.

Carte £43/91

Town plan: 37AFY-b – *Walton House, Lennox Garden Mews* ✉ *SW3 2JH – (off Walton St) –* ⊖ *South Kensington –* ✆ *(020) 7589 2062 (booking essential at dinner) – www.totosrestaurant.com*

XxX Fifth Floor at Harvey Nichols   ⅋ AK

MODERN CUISINE · FASHIONABLE The room has had more makeovers than many of its glamorous customers but now the cooking has also changed. It's still largely European in its influences but dishes are elaborately constructed and considerably more sophisticated.

Carte £24/51

Town plan: 37AGX-s – *109-125 Knightsbridge* ✉ *SW1X 7RJ –* ⊖ *Knightsbridge –* ✆ *(020) 7235 5250 – www.harveynichols.com – Closed Christmas, Easter and Sunday dinner*

XX Outlaw's at The Capital   ⅋ 🍷 AK 🎧 ⇄ 🚗
ⵣ   FISH AND SEAFOOD · FORMAL Chef Nathan Outlaw brings his award-winning formula up from Cornwall: great seafood where the quality of the fish shines through and the flavours harmonise perfectly. The well-structured wine list features the ever popular Levin Sauvignon Blanc from the owner's own estate in the Loire.

→ Lobster risotto, orange, basil and spring onion. Hake with crab, asparagus and crab dressing. Raspberry and treacle tart with clotted cream.

Menu £27/55

Town plan: 37AFX-a – *The Capital Hotel, 22-24 Basil St.* ✉ *SW3 1AT –* ⊖ *Knightsbridge –* ✆ *(020) 7591 1202 (booking essential) – www.capitalhotel.co.uk – Closed Sunday*

XX Rasoi   AK 🎧 ⇄

INDIAN · INTIMATE With outposts in Geneva, Mauritius and Dubai, Vineet Bhatia proves that Indian food is as open to innovation and interpretation as any other cuisine. His exotically decorated dining room sits within an archetypical Chelsea townhouse.

Menu £24/89 – Carte £66/99

Town plan: 37AFY-y – *10 Lincoln St* ✉ *SW3 2TS –* ⊖ *Sloane Square –* ✆ *(020) 7225 1881 – www.rasoirestaurant.co.uk – Closed 25-26 December, 1-2 January, Saturday lunch and Monday.*

XX Medlar   ⅋ 🛋 AK ⇄

MODERN CUISINE · NEIGHBOURHOOD A charming, comfortable and very popular restaurant with a real sense of neighbourhood, from two alumni of Chez Bruce. The service is engaging and unobtrusive; the cooking is quite elaborate and comes with a classical base.

Menu £28 (weekday lunch)/46

Town plan: 23PZG-x – *438 King's Rd* ✉ *SW10 0LJ –* ⊖ *South Kensington –* ✆ *(020) 7349 1900 – www.medlarrestaurant.co.uk – Closed 24-26 December and 1 January*

XX Masala Grill 🆕   🍷 AK ⇄

INDIAN · EXOTIC When the owners moved Chutney Mary to St James's after 25 years they wisely installed another Indian restaurant in her place. It's still awash with colour and vitality but is less expensive and more varied in its influences.

Carte £28/39

Town plan: 22QZG-v – *535 King's Rd* ✉ *SW10 0SZ –* ⊖ *Fulham Broadway –* ✆ *(020) 7351 7788 – www.masalagrill.co.uk – dinner only and Sunday lunch*

XX Le Colombier

FRENCH · NEIGHBOURHOOD Proudly Gallic corner restaurant in an affluent residential area. Attractive enclosed terrace. Bright and cheerful surroundings and service; traditional French cooking.

Menu £ 20 (lunch) – Carte £ 34/66

Town plan: 36ADZ-e – *145 Dovehouse St.* ⊠ *SW3 6LB* – ⊖ *South Kensington* – *𝒞 (020) 7351 1155* – *www.le-colombier-restaurant.co.uk*

XX Eight over Eight

ASIAN · FASHIONABLE Reopened after a fire, with a slightly plusher feel; still as popular as ever with the fashionable crowds. Influences stretch across South East Asia and dishes are designed for sharing.

Menu £ 35/50 – Carte £ 15/45

Town plan: 23PZG-s – *392 King's Rd* ⊠ *SW3 5UZ* – ⊖ *South Kensington* – *𝒞 (020) 7349 9934* – *www.rickerrestaurants.com* – *Closed 25 December and 1 January*

XX Painted Heron

INDIAN · FORMAL Smart, well-supported and quite formally run Indian restaurant. Nooks and crannies create an intimate atmosphere; and there's a heated cigar terrace. Fish and game dishes are the highlights of the contemporary cooking.

Menu £ 15 (lunch) – Carte £ 25/35

Town plan: 23PZG-d – *112 Cheyne Walk* ⊠ *SW10 0DJ* – ⊖ *Fulham Broadway* – *𝒞 (020) 7351 5232* – *www.thepaintedheron.com* – *Closed 1 January and lunch bank holidays*

XX Bluebird

BRITISH MODERN · DESIGN Not just for a night out with friends – with a foodstore, cellar, bakery, café and courtyard there's enough here for a day out too. Big menu to match the big room: everything from British classics to steaks, salads and shellfish.

Menu £ 20 (lunch and early dinner) – Carte £ 27/69

Town plan: 23PZG-n – *350 King's Rd.* ⊠ *SW3 5UU* – ⊖ *South Kensington* – *𝒞 (020) 7559 1000* – *www.bluebird-restaurant.co.uk*

XX Hawksmoor

MEATS · BRASSERIE The Hawksmoor people turned to rarefied Knightsbridge for their 5th London branch. Steak is still the star of the show but here there's also plenty of fish and seafood. Art deco elegance and friendly service compensate for the basement site.

Menu £ 27 (weekday lunch) – Carte £ 28/163

Town plan: 37AFX-r – *3 Yeoman's Row* ⊠ *SW3 2AL* – ⊖ *South Kensington* – *𝒞 (020) 7590 9290* – *www.thehawksmoor.com* – *Closed 24-26 December and 1 January*

XX Maze Grill Park Walk

MEATS · FASHIONABLE The site of Aubergine, where it all started for Gordon Ramsay, now specialises in steaks. Dry-aged in-house, the meats are cooked on a fierce bit of kit called a Montague grill. There's another Maze Grill close by in Royal Hospital Road.

Carte £ 24/60

Town plan: 36ACZ-x – *11 Park Walk* ⊠ *SW10 0AJ* – ⊖ *South Kensington* – *𝒞 (020) 7255 9299* – *www.gordonramsay.com/mazegrill/park-walk*

XX Brasserie Gustave

FRENCH · BRASSERIE All the traditional French favourites are here, from snails to boeuf Bourguignon and rum baba, all prepared in a way to make Escoffier proud. Studded leather seating and Art Deco-style posters complete the classic brasserie look.

Menu £ 39 – Carte £ 29/68

Town plan: 36ADY-v – *4 Sydney St* ⊠ *SW3 6PP* – ⊖ *South Kensington* – *𝒞 (020) 7352 1712* – *www.brasserie-gustave.com*

XX il trillo

ITALIAN · FRIENDLY The Bertuccelli family have been making wine and running a restaurant in the Tuscan Hills for over 30 years. Two of the brothers now run this smart local which showcases the produce and wine from their region. Delightful courtyard.

Menu £ 29 – Carte £ 29/57

Town plan: 36ACZ-s – *4 Hollywood Rd* ⊠ *SW10 9HY* – ↔ *Earl's Court*
– ℰ (020) 3602 1759 – www.iltrillo.net – dinner only and lunch Saturday-Sunday
– Closed 25-26 December

XX Colbert

FRENCH · BRASSERIE With its posters, chessboard tiles and red leather seats, Colbert bears more than a passing resemblance to a Parisian pavement café. It's an all-day, every day operation with French classics from croque monsieur to steak Diane.

Carte £ 19/65

Town plan: 37AGY-t – *50-52 Sloane Sq* ⊠ *SW1W 8AX* – ↔ *Sloane Square*
– ℰ (020) 7730 2804 (booking advisable) – www.colbertchelsea.com – Closed 25 December and dinner 24 December

XX Manicomio

ITALIAN · FASHIONABLE Modern, busy Italian, popular with shoppers and visitors to the Saatchi Gallery; the simplest dishes are the best ones. The terrific terrace fills quickly. Next door is their café and deli.

Menu £ 24 (lunch and early dinner) – Carte £ 29/46

Town plan: 37AGY-x – *85 Duke of York Sq, King's Rd* ⊠ *SW3 4LY*
– ↔ Sloane Square – ℰ (020) 7730 3366 – www.manicomio.co.uk – Closed 25-26 December

XX Good Earth

CHINESE · ELEGANT The menu might appear predictable but this long-standing Chinese has always proved a reliable choice in this area. Although there's no particular geographical bias, the cooking is carefully executed and dishes are authentic.

Carte £ 27/51

Town plan: 37AFY-h – *233 Brompton Rd.* ⊠ *SW3 2EP* – ↔ *Knightsbridge*
– ℰ (020) 7584 3658 – www.goodearthgroup.co.uk – Closed 23-31 December

XX Marco

FRENCH · BRASSERIE Marco Pierre White's brasserie at Chelsea Football Club offers an appealing range of classics, from British favourites to satisfying French and Italian fare; puddings are a highlight. Comfortable and well-run room.

Carte £ 24/44

Town plan: 22OZG-c – *Stamford Bridge, Fulham Rd.* ⊠ *SW6 1HS*
– ↔ Fulham Broadway – ℰ (020) 7915 2929 (booking advisable)
– www.marcogrill.com – dinner only – Closed Sunday-Monday

XX The Botanist

MODERN CUISINE · TRENDY Push through the busy bar to get to this stylish, comfortable restaurant. An extensive menu; the simplest dishes are usually the best ones. Open all day and useful for a bite before curtain-up at The Royal Court or Cadogan Hall.

Menu £ 21 (dinner) – Carte £ 29/54

Town plan: 37AGY-r – *7 Sloane Sq* ⊠ *SW1W 8EE* – ↔ *Sloane Square* – *ℰ (020) 7730 0077 – www.thebotanistlondon.com – Closed 25-26 December*

X Bo Lang

CHINESE · TRENDY It's all about dim sum at this diminutive Hakkasan wannabe. The kitchen has a deft touch but stick to the more traditional combinations; come with friends for the cocktails and to mitigate the effects of some ambitious pricing.

Menu £ 22 (weekday lunch) – Carte £ 25/48

Town plan: 37AFY-a – *100 Draycott Ave* ⊠ *SW3 3AD* – ↔ *South Kensington*
– ℰ (020) 7823 7887 – www.bolangrestaurant.com

X **Rabbit**

BRITISH MODERN · RUSTIC The Gladwin brothers have followed the success of The Shed with another similarly rustic and warmly run restaurant. Share satisfying, robustly flavoured plates, with game a real highlight – particularly the rabbit dishes.

Menu £ 28/42 – Carte £ 22/32

Town plan: 23QZF-r – *172 King's Rd* ⊠ *SW3 4UP* – ⊖ *Sloane Square* – ℰ *(020) 3750 0172 – www.rabbit-restaurant.com – Closed 22 December-2 January*

X **Henry Root**

FRENCH · NEIGHBOURHOOD William Donaldson satirised many of the good and the great of his day through the letters of his alter ego, Henry Root. His name lives on in this cheery local spot, with its appealing menu that includes small plates and charcuterie.

Carte £ 22/41

Town plan: 36ACZ-z – *9 Park Walk* ⊠ *SW10 0AJ* – ⊖ *South Kensington* – ℰ *(020) 7352 7040 (booking advisable) – www.thehenryroot.com – Closed 25-28 December*

X **Tom's Kitchen**

MODERN CUISINE · NEIGHBOURHOOD A converted pub, whose white tiles and mirrors help to give it an industrial feel. Appealing and wholesome dishes come in man-sized portions. The eponymous Tom is Tom Aikens.

Carte £ 26/48

Town plan: 37AFZ-b – *27 Cale St.* ⊠ *SW3 3QP* – ⊖ *South Kensington* – ℰ *(020) 7349 0202 – www.tomskitchen.co.uk – Closed 25-26 December*

X **Galvin Demoiselle**

FRENCH · SIMPLE The Galvin brothers' café overlooks Harrods food hall. The light, French-accented menu is ideal for the busy shopper. You'll find a different soup each day, salads, charcuterie, cocottes and their popular baked lobster fishcake.

Menu £ 29 – Carte £ 29/52

Town plan: 37AFX-x – *Ground Floor Food Hall, Harrods, 87-135 Brompton Rd* ⊠ *SW1X 7XL* – ⊖ *Knightsbridge* – ℰ *(020) 7893 8590 – www.galvinrestaurants.com – lunch only – Closed 25 December and Sunday dinner*

X **Geales**

FISH AND SEAFOOD · FRIENDLY Fish and chips are the main draw at this cosy, warmly run and sweetly decorated spot. Other choices can include fish pie and soft shell crab tempura, along with wholesome, homemade puddings.

Menu £ 13 (weekday lunch) – Carte £ 18/41

Town plan: 37AFZ-n – *1 Cale St* ⊠ *SW3 3QT* – ⊖ *South Kensington* – ℰ *(020) 7965 0555 – http://www.geales.com/chelsea-green/welcome – Closed 22 December-3 January and Monday*

🍴 **Admiral Codrington**

MODERN CUISINE · PUB Busy front bar and a separate, rather smart restaurant with a retractable roof. Head for the more familiar dishes from the monthly-changing menu. Beef is big here and is aged in-house; burgers are very popular. A Chelsea institution.

Carte £ 25/43

Town plan: 37AFY-v – *17 Mossop St* ⊠ *SW3 2LY* – ⊖ *South Kensington. – ℰ *(020) 7581 0005 – www.theadmiralcodrington.com – Closed 24-26 December*

🍴 **Cross Keys**

MODERN CUISINE · PUB Chelsea's oldest pub, dating from 1708, reopened in 2015 having been saved from property developers. The place has genuine character and warmth. The style of cooking is largely contemporary, although there are also dishes for traditionalists.

Menu £ 20 (weekday lunch) – Carte £ 28/50

Town plan: 23PZG-r – *1 Lawrence St* ⊠ *SW3 5NB* – ⊖ *Sloane Square* – ℰ *(020) 7351 0686 – www.thecrosskeyschelsea.co.uk – Closed 25 and dinner 24 December*

🍴 Builders Arms   AC

BRITISH TRADITIONAL · PUB Smart looking and busy pub for the Chelsea set; drinkers are welcomed as much as diners. Cooking reveals the effort put into sourcing decent ingredients; rib of beef for two is a favourite. Thoughtfully compiled wine list.

Carte £ 18/41

Town plan: 37AFZ-x – *13 Britten St ⊠ SW3 3TY –* ⊖ *South Kensington.*
– ☎ *(020) 7349 9040 (bookings not accepted) – www.geronimo-inns.co.uk*

🍴 Pig's Ear   AC

BRITISH TRADITIONAL · PUB Honest pub, with rough-and-ready ground floor bar for lunch; more intimate, wood-panelled upstairs dining room for dinner. Robust, confident and satisfying cooking with a classical bent.

Carte £ 27/43

Town plan: 23PZG-v – *35 Old Church St ⊠ SW3 5BS –* ⊖ *South Kensington.*
– ☎ *(020) 7352 2908 – www.thepigsear.info – Closed 25 December*

🍴 Lots Road Pub & Dining Room   AC

BRITISH TRADITIONAL · PUB It may be a little worn around the edges but when a kitchen occupies half the bar you know they take food seriously. The short menu may seem safe but uses good produce cooked with care and respect. Try the daily "season's eatings".

Carte £ 22/35

Town plan: 23PZG-b – *114 Lots Rd ⊠ SW10 0RJ –* ⊖ *Fulham Broadway.*
– ☎ *(020) 7352 6645 – www.lotsroadpub.com – Closed 25 December*

Earl's Court

🏨 K + K George   🌳 🛬 🕸 ℉5 🔁 AC 🛁 🚗

BUSINESS · MODERN In contrast to its period façade, this hotel's interior is stylish, colourful and contemporary. The hotel is on a quiet street, yet close to the Tube and has a large rear garden where you can enjoy breakfast in summer. Comfortable bar/lounge and a spacious restaurant serving a wide-ranging menu.

154 rooms ⊊ – ♦£ 150/330 ♦♦£ 150/375

Town plan: 35AAY-s – *1-15 Templeton Pl ⊠ SW5 9NB –* ⊖ *Earl's Court*
– ☎ *(020) 7598 8700 – www.kkhotels.com*

🏨 Twenty Nevern Square   🔁 ℅ 🅿

TOWNHOUSE · PERSONALISED Privately owned townhouse overlooking an attractive Victorian garden square. It's decorated with original pieces of hand-carved Indonesian furniture; breakfast in a bright conservatory. Some bedrooms have their own terrace.

20 rooms ⊊ – ♦£ 80/250 ♦♦£ 100/300

Town plan: 35AAY-u – *20 Nevern Sq. ⊠ SW5 9PD –* ⊖ *Earl's Court –* ☎ *(020) 7565 9555 – www.twentynevernsquare.co.uk*

🏨 Amsterdam   🛬 🔁 ℅

TOWNHOUSE · FUNCTIONAL Basement breakfast room and a small secluded garden. The brightly decorated bedrooms are light and airy. Some have smart wood floors; some boast their own balcony.

19 rooms ⊊ – ♦£ 80/160 ♦♦£ 100/220

Town plan: 35ABY-c – *7-9 Trebovir Rd. ⊠ SW5 9LS –* ⊖ *Earl's Court –* ☎ *(020) 7370 2814 – www.amsterdam-hotel.com*

🍴🍴 Garnier   AC

FRENCH · NEIGHBOURHOOD A wall of mirrors, rows of simply dressed tables and imperturbable service lend an authentic feel to this Gallic brasserie. The extensive menu of comforting French classics is such a good read, you'll find it hard to choose.

Menu £ 18/22 – Carte £ 34/56

Town plan: 35ABZ-a – *314 Earl's Court Rd ⊠ SW5 9QB –* ⊖ *Earl's Court*
– ☎ *(020) 7370 4536 – www.garnier-restaurant-london.co.uk*

Kensington

🏨 Royal Garden   ⚡ ≪ 🏊 ᴌₒ 🚪 ᴌ AC ☆ ♨ P

BUSINESS · FUNCTIONAL A tall, modern hotel with many of its rooms enjoying enviable views over the adjacent Kensington Gardens. All the modern amenities and services, with well-drilled staff. Bright, spacious Park Terrace offers an international menu as well as afternoon tea for which you're accompanied by a pianist.

394 rooms – 🛏£ 300/500 🛏🛏£ 350/500 – ⬛£ 25 – 17 suites
Town plan: 35ABX-c – *2-24 Kensington High St* ✉ *W8 4PT*
– ⊖ *High Street Kensington* – ℰ *(020) 7937 8000*
– *www.royalgardenhotel.co.uk*
Min Jiang – See restaurant listing

🏨 The Milestone   ⚡ 🏊 ᴌₒ 🚪 AC

LUXURY · PERSONALISED Elegant and enthusiastically run hotel with decorative Victorian façade and a very British feel. Charming oak-panelled sitting room is popular for afternoon tea; snug bar in former stables. Meticulously decorated bedrooms offer period detail. Ambitious cooking in discreet Cheneston's restaurant.

62 rooms ⬛ – 🛏£ 348/480 🛏🛏£ 400/1000 – 6 suites
Town plan: 35ABX-u – *1-2 Kensington Ct* ✉ *W8 5DL*
– ⊖ *High Street Kensington* – ℰ *(020) 7917 1000*
– *www.milestonehotel.com*

🏨 Baglioni   ⚡ ᴌₒ 🚪 AC ☆

LUXURY · STYLISH Opposite Kensington Palace and no escaping the fact that this is an Italian owned hotel. The interior is bold and ornate and comes with a certain swagger. Stylish bedrooms have a masculine feel and boast impressive facilities.

67 rooms – 🛏£ 300/500 🛏🛏£ 300/500 – ⬛£ 30 – 15 suites
Town plan: 36ACX-e – *60 Hyde Park Gate* ✉ *SW7 5BB*
– ⊖ *High Street Kensington* – ℰ *(020) 7368 5700*
– *www.baglionihotels.com*
Brunello – See restaurant listing

XxX Launceston Place   ⅏ AC ⇔
❀ MODERN CUISINE · NEIGHBOURHOOD Under the aegis of the D&D group, this long-standing and smoothly run neighbourhood restaurant continues to engender loyalty and goodwill from its many customers. The cooking is polished and at times original; it also produces rewardingly robust flavours.
➔ Veal sweetbread, allium, Morteau sausage and crispy potatoes. Monkfish with caramelised cauliflower, English crayfish and Indian spices. Gold Rush apple with butterscotch, crispy pastry and praline sorbet.
Menu £ 34/55
Town plan: 36ACX-a – *1a Launceston Pl* ✉ *W8 5RL* – ⊖ *Gloucester Road*
– ℰ *(020) 7937 6912 (bookings advisable at dinner)*
– *www.launcestonplace-restaurant.co.uk – Closed 19-30 December 1 January,
Tuesday lunch and Monday*

XxX Min Jiang   ⚑ ≪ AC ⇔
CHINESE · ELEGANT The cooking at this stylish 10th floor Chinese restaurant covers all provinces, but Cantonese and Sichuanese dominate. Wood-fired Beijing duck is a speciality. The room's good looks compete with the great views of Kensington Gardens.
Menu £ 40/80 – Carte £ 24/92
Town plan: 35ABX-c – *Royal Garden Hotel, 2-24 Kensington High St (10th Floor)* ✉ *W8 4PT* – ⊖ *High Street Kensington* – ℰ *(020) 7361 1988*
– *www.minjiang.co.uk*

XX Kitchen W8

😒 MODERN CUISINE · NEIGHBOURHOOD A joint venture between restaurateur Rebecca Mascarenhas and Philip Howard of The Square. Not as informal as the name suggests but still refreshingly free of pomp. The cooking has depth and personality and prices are quite restrained considering the quality of the produce and the kitchen's skill.

→ Smoked eel with Cornish mackerel, golden beetroot and sweet mustard. 55-day aged Middle White pork with smoked celeriac, charred pear and bacon dauphine. Vanilla parfait with mango, white chocolate and lime.

Menu £ 23 (lunch and early dinner)/60 – Carte £ 35/53

Town plan: 35AAX-a – *11-13 Abingdon Rd* ✉ *W8 6AH*
– ⊖ *High Street Kensington* – ℰ *(020) 7937 0120* – *www.kitchenw8.com*
– *Closed 25-26 December and bank holidays*

XX Pavilion

MODERN CUISINE · FASHIONABLE Attractive and stylish room with a smart central bar and a separate marble counter in front of the open kitchen. An appealing contemporary menu comes with a certain originality and the produce is exemplary – especially the steaks.

Menu £ 25 (lunch) – Carte £ 27/59

Town plan: 35ABX-p – *96 Kensington High St* ✉ *W8 4SG*
– ⊖ *High Street Kensington* – ℰ *(020) 7221 2000* – *www.kensingtonpavilion.com*
– *Closed Christmas-New Year*

XX Clarke's

MODERN CUISINE · NEIGHBOURHOOD Forever popular restaurant, serving a choice of dishes boasting trademark fresh, seasonal ingredients and Sally Clarke's famed lightness of touch. Has enjoyed a loyal local following for over 30 years.

Menu £ 25/39 – Carte £ 38/51

Town plan: 27ABV-c – *124 Kensington Church St* ✉ *W8 4BH*
– ⊖ *Notting Hill Gate* – ℰ *(020) 7221 9225 (booking advisable)*
– *www.sallyclarke.com* – *Closed 2 weeks August, Christmas-New Year, Sunday and bank holidays*

XX Brunello

ITALIAN · DESIGN Brunello now seems to have sensibly settled on a kitchen that is less about showiness and more about delivering recognisable Italian classics. This works because there's frankly more than enough drama in the exuberant decoration.

Menu £ 23 (lunch) – Carte £ 41/71

Town plan: 36ACX-e – *Baglioni Hotel, 60 Hyde Park Gate* ✉ *SW7 5BB*
– ⊖ *High Street Kensington* – ℰ *(020) 7368 5900* – *www.baglionihotels.com*

XX Chakra

INDIAN · ELEGANT The influences come from the Royal kitchens of the Maharajahs, particularly those from the North Western province of Lucknow. The spicing is more subtle than usual, the aroma fresher and the presentation more striking.

Menu £ 15 (lunch) – Carte £ 17/47

Town plan: 27AAV-s – *157-159 Notting Hill Gate* ✉ *W11 3LF*
– ⊖ *Notting Hill Gate* – ℰ *(020) 7229 2115 (booking advisable)*
– *www.chakralondon.com* – *Closed 25-26 December and 1 January*

XX Babylon

MODERN CUISINE · FASHIONABLE Found on the 7th floor and affording great views of the city skyline and an amazing 1.5 acres of rooftop garden. Stylish modern décor in keeping with the contemporary, British cooking.

Menu £ 24/50 – Carte £ 35/56

Town plan: 35ABX-n – *The Roof Gardens, 99 Kensington High St* ✉ *W8 5SA*
– *(entrance on Derry St)* – ⊖ *High Street Kensington* – ℰ *(020) 7368 3993*
– *www.roofgardens.virgin.com* – *Closed 24-30 December, 1-2 January and Sunday dinner*

XX Zaika

INDIAN · EXOTIC The cooking focuses on the North of India and the influences of Mughal and Nawabi, so expect rich and fragrantly spiced dishes. The softly-lit room makes good use of its former life as a bank, with its wood-panelling and ornate ceiling.

Menu £22 (lunch) – Carte £31/65

Town plan: 35ABX-r – *1 Kensington High St.* ⊠ *W8 5NP*
– ⊖ *High Street Kensington* – ℰ *(020) 7795 6533* – *www.zaikaofkensington.com*
– *Closed 25-26 December, 1 January and Monday lunch*

XX Yashin

JAPANESE · DESIGN Ask for a counter seat to watch the chefs prepare the sushi; choose 8, 11 or 15 pieces, to be served together. The quality of fish is clear; tiny garnishes and the odd bit of searing add originality.

Carte £39/81

Town plan: 35AAX-c – *1A Argyll Rd.* ⊠ *W8 7DB* – ⊖ *High Street Kensington*
– ℰ *(020) 7938 1536 (booking essential)* – *www.yashinsushi.com*
– *Closed 24-25 and 31 December, 1 January*

XX Cibo

ITALIAN · NEIGHBOURHOOD Long-standing neighbourhood Italian with local following. More space at the back of the room. Robust, satisfying cooking; the huge grilled shellfish and seafood platter a speciality.

Menu £20 (weekday lunch) – Carte £28/50

Town plan: 16MZE-b – *3 Russell Gdns* ⊠ *W14 8EZ* – ⊖ *Kensington Olympia*
– ℰ *(020) 7371 6271* – *www.ciborestaurant.net* – *Closed 1 week Christmas, Easter and bank holidays*

XX Malabar

INDIAN · NEIGHBOURHOOD Opened in 1983 in a residential Notting Hill street, but keeps up its appearance, remaining fresh and good-looking. Balanced menu of carefully prepared and sensibly priced Indian dishes.

Menu £19 (lunch and early dinner) **s** – Carte £17/39 **s**

Town plan: 27AAV-e – *27 Uxbridge St.* ⊠ *W8 7TQ* – ⊖ *Notting Hill Gate*
– ℰ *(020) 7727 8800* – *www.malabar-restaurant.co.uk*
– *Closed 1 week Christmas*

X Terrace

MODERN CUISINE · NEIGHBOURHOOD A sweet little neighbourhood restaurant, tucked away in a corner spot on a quiet residential street. The short menu changes daily and concentrates on seasonal, British-inspired dishes with classic combinations and bold flavours.

Menu £18 (weekday lunch) – Carte £28/54

Town plan: 16NZE-t – *33c Holland St* ⊠ *W8 4LX* – ⊖ *High Street Kensington*
– ℰ *(020) 7937 9252* – *www.theterraceonhollandstreet.co.uk*

X Kensington Place

MODERN CUISINE · NEIGHBOURHOOD An iconic restaurant which opened in 1987 as a big, boisterous, brasserie; these days a little less noisy but it remains well run. The menu offers a wide choice of modern European favourites, with the emphasis on very fresh fish.

Menu £25 (lunch and early dinner) – Carte £27/49

Town plan: 27AAV-z – *201-209 Kensington Church St.* ⊠ *W8 7LX*
– ⊖ *Notting Hill Gate* – ℰ *(020) 7727 3184*
– *www.kensingtonplace-restaurant.co.uk* – *Closed Sunday dinner, Monday lunch and bank holidays*

Good food at moderate prices? Look for the Bib Gourmand ⊛.

X The Shed

BRITISH MODERN · RUSTIC It's more than just a shed but does have a higgledy-piggledy charm and a healthy dose of the outdoors. One brother cooks, one manages and the third runs the farm which supplies the produce for the earthy, satisfying dishes.

Menu £ 25 (dinner) – Carte approx. £ 27

Town plan: 27ABV-s – *122 Palace Gardens Terr.* ⊠ *W8 4RT*
– ⊖ *Notting Hill Gate –* ℰ *(020) 7229 4024 – www.theshed-restaurant.com*
– Closed Monday lunch and Sunday

X Mazi

GREEK · FRIENDLY It's all about sharing at this simple, bright Greek restaurant where traditional recipes are given a modern twist to create vibrant, colourful and fresh tasting dishes. The garden terrace at the back is a charming spot in summer.

Menu £ 13 (weekday lunch) – Carte £ 28/52

Town plan: 27AAV-a – *12-14 Hillgate St* ⊠ *W8 7SR –* ⊖ *Notting Hill Gate*
– ℰ *(020) 7229 3794 – www.mazi.co.uk – Closed 24-26 December and 1-2 January*

North Kensington

🏠 The Portobello

TOWNHOUSE · PERSONALISED An attractive Victorian townhouse in an elegant terrace. Original and theatrical décor. Circular beds, half-testers, Victorian baths: no two bedrooms are the same.

21 rooms ⊡ – ♦£ 125/175 ♦♦£ 175/385

Town plan: 16NZE-n – *22 Stanley Gdns.* ⊠ *W11 2NG –* ⊖ *Notting Hill Gate*
– ℰ *(020) 7727 2777 – www.portobellohotel.com – Closed 24-27 December*

XXX Ledbury (Brett Graham)

❀❀ **MODERN CUISINE · NEIGHBOURHOOD** Brett Graham's husbandry skills and close relationship with his suppliers ensure the quality of the produce shines through and flavour combinations linger long in the memory. This smart yet un-showy restaurant comes with smooth and engaging service. Only a tasting menu is served at dinner on weekends.

→ Warm pheasant's egg with celeriac, dried ham, Arbois and truffle. Herdwick lamb with ewe's milk, Padrón and salt-baked Kabu turnip. Tartlet of strawberries with English flowers and vanilla cream.

Menu £ 50/85

Town plan: 27AAT-a – *127 Ledbury Rd.* ⊠ *W11 2AQ –* ⊖ *Notting Hill Gate*
– ℰ *(020) 7792 9090 – www.theledbury.com – Closed 25-26 December, August bank holiday and lunch Monday-Tuesday*

XX Flat Three 🆕

CREATIVE · DESIGN Basement restaurant blending the cuisines of Scandinavia, Korea and Japan. Not everything works but there's certainly ambition. They make their own soy and miso and serve more foraged ingredients than you'll find in Ray Mears' pocket.

Menu £ 65 – Carte £ 30/52

Town plan: 16MZE-k – *120-122 Holland Park Ave* ⊠ *W11 4UA –* ⊖ *Holland Park*
– ℰ *(020) 7792 8987 – www.flatthree.london – dinner only and lunch*
Friday-Saturday – Closed 2 weeks Christmas, 1 week August, Sunday and Monday

XX E&O

ASIAN · TRENDY Mean, moody and cool and that's just the customers. Sophisticated, chic and noisy, thanks to contented groups of diners. Menus scour the Far East, with dishes designed for sharing.

Carte £ 22/45

Town plan: 16MZD-a – *14 Blenheim Cres.* ⊠ *W11 1NN –* ⊖ *Ladbroke Grove*
– ℰ *(020) 7229 5454 – www.rickerrestaurants.com – Closed 25 December*

XX Edera

ITALIAN · NEIGHBOURHOOD Warm and comfortable neighbourhood restaurant with plenty of local regulars and efficient, well-marshalled service. Robust cooking has a subtle Sardinian accent and comes in generous portions.

Carte £ 33/52

Town plan: 16MZE-n – 148 Holland Park Ave. ⊠ W11 4UE – ⊖ Holland Park
– ℰ (020) 7221 6090 – www.edera.co.uk

X Dock Kitchen

MEDITERRANEAN · DESIGN What started as a 'pop-up' became a permanent feature in this open-plan former Victorian goods yard. The chef's peregrinations inform his cooking, which relies on simple, natural flavours.

Menu £ 18 (weekday lunch)/50
– Carte £ 30/44

Town plan: 16MZD-k – Portobello Dock, 342-344 Ladbroke Grove ⊠ W10 5BU
– ⊖ Ladbroke Grove – ℰ (020) 8962 1610 – www.dockkitchen.co.uk
– Closed Christmas, Sunday dinner and bank holidays

X Granger & Co Notting Hill

MODERN CUISINE · FRIENDLY When Bill Granger moved from sunny Sydney to cool Notting Hill he opened a local restaurant too. He's brought with him that delightful 'matey' service that only Aussies do, his breakfast time ricotta hotcakes and a fresh, zesty menu.

Carte £ 19/44

Town plan: 27AAU-x – 175 Westbourne Grove ⊠ W11 2SB – ⊖ Bayswater
– ℰ (020) 7229 9111 (bookings not accepted) – www.grangerandco.com
– Closed August bank holiday weekend and 25-26 December

X Polpo Notting Hill

ITALIAN · TRENDY The fourth Polpo is Russell Norman's most commercially minded one but is shares the same appealing lack of pretence – and the no booking policy. It's about the whole package, from the shared plates to the appealing vibe.

Carte £ 13/27

Town plan: 27AAV-p – 126-128 Notting Hill Gate ⊠ W11 3QG
– ⊖ Notting Hill Gate – ℰ (020) 7229 3283 – www.polpo.co.uk
– Closed 25-26 December and 1 January

X Wormwood

MEDITERRANEAN · NEIGHBOURHOOD The look is New England with a Moorish edge and it's named after the primary herb in absinthe; throw in North African dominated Mediterranean food with a creative edge and you have a restaurant doing something a little different.

Menu £ 35 (lunch)
– Carte £ 27/51

Town plan: 16NZD-w – 16 All Saints Rd ⊠ W11 1HH – ⊖ Westbourne Park
– ℰ (020) 7854 1808 – www.wormwoodrestaurant.com
– Closed 28 August-3 September 24-28 December, 1-2 January, Monday lunch and Sunday

X Electric Diner

MEATS · RUSTIC Next to the iconic Electric Cinema is this loud, brash and fun all-day operation with an all-encompassing menu; the flavours are as big as the portions. The long counter and red leather booths add to the authentic diner feel.

Carte £ 19/35

Town plan: 16MZD-e – 191 Portobello Rd ⊠ W11 2ED – ⊖ Ladbroke Grove
– ℰ (020) 7908 9696 – www.electricdiner.com
– Closed 30-31 August and 25 December

✗ John Doe Ⓝ   AC

MEATS · BISTRO The name is nothing to do with anonymity and everything to do with venison and game – wild British ingredients cooked in the big Bertha oven, using sustainable charcoal and wood from renewable forests, so that dishes burst with flavour.

Carte £ 24/41

Town plan: 16MZD-h – *46 Golborne Rd ⊠ W10 5PR –* ⊖ *Westbourne Park*
– ✆ *(020) 8969 3280 – www.johndoerestaurants.com*
– Closed 25-26 December, 30-31 August, Sunday and Monday

South Kensington

🏨 Blakes   🕈 ſ⅙ 🖭

LUXURY · DESIGN Behind the Victorian façade is one of London's first 'boutique' hotels. Dramatic, bold and eclectic décor, with oriental influences and antiques from around the world. Ambitious, Asian-influenced cooking in the intimate restaurant.

45 rooms – ♦£ 285/598 ♦♦£ 285/598 – ⏍£ 16 – 8 suites
Town plan: 36ACZ-n – *33 Rowland Gdns ⊠ SW7 3PF*
– ⊖ *Gloucester Road –* ✆ *(020) 7370 6701*
– www.blakeshotels.com

🏨 The Pelham   🕈 ſ⅙ 🖭 AC ⅀

LUXURY · STYLISH Great location if you're in town for museum visiting. It's a mix of English country house and city townhouse, with a panelled sitting room and library with honesty bar. Sweet and intimate basement restaurant with Mediterranean menu.

51 rooms – ♦£ 180/335 ♦♦£ 260/480 – ⏍£ 18 – 1 suite
Town plan: 36ADY-z – *15 Cromwell Pl ⊠ SW7 2LA*
– ⊖ *South Kensington –* ✆ *(020) 7589 8288*
– www.pelhamhotel.co.uk

🏨 Kensington   🕈 ſ⅙ 🖭 ⅍ AC ⅀ ⅏

BUSINESS · CONTEMPORARY Grand façade to this well-placed, corporate hotel fashioned from several townhouses. Appealing superior rooms and studios; quite compact singles. Pleasant drawing room with fireplace; brasserie-style dining and popular afternoon tea.

150 rooms ⏍ – ♦£ 200/400 ♦♦£ 200/400 – 24 suites
Town plan: 36ADY-x – *109-113 Queen's Gate ⊠ SW7 5LR*
– ⊖ *South Kensington –* ✆ *(020) 7589 6300*
– www.doylecollection.com

🏨 Number Sixteen   🛏 🖭 AC ⅀

TOWNHOUSE · STYLISH Elegant and delightfully furnished 19C townhouses in smart neighbourhood. Discreet entrance, comfortable sitting room, charming breakfast terrace and pretty little garden at the back. Bedrooms in an English country house style.

41 rooms – ♦£ 175/250 ♦♦£ 285/400 – ⏍£ 18
Town plan: 36ADY-d – *16 Sumner Pl. ⊠ SW7 3EG*
– ⊖ *South Kensington –* ✆ *(020) 7589 5232*
– www.firmdalehotels.co.uk

🏨 Ampersand   🕈 ſ⅙ 🖭 ⅍ AC ⅍

LUXURY · CONTEMPORARY A bright, elegant converted Victorian hotel in London's cultural centre – the nearby museums inspire the bedroom decoration. Rooms aren't the largest but they're smart and well-lit. Basement restaurant has a Mediterranean menu.

111 rooms – ♦£ 170 ♦♦£ 216/288 – ⏍£ 15 – 5 suites
Town plan: 36ADY-a – *10 Harrington Rd ⊠ SW7 3ER*
– ⊖ *South Kensington. –* ✆ *(020) 7589 5895*
– www.ampersandhotel.com

🏨 The Exhibitionist ⓝ   ☂ 🖭 🅰🅲 🍴
TOWNHOUSE · STYLISH A funky, design-led boutique hotel fashioned out of several 18C townhouses. The modern artwork changes every few months and the bedrooms are individually furnished – several have their own roof terrace.

37 rooms � – 🛏£ 240/460 🛏🛏£ 240/460 – 2 suites

Town plan: 36ADY-b – 8-10 Queensberry Pl ✉ SW7 2EA – ⊖ South Kensington
– ℰ (020) 7915 0000 – www.theexhibitionisthotel.com

🏨 The Gore   ☂ 🖭 🅰🅲 🍴 🛎
TOWNHOUSE · CLASSIC Idiosyncratic, hip Victorian house close to the Royal Albert Hall, whose charming lobby is covered with pictures and prints. Individually styled bedrooms have plenty of character and fun bathrooms. Bright and casual bistro.

50 rooms – 🛏£ 180/650 🛏🛏£ 180/650 – ☂£ 15

Town plan: 36ACX-n – 190 Queen's Gate ✉ SW7 5EX – ⊖ Gloucester Road
– ℰ (020) 7584 6601 – www.gorehotel.com

🏨 The Cranley   ☂ 🖭 🅰🅲 🍴
TOWNHOUSE · STYLISH Delightful Regency townhouse combines charm and period details with modern comforts and technology. Individually styled bedrooms; some with four-posters. Breakfast served in bedrooms.

39 rooms – 🛏£ 135/215 🛏🛏£ 155/235 – ☂£ 18 – 2 suites

Town plan: 36ACY-c – 10 Bina Gdns ✉ SW5 0LA – ⊖ Gloucester Road
– ℰ (020) 7373 0123 – www.cranleyhotel.com

🏨 The Rockwell   ☂ 🍴 🖭 🅰🅲 🍴
TOWNHOUSE · DESIGN Two Victorian houses with open, modern lobby and secluded, south-facing garden terrace. Bedrooms come in bold, warm colours; 'Garden Rooms' have their own patios. Small dining room offers easy menu of modern European staples.

40 rooms – 🛏£ 100/140 🛏🛏£ 144/210 – ☂£ 12

Town plan: 35ABY-b – 181-183 Cromwell Rd. ✉ SW5 0SF – ⊖ Earl's Court
– ℰ (020) 7244 2000 – www.therockwell.com

🏠 Aster House   🚪 🅰🅲 🍴
TOWNHOUSE · COSY An end of terrace Victorian house in a charming neighbourhood and great location for visiting museums. Pretty little rear garden; breakfast served in first floor conservatory. Ground floor bedrooms available.

13 rooms ☂ – 🛏£ 90/180 🛏🛏£ 120/350

Town plan: 36ADY-t – 3 Sumner Pl. ✉ SW7 3EE – ⊖ South Kensington
– ℰ (020) 7581 5888 – www.asterhouse.com

XxxX Bombay Brasserie   🅰🅲 🍽
INDIAN · EXOTIC Plush new look for this well-run, well-known and comfortable Indian restaurant; very smart bar and conservatory with a show kitchen. More creative dishes now sit alongside the more traditional.

Menu £ 24 (weekday lunch) – Carte £ 30/48

Town plan: 36ACY-y – Courtfield Rd. ✉ SW7 4QH – ⊖ Gloucester Road
– ℰ (020) 7370 4040 (bookings advisable at dinner) – bombayb.co.uk – Closed 25 December

XX L'Etranger   🅲🅲 🅰🅲 ⇔
CREATIVE · NEIGHBOURHOOD Eclectic menu mixes French dishes with techniques and flavours from Japanese cooking. Impressive wine and sake lists. Moody and atmospheric room; ask for a corner table.

Menu £ 25/34 – Carte £ 27/88

Town plan: 36ACX-c – 36 Gloucester Rd. ✉ SW7 4QT – ⊖ Gloucester Road
– ℰ (020) 7584 1118 (booking essential) – www.etranger.co.uk

XX Cambio de Tercio 🕸 AC 🎐 ⇔

SPANISH · COSY A longstanding, ever-improving Spanish restaurant. Start with small dishes like the excellent El Bulli inspired omelette, then have the popular Pluma Iberica. There are super sherries and a wine list to prove there is life beyond Rioja.

Carte £ 32/68 **s**

Town plan: 36ACZ-a – *163 Old Brompton Rd.* ✉ *SW5 0LJ* – ⊖ *Gloucester Road* – ☏ *(020) 7244 8970* – *www.cambiodetercio.co.uk* – *Closed 2 weeks December and 2 weeks August*

XX Yashin Ocean House 🏵 🔥 AC ⇔

JAPANESE · INDIVIDUAL The USP of this chic Japanese restaurant is 'head to tail' eating although, as there's nothing for carnivores, 'fin to scale' would be more precise. Stick with specialities like the whole dry-aged sea bream for the full umami hit.

Menu £ 20/70 – Carte £ 21/72

Town plan: 36ACZ-y – *117-119 Old Brompton Rd* ✉ *SW7 3RN* – ⊖ *Gloucester Road* – ☏ *(020) 7373 3990* – *www.yashinocean.com* – *Closed 24-25 and 31 December and 1 January*

XX Ognisko 🍷 🏵 🐶 ⇔

POLISH · BISTRO Ognisko Polskie Club was founded in 1940 in this magnificent townhouse – its restaurant is now open to the public. The gloriously traditional Polish menu celebrates cooking that is without pretence and truly from the heart.

Menu £ 20 (lunch and early dinner) – Carte £ 24/36

Town plan: 36ADX-r – *55 Prince's Gate, Exhibition Rd* ✉ *SW7 2PN* – ⊖ *South Kensington* – ☏ *(020) 7589 0101* – *www.ogniskorestaurant.co.uk* – *Closed 24-26 December and 1 January*

X Tendido Cero AC 🎐

SPANISH · TAPAS BAR It's all about the vibe here at Abel Lusa's tapas bar, just across the road from his Cambio de Tercio restaurant. Colourful surroundings, well-drilled service and a menu of favourites all contribute to the fun and lively atmosphere.

Menu £ 35/40 – Carte £ 20/61

Town plan: 36ACZ-v – *174 Old Brompton Rd.* ✉ *SW5 0LJ* – ⊖ *Gloucester Road* – ☏ *(020) 7370 3685* – *www.cambiodetercio.co.uk* – *Closed 2 weeks Christmas-New Year*

X Capote y Toros 🕸 AC 🎐

SPANISH · TAPAS BAR Expect to queue at this compact and vividly coloured spot which celebrates sherry, tapas, ham... and bullfighting. Sherry is the star; those as yet unmoved by this most underappreciated of wines will be dazzled by the variety.

Carte £ 18/45

Town plan: 36ACZ-v – *157 Old Brompton Road* ✉ *SW5 0LJ* – ⊖ *Gloucester Road* – ☏ *(020) 7373 0567* – *www.cambiodetercio.co.uk* – *dinner only* – *Closed 2 weeks Christmas, Sunday and Monday*

X Margaux 🕸 AC ⇔

MEDITERRANEAN · TRENDY Spain and Italy are the primary influences at this modern bistro. There are classics aplenty alongside more unusual dishes. The wine list provides a good choice of varietals and the ersatz industrial look is downtown Manhattan.

Menu £ 15 (weekday lunch)/55 – Carte £ 30/52

Town plan: 36ACZ-m – *152 Old Brompton Rd* ✉ *SW5 0BE* – ⊖ *Gloucester Road* – ☏ *(020) 7373 5753* – *www.barmargaux.co.uk* – *Closed 1 week Christmas*

St Pancras Renaissance

BUSINESS · STYLISH This restored Gothic jewel was built in 1873 as the Midland Grand hotel and reopened in 2011 under the Marriott brand. A former taxi rank is now a spacious lobby and all-day dining is in the old booking office. Luxury suites in Chambers wing; Barlow wing bedrooms are a little more functional.

245 rooms – ♦£ 390/450 ♦♦£ 390/450 – ⌑£ 19 – 10 suites

Town plan: 12SZC-d – *Euston Rd* ⊠ *NW1 2AR* – ⊖ *King's Cross St Pancras* – *℘ (020) 7841 3540 – www.stpancrasrenaissance.co.uk*

Gilbert Scott – See restaurant listing

Great Northern H. London

TOWNHOUSE · STYLISH Built as a railway hotel in 1854; reborn as a stylish townhouse. Connected to King's Cross' western concourse and just metres from Eurostar check-in. Bespoke furniture in each of the modern bedrooms, and a pantry on each floor.

91 rooms ⌑ – ♦£ 189/489 ♦♦£ 208/508 – 1 suite

Town plan: 12SZB-n – *Pancras Rd* ⊠ *N1C 4TB* – ⊖ *King's Cross St Pancras* – *℘ (020) 3388 0800 – www.gnhlondon.com*

Plum + Spilt Milk – See restaurant listing

Pullman London St Pancras

BUSINESS · MODERN Designed primarily for the business traveller, Pullman is a stylish and modern brand from the Accor group. The open- plan reception and chic lounge lead into a relaxed eatery offering the brasserie classics. State-of-the-art conference facilities include a theatre. Ideally located for Eurostar.

312 rooms – ♦£ 200/450 ♦♦£ 200/450 – ⌑£ 20 – 2 suites

Town plan: 12SZC-a – *100-110 Euston Rd* ⊠ *NW1 2AJ* – ⊖ *Kings Cross St Pancras* – *℘ (020) 7666 9000 – www.pullmanhotels.com*

Megaro

TOWNHOUSE · CONTEMPORARY Contemporary hotel fashioned out of a converted bank. The rooms are unfussy and the bathrooms smart. Daily 'absinthe hour' in the basement bar; simple seasonal modern European menu. Pastries for breakfast from their on-site bakery.

49 rooms – ♦£ 165/260 ♦♦£ 165/260 – ⌑£ 13

Town plan: 12SZC-x – *23-27 Euston Rd* ⊠ *WC1H 8AB* – *(entrance on Belgrove St)* – ⊖ *King's Cross St Pancras* – *℘ (020) 7843 2222 – www.hotelmegaro.co.uk*

XX Gilbert Scott

BRITISH TRADITIONAL · BRASSERIE Run under the aegis of Marcus Wareing and named after the architect of this Gothic masterpiece, the restaurant has the look of a Grand Salon but the buzz of a brasserie. It celebrates the UK's many regional and historic specialities.

Menu £ 21 (lunch and early dinner) – Carte £ 28/61

Town plan: 12SZC-d – *St Pancras Renaissance Hotel, Euston Rd* ⊠ *NW1 2AR* – ⊖ *King's Cross St Pancras* – *℘ (020) 7278 3888 – www.thegilbertscott.co.uk*

XX Plum + Spilt Milk

BRITISH MODERN · BRASSERIE Bright brasserie in the Grade II listed Great Northern hotel; ideal for those who've just arrived, or are about to leave, by train. Classic British dishes like potted shrimps and 'pie of the day'. Start with a drink in the GNH bar.

Menu £ 25 – Carte £ 21/45

Town plan: 12SZB-n – *Great Northern Hotel London, Pancras Rd* ⊠ *N1C 4TB* – ⊖ *King's Cross St Pancras* – *℘ (020) 3388 0818 – www.plumandspiltmilk.com*

✗ Grain Store   🍷 🏠 ⴲ 🔢 ⁱ◎

MODERN CUISINE · INDIVIDUAL Big, buzzy 'canteen' from Bruno Loubet and the Zetter hotel people. Eclectic, clever dishes – influenced by Bruno's experiences around the world – are packed with interesting flavours and textures; vegetables often take the lead role.

Carte £ 21/33

Town plan: 12SZB-s – *Granary Sq, 1-3 Stable St* ✉ *N1C 4AB*
– ⊖ *King's Cross St Pancras* – ℰ *(020) 7324 4466* – *www.grainstore.com*
– *Closed 24-25 December, 1 January and Sunday dinner*

✗ T.E.D ⓝ   🍷 ⴲ 🔢

BRITISH MODERN · INDIVIDUAL On a dreary stretch behind King's Cross is a bright restaurant doing its bit for the planet. T.E.D stands for "Think, eat, drink" and has impressive 'green' credentials. The seasonal food is modern in style and varied in its influences.

Menu £ 18 (weekday lunch)/28 – Carte £ 24/39

Town plan: 12SZB-e – *47-51 Caledonian Rd* ✉ *N1 9BU*
– ⊖ *King's Cross St Pancras* – ℰ *(0203) 763 2080* – *www.tedrestaurants.co.uk*
– *Closed Christmas, New Year and Sunday*

✗ Caravan   🏠 ⴲ 🔢 ⌷ 🍴

WORLD CUISINE · SIMPLE This second Caravan pitched up near King's Cross in an old granary warehouse. The industrial-chic look is matched by a great atmosphere – crowds flock here for breakfast, brunch, great coffee, pizza and globally influenced dishes.

Menu £ 30/50 – Carte £ 27/39

Town plan: 12SZB-c – *The Granary Building, 1 Granary Sq.* ✉ *N1C 4AA*
– ⊖ *King's Cross St Pancras* – ℰ *(020) 7101 7661 (booking essential)*
– *www.caravankingscross.co.uk* – *Closed Sunday dinner*

ⁱ◻ Fellow   🔢 ⇔

MODERN CUISINE · RUSTIC Anonymous façade but moody and atmospheric inside, with a cool cocktail bar. The lean menu of European dishes uses well-sourced ingredients. Fish from Cornish day boats is a highlight; cheeses are British and puds worth a flutter.

Carte £ 26/75

Town plan: 12SZB-x – *24 York Way* ✉ *N1 9AA* – ⊖ *King's Cross St Pancras.*
– ℰ *(020) 7833 4395* – *www.thefellow.co.uk* – *Closed 25-27 December*

KINGSTON UPON THAMES

Kingston-upon-Thames

✗✗ Roz ana   🍷 🔢 ⇔

INDIAN · BRASSERIE It may have smart surroundings, a cocktail bar and pleasant service but it is the cooking that marks out this Indian restaurant. Expect vibrant and satisfying dishes from across India, from monkfish Ambat to Chennai prawn Biryani.

Menu £ 23/33 – Carte £ 20/37

Town plan: 6CY-e – *6-8 Kingston Hill* ✉ *KT2 7NH* – ℰ *(020) 8546 6388*
– *www.roz-ana.com* – *Closed 24-27 December*

Surbiton

✗✗ The French Table   🔢 ⇔

MEDITERRANEAN · NEIGHBOURHOOD Husband and wife team run this lively local. Expect zesty and satisfying French-Mediterranean cooking; learn how with Saturday morning cookery lessons. They also run the bakery next door.

Menu £ 24 (lunch) – Carte £ 36/54

Town plan: 6CY-a – *85 Maple Rd* ✉ *KT6 4AW* – ℰ *(020) 8399 2365*
– *www.thefrenchtable.co.uk* – *Closed Sunday and Monday*

LAMBETH

Brixton

✗ Boqueria

SPANISH · TAPAS BAR Contemporary tapas bar, named after Barcelona's famous food market. Sit at the counter rather than in the unremarkable dining room. Highlights include the assorted cured hams and an excellent Crema Catalana.

Carte £ 15/22

Town plan: 24SZH-x – 192 Acre Ln. ⊠ SW2 5UL – ⊖ Clapham North – ✆ (020) 7733 4408 – www.boqueriatapas.com – dinner only and lunch Saturday-Sunday – Closed 25 December

Clapham Common

✗✗ Trinity

CREATIVE · FASHIONABLE Smartly decorated and smoothly run neighbourhood restaurant; ask for a table by the windows in summer. Sophisticated cooking displays some innovative combinations. Good value lunch menu.

Menu £ 22 (weekday lunch) – Carte £ 29/54

Town plan: 24RZH-a – 4 The Polygon ⊠ SW4 0JG – ⊖ Clapham Common – ✆ (020) 7622 1199 – www.trinityrestaurant.co.uk – Closed 24-30 December, Monday lunch and Sunday dinner

✗ The Manor ✪

BRITISH CREATIVE · NEIGHBOURHOOD Fans of The Dairy will like The Manor – they share ownership and menu formats and have similar cuisine styles. With its distressed looks and young, informed service, it certainly captures the zeitgeist. The innovative cooking uses all modern techniques and bursts with flavour.

Menu £ 25 (weekday lunch) – Carte approx. £ 26

Town plan: 24SZH-b – 148 Clapham Manor St ⊠ SW4 6BX – ⊖ Clapham Common – ✆ (020) 7720 4662 – www.themanorclapham.co.uk – Closed 21-27 December, 1 January, Sunday dinner, Tuesday lunch and Monday

✗ Dairy

BRITISH CREATIVE · RUSTIC The higgledy-piggledy, homemade look of this fun, lively restaurant adds to its charm. What you don't expect is such innovative cooking. The earthy, easy-to-eat food is driven by seasonality – some produce is grown on the roof.

Carte £ 22/27

Town plan: 24RZH-d – 15 The Pavement ⊠ SW4 0HY – ⊖ Clapham Common – ✆ (020) 7622 4165 (booking essential at dinner) – www.the-dairy.co.uk – Closed Christmas, Sunday dinner, Monday and Tuesday lunch

✗ Bistro Union

⊛ **BRITISH MODERN · NEIGHBOURHOOD** The little sister to Trinity restaurant is fun and affordable, with a welcoming feel and sweet staff. The menu is appealingly flexible, whether you're here for brunch or a full dinner; eschew starters in favour of their great 'snacks'.

Menu £ 26 (weekday dinner) – Carte £ 20/37

Town plan: 7EX-s – 40 Abbeville Rd ⊠ SW4 9NG – ⊖ Clapham South – ✆ (020) 7042 6400 (booking advisable) – www.bistrounion.co.uk – Closed 24-30 December and Sunday dinner

✗ May the Fifteenth

MEDITERRANEAN · RUSTIC Formerly Abbeville Kitchen – the chef took over this bistro and christened it after the date he signed the forms. The food remains as was: gutsy and wholesome, with fair prices and plenty of choice.

Carte £ 22/32

Town plan: 7EX-a – 47 Abbeville Rd ⊠ SW4 9JX – ⊖ Clapham South – ✆ (020) 8772 1110 (bookings advisable at dinner) – www.abbevillekitchen.com – dinner only and lunch Friday-Sunday – Closed 24-26 and 31 December and 1 January

Rookery

BRITISH TRADITIONAL • RUSTIC The on-trend Rookery shows that Soho doesn't have a monopoly on ersatz Brooklyn speakeasies. Come for the impressive selection of artisan beers and a short yet appealing menu; the kitchen delivers some punchy flavours.

Carte £ 20/31

Town plan: 7EX-v - *69 Clapham Common South Side ✉ SW4 9DA - ⊖ Clapham Common - ✆ (020) 8673 9162 - www.therookeryclapham.co.uk - dinner only and lunch Saturday-Sunday - Closed 25-26 December*

Zumbura

INDIAN • NEIGHBOURHOOD Going from running a furniture business to opening a restaurant seems to be working for the three friends behind this modern Indian. It's all about small plates, which are fresh tasting, subtly spiced and surprisingly light.

Carte £ 13/28

Town plan: 24RZH-z - *36a Old Town ✉ SW4 0LB - ⊖ Clapham Common - ✆ (020) 7720 7902 - www.zumbura.com - dinner only - Closed 25 December and 1 January*

Kennington

Kennington Tandoori

INDIAN • NEIGHBOURHOOD Kowsar Hoque runs this contemporary Indian restaurant with great pride and his eagerness and professionalism filters through to his staff. The food is prepared with equal care – try the seasonal specialities and the excellent breads.

Menu £ 15/30 – Carte £ 21/34

Town plan: 40ANZ-a - *313 Kennington Rd ✉ SE11 4QE - ⊖ Kennington - ✆ (020) 7735 9247 (booking advisable) - www.kenningtontandoori.com - Closed 25 December*

Lobster Pot

FRENCH • TRADITIONAL Family-run, with exuberant décor of fish tanks, portholes and even the sound of seagulls. Classic seafood menu with fruits de mer, plenty of oysters and daily specials. Good crêpes too.

Carte £ 39/64

Town plan: 40AOY-e - *3 Kennington Ln. ✉ SE11 4RG - ⊖ Kennington - ✆ (020) 7582 5556 - www.lobsterpotrestaurant.co.uk - Closed 25 December-2 January, Sunday and Monday*

Southbank

London Marriott H. County Hall

LUXURY • CLASSIC Occupying the historic County Hall building. Many of the spacious and comfortable bedrooms enjoy river and Parliament outlooks. Impressive leisure facilities. World famous views too from Gillray's, which specialises in steaks.

200 rooms – 🚹£ 420/540 🚹🚹£ 600/900 – ☕ £ 22 – 5 suites

Town plan: 40AMX-a - *Westminster Bridge Rd ✉ SE1 7PB - ⊖ Westminster - ✆ (020) 7928 5200 - www.marriott.co.uk/lonch*

Skylon

MODERN CUISINE • DESIGN Ask for a window table here at the Royal Festival Hall. Informal grill-style operation on one side, a more formal and expensive restaurant on the other, with a busy cocktail bar in the middle.

Menu £ 18/48 – Carte £ 26/54

Town plan: 32AMV-a - *1 Southbank Centre, Belvedere Rd ✉ SE1 8XX - ⊖ Waterloo - ✆ (020) 7654 7800 - www.skylon-restaurant.co.uk - Closed 25 December*

Stockwell

🍴 Canton Arms   🍽️

🐾 **BRITISH TRADITIONAL · PUB** An appreciative crowd of all ages come for the earthy, robust and seasonal British dishes which suit the relaxed environment of this pub so well. Staff are attentive and knowledgeable.

Carte £ 20/32

Town plan: 24SZG-a – *177 South Lambeth Rd* ✉ *SW8 1XP* – ⊖ *Stockwell.* – *𝒞 (020) 7582 8710 (bookings not accepted) – www.cantonarms.com – Closed Christmas-New Year, Monday lunch, Sunday dinner and bank holidays*

LEWISHAM

Blackheath

XX Chapters   🍲 🍽️ 🆒 🖥️

MODERN CUISINE · BRASSERIE A classic, bustling brasserie that keeps the locals happy, by being open all day and offering everything from Mediterranean-influenced main courses to meats cooked over charcoal. There's also a kids' menu and wines by the pichet.

Menu £ 13 (lunch and early dinner) – Carte £ 21/35

Town plan: 8HX-c – *43-45 Montpelier Vale* ✉ *SE3 0TJ* – *𝒞 (020) 8333 2666* – *www.chaptersblackheath.com – Closed 2-3 January*

Forest Hill

XX Babur   🆒

INDIAN · NEIGHBOURHOOD Good looks and innovative cooking make this passionately run and long-established Indian restaurant stand out. Influences from the south and north west feature most and seafood is a highlight - look out for the 'Treasures of the Sea' menu.

Carte £ 26/34

Town plan: 7GX-s – *119 Brockley Rise* ✉ *SE23 1JP* – ⊖ *Honor Oak Park* – *𝒞 (020) 8291 2400 – www.babur.info – Closed dinner 25 December-lunch 27 December*

Enjoy good food without spending a fortune! Look out for the Bib Gourmand 🐾 symbol to find restaurants offering good food at great prices!

MERTON

Wimbledon

🏨 Hotel du Vin at Cannizaro House 🆕   🌸 🐾 ⟨ 🛏️ 🍴 ⟩ 🆒 🧖

BUSINESS · STYLISH Previously Cannizaro House and now part of   🅿️ this growing chain of hotels. This charming part-Georgian house is surrounded by over 30 acres of parkland. The restaurant overlooks an Italian sunken garden.

49 rooms ⊠ – †£ 167 ††£ 175/235 – 2 suites

Town plan: 6DXY-x – *West Side, Wimbledon Common* ✉ *SW19 4UE* – *𝒞 (0330) 024 07 06 – www.hotelduvin.com*

X Light House

MEDITERRANEAN · NEIGHBOURHOOD The robust and flavoursome Italian dishes provide the highlights of the menu. This large, well lit room attracts plenty of locals and the service remains calm and cheery.

Menu £ 15/23 (weekdays) – Carte £ 27/38

Town plan: 6DY-n – *75-77 Ridgway* ✉ *SW19 4ST* – ⊖ *Wimbledon* – *𝒞 (020) 8944 6338 – www.lighthousewimbledon.com – Closed 25-26 December, 1 January and Sunday dinner*

🏠 Fox and Grapes ⇔ AC

BRITISH MODERN · PUB Surprisingly spacious pub, discreetly tucked away on the south side of the common. A concise menu offers simply cooked dishes which let the ingredients do the talking. Pies and burgers sit alongside Mediterranean-inspired dishes and steaks cooked on the Josper grill. Three modern bedrooms complete the picture.

Carte £ 24/42

3 rooms – ♦£ 100/125 ♦♦£ 100/125

Town plan: 6DX-v – *9 Camp Rd* ✉ *SW19 4UN* – ⊖ *Wimbledon.* – *ℰ (020) 8619 1300* – *www.foxandgrapeswimbledon.co.uk* – *Closed 25 December*

REDBRIDGE

Wanstead

✗ Provender 🛱 AC ⧉

FRENCH · BISTRO A modern, busy and bustling neighbourhood bistro courtesy of experienced restaurateur Max Renzland. The well-priced French cooking is pleasingly rustic and satisfying, with great charcuterie, appealing salads and well-timed grills.

Menu £ 17 (weekdays) – Carte £ 22/41

Town plan: 4HU-x – *17 High St* ✉ *E11 2AA* – ⊖ *Snaresbrook* – *ℰ (020) 8530 3050* – *www.provenderlondon.co.uk*

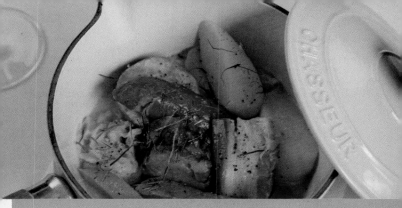

© Brasserie Chavot

RICHMOND-UPON-THAMES

Barnes

XX Sonny's Kitchen 🔣 ⇔

MODERN CUISINE · NEIGHBOURHOOD Long-time owner Rebecca Mascarenhas has been joined by Phil Howard, chef of The Square, and they're rejuvenating this much-loved neighbourhood spot. Menus are all-encompassing; the atmosphere's great and the artwork interesting.

Menu £ 18/25 – Carte £ 19/49

Town plan: 21KZH-x – *94 Church Rd* ⊠ *SW13 0DQ* – *𝓒 (020) 8748 0393*
– www.sonnyskitchen.co.uk – Closed 25 December, 1 January and bank holiday Mondays

XX Indian Zilla 🔣 🎧 ⇔

INDIAN · NEIGHBOURHOOD Bright, contemporary restaurant with attentive, friendly service. Modern menu includes a few classics; the authentic, fully-flavoured dishes display a lightness of touch.

Carte £ 20/38

Town plan: 21LZH-k – *2-3 Rocks Ln.* ⊠ *SW13 0DB*
– 𝓒 (020) 8878 3989 – www.indianzilla.co.uk
– dinner only and lunch Saturday-Sunday
– Closed 25 December

X Riva 🔣

ITALIAN · NEIGHBOURHOOD A restaurant built on customer loyalty; the regulars are showered with attention from the eponymous owner. Gutsy, no-nonsense dishes, full of flavour. Interesting all-Italian wine list.

Carte £ 33/52

Town plan: 21LZH-a – *169 Church Rd.* ⊠ *SW13 9HR* – *𝓒 (020) 8748 0434*
– Closed 2 weeks August, Christmas-New Year, Saturday lunch and bank holidays

X Olympic Café + Dining Room 🕭 🔣 🖳

BRITISH MODERN · BRASSERIE An all-day brasserie housed in what was once the world's greatest recording studio – artists like the Stones and Led Zeppelin recorded seminal albums here. No 'Goat's Head Soup', instead an appealing selection of British comfort food.

Carte £ 21/87

Town plan: 21KZH-s – *117-123 Church Rd* ⊠ *SW13 9HL*
– 𝓒 (020) 8912 5161 (bookings advisable at dinner)
– www.olympiccinema.co.uk

🍴 **Brown Dog**   🏠

BRITISH MODERN · PUB Concealed in a maze of residential streets is this homely, relaxed pub with a lived-in feel. The balanced menu offers traditional and flavoursome fare like venison pie or haddock fishcake; all done 'properly'.

Carte £ 23/38

Town plan: 21KZH-b – *28 Cross St* ⊠ *SW13 0AP* – ⊖ *Barnes Bridge (Rail).* – ℰ *(020) 8392 2200 – www.thebrowndog.co.uk – Closed 25 December*

East Sheen

🍴 **Victoria**   ⇦ 🏠 🅿

BRITISH MODERN · PUB Beautifully restored pub and a genuine local, playing its part in the community. The kitchen takes its sourcing seriously; eat in the bar or more formal conservatory overlooking the terrace. Recently refurbished bedrooms available.

Menu £ 17 (lunch and early dinner) – Carte £ 25/39

7 rooms ⊠ – †£ 100/125 ††£ 100/135

Town plan: 6CX-u – *10 West Temple Sheen* ⊠ *SW14 7RT* – ⊖ *Mortlake (Rail).* – ℰ *(020) 8876 4238 – www.thevictoria.net*

Kew

XX **The Glasshouse**   ❀ 🆔

❀ MODERN CUISINE · FASHIONABLE The Glasshouse is the very model of a modern neighbourhood restaurant and sits in the heart of lovely, villagey Kew. Food is confident yet unshowy – much like the locals – and comes with distinct Mediterranean flavours along with the occasional Asian hint. Service comes with the eagerness of youth.
➔ Assiette of rabbit with pancetta, rainbow chard, carrot purée and Madeira jus. Loin of lamb with braised shoulder, boulangère potatoes, peas and wild garlic. Dark chocolate mousse with hazelnut nougatine, bergamot and caramel ice cream.

Menu £ 30 (weekday lunch)/48

Town plan: 6CX-z – *14 Station Par.* ⊠ *TW9 3PZ* – ⊖ *Kew Gardens* – ℰ *(020) 8940 6777 – www.glasshouserestaurant.co.uk – Closed 24-26 December and 1 January*

XX **Linnea**   🆔

BRITISH MODERN · NEIGHBOURHOOD The chef-owner of this pared down yet elegant room is from Sweden – Linnea is his country's national flower. The monthly menu offers modern, unfussy dishes with Scandinavian techniques of pickling, curing and air-drying in evidence.

Carte £ 24/41

Town plan: 6CV-u – *12 Kew Grn.* ⊠ *TW9 3BH* – ⊖ *Kew Gardens* – ℰ *(020) 8940 5696 – www.linneakew.co.uk – Closed Christmas, Easter, 2 weeks August, Sunday and Monday*

XX **Kew Grill**   🆔

MEATS · TRADITIONAL It's all about steaks – Aberdeen Angus and hung for 35 days – at this long, narrow restaurant, tucked away down a side street. The look may be a tad faded but the service is warm and friendly and it's well supported by the locals.

Carte £ 22/74

Town plan: 6CV-u – *10b Kew Grn.* ⊠ *TW9 3BH* – ⊖ *Kew Gardens* – ℰ *(020) 8948 4433 (booking essential) – www.awtrestaurants.com/kewgrill – dinner only and lunch Saturday and Sunday – Closed 25 December*

Richmond

🏨 **Petersham**   ❀ ⇦ 🛏 🖵 ⅛ ❀ 🛋 🅿

HISTORIC · CLASSIC Extended over the years, a fine example of Victorian Gothic architecture, with Portland stone and self-supporting staircase. The most comfortable bedrooms overlook the Thames. Formal restaurant in which to enjoy a mix of classic and modern cooking; ask for a window table for terrific park and river views.

58 rooms – †£ 70/140 ††£ 100/205 – ⊠ £ 14 – 1 suite

Town plan: 6CX-c – *Nightingale Ln* ⊠ *TW10 6UZ* – ⊖ *Richmond* – ℰ *(020) 8940 7471 – www.petershamhotel.co.uk – Closed 25-26 December*

🏠 Bingham ✿ 🛏 AC 🍴 ⅃ P

TOWNHOUSE · MODERN A pair of conjoined and restored Georgian townhouses; a short walk from Richmond centre. Ask for a room overlooking the river and garden. Contemporary styled bedrooms; some with four-posters.

15 rooms – ♦£130/275 ♦♦£225/350 – ⌴£17

Town plan: 6CX-c – *61-63 Petersham Rd.* ✉ *TW10 6UT* – ⊖ *Richmond*
– *☏ (020) 8940 0902* – *www.thebingham.co.uk*

Bingham Restaurant – See restaurant listing

XX Bingham Restaurant 🍽 🛏 🍴 AC P

MODERN CUISINE · DESIGN Its riverside setting adds to the charm of this comfortable and enthusiastically run hotel restaurant. The various menus provide plenty of choice; the cooking is a blend of the modern and the classical and dishes are nicely balanced.

Menu £ 20 (weekday lunch) – Carte £ 25/50

Town plan: 6CX-c – *Bingham Hotel, 61-63 Petersham Rd.* ✉ *TW10 6UT*
– ⊖ *Richmond* – *☏ (020) 8940 0902* – *www.thebingham.co.uk*
– *Closed Sunday dinner*

XX Dysart Petersham 🍴 🍷 ⊖ P

MODERN CUISINE · INTIMATE A pub built in the 1900s as part of the Arts and Crafts movement but now run as quite a formal restaurant. The kitchen uses top-notch ingredients and adds subtle Asian tones to a classical base. Occasional musical recital suppers.

Menu £ 23 (weekdays)/60
– Carte £ 31/52

Town plan: 6CX-d – *135 Petersham Rd* ✉ *TW10 7AA* – *☏ (020) 8940 8005*
(booking advisable) – *www.thedysartpetersham.co.uk*
– *Closed Sunday dinner*

X Petersham Nurseries Café 🍴

MODERN CUISINE · RUSTIC On a summer's day there can be few more delightful spots for lunch, whether that's on the terrace or in the greenhouse. The kitchen uses the freshest seasonal produce in unfussy, flavoursome dishes that have a subtle Italian accent.

Carte £ 29/52

Town plan: 6CX-x – *Church Ln (off Petersham Rd)* ✉ *TW10 7AG*
– *☏ (020) 8940 5230 (booking essential)* – *www.petershamnurseries.com*
– *lunch only – Closed 25-26 December and Monday*

X Matsuba AC

JAPANESE · DESIGN Family-run Japanese restaurant with just 11 tables; understated but well-kept appearance. Extensive menu offers wide range of Japanese dishes, along with bulgogi, a Korean barbecue dish.

Carte £ 25/35

Town plan: 6CX-n – *10 Red Lion St* ✉ *TW9 1RW* – ⊖ *Richmond*
– *☏ (020) 8605 3513* – *www.matsuba-restaurant.com*
– *Closed 25-26 December, 1 January and Sunday*

X Swagat AC

INDIAN · BISTRO A very likeable little Indian restaurant, run by two friends who met while training with Oberoi hotels in India. One partner organises the warm service; the other prepares dishes with a pleasing degree of lightness and subtlety.

Menu £ 30
– Carte £ 15/32

Town plan: 6CX-b – *86 Hill Rise* ✉ *TW10 6UB* – ⊖ *Richmond*
– *☏ (020) 8940 7557 (booking essential)* – *www.swagatindiancuisine.co.uk*
– *dinner only – Closed 25 December*

LONDON ENGLAND

Teddington

✗✗ Rétro Bistrot

FRENCH · BISTRO There's substance as well as style to this French bistrot. The classic bourgeois cuisine is prepared with innate skill; service is warm and effusive; and the slick decoration, conducive to merrymaking.

Menu £10/23 – Carte £28/55

Town plan: 5BY-n – *114-116 High St* ✉ *TW11 8JB* – ✆ *(020) 8977 2239* – *www.retrobistrot.co.uk* – *Closed first 2 weeks August, first 10 days January, Sunday dinner and Monday*

✗✗ Al Borgo

ITALIAN · NEIGHBOURHOOD A refreshingly unpretentious and keenly run Italian restaurant that exudes warmth and bonhomie. Homemade focaccia and pasta are the highlights. Look out too for seasonal offerings such as the black truffle menu.

Menu £15 (weekdays) – Carte £25/48

Town plan: 5BY-e – *3 Church Rd.* ✉ *TW11 8PF* – ✆ *(020) 8943 4456* – *www.alborgo.co.uk* – *Closed 1-10 January, 20-31 March, 28 August-8 September, 25 December, Monday and Sunday dinner*

✗ Simply Thai

THAI · NEIGHBOURHOOD Simple Thai restaurant offering a huge array of dishes. Cooking is adjusted for Western tastes but makes commendable use of British ingredients; the signature dishes are a good bet. Come on a Sunday for good value street food.

Menu £16 – Carte £22/31

Town plan: 5BY-x – *196 Kingston Rd.* ✉ *TW11 9JD* – ✆ *(020) 8943 9747* – *www.simplythai-restaurant.co.uk* – *dinner only* – *Closed 25-26 December*

🍴 King's Head

MODERN CUISINE · NEIGHBOURHOOD Britain has its pubs and France its brasseries; The King's Head does its bit for the entente cordiale by combining both. Have a drink in the front bar, then enjoy rustic classics in the rear brasserie.

Menu £12 (lunch) – Carte £20/40

Town plan: 5BY-c – *123 High St* ✉ *TW11 8HG* – ⊖ *Teddington (Rail).* – ✆ *(020) 3166 2900* – *www.whitebrasserie.com*

Twickenham

✗✗ A Cena

ITALIAN · NEIGHBOURHOOD The menu at this bigger-than-you-first-think restaurant covers all parts of Italy but there's more of a northern bias in winter; pasta is a highlight. The owners may not be Italian but you can't fault their passion and enthusiasm.

Carte £16/41

Town plan: 5BX-e – *418 Richmond Rd.* ✉ *TW1 2EB* – ⊖ *Richmond* – ✆ *(020) 8288 0108* – *www.acena.co.uk* – *Closed 2 weeks August, Sunday dinner, Monday lunch and bank holidays*

🍴 Crown

BRITISH TRADITIONAL · PUB Relaxed, stylish pub with parquet floors and feature fireplaces; sit in the airy, elegant rear restaurant, with its high vaulted ceiling and garden view. Global, bound-to-please menus offer fresh, tasty, amply-sized dishes.

Carte £23/38

Town plan: 5BX-c – *174 Richmond Rd, St Margarets* ✉ *TW1 2NH* – ⊖ *St Margarets (Rail).* – ✆ *(020) 8892 5896* – *www.crowntwickenham.co.uk* – *Closed 26 December*

© HKK London

SOUTHWARK

Bermondsey

🏨 Shangri-La

LUXURY · ELEGANT When your hotel occupies floors 34-52 of The Shard, you know it's going to have the wow factor. The pool is London's highest and north-facing bedrooms have the best views. An East-meets-West theme includes the restaurant's menu and afternoon tea when you have a choice of traditional English or Asian.

202 rooms – 🛉£ 350/575 🛉🛉£ 350/575 – ☕£ 32 – 17 suites
Town plan: 34ARV-s – *The Shard, 31 St Thomas St* ✉ *SE1 9QU*
– ⊖ *London Bridge* – ✆ *(020) 7234 8000* – *www.shangri-la.com/london*

🏨 Mondrian London Ⓝ

BUSINESS · DESIGN The former Sea Containers house now has slick, stylish look evoking the golden age of the transatlantic liner. Rooms come with a bright splash of colour; Suites have balconies and Superiors, a river view. Globally influenced small plates in smart restaurant, with meat and fish from the grill & clay oven.

359 rooms – 🛉£ 195 🛉🛉£ 220/600 – ☕£ 16 – 5 suites
Town plan: 32ANV-x – *20 Upper Ground* ✉ *SE1 9PD*
– ⊖ *Southwark* – ✆ *(020) 3747 1000* – *www.mondrianlondon.com*

🏨 Hilton London Tower Bridge

BUSINESS · MODERN Usefully located new-style Hilton hotel with boldly decorated open-plan lobby. Contemporary bedrooms boast well-designed features; 4 floors of executive rooms. The Larder has an international menu.

245 rooms – 🛉£ 129/529 🛉🛉£ 129/629 – ☕£ 20
Town plan: 34ARV-e – *5 More London, Tooley St* ✉ *SE1 2BY*
– ⊖ *London Bridge* – ✆ *(020) 3002 4300* – *www.towerbridge.hilton.com*

🏨 Bermondsey Square

BUSINESS · MODERN Cleverly designed hotel in a regenerated square, with subtle '60s influences and a relaxed, hip feel. Well-equipped bedrooms, including stylish loft suites. British food and grilled meats in the open-plan GB Grill & Bar.

80 rooms – 🛉£ 99/300 🛉🛉£ 99/300 – ☕£ 14
Town plan: 20XZE-n – *Bermondsey Sq, Tower Bridge Rd* ✉ *SE1 3UN*
– ⊖ *London Bridge* – ✆ *(020) 7378 2450*
– *www.bermondseysquarehotel.co.uk*

🏨 London Bridge

BUSINESS · CONTEMPORARY Independently owned hotel with an ornate façade dating from 1915, in one of the oldest parts of London. Modern interior with contemporary bedrooms. Londinium for brasserie dining; Quarter for cocktails.

138 rooms – ♦£ 430 ♦♦£ 430 – 3 suites

Town plan: 33AQV-a – 8-18 London Bridge St ⊠ SE1 9SG – ⊖ London Bridge
– ℰ (020) 7855 2200 – www.londonbridgehotel.com

XXX Le Pont de la Tour

FRENCH · ELEGANT Providing, since 1991, seasonal French cooking, an urbane atmosphere and a wonderful riverside location, with views of Tower Bridge. Simpler dishes served in the livelier cocktail bar and grill.

Menu £ 15/25 – Carte £ 33/64

Town plan: 34ASV-c – 36d Shad Thames, Butlers Wharf ⊠ SE1 2YE
– ⊖ London Bridge – ℰ (020) 7403 8403 – www.lepontdelatour.co.uk – Closed 1 January

XX Story (Tom Sellers)

❀ **MODERN CUISINE · DESIGN** Amazing what you can create out of an old public toilet on a traffic island. In what looks like a Nordic eco-lodge, Tom Sellers offers 6 or 10 courses of earthy yet delicate, playful yet easy to eat dishes; go for 10, as 6 is too few. With just 13 tables, getting a booking is another story.
➙ Onion, apple and gin. Herdwick lamb, sheep's yoghurt and ramson. Almond and dill.

Menu £ 39 (weekday lunch)/95 (set menu only)

Town plan: 34ASV-s – 201 Tooley St. ⊠ SE1 2JX – ⊖ London Bridge – ℰ (020) 7183 2117 (booking essential) – www.restaurantstory.co.uk – Closed 2 weeks Christmas-New Year, Easter, Sunday, Monday and bank holidays

XX Magdalen

BRITISH MODERN · NEIGHBOURHOOD The clever sourcing and confident British cooking will leave you satisfied. Add genial service, an affordable lunch menu and a food-friendly wine list and you have the favourite restaurant of many.

Menu £ 17 (lunch) – Carte £ 30/42

Town plan: 34ARV-b – 152 Tooley St. ⊠ SE1 2TU – ⊖ London Bridge – ℰ (020) 7403 1342 – www.magdalenrestaurant.co.uk – Closed Sunday, Saturday lunch and bank holidays

XX Hutong

CHINESE · INTIMATE You no longer need to fly to Hong Kong to get a view with your Peking duck. On the 33rd floor of The Shard – ask to sit in 'Beijing' – you'll find a menu focusing on the more northerly Chinese regions; specialities include de-boned lamb ribs, soft shell crab and roast duck. Prices are equally vertiginous.

Menu £ 28 (weekday lunch) – Carte £ 30/62

Town plan: 34ARV-s – Level 33, The Shard, 31 St Thomas St ⊠ SE1 9RY
– ⊖ London Bridge – ℰ (020) 3011 1257 (booking essential) – www.hutong.co.uk
– Closed 25-26 December and 1 January

XX Oblix

MEATS · TRENDY From the Zuma/Roka people comes this New York grill restaurant, where meat and fish from the rotisserie, grill and Josper oven are the stars of the show. Views are far-reaching and there's live music in the adjacent lounge bar.

Menu £ 29 (weekday lunch)/58 – Carte £ 31/105

Town plan: 34ARV-s – Level 32, The Shard, St Thomas St. ⊠ SE1 9RY
– ⊖ London Bridge – ℰ (020) 7268 6700 – www.oblixrestaurant.com

✗✗ Aqua Shard

MODERN CUISINE · FASHIONABLE The Shard's most accessible restaurant covers all bases by serving breakfast, brunch, lunch, afternoon tea and dinner. If you don't mind queuing, you can even come just for a drink. The contemporary cooking makes good use of British ingredients and comes with a degree of finesse in flavour and looks.

Menu £31 (weekday lunch)/48 – Carte £36/65

Town plan: 34ARV-s – *Level 31, The Shard, 31 St Thomas St* ✉ *SE1 9RY* – ⊖ *London Bridge* – ℰ *(020) 3011 1256 – www.aquashard.co.uk – Closed 25 December and 1 January*

✗ Zucca

ITALIAN · FRIENDLY Bright and buzzy modern room, where the informed Italian cooking is driven by the fresh ingredients, the prices are more than generous and the service is sweet and responsive. The appealing antipasti is great for sharing.

Carte £24/41

Town plan: 20XZE-s – *184 Bermondsey St* ✉ *SE1 3TQ* – ⊖ *Borough* – ℰ *(020) 7378 6809 (booking essential at dinner) – www.zuccalondon.com – Closed 24 December-7 January, Sunday dinner and Monday*

✗ Blueprint Café

MODERN CUISINE · BRASSERIE Large retractable windows make the most of the river views from this bright restaurant above the Design Museum. The first change of head chef in 16 years was seamless: the cooking remains light, seasonally pertinent and easy to eat.

Menu £23/25 – Carte £30/42

Town plan: 34ASV-u – *Design Museum, Shad Thames, Butlers Wharf* ✉ *SE1 2YD* – ⊖ *London Bridge* – ℰ *(020) 7378 7031 – www.blueprintcafe.co.uk – Closed 1 January and Sunday dinner*

✗ Village East

MODERN CUISINE · TRENDY Counter dining is the focus in the main room; those celebrating can tuck themselves away in a separate bar. Cooking mixes contemporary dishes with Mediterranean-inspired plates; the confit turkey leg is the house speciality.

Carte £20/43

Town plan: 20XZE-a – *171-173 Bermondsey St* ✉ *SE1 3UW* – ⊖ *London Bridge* – ℰ *(020) 7357 6082 – www.villageeast.co.uk – Closed 24-26 December*

✗ Cantina Del Ponte

ITALIAN · RUSTIC This Italian stalwart offers an appealing mix of classic dishes and reliable favourites from a sensibly priced menu, in pleasant faux-rustic surroundings. Its pleasant terrace takes advantage of its riverside setting.

Menu £13/23 – Carte £20/50

Town plan: 34ASV-c – *36c Shad Thames, Butlers Wharf* ✉ *SE1 2YE* – ⊖ *London Bridge* – ℰ *(020) 7403 5403 – www.cantina.co.uk – Closed 25 December*

✗ Butlers Wharf Chop House

BRITISH TRADITIONAL · BRASSERIE Grab a table on the terrace in summer and dine in the shadow of Tower Bridge. Rustic feel to the interior; noisy and fun. The menu focuses on traditional English ingredients and dishes; grilled meats a speciality.

Carte £29/64

Town plan: 34ASV-n – *36e Shad Thames, Butlers Wharf* ✉ *SE1 2YE* – ⊖ *London Bridge* – ℰ *(020) 7403 3403 – www.chophouse-restaurant.co.uk – Closed 1 January*

X Vivat Bacchus London Bridge &&

MEATS · WINE BAR Wines from the South African owners' homeland feature strongly and are well-suited to the meat dishes – the strength here. Choose one of the sharing boards themed around various countries, like Italian hams or South African BBQ.

Carte £ 24/47

Town plan: 34ARV-n – *4 Hays Ln ✉ SE1 2HB – ⊖ London Bridge – 𝒞 (020) 7234 0891 – www.vivatbacchus.co.uk – Closed Christmas-New Year, Saturday lunch, Sunday and bank holidays*

X Pizarro AC 🍽 ⟵

MEDITERRANEAN · NEIGHBOURHOOD José Pizarro has a refreshingly simple way of naming his establishments: after José, his tapas bar, comes Pizarro, a larger restaurant a few doors down. Go for the small plates, like prawns with piquillo peppers and jamón.

Menu £ 35 – Carte £ 26/55

Town plan: 20XZE-r – *171-173 Bermondsey St ✉ SE1 3UW – ⊖ Borough – 𝒞 (020) 7378 9455 – www.josepizarro.com – Closed 24-28 December*

X Antico 🍷 AC

ITALIAN · NEIGHBOURHOOD Once an antiques warehouse – hence the name – Antico is fun, bright and breezy, with honest and straightforward Italian food; the homemade pasta is good. Check out the seasonal ragu, risotto and sorbet on the blackboard.

Menu £ 15 (lunch and early dinner) – Carte £ 23/38

Town plan: 20XZE-e – *214 Bermondsey St ✉ SE1 3TQ – ⊖ London Bridge – 𝒞 (020) 7407 4682 – www.antico-london.co.uk – Closed 25 December, 1 January and Monday*

X Casse Croûte

FRENCH · BISTRO Squeeze into this tiny bistro and you'll find yourself transported to rural France. A blackboard menu offers three choices for each course but new dishes are added as others run out. The cooking is rustic, authentic and heartening.

Carte £ 28/35

Town plan: 20XZE-t – *109 Bermondsey St ✉ SE1 3XB – ⊖ London Bridge – 𝒞 (020) 7407 2140 (booking essential) – www.cassecroute.co.uk – Closed Sunday dinner*

X José 🕭 AC 🍽
🏵

SPANISH · MINIMALIST Standing up while eating tapas feels so right, especially at this small, fun bar that packs 'em in like boquerones. Five dishes each should suffice; go for the daily fish dishes from the blackboard. There's a great list of sherries too.

Carte approx. £ 25

Town plan: 20XZE-v – *104 Bermondsey St ✉ SE1 3UB – ⊖ London Bridge – 𝒞 (020) 7403 4902 – www.josepizarro.com – Closed 24-26 December and Sunday dinner*

🍴 Garrison AC 🛋 ⟵

MEDITERRANEAN · PUB Known for its charming vintage look, booths and sweet-natured service, The Garrison boasts a warm, relaxed vibe. Open from breakfast until dinner, when a Mediterranean-led menu pulls in the crowd.

Carte £ 24/34

Town plan: 20XZE-z – *99-101 Bermondsey St ✉ SE1 3XB – ⊖ London Bridge. – 𝒞 (020) 7089 9355 (booking essential at dinner) – www.thegarrison.co.uk – Closed 25-26 December*

Camberwell

🍴 **Crooked Well** 🛋

MODERN CUISINE · **PUB** Warmly run pub that manages to look both new and lived-in at the same time. The kitchen mixes things up by offering sturdy classics like rabbit and bacon pie alongside more playful dishes such as a deconstructed peach Melba.

Menu £10 (weekday lunch) – Carte £23/39

Town plan: 25VZH-s – *16 Grove Ln* ⊠ *SE5 8SY* – ⊖ *Denmark Hill (Rail).*
– 𝒞(020) 7252 7798 – www.thecrookedwell.com – Closed Monday lunch and dinner on bank holiday Mondays

🍴 **Camberwell Arms**

BRITISH TRADITIONAL · **PUB** The people behind the Anchor & Hope and Canton Arms bring their successful formula to SE5: well-informed staff, a no bookings policy, a daily menu supplemented by a blackboard and simple dishes with satisfying, punchy flavours.

Carte £19/37

Town plan: 25VZH-c – *65 Camberwell Church St* ⊠ *SE5 8TR*
– ⊖ Denmark Hill (Rail). – 𝒞(020) 7358 4364 (bookings not accepted)
– www.thecamberwellarms.co.uk – Closed 27 December-2 January, Sunday dinner, Monday lunch, bank holiday Mondays and Tuesday lunch after bank holidays

East Dulwich

✗ **Toasted** 🚻 🛋

MODERN CUISINE · **NEIGHBOURHOOD** A lively wine shop and eatery with a lived-in feel. Wine bought directly from French vineyards is stored in large tanks; there are also about 200 wines on the list. The menu is short, flavours are bold and combinations quite daring.

Carte £26/44

Town plan: 26XZH-t – *38 Lordship Ln* ⊠ *SE22 8HJ* – ⊖ *East Dulwich* – 𝒞*(020) 8693 9250 – www.toasteddulwich.co.uk – Closed Sunday dinner*

🍴 **Palmerston** 🎱

MEDITERRANEAN · **PUB** A brightly run Victorian pub that has a comfortable, lived-in feel and lies at the heart of the local community. The cooking has a satisfying, gutsy edge with meat dishes, especially game, being the highlight.

Menu £14 (weekday lunch)/75 – Carte £28/50

Town plan: 26XZH-x – *91 Lordship Ln* ⊠ *SE22 8EP* – ⊖ *East Dulwich (Rail).*
– 𝒞(020) 8693 1629 – www.thepalmerston.co.uk – Closed 25-26 December and 1 January

Peckham

✗ **Artusi** Ⓝ

ITALIAN · **NEIGHBOURHOOD** An enthusiastically run Italian restaurant which shows Peckham is on the rise. The kitchen displays clear respect for the seasonal ingredients, dishes are kept honest and the prices are more than fair.

Carte £24/35

Town plan: 26XZH-a – *161 Bellenden Rd* ⊠ *SE15 4DH* – ⊖ *Peckham Rye*
– 𝒞(020) 3302 8200 (booking essential at dinner) – www.artusi.co.uk – Closed 2 weeks Christmas and bank holidays

Southwark

🏨 **citizenM** 🔲 🚻 📺 🍽 🧖

BUSINESS · **DESIGN** A new type of budget hotel with an eye for the aesthetic. Relaxing, open-plan lobby with sofas, books, tables, desks and a bar for snacks and drinks. Upstairs, the bedrooms may be pod-like but are well-lit and cleverly designed.

192 rooms – ♥£120/249 ♥♥£120/249 – ⌸ £13

Town plan: 33APV-c – *20 Lavington St* ⊠ *SE1 0NZ* – ⊖ *Southwark* – 𝒞*(020) 3519 1680 – www.citizenm.com*

⌂ **Hampton by Hilton** 🕏 🕏 🖿 📧 ♿ 🅰🅲 🕏 🛁

CHAIN HOTEL · FUNCTIONAL A useful budget hotel from Hilton, near the Old Vic and Waterloo. Crisply decorated rooms and plenty of lounge space on the ground floor. Assado is a big, bright restaurant from Cyrus Todiwala fusing Indian and Portuguese cuisine.

297 rooms ⌸ – ⫯£ 109/299 ⫯⫯£ 109/299

Town plan: 40ANX-a – *157 Waterloo Rd* ⌧ *SE1 8XA* – ⊖ *Waterloo* – ℰ *(020) 7401 8080 – http:// hamptoninn3.hilton.com/en/hotels/united-kingdom/hampton-by-*

✗✗✗ **Oxo Tower** 🕃 ≼ 🕃 🅰🅲

MODERN CUISINE · MINIMALIST Top of a converted iconic factory, providing stunning views of the Thames and beyond. Stylish, minimalist interior with huge windows. Expect quite ambitious, mostly European, cuisine.

Menu £ 34 (lunch) – Carte £ 42/71

Town plan: 32ANV-a – *Oxo Tower Wharf (8th floor), Barge House St* ⌧ *SE1 9PH* – ⊖ *Southwark* – ℰ *(020) 7803 3888 – www.harveynichols.com – Closed 25 December*

Oxo Tower Brasserie – See restaurant listing

✗✗ **Roast** 🍷 🅰🅲 🖵 🕪

BRITISH MODERN · FASHIONABLE Known for its British food and for promoting UK producers – not surprising considering the restaurant's in the heart of Borough Market. The 'dish of the day' is often a highlight; service is affable and there's live music at night.

Carte £ 31/56

Town plan: 33AQV-e – *The Floral Hall, Borough Mkt* ⌧ *SE1 1TL* – ⊖ *London Bridge* – ℰ *(020) 3006 6111 (booking essential) – www.roast-restaurant.com – Closed 25-26 December and 1 January*

✗✗ **Baltic** 🍷 ⇔

WORLD CUISINE · BRASSERIE In this converted 18C coach builder's works you'll find a big, bright restaurant specialising in Eastern European food – from Poland, Russia, Bulgaria, even Siberia. Dumplings and meat dishes stand out, as do the great vodkas.

Menu £ 18 (lunch and early dinner) – Carte £ 22/38

Town plan: 33AOV-e – *74 Blackfriars Rd* ⌧ *SE1 8HA* – ⊖ *Southwark* – ℰ *(020) 7928 1111 (bookings advisable at dinner) – www.balticrestaurant.co.uk – Closed 24-26 December and Monday lunch*

✗✗ **Union Street Café** 🍷 ♿ 🅰🅲 ⇔

ITALIAN · TRENDY Occupying a former warehouse, this Gordon Ramsay restaurant has been busy since day one and comes with a New York feel, a faux industrial look and a basement bar. The Italian menu keeps things simple and stays true to the classics.

Menu £ 19/29 – Carte £ 26/44

Town plan: 33APV-u – *47 - 51 Great Suffolk Street* ⌧ *SE1 0BS* – ⊖ *London Bridge* – ℰ *(020) 7592 7977 – www.gordonramsay.com*

✗✗ **Rabot 1745** 🍷 🕃 ♿ 🅰🅲 ⇔

MODERN CUISINE · DESIGN Want something different? How about cocoa cuisine? Rabot 1745 is from the owners of Hotel Chocolat and is named after their estate in St Lucia. They take the naturally bitter, spicy flavours of the bean and use them subtly in classically based dishes. The chocolate mousse dessert is pretty good too!

Carte £ 22/39

Town plan: 33AQV-c – *2-4 Bedal St, Borough Mkt* ⌧ *SE1 9AL* – ⊖ *London Bridge* – ℰ *(020) 7378 8226 – www.rabot1745.com – Closed 25-26 December, Sunday and Monday*

※ Oxo Tower Brasserie

MODERN CUISINE · DESIGN Less formal but more fun than the next-door restaurant. Open-plan kitchen produces modern, colourful and easy-to-eat dishes with influences from the Med. Great views too from the bar.

Menu £ 30 (lunch and early dinner) – Carte £ 31/55

Town plan: 32ANV-a – *Oxo Tower Wharf (8th floor), Barge House St*
⊠ *SE1 9PH* – ⊖ *Southwark* – ℰ *(020) 7803 3888* – *www.harveynichols.com*
– *Closed 25 December*

※ Elliot's

MODERN CUISINE · RUSTIC Open from breakfast onwards, this busy and unpretentious café sources most of its ingredients from Borough Market, in which it stands. The appealing menu is concise and the cooking is earthy, pleasingly uncomplicated and very satisfying.

Carte £ 19/31

Town plan: 33AQV-h – *12 Stoney St., Borough Market* ⊠ *SE1 9AD*
– ⊖ *London Bridge* – ℰ *(020) 7403 7436 (booking advisable)*
– *www.elliotscafe.com* – *Closed Sunday and bank holidays*

※ Tate Modern (Restaurant)

BRITISH MODERN · DESIGN Ask for a front window table facing St Paul's at this big, bright restaurant on Level 6. The menu is seasonal and the influences largely British; the kitchen has a light touch and each dish comes with a suggested wine pairing.

Menu £ 25 – Carte £ 29/42

Town plan: 33APV-s – *Tate Modern (6th floor), Bankside* ⊠ *SE1 9TG*
– ⊖ *Southwark* – ℰ *(020) 7887 8888* – *www.tate.org.uk* – *lunch only and dinner Friday-Saturday* – *Closed 24-26 December*

※ Tapas Brindisa

SPANISH · TAPAS BAR A blueprint for many of the tapas bars that subsequently sprung up over London. It has an infectious energy and the well-priced, robust dishes include Galician-style hake and black rice with squid; do try the hand-carved Ibérico hams.

Carte £ 20/32

Town plan: 33AQV-k – *18-20 Southwark St, Borough Market* ⊠ *SE1 1TJ*
– ⊖ *London Bridge* – ℰ *(020) 7357 8880 (bookings not accepted)*
– *www.brindisatapaskitchens.com*

※ Wright Brothers

FISH AND SEAFOOD · COSY Originally an oyster wholesaler; now offers a wide range of oysters along with porter, as well as fruits de mer, daily specials and assorted pies. It fills quickly and an air of contentment reigns.

Carte £ 29/71

Town plan: 33AQV-m – *11 Stoney St., Borough Market* ⊠ *SE1 9AD*
– ⊖ *London Bridge* – ℰ *(020) 7403 9554 (booking advisable)*
– *www.thewrightbrothers.co.uk* – *Closed bank holidays*

※ Arabica Bar & Kitchen ⓝ

WORLD CUISINE · RUSTIC The owner-chef once sold mezze in Borough Market so it's no surprise he opened his Levantine-inspired restaurant under a railway arch here. This fun, cavernous place serves sharing plates from Egypt, Syria, Iraq, Jordan and Lebanon.

Carte £ 15/32

Town plan: 33AQV-s – *3 Rochester Walk, Borough Mkt* ⊠ *SE1 9AF*
– ⊖ *London Bridge* – ℰ *(020) 3011 5151 (bookings advisable at dinner)*
– *www.arabicabarandkitchen.com* – *Closed 25-27 December, 1 January and Sunday October-March*

Anchor & Hope

BRITISH MODERN • PUB As popular as ever thanks to its congenial feel and lived-in looks but mostly because of the appealingly seasonal menu and the gutsy, bold cooking that delivers on flavour. No reservations so be prepared to wait at the bar.

Menu £ 15 (weekday lunch) – Carte £ 22/41

Town plan: 32ANV-n – *36 The Cut ✉ SE1 8LP – ⊖ Southwark. – ✆ (020) 7928 9898 (bookings not accepted) – www.anchorandhopepub.co.uk – Closed Christmas-New Year, Sunday dinner, Monday lunch and bank holidays*

SUTTON

Sutton

Brasserie Vacherin

FRENCH • BRASSERIE Relaxed, modern French brasserie with tiled walls, art nouveau posters and deep red banquettes. Good value midweek set price menu and à la carte of French classics. Diligent service.

Menu £ 18 (lunch and early dinner) – Carte £ 20/40

Town plan: 7EZ-x – *12 High St ✉ SM1 1HN – ✆ (020) 8722 0180 – www.brasserievacherin.co.uk*

TOWER HAMLETS

Bethnal Green

Town Hall

LUXURY • RETRO Edwardian, former council offices converted into a hotel in 2010. Its period character is balanced with modernity, with individually decorated, understated bedrooms and frequently changing art.

98 rooms – †£ 160/290 ††£ 160/290 – ☕ £ 15 – 57 suites

Town plan: 14YZB-x – *Patriot Sq ✉ E2 9NF – ⊖ Bethnal Green – ✆ (020) 7871 0460 – www.townhallhotel.com*

Corner Room • Typing Room – See restaurant listing

Typing Room

MODERN CUISINE • FASHIONABLE Jason Atherton has backed one of his protégés in a room once home to the town hall's typing pool. The open kitchen dominates the room and the cooking is clever and accomplished, with flavours that are distinct and complementary.

Menu £ 24/75 – set menu only

Town plan: 14YZB-x – *Town Hall Hotel, Patriot Sq ✉ E2 9NF – ⊖ Bethnal Green – ✆ (020) 7871 0461 – www.typingroom.com – Closed Sunday dinner and Monday*

Brawn

MODERN CUISINE • NEIGHBOURHOOD Unpretentious and simply kitted out baby sister to Terroirs; the name captures the essence of the cooking perfectly: it is rustic, muscular and makes very good use of pig. Great local atmosphere and polite, helpful service.

Carte £ 25/33

Town plan: 20XZD-z – *49 Columbia Rd. ✉ E2 7RG – ⊖ Bethnal Green – ✆ (020) 7729 5692 – www.brawn.co – Closed Christmas-New Year, Monday lunch and bank holidays*

X Corner Room   🏧 AC

CREATIVE · INTIMATE Hidden upstairs in the old town hall is this bright, intimate space – first have a drink in the little bar. The core ingredient of each dish is British and the assured cooking makes you feel you're getting a real taste of nature.

Menu £19 (lunch)/75 – Carte £20/30

Town plan: 14YZB-x – *Town Hall Hotel, Patriot Sq* ✉ *E2 9NF*
– ⊖ *Bethnal Green* – 𝒞 *(020) 7871 0461 (bookings advisable at dinner)*
– *www.cornerroom.co.uk*

X Bistrotheque   AC 🍴 ⇔

FRENCH · NEIGHBOURHOOD When the exterior is as irredeemably bleak as this, you just know it's going to be painfully cool inside. This bustling space in a converted sweatshop is great fun; its menu is French-bistro in style. Live music at weekend brunch.

Menu £20 (early dinner) – Carte £21/49

Town plan: 14YZB-s – *23-27 Wadeson St* ✉ *E2 9DR* – ⊖ *Bethnal Green*
– 𝒞 *(020) 8983 7900 (booking advisable) – www.bistrotheque.com – dinner only and lunch Saturday-Sunday – Closed 24 and 26 December*

🍴 Marksman ⓝ

BRITISH TRADITIONAL · FRIENDLY This newly decorated pub has kept its traditional looks and its quirky, brown-tiled façade; inside it's cosy, with a friendly, neighbourhood feel. Simply cooked, seasonal dishes are wonderfully fresh, perfectly balanced and full of flavour.

Carte £22/34

Town plan: 14XZB-n – *254 Hackney Rd* ✉ *E2 7SJ* – ⊖ *Hoxton* – 𝒞 *(020) 7739 7393 – www.marksmanpublichouse.com – Closed 25 December, 1 January, Sunday dinner and Monday*

Canary Wharf

🏨 Four Seasons   🏖 ⇐ 📺 🐾 🏊 🌡 🏧 AC 🍸 🚗

BUSINESS · MODERN Professionally run international hotel geared mainly to the local corporate market. The Premier rooms boast impressive views across the river. Spacious restaurant, with river-facing terrace and menu that covers all parts of Italy.

141 rooms – 🛏£220/450 🛏🛏£220/450 – ⊑ £25 – 13 suites

Town plan: 3GV-a – *Westferry Circus* ✉ *E14 8RS* – ⊖ *Canary Wharf* – 𝒞 *(020) 7510 1999 – www.fourseasons.com/canarywharf*

XX Plateau   🍸 🍴 AC 🍷 ⇔

MODERN CUISINE · DESIGN Being surrounded by tall glass buildings means you feel you're in Manhattan and the striking room has its own retro 1960s look. The Grill is for steaks from the Josper grill; the more formal restaurant for French-inspired dishes.

Menu £19/35 – Carte £33/62

Town plan: 3GV-n – *Canada Place (4th floor), Canada Square* ✉ *E14 5ER*
– ⊖ *Canary Wharf* – 𝒞 *(020) 7715 7100 – www.plateau-restaurant.co.uk – Closed 25 December, 1 January and Sunday*

XX Roka   🍸 🍴 🏧 AC

JAPANESE · FASHIONABLE You'll be hit by a wall of sound at this large and perennially busy operation in the shadow of Canary Wharf Tower. The meats cooked on the robata grill are highlights of the Japanese menu.

Menu £55 (weekdays)/79 – Carte £26/91

Town plan: 3GV-v – *4 Park Pavilion (1st Floor), 40 Canada Sqaure* ✉ *E14 5FW*
– ⊖ *Canary Wharf* – 𝒞 *(020) 7636 5228 (booking essential)*
– *www.rokarestaurant.com – Closed 25-26 December and 1 January*

LONDON ENGLAND

XX Boisdale of Canary Wharf

BRITISH TRADITIONAL · FASHIONABLE It's the 1st floor for the relaxed, art deco inspired Oyster bar, with its crustacea, burgers and top quality steaks. The grander 2nd floor has a stage for live jazz (a charge is made) and offers plenty of dishes of a Scottish persuasion.

Carte £ 21/69

Town plan: 3GV-s – Cabot Pl ⊠ E14 4QT – ⊖ Canary Wharf – ℰ (020) 7715 5818 (booking advisable) – www.boisdale.co.uk – Closed bank holidays

X Iberica Canary Wharf

SPANISH · SIMPLE Lively, modern Spanish restaurant whose narrow shop front belies its vast interior. The tapas is an appealing mix of the traditional and the more contemporary. On sunny days there's La Terraza opposite, with its lovely terrace.

Menu £ 15 (weekday lunch) – Carte £ 14/44

Town plan: 3GV-c – 12 Cabot Sq ⊠ E14 4QQ – ⊖ Canary Wharf – ℰ (020) 7636 8650 – www.ibericarestaurants.com – Closed 24-25 December, 1 January and dinner on Sunday and bank holidays

X Goodman Canary Wharf

MEATS · BRASSERIE Whether you like corn or grass fed Scottish fillet, rib on the bone or US strip loin, the helpful staff will explain the maturation process; you decide on the cut and weight. A lively brasserie with waterfront views.

Carte £ 30/115

Town plan: 3GV-e – Discovery Dock East, 3 South Quay ⊠ E14 9RU – ⊖ South Quay (DLR) – ℰ (020) 7531 0300 (booking advisable) – www.goodmanrestaurants.com – Closed 25-26 December, 1 January, Saturday lunch, Sunday and bank holidays

⏸ The Gun

BRITISH TRADITIONAL · PUB Its popularity far outweighs its size but just head to the smart dining room at the far end or to the terrace overlooking the river. The broadly British dishes are the best things on the menu – appropriate for such a historic pub.

Carte £ 26/45

Town plan: 3GV-x – 27 Coldharbour ⊠ E14 9NS – ⊖ Blackwall (DLR). – ℰ (020) 7515 5222 (booking essential) – www.thegundocklands.com – Closed 25-26 December

Spitalfields

⌂ Batty Langley's ⓝ

TOWNHOUSE · ELEGANT It looks and feels like a Georgian house, thanks to the antique furniture and attention to detail, yet even the façade was rebuilt. The luxurious rooms come with flowing drapes, reproduction fireplaces and lovely bathrooms. An oasis of composed elegance.

29 rooms – ♦£ 234 ♦♦£ 330/750 – � £ 12 – 1 suite

Town plan: 20XZD-y – 12 Folgate St ⊠ E1 6BX – ⊖ Liverpool Street – ℰ (020) 7377 4390 – www.battylangleys.com

XXX Galvin La Chapelle

❀ **FRENCH · INDIVIDUAL** The Victorian splendour of St Botolph's Hall, with its vaulted ceiling, arched windows and marble pillars, lends itself perfectly to its role as a glamorous restaurant. The food is bourgeois French with a sophisticated edge and is bound to satisfy.

→ Lasagne of Dorset crab with beurre Nantais. Tagine of Bresse pigeon, couscous, confit lemon and harissa sauce. Tarte Tatin with crème Normande.

Menu £ 29 (lunch and early dinner)/70 – Carte £ 45/73

Town plan: 34AST-v – 35 Spital Sq ⊠ E1 6DY – ⊖ Liverpool Street – ℰ (020) 7299 0400 – www.galvinrestaurants.com – Closed dinner 24-26 December and 1 January

✗ Blixen

MEDITERRANEAN · INDIVIDUAL From the same stable as The Garrison and Riding House Café comes this charmingly run and good looking restaurant with lots of natural light. An appealing European menu offers carefully prepared, keenly priced dishes. You'll want to return for breakfast or cocktails in the basement bar.

Carte £ 23/34

Town plan: 34AST-w – 65a Brushfield St ⊠ E1 6AA – ⊖ Liverpool Street
– ✆ (020) 7101 0093 – www.blixen.co.uk – Closed Sunday dinner

✗ Galvin Café a Vin

FRENCH · BISTRO In the same building as La Chapelle is this simpler yet equally worthy operation from the Galvin brothers. The room may not have the grandeur of next door but it's fun and lively and offers classic French bistro food at good prices.

Menu £ 17 (lunch and early dinner)/20 – Carte £ 27/38

Town plan: 34AST-v – 35 Spital Sq (entrance on Bishops Sq) ⊠ E1 6DY
– ⊖ Liverpool Street – ✆ (020) 7299 0404 – www.galvinrestaurants.com
– Closed 24-26 December and 1 January

✗ St John Bread and Wine

BRITISH TRADITIONAL · BISTRO Part-wine shop/bakery and local restaurant. Highly seasonal and appealing menu changes twice a day; cooking is British, uncomplicated and very satisfying. Try the less familiar dishes.

Carte £ 28/43

Town plan: 34AST-a – 94-96 Commercial St ⊠ E1 6LZ – ⊖ Liverpool Street
– ✆ (020) 7251 0848 – www.stjohnbreadandwine.com – Closed 25-26 December and 1 January

✗ Taberna do Mercado

PORTUGUESE · SIMPLE An appealingly modest little place from Nuno Mendez, serving small plates of Portuguese classics. You'll see staples elevated to a higher level: alheira, Bísaro pork and prawn rissois all deliver wonderful flavours and each dish seems to have a story.

Carte £ 22/46

Town plan: 34AST-m – Old Spitalfields Market, 107b Commercial St ⊠ E1 6BG
– ⊖ Liverpool Street – ✆ (020) 7375 0649 – www.tabernamercado.co.uk
– Closed Christmas and Sunday dinner

✗ Ottolenghi

MEDITERRANEAN · INDIVIDUAL A cross between the original Islington shop and Nopi, their Soho restaurant. The room's bright white look reminds you that the food's all about freshness. Dishes are as flavoursome as they are colourful and sharing is encouraged.

Carte £ 26/30

Town plan: 34AST-e – 50 Artillery Ln ⊠ E1 7LJ
– ⊖ Liverpool Street – ✆ (020) 7247 1999 (booking essential)
– www.ottolenghi.co.uk – Closed dinner 24-26 and 31 December, 1 January and Sunday dinner

✗ Hawksmoor

MEATS · RUSTIC Unremarkable surroundings in a modern building and it's not really about the starters or the puds. The star is the great British beef, hung for 35 days, from Longhorn cattle in the heart of the Yorkshire Moors.

Menu £ 24 (weekdays)/27 – Carte £ 23/74

Town plan: 20XZD-s – 157a Commercial St ⊠ E1 6BJ
– ⊖ Shoreditch High Street – ✆ (020) 7426 4850 (booking essential)
– www.thehawksmoor.com – Closed 24-26 December and Sunday dinner

𝖃 **Copita del Mercado** 🅝

SPANISH · TAPAS BAR Petticoat Lane is the mercado in question and is the location of this more comfortable sister to the Soho original. The menu also differs by offering a little more originality; go for the daily specials. Gin is also a speciality.

Carte £ 18/41

Town plan: 34AST-f – *60 Wentworth St* ✉ *E1 7AL* – ⊖ *Aldgate East* – *☎ (020) 7426 0218* – *www.copitadelmercado.com* – *Closed Christmas-New Year, Easter and Sunday dinner*

Whitechapel

𝖃𝖃 **Cafe Spice Namaste**

INDIAN · NEIGHBOURHOOD Fresh, vibrant and fairly priced Indian cuisine from Cyrus Todiwala, served in a colourfully decorated room that was once a magistrate's court. Engaging service from an experienced team.

Carte £ 26/37

Town plan: 34ASU-z – *16 Prescot St.* ✉ *E1 8AZ* – ⊖ *Tower Hill* – *☎ (020) 7488 9242* – *www.cafespice.co.uk* – *Closed Saturday lunch, Sunday and bank holidays*

WANDSWORTH

Balham

𝖃 **Lamberts**

BRITISH TRADITIONAL · NEIGHBOURHOOD Locals come for the relaxed surroundings, hospitable service and tasty, seasonal food. Sunday lunch is very popular. The enthusiasm of the eponymous owner has rubbed off on his team.

Menu £ 18 (weekday lunch) – Carte £ 26/39

Town plan: 6EX-n – *2 Station Par, Balham High Rd.* ✉ *SW12 9AZ* – ⊖ *Balham* – *☎ (020) 8675 2233* – *www.lambertsrestaurant.com* – *Closed 25-26 December, 1 January, Sunday dinner and Monday*

𝖃 **Harrison's**

MODERN CUISINE · BRASSERIE Lively, popular sister to Sam's Brasserie in Chiswick. Open all day, with an appealing list of favourites, from fishcakes to 'Harrison's burgers'. Weekend brunches; kids' menu; good value weekday set menus.

Menu £ 14 (weekdays)/29 – Carte £ 22/44

Town plan: 6EX-h – *15-19 Bedford Hill* ✉ *SW12 9EX* – ⊖ *Balham* – *☎ (020) 8675 6900* – *www.harrisonsbalham.co.uk* – *Closed 24-26 December*

Battersea

𝖃𝖃 **London House**

BRITISH MODERN · NEIGHBOURHOOD One doesn't associate neighbourhood restaurants with Gordon Ramsay but London House looks set to succeed. It's comfortable and well run and the classically-based dishes come with modern touches and ingredients that marry well.

Menu £ 28 – Carte £ 31/46

Town plan: 23PZH-h – *7-9 Battersea Sq, Battersea Village* ✉ *SW11 3RA* – ⊖ *Clapham Junction* – *☎ (020) 7592 8545* – *www.gordonramsay.com/londonhouse* – *dinner only and lunch Thursday-Sunday* – *Closed Monday except bank holidays*

𝖃𝖃 **Chada**

THAI · FRIENDLY A much loved local Thai restaurant which opened back in 1986 and is still run with considerable charm by its owner. The extensive menu now includes a selection of 'small eats' representing refined street food.

Carte £ 17/34

Town plan: 23QZH-x – *208-210 Battersea Park Rd.* ✉ *SW11 4ND* – ⊖ *Clapham Junction* – *☎ (020) 7622 2209* – *www.chadathai.com* – *dinner only* – *Closed Sunday and bank holidays*

X Sinabro   AC

MODERN CUISINE · NEIGHBOURHOOD The main room feels almost kitchen-like, courtesy of a wall of stainless steel; sit at the wooden counter – made by the chef-owner's father. Confidently prepared dishes rely largely on classic French flavours but are modern in style.

Menu £15 (weekday lunch) – Carte £28/45

Town plan: 23QZH-r – *28 Battersea Rd* ⊠ *SW11 1EE* – ⊖ *Clapham Junction* – *℘(020) 3302 3120* – *www.sinabro.co.uk* – *Closed 1 week August, 25 December and 1 January*

X Soif   🕸 AC
🌐
FRENCH · NEIGHBOURHOOD Great food, an appealingly louche look and a thoughtful wine list – yes, it's another terrific eaterie from the team behind Terroirs and Brawn. The cooking is robust and satisfying; anything 'piggy' is done particularly well.

Carte £27/41

Town plan: 23QZH-c – *27 Battersea Rise* ⊠ *SW11 1HG* – ⊖ *Clapham Junction* – *℘(020) 7233 1112 (booking essential at dinner)* – *www.soif.co* – *Closed Christmas and New Year, Sunday dinner, Monday lunch and bank holidays*

X Lola Rojo   🍴 AC 🍱

SPANISH · TAPAS BAR Few spots on Northcote Road are as fun as this lively, if cramped, Spanish eatery. The owner-chef comes from Valencia so paella is a sure thing but other Catalan tapas specialities are also worth seeking out.

Carte £12/23

Town plan: 23QZH-v – *78 Northcote Rd* ⊠ *SW11 6QL* – ⊖ *Clapham Junction* – *℘(020) 7350 2262 (booking essential)* – *www.lolarojo.net* – *Closed 25-26 December and lunch 1 January*

X Boqueria 🆕   🍴 AC 🍱 ⇔

SPANISH · TAPAS BAR Occupying a converted bank and smarter than the first branch in Brixton but still delivering the true flavours of Spain. Try the dishes unique to here, like the classic Mallorcan dish Coca Mallorquina and the island sausage Sobrasada.

Carte £15/23

Town plan: 23RZG-a – *278 Queenstown Rd* ⊠ *SW8 4LT* – ⊖ *Clapham Junction* – *℘(020) 7498 8247* – *www.boqueriatapas.com*

X Rosita   🍱

MEDITERRANEAN · FRIENDLY From the owners of nearby Lola Roja comes this fun sherry and tapas bar. Dishes include flavoursome meats and seafood cooked by Josper grill. There are many sherries by the glass and suggested pairings with certain dishes.

Carte £15/26

Town plan: 6EX-g – *124 Northcote Rd* ⊠ *SW11 6QU* – ⊖ *Clapham Junction* – *℘(020) 7998 9093* – *www.rositasherry.net* – *dinner only and lunch Friday-Sunday* – *Closed 25-26 December, 1 January and Monday*

X Hana   ⇔

KOREAN · SIMPLE A warm, sweet little Korean restaurant. Yang Yeum chicken and Pa Jeon pancake are popular starters; bibimbap rice dishes burst with flavour; seafood cooked on the barbeque is very good; and they do their own version of Bossam.

Carte £16/26

Town plan: 23QZH-a – *60 Battersea Rise* ⊠ *SW11 1EG* – ⊖ *Clapham Junction* – *℘(020) 7228 2496* – *www.hanakorean.co.uk* – *Closed 24-26 December*

Battersea Heliport

🏨 Crowne Plaza London Battersea   🍳 ⬩ 🍴 🐕 🎿 🧖 🛗 👥 ♿ AC 🌿

BUSINESS · DESIGN Built in 2010, in a unique riverside location   ♨ 🅿 with a heliport. Well-equipped bedrooms; those without views are bigger than those with. Impressive spa facilities. International menu in the bistro and bar.

68 rooms ☲ – 🛏£99/359 🛏🛏£99/359 – 2 suites

Town plan: 23PZH-v – *Bridges Wharf* ⊠ *SW11 3BE* – *℘(020) 7801 3500* – *www.crowneplaza.com*

Putney

✗✗ Enoteca Turi   ⬢⬢ AC ⬨

ITALIAN · FRIENDLY Giuseppe Turi's restaurant has been warming Putney hearts for nearly 25 years. The focus is on Northern Italy and dishes are full of flavour. The room has an appealing Mediterranean feel and there are no bad tables. Wine plays a big part here, with lesser known Italian producers to the fore.

Menu £19 (lunch) – Carte £29/48

Town plan: 22MZH-n – *28 Putney High St ⊠ SW15 1SQ –* ⊖ *Putney Bridge – ℰ (020) 8785 4449 – www.enotecaturi.com – Closed 25-26 December, 1 January, Sunday, Monday lunch and bank holidays*

✗ Bibo   ⌂ AC

⊛ **ITALIAN · BISTRO** Rebecca Mascarenhas is the neighbourhood restaurant expert and, with Bibo, she's hit the bullseye once again. This fun Italian comes with an appealing vibe, clued up service and well-priced food that's effortlessly easy to enjoy.

Menu £10/23 – Carte £22/34

Town plan: 22MZH-b – *146 Upper Richmond Rd ⊠ SW15 2SW –* ⊖ *East Putney – ℰ (020) 8780 0592 – www.biborestaurant.com – Closed 25-26 December and bank holidays*

⌂ Prince of Wales   ⌂

BRITISH MODERN · PUB Idiosyncratic decoration and good food make this substantial Victorian pub stand out. The daily changing menu reads well and includes British specialities like Cornish sardines as well as Spanish delicacies; simpler menu in the bar.

Carte £24/49

Town plan: 22MZH-z – *138 Upper Richmond Rd ⊠ SW15 2SP –* ⊖ *East Putney. – ℰ (020) 8788 1552 – www.princeofwalesputney.co.uk – Closed 23 December-1 January and Monday lunch except bank holidays*

Southfields

⌂ Earl Spencer   ⌂

MEDITERRANEAN · RUSTIC A handsome Edwardian pub with a bright, welcoming feel; a baseline lob away from the All England Tennis Club. Fervently seasonal cooking has a strong traditional base. The only irritant is that one has to order everything at the bar.

Carte £22/32

Town plan: 6DX-c – *260-262 Merton Rd ⊠ SW18 5JL –* ⊖ *Southfields. – ℰ (020) 8870 9244 – www.theearlspencer.com – Closed lunch Monday-Thursday*

Tooting

✗ Chicken Shop   ⬡

MEATS · RUSTIC Tooting has already taken to the second branch of Chicken Shop. The ingeniously simple idea is serving just whole, half or quarter chickens that are succulent and flavoursome, along with a few sides and a couple of puddings.

Carte £15/30

Town plan: 6EY-c – *141 Tooting High St ⊠ SW17 0SY –* ⊖ *Tooting Broadway – ℰ (020) 8767 5200 (bookings not accepted) – www.chickenshop.com*

Wandsworth

✗✗ Chez Bruce (Bruce Poole)   ⬢⬢ AC ⬨

❀ **FRENCH · BRASSERIE** Flavoursome, uncomplicated French cooking with hints of the Mediterranean prepared with innate skill; well-organised, personable service and an easy-going atmosphere - some of the reasons why Chez Bruce remains a favourite of so many.

→ Cod brandade with smoked haddock, crisp egg, wild garlic and sea kale. Anjou pigeon with stuffed onion, pearl barley, sauce poivrade and foie gras. Apple and Calvados trifle with spiced raisin fritter.

Menu £30/48

Town plan: 6EX-e – *2 Bellevue Rd ⊠ SW17 7EG –* ⊖ *Tooting Bec – ℰ (020) 8672 0114 (booking essential) – www.chezbruce.co.uk – Closed 24-26 December and 1 January*

WESTMINSTER (City of)

Regional map n° **7**-B3

Bayswater and Maida Vale

🏛 Lancaster London   🔆 ≤ 🏋 🖸 ⇄ 🔟 🎋 🏊 🅿

BUSINESS · CLASSIC An imposing 1960s hotel overlooking Hyde Park, known for its extensive conference suites. Bedrooms are bright and well-equipped. Island has an accessible, Med-influenced menu, with steaks a highlight; Nipa is their longstanding Thai restaurant.

416 rooms – 🛉£ 129/429 🛉🛉£ 129/429 – ☲ £ 16 – 22 suites
Town plan: 28ADU-e – *Lancaster Terr* ⌗ *W2 2TY*
– ⊖ *Lancaster Gate* – ℰ *(020) 7551 6000*
– *www.lancasterlondon.com*

🏛 Royal Park   🖸 🔟 🎋 🅿

TOWNHOUSE · COSY Three attractive 19C townhouses, with an appealing English feel, set back from the road, in a pleasant location near Hyde Park. Quiet lounges with period furnishings and bedrooms with four-poster beds.

48 rooms – 🛉£ 191/299 🛉🛉£ 191/299 – ☲ £ 14 – 11 suites
Town plan: 28ADU-x – *3 Westbourne Terr* ⌗ *W2 3UL*
– ⊖ *Lancaster Gate* – ℰ *(020) 7479 6600*
– *www.theroyalpark.com*

🏛 Hotel Indigo London Paddington   🔆 🏋 🖸 ⇄ 🔟 🎋

BUSINESS · MODERN Behind the period façade is a modern, corporate townhouse themed around the Golden ratio, a mathematical formula. Bright rooms have feature walls depicting scenes of the local area. All-day menu of steaks, pasta and brasserie classics.

64 rooms – 🛉£ 109/279 🛉🛉£ 129/379 – ☲ £ 20
Town plan: 28ADU-a – *16 London St* ⌗ *W2 1HL*
– ⊖ *Paddington* – ℰ *(020) 7706 4444* – *www.hotelindigo.com*

✗✗ Angelus   ⇄ 🔟 ⇄

FRENCH · BRASSERIE Hospitable owner has created an attractive French brasserie within a 19C former pub, with a warm and inclusive feel. Satisfying and honest French cooking uses seasonal British ingredients.

Menu £ 22 (lunch) – Carte £ 42/59
Town plan: 28ADU-c – *4 Bathurst St* ⌗ *W2 2SD*
– ⊖ *Lancaster Gate* – ℰ *(020) 7402 0083*
– *www.angelusrestaurant.co.uk* – *Closed 24 December-2 January*

XX Marianne

FRENCH · COSY The eponymous Marianne was a finalist on MasterChef. Her restaurant is a sweet little place with just 6 tables. A concise daily menu lets her own cooking style come through – it's classically based but keeps things quite light.

Menu £ 65/85 – set menu only

Town plan: 27AAT-m – *104a Chepstow Rd ⊠ W2 5QS – ⊖ Westbourne Park – 𝒞 (020) 3675 7750 (booking essential) – www.mariannerestaurant.com – dinner only and lunch Friday-Sunday – Closed Christmas-New Year and 26-28 August and Monday*

XX Shiori

JAPANESE · COSY Takashi & Hitomi Takagi's kaiseki restaurant brings a little of Kyoto to West London. The finest UK produce is supplemented by vegetables imported from Japan; the resulting dishes are beautifully presented, delicate, balanced and original. The small but immaculately dressed room seats just 16.

Menu £ 75/102

Town plan: 27ABU-x – *45 Moscow Rd ⊠ W2 4AH – ⊖ Bayswater – 𝒞 (020) 7221 9790 (booking essential) – www.theshiori.com – Closed Sunday and Monday*

XX Toa Kitchen

CHINESE · FRIENDLY There's an overwhelming number of Chinese restaurants on Queensway so search out Toa Kitchen and head for the "Chef's Specials" for good, authentic Cantonese dishes. Service from owner Mr Fung and his team is also a cut above average.

Carte £ 14/58

Town plan: 27ABU-t – *100 Queensway ⊠ W2 3RR – ⊖ Bayswater – 𝒞 (020) 7792 9767 – www.toakitchen.com – Closed 25 December*

X Hereford Road

BRITISH TRADITIONAL · NEIGHBOURHOOD Converted butcher's shop specialising in tasty British dishes without frills, using first-rate, seasonal ingredients; offal a highlight. Booths for six people are the prized seats. Friendly and relaxed feel.

Menu £ 14 (weekday lunch) – Carte £ 23/32

Town plan: 27ABU-s – *3 Hereford Rd ⊠ W2 4AB – ⊖ Bayswater – 𝒞 (020) 7727 1144 (booking essential) – www.herefordroad.org – Closed 24 December-3 January and 27-29 August*

X Kateh

MEDITERRANEAN · NEIGHBOURHOOD Booking is imperative if you want to join the locals who have already discovered what a little jewel they have in the form of this buzzy, busy Persian restaurant. Authentic stews, expert chargrilling and lovely pastries and teas.

Carte £ 19/36

Town plan: 28ACT-a – *5 Warwick Pl ⊠ W9 2PX – ⊖ Warwick Avenue – 𝒞 (020) 7289 3393 (booking essential) – www.katehrestaurant.co.uk – dinner only and lunch Friday-Sunday – Closed 25-26 December*

X Kurobuta Marble Arch

JAPANESE · NEIGHBOURHOOD The Aussie owner-chef's fun Japanese restaurant was influenced by izakaya. The robata grill provides the sticky BBQ pork belly for the pork buns; the black pepper soft shell crabs fly out of the kitchen; and the yuzu tart is good.

Carte £ 17/32

Town plan: 29AFU-m – *17-20 Kendal St ⊠ W2 2AW – ⊖ Marble Arch – 𝒞 (020) 3475 4158 – www.kurobuta-london.com – Closed 25 December*

Casa Malevo

ARGENTINIAN • NEIGHBOURHOOD Meat lovers should head for this warm, country style 'cocina Argentina'. Kick things off with empanadas or homemade chorizo then order a cut of premium Argentinian beef; the Malbec and bone marrow sauce hits the spot too.

Carte £ 21/44

Town plan: 29AFU-a - *23 Connaught St ✉ W2 2AY - ⊖ Marble Arch - ✆ (020) 7402 1988 - www.casamalevo.com - dinner only - Closed 24-29 December*

Truscott Arms

MODERN CUISINE • NEIGHBOURHOOD A Victorian pub resuscitated and restored by a husband and wife team. Pub classics on the ground floor; local artwork in upstairs dining room where the ambitious kitchen uses modern techniques to produce quite elaborate dishes.

Menu £ 18/36 - Carte £ 24/33

Town plan: 16NZD-a - *55 Shirland Rd ✉ W9 2JD - ⊖ Warwick Avenue. - ✆ (020) 7266 9198 - www.thetruscottarms.com*

Belgravia

Berkeley

GRAND LUXURY • STYLISH Discreet and very comfortable hotel with impressive rooftop pool and opulently decorated, immaculately kept bedrooms. Relax in the gilded, panelled Caramel Room or have a drink in the ice cool Blue Bar. Choice of two restaurants.

210 rooms - †£ 270/720 ††£ 330/840 - ☕ £ 32 - 28 suites

Town plan: 37AGX-e - *Wilton Pl ✉ SW1X 7RL - ⊖ Knightsbridge - ✆ (020) 7235 6000 - www.the-berkeley.co.uk*

✿✿ **Marcus** • **Koffmann's** - See restaurant listing

Halkin

LUXURY • STYLISH Opened in 1991 as one of London's first boutique hotels and still looking sharp today. Thoughtfully conceived bedrooms with silk walls and marbled bathrooms; everything at the touch of a button. Abundant Armani-clad staff. Small, discreet bar.

41 rooms - †£ 330/420 ††£ 370/640 - ☕ £ 28 - 6 suites

Town plan: 38AHX-b - *5 Halkin St ✉ SW1X 7DJ - ⊖ Hyde Park Corner - ✆ (020) 7333 1000 - www.comohotels.com/thehalkin*

✿ **Ametsa** - See restaurant listing

The Wellesley

TOWNHOUSE • ART DECO Stylish, elegant townhouse inspired by the jazz age, on the site of the famous Pizza on the Park. Impressive cigar lounge and bar with a super selection of whiskies and cognacs. Smart bedrooms have full butler service; those facing Hyde Park the most prized. Modern Italian food in the discreet restaurant.

36 rooms - †£ 365/555 ††£ 365/555 - ☕ £ 34 - 14 suites

Town plan: 37AGX-w - *11 Knightsbridge ✉ SW1X 7LY - ⊖ Hyde Park Corner - ✆ (020) 7235 3535 - www.thewellesley.co.uk*

Belgraves

BUSINESS • MODERN US group Thompson's first UK venture is an elegant and stylish boutique-style hotel with a hint of bohemia. Uncluttered, decently proportioned bedrooms come with oak flooring and lovely marble bathrooms. Light, Mediterranean-influenced dishes served in Pont St restaurant.

85 rooms - †£ 359/599 ††£ 360/660 - ☕ £ 20

Town plan: 37AGX-c - *20 Chesham Pl ✉ SW1X 8HQ - ⊖ Knightsbridge - ✆ (020) 7858 0100 - www.thompsonhotels.com*

🏨 Jumeirah Lowndes

BUSINESS · MODERN Compact yet friendly, modern corporate hotel within this exclusive residential area. Good levels of personal service offered. Close to the famous shops of Knightsbridge. Informal restaurant with appealing courtyard terrace.

88 rooms – ♦£ 180/595 ♦♦£ 180/595 – ⌘ £ 25 – 6 suites

Town plan: 37AGX-h – *21 Lowndes St* ✉ *SW1X 9ES* – ⊖ *Knightsbridge* – ℰ *(020) 7823 1234* – *www.jumeirah.com*

XxxX Marcus

MODERN CUISINE · FORMAL Marcus Wareing's flagship now comes with a more relaxed feel, thanks largely to the personable staff who get the tone of the service just right. The menu is flexible and dishes come with a refreshing lack of complication and are never too heavy, despite the flavours being well-defined.

→ Carrot, black garlic, chicken skin and pine nut. Rump of Herdwick mutton, calçot and radicchio. Toffee, peanut and milk chocolate nougat.

Menu £ 49/85

Town plan: 37AGX-e – *Berkeley Hotel, Wilton Pl* ✉ *SW1X 7RL* – ⊖ *Knightsbridge* – ℰ *(020) 7235 1200* – *www.marcus-wareing.com* – *Closed Sunday*

XxX Pétrus

FRENCH · ELEGANT Gordon Ramsay's Belgravia restaurant is a sophisticated and elegant affair. The service is discreet and professional; and cooking is rooted in classical techniques but isn't afraid of using influences from further afield. The superb wine list has Château Pétrus going back to 1924.

→ Aberdeen Angus tartare with truffle, quail's egg and olive oil. Fillet of Cornish brill with cuttlefish and cep bolognese. Seared pineapple with smoked coconut, lime sorbet and pineapple granité.

Menu £ 38/75

Town plan: 37AGX-v – *1 Kinnerton St* ✉ *SW1X 8EA* – ⊖ *Knightsbridge* – ℰ *(020) 7592 1609* – *www.gordonramsay.com/petrus* – *Closed 21-27 December, 1 January and Sunday*

XxX Ametsa

CREATIVE · ELEGANT Whilst the father and daughter team from the celebrated Arzak restaurant in San Sebastián are behind it, Ametsa has its own style. Most ingredients are sourced from within the British Isles but the flavours, combinations and colours are typically Basque and the dishes are wonderfully vibrant.

→ Scallops at home. Sea bass with celery illusion. Clove custard with toasted milk and pineapple ice cream.

Menu £ 28/52 – Carte £ 55/78

Town plan: 38AHX-b – *Halkin Hotel, 5 Halkin St* ✉ *SW1X 7DJ* – ⊖ *Hyde Park Corner* – ℰ *(020) 7333 1234* – *www.comohotels.com/thehalkin* – *Closed 24-26 December, 1 January, lunch 31 December, Sunday and lunch Monday*

XxX Amaya

INDIAN · DESIGN Order a selection of small dishes from the tawa griddle, tandoor or sigri grill and finish with a curry or biryani. Dishes like lamb chops are aromatic and satisfying and the cooking is skilled and consistent. This busy Indian restaurant is bright, colourful and lively; ask for a table by the open kitchen.

→ Chargrilled Madagascan prawn. Slow-roasted leg of baby lamb, cumin and garam masala. Spiced black fig brûlée with kokum sherbet.

Menu £ 23 (weekday lunch) – Carte £ 39/84

Town plan: 37AGX-k – *Halkin Arcade, 19 Motcomb St* ✉ *SW1X 8JT* – ⊖ *Knightsbridge* – ℰ *(020) 7823 1166* – *www.amaya.biz*

XxX **Koffmann's**

FRENCH · ELEGANT Pierre Koffmann, one of London's most fêted chefs, was enticed out of retirement to open this comfortable, well run and spacious restaurant. Expect classic signature dishes and plenty of gutsy flavours true to his Gascon roots.

Menu £ 28 (lunch and early dinner) – Carte £ 43/71

Town plan: 37AGX-e – *Berkeley Hotel, Wilton Pl ⊠ SW1X 7RL*
– ⊖ *Knightsbridge* – ✆ *(020) 7235 1010* – *www.the-berkeley.co.uk*

XxX **Zafferano**

ITALIAN · FASHIONABLE The immaculately coiffured regulars continue to support this ever-expanding, long-standing and capably run Italian restaurant. They come for the reassuringly familiar, if rather steeply priced dishes from all parts of Italy.

Menu £ 25 (weekday lunch) – Carte £ 40/73

Town plan: 37AGX-f – *15 Lowndes St ⊠ SW1X 9EY* – ⊖ *Knightsbridge*
– ✆ *(020) 7235 5800 (booking essential)* – *www.zafferanorestaurant.co.uk*
– *Closed 25 December*

🍺 **Pantechnicon**

BRITISH MODERN · PUB Urbane, enthusiastically run pub with a busy ground floor and altogether more formal upstairs dining room. Traditional dishes are given a modern twist; oysters and Scottish steaks are perennials.

Carte £ 29/38

Town plan: 37AGX-d – *10 Motcomb St ⊠ SW1X 8LA* – ⊖ *Knightsbridge.*
– ✆ *(020) 7730 6074 (booking advisable)* – *www.thepantechnicon.com* – *Closed 25 December*

Hyde Park and Knightsbridge

🏨 **Mandarin Oriental Hyde Park**

GRAND LUXURY · CLASSIC The Rosebery, a salon for afternoon tea, is the newest addition to this celebrated hotel which dates from 1889. The luxurious spa now includes a pool; the service is as strong as ever; and the bedrooms, many of which have views of Hyde Park, are spacious and comfortable.

194 rooms – ♦£ 414/798 ♦♦£ 414/798 – ⊆ £ 26 – 25 suites

Town plan: 37AGX-x – *66 Knightsbridge ⊠ SW1X 7LA* – ⊖ *Knightsbridge*
– ✆ *(020) 7235 2000* – *www.mandarinoriental.com/london*

❀❀ **Dinner by Heston Blumenthal • Bar Boulud** – See restaurant listing

🏨 **Bulgari**

LUXURY · STYLISH Impeccably tailored hotel making stunning use of materials like silver, mahogany, silk and marble. Luxurious bedrooms with sensual curves, sumptuous bathrooms and a great spa – and there is substance behind the style. Down a sweeping staircase to the Alain Ducasse restaurant.

85 rooms – ♦£ 510/790 ♦♦£ 510/890 – ⊆ £ 34 – 23 suites

Town plan: 37AFX-k – *171 Knightsbridge ⊠ SW7 1DW* – ⊖ *Knightsbridge*
– ✆ *(020) 7151 1010* – *www.bulgarihotels.com/london*

Rivea – See restaurant listing

XxX **Dinner by Heston Blumenthal**

❀❀ BRITISH MODERN · DESIGN Don't come expecting 'molecular gastronomy' – this is all about respect for, and a wonderful renewal of, British food, with just a little playfulness thrown in. Each one of the meticulously crafted and deceptively simple looking dishes comes with a date relating to its historical provenance.

➜ Mandarin, chicken liver parfait and grilled bread, (c.1500). Chicken with lettuce, grilled onion emulsion, spiced celeriac sauce and oyster leaves, (c.1670). Tipsy cake with spit-roast pineapple, (c.1810).

Menu £ 38 (weekday lunch) – Carte £ 63/111

Town plan: 37AGX-x – *Mandarin Oriental Hyde Park Hotel, 66 Knightsbridge ⊠ SW1X 7LA* – ⊖ *Knightsbridge* – ✆ *(020) 7201 3833* – *www.dinnerbyheston.com*

XX Bar Boulud

FRENCH • BRASSERIE Daniel Boulud's London outpost is fashionable, fun and frantic. His hometown is Lyon but he built his considerable reputation in New York, so charcuterie, sausages and burgers are the highlights.

Menu £ 19 (weekday lunch) – Carte £ 26/57

Town plan: 37AGX-x – *Mandarin Oriental Hyde Park Hotel, 66 Knightsbridge* ✉ *SW1X 7LA* – ⊖ *Knightsbridge* – ℰ *(020) 7201 3899 – www.barboulud.com*

XX Rivea

MEDITERRANEAN • DESIGN Elegant basement restaurant where blues and whites make reference to warmer climes – and also to its sister in St Tropez. Precise, unfussy cooking focuses on the French and Italian Riviera, with an interesting range of vibrant small plates.

Menu £ 35 (lunch) – Carte £ 21/42

Town plan: 37AFX-k – *Bulgari Hotel, 171 Knightsbridge* ✉ *SW7 1DW* – ⊖ *Knightsbridge* – ℰ *(020) 7151 1025 – www.rivealondon.com*

XX The Magazine

MODERN CUISINE • DESIGN Designed by Zaha Hadid, the Serpentine Sackler Gallery comprises a restored 1805 gunpowder store and a modern tensile extension. The Magazine is a bright open space with an eclectic mix of modern European.

Menu £ 22 (lunch) – Carte £ 27/51

Town plan: 28ADV-t – *Serpentine Sackler Gallery, West Carriage Dr, Kensington Gardens* ✉ *W2 2AR* – ⊖ *Lancaster Gate* – ℰ *(020) 7298 7552* – *www.magazine-restaurant.co.uk – lunch only and dinner Friday-Saturday* – *Closed Monday and dinner in winter*

XX Zuma

JAPANESE • FASHIONABLE Now a global brand but this was the original. The glamorous clientele come for the striking surroundings, bustling atmosphere and easy-to-share food. Go for the more modern dishes and those cooked on the robata grill.

Carte £ 33/79

Town plan: 37AFX-m – *5 Raphael St* ✉ *SW7 1DL* – ⊖ *Knightsbridge* – ℰ *(020) 7584 1010 (booking essential) – www.zumarestaurant.com – Closed 25 December*

Mayfair

🏨 Dorchester

GRAND LUXURY • CLASSIC One of the capital's iconic properties offering every possible facility and exemplary levels of service. The striking marbled and pillared promenade provides an elegant backdrop for afternoon tea. Bedrooms are eminently comfortable; some overlook Hyde Park. The Grill is for all things British; Alain Ducasse waves Le Tricolore; China Tang celebrates the cuisine of the Orient.

250 rooms – ♦£ 355/895 ♦♦£ 415/955 – ☑ £ 35 – 50 suites

Town plan: 30AHV-a – *Park Ln.* ✉ *W1K 1QA* – ⊖ *Hyde Park Corner* – ℰ *(020) 7629 8888 – www.dorchestercollection.com*

✸✸✸ **Alain Ducasse at The Dorchester • The Grill • China Tang** – See restaurant listing

🏨 Claridge's

GRAND LUXURY • CLASSIC Claridge's has a long, illustrious history dating back to 1812 and this iconic and very British hotel has been a favourite of the royal family over generations. Its most striking decorative feature is the art deco. The hotel also moves with the times: its restaurant was re-launched in 2014 as Fera.

197 rooms – ♦£ 480/1140 ♦♦£ 480/1140 – ☑ £ 34 – 62 suites

Town plan: 30AHU-c – *Brook St* ✉ *W1K 4HR* – ⊖ *Bond Street* – ℰ *(020) 7629 8860 – www.claridges.co.uk*

✸ **Fera at Claridge's** – See restaurant listing

Connaught

GRAND LUXURY · CLASSIC One of London's most famous hotels; restored and renovated but still retaining an elegant British feel. All the luxurious bedrooms come with large marble bathrooms and butler service. There's a choice of two stylish bars and Espelette is an all-day venue for classic French and British dishes.

121 rooms ☲ – †£ 510/840 ††£ 600/960 – 26 suites

Town plan: 30AHU-e – *Carlos Pl.* ✉ *W1K 2AL* – ⊖ *Bond Street* – ℰ *(020) 7499 7070 – www.the-connaught.co.uk*

❀❀ **Hélène Darroze at The Connaught** – See restaurant listing

Four Seasons

GRAND LUXURY · MODERN Reopened in 2011 after a huge refurbishment project and has raised the bar for luxury hotels. Striking lobby sets the scene; sumptuous bedrooms have a rich, contemporary look and boast every conceivable comfort. Great views from the stunning rooftop spa.

193 rooms – †£ 385/960 ††£ 385/960 – ☲ £ 30 – 33 suites

Town plan: 30AHV-v – *Hamilton Pl, Park Ln* ✉ *W1J 7DR* – ⊖ *Hyde Park Corner* – ℰ *(020) 7499 0888 – www.fourseasons.com/london*

Amaranto – See restaurant listing

InterContinental London Park Lane

BUSINESS · MODERN International hotel whose position facing the park is an impressive feature. Everything leads off from the large, open-plan lobby. English-style bedrooms with hi-tech equipment; luxurious suites. Casual, family-friendly Cookbook Café.

447 rooms – †£ 275/790 ††£ 275/790 – ☲ £ 28 – 48 suites

Town plan: 30AHV-k – *1 Hamilton Pl, Park Ln* ✉ *W1J 7QY* – ⊖ *Hyde Park Corner* – ℰ *(020) 7409 3131 – www.london.intercontinental.com*

Theo Randall – See restaurant listing

London Hilton

BUSINESS · CLASSIC The bedrooms at this 28 storey hotel, which celebrated 50 years in 2013, now come with a sharper and more contemporary edge. For Polynesian food and a Mai Tai, head to the iconic brand that is Trader Vic's; for casual, all-day dining, try Podium. Extensive banqueting and conference facilities.

453 rooms – †£ 322/869 ††£ 322/869 – ☲ £ 27 – 56 suites

Town plan: 30AHV-e – *22 Park Ln.* ✉ *W1K 1BE* – ⊖ *Hyde Park Corner* – ℰ *(020) 7493 8000 – www.hilton.co.uk/londonparklane*

❀ **Galvin at Windows** – See restaurant listing

Grosvenor House

BUSINESS · CLASSIC A large, landmark property occupying a commanding position by Hyde Park. Uniform, comfortable but well proportioned bedrooms in classic Marriott styling. Busy banqueting department boasts the largest ballroom in Europe. JW Steakhouse is the place for beer, bourbon and beef.

494 rooms – †£ 199/599 ††£ 199/599 – ☲ £ 29 – 73 suites

Town plan: 29AGU-g – *Park Ln* ✉ *W1K 7TN* – ⊖ *Marble Arch* – ℰ *(020) 7499 6363 – www.londongrosvenorhouse.co.uk*

The Beaumont 🆕

LUXURY · ART DECO From a 1926 former garage, restaurateurs Chris Corbin and Jeremy King fashioned their first hotel; art deco inspired, it's stunning, stylish and exudes understated luxury. The attention to detail is exemplary, from the undeniably masculine bedrooms to the lively, cool cocktail bar and busy brasserie.

73 rooms ☲ – †£ 395/480 ††£ 395/480 – 10 suites

Town plan: 30AHU-x – *Brown Hart Gdns.* ✉ *W1K 6TF* – ⊖ *Bond Street* – ℰ *(020) 7499 1001 – www.thebeaumont.com*

Colony Grill Room – See restaurant listing

45 Park Lane

LUXURY · STYLISH It was the original site of the Playboy Club and has been a car showroom but now 45 Park Lane has been reborn as The Dorchester's sister hotel. The bedrooms, all with views over Hyde Park, are wonderfully sensual and the marble bathrooms are beautiful.

46 rooms – ♦£ 495/834 ♦♦£ 495/834 – ☑ £ 19 – 10 suites

Town plan: 30AHV-r – *45 Park Ln* ✉ *W1K 1PN* – ⊖ *Hyde Park Corner* – *𝒞 (020) 7493 4545* – *www.45parklane.com*

Cut – See restaurant listing

Westbury

BUSINESS · MODERN Now as stylish as when it opened in the 1950s. Smart, comfortable bedrooms with terrific art deco inspired suites. Elegant, iconic Polo bar and bright, fresh sushi bar. All the designer brands outside the front door.

246 rooms – ♦£ 600 ♦♦£ 600 – 13 suites

Town plan: 30AIU-z – *Bond St* ✉ *W1S 2YF* – ⊖ *Bond Street* – *𝒞 (020) 7629 7755* – *www.westburymayfair.com*

❀ **Alyn Williams at The Westbury** – See restaurant listing

Brown's

LUXURY · STYLISH Opened in 1837 by James Brown, Lord Byron's butler. This urbane and very British hotel with an illustrious past offers a swish bar with Terence Donovan prints, bedrooms in neutral hues and a classic English sitting room for afternoon tea.

117 rooms – ♦£ 415/905 ♦♦£ 445/945 – ☑ £ 32 – 12 suites

Town plan: 30AIV-d – *33 Albemarle St* ✉ *W1S 4BP* – ⊖ *Green Park* – *𝒞 (020) 7493 6020* – *www.roccofortehotels.com*

Hix Mayfair – See restaurant listing

London Marriott H. Grosvenor Square

BUSINESS · FUNCTIONAL A well-appointed international hotel that benefits from an excellent location in the heart of Mayfair. Bedrooms are specifically equipped for business travellers. Ask for a Balcony room: they have access to a private roof garden.

237 rooms – ♦£ 249/599 ♦♦£ 249/599 – ☑ £ 18 – 11 suites

Town plan: 30AHU-s – *84-86 Duke St* ✉ *W1K 6JP* – ⊖ *Bond Street* – *𝒞 (020) 7493 1232* – *www.marriottgrosvenorsquare.com*

Maze Grill Mayfair – See restaurant listing

London Marriott H. Park Lane

LUXURY · DESIGN International hotel located close to Hyde Park and Oxford Street and the only one on Park Lane with a pool. Fresh, contemporary look to the bedrooms after a major refurb. Lanes offers Indian, Lebanese, Vietnamese and British dishes.

152 rooms – ♦£ 549/699 ♦♦£ 549/699 – ☑ £ 13 – 14 suites

Town plan: 29AGU-b – *140 Park Ln* ✉ *W1K 7AA* – ⊖ *Marble Arch* – *𝒞 (020) 7493 7000* – *www.londonmarriottparklane.co.uk*

Metropolitan

BUSINESS · MODERN Not quite as hip as it once was but still has an appealing, crisp and uncluttered design-led look. Decent sized bedrooms with plenty of hitech touches; an all-day menu in the Met Bar and London's original Nobu upstairs.

144 rooms – ♦£ 350/580 ♦♦£ 350/580 – ☑ £ 28 – 3 suites

Town plan: 30AHV-c – *Old Park Ln* ✉ *W1K 1LB* – ⊖ *Hyde Park Corner* – *𝒞 (020) 7447 1000* – *http://www.comohotels.com/metropolitanlondon/*

Nobu – See restaurant listing

Athenaeum

TOWNHOUSE · CONTEMPORARY 1920s building opposite the park; its smart bedrooms come in cool pastel shades and have floor to ceiling windows. Bright restaurant and a bar offering over 270 different whiskies. The hotel also organises events for kids.

164 rooms – ♥£ 295/500 ♥♥£ 295/500 – ☑£ 23 – 24 suites
Town plan: 30AHV-g – 116 Piccadilly ☒ W1J 7BJ – ⊖ Hyde Park Corner
– ℰ (020) 7499 3464 – www.athenaeumhotel.com

Chesterfield

TOWNHOUSE · CLASSIC An assuredly English feel to this Georgian house. Discreet lobby leads to a clubby bar and wood panelled library. Individually decorated bedrooms, with some antique pieces. Intimate and pretty restaurant.

107 rooms ☑ – ♥£ 195/390 ♥♥£ 220/510 – 4 suites
Town plan: 30AHV-f – 35 Charles St ☒ W1J 5EB – ⊖ Green Park – ℰ (020) 7491 2622 – www.chesterfieldmayfair.com

Alain Ducasse at The Dorchester

❀❀❀ FRENCH · ELEGANT Elegance, luxury and attention to detail are the hallmarks of Alain Ducasse's London outpost, where the atmosphere is warm and relaxed. The kitchen uses the best seasonal produce, whether British or French, to create visually striking, refined, modern dishes. The 'Table Lumière' with its shimmering curtain affords an opulent, semi-private dining experience.

→ Sauté of lobster, chicken quenelles and pasta. Simmered halibut with winkles, cockles and razor clams marinière. Baba like in Monte Carlo.

Menu £ 60/95

Town plan: 30AHV-a – Dorchester Hotel, Park Ln ☒ W1K 1QA
– ⊖ Hyde Park Corner – ℰ (020) 7629 8866 (booking essential)
– www.alainducasse-dorchester.com – Closed 9-30 August, 26-30 December, 1-5 January, 25-26 March, Saturday lunch, Sunday and Monday

Sketch (The Lecture Room & Library)

❀❀ FRENCH · LUXURY Mourad Mazouz and Pierre Gagnaire's 18C funhouse is awash with colour, energy and vim and the luxurious 'Lecture Room & Library' provides the ideal setting for the sophisticated French cooking. Relax and enjoy artfully presented, elaborate dishes that provide many varieties of flavours and textures.

→ Foie gras terrine with lime, green bean salad, langoustine consommé and rocket Chantilly. Wild turbot with black pepper. Dragon fruit syrup with lemon and olive oil jelly, lemon curd, pink praline and kirsch.

Menu £ 40/110 – Carte £ 101/129

Town plan: 30AIU-h – 9 Conduit St (1st floor) ☒ W1S 2XG – ⊖ Oxford Circus
– ℰ (020) 7659 4500 (booking essential) – www.sketch.london – Closed last 2 weeks August, Saturday lunch, Sunday and Monday

Hélène Darroze at The Connaught

❀❀ MODERN CUISINE · LUXURY From a Solitaire board of 13 marbles, each bearing the name of an ingredient, you choose 5, 7 or 9; this highlights the quality of produce used. The cooking is lighter these days yet still with the occasional unexpected flavour. The warm service ensures the wood-panelled room never feels too formal.

→ Oyster 'fine de claire' with Oscietra caviar and white coco beans. Scallop, tandoori spices, carrot, citrus and coriander. Savarin Armagnac, raspberry and pepper.

Menu £ 30/92

Town plan: 30AHU-e – Connaught Hotel, Carlos Pl. ☒ W1K 2AL
– ⊖ Bond Street – ℰ (020) 7107 8880 (booking essential)
– www.the-connaught.co.uk – Closed 3 weeks August, 1 week January, Saturday lunch, Sunday and Monday

XxxX Le Gavroche (Michel Roux Jnr) 🏛 AC ⇔

FRENCH · FORMAL Classical, rich and indulgent French cuisine is the draw at Michel Roux's renowned London institution. The large, smart basement room has a clubby, masculine feel; service is formal and structured but also has charm.

→ Mousseline de homard au champagne et caviar. Râble de lapin et galette au parmesan. Soufflé aux fruits de la passion et glace Ivoire.

Menu £ 55/126 – Carte £ 63/164

Town plan: 29AGU-c – 43 Upper Brook St ✉ W1K 7QR – ⊖ Marble Arch – ☎ (020) 7408 0881 (booking essential) – www.le-gavroche.co.uk – Closed Christmas-January, Saturday lunch, Sunday and bank holidays

XxxX Square (Philip Howard) 🏛 AC 🦶 ⇔

FRENCH · FORMAL A restaurant that demands respect, and not just because it's approaching its quarter century. The cooking is rooted in classic French cuisine but displays more than a healthy understanding of contemporary mores. The room is smart without being stuffy and the service professional yet warm.

→ White asparagus with Dorset crab, Grelot onions and beach herbs. Saddle of West Country lamb with purple garlic, thyme gnocchetti and Italian artichokes. Milk chocolate délice with salted caramel, peanuts and banana.

Menu £ 38/90 – Carte £ 75/120

Town plan: 30AIU-v – 6-10 Bruton St. ✉ W1J 6PU – ⊖ Green Park – ☎ (020) 7495 7100 – www.squarerestaurant.com – Closed 24-26 December and Sunday lunch

XxxX Fera at Claridge's 🏛 🦶 AC 🦶 ⇔

BRITISH CREATIVE · ELEGANT Earth-father, forager supreme and gastronomic alchemist Simon Rogan brings his wonderfully natural, unforced style of cooking to the capital. The deftly balanced and cleverly textured dishes deliver multi-dimensional layers of flavours and the grand room has been transformed into a thing of beauty.

→ Grilled and smoked salad with Isle of Mull truffle custard and sunflower seeds. Cornish lamb, sheep's milk, white asparagus, ramson flowers and alliums. Compressed strawberries with sweet cicely, buttermilk and sorrel.

Menu £ 39/105 – Carte £ 51/74

Town plan: 30AHU-c – Claridge's Hotel, Brook St ✉ W1K 4HR – ⊖ Bond Street – ☎ (020) 7107 8888 (booking advisable) – www.feraatclaridges.co.uk

XxxX Alyn Williams at The Westbury 🏛 🦶 AC 🦶 ⇔

MODERN CUISINE · DESIGN Confident, cheery service ensures the atmosphere never strays into terminal seriousness; rosewood panelling and a striking wine display add warmth. The cooking is creative and even playful but however elaborately constructed the dish, the combinations of flavours and textures always work.

→ Roast Scottish scallops with cauliflower and winter truffle. Wiltshire pigeon with carrot and fennel pollen. Mascarpone with caramelised apple, ginger and hibiscus.

Menu £ 30/60

Town plan: 30AIU-z – Westbury Hotel, 37 Conduit St ✉ W1S 2YF – ⊖ Bond Street – ☎ (020) 7183 6426 – www.alynwilliams.com – Closed first 2 weeks January, last 2 weeks August, Sunday and Monday

XxX Greenhouse 🏛 AC ⇔

CREATIVE · FASHIONABLE Chef Arnaud Bignon's cooking is confident, balanced and innovative and uses the best from Europe's larder; his dishes exude an exhilarating freshness. The breadth and depth of the wine list is astounding. This is a discreet, sleek and contemporary restaurant with well-judged service.

→ Cornish crab, mint jelly, cauliflower, Granny Smith apple and curry. Presa Ibérico, aubergine, Sobrasada, onion and smoked pimento. Guanaja chocolate, praline, lemon and finger lime.

Menu £ 40/110 – Carte £ 98/120

Town plan: 30AHV-m – 27a Hay's Mews ✉ W1J 5NY – ⊖ Hyde Park Corner – ☎ (020) 7499 3331 – www.greenhouserestaurant.co.uk – Closed Saturday lunch, Sunday and bank holidays

XxX **Hibiscus** (Claude Bosi)   AC ⇔

❀❀❀ CREATIVE · ELEGANT Choose 3, 6 or 8 courses and be prepared for a surprise
as the kitchen will choose the dishes. Claude Bosi's cooking is as innovative as
ever; the combinations of flavours and textures are well-judged and dishes are
underpinned by fine ingredients. The last revamp left the room brighter and
lighter.
➜ Mylor prawn, smoked butter, lemon and Beluski caviar. Cornish sea bass à la
Grenobloise. Chocolate millefeuille, Indonesian basil and star anise.
Menu £ 50/90
Town plan: 30AIU-s – *29 Maddox St* ⊠ *W1S 2PA* – ⊖ *Oxford Circus*
– *℘ (020) 7629 2999 – www.hibiscusrestaurant.co.uk*
– *Closed 3 days Christmas, Monday except December, Sunday and bank
holidays*

XxX **Umu**   ❀❀ AC

❀❀❀ JAPANESE · FASHIONABLE Stylish, discreet interior using natural materials,
with central sushi bar. Extensive choice of Japanese dishes; choose one of
the seasonal kaiseki menus for the full experience. Over 160 different labels
of sake.
➜ Line-caught squid, tosasu and ginger. Wild lobster, homemade shichimi pepper and tofu miso bisque. Japanese seasonal tiramisu, green tea, sake and blood
orange.
Menu £ 25/125 – Carte £ 41/151
Town plan: 30AIU-k – *14-16 Bruton Pl.* ⊠ *W1J 6LX* – ⊖ *Bond Street* – *℘ (020)
7499 8881 – www.umurestaurant.com – Closed Christmas, New Year, Saturday
lunch, Sunday and bank holidays*

XxX **The Grill** ❶   ❀❀ � AC ⤶

FRENCH · ELEGANT The re-launched Grill is relaxed yet formal, with an open
kitchen and a striking, hand-blown Murano glass chandelier as its centrepiece.
Grill favourites sit alongside modern day classics on the menu; sharing dishes
are a good choice, as are the speciality soufflés. Service is smooth and highly
professional.
Menu £ 39 (weekday lunch) – Carte £ 54/89
Town plan: 30AHV-a – *Dorchester Hotel, Park Ln* ⊠ *W1K 1QA*
– ⊖ *Hyde Park Corner* – *℘ (020) 7317 6531 (booking advisable)*
– *www.dorchestercollection.com*

XxX **Cut**   ⅙ AC

MEATS · DESIGN The first European venture from Wolfgang Puck, the US-based
Austrian celebrity chef, is this very slick, stylish and sexy room where glamorous
people come to eat meat. The not-inexpensive steaks are cooked over hardwood
and charcoal and finished off in a broiler.
Menu £ 45 (weekday lunch) – Carte £ 48/177
Town plan: 30AHV-r – *45 Park Lane Hotel, 45 Park Ln* ⊠ *W1K 1PN*
– ⊖ *Hyde Park Corner* – *℘ (020) 7493 4545 (booking essential)*
– *www.45parklane.com*

XxX **Murano** (Angela Hartnett)   ⅙ AC

❀ ITALIAN · FASHIONABLE Angela Hartnett's Italian influenced cooking exhibits an
appealing lightness of touch, with assured combinations of flavours, borne out of
confidence in the ingredients. This is a stylish, elegant room run by a well-organised, professional and friendly team who put their customers at ease.
➜ Sweetbreads, farfalle, broad beans and apple compote. Hake with roast cauliflower, kale, pata negra and garlic. Pistachio panna cotta, chocolate, pistachio
and mandarin.
Menu £ 33/65
Town plan: 30AHV-b – *20 Queen St* ⊠ *W1J 5PP* – ⊖ *Green Park* – *℘ (020)
7495 1127 – www.muranolondon.com – Closed Christmas and Sunday*

XxX Galvin at Windows 🍷 ≪ 👌 AC

MODERN CUISINE · FORMAL The cleverly laid out room makes the most of the spectacular views across London from the 28th floor. Relaxed service takes the edge off the somewhat corporate atmosphere. The bold cooking uses superb ingredients and the classically based food comes with a pleasing degree of flair and innovation.
→ Scallop ceviche, caviar, orange, pomelo, pickled kohlrabi and sweet soy. Fillet of sea bass with potato crust, chicken oyster and jus gras. Guanaja chocolate mousse with blood orange curd and passion fruit sorbet.

Menu £30 (weekday lunch)/70

Town plan: 30AHV-e – *London Hilton Hotel, 22 Park Ln (28th floor)* ⊠ *W1K 1BE* – ⊖ *Hyde Park Corner* – ℰ *(020) 7208 4021* – *www.galvinatwindows.com* – *Closed Saturday lunch and Sunday dinner*

XxX Benares (Atul Kochhar) 🕸 AC 🎬 ⇦

INDIAN · FORMAL No Indian restaurant in London enjoys a more commanding location or expansive interior. Atul Kochhar's influences are many and varied; his spicing is deft and he makes excellent use of British ingredients like Scottish scallops and New Forest venison. The Chef's Table has a window into the kitchen.
→ Coriander and sesame spiced scallops with ginger and grape dressing. Rump of lamb with baby spinach and chickpea stew. Rose and raspberry bhapa doi, pistachio burfi.

Menu £30/82 – Carte £45/71

Town plan: 30AIU-q – *12a Berkeley Square House, Berkeley Sq.* ⊠ *W1J 6BS* – ⊖ *Green Park* – ℰ *(020) 7629 8886* – *www.benaresrestaurant.com* – *Closed 24-26 December, 1-2 January and Sunday October-March*

XxX Tamarind AC 🎬

INDIAN · FORMAL Makes the best use of its basement location through smoked mirrors, gilded columns and a somewhat exclusive feel. The appealing northern Indian food is mostly traditionally based; kebabs and curries are the specialities, the tandoor is used to good effect and don't miss the carefully judged vegetable dishes.
→ Chickpeas, wheat crisps, blueberries and tamarind chutney. Slow-cooked lamb shank with turmeric and yoghurt. Heritage carrot cake and fudge with vanilla ice cream.

Menu £25/72 – Carte £35/67

Town plan: 30AHV-h – *20 Queen St.* ⊠ *W1J 5PR* – ⊖ *Green Park* – ℰ *(020) 7629 3561* – *www.tamarindrestaurant.com* – *Closed 25-26 December, 1 January and Saturday lunch*

XxX Kai 🕸 AC 🎬 ⇦

CHINESE · INTIMATE There are a few classics on the menu but Chef Alex Chow's strengths are his modern creations and re-workings of Chinese recipes. His dishes have real depth, use superb produce and are wonderfully balanced. The interior is unashamedly glitzy and the service team anticipate their customers' needs well.
→ Ibérico pork in a Cos lettuce wrap with plum and lime dressing, cashew, and shallots. Kagoshima Wagyu cooked on a salt block with soy, garlic and a coriander & chilli sauce. Durian and vanilla soufflé with salted caramel sauce.

Carte £39/110

Town plan: 30AHV-n – *65 South Audley St* ⊠ *W1K 2QU* – ⊖ *Hyde Park Corner* – ℰ *(020) 7493 8988 (booking essential)* – *www.kaimayfair.co.uk* – *Closed 25-26 December and 1 January*

XxX 34 🍷 AC ⇦

MEATS · BRASSERIE A wonderful mix of art deco style and Edwardian warmth makes it feel like a glamorous brasserie. A parrilla grill is used for beef – a mix of Scottish dry-aged, US prime, organic Argentinian and Australian Wagyu – as well as fish and game.

Carte £33/61

Town plan: 30AHU-b – *34 Grosvenor Sq (entrance on South Audley St)* ⊠ *W1K 2HD* – ⊖ *Marble Arch* – ℰ *(020) 3350 3434* – *www.34-restaurant.co.uk* – *Closed 25-26 December, dinner 24 December and lunch 1 January*

XxX Bentley's (Grill) 🔲 ⇔

FISH AND SEAFOOD · ELEGANT Enter into the striking bar and take the panelled staircase to the richly decorated restaurant. Carefully sourced seafood or meat dishes are enhanced by clean, crisp cooking. Unruffled service.

Menu £25 (weekday lunch) – Carte £33/74

Town plan: 30AJU-c – *11-15 Swallow St.* ⊠ *W1B 4DG* – ⊖ *Piccadilly Circus*
– 𝒞 *(020) 7734 4756* – *www.bentleys.org*
– *Closed 25 December, 1 January, Saturday lunch and Sunday*

XxX Theo Randall 🔲 🕙 🐲 ⇔

ITALIAN · FASHIONABLE Expect simple, flavoursome and seasonal Italian dishes, using much produce imported from Italy. The pleasingly rustic nature of the food is somewhat at odds with the formal service and the corporate feel of the dining room.

Menu £27/33 – Carte £46/72

Town plan: 30AHV-k – *Intercontinental Hotel, 1 Hamilton Pl, Park Ln*
⊠ *W1J 7QY* – ⊖ *Hyde Park Corner*
– 𝒞 *(020) 7318 8747* – *www.theorandall.com*
– *Closed Christmas, Easter, Saturday lunch, Sunday dinner and bank holidays*

XxX Scott's 🔲 🕙 ⇔

FISH AND SEAFOOD · FASHIONABLE Stylish yet traditional and one of London's most fashionable addresses, so getting a table can be tricky. Oak panelling is juxtaposed with vibrant artwork from young British artists. Enticing choice of top quality fish and shellfish.

Carte £39/67

Town plan: 30AHU-h – *20 Mount St* ⊠ *W1K 2HE* – ⊖ *Bond Street*
– 𝒞 *(020) 7495 7309* – *www.scotts-restaurant.com*
– *Closed 25-26 December*

XxX Corrigan's Mayfair ♿ 🔲 ⇔

BRITISH MODERN · ELEGANT Richard Corrigan's flagship celebrates British and Irish cooking, with game a speciality. The room is comfortable, clubby and quite glamorous and feels as though it has been around for years.

Menu £25 (weekday lunch)/75 – Carte £35/73

Town plan: 29AGU-a – *28 Upper Grosvenor St.* ⊠ *W1K 7EH* – ⊖ *Marble Arch*
– 𝒞 *(020) 7499 9943* – *www.corrigansmayfair.com*
– *Closed 25-30 December, Saturday lunch and bank holidays*

XxX Sartoria ♿ 🔲 ⇔

ITALIAN · FORMAL In the street renowned for English tailoring, a coolly sophisticated and stylish restaurant to suit those looking for classic Italian cooking with some modern touches thrown in. It also comes with confident service.

Menu £25 – Carte £30/62

Town plan: 30AIU-b – *20 Savile Row* ⊠ *W1S 3PR* – ⊖ *Oxford Circus*
– 𝒞 *(020) 7534 7000* – *www.sartoria-restaurant.co.uk*
– *Closed 25 December, Saturday lunch, Sunday and bank holidays*

XxX Hix Mayfair ♿ 🔲 🕙

BRITISH TRADITIONAL · FORMAL This wood-panelled dining room is lightened with the work of current British artists. Mark Hix's well-sourced menu of British classics will appeal to the hunter-gatherer in every man.

Menu £33 – Carte £34/69

Town plan: 30AIV-d – *Brown's Hotel, 33 Albemarle St* ⊠ *W1S 4BP*
– ⊖ *Green Park* – 𝒞 *(020) 7518 4004* – *www.hixmayfair.com*

> **Take note of the classification: you should not expect the same level of service in a X or 🏠 as in a XxXxX or 🏛🏛🏛.**

XxX China Tang
CHINESE · FASHIONABLE Sir David Tang's atmospheric, art deco-inspired Chinese restaurant, downstairs at The Dorchester, is always abuzz with activity. Be sure to see the terrific bar, before sharing the traditional Cantonese specialities.

Menu £ 28 (lunch) – Carte £ 28/79

Town plan: 30AHV-a – *Dorchester Hotel, Park Ln ⊠ W1K 1QA*
– ⊖ Hyde Park Corner – ℰ (020) 7629 9988 – www.chinatanglondon.co.uk
– Closed 24-25 December

XxX Amaranto
ITALIAN · FASHIONABLE It's all about flexibility as the Italian influenced menu is served in the stylish bar or the comfortable lounge, on the great terrace or in the restaurant decorated in the vivid colours of the amaranth plant.

Menu £ 20 (lunch) – Carte £ 29/55

Town plan: 30AHV-v – *Four Seasons Hotel, Hamilton Pl, Park Ln ⊠ W1J 7DR*
– ⊖ Hyde Park Corner – ℰ (020) 7499 0888
– www.fourseasons.com/london/dining

XX Araki 🟢 (Mitsuhiro Araki)
😋😋 JAPANESE · INTIMATE Mitsuhiro Araki is one of Japan's great Sushi Masters who closed his Tokyo restaurant to relocate to London because he wanted a fresh challenge. From one of 9 seats at his beautiful cypress counter, watch him deftly prepare Edomae sushi using European seafood. It's very expensive but the different cuts of tuna are stunning and the rice, grown by his father-in-law back in Japan, is also excellent.
→ Sea bream with wasabi and ponzu. 3 kinds of bluefin tuna sushi. Squid with caviar.

Menu £ 300 – set menu only

Town plan: 30AIU-e – *12 New Burlington St ⊠ W1S 3BF – ⊖ Oxford Circus*
– ℰ (020) 7287 2481 (booking essential) – www.the-araki.com – dinner only
– Closed 1 January and Monday

XX Wild Honey
😋 MODERN CUISINE · DESIGN Skilled kitchen uses seasonal ingredients at their peak to create dishes full of flavour and free from ostentation. Attractive and comfortable oak-panelled room. Personable and unobtrusive service adds to the relaxed feel.
→ Hand dived Scottish scallops, roast and dumpling, fermented ramsons. Slow-cooked shin of Limousin veal, spinach and pommes Anna. English custard tart, salted butter and golden sultanas.

Menu £ 30 (lunch and early dinner) – Carte £ 40/64

Town plan: 30AIU-w – *12 St George St. ⊠ W1S 2FB – ⊖ Oxford Circus*
– ℰ (020) 7758 9160 – www.wildhoneyrestaurant.co.uk
– Closed 25-26 December, 1 January and Sunday

XX Brasserie Chavot
😋 FRENCH · BRASSERIE Mosaic flooring, smoked mirrors, red leather seats and sparkling chandeliers add style; a satisfied buzz and great service make it fun. Eric Chavot's ability is obvious in his hearteningly rustic, refreshingly unfussy and hugely enjoyable French classics.
→ Deep-fried soft shell crab with whipped aïoli. Cassoulet de canard et cochon. Baba au rhum with crème Chantilly.

Carte £ 37/51

Town plan: 30AIU-z – *41 Conduit St ⊠ W1S 2YQ – ⊖ Bond Street*
– ℰ (020) 7183 6425 – www.brasseriechavot.com
– Closed Sunday and bank holidays

XX Pollen Street Social (Jason Atherton)
😋 CREATIVE · FASHIONABLE The restaurant where it all started for Jason Atherton when he went solo. Top quality British produce lies at the heart of the menu and the innovative dishes are prepared with great care and no little skill. The room has plenty of buzz, helped along by the 'dessert bar' and views of the kitchen pass.

→ Crab salad with apple, coriander, black garlic, lemon purée and brown crab on toast. Loin of lamb with braised neck, roast artichoke and Merguez sausage. Lincolnshire apple cake, ice wine vinegar ice cream and sweet pickled Opal apples.

Menu £ 35 (lunch) – Carte £ 56/66

Town plan: 30AIU-c – *8-10 Pollen St* ✉ *W1S 1NQ* – ⊖ *Oxford Circus* – ✆ *(020) 7290 7600 (booking essential) – www.pollenstreetsocial.com – Closed Sunday and bank holidays*

XX Bonhams 🆕   ⊕ & AC ⊡

❀ MODERN CUISINE · MINIMALIST Established in 1793, Bonhams is now one of the world's largest fine art and antique auctioneers. Its restaurant is bright, modern and professionally run. Dishes are elegant and delicate and there is real clarity to the flavours. The wine list has also been very thoughtfully compiled.
→ Flamed mackerel with pickled black radish, baby gem, avocado and sesame. Duck breast and confit leg with beetroot purée, caramelised endive, blood orange and five spice. Vanilla panna cotta, ginger-poached rhubarb and rhubarb sorbet.

Menu £ 45 (dinner) – Carte £ 30/52

Town plan: 30AHU-n – *101 New Bond St* ✉ *W1S 1SR Mayfair* – *(lower ground floor) – For breakfast before 9am and dinner entrance via Haunch of Venison Yard off Brook St* – ⊖ *Bond Street* – ✆ *(020) 7468 5868 (booking advisable) – www.bonhams.com – lunch only and set menu Thursday dinner – Closed 25-26 December, 1 January, Saturday, Sunday and bank holidays*

XX Gymkhana   ⊗ AC ⊞ 🛈 ⊡ ⇔

❀ INDIAN · INTIMATE If you enjoyed Trishna then you'll love Karam Sethi's Gymkhana – that's if you can get a table. Inspired by Colonial India's gymkhana clubs, the interior is full of wonderful detail and plenty of wry touches; ask to sit downstairs. The North Indian dishes have a wonderful richness and depth of flavour.
→ Kid goat methi keema, salli and pao. Wild muntjac biryani with pomegranate and mint raita. Rose kulfi falooda.

Menu £ 25 (lunch and early dinner)/75 – Carte £ 23/57

Town plan: 30AIV-a – *42 Albemarle St* ✉ *W1S 4JH* – ⊖ *Green Park* – ✆ *(020) 3011 5900 (booking essential) – www.gymkhanalondon.com – Closed first 2 weeks January, 25-28 December and Sunday*

XX Hakkasan Mayfair   ⊕ ⊗ & AC 🛈 ⇔

❀ CHINESE · MINIMALIST Less a copy, more a sister to the original; a sister who's just as fun but lives in a nicer part of town. This one has a funky, more casual ground floor to go with the downstairs dining room. You can expect the same extensive choice of top quality, modern Cantonese cuisine; dim sum is a highlight.
→ Crispy duck salad with pomelo, pine nut and shallot. Stir-fry black pepper ribeye beef with Merlot. Jivara bomb.

Menu £ 35/128 – Carte £ 36/75 **s**

Town plan: 30AIU-l – *17 Bruton St* ✉ *W1J 6QB* – ⊖ *Green Park* – ✆ *(020) 7907 1888 (booking essential) – www.hakkasan.com – Closed 25 December*

XX Colony Grill Room 🆕   ⊗ & AC ⊡

BRITISH TRADITIONAL · BRASSERIE Based on 1920s London and New York grill restaurants, The Beaumont's Colony Grill comes with leather booths, striking age-of-speed art deco murals and clever lighting. By making the room and style of service so defiantly old fashioned, Corbin and King have created somewhere effortlessly chic.

Carte £ 22/66

Town plan: 30AHU-x – *The Beaumont Hotel, Brown Hart Gdns.* ✉ *W1K 6TF* – ⊖ *Bond Street* – ✆ *(020) 7499 9499 (booking essential) – www.colonygrillroom.com*

XX Hawksmoor

MEATS · FASHIONABLE The best of the Hawksmoors is large, boisterous and has an appealing art deco feel. Expect top quality, 35-day aged Longhorn beef but also great seafood, much of which is charcoal grilled. The delightful staff are well organised.

Menu £ 27 (lunch and early dinner) – Carte £ 28/80

Town plan: 30AJU-m – 5a Air St ⊠ W1B 4EA – ⊖ Piccadilly Circus
– ℰ (020) 7406 3980 (booking advisable) – www.thehawksmoor.com
– Closed 24-26 December

XX Momo

MOROCCAN · EXOTIC An authentic Moroccan atmosphere comes courtesy of the antiques, kilim rugs, Berber artwork, bright fabrics and lanterns – you'll feel you're eating near the souk. Go for the classic dishes: zaalouk, briouats, pigeon pastilla, and tagines with mountains of fluffy couscous.

Menu £ 16 (weekdays)/58 – Carte £ 25/82

Town plan: 30AIU-n – 25 Heddon St. ⊠ W1B 4BH – ⊖ Oxford Circus
– ℰ (020) 7434 4040 – www.momoresto.com
– Closed 25 December and 1 January

XX Heddon Street Kitchen 🆕

MODERN CUISINE · BRASSERIE Gordon Ramsay's follow up to Bread Street is spread over two floors and is all about all-day dining: breakfast covers all tastes, there's weekend brunch, and an à la carte offering an appealing range of European dishes executed with palpable care.

Menu £ 26 – Carte £ 27/58

Town plan: 30AIU-y – 3-9 Heddon St ⊠ W1B 4BN – ⊖ Oxford Circus
– ℰ (020) 7592 1212 – www.gordonramsay.com/heddon-street
– Closed 25 December

XX Roka

JAPANESE · ELEGANT London's third Roka ventures into the rarefied surroundings of Mayfair and the restaurant's seductive looks are a good fit. All the favourites from their modern Japanese repertoire are here, with the robata grill taking centre stage.

Carte £ 21/132

Town plan: 29AGU-k – 30 North Audley St ⊠ W1K 6ZF – ⊖ Bond Street
– ℰ (020) 7305 5644 – www.rokarestaurant.com

XX Sketch (The Gallery)

MODERN CUISINE · TRENDY The striking 'Gallery' has a new look from India Mahdavi and artwork from David Shrigley. At dinner the room transmogrifies from art gallery to fashionable restaurant, with a menu that mixes the classic, the modern and the esoteric.

Carte £ 43/80

Town plan: 30AIU-h – 9 Conduit St ⊠ W1S 2XG – ⊖ Oxford Circus
– ℰ (020) 7659 4500 (booking essential) – www.sketch.london – dinner only
– Closed 25 December

XX Maze

MODERN CUISINE · FASHIONABLE This Gordon Ramsay restaurant still offers a glamorous night out, thanks to its great cocktails, effervescent atmosphere and small plates of Asian influenced food. Three or four dishes per person is about the going rate.

Menu £ 33 (lunch and early dinner) – Carte £ 35/46

Town plan: 30AHU-z – 10-13 Grosvenor Sq ⊠ W1K 6JP
– ⊖ Bond Street – ℰ (020) 7107 0000
– www.gordonramsay.com/maze

XX Nobu Berkeley St

JAPANESE · FASHIONABLE This branch of the glamorous chain is more of a party animal than its elder sibling at The Metropolitan. Start with cocktails then head upstairs for Japanese food with South American influences; try dishes from the wood-fired oven.

Menu £ 29 – Carte £ 32/121

Town plan: 30AIV-b – *15 Berkeley St.* ⊠ *W1J 8DY* – ⊖ *Green Park* – ☎ *(020) 7290 9222 (booking essential)* – *www.noburestaurants.com* – *Closed 25 December, 1 January and Sunday lunch except December*

XX Veeraswamy

INDIAN · DESIGN May have opened back in 1926 but this Indian restaurant feels fresh and is awash with vibrant colours and always full of bustle. Skilled kitchen cleverly mixes the traditional with more contemporary creations.

Menu £ 28 (weekday lunch) – Carte £ 35/65

Town plan: 30AIU-t – *Victory House, 99 Regent St* ⊠ *W1B 4RS* – *Entrance on Swallow St.* – ⊖ *Piccadilly Circus* – ☎ *(020) 7734 1401* – *www.veeraswamy.com*

XX Coya

PERUVIAN · INDIVIDUAL From the people behind Zuma and Roka comes this lively, loud and enthusiastically run basement restaurant that celebrates all things Peruvian. Try their ceviche and their skewers, as well as their Pisco Sours in the fun bar.

Menu £ 30 (lunch) – Carte £ 34/57

Town plan: 30AHV-d – *118 Piccadilly* ⊠ *W1J 7NW* – ⊖ *Hyde Park Corner* – ☎ *(020) 7042 7118 (booking advisable)* – *www.coyarestaurant.com* – *Closed 24-26 December and 1 January*

XX La Petite Maison

FRENCH · BISTRO A little piece of southern France and Ligurian Italy in Mayfair. The slickly run sister to the Nice original has a buzzy, glamorous feel, with prices to match. Just reading the menus of Mediterranean dishes will improve your tan.

Carte £ 29/69 **s**

Town plan: 30AHU-m – *54 Brooks Mews* ⊠ *W1K 4EG* – ⊖ *Bond Street* – ☎ *(020) 7495 4774 (booking essential)* – *www.lpmlondon.co.uk* – *Closed Christmas-New Year*

XX Keeper's House

BRITISH MODERN · INDIVIDUAL Built in 1860 and fully restored, this house is part of the Royal Academy. Two intimate dining rooms are lined with green baize and hung with architectural casts. The emphasis is on seasonality, freshness and contrasts in textures.

Menu £ 30 – Carte £ 29/57

Town plan: 30AIV-x – *Royal Academy of Arts, Burlington House, Piccadilly* ⊠ *W1J 0BD* – ⊖ *Green Park* – ☎ *(020) 7300 5881* – *www.keepershouse.org.uk* – *dinner only* – *Closed 25-26 December and Sunday*

XX Maze Grill Mayfair

MEATS · RETRO Next door to Maze and specialising in steaks cooked on the Josper grill. Expect a good range of aged meat, including Aberdeen Angus (28 days), Dedham Vale (31), USDA Prime (36) and Wagyu 9th Grade (49), served on wooden boards.

Menu £ 27 (lunch) – Carte £ 29/88

Town plan: 30AHU-s – *London Marriott Hotel Grosvenor Square, 10-13 Grosvenor Sq* ⊠ *W1K 6JP* – ⊖ *Bond Street* – ☎ *(020) 7495 2211* – *www.gordonramsay.com/mazegrill*

XX Goodman Mayfair

MEATS · BRASSERIE A worthy attempt at recreating a New York steakhouse; all leather and wood and macho swagger. Beef is dry or wet aged in-house and comes with a choice of four sauces; rib-eye the speciality.

Carte £ 26/97

Town plan: 30AIU-u – 26 Maddox St ⊠ W1S 1QH – ⊖ Oxford Circus
– 𝒞 (020) 7499 3776 (booking essential) – www.goodmanrestaurants.com
– Closed Sunday and bank holidays

XX Hush

MODERN CUISINE · FASHIONABLE Appealing and all-purpose European brasserie-style menu served in a busy room with smart destination bar upstairs and plenty of private dining. Tucked away in a charming courtyard, with a pleasant summer terrace.

Carte £ 21/28

Town plan: 30AHU-v – 8 Lancashire Ct., Brook St. ⊠ W1S 1EY
– ⊖ Bond Street – 𝒞 (020) 7659 1500 (booking essential) – www.hush.co.uk
– Closed 25 December and 1 January

XX Nobu

JAPANESE · FASHIONABLE Nobu restaurants are now all over the world but this was Europe's first and opened in 1997. It retains a certain exclusivity and is buzzy and fun. The menu is an innovative blend of Japanese cuisine with South American influences.

Menu £ 30
– Carte £ 24/73

Town plan: 30AHV-c – Metropolitan Hotel, 19 Old Park Ln ⊠ W1Y 1LB
– ⊖ Hyde Park Corner – 𝒞 (020) 7447 4747 (booking essential)
– www.noburestaurants.com

XX Mews of Mayfair

BRITISH MODERN · FRIENDLY This pretty restaurant, bright in summer and warm in winter, is on the first floor of a mews house, once used as storage rooms for Savile Row. Seasonal menus offer something for everyone.

Carte £ 23/57

Town plan: 30AHU-a – 10-11 Lancashire Ct (1st Floor), Brook St ⊠ W1S 1EY
– ⊖ Bond Street – 𝒞 (020) 7518 9388 – www.mewsofmayfair.com
– Closed 25 December

XX Kiku

JAPANESE · NEIGHBOURHOOD For over 35 years this earnestly run, authentically styled, family owned restaurant has been providing every style of Japanese cuisine to its homesick Japanese customers, from shabu shabu to sukiyaki, yakitori to teriyaki.

Menu £ 20 (weekday lunch) – Carte £ 28/78

Town plan: 30AIV-g – 17 Half Moon St. ⊠ W1J 7BE – ⊖ Green Park
– 𝒞 (020) 7499 4208 – www.kikurestaurant.co.uk
– Closed 25-27 December, 1 January, Sunday and lunch on bank holidays

XX Chucs Bar and Grill

ITALIAN · ELEGANT Like the shop to which it's attached, Chucs caters for those who summer on the Riviera and are not afraid of showing it. It's decked out like a yacht and the concise but not inexpensive menu offers classic Mediterranean dishes.

Carte £ 38/59

Town plan: 30AIV-r – 30b Dover St. ⊠ W1S 4NB – ⊖ Green Park
– 𝒞 (020) 3763 2013 (booking essential) – www.chucsrestaurant.com
– Closed Sunday dinner

X **Bentley's (Oyster Bar)**

FISH AND SEAFOOD · BISTRO Sit at the counter to watch white-jacketed staff open oysters by the bucket load. Interesting seafood menus feature tasty fish pies; lots of daily specials on blackboard.

Carte £ 33/70

Town plan: 30AJU-c – *11-15 Swallow St* ✉ *W1B 4DG* – ⊖ *Piccadilly Circus* – *℘ (020) 7734 4756 – www.bentleys.org – Closed 25 December and 1 January*

X **Le Boudin Blanc**

FRENCH · RUSTIC Appealing, lively French bistro in Shepherd Market, spread over two floors. Satisfying French classics and country cooking are the draw, along with authentic Gallic service. Good value lunch menu.

Menu £ 15 – Carte £ 28/58

Town plan: 30AHV-q – *5 Trebeck St* ✉ *W1J 7LT* – ⊖ *Green Park* – *℘ (020) 7499 3292 – www.boudinblanc.co.uk – Closed 24-26 December and 1 January*

X **Little Social**

FRENCH · BISTRO ason Atherton's lively French bistro, opposite his Pollen Street Social restaurant, has a clubby feel and an appealing, deliberately worn look. Service is breezy and capable and the food is mostly classic with the odd modern twist.

Menu £ 21/25 – Carte £ 34/58

Town plan: 30AIU-r – *5 Pollen St* ✉ *W1S 1NE* – ⊖ *Oxford Circus* – *℘ (020) 7870 3730 (booking essential) – www.littlesocial.co.uk* – *Closed Sunday and bank holidays*

X **Le Chabanais** ⓝ

FRENCH · BISTRO The team behind Paris's Le Chateaubriand have brought 'bistronomy' to Mayfair with this striking brass-clad bistro-deluxe. The menu is influenced by the deconstructed dishes of its French relation but with an emphasis on British ingredients.

Carte £ 31/59

Town plan: 30AHU-w – *8 Mount St* ✉ *W1K 3NF* – ⊖ *Bond Street* – *℘ (020) 7491 7078 (booking advisable) – www.lechabanaislondon.com* – *Closed 25-26 and dinner 24 December, 1 January and Sunday*

X **Kitty Fisher's** ⓝ

MODERN CUISINE · BISTRO Warm, intimate and unpretentious restaurant – the star of the show is the wood grill which gives the dishes added depth. Named after an 18C courtesan, presumably in honour of the profession for which Shepherd Market was once known.

Carte £ 32/57

Town plan: 30AHV-s – *10 Shepherd Mkt* ✉ *W1J 7QF* – ⊖ *Green Park* – *℘ (020) 3302 1661 (booking essential) – www.kittyfishers.com* – *Closed Christmas, Saturday lunch, Sunday and Monday*

X **Peyote**

MEXICAN · TRENDY From the people behind Zuma and Roka comes a 'refined interpretation of Mexican cuisine' at this fun, glamorous spot. There's an exhilarating freshness to the well-judged dishes; don't miss the great guacamole or the cactus salad.

Menu £ 24/80 – Carte £ 28/63

Town plan: 30AIU-m – *13 Cork St* ✉ *W1S 3NS* – ⊖ *Green Park* – *℘ (020) 7409 1300 (booking essential) – www.peyoterestaurant.com* – *Closed Saturday lunch and Sunday*

X **28°-50° Mayfair**

MODERN CUISINE · WINE BAR The group's third wine-bar-restaurant is possibly their best and, as this is Mayfair, almost certainly their most profitable. Modern, unfussy dishes provide great accompaniment to the thoughtfully put-together wine list.

Menu £ 20 (lunch) – Carte £ 26/39

Town plan: 30AIU-f – *17-19 Maddox St* ✉ *W1S 2QH* – ⊖ *Oxford Circus* – *℘ (020) 7495 1505 – www.2850.co.uk – Closed 25 December, 1 January and Sunday*

✗ Mayfair Chippy   🆎 ✧

BRITISH TRADITIONAL · BISTRO When it was called 'The Great British', fish and chips was the top-selling dish so the owners decided to change the restaurant name and specialise in fish dishes, along with a few other British classics. Take-away is available.

Carte £ 20/42

Town plan: 29AGU-e – *14 North Audley St* ✉ *W1K 6WE* – ↔ *Marble Arch* – 𝒞 *(020) 7741 2233* – *www.eatbrit.com* – *Closed 25 December, 1 January and Sunday dinner*

✗ Burger & Lobster   🆎

MEATS · SIMPLE Choose a burger, a lobster or a lobster roll, with chips, salad and sauces, and mousse for dessert – an ingeniously simple idea. The lobsters are Canadian and the burgers 10oz. It's a well organised bunfight in an old pub.

Menu £ 20

Town plan: 30AIV-v – *29 Clarges St* ✉ *W1J 7EF* – ↔ *Green Park.* – 𝒞 *(020) 7409 1699 (bookings not accepted)* – *www.burgerandlobster.com* – *Closed Sunday dinner and bank holidays*

🍴 Only Running Footman   🕭 🖃 ✧

BRITISH TRADITIONAL · PUB The busy ground floor bar with its appealing menu of pub classics doesn't take bookings. By contrast, upstairs is formal and its menu more European and ambitious but the simpler dishes are still the best.

Menu £ 45 – Carte £ 25/45

Town plan: 30AHV-x – *5 Charles St* ✉ *W1J 5DF* – ↔ *Green Park.* – 𝒞 *(020) 7499 2988* – *www.therunningfootmanmayfair.com*

Regent's Park and Marylebone

🏨 The Landmark London   ♨ 🖼 🕸 🕭 💪 🖃 🕭 🆎 � 🛁 🚗

BUSINESS · CLASSIC Imposing Victorian Gothic building with a vast glass-enclosed atrium which is overlooked by many of the well-equipped bedrooms. Dining options include the Winter Garden and a wood-panelled room with a global menu.

300 rooms – 🛏£ 252/780 🛏🛏£ 252/780 – ☑£ 29 – 9 suites

Town plan: 29AFT-a – *222 Marylebone Rd* ✉ *NW1 6JQ* – ↔ *Edgware Road* – 𝒞 *(020) 7631 8000* – *www.landmarklondon.co.uk*

Winter Garden – See restaurant listing

🏨 The London Edition   ♨ 🕭 🖃 🆎 �
ш 🛁

BUSINESS · DESIGN Berners, a classic Edwardian hotel, strikingly reborn through a partnership between Ian Schrager and Marriott – the former's influence most apparent in the stylish lobby and bar. Slick, understated rooms; the best ones have balconies.

173 rooms – 🛏£ 345/450 🛏🛏£ 345/450 – ☑£ 26 – 9 suites

Town plan: 31AJT-b – *10 Berners Street* ✉ *W1T 3NP* – ↔ *Tottenham Court Road* – 𝒞 *(020) 7781 0000* – *www.editionhotels.com*

Berners Tavern – See restaurant listing

🏨 Langham   ♨ 🖼 🕸 🕭 🕭 🖃 💪 🆎 🛁

LUXURY · STYLISH Was one of Europe's first purpose-built grand hotels when it opened in 1865. Now back to its best, with its famous Palm Court for afternoon tea, a stylish Artesian bar and bedrooms that are not without personality and elegance.

380 rooms – 🛏£ 360/960 🛏🛏£ 360/960 – ☑£ 30 – 24 suites

Town plan: 30AIT-n – *1c Portland Pl., Regent St.* ✉ *W1B 1JA* – ↔ *Oxford Circus* – 𝒞 *(020) 7636 1000* – *london.langhamhotels.com*

Roux at The Landau – See restaurant listing

Hyatt Regency London-The Churchill

LUXURY · MODERN Smart well-located property whose best bedrooms overlook the attractive square opposite. Elegant marbled lobby with plenty of staff. Well-appointed and refurbished bedrooms have the international traveller in mind. A British menu and afternoon tea served in The Montagu.

434 rooms – ♦£ 220/660 ♦♦£ 220/660 – ⊆£ 32 – 47 suites
Town plan: 29AGT-x – *30 Portman Sq ⊠ W1H 7BH* – ⊖ *Marble Arch*
– *℘(020) 7486 5800 – www.london.churchill.hyatt.com*

Chiltern Firehouse

TOWNHOUSE · STYLISH From Chateau Marmont in LA to The Mercer in New York, André Balazs' hotels are effortlessly cool. For his London entrance, he has sympathetically restored and extended a gothic Victorian fire station. The style comes with an easy elegance; it's an oasis of calm and hardly feels like a hotel at all.

26 rooms – ♦£ 495/1020 ♦♦£ 495/1020 – ⊆£ 20 – 6 suites –
♦♦£ 1500/4140
Town plan: 29AGT-a – *1 Chiltern St ⊠ W1U 7PA* – ⊖ *Baker Street*
– *℘(020) 7073 7676 – www.chilternfirehouse.com*
Chiltern Firehouse – See restaurant listing

Charlotte Street

LUXURY · STYLISH Stylish interior designed with a charming, understated English feel. Impeccably kept and individually decorated bedrooms. Popular in-house screening room. Colourful restaurant whose terrace spills onto Charlotte Street; grilled meats a highlight.

52 rooms – ♦£ 276/342 ♦♦£ 276/342 – ⊆£ 20 – 4 suites
Town plan: 31AJT-e – *15 Charlotte St ⊠ W1T 1RJ* – ⊖ *Goodge Street*
– *℘(020) 7806 2000 – www.charlottestreethotel.co.uk*

Sanderson

LUXURY · MINIMALIST Originally designed by Philippe Starck and his influence is still evident. The Purple Bar is dark and moody; the Long Bar is bright and stylish. Bedrooms are crisply decorated and come complete with all mod cons.

150 rooms – ♦£ 234/538 ♦♦£ 234/538 – ⊆£ 18
Town plan: 31AJT-c – *50 Berners St ⊠ W1T 3NG* – ⊖ *Oxford Circus*
– *℘(020) 7300 1400 – www.morganshotelgroup.com*

Montcalm

BUSINESS · STYLISH Named after an 18C French general, the Montcalm forms part of a crescent of townhouses with a Georgian façade. A top-to-toe refurbishment has created smart, contemporary bedrooms in lively colours. Seasonal British dishes served in Crescent restaurant.

126 rooms – ♦£ 380 ♦♦£ 380/750 – ⊆£ 20 – 17 suites
Town plan: 29AGU-m – *34-40 Great Cumberland Pl. ⊠ W1H 7TW*
– ⊖ *Marble Arch* – *℘(020) 7402 4288 – www.montcalm.co.uk*

Durrants

TRADITIONAL · CLASSIC Traditional, privately owned hotel with friendly, long-standing staff. Bedrooms are now brighter in style but still retain a certain English character. Clubby dining room for mix of British classics and lighter, European dishes.

92 rooms – ♦£ 235 ♦♦£ 300/420 – ⊆£ 20 – 4 suites
Town plan: 29AGT-e – *26-32 George St ⊠ W1H 5BJ* – ⊖ *Bond Street*
– *℘(020) 7935 8131 – www.durrantshotel.co.uk*

Dorset Square

TOWNHOUSE · CONTEMPORARY Having reacquired this Regency townhouse, Firmdale refurbished it fully before reopening it in 2012. It has a contemporary yet intimate feel and visiting MCC members will appreciate the cricketing theme, which even extends to the cocktails in their sweet little basement brasserie.

38 rooms – ♦£ 200/240 ♦♦£ 250/460 – ☷ £ 13

Town plan: 17QZD-s – 39-40 Dorset Sq ⊠ NW1 6QN – ⊖ Marylebone – ℰ (020) 7723 7874 – www.dorsetsquarehotel.co.uk

Marble Arch by Montcalm

TOWNHOUSE · STYLISH Bedrooms at this 5-storey Georgian townhouse come with the same high standards of stylish, contemporary design as its parent hotel opposite, the Montcalm, but are just a little more compact.

42 rooms – ♦£ 175/201 ♦♦£ 201/300 – ☷ £ 20

Town plan: 29AGU-s – 31 Great Cumberland Pl. ⊠ W1H 7TA – ⊖ Marble Arch – ℰ (020) 7258 0777 – www.themarblearch.co.uk

Mandeville

BUSINESS · DESIGN Usefully located hotel with a marbled reception leading into a very colourful and comfortable bar. Stylish rooms have flat screen TVs and make good use of the space available. Steaks are the highlight of the classic menu.

142 rooms – ♦£ 216/600 ♦♦£ 240/600 – ☷ £ 16 – 2 suites

Town plan: 30AHT-x – Mandeville Pl ⊠ W1U 2BE – ⊖ Bond Street – ℰ (020) 7935 5599 – www.mandeville.co.uk

No. Ten Manchester Street

TOWNHOUSE · MODERN Converted Edwardian house in an appealing, central location. Discreet entrance leads into little lounge and Italian-themed bistro; semi-enclosed cigar bar also a feature. Neat, well-kept bedrooms.

44 rooms – ♦£ 225/375 ♦♦£ 225/375 – ☷ £ 15 – 9 suites

Town plan: 29AGT-v – 10 Manchester St ⊠ W1U 4DG – ⊖ Baker Street – ℰ (020) 7317 5900 – www.tenmanchesterstreethotel.com

Sumner

TOWNHOUSE · PERSONALISED Two Georgian terrace houses in central location. Comfy, stylish sitting room; basement breakfast room. Largest bedrooms, 101 and 201, benefit from having full-length windows.

19 rooms ☷ – ♦£ 160/300 ♦♦£ 160/300

Town plan: 29AFU-k – 54 Upper Berkeley St ⊠ W1H 7QR – ⊖ Marble Arch – ℰ (020) 7723 2244 – www.thesumner.com

Locanda Locatelli

🕃 ITALIAN · FASHIONABLE Giorgio Locatelli's Italian restaurant may be into its second decade but still looks as dapper as ever. The service is smooth and the room was designed with conviviality in mind. The hugely appealing menu covers all regions; unfussy presentation and superb ingredients allow natural flavours to shine.
➜ Calf's foot salad with red onion and peppers. Roast rabbit with polenta and radicchio. Sicilian cannoli with orange sauce and pistachio ice cream.

Carte £ 34/60

Town plan: 29AGU-r – 8 Seymour St. ⊠ W1H 7JZ – ⊖ Marble Arch – ℰ (020) 7935 9088 – www.locandalocatelli.com – Closed 25-26 December and 1 January

Roux at The Landau

FRENCH · FORMAL Grand, oval-shaped hotel restaurant run under the aegis of the Roux organisation. Classical, French-influenced cooking is the order of the day, but a lighter style of cuisine using the occasional twist is also emerging.

Menu £ 35/65 – Carte £ 36/88

Town plan: 30AIT-n – Langham Hotel, 1c Portland Pl., Regent St. ⊠ W1B 1JA – ⊖ Oxford Circus – ℰ (020) 7636 1000 – www.rouxatthelandau.com – Closed Saturday lunch and Sunday

XxX **Latium** Ⓚ

ITALIAN · NEIGHBOURHOOD Bright and contemporary surroundings but with warm and welcoming service. Owner-chef from Lazio but dishes come from across Italy, often using British produce. Ravioli is the house speciality and the fassone beef is always good.

Menu £ 23 (weekdays)/36

Town plan: 31AJT-n – *21 Berners St.* ✉ *W1T 3LP* – ↔ *Oxford Circus* – ℰ *(020) 7323 9123* – *www.latiumrestaurant.com* – *Closed 25-26 December, 1 January, Saturday lunch, Sunday and bank holidays*

XxX **Orrery** 🛋 Ⓚ ↔

MODERN CUISINE · FORMAL These are actually converted stables from the 19C but, such is the elegance and style of the building, you'd never know. Featured is elaborate, modern European cooking; dishes are strong on presentation and come with the occasional twist.

Menu £ 28 (weekdays)/55

Town plan: 18RZD-a – *55 Marylebone High St* ✉ *W1U 5RB* – ↔ *Regent's Park* – ℰ *(020) 7616 8000 (booking essential)* – *www.orrery-restaurant.co.uk*

XX **Texture** (Agnar Sverrisson) 🦞 Ⓚ ↔

❀ CREATIVE · DESIGN Technically skilled but light and invigorating cooking from Icelandic chef-owner, who uses ingredients from home. Bright restaurant with high ceiling and popular adjoining champagne bar. Pleasant service from keen staff, ready with a smile.

→ Scottish scallops, coconut, ginger, lime leaf and lemongrass. Lightly salted Icelandic cod, bisque, prawns, barley and grapefruit. Skyr with vanilla, rye bread crumbs and Muscatel grapes.

Menu £ 30/79 – Carte £ 54/82

Town plan: 29AGU -p – *34 Portman St* ✉ *W1H 7BY* – ↔ *Marble Arch* – ℰ *(020) 7224 0028* – *www.texture-restaurant.co.uk* – *Closed first 2 weeks August, 1 week Easter, Christmas-New Year, Sunday and Monday*

XX **L'Autre Pied** Ⓚ 🍽

❀ MODERN CUISINE · DESIGN Chef Andy McFadden's dishes are visual and easy to eat and provide pleasing contrasts in textures; venison dishes are a particular speciality. This sibling of Pied à Terre has a more relaxed, neighbourhood atmosphere; ask for a table by the window to better enjoy the local 'village' feel.

→ Scallop ceviche with cucumber, balsamic and crème fraîche. Blackface lamb, red pepper ketchup and violet artichoke. Chocolate crémeux with honeycomb and pistachio.

Menu £ 24/75 – Carte £ 52/63

Town plan: 30AHT-k – *5-7 Blandford St.* ✉ *W1U 3DB* – ↔ *Bond Street* – ℰ *(020) 7486 9696* – *www.lautrepied.co.uk* – *Closed 4 days Christmas, 1 January and Sunday dinner*

XX **Berners Tavern** ♿ Ⓚ 🍴 ↔

BRITISH MODERN · BRASSERIE What was once a hotel ballroom is now a very glamorous restaurant, with every inch of wall filled with gilt-framed pictures. Jason Atherton has put together an appealing, accessible menu and the cooking is satisfying and assured.

Carte £ 33/117

Town plan: 31AJT-b – *The London Edition Hotel, 10 Berners St* ✉ *W1T 3NP* – ↔ *Tottenham Court Road* – ℰ *(020) 7908 7979* – *www.bernerstavern.com*

XX **Royal China Club** Ⓚ 🍽

CHINESE · ELEGANT 'The Club' is the glittering bauble in the Royal China chain but along with the luxurious feel of the room comes an appealing sense of calm. Their lunchtime dim sum is very good; at dinner try their more unusual Cantonese dishes.

Carte £ 25/70

Town plan: 29AGT-c – *40-42 Baker St* ✉ *W1U 7AJ* – ↔ *Baker Street* – ℰ *(020) 7486 3898* – *www.royalchinagroup.co.uk* – *Closed 25-27 December*

XX **Galvin Bistrot de Luxe**

FRENCH · BISTRO Firmly established modern Gallic bistro with ceiling fans, globe lights and wood-panelled walls. Satisfying and precisely cooked classic French dishes from the Galvin brothers. The elegant basement cocktail bar adds to the comfy feel.

Menu £ 22/24 – Carte £ 32/54

Town plan: 29AGT-b – 66 Baker St. ⊠ W1U 7DJ
– ⊖ Baker Street – ℰ (020) 7935 4007 – www.galvinrestaurants.com
– Closed dinner 24 December, 25-26 December and 1 January

XX **Chiltern Firehouse**

WORLD CUISINE · INDIVIDUAL How appropriate – the hottest ticket in town is a converted fire station. The room positively bursts with energy but what makes this celebrity hangout unusual is that the food is rather good. Nuno Mendes' menu is full of vibrant North and South American dishes that are big on flavour.

Carte £ 36/61

Town plan: 29AGT-a – Chiltern Firehouse Hotel, 1 Chiltern St ⊠ W1U 7PA
– ⊖ Baker Street – ℰ (020) 7073 7676 – www.chilternfirehouse.com

XX **Beast**

MEATS · ELEGANT An underground banquet hall with three exceedingly long tables set for communal dining. The main event is a perfectly cooked hunk of rib eye steak and a large platter of succulent warm king crab. Bring a big appetite and a fat wallet.

Menu £ 85 – set menu only

Town plan: 30AHU-d – 3 Chapel Pl ⊠ W1G 0BG
– ⊖ Bond Street – ℰ (020) 7495 1816 (booking essential)
– www.beastrestaurant.co.uk – Closed Sunday, lunch Monday-Wednesday and bank holidays

XX **sixtyone**

BRITISH MODERN · ELEGANT A joint venture between chef Arnaud Stevens and Searcy's, in a space leased from the Montcalm hotel. The room is stylish and slick; the modern cooking is elaborate and quite playful, although the best dishes are often the simplest.

Menu £ 18/61 – Carte £ 32/47

Town plan: 29AGU-k – 61 Upper Berkeley St ⊠ W1H 7PP
– ⊖ Marble Arch – ℰ (020) 7958 3222 – www.sixtyonerestaurant.co.uk
– Closed Sunday dinner

XX **Percy & Founders** ◍

MODERN CUISINE · BRASSERIE Where Middlesex hospital once stood is now a residential development that includes this all-day operation. It's a mix between a smart pub and a modern brasserie and the kitchen brings quite a refined touch to the seasonal menu.

Carte £ 28/51

Town plan: 30AIT -f – 1 Pearson Sq, (off Mortimer St) ⊠ W1T 3BF
– ⊖ Goodge Street – ℰ (020) 3761 0200 – www.percyandfounders.co.uk

XX **Zayna**

INDIAN · ELEGANT The keen owner spent his early years in Kashmir and Punjab hence a menu of delicacies from Pakistan and north India. Choose your preferred cooking method such as tawa, pan or grill; only halal meat and free-range chicken are used.

Carte £ 20/37

Town plan: 29AGU-x – 25 New Quebec St. ⊠ W1H 7SF
– ⊖ Marble Arch – ℰ (020) 7723 2229 – www.zaynarestaurant.co.uk

XX Archipelago   AC

CREATIVE · EXOTIC New premises for this true one-off, but the same eccentric decoration that makes you feel you're in a bazaar. The exotic menu reads like an inventory at an omnivore's safari park; it could include crocodile, zebra and wildebeest.

Carte £ 29/44

Town plan: 30AIT-e – *53 Cleveland St ⊠ W1T 4JJ –* ⊖ *Goodge Street* – ℰ *(020) 7383 3346 – www.archipelago-restaurant.co.uk – Closed 24-28 December, Saturday lunch, Sunday and bank holidays*

XX Winter Garden   AC

MEDITERRANEAN · FRIENDLY Dining options north of Marylebone Road can be limited, so the Winter Garden, in the vast atrium of the Landmark Hotel, is a useful spot for a business lunch. The kitchen has a lightness of touch and the confidence not to overcrowd a plate.

Menu £ 30/40 – Carte £ 36/50

Town plan: 29AFT-a – *The Landmark London Hotel, 222 Marylebone Rd ⊠ NW1 6JQ –* ⊖ *Edgware Road – ℰ (020) 7631 8000 – www.landmarklondon.co.uk*

XX Fischer's   AC

AUSTRIAN · INDIVIDUAL An Austrian café and konditorei that summons the spirit of old Vienna, from the owners of The Wolseley et al. Open all day; breakfast is a highlight – the viennoiserie are great. Schnitzels are also good – upgrade to a Holstein.

Carte £ 15/43

Town plan: 30AHT-b – *50 Marylebone High St ⊠ W1U 5HN –* ⊖ *Baker Street* – ℰ *(020) 7466 5501 – www.fischers.co.uk – Closed 24-25 December and 1 January*

XX The Providores   AC

CREATIVE · TRENDY Packed ground floor for tapas; upstairs for innovative fusion cooking, with spices and ingredients from around the world, including Australasia. Starter-sized dishes at dinner allow for greater choice.

Carte £ 35/47

Town plan: 30AHT-y – *109 Marylebone High St. ⊠ W1U 4RX –* ⊖ *Bond Street* – ℰ *(020) 7935 6175 – www.theprovidores.co.uk – Closed 25-26 December*

XX Iberica Marylebone   AC

SPANISH · FAMILY Some prefer the intimacy of upstairs, others the bustle of the ground floor with its bar and deli. Along with an impressive array of Iberico hams are colourful dishes to share, such as glossy black rice with cuttlefish and prawns.

Menu £ 18/36 – Carte £ 14/46

Town plan: 18RZD-x – *195 Great Portland St ⊠ W1W 5PS* – ⊖ *Great Portland Street – ℰ (020) 7636 8650 – www.ibericalondon.co.uk – Closed 24-26 December, Sunday dinner and bank holidays*

XX Levant   AC

LEBANESE · EXOTIC Come in a group to best enjoy the Lebanese and Middle Eastern specialities; it's worth ordering one of the 'Feast' menus. Belly dancing, a low slung bar, lanterns and joss sticks add to the exotic feel of this basement restaurant.

Menu £ 14/35 – Carte £ 18/41

Town plan: 30AHT-c – *Jason Ct., 76 Wigmore St. ⊠ W1U 2SJ –* ⊖ *Bond Street* – ℰ *(020) 7224 1111 – www.levant.co.uk – Closed 25-26 December*

XX Royal China   AC

CHINESE · EXOTIC Barbecued meats, assorted soups and stir-fries attract plenty of large groups to this smart and always bustling Cantonese restaurant. Over 40 different types of dim sum served during the day.

Menu £ 30/38 – Carte £ 18/74

Town plan: 29AGT- h – *24-26 Baker St ⊠ W1U 7AB –* ⊖ *Baker Street – ℰ (020) 7487 4688 – www.royalchinagroup.co.uk*

✗ Trishna (Karam Sethi)

☸ INDIAN · NEIGHBOURHOOD Double-fronted, modern Indian restaurant dressed in an elegant, understated style. The coast of southwest India provides the influences and the food is balanced, satisfying and executed with care - the Tasting menus provide a good all-round experience.

➜ Aloo tokri chaat. Dorset brown crab with butter, pepper and wild garlic. Mango bappa doi with mango and star anise chutney.

Menu £24/60 – Carte £29/51

Town plan: 29AGT-r – *15-17 Blandford St.* ✉ *W1U 3DG*
– ⊖ *Baker Street* – ✆ *(020) 7935 5624* – *www.trishnalondon.com*
– *Closed 25-28 December and 1-3 January*

✗ Portland Ⓝ

☸ MODERN CUISINE · INTIMATE A no-frills, pared down restaurant that exudes honesty. One look at the menu and you know you'll eat well: it twists and turns on a daily basis and the combinations just sound right together. Dishes are crisp and unfussy but with depth and real understanding - quite something for such a young team.

➜ Sea trout, peas, beans and lemon verbena. Pigeon with parsley root and enoki. Brown butter ice cream, fresh almonds and grilled pear.

Carte £29/39

Town plan: 30AIT-p – *113 Great Portland St* ✉ *W1W 6QQ*
– ⊖ *Great Portland Street* – ✆ *(020) 7436 3261 (booking essential)*
– *www.portlandrestaurant.co.uk* – *Closed Sunday*

✗ Lima Fitzrovia

☸ PERUVIAN · NEIGHBOURHOOD Lima is one of those restaurants that just makes you feel good about life – and that's even without the Pisco Sours. The Peruvian food at this informal, fun place is the ideal antidote to times of austerity: it's full of punchy, invigorating flavours and fantastically vivid colours.

➜ Sea bream ceviche with tiger's milk, sweet potato, red onion and cancha corn. Beef with wild black quinoa, Cuzco corn and aji panca juice. Dulce de Leche ice cream.

Menu £20 (lunch and early dinner)/55
– Carte £38/52

Town plan: 31AJT-s – *31 Rathbone Pl* ✉ *W1T 1JH*
– ⊖ *Goodge Street* – ✆ *(020) 3002 2640* – *www.limalondon.com*
– *Closed 24-27 December-3 January, Sunday dinner and bank holidays*

✗ Social Wine & Tapas Ⓝ

MEDITERRANEAN · NEIGHBOURHOOD The latest in the Jason Atherton stable, and the name says it all. Urban styling, with wines on display; sit in the moodily lit basement. A mix of Spanish and Mediterranean dishes, with some Atherton classics too; desserts are a highlight.

Carte £20/38

Town plan: 30AHU-t – *39 James St* ✉ *W1U 1DL*
– ⊖ *Bond Street* – ✆ *(020) 7993 3257 (bookings not accepted)*
– *www.socialwineandtapas.com* – *Closed 25 December*

✗ Picture

☺ BRITISH MODERN · SIMPLE An ex Arbutus and Wild Honey triumvirate have created this cool, great-value restaurant. The look may be a little stark but the delightful staff add warmth. The small plates are vibrant and colourful, and the flavours are assured.

Menu £35 – Carte £23/32

Town plan: 30AIT-t – *110 Great Portland St.* ✉ *W1W 6PQ*
– ⊖ *Oxford Circus* – ✆ *(020) 7637 7892* – *www.picturerestaurant.co.uk*
– *Closed Sunday and bank holidays*

✗ The Wallace

FRENCH · FRIENDLY Large glass-roofed courtyard on the ground floor of Hertford House, home to the splendid Wallace Collection. French-influenced menu, with fruits de mer section; terrines are the house speciality.

Menu £ 25 (lunch) – Carte £ 30/47

Town plan: 29AGT-k – *Hertford House, Manchester Sq* ✉ *W1U 3BN*
– ⊖ *Bond Street* – 𝒞 *(020) 7563 9505*
– *www.peytonandbyrne.co.uk/the-wallace-restaurant/index.html – lunch only and dinner Friday-Saturday – Closed 24-26 December*

✗ Caffé Caldesi

ITALIAN · NEIGHBOURHOOD Head upstairs at this converted corner pub for generously proportioned, big flavoured classics from across Italy - they do a very good pumpkin soufflé. The ground floor has a simpler and more accessibly priced menu.

Menu £ 15 (weekday lunch) – Carte £ 24/34

Town plan: 30AHT-s – *118 Marylebone Ln. (1st floor)* ✉ *W1U 2QF*
– ⊖ *Bond Street* – 𝒞 *(020) 7487 0753* – *www.caldesi.com*

✗ Roti Chai

INDIAN · TRENDY Representing the new wave of modern, casual Indian restaurants, in appropriately vivid colours. The ground floor is for quick and easy pan-Indian street food; downstairs is swankier and offers a contemporary update of Indian home cooking.

Carte £ 15/31

Town plan: 29AGU-v – *3 Portman Mews South* ✉ *W1H 6HS* – ⊖ *Marble Arch*
– 𝒞 *(020) 7408 0101* – *www.rotichai.com* – *Closed 25 December*

✗ Il Baretto

ITALIAN · NEIGHBOURHOOD The robata grill is the star of the show at this lively Italian restaurant. The extensive and variably priced menu offers something for everyone, from pizzas to succulent lamb chops. The basement setting adds to the 'local' feel.

Menu £ 26 – Carte £ 35/83

Town plan: 29AGT-n – *43 Blandford St.* ✉ *W1U 7HF* – ⊖ *Baker Street*
– 𝒞 *(020) 7486 7340* – *www.ilbaretto.co.uk*

✗ 28°-50° Marylebone

MODERN CUISINE · WINE BAR This second wine bar from the owners of Texture restaurant offers a great choice of wines by the glass and a terrific "Collectors' List". Most plump for the grilled meats from the coal burning oven. Service is as bright as the room.

Menu £ 20 (lunch and early dinner) – Carte £ 26/39

Town plan: 30AHT-c – *15-17 Marylebone Ln.* ✉ *W1U 2NE* – ⊖ *Bond Street*
– 𝒞 *(020) 7486 7922* – *www.2850.co.uk* – *Closed 25-26 and 31 December, 1 January and Sunday*

✗ Riding House Café

MODERN CUISINE · RUSTIC It's less a café, more a large, quirkily designed, all-day New York style brasserie and cocktail bar. The 'small plates' have more zing than the main courses. The 'unbookable' side of the restaurant is the more fun part.

Menu £ 28 – Carte £ 25/41

Town plan: 29AGT-k – *43-51 Great Titchfield St* ✉ *W1W 7PQ* – ⊖ *Oxford Circus*
– 𝒞 *(020) 7927 0840* – *www.ridinghousecafe.co.uk* – *Closed 25-26 December*

✗ Opso 🆕

GREEK · NEIGHBOURHOOD A modern Greek restaurant which has proved a good fit for the neighbourhood - and not just because it's around the corner from the Hellenic Centre. It serves small sharing plates that mix the modern with the traditional.

Menu £ 27/50 – Carte £ 21/46

Town plan: 29AGT-s – *10 Paddington St* ✉ *W1U 5QL* – ⊖ *Baker Street*
– 𝒞 *(020) 7487 5088* – *www.opso.co.uk* – *Closed Sunday dinner*

✗ Donostia

BASQUE · TAPAS BAR The two young owners were inspired by the food of San Sebastiàn to open this pintxos and tapas bar. Sit at the counter for Basque classics like cod with pil-pil sauce, chorizo from the native pig Kintoa and slow-cooked pig's cheeks.

Carte £ 19/43

Town plan: 29AFU-s – *10 Seymour Pl* ✉ *W1H 7ND*
– ⊖ *Marble Arch* – ℰ *(020) 3620 1845* – *www.donostia.co.uk*
– *Closed Chritmas, Easter and Monday lunch*

✗ Ergon

GREEK · FRIENDLY The London branch of this successful group in Greece is a bright eatery with a downstairs deli stocked with Hellenic produce. The menu is a blend of classic and modern Greek dishes designed for sharing; the wine list is all Greek too.

Carte £ 25/38

Town plan: 30AHU-g – *16 Picton Pl* ✉ *W1U 1BP*
– ⊖ *Bond Street* – ℰ *(020) 7486 9210* – *www.ergonproducts.com*

✗ Vinoteca

MODERN CUISINE · WINE BAR Follows the formula of the original: great fun, great wines, gutsy and wholesome food, enthusiastic staff and almost certainly a wait for a table. Influences from sunnier parts of Europe, along with some British dishes.

Menu £ 13 – Carte £ 21/36

Town plan: 29AFU-v – *15 Seymour Pl.* ✉ *W1H 5BD*
– ⊖ *Marble Arch* – ℰ *(020) 7724 7288 (booking advisable)*
– *www.vinoteca.co.uk* – *Closed Christmas, bank holidays and Sunday dinner*

✗ Bonnie Gull

FISH AND SEAFOOD · SIMPLE Sweet Bonnie Gull calls itself a 'seafood shack' – a reference perhaps to its modest beginnings as a pop-up. Start with an order from the raw bar then go for a classic like Cullen skink, a whole Devon cock crab or fish and chips.

Carte £ 23/56

Town plan: 30AIT-b – *21a Foley St* ✉ *W1W 6DS*
– ⊖ *Goodge Street* – ℰ *(020) 7436 0921 (booking essential)*
– *www.bonniegull.com*

✗ Lockhart

WORLD CUISINE · INDIVIDUAL Owned by two Texan couples, this fun spot specialises in the fiery flavours of Texas, Louisiana and New Mexico. Start with a mezcal-based cocktail then tuck into a wonderfully smoky meat dish like the lip-smackingly good BBQ chicken.

Carte £ 23/43

Town plan: 29AFU-t – *22-24 Seymour Pl* ✉ *W1H 7NL*
– ⊖ *Marble Arch* – ℰ *(020) 3011 5400* – *www.lockhartlondon.com*
– *Closed Sunday dinner*

✗ Yalla Yalla

LEBANESE · RUSTIC It's fun, loud and you can't book, but the name means "Hurry up!" so you won't wait long. This is Beirut street food, meant for sharing. Try homemade soujoc (spicy sausages), sawda djej (chicken livers) and a succulent lamb dish.

Carte £ 19/29

Town plan: 30AIT-v – *12 Winsley St.* ✉ *W1W 8HQ*
– ⊖ *Oxford Circus* – ℰ *(020) 7637 4748* – *www.yalla-yalla.co.uk*
– *Closed 25-26 December, 1 January and Sunday*

✗ Dinings

JAPANESE · COSY It's hard not to be charmed by this sweet little Japanese place, with its ground floor counter and basement tables. Its strengths lie with the more creative, contemporary dishes; sharing is recommended but prices can be steep.

Carte £ 36/74

Town plan: 29AFT-c – *22 Harcourt St.* ✉ *W1H 4HH* – ⊖ *Edgware Road* – ☎*(020) 7723 0666 (booking essential)* – www.dinings.co.uk – *Closed Christmas and Sunday*

✗ Zoilo

ARGENTINIAN · FRIENDLY It's all about sharing so plonk yourself at the counter and discover Argentina's regional specialities. Typical dishes include braised pig head croquettes, grilled scallops with pork belly, and refreshing watermelon salad with ricotta.

Menu £ 10 (weekdays) – Carte £ 14/42

Town plan: 30AHT-z – *9 Duke St.* ✉ *W1U 3EG* – ⊖ *Bond Street* – ☎*(020) 7486 9699* – www.zoilo.co.uk

🍴 48 Newman Street

BRITISH TRADITIONAL · NEIGHBOURHOOD The experienced team behind this Edwardian pub have created a warm, welcoming spot. The kitchen celebrates the best of British and the menu is instantly appealing. Eat in the busy bar or in the more sedate first floor dining room.

Menu £ 20 – Carte £ 17/35

Town plan: 30AJT-s – *48 Newman St* ✉ *W1T 1QQ* – ⊖ *Goodge Street.* – ☎*(020) 3667 1445* – www.newmanstreettavern.co.uk – *Closed 25-26 December and Easter Monday*

🍴 Grazing Goat

BRITISH TRADITIONAL · PUB A smart city facsimile of a country pub; it's first-come-first-served in the bar but you can book in the upstairs dining room. Proper pub classics such as pies and Castle of Mey steaks are on offer. Bedrooms with Nordic style bathrooms.

Carte £ 30/37

8 rooms – ♦£ 210 ♦♦£ 250 – ☲£ 7

Town plan: 29AGU-d – *6 New Quebec St* ✉ *W1H 7RQ* – ⊖ *Marble Arch.* – ☎*(020) 7724 7243 (booking essential at dinner)* – www.thegrazinggoat.co.uk

🍴 Portman

MODERN CUISINE · PUB The condemned on their way to Tyburn Tree gallows would take their last drink here. Now it's an urbane pub with a formal upstairs dining room. The ground floor is more fun for enjoying the down-to-earth menu.

Menu £ 35/40 – Carte £ 26/41

Town plan: 29AFU-n – *51 Upper Berkeley St* ✉ *W1H 7QW* – ⊖ *Marble Arch.* – ☎*(020) 7723 8996* – www.theportmanmarylebone.com

St James's

🏨 Ritz

GRAND LUXURY · CLASSIC World famous hotel, opened in 1906 as a fine example of Louis XVI architecture and decoration. Elegant Palm Court famed for its afternoon tea. Many of the lavishly appointed and luxurious rooms and suites overlook the park.

134 rooms – ♦£ 450/1300 ♦♦£ 450/1300 – ☲£ 39 – 45 suites

Town plan: 30AIV-c – *150 Piccadilly* ✉ *W1J 9BR* – ⊖ *Green Park* – ☎*(020) 7493 8181* – www.theritzlondon.com

Ritz Restaurant – See restaurant listing

Haymarket   ☆ ▣ ᴌ₆ ⊡ ᴔ ᴀ�ᴄ ⸝⸜ ⇔

LUXURY · STYLISH Smart and spacious hotel in John Nash Regency building, with a stylish blend of modern and antique furnishings. Large, comfortable bedrooms in soothing colours. Impressive basement pool is often used for private parties.

50 rooms – ♦£ 336/595 ♦♦£ 336/595 – ⊡ £ 20 – 3 suites
Town plan: 31AKV-x – *1 Suffolk Pl.* ⊠ *SW1Y 4HX* – ⊖ *Piccadilly Circus*
– ℰ *(020) 7470 4000* – *www.haymarkethotel.com*
Brumus – See restaurant listing

Sofitel London St James   ☆ ⬤ ᴌ₆ ⊡ ᴔ ᴀᴄ ⸝⸜

LUXURY · ELEGANT Great location for this international hotel in a Grade II former bank. The triple-glazed bedrooms are immaculately kept; the spa is one of the best around. The bar is inspired by Coco Chanel; the lounge by an English rose garden.

183 rooms – ♦£ 240/400 ♦♦£ 240/400 – ⊡ £ 25 – 18 suites
Town plan: 31AKV-a – *6 Waterloo Pl.* ⊠ *SW1Y 4AN* – ⊖ *Piccadilly Circus*
– ℰ *(020) 7747 2200* – *www.sofitelstjames.com*
Balcon – See restaurant listing

Dukes   ☆ ⑊ ᴌ₆ ⊡ ᴀᴄ ⑄ ⸝⸜

TRADITIONAL · CLASSIC The wonderfully located Dukes has been steadily updating its image over the last few years, despite being over a century old. Bedrooms are now fresh and uncluttered and the atmosphere less starchy. The basement restaurant offers a modern menu, with dishes that are original in look and elaborate in construction.

90 rooms – ♦£ 285/365 ♦♦£ 365/650 – ⊡ £ 24 – 6 suites
Town plan: 30AIV-f – *35 St James's Pl.* ⊠ *SW1A 1NY* – ⊖ *Green Park*
– ℰ *(020) 7491 4840* – *www.dukeshotel.com*

Stafford   ☆ ⑊ ᴌ₆ ⊡ ᴀᴄ ⑄ ⸝⸜

TOWNHOUSE · STYLISH Styles itself as a 'country house in the city'; its bedrooms are divided between the main house, converted 18C stables and a more modern mews. Legendary American bar a highlight; traditional British food served in the restaurant.

104 rooms – ♦£ 280/750 ♦♦£ 280/750 – ⊡ £ 25 – 15 suites
Town plan: 30AIV-u – *16-18 St James's Pl.* ⊠ *SW1A 1NJ* – ⊖ *Green Park*
– ℰ *(020) 7493 0111* – *www.thestaffordlondon.com*

St James's Hotel and Club   ☆ ⑊ ⊡ ᴀᴄ ⸝⸜

BUSINESS · MODERN 1890s house, formerly a private club in a wonderfully central yet quiet location. Modern, boutique-style interior with over 300 European works of art from the '20s to the '50s. Fine finish to the compact but well-equipped bedrooms.

60 rooms – ♦£ 295/520 ♦♦£ 295/520 – ⊡ £ 24 – 10 suites
Town plan: 30AIV-k – *7-8 Park Pl.* ⊠ *SW1A 1LS* – ⊖ *Green Park*
– ℰ *(020) 7316 1600* – *www.stjameshotelandclub.com*
– *Closed 24-29 December*
  ☸ **Seven Park Place** – See restaurant listing

Cavendish   ☆ ⪡ ⊡ ᴔ ᴀᴄ ⑄ ⸝⸜ ⇔

BUSINESS · CLASSIC There's been a hotel on this site since the 18C; this one was built in the '60s but is smart and contemporary inside. Great location, bistro-style dining with British menu and good views across London from the top five floors.

230 rooms ⊡ – ♦£ 290/480 ♦♦£ 290/480 – 2 suites
Town plan: 30AIV-p – *81 Jermyn St* ⊠ *SW1Y 6JF* – ⊖ *Piccadilly Circus*
– ℰ *(020) 7930 2111* – *www.thecavendishlondon.com*

XxXxX Ritz Restaurant 🕏 AC 🕪

BRITISH TRADITIONAL · ELEGANT Grand and lavish restaurant, with Louis XVI decoration, trompe l'oeil and ornate gilding. Delightful terrace over Green Park. Structured, formal service. Classic, traditional dishes are the highlight of the menu. Jacket and tie required.

Menu £ 49 (weekday lunch) **s** – Carte £ 69/116 **s**

Town plan: 30AIV-c – *Ritz Hotel, 150 Piccadilly* ✉ *W1J 9BR* – ⊖ *Green Park* – ☏ *(020) 7493 8181* – *www.theritzlondon.com*

XxX Seven Park Place AC ⇔

❀ **MODERN CUISINE · COSY** William Drabble's cooking is all about the quality of the produce, much of which comes from the Lake District, and his confident cooking allows natural flavours to shine. This diminutive restaurant is concealed within the hotel and divided into two; ask for the warmer, gilded back room.

→ Poached native lobster tail, cauliflower purée and Périgord truffle sauce. Assiette of Lune Valley lamb with turnips and thyme. Mango and passion fruit cream, elderflower jelly and raspberries.

Menu £ 30 (weekday lunch)/61

Town plan: 30AIV-k – *St James's Hotel and Club, 7-8 Park Pl* ✉ *SW1A 1LS* – ⊖ *Green Park* – ☏ *(020) 7316 1615 (booking essential)* – *www.stjameshotelandclub.com* – *Closed 24-29 December, Sunday and Monday*

XxX The Wolseley AC 🖵 🕪 ⇔

MODERN CUISINE · FASHIONABLE This feels like a grand and glamorous European coffee house, with its pillars and high vaulted ceiling. Appealing menus offer everything from caviar to a hot dog. It's open from early until late and boasts a large celebrity following.

Carte £ 23/78

Town plan: 30AIV-q – *160 Piccadilly* ✉ *W1J 9EB* – ⊖ *Green Park* – ☏ *(020) 7499 6996 (booking essential)* – *www.thewolseley.com* – *Closed dinner 24 December*

XxX Chutney Mary Ⓝ 🍷 AC 🕪 ⇔

INDIAN · ELEGANT After 25 years in Chelsea, one of London's pioneering Indian restaurants is now establishing itself in a more central position. Spicing is understated; classics are done well; and some regional dishes have been subtly updated.

Menu £ 30 (lunch) – Carte £ 29/61

Town plan: 30AIV-c – *73 St James's St* ✉ *SW1A 1PH* – ⊖ *Green Park* – ☏ *(020) 7629 6688* – *www.chutneymary.com* – *Closed Sunday lunch*

XX Balcon AC 🖵

FRENCH · BRASSERIE A former banking hall with vast chandeliers and a grand brasserie look. It's open from breakfast onwards and the menu features French classics like snails and cassoulet; try the charcuterie from Wales and France.

Menu £ 20 (lunch) – Carte £ 25/45

Town plan: 31AKV-a – *Sofitel London St James Hotel, 8 Pall Mall.* ✉ *SW1Y 4AN* – ⊖ *Piccadilly Circus* – ☏ *(020) 7389 7820* – *www.thebalconlondon.com*

XX Matsuri AC ⇔

JAPANESE · FRIENDLY Sweet natured service at this long-standing, traditional Japanese stalwart. Teppan-yaki is their speciality, with Scottish beef the highlight; sushi counter also available. Good value lunch menus and bento boxes.

Carte £ 33/144

Town plan: 30AIV-w – *15 Bury St.* ✉ *SW1Y 6AL* – ⊖ *Green Park* – ☏ *(020) 7839 1101* – *www.matsuri-restaurant.com* – *Closed 25 December and 1 January*

XX Le Caprice

MODERN CUISINE · FASHIONABLE For over 30 years Le Caprice's effortlessly sophisticated atmosphere and surroundings have attracted a confident and urbane clientele. Perennials on their catch-all menu include their famous burger and rich salmon fishcake.

Menu £ 25 (early dinner) – Carte £ 32/61

Town plan: 30AIV-h – *Arlington House, Arlington St.* ⊠ *SW1A 1RJ*
– ⊖ *Green Park* – *𝒞 (020) 7629 2239* – *www.le-caprice.co.uk*
– *Closed 24-26 December*

XX Sake No Hana

JAPANESE · MINIMALIST A modern Japanese restaurant within a Grade II listed '60s edifice – and proof that you can occasionally find good food at the end of an escalator. As with the great cocktails, the menu is best enjoyed when shared with a group.

Menu £ 29/65 – Carte £ 21/99

Town plan: 30AIV-n – *23 St James's St* ⊠ *SW1A 1HA*
– ⊖ *Green Park* – *𝒞 (020) 7925 8988* – *www.sakenohana.com*
– *Closed 25 December and Sunday*

XX Boulestin

FRENCH · ELEGANT Nearly a century after Xavier Marcel Boulestin opened his eponymous restaurant showcasing 'Simple French Cooking for English homes', his spirit has been resurrected at this elegant brasserie, with its lovely courtyard terrace.

Menu £ 20 (weekday dinner) – Carte £ 32/56

Town plan: 30AIV-s – *5 St James's St* ⊠ *SW1A 1EF*
– ⊖ *Green Park* – *𝒞 (020) 7930 2030* – *www.boulestin.com*
– *Closed Sunday and bank holidays*

XX Cafe Murano

ITALIAN · FASHIONABLE Angela Hartnett and her chef have created an appealing and flexible menu of delicious North Italian delicacies – the lunch menu is very good value. It's certainly no ordinary café and its popularity means pre-booking is essential.

Menu £ 18 (weekdays)/30 – Carte £ 25/58

Town plan: 30AIV-m – *33 St. James's St* ⊠ *SW1A 1HD*
– ⊖ *Green Park* – *𝒞 (0203) 371 5559 (booking essential)*
– *www.cafemurano.co.uk* – *Closed Sunday dinner*

XX Franco's

ITALIAN · FORMAL Open from breakfast until late, with café at the front leading into smart, clubby restaurant. Menu covers all parts of Italy and includes popular grill section and plenty of classics.

Menu £ 24 (lunch and early dinner) – Carte £ 38/60

Town plan: 30AIV-i – *61 Jermyn St* ⊠ *SW1Y 6LX*
– ⊖ *Green Park* – *𝒞 (020) 7499 2211 (booking essential)*
– *www.francoslondon.com* – *Closed Sunday and bank holidays*

XX Avenue

MODERN CUISINE · ELEGANT Avenue has gone all American, with a new look from Russell Sage and a contemporary menu inspired by what's cooking in Manhattan. Wine is also made more of a feature; and, of course, the cocktails at the long, lively bar are great.

Menu £ 20 (lunch and early dinner) – Carte dinner £ 27/49

Town plan: 30AIV-y – *7-9 St James's St.* ⊠ *SW1A 1EE*
– ⊖ *Green Park* – *𝒞 (020) 7321 2111* – *www.avenue-restaurant.co.uk*
– *Closed Saturday lunch, Sunday dinner and bank holidays*

XX **Mint Leaf**

INDIAN · DESIGN Cavernous and moodily lit basement restaurant incorporating trendy bar with lounge music and extensive cocktail list. Contemporary Indian cooking with curries the highlight.

Menu £ 30/58 – Carte £ 25/35

Town plan: 31AKV-k – *Suffolk Pl* ✉ *SW1Y 4HX*
– ⊖ *Piccadilly Circus* – ✆ *(020) 7930 9020* – *www.mintleaflondon.com*
– *Closed 25-26 December, 1 January and lunch Saturday-Sunday*

XX **Al Duca**

ITALIAN · FRIENDLY Cooking which focuses on flavour continues to draw in the regulars at this warm and spirited Italian restaurant. Prices are keen when one considers the central location and service is brisk and confident.

Menu £ 25/34

Town plan: 31AJV-r – *4-5 Duke of York St* ✉ *SW1Y 6LA*
– ⊖ *Piccadilly Circus* – ✆ *(020) 7839 3090* – *www.alduca-restaurant.co.uk*
– *Closed Easter, 25-26 December, 1 January, Sunday and bank holidays*

XX **Quaglino's**

MODERN CUISINE · DESIGN An updated look, a new bar and live music have added sultriness and energy to this vast, glamorous and colourful restaurant. The kitchen specialises in contemporary brasserie-style food.

Menu £ 21/30 – Carte £ 23/63

Town plan: 30AIV-j – *16 Bury St* ✉ *SW1Y 6AJ*
– ⊖ *Green Park* – ✆ *(020) 7930 6767* – *www.quaglinos-restaurant.co.uk*
– *Closed 25 December, Easter Monday and Sunday*

XX **Brumus**

MODERN CUISINE · FASHIONABLE Pre-theatre dining is an altogether less frenzied activity when you can actually see the theatre from your table. This is a modern, elegant space with switched-on staff. Stick to the good value set menu or the 'dish of the day'.

Menu £ 20 – Carte £ 22/53

Town plan: 31AKV-x – *Haymarket Hotel, 1 Suffolk Pl* ✉ *SW1Y 4HX*
– ⊖ *Piccadilly Circus* – ✆ *(020) 7470 4000* – *www.haymarkethotel.com*

X **Portrait**

MODERN CUISINE · DESIGN On the top floor of National Portrait Gallery with rooftop local landmark views: a charming spot for lunch. Modern British/European dishes; weekend brunch.

Menu £ 20 – Carte £ 34/53

Town plan: 31ALV-n – *National Portrait Gallery (3rd floor), St Martin's Pl.*
✉ *WC2H 0HE* – ⊖ *Charing Cross* – ✆ *(020) 7312 2490 (booking essential)*
– *www.npg.org.uk/portraitrestaurant* – *lunch only and dinner Thursday-Saturday*
– *Closed 24-26 December*

X **The National Dining Rooms**

BRITISH MODERN · DESIGN Set on the East Wing's first floor, you can tuck into cakes in the bakery or grab a prime corner table in the restaurant for great views and proudly seasonal British menus.

Carte £ 28/32

Town plan: 31AKV-b – *Sainsbury Wing, The National Gallery, Trafalgar Sq*
✉ *WC2N 5DN* – ⊖ *Charing Cross* – ✆ *(020) 7747 2525*
– *www.peytonandbyrne.co.uk* – *lunch only and Friday dinner*
– *Closed 24-26 December and 1 January*

On a budget? Take advantage of lunchtime prices.

X Chop Shop

MEATS • TRENDY Spread over two floors and with an ersatz industrial look, this lively spot could be in Manhattan's Meatpacking district. Start with a cocktail, then order 'jars', 'crocks' or 'planks' of mousses, meatballs and cheeses; then it's the main event – great steaks and chops.

Menu £ 22 (weekday lunch)/35 – Carte £ 17/44

Town plan: 31AKV-c – 66 Haymarket ⊠ SW1Y 4RF – ⊖ Piccadilly Circus – ℰ (020) 7842 8501 – www.chopshopuk.com

X Shoryu

JAPANESE • SIMPLE Owned by Japan Centre opposite and specialising in Hakata tonkotsu ramen. The base is a milky broth made from pork bones to which is added hosomen noodles, egg, and assorted toppings. Its restorative powers are worth queuing for. There are a two larger branches in Soho.

Menu £ 10 (weekday lunch) – Carte £ 16/37

Town plan: 31AJV-s – 9 Regent St. ⊠ SW1Y 4LR – ⊖ Piccadilly Circus (bookings not accepted) – www.shoryuramen.com – Closed 25 December and 1 January

Soho

Soho

LUXURY • STYLISH Stylish and fashionable hotel that mirrors the vibrancy of the neighbourhood. Boasts two screening rooms, a comfortable drawing room and up-to-the-minute bedrooms; some vivid, others more muted but all with hi-tech extras.

91 rooms – ♦£ 300/610 ♦♦£ 300/610 – ⊑ £ 14 – 5 suites

Town plan: 31AJU-n – 4 Richmond Mews ⊠ W1D 3DH – ⊖ Tottenham Court Road – ℰ (020) 7559 3000 – www.sohohotel.com

Refuel – See restaurant listing

Ham Yard

FAMILY • STYLISH Opened in 2014, this stylish hotel from the Firmdale group is set around a courtyard – a haven of tranquillity in the West End. Each of the rooms is different but all are supremely comfortable. There's also a great roof terrace, a theatre, a fully stocked library and bar... and even a bowling alley.

91 rooms – ♦£ 318 ♦♦£ 318 – ⊑ £ 14 – 2 suites

Town plan: 31AJU-p – 1 Ham Yard, ⊠ W1D 7DT – ⊖ Piccadilly Circus – ℰ (020) 3642 2000 – www.firmdalehotels.com

Ham Yard – See restaurant listing

Café Royal

GRAND LUXURY • HISTORIC One of the most famous names of the London social scene for the last 150 years is now a luxury hotel. The bedrooms are beautiful, elegant and discreet and the wining and dining options many and varied – they include the gloriously rococo Oscar Wilde bar, once home to the iconic Grill Room.

160 rooms – ♦£ 320/600 ♦♦£ 320/600 – ⊑ £ 32 – 25 suites

Town plan: 30AJU-r – 68 Regent St ⊠ W1B 4DY – ⊖ Piccadilly Circus – ℰ (020) 7406 3333 – www.hotelcaferoyal.com

W London

LUXURY • DESIGN An achingly trendy hotel bang in the heart of Leicester Square. A DJ plays in the lobby lounge at weekends; there's an over-subscribed bar with low slung tables and slick, über cool bedrooms in categories called 'Fantastic' or 'Spectacular'.

192 rooms – ♦£ 339 ♦♦£ 339 – ⊑ £ 18 – 15 suites

Town plan: 31AKU-b – 10 Wardour St ⊠ W1D 6QF – ⊖ Leicester Square – ℰ (020) 7758 1000 – www.wlondon.co.uk

Spice Market – See restaurant listing

🏠 Sanctum Soho 🛜 📺 🆊 🍽 ♨

TOWNHOUSE · MODERN Plenty of glitz and bling at this funky, self-styled rock 'n' roll hotel, with some innovative touches such as TVs behind mirrors. Rooftop lounge and hot tub. Relaxed and comfortable dining with plenty of classic dishes.

30 rooms – ♦£ 190/550 ♦♦£ 190/550 – ☲£ 14

Town plan: 30AIU-g – *20 Warwick St. ✉ W1B 5NF*
– ⊖ *Piccadilly Circus* – ☎ *(020) 7292 6100 – www.sanctumsoho.com*

🏠 Dean Street Townhouse 🛜 📺 🆊 🍽

TOWNHOUSE · CLASSIC In the heart of Soho and where bedrooms range from tiny to bigger; the latter have roll-top baths in the room. All are well designed and come with a good range of extras. Cosy ground floor lounge.

39 rooms – ♦£ 225/250 ♦♦£ 400/500

Town plan: 31AKU-t – *69-71 Dean St. ✉ W1D 3SE*
– ⊖ *Piccadilly Circus* – ☎ *(020) 7434 1775*
– *www.deanstreettownhouse.com*

Dean Street Townhouse Restaurant – See restaurant listing

🏠 Nadler Soho 📺 🆊 🍽 ♨

BUSINESS · CONTEMPORARY On a quiet lane, but in the heart of Soho, is a townhouse with a concept: no bar nor restaurant, just comfortable, very well-equipped bedrooms, most of which have a small kitchenette. The smart receptionists double as concierge.

78 rooms – ♦£ 185/215 ♦♦£ 220/275 – ☲£ 14 – 1 suite

Town plan: 31AJU-y – *10 Carlisle St ✉ W1D 3BR*
– ⊖ *Tottenham Court Road* – ☎ *(020) 3697 3697 – www.thenadler.com*

🏠 Hazlitt's 🆊 🍽

TOWNHOUSE · HISTORIC Dating from 1718, the former house of essayist and critic William Hazlitt still welcomes many a writer today in its role as a charming townhouse hotel. It has plenty of character and is warmly run. No restaurant so breakfast in bed really is the only option – and who is going to object to that?

30 rooms – ♦£ 222 ♦♦£ 288/834 – ☲£ 12

Town plan: 31AKU-u – *6 Frith St ✉ W1D 3JA*
– ⊖ *Tottenham Court Road* – ☎ *(020) 7434 1771 – www.hazlittshotel.com*

🍴🍴🍴 Quo Vadis 🆊 🍷 🎞 ⇔

BRITISH TRADITIONAL · FASHIONABLE Owned by the Hart brothers, this Soho institution dates from the 1920s and is as stylish and handsome as ever. The menu reads like a selection of all your favourite British dishes – game is always a highlight. They also do a good breakfast and a great value theatre menu.

Menu £ 19 – Carte £ 31/49

Town plan: 31AKU-v – *26-29 Dean St ✉ W1D 3LL*
– ⊖ *Tottenham Court Road* – ☎ *(020) 7437 9585 – www.quovadissoho.co.uk*
– *Closed 25-26 December, 1 January and bank holidays*

🍴🍴🍴 Gauthier - Soho 🆊 🍽 ⇔

FRENCH · INTIMATE Tucked away from the mischief of Soho is this charming Georgian townhouse, with dining spread over three floors. Alex Gauthier offers assorted menus of his classically based cooking, with vegetarians particularly well looked after.

Menu £ 18/60

Town plan: 31AKU-k – *21 Romilly St ✉ W1D 5AF*
– ⊖ *Leicester Square* – ☎ *(020) 7494 3111 – www.gauthiersoho.co.uk*
– *Closed Monday lunch, Sunday and bank holidays except Good Friday*

XxX Red Fort

INDIAN · FASHIONABLE A feature in Soho since 1983 but the last makeover gave it a stylish, contemporary look. Balanced Indian cooking uses much UK produce such as Herdwick lamb; look out for more unusual choices like rabbit.

Menu £ 15 – Carte £ 32/65

Town plan: 31AKU-t – 77 Dean St. ⊠ W1D 3SH – ⊖ Tottenham Court Road – ℰ (020) 7437 2525 (bookings advisable at dinner) – www.redfort.co.uk – Closed lunch Saturday-Sunday

XxX Imperial China

CHINESE · ELEGANT Sharp service and comfortable surroundings are not the only things that set this restaurant apart: the Cantonese cooking exudes freshness and vitality, whether that's the steamed dumplings or the XO minced pork with fine beans.

Menu £ 20/36 – Carte £ 16/96

Town plan: 31AKU-l – White Bear Yard, 25a Lisle St ⊠ WC2H 7BA – ⊖ Leicester Square – ℰ (020) 7734 3388 (booking advisable) – www.imperialchina-london.com – Closed 25 December

XX Yauatcha Soho

❀ CHINESE · DESIGN Refined, delicate and delicious dim sum; ideal for sharing in a group. It's over 10 years old yet the surroundings are still as slick and stylish as ever: choose the lighter, brighter ground floor or the darker, more atmospheric basement.

→ Spicy soft shell crab. Sweet and sour pork. Raspberry délice.

Menu £ 29/55 – Carte £ 16/61

Town plan: 31AJU-k – 15 Broadwick St ⊠ W1F 0DL – ⊖ Tottenham Court Road – ℰ (020) 7494 8888 – www.yauatcha.com – Closed 25 December

XX Brasserie Zédel

⊕ FRENCH · BRASSERIE A grand French brasserie, which is all about inclusivity and accessibility, in a bustling subterranean space restored to its original art deco glory. Expect a roll-call of classic French dishes and some very competitive prices.

Menu £ 13/20 – Carte £ 19/41

Town plan: 31AJU-q – 20 Sherwood St ⊠ W1F 7ED – ⊖ Piccadilly Circus – ℰ (020) 7734 4888 (booking advisable) – www.brasseriezedel.com – Closed 24-25 December and 1 January

XX Bob Bob Ricard

MODERN CUISINE · RETRO Everyone needs a little glamour now and again and this place provides it. The room may be quite small but it sees itself as a grand salon – ask for a booth. The menu is all-encompassing – oysters and caviar to pies and burgers.

Carte £ 31/94

Town plan: 31AJU-s – 1 Upper James St ⊠ W1F 9DF – ⊖ Oxford Circus – ℰ (020) 3145 1000 – www.bobbobricard.com

XX Ham Yard

MODERN CUISINE · BRASSERIE An exuberantly decorated restaurant; start with a cocktail – the bitters and syrups are homemade with herbs from the hotel's roof garden. The menu moves with the seasons and the kitchen has the confidence to keep dishes simple.

Carte £ 24/35

Town plan: 31AJU-p – Ham Yard Hotel, 1 Ham Yard, ⊠ W1D 7DT – ⊖ Piccadilly Circus – ℰ (020) 3642 2000 – www.firmdalehotels.com

XX Dean Street Townhouse Restaurant

BRITISH MODERN · BRASSERIE Georgian house now home to a fashionable bar and restaurant that is busy from breakfast onwards. Appealingly classic British food includes some retro dishes and satisfying puddings.

Menu £ 17/28 – Carte £ 28/83

Town plan: 31AKU-t – 69-71 Dean St. ⊠ W1D 3SE – ⊖ Piccadilly Circus – ℰ (020) 7434 1775 (booking essential) – www.deanstreettownhouse.com

XX **Aqua Kyoto**

JAPANESE · **TRENDY** The louder and more boisterous of the two large restaurants on the 5th floor of Aqua London. It's ideally suited to a night out with a group of friends as many of the contemporary Japanese dishes are designed for sharing.

Menu £17 (lunch)/50 – Carte £27/64 **s**

Town plan: 30AIU-x – 240 Regent St. (5th floor) ✉ W1F 7EB – (entrance on Argyll St.) – ⊖ Oxford Circus – ☏ (020) 7478 0540 – www.aquakyoto.co.uk – Closed 25 December and 1 January

XX **Vasco and Piero's Pavilion**

ITALIAN · **FRIENDLY** Regulars and tourists have been flocking to this institution for over 40 years; its longevity is down to a twice daily changing menu of Umbrian-influenced dishes rather than the matter-of-fact service or simple decoration.

Menu £17 (lunch and early dinner) – Carte £25/46

Town plan: 31AJU-b – 15 Poland St ✉ W1F 8QE – ⊖ Oxford Circus – ☏ (020) 7437 8774 (booking essential at lunch) – www.vascosfood.com – Closed Saturday lunch, Sunday and bank holidays

XX **Plum Valley** ⇔

CHINESE · **DESIGN** Its striking black façade make this modern Chinese restaurant easy to spot in Chinatown. Mostly Cantonese cooking, with occasional forays into Vietnam and Thailand; dim sum is the strength.

Menu £38 – Carte £19/37

Town plan: 31AKU-i – 20 Gerrard St. ✉ W1D 6JQ – ⊖ Leicester Square – ☏ (020) 7494 4366 – Closed 23-24 December

XX **Refuel**

BRITISH MODERN · **FASHIONABLE** At the heart of the cool Soho hotel is their aptly named bar and restaurant. With a menu to suit all moods and wallets, from Dover sole to burgers, and a cocktail list to lift all spirits, it's a fun and bustling spot.

Menu £20 – Carte £30/53

Town plan: 31AJU-n – Soho Hotel, 4 Richmond Mews ✉ W1D 3DH – ⊖ Tottenham Court Road – ☏ (020) 7559 3007 – www.sohohotel.com

XX **Spice Market**

ASIAN · **FASHIONABLE** Spread over two floors and as strikingly decorated and fun as Jean-Georges Vongerichten's original in Manhattan's Meatpacking district. Influences are from across Asia; dishes are meant for sharing and curries are a highlight.

Carte £32/50

Town plan: 31AKU-b – W London Hotel, 10 Wardour St ✉ W1D 6QF – ⊖ Leicester Square – ☏ (020) 7758 1000 – www.wlondon.co.uk

XX **HIX**

BRITISH TRADITIONAL · **FASHIONABLE** The exterior may hint at exclusivity but inside this big restaurant the atmosphere is fun, noisy and sociable. The room comes decorated with the works of eminent British artists. Expect classic British dishes and ingredients.

Menu £20 (weekday lunch)/28 – Carte £27/65

Town plan: 30AJU-l – 66-70 Brewer St. ✉ W1F 9UP – ⊖ Piccadilly Circus – ☏ (020) 7292 3518 – www.hixsoho.co.uk – Closed 25-26 December

XX **MASH**

MEATS · **BRASSERIE** A team from Copenhagen raised the old Titanic and restored the art deco to create this striking 'Modern American Steak House', offering Danish, Nebraskan and Uruguayan beef. A great bar and slick service add to the grown up feel.

Menu £25 – Carte £50/75

Town plan: 30AJU-i – 77 Brewer St ✉ W1F 9ZN – ⊖ Piccadilly Circus – ☏ (020) 7734 2608 – www.mashsteak.co.uk – Closed 23-25 December and Sunday lunch

Social Eating House

MODERN CUISINE · FASHIONABLE There's a something of a Brooklyn vibe to this Jason Atherton restaurant, with its bare brick and raw plastered walls. It's great fun, very busy and gloriously unstuffy; the menu is an eminently good read, with the best dishes being the simplest ones.
→ Smoked Lincolnshire eel, sea salt and vinegar Jersey Royals, macadamia nuts and land seaweed. Rump of Kentish salt marsh lamb, confit shoulder, miso caramel, smoked aubergine and asparagus. Jelly and ice cream.
Menu £ 23 (lunch)
– Carte £ 39/56
Town plan: 30AJU-t – *58 Poland St* ✉ *W1F 7NR*
– ⊖ *Oxford Circus* – ℰ *(020) 7993 3251 (booking advisable)*
– *www.socialeatinghouse.com* – *Closed Christmas, Sunday and bank holidays*

Arbutus

MODERN CUISINE · BISTRO A relaxed setting, enthusiastic service, a terrific wine list that doesn't break the bank, and wonderfully flavoursome cooking – what's not to like? The technically confident kitchen has an innate under-standing of the 'less is more' principle along with an appreciation of what-goes-with-what.
→ Warm crisp pig's head with potato purée, black radish and pistachio. Saddle of rabbit with peas, wild mushrooms and slow cooked shoulder 'cottage pie'. Warm chocolate soup with almond milk sorbet.
Menu £ 23 (weekday lunch)/25
– Carte £ 34/54
Town plan: 31AKU-h – *63-64 Frith St.* ✉ *W1D 3JW*
– ⊖ *Tottenham Court Road* – ℰ *(020) 7734 4545 (booking advisable)*
– *www.arbutusrestaurant.co.uk* – *Closed 25-26 December and 1 January*

Barrafina

SPANISH · TAPAS BAR For proof that great food is about great sourcing, come to this terrific, warmly run tapas bar from the Hart brothers – but be prepared to queue for gaps at the counter. Wonderful, fresh ingredients and expert cooking allow natural flavours to shine – the seafood is particularly stunning.
→ Ham croquetas. Gambas, ajetes y setas tortilla. Santiago tart.
Carte £ 11/29
Town plan: 31AKU-c – *54 Frith St.* ✉ *W1D 3SL*
– ⊖ *Tottenham Court Road* – ℰ *(020) 7813 8016 (bookings not accepted)*
– *www.barrafina.co.uk* – *Closed 25 December and 1 January*

Dehesa

MEDITERRANEAN · TAPAS BAR Repeats the success of its sister restaurant, Salt Yard, by offering flavoursome and appealingly priced Spanish and Italian tapas. Busy, friendly atmosphere in appealing corner location. Terrific drinks list too.
Carte £ 19/29
Town plan: 30AIU-i – *25 Ganton St* ✉ *W1F 9BP*
– ⊖ *Oxford Circus* – ℰ *(020) 7494 4170* – *www.dehesa.co.uk*
– *Closed Christmas*

Nopi

MEDITERRANEAN · DESIGN The bright, clean look of Yotam Ottolenghi's charm-ingly run all-day restaurant matches the fresh, invigorating food. The sharing plates take in the Mediterranean, the Middle East and Asia and the veggie dishes stand out.
Carte £ 30/44
Town plan: 30AIU-g – *21-22 Warwick St.* ✉ *W1B 5NE*
– ⊖ *Piccadilly Circus* – ℰ *(020) 7494 9584* – *www.nopi-restaurant.com*
– *Closed 25-26 December, 1 January and Sunday dinner*

✗ Ember Yard

MEDITERRANEAN · TAPAS BAR Those familiar with the Salt Yard Group will recognise the Spanish and Italian themed menus – but their 4th fun outlet comes with a focus on cooking over charcoal or wood. There's even a seductive smokiness to some of the cocktails.

Carte approx. £20

Town plan: 30AJT-y – 60 Berwick St ⊠ W1F 8DX
– ⊖ Oxford Circus – ℰ (020) 7439 8057 (booking advisable)
– www.emberyard.co.uk – Closed 25-26 December and 1 January

✗ Polpetto

ITALIAN · SIMPLE Re-opened by Russell Norman in bigger premises. The style of food is the perfect match for this relaxed environment: the small, seasonally inspired Italian dishes are uncomplicated, appealingly priced and deliver great flavours.

Carte £15/23

Town plan: 31AJU-u – 11 Berwick St ⊠ W1F 0PL
– ⊖ Tottenham Court Road – ℰ (020) 7439 8627 – www.polpetto.co.uk
– Closed Sunday

✗ Polpo Soho

ITALIAN · TAPAS BAR A fun and lively Venetian bacaro, with a stripped-down, faux-industrial look. The small plates, from arancini and prosciutto to fritto misto and Cotechino sausage, are so well priced that waiting for a table is worth it.

Carte £12/26

Town plan: 30AJU-d – 41 Beak St. ⊠ W1F 9SB
– ⊖ Oxford Circus – ℰ (020) 7734 4479 – www.polpo.co.uk
– Closed dinner 24 December, 25-26 and 31 December, 1 January and Sunday dinner

✗ Copita

MEDITERRANEAN · TAPAS BAR Perch on one of the high stools or stay standing and get stuck into the daily menu of small, colourful and tasty dishes. Staff add to the atmosphere and everything on the Spanish wine list comes by the glass or copita.

Carte £17/28

Town plan: 30AJU-a – 27 D'Arblay St ⊠ W1F 8EP
– ⊖ Oxford Circus – ℰ (020) 7287 7797 (bookings not accepted)
– www.copita.co.uk – Closed Sunday and bank holidays

✗ Palomar

WORLD CUISINE · TRENDY A hip slice of modern-day Jerusalem in the heart of theatreland, with a zinc kitchen counter running back to an intimate, wood-panelled dining room. Like the atmosphere, the contemporary Middle Eastern cooking is fresh and vibrant.

Carte £23/36

Town plan: 31AKU-s – 34 Rupert St ⊠ W1D 6DN
– ⊖ Piccadilly Circus – ℰ (020) 7439 8777 (booking advisable)
– www.thepalomar.co.uk – Closed 25-26 December and Sunday dinner

✗ Mele e Pere

ITALIAN · FRIENDLY Head downstairs – the 'apples and pears'? – to a vaulted room in the style of a homely Italian kitchen, with an appealing Vermouth bar. The owner-chef has worked in some decent London kitchens but hails from Verona so expect gutsy Italian dishes.

Menu £20 (dinner) – Carte £26/39

Town plan: 31AJU-h – 46 Brewer St ⊠ W1F 9TF
– ⊖ Piccadilly Circus – ℰ (020) 7096 2096 – www.meleepere.co.uk
– Closed 25-26 December and 1 January

Blanchette   AC 🍴 ⇔

FRENCH · SIMPLE Run by three frères, Blanchette takes French bistro food and gives it the 'small plates' treatment. It's named after their mother – the ox cheek bourguignon is her recipe. Tiles and exposed brick add to the rustic look.

Carte £ 14/22

Town plan: 30AJU-g – *9 D'Arblay St* ✉ *W1F 8DR* – ⊖ *Oxford Circus* – ℰ *(020) 7439 8100 (booking essential)* – *www.blanchettesoho.co.uk*

Bocca di Lupo   AC 🍴 ⇔

ITALIAN · TAPAS BAR Atmosphere, food and service are all best when sitting at the marble counter, watching the chefs at work. Specialities from across Italy come in large and small sizes and are full of flavour and vitality. Try also their gelato shop opposite.

Carte £ 21/46

Town plan: 31AJU-e – *12 Archer St* ✉ *W1D 7BB* – ⊖ *Piccadilly Circus* – ℰ *(020) 7734 2223 (booking essential)* – *www.boccadilupo.com* – *Closed Christmas, 1 January and 31 August*

Wright Brothers Soho   🏠 AC

FISH AND SEAFOOD · NEIGHBOURHOOD A seafood restaurant with a utilitarian look; avoid downstairs which is meant to resemble a lobster pot. Oysters are a speciality; fish is from Cornwall; and the 'surfboards' are ideal for anyone wanting a quick one course lunch.

Menu £ 22 (weekdays) – Carte £ 30/80

Town plan: 30AIU-d – *13 Kingly St.* ✉ *W1B 5PW* – ⊖ *Oxford Circus* – ℰ *(020) 7434 3611* – *www.thewrightbrothers.co.uk* – *Closed bank holidays*

10 Greek Street   🍸 AC 🍴 ⇔

MODERN CUISINE · BISTRO With just 28 seats and a dozen at the counter, the challenge is getting a table at this modishly sparse-looking bistro (no bookings taken at dinner). The chef-owner's blackboard menu comes with Anglo, Med and Middle Eastern elements.

Carte £ 27/62

Town plan: 31AKU-e – *10 Greek St* ✉ *W1D 4DH* – ⊖ *Tottenham Court Road* – ℰ *(020) 7734 4677* – *www.10greekstreet.com* – *Closed Christmas, Easter and Sunday*

Haozhan   AC

CHINESE · DESIGN Interesting fusion-style dishes, with mostly Cantonese but other Asian influences too. Specialities like jasmine ribs or wasabi prawns reveal a freshness that marks this place out from the plethora of Chinatown mediocrity.

Menu £ 15/48 – Carte £ 20/78

Town plan: 31AKU-n – *8 Gerrard St* ✉ *W1D 5PJ* – ⊖ *Leicester Square* – ℰ *(020) 7434 3838* – *www.haozhan.co.uk* – *Closed 24-25 December*

Cinnamon Soho   🍷 🏠 AC 🍴 📶

INDIAN · FRIENDLY Younger and more fun than its sister the Cinnamon Club. Has a great selection of classic and more modern Indian dishes like Rogan Josh Shepherd's pie. High Chai in the afternoon and a pre-theatre menu that's a steal.

Menu £ 10/16 – Carte £ 17/31

Town plan: 30AIU-a – *5 Kingly St* ✉ *W1B 5PF* – ⊖ *Oxford Circus* – ℰ *(020) 7437 1664* – *www.cinnamonsoho.com* – *Closed 1 January*

Duck & Rice 🆕   AC

CHINESE · INTIMATE Alan Yau is one of our most innovative restaurateurs and once again he's created something different – a modern pub with a Chinese kitchen. Beer is the thing on the ground floor; upstairs is for Chinese favourites and comforting classics.

Carte £ 35/45

Town plan: 31AJU-w – *90 Berwick St* ✉ *W1F 0QB* – ⊖ *Tottenham Court Road* – ℰ *(020) 3327 7888* – *www.theduckandrice.com*

Tapas Brindisa

SPANISH · TAPAS BAR One of the first in Soho to have a no-bookings policy. This sister to the Borough Market original also brought with it – in true tapas style – small plates using terrific produce and that great atmosphere you get when places are packed out.

Menu £13 (weekday lunch) - Carte £15/40

Town plan: 31AJU-f - 46 Broadwick St. ⊠ W1F 7AF

- ⊖ Oxford Circus - *℘* (020) 7534 1690 - www.brindisatapaskitchens.com
- Closed dinner 24-27 December

Burger & Lobster

MEATS · FASHIONABLE A sizeable place, yet as busy as the first branch in Mayfair. Choose a lobster roll in a brioche bun, a 1½lb Maine or Canadian lobster, or a 280g burger of Irish or Nebraskan beef. Bookings only taken for parties of 6 or more.

Menu £20

Town plan: 31AKU-x - 36 Dean St ⊠ W1D 4PS

- ⊖ Leicester Square - *℘* (020) 7432 4800 - www.burgerandlobster.com
- Closed 25 December and 4 January

Vinoteca

MODERN CUISINE · WINE BAR The terrific wine list mixes the classic with the esoteric and emerging markets are also covered. The food isn't forgotten – cured meats and cheeses are a highlight and dishes like venison and bacon pie also hit the spot.

Carte £26/43

Town plan: 30AJU-v - 53-55 Beak St ⊠ W1F 9SH

- ⊖ Oxford Circus - *℘* (020) 3544 7411 (booking essential) - www.vinoteca.co.uk
- Closed 24-26 December and 1 January

Antidote

MODERN CUISINE · INDIVIDUAL On the ground floor is a wine bar serving cheese, charcuterie and 'small plates'. The keenly run upstairs restaurant offers fresh, vibrant and contemporary cuisine, with the kitchen under the guidance of Mikael Jonsson of Hedone.

Menu £19/40 - Carte £34/55

Town plan: 30AIU-j - 12A Newburgh St ⊠ W1F 7RR

- ⊖ Oxford Circus - *℘* (020) 7287 8488 (booking advisable)
- www.antidotewinebar.com - Closed Sunday

Jinjuu

ASIAN · DESIGN American-born celebrity chef Judy Joo's first London restaurant is a celebration of her Korean heritage. The vibrant dishes, whether Bibimbap bowls or Ssam platters, burst with flavour and are as enjoyable as the fun surroundings.

Menu £17/42 - Carte £18/69

Town plan: 30AIU-d - 15 Kingly St ⊠ W1B 5PS

- ⊖ Oxford Circus - *℘* (020) 8181 8887 - www.jinjuu.com
- Closed 25 December

Spuntino

NORTH-AMERICAN · RUSTIC Influenced by Downtown New York, with its no-booking policy and industrial look. Sit at the counter and order classics like Mac 'n' cheese or mini burgers. The staff, who look like they could also fix your car, really add to the fun.

Carte £15/22

Town plan: 31AJU-j - 61 Rupert St. ⊠ W1D 7PW

- ⊖ Piccadilly Circus (bookings not accepted) - www.spuntino.co.uk
- Closed dinner 24 December, 25-26, 31 December and 1 January

X Bibigo

KOREAN · FRIENDLY The enthusiastically run Bibigo represents Korea's largest food company's first foray into the UK market. Watch the kitchen send out dishes such as kimchi, Bossam (simmered pork belly) and hot stone galbi (chargrilled short ribs).

Menu £ 13 (lunch) – Carte £ 20/29

Town plan: 30AJU-x – *58-59 Great Marlborough St* ⊠ *W1F 7JY* – ⊖ *Oxford Circus* – *℘ (020) 7042 5225* – *www.bibigouk.com*

X Ceviche

PERUVIAN · FRIENDLY Based on a Lima Pisco bar, Ceviche is as loud as it is fun. First try the deliriously addictive drinks based on the Peruvian spirit Pisco, and then share some thinly sliced sea bass or octopus, along with anticuchos skewers.

Menu £ 18 (weekday lunch) – Carte £ 14/24

Town plan: 31AKU-w – *17 Frith St* ⊠ *W1D 4RG* – ⊖ *Tottenham Court Road* – *℘ (020) 7292 2040 (booking essential)* – *www.cevicheuk.com*

X Cây Tre

VIETNAMESE · MINIMALIST Bright, sleek and bustling surroundings where Vietnamese standouts include Cha La Lot (spicy ground pork wrapped in betel leaves), slow-cooked Mekong catfish with a well-judged sweet and spicy sauce, and 6 versions of Pho (noodle soup).

Menu £ 22/29 – Carte £ 17/28

Town plan: 31AKU-m – *42-43 Dean St* ⊠ *W1D 4PZ* – ⊖ *Tottenham Court Road* – *℘ (020) 7317 9118 (booking advisable)* – *www.caytresoho.co.uk*

X Rosa's Carnaby

THAI · SIMPLE A bright, bustling café celebrating traditional Thai flavours, with the occasional modern twist. Perch on low stools and rub elbows with your neighbours while the unfailingly polite staff cope capably with the rush of customers.

Menu £ 20 (lunch and early dinner) – Carte £ 17/30

Town plan: 30AIU-u – *23a Ganton Street* ⊠ *W1F 9BW* – ⊖ *Oxford Circus* – *℘ (020) 7287 9617 (booking essential)* – *http://rosasthaicafe.com/* – *Closed 25 December*

X Rosa's Soho

THAI · SIMPLE The worn-in, pared down look of this authentic Thai café adds to its intimate feel. Signature dishes include warm minced chicken salad and a sweet pumpkin red curry. Tom Yam soup comes with a lovely balance of sweet, sour and spice.

Menu £ 20 – Carte £ 17/30

Town plan: 31AKU-j – *48 Dean St* ⊠ *W1D 5BF* – ⊖ *Leicester Square* – *℘ (020) 7494 1638 (booking advisable)* – *www.rosasthaicafe.com* – *Closed 25 December*

X Bone Daddies

ASIAN · FASHIONABLE Maybe ramen is the new rock 'n' roll. The charismatic Aussie chef-owner feels that combinations are endless when it comes to these comforting bowls. Be ready to queue then share a table. It's a fun place, run by a hospitable bunch.

Carte £ 17/26

Town plan: 31AJU-y – *30-31 Peter St* ⊠ *W1F 0AR* – ⊖ *Piccadilly Circus* – *℘ (020) 7287 8581 (bookings not accepted)* – *www.bonedaddies.com* – *Closed 25 December*

X Soho Kitchen & Bar

NORTH-AMERICAN · SIMPLE Most punters who pack out this appealing retro-style diner are here for the comforting American classics like mac & cheese, a hot dog or a burger. The buzz is great, the cocktails are on tap and it's open till the wee small hours.

Carte £ 17/32

Town plan: 31AKU-d – *19-21 Old Compton St.* ⊠ *W1D 5JJ* – ⊖ *Leicester Square* – *℘ (020) 7734 5656* – *www.sohodiner.com*

X Barshu

CHINESE · EXOTIC The fiery and authentic flavours of China's Sichuan province are the draw here; help is at hand as the menu has pictures. It's decorated with carved wood and lanterns; downstairs is better for groups.

Carte £ 21/52

Town plan: 31AKU-g – *28 Frith St.* ✉ *W1D 5LF* – ⊖ *Leicester Square* – ✆ *(020) 7287 8822 (booking advisable)* – *www.barshurestaurant.co.uk* – *Closed 24-26 December*

X Ba Shan

CHINESE · COSY Whilst there are some Sichuan dishes, this bigger-than-it-looks Chinese restaurant excels in specialities from Hunan. That means plenty of heat but also pickling, curing and smoking; dishes arrive when ready so sharing is best.

Carte £ 15/37

Town plan: 31AKU-f – *24 Romilly St.* ✉ *W1D 5AH* – ⊖ *Leicester Square* – ✆ *(020) 7287 3266 (booking advisable)* – *Closed 24-25 December*

X Baozi Inn

CHINESE · RUSTIC Buzzy, busy little place that's great for a quick bite, especially if you like pork buns, steaming bowls of noodles, a hit of Sichuan fire and plenty of beer or tea. You'll leave feeling surprisingly energised and rejuvenated.

Carte £ 12/18

Town plan: 31AKU-r – *25-26 Newport Court* ✉ *WC2H 7JS* – ⊖ *Leicester Square* – ✆ *(020) 7287 6877 (bookings not accepted)* – *Closed 24-25 December*

X Manchurian Legends

CHINESE · SIMPLE Try specialities from a less familiar region of China: Dongbei, the 'north east'. As winters there are long, stews and BBQ dishes are popular, as are pickled ingredients and chilli heat. Further warmth comes from the sweet natured staff.

Menu £ 16/25 – Carte £ 20/38

Town plan: 31AKU-z – *16 Lisle St* ✉ *WC2H 7BE* – ⊖ *Leicester Square* – ✆ *(020) 7287 6606* – *www.manchurianlegends.com* – *Closed Christmas*

X Koya Bar

JAPANESE · SIMPLE A simple, sweet place serving authentic Udon noodles and small plates; they open early for breakfast. Counter seating means everyone has a view of the chefs; bookings aren't taken and there is often a queue, but the short wait is worth it.

Carte £ 16/28

Town plan: 31AKU-c – *50 Frith St* ✉ *W1D 4SQ* – ⊖ *Tottenham Court Road* – ✆ *(020) 7433 4463 (bookings not accepted)* – *www.koyabar.co.uk* – *Closed Christmas*

X Beijing Dumpling

CHINESE · NEIGHBOURHOOD This relaxed little place serves freshly prepared dumplings of both Beijing and Shanghai styles. Although the range is not as comprehensive as the name suggests, they do stand out, especially varieties of the famed Siu Lung Bao.

Carte £ 10/40

Town plan: 31AKU-l – *23 Lisle St.* ✉ *WC2H 7BA* – ⊖ *Leicester Square* – ✆ *(020) 7287 6888* – *Closed 24-25 December*

X Tonkotsu

JAPANESE · RUSTIC Some things are worth queuing for. Good ramen is all about the base stock: 18 hours goes into its preparation here to ensure the bowls of soup and wheat-based noodles reach a depth of flavour that seems to nourish one's very soul.

Carte approx. £ 22

Town plan: 31AKU-p – *63 Dean St* ✉ *W1D 4QG* – ⊖ *Tottenham Court Road* – ✆ *(020) 7437 0071 (bookings not accepted)* – *www.tonkotsu.co.uk*

Ducksoup

MODERN CUISINE • TRENDY It's compact, with bar seating; decoratively it's knowingly underwhelming; and the menu is handwritten each day – yes, every 'on-trend' box is ticked here. Dishes are all about the produce and are confidently unadorned.

Carte £ 19/35

Town plan: 31AKU-a – *41 Dean St ✉ W1D 4PY – ⊖ Leicester Square – ☎ (020) 7287 4599 – www.ducksoupsoho.co.uk – Closed Christmas, Easter, Sunday dinner and bank holidays*

Pitt Cue Co.

MEATS • SIMPLE The owners started out selling their American barbecue dishes from a van before finding this tiny spot. The ribs are smoked in-house for 6 hours before roasting; the pulled pork is excellent. It's messy, filling and fun; be ready to queue.

Carte £ 18/30

Town plan: 30AIU-p – *1 Newburgh St ✉ W1F 7RB – ⊖ Oxford Circus – ☎ (020) 7287 5578 (bookings not accepted) – www.pittcue.co.uk – Closed 25-26 December,1 January, 4 April and 3 October*

Strand and Covent Garden

Savoy

GRAND LUXURY • STYLISH A legendary hotel renewed after a 3 year renovation; its luxurious bedrooms and stunning suites come in Edwardian or art deco styles. Have tea in the Thames Foyer, the hotel's heart, or drinks in the famous American Bar or the moodier Beaufort Bar. Along with the Savoy Grill is Kaspar's, an informal seafood bar and grill which replaced the River restaurant.

268 rooms – †£ 350/550 ††£ 370/570 – ☕ £ 30 – 45 suites

Town plan: 31ALU-s – *Strand ✉ WC2R 0EU – ⊖ Charing Cross – ☎ (020) 7836 4343 – www.fairmont.com/savoy*

Savoy Grill – See restaurant listing

One Aldwych

GRAND LUXURY • MODERN Former 19C bank, now a stylish hotel with lots of artwork; the lobby changes its look seasonally and doubles as a bar. Stylish, contemporary bedrooms with the latest mod cons; the deluxe rooms and suites are particularly desirable. Impressive leisure facilities. Light, accessible menu at Indigo.

105 rooms – †£ 265/450 ††£ 265/450 – ☕ £ 19 – 12 suites

Town plan: 32AMU-r – *1 Aldwych ✉ WC2B 4BZ – ⊖ Temple – ☎ (020) 7300 1000 – www.onealdwych.com*

ME London

CHAIN HOTEL • FUNCTIONAL On the site of the Gaiety theatre and Marconi House, now a striking hotel designed by Fosters + Partners. Eye-catching pyramid shaped reception; bedrooms that are crisply decorated, cleverly lit and very comfortable. Steaks in the glitzy STK; Cucina Asellina offers a contemporary setting for Italian food; Radio has a simple menu and comes with a stunning rooftop bar.

157 rooms – †£ 300/600 ††£ 330/720 – ☕ £ 25 – 16 suites

Town plan: 32AMU-a – *336-337 Strand ✉ WC2R 1HA – ⊖ Temple – ☎ (020) 7395 3400 – www.melondonuk.com*

Waldorf Hilton

HISTORIC • ELEGANT Impressive curved and columned façade: an Edwardian landmark in a great location. Stylish, contemporary bedrooms in calming colours have superb bathrooms and all mod cons. Tea dances in the Grade II listed Palm Court Ballroom. Stylish 'Homage' is popular for afternoon tea and relaxed brasserie style dining.

298 rooms – †£ 259/329 ††£ 309/369 – ☕ £ 23 – 12 suites

Town plan: 32AMU-s – *Aldwych ✉ WC2B 4DD – ⊖ Temple – ☎ (020) 7836 2400 – www.hilton.co.uk/waldorf*

🏛 St Martins Lane 🕸 ⅃ᵦ ⬆ 🅰🅲 🎎 🚗

LUXURY · DESIGN The unmistakable hand of Philippe Starck is evident at this most contemporary of hotels. Unique and stylish, from the starkly modern lobby to the state-of-the-art bedrooms, which come in a blizzard of white.
206 rooms - ♦£ 222/479 ♦♦£ 222/479 – ⌸ £ 26 – 2 suites
Town plan: 31ALU-e – 45 St Martin's Ln ✉ WC2N 3HX
– ⊖ Charing Cross – ☏ (020) 7300 5500 – www.stmartinslane.com

XxxX Savoy Grill 🅰🅲 Ⅰ👁 ℘₃ ⇔

BRITISH TRADITIONAL · ELEGANT Archives were explored, designers briefed and much money spent, with the result that the Savoy Grill has returned to the traditions that made it famous. As befits the name, it is the charcoal grilling of meats that takes centre stage.
Menu £ 38 – Carte £ 32/74
Town plan: 31ALU-s – Savoy Hotel, Strand ✉ WC2R 0EU
– ⊖ Charing Cross – ☏ (020) 7592 1600 – www.gordonramsay.com/thesavoygrill

XxX Delaunay 🗺 🅰🅲 ⇔

MODERN CUISINE · ELEGANT The Delaunay was inspired by the grand cafés of Europe but, despite sharing the same buzz and celebrity clientele as its sibling The Wolseley, is not just a mere replica. The all-day menu is more mittel-European, with great schnitzels and wieners.
Carte £ 17/67
Town plan: 32AMU-x – 55 Aldwych ✉ WC2B 4BB
– ⊖ Temple – ☏ (020) 7499 8558 (booking essential) – www.thedelaunay.com
– Closed 25 December and dinner 24 December

XxX The Ivy 🅰🅲 ℘₃ ⇔

BRITISH TRADITIONAL · FASHIONABLE This landmark restaurant has had a facelift and while the glamorous clientele remain, it now has an oval bar as its focal point. The menu offers international dishes alongside the old favourites and personable staff anticipate your every need.
Menu £ 27 – Carte £ 29/75
Town plan: 31AKU-p – 1-5 West St ✉ WC2H 9NQ
– ⊖ Leicester Square – ☏ (020) 7836 4751 – www.the-ivy.co.uk
– Closed 25 December

XX L'Atelier de Joël Robuchon 🅰🅲 ℘₃

❀ FRENCH · FASHIONABLE Creative, skilled and occasionally playful cooking; dishes may look delicate but pack a punch. Ground floor 'Atelier' comes with counter seating and chefs on view. More structured 'La Cuisine' upstairs and a cool bar above that.
➜ Salmon tartare with Sologne Imperial caviar. Free range stuffed quail with pomme purée and herb salad. Manjari chocolate mousse, dark chocolate sorbet and Oreo cookie crumb.
Menu £ 38 (lunch and early dinner)/129 – Carte £ 43/107
Town plan: 31AKU-a – 13-15 West St. ✉ WC2H 9NE
– ⊖ Leicester Square – ☏ (020) 7010 8600 – www.joelrobuchon.co.uk
– Closed 25-26 December,1 January and August bank holiday Monday

XX J. Sheekey 🅰🅲

FISH AND SEAFOOD · FASHIONABLE Festooned with photographs of actors and linked to the theatrical world since opening in 1890. Wood panels and alcove tables add famed intimacy. Accomplished seafood cooking.
Carte £ 33/74
Town plan: 31ALU-v – 28-34 St Martin's Ct. ✉ WC2 4AL
– ⊖ Leicester Square – ☏ (020) 7240 2565 (booking essential)
– www.j-sheekey.co.uk – Closed 25-26 December

XX Spring

ITALIAN · FASHIONABLE Spring occupies the 'new wing' of Somerset House that for many years was inhabited by the Inland Revenue. It's a bright, feminine space under the aegis of chef Skye Gyngell. Her cooking is Italian influenced and ingredient-led.

Menu £26 (lunch) – Carte £33/62

Town plan: 32AMU-c – *New Wing, Somerset House, Strand* ✉ *WC2R 1LA*
– *Entrance on Lancaster Pl* – ⊖ *Temple* – ℰ *(020) 3011 0115 (booking advisable)*
– *www.springrestaurant.co.uk* – *Closed Sunday dinner*

XX Rules

BRITISH TRADITIONAL · FORMAL London's oldest restaurant boasts a fine collection of antique cartoons, drawings and paintings. Tradition continues in the menu, specialising in game from its own estate.

Carte £34/65

Town plan: 31ALU-n – *35 Maiden Ln* ✉ *WC2E 7LB*
– ⊖ *Leicester Square* – ℰ *(020) 7836 5314 (booking essential)*
– *www.rules.co.uk* – *Closed 25-26 December*

XX Clos Maggiore

FRENCH · FORMAL One of London's most romantic restaurants – but be sure to ask for the enchanting conservatory with its retractable roof. The sophisticated French cooking is joined by a wine list of great depth. Good value and very popular pre/post theatre menus.

Menu £20 (weekdays)/35 – Carte £32/58

Town plan: 31ALU-z – *33 King St* ✉ *WC2E 8JD*
– ⊖ *Leicester Square* – ℰ *(020) 7379 9696* – *www.closmaggiore.com*
– *Closed 24-25 December*

XX Roka

JAPANESE · FASHIONABLE This is the fourth and largest Roka in the group. It shares the same stylish look, efficient service and modern Japanese food, although there are some dishes unique to this branch. Consider the Tasting menu for a good all-around experience.

Menu £27 (lunch) – Carte approx. £55

Town plan: 32AMU-v – *71 Aldwych* ✉ *WC2B 4HN*
– ⊖ *Temple* – ℰ *(020) 7294 7636* – *www.rokarestaurant.com*
– *Closed 25 December*

XX Les Deux Salons

FRENCH · BISTRO Sir Terence Conran took over this handily-placed site in 2015 and injected a tidy sum into its redesign. On the ground floor is a café, a bistro serving all the French classics, a bar, épicerie, and a more formal restaurant upstairs.

Menu £13/30 – Carte £23/57

Town plan: 31ALU-m – *40-42 William IV St* ✉ *WC2N 4DD*
– ⊖ *Charing Cross* – ℰ *(020) 7420 2050* – *www.lesdeuxsalons.co.uk*
– *Closed 25-26 December and 1 January*

XX Cafe Murano

ITALIAN · NEIGHBOURHOOD The second Café Murano is in the heart of Covent Garden, in a space much larger than the St James's original; head for the smart marble-topped counter at the back. Appealing menu of Northern Italian dishes cooked with care and respect.

Menu £21 – Carte £23/38

Town plan: 31ALU-o – *34-36 Tavistock St* ✉ *WC2E 7PB*
– ⊖ *Charing Cross* – ℰ *(020) 7240 3654* – *www.cafemurano.co.uk*
– *Closed Sunday dinner*

ⅩⅩ Ivy Market Grill

BRITISH TRADITIONAL · DESIGN Mere mortals can now experience a little of that Ivy glamour by eating here at the first of their diffusion line. Breakfast, a menu of largely British classics and afternoon tea keep it busy all day. There's another branch in Chelsea.

Menu £ 21 (early dinner) – Carte £ 25/47

Town plan: 31ALU-z – *1 Henrietta St ✉ WC2E 8PS*
– ⊖ *Leicester Square* – ✆ *(020) 3301 0200*
– *www.theivymarketgrill.com*

ⅩⅩ Balthazar

FRENCH · BRASSERIE Those who know the original Balthazar in Manhattan's SoHo district will find the London version of this classic brasserie uncannily familiar in looks, vibe and food. The Franglais menu keeps it simple and the cocktails are great.

Carte £ 26/65

Town plan: 31ALU-t – *4-6 Russell St. ✉ WC2B 5HZ*
– ⊖ *Covent Garden* – ✆ *(020) 3301 1155 (booking essential)*
– *www.balthazarlondon.com* – *Closed 25 December*

Ⅹ Barrafina

SPANISH · TAPAS BAR The second Barrafina is not just brighter than the Soho original – it's bigger too, so you can wait inside with a drink for counter seats to become available. Try more unusual tapas like ortiguillas, frit Mallorquin or the succulent meats.

Carte £ 11/29

Town plan: 31ALU-x – *10 Adelaide St ✉ WC2N 4HZ*
– ⊖ *Charing Cross* – ✆ *(020) 7440 1450 (bookings not accepted)*
– *www.barrafina.co.uk* – *Closed Christmas and New Year*

Ⅹ J. Sheekey Oyster Bar

FISH AND SEAFOOD · INTIMATE An addendum to J. Sheekey restaurant. Sit at the bar to watch the chefs prepare the same quality seafood as next door but at slightly lower prices; fish pie and fruits de mer are the popular choices. Open all day.

Carte £ 22/39

Town plan: 31ALU-v – *33-34 St Martin's Ct. ✉ WC2 4AL*
– ⊖ *Leicester Square* – ✆ *(020) 7240 2565* – *www.j-sheekey.co.uk*
– *Closed 25-26 December*

Ⅹ Hawksmoor

MEATS · RUSTIC Steaks from Longhorn cattle lovingly reared in North Yorkshire and dry-aged for at least 35 days are the stars of the show. Atmospheric, bustling basement restaurant in former brewery cellars.

Menu £ 24 (weekdays)/27 – Carte £ 24/73

Town plan: 31ALU-f – *11 Langley St ✉ WC2H 9JG*
– ⊖ *Covent Garden* – ✆ *(020) 7420 9390* – *www.thehawksmoor.com*
– *Closed 24-26 December*

Ⅹ Tredwell's

BRITISH MODERN · BRASSERIE A modern brasserie with a hint of art deco courtesy of Marcus Wareing. Cooking is best described as modern English; dishes show a degree of refinement, and a commendable amount of thought has gone into addressing allergen issues.

Menu £ 20 (lunch and early dinner) – Carte £ 25/44

Town plan: 31ALU-f – *4 Upper St Martin's Ln ✉ WC2H 9EF*
– ⊖ *Leicester Square* – ✆ *(020) 3764 0840* – *www.tredwells.com*
– *Closed 25-26 December*

X **Lima Floral** 🔘   🍷 🅰🅲 🉐 ⑬ ⇩

PERUVIAN · FASHIONABLE This second Lima branch has a light and airy feel by day and a cosy, candlelit vibe in the evening; regional Peruvian dishes are served alongside the more popular causa and ceviche. Basement Pisco Bar for Peruvian tapas and Pisco sours.

Menu £18 (weekday lunch) – Carte £35/47

Town plan: 31ALU-k – *14 Garrick St* ✉ *WC2E 9BJ* – ⊖ *Leicester Square* – ℰ *(020) 7240 5778* – *www.limafloral.com* – *Closed bank holiday Mondays*

X **Terroirs**   ⅋ 🅰🅲 ⑬

MEDITERRANEAN · BISTRO Eat in the ground floor bistro/wine bar or from a slightly different menu two floors below at 'Downstairs at Terroirs'. Flavoursome French cooking, with extra Italian and Spanish influences. Thoughtfully compiled wine list.

Menu £10 (lunch) – Carte £25/34

Town plan: 31ALU-h – *5 William IV St* ✉ *WC2N 4DW* – ⊖ *Charing Cross* – ℰ *(020) 7036 0660* – *www.terroirswinebar.com* – *Closed 25-26 December, 1 January, Sunday and bank holidays*

X **Opera Tavern**   ⅋ 🅰🅲 ⑬

MEDITERRANEAN · TAPAS BAR Shares the same appealing concept of small plates of Spanish and Italian delicacies as its sisters, Salt Yard and Dehesa. All done in a smartly converted old boozer which dates from 1879; ground floor bar and upstairs dining room.

Carte £13/24

Town plan: 31ALU-y – *23 Catherine St.* ✉ *WC2B 5JS* – ⊖ *Covent Garden* – ℰ *(020) 7836 3680* – *www.operatavern.co.uk* – *Closed 25 December and 1 January*

X **Polpo Covent Garden**   🅰🅲 ⑬

ITALIAN · SIMPLE First Soho, now Covent Garden gets a fun Venetian bacaro. The small plates are surprisingly filling, with delights such as pizzette of white anchovy vying with fennel and almond salad, fritto misto competing with spaghettini and meatballs.

Carte £12/26

Town plan: 31ALU-p – *6 Maiden Ln.* ✉ *WC2E 7NA* – ⊖ *Leicester Square* – ℰ *(020) 7836 8448* – *www.polpo.co.uk* – *Closed 25-26 December*

X **Bedford & Strand**

BRITISH TRADITIONAL · WINE BAR It calls itself a 'wine room and bistro' which neatly sums up both the philosophy and the style of this usefully located basement: interesting wines, reassuringly familiar French and British dishes and relaxed surroundings.

Menu £20 (lunch and early dinner) – Carte £20/41

Town plan: 31ALU-c – *1a Bedford St* ✉ *WC2E 9HH* – ⊖ *Charing Cross* – ℰ *(020) 7836 3033 (booking essential)* – *www.bedford-strand.com* – *Closed 24 December-2 January, Sunday and bank holidays*

X **Dishoom**   🍴 🅰🅲 🔌 ⑬

INDIAN · INDIVIDUAL A facsimile of a Bombay café, of the sort opened by Persian immigrants in the early 20C. Try baked roti rolls with chai, vada pav – Bombay's version of the chip butty; a curry or grilled meats. There's another branch in Shoreditch.

Menu £22/40 – Carte £13/33

Town plan: 31ALU-j – *12 Upper St Martin's Ln* ✉ *WC2H 9FB* – ⊖ *Leicester Square* – ℰ *(020) 7420 9320 (booking advisable)* – *www.dishoom.com* – *Closed 24 December dinner, 25-26 December and 1-2 January*

X Suda

THAI • FRIENDLY This shiny Thai restaurant in a new development may look like a branded chain but the quality of its food far exceeds one's expectations. Come in a group, sit upstairs, order cocktails and share plenty of dishes.

Menu £ 11/25 **s** – Carte £ 19/34

Town plan: 31ALU-d – *23 Slingsby Pl, St Martin's Courtyard ✉ WC2E 9AB – ⊖ Covent Garden – ☎ (020) 7240 8010 – www.suda-thai.com – Closed 25 December and 1 January*

X 10 Cases

FRENCH • BISTRO Cosy and inviting little bistrot offering an unpretentious daily menu of 3 starters, 3 main courses and 3 desserts, along with a very reasonably priced wine list of 10 reds and 10 whites available by the glass, carafe or bottle.

Carte £ 23/40

Town plan: 31ALU-a – *16 Endell St ✉ WC2H 9BD – ⊖ Covent Garden – ☎ (020) 7836 6801 (booking essential) – www.the10cases.co.uk – Closed Easter, Christmas-New Year and bank holidays*

X Mishkin's

NORTH-AMERICAN • RETRO The Jewish-American deli – but with cocktails – was the inspiration behind this fun spot from the Polpo people. Lox beigel, chopped liver and salt beef sit alongside nibbles like cod cheek popcorn; the Reuben sandwich hits the spot.

Carte £ 13/26

Town plan: 31ALU-w – *25 Catherine St ✉ WC2B 5JS – ⊖ Covent Garden – ☎ (020) 7240 2078 – www.mishkins.co.uk – Closed 24-26 December and 1-2 January*

Victoria

Corinthia

GRAND LUXURY • STYLISH The restored Victorian splendour of this grand, luxurious hotel cannot fail to impress. Tasteful and immaculately finished bedrooms are some of the largest in town; suites come with butlers. The stunning spa is over four floors.

294 rooms – †£ 342/1140 ††£ 342/1140 – ☕ £ 32 – 23 suites

Town plan: 31ALV-x – *Whitehall Pl. ✉ SW1A 2BD – ⊖ Embankment – ☎ (020) 7930 8181 – www.corinthia.com/london*

Northall • Massimo – See restaurant listing

Goring

LUXURY • ELEGANT Under the stewardship of the founder's great grandson, this landmark hotel has been restored and renovated while maintaining its traditional atmosphere and pervading sense of Britishness. Expect first class service and immaculate, very comfortable bedrooms, many of which overlook the garden.

69 rooms – †£ 490/710 ††£ 600/715 – ☕ £ 32 – 8 suites

Town plan: 38AIX-a – *15 Beeston Pl ✉ SW1W 0JW – ⊖ Victoria – ☎ (020) 7396 9000 – www.thegoring.com*

✿ **Dining Room at The Goring** – See restaurant listing

InterContinental London Westminster

LUXURY • CONTEMPORARY Its proximity to the seat of power is a recurring theme at this hotel which opened in 2013. Apart from its façade, little remains of the original 19C building. A cool, crisp reception area sets the tone; bedrooms are stylish and contemporary. The Smokehouse specialises in ribs, pulled pork and steaks.

256 rooms – †£ 199/699 ††£ 199/699 – ☕ £ 35 – 12 suites

Town plan: 39AKX-w – *22-28 Broadway ✉ SW1H 9JS – ⊖ St James's Park – ☎ (020) 3301 8080 – www.conradhotels.com/london*

St James' Court

LUXURY · CLASSIC Built in 1897 as serviced accommodation for visiting aristocrats. Behind the impressive Edwardian façade lies an equally elegant interior. Quietest bedrooms overlook a courtyard. Relaxed, bright Bistro 51 comes with an international menu; Bank offers brasserie classics in a conservatory.

318 rooms – ♦£ 198/594 ♦♦£ 198/594 – ☲ £ 21 – 20 suites

Town plan: 39AJX-e – *45 Buckingham Gate* ⊠ *SW1E 6BS*
– ⊖ *St James's Park* – ℰ *(020) 7834 6655* – *www.tajhotels.com/stjamescourt*

✿ **Quilon** – See restaurant listing

Taj 51 Buckingham Gate

LUXURY · CONTEMPORARY In the courtyard of the Crowne Plaza but offering greater levels of comfort and service. Contemporary in style, suites range from one to nine bedrooms. Butler service available. Restaurants located in adjacent hotel.

85 suites – ♦♦£ 300/6300 – ☲ £ 40

Town plan: 39AJX-s – *51 Buckingham Gate* ⊠ *SW1E 6AF*
– ⊖ *St James's Park* – ℰ *(020) 7769 7766* – *www.taj51buckinghamgate.co.uk*

St Ermin's

LUXURY · STYLISH Built as an apartment block in 1897 but has spent most of its life as a hotel and is a favoured spot for many a politician. A comprehensive refurbishment restored many of its original features, including the stunning rococo lobby. The restaurant specialises in meat cooked on the Josper grill.

331 rooms – ♦£ 209/499 ♦♦£ 209/499 – 41 suites

Town plan: 39AJX-a – *2 Caxton St.* ⊠ *SW1H 0QW*
– ⊖ *St James's Park* – ℰ *(020) 7222 7888* – *www.sterminshotel.co.uk*

Adam Handling at Caxton – See restaurant listing

41

LUXURY · CLASSIC Smart, discreet addendum to The Rubens hotel next door. Attractively decorated and quiet lounge where breakfast is served; comfortable bedrooms boast fireplaces and plenty of extras. Light lunches and dinners for residents only.

30 rooms ☲ – ♦£ 340/479 ♦♦£ 360/539 – 6 suites

Town plan: 38AIX-n – *41 Buckingham Palace Rd.* ⊠ *SW1W 0PS*
– ⊖ *Victoria* – ℰ *(020) 7300 0041* – *www.41hotel.com*

The Rubens at The Palace

TRADITIONAL · CLASSIC Discreet, comfortable hotel in great location for tourists. Constant reinvestment ensures bright and contemporary bedrooms. 'Old Masters' for a buffet-style carvery; fine dining in cosy 'Library'; South African themed 'bbar'.

161 rooms – ♦£ 149/259 ♦♦£ 159/269 – ☲ £ 20 – 1 suite

Town plan: 38AIX-n – *39 Buckingham Palace Rd* ⊠ *SW1W 0PS*
– ⊖ *Victoria* – ℰ *(020) 7834 6600* – *www.rubenshotel.com*

Eccleston Square

TOWNHOUSE · STYLISH Attractive townhouse in a smart square, with a crisp, contemporary interior. Bedrooms are decorated to a high standard and come full of assorted electronic gadgetry. Varied international menu in Bistrot; afternoon tea a feature.

39 rooms – ♦£ 210/350 ♦♦£ 210/350 – ☲ £ 15

Town plan: 38AIY- s – *37 Eccleston Sq* ⊠ *SW1V 1PB*
– ⊖ *Victoria* – ℰ *(020) 3489 1001* – *www.ecclestonsquarehotel.com*

Good food at moderate prices? Look for the Bib Gourmand ◉.

⌂ Artist Residence Ⓝ ⌃ AK ⌘

TOWNHOUSE · STYLISH A converted pub made into a comfortable, quirky townhouse hotel, with stylish bedrooms featuring mini Smeg fridges, retro telephones, reclaimed furniture and pop art. Cool bar and sitting room beneath the busy 64° restaurant.

10 rooms – ♦£160/375 ♦♦£160/375 – ⌷£10
Town plan: 38AIZ-r – *52 Cambridge St* ✉ *SW1V 4QQ*
– ⊖ *Victoria* – ☏ *(020) 7931 8946*
– *www.artistresidencelondon.co.uk*
64° – See restaurant listing

⌂ Lord Milner ⊞ AK ⌘

TOWNHOUSE · CLASSIC A four storey terraced house, with individually decorated bedrooms, three with four-poster beds and all with smart marble bathrooms. Garden Suite is the best room; it has its own patio. Breakfast served in your bedroom.

11 rooms – ♦£125 ♦♦£160/255 – ⌷£8.50
Town plan: 38AHY-k – *111 Ebury St* ✉ *SW1W 9QU*
– ⊖ *Victoria* – ☏ *(020) 7881 9880*
– *www.lordmilner.com*

XxX Dining Room at The Goring ⅋⅋ ⌷⌷ AK
❄

BRITISH TRADITIONAL · ELEGANT A paean to all things British and the very model of discretion and decorum – the perfect spot for those who 'like things done properly' but without the stuffiness. The menu is an appealing mix of British classics and lighter, more modern dishes, all prepared with great skill and understanding.
→ Cured sea trout with English asparagus and smoked mayonnaise. Fillet of Suffolk pork with suckling pig belly, pickled turnip, beetroot and eel fritter. Eton mess, crème fraîche and lime.
Menu £43/53
Town plan: 38AIX-a – *Goring Hotel, 15 Beeston Pl* ✉ *SW1W 0JW*
– ⊖ *Victoria* – ☏ *(020) 7396 9000*
– *www.thegoring.com* – *Closed Saturday lunch*

XxX Quilon AK I♡ ⌷
❄

INDIAN · DESIGN A meal here will remind you how fresh, vibrant, colourful and healthy Indian food can be. Chef Sriram Aylur and his team focus on India's southwest coast, so the emphasis is on seafood and a lighter style of cooking. The room is stylish and comfortable and the service team, bright and enthusiastic.
→ Coconut cream chicken with chilli and cumin. Spiced, baked black cod. Chai latte crème brûlée.
Menu £27/59 – Carte £33/59
Town plan: 39AJX-e – *St James' Court Hotel, 41 Buckingham Gate* ✉ *SW1E 6AF*
– ⊖ *St James's Park* – ☏ *(020) 7821 1899*
– *www.quilon.co.uk* – *Closed 25 December*

XxX Roux at Parliament Square ⌷ AK ⌷

MODERN CUISINE · ELEGANT Light floods through the Georgian windows of this comfortable restaurant within the offices of the Royal Institute of Chartered Surveyors. Carefully crafted, contemporary cuisine, with some interesting flavour combinations.
Menu £35 (weekday lunch)/79 – Carte £47/64
Town plan: 39ALX-x – *Royal Institution of Chartered Surveyors, Parliament Sq.*
✉ *SW1P 3AD* – ⊖ *Westminster*
– ☏ *(020) 7334 3737 (bookings advisable at lunch)*
– *www.rouxatparliamentsquare.co.uk*
– *Closed Saturday, Sunday and bank holidays*

XxX Northall   🔥 AC 🗐

BRITISH TRADITIONAL · BISTRO The Corinthia Hotel's British restaurant champions our indigenous produce, and its menu is an appealing document. It occupies two rooms: head for the more modern one with its bar and booths, which is less formal than the other section.

Menu £ 24/75 – Carte £ 26/73

Town plan: 31ALV-x – *Corinthia Hotel, Whitehall Pl.* ✉ *WC2N 5AE* – ⊖ *Embankment* – ℰ *(020) 7321 3100 – www.thenorthall.co.uk*

XxX The Cinnamon Club   🍽 AC 🗄 🕪 🗐 ⇔

INDIAN · ELEGANT Tourists and locals, politicians and business types – this smart Indian restaurant housed in the listed former Westminster Library attracts all types. The fairly elaborate dishes arrive fully garnished and the spicing is quite subtle.

Menu £ 22 (lunch and early dinner) – Carte £ 30/66

Town plan: 39AKX-c – *30-32 Great Smith St* ✉ *SW1P 3BU* – ⊖ *St James's Park* – ℰ *(020) 7222 2555 – www.cinnamonclub.com – Closed Sunday and bank holidays*

XxX Santini   🏠 AC 🗐

ITALIAN · FASHIONABLE Santini has looked after its many immaculately coiffured regulars for 30 years. The not inexpensive menu of classic Italian dishes is broadly Venetian in style; the daily specials, pasta dishes and desserts are the standout courses.

Menu £ 25 (dinner) – Carte £ 30/67

Town plan: 38AHY-v – *29 Ebury St* ✉ *SW1W 0NZ* – ⊖ *Victoria* – ℰ *(020) 7730 4094 – www.santinirestaurant.com – Closed 23-26 December, 1 January and Easter*

XxX Grand Imperial   🔥 AC ⇔

CHINESE · ELEGANT Grand it most certainly is, as this elegant restaurant is in the Grosvenor Hotel's former ballroom. It specialises in Cantonese cuisine, particularly the version found in Hong Kong; steaming and frying are used to great effect.

Menu £ 18 (weekday lunch) – Carte £ 21/110

Town plan: 38AIY-a – *Grosvenor Hotel, 101 Buckingham Palace Rd* ✉ *SW1W 0SJ* – ⊖ *Victoria* – ℰ *(020) 7821 8898 – www.grandimperiallondon.com* – *Closed 25-26 December*

XX Massimo   🔥 AC ⇔

ITALIAN · ELEGANT Opulent, visually impressive room with an oyster bar on one side. On offer are traditional dishes true to the regions of Italy; fish and seafood dishes stand out. Impressive private dining room comes with its own chef.

Menu £ 30 – Carte £ 28/57

Town plan: 31ALV-x – *Corinthia Hotel, 10 Northumberland Ave.* ✉ *WC2N 5AE* – ⊖ *Embankment* – ℰ *(020) 7321 3156 – www.corinthia.com/london* – *Closed Sunday*

XX Tinello   🗐

ITALIAN · DESIGN The brothers Sali have created a warm, friendly, romantic and very popular Italian restaurant. Their native Tuscany informs the cooking, so expect dishes like ribollita, liver crostini, and pappardelle with wild boar ragout.

Carte £ 17/50

Town plan: 37AGZ-s – *87 Pimlico Rd* ✉ *SW1W 8PH* – ⊖ *Sloane Square* – ℰ *(020) 7730 3663 (booking essential at dinner) – www.tinello.co.uk – Closed Sunday and bank holidays*

XX Adam Handling at Caxton ⓝ   🄰🄲

MODERN CUISINE · BRASSERIE The eponymous chef – a past finalist on 'MasterChef' – creates skilful, intricate and quite delicate dishes, looking to Asia for many of his influences. Small plates, steaks and a tasting menu are also on offer; lunch is a simpler affair.

Menu £ 25 (weekday lunch)/49 – Carte £ 31/59

Town plan: 39AKX-a – St. Ermin's Hotel, 2 Caxton St. ✉ SW1H 0QW
– ⊖ St James's Park – ℰ (020) 7222 7888 – www.caxtongrill.co.uk
– closed lunch Saturday-Sunday

XX Osteria Dell' Angolo   🄰🄲 ⇔

ITALIAN · NEIGHBOURHOOD At lunch, this Italian opposite the Home Office is full of bustle and men in suits; at dinner it's a little more relaxed. Staff are personable and the menu is reassuringly familiar; homemade pasta and seafood dishes are good.

Menu £ 18 (weekday lunch) – Carte £ 23/43

Town plan: 39AKY-n – 47 Marsham St ✉ SW1P 3DR – ⊖ St James's Park
– ℰ (020) 3268 1077 (booking essential) – www.osteriadellangolo.co.uk
– Closed 1-4 January, Easter, 24-28 December, Saturday lunch, Sunday and bank holidays

XX Rex Whistler   🕃🕃 ♿ 🄰🄲

BRITISH TRADITIONAL · CLASSIC The £ 45million renovation of Tate Britain included a freshening up of its restaurant and restoration of Whistler's mural, 'The Expedition in Pursuit of Rare Meats', which envelops the room. The monthly menu is stoutly British and the remarkably priced wine list has an unrivalled 'half bottle' selection.

Menu £ 27

Town plan: 39ALY-w – Tate Britain, Millbank ✉ SW1P 4RG Victoria
– ⊖ Pimlico – ℰ (020) 7887 8825 – www.tate.org.uk – lunch only
– Closed 24-26 December

XX Il Convivio   🄰🄲 ⇔

ITALIAN · NEIGHBOURHOOD Handsome Georgian townhouse with a retractable roof and Dante's poetry embossed on the walls. All of the pasta is made on the top floor; the squid ink spaghetti is a staple. Dishes are artfully presented and flavoursome.

Menu £ 18/23 – Carte £ 30/47

Town plan: 38AHY-a – 143 Ebury St ✉ SW1W 9QN – ⊖ Sloane Square
– ℰ (020) 7730 4099 – www.ilconvivio.co.uk – Closed Christmas-New Year, Easter, Sunday and bank holidays

XX Boisdale of Belgravia   🍷 🏠 🄰🄲 ⇔

BRITISH TRADITIONAL · INDIVIDUAL A proudly Scottish restaurant with acres of tartan and a charmingly higgledy-piggledy layout. Stand-outs are the smoked salmon and the 28-day aged Aberdeenshire cuts of beef. Live nightly jazz.

Menu £ 18 (lunch and early dinner) – Carte £ 27/59

Town plan: 38AHY-c – 15 Eccleston St ✉ SW1W 9LX – ⊖ Victoria
– ℰ (020) 7730 6922 – www.boisdale.co.uk – Closed 25 December, Saturday lunch, Sunday and bank holidays

XX The Ebury Restaurant & Wine Bar   🄰🄲

FRENCH · NEIGHBOURHOOD Going strong for over 50 years and as likeable as ever. Some imaginative touches but generally quite classic cooking. Dairy and gluten free menus offered, along with a keenly-priced wine list.

Menu £ 23/29 – Carte £ 28/41

Town plan: 38AHY-n – 139 Ebury St. ✉ SW1W 9QU – ⊖ Victoria
– ℰ (020) 7730 5447 – www.eburyrestaurant.co.uk
– Closed Christmas-New Year

✗ A. Wong

CHINESE · FRIENDLY Andrew Wong transformed his mother's restaurant into a modern and lively Chinese restaurant. He's taken classics from across China and introduced the odd twist here and there, whilst keeping the original combinations intact.

Menu £14 (lunch) – Carte £16/38

Town plan: 38AIY-w – *70 Wilton Rd* ✉ *SW1V 1DE* – ⊖ *Victoria*
– ☎ (020) 7828 8931 (booking essential) – www.awong.co.uk – Closed 23 December-4 January, Sunday and Monday lunch

✗ Kouzu

JAPANESE · DESIGN Occupying two floors of an attractive 19C Grade II building is this modern Japanese restaurant. Those who know Zuma or Nobu will not only recognise the style of the food but will also find the stylish surroundings familiar.

Menu £40/65 – Carte £33/114

Town plan: 38AHX-v – *21 Grosvenor Gdns* ✉ *SW1 0BD* – ⊖ *Victoria*
– ☎ (020) 7730 7043 – www.kouzu.co.uk – Closed 24-25 December, 1 January, Saturday lunch and Sunday

✗ Olivocarne

ITALIAN · INDIVIDUAL Just when you thought Mauro Sanno had this part of town sewn up he opens another restaurant. This one focuses on meat dishes, along with a selection of satisfying Sardinian specialities and is smarter and larger than his others.

Menu £18 (lunch) – Carte £31/47

Town plan: 38AHY-d – *61 Elizabeth St* ✉ *SW1W 9PP* – ⊖ *Sloane Square*
– ☎ (020) 7730 7997 – www.olivorestaurants.com

✗ Olivo

ITALIAN · NEIGHBOURHOOD Carefully prepared, authentic Sardinian specialities are the highlight at this popular Italian restaurant. Simply decorated in blues and yellows, with an atmosphere of bonhomie.

Menu £25 (weekday lunch) – Carte £33/47

Town plan: 38AHY-z – *21 Eccleston St* ✉ *SW1W 9LX* – ⊖ *Victoria*
*– ☎ (020) 7730 2505 (booking essential) – www.olivorestaurants.com
– Closed lunch Saturday-Sunday and bank holidays*

✗ Olivomare

FISH AND SEAFOOD · DESIGN Expect understated and stylish piscatorial decoration and seafood with a Sardinian base. Fortnightly changing menu, with high quality produce, much of which is available in the deli next door.

Carte £33/45

Town plan: 38AHY-b – *10 Lower Belgrave St* ✉ *SW1W 0LJ* – ⊖ *Victoria*
– ☎ (020) 7730 9022 – www.olivorestaurants.com – Closed bank holidays

✗ 64° N

MODERN CUISINE · RUSTIC A little bigger and in a more residential area than the Brighton original but with the same style of food: small sharing plates of confidently flavoured, satisfying dishes with some original touches. Sit at the large counter in front of the open kitchen if you want to see how it is all done.

Carte £20/33

Town plan: AIZ-r – *Artist Residence Hotel, 52 Cambridge St* ✉ *SW1V 4QQ*
– ⊖ Victoria – ☎ (020) 3262 0501 – www.64degrees.co.uk

🏠 Thomas Cubitt

MODERN CUISINE · PUB A pub of two halves: choose the busy ground floor bar with its accessible menu or upstairs for more ambitious, quite elaborate cooking with courteous service and a less frenetic environment.

Carte £29/44

Town plan: 38AHY-e – *44 Elizabeth St* ✉ *SW1W 9PA* – ⊖ *Sloane Square.*
– ☎ (020) 7730 6060 (booking essential) – www.thethomascubitt.co.uk

The Orange ⇦ ⌂ ⇧

MEDITERRANEAN · FRIENDLY The old Orange Brewery is as charming a pub as its stucco-fronted façade suggests. Try the fun bar or book a table in the more sedate upstairs room. The menu has a Mediterranean bias; spelt or wheat based pizzas are a speciality. Bedrooms are stylish and comfortable.

Carte £ 28/40

4 rooms ☑ – †£ 205 ††£ 240

Town plan: 38AHZ-k – *37 Pimlico Rd* ✉ *SW1W 8NE* – ⊖ *Sloane Square.*
– *𝒸 (020) 7881 9844 – www.theorange.co.uk*

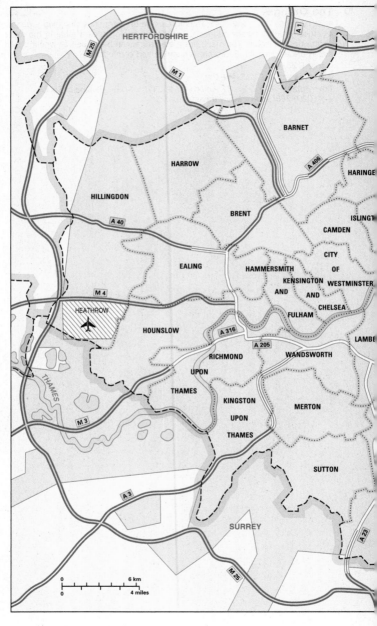

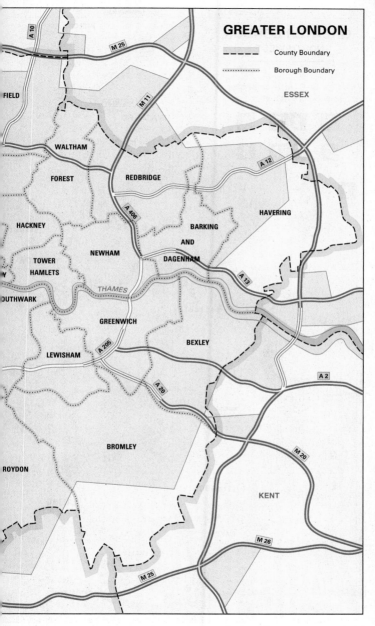

GREATER LONDON

- – – – County Boundary
- ············· Borough Boundary

ESSEX

FIELD

WALTHAM

FOREST

REDBRIDGE

HAVERING

HACKNEY

BARKING

AND

DAGENHAM

TOWER

HAMLETS

NEWHAM

SOUTHWARK

THAMES

GREENWICH

LEWISHAM

BEXLEY

BROMLEY

CROYDON

KENT

185

GREATER LONDON
NORTH-WEST

0   3 km
0   2 miles

Greater London Boundary
Through route

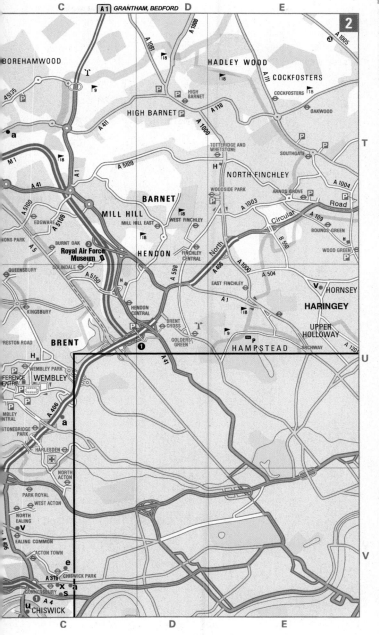

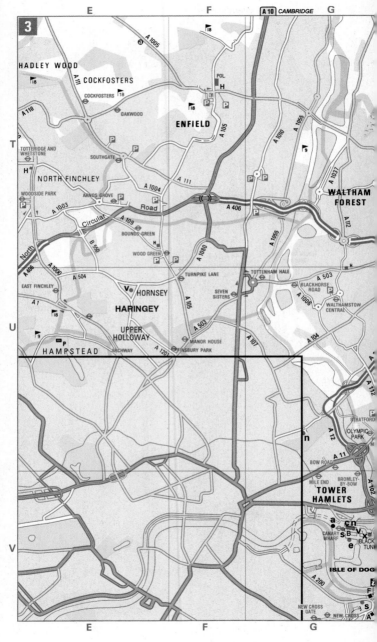

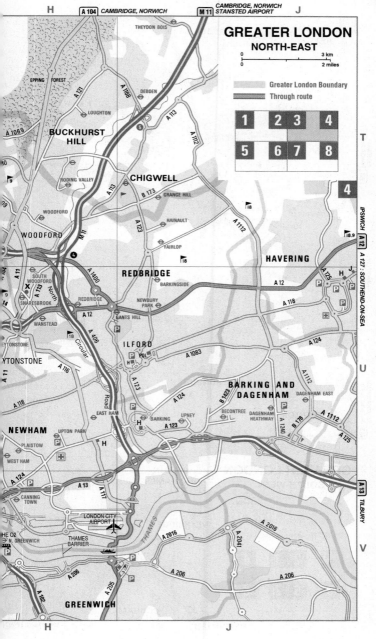

GREATER LONDON
NORTH-EAST

Greater London Boundary

Through route

1	2	3	4
5	6	7	8

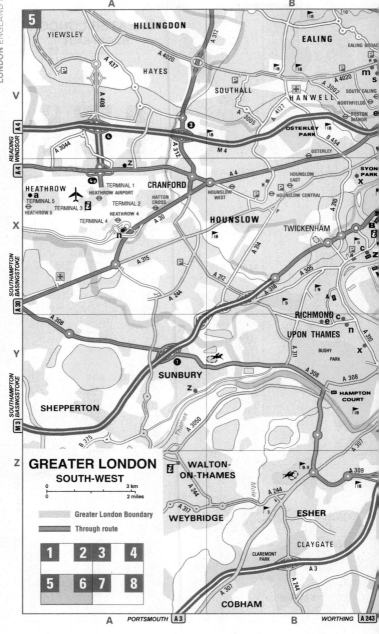

5

YIEWSLEY

HILLINGDON

EALING

EALING BROAD

HAYES

SOUTHALL

HANWELL

SOUTH EALING

NORTHFIELDS

BOSTON MANOR

V

OSTERLEY PARK

OSTERLEY

B 454

M 4

A 4

SYON PARK

HOUNSLOW EAST

HOUNSLOW CENTRAL

X

HEATHROW

TERMINAL 1

HEATHROW AIRPORT

TERMINAL 5

TERMINAL 3

TERMINAL 2

HEATHROW 5

HEATHROW 4

TERMINAL 4

CRANFORD

HATTON CROSS

A 30

HOUNSLOW WEST

TWICKENHAM

HOUNSLOW

X

A 315

A 312

A 244

A 305

RICHMOND

UPON THAMES

c

e

n

A 310

A 308

BUSHY PARK

X

Y

SUNBURY

Z

A 308

HAMPTON COURT

SHEPPERTON

Thames

A 3050

Z

WALTON-ON-THAMES

Mole

A 309

A 307

WEYBRIDGE

A 311

ESHER

CLAYGATE

CLAREMONT PARK

A 3

COBHAM

A 244

GREATER LONDON
SOUTH-WEST

0 ——— 3 km
0 ——— 2 miles

Greater London Boundary

Through route

1	2	3	4
5	6	7	8

A   PORTSMOUTH A3

B   WORTHING A 243

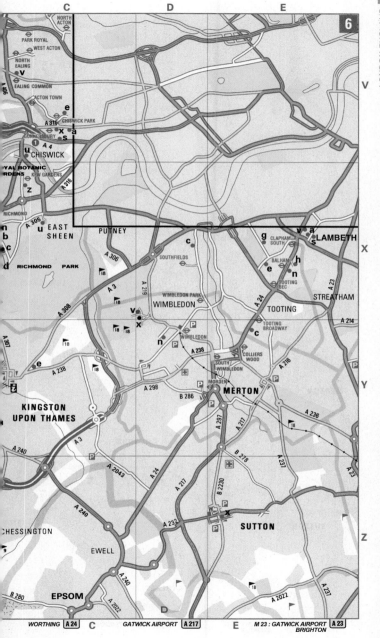

NORTH
ACTON

PARK ROYAL

WEST ACTON

NORTH
EALING **v**

EALING COMMON

A 406

ACTON TOWN

e

A 315 CHISWICK PARK

GUNNERSBURY **x s** **a**

1 A 4

u CHISWICK

YAL BOTANIC
RDENS KEW GARDENS

A 316

z

RICHMOND

A 305 **u** EAST
SHEEN

n
b

c

d RICHMOND PARK

PUTNEY

A 306

SOUTHFIELDS

A 219

A 3

18

WIMBLEDON PARK

WIMBLEDON

A 308

18

18

v **a**
s LAMBETH

g CLAPHAM
SOUTH

BALHAM **h**

e **n**

TOOTING
BEC

A 23

A 24

TOOTING

STREATHAM

A 214

18

A 307

18

v
x

18 18

n

P

P WIMBLEDON

A 238

TOOTING
BROADWAY

c

e

A 238

18

A 298

P

COLLIERS
WOOD

SOUTH
WIMBLEDON

MORDEN

MERTON

A 216

P

A 236

KINGSTON
UPON THAMES

A 240

A 3

P

B 286

A 297

A 217

B 278

18

A 237

A 23

A 2043

A 24

B 2230

CHESSINGTON

A 240

A 232

A 217

P

P

x

SUTTON

EWELL

A 240

A 2022

A 237

B 280 **EPSOM**

A 2022

D

A 2022

V

X

Y

Z

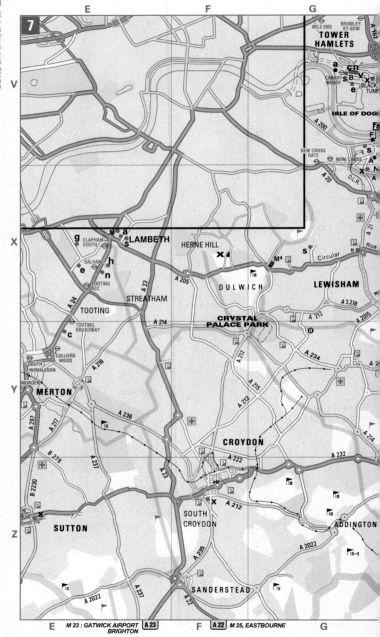

E   F   G

V

X

Y

Z

TOWER HAMLETS

MILE END

BROMLEY-BY-BOW

A 102

CANARY WHARF

BLACK TUNN

ISLE OF DOG

A 200

NEW CROSS GATE

NEW CROSS

A 20

DLR

A 21

LAMBETH

CLAPHAM SOUTH

BALHAM

TOOTING BEC

HERNE HILL

DULWICH

M4

Circular

Roa

LEWISHAM

A 205

A 2218

STREATHAM

TOOTING

A 23

A 214

CRYSTAL PALACE PARK

A 212

A 2015

TOOTING BROADWAY

c

COLLIERS WOOD

A 216

A 234

A 212

A 215

A 213

SOUTH WIMBLEDON

MORDEN

MERTON

A 297

A 217

A 236

CROYDON

A 222

A 232

A 214

A 278

B 2230

A 237

A 23

A 212

ADDINGTON

SUTTON

SOUTH CROYDON

A 235

18-9

A 2022

A 2022

A 237

SANDERSTEAD

A 22

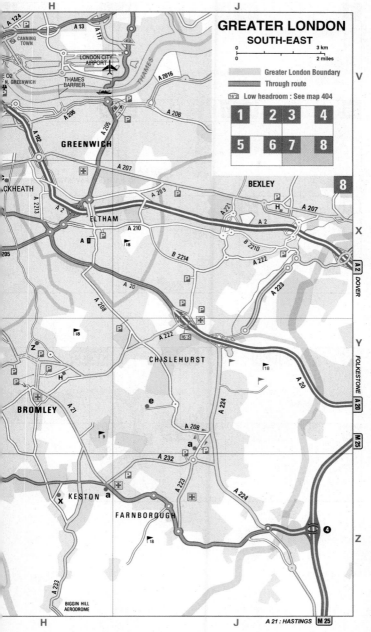

GREATER LONDON
SOUTH-EAST

0   3 km
0   2 miles

Greater London Boundary
Through route
16·2 Low headroom : See map 404

| 1 | 2 | 3 | 4 |
| 5 | 6 | 7 | 8 |

A 124
CANNING
TOWN
A 13
A 117
LONDON CITY
AIRPORT
THAMES
BARRIER
E O2
N. GREENWICH
THAMES
A 2016
A 206
A 206
A 205
A 102
GREENWICH
A 207
CKHEATH
A 2213
A 2
A 209
BEXLEY
A 207
8
X
ELTHAM
A 210
A 221
A 2
B 2210
A 1
18
B 2214
A 222
A 2 DOVER
205
A 20
A 223
A 208
P
18
A 222
16·3
Y
Z
H
CHISLEHURST
18
FOLKESTONE A 20
BROMLEY
A 21
e
A 20
9
A 224
A 208
a
M 25
A 232
a
A 223
A 224
4
KESTON
a
x
FARNBOROUGH
18
A 233
BIGGIN HILL
AERODROME
Z

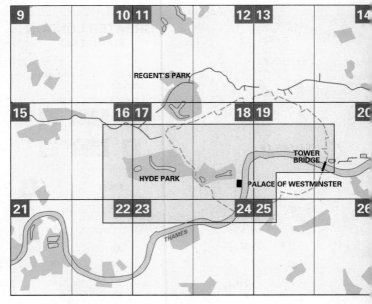

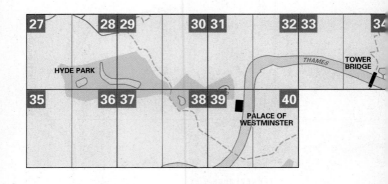

INDEX OF STREET NAMES IN LONDON CENTRE

K · L

Brent Reservoir

North Circular Road
A 406

Crest Road
Coles Green Rd
Edgware Rd
A 5
Cricklewood

Avenue
Brook Rd
Lane

NEASDEN JUNCTION
Tanfield
Dollis Hill

GLADSTONE PARK

BRENT

Mora Rd
Sheyd Rd
Heber R

A 4088
Dudden

Neasden

Neasden Lane

Kendal Rd
Park Ave North
Anson Road

Burnley Road
Sherrick Green Rd

19.3

Dollis Hill

Denzil Road
Chapter Road

Willesden Green

High Road
Lane
WILLESDEN GREEN

Pound Lane
High Road
a
Walm

A 407
357
Brondesbury

P
Peter Ave
KILBURN
Sidmouth Rd

482
Roundwood Road
WILLESDEN CEMETERY

Church Road

351
196
ROUNDWOOD PARK

Harlesden Road
Donnington Road
Mount Pleasant
Chamberlayne

A 404
352
Manor Park Rd

Doyle
Avenue
Hardinge Rd
480

Acton Lane
High Street
Wrottesley Road
Souls
Gdns
College
Clifford Gdns
KEN RIS

Harley Road
Furness Road
All
Bathurst Gdns

Oak Lane
Willesden Junction

Harrow Road
Mortim
A 404
Kensal Gre
Harrow

K · 15 · L

M   N   O

10

0   500 m
0   500 yards

Vale

Hendon Way

A 41

CHILD'S HILL

Finchley Rd

West Heath Road

The

Claremont

475

BARNET

476

Cricklewood

Lyndale Ave

Hermitage La.

477

Platt's La.

Redington Road

FENTON HOUS

ZA

KLEWOOD

Cricklewood

Lichfield Rd

Finchley

U

Heath

Drive

Frognal

A 401

ay Road

Westbere Rd

West End

Road

Frognal Lane

anson Rd

Shoot

Up

Mill

Lane

Credton Hill

Finchley

A 41

Arkwrig

n Lane

mouth

Road

Road

Hill

S

Lane

**FINCHLEY ROAD
AND FROGNAL**

atsworth

Kilburn

WEST
HAMPSTEAD

Finchl
Road

11

lesden

Road

Iverson

Rd

West
Hampstead

Broadhurst Gdns

A 4003

Lane

Mapesbury

Cavendish Ave

14'6

Broadhurst Gdns

Fairhazel

Park

Avenue

BRONDESBURY

19'6

Kilburn

West End Lane

478

Road

Canfield

Christchurch

Dyne Rd

A 5

Gascony Ave

479

Greencroft

erton

Avenue

Willesden

Lane

High

Abbey

FINCHLEY ROAD

Road

Rd

The

BRONDESBURY
PARK

Salusbury

Kingswood Rd

PADDINGTON
CEMETERY

Quex Rd

Priory

Belsize

X Road

Road

ZB

Bound

ening

Road

Rd

b

Brondesbury

Road

KILBURN
HIGH ROAD

Greville Pl.

Abb

Milman

Queen's Park

Road

Brondesbury Villas

335

Carlton

Hamilton

Harvist

Ave

Lane

POL

Kilburn Park

336

Maida Vale

Kilburn

Queen's
Park

P

Carlton

Road

Randolph

Vale

Avenue

ZC

yle Rd

Ave

Avenue

Braynton

Fernhead

Kilburn Park

Vale

Elgin

Maida
Vale

Randol

x
r

Shir

16

M   N   O

11

HAMPSTEAD HEATH

Kenwood Ladies Pond

North End Way

A 502

Spaniards Road

Vale of Health Pond

Whitestone Pond

Heath Road

East Heath Road

Heath Road

Mixed Bathing Pond

PARLIAMENT HILL

Parliament Hill

Jack Straws

Well Walk

South End Rd

208

305

FENTON HOUSE

ZA

171

227

209 324

Hampstead

479

HAMPSTEAD

Willow Rd

236

M

390 106

HAMPSTEAD HEATH

Nassington Rd

GOSPEI

Frognal

Heath St

139

a

362

Savernake Rd

Mansfield Rd

Lane

Finchley

Arkwright Road

Frognal

A 41

Fitzjohn's Av.

Rosslyn Hill

Pond St

Fleet

A 502

Lyndhurst Rd

Ornan Rd

Belsize Park

Lawn Rd

Southampton Rd

Parkhill

Malden

FINCHLEY ROAD AND FROGNAL

Netherhall Gdns

Fitzjohns Avenue

22

Lane

n a

Belsize Av.

Haverstock

Nutley Ter.

Belsize

19

Belsize Park Gardens

Finchley Road

oadhurst Gdns

10

Fairhazel Gdns

Gdns

Avenue

CAMDEN

Lancaster Grove

Eton Ave.

323

x Hill

Prince

Chalk

Chalk Farm

Canfield Gdns

Greencroft Gdns

Fairfax Road

SWISS COTTAGE

Primrose

Adelaide Road

s

e

Swiss Cottage

Adelaide Road

Road

b

CHLEY ROAD

Road

SOUTH HAMPSTEAD

Avenue

297

Elsworthy Rd

Hill

Gloucest

Regent's

s

Pa

ZB

379

PRIMROSE HILL

Boundary Road

Loudoun Rd

Finchley Road

Grove

Prince

Abbey Road

Hill

Queen's Grove

Ordnance

Avenue Rd

teville Pl.

Carlton

Marlborough Place

Queen's

Acacia Rd

Allitsen Rd

Prince Albert

Circle

ZOO

Maida Vale

Hamilton

Wellington Road

St John's Wood

79

29

Outer

REGENT'S PA

277

Road

Maida Vale

Ave

Avenue

Maida Vale

Terrace

Grove End Road

Wellington

REGENT'S PARK AND MARYLEBONE

Circus

Rd

Canal

Boating Lake

ZC

Maida

Hall

Road

LORD'S CRICKET GROUND

Road

17

Pa

QUEEN M

500 r
500 yards

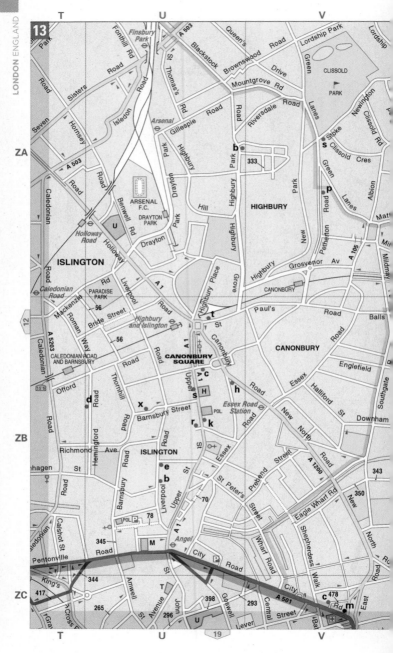

X Y

STOKE
NEWINGTON

Mount Pleasant Hill

500 m
0
500 yards

A 107

A 104

STOKE
WINGTON

Kyverdale Road

Northwold Road

Upper Clapton Road

Cleveleys Road

Chatsworth Road

ch St

Rd

Street

Rectory Road

Brooke

Maury Road

Road

Road

Lea Bridge

auld

A 10

Evering Road

Kenninghall Road

Lower

Road

POL

High Rd

RECTORY
ROAD

Clapton Way

Millfields Road

ZA

Nevill Road

Evering

Amhurst

Downs Rd

Clapton

Powerscroft Road

Rd

Walford Rd

HACKNEY

HACKNEY
DOWNS

378

Clifden Rd

Prince

George Rd

Shacklewell La

Road

Median

Barretts Grv

Cecilia

Downs Park Road

Pembury Rd

Lower Clapton Road

A 102

Boleyn

13'0

Amhurst

Dalston Lane

Homerton High

oad

Newington

Road

Road

Sandringham Road

15'0

Road

Street

Street

r

Ridley Rd

Stoke

HACKNEY
DOWNS

HACKNEY
CENTRAL

337

DALSTON
KINGSLAND

Road

Road

Morning Lane

d

Road

Dalston Lane

Graham Road

Richmond Road

h Road

Well Street

A 10

DALSTON
JUNCTION

Forest Road

Park Rd

Cassland Rd

Richmond

s

Lansdowne Drive

LONDON
FIELDS

A 107 Mare

Frampton

Kingsland

W

Middleton Road

Queensbridge Road

Well Street

ZB

13'9

Albion Drive

Road

HAGGERSTON

16'0

15'9

Mare Street

Park Road

DALSTON

Pownall Rd

Victoria Park

VICTORIA
PARK

64

Nuttall St

Whiston Road

m z

Sheep Lane

Sewardstone Rd

Street

e

HAGGERSTON
PARK

Pritchard's Rd

s

Bishop's Way

Bonner Rd

GEFFRYE
MUSEUM

HOXTON

Road

Hackney Road

CAMBRIDGE
HEATH

Ford Rd

V

n Road

Warner Pl

Green

x

Old Road

B 119 Road

Hoxton

Kingsland

z

Columbia

Old Bethnal Green

a

Carnobert St

Road

M

ZC

16'0

15'9

c

Turin S

A 1209

Green

Roman Road

Bethnal Green

Globe

X 20 Y

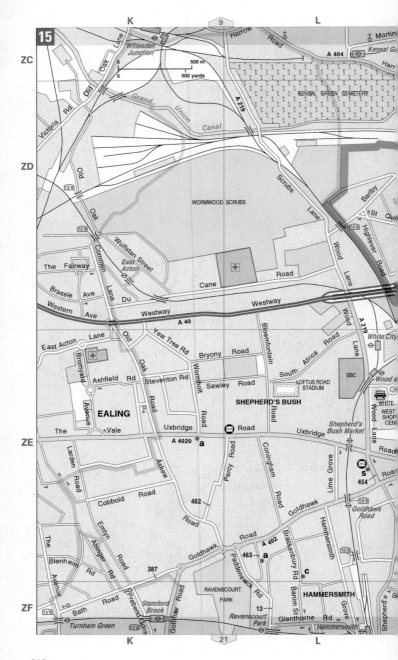

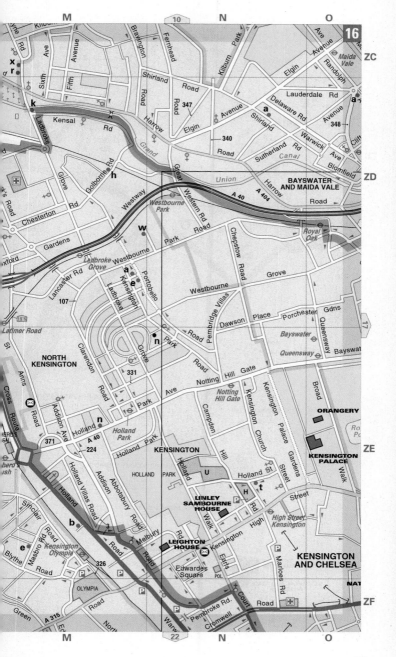

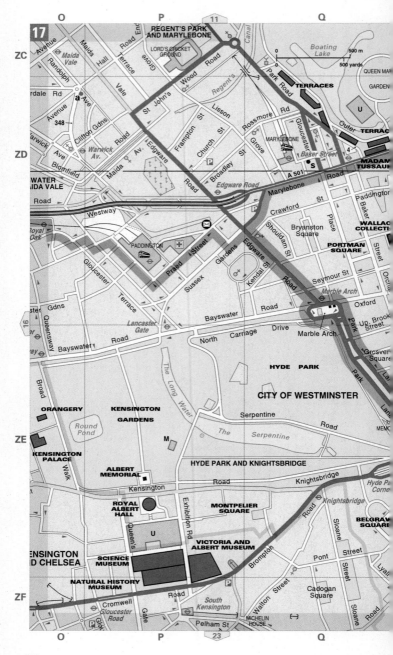

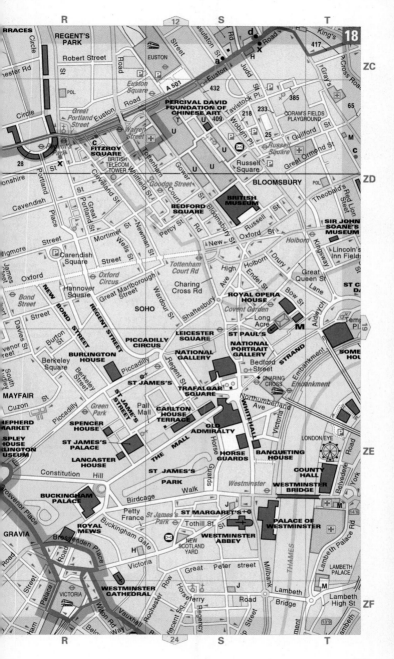

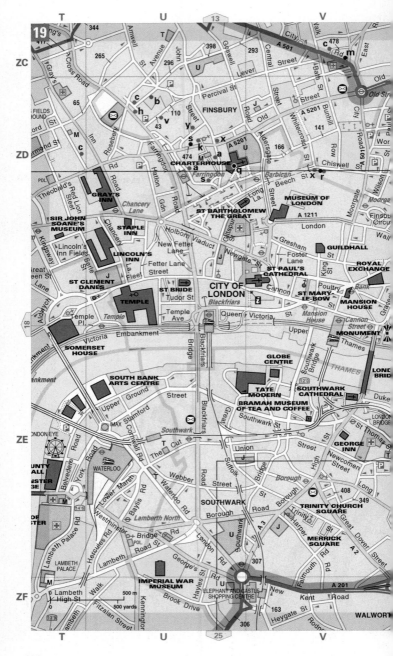

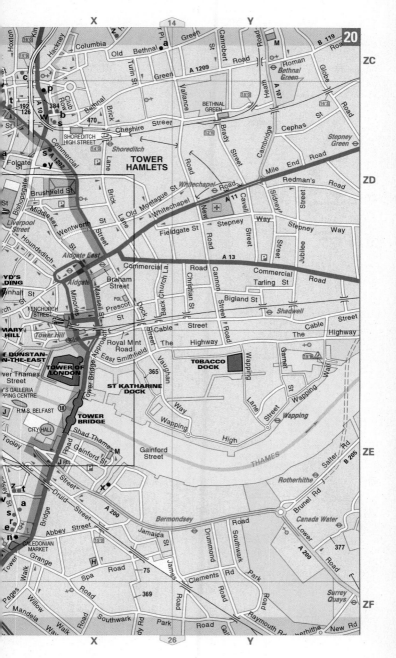

ZC

Kin
Hoxton
Columbia Old Bethnal Green Camrobert B 119 Road
M Roman Road
Bethnal
A 1209 Green
c Turin St Vallance A 107 Globe
P Old Green BETHNAL Cephas Stepney
t Club Bethnal Brick 470 GREEN Green
192 Row Cheshire Street Brady Mile End Road Redman's Road
126 384 w b SHOREDITCH Shoreditch Street ZD
s HIGH STREET TOWER Cambridge Sidney
a Commercial HAMLETS Road Cavell Stepney
Folgate S A 1202 Whitechapel Road A 11 Way Stepney Way
y Old Montague St A 13 Jubilee
Brushfield St Whitechapel Stepney Way
Bishopsgate Brick Fieldgate St Street
Liverpool Wentworth St Lane Commercial La. Road Commercial Road ZD
Street Middlesex Aldgate East Road Tarling St
Houndsditch Braham Cannon Bigland St Shadwell
LYD'S Aldgate Street Christian St Street Cable Street
DING Minories PGL Prescot Back Church St The Highway
nhall St FENCHURCH Mansell St Cable Street Road
STREET St Street Highway The Garnet
MARY HILL Tower Hill Royal Mint Vaughan TOBACCO Wapping Way
DUNSTAN- Road East Smithfield DOCK St Wapping
N-THE-EAST TOWER OF 365 Wapping Lane Wapping
ver Thames LONDON ST KATHARINE Way High
Street DOCK Wapping Street
'S GALLERIA Tower Bridge Approach THAMES
PING CENTRE 18 H.M.S. Belfast TOWER Shad Thames Gainford ZE
J BRIDGE M Street Rotherhithe Salter Rd
CITY HALL Gainford St B 205
Tooley J PGL Druid X Brunel Rd Canada Water
z Street A 200 Bermondsey Road Lower 377
v a Bridge Jamaica St Drummond Southwark A 200 Road
s r Abbey Street Park
e n Grange Clements Rd
CALEDONIAN H Road 75 James Surrey
MARKET Spa Quays
Tower 369 Road ZF
Pages Walk Willow Southwark Park Road Raymouth Rd Rotherhithe New Rd
Mandela Way

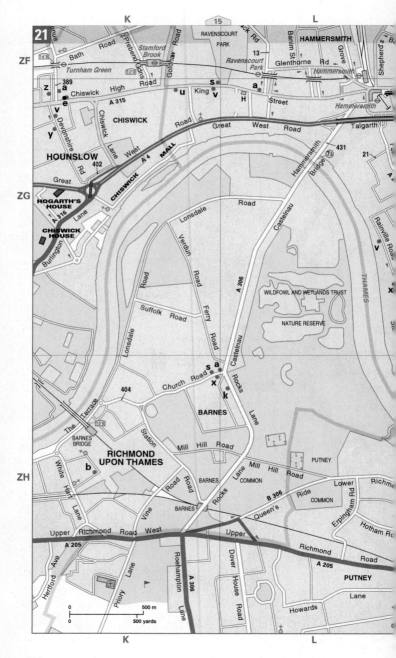

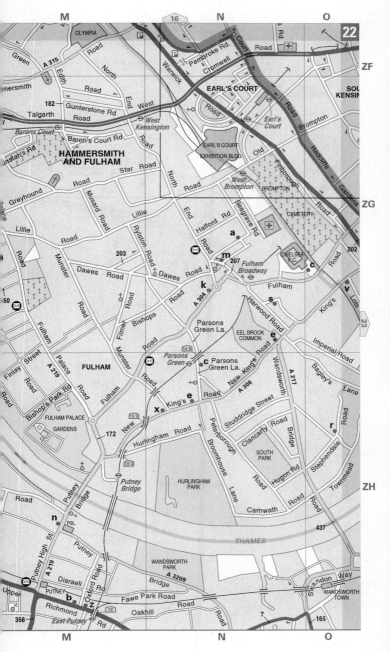

OLYMPIA

Green

A 315

Edith

mersmith

Road

North

Road

Warwick

Court

Rd

Pembroke Rd.

Cromwell

Road

ZF

EARL'S COURT

SOU
KENSIN

182

Gunterstone Rd

Talgarth

West

Road

End

Road

Earl's

Court

Brompton

Barons Court

nstan's Rd

Baron's Court Rd

West
Kensington

Road

Old

EARL'S COURT
EXHIBITION BLDG

Filmborough

Redcliffe

Gardens

ZG

**HAMMERSMITH
AND FULHAM**

Star

Road

North

Road

West
Brompton

BROMPTON

Greyhound

Musard Road

Lillie

Road

Ryston Road

Halford Rd

Road

Seagrave Rd

CEMETERY

Road

202

Lillie

Road

Road

a

203

m

207

Fulham
Broadway

CHELSEA
F.C.

c

50

Road

Munster

Dawes

Road

Dawes

Road

Fulham

v

Lots

23

Finlay Street

Fulham

Palace

Filmer

Road

Bishops

Road

Road

k

A 304

Parsons Green La.

Harwood Road

s

King's

e

EEL BROOK
COMMON

Imperial Road

FULHAM

Munster

Road

Fulham

14'6

*Parsons
Green*

c Parsons
Green La.

New

King's

Road

Wandsworth

A 308

A 217

Bagley's

Lane

Road

Bishop's Park Rd

A 219

172

New

x

e

King's

Road

Studdridge Street

Clancarty

Road

Bridge

r

Stephendale

FULHAM PALACE
GARDENS

15'0

Hurlingham

Road

Peterborough

Broomhouse

SOUTH
PARK

Hugon Rd

Townmead

Road

ZH

15'0

*Putney
Bridge*

HURLINGHAM
PARK

Lane

Road

Carnwath

Road

Road

437

Road

n

POL

Putney

THAMES

Putney

Bridge

Road

WANDSWORTH
PARK

A 3209

Bridge

Swandon Way

WANDSWORTH
TOWN

Upper

Putney High St

A 219

Disraeli

Oxford Rd

Fawe Park Road

Road

165

358

b

z

19

Richmond

East Putney

Rd

Oakhill

7

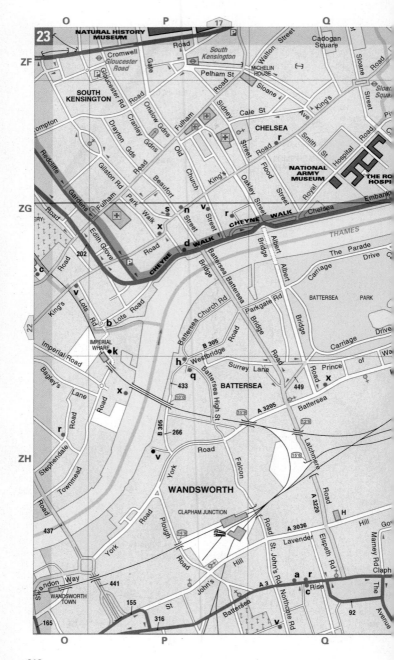

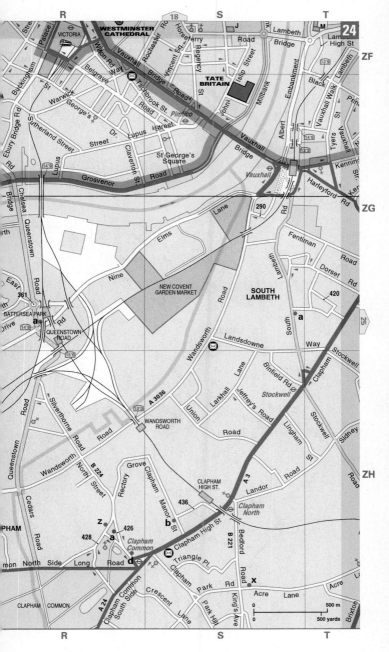

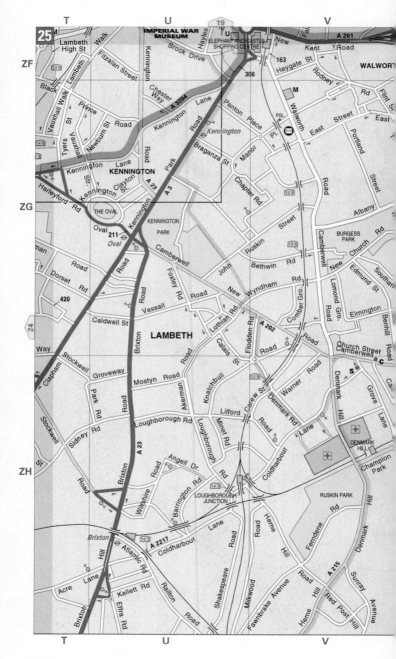

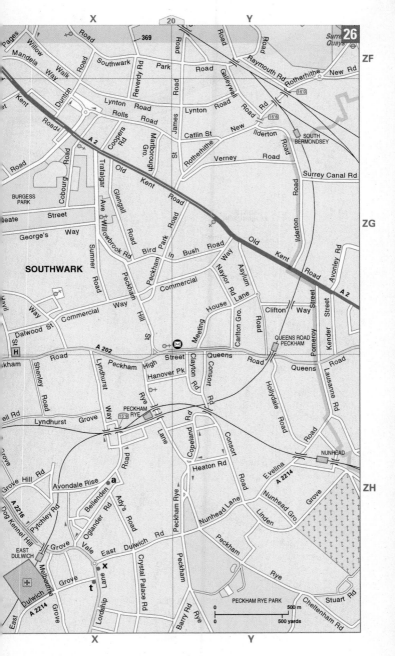

Surrey
Quays

ZF

ZG

ZH

X

Y

Pages
Willow
Road
20
369
Road
Road
Raymouth Rd
Rotherhithe
New Rd
Mandela
Way
Southwark
Reverdy Rd
Park
Road
Galleywall
Road
Rd
15'0
Kent
Dunton
Lynton
Road
James
Lynton
Road
Road
15'6
SOUTH
BERMONDSEY
Road
Rolls
Road
Coopers
Rd
Marlborough
Gro.
St
Catlin St
Rotherhithe
New
Road
Ilderton
Verney
Road
A 2
Trafalgar
Old
Kent
Road
Surrey Canal Rd
BURGESS
PARK
Cobourg
Glengall
Ave
Willowbrook Rd
Road
Bird
In
Bush
Road
Ilderton
Road
Avonley Rd
leate
Street
George's
Way
Sumner
Road
Peckham
Park
Road
Naylor Rd
Way
Asylum
Old
Kent
Road
A 2
ZG
SOUTHWARK
Peckham
Hill
Commercial
House
Lane
Clifton
Way
Kender
Street
Way
Commercial
St
Carlton Gro.
Road
QUEENS ROAD
PECKHAM
Pomeroy
Street
Dalwood St
Road
Peckham
High
Street
Meeting
Queens
Clayton
Road
Queens
Lausanne Rd
H
Shenley
Road
Lyndhurst
Hanover Pk
Consort
Road
Road
Road
kham
eil Rd
Lyndhurst
Grove
Way
Rye
PECKHAM
RYE
15'6
Lane
Copeland
Rd
Consort
Rd
Hollydale
Road
Road
NUNHEAD
rove
Grove Hill Rd
Avondale Rise
a
Bellenden
Ady's
Road
Peckham
Rye
Heaton Rd
Consort
Road
Nunhead Lane
Evelina
A 2214
Linden
Nunhead Gro.
Grove
ZH
A 2216
Pytchley Rd
Oglander
Rd
Rd
Dog Kennel Hill
EAST
DULWICH
Grove
Vale
East
Dulwich
Rd
Crystal Palace Rd
Peckham
Peckham
Rye
Melbourne
Grove
East
Dulwich
A 2214
Grove
Lane
X
t
Lordship
Barry
Rd
Rye
PECKHAM RYE PARK
Cheltenham Rd
Stuart Rd

0   500 m
0   500 yards

X

Y

221

27

AA AB

Grand Union Canal

200 m
200 yards

Bourne Terrace

BAYSWATER
AND MAIDA VALE

Harrow

Westbourne Park

Great Western Road

A 40 Westway

Harrow Road

Royal Oak

Westbourne Park Villas

T

Tavistock Rd

St Luke's Rd

Park Road

Westbourne Road

Talbot Road

Chepstow Rd

Talbot Rd

m

Westbourne Park Road

Westbourne Gdns

197

a

Ledbury Road

NORTH KENSINGTON

Hereford Road

Newton Rd

Bishop's Br

P

Colville Ter.

Artesian Road

Westbourne Grove

Queensway

Inverness

Colville Rd

Ledbury Road

Chepstow Villas

Garway

Kensington Gdns Sq.

x Grove

Villas

Hereford Road

Leinster Sq.

s

e

Porchester Road

t

U

Westbourne Road

Chepstow Villas

Pembridge Villas

Chepstow Place

Pl.

Moscow Road

Bayswater

Bark Place

x

Queensway Terrace

Portobello Road

84

Pembridge Cres.

Dawson Place

St Petersburgh Pl.

Road

P

Kensington Park Road

Pembridge Road

Pembridge Square

Ossington St

Palace Court

Queensway 328

Ladbroke Square

Pembridge Gdns

Linden Gdns

Gate

Bayswater

P

Roa

Ladbroke Road

Rd

Hill

Kensington Palace Gardens

Broad

Holland Park Ave

p Notting

e

Notting Hill Gate

s

Broad

s

Uxbridge St

a

z

Kensington

Campden Hill Square

Campden

Kensington Place

x

ORANGER

V

Aubrey Walk

Hill Rd

Bedford Gardens

c

Church St

KENSINGTON PALACE

Holland

U

Campden Hill

Campden Gro

St

Palace

KENSINGTON AND CHELSEA

Sheffield Terrace

AA 35 AB

222

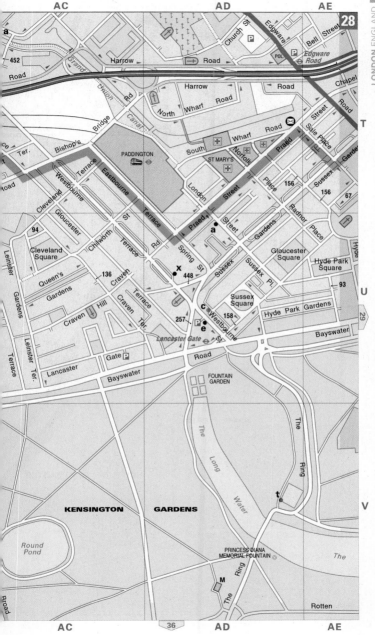

a

452
Road

Grand
Union
Canal

Church St
Edgware
Bell Street

P

Harrow Road
POL
Edgware Road

Chapel

Harrow Road

North Wharf Road

South Wharf Road

PADDINGTON

ST MARY'S

Norfolk Street

Praed Street

Sale Place

Bishop's
Bridge

Westbourne Terrace

Eastbourne Terrace

Cleveland

Gloucester

Chilworth Terrace

St

Terrace

Rd

London Street

Praed Street

Street

Sussex Gardens

156

156

Sussex Garden

67

94

Cleveland
Square

Queen's

Gardens

Craven Terrace

Craven Hill

Leinster Gardens

Craven Ter.

136

Spring St

a

x
448

Sussex

Sussex Pl.

Gloucester
Square

Gardens

Radnor Place

Hyde Park
Square

Hyde

93

Sussex Square

Hyde Park Gardens

U

Lancaster

Leinster Ter.

Terrace

Gate

Lancaster

Bayswater

c

257

P

e

Westbourne

158

Lancaster Gate

St

Road

Bayswater

Road

FOUNTAIN
GARDEN

The Ring

KENSINGTON   GARDENS

Round
Pond

The Long Water

t

V

PRINCESS DIANA
MEMORIAL FOUNTAIN

The

M

The Ring

Rotten

Road

AC

36

AD

AE

29

Bell Street

Marylebone **a** Road

Enford St

Upper York Street

Gloucester St

Baker St

Chiltern

Paddington

Edgware Road

Chapel St

Harcourt St **c**

York St

Montagu St

Pl.

Dorset St

St

Manchester St

b

St

T

Street

Sale Place

Road

Old Marylebone Rd

Crawford Pl.

Bryanston Pl.

Montagu

Baker

Blandford

Street

a

v

n

r

Crawford

St

REGENT'S PARK
AND MARYLEBONE

d

Gloucester Pl.

WALLACE
COLLECTION

h

Sussex Gardens

Edgware

Crawford Pl.

Harrowby

St

14

90

George

Street

St

156

67

Norfolk
Crescent

George Street

Great

Street

P

P

PORTMAN
SQUARE **x**

Wi

332

Upper Berkeley **s** **k**

k

m **d** **r**

Orchard St

P

m Kendal St

v **n** **k**

Cumberland

x

476 **v**

Hyde Park Square

Connaught **a**
Connaught
Square

t **P**
s

St

POL **p**

Portman St

St

Row

93

Seymour

Bryanston Pl.

Marble
Arch Oxford

Street

U

Gardens

28

400

Marble Arch

North

b

Park

Street

Lees Pl.

k

Bayswater

Road

The Ring

P

Green

149

Woods Mews

Upper **c** Brook

St

Culross St

a

g Upper Grosv

Park

HYDE PARK

CITY OF WESTMINSTER

Mou

V

Serpentine

Road

Princess

Walk

The

Serpentine

Serpentine

Road

0   200 m
0   200 yards

Rotten   Row

Rotten   Row

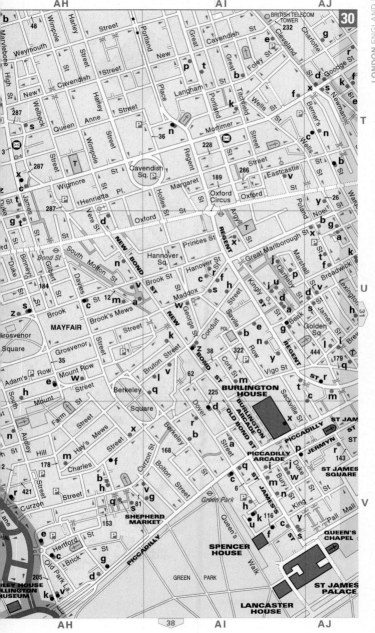

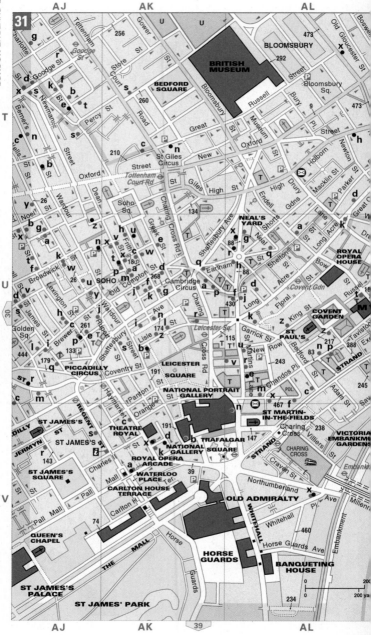

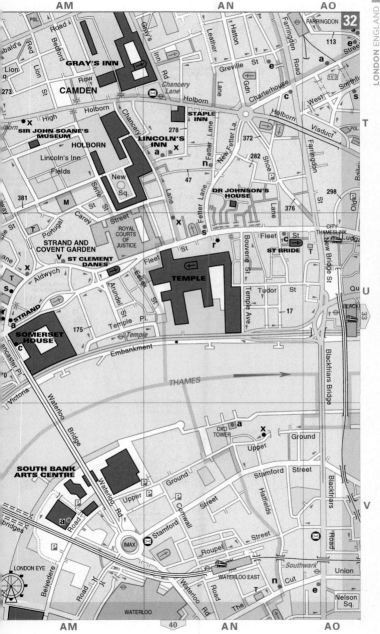

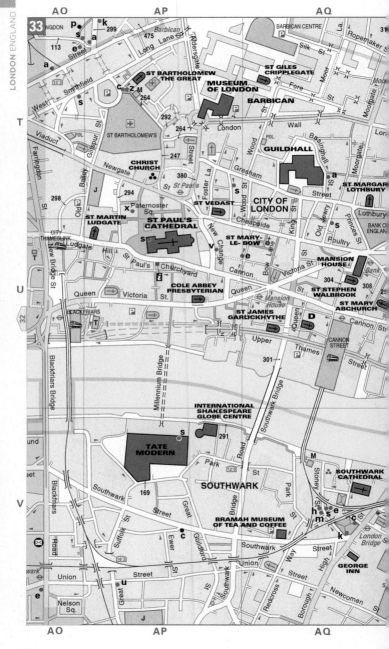

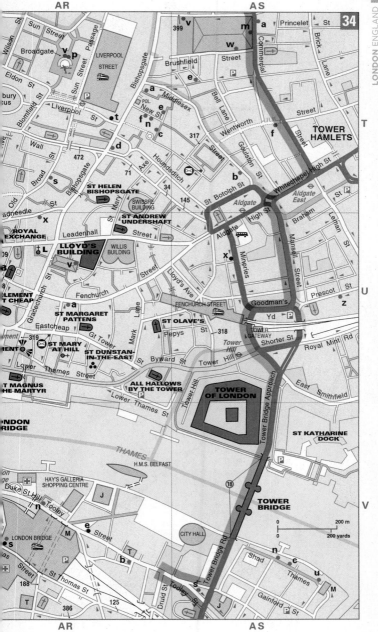

Sun Street

Wilson

Broadgate

Sun Street Passage

LIVERPOOL STREET

Bishopsgate

v 399

v p

Eldon St

Liverpool St

Blomfield

bury cus

Wall St

Broad St

Bishopsgate

Old

adneedle St

X

ROYAL EXCHANGE

L

LLOYD'S BUILDING

WILLIS BUILDING

Leadenhall Street

09

B

8

LEMENT T CHEAP

a

ST MARGARET PATTENS

Eastcheap

ment 319

ENT

ST MARY AT HILL

V

ST DUNSTAN-IN-THE-EAST

Lower Thames Street

T MAGNUS HE MARTYR

NDON RIDGE

Duke St Hill

n Tooley

LONDON BRIDGE

S

as Street

188

T

386

AR

m a Princelet St

Brick Lane

w

Brushfield Street

Commercial

P

e

Bell Lane

Wentworth

Street

Middlesex

a

e

f n

c

d

POL New St

t

472

Axe St

Houndsditch

71

34

145

St Botolph St

b

Goulston St

Street

f

TOWER HAMLETS

Whitechapel High St

Aldgate East

Braham

Leman

P

ST HELEN BISHOPSGATE

St Mary Axe

SWISSRE BUILDING

ST ANDREW UNDERSHAFT

Street

Aldgate

Aldgate High St

X

Minories

Mansell Street

Prescot St

z

Fenchurch

Gracechurch St

Lloyd's Ave

FENCHURCH STREET

Goodman's

Lime Street

Street

Lloyd's

Mark Lane

S

ST OLAVE'S

Pepys St

318

Yd

P

TOWER GATEWAY

Shorter St

Royal Mint Rd

Gt Tower St

Byward St

Tower Hill

Tower Hill

ALL HALLOWS BY THE TOWER

P

Lower Thames St

Tower Hill

TOWER OF LONDON

East Smithfield

Tower Bridge Approach

ST KATHARINE DOCK

P

THAMES

H.M.S. BELFAST

HAY'S GALLERIA SHOPPING CENTRE

J

Tooley

M

e Street

CITY HALL

Tower Bridge Rd

TOWER BRIDGE

(18)

0   200 m
0   200 yards

P

St Thomas St

b

T

n c

Shad

Thames

u

M

Druid St

Tooley St

125

J

Gainford St

P

AS

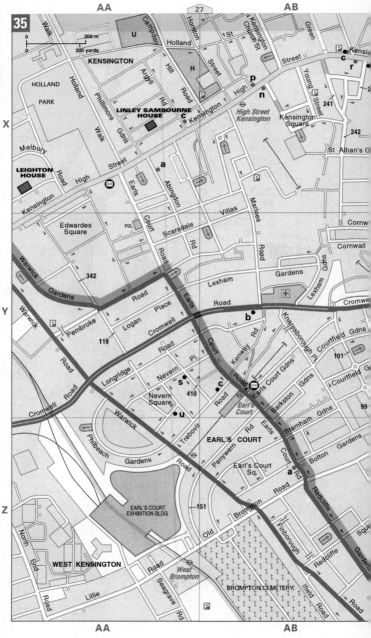

35

200 m
200 yards

U

Campden Hill Road

Holland

Horton

Kensington Church St

Green

Kensi

KENSINGTON

HOLLAND PARK

Argyll Rd

Phillimore Gdns

Hill

Holland

Road

H

Street

St

High

Street

Young Street

P

c

r

p

n

241

242

LINLEY SAMBOURNE HOUSE

c

High Street Kensington

Kensington Square

St Alban's G

X

Melbury

Phillimore Walk

Street

a

Marloes

Road

LEIGHTON HOUSE

High

Earls

Abingdon

Villas

Road

Kensington

Road

Court

Scarsdale

Rd

Cornw

Cornwall

Edwardes Square

POL

Gardens

Lexham

Gdns

342

Road

Earls

Lexham

Road

Cromwe

Y

Warwick

Gardens

Pembroke

Logan

Place

Cromwell

Road

b

Knaresborough Pl

Courtfield Gdns

101

Courtfield G

119

Road

Court

Kenway

Road

99

Longridge

Nevern

s

c

Earls Court Gdns

Barkston

Gdns

Courtfield

Warwick

Road

Nevern Square

410

Road

Earl's Court

Bramham

Gardens

u

Penywern

Rd

EARL'S COURT

Bolton

Philbeach

Trebovir

Road

Earl's Court Sq.

a

Rd

Gardens

Earls

Court

Redcliffe

Gardens

151

Brompton

Road

Squ

Z

North End

Cromwell

Road

EARL'S COURT EXHIBITION BLDG

Old

Finborough

Redcliffe

WEST KENSINGTON

Road

West Brompton

Road

Ifield

Road

Gardens

Lillie

Seagrave

Rd

P

BROMPTON CEMETERY

AA AB

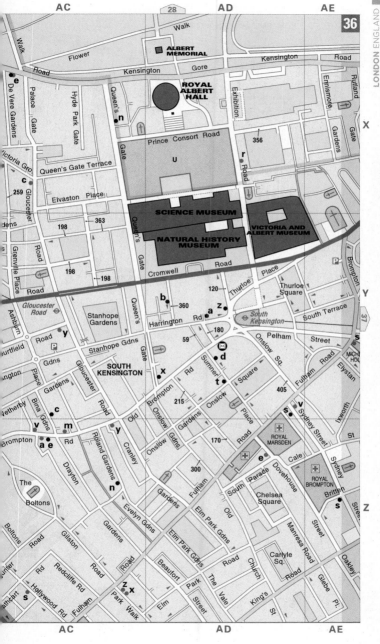

Walk

Flower

Road

ALBERT MEMORIAL

Kensington Gore

Kensington Road

e

De Vere Gardens

Palace Gate

Hyde Park Gate

Queen's

ROYAL ALBERT HALL

n

Exhibition

Kensington

Gore

Rutland

Ennismore

X

Prince Consort Road

356

Victoria Gro.

c

259

Gloucester

Queen's Gate Terrace

Elvaston Place

U

Gate

r

Road

ens

198

363

Queen's

Gloucester

SCIENCE MUSEUM

VICTORIA AND ALBERT MUSEUM

Grenville Place

Road

198

198

Gate

NATURAL HISTORY MUSEUM

Cromwell Road

Place

Brompton

Rutland Gardens

Gate

P

Gloucester Road

Stanhope Gardens

Ashburn

Road

120

Thurloe

Thurloe Square

Y

37

b

360

a z

South Terrace

South Kensington

Courtfield

Road

y

P

Stanhope Gdns

Harrington Rd

180

Pelham

Street

MICHE
HOU

ington

Place

Gdns

Gloucester

Gardens

Gate

Road

59

Onslow Sq.

Fulham

Road

Elystan

Wetherby

Bina Gdns

Road

SOUTH KENSINGTON

x

Brompton

Rd

Summer

d

t

Onslow

Square

405

St

s

v

Sydney Street

Ixworth

y

c

m

Gardens

Old

215

Onslow Gdns

Onslow

Place

s

Cale

Brompton

a e

Rd

y

Cranley

Onslow Gdns

170

Road

ROYAL MARSDEN

Sydney

Britten

Z

The Boltons

Drayton

Roland Gardens

n

Gardens

300

Fulham

South

Parade

Dovehouse

e

ROYAL BROMPTON

s

Street

Boltons

Road

Gilston

Road

Evelyn Gdns

Elm Park Gdns

Old

Chelsea Square

Manresa Road

Glebe Pl.

Oakley

hunter

Rd

Redcliffe Rd

Road

Road

Beaufort

Elm Park Gdns

Park

The Vale

Church

Carlyle Sq.

Road

athcart

s

Hollywood Rd

Fulham

Park Walk

z x

Elm

Street

King's

St

AC AD AE

37

Road　　　The　　Carriage　　Road
Knightsbridge　　　　*Knightsbridge*

x

Knightsbridge

w

e

Wilton Place

k

s

t

468

m

Lowndes

214

BELGRAVIA

Trevor Sq.

Sloane

Square

BELGI

Ennismore

Rutland

X

MONTPELIER
SQUARE

Montpelier Walk

Montpelier

Trevor Place

Trevor Sq.

x

a

c

P

Hans

Street

Basil

Crescent

Street

h

k

v

f

d

West Halkin St

Gate

Gardens

Cheval Pl.

Montpelier St

Hans

s

Road

Rd

Hans
Place

r

Cadogan Pl.

Lowndes St

Beauchamp

n

Street

Pont

Street

P

Street

c

Chesham
Place

Brompton

r

h

e

Pont

Street

Cadogan

Lyall

162

161

160

Brompton

Walton

b

Lennox
Gardens

Cadogan Square

Sloane

Place

Chesham St

Eaton Pl.

Street

Hasker St

263

Street

220

Cadogan Gdns

King's

Y

South Terrace

Walton　Rd

CHELSEA

Milner St

Moore St

Rawlings St

n

Sloane

Street

36

Street

a

v

Mossop St

Cadogan

Draycott

Street

23

c

407

Sloane

Pl.

n

Street

k

r

King's

Sloane Sq.

T T

Bourne St

Sloane Sq.

Holbein

MICHELIN
HOUSE

s

Elystan

Sloane

P

POL

Whiteheads Grove

Draycott

Avenue

s

v

King's

Road

Lower

Sloane

45

x

223

Street

d

Elystan　Place

Cheltenham

Road

Markham St

Terrace

Franklin's Row

n

Jubilee Place

Ixworth

St

b

Sydney

Street

Britten

ROYAL
BROMPTON

x

Chelsea

King's

Shawfield St

Radnor Walk

Smith

Street

BURTON'S COURT

St Leonard's Ter.

329

Hospital

THE ROY
HOSPITA

z

s

Street

Tedworth
Square

367

Christchurch St

Tite

Royal

St

Street

NATIONAL
ARMY MUSEUM

0　　　　200
0　　　200 ya

Chelsea

c

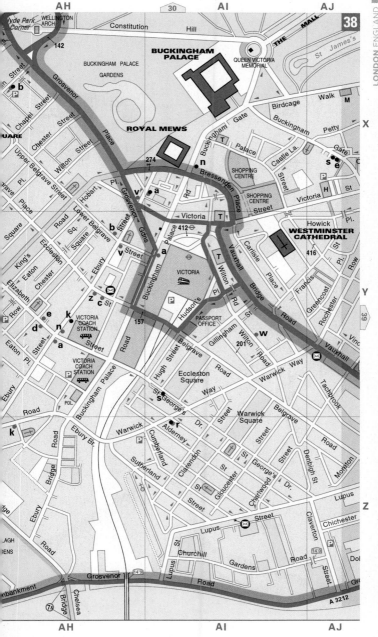

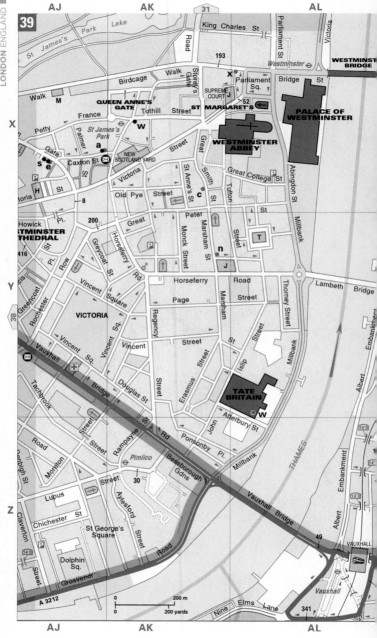

39

St James's Park Lake

31

King Charles St

193

Parliament St

Victoria

WESTMINSTER BRIDGE

St James's Park

Birdcage Walk

Storey's Gate

Westminster

X

Parliament Sq.

Bridge St

Walk

M

QUEEN ANNE'S GATE

Tothill Street

SUPREME COURT J

52

ST MARGARET'S

PALACE OF WESTMINSTER

X

France

St James's Park

W

Great

WESTMINSTER ABBEY

Petty

Palmer

Gate

a

Victoria

Street

Smith

Great College St

Abingdon St

S

Caxton St

NEW SCOTLAND YARD

St Anne's

Tufton

e

H

St

Old Pye Street

c

St

8

Howick Pl.

200

Great

Peter

St

T

WESTMINSTER CATHEDRAL

416

Pl.

Horseferry

Monck Street

Marsham

n

Street

Millbank

Francis

Greycoat

Row

Rd

J

Lambeth Bridge

Greycoat

Rochester

Vincent Square

Horseferry

Road

Thorney Street

Embankment

VICTORIA

Vincent

Page

Street

Marsham

Albert

Vincent Sq.

Vincent

Regency

Street

Islip

St

Millbank

Vauxhall

Douglas St

Street

Erasmus

John

TATE BRITAIN

W

Tachbrook

Bridge

Rampayne

Road

Ponsonby Pl.

Millbank

THAMES

Vauxhall Bridge

Road

Moreton

Street

Pimlico

Bessborough Gdns

Street

Denbigh St

30

Aylesford

Albert Embankment

49

VAUXHALL

Lupus

Street

Chichester St

St George's Square

Claverton

Street

Road

Grosvenor

Vauxhall

A 3212

Dolphin Sq.

341

Nine Elms Lane

| 0 | 200 m |
| 0 | 200 yards |

AJ   AK   AL

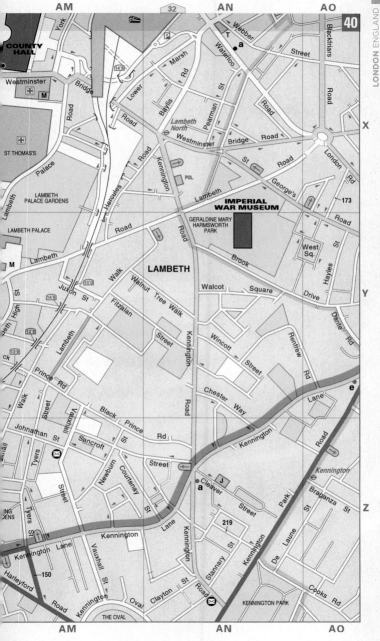

AM

AN

AO

32

COUNTY HALL

Westminster

ST THOMAS'S

York

Bridge

Road

Lower

Marsh

Rd

Waterloo

Webber

Street

Blackfriars

Road

T

a

Palace

LAMBETH PALACE GARDENS

LAMBETH PALACE

Road

Hercules

Road

Bylis

Lambeth North

Pearman

St

Westminster

Bridge

Road

St

George's

London

Rd

POL.

Lambeth

IMPERIAL WAR MUSEUM

GERALDINE MARY HARMSWORTH PARK

Road

173

Road

X

Lambeth

Lambeth

Road

Kennington

Road

Brook

West Sq.

Hayles

St

M

Juxon

St

Walk

Walnut Tree Walk

Fitzalan

Street

Kennington

Walcot

Square

Wincott

Street

Drive

Renfrew

Rd

Danfel

Rd

Y

LAMBETH

eth High

St

ck

Lambeth

Prince

Rd

Walk

Vauxhall

Black

Prince

Rd

Road

Chester

Way

Lane

e

Johnathan

St

Sancroft

Street

Kennington

Kennington

Road

Tyers

Newburn

Courtenay

St

Street

a

Cleaver

J

Street

Park

St

Kennington

Braganza

St

Z

ING DENS

Tyers

St

Lane

219

St

De

Laune

Kennington

Lane

150

Vauxhall

St

Lane

Kennington

Stannary

St

Harleyford

Road

Kennington

Oval

Clayton

St

Road

KENNINGTON PARK

Cooks

Rd

THE OVAL

AM

AN

AO

ENGLAND

A vision of England sweeps across historic buildings and rolling landscapes, but from the rugged splendour of Cornwall's cliffs to pounding Northumbrian shores, this image seeks parity with a newer picture of Albion: refined cities whose industrial past has been reshaped by a shiny, interactive reality. The country's bones and bumps are a reassuring constant: the windswept moors of the south west and the craggy peaks of the Pennines, the summery orchards of the Kentish Weald, the constancy of East Anglian skies and the mirrored calm of Cumbria's lakes.

Renewed interest in all things regional means restaurants are increasingly looking to serve dishes rooted in their locality. Think Melton Mowbray pie in Leicestershire or Lancashire hotpot in the north west – and what better place to eat cheese than where it was made? Seafood is an important part of the English diet: try shrimps from Morecambe Bay, oysters from Whitstable and Cromer crab in Norfolk. Sunday pub roasts are another quintessential part of English life – and a trip to the South West wouldn't be complete without a cream tea.

- Michelin Road map
  n° 502, 503, 504 and 713
- Michelin Green Guide:
  Great Britain

Great Britain & Ireland

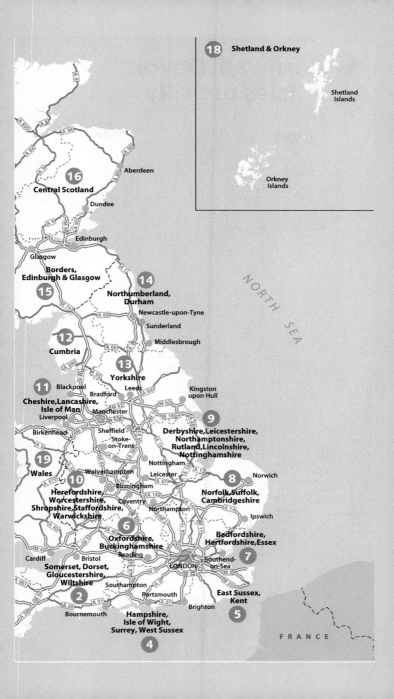

A   B

BRIST

1

Isles of Scilly

Bryher   St. Martins
Tresco
St. Mary's

Clovelly

Bude

Boscastle

Port Isaac   Camelford

CORNWALL

Rock   St Kew

2   Padstow   Treburley

Wadebridge

Watergate Bay   Bodmin

Newquay   Liskeard

Lostwithiel

St Blazey

St. Austell   Golant   Looe

St. Ewe   Fowey   Polperro

Truro   Tregony   Mevagissey

Zennor   St. Ives   Halsetown   Veryan   Portloe   Gorran Haven

Marazion   Portscatho

Penzance   Perranuthnoe   St. Mawes

Newlyn   Falmouth

Sennen Cove   Mousehole   Maenporth

Helston

Porthleven   St. Keverne

Cury

Mullion   Coverack

3

A   B

238

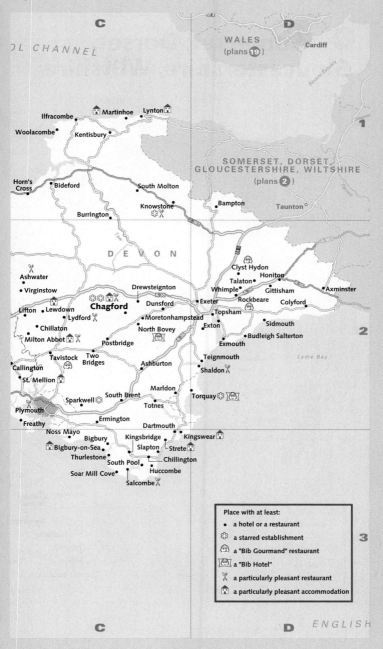

2 Somerset, Dorset, Gloucestershire, Wiltshire

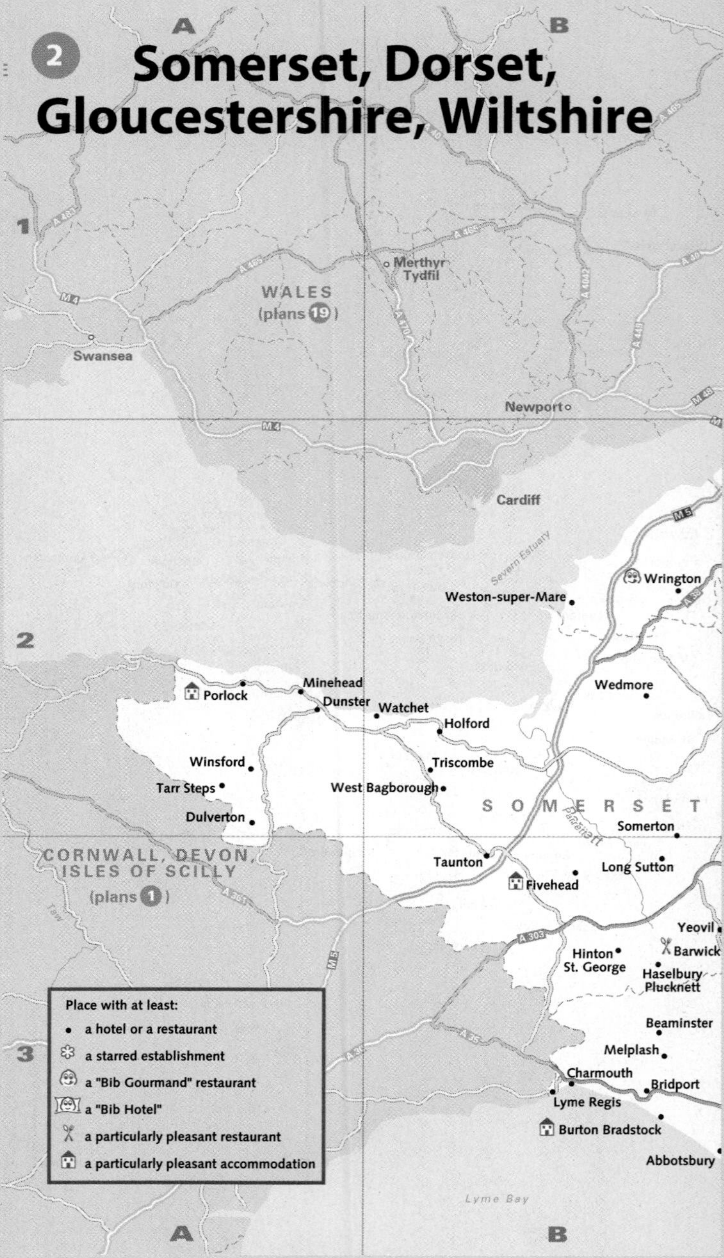

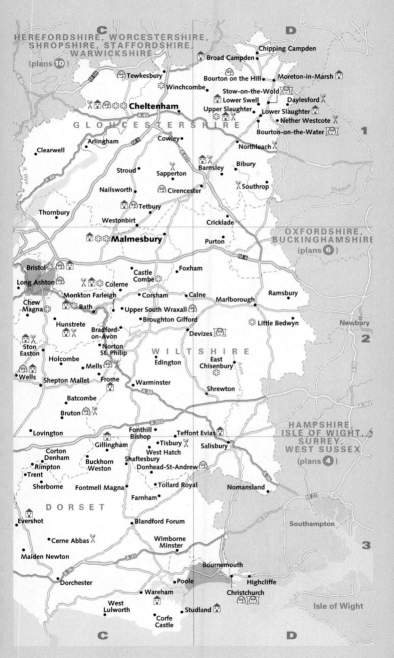

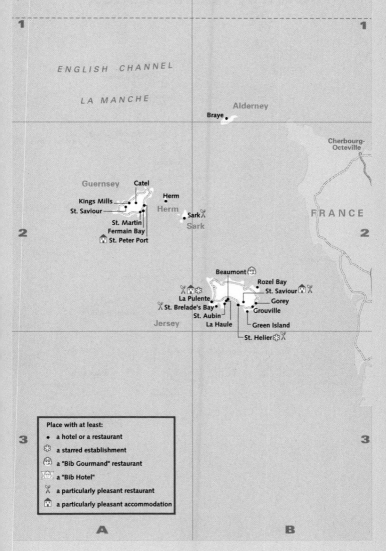

Channel Islands 3

A   B

Reading

1

SOMERSET, DORSET,
GLOUCESTERSHIRE,
WILTSHIRE
(plans 2)

Newbury

Highclere
Old Burghclere
Baughurst ✗

Hurstbourne
Tarrant
Hook
Old Basing

Longparish

Preston Candover 😊

Salisbury

✗ Stockbridge
Longstock
✗ 🏠 Sparsholt
✗ ❄ Winchester
H A M P S H I R E

2

Romsey 😊
Otterbourne
✗ West Meon

Fordingbridge
Droxford 😊

Netley Marsh
✗ 🏠
Southampton 🏠

Lyndhurst
✗ 🏠

Ringwood
Hamble-le-Rice

✗ 🏠 Brockenhurst
Beaulieu ❄ 🏠
Emsworth

Sway
New Milton
Lymington
East End
Portsmouth
Hayling
Island

Barton-
on-Sea
Gurnard

Milford-on-Sea
✗
Wootton Bridge

Bournemouth
Yarmouth
Seaview 😊
St. Helens

Shalfleet

Godshill
Shanklin

3

Isle of
Wight
Ventnor 🏠

A   B

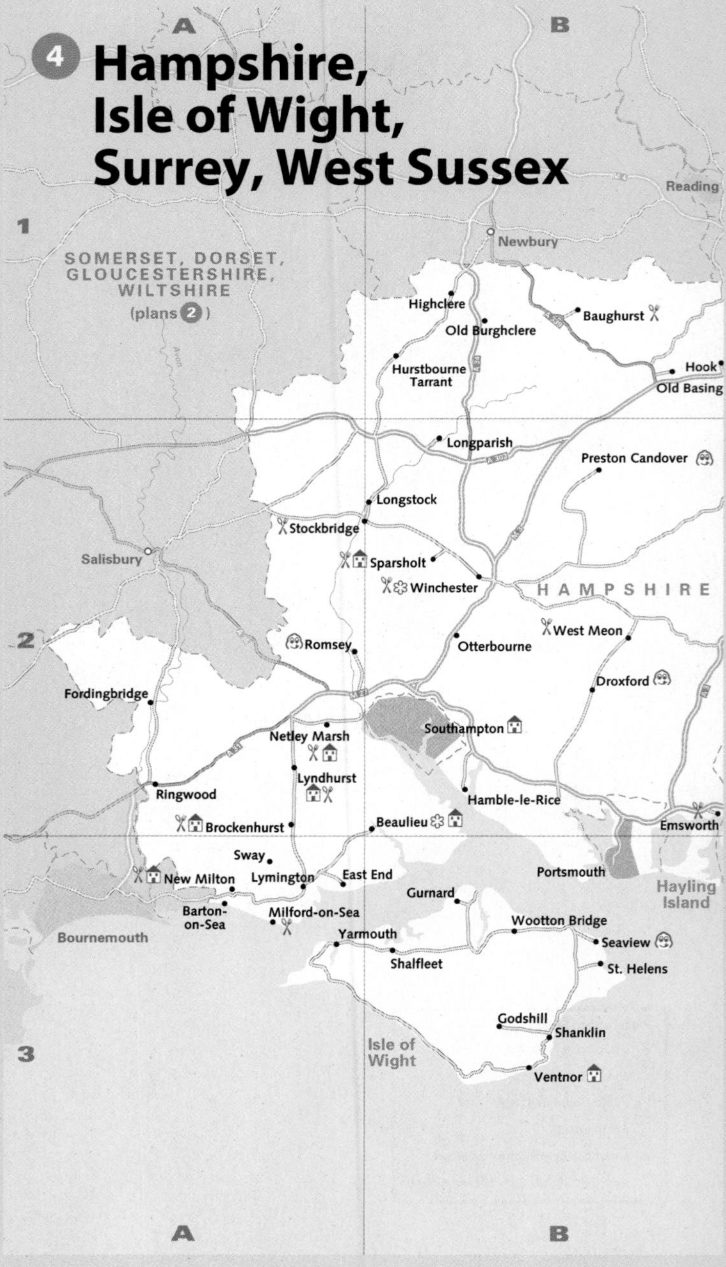

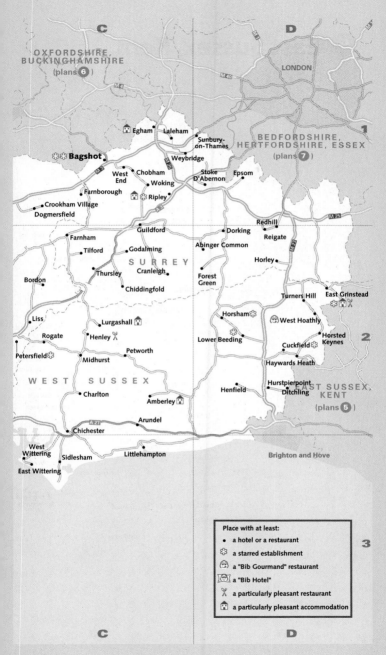

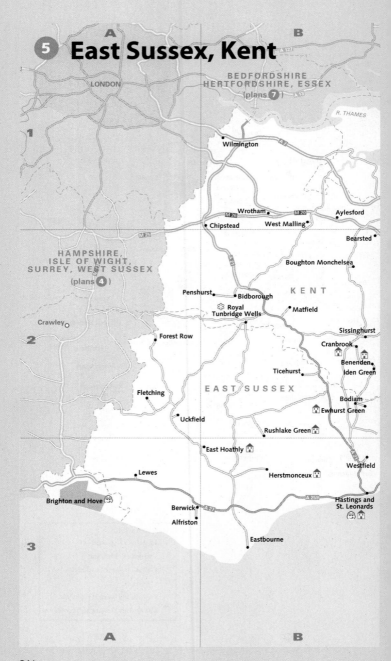

Oxfordshire, Buckinghamshire

6

A   B

HEREFORDSHIRE,
WORCESTERSHIRE,
SHROPSHIRE,
STAFFORDSHIRE,
WARWICKSHIRE
(plans 10)

1

SOMERSET, DORSET,
GLOUCESTERSHIRE,
WILTSHIRE
(plans 2)

Sibford Gower

Chipping Norton

Hethe

Churchill
Kingham

Church Enstone

Wootton

Kirtlington

Woodstock

Burford   Swinbrook

Hampton Poyle

Murcott

Crawley

Minster Lovell

Filkins   O X F O R D S H I R E

2

Clanfield

Northmoor

Oxford

Thames

Buckland Marsh   Fyfield

Abingdon

Stadhampton

Faringdon

Little Coxwell

Sutton Courtenay

Berrick Salome

East Hendred

Sparsholt

Wantage

Aston Tirrold

Swindon

Goring

Chieveley

Yattendon

Stanford Dingley

3

Kintbury

Newbury

HAMPSHIRE,
ISLE OF WIGHT,
SURREY, WEST SUSSEX
(plans 4)

A   B

Place with at least:

- •   a hotel or a restaurant
- ✿   a starred establishment
- 🎯   a "Bib Gourmand" restaurant
- 🏠   a "Bib Hotel"
- ✕   a particularly pleasant restaurant
- 🏠   a particularly pleasant accommodation

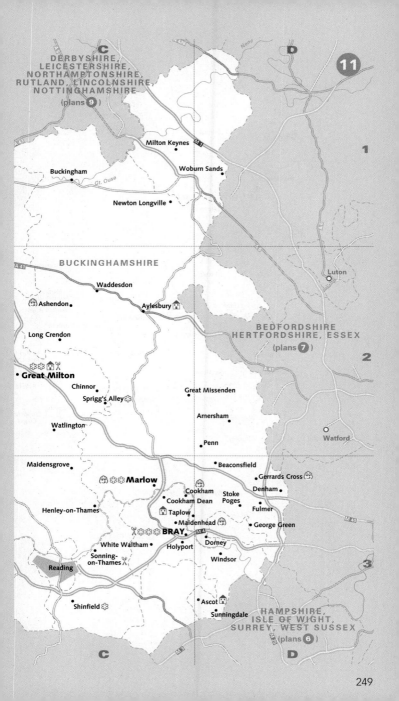

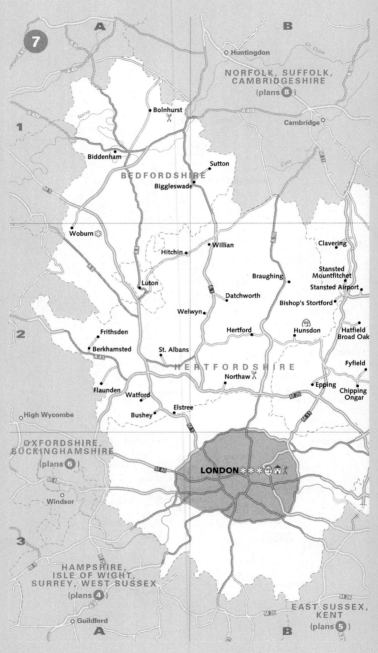

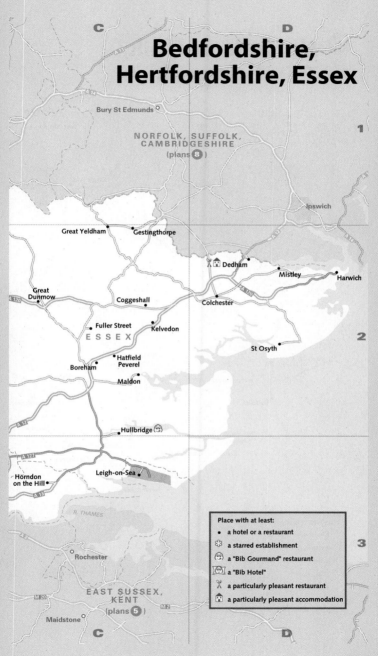

Bedfordshire, Hertfordshire, Essex

Norfolk, Suffolk, Cambridgeshire

The Wash

❄ Hunstanton
Sedgeford
Snettisham

1 DERBYSHIRE, LEICESTERSHIRE, NORTHAMPTONSHIRE, RUTLAND, LINCOLNSHIRE, NOTTINGHAMSHIRE
(plans **9**)
Spalding

King's Lynn
Grimston

Stamford

Welland

Nene

Peterborough

Elton

Stilton

C A M B R I D G E S H I R E

Great Ouse

2

Keyston 🙂 ✗

Ely

Isleham

Huntingdon

Gt. Ouse

Tuddenham

Buckden

Moulton

Caxton

Little Wilbraham ✗

Bourn

Cambridge
❄❄ ✗

Six Mile Bottom

Cam

Whittlesford

Place with at least:
- • a hotel or a restaurant
- ❄ a starred establishment
- 🙂 a "Bib Gourmand" restaurant
- 📗 a "Bib Hotel"
- ✗ a particularly pleasant restaurant
- 🏠 a particularly pleasant accommodation

3

BEDFORDSHIRE, HERTFORDSHIRE, ESSEX
(plans **7**)

Bishop's Stortford

A   B

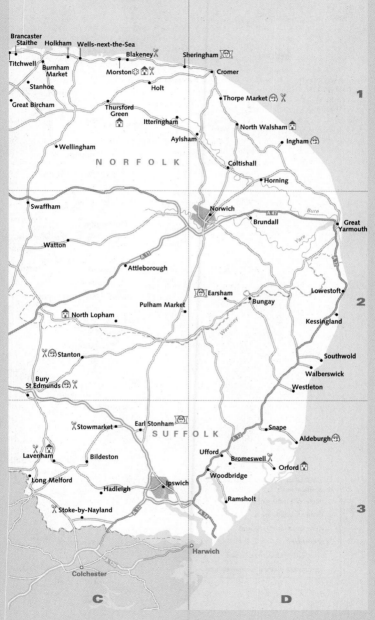

C

D

1

Brancaster Staithe
Titchwell
Holkham **Wells-next-the-Sea**
Blakeney
Sheringham
Burnham Market
Morston
Cromer
Stanhoe
Holt
Thorpe Market
Great Bircham
Thursford Green
Itteringham
North Walsham
Aylsham
Ingham
Wellingham
NORFOLK
Coltishall
Horning
Swaffham
Norwich
Brundall
Bure
Great Yarmouth
Watton
A 47
Yare
Attleborough
Earsham
Lowestoft
North Lopham
Pulham Market
Bungay
Waveney
Kessingland
Stanton
Southwold
Walberswick
Bury St Edmunds
Westleton
Stowmarket
Earl Stonham
SUFFOLK
Snape
Aldeburgh
Ufford
Lavenham
Bildeston
Bromeswell
Orford
Long Melford
Woodbridge
Hadleigh
Ipswich
Ramsholt
Stoke-by-Nayland
Harwich
Colchester

2

3

C

D

253

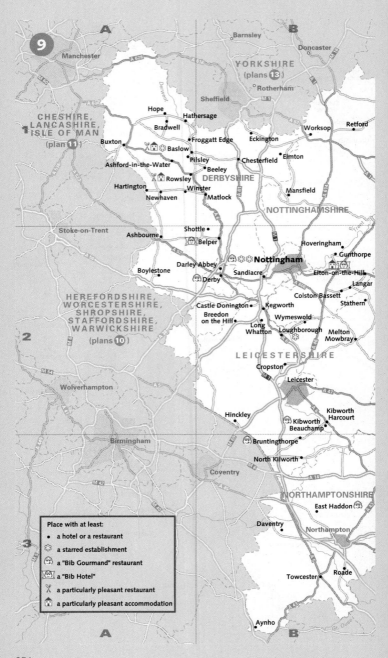

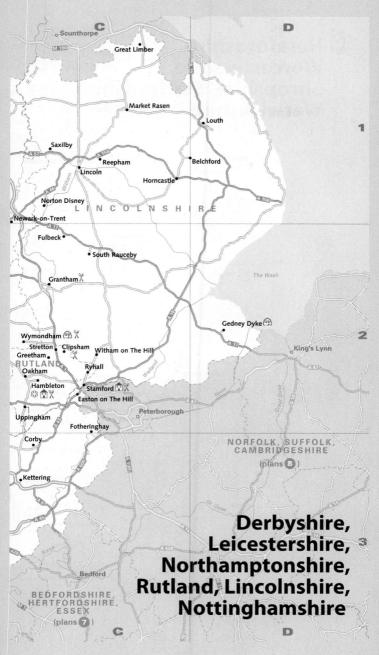

Derbyshire,
Leicestershire,
Northamptonshire,
Rutland, Lincolnshire,
Nottinghamshire

255

10 Herefordshire, Worcestershire, Shropshire, Staffordshire, Warwickshire

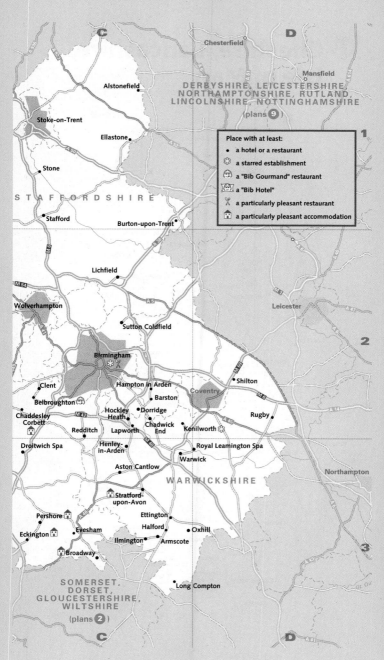

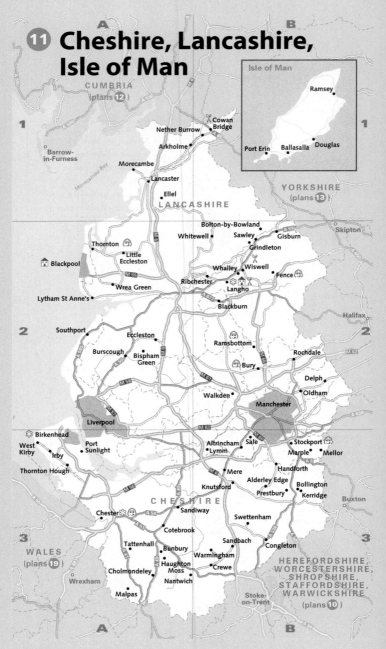

11 Cheshire, Lancashire, Isle of Man

Isle of Man

CUMBRIA
(plans 12)

Barrow-in-Furness

Cowan Bridge
Nether Burrow
Arkholme

Morecambe
Lancaster
Ellel

LANCASHIRE

Thornton
Little Eccleston

Blackpool

Wrea Green

Lytham St Anne's

Bolton-by-Bowland
Whitewell
Sawley
Gisburn
Grindleton
Whalley
Wiswell
Fence
Ribchester
Langho
Blackburn

Skipton

YORKSHIRE
(plans 13)

Halifax

Southport
Eccleston
Burscough
Bispham Green

Ramsbottom
Bury
Walkden

Rochdale
Delph
Oldham

Liverpool
Manchester

Stockport
Marple
Mellor

Birkenhead
West Kirby
Irby
Port Sunlight
Thornton Hough

Altrincham
Lymm
Sale
Mere
Knutsford

Handforth
Alderley Edge
Prestbury
Bollington
Kerridge

Buxton

Chester
Sandiway

CHESHIRE

Swettenham

Cotebrook
Tattenhall
Bunbury
Haughton Moss
Nantchwich
Warmingham
Sandbach
Congleton

HEREFORDSHIRE,
WORCESTERSHIRE,
SHROPSHIRE,
STAFFORDSHIRE,
WARWICKSHIRE
(plans 10)

WALES
(plans 19)

Wrexham

Cholmondeley
Malpas

Crewe
Stoke-on-Trent

Isle of Man:
Ramsey
Port Erin
Ballasalla
Douglas

Morecambe Bay

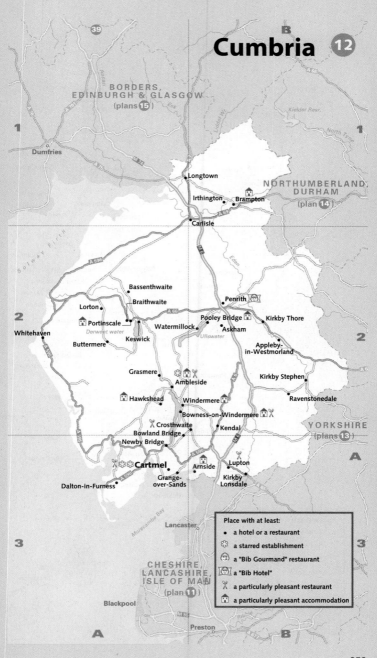

Cumbria 12 B

BORDERS,
EDINBURGH & GLASGOW
(plans 15)

1

Dumfries

NORTHUMBERLAND,
DURHAM
(plan 14)

Longtown

Irthington
Brampton

Carlisle

Solway Firth

Bassenthwaite
Penrith

Braithwaite
Kirkby Thore

Lorton
Portinscale
Pooley Bridge

Derwent water
Watermillock
Askham

Whitehaven
Keswick
Ullswater

2
Buttermere
Appleby-
in-Westmorland

Grasmere
Kirkby Stephen

Ambleside

Hawkshead
Ravenstonedale

Windermere

Bowness-on-Windermere

Crosthwaite
Kendal

Bowland Bridge
YORKSHIRE
(plans 13)

Newby Bridge

A

Cartmel
Arnside
Lupton

Dalton-in-Furness
Grange-
over-Sands
Kirkby
Lonsdale

Morecambe Bay

Lancaster

3

CHESHIRE,
LANCASHIRE,
ISLE OF MAN
(plan 11)

Blackpool

A
Preston
B

Place with at least:

● a hotel or a restaurant
❀ a starred establishment
🅱 a "Bib Gourmand" restaurant
🏠 a "Bib Hotel"
✗ a particularly pleasant restaurant
🏠 a particularly pleasant accommodation

259

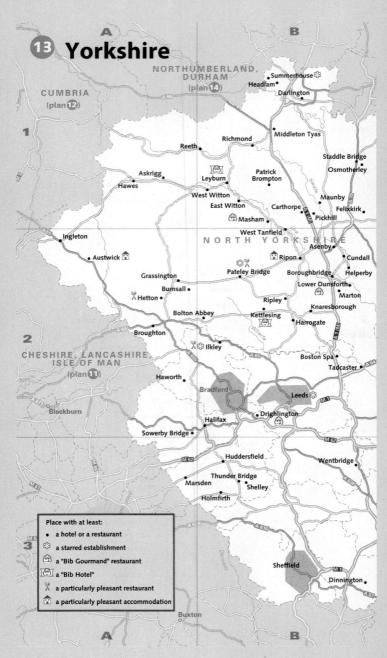

13 Yorkshire

NORTHUMBERLAND, DURHAM (plan 14)

CUMBRIA (plan 12)

Summerhouse
Headlam
Darlington

Reeth
Richmond
Middleton Tyas

Staddle Bridge
Osmotherley

Askrigg
Leyburn
Patrick Brompton

Hawes
West Witton
Maunby
East Witton
Carthorpe
Felixkirk
Masham
Pickhill

West Tanfield
Ingleton
Asenby

Austwick
Ripon
Cundall

Grassington
Pateley Bridge
Boroughbridge
Helperby

Burnsall
Lower Dunsforth
Marton

Hetton
Ripley
Knaresborough

Bolton Abbey
Kettlesing
Harrogate

Broughton

CHESHIRE, LANCASHIRE, ISLE OF MAN (plan 11)

Ilkley

Boston Spa
Tadcaster

Haworth

Blackburn
Bradford
Leeds

Halifax
Drighlington

Sowerby Bridge

Huddersfield
Wentbridge

Thunder Bridge
Marsden
Shelley

Holmfirth

Sheffield
Dinnington

Buxton

Place with at least:

- • a hotel or a restaurant
- ✿ a starred establishment
- 🍴 a "Bib Gourmand" restaurant
- 🛏 a "Bib Hotel"
- 🍴 a particularly pleasant restaurant
- 🏠 a particularly pleasant accommodation

260

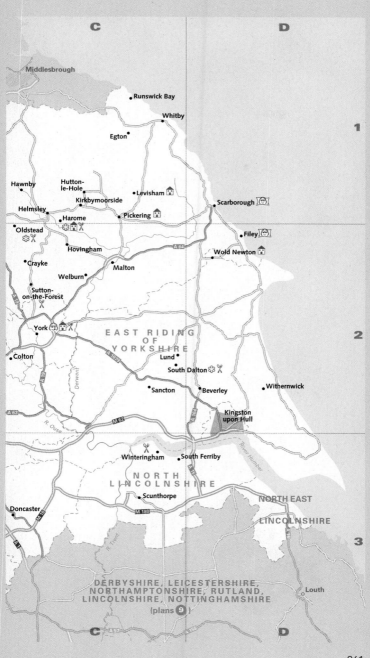

Northumberland, Durham

BORDERS, EDINBURGH & GLASGOW (plans **15**)

- Berwick-upon-Tweed
- Cornhill-on-Tweed
- Milfield
- Belford
- Bamburgh
- Seahouses
- Wooler
- Chatton
- Jedburgh
- Alnwick
- Warkworth
- Rothbury
- Eshott
- Kielder Resr.
- Kirkwhelpington
- Morpeth

NORTHUMBERLAND

- Stannington
- Barrasford
- Humshaugh
- Corbridge
- Tynemouth
- North Shields
- Haltwhistle
- Hexham
- Stocksfield
- Newcastle-upon-Tyne
- Hedley on the Hill
- Low Fell
- Sunderland
- Blanchland
- Sunniside
- Lamesley
- Newbottle
- Ouston
- Seaham

DURHAM

- Cowshill
- Eastgate
- Durham
- Castle Eden
- Middleton-in-Teesdale
- Romaldkirk
- Wynyard
- Middlesbrough
- Barnard Castle
- Winston
- Yarm
- Maltby

CUMBRIA (plan **12**)

YORKSHIRE (plans **13**)

- Thirsk
- Ripon

Place with at least:
- ● a hotel or a restaurant
- ✿ a starred establishment
- 🐷 a "Bib Gourmand" restaurant
- 🏠 a "Bib Hotel"
- ✕ a particularly pleasant restaurant
- 🏠 a particularly pleasant accommodation

FOOD NOT TO BE MISSED

STARRED RESTAURANTS

❀❀❀
Exceptional cuisine, worth a special journey!

© Restaurant Nathan Outlaw

BIB GOURMANDS ☺
Good quality, good value cooking

© Restaurant Nathan Outlaw, Port Isaac

OUR TOP PICKS

BOUTIQUE BOLTHOLES BY THE SEA

CHARMING CHOCOLATE BOX COUNTRY PUBS

ICONIC COUNTRY HOUSES

© Nathan Outlaw

REGIONAL STAND-OUTS

SOMETHING A LITTLE DIFFERENT

THE ULTIMATE IN LUXURY

ABBERLEY

Worcestershire – ✉ Worcester – Pop. 654 – Regional map n° **10**-B2

▶ London 137 mi – Birmingham 27 mi – Worcester 13 mi

🏠 The Elms

CASTLE · CLASSIC An impressive Queen Anne manor house where modern colours and fabrics blend with traditional furnishings. Bedrooms are split between the house and the old stables, and most have pleasant country views. There are plenty of facilities for families, including the Garden Café, which is child-friendly and set within the pleasant spa. Formal Brookes serves a classic menu.

23 rooms ⌂ – ♦£ 95/140 ♦♦£ 120/220

Stockton Rd ✉ WR6 6AT – West : 0.75 mi on A 443 – ℰ (01299) 896 666
– www.theelmshotel.co.uk

ABBEY DORE

Herefordshire – Regional map n° **10**-A3

▶ London 170 mi – Gloucester 39 mi – Hereford 15 mi

✗ Toi et Moi

FRENCH CLASSIC · INDIVIDUAL It's not just the views that set this charming little hillside restaurant apart. The spacious, Scandinavian lodge style building is simply but stylishly furnished; the atmosphere is delightfully relaxed; and the monthly French menu is refreshingly honest. Cooking is precise and flavours are pronounced.

Menu £ 35/40 (dinner)

Holling Grange ✉ HR2 0JJ – Northwest : 1.5 mi on Ewyas Harold Common rd
– ℰ (01981) 240 244 (booking essential) – www.toietmoi.co.uk – Closed
January-mid March and Sunday-Wednesday

ABBOTSBURY

Dorset – Pop. 481 – Regional map n° **2**-B3

▶ London 146 mi – Bournemouth 44 mi – Exeter 50 mi – Weymouth 10 mi

🏠 Abbey House

HISTORIC · COSY Characterful guesthouse-cum-tea-shop in a stunning location beside the ruins of a 15C abbey. Well-kept, classical bedrooms; one has a half-tester and one runs almost the length of the building. Unique Benedictine watermill in the gardens.

5 rooms ⌂ – ♦£ 80/100 ♦♦£ 80/125

Church St ✉ DT3 4JJ – ℰ (01305) 871 330 – www.theabbeyhouse.co.uk

ABBOTS RIPTON – Cambridgeshire ➜ See Huntingdon

ABINGDON

Oxfordshire – Pop. 38 262 – Regional map n° **6**-B2

▶ London 64 mi – Oxford 6 mi – Reading 25 mi

🏠 Rafters

FAMILY · MODERN An unassuming exterior conceals a stylish, modern hotel. Smart bedrooms have a Scandic feel and excellent facilities; one even has a water bed! The friendly owner serves homemade bread and local bacon and sausages at breakfast.

4 rooms ⌂ – ♦£ 60/120 ♦♦£ 109/154

Abingdon Rd, Marcham ✉ OX13 6NU – West : 3 mi on A 415 – ℰ (01865) 391 298
– www.bnb-rafters.co.uk

ABINGER COMMON

Surrey – Regional map n° **4**-D2

▶ London 32 mi – Croydon 26 mi – Barnet 62 mi – Ealing 44 mi

🏠 Abinger Hatch ⬅ 🏡 🅿

BRITISH MODERN · RUSTIC 18C pub in a charming hamlet – with its low beams, cosy corners and log fires it oozes country gentility. It's open throughout the day, offering snacks, sharing boards and comfort dishes; come summer, the outside kitchen is a hit.

Carte £ 24/30

*Abinger Ln ✉ RH5 6HZ – ☎ (01306) 730 737 – www.theabingerhatch.com
– Closed 25 December*

ALDEBURGH

Suffolk – Pop. 2 341 – Regional map n° **8**-D3
▶ London 97 mi – Ipswich 24 mi – Norwich 41 mi

🏨 Wentworth 🌀 ⬅ 🏡 ⬅ 🅿

TRADITIONAL · CLASSIC The friendly, engaging team know all the regulars at this family-run seaside hotel. The conservatory and large front terrace are popular spots. Extremely comfortable bedrooms come with a copy of locally set 'Orlando the Marmalade Cat'. The formal dining room serves a traditional daily menu.

35 rooms (dinner included) ⚏ – 🛆£ 88/125 🛆🛆£ 152/278
Wentworth Rd ✉ IP15 5BD – ☎ (01728) 452 312 – www.wentworth-aldeburgh.com

🏨 Brudenell 🌀 ⬅ 🏡 ⬅

HOLIDAY HOTEL · MODERN Contemporary hotel right on the beachfront, with a relaxed ambience and superb sea views; take it all in from the large terrace. New England style bedrooms come with modern bathrooms and up-to-date facilities. The informal, split-level bar-cum-restaurant offers an accessible menu of modern classics.

44 rooms ⚏ – 🛆£ 105/126 🛆🛆£ 147/352
The Parade ✉ IP15 5BU – ☎ (01728) 452 071 – www.brudenellhotel.co.uk

🏨 White Lion 🌀 ⬅

HOLIDAY HOTEL · PERSONALISED Don't be fooled by the worn exterior; inside it's smart and modern, with stylish bedrooms and several open-plan lounges, which provide the ideal spot for afternoon tea. The large brasserie serves an all-purpose daytime menu and a more structured evening selection; traditional fish dishes feature highly.

38 rooms ⚏ – 🛆£ 75/120 🛆🛆£ 120/275
Market Cross Pl ✉ IP15 5BJ – ☎ (01728) 452 720 – www.whitelion.co.uk

🍴 Lighthouse 🏡 🆎

MEDITERRANEAN · BISTRO Popular, long-standing, split-level eatery with bright yellow décor, amiable service and a laid-back feel. Menus change constantly, featuring fish from the boats 200m away and local, seasonal meats and vegetables. Cooking is rustic and flavoursome, and dishes arrive generously proportioned.

Menu £ 10 (lunch and early dinner) – Carte £ 20/35

*77 High St ✉ IP15 5AU – ☎ (01728) 453 377 (booking essential)
– www.lighthouserestaurant.co.uk – Closed lunch 1 January and
lunch 26 December*

🍴 Aldeburgh Market

FISH AND SEAFOOD · BISTRO Set in a shop brimming with local veg and fresh seafood; the best tables are in the bay window, with views across the street. Well-priced, flavoursome cooking and friendly service. Arrive early to try one of the tasty breakfasts.

Carte £ 18/24

*170-172 High St ✉ IP15 5EY – ☎ (01728) 452 520
– www.thealdeburghmarket.co.uk – lunch only – Closed 1 week January and
25 December*

ALDERLEY EDGE

Cheshire East – Pop. 5 280 – Regional map n° **11**-B3

▶ London 187 mi – Chester 34 mi – Manchester 14 mi – Stoke-on-Trent 25 mi

🏨 Alderley Edge

BUSINESS · STYLISH Well-run, early Victorian country house in an affluent village. Smart landscaped gardens; compact, fairly formal interior with modern, leather-furnished guest areas and stylish bedrooms. Good service from dedicated staff.

50 rooms – †£ 100/140 ††£ 135/310 – ⌂ £ 15 – 1 suite

Macclesfield Rd ⊠ SK9 7BJ – ℰ (01625) 583 033 – www.alderleyedgehotel.com

The Brasserie • Alderley – See restaurant listing

XXX Alderley

BRITISH MODERN · ELEGANT Smart, formal conservatory restaurant with a long-standing reputation. Modern British dishes display some interesting combinations. Good value lunch and daily evening menus. Excellent wine list with some fine vintage burgundies and clarets.

Menu £ 28 (lunch) – Carte £ 46/50

Alderley Edge Hotel, Macclesfield Rd ⊠ SK9 7BJ – ℰ (01625) 583 033 – www.alderleyedgehotel.com – Closed Sunday dinner to non residents

X The Brasserie

BRITISH TRADITIONAL · BRASSERIE Informal, French-style brasserie with mirrored walls and leather banquettes, on the ground floor of a well-run, busy hotel. Retro British dishes like prawn and crayfish cocktail, scampi in a basket and jam roly poly are given a modern twist.

Carte £ 21/30

Alderley Edge Hotel, Macclesfield Rd ⊠ SK9 7BJ – ℰ (01625) 583 033 – www.alderleyedgehotel.com – Closed Sunday

🍴 Wizard Inn

TRADITIONAL CUISINE · PUB Characterful, dog-friendly pub with flagged floors, old beams and open fires; set next to the Alderley Edge escarpment. The wide-ranging menu offers traditional pub favourites, retro British classics, and fish and meat platters.

Carte £ 17/35

Macclesfield Rd ⊠ SK10 4UB – Southeast : 1.25 mi on B 5087 – ℰ (01625) 584 000 – www.ainscoughs.co.uk – Closed 25 December

ALDFIELD – North Yorkshire ➜ See Ripon

ALFRISTON

East Sussex – ⊠ Polegate – Pop. 829 – Regional map n° **5**-A3

▶ London 66 mi – Eastbourne 9 mi – Lewes 10 mi – Newhaven 8 mi

XX Wingrove House

BRITISH MODERN · BRASSERIE This imposing colonial-style building conceals a spacious brasserie and a comfy lounge. It's personally run and has a relaxed, informal feel. Menus change quarterly and offer appealing, unfussy dishes with a modern British style. Bedrooms are stylish and understated; two have access to the heated balcony.

Menu £ 25/29

7 rooms ⌂ – †£ 100/120 ††£ 100/200

High St ⊠ BN26 5TD – ℰ (01323) 870 276 – www.wingrovehousealfriston.com – dinner only and lunch Saturday and Sunday – Closed 25 December

ALKHAM

Kent – Pop. 351 – Regional map n° **5**-D2

▶ London 72 mi – Birmingham 198 mi – Liverpool 291 mi – Leeds 264 mi

ENGLAND

Alkham Court

RURAL · HOMELY Set on a hill and surrounded by mature grounds, a delightful guesthouse with a hot tub, a sauna and a livery yard for over 20 horses. Homely, well-equipped bedrooms have stylish bathrooms. The large conservatory offers lovely views.

4 rooms ☐ – †£ 80/100 ††£ 135/170

Meggett Ln ⊠ CT15 7DG – Southwest : 1 mi by Alkham Valley Rd – ℰ (01303) 892 056 – www.alkhamcourt.co.uk

XX Marquis

MODERN CUISINE · DESIGN Fashionable former pub with a smart bar, a stylish dining room and a relaxed atmosphere. Accomplished cooking features classical combinations with original touches; portions are generous and presentation is modern. 'Foraging' and 'Tasting' menus are available. Chic, sexy bedrooms boast luxurious bathrooms.

Menu £ 20 (weekday lunch)/35 – Carte £ 31/52

10 rooms ☐ – †£ 79/99 ††£ 99/199

Alkham Valley Rd ⊠ CT15 7DF – ℰ (01304) 873 410 – www.themarquisatalkham.co.uk

ALNWICK

Northumberland – Pop. 8 116 – Regional map n° **14**-B2

▶ London 320 mi – Edinburgh 86 mi – Newcastle upon Tyne 34 mi

West Acre House ⓝ

TOWNHOUSE · PERSONALISED Proudly run Edwardian villa with a beautifully maintained 1 acre garden. Well-proportioned rooms come with bold wallpapers, Arts and Crafts features and a keen eye for detail; choose a Georgian, Edwardian, Oriental or Parisian theme.

4 rooms ☐ – †£ 110/120 ††£ 110/120

West Acres ⊠ NE66 2QA – East : 0.5 mi by A 1068 – ℰ (01665) 510 374 – www.westacrehouse.co.uk

Greycroft

TOWNHOUSE · STYLISH 19C house near the Garden and Castle, run by welcoming owners with good local knowledge. Individually styled bedrooms have good facilities and homely touches; the bright conservatory breakfast room overlooks a lovely walled garden.

6 rooms ☐ – †£ 65/70 ††£ 95/105

Croft Pl ⊠ NE66 1XU – via Prudhoe St – ℰ (01665) 602 127 – www.greycroftalnwick.co.uk – Closed Christmas and New Year

Aln House

TRADITIONAL · PERSONALISED Bay windowed, semi-detached Edwardian house with mature front and rear gardens; run by friendly, welcoming owners. Homely lounge and neatly laid breakfast room. Well-kept, individually decorated bedrooms have feature walls and bright décor.

6 rooms ☐ – †£ 65/90 ††£ 90/110

South Rd ⊠ NE66 2NZ – Southeast : 0.75 mi by B 6346 on Newcastle rd – ℰ (01665) 602 265 – www.alnhouse.co.uk – Closed 23-31 December

at North Charlton North: 6.75 mi by A1 – ⊠ Alnwick

North Charlton Farm

FAMILY · PERSONALISED A large, attractive house on a working farm, with a small 'Household and Farming' museum in one of the outbuildings. Comfy bedrooms offer lovely country views. The traditional lounge and breakfast room are filled with antiques.

3 rooms ☐ – †£ 45/50 ††£ 80/90

⊠ NE67 5HP – ℰ (01665) 579 443 – www.northcharltonfarm.co.uk – Closed Christmas

at Chathill North: 8.75 mi by A1 off B6347

🏨 Doxford Hall H. and Spa 🏠 🕸 📶 🖥 🎭 🔲 🍴 🏋 🅿

COUNTRY HOUSE · CLASSIC Georgian house with immaculately kept formal gardens, numerous comfy lounges and a smart spa – a popular venue for weddings. Bedrooms in the extension mix modern facilities and antique furnishings; those in the original house are spacious and contemporary. The wood-panelled dining room serves modern classics.

34 rooms ⌂ – ♦£ 79/200 ♦♦£ 99/280 – 1 suite
Chathill ✉ *NE67 5DN* – ℰ *(01665) 589 700* – *www.doxfordhall.com*

ALSTONEFIELD

Staffordshire – Pop. 274 – Regional map n° **10**-C1
▶ London 157 mi – Birmingham 66 mi – Liverpool 77 mi – Leeds 88 mi

🍺 The George 🚃 📶 🍴 🅿

TRADITIONAL CUISINE · PUB Simply furnished, 18C pub on the village green, with a roaring fire and a relaxed, cosy atmosphere; it has been in the same family for three generations. Daily changing menus offer well-priced, down-to-earth dishes.

Carte £ 24/48
✉ *DE6 2FX* – ℰ *(01335) 310 205* – *www.thegeorgeatalstonefield.com* – *Closed 25 December*

ALTRINCHAM

Greater Manchester – Pop. 52 419 – Regional map n° **11**-B3
▶ London 191 mi – Chester 30 mi – Liverpool 30 mi – Manchester 8 mi

🏠 Ash Farm 🕸 🚃 ⚗ 🅿

TRADITIONAL · COSY Red-brick, 18C former farmhouse with a pine-furnished breakfast room and a comfy lounge with a wood-burning stove. Some bedrooms are furnished in a traditional country house style; others are more modern. Large garden. Friendly owners.

5 rooms ⌂ – ♦£ 49/69 ♦♦£ 82/98
Park Ln, Little Bollington ✉ *WA14 4TJ – Southwest : 3.25 mi by A 56* – ℰ *(0161) 929 92 90* – *www.ashfarm.co.uk* – *Closed 22 December-2 January*

ALVESTON – Warwickshire ➜ See Stratford-upon-Avon

AMBERLEY

West Sussex – ✉ Arundel – Pop. 586 – Regional map n° **4**-C2
▶ London 56 mi – Brighton 24 mi – Portsmouth 31 mi

🏰 Amberley Castle 🏠 🕸 🚃 ⚗ ⚗ 🏋 🅿

CASTLE · HISTORIC Stunning 12C castle displaying original stonework, battlements and evidence of a moat. The charming grounds consist of lovely gardens, lakes and a croquet lawn, and are matched inside by a characterful array of rooms. Sumptuous bedrooms have a palpable sense of history; those in the main castle are the best.

19 rooms ⌂ – ♦£ 169/615 ♦♦£ 169/615 – 6 suites
✉ *BN18 9LT – Southwest : 0.5 mi on B 2139* – ℰ *(01798) 831 992*
– *www.amberleycastle.co.uk*
Queen's Room – See restaurant listing

XXX Queen's Room 🚃 ⇄ 🅿

BRITISH MODERN · ELEGANT Within the walls of a stunning 12C castle is this elegant dining room with a barrel-vaulted ceiling, lancet windows and an open fire. Ambitious modern dishes arrive artfully presented. Henry VIII's wives all visited, hence its name.

Menu £ 31/85
Amberley Castle Hotel, ✉ *BN18 9LT – Southwest : 0.5 mi on B 2139* – ℰ *(01798) 831 992 (booking essential)* – *www.amberleycastle.co.uk*

AMBLESIDE

Cumbria – Pop. 2 529 – Regional map n° **12**-A2

▶ London 276 mi – Birmingham 162 mi – Liverpool 93 mi – Leeds 121 mi

ENGLAND

🏨 The Samling

TRADITIONAL · STYLISH A former farmhouse in a stunning fellside position, looking southwards along Lake Windermere; take in the fantastic view from the outdoor hot tub. Bedrooms are highly individual and range from classical and characterful to bold and eye-catching; some are duplex suites. Service is relaxed but attentive.

11 rooms ⌂ – ♦£ 280/425 ♦♦£ 300/690 – 2 suites

Ambleside Rd ✉ LA23 1LR – South : 1.5 mi on A 591 – ☎(015394) 31 922
– www.thesamlinghotel.co.uk

🍴 **The Samling** – See restaurant listing

🏨 Nanny Brow

COUNTRY HOUSE · HISTORIC Charming Arts and Crafts house with views of the River Brathay and the Langdale Fells. Spacious, antique-furnished bedrooms sit above an elegant lounge. Original stained glass, wood panelling and impressive fireplaces feature.

14 rooms ⌂ – ♦£ 145/265 ♦♦£ 160/280

Town plan: BY-v *– Clappersgate ✉ LA22 9NF – Southwest : 1.25 mi on A 593*
– ☎(015394) 33 232 – www.nannybrow.co.uk

🏨 Riverside

TRADITIONAL · COSY A homely slate house in a peaceful riverside location; run by delightful owners. The steep, mature garden is filled with rhododendrons. Bedroom 2 has a four-poster, a whirlpool bath and water views. Breakfast is locally sourced.

6 rooms ⌂ – ♦£ 110/130 ♦♦£ 110/130

Town plan: BY-s *– Under Loughrigg ✉ LA22 9LJ – ☎(015394) 32 395*
– www.riverside-at-ambleside.co.uk – Closed 7 December-24 January

🏨 Red Bank

FAMILY · COSY Well-maintained guesthouse close to the centre of town; a former doctor's surgery. Small seating area with wood burning stove; breakfast room overlooks the garden. 3 colour-themed bedrooms with compact, modern bathrooms. Tea on arrival.

3 rooms ⌂ – ♦£ 60/90 ♦♦£ 70/90

Town plan: AZ-r *– Wansfell Rd ✉ LA22 0EG – ☎(015394) 34 637*
– www.red-bank.co.uk

✗✗ The Samling

🍴 **MODERN CUISINE · ROMANTIC** Small hotel restaurant which looks out over 66 acres of grounds and down along Lake Windermere. Cooking has a classical base and a modern, innovative touch and dishes are interesting and well-executed with a Scandic edge. The presentation is impressive and a little bit of theatre is added along the way.

→ Beef tartare with smoked hen's egg, bone marrow croutons and wild mustard. Halibut, squid pearls, sea vegetables and Asian-style broth. Chocolate and hazelnut with Amaretto, Baileys and Frangelico.

Menu £ 45/85

Ambleside Rd ✉ LA23 1LR – South : 1.5 mi on A 591 – ☎(015394) 31 922 (booking essential) – www.thesamlinghotel.co.uk

✗ Lake Road Kitchen 🆕

SCANDINAVIAN · NEIGHBOURHOOD The passionate chef-owner of this small restaurant once worked in Copenhagen and the concise daily menu features some excellent Nordic-inspired combinations. Well-crafted modern dishes use top Scandic and locally foraged produce.

Carte £ 34/43

Town plan: AZ-a *– Lake Rd ✉ LA22 0AD – ☎(015394) 22 012*
– www.lakeroadkitchen.co.uk – dinner only – Closed Monday and Tuesday

275

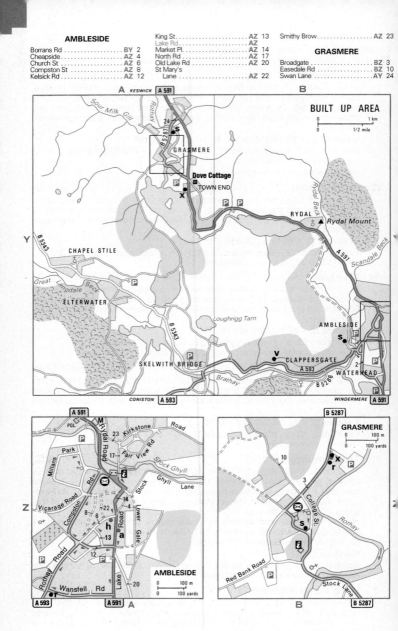

X **Old Stamp House**

MODERN CUISINE · INTIMATE Named after William Wordsworth, the 'Distributor of Stamps' for Westmorland from 1813-1843. A solid stone floor and exposed beams set the scene for an intimate experience. Cooking is modern and complex and champions Cumbrian produce.

Menu £ 19/55 – Carte £ 33/48

Town plan: AZ-h – Church St ✉ LA22 OBU – ✆ (015394) 32 775
– www.oldstamphouse.com – Closed Christmas, 3-25 January, Sunday and Monday

🍴 **Drunken Duck Inn**　　　　　↜ ≼ ⇔ 🏡 🅿

BRITISH TRADITIONAL · INDIVIDUAL Attractive pub in the heart of the beautiful Lakeland countryside, with a characterful, fire-lit bar and two more formal dining rooms. Simple lunches are followed by elaborate dinners with prices to match; cooking is generous and service, attentive. Ales are brewed on-site. Boutique, country house bedrooms – some with patios – have large squashy beds and country views.

Carte £ 28/50

17 rooms ⊑ – ♦£ 79/244 ♦♦£ 105/325

Barngates ✉ LA22 0NG – Southwest : 3 mi by A 593 and B 5286 on Tarn Hows rd – ✆ (01539) 436 347 (booking essential) – www.drunkenduckinn.co.uk – Closed 25 December

AMERSHAM (Old Town)

Buckinghamshire – Pop. 23 086 – Regional map n° **6**-D2
▶ London 34 mi – Birmingham 109 mi – Liverpool 203 mi – Leeds 189 mi

XX **Artichoke**　　　　　🄰🄲 ℐ⊘ ⇔

BRITISH CREATIVE · ELEGANT 16C red-brick house in a picturesque town. A narrow beamed room with cream-painted walls and polished tables leads through to a more modern extension complete with a semi-open kitchen. Ambitious modern dishes arrive nicely presented.

Menu £ 28 (weekdays)/68 – Carte lunch £ 41/48

9 Market Sq ✉ HP7 0DF – ✆ (01494) 726 611 (booking essential at dinner) – www.artichokerestaurant.co.uk – Closed 2 weeks late August, 1 week Easter, Christmas-New Year, Sunday and Monday

X **Gilbey's**　　　　　🏡 🄰🄲 ⇔

BRITISH TRADITIONAL · COSY Long-standing neighbourhood restaurant located in a 17C former school and consisting of three rustic rooms and a delightful terrace. It's rooted in tradition, from the furnishings to the food; homemade jams feature at afternoon tea.

Menu £ 21 (lunch and early dinner) – Carte £ 32/56

1 Market Sq ✉ HP7 0DF – ✆ (01494) 727 242 (booking essential) – www.gilbeygroup.com – Closed 23-30 December

AMPLEFORTH – North Yorkshire ➔ See Helmsley

APPLEBY-IN-WESTMORLAND

Cumbria – Pop. 2 862 – Regional map n° **12**-B2
▶ London 285 mi – Carlisle 33 mi – Kendal 24 mi – Middlesbrough 58 mi

🏠 **Appleby Manor Country House**　　　　　🏡 🦌 ≼ ⇔ 🏠 🏦 🌱 🄰🄲 🅿

FAMILY · CLASSIC A family-run Victorian gentleman's residence with mature gardens and spacious, traditional guest areas. Bedrooms are in various extensions: those in the original house are the most characterful; 'Deluxe' have whirlpool baths and TVs in the bathrooms. The formal two-roomed restaurant offers classical menus, while the smart bistro serves lighter, pub-style dishes.

31 rooms ⊑ – ♦£ 80/130 ♦♦£ 99/240

Roman Rd ✉ CA16 6JB – East : 1 mi by B 6542 and Station Rd – ✆ (017683) 51 571 – www.applebymanor.co.uk – Closed Christmas

🏠 **Tufton Arms** 🍴 🕸 ♨ **P**

TRADITIONAL · STYLISH 16C coaching inn, in an old market town; a popular place for fishing and shooting parties. Guest areas include two traditional lounges and a bar; chic bedrooms are a complete contrast with their bold, contemporary furnishings. The classical, cane-furnished restaurant offers an easy-going menu.

22 rooms ⌑ – †£ 80/125 ††£ 140/220

Market Sq ⊠ CA16 6XA – ℰ (017683) 51 593 – www.tuftonarmshotel.co.uk
– Closed 24-27 December

ARKHOLME

Lancashire – Regional map n° **11**-A1
▶ London 254 mi – Birmingham 140 mi – Liverpool 71 mi – Leeds 99 mi

🍴 **Red Well Inn** 🖘 🥪 🛏 ♿ **P**

TRADITIONAL CUISINE · PUB An attractive 16C stone inn with a rustic bar and a slightly more formal dining room. The son cooks while his parents look after the service. There's something for everyone, from a homemade scotch egg with HP sauce to a lamb and lobster combo. Stylish modern bedrooms complete the picture.

Menu £ 18/25 – Carte £ 22/45

7 rooms – †£ 75/90 ††£ 90/100

Kirkby Lonsdale Rd ⊠ LA6 1BQ – Southwest : 3 mi on B 6254 – ℰ (015242) 21 240
(booking advisable) – www.redwellinn.net

ARLINGHAM

Gloucestershire – ⊠ Gloucester – Pop. 459 – Regional map n° **2**-C1
▶ London 120 mi – Birmingham 69 mi – Bristol 34 mi – Gloucester 16 mi

✕✕ **Old Passage Inn** 🖘 🥪 ◁ 🛏 ♿ **AC P**

FISH AND SEAFOOD · FRIENDLY Sit out on the terrace or beside the window, surrounded by colourful art, and watch the famous Severn bore travel up the estuary. Extensive seafood menus offer everything from a fish pie to a fruits de mer platter or lobster direct from their saltwater tank. Simply furnished modern bedrooms share the view.

Menu £ 15 (weekday lunch) – Carte £ 36/89

2 rooms ⌑ – †£ 70/130 ††£ 110/140

Passage Rd ⊠ GL2 7JR – West : 0.75 mi – ℰ (01452) 740 547
– www.theoldpassage.com – Closed 25-26 December, Sunday dinner and Monday
and dinner Tuesday-Wednesday January-February

ARMSCOTE

Warwickshire – Regional map n° **10**-C3
▶ London 98 mi – Birmingham 45 mi – Liverpool 139 mi – Leeds 145 mi

🍴 **Fuzzy Duck** 🖘 🥪 🛏 ♿ ♻ **P**

TRADITIONAL CUISINE · PUB Siblings Adrian and Tania – also owners of the Baylis and Harding toiletries company – have taken this place from a boarded up boozer to a modern, fashionably attired dining pub. Seasonal British dishes – including plenty of pub classics – show respect for the local ingredients. Stylish boutique bedrooms.

Menu £ 15 (weekday lunch) – Carte £ 20/45

4 rooms ⌑ – †£ 110/160 ††£ 110/160

Ilmington Rd ⊠ CV37 8DD – ℰ (01608) 682 635 (booking advisable)
– www.fuzzyduckarmscote.com – Closed 1 week January, Sunday dinner and
Monday

ARNSIDE

Cumbria – Pop. 2 334 – Regional map n° **12**-A3
▶ London 257 mi – Liverpool 74 mi – Manchester 69 mi – Bradford 97 mi

🏠 Number 43

TRADITIONAL · STYLISH Stylishly converted Victorian townhouse boasting superb views over the estuary and fells. Contemporary bedrooms have smart bathrooms, quality furnishings, good facilities and plenty of extras. The comfortable open-plan lounge and dining room offers light meat and cheese sharing platters in the evening. Start the day with breakfast on the glass-enclosed terrace.

6 rooms 🛏 – ♦£ 80/140 ♦♦£ 125/185

43 The Promenade ✉ LA5 0AA – ☎ (01524) 762 761 – www.no43.org.uk

ARUNDEL

West Sussex – Pop. 3 285 – Regional map n° **4**-C2

▶ London 58 mi – Brighton 21 mi – Southampton 41 mi – Worthing 9 mi

XX Town House 🔽

MODERN CUISINE · INDIVIDUAL Early 17C house displaying original sugar glass windows and an impressively ornate Renaissance ceiling with gilded walnut panelling, taken from a Medici palace in Florence. Smartly laid, intimate dining room. Confidently executed, tried-and-tested dishes with a classical base. Quirky, well-equipped bedrooms.

Menu £ 18/30

5 rooms 🛏 – ♦£ 75/105 ♦♦£ 105/140

65 High St ✉ BN18 9AJ – ☎ (01903) 883 847 – www.thetownhouse.co.uk
– Closed 2 weeks Easter, 2 weeks October, 25-26 December, 1-2 January, Sunday and Monday

at Burpham Northeast: 3 mi by A27 – ✉ Arundel

🍴 The George at Burpham

BRITISH MODERN · RUSTIC A local consortium headed by three local businessmen saved this pub from closure and it's since been given a smart new look, to which beams, fires and a smugglers' wheel add character. The seasonal menu is full of tasty, popular classics.

Carte £ 25/44

Main St ✉ BN18 9RR – ☎ (01903) 883 131 – www.georgeatburpham.co.uk – Closed 25 December

ASCOT

Windsor and Maidenhead – Pop. 15 761 – Regional map n° **6**-D3

▶ London 37 mi – Birmingham 119 mi – Liverpool 213 mi – Leeds 214 mi

🏰 Coworth Park

LUXURY · STYLISH 18C property set in 246 acres, with its own championship polo pitches and a superb spa with a living roof of herbs and flowers. Guest areas are stylish and contemporary. Beautiful bedrooms feature bespoke furniture, marble bathrooms and excellent facilities; those in main house are the largest.

70 rooms 🛏 – ♦£ 255/750 ♦♦£ 255/750 – 21 suites

London Rd ✉ SL5 7SE – East : 2.75 mi on A 329 – ☎ (01344) 876 600 – http://
www.dorchestercollection.com/en/ascot/coworth-park

Coworth Park • Barn – See restaurant listing

XxxX Coworth Park

MODERN CUISINE · ELEGANT Bright, elegant restaurant in a beautiful mansion house, with stylish tableware, an eye-catching centrepiece and a lovely terrace offering views over the manicured gardens. The cooking is accomplished and service is professional.

Menu £ 25 (weekday lunch)/85

Coworth Park Hotel, London Rd ✉ SL5 7SE – East : 2.75 mi on A 329 – ☎ (01344) 876 600 – http://www.dorchestercollection.com/en/ascot/coworth-park – Closed Sunday dinner and Monday

XX **Ascot Grill** 🔆 AC

MEATS · FASHIONABLE Neighbourhood restaurant with a slick, minimalistic interior featuring leather, silk and velvet; full-length windows open onto a pleasant pavement terrace. Wide-ranging modern grill menu offers steak and seafood. Good value lunches.

Menu £ 19 (lunch) – Carte £ 24/49

6 Hermitage Par, High St ⊠ SL5 7HE – 𝒞 (01344) 622 285 – www.ascotgrill.co.uk – Closed 25-26 December, first week January and Sunday

X **Barn** ⇐ 🔆 ⅄ AC P

BRITISH TRADITIONAL · DESIGN A buzzy, informal alternative to this 18C mansion's fine dining restaurant. The rustic room's floor-to-ceiling windows let in plenty of light and offer views over the fields. The menu features old favourites like steak and chips.

Menu £ 25 (weekday lunch)/45 – Carte £ 32/61

Coworth Park Hotel, London Rd ⊠ SL5 7SE – East : 2.75 mi on A 329 – 𝒞 (01344) 876 600 – http://www.dorchestercollection.com/en/ascot/coworth-park

ASENBY

North Yorkshire – Regional map n° **13**-B2

▶ London 220 mi – Harrogate 21 mi – York 28 mi

🏠 **Crab Manor** 🏡 �︎ ⌂ ⅀ ⅄ P

TOWNHOUSE · STYLISH Quirky, well-run hotel in extensive grounds. Stylish bedrooms are split between a Georgian manor house and Scandinavian log cabins, and are themed around famous hotels of the world; all have access to private or shared hot tubs.

17 rooms 🖙 – 🛉£ 160 🛉🛉£ 160/250 – 3 suites

Dishforth Rd ⊠ YO7 3QL – 𝒞 (01845) 577 286 – www.crabandlobster.co.uk

Crab and Lobster – See restaurant listing

🍴 **Crab and Lobster** �︎ 🔆 ⌂ ⟷ P

FISH AND SEAFOOD · PUB Charming thatched pub with a characterful, quirky interior packed full of memorabilia. The extensive menu features traditional British favourites and, satisfyingly, plenty of seafood dishes, from fish soup to whole lobster.

Menu £ 19 (lunch) – Carte £ 35/65

Crab Manor Hotel, Dishforth Rd ⊠ YO7 3QL – 𝒞 (01845) 577 286 – www.crabandlobster.com

 Follow our inspectors @MichelinGuideUK

ASHBOURNE

Derbyshire – Pop. 8 377 – Regional map n° **9**-A2

▶ London 141 mi – Birmingham 45 mi – Manchester 46 mi – Sheffield 52 mi

🏠 **Callow Hall** 🏡 🐾 ⇐ �︎ P

TRADITIONAL · PERSONALISED Traditional Victorian country house in 30 acres of gardens, fields and woodland. Individually styled bedrooms boast original features, spacious bathrooms, and traditional fabrics and furnishings. Seasonal menus showcase local produce in classically based dishes with the occasional modern touch.

16 rooms 🖙 – 🛉£ 110/145 🛉🛉£ 160/245 – 1 suite

Mapleton Rd ⊠ DE6 2AA – West : 0.75 mi by Union St (off Market Pl) – 𝒞 (01335) 300 900 – www.callowhall.co.uk

at Shirley Southeast: 5 mi by A515 and off A52

ENGLAND

🍴 Saracen's Head

BRITISH TRADITIONAL · RUSTIC A rustic, open-plan dining pub opposite the village church, in a remote, picturesque village. Menus are chalked on blackboards above the open fire and offer an eclectic mix of generously portioned pub and restaurant-style classics.

Carte £ 20/39

Church Ln ⊠ DE6 3AS – ℰ (01335) 360 330 – www.saracens-head-shirley.co.uk

ASHBURTON

Devon – Pop. 3 346 – Regional map n° **1**-C2

▶ London 192 mi – Birmingham 187 mi – Liverpool 269 mi – Leeds 299 mi

🏚 Agaric

TOWNHOUSE · STYLISH Friendly owners welcome you to this rustic guesthouse on the main street with its comfortable, simply furnished bedrooms. The single is decorated in a Chinese style, while the best is Havana with its four-poster bed and roll top bath.

4 rooms ⌂ – �£ 58/90 ♛♛£ 120/140

36 North St ⊠ TQ13 7QD – ℰ (01364) 654 478
– www.agaricrestaurant.co.uk/bed-and-breakfast – Closed Christmas

ASHENDON

Buckinghamshire - Regional map n° **6**-C2

▶ London 82 mi – Oxford 35 mi – Northampton 59 mi

🍴 The Hundred of Ashendon 🅝

REGIONAL · FRIENDLY In Saxon times, shires were divided into 'hundreds' for military and judicial purposes. This charming 17C inn keeps the concept alive by sourcing its produce from within its 'hundred'. Great value dishes arrive in hearty portions, packed full of flavour – and influences from Matt's time at St John are clear to see. Modest bedrooms are continually being upgraded.

Carte £ 24/36

5 rooms ⌂ – ♂£ 55/65 ♛♛£ 70/85

Lower End ⊠ HP18 0HE – ℰ (01296) 651 296 – www.thehundred.co.uk – Closed 25 December, Sunday dinner and Monday

ASHFORD

Kent – Pop. 67 528 – Regional map n° **5**-C2

▶ London 56 mi – Canterbury 14 mi – Dover 24 mi – Hastings 30 mi

🏰 Eastwell Manor

LUXURY · HISTORIC Impressive manor house with Tudor origins, surrounded by beautifully manicured gardens and extensive parkland. Rebuilt in 1926 following a fire but some superb plaster ceilings and stone fireplaces remain. Characterful guest areas and luxurious bedrooms. Sizeable spa and golf course. Choice of wood-panelled restaurant complete with pianist or more casual brasserie and terrace.

42 rooms ⌂ – ♂£ 150/470 ♛♛£ 150/470 – 22 suites

Eastwell Park, Boughton Lees ⊠ TN25 4HR – North : 3 mi by A 28 on A 251
– ℰ (01233) 213 000 – www.eastwellmanor.co.uk

ASHFORD-IN-THE-WATER

Derbyshire – Regional map n° **9**-A1

▶ London 164 mi – Birmingham 87 mi – Leeds 72 mi

🏠 Riverside House

TRADITIONAL · COSY Charming former hunting lodge with gardens running down to the river. Comfy, individually styled bedrooms are named after flowers and birds: one is a four-poster and some have French doors opening onto garden terraces. Classical dining takes place over four different rooms. It has a homely feel throughout.

14 rooms ☲ – ♦£ 120/155 ♦♦£ 145/195

Fennel St ⊠ DE45 1QF – ℰ (01629) 814 275 – www.riversidehousehotel.co.uk

🏠 River Cottage

TRADITIONAL · COSY Traditional stone cottage by the River Wye, with delightful gardens and two terraces. Bedrooms mix modern and antique furnishings and mattresses are handmade. Locally sourced ingredients and homemade preserves feature at breakfast.

4 rooms ☲ – ♦£ 89/115 ♦♦£ 95/125

Buxton Rd ⊠ DE45 1QP – ℰ (01629) 813 327 – www.rivercottageashford.co.uk – Closed December and January

ASHWATER

Devon – Regional map n° **1**-C2

▶ London 217 mi – Plymouth 36 mi – Torbay 62 mi – Exeter 42 mi

✕✕ Blagdon Manor

MODERN CUISINE · ROMANTIC Former farmhouse with delightful gardens; set in a peaceful rural location and proudly run by a husband and wife team. Comfortable restaurant with lovely countryside views and a large flagged terrace for summer dining. Unfussy, seasonal cooking; dishes are classically based with a modern touch. Immaculately kept, well-equipped bedrooms have stylish modern bathrooms.

Menu £ 20/40

6 rooms ☲ – ♦£ 95/110 ♦♦£ 155/260

⊠ EX21 5DF – Northwest : 2 mi by Holsworthy rd on Blagdon rd – ℰ (01409) 211 224 (booking essential) – www.blagdon.com – Closed 2 weeks January, Monday, Tuesday and lunch Wednesday

ASKHAM – Cumbria ➜ See Penrith

ASKRIGG

North Yorkshire – ⊠ Leyburn – Pop. 1 002 – Regional map n° **13**-A1

▶ London 251 mi – Kendal 32 mi – Leeds 70 mi – Newcastle upon Tyne 70 mi

🏠 Yorebridge House

TRADITIONAL · STYLISH Stylishly restored former school in a lovely Dales setting, with a snug bar and great country views from the lounge. Bold modern bedrooms are themed around the owner's travels; those in the annexe have riverside patios and hot tubs.

12 rooms ☲ – ♦£ 175/225 ♦♦£ 200/285 – 2 suites

Bainbridge ⊠ DL8 3EE – West : 1.25 mi – ℰ (01969) 652 060 – www.yorebridgehouse.com

Yorebridge House – See restaurant listing

🏠 Skeldale House

TOWNHOUSE · HISTORIC You might recognise the handsome façade from 'All Creatures Great and Small'. Many 1860s features remain – including an impressive staircase – and the bright, spacious bedrooms are in keeping, with their period furnishings and brass beds.

5 rooms ☲ – ♦£ 80/100 ♦♦£ 80/100

Market Pl ⊠ DL8 3HG – ℰ (01969) 650 746 – www.skeldalehouse.co.uk – Closed January and Christmas

ENGLAND

XX **Yorebridge House** ⓝ   🛏 🞲 **P**

BRITISH MODERN · **ROMANTIC** Romantic restaurant set within an old school-house and offering lovely countryside views. Concise menus evolve throughout the seasons and feature locally sourced produce; dishes are modern, well-flavoured and visually appealing.

Menu £ 55

Yorebridge House H., Bainbridge ✉ DL8 3EE – West : 1.25 mi
– 𝒞 (01969) 652 060 (bookings essential for non-residents)
– www.yorebridgehouse.com – dinner only

ASTON CANTLOW

Warwickshire – Pop. 1 843 – Regional map n° **10**-C3

▶ London 104 mi – Birmingham 30 mi – Leicester 46 mi – Coventry 22 mi

🍴 **King's Head**   🛏 🞲 **P**

MODERN CUISINE · **RUSTIC** Delightful black and white timbered inn in a picturesque village. Dine in the characterful beamed bar or chic country restaurant. Choose from pub favourites and British classics with some modern twists; local game is a feature.

Carte £ 20/39

21 Bearley Rd ✉ B95 6HY – 𝒞 (01789) 488 242
– www.thekh.co.uk

ASTON TIRROLD

Oxfordshire – Regional map n° **6**-B3

▶ London 58 mi – Reading 16 mi – Streatley 4 mi

🍴 **Sweet Olive at The Chequers Inn**   🕸 🞲 **P**

FRENCH · **PUB** A charming red-brick Victorian pub at the heart of the village: cosy, welcoming and popular with the locals. The Gallic owners offer a French-influenced menu of tasty, seasonal dishes and an interesting selection of fine wines.

Carte £ 33/46

Baker St ✉ OX11 9DD – 𝒞 (01235) 851 272 (booking essential)
– www.sweet-olive.com – Closed 3 weeks July, 2 weeks February, Sunday dinner and Wednesday

ATTLEBOROUGH

Norfolk – Pop. 10 549 – Regional map n° **8**-C2

▶ London 101 mi – Norwich 19 mi – Ipswich 42 mi – Peterborough 87 mi

X **Mulberry Tree**   🞲 **P**

MODERN CUISINE · **BRASSERIE** Contemporary bar-cum-restaurant in an imposing brick-built property, with a pleasant terrace and even a bowling green. The bar menu is popular at lunchtime, while the modern à la carte offers attractively presented, globally influenced dishes. Bedrooms are stylish and very comfortable.

Carte £ 23/36

7 rooms ⌂ – 🛉£ 80 🛉🛉£ 106

Station Rd ✉ NR17 2AS – 𝒞 (01953) 452 124 – www.the-mulberry-tree.co.uk
– Closed Christmas

AUSTWICK

North Yorkshire – Pop. 463 – Regional map n° **13**-A2

▶ London 259 mi – Kendal 28 mi – Lancaster 20 mi – Leeds 46 mi

⌂ Traddock

TRADITIONAL · PERSONALISED Unusually named after a horse trading paddock; a Georgian country house with Victorian additions – once a private residence. Traditional interior with bright, airy lounges. Bedrooms boast feature beds, rural views and roll-top baths. Formal dining room serves local produce in modern versions of old classics.

12 rooms ⌑ – †£ 85/125 ††£ 95/215

✉ LA2 8BY – ☏ (015242) 51 224
– www.thetraddock.co.uk

⌂ Austwick Hall

TRADITIONAL · PERSONALISED Characterful house in a delightful village on the edge of the dales, surrounded by tiered gardens and woodland. Spacious, antique-furnished bedrooms; the Blue Room has a roll-top bath which offers views down the garden. Nothing is too much trouble for the friendly owners. Tea is served on arrival.

4 rooms ⌑ – †£ 110/140 ††£ 125/155

✉ LA2 8BS – ☏ (015242) 51 794
– www.austwickhall.co.uk

⌂ Wood View

TRADITIONAL · COSY 18C stone farmhouse by the village green, with an open-fired lounge and a cosy, low-ceilinged breakfast room with exposed beams. Simple, well-kept bedrooms have a mix of furnishings. There's even a bike store out back for cyclists.

5 rooms ⌑ – †£ 48/65 ††£ 78/86

The Green ✉ LA2 8BB – ☏ (015242) 51 190
– www.woodviewbandb.com – Restricted opening in winter

AXMINSTER

Devon – Pop. 5 761 – Regional map n° **1**-D2
▶ London 156 mi – Exeter 27 mi – Lyme Regis 5 mi – Taunton 22 mi

✗ River Cottage Canteen

REGIONAL · RUSTIC Busy restaurant, deli and coffee shop owned by Hugh Fearnley-Whittingstall. Simple, industrial-style room with mismatched furniture. Blackboards change twice-daily, offering gutsy, flavoursome country cooking and showcasing local produce.

Carte £ 19/30

Trinity Sq ✉ EX13 5AN – ☏ (01297) 631 715
– www.rivercottage.net/axminster – Closed 25-26 December, dinner Sunday, Monday and Tuesday-Wednesday October-April

AYLESBURY

Buckinghamshire – Pop. 71 977 – Regional map n° **6**-C2
▶ London 46 mi – Birmingham 72 mi – Northampton 37 mi – Oxford 22 mi

⌂ Hartwell House

HISTORIC · CLASSIC An impressive palatial house set in 90 acres of parkland: the erstwhile residence of Louis XVIII, exiled King of France, and now owned by the National Trust. It boasts ornate furnishings, luxurious lounges, an intimate spa and magnificent antique-filled bedrooms. The formal restaurant offers traditional country house cooking and afternoon tea is a speciality.

46 rooms ⌑ – †£ 175/250 ††£ 270/700 – 10 suites

Oxford Rd ✉ HP17 8NR – Southwest : 2 mi on A 418
– ☏ (01296) 747 444 – www.hartwell-house.com

AYLESFORD

Kent – Regional map n° **5**-B1

▶ London 37 mi – Maidstone 3 mi – Royal Tunbridge Wells 19 mi

XxX **Hengist**   ⌂ AC ▱

BRITISH MODERN · FASHIONABLE Pass through the rustic ground floor of this characterful 16C timbered house and head up to the boldly decorated dining rooms. Good-sized menus offer ambitious modern British dishes. In summer, sit on the terrace beside the stream.

Menu £ 15 (weekday lunch) – Carte £ 29/46

7-9 High St ✉ ME20 7AX – ℰ (01622) 885 800 – www.hengistrestaurant.co.uk – Closed 26 December, Sunday dinner and Monday

AYLSHAM

Norfolk – Pop. 6 016 – Regional map n° **8**-D1

▶ London 128 mi – Norwich 13 mi – Ipswich 57 mi – Stevenage 105 mi

🏠 **Old Pump House**   ⇔ 🅿 ▱

FAMILY · PERSONALISED This tastefully furnished Georgian house is named after the old village water pump which stands in the square outside. Spacious bedrooms have period furnishings and the open-plan lounge and breakfast room overlooks the lovely garden.

5 rooms ⌂ – ♦£ 85/100 ♦♦£ 100/125

2 Holman Rd ✉ NR11 6BY – ℰ (01263) 733 789 – www.theoldpumphouse.com – Closed Christmas

AYNHO

Northamptonshire – Pop. 651 – Regional map n° **9**-B3

▶ London 73 mi – Birmingham 66 mi – Northampton 30 mi

🏠 **Cartwright**   ✿ 🅿 🛆 🅿

BUSINESS · FUNCTIONAL Cotswold stone coaching inn dating back to the 16C. Spacious modern bedrooms are split between the main house and the courtyard; the former are more characterful, with some timbered ceilings and original fireplaces. The brasserie serves a traditional menu; the grills and cheeseboard are popular.

21 rooms ⌂ – ♦£ 120/160 ♦♦£ 130/170

1-5 Croughton Rd ✉ OX17 3BE – ℰ (01869) 811 885 – www.oxfordshire-hotels.co.uk

AYOT GREEN – Hertfordshire ➜ See Welwyn

BABBACOMBE – Torbay ➜ See Torquay

BAGSHOT

Surrey – Pop. 5 430 – Regional map n° **4**-C1

▶ London 37 mi – Reading 17 mi – Southampton 49 mi

🏨 **Pennyhill Park**   ✿ 🏊 ⟨ ⇔ 🅿 ⛲ 🔲 ⊕ 🛁 ✗ 🛆 🅿

LUXURY · CLASSIC Impressive 19C manor house in 123 acres, boasting one of Europe's best spas. Both the guest areas and bedrooms are spacious, with period furnishings and modern touches; feature bathrooms come with rain showers or glass baths. Dine in the elegant restaurant or the stylish brasserie which opens onto the garden.

123 rooms – ♦£ 225/405 ♦♦£ 225/405 – ⌂ £ 21 – 11 suites

London Rd ✉ GU19 5EU – Southwest : 1 mi on A 30 – ℰ (01276) 471 774 – www.exclusivehotels.co.uk

❀❀ **Michael Wignall at The Latymer** – See restaurant listing

ENGLAND

XxXX Michael Wignall at The Latymer

❀❀ **CREATIVE · FORMAL** Elegant hotel dining room with oak-clad walls, a glass-enclosed chef's table and top quality place settings. Precise, confident cooking uses only the best ingredients. Flavours are clearly defined yet have a delicate edge and innovative combinations marry seamlessly. Fri and Sat they only serve tasting menus.

➜ Langoustine ceviche with crab, pickled mouli, scallop taramasalata and avocado. Milk-fed lamb, braised tongue, aged balsamic and potato hash. Treacle and star anise scented salsify with buckwheat cream and biscuit, calamansi and yuzu.

Menu £ 39/91

Pennyhill Park Hotel, London Rd ⊠ GU19 5EU – Southwest : 1 mi on A30
– ☎ (01276) 486 156 (booking essential) – www.exclusivehotels.co.uk – Closed
1-21 January, Sunday, Monday, lunch Tuesday and Saturday

BALLASALLA ➜ See Man (Isle of)

BAMBURGH

Northumberland – Pop. 279 – Regional map n° **14**-B1

▶ London 337 mi – Edinburgh 77 mi – Newcastle upon Tyne 51 mi

⌂ Lord Crewe Arms

INN · COSY Smart 17C former coaching inn, privately owned and superbly set in the shadow of a famous Norman castle. Comfy, cosy bedrooms have a modern feel, yet are in keeping with the age of the building. Characterful stone-walled bar and New England style restaurant serve brasserie dishes. Efficient service.

9 rooms ⌷ – ∯£ 98/135 ∯∯£ 98/135

Front St ⊠ NE69 7BL – ☎ (01668) 214 243 – www.lord-crewe.co.uk – Closed
25 December

at Waren Mill West: 2.75 mi on B1342⊠ Belford

⌂⌂ Waren House

FAMILY · CLASSIC Personally run, antique-furnished country house set in beautiful, tranquil gardens. Bedrooms – some named after the owners' family members – mix classic and modern styles: some have four-posters and coastal views. Formal dining room boasts an ornate ceiling; traditional menus showcase local ingredients.

15 rooms ⌷ – ∯£ 85/115 ∯∯£ 110/160 – 2 suites

⊠ NE70 7EE – ☎ (01668) 214 581 – www.warenhousehotel.co.uk

BAMPTON

Devon – Pop. 1 260 – Regional map n° **1**-D1

▶ London 189 mi – Exeter 18 mi – Minehead 21 mi – Taunton 15 mi

⌂ Swan

BRITISH TRADITIONAL · INN Laid-back, modernised, open-plan pub whose history can be traced back to 1450, when it provided accommodation for craftsmen working on the local church. Unfussy pub dishes arrive neatly presented on wooden boards and showcase local produce. Smart, modern bedrooms are found on the 2nd floor.

Carte £ 20/31

3 rooms ⌷ – ∯£ 80/90 ∯∯£ 85/95

Station Rd ⊠ EX16 9NG – ☎ (01398) 332 248 – www.theswan.co – Closed
25 December

BARNARD CASTLE

Durham – Pop. 7 040 – Regional map n° **14**-A3

▶ London 258 mi – Carlisle 63 mi – Leeds 68 mi – Middlesbrough 31 mi

Homelands

TOWNHOUSE · CLASSIC Victorian terraced house just a short drive from Raby Castle. Pastel-coloured lounge filled with books and photos. Compact, individually furnished bedrooms; the largest and most peaceful is at the end of the long mature garden. Simple, home-cooked dinners of local produce, by arrangement.

5 rooms ⊊ – †£ 50/55 ††£ 80/90

85 Galgate ⊠ DL12 8ES – ℰ (01833) 638 757 – www.homelandsguesthouse.co.uk

at Greta Bridge Southeast: 4.5 mi off A66 – ⊠ Barnard Castle

Morritt

INN · PERSONALISED Attractive 19C inn on the site of an old Roman fort. The characterful interior cleverly blends the old and the new, with lovely parquet floors, antiques and feature bedsteads, offset by contemporary décor. Superb spa with a car garage theme. All-day snacks in the bar-bistro; modern menu in the restaurant.

26 rooms ⊊ – †£ 85/179 ††£ 100/179 – 1 suite

⊠ *DL12 9SE – ℰ (01833) 627 232 – www.themorritt.co.uk*

Gilroy's – See restaurant listing

XX Gilroy's

MODERN CUISINE · CLASSIC Smart hotel dining room with a lovely parquet floor, wood-panelling and bold splashes of colour here and there. Dishes are modern, attractively presented and employ some complex techniques. Start with a drink by the fire in the cosy lounge.

Menu £ 39

Morritt Hotel, ⊠ DL12 9SE – ℰ (01833) 627 232 – www.themorritt.co.uk – dinner only

at Hutton Magna Southeast: 7.25 mi by A66

⌂ Oak Tree Inn

BRITISH TRADITIONAL · COSY Small but charming whitewashed pub with six tables flanked by green settles and a bench table for drinkers. It's run by a husband and wife team; he cooks, while she serves. Cooking is hearty and flavoursome with a rustic British style.

Carte £ 32/44

⊠ *DL11 7HH – ℰ (01833) 627 371 (booking essential)*
– www.theoaktreehutton.co.uk – dinner only – Closed 24-27 and 31 December, 1 January and Monday

at Romaldkirk Northwest: 6 mi by A67 on B6277 – ⊠ Barnard Castle

⌂ Rose and Crown

BRITISH TRADITIONAL · INN Delightful Georgian inn overlooking three village greens, with a wonderfully characterful bar and a smart wood-panelled dining room. Menus focus on British pub classics and showcase local, seasonal produce. Well-equipped bedrooms are spread between the main building, the courtyard and the "Monk's House".

Carte £ 24/42 **s**

14 rooms ⊊ – †£ 100/150 ††£ 130/180

⊠ *DL12 9EB – ℰ (01833) 650 213 – www.rose-and-crown.co.uk – Closed Christmas*

BARNSLEY – Gloucestershire → See Cirencester

BARRASFORD

Northumberland – Regional map n° **14**-A2

▶ London 309 mi – Newcastle upon Tyne 29 mi – Sunderland 42 mi – Middlesbrough 66 mi

🍴 **Barrasford Arms** ⇔ 🍴 🛋 **P**

BRITISH TRADITIONAL · PUB Personally run 19C stone inn, close to Kielder Water and Hadrian's Wall. It has a traditional, homely atmosphere, with cosy fires and regular competitions for the locals. Pub classics are served at lunch, followed by more refined dishes at dinner. Bedrooms are comfortable and sensibly priced.

Menu £13 (weekday lunch)/28 – Carte £24/32

7 rooms � – ∔£67 ∔∔£87

✉ NE48 4AA – ℰ (01434) 681 237 – www.barrasfordarms.co.uk
– Closed 25-26 December, Sunday dinner, Monday lunch and bank holidays

BARSTON

West Midlands – Regional map n° **10**-C2

▶ London 110 mi – Birmingham 17 mi – Coventry 11 mi

🍴 **Malt Shovel** 🍴 🛋 & 🎬 **P**

TRADITIONAL CUISINE · FRIENDLY The Mediterranean colour scheme gives a sunny feel all year round; an impression enhanced by the cheery, long-serving staff. The menu offers plenty of pub classics but the Malt Shovel is also well known for its fish.

Carte £25/38

Barston Lane ✉ B92 0JP – West : 0.75 mi – ℰ (01675) 443 223
– www.themaltshovelatbarston.com – Closed Sunday dinner

BARTON-ON-SEA

Hampshire – Regional map n° **4**-A3

▶ London 108 mi – Bournemouth 11 mi – Southampton 24 mi – Winchester 35 mi

XX **Pebble Beach** ⇔ < 🛋 & 🎬 **P**

FISH AND SEAFOOD · BRASSERIE Head straight for the terrace of this large split-level restaurant to be rewarded with impressive views over the Solent to the Isle of Wight. Inside, the open kitchen takes pride of place and the fish tank gives a clue as to the menu. Good-sized bedrooms are smart and well-kept; the Penthouse has great views.

Carte £29/65

4 rooms ⊆ – ∔£56/196 ∔∔£90/350

Marine Dr ✉ BH25 7DZ – ℰ (01425) 627 777 – www.pebblebeach-uk.com

BARWICK – Somerset → See Yeovil

BASLOW

Derbyshire – ✉ Bakewell – Pop. 1 178 – Regional map n° **9**-A1

▶ London 158 mi – Birmingham 70 mi – Manchester 35 mi – Sheffield 14 mi

🏨 **Cavendish** ⚑ < 🛋 🍸 🕸 🔱 **P**

TRADITIONAL · PERSONALISED Elegant hotel on the Chatsworth Estate, boasting lovely parkland views. Bedrooms have a contemporary country house style and some of the furniture and paintings are from nearby Chatsworth House. The Garden Room offers an extensive menu along with afternoon teas; the formal restaurant serves classic fare.

24 rooms – ∔£155/185 ∔∔£205/235 – ⊆£20 – 1 suite

Church Ln ✉ DE45 1SP – on A 619 – ℰ (01246) 582 311 – www.cavendish-hotel.net
The Gallery – See restaurant listing

🏡 **Heathy Lea** ❶ < 🛋 🕸 **P** ⇥

COUNTRY HOUSE · HOMELY 17C farmhouse owned by the Chatsworth Estate – which has access to the grounds through its garden gate. Cosy, comfortable bedrooms have views over the farmland. The estate farm shop provides much of the produce used at breakfast.

3 rooms ⊆ – ∔£55/75 ∔∔£80/110

✉ DE45 1PQ – East : 0.75 mi on A 619 – ℰ (01246) 583 842
– www.heathylea.co.uk – Closed Christmas

XXX Fischer's at Baslow Hall

MODERN CUISINE · ELEGANT A fine Edwardian manor house with a country house feel, impressive formal grounds and a walled vegetable garden. The two dining rooms, with their ornate ceilings, offer a mix of classic and original modern dishes, prepared using skilful techniques; sit at the 'Kitchen Tasting Bench' to be part of the action. Bedrooms are charming – the garden rooms are the largest.

→ Grapefruit cured salmon and scallops with wasabi pearls and ice lettuce. Sirloin and smoked short-rib of Derbyshire beef with grilled Wye Valley asparagus. Chocolate tree trunk with lime sorbet and mint moss.

Menu £ 21 (weekday lunch)/72

11 rooms ⊡ – †£ 100/145 ††£ 150/270 – 1 suite

Calver Rd ⊠ *DE45 1RR – on A 623 – ℰ (01246) 583 259 (booking essential)*
– www.fischers-baslowhall.co.uk – Closed 25-26 and 31 December

XXX The Gallery

BRITISH MODERN · FORMAL Striking restaurant in an elegant hotel, which features a stylish mix of contemporary décor and antique furnishings. Dishes have a traditional base but techniques and presentation are modern. Service is detailed yet personable.

Menu £ 50

Cavendish Hotel, Church Ln ⊠ *DE45 1SP – on A 619 – ℰ (01246) 582 311*
– www.cavendish-hotel.net

X Rowley's

TRADITIONAL CUISINE · BRASSERIE Stone-built former blacksmith's; now a contemporary bar-restaurant with a small terrace and friendly service. Dine in the buzzy ground floor bar or more intimate upstairs rooms. Hearty, satisfying dishes have classic French roots.

Menu £ 20 (weekdays)/28 – Carte £ 28/40

Church St ⊠ *DE45 1RY – ℰ (01246) 583 880 (booking advisable)*
– www.rowleysrestaurant.co.uk – Closed 25 December, Sunday dinner and Monday

BASSENTHWAITE

Cumbria – Pop. 433 – Regional map n° **12**-A2

▶ London 300 mi – Carlisle 24 mi – Keswick 7 mi

🏠 Pheasant

INN · CLASSIC Characterful 16C coaching inn with comfy lounges and welcoming open fires. Bedrooms are spacious and retain a classic look appropriate to the building's age; some have lovely country outlooks. Have drinks amongst polished brass in the bar then make for the rustic oak-furnished bistro or more formal restaurant.

15 rooms ⊡ – †£ 95/120 ††£ 120/190

⊠ *CA13 9YE – Southwest : 3.25 mi by B 5291 on Wythop Mill Rd*
– ℰ (017687) 76 234 – www.the-pheasant.co.uk
– Closed 25 December

🏠 Overwater Hall

TRADITIONAL · CLASSIC Castellated Georgian manor house built in 1811, set in 18 acres of mature gardens. Three good-sized lounges, one with a bar. Large, boldly patterned bedrooms come with rich fabrics, homemade fruit liqueurs and spacious, good quality bathrooms. Formal dining room offers a traditional country house menu.

11 rooms ⊡ – †£ 120/140 ††£ 140/180

⊠ *CA7 1HH – Northeast : 2.5 mi by A 591, Uldale rd on Overwater rd*
– ℰ (017687) 76 566 – www.overwaterhall.co.uk
– Closed 2-16 January

X **Bistro at the Distillery**

BRITISH MODERN · BISTRO Smart modern bistro in a former cattle shed; the other farm buildings now house a shop and a working gin, vodka and whisky distillery. Extensive lunches are followed by afternoon teas, with more ambitious dishes appearing at dinner.

Menu £ 19 (lunch) – Carte £ 20/43

Bassenthwaite Lake ⊠ CA13 9SJ – West : 2.75 mi by A 591 on B 5291
– ℰ (01768) 788 852 (booking advisable) – www.bistroatthedistillery.com

BATCOMBE

Somerset – ⊠ Shepton Mallet – Pop. 439 – Regional map n° **2**-C2
▶ London 130 mi – Bournemouth 50 mi – Bristol 24 mi – Salisbury 40 mi

🍴 **Three Horseshoes Inn**

BRITISH TRADITIONAL · RUSTIC Enthusiastically run former blacksmith's workshop, hidden in a small hamlet off the beaten track, with a characterful beamed interior and a large inglenook fireplace. Menus cover all bases from pork pies and pub classics to more sophisticated dishes. Excellent cheeses. Comfortable, simply furnished bedrooms.

Carte £ 19/34

3 rooms ⌂ – ♦£ 60/75 ♦♦£ 70/85

⊠ BA4 6HE – ℰ (01749) 850 359 – www.thethreehorseshoesinn.com
– Closed 25 December

GOOD TIPS!

Known for its Georgian architecture and its Roman Baths, this city is one in which to relax and rejuvenate, so keep a look out for the spa symbol when choosing a hotel. Locally produced Bath Buns are the star of the show at afternoon tea in The Royal Crescent Hotel, in the centre of the famous terrace designed by John Wood the Younger.

BATH

Bath and North East Somerset – Pop. 94 782 – Regional map n° **2**-C2
▶ London 119 mi – Bristol 13 mi – Southampton 63 mi – Taunton 49 mi

Hotels

🏠🏠🏠 **Royal Crescent**

HISTORIC · ELEGANT Smartly refurbished, Grade I listed building at the centre of the famous sweeping terrace. Ornate plasterwork, pastel shades and gilt-framed portraits evoke feelings of the Georgian era. Wood and stone feature in the lovely spa.
45 rooms ☑ – †£ 230/495 ††£ 230/495 – 12 suites
Town plan: AV-a – *16 Royal Cres* ⊠ *BA1 2LS* – ☎ *(01225) 823 333*
– *www.royalcrescent.co.uk*
Dower House – See restaurant listing

🏠🏠🏠 **Bath Spa**

PALACE · PERSONALISED Charming Georgian mansion in landscaped gardens, with characterful period lounges and an excellent spa. Bedrooms are spacious and some have four-posters; the suites come with 24-hour butler service. The formal restaurant features impressive Corinthian columns, while the lounge-bar offers all-day dining.
129 rooms ☑ – †£ 149/320 ††£ 165/360 – 11 suites
Town plan: Y-z – *Sydney Rd* ⊠ *BA2 6JF* – ☎ *(01225) 444 424*
– *www.macdonaldhotels.co.uk/bathspa*

🏠🏠🏠 **Bath Priory**

COUNTRY HOUSE · STYLISH Charming Georgian and Victorian property in a smart residential area near Royal Victoria Park. It has a comfy country house feel, with an array of elegant, antique-filled guest areas and luxurious bedrooms which blend the traditional with the modern. A chic spa and excellent service complete the picture.
33 rooms – †£ 170/730 ††£ 170/730 – ☑ £ 25 – 6 suites
Town plan: Y-c – *Weston Rd* ⊠ *BA1 2XT* – ☎ *(01225) 331 922*
– *www.thebathpriory.co.uk*
❀ **Bath Priory** – See restaurant listing

291

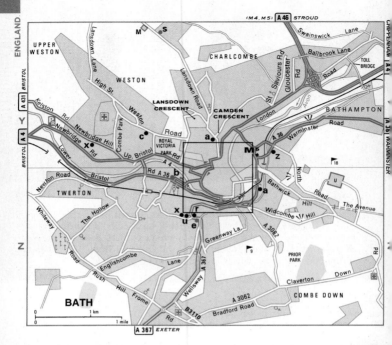

BATH

🏨 Homewood Park

🍴 🛏 🛋 ⑳ ⚡ 🅿

COUNTRY HOUSE · STYLISH 18C country house with mature gardens, a fashionable interior and a superb spa and beauty facility. Charming guest areas – many boasting open fires – have a modern country house feel; bedrooms are contemporary and have bold colour schemes. The stylish dining room serves a menu of modern classics.

21 rooms ⌛ – ♦£ 125/290 ♦♦£ 125/290 – 2 suites

Abbey Ln, Hinton Charterhouse ⊠ BA2 7TB – Southeast : 7.5 mi on A 36 – ℰ (01225) 723 731 – www.homewoodpark.co.uk

---

🏨 Queensberry

🍴 🔁 🐾 🅿

TOWNHOUSE · STYLISH A series of Georgian townhouses in one of the oldest parts of the city, run by a friendly, well-versed team. Guest areas include a charming wood-panelled lounge and a chic bar with an extensive array of unusual spirits. Funky, individually designed bedrooms have smart designer touches and a host of extras.

29 rooms – ♦£ 99/420 ♦♦£ 99/420 – ⌛£ 18

Town plan: AV-x – *Russel St ⊠ BA1 2QF – ℰ (01225) 447 928 – www.thequeensberry.co.uk*

Olive Tree – See restaurant listing

🏨 Francis

🍴 🔁 ♿ 🆎 🐾 🎣

TOWNHOUSE · HISTORIC Seven Grade I listed townhouses built between 1728 and 1736 by John Wood the Elder, overlooking the picturesque Queen Square. Contemporary interior with boldly coloured furnishings and a funky boutique style. Buzzy, brightly furnished restaurant; the lengthy menu offers satisfying French brasserie classics.

98 rooms – ♦£ 129/245 ♦♦£ 149/280 – ⌛£ 20

Town plan: AV-c – *Queen Sq ⊠ BA1 2HH – ℰ (01225) 424 105 – www.francishotel.com*

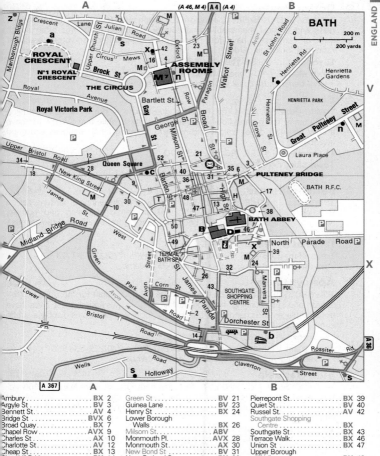

ENGLAND

BATH

🏠 Dukes

TOWNHOUSE · CLASSIC Two Grade I listed Palladian-style townhouses, built in 1789, with a friendly, informal feel. Bedrooms are named after famous Dukes and have period themes. If you've skipped dinner, they offer a late night cheese-board and port.

17 rooms 🛏 – 🛏£ 90/165 🛏🛏£ 90/165 – 4 suites

Town plan: BV-n – *Great Pulteney St* ✉ *BA2 4DN* – ✆ *(01225) 787 960*
– *www.dukesbath.co.uk* – *Closed 21-30 December*

Is breakfast included? If it is, the cup symbol 🛏 appears after the number of rooms.

⌂ Dorian House

TOWNHOUSE · MODERN Charming 19C townhouse featuring original stained glass and musical memorabilia. Individually decorated bedrooms offer a high level of comfort; 4 have four-posters. The delightful conservatory breakfast room overlooks the garden.

13 rooms ♨ – †£ 95 ††£ 109/175

Town plan: Z-u – *1 Upper Oldfield Pk* ✉ *BA2 3JX* – ✆ *(01225) 426 336*
– *www.dorianhouse.co.uk* – *Closed 24-25 December*

⌂ Grays

TOWNHOUSE · STYLISH This boutique guesthouse is run by a very hands-on family team. The ground floor bedrooms are largest, while those at the top have a cosy feel. The décor is light and modern, featuring family antiques and good attention to detail.

12 rooms ♨ – †£ 85/180 ††£ 105/200

Town plan: Z-x – *9 Upper Oldfield Pk* ✉ *BA2 3JX* – ✆ *(01225) 403 020*
– *www.graysbath.co.uk* – *Closed 24-26 December*

⌂ Paradise House

TOWNHOUSE · HOMELY Elegant 18C house with award-winning gardens, set on Beechen Cliff, overlooking the city. The interior is charming and homely, with a cosy, classical lounge and bedrooms ranging from traditional four-posters to more modern styles.

12 rooms ♨ – †£ 120/185 ††£ 120/185

Town plan: AX-s – *86-88 Holloway* ✉ *BA2 4PX* – ✆ *(01225) 317 723*
– *www.paradise-house.co.uk* – *Closed 24-25 December*

⌂ Apsley House

TOWNHOUSE · PERSONALISED Substantial 18C house built for the Duke of Wellington and still retaining many grand features. High-ceilinged guest areas have large fireplaces and chandeliers. Luxuriously appointed bedrooms display a subtle contemporary style.

12 rooms ♨ – †£ 90/180 ††£ 99/240

Town plan: Y-x – *141 Newbridge Hill* ✉ *BA1 3PT* – ✆ *(01225) 336 966*
– *www.apsley-house.co.uk* – *Closed 24-26 December*

⌂ Villa Magdala

TOWNHOUSE · CONTEMPORARY Victorian house named after Napier's 1868 victory, in an attractive residential area, overlooking a park. Smart, modern interior with two impressive staircases. Stylish, airy bedrooms have shuttered windows and feature wallpapers.

20 rooms ♨ – †£ 110/195 ††£ 110/195

Town plan: BV-r – *Henrietta Rd* ✉ *BA2 6LX* – ✆ *(01225) 466 329*
– *www.villamagdala.co.uk* – *Closed 1 week Christmas*

⌂ One Three Nine

LUXURY · MODERN Detached Victorian house within walking distance of the city centre. A contemporary black and white sitting room and chic breakfast room set the tone. Sizeable bedrooms are equally stylish; some have four-poster beds and spa baths.

10 rooms ♨ – †£ 110/180 ††£ 110/195

Town plan: Z-r – *139 Wells Rd* ✉ *BA2 3AL* – ✆ *(01225) 314 769*
– *www.139bath.co.uk* – *Closed 24-25 December*

⌂ Brindleys

TOWNHOUSE · DESIGN Victorian house tucked away in a residential street and concealing a surprisingly chic interior. Cosy lounge and neatly laid breakfast room. Tastefully decorated bedrooms in colour themes ranging from lavender to monochrome.

6 rooms ♨ – †£ 95/170 ††£ 115/190

Town plan: Z-a – *14 Pulteney Gdns* ✉ *BA2 4HG* – ✆ *(01225) 310 444*
– *www.brindleysbath.co.uk* – *Closed 24-26 December*

Hill House

TOWNHOUSE · PERSONALISED A former hotel, pub and wine merchant's, this Georgian townhouse retains much of its original character, but with all the comfort expected by the modern traveller. Good-sized, contemporary bedrooms; those at the rear have city views.

6 rooms ⌕ – ♦£ 80/115 ♦♦£ 105/145

Town plan: Y-a – *25 Belvedere* ✉ *BA1 5ED* – ℰ *(01225) 920 520*
– *www.hillhousebath.co.uk*

Restaurants

XхX Bath Priory

MODERN CUISINE · FORMAL Elegant hotel restaurant made up of several areas: a smart cocktail bar; an airy dining room overlooking the gardens; and a contemporary orangery and terrace. Cooking is refined and accomplished, delivering robust flavours in interesting, classically based dishes. A superb wine list accompanies.

→ Seared scallops with St George's mushrooms, apple and hazelnuts. Plate of local pig cheek, shoulder and belly with cheese mash, spring onions and paprika jus. Salted caramel fondant with butterscotch and banana sorbet.

Menu £ 28/80

Town plan: Y-c – *Bath Priory Hotel, Weston Rd* ✉ *BA1 2XT* – ℰ *(01225) 331 922*
– *www.thebathpriory.co.uk*

XхX Dower House

MODERN CUISINE · ELEGANT Across the garden of a smart hotel is this elegant restaurant with gold and blue hues and a feature wall of hand-stitched silk. Dishes are modern and very visual; desserts are a highlight. 'Wine walls' display their finest bottles.

Menu £ 40 – Carte £ 54/60

Town plan: AV-a – *Royal Crescent Hotel, 16 Royal Cres* ✉ *BA1 2LS* – ℰ *(01225) 823 333* – *www.royalcrescent.co.uk* – *dinner only*

XX Olive Tree

MODERN CUISINE · INTIMATE A stylish, well-run restaurant in the basement of a boutique hotel, with a small bar and three dining rooms – all on different levels. Refined, classic dishes are created using fine ingredients and delivered in a modern style.

Carte £ 37/51

Town plan: AV-x – *Queensberry Hotel, Russel St* ✉ *BA1 2QF* – ℰ *(01225) 447 928* – *www.olivetreebath.co.uk* – *dinner only and lunch Friday-Sunday*

XX Allium Brasserie

MODERN CUISINE · BRASSERIE A distinctly modern hotel restaurant, close to the river in the city centre. Confident, well-presented brasserie cooking is skilful and ambitious, with influences ranging from Britain to Asia and the Med. Dine alfresco in the summer.

Menu £ 18 (lunch and early dinner) – Carte £ 32/48

Town plan: BX-x – *Abbey Hotel, 1 North Par* ✉ *BA1 1LF* – ℰ *(01225) 461 603* *(booking advisable)* – *www.abbeyhotelbath.co.uk*

XX Menu Gordon Jones

MODERN CUISINE · SIMPLE Tiny restaurant comprising 8 tables and an open kitchen. Daily tasting menus showcase some unusual British ingredients such as beef tendons or rabbit kidneys. Complex modern dishes have interesting texture and flavour combinations.

Menu £ 40/60 – *set menu only*

Town plan: Z-e – *2 Wellsway* ✉ *BA2 3AQ* – ℰ *(01225) 480 871 (booking essential at dinner)* – *www.menugordonjones.co.uk* – *Closed 2 weeks July, 2 weeks Christmas-New Year, Sunday and Monday*

XX Mint Room

INDIAN · DESIGN Smart, spacious Indian restaurant with a distinctly modern, glitzy style. The experienced chef offers an impressive collection of appealing, well-presented dishes which display original and contemporary twists. Knowledgeable service.

Carte £ 23/32

Town plan: Z-b – *Lower Bristol Rd* ✉ *BA2 3EB* – ℰ *(01225) 446 656*
– *www.themintroom.co.uk*

X Graze

MEATS · BRASSERIE Buzzy, modern, industrial-style restaurant next to Bath Spa Station, in the Vaults development; its terrace is a must for railway enthusiasts. The grill menu features steak cooked in the Josper oven. Superb ales from their own brewery.

Menu £ 10 (weekday lunch) – Carte £ 22/40

Town plan: BX-b – *Unit 5, 9 Brunel Sq* ✉ *BA1 1SX* – ℰ *(01225) 429 392*
– *www.bathales.com* – *Closed 25 December*

X Casanis

FRENCH CLASSIC · NEIGHBOURHOOD Sweet Gallic bistro tucked away in the shadow of the Assembly Rooms; run by a French chef and his charming wife. Small, cosy interior and lovely rear courtyard. Authentic, tasty cooking with a focus on classics from the south west.

Menu £ 18 (weekdays) – Carte £ 26/41

Town plan: A/BV-n – *4 Saville Row* ✉ *BA1 2QP* – ℰ *(01225) 780 055 (booking essential)* – *www.casanis.co.uk* – *Closed 2 weeks January, 1 week July-August, 25-26 December, Sunday and Monday*

Marlborough Tavern

BRITISH TRADITIONAL · NEIGHBOURHOOD 18C pub on the edge of Victoria Park, close to the Royal Crescent. Chic, fashionable interior with boldly patterned wallpapers and contemporary art. Carefully sourced ingredients feature in pub classics and interesting specials.

Carte £ 22/42

Town plan: AV-z – *35 Marlborough Buildings* ✉ *BA1 2LY* – ℰ *(01225) 423 731*
– *www.marlborough-tavern.com* – *Closed 25 December*

Chequers

TRADITIONAL CUISINE · NEIGHBOURHOOD Set in a smart residential street amid elegant Georgian terraces, with a simply furnished bar and a cosy dining room. Cooking is sophisticated and presentation is elaborate. Lunch is good value and desserts are a little different.

Carte £ 22/43

Town plan: AV-s – *50 Rivers St* ✉ *BA1 2QA* – ℰ *(01225) 360 017*
– *www.thechequersbath.com* – *Closed 25 December*

White Hart

TRADITIONAL CUISINE · SIMPLE Appealing pub on south east edge of the city centre, with a local following and a neighbourhood feel. Generous portions of hearty cooking; smaller tapas plates are also popular.

Menu £ 13 (weekday lunch)/25 – Carte £ 27/35

Town plan: BX-s – *Widcombe Hill* ✉ *BA2 6AA* – ℰ *(01225) 338 053 (booking essential at dinner)* – *www.whitehartbath.co.uk* – *Closed 25-26 December, Sunday dinner and bank holidays*

Hare & Hounds

TRADITIONAL CUISINE · PUB A huge pub, more suited to a celebration with friends than a romantic dinner for two. Its hillside location affords superb views and its gardens and terrace come into their own in summer. Menus offer modern versions of classic dishes.

Carte £ 22/32

Town plan: Y-s – *Lansdown Rd* ✉ *BA1 5TJ* – ℰ *(01225) 482 682*
– *www.hareandhoundsbath.com*

at Box Northeast: 4.75 mi on A4 -(Y)⊠ Bath

ⓘ The Northey ⇔ 🛏 🍴 🖥 🅿

BRITISH MODERN · INDIVIDUAL Traditional-looking, family-run coaching inn with an open-plan interior, a large dining room and a vast bar. Appealing monthly menus feature unfussy, seasonal British cooking. Seafood dishes – particularly the mussels – are a strength. Smart, contemporary bedrooms have bathrooms to match.
Carte £ 24/51
5 rooms ⌂ – †£ 95/160 ††£ 99/160
Bath Rd ⊠ SN13 8AE – ℰ (01225) 742 333 – www.ohhcompany.co.uk
– Closed 25-26 December

at Colerne Northeast: 6.5 mi by A4 – Plan: Y – Batheaston rd and Bannerdown Rd
⊠ Chippenham

🏨🏨 Lucknam Park 🕈 🖄 ⇚ 🛏 🖾 🐶 🛁 🏋 🕭 🅿

GRAND LUXURY · CLASSIC Grand Palladian mansion with a mile-long tree-lined drive, rich, elegant décor, luxurious furnishings and sumptuous fabrics. Extremely comfortable, classically furnished bedrooms. Top class facilities include an impressive modern spa and well-being centre, a renowned equestrian centre and a cookery school.
42 rooms – †£ 285/835 ††£ 285/835 – ⌂ £ 25 – 5 suites
⊠ SN14 8AZ – North : 0.5 mi on Marshfield rd – ℰ (01225) 742 777
– www.lucknampark.co.uk
🕸 **The Park • Brasserie** – See restaurant listing

XxxX The Park ⇐ 🛏 🅿

🕸 BRITISH MODERN · ELEGANT An aperitif in the elegant library of this impressive mansion is a fine prelude to a formal dinner in the opulent dining room. Service is professional and the kitchen, knowledgeable. Classical menus display modern European influences, with dishes expertly crafted from top quality produce; some from the estate.
➜ Poached langoustine, potato mousse, Exmoor caviar and gribiche dressing. Brecon lamb two ways with smoked Roscoff onion risotto and violet artichokes. Caraibe chocolate bar, salted caramel ice cream, honey-roast peanuts and glazed bananas.
Menu £ 80 (weekdays)/105
Lucknam Park Hotel, ⊠ SN14 8AZ – North : 0.5 mi on Marshfield rd
– ℰ (01225) 742 777 (booking essential) – www.lucknampark.co.uk
– dinner only and Sunday lunch – Closed Sunday dinner and Monday

XX Brasserie 🛏 🍴 🆎 🅿

INTERNATIONAL · FASHIONABLE Stylish brasserie in a beautiful courtyard setting in Lucknam Park's state-of-the-art spa, with a spacious bar-lounge and an airy, open-plan dining room with full-length windows. Precise, modern cooking in well-judged combinations; many healthy options are available. Barbecues on the charming terrace in summer.
Menu £ 22 (lunch) – Carte £ 26/47
Lucknam Park Hotel, ⊠ SN14 8AZ – North : 0.5 mi on Marshfield rd
– ℰ (01225) 742 777 – www.lucknampark.co.uk

 Don't confuse the classification X with the stars 🕸!
The number of X denotes levels of comfort and service, while
stars are awarded for the cooking.

at Monkton Combe Southeast: 4.5 mi by A36 – Plan: Y – ⊠ Bath

🏠 **Wheelwrights Arms**　　　⇆ 🏡 ♿ 🖳 🅿

TRADITIONAL CUISINE · PUB Relax to the sound of birdsong at this charming stone inn; part of which was once a carpenter's workshop. Concise menus offer traditional dishes and some more creative specials. Order 48 hours ahead for the Sunday special, a 'carve-it-yourself' rib of beef. Individually designed bedrooms are warm and welcoming.

Menu £ 12 (weekday lunch) – Carte £ 24/36 **s**

7 rooms � – ♦£ 75/85 ♦♦£ 85/150

Church Ln ⊠ BA2 7HB – ℰ (01225) 722 287 – www.wheelwrightsarms.co.uk
– Closed dinner 25-26 December and 1 January

at Combe Hay Southwest: 5 mi by A367 – ⊠ Bath

🏠 **Wheatsheaf**　　　🐾 ⇆ 🛏 🏡 🅿

BRITISH MODERN · COSY It began life as a farmhouse in 1576 but now boasts chic, uber-modern styling typified by pink flocked wallpaper and vivid artwork; and a relaxed atmosphere helped on its way by open fires, comfy low sofas and the pub's resident spaniels. Flavourful, seasonal food is presented in a contemporary style. Bedrooms have a spacious, modern feel; Buttercup is the largest.

Menu £ 15 (weekday lunch) – Carte £ 25/46

3 rooms ⊏ – ♦£ 100/120 ♦♦£ 120/150

⊠ BA2 7EG – ℰ (01225) 833 504 – www.wheatsheafcombehay.com – Closed 10 days January, Sunday dinner and Monday except bank holidays

BAUGHURST

Hampshire – Regional map n° **4**-B1

▶ London 61 mi – Camberley 28 mi – Farnborough 27 mi

🏠 **Wellington Arms**　　　⇆ 🛏 🏡 🅿

TRADITIONAL CUISINE · PUB This smart cream pub has its own herb and vegetable beds, keeps its own sheep, pigs, chickens and bees, and sources the rest of its meats from within 20 miles. Menus feature 6 dishes per course – supplemented by a selection of blackboard specials – and cooking is generous and satisfying. Smart, rustic bedrooms come with slate floors, sheepskin rugs and big, comfy beds.

Menu £ 16 (weekday lunch) – Carte £ 21/47

4 rooms ⊏ – ♦£ 95/200 ♦♦£ 95/200

Baughurst Rd ⊠ RG26 5LP – Southwest : 0.5 mi – ℰ (0118) 982 01 10 (booking essential) – www.thewellingtonarms.com – Closed Sunday dinner

BEACONSFIELD

Buckinghamshire – Pop. 13 797 – Regional map n° **6**-D3

▶ London 26 mi – Aylesbury 19 mi – Oxford 32 mi – Croydon 37 mi

🏨 **Crazy Bear**　　　🏋 ⌁ 🕮 🗏 🛋 🅿

LUXURY · DESIGN A discreet, unique hotel with sumptuous, over-the-top styling and idiosyncratic furnishings. Moody, masculine bedrooms blend original features with rich fabrics; some slightly less flamboyant bedrooms are located over the road. The lavishly styled 'English' restaurant offers extensive menus and uses produce from their farm shop, while sexy 'Thai' serves Asian cuisine.

25 rooms ⊏ – ♦£ 290/490 ♦♦£ 290/490

75 Wycombe End ⊠ HP9 1LX – ℰ (01494) 673 086 – www.crazybeargroup.co.uk
Thai – See restaurant listing

XX Thai

THAI • FASHIONABLE Part of the Crazy Bear but in a separate building. It's extravagant, sexy and atmospheric, with chandeliers, flock wallpaper, snakeskin handrails and studded leather chairs. Thai dishes dominate, but influences are drawn from all over Asia.

Menu £ 43/63 – Carte £ 25/99

Crazy Bear Hotel, 73 Wycombe End ✉ HP9 1LX – ✆ (01494) 673 086 (booking essential) – www.crazybeargroup.co.uk – Closed Sunday lunch and Monday

at Seer Green Northeast: 2.5 mi by A355

Jolly Cricketers

BRITISH TRADITIONAL • PUB Charming Victorian pub filled with a host of cricketing memorabilia; even the menu is divided into 'Openers', 'Main Play' and 'Sticky Wicket'. Cooking pleasingly balances the classics with more modern choices. Staff are welcoming.

Carte £ 25/41

24 Chalfont Rd ✉ HP9 2YG – ✆ (01494) 676 308 (booking advisable) – www.thejollycricketers.co.uk – closed Sunday dinner

at Wooburn Common Southwest: 3.5 mi by A40 – ✉ Beaconsfield

Chequers Inn

INN • CLASSIC Attractive 17C inn which has been family-owned and run since 1975. Good-sized bedrooms have flowery feature walls and display old pine furnishings collected from antique shops. Enjoy drinks in the spacious leather-furnished lounge, snacks in the cosy beamed bar or more ambitious dishes in the restaurant.

17 rooms – †£ 95/100 ††£ 100/140 – ☕ £ 10

Kiln Ln ✉ HP10 0JQ – Southwest : 1 mi on Bourne End rd – ✆ (01628) 529 575 – www.chequers-inn.com

BEAMINSTER

Dorset – Pop. 2 957 – Regional map n° **2**-B3

▶ London 154 mi – Exeter 45 mi – Taunton 30 mi – Weymouth 29 mi

BridgeHouse

TRADITIONAL • PERSONALISED Hugely characterful 13C priests' house. Relax by an inglenook fireplace in one of the traditional flag-floored lounges. Bedrooms in the main house are spacious and have original features; those in the 'Coach-House' are more modern.

13 rooms ☕ – †£ 95/235 ††£ 95/290

3 Prout Bridge ✉ DT8 3AY – ✆ (01308) 862 200 – www.bridge-house.co.uk

Beaminster Brasserie – See restaurant listing

XX Beaminster Brasserie

MODERN CUISINE • BRASSERIE Start with a fireside drink in the bar of this charming hotel, then head for the Georgian dining room, the conservatory or the covered terrace. Menus showcase local produce and dishes are fresh, vibrant and attractively presented.

Menu £ 14 (weekday lunch) – Carte £ 25/48

BridgeHouse Hotel, 3 Prout Bridge ✉ DT8 3AY – ✆ (01308) 862 200 – www.bridge-house.co.uk

BEARSTED

Kent – Regional map n° **5**-B2

▶ London 39 mi – Dover 40 mi – Royal Tunbridge Wells 22 mi

XX Fish On The Green   🏠 AK P

FISH AND SEAFOOD · NEIGHBOURHOOD Tucked away on a corner of the green is this simply decorated restaurant with a pleasant terrace. Professional cooking focuses on fresh, tasty local seafood. The lunch menu is good value and service is polite and knowledgeable.

Menu £ 17 (lunch)/20 – Carte £ 33/47

Church Ln ✉ ME14 4EJ – ℰ (01622) 738 300 – www.fishonthegreen.com – Closed 25 December-mid January, Sunday dinner and Monday

BEAULIEU

Hampshire – ✉ Brockenhurst – Pop. 726 – Regional map n° **4**-B2

▶ London 102 mi – Bournemouth 24 mi – Southampton 13 mi – Winchester 23 mi

🏠🏠 Montagu Arms   🏠 🛏 ⚜ 🏊 P

INN · CLASSIC With its characterful parquet floors and old wood panelling, this charming 18C inn has a timeless elegance. Traditional country house bedrooms marry antique furniture with modern facilities, and service is discreet and personalised. The wicker-furnished conservatory and terrace overlook the lovely gardens.

22 rooms ☑ – ∦£ 145/170 ∦∦£ 169/219 – 4 suites

Palace Ln ✉ SO42 7ZL – ℰ (01590) 612 324 – www.montaguarmshotel.co.uk

❀ **The Terrace • Monty's Inn** – See restaurant listing

XXX The Terrace   🛏 🏠 I♡ ⇔ P

❀ **BRITISH MODERN · FORMAL** This elegant dining room is found at the heart of an alluring 18C inn; head to the terrace for views across the lovely gardens. Service is polite and efficient, and only top quality produce is used in the refined, precisely prepared dishes. Cooking has a classical base and modern touches.

➜ Spiced scallops with cauliflower purée, apple, coriander and cumin velouté. Roast duck breast, smoked bacon, chicory and creamed potatoes. Seville orange soufflé with Sichuan-spiced chocolate ice cream.

Menu £ 30 (weekday lunch)/75

Montagu Arms Hotel, Palace Ln ✉ SO42 7ZL – ℰ (01590) 612 324 – www.montaguarmshotel.co.uk – Closed Monday and lunch Tuesday

X Monty's Inn   🛏 P

BRITISH TRADITIONAL · INN Set within a large red-brick inn in a delightful village, this laid-back bar-restaurant is the perfect spot for a pint and a home-cooked classic. The eggs are from their own chickens while meats are free range and from nearby farms.

Carte £ 21/38

Montagu Arms Hotel, Palace Ln ✉ SO42 7ZL – ℰ (01590) 612 324 – www.montaguarmshotel.co.uk

BEAUMONT – Saint Peter ➜ See Channel Islands (Jersey)

BEELEY

Derbyshire – Pop. 165 – Regional map n° **9**-B1

▶ London 160 mi – Derby 26 mi – Matlock 5 mi

🍴 Devonshire Arms   🐾 ⇔ 🏠 I♡ P

BRITISH TRADITIONAL · INN Stone inn with a hugely characterful low-beamed bar and a bright modern brasserie extension with views of the village and stream. Have afternoon tea or choose from the lengthy classically based main menu; estate game is a speciality. Bedrooms in the inn and next door are cosy; those opposite are more modern.

Carte £ 27/41

14 rooms – ∦£ 99/119 ∦∦£ 119/139 – ☑ £ 14

Devonshire Sq ✉ DE4 2NR – ℰ (01629) 733 259 (booking advisable) – www.devonshirebeeley.co.uk

BELBROUGHTON

Worcestershire – Pop. 1 272 – Regional map n° **10**-C2
▶ London 122 mi – Sheffield 108 mi – Kingston upon Hull 156 mi – Derby 64 mi

🏠 **The Queens** 🛏 ㅤ

BRITISH TRADITIONAL · FRIENDLY This 16C pub might have been refurbished but a traditional feel remains – a conscious effort by the owners to respect the locals' preferences. Refined, attractive dishes range from hearty pub favourites to flavoursome classics. Themed evenings include 'Pie', 'Surf & Turf' and 'Fizz & Chips' Nights.

Menu £ 13 (weekdays) – Carte £ 23/35

Queens Hill ⊠ DY9 ODU – ℰ (01562) 730 276 (bookings advisable at dinner) – www.thequeensbelbroughton.co.uk – closed Sunday dinner – Closed 25 December

BELCHFORD

Lincolnshire – ⊠ Horncastle – Regional map n° **9**-C1
▶ London 169 mi – Horncastle 5 mi – Lincoln 28 mi

🏠 **Blue Bell Inn** 🛏

TRADITIONAL CUISINE · PUB Welcoming pub in a tiny village in the Lincolnshire Wolds. Traditional bar with a copper-topped counter and sofas leads to a bright red dining room. Menus cover all bases, offering honest, home-cooked dishes which are big on flavour.

Carte £ 18/35

1 Main Rd ⊠ LN9 6LQ – ℰ (01507) 533 602 – www.bluebellbelchford.co.uk – Closed 12-26 January

BELFORD

Northumberland – Pop. 1 258 – Regional map n° **14**-A1
▶ London 335 mi – Edinburgh 71 mi – Newcastle upon Tyne 49 mi

🏠 **Market Cross**

TOWNHOUSE · PERSONALISED 200 year old stone townhouse close to the medieval cross in the market square; run by friendly, welcoming owners. Bright modern bedrooms come in neutral hues and feature Nespresso machines and complimentary sherry and Lindisfarne Mead. Local produce features at breakfast; dinner is by arrangement.

4 rooms 🔄 – ♥£ 60/100 ♥♥£ 80/110

1 Church St ⊠ NE70 7LS – ℰ (01668) 213 013 – www.marketcrossbelford.co.uk – Closed 21-28 December

BELPER

Derbyshire – Pop. 23 417 – Regional map n° **9**-B2
▶ London 141 mi – Birmingham 59 mi – Leicester 40 mi – Manchester 55 mi

🏠 **Chevin Green Farm**

FAMILY · PERSONALISED Chevin Green has been in the family since 1929, when it was a working farm; the outbuildings are now homes, and the residents' families supply fresh produce to the farmhouse. The delightful owners have a passion for tea, so you'll find a great selection, alongside tea-themed artwork, ornaments and furnishings.

5 rooms 🔄 – ♥£ 70/75 ♥♥£ 85/90

Chevin Rd ⊠ DE56 2UN – West : 2 mi by A 517 and Farnah Green Rd – ℰ (01773) 822 328 – www.chevingreenfarm.com

BENENDEN

Kent – Pop. 787 – Regional map n° **5**-B2
▶ London 55 mi – Hastings 23 mi – Royal Tunbridge Wells 19 mi

☖ **Ramsden Farm** ⚐ ⪡ ☖ ⚙ **P** ⇄

FAMILY · PERSONALISED Attractive clapperboard house with a refreshingly re-laxed air and modern styling. Bedrooms are spacious, with a slight New England look, and the luxurious bathrooms have underfloor heating. Have breakfast in the country kitchen or out on the terrace and take in lovely garden and country-side views.

3 rooms ☟ – ♦£ 90/115 ♦♦£ 95/120

Dingleden Ln ⊠ TN17 4JT – Southeast : 1 mi by B 2086 – ℰ (01580) 240 203
– www.ramsdenfarmhouse.co.uk

BEPTON – West Sussex → See Midhurst

BERKHAMSTED
Hertfordshire – Pop. 20 641 – Regional map n° **7**-A2
▶ London 34 mi – Aylesbury 14 mi – St Albans 11 mi

✗✗ **The Gatsby** ⚐ ☖

BRITISH MODERN · INDIVIDUAL Charming cinema built in 1938 and sympatheti-cally converted to incorporate a trendy art deco bar and glamorous restaurant. Dine among elegant columns and ornate plasterwork. Menus offer detailed, clas-sically based dishes with modern twists.

Menu £ 15 (lunch and early dinner) – Carte £ 30/48

97 High St ⊠ HP4 2DG – ℰ (01442) 870 403 – www.thegatsby.net – Closed
25-26 December

ᛙ **Old Mill** ⚐ ⪦ ☖ **P**

TRADITIONAL CUISINE · PUB An imposing red-brick building on the Grand Un-ion Canal; its still-turning waterwheel a testament to its industrial past. All-en-compassing menus move with the seasons; the deli boards and grass-fed, dry-aged steaks are a feature.

Menu £ 13 (weekday lunch) – Carte £ 23/42

London Rd ⊠ HP4 2NB – ℰ (01442) 879 590 – www.theoldmillberkhamsted.co.uk
– Closed 25 December

BERRICK SALOME
Oxfordshire – Pop. 326 - Regional map n° **6**-C2
▶ London 50 mi – Oxford 13 mi – Aylesbury 22 mi

ᛙ **Chequers** ⓝ ⪦ ⚐ **P**

BRITISH TRADITIONAL · FRIENDLY Delightful 17C pub with a spacious garden and a warm, welcoming interior with fresh flowers and candles on the tables and warming open fires. Hearty menus list British classics and at lunchtime they offer a good value 2 course menu.

Menu £ 18 (weekdays) – Carte £ 25/41

⊠ OX10 6JN – ℰ (01865) 891 118 – www.chequersberricksalome.co.uk – Closed
25 December, Sunday dinner, Tuesday

BERWICK
East Sussex – Regional map n° **5**-A3
▶ London 65 mi – Eastbourne 9 mi – Brighton and Hove 17 mi

✗✗ **Restaurant at the English Wine Centre** ⇔ ⪦ ⚐ ☖ **P**

BRITISH MODERN · DESIGN A collection of delightful 16C and 17C barns; one houses a shop selling over 140 English wines and this pretty, intimate restaurant, where the sweet-natured staff serve traditional English dishes with a modern touch. Stylish bedrooms are situated in another building and have views over the South Downs.

Carte £ 23/40

5 rooms ☟ – ♦£ 75/120 ♦♦£ 135/175

Alfriston Rd ⊠ BN26 5QS – ℰ (01323) 870 164 (booking essential)
– www.englishwine.co.uk – lunch only and dinner Friday-Saturday – Closed last
2 weeks February, Christmas-New Year and Monday

BERWICK-UPON-TWEED

Northumberland – Pop. 13 265 – Regional map n° **14**-A1

London 349 mi – Edinburgh 57 mi – Newcastle upon Tyne 63 mi

Granary ⓝ

TOWNHOUSE · PERSONALISED Discreet Georgian house on a side street near the river. Guest areas are on the first floor; breakfast features organic and Fairtrade produce. The 2nd floor bedrooms are bright and modern with eye-catching art and thoughtful extras.

3 rooms – †£ 96 ††£ 96/138

11 Bridge St ⊠ TD15 1ES – ℰ (01289) 304 403 – www.granaryguesthouse.co.uk

BEVERLEY

East Riding of Yorkshire – ⊠ Kingston-Upon-Hull – Pop. 30 587 – Regional map n° **13**-D2

London 188 mi – Kingston-upon-Hull 8 mi – Leeds 52 mi – York 29 mi

XX Whites

CREATIVE · NEIGHBOURHOOD A small, keenly run neighbourhood restaurant by the old city walls; its plain décor contrasts nicely with its black wood tables and eye-catching glass art. Ambitious, creative, modern cooking is delivered in set menus of either 4 or 9 courses. Smart, contemporary bedrooms and rooftop terrace breakfasts.

Menu £ 25 (weekdays)/50

4 rooms – †£ 80 ††£ 95

12a North Bar Without ⊠ HU17 7AB – ℰ (01482) 866 121 (booking advisable) – www.whitesrestaurant.co.uk – dinner only and Saturday lunch – Closed 1 week Christmas, 1 week August, Sunday and Monday

at Tickton Northeast: 3.5 mi by A1035 – ⊠ Kingston-Upon-Hull

Tickton Grange

COUNTRY HOUSE · CLASSIC A warm, welcoming, family-run hotel in an extended Georgian house – a popular wedding venue. Bedrooms are smart, stylish and up-to-date, while the spacious sitting room looks out over the immaculately kept gardens. Ambitious, modern cooking is served in the contemporary ground floor restaurant.

21 rooms – †£ 93/115 ††£ 120/145

⊠ HU17 9SH – on A 1035 – ℰ (01964) 543 666 – www.beverleyticktongrange.co.uk

at South Dalton Northwest: 5 mi by A164 and B1248 – ⊠ Beverley

Pipe and Glass Inn (James Mackenzie)

BRITISH MODERN · FRIENDLY Warm, bustling and inviting pub; very personally run by its experienced owners. Dishes are generously proportioned, carefully executed and flavourful, with judicious use of local, seasonal and traceable produce. Luxurious designer bedrooms boast the latest mod cons and have their own patios overlooking the estate woodland; breakfast is served in your room.

→ Crisp monkfish cheeks with Jerusalem artichoke, ham hock and sorrel. Rump of lamb, mutton belly fritter, spring vegetables and barley 'Hotchpotch'. Warm raspberry and pistachio Bakewell tart with raspberry sorbet.

Carte £ 22/55

5 rooms – †£ 135/175 ††£ 170/210

West End ⊠ HU17 7PN – ℰ (01430) 810 246 – www.pipeandglass.co.uk – Closed 2 weeks January, Sunday dinner and Monday except bank holidays

BEWDLEY

Worcestershire – Pop. 8 571 – Regional map n° **10**-B2

London 130 mi – Birmingham 30 mi – Liverpool 91 mi – Bristol 77 mi

🏠 Kateshill House

TOWNHOUSE · PERSONALISED This elegant Georgian manor house is surrounded by beautiful gardens; where you'll find a tree from the reign of King Henry VIII. Sumptuous, contemporary furnishings provide a subtle contrast to the house's original features.

8 rooms 🖵 – **†**£ 75/85 **††**£ 90/120

Redhill ✉ DY12 2DR – South : 0.25 mi on B 4194 – ✆ (01299) 401 563
– www.kateshillhouse.co.uk

BIBURY

Gloucestershire – ✉ Cirencester – Pop. 570 – Regional map n° **2**-D1
▶ London 86 mi – Gloucester 26 mi – Oxford 30 mi

🏨 Swan

INN · STYLISH Set in a delightful village, this ivy-clad coaching inn has a trout stream running through the garden and a cosy, characterful interior. Bedrooms mix cottagey character with contemporary touches; the best are in the annexes. The brasserie has an unusual log wall and opens onto a lovely flag-stoned courtyard.

22 rooms 🖵 – **†**£ 150/210 **††**£ 170/210 – 4 suites

✉ GL7 5NW – ✆ (01285) 740 695 – www.cotswold-inns-hotels.co.uk/swan

🏠 Cotteswold House

FAMILY · PERSONALISED This pleasant guesthouse is set just outside picturesque Bibury and provides an ideal base for exploring the area. The Victorian façade conceals traditional, spotlessly kept bedrooms and the friendly owner offers a warm welcome.

3 rooms 🖵 – **†**£ 65/70 **††**£ 90/95

Arlington ✉ GL7 5ND – on B 4425 – ✆ (01285) 740 609
– www.cotteswoldhouse.net

BIDBOROUGH

Kent – Regional map n° **5**-B2
▶ London 35 mi – Brighton 37 mi – Oxford 100 mi

🍴 Kentish Hare

MODERN CUISINE · NEIGHBOURHOOD Saved from development by local residents Lord and Lady Mills of Olympic Committee fame and run by the Tanner brothers, this smart pub features a hare theme, quirky wallpaper and an open kitchen. Tasty steaks from the Kamado grill.

Menu £ 18 (weekdays) – Carte £ 25/48

95 Bidborough Ridge ✉ TN3 0XB – ✆ (01892) 525 709
– www.thekentishhare.com – Closed Sunday dinner and Monday except bank holidays

BIDDENDEN

Kent – Pop. 1 303 – Regional map n° **5**-C2
▶ London 52 mi – Ashford 13 mi – Maidstone 16 mi

🏠 Barclay Farmhouse

TRADITIONAL · HOMELY A converted farmhouse and barn conversion in an acre of neat gardens, complete with a duck pond. Comfortable bedrooms feature French oak furniture and characterful beams; extra touches include chocolate truffles on your pillow.

3 rooms 🖵 – **†**£ 70/75 **††**£ 90/95

Woolpack Corner ✉ TN27 8BQ – South : 0.5 mi by A 262 on Benenden rd
– ✆ (01580) 292 626 – www.barclayfarmhouse.co.uk

✗ West House (Graham Garrett) 🅸🅿

🏵 **BRITISH MODERN · RUSTIC** Characterful beamed restaurant with contemporary oil paintings and a wood-burning stove – one of a row of old weavers' cottages in a picturesque village. Original, modern dishes display global influences and the occasional playful touch, and top quality ingredients allow the natural flavours to shine through.

➜ Grilled potato gnocchi with confit cep, onion broth, chestnut and parmesan. Roast haunch of Sika deer, mashed swede and wild mushrooms. Milk jelly, mousse, nuggets and crisps with buttermilk sorbet.

Menu £ 25/40

28 High St ✉ *TN27 8AH* – ℰ *(01580) 291 341* – *www.thewesthouserestaurant.co.uk*
– *Closed Christmas, Saturday lunch, Sunday dinner and Monday*

🍴 The Three Chimneys �🅿

TRADITIONAL CUISINE · PUB Delightful pub with a charming terrace and garden, dating back to 1420 and boasting a roaring fire, dimly lit low-beamed rooms and an old world feel. Dishes are mainly British based; there are some tempting local wines, ciders and ales too.

Carte £ 24/37

Hareplain Rd ✉ *TN27 8LW* – *West : 1.5 mi by A 262* – ℰ *(01580) 291 472 (booking essential)* – *www.thethreechimneys.co.uk*

BIDDENHAM
Bedford – Regional map n° **7**-A1
▶ London 50 mi – Cambridge 33 mi – Northampton 20 mi

🍴 Three Tuns 🚘🛋🅿

TRADITIONAL CUISINE · NEIGHBOURHOOD Set in a leafy residential suburb; if you're lost, look up above the rooftops for the majestic Canadian redwood tree. It's part-16C and part-19C, with a lovely terrace. Cooking is classical, seasonal and everything is homemade.

Menu £ 15 (weekday lunch) – Carte £ 22/40

57 Main Rd ✉ *MK40 4BD* – ℰ *(01234) 354 847*
– *www.thethreetunsbiddenham.co.uk* – *Closed Sunday dinner*

BIDEFORD
Devon – Pop. 18 029 – Regional map n° **2**-C1
▶ London 231 mi – Exeter 43 mi – Plymouth 58 mi – Taunton 60 mi

🏚 Yeoldon House 🆕 ✿🐾≤🚘🅿

COUNTRY HOUSE · HOMELY 19C house featuring original stained glass and wood-panelling; run by a delightful owner. It's set in a peaceful riverbank location and the landscaped gardens offer lovely walks. Some of the cosy bedrooms have balconies with river views. The formal dining room serves a modern seasonal menu.

9 rooms 🖙 – ♦£ 85 ♦♦£ 135

Durrant Lane, Northam ✉ *EX39 2RL* – *North : 1.5 mi by B 3235 off A 386*
– ℰ *(01237) 474 400* – *www.yeoldonhousehotel.co.uk* – *Closed Christmas*

BIGBURY
Devon – Regional map n° **1**-C3
▶ London 195 mi – Exeter 41 mi – Plymouth 22 mi

✗ Oyster Shack 🛋🛗🅿

FISH AND SEAFOOD · NEIGHBOURHOOD Former oyster farm with a small oyster bar and lounge, and a large terrace. The brightly decorated room is hung with fishing nets and centred around a large fish tank. Cooking is fresh and un-fussy, focusing on shellfish and the daily catch.

Carte £ 23/47

Milburn Orchard Farm, Stakes Hill ✉ *TQ7 4BE* – *East : 1 mi by Easton rd on Tidal rd* – ℰ *(01548) 810 876 (booking essential)* – *www.oystershack.co.uk*
– *Closed 4 January-2 February and Sunday dinner in winter*

BIGBURY-ON-SEA

Devon – ⊠ Kingsbridge – Pop. 220 – Regional map n° **1**-C3
▶ London 196 mi – Exeter 42 mi – Plymouth 23 mi

🏠 Burgh Island   ❄ ⅏ ≼ 👜 🛖 ✕ 🖵 ✆ **P**

HISTORIC · ART DECO Grade II listed house on its own island, accessed using the hotel's Land Rover (or tractor at high tide!). It has classic art deco styling throughout, from the guest areas to the individually designed bedrooms; some rooms have small balconies and most have excellent bay views. 1930s themed 'black tie' dinners take place in the ballroom; there's live music Weds and Sat.

25 rooms (dinner included) ⅏ – ♦£ 310 ♦♦£ 400/640 – 10 suites
⊠ TQ7 4BG – South : 0.5 mi by hotel transport
– ✆ (01548) 810 514 – www.burghisland.com
– Closed 2-15 January

🏠 Henley   ❄ ⅏ ≼ 👜 **P**

TRADITIONAL · PERSONALISED Charming hotel affording superb views over Burgh Island and towards Bolt Tail. Homely lounge and wicker-furnished conservatory. Comfortable bedrooms cross New England and English Country styles; Room 6 boasts the best views. Concise, unfussy menus feature locally sourced ingredients.

5 rooms ⅏ – ♦£ 90 ♦♦£ 120/150
Folly Hill ⊠ TQ7 4AR
– ✆ (01548) 810 240 – www.thehenleyhotel.co.uk
– Mid March-October

BIGGLESWADE

Central Bedfordshire – Pop. 16 551 – Regional map n° **7**-B1
▶ London 47 mi – Bedford 12 mi – Cambridge 23 mi

✕✕ Croft Kitchen 🆕   🄰🄲

BRITISH MODERN · FRIENDLY Two enthusiastic brothers, of Indian and Scottish descent, run this simple little restaurant – one cooks and one serves. Creative modern dishes are attractively presented and subtle Indian spicing adds another dimension to the cooking.

Menu £ 28 (weekdays)/70
– Carte £ 35/49
28 Palace St ⊠ SG18 8DP
– ✆ (01767) 601 502 – www.thecroftbiggleswade.com
– Closed Monday-Tuesday, Sunday dinner and lunch Wednesday-Thursday

BILDESTON

Suffolk – Regional map n° **8**-C3
▶ London 85 mi – Bury St Edmunds 18 mi – Ipswich 15 mi

🏠 Bildeston Crown   ❄ 🏡 ⅃ **P**

INN · CONTEMPORARY Hugely characterful 15C wool merchant's, with a lovely rear courtyard. Stylish, modern interior with warm colours and open fires. Bedrooms vary from florally feminine to bright and bold; all are luxurious with designer furniture and chic bathrooms. Sumptuous, formal 'Ingrams' serves creative modern dishes; the charming beamed dining room offers a more classical menu.

12 rooms ⅏ – ♦£ 80/90 ♦♦£ 100/200
104 High St ⊠ IP7 7EB
– ✆ (01449) 740 510 – www.thebildestoncrown.com

BIRKENHEAD

Merseyside – Pop. 142 968 – Regional map n° **11**-A3

▶ London 208 mi – Liverpool 3 mi – Manchester 37 mi – Stoke-on-Trent 52 mi

XxX **Fraiche** (Marc Wilkinson)

❀ CREATIVE · DESIGN Enter into the cosy bar, where seasonal images are projected onto the wall, then head through to the boldly decorated restaurant which seats just 10 diners. Cooking is innovative and presentation is key – the colours of the ingredients and the shape and style of the crockery both play their part.

➜ Scallop tartare, pink grapefruit and pressed avocado. Duck breast with pickled cherries and kohlrabi. Pineapple sorbet with hibiscus-infused pineapple and sesame crisp.

Menu £ 85 – set menu only

11 Rose Mount, Oxton ✉ *CH43 5SG – Southwest : 2.25 mi by A 552 and B 5151 – ✆ (0151) 652 29 14 (booking essential) – www.restaurantfraiche.com – dinner only and Sunday lunch – Closed 25 December, 1-7 July, Sunday dinner, Monday and Tuesday*

GOOD TIPS!

Known as a city of cars, canals and chocolate, the 'Second City of the Kingdom' is also a centre for culinary excellence, boasting five Michelin-starred restaurants. 21C Brum is a major convention and retail destination, and redevelopment continues apace; hotels like Malmaison and Hotel Indigo providing luxury accommodation for its many visitors.

BIRMINGHAM

West Midlands – Pop. 1 085 810 – Regional map n° **10**-C2
▶ London 122 mi – Bristol 91 mi – Newcastle upon Tyne 207 mi

Hotels

🏨 **Hyatt Regency**   ⚘ ⪡ 🔲 🚇 ♨ 🛋 🔄 ⅋ 🆎 🕸 🔱

BUSINESS · CONTEMPORARY An eye-catching, mirror-fronted, tower block hotel in a prime city centre location, with a covered link to the International Convention Centre. Spacious bedrooms have floor to ceiling windows and an excellent level of facilities. Aria restaurant, in the atrium, offers modern European menus.
325 rooms – ♚£ 117/219 ♚♚£ 117/219 – ☑ £ 18 – 4 suites
Town plan: **5KZ-a** – *2 Bridge St* ✉ *B1 2JZ* – ℰ *(0121) 643 12 34*
– *www.birmingham.regency.hyatt.com*

🏨 **Hotel Du Vin**   ⚘ 🚇 ♨ 🛋 🔄 🆎 🔱 🚗

BUSINESS · DESIGN Characterful former eye hospital with a relaxed, boutique style. Richly hued bedrooms are named after wine companies and estates; one suite boasts an 8 foot bed, 2 roll-top baths and a gym. Kick-back in the small cellar pub or comfy champagne bar. The classical bistro has a lively buzz and a French menu.
66 rooms ☑ – ♚£ 120/185 ♚♚£ 130/195
Town plan: **6LY-e** – *25 Church St* ✉ *B3 2NR* – ℰ *(0844) 7364 250*
– *www.hotelduvin.com*

🏨 **Hotel La Tour**   ⚘ 🛋 🔄 🔄 🆎 🕸 🔱

BUSINESS · MODERN Striking modern building with a stylish lobby featuring state-of-the-art self-check-in terminals. With their media hubs and TV recording facilities, bedrooms are ideal for business travellers; the smart bathrooms are shower-only. There are extensive events facilities, and a chic café, bar and brasserie.
174 rooms – ♚£ 85/249 ♚♚£ 89/359 – ☑ £ 16
Town plan: **6MY-a** – *Albert St* ✉ *B5 5JE* – ℰ *(0121) 718 8000*
– *www.hotel-latour.co.uk* – Closed 23-30 December

INDEX OF STREET NAMES IN BIRMINGHAM

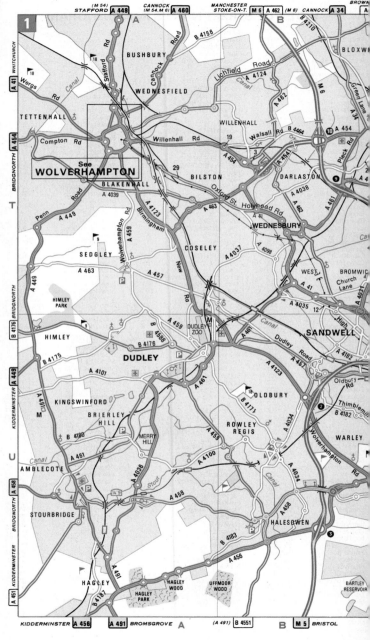

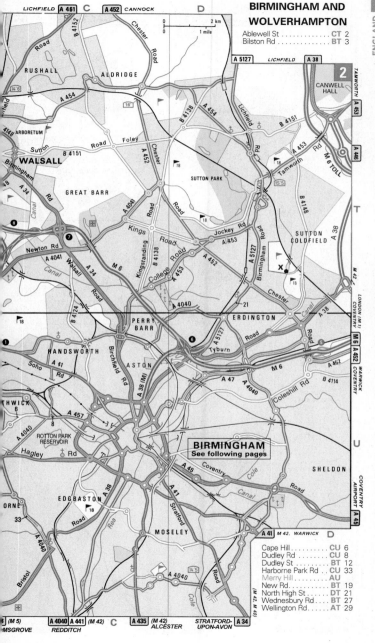

LICHFIELD **A 461** C   **A 452** CANNOCK   D

A 5127 LICHFIELD **A 38**

CANWELL HALL

RUSHALL   ALDRIDGE

ARBORETUM

WALSALL

GREAT BARR

SUTTON PARK

SUTTON COLDFIELD

PERRY BARR

ERDINGTON

HANDSWORTH

ASTON

Tyburn

ROTTON PARK RESERVOIR

BIRMINGHAM
See following pages

SHELDON

EDGBASTON

MOSELEY

A 4040 **A 441** (M 42) C   **A 435** (M 42) ALCESTER   STRATFORD-UPON-AVON **A 34**

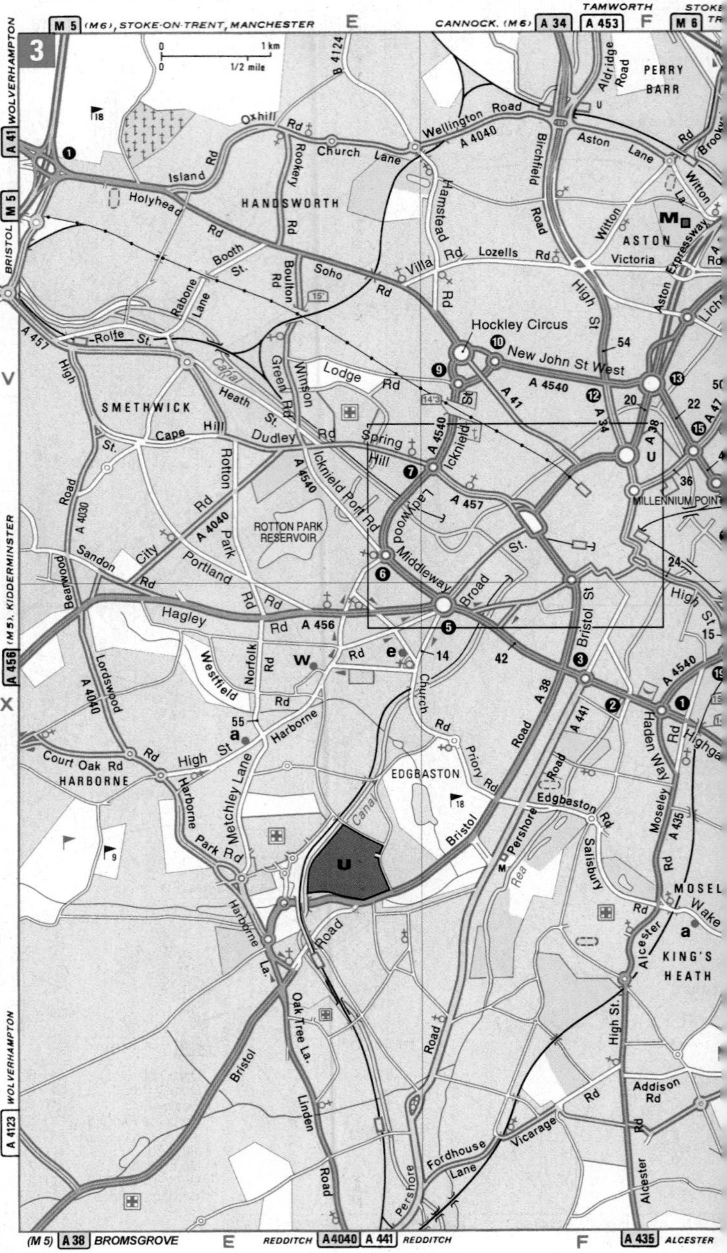
M 5 (M6), STOKE-ON-TRENT, MANCHESTER
E
CANNOCK. (M6) A 34
TAMWORTH A 453
F
STOKE M 6
3
0 1 km
0 1/2 mile
A 41 WOLVERHAMPTON
M 5 BRISTOL
A 456 (M5). KIDDERMINSTER
A 4123 WOLVERHAMPTON
V
X
(M 5) A 38 BROMSGROVE
REDDITCH A4040 A 441 REDDITCH
A 435 ALCESTER
PERRY BARR
Aldridge Road
Wellington Road
A 4040
Birchfield Road
Aston Lane
Witton La.
Oxhill Rd
Rookery Rd
Church Lane
Island Rd
Holyhead Rd
HANDSWORTH
Hamstead Rd
Villa Rd
Lozells Rd
Witton
ASTON
Victoria
Aston Expressway
Booth St.
Soho Rd
Boulton Rd
Rabone Lane
High St
Hockley Circus
New John St West
A 4540
A 41
A 34
A 457
Rolfe St.
Canal
Lodge Rd
Green Rd
Winson
Heath St.
SMETHWICK
Cape Hill
Dudley Rd
Spring Hill
Icknield St
A 38
U
MILLENNIUM POINT
Rotton Park
Icknield Port Rd
Ladywood
Middleway
ROTTON PARK RESERVOIR
City Rd
Portland Rd
Sandon Rd
Bearwood Road
A 4030
Broad St.
Bristol St
Hagley Rd
A 456
Westfield Rd
Norfolk Rd
Lordswood Rd
A 4040
Church Rd
Harborne Rd
High St
Court Oak Rd
HARBORNE
Metchley Lane
Harborne Park Rd
EDGBASTON
Priory Rd
Bristol Rd
Pershore Road
Edgbaston Rd
Salisbury Rd
Haden Way
Highgate
Moseley Rd
A 435
MOSELEY
Wake Green
Alcester Rd
KING'S HEATH
High St.
Harborne La.
Oak Tree La.
Linden Road
Bristol Rd
Fordhouse Lane
Vicarage Rd
Addison Rd
Alcester Rd
Pershore Rd
Rea
Hockley
Rea

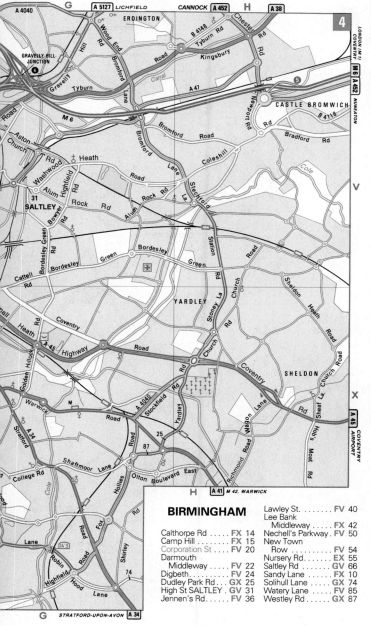

BIRMINGHAM

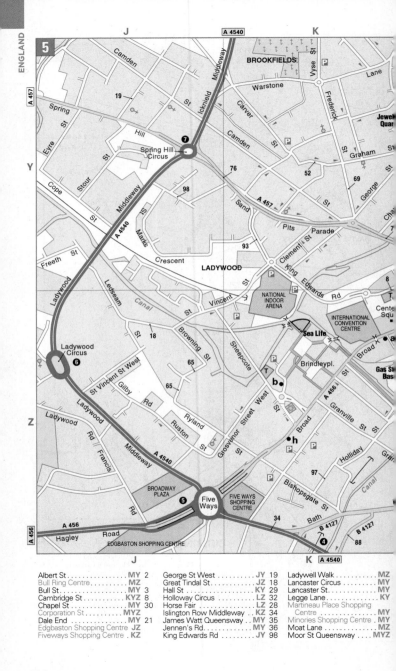

BROOKFIELDS

Camden

Warstone

Carver

Camden

Spring Hill Circus **7**

LADYWOOD

NATIONAL INDOOR ARENA

INTERNATIONAL CONVENTION CENTRE

Sea Life

Ladywood Circus **6**

Brindleypl.

Gas St Bas

St Vincent St West

Gilby

Rd

Ryland

Ruston

Grosvenor Street West

Broad

Granville St

Holliday

BROADWAY PLAZA

5

Five Ways

FIVE WAYS SHOPPING CENTRE

Bishopsgate St

Bath

Hagley Road

EDGBASTON SHOPPING CENTRE

A 456

B 4127

B 4127

4

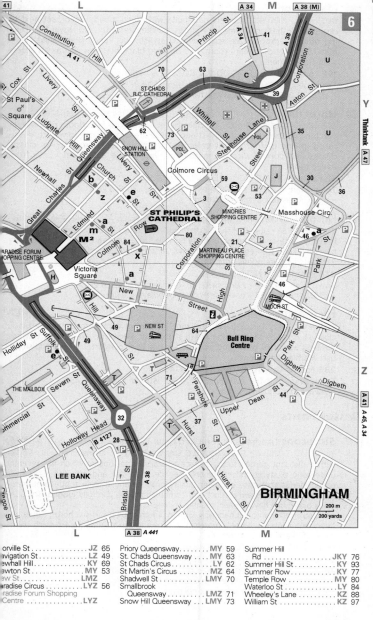

ENGLAND

Constitution Hill
Canal
A 41
70
63
A 34
41
41
Princip St
Corporation St
C
39
Cox St
Livery St
St Paul's
Square
Ludgate
Hill
Newhall
Queensway
Church St
Livery St
SNOW HILL
STATION
62
73
POL
Colmore Circus
59
Whittall St
Steelhouse Lane
Street
Aston St
35
U
U
30
36
Great Charles
b
z
e
a
a
m
M²
Edmund St
Colmore Row
ST PHILIP'S
CATHEDRAL
3
MINORIES
SHOPPING CENTRE
53
J
Masshouse Circ.
46 a
46
St
PARADISE FORUM
SHOPPING CENTRE
H
Victoria
Square
a
x
84
80
Corporation St
21
MARTINEAU PLACE
SHOPPING CENTRE
2
Park St
New
Street
High St
46
MOOR ST
Hill St
49
49
NEW ST
64
Bull Ring
Centre
Park St
Digbeth
Holliday St
Suffolk St
THE MAILBOX
e
Severn St
Queensway
Smallbrook
Queensway
T
T
71
Pershore St
Upper Dean St
44
Digbeth
Commercial St
Holloway Head
32
B 4121
28
Bristol St
Hurst St
37
Hurst St
LEE BANK
A 38
A 441

BIRMINGHAM

0   200 m
0   200 yards

⌂ Malmaison ⚑ 🏨 🕸 ⚙ ☰ ⚐ ⟲ ÅC 🛁

BUSINESS · MODERN A smart new-build with dark, moody décor, set next to designer clothes and homeware shops, on the site of the old Royal Mail sorting office. Bedrooms are spacious and stylish; the Penny Black suite has a mini-cinema and a steam room. The bustling black brasserie serves an accessible British menu.

192 rooms ⌑ – ♦£ 80/200 ♦♦£ 80/250 – 1 suite
Town plan: 6LZ-e – *Mailbox, 1 Wharfside St* ✉ *B1 1RD*
– ✆ *(0121) 246 50 00* – *www.malmaison.com*

⌂ Hotel Indigo ⚑ ⩻ 🏨 🕸 ⚙ ☰ ⚐ ⟲ ÅC 🅟 🚗

BUSINESS · DESIGN Stylish, modern hotel on the top two floors of the eye-catching 'Cube'. Appealingly styled guest areas and bedrooms are decorated in one of four bright colours. The smart steakhouse serves classic dishes and comes with a champagne bar, terrace and great views from every table.

52 rooms – ♦£ 89/200 ♦♦£ 89/200 – ⌑ £ 14
Town plan: 6LZ-x – *The Cube* ✉ *B1 1PR* – ✆ *(0121) 643 20 10*
– *www.hotelindigobirmingham.com*

⌂ Hilton Garden Inn Birmingham ⚑ ⚙ ☰ ⚐ ⟲ ÅC 🅟 🛁

BUSINESS · STYLISH Stylish, modern business hotel in the heart of the lively Brindley Place development. Brightly coloured reception and small, contemporary bar. Well-kept, well-equipped bedrooms; facilities include Apple iMac computers. Popular City Café opens onto a terrace.

238 rooms ⌑ – ♦£ 59/195 ♦♦£ 69/205
Town plan: 5KZ-b – *1 Brunswick Sq, Brindley Place* ✉ *B1 2HW*
– ✆ *(0121) 643 10 03* – *www.birminghambrindleyplace.hgi.com*

⌂ Hampton by Hilton ⚙ ☰ ⚐ ⟲ ÅC 🅟 🅿

CHAIN HOTEL · FUNCTIONAL The top 17 floors of a modern 20 storey block, close to Brindley Place in the heart of the city. Bedrooms are geared towards business travellers, with good work desks, free wi-fi, comfortable beds and smart, part-marbled bathrooms.

285 rooms ⌑ – ♦£ 49/149 ♦♦£ 49/149
Town plan: 5KZ-h – *200 Broad St* ✉ *B15 1SU* – ✆ *(0121) 329 7450*
– *www.hamptonbyhilton.com*

Restaurants

XxX Simpsons (Andreas Antona and Luke Tipping) ⇦ 🍴 🏮 ⟲ ÅC 🍴

❀ **MODERN CUISINE · FASHIONABLE** Smart Georgian mansion ⇦ 🅿
with a pleasant garden-facing terrace and a summer house; which has recently undergone a stylish refurbishment. Service is formal and efficient. Classically based menus showcase excellent quality produce and display subtle contemporary twists; flavours are distinct and combinations are carefully judged. The spacious bedrooms have French country styling.

➔ Crab risotto, smoked haddock, Granny Smith apples and sea herbs. Squab pigeon with cabbage, onions, morels, wild rice and sauce Albufera. Rhubarb crumble soufflé and rhubarb sorbet.

Menu £ 45 (lunch) – Carte £ 48/65
3 rooms ⌑ – ♦£ 125/175 ♦♦£ 125/175
Town plan: 3EX-e – *20 Highfield Rd, Edgbaston* ✉ *B15 3DU*
– ✆ *(0121) 454 34 34* – *www.simpsonsrestaurant.co.uk*
– *Closed Sunday dinner and bank holidays*

The symbol ❀ denotes a particularly interesting wine list.

XxX **Purnell's** (Glynn Purnell) &. AC ⇔

MODERN CUISINE · DESIGN A well-regarded restaurant with a passionate owner and a keen local following – you're encouraged to relax and enjoy your time here. Start with a drink in the large bar, then move to the sleek dining room. Cooking is modern and refined; choose from the 'Now' or 'Reminisce' menu. Service is smooth and friendly.

→ Salad of Cornish crab with sumac honeycomb "Ice"berg lettuce. Vanilla and cardamom confit pork belly with crisp pickled apple and Savoy salt. Mint chocolate chip with aerated chocolate.

Menu £ 32 (weekday lunch)/85

Town plan: 6LY-b – *55 Cornwall St* ✉ *B3 2DH* – *℘ (0121) 212 97 99 – www.purnellsrestaurant.com – Closed 2 weeks August, 1 week Easter, 1 week Christmas, Saturday lunch, Sunday and Monday*

XxX **Opus at Cornwall Street** ♥ &. AC ⇔

MODERN CUISINE · DESIGN Very large and popular restaurant with floor to ceiling windows; enjoy an aperitif in the cocktail bar before dining in the stylish main room or at the chef's table in the kitchen. Daily changing menu of modern brasserie dishes.

Menu £ 14 (weekdays) – Carte £ 26/44

Town plan: 6LY-z – *54 Cornwall St* ✉ *B3 2DE* – *℘ (0121) 200 2323 – www.opusrestaurant.co.uk – Closed 24 December-3 January, Saturday lunch, Sunday dinner and bank holidays*

XX **adam's** (Adam Stokes) &. AC

MODERN CUISINE · INDIVIDUAL A bright, contemporary restaurant with a huge trompe l'oeil of a Victorian columned hallway. Menus range from a 3-choice, 3 course set lunch menu to a 5 or 9 course tasting menu with wine pairings. Cooking is intricate, innovative and attractively presented, relying on top quality seasonal ingredients.

→ Cauliflower with smoked eel and mint. Venison, pearl barley and charred onions. Rhubarb with cardamom and blood orange.

Menu £ 32 (weekday lunch)/80

Town plan: 6LZ-a – *21a Bennetts Hill* ✉ *B2 5QP* – *℘ (0121) 643 3745 (booking advisable) – www.adamsrestaurant.co.uk – Closed Christmas-New Year, Sunday and Monday*

XX **Turners** (Richard Turner) &. AC

MODERN CUISINE · NEIGHBOURHOOD Busy neighbourhood restaurant in a suburban parade, smartly decorated with etched mirrors and velvet chairs; there are just 8 neatly set tables. Visually impressive, confidently crafted, flavoursome dishes use top quality seasonal ingredients. Cooking is classically based but has a modern touch.

→ Ceviche of scallop with salt baked beetroot, apple, yoghurt and horseradish. Tasting of new season lamb, wild garlic, morels and lamb jus. Rhubarb crumble soufflé and custard ice cream.

Menu £ 35/55

Town plan: 3EX-a – *69 High St, Harborne* ✉ *B17 9NS* – *℘ (0121) 426 44 40 (booking essential) – www.turnersrestaurantbirmingham.co.uk – dinner only and lunch Friday-Saturday – Closed Sunday and Monday*

XX **Carters of Moseley** (Brad Carter) &. AC I◯

BRITISH MODERN · NEIGHBOURHOOD Lovely little neighbourhood restaurant with black ash tables and a glass-fronted cabinet running down one wall. Each dish is made up of three key components – which can include some unusual ingredients; combinations are well-balanced and flavours are intense. The young team are friendly and engaging.

→ Devilled crab with Jersey Royals and samphire. Cornish lamb with sea vegetables and seaweed sauce. Wye Valley rhubarb and custard.

Menu £ 28/50 – set menu only

Town plan: 3FX-a – *2c St Mary's Row, Wake Green Rd* ✉ *B13 9EZ* – *℘ (0121) 449 8885 (booking advisable) – www.cartersofmoseley.co.uk – Closed 1-7 January, 10-23 August, Monday and Tuesday*

XX Waters on the Square   🄰🄲

CLASSIC CUISINE · NEIGHBOURHOOD Bright red chairs stand out against white walls at this unassuming neighbourhood restaurant. It's run by a well-regarded local chef and cooking is good value and classically based; dessert is a tasting plate of five mini treats.

Menu £15 (weekday lunch)/30

Town plan: 3EX-w – *Chad Sq., Hawthorne Rd, Edgbaston* ✉ *B15 3TQ* – ✆ *(0121) 454 5436 (booking essential)* – *www.watersonthesquare.com* – *Closed Monday*

XX Lasan   🄰🄲 ⅑🕅

INDIAN · DESIGN An industrial-style restaurant in an old Jewellery Quarter art gallery. Original cooking takes authentic Indian flavours and delivers them in creative modern combinations; there are some particularly interesting vegetarian choices.

Carte £27/57

Town plan: 5KY-a – *3-4 Dakota Buildings, James St, St Pauls Sq* ✉ *B3 1SD* – ✆ *(0121) 212 36 64* – *www.lasan.co.uk* – *Closed 25 December*

XX Purnell's Bistro   🍽 🄰🄲

MODERN CUISINE · BRASSERIE Just around the corner from Glynn Purnell's eponymous restaurant is his bistro – a simply styled, low-ceilinged eatery fronted by a lively cocktail bar. Cooking is clever and modern and dishes arrive in original combinations.

Menu £20 (weekdays) – Carte £26/35

Town plan: 6LY-a – *Ground Floor, Newater House, 11 Newhall St* ✉ *B3 3NY* – ✆ *(0121) 200 1588* – *www.purnellsbistro-gingers.com* – *Closed 25-30 December and Sunday dinner*

XX Asha's   🍽 ⅆ 🄰🄲 ⅑🕅 ⇔

INDIAN · EXOTIC A stylish, passionately run Indian restaurant with exotic décor; owned by renowned artiste/gourmet Asha Bhosle. Extensive menus cover most parts of the Subcontinent, with everything cooked to order. Tandoori kebabs are a speciality.

Carte £27/68

Town plan: 6LY-m – *12-22 Newhall St* ✉ *B3 3LX* – ✆ *(0121) 200 27 67* – *www.ashasuk.co.uk* – *Closed 26 December, 1 January and lunch Saturday-Sunday*

XX Fumo   🍽 ⅆ 🄰🄲 🍴

ITALIAN · TAPAS BAR Set in a smart area; an elegant Italian restaurant with a 1930s edge and a lovely bar. Tables are closely set and waiters bustle around delivering good value 'cicchetti' – tasty Venetian small plates that are designed for sharing.

Carte £18/35

Town plan: 6LY-x – *1 Waterloo St* ✉ *B2 5PG* – ✆ *(0121) 643 8979 (bookings not accepted)* – *www.sancarlofumo.co.uk*

BISHOP'S STORTFORD

Hertfordshire – Pop. 37 838 – Regional map n° **7**-B2

▶ London 34 mi – Cambridge 27 mi – Chelmsford 19 mi – Colchester 33 mi

X Water Lane 🆕   ⅆ 🄰🄲

BRITISH TRADITIONAL · BISTRO Atmospheric restaurant set over two floors – with a cellar bar below – in the converted 18C Hawkes Brewery. Menus offer a range of rustic British and American dishes, from bubble and squeak to Bourbon-glazed ribs with chipotle slaw.

Carte £21/34

31 Water Ln ✉ *CM23 2JZ* – ✆ *(01279) 211 888* – *www.waterlane.co* – *Closed Monday*

ENGLAND

X **Lemon Tree** AC P

REGIONAL · FRIENDLY A friendly, passionately run little restaurant in a 200 year old house hidden in the town centre. Choose from several characterful dining areas. Seasonal menus offer unfussy classical dishes; the 'Taste of ...' menus are good value.

Menu £ 15 (lunch and early dinner) – Carte £ 21/44

14-16 Water Ln ⊠ CM23 2JZ – ℰ (01279) 757 788 – www.lemontree.co.uk – Closed 25-27 December, 1-2 January and bank holidays

BISPHAM GREEN

Lancashire – Regional map n° **11**-A2

▶ London 212 mi – Liverpool 22 mi – Preston 15 mi

🍴 **Eagle & Child** ⓝ 🖨 🛜 P

BRITISH TRADITIONAL · COSY A 16C inn with all the requisite character of a 'proper' pub; sit in the charmingly small snug. Quality seasonal ingredients are used to create unfussy, boldly flavoured dishes. Before you leave, visit the delightful farm shop next door.

Carte £ 20/47

Maltkiln Ln ⊠ L40 3SG – ℰ (01257) 462 297 – www.ainscoughs.co.uk

BLACKBURN

Blackburn with Darwen – Pop. 117 963 – Regional map n° **11**-B2

▶ London 228 mi – Leeds 47 mi – Liverpool 39 mi – Manchester 24 mi

🍴 **Clog & Billycock** 🛜 & P

BRITISH TRADITIONAL · PUB Spacious, modern, open-plan pub. Extensive menus offer plenty of choice and display a strong Lancastrian slant; cooking is rustic and generous. Most produce is sourced from within 25 miles.

Menu £ 13 (weekdays)/21 – Carte £ 19/39

Billinge End Rd, Pleasington ⊠ BB2 6QB – West : 2 mi by A 677 – ℰ (01254) 201 163 – www.theclogandbillycock.com

at Langho North: 4.5 mi on A666 – ⊠ Whalley

🏛 **Northcote** 🍃 🖨 & 🛜 AC 💱 🎵 P

COUNTRY HOUSE · ELEGANT This smart Victorian house sits on the edge of the Ribble Valley and is continually evolving and expanding. The individually designed bedrooms are spacious, stylish and sophisticated; all have queen or king-sized beds and some have garden terraces. Have afternoon tea beside the fire in the lounge.

26 rooms ⌂ – �£ 255/600 ♙♙£ 255/600 – 1 suite

Northcote Rd ⊠ BB6 8BE – North : 0.5 mi on A 59 at junction with A 666 – ℰ (01254) 240 555 – www.northcote.com

❀ **Northcote** – See restaurant listing

XXX **Northcote** (Nigel Haworth) 🕸 🖨 & AC 🕪 🔄 P

❀ BRITISH MODERN · ELEGANT Elegant restaurant within a smart Victorian house. Refined, sophisticated cooking shows depth of flavour and a lightness of touch. Local and garden ingredients are the stars of the show. Watch the chefs in action from the glass-walled kitchen table or join them by taking part in one of the cookery classes.

➔ Black pudding and buttered pink trout with mustard and nettle sauce. Milk-fed lamb, Jersey Royals, cabbage, spring vegetables and onion foam. Valrhona chocolate cylinder with smoked hazelnut praline and salted sheeps' milk ice cream.

Menu £ 32 (weekday lunch)/60 – Carte £ 39/86

Northcote Hotel, Northcote Rd ⊠ BB6 8BE – North : 0.5 mi on A 59 at junction with A 666 – ℰ (01254) 240 555 (booking essential) – www.northcote.com

at Mellor Northwest: 3.25 mi by A677 – ⊠ Blackburn

Stanley House

LUXURY · DESIGN Attractive part-17C manor house boasting superb country views and a smart spa with four types of sauna. Bedrooms in the main house are elegant and feature original beams and mullioned windows; the 'Woodland Rooms' are more contemporary. Stylish 'Grill on the Hill' offers modern favourites and views over the garden to the coast; 'Mr Fred's' serves simpler fare.

30 rooms ⊠ – ♦£ 150/250 ♦♦£ 180/280

⊠ BB2 7NP – Southwest : 0.75 mi by A 677 and Further Ln – ℰ (01254) 769 200
– www.stanleyhouse.co.uk

Millstone

INN · COSY Characterful sandstone inn set in a charming Ribble Valley village. Bedrooms offer modern comforts and have a cottagey feel, while the dining room blends contemporary styling with traditional features. Classic dishes change with the seasons; the steak is a perennial favourite. Service is cheery.

23 rooms ⊠ – ♦£ 78/138 ♦♦£ 88/148 – 1 suite

Church Ln ⊠ BB2 7JR – ℰ (01254) 813 333 – www.millstonehotel.co.uk

BLACKPOOL

Blackpool – Pop. 147 663 – Regional map n° **11**-A2

▶ London 246 mi – Leeds 88 mi – Liverpool 56 mi – Manchester 51 mi

Number One South Beach

LUXURY · DESIGN Modernised hotel close to the promenade, that's run with a passion and features bright, bold colour schemes. Striking, contemporary bedrooms – two with four-posters – come with smart bathrooms boasting whirlpool baths and TVs. Concise menus are largely made up of free range, organic and fair trade produce.

13 rooms ⊠ – ♦£ 81/150 ♦♦£ 125/159 – 1 suite

Town plan: BZ-v – 4 Harrowside West ⊠ FY4 1NW – ℰ (01253) 343 900
– www.numberonehotels.com

Redstone

TOWNHOUSE · CONTEMPORARY A very stylish, intimate hotel close to the famous Pleasure Beach, with a small lounge and bijou basement bar. Smart bedrooms have good mod cons. Breakfast on soufflé omelette or Manx kippers while sat beside a baby grand piano.

8 rooms ⊠ – ♦£ 90/100 ♦♦£ 90/125

Town plan: BZ-a – 9 Alexandra Rd ⊠ FY1 6BU – ℰ (01253) 283 387
– www.theredstoneblackpool.co.uk – Closed 17-28 December

Number One St Lukes

LUXURY · DESIGN Boutique guesthouse close to the promenade and Pleasure Beach; run by a very charming owner. Bedrooms are named after the town's piers: 'North' has an African feel and 'Central', a white four-poster and more feminine touch. They also have an outdoor hot tub and a mini pitch and putt green.

3 rooms ⊠ – ♦£ 75/120 ♦♦£ 100/130

Town plan: AZ-a – 1 St Lukes Rd ⊠ FY4 2EL – ℰ (01253) 343 901
– www.numberoneblackpool.com

Langtrys

FAMILY · PERSONALISED Smart guesthouse in a peaceful residential area. Bedrooms have warm fabrics, modern facilities and extras such as robes, clothes brushes and items travellers often forget. Bathrooms have underfloor heating and one even has a TV!

6 rooms ⊠ – ♦£ 70/90 ♦♦£ 100/130

Town plan: Y-x – 36 King Edward Ave ⊠ FY2 9TA – ℰ (01253) 352 031
– www.langtrysblackpool.co.uk

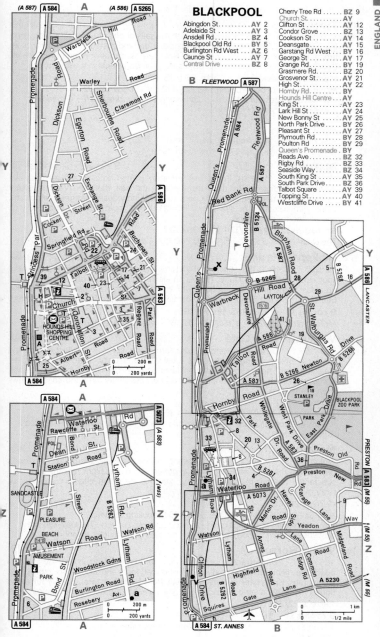

BLACKPOOL

ENGLAND

LANCASTER

PRESTON

321

at Thornton Northeast: 5.5 mi by A584 – Plan: BY – on B5412 – ⊠ Blackpool

XX **Twelve**

BRITISH MODERN · DESIGN Set beneath the sails of one of Europe's tallest working windmills is this passionately run cocktail bar and restaurant – which has an urban, industrial feel courtesy of brick walls, exposed pipework and grey beams. Good value menus offer modern dishes with the occasional innovative touch.

Menu £ 18 (weekdays) – Carte £ 31/45

Marsh Mill, Fleetwood Rd North ⊠ FY5 4JZ – ℰ (01253) 821 212
– www.twelve-restaurant.co.uk – dinner only and Sunday lunch – Closed first
2 weeks January and Monday

BLAKENEY

Norfolk – ⊠ Holt – Pop. 801 – Regional map n° **8**-C1
▶ London 127 mi – King's Lynn 37 mi – Norwich 28 mi

🏨 **Blakeney**

TRADITIONAL · CLASSIC Traditional, privately owned hotel in a great quayside location, affording views over the estuary and salt marshes. Various comfy lounges and a bar with subtle modern touches. Individually designed bedrooms, some with balconies or sea views. Formal dining room offers a good outlook and a wide-ranging menu.

64 rooms ⊇ – †£ 95/174 ††£ 190/328

The Quay ⊠ NR25 7NE – ℰ (01263) 740 797 – www.blakeneyhotel.co.uk

🏠 **Blakeney House**

FAMILY · HOMELY This substantial Victorian house is tucked away in a peaceful spot close to Blakeney Quay. There's an elegant dining room offering a delicious breakfast menu and a lounge hung with modern seascapes. Cosy bedrooms have been smartly refurbished by the welcoming owner – several have coastal themes.

9 rooms ⊇ – †£ 75/165 ††£ 75/165

High St ⊠ NR25 7NX – ℰ (01263) 740 561 – www.blakeneyhouse.com

X **Wiveton Farm Café**

REGIONAL · RURAL An extension of a farm shop, set down a dusty track and run by a smiley young team. Light breakfasts and tasty, salad-based lunches; weekends see more substantial breakfasts and 'Norfolk' tapas in the evenings. Unfussy preparation of local and farm produce. Glorious farm and coastal views from the terrace.

Carte £ 18/32

⊠ NR25 7TE – West : 0.5 mi on A149 – ℰ (01263) 740 515
– www.wivetonhall.co.uk – lunch only and dinner Thursday-Saturday – Closed
January-Easter

X **Moorings**

TRADITIONAL CUISINE · BISTRO Bright, relaxed village bistro just a stone's throw from the quay and run by an experienced couple. Light lunches and more substantial dinners featuring unfussy, seasonal dishes in classic combinations; tasty, homemade, old school puddings.

Carte £ 25/40

High St ⊠ NR25 7NA – ℰ (01263) 740 054 (booking essential)
– www.blakeney-moorings.co.uk – Closed 3 weeks January, Tuesday-Thursday
November-March, Sunday except bank holidays and Monday dinner

🍺 **White Horse**

REGIONAL · PUB Attractive brick and flint former coaching inn set by the harbour. The menu champions all things seasonal, local and British, so expect lobsters, crabs, Brancaster oysters and meat from Norfolk estates. Simply furnished bedrooms come in various shapes and sizes; one has a great view of the marshes.

Carte £ 22/31

9 rooms ⊇ – †£ 99/129 ††£ 99/129

4 High St ⊠ NR25 7AL – ℰ (01263) 740 574 (booking advisable)
– www.blakeneywhitehorse.co.uk – Closed 25 December

at Cley next the Sea East: 1.5 mi on A149 – ⊠ Holt

⌂ Cley Windmill ⬠ ⬠ ⬠ ⬠ ⬠ ⬠ ⬠ **P**

HISTORIC · COSY With its views over the marshes and river, this restored 18C windmill is a birdwatcher's paradise. Snug, characterful bedrooms are split between the mill, the stables and the boatshed. The flagstoned dining room offers a set menu of homemade country dishes and the tea room opens in the summer months.

9 rooms ⬠ – ♦£ 129/199 ♦♦£ 159/219
The Quay ⊠ *NR25 7RP* – ℰ *(01263) 740 209* – *www.cleywindmill.co.uk*

at Wiveton South: 1 mi by A149 on Wiveton Rd

⌂ Wiveton Bell ⬠ ⬠ **P**

BRITISH   TRADITIONAL · FASHIONABLE Modernised pub featuring beams, stripped floors and wood-burning stoves; with picnic tables out the front and a beautifully landscaped rear terrace. Seasonal menu offers pub classics, carefully crafted from quality local ingredients. Stylish, cosy bedrooms have smart bathrooms; continental breakfasts.

Carte £ 27/37

4 rooms ⬠ – ♦£ 95/130 ♦♦£ 85/140
Blakeney Rd ⊠ *NR25 7TL* – ℰ *(01263) 740 101 (booking essential)*
– *www.wivetonbell.com*

> If you are looking for particularly pleasant accommodation,
> book a hotel shown in red: ⌂...🏠🏠.

at Morston West: 1.5 mi on A149 – ⊠ Holt

⌂⌂ Morston Hall ⬠ ⬠ ⬠ **P**

LUXURY · CLASSIC Attractive, personally run country house with manicured gardens, set in a small coastal hamlet. Comfy guest areas feature antiques and paintings. Bedrooms are split between the main house and an annexe – the latter are larger and have subtle contemporary touches. Service is keen and friendly.

13 rooms (dinner included) ⬠ – ♦£ 260/300 ♦♦£ 380/400
The Street ⊠ *NR25 7AA* – ℰ *(01263) 741 041* – *www.morstonhall.com*
– *Closed 1-29 January and 24-26 December*
❀ **Morston Hall** – See restaurant listing

✗✗ Morston Hall (Galton Blackiston) ⬠ **P**

❀ **CLASSIC CUISINE · ELEGANT** Set in an attractive country house surrounded by landscaped gardens: choose between a traditionally furnished room or a beautiful conservatory. The set 7 course daily menu (served at 8pm), offers well-balanced seasonal dishes. Cooking is classically based, sophisticated and exhibits a delicate, modern touch.

➔ Butter-poached Brancaster lobster, sea beets and oyster sauce. Loin of Norfolk lamb, haggis croustillant, spring carrot, mint jelly and lamb jus. Gariguette strawberries, yoghurt mousse and buttermilk panna cotta.

Menu £ 66 – set menu only
Morston Hall Hotel, The Street ⊠ *NR25 7AA*
– ℰ *(01263) 741 041 (booking essential)* – *www.morstonhall.com*
– *dinner only and Sunday lunch* – *Closed 1-29 January and 24-26 December*

BLANCHLAND

Northumberland – Regional map n° **14**-A2
▶ London 286 mi – Newcastle upon Tyne 29 mi – Carlisle 50 mi

🏠 Lord Crewe Arms ✿ 🛏 👌 🅿

TRADITIONAL · CONTEMPORARY This 12C abbot's priory has also spent time as a hunting lodge and a lead miners' hostelry. Its hugely characterful guest areas don't disappoint; smell the chicken roasting over the open fire in the barrel-ceilinged bar. Bedrooms have a modern country charm and come with bespoke furnishings and walkers' packs.

21 rooms 🖙 – 🛉£ 120/230 🛉🛉£ 150/260 – 3 suites
The Square ✉ DH8 9SP – ☏ (01434) 675 469
– www.lordcrewearmsblanchland.co.uk
Bishop's Dining Room – See restaurant listing

🍴 Bishop's Dining Room 🛏 ☂ 🍴 🅿

BRITISH TRADITIONAL · RUSTIC Bright, hunting-themed restaurant in a characterful hotel; the monks from the neighbouring abbey once dined here. Menus offer robust, flavoursome British dishes which feature kitchen garden, spit-roast and home-smoked produce.

Carte £ 19/28
Lord Crewe Arms Hotel, The Square ✉ DH8 9SP – ☏ (01434) 675 469
– www.lordcrewearmsblanchland.co.uk

BLANDFORD FORUM
Dorset – Pop. 11 694 – Regional map n° **2**-C3
▶ London 124 mi – Bournemouth 17 mi – Dorchester 17 mi – Salisbury 24 mi

at Tarrant Launceston Northeast: 5.5 mi by A354

🏠 Launceston Farmhouse 🐾 🛏 🗽 ✿ 🛗 🅿

FAMILY · PERSONALISED Charming guesthouse on a working cattle farm, which is the friendly owner's childhood home. Stylish bedrooms can be reached via a wrought iron spiral staircase and feature period furniture, modern bathrooms and homely extras.

6 rooms 🖙 – 🛉£ 75/125 🛉🛉£ 100/125
✉ DT11 8BY – ☏ (01258) 830 528 – www.launcestonfarm.co.uk

at Farnham Northeast: 7.5 mi by A354 – ✉ Blandford Forum

🏠 Farnham Farm House 🐾 ≤ 🛏 🗽 ✿ 🅿

FAMILY · COSY Welcoming farmhouse on a 300 acre working farm, complete with a swimming pool and a holistic therapy centre. Homely, immaculately kept bedrooms have country views. Enjoy tea and cake on arrival; the eggs are from their own hens.

3 rooms 🖙 – 🛉£ 80 🛉🛉£ 85/100
✉ DT11 8DG – North : 1 mi by Shaftesbury rd – ☏ (01725) 516 254
– www.farnhamfarmhouse.co.uk – Closed 25-26 December

BLEDINGTON – Gloucestershire ➜ See Stow-on-the-Wold

BODIAM
East Sussex – Regional map n° **5**-B2
▶ London 58 mi – Cranbrook 7 mi – Hastings 13 mi

🍴🍴 Curlew 🗽 🍽 🅿

BRITISH MODERN · DESIGN Contemporary restaurant behind a white clapperboard pub façade, with funky cow print wallpaper and a Scandinavian feel. Menus are modern, the wine list promotes organic and biodynamic wines, and service is smooth and professional.

Menu £ 25 (weekdays) – Carte £ 38/50
Junction Rd ✉ TN32 5UY – Northwest : 1.5 mi at junction with B 2244 – ☏ (01580) 861 394 – www.thecurlewrestaurant.co.uk – Closed 26 December, 1 January and Monday

BODMIN

Cornwall – Pop. 14 614 – Regional map n° **1**-B2

▶ London 270 mi – Newquay 18 mi – Plymouth 32 mi – Truro 23 mi

⌂ **Trehellas House** ✿ ⟨⟩ ⊼ **P**

TRADITIONAL · COSY Former posting inn, built by the Lordship of Pencarrow Manor to house officers from the local garrison. Cosy bedrooms with smart wood furnishings and understated décor. Popular restaurant offers extensive menu of local produce with venison a speciality. Good value 'steak and dessert' menu.

12 rooms ⌷ – ♦£ 50/75 ♦♦£ 75/175

Washaway ✉ *PL30 3AD – Northwest : 3 mi on A 389*
– ☎ (01208) 72 700 – www.trehellashouse.co.uk

⌂ **Bokiddick Farm** ⟨⟩ ⚸ **P**

TRADITIONAL · RUSTIC A traditional farmhouse on a 180 acre working dairy farm – a warm welcome is guaranteed and they serve cream teas on arrival. Homely, spotlessly kept bedrooms come with super king sized beds and country views; the largest rooms are in the old barn. Hearty breakfasts are taken overlooking the garden.

3 rooms ⌷ – ♦£ 50/55 ♦♦£ 85/90

Lanivet ✉ *PL30 5HP – South : 5 mi by A 30 following signs for Lanhydrock and Bokiddick – ☎ (01208) 831 481 – www.bokiddickfarm.co.uk*
– Closed Christmas

BOLLINGTON

Cheshire East – ✉ Cheshire – Pop. 7 373 – Regional map n° **11**-B3

▶ London 178 mi – Birmingham 69 mi – Leeds 58 mi – Manchester 22 mi

✗✗ **Oliver at Bollington Green**

MODERN CUISINE · BISTRO Bright and friendly, family-run neighbourhood restaurant just off the main road, opposite a tiny village green. Interesting menus of refined, balanced, flavoursome dishes, with the breads, ice-creams and chocolates all homemade.

Menu £ 20 (weekdays) – Carte £ 27/42

22 High St ✉ *SK10 5PH – ☎ (01625) 575 058 (booking advisable)*
– www.oliveratbollingtongreen.com – dinner only and Sunday lunch – Closed Sunday dinner, Monday and Tuesday

BOLNHURST

Bedford – Regional map n° **7**-A1

▶ London 64 mi – Bedford 8 mi – St Neots 7 mi

⌂ **Plough at Bolnhurst** ⟨⟩ ⌂ **P**

BRITISH MODERN · INN Charming whitewashed pub with a rustic bar, a modern restaurant, a lovely garden and a bustling atmosphere. Menus change with the seasons but always feature 28-day aged Aberdeenshire steaks, dishes containing Mediterranean ingredients like Sicilian black olives, and a great selection of wines and cheeses.

Menu £ 22 (weekday lunch) – Carte £ 30/50

Kimbolton Rd ✉ *MK44 2EX – South : 0.5 mi on B 660*
– ☎ (01234) 376 274 – www.bolnhurst.com
– Closed 2 weeks January, Sunday dinner and Monday

BOLTON ABBEY

North Yorkshire – ✉ Skipton – Pop. 117 – Regional map n° **13**-B2

▶ London 216 mi – Harrogate 18 mi – Leeds 23 mi – Skipton 6 mi

🏰 Devonshire Arms H. & Spa

LUXURY · CLASSIC A period coaching inn with a popular spa, set on the Duke and Duchess of Devonshire's 30,000 acre estate in the Yorkshire Dales. Comfy lounges display part of the owners' vast art collection and dogs are welcome too. Bedrooms in the wing are bright, modern and compact; those in the inn are more traditional.

40 rooms ⌁ – †£160/350 ††£160/450 – 2 suites

✉ BD23 6AJ – ℰ (01756) 710 441 – www.thedevonshirearms.co.uk

Burlington • Brasserie – See restaurant listing

✗✗✗ Burlington

BRITISH MODERN · FORMAL Elegant, antique-filled hotel dining room hung with impressive oils; sit in the conservatory to overlook the Italian garden. Elaborate modern dishes utilise fine ingredients, with much coming from the kitchen garden and estate.

Menu £65

Devonshire Arms H. & Spa, ✉ BD23 6AJ – ℰ (01756) 710 441 (booking essential) – www.burlingtonrestaurant.co.uk – dinner only – Closed Monday

✗✗ Brasserie

BRITISH MODERN · BRASSERIE Funky hotel brasserie with an attractive wine cellar; set opposite the kitchen garden. Sit on stripy banquettes in the bar or on red velour chairs in the dining room. The extensive à la carte offers satisfying brasserie classics.

Carte £26/59

Devonshire Arms H. & Spa, ✉ BD23 6AJ – ℰ (01756) 718 105 – www.devonshirebrasserie.co.uk

BOLTON-BY-BOWLAND

Lancashire – Regional map n° **11**-B2

▶ London 246 mi – Blackburn 17 mi – Skipton 15 mi

🏠 Middle Flass Lodge

TRADITIONAL · RUSTIC This cosy lodge started life as barn and cow byre, before being transformed into a lodge by its friendly owners. It's delightfully located in the heart of the Forest of Bowland and the comfy, classical bedrooms offer lovely country outlooks. Local, seasonal produce informs the regularly changing menu.

7 rooms ⌁ – †£55/60 ††£76/80

Settle Rd ✉ BB7 4NY – North : 2.5 mi by Clitheroe rd on Settle rd – ℰ (01200) 447 259 – www.middleflasslodge.co.uk

BORDON

Hampshire – Pop. 16 035 – Regional map n° **4**-C2

▶ London 54 mi – Croydon 57 mi – Barnet 67 mi – Ealing 49 mi

🏠 Groomes

TRADITIONAL · MODERN A former farmhouse set in 185 acres, which has been made 'green' by the installation of biomass boilers and solar panels. Spacious, modern bedrooms come with roll-top baths; it even has its own games room. Dining takes place at two communal tables – local produce features in dishes cooked on the Aga.

6 rooms ⌁ – †£90/130 ††£120/150

Frith End ✉ GU35 0QR – North : 2.75 mi by A 325 on Frith End Sand Pit rd – ℰ (01420) 489 858 – www.groomes.co.uk

BOREHAM

Essex – Regional map n° **7**-C2

▶ London 42 mi – Colchester 20 mi – Cambridge 54 mi

⌂ **Lion Inn** ☆ 🍴 ♿ AC 🛁 🏋 P

INN · DESIGN Keenly run, extended former pub with eco-friendly credentials and a French feel. Soundproofed bedrooms blend contemporary fabrics with reproduction furniture. Large open-plan lounge/brasserie with buzzy atmosphere; short menu of appealing, pub-style dishes.

23 rooms ⌂ – ♥£ 95/175 ♥♥£ 110/250

Main Rd ✉ CM3 3JA – 𝒞 (01245) 394 900
– www.lioninnhotel.co.uk – Closed 25, 26 ,31 December and 4-11 January

BOROUGHBRIDGE

North Yorkshire – Pop. 3 610 – Regional map n° **13**-B2
▶ London 215 mi – Leeds 19 mi – Middlesbrough 36 mi – York 16 mi

XX **thediningroom** 🍴

BRITISH MODERN · INTIMATE Characterful bow-fronted cottage concealing an opulent bar-lounge and an intimate beamed dining room. Wide-ranging menus offer boldly flavoured, Mediterranean-influenced dishes and chargrilled meats. In summer, head for the terrace.

Menu £ 16 (weekdays) – Carte £ 25/47

20 St James's Sq ✉ YO51 9AR – 𝒞 (01423) 326 426 (booking essential)
– www.thediningroomonline.co.uk – dinner only and Sunday lunch
– Closed 26 December, 1 January, Sunday dinner and Monday

XX **Grantham Arms** 🍴 🍷 🍴 P

MODERN CUISINE · FRIENDLY An intimate, glitzy restaurant with deep purple décor, chandeliers, an atmospheric cocktail bar and a 'gin bible' offering over 20 varieties. Modern cooking uses good texture and flavour combinations and everything is made on-site. Smart bedrooms have contemporary oak furnishings and Egyptian cotton linen.

Carte £ 18/35

7 rooms ⌂ – ♥£ 50/80 ♥♥£ 70/100

Milby ✉ YO51 9BW – North : 0.25 mi on B 6265
– 𝒞 (01423) 323 980 – www.granthamarms.co.uk

at Roecliffe West: 1 mi

🍴 **Crown Inn** 🍴 🍴 P

REGIONAL · INN 14C inn in a delightful position by the village green. Menus offer pub classics alongside more ambitious dishes; if you can't decide on a dessert, try them all with the assiette of puddings. Well-appointed bedrooms come with feature beds, roll top baths and plenty of extra touches.

Carte £ 26/43

4 rooms ⌂ – ♥£ 75/90 ♥♥£ 80/120

✉ YO51 9LY – 𝒞 (01423) 322 300
– www.crowninnroecliffe.co.uk

at Lower Dunsforth Southeast : 4.25 mi by B 6265

🍴 **The Dunsforth** 🍴 P
🌾

BRITISH MODERN · PUB You can tailor your experience at this contemporary pub: if you like things lively, sit in its fire-lit front rooms; for a more intimate meal head for the smart restaurant. Menus offer admirable choice and value for money, and seasonality and freshness are key. Most dishes come with a modern twist.

Menu £ 18/45 – Carte £ 25/56

Mary Ln ✉ YO26 9SA – 𝒞 (01423) 320 700
– www.thedunsforth.co.uk – Closed Sunday dinner and Monday-Tuesday

BOSCASTLE

Cornwall – Regional map n° **1**-B2

▶ London 260 mi – Bude 14 mi – Exeter 59 mi – Plymouth 43 mi

Boscastle House
⇐ 🚗 🎇 🅿

FAMILY · STYLISH Modern styling in a detached Victorian house with a calm, relaxing air. Bedrooms are light and spacious, with roll-top baths and walk-in showers. Hearty breakfasts feature home-baked muffins and banana bread. Tea and cake on arrival.

6 rooms ⌂ – ♦£ 60 ♦♦£ 100/120

Tintagel Rd ⊠ PL35 OAS – South : 0.75 mi on B 3263 – ℰ (01840) 250 654
– www.boscastlehouse.com – Closed 2 weeks Christmas

Old Rectory
🐾 🚗 🅿

HISTORIC · PERSONALISED Lovely house with a Victorian walled garden. Characterful bedrooms: one has a wood stove; another, a super king sized bed and whirlpool bath. Breakfasts include bacon and sausages from the owner's pigs. Thomas Hardy once stayed here.

4 rooms ⌂ – ♦£ 53/99 ♦♦£ 75/110

St Juliot ⊠ PL35 OBT – Northeast : 2.5 mi by B 3263 – ℰ (01840) 250 225
– www.stjuliot.com – Closed Christmas

BOSHAM – West Sussex ➜ See Chichester

BOSTON SPA

West Yorkshire – Pop. 4 662 – Regional map n° **13**-B2

▶ London 127 mi – Harrogate 12 mi – Leeds 12 mi – York 16 mi

Four Gables
🐾 🚗 🎇 🅿 🚭

TRADITIONAL · ART DECO Grade II listed Arts and Crafts house with a smartly manicured garden and croquet lawn; hidden away down a private road. Cosy bedrooms have good comforts. Breakfast includes homemade breads and jams, as well as eggs from their hens.

4 rooms ⌂ – ♦£ 52/65 ♦♦£ 75/95

Oaks Ln ⊠ LS23 6DS – West : 0.25 mi by A 659 – ℰ (01937) 845 592
– www.fourgables.co.uk – Closed Christmas-New Year

BOUGHTON MONCHELSEA

Kent – Pop. 2 863 – Regional map n° **5**-B2

▶ London 40 mi – Maidstone 4 mi – Sevenoaks 23 mi

XX Mulberry Tree
🚗 🏡 🅿

BRITISH MODERN · FRIENDLY This rurally located restaurant has lovely gardens, a large paved terrace and a surprisingly stylish interior. Modern British menus feature confidently prepared, imaginatively presented dishes and ingredients are well-sourced.

Menu £ 17 (weekdays) – Carte £ 30/40

Hermitage Ln. ⊠ ME17 4DA – South : 1.5 mi by Park Lane and East Hall Hill
– ℰ (01622) 749 082 – www.themulberrytreekent.co.uk – Closed first 2 weeks
January, Sunday dinner and Monday

BOURN

Cambridgeshire – Pop. 669 – Regional map n° **8**-A3

▶ London 58 mi – Croydon 87 mi – Barnet 44 mi – Ealing 57 mi

Willow Tree
🍴 🚗 🏡 🅿

BRITISH MODERN · PUB Quirky pub with a life-sized cow model outside and gilt mirrors, chandeliers and Louis XV style furniture inside. Menus range from old pub classics to much more ambitious modern dishes; afternoon tea and a 'Deckchair' menu served May-Sept.

Menu £ 23/29 – Carte £ 20/34

29 High St ⊠ CB23 2SQ – ℰ (01954) 719 775 – www.thewillowtreebourn.com

BOURNEMOUTH

Bournemouth – Pop. 187 503 – Regional map n° **2**-D3

▶ London 114 mi – Bristol 76 mi – Southampton 34 mi

🏨 Bournemouth Highcliff Marriott

CHAIN HOTEL · CLASSIC Set on the clifftop, this grand old seaside hotel has a funicular linking it directly to the beach. Smart guest areas and airy modern bedrooms; some with lovely sea views. Leisure club boasts a tennis court and indoor and outdoor pools. Stylish grill restaurant offers a modern steak and seafood based menu.

160 rooms ⊠ – ♦£ 99/160 ♦♦£ 120/220 – 3 suites

Town plan: CZ-z – *St Michael's Rd, West Cliff* ⊠ BH2 5DU – ℰ *(01202) 557 702*
– *www.bournemouthhighcliffmarriott.co.uk*

🏨 Miramar

FAMILY · CLASSIC Late Edwardian villa intended as a summer residence for the Austrian ambassador – until WW1 intervened. Close to town yet boasting peaceful, award winning gardens and superb sea views. Large, classical bedrooms; some with balconies. Traditional dinner menu and snacks in the bar or on the terrace.

43 rooms ⊠ – ♦£ 35/75 ♦♦£ 96/220

Town plan: DZ-u – *19 Grove Rd, East Overcliff* ⊠ BH1 3AL – ℰ *(01202) 556 581*
– *www.miramar-bournemouth.com*

🏨 Green House

TRADITIONAL · DESIGN Bright, eco-friendly hotel in a small Victorian property, run by an enthusiastic team. Contemporary interior features reclaimed and eco-furnishings, including chairs made from old video game consoles and vegetable ink wallpapers.

32 rooms ⊠ – ♦£ 99/129 ♦♦£ 129/179

Town plan: DZ-n – *4 Grove Rd* ⊠ BH1 3AX – ℰ *(01202) 498 900*
– *www.thegreenhousehotel.com*

Arbor – See restaurant listing

🏨 Chocolate

HOLIDAY HOTEL · PERSONALISED A unique, chocolate-themed hotel, owned by a chocolatier who runs regular workshops. Contemporary bedrooms come in browns and creams. The small lounge-bar features an automatic cocktail machine – they even serve 'choctails'.

15 rooms – ♦£ 65 ♦♦£ 90/180

Town plan: CZ-a – *5 Durley Rd* ⊠ BH2 5JQ – ℰ *(01202) 556 857*
– *www.thechocolateboutiquehotel.co.uk* – *Closed 2-27 December*

🏨 Urban Beach

TOWNHOUSE · DESIGN A laid-back hotel with a large heated terrace; set close to the sea and the town. A beach shack style exterior conceals spacious designer bedrooms with stylish modern bathrooms. The small reception is located in the trendy bar-cum-bistro, which offers a large menu of steaks and modern classics.

12 rooms ⊠ – ♦£ 72 ♦♦£ 100/180

Town plan: DX-a – *23 Argyll Rd* ⊠ BH5 1EB – ℰ *(01202) 301 509*
– *www.urbanbeach.co.uk*

XX Edge

BRITISH MODERN · FASHIONABLE Stylish restaurant on the top levels of an apartment block, with floor to ceiling windows and excellent views over the town and Poole Bay. Seafood menus feature intricate modern dishes which are styled on classical combinations.

Menu £ 20 (lunch) – Carte £ 29/47

Town plan: CX-s – *2 Studland Rd, (4th Floor), Alum Chine* ⊠ BH4 8JA
– ℰ *(01202) 757 007 (booking essential)* – *www.edgerestaurant.co.uk*

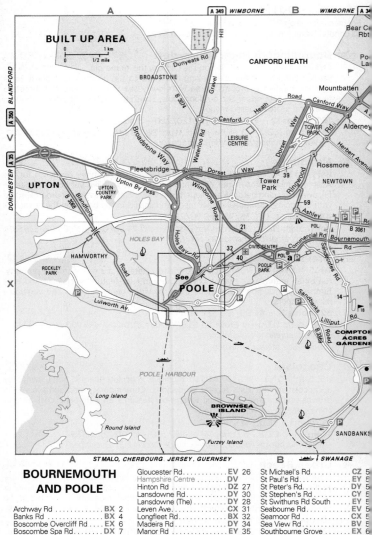

ST MALO, CHERBOURG, JERSEY, GUERNSEY   SWANAGE

BOURNEMOUTH AND POOLE

XX Arbor

MODERN CUISINE · MINIMALIST Large restaurant in an eco-friendly hotel; it upholds a 'sustainable' ethos with FSC timber on the floors, low energy induction cookers in the kitchen and honey bees on the roof. Modern menus display innovative touches; produce is local.

Menu £ 20 (lunch)/20 – Carte £ 25/43

Town plan: DZ-n – *Green House Hotel, 4 Grove Rd ✉ BH1 3AX – 𝒞 (01202) 498 900 – www.arbor-restaurant.co.uk*

XX Plates & Co 𝒸

MODERN CUISINE · INDIVIDUAL Grand 18C church with antique oak panelling and stunning stained glass; the kitchen is in the old chancel. Modern British cooking is fresh and flavoursome; lighter options are available in the small outside area. Lunch is good value.

Menu £ 15 (lunch)/19 – Carte £ 17/44

Town plan: CX-x – *Lansdeer Rd, Westbourne ✉ BH4 9EH – 𝒞 (01202) 765 696 – www.platesandco.com – Closed 25-26 December ,Monday and Sunday dinner*

X West Beach

FISH AND SEAFOOD · BISTRO Popular beachfront restaurant with folding glass doors opening onto a terrace. Seafood menus feature fish caught in front of the building; look for the buoys where the nets lie. They also offer an express lunch and summer takeaways.

Carte £ 27/42

Town plan: DZ-c – *Pier Approach ✉ BH2 5AA – 𝒞 (01202) 587 785 (booking essential) – www.west-beach.co.uk – Closed 25 December*

at Southbourne East : 3.75 mi. by A 35 – EV – on B 3059

🏠 Cliff House ⓝ

BUSINESS · PERSONALISED A smartly refurbished 120 year old house which retains some of its Victorian features. Its elegant, modern bar-lounge leads onto a landscaped garden and terrace, while the comfortable bedrooms vary in size and feature 'Smart' TVs and coffee machines. The menu offers something for everyone.

14 rooms ☲ – ♦£ 50/75 ♦♦£ 90/150

13 Belle Vue Rd ✉ BH6 3DA – 𝒞 (01202) 424 701 – www.cliffhouse-hotel.com

BOURTON-ON-THE-HILL – Gloucestershire ➜ See Moreton-in-Marsh

BOURTON-ON-THE-WATER

Gloucestershire – Pop. 3 296 – Regional map n° **2**-D1

▶ London 91 mi – Gloucester 24 mi – Birmingham 47 mi – Oxford 36 mi

🏠 Dial House

COUNTRY HOUSE · CLASSIC The oldest stone-built house in this charming Cotswold village, with lovely lawned gardens and a tranquil feel. Bedrooms in the original house have character; those in the coach house are more contemporary. The atmospheric dining room serves light lunches and more ambitious modern dinners.

14 rooms ☲ – ♦£ 129/229 ♦♦£ 139/259

The Chestnuts, High St ✉ GL54 2AN – 𝒞 (01451) 822 244 – www.dialhousehotel.com – Closed 1 week January

🏠 Coombe House

TRADITIONAL · PERSONALISED Spacious 1920s detached house, not far from the delightful village centre. There's a traditional lounge and a first floor terrace for sunnier days; the breakfast room boasts full-length leaded windows and overlooks the attractive garden. Homely, immaculately kept bedrooms offer good comforts.

4 rooms ☲ – ♦£ 60/70 ♦♦£ 75/90

Rissington Rd ✉ GL54 2DT – 𝒞 (01451) 821 966 – www.coombehouse.net – Restricted opening in winter

at Lower Slaughter Northwest: 1.75 mi by A429 – ⊠ Cheltenham

🏛 Lower Slaughter Manor 🕿 🏊 🖃 🍴 🕍 🅿

LUXURY · CLASSIC Beautiful part-17C manor house in warm Cotswold stone, surrounded by delightful grounds and filled with antiques and oil paintings. Elegant bedrooms are split between the house and the stables: the former are more individually styled; the latter are more modern – two have private outdoor hot tubs.

19 rooms � – ♦£ 149/539 ♦♦£ 169/559

⊠ GL54 2HP – ☎ (01451) 820 456 – www.lowerslaughter.co.uk

Sixteen58 – See restaurant listing

🏛 Slaughters Country Inn 🕿 🖃 🕭 🕍 🅿

INN · CONTEMPORARY Originally a crammer school for Eton College, this stone-built manor house is a good choice for families – and they welcome dogs too! It's relaxed and understated, with modern styling; the cosy bedrooms have feature walls and up-to-date facilities. The pub and restaurant serve British classics.

31 rooms ⊡ – ♦£ 75/330 ♦♦£ 85/340 – 7 suites

⊠ GL54 2HS – ☎ (01451) 822 143 – www.theslaughtersinn.co.uk

The Pub at Slaughters Country Inn – See restaurant listing

✕✕✕ Sixteen58 🖃 🕿 🕭 🕼 ↔ 🅿

MODERN CUISINE · FORMAL Elegant dining room in a bright, airy extension of a fine manor house hotel, overlooking the lovely gardens. Immaculately laid tables have beautiful floral displays. Menus offer accomplished modern dishes with a classical base.

Menu £ 26 (weekdays)/65

Lower Slaughter Manor, ⊠ GL54 2HP – ☎ (01451) 820 456
– www.lowerslaughter.co.uk

🍴 The Pub at Slaughters Country Inn 🖃 🕿 🕭 🅿

BRITISH TRADITIONAL · TRADITIONAL A trio of characterful rooms with wonky low ceilings and stone floors, within a hotel in a charming Cotswold village. The appealing menu offers hearty dishes and puddings that stray from the norm. Have afternoon tea on the terrace.

Carte £ 25/37

⊠ GL54 2HS – ☎ (01451) 822 143 – www.theslaughtersinn.co.uk

at Upper Slaughter Northwest: 2.5 mi by A429 – ⊠ Bourton-On-The-Water

🏛 Lords of the Manor 🕿 🏊 🖃 🕿 🕍 🅿

LUXURY · CLASSIC Charming 17C former rectory in a pretty Cotswold village, with beautiful gardens, superb views and a real sense of tranquility. Two luxurious sitting rooms and a bar with a 'nature' colour theme. Bedrooms have a fitting country house style and subtle contemporary touches. Staff are diligent and affable.

24 rooms ⊡ – ♦£ 249/545 ♦♦£ 249/545 – 2 suites

⊠ GL54 2JD – ☎ (01451) 820 243 – www.lordsofthemanor.com

❀ **Lords of the Manor** – See restaurant listing

✕✕✕ Lords of the Manor 🖃 🕿 🅿

❀ **MODERN CUISINE · FORMAL** Plush, formal dining room in a beautiful country house in a tranquil Cotswold village; enjoy an aperitif in the luxurious sitting rooms. Accomplished, understated dishes use well-judged, classical combinations and are executed using modern techniques. Service is professional and very personable.

→ Port marinated foie gras with apples, sweet wine jelly and gingerbread purée. Braised lardo-glazed halibut with celeriac, spring greens and oxtail. Hazelnut dacquoise, caramel ganache, chocolate mousse and bitter orange sorbet.

Menu £ 73

Lords of the Manor Hotel, ⊠ GL54 2JD – ☎ (01451) 820 243 (booking essential)
– www.lordsofthemanor.com – dinner only and Sunday lunch

BOWLAND BRIDGE

Cumbria – Regional map n° **12**-A2_3

🄿 London 269 mi – Liverpool 86 mi – Preston 48 mi – Blackpool 60 mi

🍴 Hare and Hounds

REGIONAL · PUB Charming, 17C Lakeland pub in a delightful village. Large front terrace leads through into a rustic, open-fired inner hung with old village photos and hop bines. Menus offer typical, hearty favourites and most produce is locally sourced. Bedrooms are well-equipped and elegant; some boast roll-top baths.

Carte £ 20/31

5 rooms ☑ – ♦£ 95/165 ♦♦£ 95/165

✉ LA11 6NN – ✆ (015395) 68 333 – www.hareandhoundsbowlandbridge.co.uk
– Closed 25 December

BOWNESS-ON-WINDERMERE – Cumbria ➜ See Windermere

BOX – Wiltshire ➜ See Bath

BOYLESTONE
Derbyshire – Regional map n° **9**-A2
▶ London 142 mi – Derby 18 mi – Stoke on Trent 24 mi

XX Lighthouse ♿ 🅿

BRITISH MODERN · DESIGN It may not be near the coast, but the Lighthouse does attract your attention. The self-taught chef prepares ambitious, complex dishes with good combinations of flavours and textures; the tasting menu, in particular, is a hit.

Carte £ 40/46

New Rd ✉ DE6 5AA – behind Rose & Crown public house – ✆ (01335) 330 658
– www.the-lighthouse-restaurant.co.uk – dinner only and Sunday lunch – Closed Sunday dinner and Monday-Wednesday

BRADFORD-ON-AVON
Wiltshire – Pop. 9 149 – Regional map n° **2**-C2
▶ London 118 mi – Bristol 24 mi – Salisbury 35 mi – Swindon 33 mi

🏨 Woolley Grange

COUNTRY HOUSE · CLASSIC Fine Jacobean manor house that's geared towards families, with a crèche, a kids' club, a games room and outdoor activities. For adults, there's a chic spa and some lovely country views. Smart bedrooms come in many styles. Accomplished, classical cooking is served in the restaurant and more relaxed orangery.

25 rooms ☑ – ♦£ 120/180 ♦♦£ 190/560 – 6 suites

Woolley Green ✉ BA15 1TX – Northeast : 0.75 mi by B 3107 on Woolley St
– ✆ (01225) 864 705 – www.woolleygrangehotel.co.uk

XxX Three Gables

MODERN CUISINE · ELEGANT Personally and passionately run restaurant in a 350 year old house, with a lovely terrace and charming exposed stone and wattle and daub walls. Skilful, accomplished cooking; interesting, original dishes are based on classical combinations.

Menu £ 18/33 – Carte £ 28/47

St Margaret's St ✉ BA15 1DA – ✆ (01225) 781 666 – www.thethreegables.com
– Closed 1-15 January, 25-26 December, Sunday and Monday

at Winsley West: 2 mi by A363 off B3108

🏨 Stillmeadow

FAMILY · COSY The name sums it up well, as it has a charming wildflower garden and is located on the edge of a small hamlet. Tasteful furnishings provide a good degree of luxury and comfort. Bedrooms are colour-themed and have thoughtful touches.

4 rooms ☑ – ♦£ 90 ♦♦£ 100

18 Bradford Rd ✉ BA15 2HW – ✆ (01225) 722 119 – www.stillmeadow.co.uk
– Closed 23 December-2 January

BRADWELL

Derbyshire – Pop. 1 416 – Regional map n° **9**-A1

▶ London 170 mi – Birmingham 99 mi – Liverpool 66 mi – Leeds 48 mi

🍴 **Samuel Fox Country Inn**   ⇔ 🏠 **P**

BRITISH TRADITIONAL · **PUB** Attractive, light-stone pub with smart bedrooms and a dramatic, hilly backdrop: named after the inventor of the steel-ribbed umbrella, who was born in the village. Classic dishes have modern touches; Spanish influences hint at the chef's time in Andalucia. On Fridays, try the 'secret supper' small plates.

Menu £ 19 (weekday lunch)/49 – Carte £ 26/38

4 rooms ⌑ – ♦£ 70/95 ♦♦£ 95/130

Stretfield Rd ⊠ *S33 9JT* – *℘ (01433) 621 562* – *www.samuelfox.co.uk*
– *Closed 4-14 January*

BRAITHWAITE – Cumbria ➜ See Keswick

BRAMPFORD SPEKE – Devon ➜ See Exeter

BRAMPTON

Cumbria – Pop. 4 229 – Regional map n° **12**-B1

▶ London 317 mi – Carlisle 9 mi – Newcastle upon Tyne 49 mi

🏠 **Farlam Hall**   ⇗ 🦢 ⇐ 🛏 **P**

TRADITIONAL · **PERSONALISED** Well-run, family-owned Victorian country house, whose origins can be traced back to the 1600s. Bedrooms are furnished with antiques but also have Bose radios. The sumptuous formal dining room has romantic lake views, a traditional daily menu and attentive service. Enjoy afternoon tea in the comfy, curio-filled lounges, overlooking the immaculately kept ornamental gardens.

12 rooms (dinner included) ⌑ – ♦£ 118/148 ♦♦£ 310/370

⊠ *CA8 2NG – Southeast : 2.75 mi on A 689* – *℘ (016977) 46 234*
– *www.farlamhall.co.uk – Closed 4-22 January and 25-30 December*

BRANCASTER STAITHE

Norfolk – Regional map n° **8**-C1

▶ London 131 mi – King's Lynn 25 mi – Boston 57 mi – East Dereham 27 mi

🍴 **White Horse**   ⇔ ⇐ 🏠 **P**

REGIONAL · **PUB** The rear views over the marshes and Scolt Head Island really make this pub. Choose from old favourites, tapas-style dishes and a few more ambitious offerings on the bar menu; or seasonally changing dishes supplemented by daily specials on the à la carte. Smart, New England style bedrooms – some with terraces.

Carte £ 24/32

15 rooms ⌑ – ♦£ 140 ♦♦£ 180

⊠ *PE31 8BY* – *℘ (01485) 210 262 (booking essential)*
– *www.whitehorsebrancaster.co.uk*

BRAUGHING

Hertfordshire – Pop. 854 – Regional map n° **7**-B2

▶ London 33 mi – Hertford 12 mi – Stevenage 18 mi

🍴 **Golden Fleece**   🛏 🏠 **P**

BRITISH TRADITIONAL · **INN** Proudly run, part-16C pub with a spacious garden, a pretty terrace overlooking the village and striking period features including a vast inglenook fireplace. Tasty, comforting, country-style dishes; gluten and dairy free options available.

Carte £ 21/36

20 Green End ⊠ *SG11 2PG* – *℘ (01920) 823 555*
– *www.goldenfleecebraughing.co.uk – Closed 25-26 December and Sunday dinner*

BRAY

Windsor and Maidenhead – ✉ Maidenhead – Pop. 8 121 – Regional map n° **6**-C3

▶ London 30 mi – Oxford 36 mi – Bristol 93 mi

see Maidenhead Plan

XxxX **Waterside Inn** (Alain Roux)

❀❀❀ FRENCH CLASSIC • **ELEGANT** An illustrious restaurant in a glorious spot on a bank of the Thames, with a relaxed, rustic dining room and a delightful terrace ideal for aperitifs. Service is charming and expertly structured. Carefully considered French menus reflect the seasons and use top quality luxury ingredients in perfectly judged, sophisticated combinations. Bedrooms are chic and sumptuous.

→ Tronçonnettes de homard poêlées minute au Porto blanc. Filets de lapereau grillés sur un fondant de céleri-rave, sauce à l'armagnac et aux marrons glacés. Soufflé chaud aux mirabelles.

Menu £ 62 (weekday lunch)/160 – Carte £ 121/167

11 rooms ⌂ – †£ 240/395 ††£ 240/395 – 2 suites

Town plan: X-s – *Ferry Rd* ✉ *SL6 2AT* – ℰ *(01628) 620 691 (booking essential)*
– www.waterside-inn.co.uk – Closed 26 December-28 January, Monday-Tuesday

XX **Caldesi in Campagna**

ITALIAN • **INTIMATE** Sister of Café Caldesi in London, is this chic, sophisticated restaurant with a cosy conservatory and a lovely covered terrace – complete with a wood-fired oven. Flavoursome Italian dishes feature Tuscan and Sicilian specialities.

Menu £ 17 (weekday lunch) – Carte £ 29/58

Town plan: X-x – *Old Mill Ln* ✉ *SL6 2BG* – ℰ *(01628) 788 500*
– www.caldesi.com – Closed Sunday dinner and Monday

⒯ **Hinds Head**

❀ BRITISH TRADITIONAL • **RUSTIC** Listed 15C pub at the heart of a pretty village; its dark wood panelling and log fires giving it a characterful Georgian feel. Prime seasonal produce is used to create rich, satisfying dishes that are down-to-earth, fiercely British, carefully presented and big on flavour. Service is informed and engaging.

→ Hash of snails. Chicken, ham and leek pie with mashed potato. Caramelised butter loaf with apple.

Menu £ 48 – Carte £ 33/58

Town plan: X-e – *High St* ✉ *SL6 2AB* – ℰ *(01628) 626 151 (booking essential)*
– www.hindsheadbray.com – Closed 25 December and Sunday dinner

⒯ **Royal Oak**

❀ BRITISH TRADITIONAL • **DESIGN** A warm, welcoming beamed dining pub with a smart extension and an elegantly manicured herb garden. The appealing menu champions seasonal British produce. Cooking is skilled, confident and sensibly avoids over-elaboration; fish and game are handled deftly. Formal service provides a sense of occasion.

→ Roe deer carpaccio, foie gras, pickled shimeji mushrooms and Périgord truffle. Scottish halibut with chorizo, cockles and mussels. Cox's apple with apple sorbet and Calvados.

Menu £ 20 (weekday lunch)/25 – Carte £ 28/47

Paley Street ✉ *SL6 3JN – Southwest : 3.5 mi by A 308 and A 330 on B 3024*
– ℰ (01628) 620 541 – www.theroyaloakpaleystreet.com – Closed Sunday dinner

⒯ **Crown**

BRITISH TRADITIONAL • **PUB** Charmingly restored 16C building; formerly two cottages and a bike shop! Drinkers mingle with diners, and dark columns, low beams and roaring fires create a cosy atmosphere. Carefully prepared British dishes are robust and flavoursome.

Carte £ 28/45

Town plan: X-a – *High St* ✉ *SL6 2AH* – ℰ *(01628) 621 936*
– www.thecrownatbray.com – Closed 25 December and Sunday dinner

BRAYE → See Channel Islands (Alderney)

BREEDON ON THE HILL
Leicestershire – ✉ Castle Donington – Pop. 686 – Regional map n° **9**-B2
▶ London 121 mi – Birmingham 35 mi – Sheffield 57 mi – Manchester 95 mi

🍴 Three Horseshoes Inn   🍽 & 🅿

TRADITIONAL CUISINE · PUB Enter through the rear courtyard, past the antique shop, farm shop and chocolatier. It's more dining pub than village local but it has plenty of character courtesy of its quarry-tiled bar and cosy beamed rooms. Cooking is classical.
Carte £ 21/40
*44-46 Main St ✉ DE73 8AN – ✆ (01332) 695 129 – www.thehorseshoes.com
– Closed 25-26 December, 1 January, Sunday dinner and Monday*

BRIDGNORTH
Shropshire – Pop. 12 315 – Regional map n° **10**-B2
▶ London 146 mi – Birmingham 26 mi – Shrewsbury 20 mi – Worcester 29 mi

🏠 Old Vicarage   🌸 🐾 🖨 & 🅿

TRADITIONAL · CLASSIC Red-brick Edwardian vicarage in a quiet village; a popular place for weddings. From the lounge to the bedrooms it has a country house feel – many of the latter display impressive antiques; those in the coach house have spa baths. The smart restaurant has a tiled floor, a glass roof and pleasant garden views.
14 rooms ⊒ – †£ 65/85 ††£ 85/130
*Worfield ✉ WV15 5JZ – Northeast : 4 mi by A 454 – ✆ (01746) 716 497
– www.oldvicarageworfield.com*

BRIDPORT
Dorset – Pop. 13 737 – Regional map n° **2**-B3
▶ London 150 mi – Exeter 38 mi – Taunton 33 mi – Weymouth 19 mi

🏠 Bull   🌸 🍽 🧺 🎱 🅿

INN · STYLISH Stylishly refurbished, 16C coaching inn with a grand Victorian ballroom and a well-equipped games room. Chic bedrooms – upstairs and in a mews – are decorated with local auction house finds and artefacts from Parisian flea markets. Appealing classics in the bar; pizzas, pies and ciders in the former stables.
19 rooms ⊒ – †£ 90/115 ††£ 100/200
34 East St ✉ DT6 3LF – ✆ (01308) 422 878 – www.thebullhotel.co.uk

✗ Riverside   ⪜ 🍽

FISH AND SEAFOOD · BISTRO Long-standing seafood restaurant with harbour views; accessed via a bridge. Good value daily menu offers extremely fresh, straightforward dishes crafted from local produce. Plenty of choice.
Menu £ 23 (weekdays)/28 – Carte £ 26/56
West Bay ✉ DT6 4EZ – South : 1.75 mi by B 3157 – ✆ (01308) 422 011 (booking essential) – www.thefishrestaurant-westbay.co.uk – Closed December-mid February, Sunday dinner and Monday except bank holidays

at Burton Bradstock Southeast: 2 mi by B3157

🏠 Norburton Hall   🐾 ⪜ 🧺 🎱 🅿

TRADITIONAL · CLASSIC Originally a 17C farmhouse; extended and turned into an Arts and Crafts gem in 1902. Woodwork, ornate carvings and period furniture abound. Comfortable bedrooms offer good quality bedding and modern bathrooms. 6 acres of mature grounds, with barbecue available. Charming owners.
3 rooms ⊒ – †£ 100/200 ††£ 130/220
Shipton Ln ✉ DT6 4NQ – North : 0.25 mi on Shipton Gorge rd – ✆ (01308) 897 007 – www.norburtonhall.com

GOOD TIPS!

The jewel of the south coast is a city that knows how to have a good time, with plenty of cool, quirky hotels and restaurants. Those here to party should stay at the contemporary MyHotel in the vibrant North Laine. Terre à Terre is a vegetarian's dream; pescatarians should book a table at Little Fish Market, while carnivores can head for Coal Shed.

BRIGHTON AND HOVE

Brighton and Hove – Pop. 229 700 – Regional map n° **5**-A3
▶ London 53 mi – Portsmouth 48 mi - Southampton 61 mi

Hotels

Hotel du Vin

BUSINESS · STYLISH Made up of various different buildings; the oldest being a for-mer wine merchant's. Kick-back in the cavernous, gothic-style bar-lounge or out on the terrace. Bedrooms are richly decorated and have superb monsoon showers. The relaxed brasserie, with its hidden courtyard, serves French bistro classics.
49 rooms ☲ – ♦£ 105/550 ♦♦£ 105/550
Town plan: CZ-a – *2-6 Ship St* ✉ *BN1 1AD* – ℰ *(01273) 718 588*
– www.hotelduvin.com

Drakes

TOWNHOUSE · DESIGN A pair of 18C townhouses on the promenade, with a smart cocktail bar. Chic, well-equipped bedrooms have wooden feature walls and sea or city views – one even has a bath in the bay window! Minimum 2 night stay at weekends.
20 rooms – ♦£ 145/180 ♦♦£ 145/430 – ☲£ 15
Town plan: CZ-u – *43-44 Marine Par* ✉ *BN2 1PE* – ℰ *(01273) 696 934*
– www.drakesofbrighton.com
The Restaurant at Drakes – See restaurant listing

Myhotel Brighton

CHAIN HOTEL · MODERN Contemporary hotel in the heart of town – a hit with the younger crowd. It has a wacky designer interior with a funky bar and a mod-ern bar-cum-breakfast room. Quirky, minimalist bedrooms come with the latest technological extras.
80 rooms – ♦£ 70/350 ♦♦£ 70/350 – ☲£ 10
Town plan: CY-z – *17 Jubilee St* ✉ *BN1 1GE* – ℰ *(01273) 900 300*
– www.myhotels.com

A Room with a View

TOWNHOUSE · STYLISH Snuggle into a Hungarian goose down duvet and, if your room is at the front of this Regency townhouse, enjoy the views out over the Channel. All have Nespresso machines and a soft drink mini-bar; Room 10 has a roof terrace.

9 rooms 🍴£ 59/75 👫£ 79/275

Town plan: **CZ-u** – *41 Marine Par.* ✉ *BN2 1PE*
– ✆ *(01273) 682 885* – *www.aroomwithaviewbrighton.com*

Kemp Townhouse

TOWNHOUSE · MODERN Stylish 19C townhouse with a tastefully decorated breakfast room. Bedrooms have a modern, uncluttered style and feature compact wet rooms; rooms facing the front are larger and more comfortable – two have four-poster beds.

9 rooms 🍴£ 75/95 👫£ 125/215

Town plan: **CZ-n** – *21 Atlingworth St* ✉ *BN2 1PL*
– ✆ *(01273) 681 400* – *www.kemptownhousebrighton.com*
– *Closed 24-26 December*

Twenty One

TOWNHOUSE · MODERN A smart, well-run Regency townhouse, set back from the promenade. Immaculate, modern bedrooms come with bathrobes and a tea tray bursting with goodies. Fresh coffee is served on arrival and there's plenty of choice at breakfast.

7 rooms 🍴£ 65/80 👫£ 105/159

Town plan: **CV-e** – *21 Charlotte St* ✉ *BN2 1AG*
– ✆ *(01273) 686 450* – *www.thetwentyone.co.uk*

Fab Guest

TOWNHOUSE · DESIGN Don't be fooled by the classic Georgian exterior; inside it's stylish and modern, with minimalist bedrooms displaying a mix of antiques and bespoke furnishings by local artists. There's no reception and no keys – just access codes.

14 rooms 🍴£ 69/89 👫£ 109/159

Town plan: **CV-z** – *9 Charlotte St* ✉ *BN2 1AG*
– ✆ *(01273) 625 505* – *www.fabguest.co.uk*
– *Closed Christmas*

brightonwave

TOWNHOUSE · MODERN You're guaranteed a very personal welcome at this Victorian townhouse. Bedrooms have a contemporary edge: ask for one of the larger, front facing rooms. An ever-changing display of colourful local artwork adorns the walls.

8 rooms 🍴£ 65/75 👫£ 90/125

Town plan: **CZ-s** – *10 Madeira Pl* ✉ *BN2 1TN*
– ✆ *(01273) 676 794* – *www.brightonwave.com*
– *Closed 14-26 December*

Restaurants

ⅩⅩ Salt Room ⓝ

FISH AND SEAFOOD · FASHIONABLE This city hotspot has a lovely 'rustic-meets-industrial' style and has views from many of its tables and the terrace. Menus focus on seafood, with some fish cooked whole on the Josper grill. Service is attentive and personable.

Menu £ 15 (weekday lunch) – Carte £ 28/39

Town plan: **BZ-s** – *106 Kings Rd* ✉ *BN1 2FY*
– ✆ *(01273) 929 488* – *www.saltroom-restaurant.co.uk*
– *Closed 25 and 26 December*

BRIGHTON AND HOVE

BUILT UP AREA

0   1 km

CENTRE

BRIGHTON

HOVE

ROYAL PAVILION

THE LANES

ST ANN'S WELL GARDENS

CHURCHILL SQ SHOPPING CENTRE

THE BRIGHTON CENTRE

XX The Restaurant at Drakes   🅰🅲 ⇔

BRITISH MODERN · DESIGN Two small, intimate dining rooms in the basement of a townhouse hotel. Menus feature luxury ingredients and have a classical bent. With the soft, moody atmosphere and elegantly laid tables, there's a formal feel, even at lunch.

Menu £ 25/60

Town plan: CZ-u – *Drakes Hotel, 43-44 Marine Par* ✉ *BN2 1PE*
– *𝒞 (01273) 696 934 (booking advisable) – www.therestaurantatdrakes.co.uk*

XX Gingerman   🅰🅲

MODERN CUISINE · NEIGHBOURHOOD There's a homespun feel to the decoration and an intimacy to the atmosphere at this long-standing neighbourhood restaurant. Classically based dishes have modern touches, with French and Mediterranean flavours to the fore.

Menu £ 18/37

Town plan: BZ-a – *21a Norfolk Sq* ✉ *BN1 2PD*
– *𝒞 (01273) 326 688 (booking essential) – www.gingermanrestaurants.com*
– *Closed 2 weeks winter, 25 December and Monday*

XX Coal Shed   🅰🅲

MEATS · NEIGHBOURHOOD A keenly run, rustic steakhouse hidden away in the Brighton Lanes district. Cooking centres around the charcoal oven; they specialise in 35-day matured organic steaks but there's also a tasty selection of fresh fish dishes to try.

Menu £ 13 (lunch and early dinner)/40 – Carte £ 27/58

Town plan: BZ-x – *8 Boyces St* ✉ *BN1 1AN*
– *𝒞 (01273) 322 998 – www.coalshed-restaurant.co.uk*
– *Closed 25-26 December*

XX 24 St Georges   🅰🅲

MODERN CUISINE · BRASSERIE Shabby chic restaurant on the edge of Kemp Town, run by keen owners; its three adjoining rooms have a stylish, contemporary feel. Seasonal menus offer complex, technically skilled dishes. The staff are welcoming and knowledgeable.

Menu £ 23 (weekdays)/32 – Carte £ 27/42

Town plan: CV-x – *24 St George's Rd* ✉ *BN2 1ED*
– *𝒞 (01273) 626 060 (booking advisable) – www.24stgeorges.co.uk – dinner only and Saturday lunch – Closed 25-26 December, 1-2 January, Sunday and Monday*

X Chilli Pickle   🛋 🔥 🅰🅲

🏵 INDIAN · BISTRO Simple restaurant with a relaxed, buzzy vibe and friendly, welcoming service. The passionate chef uses good quality ingredients to create oft-changing menus of thoughtfully prepared, authentic Indian dishes with delicate spicing. Beside the terrace they also have a cart selling street food style snacks.

Menu £ 14 (lunch)/28 – Carte £ 19/32

Town plan: CY-z – *17 Jubilee St* ✉ *BN1 1GE*
– *𝒞 (01273) 900 383 – www.thechillipickle.com*
– *Closed 25-26 December*

X Terre à Terre   🛋 🅰🅲 🍷

VEGETARIAN · NEIGHBOURHOOD Relaxed, friendly restaurant decorated in warm burgundy colours. Appealing menu of generous, tasty, original vegetarian dishes which include items from Japan, China and South America. Mini épicerie sells wine, pasta and chutney.

Menu £ 29/31 – Carte £ 26/33

Town plan: CZ-e – *71 East St* ✉ *BN1 1HQ*
– *𝒞 (01273) 729 051 (booking essential) – www.terreaterre.co.uk*
– *Closed 25-26 December*

✗ Sam's of Brighton

MODERN CUISINE · BISTRO An established neighbourhood bistro where brown leather stands out against plain walls. The concise à la carte offers seasonal dishes and there's a good value set lunch and early evening menu. At weekends, they also serve brunch.

Menu £17 (lunch and early dinner) – Carte £27/37

Town plan: CV-a – *1 Paston Pl* ✉ *BN2 1HA* – ✆ *(01273) 676 222*
– *www.samsofbrighton.co.uk* – *Closed 25 and 26 December and Monday*

✗ 64°

BRITISH MODERN · SIMPLE If you like things fun and fuss-free, then this intimate modern restaurant is the place for you! Menus are divided into four – 'Meat', 'Fish', 'Veg' and 'Dessert' – and each section also has four choices. Cooking is simple but well-textured and flavoursome; most of the dining takes place at the counter.

Carte £20/49

Town plan: CZ-c – *53 Meeting House Ln.* ✉ *BN1 1HB* – ✆ *(01273) 770 115*
(booking essential) – *www.64degrees.co.uk* – *Closed 25 December*

✗ Little Fish Market

FISH AND SEAFOOD · SIMPLE Fish is the focus at this simple little restaurant in a converted fishmonger's, which sits opposite the former Victorian fish market. The menu offers refined, interesting modern seafood dishes. The owner cooks alone in the kitchen.

Menu 50

Town plan: BY-m – *10 Upper Market St, Hove* ✉ *BN3 1AS* – ✆ *(01273) 722 213*
(booking essential) – *www.thelittlefishmarket.co.uk* – *dinner only and Saturday lunch* – *Closed 1 week April, 1 week August, 1 week September, 1 week December, Sunday and Monday*

🍺 Ginger Dog

BRITISH MODERN · PUB Charming Victorian pub with a shabby-chic, canine-theme, a welcoming atmosphere and a relaxed feel. Fresh produce is to the fore; dishes are mostly British-based but with the odd nod to Italy. A ginger 'dog' biscuit is served with coffee.

Menu £13 (weekdays) – Carte £26/40

Town plan: CV-s – *12 College Pl* ✉ *BN2 1HN* – ✆ *(01273) 620 990*
– *www.gingermanrestaurants.com* – *Closed 25 December*

🍺 Ginger Pig

BRITISH TRADITIONAL · PUB Smart building by the seafront – formerly a hotel – boasting a mortar ship relief and a beautifully restored revolving door. Menus offer precise, flavoursome British dishes and vegetarians are well-catered for. Good value set lunch menu.

Menu £13 (weekdays)/35 – Carte £26/38

Town plan: AV-c – *3 Hove St, Hove* ✉ *BN3 2TR* – ✆ *(01273) 736 123*
– *www.gingermanrestaurants.com* – *Closed 25 December*

BRISTOL

City of Bristol – Pop. 535 907 – Regional map n° **2**-C2
▶ London 121 mi – Birmingham 91 mi – Cardiff 43 mi

Hotels

🏨 Hotel du Vin   ⌂ 🔼 AC ⚒

BUSINESS · DESIGN Characterful 18C former sugar refinery with classical Hotel du Vin styling and a wine-theme running throughout. Dark-hued bedrooms and duplex suites boast Egyptian cotton linen – one room has twin roll-top baths. Cosy lounge-bar; French brasserie with a pleasant courtyard terrace for bistro classics.
40 rooms – ♦£ 109/185 ♦♦£ 119/395 – ⌂ £ 17
Town plan: CY-e – *The Sugar House* ⊠ *BS1 2NU* – 𝒞 *(0844) 736 42 52*
– *www.hotelduvin.com*

🏨 Mercure Bristol Brigstow   ⌂ 🔼 ⚒ 🍽 ⚒

BUSINESS · MODERN Modern city centre hotel overlooking the River Avon. Stylishly furnished, curvaceous bedrooms have bold colour schemes and luxurious bathrooms, with a TV above the bath. Some have balconies; others, coffee machines and river views. Smart, contemporary 'Ellipse' serves a menu of European classics.
116 rooms – ♦£ 99/359 ♦♦£ 109/369 – ⌂ £ 10 – 1 suite
Town plan: CY-n – *5-7 Welsh Back* ⊠ *BS1 4SP* – 𝒞 *(0117) 929 10 30*
– *www.mercure.com*

Enjoy good food without spending a fortune! Look out for the Bib Gourmand ⊛ symbol to find restaurants offering good food at great prices!

INDEX OF STREET NAMES IN BRISTOL

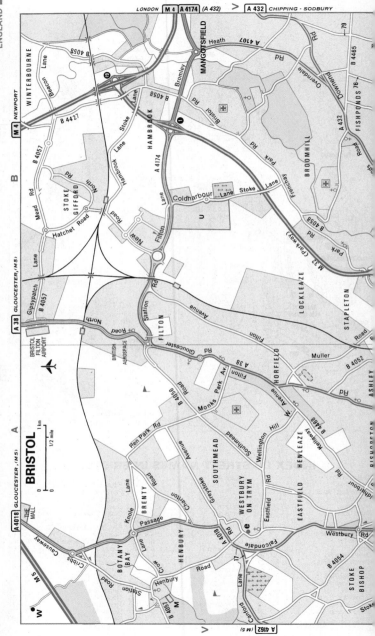

LONDON M 4 A 4174 (A 432) > A 432 CHIPPING · SODBURY

MANGOTSFIELD

Heath

A 4107

Bromley

WINTERBOURNE

Beacon Lane

B 4058

M 4 NEWPORT

B 4427

Stoke Lane

Hambrook Lane

B 4058

HAMBROOK

A 4174

North Road

STOKE GIFFORD

Mead Rd

B 4057

Hatchet Road

Lane

New Road

Filton Lane

Coldharbour Lane Stoke Lane

Overndale Rd

B 4465

FISHPONDS 78

A 432

BROOMHILL

Bristol Rd

Frenchay Park Rd

Park Rd

B 4058

M 32 (Parkway)

A 38 GLOUCESTER (M 5)

Gipsypatch

B 4057

Station Rd

North Road

Avenue

FILTON

Filton Avenue

LOCKLEAZE

STAPLETON

Road

BRISTOL FILTON AIRPORT

BRITISH AEROSPACE

Gloucester Rd

A 38

Muller

B 4052

ASHLEY

HORFIELD

B 4468

B 4469

Rd

BISHOPSTON

Ishibrook Rd

A 4018 GLOUCESTER (M 5)

BRISTOL

1 km

1/2 mile

0

Pen Park Rd

B 4055

Monks Park Av

Filton Av

Avenue

SOUTHMEAD

Southmead

Wellington Hill

HENLEAZE

Kellaway

THE MALL

Charlton Rd

Knole Lane

BRENTRY

Passage

Greystoke Avenue

Eastfield Rd

EASTFIELD

WESTBURY ON TRYM

A 4018 Rd

Westbury Rd

Westbury

B 4054

M 5

Crow Lane

Causeway

Cribbs

BOTANY BAY

HENBURY

Crow Road

Henbury

Station Road

B 4057

Falcondale Lane

Canford

STOKE BISHOP

Stoke

A 4162 (M 5)

346

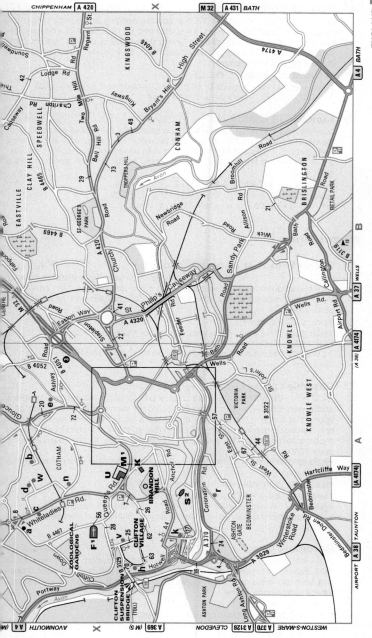

Berwick Lodge

COUNTRY HOUSE · PERSONALISED A popular wedding and events venue, run by gregarious, hands-on owners. It's surrounded by 18 acres of grounds and offers views over Avonmouth and the Severn Bridge. Inside, original features combine with Eastern furnishings and mosaic tiles. The intimate restaurant has fine chandeliers and a modern menu.

14 rooms ⌂ – ♦£ 85/95 ♦♦£ 125/165
Town plan: AV-w – *Berwick Dr* ⊠ *BS10 7TD* – *Northwest 5 mi by A 4018*
– 𝒞 *(0117) 958 1590* – *www.berwicklodge.co.uk*

Number 38 Clifton

TOWNHOUSE · STYLISH Built in 1820, this substantial townhouse overlooks both the city and the Clifton Downs. Boutique bedrooms have coloured wood-panelled walls, Roberts radios and smart bathrooms with underfloor heating; the most luxurious are the loft suites, complete with copper baths. The rear terrace makes a great suntrap.

9 rooms ⌂ – ♦£ 110/200 ♦♦£ 115/225
Town plan: AX-a – *38 Upper Belgrave Rd* ⊠ *BS8 2XN*
– 𝒞 *(01179) 466 905* – *www.number38clifton.com*

Restaurants

XXX Second Floor at Harvey Nichols

MODERN CUISINE · DESIGN A spacious and elegant light-filled restaurant with stylish gold décor. Good value lunch menu and concise à la carte offering original, modern dishes. Chic lounge bar for cocktails and light bites. Attentive service.

Menu £ 20 – Carte £ 31/42
Town plan: DY-a – *27 Philadelphia St, Quakers Friars, Cabot Circus*
⊠ *BS1 3BZ* – 𝒞 *(0117) 916 8898* – *www.harveynichols.com*
– *Closed 25 December, 1 January, Easter Sunday, Sunday and Monday dinner*

XX Casamia (Jonray and Peter Sanchez-Iglesias)

CREATIVE · INDIVIDUAL Casamia is very passionately run by two brothers and a well-informed team. The set 13 course menu (with the option of 6 courses at lunch) changes with the seasons and is inspired by the brothers' childhood memories. Ambitious, skilful, highly innovative cooking uses modern techniques. The restaurant is set to move to the city centre in early 2016.
→ Squid with wild garlic. Monkfish, spring greens and cider sauce. Passion fruit and tarragon.

Menu £ 38 (weekday lunch)/88 – set menu only
Town plan: AV-e – *38 High St, Westbury-on-Trym* ⊠ *BS9 3DZ*
– *Northwest : 4 mi by A 4018* – 𝒞 *(0117) 959 28 84 (booking essential)*
– *www.casamiarestaurant.co.uk* – *Closed Sunday, Monday and Tuesday after bank holidays*

XX Bordeaux Quay

MODERN CUISINE · BRASSERIE Huge harbourside emporium which aims to be 100% organic. It houses a deli, a bakery, a bar and a laid-back brasserie. Above is a linen-laid restaurant which opens at the weekend and offers adventurous Mediterranean-style cuisine.

Carte £ 20/44
Town plan: CZ-e – *V Shed, Canons Way* ⊠ *BS1 5UH*
– 𝒞 *(0117) 943 12 00* – *www.bordeaux-quay.co.uk*
– *Closed 25-26 December*

✗✗ Spiny Lobster   AK

FISH AND SEAFOOD · BRASSERIE Bringing a taste of the sea to the city. Pass the daily catch displayed on a marble slab (this was once a fishmonger's) on your way to the leather-furnished dining room. Simply prepared dishes are cooked in the Josper oven.

Menu £ 18 (lunch) – Carte £ 25/44

Town plan: AX-c – *128 Whiteladies Rd* ⊠ *BS8 2RS* – ℰ *(0117) 973 73 84* – *www.thespinylobster.co.uk* – *Closed 24 December-4 January, Sunday and Monday*

✗ wilks (James Wilkins)

✿ BRITISH MODERN · FRIENDLY An appealing neighbourhood restaurant with a relaxed atmosphere and a simple understated style. Well-balanced dishes display a lightness of touch and a real understanding of flavours – they are also refreshingly lacking in over-adornment. The meringue-based desserts have become something of a speciality.

➔ Scallop sashimi with English wasabi, sesame, apple and ginger. Fillet of wild turbot with leeks, garlic, Jersey Royal cream and morels. Cocoa meringue with coffee ice cream.

Menu £ 19 (lunch and early dinner) – Carte £ 38/50

Town plan: AX-d – *1 Chandos Rd* ⊠ *BS6 6PG* – ℰ *(0117) 973 79 99 (booking essential at dinner)* – *www.wilksrestaurant.co.uk* – *Closed 21 December-10 January, 1-21 August, Monday and Tuesday*

✗ Flinty Red   🍷 AK 📖

🕸 MEDITERRANEAN · BISTRO The combined effort of two couples; one pair are independent wine merchants, the other, chefs. Unfussy cooking relies on quality local produce and features some lesser-known cuts; dishes are largely Mediterranean but with some Asian influences. The rustic room is overseen by a friendly, knowledgeable team.

Menu £ 10 (lunch) – Carte £ 17/35

Town plan: AX-n – *34 Cotham Hill* ⊠ *BS6 6LA* – ℰ *(0117) 923 87 55 (booking essential)* – *www.flintyred.co.uk* – *Closed 1-7 January, 25-28 December, Monday lunch and Sunday*

✗ Riverstation   🍷 🏠 🖥 ✿

MODERN CUISINE · BRASSERIE Striking building where you can watch the canal boats passing by. The busy bar specialises in cocktails and offers a menu of Mediterranean and Asian inspired dishes. The upstairs restaurant and terrace serve modern European fare.

Menu £ 16 (weekday lunch) – Carte £ 28/37

Town plan: CZ-c – *The Grove, Harbourside* ⊠ *BS1 4RB* – ℰ *(0117) 914 44 34* – *www.riverstation.co.uk* – *Closed 24-26 December*

✗ Wallfish Bistro

CLASSIC CUISINE · BISTRO This friendly bistro is named after the West Country word for 'snail' and, satisfyingly, you'll find Herefordshire Wallfish on the menu. Careful, classical cooking focuses on good ingredients; fish from the day boats is popular.

Menu £ 14 (weekdays) – Carte £ 22/57

Town plan: AX-h – *112 Princess Victoria St, Clifton Village* ⊠ *BS8 4DB* – ℰ *(0117) 973 5435 (booking advisable)* – *www.wallfishbistro.co.uk* – *Closed 24-31 December, Monday and Tuesday*

✗ Bell's Diner & Bar Rooms   📖

MEDITERRANEAN · BISTRO A bustling city institution, which still retains evidence of its former grocer's shop days. Flavoursome, Mediterranean-style cooking shows a good understanding of ingredients; be sure to try the slow-cooked cauliflower in yoghurt.

Carte £ 21/40

Town plan: AX-e – *1-3 York Rd, Montpelier* ⊠ *BS6 5QB* – ℰ *(0117) 924 0357 (bookings advisable at dinner)* – *www.bellsdiner.com* – *Closed 25-26 December, 1 January, Sunday and lunch Monday*

✗ No Man's Grace ⓝ   🛱 🆂 🎍

BRITISH MODERN · NEIGHBOURHOOD Simple neighbourhood restaurant run by an experienced young chef. Small plates feature 3 or 4 ingredients in boldly flavoured combinations with a classic heart and a modern touch. For something sweeter, pay a visit to the dessert bar, where every dish is matched with a dessert wine and a cocktail.

Carte £ 11/17

Town plan: AX-w - 6 Chandos Rd ⊠ BS6 6PE - ℰ (0117) 974 4077
- www.nomansgrace.com - Closed 2 weeks August, 1st week January, Sunday dinner, Monday and Tuesday

✗ Birch ⓝ   🛱

BRITISH TRADITIONAL · SIMPLE Simple neighbourhood restaurant on a long terraced street. Chef Sam's time at St John shows in his concise menu of rustic British dishes, which use lesser-known produce and are packed with flavour. Service is charming and attentive.

Carte £ 23/31

Town plan: AX-a - 47 Raleigh Rd ⊠ BS3 1QS - ℰ (0117) 902 83 26 (booking essential) - www.birchbristol.co - dinner only - Closed 3 weeks August, 2 weeks Christmas-New Year and Sunday-Tuesday

🍴 Pump House   🛱 ♿ 🅿

MODERN CUISINE · INDIVIDUAL Cavernous Victorian pumping station for the adjacent docks; now a rustic pub with a smart mezzanine restaurant. Modern classics change with seasons; Weds-Sat there's also a more refined tasting menu. Watch the boats from the terrace.

Menu £ 55 - Carte £ 25/39

Town plan: AX-k - Merchants Rd ⊠ BS8 4PZ - ℰ (0117) 927 2229
- www.the-pumphouse.com - Closed 25 December

🍴 Albion Public House and Dining Rooms   🛱 ♧

TRADITIONAL CUISINE · TRENDY Trendy Grade II listed pub with a fun, friendly and informal feel and a canopy-covered terrace. Lunch sees sandwiches, 'brunch' dishes and traditional mains, while the evening à la carte offers satisfying seasonal cooking.

Carte £ 20/32

Town plan: AX-v - Boyces Ave, Clifton Village ⊠ BS8 4AA - ℰ (0117) 973 35 22 (booking essential) - www.thealbionclifton.co.uk - Closed 25-26 December and dinner Sunday-Monday

🍴 Kensington Arms   🛱 ♿ ♧

BRITISH TRADITIONAL · PUB Charming, Victorian-style neighbourhood pub, with a traditional bar and an impressive, high-ceilinged dining room. Daily menus have a strong British and seasonal base; in winter you'll find hearty, nourishing dishes and proper puddings.

Carte £ 20/44

Town plan: AX-b - 35-37 Stanley Rd ⊠ BS6 6NP - ℰ (0117) 944 64 44
- www.thekensingtonarms.co.uk - Closed 25-26 December and Sunday dinner

at Long Ashton Southwest: 2.5 mi by A370 off B3128

🍴 Bird in Hand   🛱 ♿

BRITISH TRADITIONAL · COSY Tiny country pub with three small but smartly decorated rooms. Quirky touches include an antelope's head and a wall covered in pages from Mrs Beeton's Book of Household Management. Menus offer tasty, carefully cooked British dishes which let local and foraged ingredients speak for themselves.

Carte £ 27/33

17 Weston Rd ⊠ BS41 9LA - ℰ (01275) 395 222 (booking essential at dinner)
- www.bird-in-hand.co.uk - Closed 25 December

BROAD CAMPDEN – Gloucestershire → See Chipping Campden

BROADCLYST – Devon → See Exeter

BROADSTAIRS
Kent – Pop. 23 632 – Regional map n° **5**-D1
▶ London 77 mi – Canterbury 18 mi – Ramsgate 2 mi

🏠 Belvidere Place
TOWNHOUSE · PERSONALISED Centrally located Georgian house with a charming owner, green credentials and an eclectic, individual style. Bohemian, shabby-chic lounge boasts a retro football table. Spacious bedrooms mix modern facilities with older antique furnishings.
5 rooms ⌑ – ♦£130 ♦♦£160/180
Belvidere Rd ⊠ CT10 1PF – ℰ(01843) 579 850 – www.belvidereplace.co.uk

✗ Albariño
SPANISH · TAPAS BAR Run by a husband and wife team and named after her favourite wine. Freshly prepared, full-flavoured tapas dishes; 3 per person will suffice – let the chef choose. Counter seating for 7. Good views of the Channel.
Carte £13/20
29 Albion St ⊠ CT10 1LX – ℰ(01843) 600 991 – www.albarinorestaurant.co.uk
– dinner only and Saturday lunch – Closed 21-31 December and Sunday

✗ Wyatt & Jones
BRITISH MODERN · BISTRO Follow the narrow road under the arch, towards the harbour; here you'll find 3 old fishermen's cottages with pleasant sea views. Appealing menus keep things regional, with local lobsters a speciality; start with some tempting nibbles.
Menu £18 (weekday lunch) – Carte £24/33
23-27 Harbour St ⊠ CT10 1EU – ℰ(01843) 865 126 – www.wyattandjones.co.uk
– Closed Sunday dinner

BROADWAY
Worcestershire – Pop. 2 496 – Regional map n° **10**-C3
▶ London 93 mi – Birmingham 36 mi – Cheltenham 15 mi – Oxford 38 mi

🏰 Buckland Manor
HISTORIC · CLASSIC With its 13C origins, beautiful gardens and peaceful hamlet setting, this is one of England's most charming country houses. The elegant interior comprises tastefully appointed country house bedrooms and traditionally furnished lounges featuring wood panelling and big open fires. The formal restaurant has garden views and offers classical cooking with modern touches.
15 rooms ⌑ – ♦£195/550 ♦♦£215/595
Buckland ⊠ WR12 7LY – Southwest : 2.25 mi by B 4632 – ℰ(01386) 852 626
– www.bucklandmanor.com

🏰 Dormy House
LUXURY · CONTEMPORARY Behind the original farmhouse façade you'll find a funky, modern interior and a luxurious spa. The odd beam and fireplace remain but bold contemporary fabrics and designer furnishings feature now too. Wood and stone play a big part and the atmosphere is laid-back. The Potting Shed has a pub-like feel and the stylish restaurant offers a more sophisticated alternative.
38 rooms ⌑ – ♦£240/500 ♦♦£250/510 – 10 suites
Willersey Hill ⊠ WR12 7LF – East : 4 mi by A 44 – ℰ(01386) 852 711
– www.dormyhouse.co.uk

351

Lygon Arms

HISTORIC · CLASSIC One of the most famous coaching inns in the country, with a hugely characterful interior of wood panelling, inglenook fireplaces and assorted comfy corners. Bedrooms vary in size and shape; those in the newer wing have a more contemporary style. Cosy brasserie serves modern British dishes; the impressive Great Hall has a 17C minstrels' gallery and a modern European menu.

78 rooms ☑ – †£ 90/200 ††£ 140/350 – 6 suites
High St ✉ *WR12 7DU* – ℘ *(01386) 852 255* – *www.thehotelcollection.co.uk*

Foxhill Manor

COUNTRY HOUSE · DESIGN Once home to Henry Maudslay, who died in the Dam Busters raid; a Grade II listed Arts and Crafts house, where guests are made to feel as if they're staying in a private home. Striking bedrooms have first class facilities – 'Oak' has his and hers baths with a view. Modern 4 course menus are discussed with the chef; after dinner, relax on bean bags in front of the 74" TV.

8 rooms ☑ – †£ 295/650 ††£ 295/650 – 2 suites
Farncombe Estate ✉ *WR12 7LJ – East : 3.75 mi by A 44*
– ℘ (01386) 852 711 – www.foxhillmanor.com

Broadway

HISTORIC · STYLISH 16C inn on the village green – once an abbots' retreat – with warmly decorated modern bedrooms and a horse racing theme. Relax in the timbered bar with its minstrels' gallery or have afternoon tea by the inglenook fireplace in the sitting room. The airy courtyard brasserie offers an extensive seasonal menu.

17 rooms ☑ – †£ 170/190 ††£ 170/240
The Green ✉ *WR12 7AA* – ℘ *(01386) 852 401*
– www.cotswold-inns-hotels.co.uk/broadway

East House

HISTORIC · STYLISH Beautifully furnished, 18C former farmhouse in lovely mature gardens, with wood-burning stoves and a welcoming feel. Sumptuous beamed bedrooms mix antique furniture with modern technology; superb bathrooms have underfloor heating. The Jacobean Suite is the biggest room, with a four-poster and garden views.

4 rooms ☑ – †£ 185/225 ††£ 185/225
162 High St ✉ *WR12 7AJ* – ℘ *(01386) 853 789*
– www.easthouseuk.com

Mill Hay House

HISTORIC · ELEGANT This lovely 17C house, tucked away on the edge of the village, comes with beautiful gardens overlooking a lake. With just three individually furnished bedrooms, the atmosphere is intimate, and guests are treated as family friends.

3 rooms ☑ – †£ 155/225 ††£ 175/245
Snowshill Rd ✉ *WR12 7JS – South : 0.5 mi* – ℘ *(01386) 852 498*
– www.millhay.co.uk – Closed Christmas-New Year

Windrush House

FAMILY · STYLISH Welcoming guesthouse in a pretty village. Individually decorated bedrooms have bold feature walls: some use Laura Ashley designs and have wrought iron beds; four-poster 'Snowshill' is the best. Homemade jams feature at breakfast.

5 rooms ☑ – †£ 70/90 ††£ 90/110
Station Rd ✉ *WR12 7DE* – ℘ *(01386) 853 577*
– www.windrushhouse.com

🏠 Olive Branch   ⚄ P

TOWNHOUSE · COSY Welcoming guesthouse run by an experienced husband and wife team. Pleasantly cluttered bedrooms with thoughtful extras; one has a small veranda. Rustic, characterful dining room with homemade cakes, breads and muesli at breakfast.

8 rooms ⌂ – ♦£ 68/75 ♦♦£ 98/121

78 High St ✉ *WR12 7AJ –* ☎ *(01386) 853 440*
– www.theolivebranch-broadway.com

XX Russell's   ⟺ 🛋 ⚄ AC ⚄ P

BRITISH MODERN · FASHIONABLE Attractive Cotswold stone house in the centre of the village, with a smart, modern, brasserie-style interior and both a front and rear terrace. Seasonal menus of modern dishes, with a well-priced set menu. Casual service. Stylish, modern bedrooms boast good facilities.

Menu £ 14 (lunch and early dinner) – Carte £ 28/50

7 rooms ⌂ – ♦£ 120/300 ♦♦£ 120/300

20 High St ✉ *WR12 7DT –* ☎ *(01386) 853 555 – www.russellsofbroadway.co.uk*
– Closed Sunday dinner and bank holidays

BROCKENHURST

Hampshire – Pop. 3 552 – Regional map n° **4**-A2
▶ London 99 mi – Bournemouth 17 mi – Southampton 14 mi – Winchester 27 mi

🏠 The Pig   ⚘ ⚶ 🛏 ⚄ ⚄ P

COUNTRY HOUSE · STYLISH This smart manor house hotel follows a philosophy of removing barriers and bringing nature indoors. Characterful bedrooms are divided between the house and a stable block, and boast distressed wood floors, chunky furnishings and large squashy beds. The comfy lounges and dining room have a shabby-chic style.

29 rooms – ♦£ 149/385 ♦♦£ 149/385 – ⌂ £ 15

Beaulieu Rd ✉ *SO42 7QL – East : 1 mi on B 3055 –* ☎ *(01590) 622 354*
– www.thepighotel.com

The Pig – See restaurant listing

🏠 New Park Manor   ⚘ ⚶ ⟨ 🛏 ⚒ ▥ ⚙ ⚶ ♨ 🏋 ⚄ P

TRADITIONAL · CLASSIC This elegantly proportioned former hunting lodge was built by Charles II on his return from France. Bedrooms fuse modern comforts with traditional features. Children are well-catered for with a crèche, a cinema and games rooms, while for adults there's an impressive spa. The restaurant offers relaxed dining.

21 rooms ⌂ – ♦£ 115/195 ♦♦£ 135/315 – 1 suite

Lyndhurst Rd ✉ *SO42 7QH – North : 1.5 mi on A 337 –* ☎ *(01590) 623 467*
– www.newparkmanorhotel.co.uk

🏠 Cloud   ⚘ ⚄ ♨ P

FAMILY · COSY Well-kept hotel made up of four cottages, set on the edge of a pretty New Forest village. It has a homely feel, from the cosy lounges to the immaculately kept bedrooms; a collection photos attest to the owner's past as a tiller girl. The theatrical-themed restaurant and conservatory offer traditional menus.

18 rooms ⌂ – ♦£ 84/90 ♦♦£ 128/180

Meerut Rd ✉ *SO42 7TD –* ☎ *(01590) 622 165 – www.cloudhotel.co.uk*
– Closed 27 December-13 January

🏠 Cottage Lodge   ⚘ 🛏 ⚄ P

FAMILY · COSY Cosy, low-ceilinged former forester's cottage in a charming village where New Forest ponies wander freely. Rustic furnishings include some four-poster beds made from local trees. Traditional, hearty dinners use organic produce. The building dates from 1650 and is part-constructed from a decommissioned ship.

15 rooms ⌂ – ♦£ 49/99 ♦♦£ 55/175

Sway Rd ✉ *SO42 7SH –* ☎ *(01590) 622 296 – www.cottagelodge.co.uk – Closed 19-26 December*

🏠 Daisybank Cottage   🖙 ⊘ 🅿

TRADITIONAL · STYLISH A charming Arts and Crafts house built in 1902. Modern bedrooms come with seating areas; one room opens onto an internal courtyard and another, onto a terrace. Aga-cooked breakfasts come in English, Irish and American versions.

7 rooms 🖙 – ♦£ 85/125 ♦♦£ 100/140

Sway Rd ⊠ SO42 7SG – South : 0.5 mi on B 3055 – ℰ (01590) 622 086
– www.bedandbreakfast-newforest.co.uk

✗✗ The Pig   🐴 🍷 🖙 🏠 ⅙ ⇔ 🅿

BRITISH TRADITIONAL · BRASSERIE A delightful conservatory with plants dotted about, an eclectic collection of old tables and chairs, and a bustling atmosphere. The forager and kitchen gardener supply what's best and any ingredients they can't get themselves are sourced from within 25 miles. Cooking is unfussy, wholesome and British-based.

Carte £ 22/45

The Pig Hotel, Beaulieu Rd ⊠ SO42 7QL – East : 1 mi on B 3055 – ℰ (01590) 622 354 – www.thepighotel.com

BROUGHTON

North Yorkshire – Regional map n° **13**-A2
▶ London 228 mi – Sheffield 71 mi – Kingston upon Hull 94 mi – Derby 106 mi

🍴 Bull   🏠 ⅙ 🅿

REGIONAL · PUB Part of Ribble Valley Inns, a burgeoning pub company which proudly promotes local and very British ingredients and dishes. This solid, sizeable pub boasts log fires, beams and stone floors.

Menu £ 15 (weekdays) – Carte £ 19/39

⊠ BD23 3AE – ℰ (01756) 792 065 – www.thebullatbroughton.com

BROUGHTON GIFFORD

Wiltshire – Regional map n° **2**-C2
▶ London 109 mi – Bristol 31 mi – Cardiff 64 mi – Southampton 81 mi

🍴 The Fox   🖙 🏠 🅿

BRITISH TRADITIONAL · COSY Raising the profile of this pub, both locally and farther afield, has been a labour of love for its young owner. Cooking is simple, unfussy and fresh, and uses what's in the garden: salad leaves, fruits, chickens and pigs.

Menu £ 17 (weekday lunch) – Carte £ 25/46

The Street ⊠ SN12 8PN – ℰ (01225) 782 949
– www.thefox-broughtongifford.co.uk – Closed 26-27 December, 1-2 January, Sunday dinner and Monday

BRUNDALL

Norfolk – Pop. 4 019 – Regional map n° **8**-D2
▶ London 118 mi – Great Yarmouth 15 mi – Norwich 8 mi

✗✗ Lavender House   ⇔ 🅿

MODERN CUISINE · FRIENDLY Characterful thatched cottage with low beamed ceilings and inglenook fireplaces. Cooking has a rustic, north Italian style – good quality ingredients feature in gutsy dishes and flavours are clearly defined. They also run cookery courses.

Menu £ 60

39 The Street ⊠ NR13 5AA – ℰ (01603) 712 215 (booking advisable)
– www.thelavenderhouse.co.uk – dinner only and Sunday lunch
– Closed 26 December-9 January, Sunday dinner and Monday-Wednesday

BRUNTINGTHORPE

Leicestershire – Regional map n° **9**-B3
▶ London 96 mi – Leicester 10 mi – Market Harborough 15 mi

The Joiners

BRITISH TRADITIONAL · RUSTIC Beams and a tiled floor bring 17C character to this dining pub, but touches like designer wallpaper and fresh flowers give it a chic overall feel. There's plenty of choice on the good value menus and dishes might include pork rillettes or pot-roast pheasant. Experienced staff run the show with a steady hand.

Menu £ 14/22 – Carte £ 26/39

Church Walk ⊠ LE17 5QH – ℰ (0116) 247 82 58 (booking essential)
– www.thejoinersarms.co.uk – Closed Sunday dinner and Monday

BRUSHFORD – Somerset → See Dulverton

BRUTON

Somerset – Pop. 2 984 – Regional map n° **2**-C2

▶ London 118 mi – Bristol 27 mi – Salisbury 35 mi – Taunton 36 mi

At The Chapel

MEDITERRANEAN · FASHIONABLE Stylish, informal restaurant in a former 18C chapel, with a bakery to one side and a wine shop to the other. Well-priced, daily menus offer rustic, Mediterranean-influenced dishes; specialities include wood-fired breads, pizzas and cakes. Luxurious bedrooms have king-sized beds, 46" TVs and Egyptian cotton linen. Chic club lounge and cocktail bar opens at weekends.

Carte £ 24/42

8 rooms ⊡ – †£ 100/150 ††£ 100/250
High St ⊠ BA10 0AE – ℰ (01749) 814 070 (booking advisable)
– www.atthechapel.co.uk

Roth Bar & Grill 🆕

BRITISH TRADITIONAL · RUSTIC The converted outbuildings of a working farm now house the Hauser & Wirth art gallery and this charming restaurant. Farm produce and artisan breads feature in substantial dishes; try the bespoke cocktails and caramelised lemonade.

Carte £ 21/39

Durslade Farm, Dropping Ln ⊠ BA10 0NL – Southeast : 0.5 mi on B 3081
– ℰ (01749) 814 700 (booking advisable) – www.rothbarandgrill.co.uk – lunch only and dinner Friday and Saturday – Closed first week January, 25-26 December and Monday except bank holidays

BRYHER → See Scilly (Isles of)

BUCKDEN

Cambridgeshire – ⊠ Huntingdon – Pop. 2 385 – Regional map n° **8**-A2

▶ London 65 mi – Bedford 15 mi – Cambridge 20 mi – Northampton 31 mi

George

HISTORIC · PERSONALISED Delightfully restored part black and white, part red-brick coaching inn. Original flag floors mix with modern furnishings, creating a stylish, understated feel. The simple yet tastefully decorated bedrooms are named after famous 'Georges'. Classic brasserie dishes feature in the restaurant.

12 rooms ⊡ – †£ 95/150 ††£ 120/150
High St ⊠ PE19 5XA – ℰ (01480) 812 300 – www.thegeorgebuckden.com

BUCKHORN WESTON

Dorset – Regional map n° **2**-C3

▶ London 117 mi – Poole 36 mi – Bath 33 mi – Weymouth 37 mi

🛏 Stapleton Arms

BRITISH TRADITIONAL · PUB A welcoming, well-run pub with a homely, shabby-chic style. Menus showcase pub classics, with the occasional international influence, and snacks like pork pies can be wrapped up and taken home. Spacious bedrooms boast Egyptian cotton linen, smart bathrooms and a mix of modern and antique furnishings.

Carte £ 24/33

4 rooms ⬚ – †£ 70/100 ††£ 90/120

Church Hill ⊠ SP8 5HS – ℰ (01963) 370 396 – www.thestapletonarms.com – Closed 25 December

BUCKINGHAM

Buckinghamshire – Pop. 12 890 – Regional map n° **6**-C1
▶ London 64 mi – Birmingham 61 mi – Northampton 20 mi – Oxford 25 mi

🏠 Villiers

BUSINESS · CLASSIC Proudly run hotel on a central street in a quaint market town. Bright, modern meeting rooms and a cosy lounge; the bar has a charming open fire. Bedrooms vary in style: all have modern facilities; some have original beams and some are duplex suites. The restaurant serves a mix of classical and modern dishes.

49 rooms ⬚ – †£ 85/140 ††£ 90/160 – 4 suites

3 Castle St ⊠ MK18 1BS – ℰ (01280) 822 444 – www.oxfordshire-hotels.co.uk

BUCKLAND MARSH

Oxfordshire – Pop. 2 243 – Regional map n° **6**-A2
▶ London 76 mi – Faringdon 4 mi – Oxford 15 mi

🛏 Trout at Tadpole Bridge

BRITISH TRADITIONAL · PUB This pub's lawned gardens run down to the Thames, where it has its own private moorings and an electric punt available for hire. Menus offer an appealing mix of pub classics and modern British dishes, alongside a selection of tapas. Bedrooms are traditionally decorated and generously sized.

Carte £ 19/41

6 rooms ⬚ – †£ 85/95 ††£ 130/160

⊠ SN7 8RF – ℰ (01367) 870 382 – www.troutinn.co.uk – Closed 25-26 December

BUDE

Cornwall – Pop. 5 091 – Regional map n° **1**-B2
▶ London 252 mi – Exeter 51 mi – Plymouth 50 mi – Truro 53 mi

🏠 Falcon

HOLIDAY HOTEL · CLASSIC A formally run whitewashed hotel overlooking the Bude Canal; purportedly the oldest coaching house in North Cornwall. Homely, classically styled bedrooms have contemporary touches. The traditional restaurant and spacious bar are smartly dressed in red velour; look out for the old photos in the latter.

30 rooms ⬚ – †£ 63/68 ††£ 125/135 – 1 suite

Breakwater Rd ⊠ EX23 8SD – ℰ (01288) 352 005 – www.falconhotel.com – Closed 25 December

🏠 Beach

HOLIDAY HOTEL · CONTEMPORARY Spacious New England style hotel with views over the Atlantic Ocean and a pleasingly laid-back feel. Contemporary bedrooms have limed oak furnishings and all the latest mod cons; 'Deluxe' boast roll-top baths and either a terrace or a balcony. The smart brasserie offers a menu of classic dishes and grills.

16 rooms – †£ 95/170 ††£ 95/190 – ⬚ £ 13

Summerleaze Cres. ⊠ EX23 8HL – ℰ (01288) 389 800 – www.thebeachatbude.co.uk

BUDLEIGH SALTERTON

Devon – Pop. 5 185 – Regional map n° **1**-D2

▶ London 182 mi - Exeter 16 mi - Plymouth 55 mi

Heath Close

FAMILY · PERSONALISED Smart detached house with a lovely rear garden. The open-plan lounge and dining room are stylish and modern. Good-sized bedrooms display personal touches and bathrooms have underfloor heating. The welcoming owners offer tea and cake on arrival and traditional home-cooked dinners on Friday and Saturday.

5 rooms ⌷ – ♦£ 75 ♦♦£ 105

3 Lansdowne Rd ✉ EX9 6AH – West : 1 mi by B 3178 – ℰ (01395) 444 337
– www.heathclose.com

Rosehill

VILLA · HOMELY After a tasty breakfast of French toast, eggs royale or smoked salmon, relax on the veranda, by the monkey puzzle tree. Bright, airy bedrooms come with king-sized beds and homemade treats. The owner also runs cookery courses.

4 rooms ⌷ – ♦£ 105/145 ♦♦£ 105/145

30 West Hill ✉ EX9 6BU – ℰ (01395) 444 031
– www.rosehillroomsandcookery.co.uk – Closed Christmas

Long Range

FAMILY · HOMELY Spotlessly kept guesthouse with a large garden, set on a quiet street. Choice of two lounges; one in a conservatory and complete with a small bar. Unfussy, brightly coloured bedrooms have good facilities; those to the rear can see the sea.

9 rooms ⌷ – ♦£ 66/78 ♦♦£ 100/140

5 Vales Rd ✉ EX9 6HS – by Raleigh Rd – ℰ (01395) 443 321
– www.thelongrangehotel.co.uk – Restricted opening in winter

BUNBURY

✉ Tarporley – Pop. 1 308 – Regional map n° **11**-A3

▶ London 183 mi - Birmingham 68 mi - Liverpool 39 mi - Sheffield 87 mi

Yew Tree Inn

BRITISH TRADITIONAL · PUB Handsome part red brick, part black and white timbered pub with a pleasingly relaxed feel, a lovely terrace and numerous snug, quirky rooms. They host a monthly farmers market and cooking is – unsurprisingly – seasonal and local.

Carte £ 20/33

Long Ln, Spurstow ✉ CW6 9RD – ℰ (01829) 260 274
– www.theyewtreebunbury.com

BUNGAY

Suffolk – Pop. 5 127 – Regional map n° **8**-D2

▶ London 108 mi - Beccles 6 mi - Ipswich 38 mi

Castle Inn

REGIONAL · PUB Sky-blue pub, formerly known as The White Lion, with an open-plan dining area and an intimate rear bar. Fresh, simple and seasonal country based cooking; the Innkeeper's platter of local produce is a perennial favourite. Tasty homemade cakes and cookies on display. Homely, comfortable bedrooms.

Menu £ 16 (lunch) – Carte dinner £ 22/34

4 rooms ⌷ – ♦£ 70/80 ♦♦£ 95/100

35 Earsham St ✉ NR35 1AF – ℰ (01986) 892 283 – www.thecastleinn.net – Closed 25 December, Sunday dinner and Monday in winter

357

BURFORD

Oxfordshire – Pop. 1 171 – Regional map n° **6**-A2

▶ London 76 mi – Birmingham 55 mi – Gloucester 32 mi – Oxford 20 mi

🏠 Bay Tree   ✿ ⇔ ☎ ♨ P

HISTORIC · COSY Characterful 16C wisteria-clad house with low beamed ceilings and antique furnishings. Delightful bedrooms split between main house and adjacent cottage. Charming bar and lounges with vast stone fireplaces and a snack menu. Restaurant offers ambitious, modern dishes overlooking the beautiful landscaped garden.

21 rooms �a – †£ 89/180 ††£ 99/200 – 3 suites
Sheep St ✉ OX18 4LW – ✆ (01993) 822 791
– www.cotswold-inns-hotels.co.uk/baytree

🏠 Burford House   ⇔

TRADITIONAL · STYLISH The welcome is warm at this delightful part-timbered 17C house, where spacious, comfy bedrooms – including 3 four-posters – mix traditional styling with contemporary touches. Cosy sitting rooms and a lovely terrace for afternoon tea.

8 rooms �a – †£ 95/180 ††£ 145/240
99 High St ✉ OX18 4QA – ✆ (01993) 823 151 – www.burfordhouse.co.uk

🍴 Lamb Inn   ⇔ ⇔ ☎ ℣ P

BRITISH TRADITIONAL · COSY Delightful collection of 15C weavers' cottages with a gloriously cosy feel. The elegant, candlelit dining room offers a tasting menu and an à la carte of classic dishes; a simpler menu is served in the bar and sitting rooms. Chatty service. Charming, individually furnished bedrooms; 'Rosie' has a private garden.

Menu £ 25/42
17 rooms ☎ – †£ 150/190 ††£ 170/210
Sheep St ✉ OX18 4LR – ✆ (01993) 823 155
– www.cotswold-inns-hotels.co.uk/lamb

at Swinbrook East: 2.75 mi by A40 – ✉ Burford

🍴 Swan Inn   ⇔ ⇔ ☎ P

BRITISH MODERN · PUB Wisteria-clad, honey-coloured pub on the riverbank, boasting a lovely garden filled with fruit trees. The charming interior displays an open oak frame and exposed stone walls hung with old lithographs and handmade walking sticks. The daily menu showcases the latest local produce and features modern takes on older recipes. Well-appointed bedrooms have a luxurious feel.

Carte £ 23/44
11 rooms ☎ – †£ 90/150 ††£ 125/195
✉ OX18 4DY – ✆ (01993) 823 339 – www.theswanswinbrook.co.uk – Closed 25-26 December

at Shilton Southeast : 2.5 mi by A40 off B4020

🍴 Rose & Crown   ☎ P

TRADITIONAL CUISINE · RUSTIC Charming Cotswold stone pub with flickering fires, exposed beams and a welcoming owner. Meats are from local farms and game, from nearby shoots. Gutsy country cooking is full of flavour and reasonably priced; Sunday lunch is popular.

Carte £ 21/40
Shilton ✉ OX18 4AB – ✆ (01993) 842 280 – www.shiltonroseandcrown.com
– Closed 25 December

BURNHAM MARKET

Norfolk – Pop. 877 – Regional map n° **8**-C1

▶ London 128 mi – Cambridge 71 mi – Norwich 36 mi

🏨 **Hoste**   ⚜ 🛏 🏠 🖥 🅿

INN · PERSONALISED Personally and passionately run inn, at the heart of a picturesque village. Stylish, luxurious bedrooms are split between the main building and two annexes, and there's a smart beauty and wellness spa in the wing. The extensive restaurant comprises an appealing bar, five dining rooms and a courtyard garden.

62 rooms ☑ – †£ 85/275 ††£ 130/350 – 6 suites
The Green ✉ *PE31 8HD* – ☎ *(01328) 738 777* – *www.thehoste.com*

BURNSALL

North Yorkshire – ✉ Skipton – Pop. 108 – Regional map n° **13**-A2
▶ London 223 mi – Bradford 26 mi – Leeds 29 mi

🏠 **Devonshire Fell**   ⚜ ≼ 🛏 🖥 🅿

TRADITIONAL · PERSONALISED Stone-built hotel – once a 19C gentleman's club for mill owners – set in a lovely hillside location and decorated with bold colours and striking, contemporary artwork. Spacious, modern bedrooms have dale views. Modern British menu served in the formal conservatory and funky, open-plan bar and bistro.

16 rooms – †£ 99/189 ††£ 99/189 – ☑ £ 10
✉ *BD23 6BT* – ☎ *(01756) 729 000* – *www.devonshirefell.co.uk*

🍴 **Red Lion**   ⇦ ≼ 🛏 🔄 🏠 ও 🅿

BRITISH TRADITIONAL · INN Appealing stone inn on the riverbank with a cosy bar, laid-back lounge and a formally dressed dining room. Extensive menus offer pub favourites and local meat, fish and game, along with daily specials. Classic bedrooms have modern overtones; the annexe rooms are more contemporary.
Carte £ 27/34

25 rooms ☑ – †£ 60/68 ††£ 115/158
✉ *BD23 6BU* – ☎ *(01756) 720 204* – *www.redlion.co.uk*

BURPHAM – West Sussex ➡ See Arundel

BURRINGTON

Devon – Pop. 533 – Regional map n° **1**-C1
▶ London 260 mi – Barnstaple 14 mi – Exeter 28 mi – Taunton 50 mi

🏨 **Northcote Manor**   ⚜ 🦢 ≼ 🛏 🍽 ও 🖥 🅿

HISTORIC · HOMELY Creeper-clad hall in the Torr Valley, dating from 1716. Fine fabrics and antiques feature in the elegant, individually styled rooms; well-judged attention to detail lends an air of idyllic calm. The country house restaurant features eye-catching murals.

16 rooms ☑ – †£ 120/180 ††£ 170/280 – 7 suites
✉ *EX37 9LZ* – *Northwest : 2 mi on A 377* – ☎ *(01769) 560 501*
– *www.northcotemanor.co.uk*

BURSCOUGH

Lancashire – Regional map n° **11**-A2
▶ London 215 mi – Liverpool 16 mi – Birmingham 101 mi

🍴 **Blue Mallard**   🏠 ও

BRITISH MODERN · FRIENDLY Beside the towpath you'll find a restored Victorian wharf filled with small artisan businesses and this unfussy first floor restaurant. Cooking is fresh, local and flavoursome, with a modern edge; the set menu offers great value.
Menu £ 17 (weekday lunch) – Carte £ 23/36
Burscough Wharf, Liverpool Rd North ✉ *L40 5RZ* – ☎ *(01704) 893 954*
– *www.thebluemallard.co.uk* – *Closed Monday dinner*

ENGLAND

BURTON BRADSTOCK – Dorset → See Bridport

BURTON-UPON-TRENT
Staffordshire – Pop. 72 299 – Regional map n° **10**-C1
▶ London 128 mi – Birmingham 29 mi – Leicester 27 mi – Nottingham 27 mi

🏠 Dovecliff Hall ⚜ 🐾 ≼ 🍴 🏊 **P**
TRADITIONAL · CLASSIC Imposing red-brick Georgian manor house in 7 acres of gardens, overlooking the River Dove. Characterful guest areas with antiques and drapes. Bedrooms combine traditional styling with modern facilities and all have pleasant country views. Menu of classics in the orangery restaurant.
15 rooms ☲ – 🛏£ 75/110 🛏🛏£ 75/195
Dovecliff Rd ✉ DE13 0DJ – North : 3.75 mi by A 5121 – ℰ (01283) 531 818
– www.dovecliffhallhotel.co.uk

✗ 99 Station Street
BRITISH TRADITIONAL · NEIGHBOURHOOD Amongst the vast brewing towers is this bright, boldly decorated neighbourhood restaurant, run by two experienced locals. They make everything on the premises daily and showcase regional ingredients; try the mature rare breed meats.
Menu £ 14 (weekday lunch) – Carte £ 24/36
99 Station St ✉ DE14 1BT – ℰ (01283) 516 859 – www.99stationstreet.com
– Closed Monday, Tuesday, Sunday dinner and Wednesday lunch

BURY
Greater Manchester – Pop. 77 211 – Regional map n° **11**-B2
▶ London 211 mi – Leeds 45 mi – Liverpool 35 mi – Manchester 9 mi

✗ Waggon ⟳ **P**
🐨 **BRITISH TRADITIONAL · NEIGHBOURHOOD** Unassuming former pub on a main road. The focus here is firmly on the food, which is well-cooked and well-priced. Classically based dishes change with the seasons; there's fresh fish daily, an excellent value midweek market menu and popular themed gourmet nights. A young team are guided by the charming owner.
Menu £ 16 (lunch and early dinner) – Carte £ 20/41
131 Bury and Rochdale Old Rd, Birtle ✉ BL9 6UE – East : 2 mi on B 6222
– ℰ (01706) 622 955 – www.thewaggonatbirtle.co.uk – dinner only and lunch Thursday, Friday and Sunday – Closed 2 weeks summer, first week January, Monday and Tuesday

BURY ST EDMUNDS
Suffolk – Pop. 41 113 – Regional map n° **8**-C2
▶ London 79 mi – Cambridge 27 mi – Ipswich 26 mi – Norwich 41 mi

🏠 Angel ⚜ 🖭 ⅙ 🏊 **P**
INN · CLASSIC The creeper-clad Georgian façade hides a surprisingly stylish hotel. Relax in the atmospheric bar or smart lounges. Individually designed bedrooms offer either classic four-poster luxury or come with funky décor and iPod docks.
78 rooms ☲ – 🛏£ 120/333 🛏🛏£ 120/333 – 6 suites
3 Angel Hill ✉ IP33 1LT – ℰ (01284) 714 000 – www.theangel.co.uk
Eaterie – See restaurant listing

✗✗ Maison Bleue 🦞
FISH AND SEAFOOD · NEIGHBOURHOOD Passionately run neighbourhood restaurant in a converted 17C house, with a smart blue canopy, wooden panelling and impressive fish sculptures. Menus focus on seafood; cooking is modern in style but with classic influences and Gallic and Asian touches; you must try the excellent French cheeses.
Menu £ 20 (weekdays)/35 – Carte £ 35/54
30-31 Churchgate St ✉ IP33 1RG – ℰ (01284) 760 623 – www.maisonbleue.co.uk
– Closed 3 weeks January, 2 weeks summer, Sunday and Monday

X **Eaterie** 🅿

BRITISH TRADITIONAL · BRASSERIE An airy two-roomed bistro in an attractive 15C coaching inn where Dickens once stayed. Impressive modern chandelier and display of the owner's contemporary art. Tasty, modern, British brasserie-style dishes use local produce.

Menu £ 22 (lunch) – Carte dinner £ 22/49

Angel Hotel, 3 Angel Hill ⊠ IP33 1LT – ℰ (01284) 714 000 – www.theangel.co.uk

X **Pea Porridge**

⊕ BRITISH MODERN · BISTRO Run by an efficient team; a charming former bakery in two 19C cottages – keep an eye out for the old bread oven. Tasty country cooking is led by the seasons and has a strong Mediterranean bias. Biodynamic and organic old world wines feature. Its unusual name is a reference to the old town green.

Menu £ 19 (weekdays)/22 – Carte £ 27/36

28-29 Cannon St ⊠ IP33 1JR – ℰ (01284) 700 200 (booking advisable) – www.peaporridge.co.uk – Closed first week Janaury, 2 weeks summer, last week December, Sunday-Monday and lunch Tuesday and Wednesday

at Ixworth Northeast: 7 mi by A143 – ⊠ Bury St Edmunds

XX **Theobalds**

BRITISH TRADITIONAL · NEIGHBOURHOOD Part-16C cottage in a charming village, with a cosy, fire-lit lounge and a beamed dining room. It's professionally run by a husband and wife and a jolly chef. Seasonal menus offer heartwarming, well-presented, traditional dishes.

Menu £ 29/37

68 High St ⊠ IP31 2HJ – ℰ (01359) 231 707 – www.theobaldsrestaurant.co.uk – dinner only and lunch Friday and Sunday – Closed 1 week early summer, Monday and dinner Sunday

at Whepstead South: 4.5 mi by A143 on B1066

🛏 **White Horse** 🏠 🏡 ♿ 🅿

TRADITIONAL CUISINE · PUB Cheerfully run, 17C village pub; sit in a characterful beamed room, the brighter 'Gallery' displaying local artwork or a room opening onto the garden. The kitchen's strength is conventional dishes like fish and chips and homemade sausages.

Carte £ 23/30

Rede Rd ⊠ IP29 4SS – ℰ (01284) 735 760 – www.whitehorsewhepstead.co.uk – Closed Sunday dinner

at Horringer Southwest: 3 mi on A143 – ⊠ Bury St Edmunds

🏨 **Ickworth** 🌳 🦌 ⬳ 🏠 🔲 ✗ 🖼 🏃 🏋 🅿

HISTORIC · CLASSIC This family-orientated hotel occupies the east wing of a grand 200 year old mansion set in 1,800 acres: former home of the 7th Marquess of Bristol and now owned by the National Trust. It features huge art-filled lounges, antique-furnished bedrooms and luxurious suites. Dine in the formal restaurant or in the impressive orangery, which serves relaxed meals and high teas.

39 rooms ⊊ – †£ 175/265 ††£ 225/475 – 12 suites

⊠ IP29 5QE – ℰ (01284) 735 350 – www.ickworthhotel.co.uk

BURYTHORPE – North Yorkshire → See Malton

BUSHEY

Hertfordshire – Pop. 25 328 – Regional map n° **7**-A2

▶ London 18 mi – Luton 21 mi – Watford 3 mi

Plan : see Greater London (North-West) 1

✕✕ Alpine

ITALIAN · FAMILY Long-standing family restaurant with low lighting, bold wallpaper and contemporary fabrics. Honest Italian menu displays influences from Sicily and Emilia-Romagna, ranging from family classics to more modern interpretations; homemade pasta.

Menu £ 20/24 – Carte £ 23/40

Town plan: BT-c – *135 High Rd* ⊠ *WD23 1JA* – ℰ *(020) 8950 2024*
– *www.thealpinerestaurant.co.uk* – *Closed Monday*

BUTTERMERE

Cumbria – ⊠ Cockermouth – Pop. 139 – Regional map n° **12**-A2
▶ London 306 mi – Carlisle 35 mi – Kendal 43 mi

🏠 Wood House

TRADITIONAL · CLASSIC Charming part-16C house with Victorian additions and lovely gardens, in a wonderfully serene lakeside setting. Welcoming owners, stunning views and no TVs to disturb the peace! Classical lounge and cosy dining room with communal antique table, silver cutlery and cut crystal glassware.

3 rooms ⌂ – **†**£ 80 **††**£ 130

⊠ *CA13 9XA* – *Northwest : 0.5 mi on B 5289* – ℰ *(017687) 70 208*
– *www.wdhse.co.uk* – *March-October*

BUXTON

Derbyshire – Pop. 22 115 – Regional map n° **9**-A1
▶ London 172 mi – Derby 38 mi – Manchester 25 mi – Stoke-on-Trent 24 mi

🏠 Buxton's Victorian

TOWNHOUSE · COSY Charming townhouse built in 1860 by the Duke of Devonshire, overlooking the boating lake and bandstand in the Pavilion Gardens. Traditional bedrooms are furnished with antiques and come with complimentary Buxton water and sherry.

4 rooms ⌂ – **†**£ 65/70 **††**£ 88/106

3A Broad Walk ⊠ *SK17 6JE* – ℰ *(01298) 78 759* – *www.buxtonvictorian.co.uk*
– *Closed Christmas-New Year*

CALLINGTON

Cornwall – Pop. 4 698 – Regional map n° **1**-C2
▶ London 237 mi – Exeter 53 mi – Plymouth 15 mi – Truro 46 mi

🏠 Cadson Manor

COUNTRY HOUSE · HOMELY Welcoming guesthouse on a 600 year old working farm, with views over an iron age settlement. Cosy, individually furnished bedrooms feature antiques, fresh flowers and a decanter of sherry. Rayburn-cooked breakfasts include weekly specials.

4 rooms ⌂ – **†**£ 85 **††**£ 110/125

⊠ *PL17 7HW* – *Southwest : 2.75 mi by A 390* – ℰ *(01579) 383 969*
– *www.cadsonmanor.co.uk* – *Closed Christmas*

✕✕ Langmans

BRITISH MODERN · INDIVIDUAL Quaint, double-fronted shop conversion run by a husband and wife team. Pre-dinner drinks in the lounge are followed by a 6 course tasting menu in the formal rear dining room. Refined cooking with a good selection of Cornish cheeses.

Menu £ 43 – set menu only

3 Church St ⊠ *PL17 7RE* – ℰ *(01579) 384 933 (booking essential)*
– *www.langmansrestaurant.co.uk* – *dinner only* – *Closed Sunday-Wednesday*

CALNE

Wiltshire – Pop. 17 274 – Regional map n° **2**-C2
▶ London 91 mi – Bristol 33 mi – Southampton 63 mi – Swindon 17 mi

🏨 Bowood ☆ ⋙ 🍴 🖼 📺 ⑩ 🏯 ♨ 🎨 ⬆ ⬇ ♿ 🅰 💈 🛎 🅿

LUXURY · MODERN Smart, professionally run, purpose-built hotel in the grounds of Lord and Lady Lansdowne's Estate. Contemporary country house styling. Spacious bedrooms; some with balconies. Modern British cooking in formal Shelburne, with its attractive terrace. Brasserie menu served in the golf clubhouse.

43 rooms ⌑ – †£ 120/240 ††£ 130/280

Derry Hill ✉ SN11 9PQ – West : 3 mi by A 4 on Derry Hill rd – ℰ (01249) 822 228 – www.bowood-hotel.co.uk

at Compton Bassett Northeast: 4.5 mi by A4

🍴 White Horse Inn ⇦ 🍴 🛋 🅿

BRITISH MODERN · FRIENDLY A truly welcoming, 18C pub. The cosy bar has a wood burning stove and a jolly atmosphere and there's also a rustic dining room. All-encompassing menus offer everything from a croque monsieur to loin of venison from their own farm. Simply furnished, well-priced bedrooms are set across the large garden.

Carte £ 26/45

8 rooms ⌑ – †£ 75/85 ††£ 85/105

✉ SN11 8RG – ℰ (01249) 813 118 – www.whitehorse-comptonbassett.co.uk
– Closed 25 December, Sunday dinner and Monday

CAMBER – East Sussex ➜ See Rye

CAMBRIDGE

Cambridgeshire – Pop. 123 867 – Regional map n° **8**-B3

▶ London 55 mi – Coventry 88 mi – Ipswich 54 mi – Kingston-upon-Hull 137 mi

Hotels

🏨 Hotel du Vin ✿ ⬚ 🖪 🖳 🏵

TOWNHOUSE · STYLISH Stylish hotel set over a row of 16C and 17C ex-university owned buildings. Original quarry tiled floors and wood-panelled walls feature, along with plenty of passages, nooks and crannies. Chic, modern bedrooms – one even has its own cinema. Clubby bar and an appealing brasserie with a Gallic-led menu.

41 rooms – ♦£ 185/220 ♦♦£ 205/255 – ⬚ £ 17

Town plan: Z-e – *15-19 Trumpington St* ⊠ *CB2 1QA* – *℘ (01223) 227 330* – *www.hotelduvin.com*

🏨 Hotel Felix ✿ 🐾 🍸 ⬚ 🏵 🖳 🅿

BUSINESS · DESIGN A substantial Victorian mansion which was once a private house; set in 3 acres of gardens. Stylish lounge and bar hung with modern art. Spacious, comfortable, boutique bedrooms offer good mod cons: four are in the main house; the rest, in the extensions. Contemporary restaurant serves modern British cooking.

52 rooms ⬚ – ♦£ 168/178 ♦♦£ 212/325

Whitehouse Ln, Huntingdon Rd ⊠ *CB3 0LX* – *Northwest : 1.5 mi by A 1307* – *℘ (01223) 277 977* – *www.hotelfelix.co.uk*

🏨 Varsity H. & Spa ✿ 🐿 🏋 ⬚ 🖪 🖳 🏵 ✀

TOWNHOUSE · DESIGN A boutique hotel just back from the River Cam, with a stylish roof terrace and a tranquil lounge offering complimentary drinks. Well-appointed bedrooms; some boast coffee machines and balconies. The informal restaurant is set over two floors with a view of the Cam and a menu of steak and fish.

48 rooms ⬚ – ♦£ 140/199 ♦♦£ 140/395

Town plan: Y-x – *Thompson's Ln* ⊠ *CB5 8AQ* – *℘ (01223) 306 030* – *www.thevarsityhotel.co.uk*

ge St . . . . **Y 2**
ham's Lane . . . . . . **X 5**
e Exchange St. . . . **Z 6**
ning St . . . . **Z 7**
School Lane . . . . . **Z 12**
on Centre . . . . **Y**
son St . . . . **Z 14**
's Parade . . . . **Z 15**
Yard Centre . . . . . . **Z**
ingley Rd . . . . **X 16**
dalene St . . . . **Y 17**
et Hill . . . . **YZ 18**
et St . . . . **Y 19**

Milton Rd. . . . . **Y 20**
Newmarket Rd . . . . . **Y 21**
Northampton St . . . . **Y 22**
Parker St . . . . **Z 23**
Peas Hill . . . . **Z 25**
Pembroke St . . . . . . **Z 26**
Petty Cury . . . . **Y 27**
Rose Crescent . . . . . **Y 28**
St Andrew's St . . . . . **Z 30**
St John's St. . . . . . . **Y 31**
Short St . . . . **Z 32**
Sidney St . . . . **Y 34**
Trinity St. . . . . **Y 36**
Trumpington Rd . . . . **Z 37**
Wheeler St . . . . **Z 39**

COLLEGES

ist's . . . . **Y A**
urchill . . . . **X B**
re . . . . **Z B**
e Hall . . . . **X N**
pus Christi . . . . . **Z G¹**
win . . . . **Z D**
rning . . . . **Z E¹**
manuel . . . . **Z F**
william . . . . **Y G**
nville and Caius . . **Y G²**
ues Hall . . . . **Z K**
us . . . . **Y K**
g's . . . . **Z**

Lucy Cavendish . . . **Y O¹**
Magdalene . . . . . . **Y N**
Newnham . . . . **X E²**
New Hall . . . . **Y N**
Pembroke. . . . . **Z O²**
Peterhouse . . . . . . **Z**
Queen's . . . . **Z**
Robinson . . . . **X K**
St Catharine's . . . . **Z R**
St Edmund's House **Y U**
St John's . . . . **Y**
Selwyn . . . . **X F**
Sidney Sussex . . . . **Y P**
Trinity . . . . **Y**
Trinity Hall. . . . . . . **Y V**
Wolfson . . . . **X U**

Restaurants

✗✗✗ **Midsummer House** (Daniel Clifford)

ᗀ ᗣ ᗤ ᗥ

❀❀ MODERN CUISINE · ELEGANT A stylish restaurant in an idyllic location on Midsummer Common; enjoy an aperitif in the first floor lounge overlooking the River Cam. Set 7 or 10 course menus (with 5 courses also available at lunch). Creative, highly accomplished cooking showcases top quality produce, and flavours are well-balanced, with the main ingredient of each dish allowed to shine.
→ Beetroot baked on open coals with quinoa, goat's cheese and mizuna. Pot-roasted black leg chicken with leek purée and pickled mushrooms. Yorkshire rhubarb, Chantilly, caramelised Bramley apple and meringues.
Menu £ 48 (lunch)/105
Town plan: Y-a – *Midsummer Common* ✉ *CB4 1HA* – ✆ *(01223) 369 299*
– www.midsummerhouse.co.uk – Closed 2 weeks December, Sunday, Monday and lunch Tuesday

✗✗ **Alimentum** (Mark Poynton)

ᗀ ᗩ ᗪ ᗥ

❀ FRENCH MODERN · MINIMALIST Sleek, stylish restaurant with a spacious cocktail bar and a striking red & black dining room with bold feature walls. Top quality ingredients are showcased in skilfully crafted dishes. Cooking is classically based, with clearly defined flavours and innovative modern touches. Good value early evening menu.
→ Roast and braised Norfolk quail, broccoli, peanut and lime. Sea bass with cauliflower, langoustine, goat's cheese and Pedro Ximénez sauce. Apricot and almond Battenberg, apricot sorbet, Amaretto and apricot cannelloni.
Menu £ 27 (lunch and early dinner)/53
Town plan: X-a – *152-154 Hills Rd* ✉ *CB2 8PB* – ✆ *(01223) 413 000*
– www.restaurantalimentum.co.uk – Closed 23-30 December and bank holiday Mondays

✗✗ **Restaurant 22**

ᗪ ᗥ

FRENCH · NEIGHBOURHOOD A converted Victorian townhouse with a formal dining room; personally run, with ten tables set with flowers and candles. Monthly changing, four course menu of classically based, flavourful cooking with Italian influences.
Menu £ 38
Town plan: Y-c – *22 Chesterton Rd* ✉ *CB4 3AX* – ✆ *(01223) 351 880 (booking essential)* – *www.restaurant22.co.uk* – *dinner only – Closed 24 December-2 January, Sunday and Monday*

✗✗ **Cotto**

CLASSIC CUISINE · FRIENDLY Personally run, first floor restaurant with illuminated canvasses lining the walls. Weekly changing, fixed price menu; classic cooking showcases excellent ingredients. The chef-owner is a chocolatier by trade so the chocolates are a must!
Menu £ 55 **s**
Town plan: Z-a – *183 East Rd* ✉ *CB1 1BG* – ✆ *(01223) 302 010 (booking essential)* – *www.cottocambridge.co.uk* – *dinner only – Closed August, 23 December-10 January, Sunday-Tuesday*

✗ **Fitzbillies**

ᗪ

BRITISH MODERN · BISTRO Originally a 1921 cake shop famed for its Chelsea buns; now an upmarket café which retains its dark wood, art deco façade. The concise, weekly changing menu offers traditional, flavourful dishes. Excellent baked goods.
Carte £ 23/35
Town plan: Z-x – *51-52 Trumpington St* ✉ *CB2 1RG* – ✆ *(01223) 352 500*
– www.fitzbillies.com – Closed dinner Sunday-Wednesday

at Horningsea Northeast: 4 mi by A1303 – Plan: X – and B1047 on Horningsea rd
✉ Cambridge

✗ Crown & Punchbowl

BRITISH MODERN · PUB Homely restaurant in an old pub, complete with beams, open fires and chunky wooden tables. Cooking is modern and ambitious and there's always a fresh scallop dish on offer, as well as fish specials on the blackboard. Take time to relax on the terrace before heading for one of the simply furnished bedrooms.

Carte £ 26/43

5 rooms ⬚ – †£ 80 ††£ 100

High St ✉ CB25 9JG – ☏ (01223) 860 643
– www.cambscuisine.com – Closed 26 December-1 January,
dinner Sunday and bank holiday Monday

at Madingley West: 4.5 mi by A1303 – Plan: X – ✉ Cambridge

🍽 Three Horseshoes

MODERN CUISINE · PUB An appealing thatched pub with a lively bar and a more formal conservatory restaurant overlooking the garden. Ambitious, modern dishes have international influences and the wine list is well-chosen, with plenty by the glass.

Carte £ 25/41

High St ✉ CB23 8AB – ☏ (01954) 210 221 (booking advisable)
– www.threehorseshoesmadingley.com – Closed Sunday dinner
November-February

at Little Wilbraham East: 7.25 mi by A1303 – Plan: X – ✉ Cambridge

🍽 Hole in the Wall

🏠 🅿

BRITISH MODERN · PUB A charming 16C pub with a cosy, fire-lit, beamed bar. The regularly changing, seasonal menu offers European flavours presented in a modern fashion; dishes are prepared with zeal by the young chef-owner, a past MasterChef finalist. Excellent value lunch menu; tasting menus available in the evening.

Menu £ 20/30

2 High St ✉ CB21 5JY – ☏ (01223) 812 282 (booking advisable)
– www.holeinthewallcambridge.com – Closed 2 weeks January, Sunday dinner,
Monday and Tuesday lunch

CAMELFORD

Cornwall – Pop. 2 335 – Regional map n° **1**-B2
▶ London 376 mi – Truro 57 mi – Plymouth 69 mi

🏠 Pendragon Country House 🆕

COUNTRY HOUSE · HOMELY This former vicarage is run by an extremely enthusiastic couple and offers views across the fields to the church it once served. There's always a jigsaw on the go in the period furnished drawing room and Cornish artwork features throughout. Home-baked breads, homemade cake and local produce feature.

7 rooms ⬚ – †£ 60/65 ††£ 95/140

Davidstow ✉ PL32 9XR – Northeast : 3.5 mi by A 39 on A 395
– ☏ (01840) 261 131 – www.pendragoncountryhouse.com
– Closed 23-27 December

CANTERBURY

Kent – Pop. 54 880 – Regional map n° **5**-D2
London 59 mi – Brighton 76 mi – Dover 15 mi – Maidstone 28 mi

Abode Canterbury

HISTORIC · STYLISH Centrally located former coaching inn; heavily beamed, yet with a stylish, boutique feel. Comfy champagne bar and atmospheric first floor lounge. Contemporary bedrooms come in 4 categories: 'Enviable' and 'Fabulous' are the most luxurious.

72 rooms – £ 95/155 £ 95/250 – £ 12 – 1 suite

Town plan: Y-a – *30-33 High St* ✉ *CT1 2RX* – *(01227) 766 266*
– *www.abodecanterbury.co.uk*

County – See restaurant listing

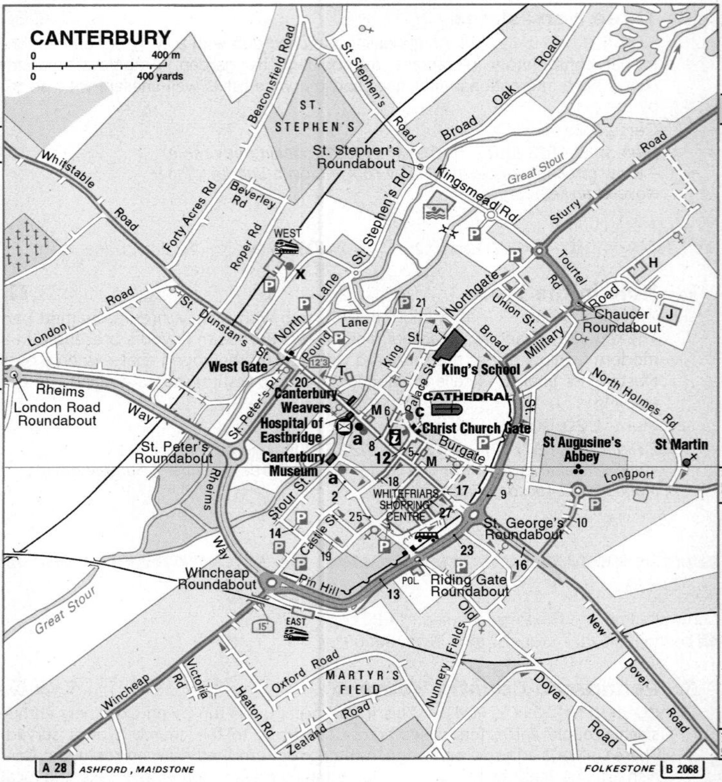

Beercart Lane . . . . . YZ 2
Borough (The) . . . . . Y 4
Burgate . . . . . Y
Butchery Lane . . . . . Y 5
Guildhall St . . . . . Y 6
High St . . . . . Y 8
Lower Bridge St. . . . . . Z 9
Lower Chantry Lane . . . . . Z 10
Mercery Lane . . . . . Y 12
Palace St . . . . . Y
Rhodaus Town. . . . . . Z 13
Rosemary Lane . . . . . Z 14
St George's Pl. . . . . . Z 16
St George's St . . . . . Z 17
St Margaret's St . . . . . YZ 18
St Mary's St . . . . . Z 19
St Peter's St. . . . . . Y 20
St Redigund's St . . . . . Y 21
Upper Bridge St. . . . . . Z 23
Watling St. . . . . . Z 25
Whitefriars Shopping Centre . . . . . Z
Whitefriars St. . . . . . Z 27

XX Deesons

BRITISH TRADITIONAL · TRADITIONAL Charming building in the shadow of the cathedral. The rustic interior consists of several different areas with old wood furnishings and funky modern wallpaper. Hearty British cooking uses ingredients from the owner's smallholding.

Menu £15 (lunch)/23 – Carte £21/42

Town plan: Y-c – *25-27 Sun St* ✉ *CT1 2HX* – ✆ *(01227) 767 854*
– *www.deesonsrestaurant.co.uk* – *Closed 25-26 December*

XX County

BRITISH MODERN · DESIGN Spacious, modern restaurant divided in two by a smart, glass-walled wine cellar. Accomplished, contemporary cooking is stylishly presented, with classic combinations of ingredients interpreted in a modern fashion. Private chef's table.

Carte £27/38

Town plan: Y-a – *Abode Canterbury Hotel, High St* ✉ *CT1 2RX* – ✆ *(01227) 826 684* – *www.abodecanterbury.co.uk* – *Closed Sunday dinner*

XX Ambrette 🆕

INDIAN · TRENDY This modern restaurant is hidden away, just off the main street. A striking tiled floor leads through to a spacious, moodily lit room. Local ingredients – some foraged from the woods – feature in deftly spiced Anglo-Indian dishes.

Menu £20 (lunch) – Carte £26/39

Town plan: Z-a – *14-15 Beer Cart Ln* ✉ *CT1 2NY* – ✆ *(01227) 200 777*
– *www.theambrette.co.uk*

X Goods Shed

BRITISH TRADITIONAL · RUSTIC Daily farmers' market and food hall in an early Victorian locomotive shed, selling an excellent variety of organic, free range and homemade produce. Hearty, rustic, daily changing dishes are served at scrubbed wooden tables.

Carte £27/46

Town plan: Y-x – *Station Rd West, St Dunstans* ✉ *CT2 8AN* – ✆ *(01227) 459 153*
– *www.thegoodsshed.net* – *Closed 25-26 December, 1-2 January, Sunday dinner and Monday*

at Lower Hardres South: 3 mi on B2068 – Plan: Z – ✉ Canterbury

🍴 Granville

BRITISH TRADITIONAL · RUSTIC Sizeable family-run pub on a village T-junction. The open-plan interior has a high ceiling, exposed rafters and a Scandinavian feel. Constantly evolving blackboard menus offer unfussy, generous dishes; veg is from their allotment.

Carte £24/40

Street End ✉ *CT4 7AL* – ✆ *(01227) 700 402* – *www.thegranvillecanterbury.co.uk*
– *Closed 25 December, Sunday dinner and Monday*

CARBIS BAY – Cornwall ➜ See St Ives

CARLISLE

Cumbria – Pop. 75 306 – Regional map n° **12**-B1
▶ London 317 mi – Blackpool 95 mi – Edinburgh 101 mi – Glasgow 100 mi

🏠 Warwick Hall

COUNTRY HOUSE · HOMELY Impressive sandstone house in a 270 acre riverside setting. The extremely spacious interior includes a charming lobby and an elegant drawing room. A sweeping stone staircase leads to period-furnished bedrooms – some with kitchens.

9 rooms ☑ – †£ 98/138 ††£ 118/158
Warwick-on-Eden ✉ *CA4 8PG* – *East : 4.75 mi on A 69* – ✆ *(01228) 561 546*
– *www.warwickhall.co.uk*

CARLYON BAY – Cornwall → See St Austell

CARTHORPE

North Yorkshire – Regional map n° **13**-B1
▶ London 228 mi – Leeds 49 mi – Middlesbrough 40 mi – York 34 mi

🍴 Fox and Hounds 🕙 🅿

BRITISH TRADITIONAL · PUB Traditional country pub with an open-fired bar and a dining room filled with equine, farming and blacksmith paraphernalia. Good-sized menu offers unfussy, home-cooked dishes. Local, organic and homemade products are also for sale.
Menu £ 16 (weekdays) – Carte £ 21/43
✉ DL8 2LG – ☎ (01845) 567 433 – www.foxandhoundscarthorpe.co.uk – Closed first 2 weeks January, 25 December and Monday

CARTMEL – Cumbria → See Grange-over-Sands

CASTLE COMBE

Wiltshire – ✉ Chippenham – Pop. 347 – Regional map n° **2**-C2
▶ London 110 mi – Bristol 23 mi – Chippenham 6 mi

🏨 Manor House H. and Golf Club 🐾 🐕 ⇦ 🔌 📷 ✕ & 🏋 🅿

LUXURY · ELEGANT Fine period manor house in 365 acres of formal gardens and parkland. The interior exudes immense charm and style, with characterful oak panelling and a host of open-fired lounges. Uniquely styled, luxurious bedrooms are split between the main house and mews cottages. Book ahead for one of the event days.
48 rooms ☲ – ♦£ 270/650 ♦♦£ 270/650 – 7 suites
✉ SN14 7HR – ☎ (01249) 782 206 – www.manorhouse.co.uk
❀ **Bybrook** – See restaurant listing

🏠 Castle Inn 🐾 🍴 ✕

HISTORIC · COSY Delightful 12C former inn in a charming village, with two small, cosy lounges and a pubby dining room – where rustic features blend with contemporary touches. Menus range from old favourites to more sophisticated dishes. Bedrooms mix old beams with modern furnishings; some have four-posters.
11 rooms ☲ – ♦£ 80/145 ♦♦£ 135/199
✉ SN14 7HN – ☎ (01249) 783 030 – www.castle-inn.info – Closed 25 December

🍴🍴🍴 Bybrook ⇦ 🍴 🅿

❀ **BRITISH MODERN · ELEGANT** Spacious dining room within a charming 14C manor house, in 365 acres of formal gardens and parkland. Large, well-spaced tables are immaculately laid. Menus offer refined, carefully prepared dishes with a classical base and modern overtones, and feature local and kitchen garden produce. Smooth service.
→ Ravioli of chicken with Montgomery cheddar velouté and crispy shallots. Breast of Creedy Carver duck, sweet potato, baby turnip, maple, sesame and ponzu. Vanilla cheesecake with cardamom ice cream and saffron-poached pineapple.
Menu £ 30/78
Manor House Hotel and Golf Club, ✉ SN14 7HR – ☎ (01249) 782 206
– www.manorhouse.co.uk – Closed lunch Monday and Tuesday

CASTLE DONINGTON

Leicestershire – ✉ Derby – Pop. 6 416 – Regional map n° **9**-B2
▶ London 121 mi – Leeds 82 mi – Sheffield 52 mi – Manchester 96 mi

🏨 **Radisson Blu East Midlands Airport**

ENGLAND

BUSINESS · MODERN An ultra-modern airport hotel with admirable green credentials and a well-equipped gym. Spacious bedrooms have feature walls, modern facilities and good soundproofing; some boast runway views. A European menu is served in the light, airy restaurant; watch the planes taking off and landing while you dine.

218 rooms � – ♦£ 79/211 ♦♦£ 91/223 – 1 suite

Herald Way, Pegasus Business Pk ⊠ DE74 2TZ – Southeast : 4 mi by A 453 – ℰ (01509) 670 575 – www.radissonblu.com

CASTLE EDEN

Durham – Regional map n° **14**-B3

▶ London 265 mi – Newcastle upon Tyne 28 mi – York 62 mi

🍴 **Castle Eden Inn**

BRITISH TRADITIONAL · PUB A former coaching inn on what was once the main road to London: local gossip says that Dick Turpin was once tied up outside! The experienced owners offer a wide choice of dishes and the 'monthly specials' menu offers great value.

Menu £ 12/15 – Carte £ 25/37

Stockton Rd ⊠ TS27 4SD – ℰ (01429) 835 137 – www.castleedeninn.com – Closed Sunday dinner

CATEL/CASTEL → See Channel Islands (Guernsey)

CAXTON

Cambridgeshire – Pop. 572 – Regional map n° **8**-A3

▶ London 58 mi – Cambridge 15 mi – Bedford 22 mi

🍴 **No 77** 🆕

THAI · PUB The cream and blue exterior of No 77 leads to a rustic interior with blue velvet cushioned chairs from an old cinema. An extensive list of Thai dishes includes popular Kantok sharing platters and there's a cinema club on Sundays.

Menu £ 15 (weekday lunch)/25 – Carte £ 15/24

77 Ermine St ⊠ CB23 3PQ – ℰ (01954) 269 577 – www.77cambridge.com – Closed Tuesday lunch and Monday

CERNE ABBAS

Dorset – Regional map n° **2**-C3

▶ London 132 mi – Bristol - 60 mi – Cardiff 115 mi – Southampton 58 mi

🍴 **New Inn**

BRITISH TRADITIONAL · FRIENDLY An elegantly dressed, 16C part-flint inn on the main street of this delightful village, home to the famous Chalk Giant. This charming pub has a relaxing ambience, genial staff and an appealing menu of tasty, traditional dishes. Spacious, stylish bedrooms are split between the pub and the courtyard; some are duplex suites with a freestanding bath in the room.

Carte £ 25/46

12 rooms ☲ – ♦£ 95/170 ♦♦£ 95/170

14 Long St ⊠ DT2 7JF – ℰ (01300) 341 274 – www.thenewinncerneabbas.co.uk – Closed 25-26 December

CHADDESLEY CORBETT

Worcestershire – Pop. 1 440 – Regional map n° **10**-B2

▶ London 123 mi – Birmingham 26 mi – Leicester 62 mi – Coventry 35 mi

⌂⌂⌂ Brockencote Hall ☂ ⌖ 🖢 ✻ 🕭 🕿 🛎 🅿

HISTORIC · CONTEMPORARY Professionally run 19C mansion with the feel of a French château; its long driveway leads past a lake and grazing cattle. Inside, period features blend well with contemporary country house furnishings and bold colour schemes. Bedrooms are spacious and well-equipped and some have pleasant park views.

21 rooms 🖙 – ♦£ 95/325 ♦♦£ 135/435

✉ DY10 4PY – On A 448 – 𝒞 (01562) 777 876 – www.brockencotehall.com

The Chaddesley – See restaurant listing

XxX The Chaddesley 🖢 🕭 🅿

MODERN CUISINE · ELEGANT Elegant restaurant in an impressive 19C mansion. Smartly laid tables overlook the gardens; in summer, head for the terrace. Accomplished cooking relies on classic combinations but uses modern techniques and dishes are nicely presented.

Menu £ 23 (weekdays)/60 **s**

Brockencote Hall Hotel, ✉ DY10 4PY – On A 448 – 𝒞 (01562) 777 876
– www.brockencotehall.com

CHADWICK END

West Midlands – Regional map n° **10**-C2
▶ London 106 mi – Birmingham 13 mi – Leicester 40 mi – Stratford-upon-Avon 16 mi

🍴 Orange Tree 🖢 🕭 🅿

INTERNATIONAL · PUB This impressively smart pub has a unique style: cosy, rustic and contemporary by turns, with a bit of kitsch thrown in for good measure. Expect global influences alongside the more traditional pizza, pie or risotto.

Menu £ 13 (lunch and early dinner) – Carte £ 21/37

Warwick Rd ✉ B93 0BN – on A 4141 – 𝒞 (01564) 785 364 (booking advisable)
– www.lovelypubs.co.uk

CHAGFORD

Devon – Pop. 1 020 – Regional map n° **1**-C2
▶ London 218 mi – Exeter 17 mi – Plymouth 27 mi

⌂⌂⌂⌂ Gidleigh Park ☂ ⌖ ⩶ 🖢 ⟍ ✻ 🕭 🕿 🅿

LUXURY · STYLISH An impressive black & white, timbered Arts and Crafts house with lovely tiered gardens and Teign Valley views. Luxurious sitting and drawing rooms have a classic country house feel but a contemporary edge. Wonderfully comfortable bedrooms echo this and come in an appealing mix of styles. Service is superb.

23 rooms 🖙 – ♦£ 215/1265 ♦♦£ 240/1290 – 1 suite

✉ TQ13 8HH – Northwest : 2 mi by Gidleigh Rd – 𝒞 (01647) 432 367
– www.gidleigh.co.uk – Closed 3-15 January

❀❀ **Gidleigh Park** – See restaurant listing

XxXX Gidleigh Park (Michael Caines) ❀❀ ⩶ 🖢 🍴 🅿

❀❀ **FRENCH CLASSIC · FORMAL** Formal restaurant in a beautifully restored Edwardian house set in 100 acres of parkland. Classic French menus showcase top quality local produce and veg from the kitchen garden in skilfully prepared combinations. The tasting menu features Michael Caines' signature dishes and the wine list is top notch.

→ Scallops and celeriac purée with soy and truffle vinaigrette. Lamb, boulangère potatoes, fennel purée and confit shoulder. Chocolate and orange mousse with orange sorbet.

Menu £ 46/143

Gidleigh Park Hotel, ✉ TQ13 8HH – Northwest : 2 mi by Gidleigh Rd – 𝒞 (01647) 432 367 (booking essential) – www.gidleigh.co.uk – Closed 3-15 January

at Sandypark Northeast: 2.25 mi on A382 – ⊠ Chagford

🏠 Mill End

TRADITIONAL · PERSONALISED Whitewashed former mill off a quiet country road: once home to Frank Whittle, inventor of the jet engine. Comfy, cosy lounges with beams and open fires. Contemporary bedrooms have bold feature walls and colourful throws. Bright dining room offers classical dishes prepared using local produce.

15 rooms ⌕ – ♦£ 75/195 ♦♦£ 90/210 – 1 suite

⊠ TQ13 8JN – On A 382 – ℰ (01647) 432 282 – www.millendhotel.com – Closed 5-21 January

🏠 Parford Well

TRADITIONAL · COSY Well-kept guesthouse with superb mature gardens. Homely lounge with a wood-burning stove, books and games. Two small breakfast rooms; one communal and one with a table for two. Individually decorated bedrooms offer pleasant country views.

3 rooms ⌕ – ♦£ 80/110 ♦♦£ 90/110

⊠ TQ13 8JW – On Drewsteignton rd – ℰ (01647) 433 353 – www.parfordwell.co.uk – restricted opening in winter

at Easton Northeast: 1.5 mi on A382 – ⊠ Chagford

🏠 Easton Court

TRADITIONAL · COSY This Devonshire Longhouse was once a regular haunt of writer Evelyn Waugh. Some of the spacious, simply styled bedrooms look out over the grounds. The sun rises over the hills in the summer, so breakfast in the garden is a must.

5 rooms ⌕ – ♦£ 55/65 ♦♦£ 75/85

Easton Cross ⊠ TQ13 8JL – ℰ (01647) 433 469 – www.easton.co.uk

CHANNEL ISLANDS

Regional map n° **3**-B2

ALDERNEY

Alderney – Pop. 2 400 – Regional map n° **3**-B1

Braye

🏠 **Braye Beach** 🏠 🕭 ← 🛖 🖃 🕅 🔏 **P**

HOLIDAY HOTEL · MODERN Stylish hotel on Braye beach, just a stone's throw from the harbour. The vaulted basement houses two lounges and a 19-seater cinema; above is a modern bar with a delightful terrace. Bedrooms are beech-furnished, and some have balconies and bay views. The formal restaurant showcases local island seafood.

27 rooms 😴 – ♥£ 95/165 ♥♥£ 100/250

Braye St. ✉ *GY9 3XT –* 𝒞 *(01481) 824 300 – www.brayebeach.com*

GUERNSEY

Guernsey – Pop. 58 867 – Regional map n° **3**-A2

Castel

🏠 **Cobo Bay** 🏠 ← 🛖 🕅 🖃 🔏 **P**

FAMILY · MODERN Modern hotel set on the peaceful side of the island and well run by the 3rd generation of the family. Bright, stylish bedrooms come with fresh fruit, irons, safes and bathrobes – some have large balconies overlooking the sandy bay. Smart dining room; sit on the spacious terrace for lovely sunset views.

34 rooms 😴 – ♥£ 59/219 ♥♥£ 99/225

Cobo Coast Rd ✉ *GY5 7HB –* 𝒞 *(01481) 257 102 – www.cobobayhotel.com*
– Closed January-February

Fermain Bay

🏠 **Fermain Valley** 🏠 ← 🛖 🖾 🕅 🖃 🕹 🔏 **P**

LUXURY · MODERN Stylish hotel with beautiful gardens, hidden in a picturesque valley and affording pleasant bay views through the trees. Well-equipped bedrooms are widely dispersed; the 'Gold' rooms have balconies. Dine with a view in Ocean or from a steakhouse menu – accompanied by cocktails – in contemporary Rock Garden.

45 rooms 😴 – ♥£ 110/220 ♥♥£ 125/235

Fermain Ln ✉ *GY1 1ZZ –* 𝒞 *(01481) 235 666 – www.fermainvalley.com*

Kings Mills

ⓘ Fleur du Jardin　　　　⇆ 🍴🛏🚗⊐ 🅿

TRADITIONAL CUISINE · INN Attractive inn with a stylish terrace, lovely land-scaped gardens and several charming, adjoining rustic rooms. The menu ranges from homemade burgers to sea bass and tasty island seafood specials. Stylish bedrooms have a New England theme, and there's even a heated outdoor pool.

Menu £ 15 (lunch and early dinner) – Carte £ 21/36

13 rooms ☲ – ♥£ 60/90 ♥♥£ 80/130 – 2 suites

Grand Moulins ✉ GY5 7JT – ℰ *(01481) 257 996 – www.fleurdujardin.com – Closed dinner 25 December and 1 January*

St Martin

▶ St Peter Port 2 mi

🏨 Bella Luce　　　　🌿 🐾 🍴⊐ 🕐 🎾 🅿

COUNTRY HOUSE · STYLISH Originally a Norman manor house; now a hotel with a cosy beamed bar, a cellar-like lounge and a stylish, intimate interior fea-turing voluptuous velvets. Opulent bedrooms have modern bathrooms and the pleasant gardens come with a pool. The restaurant offers an eclectic array of modern dishes.

23 rooms ☲ – ♥£ 118/223 ♥♥£ 118/223

La Fosse ✉ GY4 6EB – ℰ *(01481) 238 764 – www.bellalucehotel.com*

🏨 La Barbarie　　　　🌿 🐾 🍴🛏⊐ 🎾 🅿

TRADITIONAL · CONTEMPORARY An attractive stone-built former priory with an outdoor swimming pool and a cosy, cottagey style. Go for a spacious 'Superior' room or the 'Suite', which overlooks the pool. The characterful bar-lounge has oak beams and an open fire; in contrast, the dining room is bright and modern. Seafood dishes feature.

31 rooms ☲ – ♥£ 83/122 ♥♥£ 95/164 – 1 suite

Saints Bay ✉ GY4 6ES – ℰ *(01481) 235 217 – www.labarbariehotel.com – March-October*

✕✕ Auberge　　　　⇆ 🍴🛏 🅿

MODERN CUISINE · FRIENDLY Long-standing restaurant in a great location. Sim-ple interior with a bar and well-spaced tables; concertina doors open onto a lovely terrace, which offers views across to the other islands. Classical menu fea-tures plenty of island seafood.

Menu £ 13 (lunch and early dinner) – Carte £ 25/41

Jerbourg Rd ✉ GY4 6BH – ℰ *(01481) 238 485 (booking essential) – www.theauberge.gg – Closed 24 December-1 February and Sunday dinner*

St Peter Port

🏨 Old Government House H. & Spa　🌿 🍴⊐ 🕐 🛁 💆 📺 🔓 🆎 🛎

LUXURY · CLASSIC Fine, classically furnished 18C building, with 🅿 many of its original features restored, including a glorious ballroom. Individually styled bedrooms have padded walls, modern bathrooms and a personal touch. Relax in the well-equipped spa or outdoor pool. Authentic Indian cooking in The Curry Room. The smart yet informal brasserie has a delightful terrace.

62 rooms ☲ – ♥£ 188/515 ♥♥£ 188/515 – 1 suite

Town plan: Y-a – *St Ann's Pl* ✉ GY1 2NU – ℰ *(01481) 724 921 – www.theoghhotel.com*

🏨 Duke of Richmond　　　🌿 ⇆ ⊐ 📺 🆎 🛎

BUSINESS · CONTEMPORARY Contemporary hotel with a bright reception area and a stylish lounge ideal for afternoon tea. Smart, modern bedrooms; some with balconies. Relax in the secluded pool or on the patio overlooking the 19C Candie Gardens. A chic bar with leopard print furnishings leads to the restaurant and terrace.

73 rooms ☲ – ♥£ 143/408 ♥♥£ 143/408 – 1 suite

Town plan: Y-s – *Cambridge Pk.* ✉ GY1 1UY – ℰ *(01481) 726 221 – www.dukeofrichmond.com*

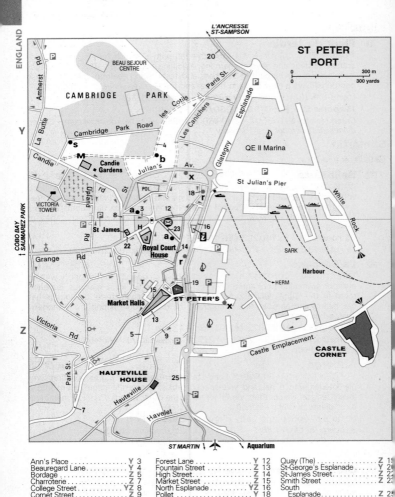

ST PETER PORT

L'ANCRESSE ST-SAMPSON

BEAU SEJOUR CENTRE

CAMBRIDGE PARK

Cambridge Park Road

QE II Marina

St Julian's Pier

Candie Gardens

VICTORIA TOWER

St James

Royal Court House

SARK

Harbour

HERM

Market Halls

ST PETER'S

CASTLE CORNET

Castle Emplacement

HAUTEVILLE HOUSE

ST MARTIN

Aquarium

🏠 La Frégate 🆕

🡥 ≤ 🍴 ⊟ ℅ 🛎 P

TOWNHOUSE · HOMELY Greatly extended 18C property offering stunning panoramic views across the harbour and out towards the island of Herm. Bedrooms have a clean contemporary style; go for one with a balcony or terrace. Extensive menus feature modern international dishes. Breakfast on the terrace is hard to beat.

22 rooms ☲ – 🛉£100 🛉🛉£195/250 – 1 suite

Town plan: Y-b – Beauregard Ln, Les Cotils ✉ GY1 1UT – ℰ (01481) 724 624
– www.lafregatehotel.com

The symbol 🜲 guarantees a peaceful night's sleep.

ENGLAND

🏛 **Duke of Normandie**

BUSINESS · FUNCTIONAL A former German HQ during the WW2 invasions; superbly located in the centre of town. Modern designer bedrooms display bright colours and have a comfy, cosy feel; some are set in the courtyard. The smart lounge and bar are decorated with historical island memorabilia and serve traditional international dishes.

37 rooms 🖙 – ♟£ 49/89 ♟♟£ 89/159
Town plan: Z-a – *Lefebvre St* ✉ GY1 2JP
– 𝒞 (01481) 721 431 – www.dukeofnormandie.com

✗✗ **Nautique**

FRENCH · FORMAL A former sailmaker's warehouse on the quayside with a stylish, nautically themed interior and a pleasant marina view; ask for a window seat. The large menu offers generously sized classic dishes, with daily fish specials a feature.

Menu £ 16 (weekday lunch) – Carte £ 29/47
Town plan: Z-r – *Quay Steps* ✉ GY1 2LE
– 𝒞 (01481) 721 714 – www.lenautiquerestaurant.co.uk
– Closed Saturday lunch and Sunday

✗✗ **Pier 17**

BRITISH TRADITIONAL · FASHIONABLE Set at the end of a substantial stone pier in the centre of Guernsey harbour. The conservatory extension affords superb water views and the two terraces catch the last of the sun's rays. Tasty, traditionally based, seasonal dishes.

Carte £ 25/43
Town plan: Z-x – *Albert Pier* ✉ GY1 1AD
– 𝒞 (01481) 720 823 – www.pier17restaurant.com
– Closed 25-26 December and Sunday

✗✗ **Red**

MEATS · FASHIONABLE Popular harbourfront restaurant run by an experienced owner; the first floor cocktail lounge is a real hit. Its name refers to 'red' wines and 'red' meat, with the large menu focusing on top quality chargrilled Scottish steaks.

Menu £ 16 (lunch) – Carte £ 20/43
Town plan: Y-r – *61 Le Poulet* ✉ GY1 1WL
– 𝒞 (01481) 700 299 (booking essential) – www.red.gg
– Closed 25 December, Saturday lunch and Sunday

✗✗ **Absolute End** ⓝ

MODERN CUISINE · FORMAL This cosy, formal restaurant is located at the quieter end of town. Menus offer a good selection of hearty, classically based seafood dishes. The linen-clad dining room leads up to a small first floor bar-lounge and roof terrace.

Menu £ 16 (lunch) – Carte £ 23/41
St Georges Esplanade ✉ GY1 2BG – 𝒞 (01481) 723 822 (booking advisable)
– www.absoluteendrestaurant.com – Closed Sunday

✗✗ **Pavilion in the Park** ⓝ

MODERN CUISINE · BRASSERIE Light, spacious restaurant set within the St Pierre Park hotel, overlooking the gardens. The larger-than-life chef prepares extensive all-day menus using the best of the island's produce. Champagne afternoon teas are a feature.

Menu £ 16/28 – Carte £ 22/30
St Pierre Park, Rohais ✉ GY1 1FD – West : 1.5 mi by Grange Rd
– 𝒞 (01481) 736 676 – www.thepavilion.co.gg – lunch only and dinner
Friday-Saturday – Closed Tuesday

🏠 Swan Inn

BRITISH TRADITIONAL · PUB Smart Victorian pub with a bottle-green façade, a traditional bar complete with a coal fire and a formal first floor dining room. The same menu is served throughout, offering plenty of choice, with hearty main courses and nursery puddings.

Carte £ 21/30

Town plan: Y-x – *St Julian's Ave* ✉ *GY1 1WA* – *℘ (01481) 728 969 – Closed 25 December, Sunday in winter and Monday including bank holidays*

St Saviour

▶ St Peter Port 4 mi

🏠 Farmhouse

LUXURY · MODERN Former farm restyled in a boutique vein. Stylish, sumptuous bedrooms come with hi-tech amenities and the bathrooms have heated floors. The pleasant garden features a pool, a terrace and a kitchen garden. Contemporary cooking has an international edge and uses the island's finest produce in eclectic ways.

14 rooms ⌑ – †£ 119/179 ††£ 179/279
Route des Bas Courtils ✉ *GY7 9YF* – *℘ (01481) 264 181 – www.thefarmhouse.gg*

HERM

Herm – Pop. 60 – Regional map n° **3**-A2

🏠 White House

TRADITIONAL · PERSONALISED The only hotel on this tranquil, car-free island. Comfy, airy bedrooms are split between the house and various annexes; there are no clocks, TVs or radios. The open-fired lounge offers bay and island views; vast tropical gardens come with tennis courts and a pool. Traditional dining room offers plenty of seafood; popular pub-cum-brasserie serves more modern dishes.

40 rooms (dinner included) ⌑ – †£ 69/114 ††£ 138/228
✉ *GY1 3HR* – *℘ (01481) 750 075 – www.herm.com – Closed October-March*

JERSEY

C.I. – Pop. 85 150 – Regional map n° **3**-B2

Beaumont

✕✕ Mark Jordan at the Beach

MEDITERRANEAN · NEIGHBOURHOOD Modern brasserie with a small lounge and bar; a paved terrace with bay views; and a dining room with heavy wood tables, modern seashore paintings and animal ornaments. Menus showcase island produce and fish from local waters. Cooking is refined but hearty, mixing tasty brasserie and restaurant style dishes.

Menu £ 25/28 – Carte £ 28/43
La Plage, La Route de la Haule ✉ *JE3 7YD* – *℘ (01534) 780 180
– www.markjordanatthebeach.com – Closed 5-20 January and Mondays except in summer*

Gorey

▶ St Helier 4 mi

🏠 Moorings

TRADITIONAL · PERSONALISED Keenly run hotel below the ramparts of Mont Orgueil castle, overlooking the harbour. Leather-furnished first floor lounge. Modern bedrooms in cream, brown and purple colour schemes; some have small balconies. Formal restaurant or casual bistro and terrace for comfort dishes and seafood specials.

15 rooms ⌑ – †£ 58/87 ††£ 115/164
Gorey Pier ✉ *JE3 6EW* – *℘ (01534) 853 633 – www.themooringshotel.com*
Walker's – See restaurant listing

ENGLAND

✗✗ Sumas

MODERN CUISINE · TRENDY A well-known restaurant in a whitewashed house, with a smart heated terrace affording lovely harbour views. Modern European dishes feature island produce. The monthly changing lunch and midweek dinner menus represent good value.

Menu £22 (weekdays) – Carte £28/45

Gorey Hill ⊠ JE3 6ET – 𝒞 (01534) 853 291 (booking essential)
– www.sumasrestaurant.com – Closed 23 December-20 January and Sunday dinner

✗✗ Walker's

TRADITIONAL CUISINE · FORMAL Formal hotel restaurant with a modern lounge, harbour views and local artwork on display. Good value menus offer well-prepared, unashamedly traditional dishes in tried-and-tested combinations and feature the odd personal twist.

Menu £25

Moorings Hotel, Gorey Pier ⊠ JE3 6EW – 𝒞 (01534) 853 633
– www.themooringshotel.com – dinner only and Sunday lunch

✗ Crab Shack Gorey

FISH AND SEAFOOD · FASHIONABLE Laid-back, friendly restaurant with a decked terrace and superb views over the harbour. The pared-down, rustic interior is decorated with nautical memorabilia. Unfussy menus have a Mediterranean edge and focus on locally caught seafood.

Carte £17/32

La Route de la Cote ⊠ JE3 6DR – 𝒞 (01534) 850 830 (booking advisable)
– www.jerseycrabshack.com – Closed 25-26 December and 1 January

�🍴 Bass and Lobster

TRADITIONAL CUISINE · PUB A bright, modern 'foodhouse' close to the beach, with a small decked terrace. Seasonal island produce is simply cooked to create immensely flavourful dishes; fresh, tasty seafood and shellfish dominate the menu. Smooth, effective service.

Menu £26 – Carte £27/40

Gorey Coast Rd ⊠ JE3 6EU – 𝒞 (01534) 859 590 – www.bassandlobster.com
– Closed 25-26 December, 1 January, Sunday and Monday except Sunday lunch October-April

Green Island

✗ Green Island

MEDITERRANEAN · FRIENDLY Friendly, personally run restaurant with a terrace and beachside kiosk; the southernmost restaurant in the British Isles. Mediterranean-influenced dishes and seafood specials showcase island produce. Flavours are bold and perfectly judged.

Menu £20/25 – Carte £31/47

St Clement ⊠ JE2 6LS – 𝒞 (01534) 857 787 (booking essential)
– www.greenisland.je – Closed 23 December-1 March, Sunday dinner and Monday

Grouville

▶ St Helier 3 mi

✗ Café Poste

MEDITERRANEAN · BISTRO Popular all-day restaurant – formerly a post office – with a vast array of curios, a wood burning stove and a French country kitchen feel. Choose from an eclectic Mediterranean menu and daily specials; breakfast is served at weekends.

Menu £20 (lunch and early dinner) – Carte £27/44

La Rue de la ville es Renauds ⊠ JE3 9FY – 𝒞 (01534) 859 696
– www.cafeposte.co.uk – Closed 11-27 November, Monday and Tuesday

La Haule

🏠 La Haule Manor ⟨ 🛏 ⌇ ✦ 🅿

TOWNHOUSE · STYLISH Attractive Georgian house overlooking the fort and bay, with a lovely terrace, a good-sized pool and neat lawned gardens. Stylish guest areas and spacious bedrooms mix modern and antique furnishings; those in the wing are the largest.

16 rooms ⌷ – †£75/198 ††£97/198

St Aubin's Bay ✉ JE3 8BS – ℰ (01534) 741 426 – www.lahaulemanor.com
– Closed December-February

La Pulente

▶ St Helier 7 mi

🏨 Atlantic ⟨🏊 🐾 ✦ 🛏 ⌇ 🔲 🏔 🛁 🍽 🖼 ✦ 🛗 🅿

LUXURY · STYLISH Stylish hotel with well-manicured grounds, set in a superb location overlooking St Ouen's Bay. Public areas are understated, with tiled floors, exposed brick, water features and a relaxed, intimate feel. Bedrooms are cool and fresh: some have a patio; others, a balcony. Attentive, personable staff.

50 rooms ⌷ – †£100/250 ††£150/550 – 1 suite

Le Mont de la Pulente ✉ JE3 8HE – on B 35
– ℰ (01534) 744 101 – www.theatlantichotel.com
– Closed 5 January-5 February

  ✿ **Ocean** – See restaurant listing

XxX Ocean ⟨ 🛏 🍴 🏠 🅿

✿ **MODERN CUISINE · LUXURY** Elegant, well-run dining room with a fresh, understated feel, set in a stunning position overlooking St Ouen's Bay. Delicious, well-crafted dishes make use of fine ingredients from the island and display a real understanding of flavour. Smooth, professional service and a relaxed, friendly atmosphere.

➜ Squab pigeon with pearl barley risotto, corn kernels and an offal brochette. Line caught sea bass, borlotti bean cassoulet, roast artichoke heart and lobster tortellini. Caramelised lemon tart with raspberry sorbet.

Menu £25/65

Atlantic Hotel, Le Mont de la Pulente ✉ JE3 8HE – on B 35
– ℰ (01534) 744 101 (booking essential) – www.theatlantichotel.com/dining
– Closed 5 January-5 February

Rozel Bay

▶ St Helier 6 mi

🏨 Chateau La Chaire ⟨🏊 🐾 🛏 🏠 🅿

HISTORIC · CLASSIC Attractive 19C house surrounded by peaceful gardens and mature woodland. Traditionally styled guest areas and more modern, well-equipped bedrooms: 2nd floor rooms are cosy; 1st floor rooms are larger and some have balconies. Formal restaurant with a conservatory and terrace offers classics with a twist.

14 rooms ⌷ – †£95/145 ††£125/325 – 2 suites

Rozel Valley ✉ JE3 6AJ – ℰ (01534) 863 354 – www.chateau-la-chaire.co.uk

🍴 Rozel ❶ 🛏 🏠 🖥 🅿

TRADITIONAL CUISINE · PUB Cosy pub run by the same as owners as the neighbouring hotel. The upstairs dining room has distant sea views but come summer, the garden is the place to be. Cooking is traditional and homely and ales are from the island's Liberation Brewery.

Carte £19/30

Rozel Valley ✉ JE3 6AJ – ℰ (01534) 863 438 – www.rozelpubanddining.co.uk

St Aubin

▶ St Helier 4 mi

🏨 Somerville   ⌂ ⟨ ⬢ ☴ ▣ ⊛ ℗

TRADITIONAL · CLASSIC An imposing 19C hotel affording excellent views over the village and the bay. Smart modern guest areas lead out to a well-kept garden with a pleasant poolside terrace. Bright bedrooms vary in shape and size; go for one with a view. The large restaurant offers classical menus and a great outlook.

59 rooms ☟ – **♦**£ 67/130 **♦♦**£ 95/250

Mont du Boulevard ✉ *JE3 8AD – South : 0.75 mi via harbour – 𝒞 (01534) 741 226 – www.dolanhotels.com*

🏠 Panorama   ⟨ ⬢ ⊛

TRADITIONAL · PERSONALISED Immaculate hotel with Georgian origins, colourful gardens and stunning views over the fort and bay. It's largely traditional throughout. Afternoon tea is served in the conservatory on arrival and over 1,400 teapots are on display.

14 rooms ☟ – **♦**£ 56/132 **♦♦**£ 108/176

La Rue du Crocquet ✉ *JE3 8BZ – 𝒞 (01534) 742 429 – www.panoramajersey.com – Closed November-early April*

St Brelade's Bay

▶ St Helier 6 mi

🏨 L'Horizon Beach H & Spa   ⌂ ⟨ ▢ ⊛ ♨ ℔ ℅ ▣ ⅋ ⚲ ⊛ 🛁 ℗

LUXURY · STYLISH Long-standing hotel located right on the beachfront and boasting stunning views over the bay. Luxurious interior with extensive guest areas and subtle modern styling. Choose a deluxe bedroom, as they come with balconies and sea views. Stylish, formal restaurant; modern British menus focus on local seafood.

106 rooms ☟ – **♦**£ 75/200 **♦♦**£ 95/305 – 6 suites

✉ *JE3 8EF – 𝒞 (01534) 743 101 – www.handpickedhotels.co.uk/lhorizon*

🏨 St Brelade's Bay   ⌂ ⟨ ⬢ ☴ ▢ ♨ ℔ ℅ ▣ ⚲ ⊛ 🛁 ℗

FAMILY · STYLISH Smart seafront hotel with charming tropical gardens and panoramic views across the bay. A modernised lounge and contemporary bedrooms fit well alongside original parquet floors and ornate plaster ceilings. Excellent health club. Formal restaurant offers impressive sea views and a classical menu.

74 rooms ☟ – **♦**£ 93/145 **♦♦**£ 140/290 – 5 suites

La Route de la Baie ✉ *JE3 8EF – 𝒞 (01534) 746 141 – www.stbreladesbayhotel.com*

✗ Oyster Box   ⟨ ⌂ ⅋ 🆊

FISH AND SEAFOOD · BRASSERIE Glass-fronted eatery with pleasant heated terrace, set on the promenade and affording superb views over St Brelade's Bay. Stylish, airy interior hung with sail cloths and fishermen's floats. Laid-back, friendly service. Accessible seasonal menu features plenty of fish and shellfish; oysters are a speciality.

Menu £ 20/27 – Carte £ 29/48

La Route de la Baie ✉ *JE3 8EF – 𝒞 (01534) 850 888 (booking essential) – www.oysterbox.co.uk – Closed 25-26 December, 1 January, dinner Sunday-Monday October-April and Monday lunch*

✗ Crab Shack St Brelade's Bay   ⟨ ⌂ ⅋ 🆊

FISH AND SEAFOOD · BISTRO A scaled down version of next door Oyster Box, superbly sited on the beachfront; sit in a cosy booth or on a bench outside. Accessible modern dishes of prime island produce, with seafood a speciality. Relaxed, family-friendly atmosphere.

Carte £ 15/29

La Route de la Baie ✉ *JE3 8EF – 𝒞 (01534) 850 855 (booking advisable) – www.jerseycrabshack.com – Closed 25-26 December, 1 January and Monday dinner except bank holidays*

Grand Jersey

LUXURY · MODERN Welcoming hotel with a large terrace overlooking the bay. The stylish interior incorporates a chic champagne bar, a well-equipped spa and a corporate cinema. Contemporary bedrooms come in bold colours; some have balconies and sea views. Watch TV footage from the kitchen in intimate Tassili; Victoria's serves brasserie dishes.

123 rooms ☑ – †£109/155 ††£119/246

Town plan: Y-u – *The Esplanade* ✉ JE2 3QA – ℰ *(01534) 722 301*
– *www.grandjersey.com*

Club Hotel & Spa

LUXURY · MODERN Modern hotel with stylish guest areas, an honesty bar and a split-level breakfast room. Contemporary bedrooms have floor to ceiling windows and good facilities. Relax in the smart spa or on the terrace beside the small outdoor pool.

46 rooms ☑ – †£89/445 ††£89/445 – 4 suites

Town plan: Z-e – *Green St* ✉ JE2 4UH – ℰ *(01534) 876 500*
– *www.theclubjersey.com* – *Closed 24-30 December*

❀ **Bohemia** – See restaurant listing

Royal Yacht

BUSINESS · DESIGN This is an unusual combination of an old whitewashed building and a vast modern extension. The spacious interior boasts a large bar, good conference facilities and a superb spa. Bedrooms are contemporary; the best have balconies and harbour views. Take in lovely vistas from the formal first floor restaurant and terrace; steaks are a speciality in the cosy beamed grill.

109 rooms ☑ – †£150/750 ††£205/750 – 2 suites

Town plan: Z-b – *Weighbridge* ✉ JE2 3NF – ℰ *(01534) 720 511*
– *www.theroyalyacht.com*

XX Bohemia

❀ **MODERN CUISINE · FASHIONABLE** Marble-fronted hotel restaurant with a chic cocktail bar and an intimate dining room. The emphasis is on tasting menus, with both pescatarian and vegetarian options available. Cooking is modern, vibrant and has a lightness of touch; original texture and flavour combinations feature.

→ Foie gras cream with orange, sea buckthorn, pistachio and duck salad. Suckling pig with onion, prune and black pudding. Rhubarb, champagne, hibiscus.

Menu £25 (weekday lunch)/59

Town plan: Z-e – *Club Hotel & Spa, Green St* ✉ JE2 4UH – ℰ *(01534) 880 588* *(booking advisable)* – *www.bohemiajersey.com* – *Closed 24-30 December*

XX Ormer by Shaun Rankin

❀ **MODERN CUISINE · DESIGN** This tasteful restaurant features attractive wood panelling and turquoise banquettes, and is named after a rare shellfish found in local waters. Cooking is refined and assured and uses only the very best seasonal island produce. Inside, it's intimate yet buzzy, and there's a pavement terrace for warmer days.

→ Lobster and scallop ravioli with ginger, coriander, crab and tomato bisque. Loin of venison with quinoa, parsnip, chocolate tortellini and Medjool date. Rhubarb soufflé with baked vanilla cheesecake ice cream and mascarpone.

Menu £25/75 – Carte £35/59

Town plan: Z-o – *7-11 Don St* ✉ JE2 4TQ – ℰ *(01534) 725 100 (booking advisable)* – *www.ormerjersey.com* – *Closed 2 weeks Christmas-New Year and Sunday*

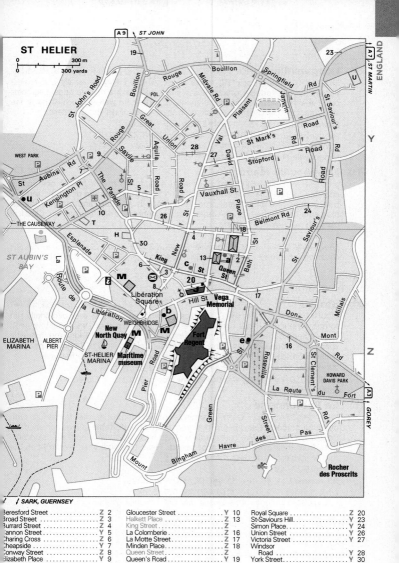

✗ Banjo ⇦ 🍽 ⬇ 🔽 🛗 AC ⇨

INTERNATIONAL · BRASSERIE Substantial former gentlemen's club with an ornate façade; the banjo belonging to the owner's great grandfather is displayed in a glass-fronted wine cellar. The appealing, wide-ranging menu features everything from brasserie classics to sushi. Stylish bedrooms have Nespresso machines and Bose sound systems.

Menu £ 24 (weekdays) – Carte £ 25/49

4 rooms – 🛏£ 80/170 🛏🛏£ 80/170 – 🍽 £ 12

Town plan: Z-a – 8 Beresford St ⊠ JE2 4WN – 𝒞 (01534) 850 890
– www.banjojersey.com – Closed 25-26 December and Sunday

St Saviour

▶ St Helier 1 mi

🏠 Longueville Manor   ☆ 🛏 ⌁ 𝄞 ✕ 🖭 ♨ 🅿

LUXURY · CLASSIC Iconic 13C manor house, which is very personally and professionally run. Comfortable, country house guest areas have a modern edge. Bedrooms
come in either classic or contemporary styles and all are well-equipped. Relax in the
lovely pool, on the charming terrace or in the 6 acres of delightful gardens.

28 rooms ☲ – ♦£ 120/475 ♦♦£ 195/575 – 2 suites
*Longueville Rd ✉ JE2 7WF – on A 3 – ℰ (01534) 725 501
– www.longuevillemanor.com – Closed 4-21 January*
Longueville Manor – See restaurant listing

✕✕✕ Longueville Manor   🐝 🛏 🏠 🅿

MODERN CUISINE · ELEGANT Set within a charming manor house; dine in the
characterful 15C oak-panelled room, the brighter Garden Room or on the terrace.
Daily menus champion island produce; seafood is a feature and many of the ingredients are foraged for or come from the impressive kitchen garden. Classical
dishes have a modern edge.

Menu £ 27/57 **s**
*Longueville Manor Hotel, Longueville Rd ✉ JE2 7WF – on A 3 – ℰ (01534) 725 501
(booking advisable) – www.longuevillemanor.com – Closed 4-21 January*

SARK

Sark – Pop. 550 – Regional map n° **3**-A2

🏠 Stocks   ☆ 🐝 🛏 🏠 ⌁ 𝄞

COUNTRY HOUSE · ELEGANT Set facing a wooded valley; a very personally run
former farmhouse that's undergone a smart transformation. Immaculately kept,
well-equipped, classical bedrooms. Small gym, arty island shop and fantastic
wine cellar. Formal gardens have a split-level pool and jacuzzi. Eat in the panelled
dining room, in the bistro or on the terrace; local island produce features.

23 rooms ☲ – ♦£ 110/295 ♦♦£ 135/350 – 5 suites
*✉ GY10 1SD – ℰ (01481) 832 001 – www.stockshotel.com – Closed
January-February*

✕✕ La Sablonnerie   🖘 🐝 🛏 🏠

FISH AND SEAFOOD · COSY Charming, whitewashed 16C former farmhouse with
beautiful gardens. Cosy, beamed interior with a comfortable lounge for aperitifs.
Regularly changing, five course menu offers a classic style of cooking using produce from their own farm. Prompt service. Neat, tidy bedrooms; Room 14, in the
former stables, is the best.

Carte £ 27/48
22 rooms ☲ – ♦£ 48/155 ♦♦£ 96/310 – 2 suites
*Little Sark ✉ GY9 0SD – ℰ (01481) 832 061 (booking essential)
– www.lasablonnerie.com – Closed mid October-mid April*

CHANNEL TUNNEL – Kent → See Folkestone

CHARLTON

West Sussex – Regional map n° **4**-C2
▶ London 72 mi – Birmingham 165 mi – Leeds 258 mi – Sheffield 228 mi

🏠 Fox Goes Free   🖘 🛏 🏠 🅿

TRADITIONAL CUISINE · RUSTIC Charming 17C flint pub with a superb garden
and terrace and a lovely outlook. Original features include exposed stone walls,
low beamed ceilings and brick floors. Dishes range from simple pub classics to
more substantial local offerings; some are to share. Clean, unfussy bedrooms; a
few with low beamed ceilings.

Carte £ 20/32
5 rooms ☲ – ♦£ 70/180 ♦♦£ 95/180
✉ PO18 0HU – ℰ (01243) 811 461 – www.thefoxgoesfree.com

CHARMOUTH

Dorset – ✉ Bridport – Pop. 1 352 – Regional map n° **2**-B3
▶ London 157 mi – Dorchester 22 mi – Exeter 31 mi – Taunton 27 mi

🏠 White House

FAMILY · PERSONALISED Charming Regency house; personally run by a friendly couple. Spacious, comfy bedrooms retain some period features – one has a cast iron bed – and all have modern bathrooms, fresh flowers, iPod docks and seasonal fruit. The wood-furnished dining room offers concise modern menus of local produce.

4 rooms ☟ – ♦£ 90/180 ♦♦£ 125/180
2 Hillside, The Street ✉ DT6 6PJ – ℰ (01297) 560 411 – www.whitehousehotel.com – Restricted opening in winter

🏘 Abbots House

TOWNHOUSE · STYLISH This cosy guesthouse dates back to 1480 and was originally an annexe of Forde Abbey. It has a beamed, wood-panelled lounge and a conservatory breakfast room overlooking a model railway in the garden. Bedrooms are bright and modern.

4 rooms ☟ – ♦£ 110/130 ♦♦£ 120/150
The Street ✉ DT6 6QF – ℰ (01297) 560 339 – www.abbotshouse.co.uk – Closed January and last 2 weeks December

CHATHILL – Northumberland → See Alnwick

CHATTON

Northumberland – Pop. 438 – Regional map n° **14**-A1
▶ London 336 mi – Sunderland 63 mi – Newcastle upon Tyne 52 mi – South Shields 57 mi

🏘 Chatton Park House

TRADITIONAL · PERSONALISED Charming 1730s house in 6 acres of formal gardens. It has a smart parquet-floored hallway, a huge open-fired sitting room and spacious bedrooms which blend modern décor and original features. Excellent breakfasts use local produce.

5 rooms ☟ – ♦£ 100/189 ♦♦£ 129/199
✉ NE66 5RA – East : 1 mi on B 6348 – ℰ (01688) 215 507 – www.chattonpark.com – Closed 23 December-7 February

CHELMONDISTON – Suffolk → See Ipswich

GOOD TIPS!

This pretty spa town on the edge of the Cotswolds is renowned for its splendid Regency architecture, two examples being the elegant, Grade II listed Montpellier Chapter Hotel and the chic, centrally located Hotel du Vin. The grounds of the magnificent, part-15C Ellenborough Park Hotel stretch down to Cheltenham's famous racecourse, home of the Gold Cup.

© Le Champignon Sauvage

CHELTENHAM

Gloucestershire – Pop. 116 447 – Regional map n° **2**-C1
▶ London 99 mi – Birmingham 48 mi – Gloucester 9 mi

Hotels

🏚🏚🏚 **Ellenborough Park** 🕭 🐾 🛏 🥤 🏊 💷 🛜 🖵 🖪 🕭 🅰🅲 🈯 🅿

LUXURY · STYLISH Part-15C timbered manor house, with stone annexes, an understated Indian-themed spa and large grounds stretching down to the racecourse. Beautifully furnished guest areas have an elegant, classical style. Nina Campbell designed bedrooms have superb bathrooms, the latest mod cons and plenty of extras. Dine in the sophisticated restaurant or informal brasserie.
61 rooms ☲ – †£ 230/575 ††£ 230/575
Town plan: AX-a – *Southam Rd* ⊠ *GL52 3NJ – Northeast : 2.75 mi on B 4632* – 𝒞 *(01242) 545 454 – www.ellenboroughpark.com*
The Beaufort – See restaurant listing

🏚🏚 **Hotel du Vin** 🕭 🖵 🕭 🅰🅲 🅿

TOWNHOUSE · STYLISH Attractive Regency house in an affluent residential area. Inside it's chic and laid-back, with a leather-furnished bar and a comfy lounge. Some of the individually designed, well-equipped, wine-themed bedrooms have baths in the room. The French bistro features an eye-catching wine glass chandelier.
49 rooms ☲ – †£ 115/185 ††£ 155/595 – 1 suite
Town plan: BY-c – *Parabola Rd* ⊠ *GL50 3AQ – 𝒞 (01242) 588 450* – *www.hotelduvin.com*

On a budget? Take advantage of lunchtime prices.

CHELTENHAM

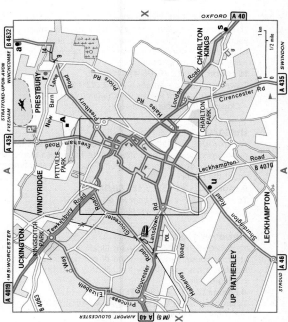

🏨 Montpellier Chapter

TOWNHOUSE · STYLISH Chic Regency townhouse, where stylish modern guest areas are hung with an impressive collection of contemporary art. Light wood furnished bedrooms come with Nespresso machines, complimentary mini bars and in-room info on an iPod touch. Dine on British dishes at marble-topped tables or on one of two terraces.

61 rooms ☲ – ♦£120/500 ♦♦£120/500
Town plan: BX-r – *Bayshill Rd* ⊠ *GL50 3AS*
– ☎ *(01242) 527 788* – *www.themontpellierchapterhotel.com*

🏠 No 38 The Park

TOWNHOUSE · DESIGN Behind the attractive Georgian façade is a very original, tastefully designed hotel with a relaxed atmosphere and supremely comfortable furnishings. Bedrooms come with coffee machines and vast walk-in showers or feature baths.

13 rooms ☲ – ♦£125/240 ♦♦£125/240
Town plan: CY-x – *38 Eversham Rd* ⊠ *GL52 2AH*
– ☎ *(01242) 248 656* – *www.no38thepark.com*

🏠 Beaumont House

TOWNHOUSE · CONTEMPORARY Your hosts here are warm and welcoming, just like the hotel. The lounge and breakfast room are comfortably and classically furnished, while the bedrooms are more contemporary; there are two themed rooms – Africa and Asia.

16 rooms ☲ – ♦£78/220 ♦♦£95/290
Town plan: AX-u – *56 Shurdington Rd* ⊠ *GL53 0JE*
– ☎ *(01242) 223 311* – *www.bhhotel.co.uk*

🏠 Wyastone Townhouse

TOWNHOUSE · CONTEMPORARY Nothing is too much trouble for the charming young owner of this attractive townhouse. Inside, contemporary décor blends with period features. Bedrooms – split between the house and the courtyard – are surprisingly spacious.

16 rooms ☲ – ♦£75/95 ♦♦£105/165
Town plan: BY-a – *Parabola Rd* ⊠ *GL50 3BG*
– ☎ *(01242) 245 549* – *www.wyastonehotel.co.uk*
– *Closed 23 December-1 January*

🏨 Butlers

TOWNHOUSE · PERSONALISED The bedrooms of this tastefully furnished Victorian townhouse are named after famous butlers – a theme which continues in the classical lounge and breakfast room. There's also an interesting collection of hats about the place!

9 rooms ☲ – ♦£75/85 ♦♦£88/110
Town plan: BY-v – *Western Rd* ⊠ *GL50 3RN*
– ☎ *(01242) 570 771* – *www.butlers-hotel.co.uk*

🏨 Hanover House

TOWNHOUSE · CLASSIC Edward Elgar's wife once lived in this Victorian Italianate townhouse, hence the name of the bedrooms – Alice Elgar, Tennyson and Rossetti. It has a real family feel courtesy of its bright furnishings and warm, welcoming owners.

4 rooms ☲ – ♦£75/90 ♦♦£100/120
Town plan: BY-u – *65 St George's Rd* ⊠ *GL50 3DU*
– ☎ *(01242) 541 297* – *www.hanoverhouse.org*
– *Closed Christmas-New Year and Easter*

ENGLAND

Georgian House   ⚄ 🅿

TRADITIONAL · CLASSIC The experienced owner of this terraced Georgian townhouse looks after his guests very personally – which is why so many come back time and again. The décor and furnishings respect the house's age; one of the rooms is a four-poster.

3 rooms �) – 🛉£ 75/95 🛉🛉£ 90/115

Town plan: BZ-s – *77 Montpellier Terr* ✉ *GL50 1XA*
– ☎ *(01242) 515 577 – www.georgianhouse.net*
– *Closed 19 December-15 January*

Detmore House   ⚓ 🖙 ⚄ 🅿

COUNTRY HOUSE · CONTEMPORARY Peace and tranquility reign at this 1840s country house, which is accessed via a private drive and offers pleasant rural views. Bedrooms are modern and comfortable – 'Oak' is the best. Breakfast is served at a fine oak table.

4 rooms �) – 🛉£ 65/95 🛉🛉£ 95/105

Town plan: AX-s – *London Rd, Charlton Kings* ✉ *GL52 6UT*
– ☎ *(01242) 582 868 – www.detmorehouse.com*

Restaurants

XXX **Le Champignon Sauvage** (David Everitt-Matthias)   🆎

✿✿ **MODERN CUISINE · INTIMATE** The chef has cooked here passionately and proudly for over 25 years, creating dishes with classic French roots and a personal touch. Visually impressive and boldly flavoured, they often feature foraged ingredients such as dandelion or burdock. Tasting menu available evenings, Tues to Sat (order before 8.15pm).

→ Pigeon breast and pastilla with pistachio and cherry & rosehip purée. Poached megrim sole with beurre noisette and roast cauliflower cream. Mango with spiced cream and Thai green curry sorbet.

Menu £ 35 (weekdays)/63

Town plan: BZ-a – *24-28 Suffolk Rd* ✉ *GL50 2AQ*
– ☎ *(01242) 573 449 – www.lechampignonsauvage.co.uk*
– *Closed 3 weeks June, 10 days Christmas, Sunday and Monday*

XXX **The Beaufort**   🖙 ♿ 🆎 🎦 🅿

MODERN CUISINE · FORMAL With its Tudor stone fireplaces, original oak wood panelling and stained glass windows, this characterful hotel restaurant lends itself to sophisticated dining. Cooking is modern and accomplished and relies on local ingredients.

Menu £ 45/75 **s**

Town plan: AX-a – *Ellenborough Park Hotel, Southam Rd* ✉ *GL52 3NJ*
– *Northeast : 2.75 mi on B 4632* – ☎ *(01242) 545 454*
– *www.ellenboroughpark.com – dinner only and Sunday lunch*
– *Closed Sunday dinner and Monday*

XXX **Lumière**   🆎

MODERN CUISINE · INTIMATE Friendly, personally run restaurant; its unassuming exterior concealing a long, stylish room decorated with mirrors. Seasonal dishes are modern and intricate with the occasional playful twist – desserts are often the highlight.

Menu £ 28/60

Town plan: BCY-z – *Clarence Par* ✉ *GL50 3PA*
– ☎ *(01242) 222 200 (booking essential) – www.lumiere.cc*
– *dinner only and lunch Friday-Saturday*
– *Closed 2 weeks January, 2 weeks summer, Sunday and Monday*

XX Curry Corner   🕎 AC 🕪 ⇔

BANGLADESHI · NEIGHBOURHOOD Long-standing, family-run restaurant in a smart Regency townhouse. Authentic, flavoursome dishes take their influences from across Bangladesh, India and Persia. Imported spices are ground and roasted every morning.

Menu £ 25 – Carte £ 23/40

Town plan: CY-a – *133 Fairview Rd ⊠ GL52 2EX –* 𝒞 *(01242) 528 449 – www.thecurrycorner.com – Closed 25 December, Friday lunch and Monday except bank holidays*

XX Daffodil   🍷 & AC 🖳

BRITISH MODERN · BRASSERIE Delightful 1920s art deco cinema, with original tiling still on display in the entrance. The kitchens are in the former screen area, the tables are in the old stalls, and the stylish lounge is up on the balcony. Classical brasserie dishes include steaks from the Josper grill. Service is slick and attentive.

Menu £ 16 (lunch and early dinner) – Carte £ 25/47

Town plan: BZ-u – *18-20 Suffolk Par ⊠ GL50 2AE –* 𝒞 *(01242) 700 055 – www.thedaffodil.com – Closed 1-7 January, 25-26 December and Sunday*

XX Prithvi   AC 🕪

INDIAN · DESIGN This smart Indian restaurant is a refreshing break from the norm, with its ambitious owner, designer décor, detailed service and refined cooking. Reinvented Indian and Bangladeshi dishes are presented in a sophisticated manner.

Menu £ 16/39 – Carte £ 26/35

Town plan: CZ-s – *37 Bath Rd ⊠ GL53 7HG –* 𝒞 *(01242) 226 229 (booking essential at dinner) – www.prithvirestaurant.com – Closed 21 December-4 January*

XX Bhoomi   AC 🕪 ⇔

INDIAN · CLASSIC Its name means 'earth' in the Keralan dialect and the cooking focuses on southeast India (from where the young owner and chef originate). Preparation and presentation has been subtly modernised but the essence of each dish remains.

Carte £ 19/35

Town plan: BZ-b – *52 Suffolk Rd ⊠ GL50 2AQ –* 𝒞 *(01242) 222 010 – www.bhoomi.co.uk – Closed 25-30 December, Monday and lunch Tuesday-Wednesday*

XX Koloshi   � & 🕪 P

INDIAN · DESIGN Former pub, set by the reservoir; now a spacious Indian restaurant, its name meaning 'water carrying vessel' in Hindi. Visual, vibrant cooking is full of flavour; good vegetarian selection. Smartly attired staff provide professional service.

Menu £ 10/55 – Carte £ 20/32

London Rd ⊠ GL54 4HG – Southeast : 2.5 mi on A 40 – 𝒞 *(01242) 516 400 – www.koloshi.co.uk – Closed 25-26 December and Monday*

X 131 The Promenade   ⇔ 🍷 🕎 & ⇔

MEATS · INDIVIDUAL The columned exterior of this fine 1820s building overlooks an attractive park. Inside, original features remain but it now has a cool, contemporary style, with impressive modern artwork featuring throughout. The menu lists well-prepared, unfussy classics, with steaks cooked on the Josper grill a feature at dinner. Bedrooms are individually and tastefully furnished.

Carte £ 23/81

11 rooms ⌲ – †£ 150/240 ††£ 150/240

Town plan: BZ-z – *131 Promenade ⊠ GL50 1NW –* 𝒞 *(01242) 822 939 (booking essential) – www.no131.com*

X Purslane

BRITISH MODERN · INTIMATE A stylishly minimalistic neighbourhood restaurant with relaxed, efficient service. Fresh seafood from Cornwall and Scotland is combined with good quality, locally sourced ingredients to produce interesting, original dishes.

Menu £ 24 (lunch and early dinner)/35

Town plan: CY-p – *16 Rodney Rd* ⊠ *GL50 1JJ* – ℰ *(01242) 321 639*
– *www.purslane-restaurant.co.uk* – *Closed 2 weeks January, 2 weeks August, Sunday and Monday*

X The Tavern &. &

⊛ **MEATS · FASHIONABLE** Rustic, all-day eatery with a strong American theme, split over two floors and featuring large tables and bench seating suited to sharing. Stools sit around the open kitchen make up the chef's table. Accessible menu offers the likes of sliders, chilli cheese dogs and steaks to share. Chatty service.

Menu £ 10 (weekday lunch) – Carte £ 20/39

Town plan: BY-e – *5 Royal Well Pl* ⊠ *GL50 3DN* – ℰ *(01242) 221 212*
– *www.thetaverncheltenham.com* – *Closed 25-26 December*

X Svea

SWEDISH · SIMPLE A homely city centre café with pretty gingham-clothed tables, serving fresh, authentic Swedish cooking and monthly smorgasbords. As is tradition in Sweden, lunch is simpler, with light snacks, open sandwiches and homemade cakes.

Carte £ 25/33

Town plan: CY-s – *24 Rodney Rd* ⊠ *GL50 1JJ* – ℰ *(01242) 238 134*
– *www.sveacafe.co.uk* – *Closed Sunday-Monday and dinner Tuesday-Wednesday*

ⓘ Royal Oak ⬚ ⬚

BRITISH TRADITIONAL · RUSTIC This was once owned by batting legend Tom Graveney, hence the 'Pavilion' function room. Lunch offers tasty, satisfying dishes like kedgeree, while dinner steps things up a level. Sit in the cosy bar, dark wood dining room or heated garden.

Carte £ 25/40

Town plan: AX-r – *The Burgage, Prestbury* ⊠ *GL52 3DL* – ℰ *(01242) 522 344*
– *www.royal-oak-prestbury.co.uk* – *Closed 25 December*

at Shurdington Southwest: 3.75 mi on A46 – Plan: AX – ⊠ Cheltenham

⬛ Greenway ⬚ ⬚ ⬚ ⬚ ⬚ ⬚ ⬚ P

COUNTRY HOUSE · CLASSIC 16C ivy-clad manor house, set in 8 acres of peaceful grounds and offering pleasant views over the hills. Comfy drawing rooms and well-equipped bedrooms have a pleasant country house style. Enjoy a laid-back brasserie-style lunch on the terrace of the lovely spa. The oak-panelled restaurant offers classic dishes with modern overtones and overlooks the lily pond.

21 rooms ⬚ – ♦£ 139/209 ♦♦£ 169/499 – 1 suite
⊠ *GL51 4UG* – ℰ *(01242) 862 352* – *www.thegreenwayhotelandspa.com*

at Piff's Elm Northwest: 4 mi on A4019 – Plan: AX

ⓘ Gloucester Old Spot ⬚ &. P

BRITISH TRADITIONAL · RUSTIC Cosy, relaxing inn with a snug, quarry-tiled bar, a baronial dining room and open fires aplenty. Menus offer tasty, seasonal dishes, with rare breed pork a speciality. Nursery puddings. Cheery, welcoming staff.

Menu £ 14 (lunch) – Carte £ 26/35

Tewkesbury Rd ⊠ *GL51 9SY* – ℰ *(01242) 680 321*
– *www.thegloucesteroldspot.co.uk* – *Closed 25-26 December*

GOOD TIPS!

There is evidence of Chester's Roman origins all around the city; not least, its two miles of ancient walls. It is also known for its black & white half-timbered buildings, like the Grade II listed Chester Grosvenor Hotel – home to Simon Radley's Michelin starred restaurant – and its racecourse, overlooked by Michael Caine's restaurant at the Abode.

CHESTER

Cheshire West and Chester – Pop. 86 011 – Regional map n° **11**-A3

▶ London 207 mi – Birkenhead 7 mi – Birmingham 91 mi – Liverpool 21 mi

Hotels

🏨 **Chester Grosvenor**   🍴 🍸 🐕 ⅃ѕ ⬇ 🔥 🅰 ✂ 🛁 🅿

GRAND LUXURY · CLASSIC 19C hotel with a grand, black and white timbered façade, a stunning Rococo chocolate shop and a buzzy lounge serving all-day snacks. Stylish bedrooms blend traditional furnishings and modern fabrics; luxurious, marble-floored bathrooms.

80 rooms 🍽 – ♦£ 165/330 ♦♦£ 190/330 – 6 suites

Town plan: B-a – *Eastgate* ⊠ CH1 1LT – ℰ (01244) 324 024 – *www.chestergrosvenor.com* – *Closed 25 December*

❀ **Simon Radley at Chester Grosvenor • La Brasserie** – See restaurant listing

🏨 **DoubleTree by Hilton H. & Spa Chester**   🍴 🛋 🖼 🍸 🐕 ⅃ѕ

BUSINESS · STYLISH Smart, stylish hotel offering   ⬇ 🔥 🅰 ✂ 🛁 🅿 sleek, spacious bedrooms with super king-sized beds, bright white décor and modern facilities. State-of-the-art conference facilities and superb spa with a well-equipped leisure club. Contemporary steakhouse in the 18C manor house; informal brasserie overlooks the courtyard.

140 rooms 🍽 – ♦£ 105/190 ♦♦£ 118/203

Town plan: A-s – *Warrington Rd* ⊠ CH2 3PD – *Northeast : 2 mi on A 56* – ℰ (01244) 408 800 – *www.doubletreechester.co.uk*

Take note of the classification: you should not expect the same level of service in a 🍴 or 🏠 as in a 🍴🍴🍴🍴🍴 or 🏨🏨🏨🏨🏨.

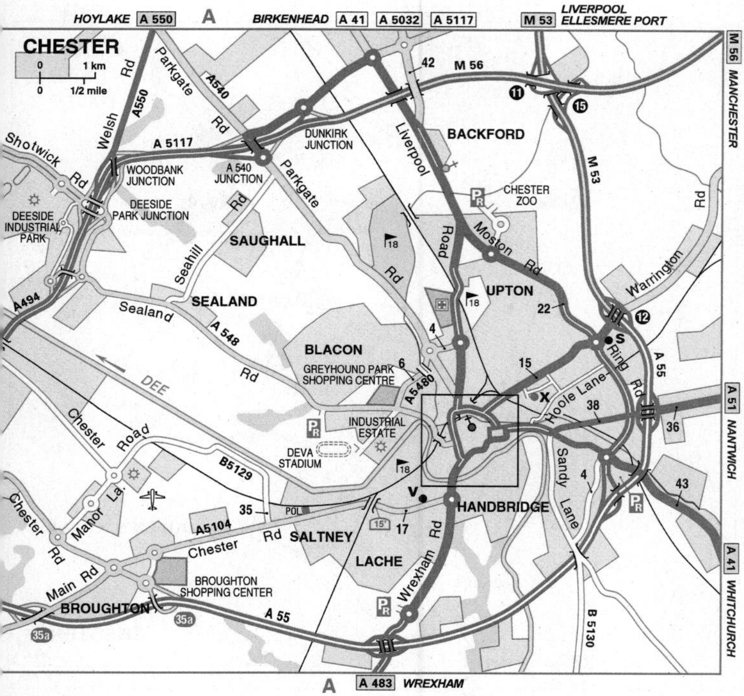
HOYLAKE A 550
A
BIRKENHEAD A 41 A 5032 A 5117
LIVERPOOL
M 53 ELLESMERE PORT
CHESTER
0 1 km
0 1/2 mile
M 56 MANCHESTER
A 51 NANTWICH
A 41 WHITCHURCH
A
A 483 WREXHAM
42
M 56
Parkgate
A540
Rd
Welsh
A550
Rd
A 5117
Shotwick
Rd
WOODBANK JUNCTION
A 540 JUNCTION
DUNKIRK JUNCTION
DEESIDE PARK JUNCTION
DEESIDE INDUSTRIAL PARK
Liverpool
Road
BACKFORD
CHESTER ZOO
M 53
Moston
Rd
SAUGHALL
Seahill
Rd
SEALAND
Sealand
A 548
Rd
A494
UPTON
22
Warrington
Rd
BLACON
GREYHOUND PARK SHOPPING CENTRE
6
4
15
A5480
Hoole Lane
Ring
Rd
A 55
38
36
DEE
INDUSTRIAL ESTATE
DEVA STADIUM
Chester
Road
B5129
Manor
La.
Chester
Rd
35
POL
A5104
Chester
Rd
SALTNEY
17
15'
HANDBRIDGE
Sandy
Lane
4
43
LACHE
Wrexham
Rd
Main Rd
BROUGHTON
BROUGHTON SHOPPING CENTER
A 55
35a
B 5130

aldy Valley Rd . . . . A 4
ountess Way . . . . A 5
eva Link. . . . . A 6
ireyhound Park
Shopping Centre . . . . A
Hoole Rd . . . . A 15
Hough Green. . . . . A 17
Long Lane . . . . A 22
Saltney Ferry
Rd. A 35
Tarvin Rd . . . . A 36
Vicar's Cross
Rd. A 38
Whitby Lane . . . . A 42
Whitchurch Rd . . . . A 43

Abode Chester

BUSINESS • MODERN Contemporary hotel opposite the castle, just a short walk from the city. There are four categories of bedroom: 'Enviable' and 'Fabulous' are the best – ask for a room with a racecourse view. The ground floor MC Café Bar & Grill offers a brasserie menu; chic Michael Caines offers modern French fare.

84 rooms – †£ 80/200 ††£ 80/600

Town plan: B-z – *Grosvenor Rd* ✉ *CH1 2DJ*
– *✆ (01244) 347 000 – www.abodehotels.co.uk/chester*

Michael Caines – See restaurant listing

Oddfellows

TOWNHOUSE • DESIGN Originally an Oddfellows Hall built in 1676 to help the poor, but its name also suits its unique, quirky styling. Well-equipped, contemporary bedrooms include some duplex suites: one room has a circular bed; another, a double roll-top bath.

18 rooms – †£ 109/162 ††£ 109/162 – ☕ £ 12

Town plan: B-c – *20 Lower Bridge St* ✉ *CH1 1RS*
– *✆ (01244) 895 700 – www.oddfellowschester.com*
– *Closed 25 December*

The Garden by Oddfellows – See restaurant listing

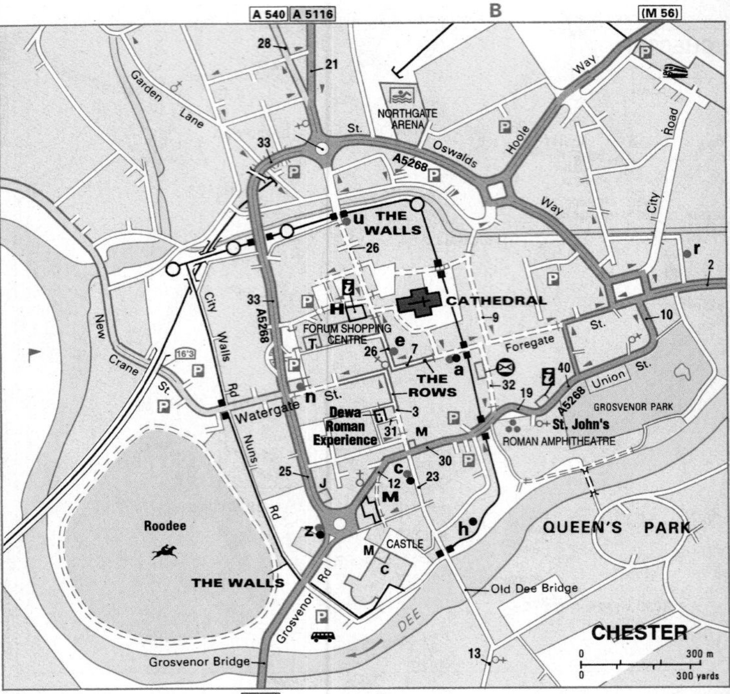

B

⌂ Edgar House Ⓝ

TOWNHOUSE • STYLISH A charming 17C house by the city walls, in the historic heart of Chester. The delightful garden overlooks the River Dee and the bright, modern bedrooms have raised beds so you can see the water. An honesty bar is housed in an old telephone box and the rustic dining room offers a traditional menu.

7 rooms – 👤£ 149/259 👥£ 149/259 – ☕£ 15

Town plan: B-h – *22 City Walls ✉ CH1 1SB – ✆ (01244) 347 007 – www.edgarhouse.co.uk – Closed 2 weeks Janaury*

Mitchell's of Chester

TOWNHOUSE • CLASSIC Proudly run Victorian house with homely bedrooms, thoughtful extras and smart, compact shower rooms; those on the first floor are the best. Classical lounge complete with a parrot. Spacious breakfast room; try the homemade preserves.

3 rooms ☕ – 👤£ 70/105 👥£ 92/105

Town plan: A-v – *28 Hough Grn ✉ CH4 8JQ – Southwest : 1 mi by A 483 on A 5104 – ✆ (01244) 679 004 – www.mitchellsofchester.com – Closed 18 December-3 January*

Restaurants

XXXX Simon Radley at Chester Grosvenor

❀ MODERN CUISINE · LUXURY Elegant restaurant with a fresh, classic feel, a stylish cocktail lounge and an impressive wine cellar. Confident cooking shows respect for ingredients, bringing together clean, clear flavours in sophisticated dishes that display interesting, innovative touches. Formal and detailed service.
→ Torched obsiblue prawns, Devon cock crab and langoustine. Squab pigeon with pistachio, dates, dandelions and coffee. Tête de Moine with sweet barbecue pears, walnuts, candied celery and Alpine cheese.

Menu £ 75/99

Town plan: B-a – *Chester Grosvenor Hotel, Eastgate* ⊠ *CH1 1LT* – *✆ (01244) 324 024* – *www.chestergrosvenor.com* – *dinner only* – *Closed 25 December, Sunday and Monday*

XX Michael Caines

BRITISH MODERN · FASHIONABLE A stylish spot on the fifth floor of a hotel, where you can enjoy far-reaching views over the castle and racecourse. Menus combine a French base with a modern edge; the tasting menu best demonstrates the flavourful, artistic cooking.

Menu £ 15 (lunch) – Carte £ 29/47

Town plan: B-z – *Abode Chester Hotel, Grosvenor Rd* ⊠ *CH1 2DJ* – *✆ (01244) 405 820* – *www.michaelcaines.com* – *Closed first week January*

XX Upstairs at the Grill

MEATS · INDIVIDUAL Smart restaurant offering prime quality steaks – including porterhouse and bone-in fillet or rib-eye; the 5 week dry-aged cuts are from premium Welsh beef. Eat in the moody cocktail bar or downstairs amongst the cow paraphernalia.

Carte £ 22/51

Town plan: B-n – *70 Watergate St* ⊠ *CH1 2LA* – *✆ (01244) 344 883* – *www.upstairsatthegrill.co.uk* – *dinner only and lunch Thursday-Sunday* – *Closed 25 December and 1 January*

XX La Brasserie

INTERNATIONAL · BRASSERIE Parisian brasserie with a large, hand-painted glass skylight, mirrors, brass rails and colourful light fittings; sit on a leather banquette or in a booth. Refined British, French and Mediterranean dishes are cooked on the Josper grill.

Carte £ 31/51

Town plan: B-a – *Chester Grosvenor Hotel, Eastgate* ⊠ *CH1 1LT* – *✆ (01244) 324 024* – *www.chestergrosvenor.com* – *Closed 25 December*

XX The Garden by Oddfellows

MEDITERRANEAN · TRENDY Set in an impressive Georgian hotel; have a drink in the quirky bar then head to the garden-themed restaurant with its bird motifs, flower displays, butterfly-filled glass boxes and large terrace. Unfussy, Mediterranean-influenced menus.

Carte £ 28/44 **s**

Town plan: B-c – *Oddfellows Hotel, 20 Lower Bridge St* ⊠ *CH1 1RS* – *✆ (01244) 895 700* – *www.oddfellowschester.com* – *Closed 25 December*

X Joseph Benjamin

☺ MODERN CUISINE · BISTRO This personally and passionately run bistro is named after its owners, Joe and Ben. The light, simple décor mirrors the style of cooking and the monthly menu offers tasty, well-judged dishes. They serve breakfast, lunch, coffee and homemade pastries and, from Thursday to Saturday, intimate candlelit dinners.

Carte £ 18/32

Town plan: B-u – *134-140 Northgate St* ⊠ *CH1 2HT* – *✆ (01244) 344 295* *(booking essential)* – *www.josephbenjamin.co.uk* – *lunch only and dinner Thursday-Saturday* – *Closed 25 December-1 January and Monday*

X **Chef's Table** Ⓝ

BRITISH MODERN · SIMPLE Intimate café-cum-bistro in the city centre. They open from early 'til late, offering breakfast, snacks, sandwiches and full meals – there are no real boundaries! The vibe is pleasingly laid-back and they will do anything to help.

Menu £ 15 (lunch) – Carte £ 26/39

Town plan: B-e – *4 Music Hall Passage* ⊠ *CH1 2EU* – ℰ *(01244) 403 040 (booking essential) – www.chefstablechester.co.uk – Closed 24 December-2 January, Sunday and Monday*

X **Sticky Walnut**

BRITISH MODERN · SIMPLE Run by a confident young team, a quirky, slightly bohemian restaurant in a residential parade of shops. Concise menus feature quality ingredients in a mix of British, French and Italian dishes; the breads and pastas are all homemade.

Carte £ 22/37

Town plan: A-x – *11 Charles St* ⊠ *CH2 3AZ* – ℰ *(01244) 400 400 (booking essential at dinner) – www.stickywalnut.com – Closed 25-26 December*

X **Artichoke**

MODERN CUISINE · BISTRO Sit outside beside the canal towpath or inside the Victorian mill building, where you'll find original beams, bare brick walls and a contemporary cocktail bar. Cooking ranges from homemade cakes to seasonal 3 course meals.

Carte £ 22/35

Town plan: B-r – *The Steam Mill, Steam Mill St* ⊠ *CH3 5AN* – ℰ *(01244) 329 229 – www.artichokechester.co.uk – Closed 25-26 December*

X **Porta**

SPANISH · TAPAS BAR Close to the city wall, behind a narrow terrace, is this cosy, characterful little tapas bar. It has no phone number or reservation system, but it does offer generous, tasty dishes which are served by a friendly young team.

Carte approx. £ 20

Town plan: B-u – *140 Northgate St* ⊠ *CH1 2HT* – ℰ *(01244) 344 295 (bookings not accepted) – www.portatapas.co.uk – dinner only – Closed 25 December-1 January*

CHESTERFIELD

Derbyshire – Pop. 88 483 – Regional map n° **9**-B1

▶ London 149 mi – Birmingham 72 mi – Liverpool 77 mi – Manchester 44 mi

🏠 **Casa**

BUSINESS · MODERN Modern hotel with 11 state-of-the-art meeting rooms and a smart bar with a heated terrace. Sizeable bedrooms are furnished in autumnal colours and come with useful extras; some of the suites have balconies and out-door hot tubs.

100 rooms ⊑ – †£ 100/135 ††£ 115/150

Lockoford Ln ⊠ *S41 7JB – North : 1 mi off A 61 –* ℰ *(01246) 245 999 – www.casahotels.com*

Cocina – See restaurant listing

XX **Cocina**

MEDITERRANEAN · BRASSERIE Stylish hotel restaurant with a well-stocked cocktail bar. Mediterranean menus have a strong Spanish influence; try the tapas or mature steaks from the Josper oven. The organic rare breed beef comes from the owners' 350 acre farm.

Menu £ 22 (early dinner) – Carte £ 19/47

Casa Hotel, Lockoford Ln ⊠ *S41 7JB – North : 1 mi off A 61 –* ℰ *(01246) 245 999 – www.casahotels.com*

CHEW MAGNA

Bath and North East Somerset – Pop. 1 149 – Regional map n° **2**-C2
▶ London 128 mi – Bristol 9 mi – Cardiff 52 mi – Swindon 49 mi

✗ Salt & Malt ⓝ   ⩺ 🛋 ㆔ 🄰🄲 🖵 🄿

FISH AND SEAFOOD · FRIENDLY Smart lakeside eatery with lovely views over the water. They're open all day for breakfast, coffee and cakes, light lunches and cream teas. The evening menu steps things up a gear; fish and chips are the focus and the thing to go for.

Carte £14/23

Walley Ln, Chew Stoke ✉ BS40 8TF – South : 1.25 mi by Bishop Sutton rd and Denny Rd – ℰ (01275) 333 345 – www.saltmalt.com – Closed Sunday dinner

🍴 Pony & Trap (Josh Eggleton)   🍺 🛋 🄿
❀

BRITISH MODERN · COSY A cosy whitewashed pub with a characterful bar featuring church pews and an old range – and superb countryside views from the rustic dining room and terrace. Twice-daily menu of extremely fresh, seasonal produce, including locally sourced, hung and smoked meats and fish. Classical cooking with bold flavours.

→ Glazed pork belly, crab, consommé, celeriac and apple. Poached halibut, on the bone with sea beets, clams and red wine sauce. Bay leaf custard slice with rhubarb sorbet.

Carte £22/42

Knowle Hill, New Town ✉ BS40 8TQ – South : 1.25 mi on Bishop Sutton rd – ℰ (01275) 332 627 (booking essential) – www.theponyandtrap.co.uk – Closed 25 December, Monday except December and bank holidays

CHICHESTER

West Sussex – Pop. 28 657 – Regional map n° **4**-C2
▶ London 69 mi – Brighton 31 mi – Portsmouth 18 mi – Southampton 30 mi

🏨 Goodwood   ☆ 🍴 🎬 🖥 🐜 🛦 🎿 ℅ 🄰🄲 🛁 🄿

BUSINESS · CONTEMPORARY Refurbished hotel on the Goodwood Estate, with luxurious, English-style bedrooms in subtle, contemporary colour schemes; modern furniture and motor racing photos abound. Well-equipped spa. Smart Richmond Arms serves a seasonal menu, with many ingredients from the estate. Informal Bar & Grill overlooks the golf course and offers modern classics.

91 rooms ☲ – ♦£115/180 ♦♦£125/192 – 5 suites

Goodwood ✉ PO18 0QB – Northeast : 4 mi by A 285 and Lavant rd – ℰ (01243) 775 537 – www.goodwood.com

🏨 Ship   ☆ 🗐 ⬆ ℅ 🛁 🄿

BUSINESS · MODERN Grade II listed former home to one of Nelson's men. Some impressive Georgian features remain, including a cantilevered wrought iron staircase. Stylish, up-to-date bedrooms and a spacious, contemporary bar. Airy brasserie offers a modern European menu, with meat and game from the nearby estate.

37 rooms ☲ – ♦£99/190 ♦♦£125/300

Town plan: BY-s – *57 North St ✉ PO19 1NH – ℰ (01243) 778 000 – www.theshiphotel.net*

✗✗ Brasserie Blanc   🛋 🄰🄲

FRENCH CLASSIC · BRASSERIE Classically styled brasserie with a lovely terrace, tucked away in a modern flag-stoned square. There's an impressive open kitchen and a display of artisan provisions for sale. Tasty, rustic French cooking uses local produce.

Menu £15 (lunch) – Carte £18/40

Town plan: BZ-z – *Richmond House, The Square ✉ PO19 7SJ – ℰ (01243) 534 200 – www.brasserieblanc.com*

397

CHICHESTER

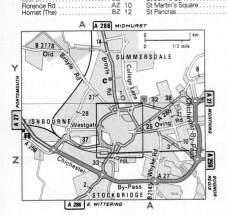

✕ Amelie and Friends 📶

MODERN CUISINE · SIMPLE City centre brasserie-style restaurant with contemporary white décor; sit in the smaller room overlooking the walled garden terrace. The cheerful, efficient team serve everything from brasserie classics through to Asian-inspired dishes.
Carte £ 21/43

Town plan: BY-x – *31 North St* ✉ *PO19 1LY*
– *𝒞 (01243) 771 444 (booking essential at dinner)*
– *www.amelieandfriends.com* – *Closed Sunday dinner*

at Mid Lavant North: 2 mi on A286

🏠 Rooks Hill ⊛ P

COUNTRY HOUSE · PERSONALISED Grade II listed house with a pleasant view across to the Goodwood estate. Relax on the charming courtyard terrace or next to the wood burner in the cosy sitting room. Individually decorated bedrooms have contemporary touches.
3 rooms ⊇ – ♦£ 90/125 ♦♦£ 120/175
Lavant Rd ✉ *PO18 OBQ* – *𝒞 (01243) 528 400*
– *www.rookshill.co.uk*

🍴 Earl of March 🏡 ⇄ P

TRADITIONAL CUISINE · PUB 18C inn with a perfect blend of country character and contemporary styling; its terrace offers amazing views of the South Downs. Good quality, seasonal produce is used in classic British dishes.
Menu £ 22 (lunch and early dinner) **s** – Carte £ 28/43 **s**
✉ *PO18 OBQ* – *𝒞 (01243) 533 993*
– *www.theearlofmarch.com*

The symbol ⊛ denotes a particularly interesting wine list.

ENGLAND

at East Lavant North: 2.5 mi off A286 – Plan: AY – ✉ Chichester

🏠 **Royal Oak Inn**

TRADITIONAL CUISINE · PUB 18C inn with a rustic, laid-back feel; arrive early for a spot by the fire. Cooking is fairly refined but steaks play an important role. There are interesting vegetarian options, a good cheese selection and plenty of wines by the glass. Spacious bedrooms are comfy and well-equipped; breakfast is a treat.

Carte £ 22/40

8 rooms ☞ – ♦£ 90/145 ♦♦£ 125/230

Pook Ln ✉ PO18 0AX – ℰ (01243) 527 434 – www.royaloakeastlavant.co.uk

at Tangmere East: 2 mi by A27 – Plan: AY – ✉ Chichester

✕✕ **Cassons**

MODERN CUISINE · RUSTIC Passionately run restaurant with exposed brick, wooden beams and a rustic feel. Boldly flavoured dishes are generously proportioned. Cooking is classically based but employs modern techniques. The regular gourmet evenings are a hit.

Menu £ 39 (dinner) – Carte lunch £ 39/45

Arundel Rd ✉ PO18 0DU – Northwest : 0.25 mi off A 27 (westbound) – ℰ (01243) 773 294 – www.cassonsrestaurant.co.uk – Closed 25-30 December, Tuesday lunch, Sunday dinner and Monday

at Bosham West: 4 mi by A259 – Plan: AZ – ✉ Chichester

🏨 **Millstream**

TRADITIONAL · CLASSIC Genuine, old-fashioned hospitality and classic comforts mean that most guests are on return visits to this pretty hotel, with its well-tended garden and fast-flowing stream. Cosy bar, comfy sitting room and traditionally furnished, immaculately kept bedrooms. Classic menu with modern touches in the light, airy restaurant. Brasserie dishes in contemporary Marwick's.

35 rooms ☞ – ♦£ 99/139 ♦♦£ 159/229 – 2 suites

Bosham Ln ✉ PO18 8HL – ℰ (01243) 573 234 – www.millstreamhotel.com

at Funtington Northwest: 4.75 mi by B2178 – Plan: AY on B2146 – ✉ Chichester

✕✕ **Hallidays**

CLASSIC CUISINE · INTIMATE Charming thatched cottage with a low-beamed ceiling and a homely feel. The experienced chef knows about sourcing good, local ingredients and his menu changes weekly. Skilful, classical cooking.

Menu £ 37 (dinner) – Carte lunch £ 30/42

Watery Ln ✉ PO18 9LF – ℰ (01243) 575 331 – www.hallidays.info.co.uk – Closed 2 weeks August, 1 week March, 1 week Christmas-New Year, Saturday lunch, Sunday dinner, Monday and Tuesday

at West Ashling Northwest: 4.5 mi by B2178 and B2146

🏠 **Richmond Arms**

INTERNATIONAL · RUSTIC Appealing, laid-back country pub opposite a duck pond in a lovely little village. The menu offers an appealing mix, from freshly sliced hams and local steaks to game from the family estate in Anglesey; many meats are cooked on the rotisserie or the Japanese robata grill. Two luxurious bedrooms are above.

Carte £ 23/45

2 rooms ☞ – ♦£ 115 ♦♦£ 125

Mill Rd ✉ PO18 8EA – ℰ (01243) 572 046 – www.therichmondarms.co.uk – Closed Christmas-New Year, last week July, first week November, Sunday dinner, Monday and Tuesday

CHIDDINGFOLD
Surrey – Pop. 2 211 – Regional map n° **4**-C2
▶ London 47 mi – Guildford 10 mi – Haslemere 5 mi

🍴 **Swan Inn**   ⇦ 🌳 ⚒ 🏧 🅿

MODERN CUISINE · INDIVIDUAL Elegant tile-hung pub with a 200 year old history and an up-to-date interior. The local Surrey set pop in for crab cakes or the 'terrine of the day' at lunch; the à la carte changes daily, depending on the latest local produce available. Bedrooms are cool and contemporary.

Carte £ 22/39

10 rooms 🖴 – **†**£ 100/190 **††**£ 100/190

Petworth Rd ✉ GU8 4TY – ℘ (01428) 684 688
– www.theswaninnchiddingfold.com

CHIEVELEY
West Berkshire – Regional map n° **6**-B3
▶ London 60 mi – Newbury 5 mi – Swindon 25 mi

🍴 **Crab & Boar** Ⓝ   ⇦ 🍴 🌳 ⚒ 🗓 ✿ 🅿

BRITISH TRADITIONAL · INN A pretty pub with a thatch and red tile roof, leaded windows, rustic timbers and a sunny front terrace. British dishes are rooted in tradition with a modern edge, and include plenty of fresh seafood and game in season. Grill dishes are a hit and Sunday lunch is an event. Stylish bedrooms; some with hot tubs.

Carte £ 26/45

14 rooms 🖴 – **†**£ 110/210 **††**£ 110/210

Wantage Rd ✉ RG20 8UE – West : 2.5 mi by School Rd on B 4494 – ℘ (01635) 247 550 – www.crabandboar.com

CHILLATON – Devon ➜ See Tavistock

CHILLINGTON
Devon – Regional map n° **1**-C3
▶ London 217 mi – Plymouth 26 mi – Torbay 20 mi – Torquay 22 mi

🏠 **whitehouse**   🍴 🅿

COUNTRY HOUSE · STYLISH Attractive Georgian house run in a relaxed manner. Stylish bedrooms are boldly decorated and feature a mix of modern and retro furnishings; all have heavy handmade beds and smart bathrooms. The breakfast room overlooks the gardens.

6 rooms 🖴 – **†**£ 190/260 **††**£ 190/260

✉ TQ7 2JX – ℘ (01548) 580 505 – www.whitehousedevon.com

CHINNOR
Oxfordshire – Pop. 5 473 – Regional map n° **6**-C2
▶ London 45 mi – Oxford 19 mi – Birmingham 88 mi

at Sprigg's Alley Southeast: 2.5 mi by Bledlow Ridge rd – ✉ Chinnor

🍴 **Sir Charles Napier**   🅿 🍴 🌳 🅿
❀

BRITISH MODERN · COSY An attractive flint pub in a small hillside hamlet, with a hint of eccentricity in its décor. In summer, relax on the pleasant terrace or in the delightful gardens; in winter, sit beside the log fire. Boldly flavoured dishes are prepared with skill and capture flavours to their full.

➜ Scallops with tandoori-spiced pork belly and lime pickle purée. Honey and ginger glazed Goosnargh duck, confit leg wontons, rhubarb and sweet wine jus. Salted caramel with chocolate & peanut terrine and lime ice cream.

Menu £ 20 (weekday lunch)/65 – Carte £ 38/56

Sprigs Holly ✉ OX39 4BX – ℘ (01494) 483 011 (booking advisable)
– www.sircharlesnapier.co.uk – Closed 24-26 December, Sunday dinner and Monday except bank holidays

CHIPPING CAMPDEN

Gloucestershire – Pop. 2 037 – Regional map n° **2**-D1

▶ London 93 mi – Gloucester 35 mi – Birmingham 44 mi – Bristol 67 mi

Cotswold House H. and Spa

TOWNHOUSE · CONTEMPORARY A set of stylish Regency townhouses with lovely gardens, boldly decorated lounges hung with eclectic modern art, and a fine spiral staircase winding upwards towards luxurious modern bedrooms. Eat in the laid-back grill restaurant.

25 rooms ♫ – †£ 93/420 ††£ 100/420 – 3 suites
The Square ⊠ GL55 6AN – ℰ (01386) 840 330 – www.cotswoldhouse.com
Cotswold Grill – See restaurant listing

Noel Arms

INN · CONTEMPORARY Pick a characterful beamed bedroom in the main building (one has an ornate carved bed dating from 1657), or go for one with a touch more modernity in the newer extension. The wood-panelled bar might be traditional but the conservatory lounge and boldly coloured restaurant are more contemporary.

28 rooms ♫ – †£ 70/190 ††£ 75/215
High St ⊠ GL55 6AT – ℰ (01386) 840 317
– www.bespokehotels.com/noelarmshotel

Kings

TOWNHOUSE · STYLISH Beautiful Cotswold stone townhouse with a stylish boutique interior. Bedrooms in the main house mix antiques with modern facilities – some boast sleigh beds; rooms in the cottage at the end of the garden are more up-to-date.

18 rooms ♫ – †£ 110/275 ††£ 130/305
The Square ⊠ GL55 6AW – ℰ (01386) 840 256 – www.kingscampden.co.uk
Kings – See restaurant listing

Seymour House

TOWNHOUSE · PERSONALISED Welcoming Cotswold stone house with early 18C origins, a lovely garden and a pretty breakfast terrace. It's tastefully furnished throughout, with a classical, understated style; fine furnishings, artwork and antiques feature.

5 rooms ♫ – †£ 90 ††£ 120/140
High St ⊠ GL55 6AG – ℰ (01386) 840 064 – www.seymourhousebandb.co.uk
– Closed Christmas-New Year

XX Kings

MODERN CUISINE · RUSTIC An appealing, rustic restaurant in a stylish boutique townhouse. Exposed stone walls, wooden beams and a large inglenook fireplace feature. Modern British menus use top quality ingredients and dishes are refined and flavoursome.

Menu £ 18/33
Kings Hotel, The Square ⊠ GL55 6AW – ℰ (01386) 840 256
– www.kingscampden.co.uk

X Chef's Dozen

BRITISH MODERN · FRIENDLY This intimate restaurant and shady terrace sit close to the square and are run by a local chef with a passion for fine organic and wild ingredients. Dishes are modern, creative and attractive; this is inspired field-to-fork cooking.

Menu £ 19 (weekday lunch)/58
Island House, High St ⊠ GL55 6AL – ℰ (01386) 840 598 (booking advisable)
– www.thechefsdozen.co.uk – Closed 24 January-10 February,
25-26 December, Sunday, Monday and Tuesday lunch

✗ Cotswold Grill

TRADITIONAL CUISINE · BISTRO This relaxed, informal restaurant is found within a Regency townhouse hotel. Open all day, it serves breakfast and after-noon tea as well as an appealing, bistro-style menu of modern dishes including steaks, burgers and charcuterie.

Carte £ 25/45

Cotswold House H. and Spa, The Square ✉ *GL55 6AN –* ✆ *(01386) 840 330 – www.cotswoldhouse.com*

ⓘ Eight Bells Inn

BRITISH TRADITIONAL · COSY Characterful country pub just off the historic high street in an old wool merchant's town. Cooking is classical – homemade pies and winter casseroles fill you up, puddings are comforting and specials are just that, so arrive early. Bedrooms are traditionally furnished; mind your head on the beams!

Carte £ 25/37

6 rooms ☑ – ♦£ 65/85 ♦♦£ 80/140

Church St ✉ *GL55 6JG –* ✆ *(01386) 840 371 – www.eightbellsinn.co.uk – Closed 25 December*

---

at Mickleton North: 3.25 mi by B4035 and B4081 on B4632 – ✉ Chipping Campden

🏠 Three Ways House

COUNTRY HOUSE · CONTEMPORARY This privately owned 1870s Cotswold ho-tel plays host to the famous 'Pudding Club' meetings – they do 'Pudding Breaks' and you can even stay in a pudding-themed room! Bedrooms are contemporary and individually designed; some have private patios. The formal, arcaded restau-rant showcases local produce.

48 rooms ☑ – ♦£ 88/130 ♦♦£ 155/260

✉ *GL55 6SB –* ✆ *(01386) 438 429 – www.threewayshousehotel.com*

---

at Ebrington East: 2 mi by B4035

ⓘ Ebrington Arms

BRITISH TRADITIONAL · COSY Proper village local with a beamed, flag-floored bar at its hub, set in a charming chocolate box village. The blackboard menu of-fers pub classics; the à la carte, a choice of more elaborate dishes. Bedrooms have country views; Room 3, with its four-poster bed and luxury bathroom, is the best.

Menu £ 15 (weekday lunch)/19 – Carte £ 26/38

5 rooms ☑ – ♦£ 105/160 ♦♦£ 115/170

✉ *GL55 6NH –* ✆ *(01386) 593 223 – www.theebringtonarms.co.uk*

---

at Broad Campden South: 1.25 mi by B4081 – ✉ Chipping Campden

🏠 Malt House

COUNTRY HOUSE · PERSONALISED This attractive Cotswold stone guesthouse started life as a 16C malt house and two old cottages. Inside, characterful guest areas have exposed beams, inglenook fireplaces and Arts and Crafts furnishings; outside there's a lovely summerhouse, a croquet lawn and a wild flower meadow. Bedrooms are comfy and cosy. Breakfast and dinner feature fruit from the garden.

8 rooms ☑ – ♦£ 100 ♦♦£ 150/170

✉ *GL55 6UU –* ✆ *(01386) 840 295 – www.thecotswoldmalthouse.com*

---

at Weston-sub-Edge Northwest : 3 mi. by B 4081 and B 4035 on B 4632

ⓘ Seagrave Arms

BRITISH MODERN · PUB A handsome building of Cotswold stone, with a cosy, fire-warmed bar and two traditional dining rooms. Attractively presented, refined modern dishes use well-judged combinations of ingredients from the local larder. Bedrooms are classic in style; opt for the suite, with its spacious bathroom and roll-top bath.

Carte £ 24/46

8 rooms ☑ – ♦£ 70/155 ♦♦£ 80/165

Friday St ✉ *GL55 6QH –* ✆ *(01386) 840 192 – www.seagravearms.co.uk*

CHIPPING NORTON

Oxfordshire – Pop. 5 719 – Regional map n° **6**-A1
▶ London 77 mi – Oxford 22 mi – Stow-on-the-Wold 9 mi

✗ Wild Thyme

BRITISH TRADITIONAL · COSY A cosy, keenly run restaurant with rustic tables; No. 10, in the window, is the best. Wholesome regional British cooking has Mediterranean influences, with tasty homemade breads and game in season. Simply appointed bedrooms; the friendly owners go out of their way to ensure their guests' comfort.

Menu £ 20 (weekday lunch)/38

3 rooms ⌂ – ♦£ 65/75 ♦♦£ 75/85

10 New St ⌂ OX7 5LJ – ℰ (01608) 645 060 (booking advisable)
– www.wildthymerestaurant.co.uk – Closed first week January, Sunday and lunch Monday

CHIPPING ONGAR

Essex – Pop. 6 093 – Regional map n° **7**-B2
▶ London 28 mi – Chelmsford 12 mi – Harlow 10 mi

✗✗ Smith's

FISH AND SEAFOOD · BRASSERIE Long-standing, locally acclaimed seafood restaurant with a buzzy atmosphere. The à la carte and extensive daily set menu offer dishes ranging from Cornish squid to Scottish smoked salmon. Lobster, cooked several ways, is a speciality.

Menu £ 22 (weekdays)/30 – Carte £ 31/63

Fyfield Rd ⌂ CM5 0AL – ℰ (01277) 365 578 (booking essential)
– www.smithsrestaurants.com – Closed 25-26 December 1 January and Monday lunch

CHIPSTEAD

Kent – Regional map n° **5**-B1
▶ London 27 mi – Maidstone 37 mi – Dartford 28 mi

⌂ George & Dragon

BRITISH MODERN · PUB Superbly set, 450 year old inn with a beamed bar and a wonky-floored upstairs dining room. Delightful garden with terrace and children's play area. The menu is a roll call of seasonal English classics; herbs and salad are home-grown.

Carte £ 21/37

39 High St ⌂ TN13 2RW – ℰ (01732) 779 019 – www.georgeanddragonchipstead.com

CHOBHAM

Surrey – Pop. 2 771 – Regional map n° **4**-C1
▶ London 32 mi – Birmingham 127 mi – Bristol 98 mi – Croydon 31 mi

✗✗✗ Stovell's

BRITISH MODERN · INTIMATE The husband and wife team at this elegant 16C Tudor farmhouse have put Chobham firmly on the culinary map. Creative, often intricate dishes use top quality ingredients; highlights include dishes from the wood-fired grill.

Menu £ 21/42

125 Windsor Rd ⌂ GU24 8QS – North : 0.75 mi on B 383 – ℰ (01276) 858 000
(booking essential) – www.stovells.com – Closed first 2 weeks January,
21-23 August, 26-27 December, Saturday lunch, Sunday dinner and Monday

CHOLMONDELEY

Cheshire East – Regional map n° **11**-A3
▶ London 178 mi – Birmingham 65 mi – Leeds 86 mi – Sheffield 90 mi

⌂ Cholmondeley Arms

BRITISH TRADITIONAL · RUSTIC The eponymous estate's old schoolhouse, with high, vaulted ceilings, large windows and roaring fires. Modern pub favourites might include calves' liver or homemade lamb faggots. Gin lovers will be in clover with more than 200 from which to choose. The 6 comfy bedrooms are in the Old Headmaster's House.

Carte £ 22/34

6 rooms ⌂ – ♦£ 65/85 ♦♦£ 85/100

Wrenbury Rd ⌂ SY14 8HN – ℰ (01829) 720 300 – www.cholmondeleyarms.co.uk

CHORLTON-CUM-HARDY – Greater Manchester → See Manchester

CHRISTCHURCH
Dorset – Pop. 54 210 – Regional map n° **2**-D3
▶ London 111 mi – Bournemouth 6 mi – Salisbury 26 mi – Southampton 24 mi

⛨ Christchurch Harbour
⚘ ⬳ ⌂ ⬚ ⊚ ⟫ ⊞ ⭐ ⊞ ⭳ Ⓜ ⚒ ⭐ 🅿

FAMILY · PERSONALISED Don't be fooled by the unassuming exterior; inside is a cool, chic hotel with a smart basement spa – its waterside location reflected in the modern, nautical-inspired décor. Some bedrooms have waterfront terraces or balconies. Both of the restaurants open onto delightful terraces with far-reaching views.

64 rooms ⚏ – ♦£130/198 ♦♦£130/198
95 Mudeford ⊠ BH23 3NT – ℰ (01202) 483 434
– www.christchurch-harbour-hotel.co.uk
Jetty – See restaurant listing

⛨ Captain's Club
⚘ ⬳ ⌂ ⊚ ⟫ ⊞ ⭳ Ⓜ ⚒ 🅿

BUSINESS · DESIGN Striking modern building with art deco and nautical influences, set in a lovely riverside spot – floor to ceiling windows offer fantastic views. Bedrooms are sleek and contemporary; some are three-roomed suites. The restaurant offers all-day menus. Relax in the stylish spa or out on the water in their boat.

29 rooms ⚏ – ♦£179/269 ♦♦£199/269 – 12 suites
Wick Ferry, Wick Ln ⊠ BH23 1HU – ℰ (01202) 475 111
– www.captainsclubhotel.com

⛨ Kings Arms
⚘ ⊞ ⭳ ⚒

TOWNHOUSE · STYLISH This lovingly restored Georgian inn stands opposite the bowling green and castle ruins, and has been given a smart modern makeover. Guest areas have a chic yet characterful feel and the boutique-style bedrooms are well-appointed.

20 rooms (dinner included) ⚏ – ♦£68/119 ♦♦£75/169
18 Castle St ⊠ BH23 1DT – ℰ (01202) 588 933 – www.thekings-christchurch.co.uk
⚘ **Kings Arms** – See restaurant listing

⛨ Druid House
⌂ ⚒ 🅿

FAMILY · PERSONALISED Hidden behind an unassuming exterior, a bright, well-kept house that's passionately run and great value for money. Bedrooms are bright and modern; some of those in the newer wing open out onto a small terrace. Excellent breakfasts include a buffet and hot specials such as muffins with poached eggs and bacon.

10 rooms ⚏ – ♦£65/110 ♦♦£85/135
26 Sopers Ln ⊠ BH23 1JE – ℰ (01202) 485 615 – www.druid-house.co.uk

XX Splinters
✧

CLASSIC CUISINE · BISTRO A very traditional, family-run restaurant, named after the splinters the carpenters got when building the booths! Choose from several cosy, characterful rooms. Cooking is wholesome and classical, with rich, tasty sauces a feature.

Menu £14/21 – Carte £29/49
12 Church St ⊠ BH23 1BW – ℰ (01202) 483 454 – www.splinters.uk.com
– Closed 1-13 January, Sunday and Monday

XX Jetty
⬳ ⌂ ⭳ Ⓜ 🅿

BRITISH MODERN · DESIGN Set within the grounds of the Christchurch Harbour hotel, this contemporary, eco-friendly restaurant offers fantastic water views. Appealing menus reflect what's available locally, with fish from nearby waters and game from the forest.

Menu £19 (weekdays)/25 – Carte £32/70
Christchurch Harbour Hotel, 95 Mudeford ⊠ BH23 3NT – East : 2 mi – ℰ (01202)
400 950 – www.thejetty.co.uk

✗ Kings Arms

BRITISH MODERN · BRASSERIE Smart, spacious hotel brasserie offering gutsy, no frills cooking that's packed with flavour. The Josper grill plays a big role, as does the good value £15 weekly menu, which is made up of produce sourced from within 15 miles. Friday is 'Fizz 'n' Chips' night and they also offer afternoon tea.

Menu £15 (lunch and early dinner) – Carte £24/40
Kings Arms Hotel, 18 Castle St ⊠ BH23 1DT – ℰ (01202) 588 933
– www.thekings-christchurch.co.uk

CHURCHILL

Oxfordshire – ⊠ Chipping Norton – Pop. 502 – Regional map n° **6**-A1
▶ London 79 mi – Birmingham 46 mi – Cheltenham 29 mi – Oxford 23 mi

⑩ Chequers

TRADITIONAL CUISINE · PUB Welcoming sandstone pub in the heart of the village; it's a vital part of the community and the owners have got the formula just right. The bar is stocked with local ales; gutsy, traditional dishes include steaks cooked on the Josper grill.

Carte £15/40
Church Rd ⊠ OX7 6NJ – ℰ (01608) 659 393 – www.thechequerschurchill.com
– Closed 25 December and dinner 26 December and 1 January

CHURCH ENSTONE

Oxfordshire – ⊠ Chipping Norton – Regional map n° **6**-B1
▶ London 72 mi – Banbury 13 mi – Oxford 38 mi

⑩ Crown Inn

BRITISH TRADITIONAL · PUB 17C inn set among pretty stone houses in a picturesque village. Sit in the slate-floored conservatory, the beamed dining room or the rustic bar. Meat, fruit and veg come from local farms; seafood is a speciality, as is the steak pie.

Carte £18/34
Mill Ln ⊠ OX7 4NN – ℰ (01608) 677 262 – www.crowninnenstone.co.uk – Closed 25-26 December, 1 January and Sunday dinner

CIRENCESTER

Gloucestershire – Pop. 16 325 – Regional map n° **2**-D1
▶ London 97 mi – Bristol 37 mi – Gloucester 19 mi – Oxford 37 mi

🏰 Kings Head ⑪

HISTORIC · DESIGN Former coaching inn of local stone, overlooking the Market Place. Original features attest to its age, but after years of refurbishment, it is now a stylish, modern hotel offering spacious, comfortable bedrooms with all the latest mod cons.

45 rooms ⌑ – ♦£135/265 ♦♦£150/280
24 Market Pl ⊠ GL7 2NR – ℰ (01285) 700 900 – www.kingshead-hotel.co.uk
Kings Head – See restaurant listing

🏠 Fleece at Cirencester

INN · COSY Charming, centrally located 18C coaching inn with an open-plan coffee shop and a cosy open-fired sitting room. Spacious modern bedrooms are individually furnished and well-kept; Rooms 1 and 4 are the best. The simple bistro dining room serves an accessible menu, with choices including deli boards and steaks.

28 rooms ⌑ – ♦£85/91 ♦♦£98/165
Market Pl ⊠ GL7 2NZ – ℰ (01285) 650 231 – www.thefleececirencester.co.uk

🏠 No 12

TOWNHOUSE · PERSONALISED This 16C townhouse provides plenty of contrasts with its Georgian façade and modern interior. Large bedrooms blend stylish furnishings with original features. Local organic products are used at breakfast and there's a delightful garden.

4 rooms ⌂ – 🛏£ 100 🛏🛏£ 130
12 Park St ⌂ GL7 2BW – ℰ (01285) 640 232
– www.no12cirencester.co.uk

🏠 Old Brewhouse

TOWNHOUSE · PERSONALISED 17C former brewhouse in busy central spot, with a characterful cluttered interior and two stone-walled breakfast rooms. Choose between cottage-style bedrooms – most with wrought iron beds – or more modern rooms set around a small courtyard.

9 rooms ⌂ – 🛏£ 75/85 🛏🛏£ 89/98
7 London Rd ⌂ GL7 2PU – ℰ (01285) 656 099
– www.theoldbrewhouse.com – Closed 24 December-2 January

XX Kings Head ⓝ

MODERN CUISINE · BRASSERIE A popular, modern restaurant on the ground floor of a stylish hotel; start with a cocktail at the bar or by the inglenook in the clubby lounge. The menu offers sharing boards, hearty classics and Cotswold beef cooked on the Robata grill.

Carte £ 23/76
Kings Head Hotel, 24 Market Pl ⌂ GL7 2NR
– ℰ (01285) 700 900 (booking advisable) – www.kingshead-hotel.co.uk

X Made by Bob

MEDITERRANEAN · FASHIONABLE The name says it all: Bob makes most of the products himself – be it for the informal eatery or the crammed deli – and the rest of the ingredients are organic and locally sourced. Service is bright and breezy, and the flexible daily menus are appealing. If you can't find a seat, they also do takeaway.

Carte £ 21/40
The Corn Hall, 26 Market Pl ⌂ GL7 2NY
– ℰ (01285) 641 818 (bookings not accepted) – www.foodmadebybob.com
– lunch only and dinner Thursday-Friday – Closed 25-26 December, 1 January and Sunday

X Jesse's Bistro

TRADITIONAL CUISINE · COSY Rustic bistro where guests can interact with the team in the open-plan kitchen. Well-crafted, generously proportioned dishes feature fish from Cornwall and meats from their adjoining butcher's shop – many are cooked in the wood-fired oven.

Menu £ 19 (weekdays) – Carte £ 26/54
14 Blackjack St ⌂ GL7 2AA – ℰ (01285) 641 497
– www.jessesbistro.co.uk – Closed Monday dinner and Sunday

at Barnsley Northeast: 4 mi by A429 on B4425 – ⌂ Cirencester

🏠 Barnsley House

HISTORIC · STYLISH 17C Cotswold manor house with a wonderfully relaxed vibe, set in the midst of beautiful gardens styled by Rosemary Verey. A very stylish interior blends original features with modern touches, from the open-fired lounges to the chic bedrooms; there's also a spa and even a cinema in the grounds.

18 rooms ⌂ – 🛏£ 282/532 🛏🛏£ 300/550 – 8 suites
⌂ GL7 5EE – ℰ (01285) 740 000 – www.barnsleyhouse.com
The Potager – See restaurant listing

XX The Potager   🍴 ♿ 🅿

MEDITERRANEAN · INDIVIDUAL Understated hotel restaurant with a pleasant garden outlook and a laid-back feel. Influencing more than just the name, the kitchen gardens inform what's on the menu each day. Unfussy cooking has Mediterranean overtones; don't miss the freshly baked breads with herb-infused oils and salsa verde.

Carte £ 25/53

Barnsley House Hotel, ⊠ GL7 5EE – 𝒞 (01285) 740 000
– www.barnsleyhouse.com

🍴 Village Pub   🅿

BRITISH TRADITIONAL · DESIGN With an interior straight out of any country homes magazine, this place has the cosy, open-fired, village pub vibe down to a tee. It has four intimate rooms and a carefully manicured terrace. Appealing modern British dishes and irresistible nibbles feature locally sourced meats, charcuterie from Highgrove and comforting desserts. Bedrooms are tastefully styled.

Carte £ 28/40

6 rooms 🖙 – 🛏£ 140/170 🛏🛏£ 140/170
⊠ GL7 5EF – 𝒞 (01285) 740 421 (booking essential) – www.thevillagepub.co.uk

at Sapperton West: 5 mi by A419 – ⊠ Cirencester

🍴 The Bell   🅿

TRADITIONAL CUISINE · RUSTIC Charming and characterful Cotswold pub with flagged floors, exposed stone, an abundance of beams and warming log fires. Menus offer the expected burger or fish and chips, as well as dishes which show off more of the chef's skills.

Carte £ 23/37

⊠ GL7 6LE – 𝒞 (01285) 760 298 – www.bellsapperton.co.uk – Closed
25 December and Sunday dinner

CLANFIELD

Oxfordshire – Pop. 1 709 – Regional map n° **6**-A2
▶ London 75 mi – Oxford 24 mi – Ealing 68 mi – Coventry 56 mi

🏠 Cotswold Plough   🅿

TRADITIONAL · CLASSIC Charming16C wool merchant's house in the heart of a pretty village, with an antique-furnished lounge and a characterful bar boasting two open fires and over 180 types of gin. Bedrooms in the main house are cosy with mullioned windows; those in the extension are more spacious. 3 of the rooms have four-posters.

11 rooms 🖙 – 🛏£ 89/135 🛏🛏£ 115/175
Bourton Rd ⊠ OX18 2RB – on A 4095 – 𝒞 (01367) 810 222
– www.cotswoldploughhotel.com – Closed 24-27 December
Cotswold Plough – See restaurant listing

XX Cotswold Plough   🅿

BRITISH TRADITIONAL · FRIENDLY Set within a 16C hotel, a lovely three-roomed restaurant with beamed ceilings, relaxed service and a comfortingly traditional feel. Classical menus provide plenty of appeal and all of the wines are available by the glass or carafe.

Carte £ 22/39

Cotswold Plough Hotel, Bourton Rd ⊠ OX18 2RB – on A 4095 – 𝒞 (01367) 810 222
– www.cotswoldploughhotel.com – Closed 24-27 December

CLAVERING

Essex – ⊠ Saffron Walden – Pop. 882 – Regional map n° **7**-B2
▶ London 44 mi – Cambridge 25 mi – Colchester 44 mi – Luton 29 mi

🍴 Cricketers

INTERNATIONAL · INN Deceptively spacious pub set close to the cricket pitch in a sleepy village. Bread is baked daily, specials are chalked on a board above the fire and the cooking mixes British and Italian influences. The owners' son, Jamie Oliver, supplies fruit, veg and herbs from his organic garden. Bedrooms are welcoming.
Carte £ 20/38

20 rooms 🍽 - 🛏£ 68/75 🛏🛏£ 95/120
✉ CB11 4QT - 𝒞 (01799) 550 442 (booking essential) - www.thecricketers.co.uk
- Closed 25-26 December

CLEARWELL

Gloucestershire - Regional map n° **2**-C1
▶ London 138 mi - Birmingham 85 mi - Bristol 31 mi - Cardiff 46 mi

🏠 Tudor Farmhouse

COUNTRY HOUSE · CONTEMPORARY A group of converted farm buildings in the heart of the Forest of Dean. Two cosy dining rooms serving carefully prepared, interesting dishes are found in the old farmhouse and, above them, characterful bedrooms with old beams and wonky floors. More modern bedrooms are housed in two of the outbuildings.
20 rooms 🍽 - 🛏£ 100/230 🛏🛏£ 100/230 - 5 suites
High St ✉ GL16 8JS - 𝒞 (01594) 833 046 - www.tudorfarmhousehotel.co.uk

CLEESTANTON - Shropshire → See Ludlow

CLENT

Worcestershire - Regional map n° **10**-C2
▶ London 127 mi - Birmingham 12 mi - Hagley 2 mi

🍴 Bell & Cross

TRADITIONAL CUISINE · PUB Charming pub with colourful window boxes and country views. Huge choice of dishes: lunch offers light bites and pub classics, while more substantial dishes appear on the à la carte. Influences range from Asia to the Med.
Menu £ 15 (lunch and early dinner) - Carte £ 22/36
Holy Cross ✉ DY9 9QL - Southwest : 0.5 mi - 𝒞 (01562) 730 319
- www.bellandcrossclent.co.uk - Closed 25 December and dinner 26 December and 1 January

CLEY-NEXT-THE-SEA - Norfolk → See Blakeney

CLIFTON - Cumbria → See Penrith

CLIPSHAM

Rutland - Regional map n° **9**-C2
▶ London 101 mi - Leicester 35 mi - Coventry 72 mi - Nottingham 38 mi

🍴 Olive Branch & Beech House

BRITISH TRADITIONAL · PUB Characterful village pub made up of a series of small rooms which feature open fires and exposed beams. The selection of rustic British dishes changes daily, reflecting the seasons and keeping things fiercely local. These are accompanied by real ales, homemade lemonade and vodka made from hedgerow berries. Bedrooms, across the road, are cosy and thoughtfully finished.
Menu £ 20/30 - Carte £ 26/43
6 rooms 🍽 - 🛏£ 98/113 🛏🛏£ 115/195
Main St ✉ LE15 7SH - 𝒞 (01780) 410 355 (booking essential)
- www.theolivebranchpub.com

CLOVELLY

Devon – ✉ Bideford – Pop. 439 – Regional map n° **1**-B1
▶ London 241 mi – Barnstaple 18 mi – Exeter 52 mi – Penzance 92 mi

⌂ **Red Lion**   ☆ ⇐ 🏠 **P**

TRADITIONAL · COSY Traditional inn set in a wonderful location under the cliffs, right on the harbourfront. Good-sized, comfortable bedrooms all have sea views; the newest and largest rooms are in the converted sail loft. Classic dishes and a superb vista in the dining room; lighter snacks in the bar.
17 rooms ⊆ – †£ 102/115 ††£ 155/185
The Quay ✉ *EX39 5TF* – ☏ *(01237) 431 237* – *www.clovelly.co.uk*

CLYST HYDON

Devon – Regional map n° **1**-D2
▶ London 188 mi – Bristol 74 mi – Exeter 12 mi

🍴 **Five Bells Inn**   🍺 🏠 ⚙ **P**

BRITISH TRADITIONAL · PUB Pretty, thatched, Grade II listed pub, deep in the Devon countryside. Experienced chef uses the finest local ingredients in well-balanced dishes with real clarity of flavour. Blackboard of pub favourites and a more creative à la carte. Set lunch menu is excellent value for money. Smooth, friendly service.
Menu £ 15 (weekday lunch) – Carte £ 28/40
✉ *EX15 2NT – West : 0.5 mi on Clyst St Lawrence rd*
– ☏ *(01884) 277 288 (bookings advisable at dinner)*
– *www.fivebells.uk.com*

COALPORT – Telford and Wrekin ➜ See Ironbridge

COGGESHALL

Essex – ✉ Colchester – Pop. 3 919 – Regional map n° **7**-C2
▶ London 49 mi – Braintree 6 mi – Chelmsford 16 mi – Colchester 9 mi

✗✗ **Ranfield's Brasserie**   🍴

INTERNATIONAL · BRASSERIE Characterful 16C building on the market square; its walls packed with pictures and prints. Globally-influenced dishes are made up of lots of different ingredients. Service is warm and welcoming and it has a loyal local following.
Menu £ 15 (lunch and early dinner) – Carte £ 24/74
4-6 Stoneham St ✉ *CO6 1TT* – ☏ *(01376) 561 453* – *www.baumannsbrasserie.co.uk*
– *Closed first 2 weeks January and Monday*

at Pattiswick Northwest: 3 mi by A120 (Braintree Rd) – ✉ Coggeshall

🍴 **Compasses at Pattiswick**   🍺 🏠 ⚙ ⇔ **P**

REGIONAL · PUB Remote pub with far-reaching views; make the most of these with a seat in the garden. Smart, spacious interior with open fires, chatty staff and a warm, relaxing feel. Wide-ranging menu of traditional English dishes and nursery puddings.
Menu £ 15 (weekdays) – Carte £ 19/36
Compasses Rd ✉ *CM77 8BG* – ☏ *(01376) 561 322*
– *www.thecompassesatpattiswick.co.uk*

COLCHESTER

Essex – Pop. 119 441 – Regional map n° **7**-D2
▶ London 52 mi – Cambridge 48 mi – Ipswich 18 mi

XX Memoirs

BRITISH MODERN · ELEGANT The town's old Victorian library is a grand, impressive place, with high beamed ceilings, wood-panelled walls and a big stone tablet depicting the Great Exhibition of 1853. The equally large menu of classics has Portuguese touches.

Menu £ 15 (weekdays)/35 – Carte £ 27/86

*65 West Stockwell St ⊠ CO1 1HE – ℰ (01206) 562 400
– www.memoirscolchester.co.uk – Closed Sunday*

X Church Street Tavern

BRITISH TRADITIONAL · BRASSERIE Modern brasserie run in a relaxed, efficient manner. The trendy, shabby-chic bar serves cocktails and light bites. The upstairs restaurant offers British classics with Mediterranean influences; the early evening menu is great value.

Menu £ 19 (weekdays) – Carte £ 21/33

*3 Church St ⊠ CO1 1NF – ℰ (01206) 564 325 – www.churchstreettavern.co.uk
– Closed 25-26 December, first week January and Sunday dinner*

COLERNE – Wiltshire → See Bath

COLSTON BASSETT

Nottinghamshire – ⊠ Nottingham – Pop. 239 – Regional map n° **9**-B2
▶ London 129 mi – Leicester 23 mi – Lincoln 40 mi – Nottingham 15 mi

Ⓘ The Martins Arms

TRADITIONAL CUISINE · FORMAL Creeper-clad pub in a charming village, with a cosy, fire-lit bar and period furnished dining rooms. The menu has a meaty, masculine base, with a mix of classical and more modern dishes, and plenty of local game in season.

Carte £ 30/50

School Ln ⊠ NG12 3FD – ℰ (01949) 81 361 – www.themartinsarms.co.uk – Closed dinner 25 December and 1 January

COLTISHALL

Norfolk – ⊠ Norwich – Pop. 2 310 – Regional map n° **8**-D1
▶ London 125 mi – Norwich 8 mi – Ipswich 54 mi – Lowestoft 31 mi

ⒾⒾ Norfolk Mead

TRADITIONAL · CLASSIC Former Georgian merchant's house in 8 acres of grounds, complete with an otter lake and a walled garden. Smart modern bedrooms come in neutral hues: one has a balcony; another, a courtyard; and many have rain showers. The stylish two-roomed bistro offers complex dishes and views over the meadow to the river.

13 rooms ⊵ – ♦£ 130/190 ♦♦£ 130/190

Church Loke ⊠ NR12 7DN – ℰ (01603) 737 531 – www.norfolkmead.co.uk

COLTON

North Yorkshire – Regional map n° **13**-C2
▶ London 199 mi – Leeds 20 mi – York 10 mi

Ⓘ Ye Old Sun Inn

BRITISH TRADITIONAL · PUB Rustic, family-run pub with warming open fires and a small deli. The owners are great ambassadors for local suppliers and seasonal produce, and give regular cookery demonstrations. The smart bedroom is located in the old barn next door.

Carte £ 21/40

1 rooms ⊵ – ♦£ 70 ♦♦£ 120

Main St ⊠ LS24 8EP – ℰ (01904) 744 261 – www.yeoldsuninn.co.uk – Closed 26 and dinner 31 December

COLWALL → See Great Malvern

COLYFORD

Devon – ✉ Colyton – Regional map n° **1**-D2
▶ London 168 mi – Exeter 21 mi – Taunton 30 mi – Torquay 46 mi

🏠 **Swallows Eaves**   ✿ 🐾 🚗 ⚡ **P**

TRADITIONAL · PERSONALISED Smart creamwashed house clad with wisteria, located in the heart of a pretty village. Bright bedrooms come with books, wi-fi and views over the gardens or the Axe Valley. Relax in the comfy lounge or out on the terrace. The light, airy restaurant serves traditional dishes of locally sourced produce.

7 rooms 😋 – ♦£ 80/90 ♦♦£ 110/145
Swan Hill Rd ✉ EX24 6QJ – ℰ (01297) 553 184
– www.swallowseaves.co.uk

COMBE HAY – Bath and North East Somerset → See Bath

COMPTON BASSETT – Wiltshire → See Calne

CONDOVER – Shropshire → See Shrewsbury

CONGLETON

Cheshire East – Pop. 26 178 – Regional map n° **11**-B3
▶ London 183 mi – Liverpool 50 mi – Manchester 25 mi – Sheffield 46 mi

✕✕ **Pecks**   🍴 🅰🅲 ⇔ **P**

TRADITIONAL CUISINE · NEIGHBOURHOOD Airy, modish restaurant with a unique style. A la carte lunches are followed by monthly changing 5 and 7 course set dinners at 8pm sharp. Traditional homemade dishes use good produce and arrive in generous portions.

Menu £ 39/49 (dinner) – Carte lunch £ 27/47
Newcastle Rd, Moreton ✉ CW12 4SB – South : 2.75 mi on A 34
– ℰ (01260) 275 161 – www.pecksrest.co.uk
– Closed 25-30 December, Sunday dinner and Monday

CONSTANTINE BAY – Cornwall → See Padstow

COOKHAM

Windsor and Maidenhead – ✉ Maidenhead – Pop. 5 304 – Regional map n° **6**-C3
▶ London 32 mi – High Wycombe 7 mi – Oxford 31 mi – Reading 16 mi

🏠 **White Oak**   🍴 🏡 **P**

🐸 **BRITISH TRADITIONAL · FRIENDLY** One could argue about whether this is a contemporary pub or a pubby restaurant, as it's set up quite formally, but what is in no doubt is the warmth of the welcome and the affection in which the place is held by its many regulars. Cooking is carefully executed and full of flavour. Great value 'Menu Auberge'.

Menu £ 12/19 – Carte £ 24/41
Pound Ln ✉ SL6 9QE – ℰ (01628) 523 043
– www.thewhiteoak.co.uk
– Closed Sunday dinner

COOKHAM DEAN

Windsor and Maidenhead – Regional map n° **6**-C3
▶ London 32 mi – High Wycombe 7 mi – Oxford 31 mi – Reading 16 mi

🏠 Sanctum on the Green   ☆ 🛋 🏊 🅿

TOWNHOUSE · STYLISH Hidden away on the side of the green, a part-timbered property with large decked terraces, lovely gardens and a heated outdoor pool. Contemporary furnishings contrast with old beams. Stylish, boutique bedrooms come in bold colours. Two lounges and an open-plan bar and dining area; tasty, classical cooking.

9 rooms ⌧ – †£ 99/245 ††£ 99/245
The Old Cricket Common ⌧ SL6 9NZ – ℰ (01628) 482 638
– www.sanctumonthegreen.com

CORBRIDGE

Northumberland – Pop. 2 946 – Regional map n° **14**-A2
▶ London 300 mi – Hexham 3 mi – Newcastle upon Tyne 18 mi

🍴 Duke of Wellington   ⇔ ⇐ 🏡 ⅏ 🅿

BRITISH TRADITIONAL · DESIGN Smart, modern country style pub looking out over the Tyne Valley – head straight for the terrace on sunnier days. Pub classics sit alongside more adventurous dishes such as saddle of roe deer; breakfast includes local eggs Benedict. Stylish, luxurious bedrooms feature characterful exposed beams.

Menu £ 18 (weekdays) – Carte £ 19/36 **s**
7 rooms ⌧ – †£ 80 ††£ 120
Newton ⌧ NE43 7UL – East : 3.5 mi by A 69 – ℰ (01661) 844 446
– www.thedukeofwellingtoninn.co.uk

CORBY

Northamptonshire – Pop. 54 927 – Regional map n° **9**-C3
▶ London 100 mi – Leicester 26 mi – Northampton 22 mi – Peterborough 24 mi

🏠 Hampton by Hilton   🕰 🖭 ⅏ 🖾 🛁 🅿

BUSINESS · FUNCTIONAL Smart hotel on a business park close to Rockingham Motor Speedway. Modern bedrooms have big comfy beds and are ideal for business travellers; contemporary bathrooms have large walk-in showers. There's a bar and snack shop but no restaurant.

88 rooms ⌧ – †£ 49/129 ††£ 49/129
Rockingham Leisure Park, Princewood Rd ⌧ NN17 4AP – Northwest : 2.5 mi by Rockingham Rd off A 6116 – ℰ (01536) 211 001
– www.hamptonbyhilton.co.uk/corby

CORFE CASTLE

Dorset – ⌧ Wareham – Pop. 1 355 – Regional map n° **2**-C3
▶ London 129 mi – Bournemouth 18 mi – Weymouth 23 mi

🏠 Mortons House   ☆ 🛋 🏡 ⅏ 🍴 🅿

FAMILY · PERSONALISED An Elizabethan manor house built in the shape of an "E" to honour the Queen. The castle ruins are close above it and a steam railway runs just below. Bedrooms are classical and well-kept; one has a Victorian bath and four are in an annexe. Have lunch in the bar or lounges and dinner in the panelled restaurant.

23 rooms ⌧ – †£ 80/110 ††£ 160 – 2 suites
45 East St ⌧ BH20 5EE – ℰ (01929) 480 988 – www.mortonshouse.co.uk

CORNHILL-ON-TWEED

Northumberland – Pop. 347 – Regional map n° **14**-A1
▶ London 345 mi – Edinburgh 49 mi – Newcastle upon Tyne 59 mi

🏚 Tillmouth Park

COUNTRY HOUSE · HISTORIC Late Victorian country house set in 15 acres of prime shooting and fishing country. The welcoming interior comes with grand staircases, wood panelling and characterful stained glass. Traditional guest areas have lovely views; the most popular bedrooms boast four-poster beds. Cooking is fittingly classical.

14 rooms 🖵 – †£ 62/225 ††£ 175/225

✉ TD12 4UU – Northeast : 2.5 mi on A 698 – ☎ (01890) 882 255
– www.tillmouthpark.co.uk – Closed 2 January-2 April

🏠 Coach House

FAMILY · COSY Keenly run hotel close to the Flodden battleground, consisting of a 1680s dower house and a collection of old farm buildings set around a court-yard. The stable block houses a lounge with an honesty bar and the largest, most modern bedrooms. The cosy breakfast-cum-dining room is in the original house.

11 rooms 🖵 – †£ 50 ††£ 100/110

Crookham ✉ TD12 4TD – East : 4 mi on A 697 – ☎ (01890) 820 293
– www.coachhousecrookham.com

CORSE LAWN – Worcestershire ➜ See Tewkesbury (Glos.)

CORSHAM
Wiltshire – Pop. 13 432 – Regional map n° **2**-C2
▶ London 103 mi – Bristol 31 mi – Cardiff 64 mi – Swansea 100 mi

🍴 Methuen Arms

BRITISH MODERN · INN This 17C coaching inn is named after the family who own nearby Corsham Court. Eat in the 'Little Room' by the bar, the open-fired 'Nott Room' or the characterful restaurant. Good ingredients feature in tasty dishes; they even serve breakfast and afternoon teas. Comfy, boutique-style bedrooms await.

Menu £ 18 (weekdays) – Carte £ 27/46

14 rooms 🖵 – †£ 85/135 ††£ 110/175

2 High St ✉ SN13 0HB – ☎ (01249) 717 060 – www.themethuenarms.com

CORTON DENHAM
Somerset – ✉ Sherborne – Pop. 210 – Regional map n° **2**-C3
▶ London 123 mi – Bristol 36 mi – Cardiff 110 mi – Southampton 84 mi

🍴 Queens Arms

BRITISH MODERN · PUB Relaxed, bohemian pub with open fires and a hotch-potch of tables that include a glass-topped cartwheel. One menu offers pub fa-vourites; the other displays a more interesting array of dishes. Appealing selection of ciders, beers and whiskies. Bedrooms are modern, with good facilities – some have slipper baths.

Carte £ 24/49

8 rooms 🖵 – †£ 85/135 ††£ 115/135

✉ DT9 4LR – ☎ (01963) 220 317 (booking advisable) – www.thequeensarms.com

COTEBROOK
Cheshire West and Chester – Regional map n° **11**-A3
▶ London 186 mi – Chester 13 mi – Manchester 33 mi

🍴 Fox and Barrel

BRITISH TRADITIONAL · PUB Well-run pub with wood-panelled walls, heaving bookshelves and a smart terrace. The constantly evolving menu offers originality and interest, with sensibly priced dishes arriving neatly presented and gener-ously sized.

Carte £ 20/34

Foxbank ✉ CW6 9DZ – ☎ (01829) 760 529 – www.foxandbarrel.co.uk – Closed dinner 25-26 December and 1 January

COVERACK

Cornwall – Regional map n° **1**-A3

▶ London 300 mi – Penzance 25 mi – Truro 27 mi

⌂ **Bay** ♔ ← 🖨 ⅙ 🅿

COUNTRY HOUSE · COSY Imposing, family-run country house located in a pretty fishing village and boasting views over the bay. Homely lounge and bar. Spotless, modern bedrooms with a slight New England edge. Dining room and conservatory offer a classical daily menu and local seafood specials.

13 rooms (dinner included) ☲ – ♦£ 75/195 ♦♦£ 110/250

North Corner ✉ *TR12 6TF – ℰ (01326) 280 464 – www.thebayhotel.co.uk – Closed 1-22 December and 3 January-mid March*

COWAN BRIDGE

Lancashire – Regional map n° **11**-B1

▶ London 263 mi – Carlisle 61 mi – Lancaster 18 mi

XX **Hipping Hall** ← 🖨 🅿

MODERN CUISINE · ROMANTIC Charming part-15/16C house – a former blacksmith's – named after the stepping (or 'hipping') stones over the beck by the old washhouse. The formal, airy restaurant has a superb beamed ceiling, a minstrel's gallery and an almost baronial feel. Well-executed modern dishes use top quality local ingredients. Sleek white bedrooms feature deep pile carpets and modern bathrooms.

Menu £ 30/55

15 rooms ☲ – ♦£ 159/319 ♦♦£ 159/319 – 2 suites

on A 65 ✉ *LA6 2JJ – ℰ (01524) 271 187 – www.hippinghall.com – dinner only and lunch Saturday-Sunday – Closed 7-10 January*

COWLEY

Gloucestershire – Regional map n° **2**-C1

▶ London 105 mi – Swindon 28 mi – Gloucester 14 mi – Cheltenham 6 mi

🏨 **Cowley Manor** ♔ ⅗ 🖨 🛋 🗔 ⊕ 🏊 🖥 🎱 ※ 🛁 🅿

LUXURY · CONTEMPORARY Impressive Regency house in 55 acres, with beautiful formal gardens, a superb spa, and lake views from some of the bedrooms. Original features and retro furnishings mix with bold colours and modern fittings to create a laid-back, understated vibe. The carved wood panelling in the restaurant is a feature.

30 rooms ☲ – ♦£ 225/575 ♦♦£ 225/575 – 8 suites

✉ *GL53 9NL – ℰ (01242) 870 900 – www.cowleymanor.com*

COWSHILL

Durham – Regional map n° **14**-A3

▶ London 295 mi – Newcastle upon Tyne 42 mi – Stanhope 10 mi – Wolsingham 16 mi

🏠 **Low Cornriggs Farm** ♔ ⅗ ← 🖨 ※ 🅿 🍽

FAMILY · COSY Extended stone farmhouse dating back 300 years and offering lovely views over Weardale. Cosy flag-floored lounge with an open fire. Dine in the conservatory in summer or the beamed dining room in winter; steak pie is a speciality. Pine-furnished bedrooms have up-to-date facilities and neat, compact bathrooms.

3 rooms ☲ – ♦£ 47 ♦♦£ 70

Weardale ✉ *DL13 1AQ – Northwest : 0.75 mi on A 689 – ℰ (01388) 537 600 – www.cornriggsfarm.co.uk – Closed 20 December-5 January*

CRADLEY – Herefordshire ➜ See Great Malvern

CRANBROOK

Kent – Pop. 4 225 – Regional map n° **5**-B2

▶ London 53 mi – Hastings 19 mi – Maidstone 15 mi

Cloth Hall Oast

🐾 🖼 🗏 🎉 P 🚗

HISTORIC · PERSONALISED Superbly restored oast house that was rebuilt in 2001. Antiques, family photos and fine artwork fill the drawing room. Bedrooms are well-equipped but retain some original character; one boasts a splendid four-poster bed. Communal breakfasts at an antique table set below restored rafters in the main hall.

3 rooms ⌂ – ∮£ 65/75 ∮∮£ 95/125

Coursehorn Ln ⊠ TN17 3NR – East : 1 mi by Tenterden rd
– ℰ (01580) 712 220 – www.clothhalloast.co.uk
– Closed Christmas

CRANLEIGH

Surrey – Pop. 9 905 – Regional map n° **4**-C2
▶ London 40 mi – Birmingham 150 mi – Leeds 233 mi – Sheffield 203 mi

XX Restaurant 107

A/C

MODERN CUISINE · INTIMATE The hands-on owner looked at 106 other places before deciding this light, airy first floor restaurant was the one for him. Like the subtly made-over room, the classically based dishes have a modern edge. Live music nights feature.

Menu £ 10 – Carte £ 25/41

180 High St (1st Floor) ⊠ GU6 8RG
– ℰ (01483) 276 272 – www.restaurant107.co.uk
– Closed Saturday lunch, Sunday dinner and Monday

CRAWLEY

Oxfordshire – Regional map n° **6**-A2
▶ London 111 mi – Oxford 23 mi – Cheltenham 46 mi

🍴 Lamb Inn Ⓝ

🖼 🛋 🕸 P

BRITISH MODERN · FRIENDLY Pretty stone pub in a charming village – a hit with one and all. Roaring log fires and a friendly team welcome you into the charming bar, where old milk churns act as tables. Top quality regional produce includes some rare breeds.

Carte £ 31/39

Steep Hill ⊠ OX29 9TW – ℰ (01993) 708 792
– www.lambcrawley.co.uk – Closed Sunday dinner and Monday

CRAYKE

North Yorkshire – Regional map n° **13**-C2
▶ London 217 mi – Sheffield 70 mi – York 16 mi

🍴 Durham Ox

🛋 🔄 P

REGIONAL · PUB Characterful 300 year old family-run pub, set in a sleepy hamlet next to Crayke Castle. Menus change regularly and offer hearty dishes of fresh seafood, local meats and Crayke game – with 40-day dry-aged steaks the speciality. Bedrooms are set in old farm cottages; the split-level suite has a jacuzzi bath.

Menu £ 15 (weekday lunch) – Carte £ 22/51

6 rooms ⌂ – ∮£ 100/120 ∮∮£ 120/150

Westway ⊠ YO61 4TE – ℰ (01347) 821 506 (booking essential)
– www.thedurhamox.com

CREWE

Cheshire East – Pop. 71 722 – Regional map n° **11**-B3
▶ London 174 mi – Birmingham 57 mi – Manchester 36 mi

🏛 Crewe Hall
🛜 🛗 ▥ ⊛ 🎴 ⬥ ✕ ▣ ⛟ 🅰 ⊛ 🅿

BUSINESS · HISTORIC A tree-lined drive leads up to this impressive 19C mansion designed by Edward Barry. Dramatic Jacobean features provide plenty of character in the main house and lovely chapel, while bedrooms and events rooms in the extensions are stylish and contemporary. The modern brasserie offers a menu to match.

117 rooms ⌕ – **♦**£ 89/139 **♦♦**£ 99/149 – 4 suites
*Weston Road ✉ CW1 6UZ – Southeast : 1.75 mi on A 5020 – ℰ (01270) 253 333
– www.qhotels.co.uk*

CRICKLADE

Wiltshire – Regional map n° **2**-D1
▶ London 89 mi – Birmingham 86 mi – Bristol 54 mi – Cardiff 87 mi

🍴 Red Lion
⇔ 🛗 🛋

BRITISH TRADITIONAL · RUSTIC Traditional 17C pub just off the Thames path with a characterful, low-beamed bar. Classic cooking makes good use of local produce; burgers are a speciality. They smoke some of their own meats and fish and even brew their own ales on-site. Comfortable, well-equipped bedrooms are found in the old stables.
Carte £ 21/36
5 rooms ⌕ – **♦**£ 85 **♦♦**£ 85
74 High St ✉ SN6 6DD – ℰ (01793) 750 776 – www.theredlioncricklade.co.uk

CROCKERTON – Wiltshire ➜ See Warminster

CROMER

Norfolk – Pop. 7 949 – Regional map n° **8**-D1
▶ London 132 mi – Kings Lynn 43 mi – Norwich 23 mi

𝑋 No1 Cromer
⇔ 🅰

FISH AND CHIPS · SIMPLE This is fish and chips with a difference: looking over the beach and pier and offering everything from fresh fish and battered local sausages to cockle popcorn and mushy pea fritters. Potatoes are from their farm and the varieties change throughout the year. Head up to the bistro for the best views.
Carte £ 20/28
*1 New St ✉ NR27 9HP – ℰ (01263) 512 316 – www.no1cromer.com – Closed
24-25 December and Monday except June-September*

CROOKHAM VILLAGE

Hampshire – Pop. 3 648 – Regional map n° **4**-C1
▶ London 43 mi – Sheffield 191 mi – Kingston upon Hull 219 mi – Peterborough 115 mi

🍴 Exchequer
🛋 🅿

BRITISH TRADITIONAL · INN Slick, modern pub with an inviting drinkers' area and a smart conservatory-style room. The menu offers mainly gutsy British staples but there's also a nod to the East; the blackboard best displays the kitchen's abilities. Service is keen.
Carte £ 31/35
*Crondall Rd ✉ GU51 5SU – ℰ (01252) 615 336 – www.exchequercrookham.co.uk
– Closed 25 December*

CROPSTON

Leicestershire – Regional map n° **9**-B2
▶ London 106 mi – Birmingham 49 mi – Sheffield 67 mi – Leicester 6 mi

🏠 Horseshoe Cottage Farm   ⚘ 🛋 🚗 🗺 🅿

FAMILY · CLASSIC Well-run, extended farmhouse and outbuildings, beside Bradgate Country Park. Traditional bedrooms with beams, exposed stonework and coordinating fabrics. Small breakfast room and a larger, high-ceilinged drawing room, with a solid oak table where communal dinners are served; local and garden produce feature.

3 rooms ⌧ – ♦£ 65/70 ♦♦£ 100/105

Roecliffe Rd, Hallgates ⊠ LE7 7HQ – Northwest : 1 mi on Woodhouse Eaves rd
– ☏ (0116) 235 00 38 – www.horseshoecottagefarm.com

CROSTHWAITE – Cumbria ➜ See Kendal

CRUDWELL – Wiltshire ➜ See Malmesbury

CUCKFIELD
West Sussex – Pop. 3 500 – Regional map n° **4**-D2
▶ London 37 mi – Croydon 27 mi – Barnet 51 mi – Ealing 48 mi

🏠 Ockenden Manor   

HISTORIC · STYLISH Part-Elizabethan manor house in 9 acres of parkland. Kickback in the cosy panelled bar or beside the grand fireplace in the elegant drawing room. Stay in a characterful period bedroom or one of the modern rooms above the chic spa.

28 rooms ⌧ – ♦£ 139/390 ♦♦£ 189/390 – 3 suites

Ockenden Ln ⊠ RH17 5LD – ☏ (01444) 416 111
– www.ockenden-manor.co.uk

❀ **Ockenden Manor** – See restaurant listing

✗✗✗ Ockenden Manor   🛋 ⅙ 🅿

❀ **MODERN CUISINE · ELEGANT** Contemporary orangery dining room opening onto the manor house gardens and affording pleasant views over the South Downs. The passionate chef uses seasonal local produce to create appealing, original menus. Cooking is refined, flavours are well-balanced and dishes show good attention to detail.

➜ Skye langoustines with buttered lettuce, cauliflower and crispy pork belly. Sussex monkfish with Parma ham, braised fennel, onion purée and wild garlic. Caramelised lemon tart and blackcurrant sorbet.

Menu £ 20 (weekday lunch)/60

Ockenden Manor Hotel, Ockenden Ln ⊠ RH17 5LD
– ☏ (01444) 416 111 (booking essential) – www.ockenden-manor.co.uk

CUNDALL
North Yorkshire – Regional map n° **13**-B2
▶ London 222 mi – Leeds 36 mi – York 29 mi

🏠 Cundall Lodge Farm   ⋖ 🛋 🚗 🅿

FAMILY · HOMELY Grade II listed Georgian farmhouse on a working arable farm; its 150 acres include a stretch of the River Swale. Country bedrooms come with homemade shortbread and Roberts radios. The friendly owners have great local knowledge.

3 rooms ⌧ – ♦£ 55/65 ♦♦£ 85/95

⊠ YO61 2RN – Northwest : 0.5 mi on Asenby rd
– ☏ (01423) 360 203 – www.cundall-lodgefarm.co.uk
– Closed January and Christmas

CURY – Cornwall ➜ See Helston

DALTON-IN-FURNESS
Cumbria – Pop. 7 827 – Regional map n° **12**-A3
▶ London 283 mi – Barrow-in-Furness 3 mi – Kendal 30 mi – Lancaster 41 mi

🏠 Clarence House   ☂ ⛵ ♨ 🅿

FAMILY · HOMELY The majority of guests here are repeat customers – which says a lot about the way the family run it. Relax in the peaceful, mature gardens or in one of the plush sitting rooms. Some bedrooms come with jacuzzis or four-posters.

28 rooms ☄ – ♛£ 105 ♛♛£ 140
Skelgate ✉ *LA15 8BQ –* ☎ *(01229) 462 508 – www.clarencehouse-hotel.com
– Closed 26 December*
Clarence House – See restaurant listing

XX Clarence House   🅿

BRITISH MODERN · FAMILY This is a proper country house hotel restaurant with luxurious furnishings and willing service. Dishes are traditionally based but are modern in their execution. They use the finest Cumbrian meats, so steak is always a good bet.

Carte £ 25/48
Clarence House Hotel, Skelgate ✉ *LA15 8BQ –* ☎ *(01229) 462 508
– www.clarencehouse-hotel.co.uk – Closed 26 December*

DARGATE – Kent → See Faversham

DARLEY ABBEY – Derby → See Derby

DARLINGTON
Darlington – Pop. 92 363 – Regional map n° **13**-B1
▶ London 251 mi – Leeds 61 mi – Newcastle upon Tyne 35 mi

🏠 Houndgate Townhouse   ☂ 🏠 ⊡ ♿ 🍽

TOWNHOUSE · CONTEMPORARY This smart Georgian townhouse – formerly a registry office – is set on a quiet square in the heart of town. Inside, stylish colour schemes and contemporary furnishings create a boutique feel; bedroom Two has a bath in the room. The bistro has comfy booths, a terrace and a menu of modern classics.

8 rooms ☄ – ♛£ 80/135 ♛♛£ 90/145
11 Houndgate ✉ *DL1 5RF –* ☎ *(01325) 486 011 – www.houndgatetownhouse.co.uk*

🏠 Clow Beck House   ☂ 🐾 ⪕ ⛵ 🔄 ♿ 🍽 🅿

FAMILY · COSY Collection of converted farm buildings not far from the River Tees. Welcoming owners and a homely interior. Immaculately kept, tastefully furnished bedrooms come with iPod docks, bathrobes and chocolates; the larger ones have dressing rooms. Home-cooked dinners, with a puzzle supplied while you wait.

13 rooms ☄ – ♛£ 90 ♛♛£ 140
Monk End Farm, Croft-on-Tees ✉ *DL2 2SP – South : 5.25 mi by A 167 off Barton rd –* ☎ *(01325) 721 075 – www.clowbeckhouse.co.uk – Closed 24 December-3 January*

at Hurworth-on-Tees South: 5.5 mi by A167

🏨 Rockliffe Hall   ☂ 🐾 ⛵ 🖼 🔲 🌐 🏋 ♨ ⊡ ♿ 🎹 🍽 ♨ 🅿

LUXURY · STYLISH Impressive red-brick manor house in 376 acres of grounds, complete with a championship golf course and extensive, state-of-the-art leisure facilities. The original Victorian house has grand guest areas and characterful bedrooms; rooms in the extensions are more modern. Dining options include an ambitious restaurant menu, modern brasserie dishes, classics and grills.

61 rooms ☄ – ♛£ 210/295 ♛♛£ 265/440
✉ *DL2 2DU –* ☎ *(01325) 729 999 – www.rockliffehall.com*
The Orangery – See restaurant listing

XxX The Orangery 🅝   🖵 & 🕪 🅿

MODERN CUISINE · ELEGANT An elegant glass extension to the original hall of a smart country house hotel. Choose from three 5 course menus – 'Sea' ,'Land & Sea' and a vegetarian menu. Dishes are carefully crafted and eye-catching, with contrasting textures and flavours.

Menu £ 55 – set menu only

Rockcliffe Hall Hotel, ✉ DL2 2DU – ℰ (01325) 729 999 – www.rockliffehall.com
– dinner only – Closed Sunday and Monday

🍴 Bay Horse   🔭 🕪 ⇔ 🅿

MODERN CUISINE · PUB A smart and cosy dining pub in a delightful village, with beams, open fires, antique furnishings and a warm, welcoming feel. Wide-ranging menus offer ambitious dishes with distinctive flavours, and friendly locals provide charming service.

Menu £ 17 (weekday lunch)/25 – Carte £ 31/49

45 The Green ✉ DL2 2AA – ℰ (01325) 720 663 – www.thebayhorsehurworth.com
– Closed 25-26 December

at Summerhouse Northwest: 6.5 mi by A68 on B6279

XX Raby Hunt (James Close)   ⇔ 🅿
❀   **BRITISH MODERN · CLASSIC** A former inn in a rural hamlet, where the Raby Castle hunt hounds were once kennelled; now a stylishly decorated, family-run restaurant with a small modern bar and an elegant dining room. The passionate, self-taught chef uses first class ingredients to create unfussy modern dishes with bold flavours and a confident touch. Bedrooms are comfortable and contemporary.
➜ Raw beef with pickled ramson capers, anchovy and basil emulsions. Deer with caramelised cauliflower, venison ragu and kale. Liquorice with lime, sheep's yoghurt ice cream and fennel.

Menu £ 35/80

2 rooms ⌖ – ♦£ 125/150 ♦♦£ 125/150

✉ DL2 3UD – ℰ (01325) 374 237 (booking essential)
– www.rabyhuntrestaurant.co.uk – Closed 1 week spring, 1 week
autumn, 25-26 December, 1 January and Sunday-Tuesday

at Headlam Northwest: 8 mi by A67 – ✉ Gainford

🏨 Headlam Hall   🕊 🦆 ⇐ 🖥 🖼 🖵 💮 🎋 🛁 🎾 & 🏊 🅿

FAMILY · HISTORIC Family-run manor house with delightful walled gardens, set in a secluded countryside spot. Spacious sitting rooms are furnished with antiques. Well-equipped bedrooms are a mix of the traditional (in the original house) and the more contemporary. The bright conservatory restaurant offers classic dishes.

39 rooms ⌖ – ♦£ 100/140 ♦♦£ 130/170 – 3 suites

✉ DL2 3HA – ℰ (01325) 730 238 – www.headlamhall.co.uk – Closed
24-27 December

DARTMOUTH

Devon – Pop. 6 008 – Regional map n° **1**-C3
▶ London 236 mi – Exeter 36 mi – Plymouth 35 mi

🏨 Dart Marina   🕊 ⇐ 🖥 💮 🛁 🖵 & 🅿

TRADITIONAL · DESIGN Once an old boat works and chandlery, now a relaxed, modern hotel with a small spa and leisure centre. Smart, contemporary bedrooms have lovely outlooks over either the river or marina – many also boast balconies. The stylish, formal restaurant offers up-to-date versions of British classics.

49 rooms ⌖ – ♦£ 115/155 ♦♦£ 170/425

Sandquay Rd ✉ TQ6 9PH – ℰ (01803) 832 580 – www.dartmarina.com

🏨 Royal Castle ⎙ ⇐ 🅿

TRADITIONAL · CLASSIC Iconic 15C coaching inn consisting of two separate buildings joined by a smart glass atrium. Boldly coloured bedrooms offer good comforts – some have jacuzzi baths. Choice of two bars: one for drinkers and one serving all-day dishes. The restaurant offers modern takes on old classics and has great views.

24 rooms ⌂ – ♦£ 160/175 ♦♦£ 210/235

11 The Quay ⊠ *TQ6 9PS –* ℰ *(01803) 833 033 – www.royalcastle.co.uk*

✗✗ Seahorse ⎙ 🄰🄲

FISH AND SEAFOOD · FORMAL Smart restaurant in a lovely spot on the embankment; sit outside looking over the estuary or inside, beside the glass-walled kitchen. Seafood orientated menus have a Mediterranean bias; whole fish cooked on the Josper grill are a hit.

Menu £ 20 (lunch and early dinner) – Carte £ 31/52

5 South Embankment ⊠ *TQ6 9BH –* ℰ *(01803) 835 147 (booking essential) – www.seahorserestaurant.co.uk – Closed Monday and Sunday dinner*

✗ Rockfish 🄰🄲

FISH AND SEAFOOD · NEIGHBOURHOOD Buzzy 'beach shack' style eatery run by a chatty team. Good old comfort dishes arrive in paper-lined baskets and rely on sustainable produce. Closely set tables have paper cloths proclaiming 'fish so fresh, tomorrow's are still in the sea'.

Carte £ 17/34

8 South Embankment ⊠ *TQ6 9BH –* ℰ *(01803) 832 800 (bookings not accepted) – www.rockfishdevon.co.uk – Closed 25 December*

at Kingswear East: via lower ferry – ⊠ Dartmouth

🏠 Nonsuch House ⎙ ⇐ 🖴 ⁘

TOWNHOUSE · CLASSIC Charming Edwardian house run by friendly hands-on owners; boasting lovely views over the castle, town and sea. Bright Mediterranean-style décor blends nicely with original features. Bedrooms are spacious and well-appointed and one has a small balcony. Tea and homemade cake on arrival; local, seasonal cooking and excellent views from the conservatory dining room.

4 rooms ⌂ – ♦£ 75/150 ♦♦£ 115/195

Church Hill ⊠ *TQ6 0BX – from lower ferry take first right onto Church Hill before Steam Packet Inn –* ℰ *(01803) 752 829 – www.nonsuch-house.co.uk – Closed January*

at Strete Southwest: 4.5 mi on A379 – ⊠ Dartmouth

🏨 Strete Barton House ⎙ ⇐ 🖴 ⁘ 🅿

HISTORIC · PERSONALISED Attractive part-16C manor house in a quiet village, with partial views over the rooftops to the sea. The contemporary interior has a personal style; bedrooms come with bold feature walls and modern facilities. Homemade cake is served on arrival and top quality local ingredients feature at breakfast.

6 rooms ⌂ – ♦£ 105/160 ♦♦£ 105/160

Totnes Rd ⊠ *TQ6 0RU –* ℰ *(01803) 770 364 – www.stretebarton.co.uk – Closed 2 weeks January*

✗ Laughing Monk

TRADITIONAL CUISINE · BISTRO Built in 1839 as the village schoolhouse; the original wooden floor and a huge stone fireplace remain. Tasty, traditional dishes feature meats from nearby farms and seafood from local waters; cooking is unfussy and uses classical pairings.

Carte £ 26/50

Totnes Rd ⊠ *TQ6 0RN –* ℰ *(01803) 770 639 – www.thelaughingmonkdevon.co.uk – dinner only – Closed December, January, Sunday and Monday*

DATCHWORTH

Hertfordshire – Regional map n° **7**-B2

▶ London 31 mi – Luton 15 mi – Stevenage 6 mi

⌂ **Coltsfoot Country Retreat** 　　🛎🐕🚗🏠🛗🛜🅿

RURAL · HISTORIC A former farmhouse dating back to the 16C; now a contemporary hotel and a popular wedding venue. Some of the spacious bedrooms have terraces; Room 15 is where the prize bull was once kept. The bar and restaurant are in a converted barn and offer pleasant country views; menus are classical with a modern twist.

15 rooms ☐ – ♦£ 118/175 ♦♦£ 138/199

Coltsfoot Lane, Bulls Green ✉ *SG3 6SB – South 0.75 mi by Bramfield Rd, turning at 'The Horns' –* ✆ *(01438) 212 800 – www.coltsfoot.com*

🍽 **Tilbury** 　　🚗🏠🅿

TRADITIONAL CUISINE · TRADITIONAL Charming 18C inn run by two brothers, set just off the village green. There's something for everyone here: pub classics will please traditionalists, while dishes like maple-roasted guinea fowl really showcase the kitchen's skills.

Menu £ 15 (weekdays) – Carte £ 23/43

1 Watton Rd ✉ *SG3 6TB –* ✆ *(01483) 815 550 – www.thetilbury.co.uk – Closed Monday and Sunday dinner*

DAVENTRY

Northamptonshire – Pop. 23 879 – Regional map n° **9**-B3

▶ London 79 mi – Coventry 23 mi – Leicester 31 mi – Northampton 13 mi

⌂ **Fawsley Hall** 　　🛎🐕🏊🚗🖼♨🜨🏋🎾🛗🛜🧖🅿

LUXURY · CLASSIC Set in 2,000 peaceful acres, a luxurious Tudor manor house with Georgian and Victorian extensions. Have afternoon tea in the Great Hall or unwind in the exclusive leisure club and spa. Smart, well-appointed bedrooms vary from wing to wing. Have lunch in the courtyard and dinner in the atmospheric restaurant.

60 rooms ☐ – ♦£ 125/500 ♦♦£ 125/500 – 2 suites

Fawsley ✉ *NN11 3BA – South : 6.5 mi by A 45 off A 361 –* ✆ *(01327) 892 000 – www.handpicked.co.uk/fawsley*

at Staverton Southwest: 2.75 mi by A45 off A425 – ✉ Daventry

⌂ **Colledges House** 　　🚗🛜🅿

TRADITIONAL · PERSONALISED Lovely 17C thatched cottage and barn, run by an equally charming owner. The cosy lounge is filled with antiques and curios; the conservatory is a pleasant spot come summer. Traditional bedrooms have floral fabrics and good extras.

3 rooms ☐ – ♦£ 70 ♦♦£ 99

Oakham Ln ✉ *NN11 6JQ – off Glebe Ln –* ✆ *(01327) 702 737 – www.colledgeshouse.co.uk*

DAYLESFORD – Gloucestershire ➔ See Stow-on-the-Wold

DEAL

Kent – Pop. 30 555 – Regional map n° **5**-D2

▶ London 78 mi – Canterbury 19 mi – Dover 8 mi – Margate 16 mi

⌂ **Dunkerley's** 　　🛎🛜

FAMILY · HOMELY Very welcoming hotel in a good spot just off the main street, opposite the beach and pier. Bedrooms are a mix of styles: some are modern, some are more classical and some have feature wallpaper; four of them come with spa baths.

16 rooms ☐ – ♦£ 80/110 ♦♦£ 120/150

19 Beach St ✉ *CT14 7AH –* ✆ *(01304) 375 016 – www.dunkerleys.co.uk*

Dunkerley's – See restaurant listing

🏠 Number One   🍴

TOWNHOUSE · MODERN Stylish guesthouse near the promenade, run by an enthusiastic owner. Bedrooms have bold wallpapers, fine linen and luxury bathrooms with tower showers. A delightful breakfast room hosts award-winning breakfasts of Kentish produce.

4 rooms ☑ – 🛏£ 67/95 🛏🛏£ 77/105

1 Ranelagh Rd ✉ *CT14 7BG* – ✆ *(01304) 364 459* – *www.numberonebandb.co.uk*

✕✕ Dunkerley's   🍴 AC

FISH AND SEAFOOD · INTIMATE Traditional hotel restaurant with original stained glass windows, a terrace and views over the Channel. Cooking is hearty, with plenty of seafood on offer. Specials usually come from the day boats and there's a good range of wines.

Menu £ 12/29

Dunkerley's Hotel, 19 Beach St ✉ *CT14 7AH* – ✆ *(01304) 375 016*
– www.dunkerleys.co.uk

✕ Victuals & Co

BRITISH MODERN · BISTRO Found down a narrow passageway, this enthusiastically run restaurant is named after the victuallers who supplied the local ships. Classic dishes are given modern twists; try some small plates followed by a tasting plate at lunch.

Menu £ 16 (weekday dinner)/42 – Carte £ 26/45

St Georges Passage ✉ *CT14 6TA* – ✆ *(01304) 374 389* – *www.victualsandco.com*
– Closed Monday-Tuesday and lunch Wednesday-Thursday

at Worth Northwest: 5 mi by A258

🏠 Solley Farm House   🚪 🍴 P

FAMILY · PERSONALISED Attractive 300 year old house overlooking the duck pond and run by a charming owner. In the beamed lounge, a vast inglenook fireplace takes centre stage; colour-themed bedrooms come with great extras. Have breakfast on the terrace.

3 rooms ☑ – 🛏£ 95/105 🛏🛏£ 140/155

The Street ✉ *CT14 0DG* – ✆ *(01304) 613 701* – *www.solleyfarmhouse.co.uk*

DEDHAM

Essex – ✉ Colchester – Pop. 719 – Regional map n° **7**-D2
▶ London 63 mi – Chelmsford 30 mi – Colchester 8 mi – Ipswich 12 mi

🏠 Maison Talbooth   🎾 🕸 ⚞ 🚪 ⟁ 🍴 P

LUXURY · PERSONALISED Charming, part-Georgian house in rolling countryside, with a modern, country house feel and views over the river valley. Individually decorated bedrooms boast quality furnishings and come in a mix of classical and contemporary styles. Seek out the tennis court and lovely, year-round heated swimming pool.

12 rooms ☑ – 🛏£ 225/425 🛏🛏£ 225/425

Stratford Rd ✉ *CO7 6HN – West : 0.5 mi* – ✆ *(01206) 322 367*
– www.milsomhotels.com

Le Talbooth – See restaurant listing

🏠 Milsoms   🎾 🚪 🍴 🛁 P

TRADITIONAL · MODERN A late 19C country house with modern additions, overlooking Dedham Vale; its interior is stylish and contemporary, with comfortable and well-equipped New England style bedrooms. All-day dining from an appealing menu in the airy bar-restaurant with its covered terrace.

15 rooms ☑ – 🛏£ 135/210 🛏🛏£ 135/210

Stratford Rd ✉ *CO7 6HW – West : 0.75 mi* – ✆ *(01206) 322 795*
– www.milsomhotels.com

XxX Le Talbooth

BRITISH MODERN · LUXURY Delightful hotel restaurant with numerous private rooms and a lovely terrace, in an attractive riverside setting. To celebrate its 60th birthday, it was cleverly and subtly updated, with a zinc bar and stunning Italian chandeliers. Menus are light and modern, and are accompanied by a well-chosen wine list.

Menu £ 31 (weekday lunch) – Carte £ 40/62

Maison Talbooth Hotel, Gun Hill ⊠ CO7 6HN – West : 0.75 mi – ℰ (01206) 323 150 – www.milsomhotels.com – Closed Sunday dinner October-May

🏠 Sun Inn

ITALIAN · INN Brightly painted 15C pub in the heart of a picturesque village. Relaxed dining room and beautiful wooden bar stocked with real ales and homemade sausage rolls. Hearty, rustic Italian dishes – many available in two sizes – and a large selection of tasty antipasti. Rustic bedrooms; two have a New England feel.

Carte £ 20/33

7 rooms ⊆ – ♥£ 85/120 ♥♥£ 135

High St ⊠ CO7 6DF – ℰ (01206) 323 351 – www.thesuninndedham.com – Closed 25-26 December

DELPH

Greater Manchester – Pop. 2 224 – Regional map n° **11**-B2

▶ London 215 mi – Manchester 13 mi – Oldham 6 mi

🏠 Old Bell Inn ⓝ

BRITISH TRADITIONAL · TRADITIONAL 18C coaching inn set high up on the moors, with a cosy bar, a smart modern brasserie and well-kept bedrooms. Choose from sharing platters, hearty pub favourites, 35 day matured steaks and more modern set menus. Their gin selection features over 500 different types and is the biggest in the world.

Menu £ 25 (lunch and early dinner) – Carte £ 22/43

18 rooms ⊆ – ♥£ 58/70 ♥♥£ 95/120

Huddersfield Rd ⊠ OL3 5EG – ℰ (01457) 870 130 – www.theoldbellinn.co.uk

DENHAM

Buckinghamshire – Pop. 1 432 – Regional map n° **6**-D3

▶ London 20 mi – Buckingham 42 mi – Oxford 41 mi – Croydon 26 mi

🏠 Swan Inn

BRITISH TRADITIONAL · PUB Located in a picture postcard village; a wisteria-clad, red-brick Georgian pub with a pleasant terrace and mature gardens. Menus change with the seasons and offer plenty of interest – the side dishes are appealing and pudding is a must.

Carte £ 22/39

Village Rd ⊠ UB9 5BH – ℰ (01895) 832 085 (booking essential) – www.swaninndenham.co.uk – Closed 25-26 December

DERBY

Derby – Pop. 255 394 – Regional map n° **9**-B2

▶ London 132 mi – Birmingham 40 mi – Coventry 49 mi – Leicester 29 mi

🏨 Cathedral Quarter

TRADITIONAL · PERSONALISED Boutique-style hotel retaining many original Victorian features including mosaic floors, ornate ceilings and marble pillars. Bedrooms vary in size but all are furnished in a contemporary style. The first floor restaurant has wood panelling, an 8-seater chef's table and a menu of ambitious modern dishes.

38 rooms ⊆ – ♥£ 69/89 ♥♥£ 99/249

Town plan: Y-x – *16 St. Mary's Gate ⊠ DE1 3JR – ℰ (01332) 546 080 – www.cathedralquarterhotel.com*

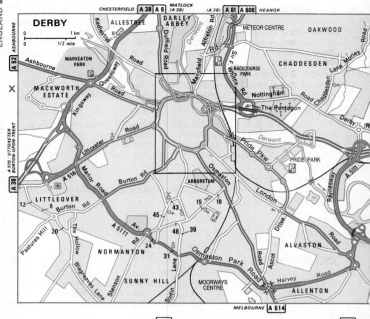

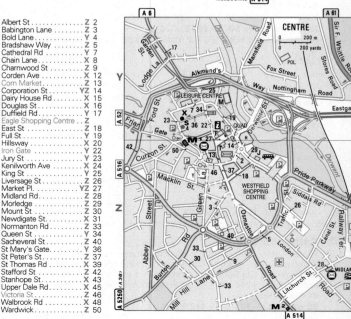

424

X **Ibérico World Tapas**   🕭 AC 🗏

MEDITERRANEAN · FRIENDLY It's all in the name: the main concept is Spanish, with plenty of tapas dishes and Spanish classics, but there's also a more global feel, courtesy of Mediterranean-style décor and some dishes with Asian origins. The imported hams are a must-try, and the lunch and early evening menus are excellent value.

Menu £12 (weekdays)/24 – Carte £14/39

Town plan: Y-s – *9-11 Bold Ln* ⊠ *DE1 3NT* – ℰ *(01332) 345 456*
– www.ibericotapas.com/derby – Closed Sunday

at Darley Abbey North: 2.5 mi off A6 – Plan: X – ⊠ Derby

XX **Darleys**   AC 🕭 P

MODERN CUISINE · FRIENDLY Popular weir-side restaurant, located in the old canteen of a 19C silk mill. Start with drinks in the modern bar-lounge or on the attractive terrace. Good value lunches are followed by more ambitious European dishes in the evening.

Menu £23 (lunch) – Carte £36/44

Darley Abbey Mill ⊠ *DE22 1DZ* – ℰ *(01332) 364 987 (booking advisable)*
– www.darleys.com – Closed 25 December-15 January, Sunday dinner and bank holidays

DEVIZES

Wiltshire – Pop. 18 064 – Regional map n° **2**-C2

▶ London 98 mi – Bristol 38 mi – Salisbury 25 mi – Southampton 50 mi

🏠 **Blounts Court Farm**   🐎 🖙 🌿 P

COUNTRY HOUSE · PERSONALISED Delightfully run farmhouse on a 150 acre working farm; the village cricket team play in one of their fields! The snug interior consists of a cosy lounge and a spacious breakfast room filled with clocks and curios. Warm, well-kept bedrooms show good attention to detail. Pastel artwork and country photos abound.

3 rooms ⊡ – ♦£52/58 ♦♦£82/88

Coxhill Ln, Potterne ⊠ *SN10 5PH* – *South : 2.25 mi by A 360* – ℰ *(01380) 727 180*
– www.blountscourtfarm.co.uk

at Rowde Northwest: 2 mi by A361 on A342 – ⊠ Devizes

🍴 **George & Dragon**   ⇔ 🖙 🏡 P

FISH AND SEAFOOD · PUB Rustic and cosy 16C coaching inn with open fires, solid stone floors and wooden beams. The oft-changing menu has a strong emphasis on seafood, with fish delivered daily from Cornwall. Old-world charm meets modern facilities in the individually designed bedrooms.

Menu £17 (weekdays)/20 – Carte £25/36

3 rooms ⊡ – ♦£75/125 ♦♦£75/125

High St ⊠ *SN10 2PN* – ℰ *(01380) 723 053*
– www.thegeorgeanddragonrowde.co.uk – Closed Sunday dinner

DIDSBURY – Greater Manchester → See Manchester

DINNINGTON

South Yorkshire – Pop. 19 860 – Regional map n° **13**-B3

▶ London 40 mi – Birmingham 150 mi – Leeds 233 mi – Sheffield 203 mi

🏠 **Throapham House**   🖙 🌿 P

COUNTRY HOUSE · PERSONALISED Comfy 19C house run by a friendly couple. Well-equipped, individually decorated bedrooms come with extra touches; Bradwell, with its beams, is the most characterful. Spacious first floor lounge. Home-made jams feature at breakfast.

3 rooms ⊡ – ♦£65/85 ♦♦£85/110

Oldcotes Rd, Throapham ⊠ *S25 2QS* – *North : 1.5 mi by B 6060 on B 6463*
– ℰ (01909) 562 208 – www.throapham-house.co.uk

DITCHLING
East Sussex – Pop. 1 476 – Regional map n° **4**-D2
▶ London 48 mi – Brighton and Hove 10 mi – Hastings 40 mi

Tovey Lodge
FAMILY · PERSONALISED Well-appointed guesthouse with mature gardens and views over the South Downs. Smart bedrooms have modern facilities; Maple, with its balcony, is the best. Beyond the communal breakfast room you'll find a swimming pool and sauna.
5 rooms ☑ – †£ 65/155 ††£ 85/190
Underhill Ln ✉ BN6 8XE – South : 1 mi by B 2112 off Ditchling Beacon rd – ℰ (01273) 256 156 – www.toveylodge.co.uk – Closed January

DODDINGTON
Kent – Regional map n° **5**-C2
▶ London 50 mi – Maidstone 15 mi – Faversham 7 mi

Old Vicarage
FAMILY · CLASSIC Grade II listed former vicarage with 16C origins, where wooden beams and exposed stone blend with modern furnishings. There's an impressive galleried hall and a striking antique dining table where the excellent breakfasts are taken. Good-sized bedrooms feature coffee machines and Bose sound systems.
5 rooms ☑ – †£ 60/72 ††£ 85/105
Church Hill ✉ ME9 0BD – ℰ (01795) 886 136 – www.oldvicaragedoddington.co.uk – Closed 24 December-2 January

DOGMERSFIELD
Hampshire – Regional map n° **4**-C1
▶ London 44 mi – Farnham 6 mi – Fleet 2 mi

Four Seasons
LUXURY · CLASSIC An attractive part-Georgian house in 350 acres of parkland, where you can try your hand at all manner of outdoor pursuits. Luxurious bedrooms are well-equipped and come with marble bathrooms. A superb spa is found in the converted coach house. The contemporary restaurant offers classic dishes presented in a modern style, while the casual bistro offers steaks and grills.
133 rooms ☑ – †£ 285/490 ††£ 285/490 – 22 suites
Dogmersfield Park, Chalky Ln ✉ RG27 8TD – ℰ (01252) 853 000 – www.fourseasons.com/hampshire

DONCASTER
South Yorkshire – Pop. 109 805 – Regional map n° **13**-C3
▶ London 173 mi – Kingston-upon-Hull 46 mi – Leeds 30 mi – Nottingham 46 mi

Mount Pleasant
BUSINESS · CONTEMPORARY Well-run hotel with smart, spacious, individually styled bedrooms – many with feature beds, jacuzzi baths and even saunas; try a room with a four-poster or glass bed. Good range of beauty treatments in the spa. Characterful bar and a formal restaurant with an impressive wall tapestry; extensive, classic menu.
68 rooms ☑ – †£ 79/149 ††£ 99/259 – 2 suites
Great North Rd ✉ DN11 0HW – Southeast : 6 mi on A 638 – ℰ (01302) 868 696 – www.mountpleasant.co.uk – Closed 24-25 December

DONHEAD-ST-ANDREW
Wiltshire – Regional map n° **2**-C3
▶ London 115 mi – Bournemouth 34 mi – Poole 32 mi – Bath 37 mi

🍴 The Forester ⟵ 🏠 P

BRITISH TRADITIONAL · RUSTIC Gloriously rustic, 13C thatched pub, hidden down narrow lanes in a delightful village. Exposed stone walls and vast open fires feature throughout. Seasonal menus showcase well-prepared, flavoursome dishes with a classical country base and a refined edge; they also offer a daily seafood selection.

Menu £19/24 – Carte £24/37

Lower St ⊠ SP7 9EE – 𝒞(01747) 828 038
– www.theforesterdonheadstandrew.co.uk – Closed Sunday dinner

Your discoveries and comments help us improve the guide. Please let us know about your experiences - good or bad!

DORCHESTER

Dorset – Pop. 19 060 – Regional map n° **2**-C3
▶ London 135 mi – Bournemouth 27 mi – Exeter 53 mi – Southampton 53 mi

🏠 Little Court ⟵ ⊐ ✻ ⅋ P

TRADITIONAL · CLASSIC Lutyens-style house boasting Edwardian wood and brickwork, leaded windows and mature gardens with a pool and tennis court. Bedrooms display original features and modern furnishings; one has a four-poster bed.

8 rooms ⊠ – ♦£89/109 ♦♦£99/169

5 Westleaze, Charminster ⊠ DT2 9PZ – North : 1 mi by B3147, turning right at Loders garage – 𝒞(01305) 261 576 – www.littlecourt.net
– Closed 22 December-2 January

🏠 Westwood House ⅋

TOWNHOUSE · COSY Georgian townhouse built in 1815 by Lord Illchester. Spotlessly kept bedrooms have bold colours, king-sized beds and fridges containing fresh milk. The sunny drawing room opens onto a conservatory where hearty breakfasts are served.

6 rooms ⊠ – ♦£65/75 ♦♦£80/95

29 High St West ⊠ DT1 1UP – 𝒞(01305) 268 018
– www.westwoodhouse.co.uk – Closed 31 December-5 January

✕✕ Sienna 🆕 AC

REGIONAL · COSY This unassuming high street restaurant was recently taken over by a young MasterChef quarter finalist. His ambitious cooking is modern both in flavour and presentation. It has just five tables, so be sure to book ahead.

Menu £65 – Carte £26/34

36 High West St ⊠ DT1 1UP – 𝒞(01305) 250 022 (booking essential)
– www.siennarestaurant.co.uk – Closed 25-26 December, 1 January, Sunday and Monday

✕✕ Yalbury Cottage ⟷ ⟵ P

BRITISH MODERN · INTIMATE This proudly run restaurant is in an old thatched cottage and has a snug beamed interior. Cooking is gutsy and flavoursome, and produce is sourced from within 9 miles. In summer, try the English tapas, which features cured meats, cheese and bread baked in plant pots. Well-kept cottagey bedrooms are in a wing.

Menu £33/38

8 rooms ⊠ – ♦£75/85 ♦♦£99/120

Lower Bockhampton ⊠ DT2 8PZ – East : 3.75 mi by A 35
– 𝒞(01305) 262 382 – www.yalburycottage.com – dinner only and Sunday lunch residents only Sunday-Monday dinner
– Closed Christmas-mid January

at Winterbourne Steepleton West: 4.75 mi by B3150 and A35 on B3159
– ⊠ Dorchester

🏠 **Old Rectory**

TRADITIONAL · PERSONALISED A proudly run, attractive stone rectory in a pretty village. It's immaculately kept, from the comfy lounge and conservatory breakfast room to the homely bedrooms and smart bathrooms. Cross the brook to enter the mature gardens.

4 rooms ⌇ – †£70 ††£80/110

⊠ DT2 9LG – 𝒞 (01305) 889 468 – www.theoldrectorybandb.co.uk – Closed 1 week Christmas

DORKING

Surrey – Pop. 17 098 – Regional map n° **4**-D2
▶ London 26 mi – Brighton 39 mi – Guildford 12 mi – Worthing 33 mi

✗ **Two to Four** 🔲 ⇔

MODERN CUISINE · COSY This 17C, Grade II listed property sports contemporary décor, although beams bear witness to its history and help give it a pleasant rustic feel. Friendly and informal; cosy in the evening. Menu is British at its core but with influences from all over; dishes are unfussy and well-presented.

Menu £12 (weekday lunch)/19 – Carte £30/54

2-4 West St ⊠ RH4 1BL – 𝒞 (01306) 889 923 – www.2to4.co.uk – Closed 25 December-early January and Sunday

DORNEY

Buckinghamshire – Pop. 278 – Regional map n° **6**-D3
▶ London 27 mi – Birmingham 111 mi – Bristol 97 mi – Croydon 35 mi

🍴 **Palmer Arms**

MODERN CUISINE · PUB Run by a keen young couple; it's the food, not the furnishings, that matter here. Menus display a well-balanced mix of pub favourites and some more adventurous dishes. The private dining room offers far-reaching views.

Carte £21/41

Village Rd ⊠ SL4 6QW – 𝒞 (01628) 666 612 (booking advisable)
– www.thepalmerarms.com

DORRIDGE

West Midlands – ⊠ Birmingham – Regional map n° **10**-C2
▶ London 109 mi – Birmingham 11 mi – Warwick 11 mi

✗✗ **Forest**

BRITISH MODERN · DESIGN Surprisingly stylish restaurant located opposite the railway station in a 19C hotel: choose the bar-lounge for unfussy classics or head to the dining room for ambitious dishes with interesting modern twists. Cooking is accomplished and well-judged. Comfortable, contemporary bedrooms complete the picture.

Menu £14 (lunch and early dinner) – Carte £25/35

12 rooms – †£92/120 ††£92/120 – ⌇£8

25 Station Approach ⊠ B93 8JA – 𝒞 (01564) 772 120 – www.forest-hotel.com
– Closed 25 December and Sunday dinner

DOUGLAS – Douglas ➔ See Man (Isle of)

DOVER

Kent – Pop. 41 709 – Regional map n° **5**-D2
▶ London 76 mi – Eastbourne 68 mi – Maidstone 43 mi

DOVER

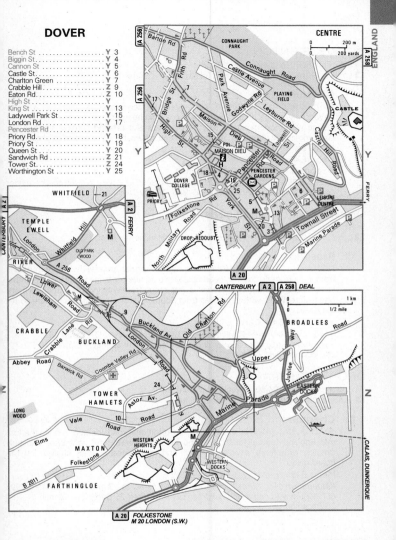

Wallett's Court

HISTORIC · COSY Family-run country house with 16C origins, in a peaceful setting. Guest areas are heavily beamed and bedrooms are traditional and characterful. The annexe rooms are more modern, with the converted grain store and Victorian bath house the most unusual. Classic menus are offered in the atmospheric restaurant.

18 rooms ⌂ – †£ 95 ††£ 150/250
West Cliffe, St Margaret's at Cliffe ⊠ *CT15 6EW*
– Northeast : 3.5 mi by A 258 on St Margaret's at Cliffe rd
– ☎ (01304) 852 424
– www.wallettscourt.com

DOWNTON – Hampshire → See Lymington

DREWSTEIGNTON

Devon – Pop. 668 – Regional map n° **1**-C2

▶ London 190 mi – Plymouth 56 mi – Torbay 35 mi – Exeter 15 mi

XX **Old Inn**   ⇦

BRITISH MODERN · INTIMATE Olive green former pub in the centre of a lovely Devonshire village. It has two small, cosy dining rooms and a parquet–floored lounge with modern art for sale on the walls and a wood-burning stove in the large inglenook fireplace. A concise menu offers hearty, classical dishes. Bedrooms are simply furnished.

Menu £ 49

3 rooms ⌷ – ♦£ 70/80 ♦♦£ 90/100

✉ EX6 6QR – ℰ *(01647) 281 276 (booking essential) – www.old-inn.co.uk – dinner only and lunch Friday-Saturday – Closed Sunday-Tuesday*

DRIGHLINGTON see Leeds Plan

West Yorkshire – Regional map n° **13**-B2

▶ London 196 mi – Leeds 7 mi – Sheffield 41 mi – Manchester 35 mi

XX **Prashad**   ৬ 🅰🅺 🏵 ⇦ 🅿

🏵 INDIAN VEGETARIAN · INDIVIDUAL Stylish former pub with wooden panels from India fronting the bar; head upstairs to admire the huge picture of a Mumbai street scene. Authentic vegetarian dishes range from enticing street food to more original creations, with influences from Southern India and Gujarat; be sure to try the dosas.

Menu £ 25/34 – Carte £ 21/37

Town plan: BU-a – *137 Whitehall Rd* ✉ *BD11 1AT* – ℰ *(0113) 285 20 37 – www.prashad.co.uk – dinner only and lunch Friday-Sunday – Closed 25 December and 1 January*

DROITWICH SPA

Worcestershire – Pop. 23 504 – Regional map n° **10**-C3

▶ London 129 mi – Birmingham 20 mi – Bristol 66 mi – Worcester 6 mi

� **Chequers**   ⇛ 🛋 🅿

TRADITIONAL CUISINE · PUB Cosy and traditional roadside pub, run by the former England football team chef and his wife. Menus offer light bites and pub classics, with more adventurous fish and offal-based specials chalked on the board daily.

Menu £ 15 (weekdays) – Carte £ 21/36

Kidderminster Rd, Cutnall Green ✉ *WR9 0PJ* – *North : 3 mi on A 442* – ℰ *(01299) 851 292 – www.chequerscutnallgreen.co.uk – Closed 25 December, dinner 26 December and 1 January*

DROXFORD

Hampshire – Pop. 675 – Regional map n° **4**-B2

▶ London 79 mi – Southampton 21 mi – Portsmouth 16 mi – Basingstoke 37 mi

� **Bakers Arms**   🛋 🅿

🏵 BRITISH MODERN · PUB Proudly run, charming village pub with leather sofas, a roaring log fire and walls hung with old beer adverts, Victorian photographs and stag heads. Unfussy, filling dishes rely on local produce, with veg grown by the owners and bread baked daily in-house. Beers are from the local Droxford-based brewery.

Menu £ 15 (weekdays) – Carte £ 24/34

High St ✉ *SO32 3PA* – ℰ *(01489) 877 533 – www.thebakersarmsdroxford.com – Closed Sunday dinner*

DULVERTON

Somerset – Pop. 1 052 – Regional map n° **2**-A2

▶ London 198 mi – Barnstaple 27 mi – Exeter 26 mi – Minehead 18 mi

🗓 Woods   🍷 🏠

BRITISH MODERN · PUB Former bakery, with a cosy, hugely characterful interior. Tasty, carefully prepared dishes offer more than just the usual pub fare. Provenance is taken seriously, with quality local ingredients including meat from the owner's farm.

Carte £ 23/33

4 Banks Sq ⊠ TA22 9BU – ℰ (01398) 324 007 (bookings advisable at dinner) – www.woodsdulverton.co.uk – Closed 25 December, dinner 26 December and 1 January

at Brushford South: 1.75 mi on B3222 – ⊠ Dulverton

🏠 Three Acres Country House   🌿 🚪 🍽 **P**

TRADITIONAL · PERSONALISED Remotely set guesthouse boasting nearly 3 acres of mature gardens and parkland. Comfy lounge, small bar, pine-furnished breakfast room and pleasant terrace. Large, cosy bedrooms with country views.

6 rooms ⌸ – ♦ £ 60/75 ♦♦ £ 90/120

⊠ *TA22 9AR – ℰ (01398) 323 730 – www.threeacresexmoor.co.uk*

DUNSFORD

Devon – Regional map n° **1**-C2

▶ London 206 mi – Plymouth 40 mi – Exeter 8 mi

🏠 Weeke Barton   🌤 🌿 🚪 **P** 🍴

HISTORIC · CONTEMPORARY The owners of this 15C Devonshire longhouse are friendly and laid-back, and the place itself has a funky yet cosy feel. The interior combines old world character with stylish furnishings and bedrooms are modern and minimalistic. Rustic, home-cooked dishes feature in the communal dining room.

5 rooms ⌸ – ♦ £ 100/120 ♦♦ £ 110/130

⊠ *EX6 7HH – Southeast : 1.5 mi by B 3212 and Christow rd, turning right up unmarked road after river bridge – ℰ (01647) 253 505 – www.weekebarton.com – Closed Christmas and New Year*

DUNSTER

Somerset – Pop. 408 – Regional map n° **2**-A2

▶ London 185 mi – Minehead 3 mi – Taunton 23 mi

🏠 Spears Cross   🍽 **P**

HISTORIC · CLASSIC Built in 1460 and reputedly the oldest house in the street. Charming bedrooms feature traditional William Morris and Sanderson furnishings – one room has elm panelling. They also offer over 120 wines and malt whiskies for sale.

4 rooms ⌸ – ♦ £ 72 ♦♦ £ 100/110

West St ⊠ TA24 6SN – ℰ (01643) 821 439 – www.spearscross.co.uk

🏠 Exmoor House   🍽

TRADITIONAL · COSY Georgian terraced house in the centre of a historic town, run by warm, welcoming owners; look out for their year-round Christmas shop! The comfy lounge, spacious breakfast room and cosy bedrooms come in bright, contemporary tones.

6 rooms ⌸ – ♦ £ 55/62 ♦♦ £ 75/90

12 West St ⊠ TA24 6SN – ℰ (01643) 821 268 – www.exmoorhousedunster.co.uk – Closed 2 January-29 February

ENGLAND

DURHAM
Durham – Pop. 47 785 – Regional map n° **14**-B3
▶ London 267 mi – Leeds 77 mi – Middlesbrough 23 mi – Newcastle upon Tyne 20 mi

⌂ The Town House

TOWNHOUSE · DESIGN Attractive Georgian townhouse with lavishly decorated rooms: the lounge has purple velvet furnishings and there's a mahogany bar. Sumptuous bedrooms feature bathrooms with underfloor heating; those in the garden annexe have hot tubs. Intimate restaurant serving classic British dishes, with steaks a speciality.

11 rooms 🖙 – †£ 99/250 ††£ 99/250

Town plan: B-x – *34 Old Elvet* ⊠ *DH1 3HN* – ℰ *(0191) 384 10 37*
– *www.thetownhousedurham.com* – *Closed 1 January*

⌂ Castle View

TOWNHOUSE · COSY Attractive Georgian townhouse beside a Norman castle on a steep cobbled hill; reputedly a former vicarage. Large bedrooms have modern monochrome colour schemes, good facilities and smart bathrooms. Have breakfast on the terrace in summer.

5 rooms 🖙 – †£ 70/80 ††£ 100/120

Town plan: A-e – *4 Crossgate* ⊠ *DH1 4PS* – ℰ *(0191) 386 88 52*
– *www.castle-view.co.uk* – *Closed 18 December-13 January*

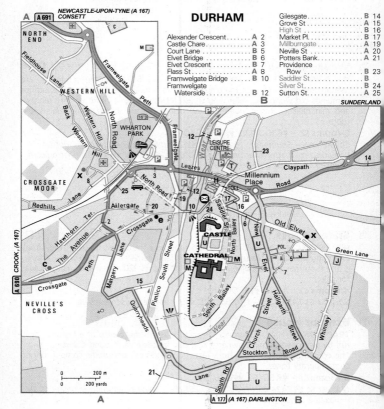

DURHAM

Alexander Crescent	A 2
Castle Chare	A 3
Court Lane	B 5
Elvet Bridge	B 6
Elvet Crescent	B 7
Flass St	A 8
Framwelgate Bridge	B 10
Framwelgate Waterside	B 12
Gilesgate	B 14
Grove St	A 15
High St	B 16
Market Pl.	B 17
Millburngate	A 19
Neville St	A 20
Potters Bank	A 21
Providence Row	B 23
Saddler St	B
Silver St.	B 24
Sutton St.	A 25

XX **Bistro 21** 🏠 📶 ⇔ 🅿

🕸 BRITISH MODERN · RUSTIC Brightly painted restaurant with an internal courtyard and a herb garden. Formerly a manor house outbuilding, the rustic main
room has high windows and French farmhouse styling; the bar is in a smaller
vaulted room. Cooking is satisfying and filling, and centres around good old British classics.

Menu £ 19 (lunch and early dinner) – Carte £ 26/39

*Aykley Heads House, Aykley Heads ⊠ DH1 5TS – Northwest : 1.5 mi by A 691 and
B 6532 – ℰ (0191) 384 43 54 (booking essential) – www.bistrotwentyone.co.uk
– Closed Christmas, Sunday dinner and bank holiday Mondays*

XX **DH1** Ⓝ 🔥 📶 🅿

MODERN CUISINE · INTIMATE An intimate restaurant on the lower floor of a
large Victorian house overlooking the city. An array of choices mean everything
from a weekly market menu to a vegetarian tasting menu; dishes are modern
and full of flavour.

Menu £ 25/60 – Carte approx. £ 40

Town plan: A-c – *The Avenue ⊠ DH1 4DX – ℰ (0191) 384 6655
– www.restaurantdh1.co.uk – dinner only – Closed 2 weeks October, first week
January, 25-26 December, Sunday and Monday*

XX **Finbarr's** 🏠 🔥 🖵 🅿

BRITISH MODERN · FRIENDLY Hidden away in a hotel just outside the city, a
spacious restaurant with monochrome photos and well-spaced, smartly laid tables. Modern menus display international influences; the set menu provides good
value. Smooth, professional service.

Menu £ 17 (weekdays) – Carte £ 23/49

Town plan: A-x – *Waddington St, Flass Vale ⊠ DH1 4BG – ℰ (0191) 370 9999
(booking advisable) – www.finbarrsrestaurant.co.uk – Closed 25-26 December*

EARL STONHAM

Suffolk – Regional map n° **8**-C3

▶ London 91 mi – Ipswich 12 mi – Colchester 33 mi – Clacton-on-Sea 38 mi

🏠 **Bays Farm** 🐾 🚗 🛜 🅿

🏡 FAMILY · PERSONALISED A delightful 17C farmhouse run by a charming
host; surrounded by 3 acres of attractive gardens. There's a characterful lounge
and a beamed dining room. Bedrooms are individually styled – the annexed 'Hayloft' is the most luxurious. Breakfast features local and garden produce, and
homemade bread and jam.

4 rooms ⊑ – 🛏£ 65/110 🛏🛏£ 75/120

*Forward Grn ⊠ IP14 5HU – Northwest : 1 mi by A1120 on Broad Green rd
– ℰ (01449) 711 286 – www.baysfarmsuffolk.co.uk*

🍴 **Shepherd & Dog** 🅿

BRITISH MODERN · ELEGANT An unexpected find in sleepy Suffolk: relax in the
lounge, enjoy traditional pub dishes in the bar or head to the snazzily named
'Eaterie', which serves modern cooking in a formal style to match its smart, contemporary décor.

Carte £ 27/41

*Forward Green ⊠ IP14 5HN – Northwest : 0.5 mi on A 1120 – ℰ (01449) 711 685
– www.theshepherdanddog.com – Closed Monday*

EAST CHILTINGTON – East Sussex ➡ See Lewes

EAST CHISENBURY

Wiltshire – Regional map n° **2**-D2

▶ London 92 mi – Bristol 51 mi – Southampton 53 mi – Reading 51 mi

⌂ **Red Lion Freehouse** (Guy Manning)   ⇦ 🛏 🌳 **P**

❀ CLASSIC CUISINE · SIMPLE Delightful thatched pub off the beaten track, with simple country styling and a cosy, characterful feel. Daily menus focus on carefully sourced, seasonal ingredients and the down-to-earth dishes are stunning in their simplicity, precisely composed and packed with flavour. Set opposite, the smart, well-equipped bedrooms come with private terraces; all have river views.
→ Roast lettuce soup with ewe's curd & lovage ravioli, walnut and radish. Saddle of Wiltshire lamb with Jersey Royals, asparagus and morels. Cocoa pound cake, confit fennel, warm chocolate pudding and orange blossom ice cream.
Menu £ 18 (weekday lunch)/24 – Carte £ 27/52
5 rooms ⌂ – †£ 150/250 ††£ 150/250
✉ SN9 6AQ – ☎ (01980) 671 124 (booking advisable)
– www.redlionfreehouse.com

EAST CLANDON – Surrey → See Guildford

EAST END
Hampshire – Regional map n° **4**-A3
▶ London 100 mi – Bristol 85 mi – Southampton 21 mi

⌂ **East End Arms**   ⇦ 🌳 **P**

BRITISH TRADITIONAL · RUSTIC Traditional country pub owned by John Illsley of Dire Straits. Shabby locals bar and classical pine-furnished dining room; great display of music-based photos. Concise menus of satisfying British dishes. Modern, cottage-style bedrooms provide a smart contrast.
Carte £ 22/38
5 rooms ⌂ – †£ 71 ††£ 99/120
Lymington Rd ✉ SO41 5SY – ☎ (01590) 626 223 – www.eastendarms.co.uk
– Closed dinner Sunday

EAST GRINSTEAD
West Sussex – Pop. 29 084 – Regional map n° **4**-D2
▶ London 48 mi – Brighton 30 mi – Eastbourne 32 mi – Lewes 21 mi

🏨 **Gravetye Manor**   ✿ 🐦 ⇦ 🛏 🔄 🎾 **P**

LUXURY · CLASSIC A quintessential English country house set in a forest and surrounded by 35 acres of glorious gardens. Ornate Elizabethan ceilings and fireplaces dominate beautifully furnished lounges, which provide the perfect spot for afternoon tea. Bedrooms are luxurious and service is personalised and detailed.
17 rooms ⌂ – †£ 170/210 ††£ 260/495 – 1 suite
Vowels Ln ✉ RH19 4LJ – Southwest : 4.5 mi by B 2110 taking second turn left towards West Hoathly – ☎ (01342) 810 567 – www.gravetyemanor.co.uk – Closed 4-7 January
❀ Gravetye Manor – See restaurant listing

XxX **Gravetye Manor**   ⇦ 🛏 🔄 **P**

❀ BRITISH MODERN · FORMAL A charming country house dining room with wood-panelled walls, fresh flowers and a cosy, traditional feel. Classically based menus use excellent quality produce from the kitchen garden to create refined, flavourful dishes, with desserts a highlight. Well-chosen wine list and polished, professional service.
→ Orkney scallops with heritage carrots, cardamom yoghurt and spiced carrot cake. Sea bass with smoked eel, confit leek, fennel farfalle and eel velouté. Rhubarb soufflé with clotted cream ice cream.
Menu £ 30 – Carte £ 58/71
Gravetye Manor Hotel, Vowels Ln ✉ RH19 4LJ – ☎ (01342) 810 567 (booking essential) – www.gravetyemanor.co.uk – Closed 4-7 January

EAST HADDON
Northamptonshire – Regional map n° **9**-B3
▶ London 76 mi – Birmingham 47 mi – Leicester 32 mi – Coventry 34 mi

🏮 Red Lion   ⇔ 🍴 🛏 ⌚ ⌖ P

TRADITIONAL CUISINE · PUB Thatched honey-stone inn at the heart of an attractive village, boasting pretty gardens and a pleasing mix of exposed wood, brick and slate. Drinkers are welcome but it's the food that's the focus here, with a seasonal menu offering an eclectic mix of tasty dishes including perennial favourite, slow-cooked red wine beef. Enthusiastic service and chic, cosy bedrooms.

Carte £ 21/40

7 rooms ⌂ – ♦£ 80/95 ♦♦£ 95/110

*Main St ⌧ NN6 8BU – ℰ (01604) 770 223 – www.redlioneasthaddon.co.uk
– Closed 25 December*

EAST HENDRED
Oxfordshire – Regional map n° **6**-B3
▶ London 70 mi – Oxford 18 mi – Swindon 30 mi

🏮 Eyston Arms   🛏 ⌖ P

INTERNATIONAL · PUB Set in a largely estate-owned village; an inviting modern pub where several low-beamed rooms are set around an inglenook fireplace. Local workers pop in for the 'business dish of the day' and Maria's blackboard lists the specials.

Carte £ 26/36

*High St ⌧ OX12 8JY – ℰ (01235) 833 320 – www.eystonarms.co.uk – Closed
25 December and Sunday dinner*

EAST HOATHLY
East Sussex – Pop. 893 – Regional map n° **5**-B3
▶ London 60 mi – Brighton 16 mi – Eastbourne 13 mi – Hastings 25 mi

🏠 Old Whyly   ⌂ 🌿 ⛲ ⟁ ⌘ ✗ P 🚲

TRADITIONAL · PERSONALISED Charming red-brick house built in 1760, set in beautiful grounds and very personally run by its delightful owner. Guest areas mix the classic and the contemporary. Bedrooms are individually designed around a subtle theme: choose from Tulip, French or Chinese. The minimalist dining room offers a daily changing 3 course dinner, and homemade yoghurts and jams at breakfast.

4 rooms ⌂ – ♦£ 85/100 ♦♦£ 95/145

*London Rd ⌧ BN8 6EL – Northwest : 0.5 mi, turning right by post box on right
and then taking centre drive – ℰ (01825) 840 216 – www.oldwhyly.co.uk*

EAST KENNETT – Wiltshire → See Marlborough

EAST LAVANT – West Sussex → See Chichester

EAST WITTERING
West Sussex – Pop. 5 647 – Regional map n° **4**-C3
▶ London 86 mi – Birmingham 178 mi – Leeds 272 mi – Sheffield 242 mi

✗ Samphire   🛏

MODERN · SIMPLE A smart, keenly run restaurant set 100 metres from the sea; a new extension gives more light and a sea view. Fresh, locally caught seafood and fish – with a wide range of meat dishes too. Straightforward, tasty, good value cooking.

Menu £ 16 (lunch) – Carte £ 24/40

*57 Shore Rd ⌧ PO20 8DY – ℰ (01243) 672 754
– www.samphireeastwittering.co.uk – Closed 2 weeks January, Christmas and
Sunday*

EAST WITTON
North Yorkshire – ⌧ Leyburn – Regional map n° **13**-B1
▶ London 238 mi – Leeds 45 mi – Middlesbrough 30 mi – York 39 mi

📁 **Blue Lion**   ⇦ 🍴 🛋 ♿ 🕙 **P**

REGIONAL · PUB Charming, characterful countryside pub. Daily-changing menu features a tasty mix of classic and modern dishes, all with seasonality and traceability at their core. Bedrooms – in the pub and outbuildings – are warm and cosy.
Menu £ 16 (weekday lunch) – Carte £ 25/46 **s**

15 rooms ⊆ – †£ 69/104 ††£ 94/145

✉ DL8 4SN – ℰ (01969) 624 273 (booking essential) – www.thebluelion.co.uk

EASTBOURNE

East Sussex – Pop. 109 185 – Regional map n° **5**-B3
▶ London 68 mi – Brighton 25 mi – Dover 61 mi – Maidstone 49 mi

🏨 **Grand**   🍴 ≪ 🛋 🏊 🖥 🌐 🏠 🛋 🎣 ♿ 📶 🎱 **P**

LUXURY · CLASSIC Built in 1875 and offering all its name promises, the Grand retains many original features including ornate plasterwork, columned corridors and a Great Hall. The delightful gardens feature a superb outdoor pool and a sun terrace. Bedrooms are classical; pay the extra for a sea view. Dining is a formal affair.

152 rooms ⊆ – †£ 145/240 ††£ 300/395 – 13 suites

Town plan: Z-x – King Edward's Par. ✉ BN21 4EQ – ℰ (01323) 412 345
– www.grandeastbourne.com

Mirabelle – See restaurant listing

🏠 **Waterside**   🚫

BUSINESS · MODERN Modern seafront hotel with views of the beach and pier; take in the view from the boldly wallpapered cocktail bar. Bedrooms vary in size and have unusual feature walls; some of the baths are in the rooms and come with a view.

19 rooms ⊆ – †£ 80/150 ††£ 80/150

Town plan: Z-a – 11-12 Royal Par ✉ BN22 7AR – ℰ (01323) 646 566
– www.watersidehoteleastbourne.co.uk

🏡 **Ocklynge Manor**   🍴 🚫 **P** 🚭

HISTORIC · PERSONALISED Sit in the small summerhouse and admire the beautiful mature gardens of this charming, traditional guesthouse. Mabel Lucie Attwell – the illustrator of 'Peter Pan and Wendy' – once lived here. Homemade cake is served on arrival.

3 rooms ⊆ – †£ 60/90 ††£ 100/120

Town plan: Z-s – Mill Rd ✉ BN21 2PG – ℰ (01323) 734 121
– www.ocklyngemanor.co.uk

🏡 **Brayscroft**   🍴 🚫

TOWNHOUSE · CLASSIC Cosy Edwardian house located close to the seafront, gardens and pier. The traditional lounge and dining room display antiques and Italian artwork. Bedrooms are comfy and classically styled. Evening meals – by arrangement – are tailored to each guest and feature fresh, local, free range ingredients.

6 rooms ⊆ – †£ 40/45 ††£ 80/90

Town plan: Z-n – 13 South Cliff Ave ✉ BN20 7AH – ℰ (01323) 647 005
– www.brayscrofthotel.co.uk

🏡 **Southcroft**   🍴 🚫

TRADITIONAL · HOMELY A terraced Edwardian guesthouse in a quiet residential area close to the promenade. The homely lounge is filled with books, games and lots of local information and the bedrooms are cosy and well-kept. Have your morning coffee out on the patio; home-cooked dinners are served by arrangement.

6 rooms ⊆ – †£ 40/45 ††£ 80/100

Town plan: Z-n – 15 South Cliff Ave ✉ BN20 7AH – ℰ (01323) 729 071
– www.southcrofthotel.co.uk

EASTBOURNE

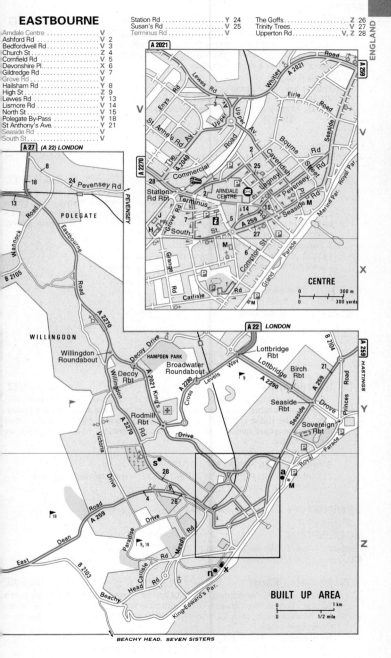

CENTRE

BUILT UP AREA

BEACHY HEAD, SEVEN SISTERS

437

XxxX **Mirabelle** 🕮 🛏 🕭 🅰 🅿

BRITISH TRADITIONAL · ELEGANT This traditional hotel restaurant features plush fabrics and tables laid with monogrammed silverware. The dress code is formal and the team are professional. Rich, well-executed cooking follows the seasons and has a modern touch.

Menu £ 26/43

Town plan: Z-x – *Grand Hotel, King Edward's Par.* ✉ BN21 4EQ – ℰ *(01323) 412 345 (booking essential) – www.grandeastbourne.com – Closed Sunday-Monday and Tuesday January-February*

EASTGATE
Durham – Regional map n° **14**-A3
▶ London 288 mi – Bishop Auckland 20 mi – Newcastle upon Tyne 35 mi – Stanhope 3 mi

⌂ **Horsley Hall** 🕭 🕮 ⇐ 🛏 🕭 🧼 🅿

HISTORIC · PERSONALISED Characterful 14C hunting lodge built for the Bishop of Durham, featuring impressive stained glass and a baronial hallway. Two of the cosy bedrooms have Edwardian bathrooms and many offer valley views. Have afternoon tea in the revolving garden pod and dinner under an ornate ceiling; game is a speciality.

9 rooms 🖙 – 🛉£ 85/95 🛉🛉£ 130/150

✉ DL13 2LJ – *Southeast : 1 mi by A 689* – ℰ *(01388) 517 239*
– www.horsleyhall.co.uk – Closed 21 December-17 January

EASTON – Devon ➜ See Chagford

EASTON – Somerset ➜ See Wells

EASTON ON THE HILL
Northamptonshire – Pop. 1 015 – Regional map n° **9**-C2
▶ London 94 mi – Birmingham 75 mi – Leicester 30 mi – Coventry 61 mi

🏠 **Exeter Arms** ⇦ 🛏 🕭 🅿

BRITISH TRADITIONAL · RUSTIC Sympathetically restored pub adorned with copper pans, enamel signs and hop bines. Eat either in the snug candlelit restaurant or in the stylish conservatory which opens out onto a terrace. Hearty dishes arrive in generous portions, with the occasional modern touch. Bedrooms are well-appointed.

Carte £ 23/35

6 rooms 🖙 – 🛉£ 70/100 🛉🛉£ 80/110

21 Stamford Rd ✉ PE9 3NS – ℰ *(01780) 756 321 – www.theexeterarms.net*
– Closed Sunday dinner

EBRINGTON – Gloucestershire ➜ See Chipping Campden

ECCLESTON
Lancashire – Pop. 4 708 – Regional map n° **11**-A2
▶ London 219 mi – Birmingham 103 mi – Liverpool 29 mi – Preston 11 mi

🏠 **Parr Hall Farm** 🛏 🧼 🅿

FAMILY · RUSTIC Welcoming, red-brick former farmhouse. Bedrooms are in the adjacent barn conversion and come with pine furnishings, country style fabrics and modern bathrooms. Continental breakfasts are taken under low-beams in the original house.

10 rooms 🖙 – 🛉£ 45 🛉🛉£ 70

Parr Ln. ✉ PR7 5SL – ℰ *(01257) 451 917 – www.parrhallfarm.com*

ECKINGTON – Worcestershire → See Pershore

ECKINGTON

Derbyshire – Pop. 16 684 – Regional map n° **9**-B1

▶ London 155 mi – Leeds 49 mi – Sheffield 10 mi – Manchester 58 mi

🏮 Devonshire Arms

BRITISH TRADITIONAL · DESIGN Smartly updated inn with several modern rooms and a small terrace. Fresh, seasonal ingredients are at the core of the hearty menu. They like to keep things local, with eggs coming from down the road and meat from the butcher who lives opposite.

Menu £ 28 (weekdays) – Carte £ 26/42

Lightwood Ln, Middle Handley ⊠ S21 5RN – Southwest : 2 mi by B 6052 on Middle Handley rd – ℰ (01246) 434 800
– www.devonshirearmsmiddlehandley.com – Closed Monday except bank holiday lunch and dinner Sunday

🏮 Inn at Troway

BRITISH TRADITIONAL · PUB Early Victorian pub in a picturesque location, offering delightful views over rolling countryside. The extensive menu offers hearty, satisfying dishes and desserts often have a playful element. There's a fine selection of local ales.

Carte £ 18/30

Snowdon Ln, Troway ⊠ S21 5RU – West : 3.5 mi by B 6052 on B 6056
– ℰ (01246) 417 666 – www.relaxeatanddrink.co.uk

EDINGTON

Wiltshire – Regional map n° **2**-C2

▶ London 105 mi – Bristol 43 mi – Cardiff 76 mi – Southampton 64 mi

🏮 Three Daggers

BRITISH MODERN · COSY Attractive pub with original wood beams and flagstones, and a large conservatory overlooking the garden. The accessible menu always features a homemade soup and a 'pie of the day', and the Huntsman's and Fisherman's sharing platters are extremely popular. Charming bedrooms feature bespoke oak furnishings.

Menu £ 25 (dinner) – Carte £ 23/38

9 rooms ⊿ – ♦£ 85/165 ♦♦£ 85/165

47 Westbury Rd ⊠ BA13 4PG – ℰ (01380) 830 940
– www.threedaggers.co.uk

EGHAM

Surrey – Pop. 25 996 – Regional map n° **4**-C1

▶ London 22 mi – Croydon 24 mi – Barnet 35 mi – Ealing 17 mi

🏰 Great Fosters

BUSINESS · ELEGANT Striking Elizabethan manor built as a hunting lodge for Henry VIII, boasting 50 acres of gardens, a beautiful parterre and an amphitheatre. The charming interior displays characterful original detailing. Bedrooms come with feature beds and a flamboyant touch; those in the annexes are more modern. Dine on steaks from the Josper grill or more formally in the Tudor Room.

43 rooms – ♦£ 150/175 ♦♦£ 185/450 – ⊿ £ 20 – 3 suites

Stroude Rd ⊠ TW20 9UR – South : 1.25 mi by B 388
– ℰ (01784) 433 822 – www.greatfosters.co.uk

Tudor Room – See restaurant listing

XxX **Tudor Room** ❶   🕷 🖳 � & 🅿

MODERN CUISINE · INTIMATE Intimate hotel dining room with mullioned windows, burgundy décor and a large tapestry hung on one wall. The kitchen garden provides many of the ingredients showcased on the 4 course menu. Cooking is classical with modern twists.

Menu £ 58

*Stroude Rd ⊠ TW20 9UR – South : 1.25 mi by B 388 – ℰ (01784) 433 822
(booking essential) – www.greatfosters.co.uk – dinner only and Friday lunch
– Closed Sunday-Wednesday*

EGTON

North Yorkshire – Regional map n° **13**-C1

▶ London 250 mi – Birmingham 180 mi – Leeds 72 mi – Sheffield 107 mi

🕪 **Wheatsheaf Inn**   🍴 🅿

BRITISH TRADITIONAL · INN Family-run, late 17C inn on the edge of the picturesque North Yorkshire Moors. Menu offers a real taste of Yorkshire with fresh, hearty dishes like lambs' kidneys, local steak, Whitby scampi and game sourced from within 2 miles.

Carte £ 22/35

*⊠ YO21 1TZ – ℰ (01947) 895 271 – www.wheatsheafegton.com – Closed
25 December and Monday*

ELDERSFIELD

Worcestershire – Regional map n° **10**-B3

▶ London 124 mi – Birmingham 63 mi – Liverpool 145 mi – Bristol 52 mi

🕪 **Butchers Arms** (James Winter)   🖳 🅿

✿ BRITISH MODERN · RUSTIC This sweet red-brick pub has a small bar for the local drinkers and two cosy, intimate dining rooms. The chef – who cooks alone – has a terrific appreciation of market produce and knows how to get the best out of his ingredients. Constantly evolving dishes are refined, classical and packed with flavour.

→ Seared scallop with steamed pork dumpling and slow roasted pork shoulder. Turbot roasted on the bone with lobster tortellini, bisque sauce and buttered spinach. Pistachio and pink praline macaroons with pistachio ice cream.

Carte £ 39/51

*Lime Street ⊠ GL19 4NX – Southeast : 1 mi – ℰ (01452) 840 381 (booking
essential) – www.thebutchersarms.net – dinner only and lunch Friday-Sunday
– Closed 1 week early January, 1 week late August, Sunday dinner, Monday and
bank holidays*

ELLASTONE

Staffordshire – Regional map n° **10**-C1

▶ London 148 mi – Birmingham 49 mi – Stoke-on-Trent 22 mi

🕪 **Duncombe Arms**   🖳 🍴 & 🅿

BRITISH TRADITIONAL · COSY A stylish dining pub owned by the Hon. Johnny Greenall – of the famous brewery family: his wife, Laura, is a descendant of the Duncombe family after which the pub is named. Food keeps to a core of classic pub dishes.

Menu £ 22/30 – Carte £ 22/45

Main Road ⊠ DE6 2GZ – ℰ (01335) 324 275 – www.duncombearms.co.uk

ELLEL

Lancashire – Regional map n° **11**-A1

▶ London 240 mi – Leeds 85 mi – Sheffield 95 mi – Manchester 51 mi

Bay Horse Inn

REGIONAL · PUB Cosy, homely pub in a pleasant rural location, with a characterful interior and an attractive terrace. Seasonal, locally sourced produce is crafted into classic, tried-and-tested dishes. The Lancashire cheeseboard is a speciality.

Menu £ 10 (weekdays)/24 **s** – Carte £ 22/41 **s**

Bay Horse Ln, Bay Horse ⊠ LA2 0HR – South 1.5 mi by A 6 on Quernmore rd – ℰ (01524) 791 204 – www.bayhorseinn.com – Closed Monday except bank holiday lunch and Tuesday

ELMTON

Derbyshire – Regional map n° **9**-B1

▶ London 155 mi – Birmingham 78 mi – Leeds 51 mi – Sheffield 21 mi

Elm Tree

TRADITIONAL CUISINE · PUB 18C stone pub with a brightly lit bar, characterful beamed rooms, a wood-burning stove and a large garden. The good value menu offers pub classics presented in a modern manner, with most ingredients sourced from within 10 miles.

Menu £ 18 (weekday lunch) – Carte £ 18/41

⊠ S80 4LS – ℰ (01909) 721 261 – www.elmtreeelmton.co.uk – Closed Tuesday

ELSTREE see Greater London (North West) Plan 2

Hertfordshire – Pop. 1 986 – Regional map n° **7**-A2

▶ London 24 mi – Hertford 32 mi – Watford 11 mi

Laura Ashley-The Manor H. Elstree

HISTORIC · STYLISH An eye-catching, timbered Edwardian house which showcases the latest fabrics, furnishings and fittings from the famous company. Well-equipped bedrooms: the largest and most characterful are in the main house. The intimate, formal restaurant offers modern cooking and views over the extensive gardens.

49 rooms ⊠ – **†**£ 99/149 **††**£ 109/159

Town plan: CT-a – *Barnet Ln ⊠ WD6 3RE – ℰ (020) 8327 4700 – www.lauraashleyhotels.com/elstree*

ELTON

Cambridgeshire – Regional map n° **8**-A2

▶ London 84 mi – Peterborough 11 mi – Bedford 40 mi – Kettering 24 mi

Crown Inn

BRITISH TRADITIONAL · PUB 17C honey-stone pub in a delightful country parish, with a thatched roof, a cosy inglenook fireplace in the bar and a laid-back feel. Extensive menus offer homely British dishes which arrive in generous portions. Bedrooms are smart and individually styled – some have feature beds or roll-top baths.

Menu £ 13 (weekday lunch) – Carte £ 21/34

8 rooms ⊠ – **†**£ 68/75 **††**£ 110/145

8 Duck St ⊠ PE8 6RQ – ℰ (01832) 280 232 – www.thecrowninn.org

ELTON-ON-THE-HILL

Nottinghamshire – Regional map n° **9**-B2

▶ London 121 mi – Nottingham 15 mi – Lincoln 35 mi

The Grange

FAMILY · COSY What better way to start your holiday than in this charming Georgian farmhouse with a slice of homemade cake? The owners are lovely, the gardens are delightful and the country views are superb. Bedrooms are homely and come with good facilities and thoughtful touches; one is accessed via a spiral staircase.

3 rooms ⊠ – **†**£ 49/59 **††**£ 80/89

Sutton Ln. ⊠ NG13 9LA – ℰ (07887) 952 181 – www.thegrangebedandbreakfastnotts.co.uk

ELY

Cambridgeshire – Pop. 19 090 – Regional map n° **8**-B2

▶ London 74 mi – Cambridge 16 mi – Norwich 60 mi

🏠 Poets House

🕤 🛏 🗗 ♿ 🗚 ⅏ 🏋 **P**

TOWNHOUSE · MODERN A series of 19C townhouses opposite the cathedral. Spacious, boutique bedrooms come with beautiful bathrooms and extras such as local vodka and gin. The modern bar overlooks the pretty walled garden and also offers afternoon tea.

21 rooms ⌂ – †£ 169/199 ††£ 169/249

St Mary's St ✉ *CB7 4EY –* ℰ *(01353) 887 777 – www.poetshouse.com*

Dining Room – See restaurant listing

XX Dining Room

🛏 ♿ 🗚 🎧 **P**

MODERN CUISINE · FASHIONABLE Pretty hotel dining room which blends original features with contemporary décor. Ambitious modern dishes are attractively presented and full of flavour; there are plenty of vegetarian options too. Some tables have cathedral views.

Carte £ 28/46

Poets House Hotel, St Mary's St ✉ *CB7 4EY –* ℰ *(01353) 887 777*
– www.poetshouse.com

at Sutton Gault West: 8 mi by A142 off B1381 – ✉ Ely

🍴 Anchor Inn

⇔ 🛏 🛋 **P**

REGIONAL · PUB Riverside pub dating back to 1650 and the creation of the Hundred Foot Wash. Tempting menu complemented by daily fish specials. For a pleasant river outlook head for the wood-panelled rooms to the front of the bar. Neat, pine-furnished bedrooms include two suites; one with river views.

Menu £ 14 (weekday lunch) – Carte £ 25/37

4 rooms ⌂ – †£ 60/90 ††£ 80/155

✉ *CB6 2BD –* ℰ *(01353) 778 537 – www.anchor-inn-restaurant.co.uk*

at Little Thetford South: 2.75 mi by A10 – ✉ Ely

🏠 Springfields

🛏 ⅏ **P** 🚭

TRADITIONAL · PERSONALISED Delightfully run, curio-filled bungalow in pleasant gardens. Immaculately kept bedrooms have different coloured Toile de Jouy wallpapers and plenty of extra touches. Enjoy breakfast among the Cranberry Glass collection or in the courtyard.

3 rooms ⌂ – †£ 60 ††£ 85

Ely Rd ✉ *CB6 3HJ – North : 0.5 mi on A 10 –* ℰ *(01353) 663 637*
– www.smoothhound.co.uk/hotels/springfields – Closed Christmas-New Year

EMSWORTH

Hampshire – Pop. 18 777 – Regional map n° **4**-B2

▶ London 75 mi – Brighton 37 mi – Portsmouth 10 mi – Southampton 22 mi

XX 36 on the Quay

⇔ ⇐ ♿ ⟳

BRITISH MODERN · ELEGANT Long-standing, intimate restaurant and conservatory bar-lounge in a quayside cottage with pleasant harbour views. Concise menus offer elaborate modern dishes in some unusual combinations and foraged ingredients feature highly. Stylish bedrooms have good comforts; be ready to order breakfast at check-in.

Menu £ 24/58

7 rooms ⌂ – †£ 55/90 ††£ 90/200

47 South St, The Quay ✉ *PO10 7EG –* ℰ *(01243) 375 592 (booking essential)*
– www.36onthequay.co.uk – closed Sunday and Monday – Closed first
2 weeks January, 1 week May, 1 week October and 24-26 December

X **Fat Olives**

BRITISH MODERN · RUSTIC This sweet 17C fisherman's cottage sits in a character-ful coastal town, in a road leading down to the harbour. It's run by a charming cou-ple and has a rustic modern feel, courtesy of locally crafted tables and upholstered chairs. Classic British dishes have a modern edge and rely on small local suppliers.

Menu £ 20 (lunch) – Carte £ 30/41

30 South St ⊠ PO10 7EH – 𝒞 (01243) 377 914 (booking essential)
– www.fatolives.co.uk – Closed 2 weeks late June, 1 week Christmas, 1 week spring, Sunday and Monday

EPPING

⊠ Essex – Pop. 10 289 – Regional map n° **7**-B2
▶ London 23 mi – Colchester 41 mi – Watford 31 mi

XX **Haywards**

MODERN CUISINE · INTIMATE This proudly run restaurant is the realisation of a couple's dream. A hammerbeam ceiling and cherry wood tables set the scene. Appealing dishes follow the seasons and flavours are well-balanced. Service is ex-tremely welcoming.

Menu £ 23/55 – Carte £ 40/46

111 Bell Common ⊠ CM16 4DZ – Southwest : 1 mi by B 1393 and Theydon Rd
– 𝒞 (01992) 577 350 – www.haywardsrestaurant.co.uk – Closed 1-27 January and Sunday dinner-Wednesday lunch

EPSOM

Surrey – Pop. 31 474 – Regional map n° **4**-D1
▶ London 14 mi – Croydon 9 mi – Barnet 29 mi – Ealing 18 mi

🏠 **Chalk Lane**

COUNTRY HOUSE · COSY Personally run hotel in a residential area; comfortable and welcoming, with a charming, traditionally furnished interior to match its Vic-torian heritage. Individually styled bedrooms – one with a four-poster. More mod-ern dining room serves a menu inspired by classic French cooking.

21 rooms � – †£ 85/105 ††£ 125/200

Chalk Ln ⊠ KT18 7BB – Southwest : 0.5 mi by A 24 and Woodcote Rd – 𝒞 (01372) 721 179 – www.chalklanehotel.com

XXX **Le Raj**

BANGLADESHI · FORMAL A local institution with a larger-than-life owner, a comfortable bar-lounge and a smart, wood-panelled restaurant. Waiters in bow ties and white gloves serve carefully prepared, well-presented, authentic Bangla-deshi cooking.

Carte £ 21/37

211 Fir Tree Rd, Epsom Downs ⊠ KT17 3LB – Southeast : 2 mi by B 289 and B 284 on B 291 – 𝒞 (01737) 371 371 – www.lerajrestaurant.co.uk

ERMINGTON

Devon – Regional map n° **1**-C2
▶ London 216 mi – Plymouth 11 mi – Salcombe 15 mi

XX **Plantation House**

MODERN CUISINE · INTIMATE Georgian former rectory in a pleasant country spot, with a small drinks terrace, an open-fired lounge and two dining rooms: one formal, with black furnishings; one more relaxed, with polished wood tables. Interesting modern menus feature local produce. Stylish bedrooms come with fresh milk and homemade cake.

Menu £ 36 **s**

8 rooms ⊇ – †£ 75/185 ††£ 125/230

Totnes Rd ⊠ PL21 9NS – Southwest : 0.5 mi on A 3121 – 𝒞 (01548) 831 100 (bookings essential for non-residents) – www.plantationhousehotel.co.uk – dinner only

ESHOTT → See Morpeth

ETTINGTON

Warwickshire – Pop. 1 039 – Regional map n° **10**-C3

▶ London 95 mi – Birmingham 41 mi – Leicester 48 mi – Coventry 23 mi

🍴 Chequers Inn

TRADITIONAL CUISINE · PUB Chandeliers, brushed velvet furniture and Regency chairs set at chequered tables mean this is not your typical pub. Menus display a broad international style; dishes range from British classics to others with a Mediterranean bent.

Carte £ 21/37

91 Banbury Rd ⊠ CV37 7SR – ℰ (01789) 740 387
– www.the-chequers-ettington.co.uk – Closed Sunday dinner and Monday

EVERSHOT

Dorset – ⊠ Dorchester – Pop. 225 – Regional map n° **2**-C3

▶ London 149 mi – Bournemouth 39 mi – Dorchester 12 mi – Salisbury 53 mi

🏨 Summer Lodge

LUXURY · PERSONALISED Attractive former dower house in mature gardens, featuring a smart wellness centre, a pool and a tennis court. Plush, individually designed bedrooms come with marble bathrooms and the country house guest areas display heavy fabrics and antiques – the drawing room was designed by Thomas Hardy. The formal dining room offers classical cuisine and a superb wine list.

24 rooms � – ♦£ 215/360 ♦♦£ 245/760 – 4 suites
9 Fore St ⊠ DT2 0JR – ℰ (01935) 482 000 – www.summerlodgehotel.com

🏠 Acorn Inn

TRADITIONAL · CLASSIC Historic inn mentioned in 'Tess of the d'Urbervilles'. Individually styled bedrooms boast fabric-covered walls, good facilities and modern bathrooms. Guest areas include a characterful residents' lounge, a locals bar with a skittle alley and a classical restaurant.

10 rooms ⊡ – ♦£ 89/210 ♦♦£ 99/210
28 Fore St ⊠ DT2 0JW – ℰ (01935) 83 228 – www.acorn-inn.co.uk

🏠 Wooden Cabbage

TRADITIONAL · COSY Attractive former gamekeeper's cottage. Spacious guest areas include a cosy dining room used in winter and an airy conservatory used in summer. Pretty bedrooms boast good facilities and lovely countryside views. Meals (by arrangement) feature home-grown produce.

3 rooms ⊡ – ♦£ 90/100 ♦♦£ 110/120
East Chelborough ⊠ DT2 0QA – West : 3.25 mi by Beaminter rd and Chelborough rd on East Chelborough rd – ℰ (01935) 83 362 – www.woodencabbage.co.uk

EVESHAM

Worcestershire – Pop. 23 576 – Regional map n° **10**-C3

▶ London 99 mi – Birmingham 30 mi – Cheltenham 16 mi

🏨 The Wood Norton

COUNTRY HOUSE · ELEGANT Beautifully panelled country house in the shadow of the Malvern Hills; once a French duke's hunting lodge and then a BBC training centre. Bedrooms in the main house are characterful and those in the mews are more modern; all have unique photos from old BBC shows. The intimate restaurant overlooks the parterre.

50 rooms ⊡ – ♦£ 99/430 ♦♦£ 99/430 – 2 suites
Worcester Rd ⊠ WR11 4YB – Northwest : 2.5 mi by B 4624 on A 44 – ℰ (01386) 765 611 – www.thewoodnorton.com

EWHURST GREEN

East Sussex – Regional map n° **5**-B2

London 61 mi – Eastbourne 24 mi – Royal Tunbridge Wells 22 mi

🏠 Prawles Court   ⟍ ⌂ ⅏ P

COUNTRY HOUSE · PERSONALISED This lovely red-brick Arts and Crafts house is surrounded by 27 acres of beautiful gardens and grounds. It was designed by Nathaniel Lloyd and the guest areas retain a comfy, period style. Bedrooms are spacious and hugely impressive, featuring luxurious fabrics and furnishings, and a good range of facilities.

4 rooms � – †£ 110/125 ††£ 140/170

Shoreham Ln. ⊠ *TN32 5RG – Southwest : 1 mi – ℰ (01580) 830 136
– www.prawlescourt.com – Closed December and January, mid week November,
February and March, (minimum 2 nights stay at weekends)*

EXETER

Devon – Pop. 113 507 – Regional map n° **1**-D2

London 201 mi – Bournemouth 83 mi – Bristol 83 mi – Plymouth 46 mi

🏨 Abode Exeter   ⟨symbols⟩

HISTORIC · MODERN An attractive Georgian property in the shadow of the cathedral. The stylish interior features an all-day café, a pub and a chic cocktail bar. Some of the smart, boldly coloured bedrooms have roll-top baths with cathedral views.

52 rooms – †£ 75/154 ††£ 75/154 – � £ 12 – 1 suite

Town plan: Y-z – *Cathedral Yard* ⊠ *EX1 1HD – ℰ (01392) 319 955
– www.abodehotels.co.uk*

Michael Caines – See restaurant listing

🏨 Magdalen Chapter   ⟨symbols⟩

HISTORIC · DESIGN Converted Victorian eye hospital; now a stylish, modern hotel with a garden and a small spa tucked away to the rear. Chic, understated bedrooms come with mood lighting, espresso machines and iPads loaded with the hotel's information.

59 rooms ⊠ – †£ 90/110 ††£ 120/300

Town plan: Z-a – *Magdalen St* ⊠ *EX2 4HY – ℰ (01392) 281 000
– www.themagdalenchapter.com*

Magdalen Chapter – See restaurant listing

🏨 Southernhay House   ⟨symbols⟩

TOWNHOUSE · STYLISH Attractive Georgian townhouse with original ceiling roses and ornate coving. Smart, compact guest areas include a stylish lounge and a bar with bright blue furniture. Warmly decorated bedrooms have sumptuous beds, luxurious fabrics and chic bathrooms. Small dining room offers British-based menus.

10 rooms ⊠ – †£ 150/240 ††£ 150/240

Town plan: Z-x – *36 Southernhay East* ⊠ *EX1 1NX – ℰ (01392) 435 324
– www.southernhayhouse.com*

XX Michael Caines   ⟨symbols⟩

INTERNATIONAL · FRIENDLY Contemporary restaurant with well-spaced tables, set within a famous hotel; sit by the window for cathedral views. Modern British menus offer tasty, well-presented dishes comprising lots of different ingredients. Service is formal.

Menu £ 18/30 – Carte £ 26/52

Town plan: Y-z – *Abode Exeter Hotel, Cathedral Yard* ⊠ *EX1 1HD – ℰ (01392)
223 638 – www.michaelcaines.com*

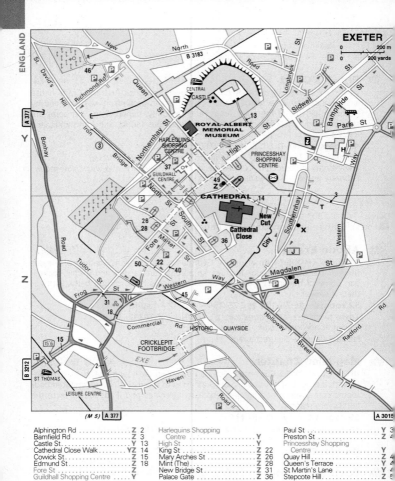

EXETER

✗✗ Magdalen Chapter 🍴 🛏 ♿ AC ⇔

TRADITIONAL CUISINE · FASHIONABLE An impressive steel and glass extension to a 19C hotel, with a curved wood roof and a delightful terrace. The large menu of brasserie classics mixes British, French, Spanish and Italian influences. Produce is carefully sourced.

Menu £ 17/32 – Carte £ 23/47

Town plan: Z-a – *Magdalen Chapter Hotel, Magdalen St* ✉ *EX2 4HY* – 𝒞 *(01392) 281 000* – *www.themagdalenchapter.com*

🏠 Rusty Bike ♿

BRITISH TRADITIONAL · PUB A bohemian pub which appeals to lovers of traditional British food. Daily changing menus feature hearty, masculine dishes. They butcher rare breed pigs on-site, cure their own bresaola and smoke their own ham. Sit in the cosy snug.

Carte £ 26/40

Town plan: V-x – *67 Howell Rd* ✉ *EX4 4LZ* – 𝒞 *(01392) 214 440* – *www.rustybike-exeter.co.uk* – *dinner only and Sunday lunch*

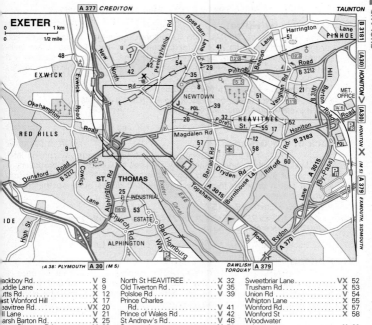

at Brampford Speke North: 5 mi by A377

🛏 Lazy Toad Inn   ⇦ 🍴 🛋 & 🅿

REGIONAL · COSY A sweet, Grade II listed pub with a beautiful walled garden and a charming cobbled courtyard. Much of the produce comes from their poly-tunnel, vegetable plot and orchard, opposite, and lamb from their smallholding features in spring. Fresh flowers and homemade biscuits welcome you in the comfy bedrooms.

Carte £ 25/32

5 rooms 🖵 – 🛉£ 68/88 🛉🛉£ 95/115

✉ EX5 5DP – ℰ (01392) 841 591 – www.thelazytoad.com
– Closed 1 week January, Sunday dinner and Monday

at Broadclyst Northeast: 4.5 mi by B3212 on B3181

XX The HH   ⇔ 🅿

MODERN CUISINE · RUSTIC Pleasant little restaurant which resembles a cottage. The interior blends the rustic and the contemporary, with its wooden beams, in-glenook fireplace and up-to-date décor. Interesting modern dishes are well presented and flavours are clear.

Menu £ 19 (weekday lunch)/27
– Carte £ 26/36

✉ EX5 3ET – ℰ (01392) 461 472 – www.the-hh.co.uk
– Closed Christmas-New Year, Monday and Tuesday

at Exeter Airport East: 5.5 mi by B3183 – Plan: V – A30 and B3184

🏨 Hampton by Hilton   ⛄ 🕴 📶 🗓 🔥 🗚 🎿 🅿

CHAIN HOTEL · FUNCTIONAL With its modern, open-plan business area and bar-lounge, the Hampton is ideal for corporate travellers. Bedrooms are well-soundproofed and come in raspberry, lemon or lime: all have work stations and spacious walk-in showers. Marco Pierre White's chic restaurant offers dishes from Italy and New York.

120 rooms ⌷ – 🛉£ 65/125 🛉🛉£ 65/125

✉ EX5 2LJ – East : 0.5 mi by Westcott rd – ℰ (01392) 348 348
– www.exeterairport.hamptonbyhilton.com

at Rockbeare East: 7.5 mi by B3183 – Plan: V – A30 and B3184 on B3174 – ✉ Exeter

🍴 Jack in the Green   🛏 🎍 🔥 🗚 🎮 🅿

BRITISH TRADITIONAL · PUB Green-painted pub with a warm, welcoming interior. Cooking is taken seriously and they are keen to support local producers. A vast array of menus feature both pub and restaurant style dishes, and you can mix and match between them; the 6 highlighted dishes make up the 'Totally Devon' set menu.

Menu £ 25 – Carte £ 34/45

London Rd ✉ EX5 2EE – ℰ (01404) 822 240 – www.jackinthegreen.uk.com
– Closed 25 December-3 January

at Kenton Southeast: 7 mi by A3015 – Plan: X – on A379 – ✉ Exeter

XX Rodean

BRITISH TRADITIONAL · NEIGHBOURHOOD Family-run restaurant – once a butcher's shop – overlooking a tiny village green. Small bar-lounge and two traditional dining rooms with beams and dark wood panelling. Constantly evolving menus have a classical base and a personal touch.

Menu £ 18 – Carte £ 33/46

The Triangle ✉ EX6 8LS – ℰ (01626) 890 195 (booking advisable)
– www.rodeanrestaurant.co.uk – dinner only and Sunday lunch – Closed Sunday dinner and Monday

EXETER AIRPORT – Devon → See Exeter

EXMOUTH

Devon – Pop. 34 432 – Regional map n° **1**-D2
▶ London 175 mi – Cardiff 114 mi – Plymouth 52 mi – Torbay 30 mi

X Les Saveurs   ⇗

TRADITIONAL CUISINE · BISTRO Traditional restaurant owned and run by a French chef and his family. Menus are unashamedly classical and feature dishes from their homeland; seafood features highly - most of it caught by the chef himself. Don't miss the lemon tart.

Carte £ 33/44

9 Tower St ✉ EX8 1NT – ℰ (01395) 269 459 – www.lessaveurs.co.uk – dinner only
– Closed early January-mid February, Sunday and Monday

EXTON

Devon – Regional map n° **1**-D2
▶ London 176 mi – Exmouth 4 mi – Topsham 3 mi

🍴 Puffing Billy   🎍 🔥 🗚 🅿

BRITISH TRADITIONAL · PUB Bright, modern, open-plan country dining pub with high vaulted ceilings, a semi-circular bar and a friendly, welcoming atmosphere. The eclectic menu offers tasty, globally influenced dishes, pub classics and local specialities.

Menu £ 15 (weekdays) – Carte £ 21/32

Station Rd ✉ EX3 0PR – ℰ (01392) 877 888 – www.thepuffingbilly.co.uk – Closed 25 December

FALMOUTH

Cornwall – Pop. 22 686 – Regional map n° **1**-A3

▶ London 308 mi – Penzance 26 mi – Plymouth 65 mi – Truro 11 mi

🏠 Greenbank

☆ ≤ 🖽 🍴 🚗

HOLIDAY HOTEL · MODERN 17C harbourside coaching inn, where flagstone floors and a sweeping staircase contrast with bold modern colours and contemporary furnishings. Spacious bedrooms are decked out in light wood; the Master Suite has a balcony and a bath with harbour views. The all-day restaurant serves modern, seasonal fare.

60 rooms 🖙 – 🛉£ 89/109 🛉🛉£ 109/229

Town plan: A-a – *Harbourside* ✉ TR11 2SR – 𝒞 *(01326) 312 440*
– *www.greenbank-hotel.co.uk*

🏠 St Michael's H & Spa

☆ ≤ 🛏 🖽 🌐 ♨ 🛁 🔥 🍴 🅿

HOLIDAY HOTEL · STYLISH Contemporary hotel with a nautical theme, from the reception desk 'boat' to the New England style bedrooms – some of which have balconies and sea views. Sea-blue décor, atmospheric lighting, friendly staff and a relaxed atmosphere.

61 rooms 🖙 – 🛉£ 50/127 🛉🛉£ 100/254

Town plan: B-c – *Gyllyngvase Beach* ✉ TR11 4NB – 𝒞 *(01326) 312 707*
– *www.stmichaelshotel.co.uk*

Flying Fish – See restaurant listing

🏠 Dolvean House

🌿 🅿

TOWNHOUSE · CLASSIC Victorian house built in 1870; its homely lounge has lots of local guide books and magazines. Neat breakfast room. Good-sized bedrooms with thoughtful touches; Room 9, with a big bay window, is the best.

10 rooms 🖙 – 🛉£ 45/85 🛉🛉£ 80/100

Town plan: B-n – *50 Melvill Rd* ✉ TR11 4DQ – 𝒞 *(01326) 313 658*
– *www.dolvean.co.uk – Closed first 2 weeks November and 22-28 December*

🏠 Chelsea House

≤ 🛏 🌿

TOWNHOUSE · PERSONALISED Edwardian house in a quiet residential area close to the beaches. Pine-furnished breakfast room. Spacious, modern bedrooms, some with nautically themed décor and three with balconies; top floor rooms have the best views.

9 rooms 🖙 – 🛉£ 40/50 🛉🛉£ 60/130

Town plan: B-e – *2 Emslie Rd* ✉ TR11 4BG – 𝒞 *(01326) 212 230*
– *www.chelseahousehotel.com*

XX Flying Fish

≤ 🛏 🅿

BRITISH TRADITIONAL · DESIGN Glass-fronted hotel restaurant overlooking the bay, with cool, azure-blue décor and stylish, atmospheric lighting. Deli dishes, sandwiches and salads at lunch; more elaborate, adventurous dinner dishes. Warm, friendly service.

Menu £ 27 (dinner) – Carte £ 26/57

Town plan: B-c – *St Michael's Hotel & Spa, Gyllyngvase Beach* ✉ TR11 4NB
– 𝒞 *(01326) 312 707 (bookings essential for non-residents)*
– *www.stmichaelshotel.co.uk*

X Rick Stein's Fish

🅰🅲 📖

FISH AND SEAFOOD · BISTRO With their own special beef dripping batter and fish chilli burgers to takeaway, this is more than your usual fish 'n' chips. Head inside and alongside your favourites you'll find the likes of dressed crab, fruits de mer and cod curry.

Menu £ 15 (lunch)/20 – Carte £ 25/52

Town plan: B-a – *Discovery Quay* ✉ TR11 3XA – 𝒞 *(01841) 532 700 (booking advisable) – www.rickstein.com – Closed 25-26 December and Sunday-Monday in winter*

449

FALMOUTH

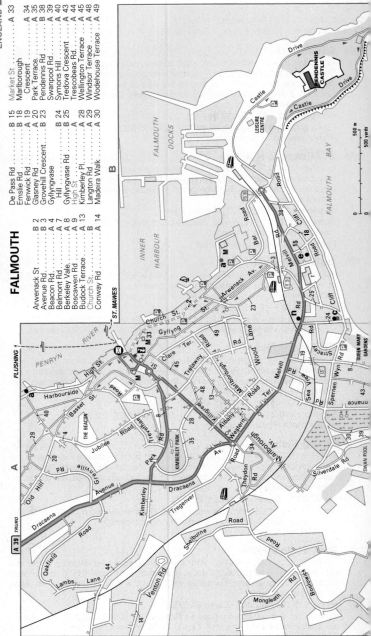

at Maenporth Beach South: 3.75 mi by Pennance Rd

X **Cove** ≤ 🏠 🕭 🗚 **P**

MODERN CUISINE · ROMANTIC Bright, stylish restaurant in a smart glass-fronted building overlooking the beach, the cove and St Anthony's Head. The modern dining room is decorated in purple and there's a lovely split-level terrace with a retractable roof. Menus are contemporary, with a strong seafood base and some Asian influences.

Menu £ 24 - Carte £ 23/36

Maenporth Beach ⊠ *TR11 5HN* – ℰ *(01326) 251 136*
– www.thecovemaenporth.co.uk – Closed 25 December

FARINGDON

Oxfordshire – Pop. 7 121 – Regional map n° **6**-A2

London 81 mi – Newbury 29 mi – Oxford 19 mi – Swindon 12 mi

🏠 **Sudbury House** 🆕 🕭 🗚 🗓 🔄 **P**

BUSINESS · FUNCTIONAL Corporate hotel in 9 acres of grounds, not far from the Folly Tower. The eight meeting rooms include a 100-seater tiered lecture theatre. Bedrooms are modern and functional with smart bathrooms. Have snacks in the bar, wood-fired specialities in relaxed Magnolia or more elaborate dishes in Restaurant 56.

49 rooms ⊇ – 🛉£ 80/150 🛉🛉£ 90/160

56 London St. ⊠ *SN7 7AA* – ℰ *(01367) 241 272*
– www.sudburyhouse.co.uk

Restaurant 56 – See restaurant listing

XxX **Restaurant 56** 🕭 🔄 **P**

MODERN CUISINE · ELEGANT Georgian manor house in the grounds of a corporate hotel – its wood-panelling and red fabrics give it a smart, formal feel. Attractive dishes are crafted from good quality produce; cooking is classically based with a modern edge.

Menu £ 20 (weekdays)/60 – Carte £ 46/57

Sudbury House Hotel, 56 London St ⊠ *SN7 7AA*
– ℰ (01367) 241 272 (booking advisable) – www.restaurant56.co.uk
– Closed Sunday and Monday

FARNBOROUGH

Hampshire – Pop. 65 034 – Regional map n° **4**-C1

London 41 mi – Reading 17 mi – Southampton 44 mi – Winchester 33 mi

🏠 **Aviator** 🕭 ≤ 🗓 🗓 🕭 🗚 🔄 🔄 **P**

BUSINESS · STYLISH Eye-catching modern hotel overlooking Farnborough Airport and boasting an unusual circular atrium, a smart first-floor lounge-bar and a small deli. Sleek, good-sized bedrooms feature light wood and modern facilities. The contemporary restaurant serves modern British dishes and steaks from the Josper grill.

169 rooms ⊇ – 🛉£ 145/245 🛉🛉£ 155/470

55 Farnborough Rd ⊠ *GU14 6EL* – *Southwest : 1 mi on A 325*
– ℰ (01252) 555 890 – www.aviatorbytag.com

FARNHAM – Dorset ➔ See Blandford Forum

FARNHAM

Surrey – Pop. 25 604 – Regional map n° **4**-C2

London 45 mi – Reading 22 mi – Southampton 39 mi – Winchester 28 mi

🍴 **Wheatsheaf**   斦 ఉ

TRADITIONAL CUISINE · PUB Meat is the speciality here, with tasty homemade burgers and steaks which use 21 day matured grassland beef from the local Surrey Farm. The smart, narrow dining room seems to stretch back for miles. Keen young staff know their stuff.

Menu £ 21 – Carte £ 24/37

19 West St ✉ GU9 7DR – 𝒞 (01252) 717 135 – www.thewheatsheaffarnham.co.uk – Closed 25 December

FAVERSHAM

Kent – Pop. 19 829 – Regional map n° **5**-C1

▶ London 52 mi – Dover 26 mi – Maidstone 21 mi – Margate 25 mi

XXX **Read's**   錄 ⇐ 喘 斦 ⇔ 🅿

TRADITIONAL CUISINE · ELEGANT An elegant Georgian manor house in landscaped grounds, with traditional country house styling, antique furnishings and lovely oil paintings. Classically based dishes have subtle modern touches and make use of seasonal produce from the walled kitchen garden and the nearby quay. Comfortable bedrooms are full of period charm and thoughtful extras provide a sense of luxury.

Menu £ 26/60

6 rooms 🛏 – ♦£ 125/185 ♦♦£ 165/195

Macknade Manor, Canterbury Rd ✉ ME13 8XE – East : 1 mi on A 2 – 𝒞 (01795) 535 344 – www.reads.com – Closed 2 weeks early September, 1 week early January, 25-26 December, Sunday and Monday

at Dargate East: 6 mi by A2 off A299

🍴 **The Dove**   喘 斦 🅿

BRITISH TRADITIONAL · PUB Red-brick Victorian pub in the heart of a sleepy hamlet, on the aptly named Plum Pudding Lane. Open fires, wood floors and old black and white photos give it a cosy, rustic feel. Dishes would be equally at home in a restaurant.

Carte £ 24/46

Plum Pudding Ln ✉ ME13 9HB – 𝒞 (01227) 751 360 (booking advisable) – www.thedovedargate.co.uk – Closed first week January, Sunday dinner, Tuesday lunch and Monday

at Oare Northwest: 2.5 mi by A2 off B2045

🍴 **Three Mariners**   喘 斦 🅿

BRITISH TRADITIONAL · PUB Welcoming 500 year old pub set in a sleepy hamlet and boasting views across the marshes to the estuary. Constantly evolving menus offer an extensive range of British and Mediterranean-influenced dishes.

Menu £ 14 (weekday lunch)/21 – Carte £ 23/34

2 Church Rd ✉ ME13 0QA – 𝒞 (01795) 533 633 – www.thethreemarinersoare.co.uk – Closed dinner 24-25 December

FELIXKIRK

North Yorkshire – Regional map n° **13**-B1

▶ London 228 mi – Harrogate 29 mi – Darlington 27 mi

🍴 **Carpenter's Arms**   ⇐ 喘 斦 ఉ 🔌 🅿

BRITISH TRADITIONAL · PUB A proper village pub with 18C origins, set in a village mentioned in the Domesday Book. Choose from blackboard specials or a wide-ranging menu of seasonal dishes, and be sure to save room for pudding. Stylishly appointed, well-equipped bedrooms overlook the Vale of Mowbray – as does the lovely terrace.

Carte £ 22/41

10 rooms 🛏 – ♦£ 100/165 ♦♦£ 120/185

✉ YO7 2DP – 𝒞 (01845) 537 369 – www.thecarpentersarmsfelixkirk.com

FENCE

Lancashire – Pop. 1 459 – Regional map n° **11**-B2

▶ London 240 mi – Skipton 17 mi – Burnley 5 mi

White Swan

BRITISH MODERN · SIMPLE Traditional pub owned by Timothy Taylor's brewery; you're always guaranteed a perfect, crystal-clear pint here – and the food is just as good. Concise set menus offer a daily selection of well-crafted, flavoursome modern dishes. The cheeseboard with homemade crackers and truffle honey is well worth a try.

Menu £ 25 (lunch) – Carte £ 26/36

300 Wheatley Lane Rd ⊠ BB12 9QA – ℰ (01282) 611 773
– www.whiteswanatfence.co.uk – Closed Monday

FERMAIN BAY → See Channel Islands (Guernsey)

FERRENSBY – North Yorkshire → See Knaresborough

FILEY

North Yorkshire – Pop. 6 530 – Regional map n° **13**-D2

▶ London 240 mi – Leeds 66 mi – York 40 mi

All Seasons

TOWNHOUSE · PERSONALISED This unassuming Victorian terraced house – just a stone's throw from the sea – conceals a smart, stylish interior, where no detail is forgotten. The cosy lounge is filled with magazines and local info, and bedrooms are bright, comfy and immaculately kept. You are welcomed with homemade cake and brownies.

6 rooms � – †£ 60/97 ††£ 80/117

11 Rutland St ⊠ YO14 9JA – ℰ (01723) 515 321 – www.allseasonsfiley.co.uk
– Closed 24-26 December

FILKINS

Oxfordshire – Pop. 434 – Regional map n° **6**-A2

▶ London 78 mi – Birmingham 72 mi – Manchester 152 mi – Bristol 59 mi

Five Alls

BRITISH TRADITIONAL · PUB Like its curious logo, this pub has it all: an open-fired bar where they serve snacks and takeaway burgers; a locals bar stocked with fine ales; three antique-furnished dining rooms; and a terrace and a garden with an Aunt Sally area. The menu is satisfyingly traditional and bedrooms are modern and cosy.

Carte £ 25/43

9 rooms ⊠ – †£ 90/180 ††£ 90/180

⊠ GL7 3JQ – ℰ (01367) 860 875 – www.thefiveallsfilkins.co.uk – Closed
25 December and Sunday dinner

FIVEHEAD

Somerset – Pop. 609 – Regional map n° **2**-B3

▶ London 140 mi – Bristol 63 mi – Cardiff 84 mi – Bournemouth 77 mi

Langford Fivehead

LUXURY · ELEGANT Beautiful 1453 country house on the Somerset Levels, surrounded by landscaped gardens – and very personally run. Tastefully furnished lounges have a classic English style and the luxurious bedrooms are furnished with antiques; one has a particularly impressive ceiling. Choose from a concise menu in the open-fired dining room; classic dishes have a subtle modern edge.

6 rooms ⊠ – †£ 100/275 ††£ 145/290

Lower Swell ⊠ TA3 6PH – East : 0.5 mi by Westport rd on Swell rd – ℰ (01460)
282 020 – www.langfordfivehead.co.uk – Closed 2 January-3 February and
25-26 December

FLAUNDEN

Hertfordshire – Pop. 5 468 – Regional map n° **7**-A2
▶ London 35 mi – Reading 43 mi – Luton 23 mi – Milton Keynes 42 mi

⌂ Bricklayers Arms   🛏 🏠 **P**

TRADITIONAL CUISINE · **INN** Smart pub tucked away in a small hamlet. There are no snacks, just hearty, French-inspired dishes and old-school puddings. The wine list is a labour of love, featuring boutique Australian wines, and Sunday lunch is a real family affair.
Menu £ 17 (weekdays) – Carte £ 26/46
Hogpits Bottom ⊠ *HP3 0PH* – ☎ *(01442) 833 322* – *www.bricklayersarms.com*
– Closed 25 December

FLETCHING

East Sussex – Pop. 301 – Regional map n° **5**-A2
▶ London 45 mi – Brighton 20 mi – Eastbourne 24 mi – Maidstone 20 mi

⌂ Griffin Inn   ⇦ 🛏 🏠 **P**

BRITISH TRADITIONAL · **CLASSIC** Hugely characterful coaching inn, under the same ownership for over 30 years. There's a sizeable garden and a terrace with a wood-burning oven for summer BBQs. Menus feature British classics and some Mediterranean influences. Individually decorated bedrooms are accessed via narrow, sloping corridors.
Carte £ 26/41
13 rooms ⊡ – ♦£ 70/80 ♦♦£ 85/155
⊠ *TN22 3SS* – ☎ *(01825) 722 890* – *www.thegriffininn.co.uk* – *Closed 25 December*

FOLKESTONE

Kent – Pop. 51 337 – Regional map n° **5**-D2
▶ London 76 mi – Brighton 76 mi – Dover 8 mi – Maidstone 33 mi

⌂ Relish   🏊

TOWNHOUSE · **DESIGN** A fine Regency house with a spacious, stylish interior. Contemporary bedrooms are named after their colour scheme or view – one has a four-poster bed. The smart lounge and breakfast room lead to a terrace overlooking the gardens.
10 rooms ⊡ – ♦£ 75 ♦♦£ 98/150
Town plan: Z-n – *4 Augusta Gdns* ⊠ *CT20 2RR* – ☎ *(01303) 850 952*
– www.hotelrelish.co.uk – *Closed 23-30 December*

⌂ 10 to12 Folkestone 🆕

TOWNHOUSE · **FUNCTIONAL** Classic Victorian end-of-terrace house, close to the seafront. It's run by friendly owners and is the perfect place to stop before getting the ferry. Bedrooms are particularly spacious and are appointed in a simple, modern manner.
10 rooms ⊡ – ♦£ 100 ♦♦£ 110/120
Town plan: Z-a – *10-12 Langhorne Gdns* ⊠ *CT20 2EA* – ☎ *(01303) 21012 7*
– www.10to12folkestone.co.uk – *Closed 1 week Christmas*

XX Rocksalt   ⇦ ≪ 🏠 ⌂ **AC** ⇧

FISH AND SEAFOOD · **DESIGN** Set within a stylish harbourfront eco-building affording lovely sea views. Smart cantilevered dining room with full-length windows opening onto a terrace; semi open air bar upstairs. Menus mix seafood and local meats; veg is from their farm. Nearby, bedrooms boast antique beds, Egyptian cotton linen and wet rooms.
Menu £ 25 (weekday lunch) – Carte £ 28/58
4 rooms ⊡ – ♦£ 85/115 ♦♦£ 85/115
Town plan: Z-x – *4-5 Fish Market* ⊠ *CT19 6AA* – ☎ *(01303) 212 070*
– www.rocksaltfolkestone.co.uk – *Closed Sunday dinner*

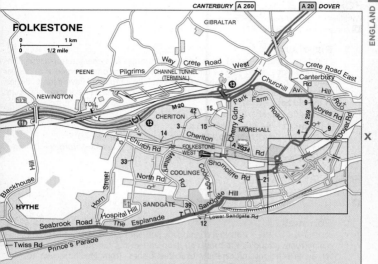

FOLKESTONE

CANTERBURY A 260   A 20 DOVER

GIBRALTAR

A 259   A 260 (A 20)

CENTRE

0   400 m
0   400 yards

FONTHILL BISHOP

Wiltshire – Regional map n° **2**-C2

▶ London 101 mi – Exeter 77 mi – Cheltenham 85 mi

✗ Riverbarn ⟵ 🛋 🖼 ♿ 🅿

MODERN CUISINE · SIMPLE Two riverside cottages in a characterful village. Dining takes places in a series of beamed, low-ceilinged rooms adorned with copper pans and prints. Two brothers create carefully prepared, flavoursome dishes, which their parents bring to the table. Simple, comfortable bedrooms are found in the old barn.

Menu £ 18 (lunch)/65 – Carte £ 27/44

3 rooms ☲ – ♦£ 60/75 ♦♦£ 75/85

✉ SP3 5SF – ✆ (01747) 820 232 *(bookings advisable at dinner) – www.theriverbarn.org.uk – lunch only and dinner Thursday-Saturday – Closed 26 December-mid January and Monday*

FONTMELL MAGNA

Dorset – Pop. 333 – Regional map n° **2**-C3

▶ London 115 mi – Bristol 60 mi – Cardiff 93 mi – Southampton 52 mi

🍴 Fontmell ⟵ 🖼 🅿

MODERN CUISINE · PUB Stylish, modern pub with a simple front bar; the smart dining room straddles the brook, so keep an eye out for otters. Daily menus offer an eclectic mix of carefully executed dishes, from Mediterranean to Thai. Bedrooms are named after butterflies; Mallyshag is particularly spacious, with a roll-top bath.

Carte £ 21/42

6 rooms ☲ – ♦£ 75/145 ♦♦£ 85/155

✉ SP7 0PA – ✆ (01747) 811 441 – *www.thefontmell.com – Closed 26 December*

FORDINGBRIDGE

Hampshire – Pop. 4 474 – Regional map n° **4**-A2

▶ London 101 mi – Bournemouth 17 mi – Salisbury 11 mi – Southampton 22 mi

⌂ Three Lions 🍴 🐾 🛋 🅿

FAMILY · COSY A former farmhouse and pub in a small hamlet. Homely bedrooms are split between this and various outbuildings; those in the garden are the largest and come with French windows and outdoor seating. Blackboard menus offer classically inspired Anglo-French dishes crafted from local seasonal produce.

7 rooms ☲ – ♦£ 79 ♦♦£ 125

Stuckton Rd, Stuckton ✉ *SP6 2HF – Southeast : 1 mi by B 3078 – ✆ (01425) 652 489 – www.thethreelionsrestaurant.co.uk – Closed last 2 weeks February*

FOREST GREEN

Surrey – ✉ Dorking – Pop. 1 843 – Regional map n° **4**-D2

▶ London 34 mi – Guildford 13 mi – Horsham 10 mi

🍴 Parrot Inn 🛋 🖼 🅿

TRADITIONAL CUISINE · RUSTIC Traditional 17C pub set on the village green. Well-priced, generously proportioned dishes use produce from the pub's own farm. Homemade bread, cheese, cakes and preserves for sale.

Carte £ 21/35

✉ RH5 5RZ – ✆ (01306) 621 339 – *www.theparrot.co.uk – Closed 25 December and Sunday dinner*

FOREST ROW

East Sussex – Pop. 4 096 – Regional map n° **5**-A2

▶ London 35 mi – Brighton 26 mi – Eastbourne 30 mi – Maidstone 32 mi

🏨 Ashdown Park

LUXURY · CLASSIC Impressive Victorian building on the edge of Ashdown Forest. The spacious country house interior boasts grand staircases, impressive halls and open-fired lounges with parkland views. Elegant classical bedrooms feature antique furnishings. The traditional, formal restaurant has a pleasant estate outlook.

106 rooms ⊊ – ♦£170/380 ♦♦£170/380 – 3 suites

Colemans Hatch Rd, Wych Cross ⊠ *RH18 5JR – South : 3.25 mi by A 22 – ℰ (01342) 824 988 – www.ashdownpark.com*

FOTHERINGHAY

Northamptonshire – Regional map n° **9**-C2

◗ London 87 mi – Northampton 34 mi – Peterborough 12 mi

🍴 Falcon Inn

TRADITIONAL CUISINE · PUB An attractive stone inn with a nice terrace and garden. Good ingredients feature in a wide range of flavoursome dishes and local game is a feature. You'll find the regulars playing darts in the tap bar and diners in the conservatory.

Menu £14 (weekdays) – Carte £25/37

Fotheringhay ⊠ *PE8 5HZ – ℰ (01832) 226 254 – www.thefalcon-inn.co.uk*

FOWEY

Cornwall – Pop. 2 131 – Regional map n° **1**-B2

◗ London 277 mi – Newquay 24 mi – Plymouth 34 mi – Truro 22 mi

🏨 Fowey Hall

COUNTRY HOUSE · HOMELY Striking 19C manor house with an ornate, period-furnished lounge and a mix of traditional and modern bedrooms. Families are well-catered for and an informal feel pervades. Oak-panelled restaurant for adults; conservatory for those with children. Set menu has modern touches; less formal à la carte.

36 rooms ⊊ – ♦£165/700 ♦♦£185/700 – 11 suites

Hanson Dr ⊠ *PL23 1ET – West : 0.5 mi off A 3082 – ℰ (01726) 833 866 – www.foweyhallhotel.co.uk*

🏠 Old Quay House

TOWNHOUSE · CONTEMPORARY 19C former seamen's mission in a pretty harbour village; now a characterful boutique hotel with a friendly, laid-back feel. Bedrooms are individually decorated and have a contemporary, understated style; most have balconies and water views. Be sure to spend some time on the lovely terrace beside the river.

11 rooms ⊊ – ♦£160/195 ♦♦£190/335

28 Fore St ⊠ *PL23 1AQ – ℰ (01726) 833 302 – www.theoldquayhouse.com – Closed 1-20 December*

Q – See restaurant listing

🍴🍴 Q

MODERN CUISINE · FRIENDLY Light, bright hotel restaurant with wood framed mirrors, wicker furnishings and a glorious terrace with harbour views. Light lunches and more sophisticated dinners of modern, flavoursome dishes; fish is from Looe and shellfish, from Fowey.

Menu £30 (dinner) – Carte lunch £28/49

Old Quay House Hotel, 28 Fore St ⊠ *PL23 1AQ – ℰ (01726) 833 302 – www.theoldquayhouse.com – Closed 1-20 December and lunch October-April*

🍴 The Globe 🆕

BRITISH TRADITIONAL · COSY 400 year old posting house run by lifelong friends and refurbished by local craftsmen. The food keeps things local too, with bread from the adjacent bakery, meats from a nearby farm, wild garlic from the fields and beer from St Austell.

Menu £15 (weekday lunch) – Carte £26/34

24 Fore St ⊠ *PL23 1AQ – ℰ (01726) 337 076 – www.theglobefowey.co.uk*

at Golant North: 3 mi by B3269 – ✉ Fowey

ⓗ **Cormorant**   ✿ ⌕ ≼ ⇤ ⌂ ▣ ⌷ ⑩ ▣

HOLIDAY HOTEL · PERSONALISED Well-run hotel in a superb waterside position. At only one room deep, all of its bedrooms overlook the estuary; the superior rooms boast balconies. Appealing seasonal menus feature local meats and seafood dishes. Light lunches offered in the formal restaurant or on the terrace.

14 rooms 🖵 – ♦£ 80/230 ♦♦£ 80/230

✉ PL23 1LL – ℰ (01726) 833 426 – www.cormoranthotel.co.uk

FOXHAM

Wiltshire – Regional map n° **2**-C2

▶ London 94 mi – Bristol 28 mi – Cardiff 61 mi – Southampton 81 mi

ⓘ **Foxham Inn**   ⇆ ⌂ ⅙ ▣

CLASSIC CUISINE · SIMPLE Family-run pub in a sleepy Wiltshire village. A semi-covered terrace overlooks the fields and inside there's a cosy bar and a light, airy restaurant in a conservatory extension. Dishes are uniformly priced, and everything from the condiments to the ice creams is homemade. Bedrooms are warm and homely.

Menu £ 16 (weekday lunch) – Carte £ 26/39

2 rooms 🖵 – ♦£ 75/85 ♦♦£ 90/100

✉ SN15 4NQ – ℰ (01249) 740 665 (booking advisable) – www.thefoxhaminn.co.uk
– Closed 2 weeks early January and Monday

FREATHY

Cornwall – Regional map n° **1**-C2

▶ London 235 mi – Plymouth 9 mi – Tavistock 22 mi

✗ **The View**   ≼ ⌂ ▣

BRITISH MODERN · SIMPLE Charming and informal converted café perched on a cliff, with coastal views. Relaxed daytime vibe; more atmospheric in the evening. Assured, confident, generous cooking and friendly service. Plenty of seafood and tasty homemade bread.

Menu £ 14 (lunch) – Carte £ 31/39

✉ PL10 1JY – East : 1 mi – ℰ (01752) 822 345 – www.theview-restaurant.co.uk
– Closed February, Monday and Tuesday

FRILSHAM – West Berkshire ➜ See Yattendon

FRITHSDEN

Hertfordshire – Regional map n° **7**-A2

▶ London 33 mi – St Albans 11 mi – Aylesbury 16 mi

ⓘ **Alford Arms**   ⌂ ▣

BRITISH TRADITIONAL · INN Attractive Victorian pub beside the village green. The traditional British menu follows the seasons closely, with salads and fish featuring in the summer and game and comfort dishes in the winter; have a look at the tempting specials board.

Carte £ 20/37

✉ HP1 3DD – ℰ (01442) 864 480 – www.alfordarmsfrithsden.co.uk – Closed
25-26 December

FROGGATT

Derbyshire – Regional map n° **9**-A1

▶ London 167 mi – Bakewell 6 mi – Sheffield 11 mi

ⓘ **Chequers Inn**   ⇆ ⌂ ▣

BRITISH TRADITIONAL · PUB Traditional 16C inn built right into the stone boulders of Froggatt Edge and boasting a direct path up to the peak. Cooking is unfussy, tasty and largely classical, with more imaginative specials on the blackboard. Comfortable bedrooms; Number One, to the rear, is the quietest.

Carte £ 26/35

6 rooms 🖵 – ♦£ 89/119 ♦♦£ 89/119

Hope Valley ✉ S32 3ZJ – on A 625 – ℰ (01433) 630 231
– www.chequers-froggatt.com – Closed 25 December

FROME

Somerset – Pop. 26 203 – Regional map n° **2**-C2

London 118 mi – Bristol 24 mi – Southampton 52 mi – Swindon 44 mi

🏛 **Babington House**

LUXURY · STYLISH Behind this country house's classic Georgian façade is a cool, fashionable hotel with bold colour schemes and a bohemian feel. Kick-back in the luxurious lounges or relax in the beautiful spa with its superb fitness area and pool. Bedrooms are modern and understated. The newly built but classic-looking Orangery offers an accessible menu of Italian-influenced dishes.

33 rooms – †£ 250/570 ††£ 250/570 – �)£ 17 – 11 suites

Babington ✉ BA11 3RW – Northwest : 6.5 mi by A 362 on Vobster rd – ℰ (01373) 812 266 – www.babingtonhouse.co.uk

FULBECK

Lincolnshire – Regional map n° **9**-C2

London 123 mi – Birmingham 83 mi – Leeds 80 mi – Sheffield 54 mi

🍴 **Hare & Hounds**

BRITISH TRADITIONAL · PUB Built in 1680 as a house, this charmingly decorated pub has been enthusiastically adopted by the locals. The ethos of 'simple pub classics done well' goes down a storm – the menus are refreshingly concise and local produce is to the fore. Smart, comfortable bedrooms in the old stables; popular jazz evenings.

Carte £ 20/36

8 rooms ☟ – †£ 60/65 ††£ 80/85

The Green ✉ NG32 3JJ – ℰ (01400) 273 322 – www.hareandhoundsfulbeck.com – Closed 25 December and Sunday dinner

FULLER STREET

Essex – Pop. 50 – Regional map n° **7**-C2

London 52 mi – Birmingham 141 mi – Leicester 112 mi – Coventry 123 mi

🍴 **Square & Compasses**

BRITISH MODERN · PUB A hugely characterful pub hidden down rural lanes: run with a passion by its welcoming owners. One menu lists classic dishes; the other features more adventurous choices, including fish caught off the Essex coast and local game in season.

Carte £ 19/33

✉ CM3 2BB – ℰ (01245) 361 477 (booking essential) – www.thesquareandcompasses.co.uk

FULMER

Buckinghamshire – Pop. 230 – Regional map n° **6**-D3

London 21 mi – Croydon 49 mi – Barnet 30 mi – Ealing 13 mi

🍴 **Black Horse**

BRITISH TRADITIONAL · PUB Whitewashed village pub with thick walls, cosy alcoves, a wood-burning stove and a gem of a garden for sunny days. The stylish, formal dining area is hung with delightful portraits. Dishes include sharing boards, small plates and grills. Uniquely styled bedrooms have spacious, modern bathrooms.

Menu £ 13 – Carte £ 21/42

2 rooms – †£ 120/150 ††£ 120/150

Windmill Rd ✉ SL3 6HD – ℰ (01753) 663 183 – www.theblackhorsefulmer.co.uk – Closed 25 December and Sunday dinner

FUNTINGTON – West Sussex ➜ See Chichester

FYFIELD

Essex – Pop. 737 – Regional map n° **7**-B2

▶ London 33 mi – Cambridge 44 mi – Chelmsford 14 mi

🍴 **Queens Head**   🖼 🏠 ♿ **P**

MODERN CUISINE · PUB Characterful village pub with a pretty rear garden leading down to the river. The inviting interior features original 16C beams and fireplaces. Menus change regularly and offer a good choice of classics and blackboard specials.

Menu £ 20 (weekdays) – Carte £ 22/39

Queen St ✉ CM5 0RY – ✆ (01277) 899 231 – www.thequeensheadfyfield.co.uk – Closed 26 December and Monday

FYFIELD – Oxfordshire ➜ See Oxford

GEDNEY DYKE

Lincolnshire – Pop. 320 – Regional map n° **9**-D2

▶ London 112 mi – Birmingham 112 mi – Sheffield 91 mi – Cambridge 32 mi

🍴🍴 **Chequers**   🏠 ♿ **P**

🐌 **BRITISH MODERN · FORMAL** Formerly a pub, now a stylish modern bar and restaurant with a smart conservatory extension opening onto a pavement terrace. The chef is keen to use the wealth of produce on his doorstep. Preparation is precise and cooking is refined and flavoursome; the set menus represent particularly good value.

Menu £ 20 (weekday lunch) – Carte dinner £ 22/41

Main St ✉ PE12 0AJ – ✆ (01406) 366 700 – www.the-chequers.co.uk – Closed first 2 weeks January, Sunday dinner, Monday and Tuesday

GEORGE GREEN

Buckinghamshire – Pop. 950 – Regional map n° **6**-D3

▶ London 56 mi – Croydon 49 mi – Barnet 78 mi – Ealing 60 mi

🏨 **Pinewood**   🏠 🖼 🔄 ♿ 🖼 🗠 🗠 **P**

BUSINESS · MODERN Modern, purpose-built hotel set in 4 acres; named after the nearby film studios and within easy reach of 3 motorways. Good-sized, well-equipped bedrooms are split between the house and an adjacent annexe. The simply decorated dining room serves a wide-ranging menu; go for a pizza from the wood-fired oven.

49 rooms ⌂ – ♦£ 79/139 ♦♦£ 89/159

Wexham Park Ln, Uxbridge Rd ✉ SL3 6AP – on A 412 – ✆ (01753) 896 400 – www.pinewoodhotel.co.uk – Closed 24-28 December

GERRARDS CROSS

Buckinghamshire – Pop. 20 633 – Regional map n° **6**-D3

▶ London 22 mi – Birmingham 106 mi – Bristol 112 mi – Cardiff 145 mi

🍴 **Three Oaks**   🖼 🏠 **P**

🐌 **BRITISH MODERN · PUB** An appealing, well-run pub in a rural location, with several stylishly decorated rooms: dine in the brighter room overlooking the terrace and pretty garden. Cooking is tasty, satisfying and seasonal, and they offer particularly good value set lunch and dinner menus. The bright young staff are eager to please.

Menu £ 12/19 (weekdays) – Carte £ 23/39

Austenwood Ln ✉ SL9 8NL – Northwest : 0.75 mi by A 413 on Gold Hill rd – ✆ (01753) 899 016 – www.thethreeoaksgx.co.uk – Closed Sunday dinner

GESTINGTHORPE

Essex – Regional map n° **7**-C2

▶ London 65 mi – Colchester 20 mi – Ipswich 29 mi

🍽️ **Pheasant** ⇐ 🛏 🅿️

BRITISH TRADITIONAL · **PUB** A true country inn centring around sustainability, where they grow vegetables and keep chickens and bees. Simple cooking offers traditional, heartwarming dishes and the inviting, low-beamed bar and takeaway fish & chips keep the locals happy. Stylish, modern bedrooms; those to the rear have country views.

Carte £ 25/37

5 rooms ⌑ – 🛏£ 85/130 🛏🛏£ 95/185

✉ CO9 3AU – South : 0.75 mi by Church St on Halstead rd – ✆ (01787) 465 010 – www.thepheasant.net – Closed January and Monday in winter

GILLINGHAM

Dorset – Pop. 11 278 – Regional map n° **2**-C3

▶ London 116 mi – Bournemouth 34 mi – Bristol 46 mi – Southampton 52 mi

🏠 **Stock Hill Country House** 🌿 🦢 🛏 🏠 🍽 🏊 🅿️

TRADITIONAL · **CLASSIC** Personally-run Georgian country house with later extensions, set in attractive mature grounds. Classical lounges boast heavy fabrics and antiques. Spacious bedrooms – in the main house and stables – display a mix of cottagey and country house styles; all have good facilities. The formal two-roomed restaurant has its own kitchen garden and serves Austrian cuisine.

9 rooms (dinner included) ⌑ – 🛏£ 95/145 🛏🛏£ 195/280

Stock Hill ✉ SP8 5NR – West : 1.5 mi on B 3081 – ✆ (01747) 823 626 – www.stockhillhouse.co.uk

GISBURN

Lancashire – Regional map n° **11**-B2

▶ London 242 mi – Bradford 28 mi – Skipton 12 mi

🏠 **Park House** 🛏 🏊 🅿️

TOWNHOUSE · **CLASSIC** Imposing Victorian house with a classical open-fired drawing room and a small library leading to a hidden stepped garden. Bedrooms mix antique and more modern furnishings. Good breakfast selection; tea and homemade cake served on arrival.

6 rooms ⌑ – 🛏£ 55/95 🛏🛏£ 65/110

13 Church View ✉ BB7 4HG – ✆ (01200) 445 269 – www.parkhousegisburn.co.uk – Closed December-February

🍴 **La Locanda**

ITALIAN · **NEIGHBOURHOOD** Charming low-beamed, flag-floored cottage run by a keen couple. Comfy lounge serving Italian drinks, with the dining room above. Extensive menu of hearty homemade dishes; try the tasty pastas. Good quality local and imported produce.

Menu £ 15 (lunch and early dinner) – Carte £ 18/33

Main St ✉ BB7 4HH – ✆ (01200) 445 303 – www.lalocanda.co.uk – Closed 25 December, 1 January and lunch Monday-Wednesday

GITTISHAM – Devon ➡ See Honiton

GLINTON – Peterborough ➡ See Peterborough

GODALMING

Surrey – Pop. 22 689 – Regional map n° **4**-C2

▶ London 39 mi – Guildford 5 mi – Southampton 48 mi

🍴🍴 **La Luna** 🌸 🅰️🅲 ⇐

ITALIAN · **BRASSERIE** Contemporary Italian restaurant whose passionate owner looks after his guests with great enthusiasm. Classic Italian dishes use excellent ingredients. Particularly good selection of authentic antipasti and pasta.

Menu £ 15 (weekday lunch) – Carte £ 25/40

10-14 Wharf St ✉ GU7 1NN – ✆ (01483) 414 155 – www.lalunarestaurant.co.uk – Closed Sunday and Monday

at Lower Eashing West: 1.75 mi by A3100

📖 Stag on the River ⇔ 🛏 🛋 🅿

MODERN CUISINE · COSY Pretty 16C former mill with a smart modern feel and a terrace overlooking the old millstream. Menus offer hearty, traditional dishes and sharing plates – the 8hr roasted pork belly is a popular choice. Attractively appointed, contemporary bedrooms come with a complimentary bottle of locally brewed beer.
Carte £ 20/41
7 rooms ☑ – †£ 65/95 ††£ 95/125
Lower Eashing Rd ⊠ GU7 2QG – ℰ (01483) 421568
– www.stagontherivereashing.co.uk – Closed 25 December

GODSHILL – Isle of Wight ➜ See Wight (Isle of)

GOLANT Cornwall ➜ See Fowey

GOREY ➜ See Channel Islands (Jersey)

GORING

Oxfordshire – Pop. 4 193 – Regional map n° **10**-B3
▶ London 56 mi – Oxford 16 mi – Reading 12 mi

📖 Miller of Mansfield ⓝ ⇔ 🛋

BRITISH MODERN · FRIENDLY A large 18C coaching inn on the banks of the Thames; sit in one of two cosy rooms or out on the terrace. Dishes range from homemade sausage rolls to poached lobster salad. The homemade bread and skilfully prepared desserts are a highlight. Bedrooms successfully blend modern furnishings with original features.
Menu £ 13 (weekday lunch) – Carte £ 28/42
13 rooms – †£ 80/110 ††£ 110/195
High St ⊠ RG8 9AW – ℰ (01491) 872829 – www.millerofmansfield.com

Good food at moderate prices? Look for the Bib Gourmand ⊛.

GORRAN HAVEN

Cornwall – Regional map n° **1**-B3
▶ London 260 mi – Plymouth 53 mi – Torbay 80 mi – Torquay 83 mi

🏨 Llawnroc ✧ 🗞 🖭 👌 🗚 🅿

FAMILY · MODERN Unpretentious boutique hotel that's popular with families – enjoy tea on the terrific terrace. Boldly coloured, well-equipped bedrooms feature plenty of contemporary design touches; bathrooms have drench showers and Voya seaweed toiletries. Unfussy bistro dishes are served in the minimalist restaurant.
18 rooms ☑ – †£ 80/250 ††£ 80/250
Chute Ln ⊠ PL26 6NU – ℰ (01726) 843461 – www.thellawnrochotel.co.uk
– Closed 25-26 December and restricted opening in winter

GRANGE-OVER-SANDS

Cumbria – Pop. 4 788 – Regional map n° **12**-A3
▶ London 268 mi – Kendal 13 mi – Lancaster 24 mi

🏰 **Netherwood** ⌂ ⪦ 🛏 🖼 🎛 🖥 ⬇ 🛎 P

BUSINESS · CLASSIC Impressive castellated Victorian mansion on the hillside, affording lovely bay views. Traditional guest areas display wood panelling and original features. Bedrooms are simple and well-maintained; the most contemporary rooms are in the annexe. Formal dining comes with a great outlook.

34 rooms ⛁ – 🛉£ 70/130 🛉🛉£ 120/240
Lindale Rd ⊠ *LA11 6ET –* ℰ *(015395) 32 552*
– www.netherwood-hotel.co.uk

🏠 **Clare House** ⌂ ⪦ 🛏 🛎 P

FAMILY · PERSONALISED Family-run Victorian house set in lovely gardens, overlooking Morecambe Bay. Two classical sitting rooms. Stylish, boldly coloured bedrooms in the main house and smaller, simpler rooms with balconies in the wing. The smart, modern dining room offers traditional daily menus.

18 rooms (dinner included) ⛁ – 🛉£ 74/82 🛉🛉£ 148/164
Park Rd ⊠ *LA11 7HQ –* ℰ *(015395) 33 026*
– www.clarehousehotel.co.uk – Closed 14 December-21 March

at Cartmel Northwest: 3 mi – ⊠ Grange-Over-Sands

XXX **L'Enclume** (Simon Rogan) ⪤ 🛏 🅰

✿✿ CREATIVE · RUSTIC A very well run, stone-built former smithy in an attractive village. Inventive modern cooking has a superb balance of textures and flavours and a pleasing lightness; home-grown and foraged ingredients feature. Smart, comfortable bedrooms are spread about the village; breakfast is taken at Rogan and Company.
➜ Milk-fed Holker lamb with whey onions, ramson and potato. Langoustine, parsnip, scurvy grass and radish. Apple and gingerbread with birch sap, pear and oats.
Menu £ 45/120 – set menu only
16 rooms ⛁ – 🛉£ 89/179 🛉🛉£ 119/199
Cavendish St ⊠ *LA11 6PZ –* ℰ *(015395) 36 362 (booking essential)*
– www.lenclume.co.uk – Closed 5-11 December and Monday lunch

X **Rogan and Company**

BRITISH MODERN · NEIGHBOURHOOD The informal cousin to L'Enclume, set in a converted cottage by a lovely stream. The open-plan interior has dark wood beams and a minimalist feel; watch the chefs in the large kitchen pass. Modern dishes rely on local, seasonal produce.
Menu £ 28/41
The Square ⊠ *LA11 6QD –* ℰ *(015395) 35 917*
– www.roganandcompany.co.uk

GRANTHAM
Lincolnshire – Pop. 41 998 – Regional map n° **9**-C2
▶ London 113 mi – Leicester 31 mi – Lincoln 29 mi – Nottingham 24 mi

XX **Harry's Place** P

BRITISH TRADITIONAL · COSY Long-standing, intimate restaurant in a former farmhouse: it consists of just 3 tables and is personally run by a dedicated and delightful husband and wife team. Warm, welcoming feel, with fresh flowers, candles and antiques. Classically based menus offer 2 choices per course. Good cheese selection.
Carte £ 57/70
17 High St, Great Gonerby ⊠ *NG31 8JS – Northwest : 2 mi on B 1174*
– ℰ *(01476) 561 780 (booking essential) – Closed 25 December-1 January, 2 weeks August, Sunday and Monday*

at Hough-on-the-Hill North: 6.75 mi by A607 – ⊠ Grantham

XX Brownlow Arms ⇦ 🏠 🔲 🅿

BRITISH MODERN · INN Characterful former shooting lodge for the nearby Belton Estate, with wood-panelled walls and large open fireplaces. Lengthy menu and specials list offer classically based dishes with modern presentation. Lovely terrace and friendly service. Delightful bedrooms are furnished with contemporary fabrics and period pieces.

Carte £ 29/48

7 rooms ⌷ – †£ 70/100 ††£ 110/120
High Rd ⊠ NG32 2AZ – ℰ (01400) 250 234 – www.thebrownlowarms.com
– dinner only and Sunday lunch – Closed Sunday dinner and Monday

GRASMERE see Ambleside plan

Cumbria – ⊠ Ambleside – Regional map n° **12**-A2
▶ London 282 mi – Carlisle 43 mi – Kendal 18 mi

Plan : see Ambleside

🏠 Rothay Garden ⌂ 🛏 🏠 ⅗ 🅿

COUNTRY HOUSE · STYLISH Slate-built Lakeland house with modern extensions, which include a spa and a copper-roofed conservatory restaurant with a lovely outlook and a classically based menu. Bedrooms are stylish and contemporary – many have king-sized beds and some have balconies or patios; the Loft Suites are the best.

30 rooms ⌷ – †£ 105/150 ††£ 131/271
Town plan: AY-s – *Broadgate ⊠ LA22 9RJ – ℰ (015394) 35 334*
– www.rothaygarden.com

🏠 Daffodil ⌂ ⇦ 🛏 ◉ 🏠 🔲 ⅗ 🔲 🔲 🅿

BUSINESS · CONTEMPORARY Smart corporate hotel with lake and mountain views, set opposite the Wordsworth Museum. The small spa specialises in Rasul mud treatments. Bedrooms have multi-media panels, Molton Brown toiletries and king, super king or emperor sized beds. Light lunches, followed by hearty, traditional dishes in the evening.

78 rooms ⌷ – †£ 120/350 ††£ 130/380 – 13 suites
Town plan: AY-x – *Keswick Rd ⊠ LA22 9PR – on A 591 – ℰ (015394) 63 550*
– www.daffodilhotel.co.uk

🏠 Moss Grove Organic 🅿

TRADITIONAL · STYLISH Laid-back house with a stylish interior featuring many reclaimed furnishings. Funky bedrooms boast large beds, Bose sound systems and whirlpool baths. Organic breakfasts include tasty veggie options; help yourself from the kitchen.

11 rooms ⌷ – †£ 84/160 ††£ 99/259
Town plan: BZ-s – *⊠ LA22 9SW – ℰ (015394) 35 251 – www.mossgrove.com*
– Closed 24-25 December

🏠 Grasmere ⌂ 🛏 🅿

TRADITIONAL · PERSONALISED Small Victorian house close to the village centre, with the River Rothay running through the garden. The spacious lounge and bar are traditionally decorated; similarly styled bedrooms are named after writers and some have antique beds. The classically furnished dining room overlooks the garden.

11 rooms ⌷ – †£ 62/67 ††£ 114/144
Town plan: BZ-r – *Broadgate ⊠ LA22 9TA*
– ℰ (015394) 35 277 – www.grasmerehotel.co.uk
– Restricted opening in winter

⌂ Oak Bank

TRADITIONAL · PERSONALISED Passionately run Victorian house with a pretty rear garden. Relax beside the converted range in the sitting room or next to the open fire in the lounge-bar. Modern bedrooms have comfortable beds, bold fabrics and bright colours.

13 rooms ⌑ – †£ 89/123 ††£ 98/183

Town plan: BZ-x – *Broadgate* ⊠ *LA22 9TA* – ℰ *(015394) 35 217*
– www.lakedistricthotel.co.uk – Closed 2-21 January,1-5 May, 7-18 August and 20-26 December

Dining Room – See restaurant listing

XX Dining Room

MODERN CUISINE · FORMAL Split-roomed hotel restaurant in a Victorian house, with a pleasant conservatory overlooking the garden. The concise daily menu features interesting modern dishes crafted from seasonal Lakeland produce; everything is made in-house.

Menu £ 28 (lunch)/60

Town plan: BZ-x – *Oak Bank Hotel, Broadgate* ⊠ *LA22 9TA* – ℰ *(015394) 35 217 (booking essential) – www.lakedistricthotel.co.uk – Closed 2-21 January, 1-5 May, 7-18 August and 20-26 December*

GRASSINGTON

North Yorkshire – ⊠ Skipton – Pop. 1 126 – Regional map n° **13**-A2
▶ London 240 mi – Bradford 30 mi – Burnley 28 mi – Leeds 37 mi

⌂ Ashfield House

TRADITIONAL · PERSONALISED Bright, cheery hotel with a larger-than-life owner. Formerly three 1604 lead miners' cottages, its old beams and mullioned windows blend well with the Mediterranean colours. The cottage bedroom boasts a spiral staircase and terrace.

8 rooms ⌑ – †£ 80/120 ††£ 88/200

Summers Fold ⊠ *BD23 5AE* – *off Main St* – ℰ *(01756) 752 584*
– www.ashfieldhouse.co.uk – Closed 23-27 December

▥ Grassington Lodge

TRADITIONAL · STYLISH Stone house close to the square, with a sleek breakfast room and two lounges; one offering complimentary sherry, the other with a large DVD collection and a laptop. Bedrooms are modern and unfussy; those in the eaves are the best.

12 rooms ⌑ – †£ 70/165 ††£ 80/165

8 Wood Ln ⊠ *BD23 5LU* – ℰ *(01756) 752 518* – *www.grassingtonlodge.co.uk*
– Closed 5 January-first week February

XX Grassington House

BRITISH MODERN · BRASSERIE Georgian house with a large bar-lounge, two dining rooms and delightful service. Classical menus display Mediterranean touches and include their home-bred pork. Smart, modern bedrooms; No.6 has a roll-top bath in the room. Home-cured bacon or sausages are offered at breakfast and they host regular wine dinners.

Menu £ 15 (lunch and early dinner)/40 – Carte £ 23/40

9 rooms ⌑ – †£ 105 ††£ 120/140

5 The Square ⊠ *BD23 5AQ* – ℰ *(01756) 752 406*
– www.grassingtonhousehotel.co.uk – Closed 25 December

GREAT BIRCHAM

Norfolk – Regional map n° **8**-C1
▶ London 115 mi – Hunstanton 10 mi – King's Lynn 15 mi

🏠 King's Head

INN · STYLISH This family run inn dates from the Edwardian era and is well-located for the north Norfolk coast and the Sandringham Estate. Individually decorated bedrooms are contemporary in style. Enjoy a G&T from the 'gin wall' in the cosy bar then dine on pub classics either here or in the restaurant.

12 rooms ⌕ – ♦£ 89/125 ♦♦£ 125/175

✉ PE31 6RJ – ℰ (01485) 578 265 – www.the-kings-head-bircham.co.uk

GREAT DUNMOW

Essex – Pop. 7 749 – Regional map n° **7**-C2

▶ London 42 mi – Cambridge 27 mi – Chelmsford 13 mi – Colchester 24 mi

✗ Square 1

MODERN CUISINE · FRIENDLY Pretty little whitewashed building; once a 14C monastic reading room. Much original character remains in the form of exposed beams and low ceilings; which contrast with vibrant modern art. Unfussy monthly menu has Mediterranean leanings.

Menu £ 13 (lunch) – Carte £ 22/38

15 High St. ✉ CM6 1AB – ℰ (01371) 859 922 – www.square1restaurant.co.uk
– Closed 25-26 December and Sunday dinner

GREAT LIMBER

Lincolnshire – Pop. 271 – Regional map n° **9**-C1

▶ London 172 mi – Lincoln 31 mi – Grimsby 13 mi

🍴 New Inn

MODERN CUISINE · INN Smart modern pub with a stylish terrace. The bar is a hit with the locals, while the lounge is the perfect spot for a fireside G&T before dinner in the contemporary restaurant. Carefully prepared, sophisticated dishes have a modern touch. Smart bedrooms exceed expectations; some are in a barn conversion.

Carte £ 25/41

10 rooms – ♦£ 78/135 ♦♦£ 78/135 – ⌕ £ 10

2 High St ✉ DN37 8JL – ℰ (01469) 569 998 – www.thenewinngreatlimber.co.uk

GREAT MALVERN

Worcestershire – Pop. 36 770 – Regional map n° **10**-B3

▶ London 127 mi – Birmingham 34 mi – Cardiff 66 mi – Gloucester 24 mi

🏠 Cotford

TOWNHOUSE · CONTEMPORARY The owners of this 1851 Gothic-style house (built for the Bishop of Worcester), put a lot of effort into getting things right. It mixes the traditional and the contemporary and has stylish bedrooms and a chic black and pink bar.

15 rooms ⌕ – ♦£ 70/89 ♦♦£ 130/145

Town plan: B-s – 51 Graham Rd ✉ WR14 2HU – ℰ (01684) 572 427
– www.cotfordhotel.co.uk

L' Amuse Bouche – See restaurant listing

✗✗ L' Amuse Bouche

BRITISH MODERN · FASHIONABLE Start with an aperitif in the stylish bar or traditional lounge of this Gothic hotel, then head for the contemporary dining room overlooking the gardens. Boldly flavoured, classically based dishes have a subtle modern touch.

Carte £ 30/41

Town plan: B-s – Cotford Hotel, 51 Graham Rd ✉ WR14 2HU – ℰ (01684) 572 427 – www.cotfordhotel.co.uk – dinner only and Sunday lunch

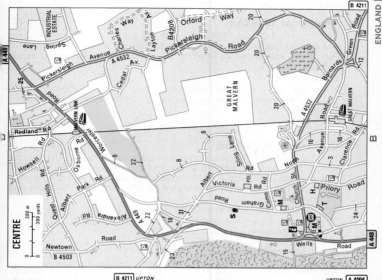

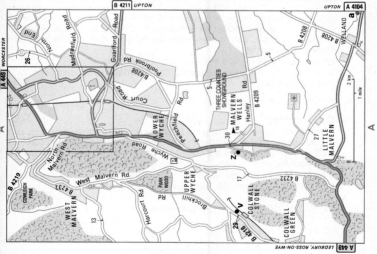

GREAT MALVERN

at Welland Southeast: 5 mi on B4208

🍴 **The Inn at Welland** 　　　🛏 🏠 ♿ 🅿

BRITISH TRADITIONAL · COSY Light, open and stylish, with charming features and designer touches; its owners have turned this pub from wreck to "by 'eck!" Pub classics and sandwiches sit alongside generously portioned modern British dishes on the menu.

Carte £ 25/38

Town plan: A-a – *Hook Bank* ✉ *WR13 6LN* – *East : 1 mi on A 4104* – ✆ *(01684) 592 317* – *www.theinnatwelland.co.uk* – *Closed 25-26 December, Sunday dinner and Monday*

at Malvern Wells South: 2 mi on A449 – ✉ Malvern

🏠 **Cottage in the Wood** 　　🌲 🦢 ⪡ 🛏 ♿ 📺 🅿

TRADITIONAL · PERSONALISED Three superbly set properties with far-reaching views across the vale. Bedrooms in the original cottage and Beech House are cosy and traditional; those in The Pinnacles are larger and some have balconies. The bright restaurant offers an extensive modern menu, over 700 wines and great views.

30 rooms ☲ – 🛏£ 79/121 🛏🛏£ 99/198

Town plan: A-z – *Holywell Rd* ✉ *WR14 4LG* – ✆ *(01684) 588 860* – *www.cottageinthewood.co.uk*

at Colwall Southwest: 3 mi on B4218 – ✉ Great Malvern

🏠 **Colwall Park** 　　　🌲 🛏 🦢 🛝 🅿

TRADITIONAL · CLASSIC Personally run Edwardian house with an attractive mock-Tudor façade. From the cosy lounges to the comfy bedrooms it has a traditional style but also displays contemporary touches. Modern menus in the high ceilinged restaurant, with locally sourced ingredients including salad leaves and herbs from the garden.

22 rooms ☲ – 🛏£ 60/105 🛏🛏£ 85/200 – 1 suite

Town plan: A-v – *Walwyn Rd* ✉ *WR13 6QG* – ✆ *(01684) 540 000* – *www.colwall.co.uk*

at Cradley West: 4 mi by B4219 and A4103

🏠 **Old Rectory** 　　　🌲 🦢 🦢 🛏 🅿

FAMILY · HOMELY A welcoming red-brick former rectory in mature gardens; built in 1790 and set right next to the church. Spacious, individually styled bedrooms. Food plays a big role: jams are homemade and vegetables are from the garden, while breakfast includes eggs 7 ways, 6 fish dishes and locally cured bacon.

6 rooms ☲ – 🛏£ 100 🛏🛏£ 140/150

✉ *WR13 5LQ* – ✆ *(01886) 880 109* – *www.oldrectorycradley.com*

GREAT MILTON – Oxfordshire ➜ See Oxford

GREAT MISSENDEN

Buckinghamshire – Pop. 7 980 – Regional map n° **6**-C2

▶ London 34 mi – Aylesbury 10 mi – Maidenhead 19 mi – Oxford 35 mi

🍴 **Nags Head** 　　　⟵ 🛏 🅿

BRITISH TRADITIONAL · PUB Traditional 15C inn whose features include original oak beams, thick brick walls and an inglenook fireplace. Gallic charm mixes with British classics on the interesting menus and service is keen and cheerful. Bedrooms are stylish and modern (Number One is the best), and breakfasts are tasty.

Menu £ 17 (weekdays) – Carte £ 24/50

5 rooms ☲ – 🛏£ 75/95 🛏🛏£ 95/115

London Rd ✉ *HP16 0DG* – *Southeast : 1.5 mi by A 413 and Holmer Green rd.* – ✆ *(01494) 862 200* – *www.nagsheadbucks.com* – *Closed 25 December*

GREAT YARMOUTH

Norfolk – Pop. 38 693 – Regional map n° **8**-D2

▶ London 126 mi – Cambridge 81 mi – Ipswich 53 mi – Norwich 20 mi

XX Andover House

MODERN CUISINE · BRASSERIE Modernised, listed Victorian property with a crisp, chic style and friendly, well-drilled service. Constantly evolving à la carte of modern, well-presented and accomplished dishes, with the occasional Asian touch. Simple, modern bedrooms; some with four-posters, some with large bay windows.

Carte £ 25/32 **s**

20 rooms – ♦£ 67/79 ♦♦£ 87/99 – ☑ £ 5 – 4 suites

28-30 Camperdown ✉ NR30 3JB – ℰ (01493) 843 490
– www.andoverhouse.co.uk – dinner only

GREAT YELDHAM

Essex – Pop. 1 844 – Regional map n° **7**-C2

▶ London 64 mi – Cambridge 28 mi – Colchester 20 mi

XX White Hart

BRITISH MODERN · ROMANTIC Charming 16C house with a characterful interior. The large, open-fired bar with its wonky floors and exposed beams serves unfussy favourites, while the elegant restaurant offers a refined, modern menu of skilfully prepared dishes which are full of flavour. Bedrooms are stylish, modern and comfortable.

Carte £ 30/49

13 rooms ☑ – ♦£ 70/80 ♦♦£ 90/180

Poole St ✉ CO9 4HJ – ℰ (01787) 237 250 (booking advisable)
– www.whitehartyeldham.co.uk – Closed dinner 25-26 December, Monday and lunch Tuesday

GREEN ISLAND → See Channel Islands (Jersey)

GREETHAM

Rutland – Regional map n° **9**-C2

▶ London 101 mi – Birmingham 86 mi – Nottingham 38 mi

⌂ Wheatsheaf Inn

BRITISH TRADITIONAL · FAMILY The aroma of fresh bread is the first thing you notice at this simple, family-friendly country pub. Cooking is unfussy and traditionally based; cheaper cuts keep prices sensible and desserts are a must. It's run by a charming couple.

Menu £ 17 (weekday lunch) – Carte £ 23/33

1 Stretton Rd ✉ LE15 7NP – ℰ (01572) 812 325 – www.wheatsheaf-greetham.co.uk
– Closed first 2 weeks January, Sunday dinner and Monday except bank holidays

GRETA BRIDGE – Durham → See Barnard Castle

GRETTON – Gloucestershire → See Winchcombe

GRIMSTON – Norfolk → See King's Lynn

GRINDLETON

Lancashire – Pop. 435 – Regional map n° **11**-B2

▶ London 238 mi – Birmingham 125 mi – Leeds 44 mi – Sheffield 85 mi

⌂ Duke of York Inn

REGIONAL · PUB Keenly run, ivy-clad pub in the heart of the Trough of Bowland, with views to Pendle Hill. Characterful, rustic bar and light, contemporary dining room. Excellent choice on the seasonal menu, with plenty of regional dishes and fish.

Carte £ 22/39

Brow Top ✉ BB7 4QR – ℰ (01200) 441 266 – www.dukeofyorkgrindleton.com – Closed 25 December, Monday except bank holidays and Tuesday following bank holidays

GRINSHILL – Shropshire → See Shrewsbury

GROUVILLE → See Channel Islands (Jersey)

GUILDFORD
Surrey – Pop. 77 057 – Regional map n° **4**-C1
▶ London 33 mi – Brighton 43 mi – Reading 27 mi – Southampton 49 mi

🏨 **Radisson Blu Edwardian Guildford** 🛜 📶 🛁 🚗 🔄 🛗 ⬆ 🅰🅚 🏊 ♨
BUSINESS · DESIGN A smart, glass-fronted hotel in the heart of the town; notable for its modern design and subtle theatrical theme. Well-sound-proofed, contemporary bedrooms offer high levels of comfort and the latest technology. As its name suggests, the modern brasserie offers a choice between steak and lobster.
183 rooms ⌂ – ♦£ 99/350 ♦♦£ 110/375
Town plan: Y-x – *3 Alexandra Terr, High St* ✉ *GU1 3DA* – ✆ *(01483) 792 300*
– *www.radissonblu-edwardian.com/guildford*

🍴 **CAU** 🅰🅚
MEATS · DESIGN The name stands for Carne Argentina Unica and beef reigns supreme; go for a steak, as it's what they do best. Staff are attentive, the atmosphere's lively, prices are reasonable and the surroundings, trendy and bright.
Carte £ 19/35
Town plan: Y-s – *274 High St* ✉ *GU1 3JL* – ✆ *(01483) 459 777 (bookings advisable at dinner)* – *www.caurestaurants.com* – *Closed 25-26 December and 1 January*

at East Clandon Northeast: 4.75 mi by A25 off A246

🍺 **Queen's Head** 🛏 🛜 🅿
TRADITIONAL CUISINE · FASHIONABLE Charming 17C pub with a large garden where village celebrations are held. Four rooms feature open fires, faux-beams and bovine-themed pictures. Simple menus offer something for everyone, from sharing boards to a steak and ale pie.
Menu £ 18 (weekday lunch) – Carte £ 23/35
The Street ✉ *GU4 7RY* – ✆ *(01483) 222 332* – *www.queensheadeastclandon.co.uk*
– *Closed 25 December*

at West Clandon Northeast: 4.75 mi by A25 and A246 on A247

🍺 **Onslow Arms** 🛏 🛜 ⬆ 🅿
BRITISH TRADITIONAL · FRIENDLY Smartly refurbished pub, with old beams, copper artefacts and open fires giving a clue as to its true age. The same menu is served throughout, offering sharing platters, light bites and more sophisticated dishes in the evening.
Carte £ 21/40
The Street ✉ *GU4 7TE* – ✆ *(01483) 222 447* – *www.onslowarmsclandon.co.uk*

at Shere East: 6.75 mi by A246 off A25 – Plan: Z – ✉ Guildford

🍴🍴 **Kinghams** 🛜 🅿
BRITISH MODERN · RUSTIC Characterful 17C creeper-clad cottage with a cosy low-beamed interior and a pleasant terrace. Cooking has a classic foundation, with plenty of fish specials and game in season. The good value 2 course menu includes a side dish too.
Menu £ 18 (weekdays) – Carte £ 31/44
Gomshall Ln ✉ *GU5 9HE* – ✆ *(01483) 202 168* – *www.kinghams-restaurant.co.uk*
– *Closed 25 December-5 January, Sunday dinner and Monday*

GUILDFORD

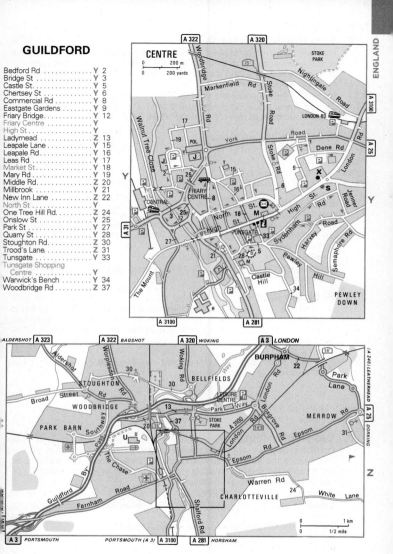

GULVAL – Cornwall ➜ See Penzance

GULWORTHY – Devon ➜ See Tavistock

GUNTHORPE

Nottinghamshire – Pop. 646 – Regional map n° **9**-B2

◼ London 132 mi – Nottingham 12 mi – Newark-on-Trent 13 mi

471

X **Tom Brown's Brasserie** Ⓝ   🛱 & 🎢 🅿

MODERN CUISINE · BRASSERIE Stylish modern restaurant in an old Victorian schoolhouse beside the river. Tables are spread over several different areas – including a mezzanine – and the team are friendly and efficient. Dishes are fresh, tasty and well-presented.

Menu £ 17 (lunch and early dinner) – Carte £ 25/48

The Old School House, Trentside ⊠ NG14 7FB – 𝒞 (0115) 966 36 42
– www.tombrowns.co.uk – Closed dinner 25-26 December and 1 January

GURNARD → See WIGHT (Isle of)

HADLEIGH

Suffolk – Pop. 8 150 – Regional map n° **8**-C3
▶ London 72 mi – Cambridge 49 mi – Colchester 17 mi – Ipswich 10 mi

🏠 **Edge Hall**   🖨 ⅋ 🅿 ⌁

FAMILY · CLASSIC A lovely Queen Anne style house with a Georgian brick façade, dating from 1453 – supposedly the oldest house in the village. Bedrooms are spacious and furnished with antiques. The breakfast room overlooks the delightful garden.

6 rooms ⌂ – ♥£ 60/75 ♥♥£ 90/125

2 High St ⊠ IP7 5AP – 𝒞 (01473) 822 458 – www.edgehall.co.uk – Closed 23-29 December

🍴 **Hadleigh Ram** Ⓝ   🛱 & ⌂

MODERN CUISINE · RUSTIC Stylish, contemporary dining pub with neatly laid tables. Elaborate modern cooking features lots of ingredients in some original combinations. If you've come just for a drink you'll feel most at home on the attractive terrace.

Carte £ 25/40

5 Market Pl ⊠ IP7 5DL – 𝒞 (01473) 822 880 – www.thehadleighram.co.uk – Closed 26-27 December and Sunday dinner

HALFORD

Warwickshire – Pop. 301 – Regional map n° **10**-C3
▶ London 94 mi – Oxford 43 mi – Stratford-upon-Avon 8 mi

🏠 **Old Manor House**   ⌇ 🖨 ⊸ 🎢 ⅋ 🅿

COUNTRY HOUSE · HISTORIC Characterful part-timbered house in a pleasant spot next to the River Stour. Well-appointed drawing room with garden views and an antique-furnished breakfast room with a large inglenook. Appealing period style bedrooms have rich fabrics.

3 rooms ⌂ – ♥£ 65/85 ♥♥£ 95/110

Queens St ⊠ CV36 5BT – 𝒞 (01789) 740 264 – www.oldmanor-halford.co.uk

HALFWAY BRIDGE – West Sussex → See Petworth

HALIFAX

West Yorkshire – Pop. 88 134 – Regional map n° **13**-B2
▶ London 205 mi – Bradford 8 mi – Burnley 21 mi – Leeds 15 mi

🏨 **Holdsworth House**   ⌂ ⌇ 🖨 🛱 & 🎐 🅿

HISTORIC · COSY Attractive 17C property with beautiful gardens and a parterre within its old stone walls. Characterful rooms feature original wood panelling and mullioned windows; bedrooms are contemporary. The three-roomed restaurant offers a mix of homely classics and more refined dishes – all use local produce.

39 rooms ⌂ – ♥£ 69/145 ♥♥£ 89/165 – 5 suites

Holdsworth Rd ⊠ HX2 9TG – North : 3 mi by A 629 and Shay Ln – 𝒞 (01422) 240 024 – www.holdsworthhouse.co.uk

X **Ricci's Tapas & Cicchetti** Ⓝ 🛋 🖥

MEDITERRANEAN · FASHIONABLE Modern tapas restaurant with a buzzy vibe, run by a bright, breezy team. Sit on the spacious terrace, at a wooden table or on white leather stools at the metal-topped bar. The Spanish and Italian small plates are perfect for sharing.
Carte £ 23/36
F Mill, Ground Floor, Dean Clough, (Gate 9) ⊠ HX3 5AX – 𝒞 (01422) 410 204
– www.riccistapasandcicchetti.co.uk – Closed Sunday

🏚 **Shibden Mill Inn** 🛋 🛋 ❖ 🅿

BRITISH MODERN · COSY A former corn mill set in a tranquil, deep-sided valley, with beamed ceilings, welcoming fires and lots of cosy corners. Menus offer plenty of choice, with pub favourites alongside more ambitious dishes. Well-drilled staff. Comfy, individually furnished bedrooms; choose Room 14 if it's luxury you're after.
Menu £ 17 (lunch and early dinner) **s** – Carte £ 22/35 **s**
11 rooms � – ♦£ 95/165 ♦♦£ 100/195
Shibden Mill Fold ⊠ HX3 7UL – 𝒞 (01422) 365 840 – www.shibdenmillinn.com
– Closed 25-26 December and 1 January

HALSETOWN – Cornwall ➜ See St Ives

HALTWHISTLE
Northumberland – Pop. 3 791 – Regional map n° **14**-A2
▶ London 335 mi – Carlisle 22 mi – Newcastle upon Tyne 37 mi

🏠 **Centre of Britain** 🏠 ♨ 🅿

INN · COSY Yellow-painted former coaching inn in the town centre, with a pele tower dating from the 16C. Simple, well-kept bedrooms; those in the main house are larger and more characterful, while the cosy duplex chalet rooms are ideal for walkers, cyclists and guests with dogs. Traditional menus.
12 rooms ⊠ – ♦£ 64/79 ♦♦£ 79/110
Main St ⊠ NE49 0BH – 𝒞 (01434) 322 422 – www.centre-of-britain.org.uk

🏚 **Ashcroft** 🛋 ♨ 🅿

FAMILY · CLASSIC A family-run early Victorian vicarage, with beautiful award-winning gardens. The spacious interior retains many of its original features and smoothly blends the classic with the contemporary. Some of the bedrooms have roof terraces.
9 rooms ⊠ – ♦£ 69/99 ♦♦£ 80/110
Lantys Lonnen ⊠ NE49 0DA – 𝒞 (01434) 320 213
– www.ashcroftguesthouse.co.uk – Closed 25 December

HAMBLE-LE-RICE
Hampshire – Pop. 4 695 – Regional map n° **4**-B2
▶ London 87 mi – Birmingham 149 mi – Leeds 243 mi – Sheffield 213 mi

🏚 **Bugle** 🛋 ⅋ ❖

BRITISH TRADITIONAL · PUB Set in a charming spot in a quaint little village, this Grade II listed building is popular with the sailing community and has views over the marina. Menus offer soups, salads and sandwiches, small plates and traditional pub dishes.
Menu £ 15 (weekday lunch) – Carte £ 21/39 **s**
High St ⊠ SO31 4HA – 𝒞 (023) 8045 3000 (booking advisable)
– www.idealcollection.co.uk/buglehamble

HAMBLETON – Rutland ➜ See Oakham

HAMPTON IN ARDEN

West Midlands – Pop. 1 678 – Regional map n° **10**-C2

▶ London 113 mi – Birmingham 15 mi – Coventry 11 mi

🏠 Hampton Manor ☆ 🖨 🕭 🎦 🌱 🐴 🅿

HISTORIC · STYLISH Early Victorian manor house in 45 acres; built for Sir Robert Peel's son. Contemporary décor blends with characterful original plasterwork and wooden panelling in the guest areas. Spacious modern bedrooms have superb bathrooms.

15 rooms – ♦£ 150/340 ♦♦£ 150/340 – 🖵 £ 15 – 3 suites
Shadowbrook Ln ✉ *B92 ODQ* – ℰ *(01675) 446 080* – *www.hamptonmanor.eu*
Peel's – See restaurant listing

XxX Peel's 🖨 🕭 🕅 ↔ 🅿

BRITISH CREATIVE · ELEGANT Elegant dining room situated within an impressive manor house and featuring beautiful plasterwork, oak panelling and hand-painted Chinoiserie wallpaper. Modern menus feature refined, original combinations. Service is pitched perfectly.

Menu £ 55/75 – Carte £ 41/56
Hampton Manor Hotel, Shadowbrook Ln ✉ *B92 ODQ* – ℰ *(01675) 446 080*
(booking essential) – *www.hamptonmanor.eu* – *dinner only* – *Closed
Sunday and Monday*

HAMPTON POYLE

Oxfordshire – Pop. 106 – Regional map n° **6**-B2

▶ London 68 mi – Birmingham 72 mi – Barnet 71 mi – Ealing 57 mi

🍴 Bell at Hampton Poyle ↩ 🛋 🕭 🅿

MEDITERRANEAN · PUB Almost Mediterranean in its style, with a very visual kitchen that includes a wood-burning oven. The seasonal menu offers everything from meze, homemade pizza and charcuterie boards to pub staples, steaks and seafood. Bright, fresh bedrooms are located above the bar and in a neighbouring cottage.

Menu £ 10 (weekdays) – Carte £ 17/46
9 rooms 🖵 – ♦£ 95/130 ♦♦£ 120/155
11 Oxford Rd ✉ *OX5 2QD* – ℰ *(01865) 376 242*
– www.thebellathamptonpoyle.co.uk

HANDFORTH

Cheshire East – Regional map n° **11**-B3

▶ London 187 mi – Manchester 11 mi – Macclesfield 9 mi

🏠 Pinewood on Wilmslow 🆕 ☆ 🖃 🐴 🅿

BUSINESS · FUNCTIONAL Well-run hotel, handily located for the airport. Smart guest areas lead up to modern, well-equipped bedrooms; the Balcony rooms have king-sized beds, bathrobes and outdoor seating areas overlooking landscaped gardens. The airy, open-plan bar and dining room offer modern menus with global influences.

70 rooms – ♦£ 70/110 ♦♦£ 90/130
Wilmslow Rd ✉ *SK9 3LF* – ℰ *(01625) 529 211* – *www.pinewood-hotel.co.uk*

HAROME – North Yorkshire ➔ See Helmsley

HARROGATE

North Yorkshire – Pop. 73 576 – Regional map n° **13**-B2

▶ London 211 mi – Bradford 18 mi - Leeds 15 mi – Newcastle upon Tyne 76 mi

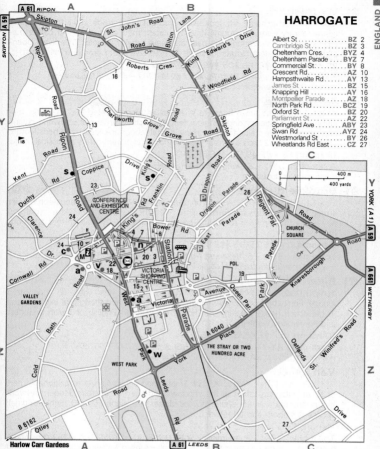

HARROGATE

Rudding Park

🛜 ⚄ 🖼 🕪 ⚃ 🖨 🚻 🧖 🅿

LUXURY · DESIGN Grade I listed manor house in 250 acres. Sleek bedrooms are in a wing; the best boast media hubs, touch lighting and jacuzzis. Relax in the spa, the cinema or on one of the terraces. The old Victorian church is used for events.

88 rooms 🖙 – 🛏£140/389 🛏🛏£165/462 – 8 suites

Rudding Park, Follifoot ⊠ HG3 1JH – Southeast : 3.75 mi by A 661 – 𝒞 (01423) 871 350 – www.ruddingpark.com

Clocktower – See restaurant listing

Hotel du Vin

🛜 🕪 🖨 🚻 🧖

TOWNHOUSE · DESIGN A smart hotel with a small basement spa, in a terrace of Georgian houses overlooking the green. The contemporary, boutique-style interior has wine-themed décor; the two attic bedrooms boast huge bathrooms with 'his and hers' roll-top baths. The stylish bistro has an open courtyard and a Gallic menu.

48 rooms – 🛏£79/250 🛏🛏£89/500 – 🖙£17

Town plan: BZ-a – *Prospect Pl ⊠ HG1 1LB – 𝒞 (01423) 856 800 – www.hotelduvin.com*

West Park

INN · STYLISH It might still look like a pub but once inside you'll find a stylish, contemporary hotel. Bedrooms have the latest mod cons, including coffee machines; the suites overlook the park and have small balconies. The lively open-plan bar and modern restaurant serve an extensive list of brasserie favourites.

25 rooms ⌂ – ♦£ 99/205 ♦♦£ 119/275 – 2 suites
Town plan: BZ-w – *19 West Park Rd ⊠ HG1 1BJ – ℰ (01423) 524 471*
– www.thewestparkhotel.com

Ascot House

FAMILY · HOMELY Once home to W H Baxter, who invented the 'knapping' machine used in road-making. Original features include ornate plasterwork, coving and an impressive stained glass window. Floral fabrics and king-sized beds feature upstairs – Room 22 has a turret. The traditional restaurant offers a classical menu.

19 rooms ⌂ – ♦£ 49/75 ♦♦£ 69/130
Town plan: BY-z – *53 King's Rd ⊠ HG1 5HJ – ℰ (01423) 531 005*
– www.ascothouse.com

Brookfield House

TOWNHOUSE · STYLISH A well-run, three-storey Victorian townhouse on a quiet street. Modern bedrooms come in light hues: the first floor rooms are bright and airy, while the top floor rooms are cosy and intimate – all have fridges and ironing boards.

6 rooms ⌂ – ♦£ 75/95 ♦♦£ 85/110
Town plan: BY-s – *5 Alexandra Rd ⊠ HG1 5JS – ℰ (01423) 506 646*
– www.brookfieldhousehotel.co.uk – Closed 2 weeks Christmas-New Year

Bijou

TOWNHOUSE · PERSONALISED Well-run Victorian villa with an open-fired lounge. Funky bedrooms have minimalist furnishings and thoughtful extras; those in the coach house are largest. Choose between an English or Italian breakfast and homemade waffles.

10 rooms ⌂ – ♦£ 45/59 ♦♦£ 64/124
Town plan: AY-s – *17 Ripon Rd ⊠ HG1 2JL – ℰ (01423) 567 974*
– www.thebijou.co.uk – Closed 24-27 December

✗✗ Van Zeller

BRITISH MODERN · FASHIONABLE Smart shop conversion in a fashionable part of town, with two tables in the windows and the rest upstairs. Modern artwork hangs on cream walls. Well-executed dishes are elaborate and highly original; service is smooth and attentive.

Menu £ 35/50
Town plan: AZ-v – *8 Montpellier St ⊠ HG1 2TQ – ℰ (01423) 508 762 (booking advisable) – www.vanzellerrestaurants.co.uk – Closed 1 week January, Sunday and Monday*

✗✗ Quantro

INTERNATIONAL · FRIENDLY A busy, buzzy brasserie with a keenly priced, internationally influenced menu which offers something for everyone. The sharing platters are a sure-fire hit and a choice of dish size on the à la carte suits the local workers.

Menu £ 17 (lunch and early dinner) – Carte £ 26/36
Town plan: AZ-a – *3 Royal Par ⊠ HG1 2SZ – ℰ (01423) 503 034*
– www.quantro.co.uk – Closed 25-26 December, 1 January and Sunday

✗✗ Orchid

ASIAN · FASHIONABLE Below the chic cocktail bar is a spacious room with etched glass screens, Asian artefacts and a TV screening live kitchen action. The extensive pan-Asian menu indicates the dishes' origins and spiciness; Sunday lunch is a buffet.

Menu £ 14 (weekday lunch) – Carte £ 19/40
Town plan: AZ-c – *28 Swan Rd ⊠ HG1 2SE – ℰ (01423) 560 425*
– www.orchidrestaurant.co.uk – Closed 25-26 December and Saturday lunch

XX **Clocktower**

BRITISH TRADITIONAL · FASHIONABLE Set in the old stables and named after the adjoining clocktower: a contemporary hotel dining room with an impressive pink chandelier. Menus offer an array of modern dishes; most ingredients are from within 20 miles.

Menu £ 30 **s** – Carte £ 41/58 **s**

Rudding Park Hotel, Rudding Park, Follifoot ⊠ HG3 1JH – Southeast : 3.75 mi by A 661 – ℰ (01423) 871 350 – www.ruddingpark.co.uk

X **Norse**

SCANDINAVIAN · SIMPLE During the day it's a café called Baltzersen's; in the evening it reopens as Norse. Choose 2 or 3 savoury dishes plus a dessert from the concise menu. Flavoursome Nordic cooking includes the likes of Norwegian skrei and woof fish.

Carte £ 19/40

Town plan: BZ-n – *22 Oxford St ⊠ HG1 1PU – ℰ (01423) 202 363 – www.norserestaurant.co.uk – dinner only – Closed 4 days Christmas-New Year, Sunday and Monday*

at Kettlesing West: 6 5 mi by A59 – Plan: AY – ⊠ Harrogate

Knabbs Ash

TRADITIONAL · COSY This welcoming stone-built farmhouse is set on a small-holding overlooking Nidderdale and Knabbs Moor. There's a cosy lounge, a pine-furnished breakfast room and three light and airy bedrooms – these have a 'Country Living' style and come with plenty of extras, including a complimentary decanter of Madeira.

3 rooms � – †£ 65 ††£ 80/90

Skipton Rd ⊠ HG3 2LT – on A 59 – ℰ (01423) 771 040 – www.knabbsash.co.uk

Cold Cotes

TRADITIONAL · COSY A remotely set former farmhouse bordered by colourful, superbly-tended gardens and the owners' plant nursery. Smart bedrooms provide good comforts – those in the main house are small suites; Room 6, in the old barn, is the best.

6 rooms ⊠ – †£ 75/85 ††£ 89/99

Cold Cotes Rd, Felliscliffe ⊠ HG3 2LW – West : 1 mi by A 59 – ℰ (01423) 770 937 – www.coldcotes.com – Closed February

HARTINGTON

Derbyshire – ⊠ Buxton – Pop. 1 604 – Regional map n° **9**-A1

▶ London 168 mi – Derby 36 mi – Manchester 40 mi – Sheffield 34 mi

Biggin Hall

TRADITIONAL · COSY Characterful house with traditional, rustic appeal. Many guests follow the Tissington and High Peak Trails: bike storage and picnics are offered. Classical, low-beamed bedrooms in the main house; brighter rooms in the barns. Pleasant garden views from the dining room and homely cooking.

21 rooms ⊠ – †£ 80/140 ††£ 90/172

Biggin ⊠ SK17 0DH – Southeast : 2 mi by B 5054 – ℰ (01298) 84 451 – www.bigginhall.co.uk

HARTLEBURY

Worcestershire – Pop. 2 253 – Regional map n° **10**-B2

▶ London 135 mi – Birmingham 33 mi – Cardiff 93 mi – Leicester 72 mi

🍽 White Hart

BRITISH TRADITIONAL · PUB Proudly run, proper village local. Carefully prepared, classically based dishes rely on quality produce; go for one of the blackboard specials. Relax in the large garden and, if you enjoy live music, come for the annual beer festival.

Menu £ 20 (lunch and early dinner) – Carte £ 20/34

✉ DY11 7TD – ℰ (01299) 250 286 – www.thewhitehartinhartlebury.co.uk – Closed 25 December and Sunday dinner

HARWICH

Essex – Pop. 19 738 – Regional map n° **7**-D2

▶ London 78 mi – Chelmsford 41 mi – Colchester 20 mi – Ipswich 23 mi

🏨 Pier at Harwich

TOWNHOUSE · PERSONALISED Victorian hotel in a pleasant quayside spot – built to accommodate rail travellers waiting to board their cruise liners and an ideal place to stay if you're catching the ferry. Stylish, 'New England' style bedrooms; some boast port views. Smart seafood restaurant or casual all-day dining overlooking the pier.

14 rooms ☟ – †£ 120/200 ††£ 120/200

The Quay ✉ CO12 3HH – ℰ (01255) 241 212 – www.milsomhotels.com

Harbourside – See restaurant listing

XX Harbourside

FISH AND SEAFOOD · CLASSIC Comfortable hotel dining room boasting crisp linen-laid tables and attractive port and North Sea views. Seafood-orientated menu offers everything from the traditional to the more contemporary.

Menu £ 21 (weekday lunch) – Carte £ 31/45 **s**

Pier at Harwich Hotel, The Quay ✉ CO12 3HH – ℰ (01255) 241 212
– www.milsomhotels.com – Closed Monday and Tuesday

HASELBURY PLUCKNETT

Somerset – Pop. 744 – Regional map n° **2**-B3

▶ London 140 mi – Taunton 24 mi – Yeovil 8 mi

🍽 White Horse ⓝ

MEDITERRANEAN · PUB Traditional village pub with dried hops hung on exposed beams, a mix of wood and flagged floors, and a fire at either end. Most produce comes from within 50 miles; alongside British classics, you'll find Gallic and Mediterranean dishes.

Menu £ 19 – Carte £ 20/41

North St ✉ TA18 7RJ – ℰ (01460) 78 873 – www.thewhitehorsehaselbury.co.uk
– Closed Sunday dinner and Monday

HASTINGS and ST LEONARDS

East Sussex – Pop. 91 053 – Regional map n° **5**-B3

▶ London 65 mi – Brighton 37 mi – Folkestone 37 mi – Maidstone 34 mi

🏠 Zanzibar

TOWNHOUSE · DESIGN An enthusiastically run Victorian seafront property with a stylish boutique interior. The lounge and bar lead to a delightful terrace and garden. Bedrooms are named and themed after places the owner has visited and have intimate lighting and good mod cons. Modern, seasonal menus also have global influences.

8 rooms ☟ – †£ 95/265 ††£ 99/275

Town plan: AZ-c – 9 Eversfield Pl ✉ TN37 6BY – ℰ (01424) 460 109
– www.zanzibarhotel.co.uk

HASTINGS ST. LEONARDS

ENGLAND

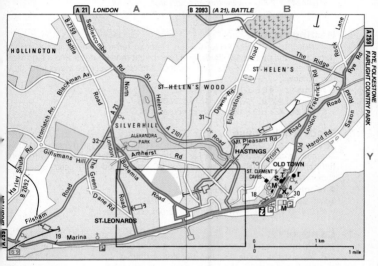

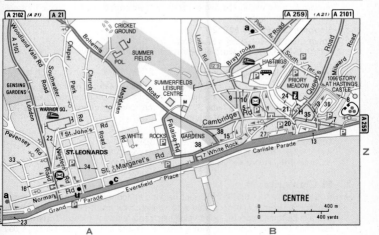

Old Rectory

TOWNHOUSE · ELEGANT Delightful Georgian house with beautiful tiered gardens to the rear, just a short walk from the sea. No expense has been spared inside, with hand-painted walls, bespoke designer furnishings and luxurious bedrooms featuring roll-top baths. The charming owner makes the bread, muesli and sausages for breakfast.

8 rooms ⌂ – †£ 80/125 ††£ 99/160

Town plan: BY-r – *Harold Rd, Old Town* ✉ *TN35 5ND*
– *℘ (01424) 422 410 – www.theoldrectoryhastings.co.uk*
– *Closed 2 weeks January and 1 week Christmas*

Hastings House

TOWNHOUSE · STYLISH Personally-run Victorian terraced house, just a stone's throw from the promenade. Bedrooms have bright modern décor and a high level of mod cons; rooms 3, 5 and 7 are the best and offer lovely sea views from their bay windows.

8 rooms ⌂ – †£ 80/100 ††£ 99/145

Town plan: AZ-u – *9 Warrior Sq.* ✉ *TN37 6BA*
– *℘ (01424) 422 709 – www.hastingshouse.co.uk*

Black Rock House

TOWNHOUSE · ELEGANT Smart Victorian villa hidden away in a residential area. The cool, contemporary interior has stripped wooden floors and stylish modern furnishings; individually designed bedrooms have good mod cons. Breakfasts showcase local produce.

5 rooms ⌂ – †£ 85/90 ††£ 120/135

Town plan: BZ-a – *10 Stanley Rd* ✉ *TN34 1UE*
– *℘ (01424) 438 448 – www.hastingsaccommodation.com*

Laindons

TOWNHOUSE · CONTEMPORARY Grade II listed Georgian townhouse in a lovely Old Town street; inside it's been transformed into a stylish designer hotel with modern Scandic décor. The owner roasts his own coffee and has opened a small coffee shop at the front.

5 rooms ⌂ – †£ 105 ††£ 120

Town plan: BY-s – *23 High St* ✉ *TN34 3EY*
– *℘ (01424) 437 710 – www.thelaindons.com – Closed Christmas*

XX Webbe's Rock-a-Nore

FISH AND SEAFOOD · BRASSERIE Bright, modern seafood restaurant with an open kitchen, a marble-topped horseshoe bar, and a large terrace overlooking the Stade and its fishing huts. Straightforward cooking offers small plates and classics, dictated by the daily catch.

Carte £ 21/41

Town plan: BY-x – *1 Rock-a-Nore* ✉ *TN34 3DW*
– *℘ (01424) 721 650 – www.webbesrestaurants.co.uk*
– *Closed 4-11 January and 24-26 December*

X St Clements

MODERN CUISINE · BISTRO Pleasant neighbourhood restaurant run by an experienced chef-owner and decorated with striking local art. It offers a comprehensive à la carte and concise, good value lunch and midweek menus. Tasty modern European cooking is unfussy with a rustic edge and fish from the Hastings day boats plays a key role.

Menu £ 15/24 – Carte £ 27/39

Town plan: AZ-a – *3 Mercatoria, St Leonards on Sea* ✉ *TN38 0EB*
– *℘ (01424) 200 355 – www.stclementsrestaurant.co.uk*
– *Closed 25-26 December, 1 January, Sunday dinner and Monday*

HATCH BEAUCHAMP – Somerset ➜ See Taunton

HATFIELD BROAD OAK
Essex – Pop. 916 – Regional map n° **7**-B2
▶ London 35 mi – Bishop's Stortford 8 mi – Colchester 34 mi

🏚 Duke's Head 　　　　　　　　　🛏 🅿
BRITISH TRADITIONAL · COSY 17C pub with a large terrace and pleasant garden, run by an enthusiastic couple who support local clubs and host village events. Choose from a selection of well-crafted, generously sized dishes, or enjoy nibbles on a sofa by the fire.
Carte £ 22/32
High St ⊠ CM22 7HH – 𝒞 (01279) 718 598 – www.thedukeshead.co.uk – Closed 25-26 December

HATFIELD PEVEREL
Essex – Pop. 3 251 – Regional map n° **7**-C2
▶ London 39 mi – Chelmsford 8 mi – Maldon 12 mi

✗✗ Blue Strawberry Bistrot 　　　　　　　🏡 🅿
BRITISH TRADITIONAL · INTIMATE A creeper-clad, red-brick restaurant with a labyrinth of characterful, old-fashioned rooms full of ornaments. Extensive menus offer traditional, keenly priced cooking which is wholesome and satisfying. Polite service.
Menu £ 15/20 (weekdays) – Carte £ 22/40
The Street ⊠ CM3 2DW – 𝒞 (01245) 381 333 – www.bluestrawberrybistrot.co.uk – Closed 26 December and Sunday dinner

HATHERSAGE
Derbyshire – Pop. 2 018 – Regional map n° **9**-A1
▶ London 177 mi – Derby 39 mi – Manchester 34 mi – Sheffield 11 mi

🏨 George 　　　　　　　　　🍸 🐾 🔥 🅿
TRADITIONAL · COSY Eye-catching 14C coaching inn where modern furnishings blend nicely with traditional stone walls and exposed beams. Relax in the open-fired lounge or small cocktail bar. Smart, pastel-hued bedrooms are bright and contemporary.
24 rooms ⌂ – ♦£ 65 ♦♦£ 95/198
Main Rd ⊠ S32 1BB – 𝒞 (01433) 650 436 – www.george-hotel.net
George's – See restaurant listing

✗✗ George's 　　　　　　　　　　　　　🅿
BRITISH TRADITIONAL · FORMAL Formally laid restaurant decorated in subtle pastel shades and set within a 14C coaching inn. Extensive menus have a largely British base and dishes are classically grounded with modern touches. Cooking is refined and flavoursome.
Menu £ 20/37
George Hotel, Main Rd ⊠ S32 1BB – 𝒞 (01433) 650 436 – www.george-hotel.net

HAUGHTON MOSS
Cheshire East – Regional map n° **11**-A3
▶ London 180 mi – Manchester 41 mi – Chester 17 mi

🏚 Nag's Head 　　　　　　　🛏 🏡 ♿ 🅿
BRITISH TRADITIONAL · PUB Characterful timbered pub in a peaceful hamlet; sit at a table made from a shotgun or in the delightful garden overlooking the bowling green. Local produce features in regional specialities, pub classics and dishes from the charcoal grill.
Menu £ 13/21 (weekdays) – Carte £ 21/42
Long Ln ⊠ CW6 9RN – 𝒞 (01829) 260 265 – www.nagsheadhaughton.co.uk

481

HAWES

North Yorkshire – Pop. 887 – Regional map n° **13**-A1

▶ London 253 mi – Kendal 27 mi – Leeds 72 mi – Newcastle upon Tyne 76 mi

🏠 Stone House

TRADITIONAL · COSY Characterful stone house built in 1908. Guest areas include a pleasant drawing room with an oak-panelled fireplace and a small billiard-room-cum-library. Bedrooms vary in size and décor; some have conservatories and are ideal for those with dogs. The traditional beamed dining room offers a classical menu.

24 rooms ☲ – 🛉£ 75/200 🛉🛉£ 150/200 – 2 suites

Sedbusk ✉ DL8 3PT – North : 1 mi by Muker rd – ☎ (01969) 667 571
– www.stonehousehotel.co.uk – Closed January and mid-week December

HAWKSHEAD

Cumbria – ✉ Ambleside – Pop. 570 – Regional map n° **12**-A2

▶ London 283 mi – Carlisle 52 mi – Kendal 19 mi

🏠 West Vale

FAMILY · STYLISH Welcoming slate house boasting lovely countryside views; run by keen owners. Two comfy lounges and a smart country house style room for hearty breakfasts. Good-sized bedrooms have a warm, boutique style; 7 and 8, on the top floor, are the best. Tea and cake on arrival, and plenty of extra touches.

7 rooms ☲ – 🛉£ 90/105 🛉🛉£ 90/170

Far Sawrey ✉ LA22 0LQ – Southeast : 2 mi on B 5285 – ☎ (015394) 42 817
– www.westvalecountryhouse.co.uk – Closed 25-26 December and restricted opening 3 January-4 February

HAWNBY

North Yorkshire – ✉ Helmsley – Regional map n° **13**-C1

▶ London 245 mi – Middlesbrough 27 mi – Newcastle upon Tyne 69 mi – York 30 mi

🏠 Laskill Country House

TRADITIONAL · PERSONALISED Delightful manor-style house in popular shooting and walking area. Comfy lounge, small function suite and good-sized bedrooms with countryside views. Communal dining; wholesome home-cooked meals, with meat from the family's farms.

3 rooms ☲ – 🛉£ 48/65 🛉🛉£ 95/125

Easterside, Laskill ✉ YO62 5NB – Northeast : 2.25 mi by Osmotherley rd
– ☎ (01439) 798 265 – www.laskillcountryhouse.co.uk – Closed 24-25 December

HAWORTH

West Yorkshire – ✉ Keighley – Pop. 6 379 – Regional map n° **13**-A2

▶ London 213 mi – Burnley 22 mi – Leeds 22 mi – Manchester 34 mi

🏠 Ashmount Country House

COUNTRY HOUSE · PERSONALISED Substantial Victorian house built by the Brontë sisters' physician. Luxurious bedrooms have state-of-the-art bathrooms – some with hot tubs. Original features include impressive stained glass paintings and an intricate plaster ceiling in the dining room; menus mix classics with more modern dishes.

12 rooms ☲ – 🛉£ 75/150 🛉🛉£ 80/255

Mytholmes Ln ✉ BD22 8EZ – ☎ (01535) 645 726 – www.ashmounthaworth.co.uk

🏠 Old Registry

TOWNHOUSE · COSY Stone-built former registrar's office at the bottom of the village's cobbled main street. Individually decorated bedrooms feature rich fabrics and antiques, and some have four-poster beds. Dine surrounded by Brontë memorabilia – local ingredients feature in traditionally based dishes.

8 rooms ☲ – 🛉£ 65/125 🛉🛉£ 80/125

2-6 Main St ✉ BD22 8DA – ☎ (01535) 646 503
– www.theoldregistryhaworth.co.uk – Closed 24-26 December

HAYDON BRIDGE – Northumberland ➜ See Hexham

HAYLING ISLAND
Hampshire – Pop. 14 842 – Regional map n° **4**-B3
▶ London 77 mi – Brighton 45 mi – Southampton 28 mi

🏠 **Cockle Warren Cottage**   🖙 ⌿ 🅿
FAMILY · PERSONALISED Set just across from the beach, this welcoming guest-house has a fish pond and fountain in the front courtyard and a lovely south-facing terrace and outdoor pool to the rear. Bedrooms are comfy and the owner is extremely welcoming.

6 rooms ⌂ – ♦£ 50/70 ♦♦£ 70/90
36 Seafront ✉ PO11 9HL – ℰ (023) 9246 4961 – www.cocklewarren.co.uk

HAYWARDS HEATH
West Sussex – Pop. 33 845 – Regional map n° **4**-D2
▶ London 39 mi – Croydon 30 mi – Barnet 53 mi – Ealing 50 mi

✗✗ **Jeremy's at Borde Hill**   🖙 🏠 🅿
MODERN CUISINE · INDIVIDUAL Converted stable block with exposed rafters, contemporary sculptures, vivid artwork and delightful views towards the Victorian walled garden. Interesting, modern European dishes and a good value 'menu of the day'. Regular gourmet nights.

Menu £ 22 (weekdays) – Carte £ 30/46
Borde Hill Gdns ✉ RH16 1XP – North : 1.75 mi by B 2028 and Balcombe Rd on Borde Hill Ln. – ℰ (01444) 441102 – www.jeremysrestaurant.com – Closed 1-15 January, Monday except bank holidays and Sunday dinner

HEADLAM – Durham ➜ See Darlington

HEATHROW AIRPORT – Greater London ➜ See London

HEDLEY ON THE HILL
Northumberland – Regional map n° **14**-A2
▶ London 293 mi – Newcastle upon Tyne 16 mi – Sunderland 26 mi – South Shields 26 mi

🍴 **Feathers Inn**   🏠 🅿
BRITISH TRADITIONAL · PUB Traditional stone inn set on a steep hill in the heart of a rural village. Daily changing menu of hearty British classics, cooked using carefully sourced regional produce, with meat and game to the fore. Relaxed, friendly atmosphere.

Carte £ 18/33
✉ NE43 7SW – ℰ (01661) 843 607 – www.thefeathers.net – Closed first 2 weeks January, Monday except bank holidays and Sunday dinner

HELMSLEY
North Yorkshire – Pop. 1 515 – Regional map n° **13**-C1
▶ London 239 mi – Leeds 51 mi – Middlesbrough 28 mi – York 24 mi

🏰 **Black Swan**   ✿ 🖙 🖾 🅿
HISTORIC · PERSONALISED Set overlooking the historic marketplace, The Black Swan is one of the country's best known coaching inns. The charming interior features beamed lounges, a modern bar and a tea shop. Bedrooms are a mix of characterful and contemporary.

45 rooms ⌂ – ♦£ 130/180 ♦♦£ 145/195 – 1 suite
Market Pl ✉ YO62 5BJ – ℰ (01439) 770 466 – www.blackswan-helmsley.co.uk
Gallery – See restaurant listing

🏠 Feversham Arms

TRADITIONAL · CLASSIC 19C former coaching inn with a lovely stone façade. Relax on the terrace beside the outdoor pool; the spa is superb and boasts a salt vapour room and an ice cave. Be sure to book one of the stylish newer bedrooms; many have stoves or fires.

33 rooms 🍽 – 🛉£ 110/430 🛉🛉£ 120/430 – 20 suites
1-8 High St ✉ *YO62 5AG* – ✆ *(01439) 770 766*
– www.fevershamarmshotel.com
Feversham Arms – See restaurant listing

🏠 No.54

TOWNHOUSE · COSY Charming Victorian stone cottage located just off the main square. Simply decorated, cosy bedrooms are well-equipped and set around a rear courtyard. Friendly owner offers communal breakfasts of fresh, local produce.

3 rooms 🍽 – 🛉£ 70/85 🛉🛉£ 100/130
54 Bondgate ✉ *YO62 5EZ* – ✆ *(01439) 771 533*
– www.no54.co.uk – Closed Christmas-New Year

🏠 Carlton Lodge

TOWNHOUSE · CLASSIC Late 19C house on the edge of town, fronted by a colourful garden. Spacious, simply appointed bedrooms are immaculately kept and have a homely feel. The owners have good local knowledge; breakfast ingredients are regionally sourced.

8 rooms 🍽 – 🛉£ 65/75 🛉🛉£ 95/110
Bondgate ✉ *YO62 5EY* – ✆ *(01439) 770 557*
– www.carlton-lodge.com – Closed January

✗✗ Feversham Arms

MODERN CUISINE · BRASSERIE Modern hotel restaurant with a pleasingly laid-back style. In summer, have lunch in the garden or on the poolside terrace. Dishes feature the latest local produce and cooking is refined and accurate; the tasting menu is worth a try.

Menu £ 45 – Carte £ 42/61 – bar lunch Monday-Saturday
Feversham Arms Hotel, 1-8 High St ✉ *YO62 5AG*
– ✆ (01439) 770 766 – www.fevershamarmshotel.com

✗✗ Gallery

CREATIVE · ELEGANT Bright modern restaurant within a historic 15C coaching inn; its walls filled with artwork for sale. At dinner, the plate becomes the canvas. Attractive, innovative dishes have the odd Asian influence; the tasting menu is a highlight.

Menu £ 29/45
Black Swan Hotel, Market Pl ✉ *YO62 5BJ*
– ✆ (01439) 770 466 – www.blackswan-helmsley.co.uk

 🐦 **Follow our inspectors @MichelinGuideUK**

at Nawton East: 3.25 mi on A170 – ✉ York

🏠 Plumpton Court

FAMILY · COSY 17C stone-built house with a small open-fired bar and a homely lounge. Comfy, cosy, simply furnished bedrooms with modern bathrooms. The cottage-style breakfast room offers local bacon and sausages. Relax in the secluded garden.

6 rooms 🍽 – 🛉£ 60/65 🛉🛉£ 78/82
High St ✉ *YO62 7TT* – ✆ *(01439) 771 223*
– www.plumptoncourt.com – Restricted opening January-February

at Wombleton East: 4 mi by A170

🏠 **Plough Inn**   🛖 ⇔ **P**

TRADITIONAL CUISINE · PUB 16C inn, popular with locals, serving tasty traditional dishes, including game in season. Prices are laudably low and service,
friendly and relaxed. Sit in the hugely characterful restaurant, which is kept cosy
by wood burners.

Carte £ 24/36

Main St ✉ *YO62 7RW* – ✆ *(01751) 431 356*
– www.theploughinnatwombleton.co.uk
– Closed 25 December and Monday lunch

at Harome Southeast: 2.75 mi by A170 – ✉ York

🏨 **Pheasant**   🏖 🛏 🕸 **P**

TRADITIONAL · STYLISH An attractive hotel in a picturesque hamlet, with a delightful duck pond and a mill stream close by. Beautiful, very comfortable lounges
and spacious, well-furnished bedrooms; Rudland – running the width of the building and with views of the pond – is one of the best. Pleasant service. Excellent
breakfasts.

16 rooms ⌑ – ♦£ 80/200 ♦♦£ 170/330
Mill St ✉ *YO62 5JG* – ✆ *(01439) 771 241*
– www.thepheasanthotel.com
Pheasant – See restaurant listing

🏠 **Cross House Lodge**   🏖 🛏 🕸 **P**

TOWNHOUSE · DESIGN These sympathetically converted farm buildings have a
rustic ski-chalet style and ultra-stylish, individually decorated bedrooms; one
boasts a snooker table; another, a bed suspended on ropes. Relax in the open-
plan, split-level lounge; excellent breakfasts are taken in the dramatic beamed
'Wheelhouse'.

9 rooms ⌑ – ♦£ 150/260 ♦♦£ 150/260
High St ✉ *YO62 5JE* – ✆ *(01439) 770 397*
– www.thestaratharome.co.uk
🌸 **Star Inn** – See restaurant listing

XX **Pheasant**   🛏 🛖 🍽 **P**

BRITISH MODERN · FORMAL Elegant hotel dining room with both classical and
contemporary touches – along with a less formal conservatory and a lovely terrace overlooking the village duck pond. Appealing menus of seasonal dishes
with a classical base and a modern touch. Skilful, knowledgeable cooking;
smooth, assured service.

Menu £ 29/36 – Carte £ 37/54

Pheasant Hotel, Mill St ✉ *YO62 5JG* – ✆ *(01439) 771 241*
– www.thepheasanthotel.com

🏠 **Star Inn** (Andrew Pern)   🍴 🛏 🛖 🕭 ⇔ **P**
🌸 BRITISH MODERN · RUSTIC 14C thatched pub with a delightful terrace, a low-
ceilinged bar and a brasserie-like restaurant with a chef's table. Dishes have assured flavours and a skilled, classical style; they use the very best of local produce, including veg from the kitchen garden and meats from their own pigs and
chickens.
→ Black pudding and foie gras with watercress salad and apple & vanilla chutney. Roe deer with honey-roast fig, date purée, cavolo nero and thyme juices.
Yorkshire rhubarb and gingerbread cheesecake with blood orange and lemon
balm cress.

Menu £ 25 (weekdays) – Carte £ 33/60

High St ✉ *YO62 5JE* – ✆ *(01439) 770 397 (booking essential)*
– www.thestaratharome.co.uk – Closed Monday lunch except bank holidays

at Ampleforth Southwest: 4.5 mi by A170 off B1257 – ⊠ Helmsley

🏠 Shallowdale House   🏠 🐾 ⇐ 🛏 ⚲ 🅿

TRADITIONAL · CLASSIC A remotely set, personally run house with a well-tended garden and stunning views of the Howardian Hills. Charming, antique-furnished interior, with an open-fired sitting room and good-sized bedrooms decorated in bright, Mediterranean tones. Four course set menu of home-cooked fare.

3 rooms ⊡ – **†**£ 100/125 **††**£ 120/150

⊠ YO62 4DY – West : 0.5 mi – *ℰ* (01439) 788 325 – www.shallowdalehouse.co.uk
– Closed Christmas-New Year

at Scawton West : 5 m. by B 1257 – ⊠ Helmsley

XX The Hare Inn Ⓝ ⓞ   & 🅿

MODERN CUISINE · INN This 13C inn has a rustic feel courtesy of its beams and exposed brick but, despite its appearance, this is a restaurant not a pub. The self-taught chef offers attractively presented, creative modern dishes which are full of flavour.

Menu £ 25/65 – set menu only

⊠ YO7 2HG – *ℰ* (01845) 597 769 (booking advisable) – www.thehare-inn.com
– Closed 3 weeks January, 1 week November, Sunday dinner, Monday and Tuesday

HELPERBY

North Yorkshire – Regional map n° **13**-B2
▶ London 220 mi – Leeds 36 mi – Sheffield 70 mi – Manchester 81 mi

🏠 Oak Tree Inn   ⇆ 🏠 & ⇔ 🅿

BRITISH TRADITIONAL · INN A pub of two halves, with a large bar, a tap room and two snugs in the main building, and a smart dining room in the old hay barn. Cooking is based around the Bertha charcoal oven, with steaks, chops, poultry and fish to the fore. Smart modern bedrooms come with 'Yorkie' bars and jacuzzi baths.

Carte £ 19/42

6 rooms ⊡ – **†**£ 55/140 **††**£ 55/140
Raskelf Rd ⊠ YO61 2PH – *ℰ* (01423) 789 189 – www.theoaktreehelperby.com

HELSTON

Cornwall – Pop. 11 311 – Regional map n° **1**-A3
▶ London 280 mi – Birmingham 275 mi – Croydon 288 mi – Barnet 293 mi

at Trelowarren Southeast: 4 mi by A394 and A3083 on B3293 – ⊠ Helston

X New Yard   🏠 🅿

BRITISH MODERN · RUSTIC Converted 17C stable building adjoining a craft gallery. Spacious, rustic room with timbered walls and doors opening onto the terrace. Seasonal menu uses quality Cornish produce; breads and ice creams are homemade. Friendly service.

Carte £ 19/31

Trelowarren Estate ⊠ TR12 6AF – *ℰ* (01326) 221 595 (bookings advisable at dinner) – www.trelowarren.com – Closed 3 weeks January, Monday and Tuesday October-Easter

at Cury South: 5 mi by A394 off A3083

🏠 Colvennor Farmhouse   🐾 🛏 ⚲ 🅿 ⤢

TRADITIONAL · CLASSIC Part-17C farmhouse in a peaceful location, boasting a lovely mature garden and paddock to the rear. Homely lounge features a wood burning stove. Simple, wood-furnished bedrooms are of a reasonable size. Linen-laid breakfast room.

3 rooms ⊡ – **†**£ 52/58 **††**£ 68/78
⊠ TR12 7BJ – *ℰ* (01326) 241 208 – www.colvennorfarmhouse.com

HEMINGFORD GREY – Cambridgeshire → See Huntingdon

HENFIELD
West Sussex – Pop. 4 527 – Regional map n° **4**-D2
▶ London 47 mi – Brighton 10 mi – Worthing 11 mi

🍴 Ginger Fox   ♿ 🌳 ⇄ 🅿
CLASSIC CUISINE · PUB Spot the fox running across the thatched roof and you know you're in the right place. Monthly changing menu offers good value, flavourful dishes, with a popular vegetarian tasting plate. Desserts are a highlight, so save space.
Menu £ 15 (weekday lunch) – Carte £ 23/41
Muddleswood Rd, Albourne ✉ BN6 9EA – Southwest : 3 mi on A 281
– ℰ (01273) 857 888 – www.gingermanrestaurants.com
– Closed 25 December

HENLADE – Somerset → See Taunton

HENLEY – West Sussex → See Midhurst

HENLEY-IN-ARDEN
Warwickshire – Pop. 2 846 – Regional map n° **10**-C3
▶ London 104 mi – Birmingham 15 mi – Stratford-upon-Avon 8 mi – Warwick 8 mi

🍴 Bluebell   🌳 🅿
BRITISH MODERN · ROMANTIC Part-timbered pub on the high street, displaying an unusual mix of rustic character and formal elegance. The experienced chef uses the best local ingredients in honest, seasonal dishes and there's a wide range of wines, beers and cocktails.
Menu £ 20 – Carte £ 27/46
93 High St ✉ B95 5AT
– ℰ (01564) 793 049 – www.bluebellhenley.co.uk
– Closed Monday

HENLEY-ON-THAMES
Oxfordshire – Pop. 11 494 – Regional map n° **6**-C3
▶ London 40 mi – Oxford 23 mi – Croydon 44 mi – Barnet 46 mi

🏨 Hotel du Vin   ⚘ ♿ 🅰 � 🅿
BUSINESS · MODERN Characterful 1857 building that was formerly the Brakspear Brewery. Stylish bedrooms include airy doubles and duplex suites: one features two roll-top tubs and a great view of the church; others boast heated balconies and outdoor baths. Choose from a list of brasserie classics and over 400 wines in the bistro.
43 rooms – †£ 130/300 ††£ 130/300 – ♙ £ 17 – 2 suites
New St. ✉ RG9 2BP – ℰ (01491) 848 400
– www.hotelduvin.com

✗✗ Shaun Dickens at The Boathouse   🌳 ♿ 🅰
BRITISH MODERN · FRIENDLY This modern restaurant is sure to please with its floor to ceiling glass doors and decked terrace overlooking the Thames. The young chef-owner offers an array of menus; attractively presented dishes centre around local ingredients.
Menu £ 26/70 – Carte £ 39/48
Station Rd ✉ RG9 1AZ
– ℰ (01491) 577 937 – www.shaundickens.co.uk
– Closed Monday and Tuesday

X **Luscombes at The Golden Ball**

TRADITIONAL CUISINE · FRIENDLY A pretty former pub – now a cosy restaurant that's popular with the locals. Appealing menus offer tasty, well-executed modern classics; the afternoon tea with homemade preserves is a hit. Service is friendly and attentive.

Menu £ 14 (weekday lunch)/25 – Carte £ 27/41

Lower Assendon ✉ RG9 6AH – Northwest : 0.75 mi by A 4130 on B 480
– ☎ (01491) 574 157 – www.luscombes.co.uk

🍴 **Three Tuns** 🈁 ♿

BRITISH TRADITIONAL · PUB Pretty, red-brick, town centre pub with a lively, open-fired front bar and a formal dining room for a more intimate meal. Seasonal, traditional dishes are well-presented, satisfying and full of flavour. Homemade bread. Friendly service.

Menu £ 11 (weekday lunch)/16 – Carte £ 25/41

5 Market Pl ✉ RG9 2AA – ☎ (01491) 410 138
– www.threetunshenley.co.uk
– Closed 25 December and Sunday dinner

at Stonor North: 4 mi by A4130 on B480

🍴 **Quince Tree** 🈁♿⇆🅿

BRITISH MODERN · PUB Delightfully set in a fold of the Chiltern Hills, with smart gardens, a sunny terrace and an adjoining café and deli. Cooking ranges from pub classics with a twist to more original dishes. Sit in the main room or the formal restaurant.

Carte £ 21/51

✉ RG9 6HE – ☎ (01491) 639 039 (booking advisable)
– www.thequincetree.com – Closed 25 December, 1 January and dinner Sunday-Monday

at Shiplake South: 2 mi on A4155

XX **Orwells** 🈁 🅿

BRITISH MODERN · RUSTIC This 18C building may look like a rural inn but inside it has a modern, formal feel. Creative cooking uses top quality produce and flavours are pronounced. It's named after George Orwell, who spent his childhood in the area.

Menu £ 15 (weekdays)/25 – Carte £ 35/50

Shiplake Row ✉ RG9 4DP – West 0.5 mi on Binfield Heath rd.
– ☎ (01189) 403 673 – www.orwellsatshiplake.co.uk
– Closed first 2 weeks January, first 2 weeks September, 1 week June, Sunday dinner, Tuesday and Monday except bank holidays

🍴 **Plowden Arms**

BRITISH TRADITIONAL · FAMILY An appealing pub with a delightful garden; inside, open fires, flickering candles and hop bines set the scene. The large blackboard offers tasty snacks and the interesting main menu features a number of Eliza Acton inspired dishes.

Menu £ 19 (weekdays) – Carte £ 21/42

Reading Rd ✉ RG9 4BX – ☎ (01189) 402 794
– www.plowdenarmsshiplake.co.uk
– Closed Mondays except bank holidays

HEREFORD

Herefordshire – Pop. 60 415 – Regional map n° **10**-B3

▶ London 133 mi – Birmingham 51 mi – Cardiff 56 mi

HEREFORD

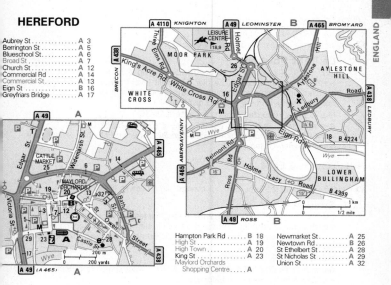

🏠 Castle House

🔆 🍸 🖥 🔌 ♿ ✂️ 🅿️

TOWNHOUSE · STYLISH This elegant Georgian house sits close to the cathedral. An impressive staircase leads to warmly furnished bedrooms of various sizes; some overlook the old castle moat. More contemporary rooms can be found in nearby 'Number 25'.

24 rooms ⌕ – ♦£110/130 ♦♦£150/230

Town plan: A-e – Castle St ⌧ HR1 2NW – ℰ (01432) 356 321
– www.castlehse.co.uk

Castle House – See restaurant listing

🏠 Brandon Lodge

🍸 ✂️ 🅿️

TRADITIONAL · CLASSIC Well-run, good value hotel with a welcoming owner. Bedrooms are split between the main house and the garden wing; the latter are more spacious, but all have good facilities. Neatly linen-laid breakfast room; comfy bar and lounge.

10 rooms ⌕ – ♦£55/60 ♦♦£70/80

Ross Rd ⌧ HR2 8BH – South : 1.25 mi on A 49 – ℰ (01432) 355 621
– www.brandonlodge.co.uk

🏠 Somerville House

🍸 ✂️ 🅿️

TOWNHOUSE · CONTEMPORARY Victorian villa with cathedral and hill views and an enclosed garden; home-grown apples, plums and pears are used to make their breakfast preserves. Spacious first floor rooms; those in the roof are smaller. Good facilities and a mini-bar.

12 rooms ⌕ – ♦£60/87 ♦♦£79/115

Town plan: B-x – 12 Bodenham Rd ⌧ HR1 2TS – ℰ (01432) 273 991
– www.somervillehouse.net

✗✗ Castle House

🍸 🍴 🆊 🅿️

MODERN CUISINE · FORMAL This elegant restaurant looks out over the hotel gardens and across the old moat of Hereford Castle. Classic dishes are reinvented in a modern manner and ingredients from Herefordshire feature highly. Menus offer plenty of choice.

Carte £25/44

Town plan: A-e – Castle House Hotel, Castle St ⌧ HR1 2NW – ℰ (01432) 356 321
– www.castlehse.co.uk

HERNE BAY

Kent – Pop. 38 385 – Regional map n° **5**-D1

▶ London 65 mi – Maidenhead 33 mi – Dover 25 mi

✗ Le Petit Poisson

FISH AND SEAFOOD · NEIGHBOURHOOD Head for the terrace of this white-washed building opposite the pier. The split-level interior boasts flagged floors, exposed brick and eye-catching mosaic art. Constantly evolving blackboard menus offer tasty, unfussy seafood dishes.

Menu £ 12 (weekday lunch) – Carte £ 21/36

Pier Approach, Central Par. ✉ CT6 5JN – ℰ (01227) 361 199
– www.lepetitpoisson.co.uk – Closed Sunday dinner and Monday except bank holidays when closed Tuesday

HERSTMONCEUX

East Sussex – Pop. 1 130 – Regional map n° **5**-B3

▶ London 63 mi – Eastbourne 12 mi – Hastings 14 mi – Lewes 16 mi

✗✗✗ Sundial

FRENCH CLASSIC · FORMAL With its original leaded windows and beamed ceiling, this characterful 16C cottage is a real hit with the locals. Service is structured and the room is formally laid. Rich, classic French dishes use luxurious seasonal ingredients.

Menu £ 27/42

Gardner St ✉ BN27 4LA – ℰ (01323) 832 217 – www.sundialrestaurant.co.uk
– Closed Sunday dinner and Monday

at Wartling Southeast: 3.75 mi by A271 on Wartling rd ✉ Herstmonceux

🏠 Wartling Place

COUNTRY HOUSE · CLASSIC A charming part-Georgian house set in three acres of mature grounds and run by a delightful owner. Two of the spacious bedrooms have four-poster beds; DAB radios and iPod docks provide a contrast to the antique furniture. Homely guest areas include an open-fired lounge and a communal dining area.

4 rooms ⌷ – †£ 90/110 ††£ 115/175

✉ BN27 1RY – ℰ (01323) 832 590 – www.wartlingplace.co.uk

HERTFORD

Hertfordshire – Regional map n° **7**-B2

▶ London 25 mi – Bishop's Stortford 16 mi – Stevenage 11 mi

🏠 Rigsby's 🆕

HISTORIC · STYLISH A red-brick Georgian townhouse, run in a relaxed, friendly manner. Bedrooms are the strong point here: smart and stylish, they offer good facilities and have a subtle New England style. Those in the main house are the largest.

7 rooms ⌷ – †£ 88/90 ††£ 100/125

25 St Andrew St ✉ SG14 1HZ – ℰ (01992) 535 999 – www.rigsbysguesthouse.com
– Closed 3 days Christmas

HETHE

Oxfordshire – Regional map n° **6**-B1

▶ London 114 mi – Oxford 36 mi – Northampton 45 mi

🍴 Muddy Duck 🆕

MODERN CUISINE · FRIENDLY An unpretentious local with a happy feel and ultra-smiley staff, this modernised mellow stone pub stays true to its traditional roots. Pub staples and more adventurous choices on the menu, with dishes from the wood-fired oven in summer.

Carte £ 24/54

Main St ✉ OX27 8ES – ℰ (01869) 278 099 – www.themuddyduckpub.co.uk

HETTON

North Yorkshire – Regional map n° **13**-N2
▶ London 229 mi – Leeds 31 mi – York 48 mi
see Regional map n 22-N2

XXX **Angel Inn**   ⅋ ⇔ ⅏ ⇔ **P**

BRITISH TRADITIONAL · FORMAL Formal restaurant comprising two smartly laid dining rooms with an intimate, romantic feel; now something of a local institution and surprisingly busy considering its rural location. Classically based cooking displays a few modern touches. Attentive, professional team. Antique-furnished bedrooms in the 'Barn Lodgings'; more modern rooms in 'Sycamore Bank' cottage.
Carte £ 28/44

9 rooms ⌂ – ♦£ 135/185 ♦♦£ 150/200

✉ BD23 6LT – ℰ (01756) 730 263 (booking essential) – www.angelhetton.co.uk
– dinner only and Sunday lunch – Closed 4 days January and 25 December
Brasserie at Angel Inn – See restaurant listing

⅃⌂ **Brasserie at Angel Inn**   ⅋ ⌂ ⌸ **P**

REGIONAL · PUB 18C stone inn, its characterful interior featuring old beams, wood-burning stoves and log fires. Despite its rural location, it's a popular place, and the staff cope well with the numbers. Seasonally changing menus offer hearty dishes of local produce and even some Yorkshire tapas.
Menu £ 15 (weekday lunch) – Carte £ 23/43

✉ BD23 6LT – ℰ (01756) 730 263 (booking essential) – www.angelhetton.co.uk
– Closed 4 days January and 25 December

HEXHAM

Northumberland – Pop. 11 388 – Regional map n° **14**-A2
▶ London 304 mi – Carlisle 37 mi – Newcastle upon Tyne 21 mi

XX **Bouchon**   ⇔

FRENCH CLASSIC · INTIMATE Well-run French restaurant with a simply styled ground floor room and a more romantic first floor with opulent purple furnishings. Excellent value set price lunch menu and more ambitious à la carte. Classic French dishes use local produce.
Menu £ 16 (lunch) – Carte £ 22/37

4-6 Gilesgate ✉ NE46 3NJ – ℰ (01434) 609 943 – www.bouchonbistrot.co.uk
– Closed 24-26 December, Sunday and bank holidays

⅃⌂ **Rat Inn**   ⌂ **P**

BRITISH TRADITIONAL · PUB Traditional 18C drovers' inn with old wood beams and an open range. The daily changing blackboard menu features wholesome pub classics; the rib of beef for two is a must. The multi-levelled garden boasts arbours and Tyne Valley views.
Carte £ 19/38

Anick ✉ NE46 4LN – Northeast : 1.75 mi by A 6079 – ℰ (01434) 602 814
– www.theratinn.com – Closed 25 December, Monday except bank holidays and Sunday dinner

at Slaley Southeast: 5.5 mi by B6306 ✉ Hexham

🏰 **Slaley Hall**   ⇪ ⅍ ⇐ ⅏ ▣ ⬚ ⑩ ⅏ ⅃ ⊡ ⅙ ⅏ ⅍ ⅍ **P**

COUNTRY HOUSE · CLASSIC Extended Edwardian manor house set in 1,000 acres and boasting two championship golf courses, a spa and extensive leisure facilities. Spacious, stylish guest areas. Largely traditional bedrooms, with 'Double Deluxe' being more contemporary. Classical dishes served in formal, cosy Duke's; Brasserie menu in Hadrian's; British favourites offered in clubby Claret Jug.

142 rooms ⌂ – ♦£ 105/125 ♦♦£ 115/145 – 2 suites

✉ NE47 0BX – Southeast : 2.25 mi – ℰ (01434) 673 350 – www.qhotels.co.uk

at Haydon Bridge West: 7.5 mi on A69 – ⊠ Hexham

🏰 **Langley Castle** ⇧ 🐾 🦽 ⅙ 🅰 🐾 🛌 🅿

CASTLE · HISTORIC Impressive 14C castle in 12 acres; its charming guest areas feature stone walls, tapestries and heraldic shields. Characterful bedrooms, some with four-posters; Castle View rooms are more uniform in style. Modern, international menus in the romantic dining room or in the glass cube overlooking the gardens.

27 rooms ⊆ – †£ 130/220 ††£ 159/279

Langley-on-Tyne ⊠ NE47 5LU – South : 2 mi by Alston rd on A 686 – ℰ (01434) 688 888 – www.langleycastle.com

HEYTESBURY – Wiltshire → See Warminster

HIGHCLERE

Hampshire – ⊠ Newbury – Pop. 2 409 – Regional map n° **4**-B1
▶ London 69 mi – Newbury 5 mi – Reading 25 mi

🍴 **Yew Tree** ⇦ 🏠 🅿

BRITISH MODERN · INN Attractive 17C whitewashed inn, with a pretty terrace, a welcoming open-fired bar and three low-beamed dining rooms. Classically based dishes come in a choice of sizes and are given modern twists; the vegetarian dishes provide interest. Cosy bedrooms come with good mod cons and smart wet rooms.

Carte £ 24/49

8 rooms ⊆ – †£ 95/130 ††£ 95/130

Hollington Cross, Andover Rd ⊠ RG20 9SE – South : 1 mi on A 343 – ℰ (01635) 253 360 – www.theyewtree.co.uk

HIGHCLIFFE

Dorset – Regional map n° **2**-D3
▶ London 112 mi – Bournemouth 10 mi – Salisbury 21 mi – Southampton 26 mi

🏰 **Lord Bute** ⇧ 🅰 🛌 🅿

BUSINESS · PERSONALISED Some of the suites in this elegant hotel stand where the original 18C entrance lodges to Highcliffe Castle (home of Lord Bute), were once located. Bedrooms are well-appointed and decorated in a contemporary style. The smart restaurant and courtyard offer classical menus and host jazz and cabaret evenings.

13 rooms ⊆ – †£ 115/235 ††£ 115/235 – 2 suites

179-185 Lymington Rd ⊠ BH23 4JS – ℰ (01425) 278 884 – www.lordbute.co.uk

HIGHER BURWARDSLEY – Cheshire West and Chester → See Tattenhall

HINCKLEY

Leicestershire – Pop. 45 249 – Regional map n° **9**-B2
▶ London 103 mi – Birmingham 31 mi – Leicester 14 mi

🍴🍴 **34 Windsor St** ⓝ 🏠 🅰 🅿

MODERN CUISINE · FASHIONABLE This stylish modern restaurant is well-run by an experienced, hands-on owner. It has a relaxed feel and a smart chill-out terrace to the rear. Cooking is also contemporary; the 8 course tasting menu shows the kitchen's ambition.

Carte £ 24/45

34 Windsor St ⊠ LE10 2EF – Southeast : 2.25 mi by B 4669 off B 578 – ℰ (01455) 234 342 – www.34windsorst.com – Closed 1-4 January, Sunday dinner and Monday

HINTLESHAM – Suffolk → See Ipswich

HINTON ST GEORGE
Somerset – Regional map n° **2**-B3
▶ London 138 mi – Taunton 21 mi – Weymouth 41 mi – Yeovil 13 mi

🛏 Lord Poulett Arms   ⬅ 🍴 🏠

BRITISH MODERN · **RURALLY** 17C inn with a lavender-framed terrace, a boules
pitch, an untamed garden and a country interior filled with hop bines and candles. A refreshing mix of classic and modern dishes; cooking is full of flavour
and there's a fine selection of real ales. Smart, stylish bedrooms have Roberts radios instead of TVs.
Menu £ 12 (lunch and early dinner) – Carte £ 27/37
5 rooms ☞ – ♦£ 60/65 ♦♦£ 85/95
*High St ⊠ TA17 8SE – ℰ (01460) 73 149 – www.lordpoulettarms.com – Closed
25-26 December and 1 January*

HITCHIN
Hertfordshire – Pop. 34 266 – Regional map n° **7**-A2
▶ London 40 mi – Bedford 14 mi – Cambridge 26 mi – Luton 9 mi

✗ hermitage rd   🍸 🏧

BRITISH MODERN · **BRASSERIE** A vast, open-plan brasserie with a cocktail bar
and a vibrant, buzzy atmosphere; sit in the booths at the back. The menu offers
something for everyone, with mussels or oysters from their own beds, sharing
boards and some great steaks.
Carte £ 20/35
*20-21 Hermitage Rd ⊠ SG5 1BT – ℰ (01462) 433 603 (booking essential)
– www.hermitagerd.co.uk – Closed 25-26 December*

🛏 Radcliffe Arms   🐾 🏠 ♿ 🏧 🖥 ⇄ 🅿

BRITISH MODERN · **NEIGHBOURHOOD** A friendly and relaxed neighbourhood
pub named after a local family, with a central bar, gravity fed ales and a good
spirit and wine selection. Tasty cooking focuses on well-presented, restaurant-
style dishes. Breakfast is served from 8am.
Carte £ 26/46
*31 Walsworth Rd ⊠ SG4 9ST – ℰ (01462) 456 111 – www.radcliffearms.com
– Closed 26 December*

HOCKLEY HEATH
West Midlands – ⊠ Solihull – Pop. 1 604 – Regional map n° **10**-C2
▶ London 117 mi – Birmingham 11 mi – Coventry 17 mi

🏯 Nuthurst Grange Country House   🌳 🍴 ♿ 🥂 ⛵ 🅿

COUNTRY HOUSE · **STYLISH** With its lovely mature grounds and walled herb
garden, this attractive part-Edwardian former farmhouse is a popular wedding
venue. Spacious, country house style bedrooms are individually furnished; some
have four-poster beds. The traditional dining room prepares classic dishes with a
modern twist.
19 rooms ☞ – ♦£ 132 ♦♦£ 143
*Nuthurst Grange Ln ⊠ B94 5NL – South : 0.75 mi by A 3400 – ℰ (01564) 783 972
– www.nuthurst-grange.co.uk – Closed 24-26 December*

HOLCOMBE
Somerset – Regional map n° **2**-C2
▶ London 119 mi – Birmingham 106 mi – Leeds 228 mi – Sheffield 198 mi

🍴 Holcombe Inn

BRITISH MODERN · RUSTIC Charming 17C inn set in the heart of the Somerset countryside, with a lovely south-facing garden and a peaceful air. Menus offer quite a range of dishes, from good old pub classics to more sophisticated offerings. Bedrooms are luxuriously appointed; some boast views over Downside Abbey.

Carte £ 26/47

10 rooms 😋 – 🛏£ 75/120 🛏🛏£ 100/145

Stratton Rd ✉ BA3 5EB – West : 0.25 mi on Stratton-on-the-Fosse rd – ℰ (01761) 232 478 – www.holcombeinn.co.uk

HOLFORD

Somerset – ✉ Bridgwater – Pop. 307 – Regional map n° **2**-B2

▶ London 171 mi – Bristol 48 mi – Minehead 15 mi – Taunton 22 mi

🏠 Combe House

COUNTRY HOUSE · CONTEMPORARY Hidden up a narrow lane is this smart country house, with an old water wheel and mill alongside. It might be rustic outside but inside it's bright and modern. Bedrooms feature bold, contemporary fabrics and white furnishings, and there's a pleasant spa. The split-level restaurant offers modern classics.

18 rooms 😋 – 🛏£ 85/99 🛏🛏£ 99/159

✉ TA5 1RZ – Southwest : 0.75 by road next to Plough pub and Holford rd. – ℰ (01278) 741 382 – www.combehouse.co.uk

HOLKHAM

Norfolk – Regional map n° **8**-C1

▶ London 124 mi – King's Lynn 32 mi – Norwich 39 mi

🏠 Victoria

INN · MODERN Located close to the beach, at the gates of Holkham Hall, an extended flint inn with large lawned gardens and pleasant country views. A relaxed, modern style pervades and bedrooms have a stylish, homely feel. Dine on traditional British dishes while overlooking the marshes of the adjacent nature reserve.

20 rooms 😋 – 🛏£ 90/150 🛏🛏£ 120/280

Park Rd ✉ NR23 1RG – ℰ (01328) 711 008 – www.holkham.co.uk/victoria

HOLLINGBOURNE

Kent – Regional map n° **5**-C2

▶ London 43 mi – Maidstone 7 mi – Faversham 23 mi

🍴 The Windmill

BRITISH TRADITIONAL · PUB This pub is as characterful as they come, with a giant inglenook and beams so low you have to watch your head. Hearty British dishes fittingly form the core of the menu, with bar snacks, comforting puddings-and sharing roasts on Sundays.

Menu £ 15 (weekday lunch) – Carte £ 25/36

32 Eyhorne St ✉ ME17 1TR – ℰ (01622) 889 000 – www.thewindmillbyrichardphillips.co.uk

HOLMFIRTH

West Yorkshire – Pop. 21 706 – Regional map n° **13**-B3

▶ London 187 mi – Leeds 35 mi – Sheffield 32 mi – Manchester 25 mi

🏠 Sunnybank

TOWNHOUSE · ELEGANT Attractive Victorian house with lovely gardens and great views; hidden up a narrow road in the village where 'Last of the Summer Wine' was filmed. Cosy bedrooms have a personal touch. Look out for the original stained glass window.

6 rooms 😋 – 🛏£ 68/105 🛏🛏£ 78/115

78 Upperthong Ln ✉ HD9 3BQ – Northwest : 0.5 mi by A 6024 – ℰ (01484) 684 065 – www.sunnybankguesthouse.co.uk

HOLT

Norfolk – Pop. 3 550 – Regional map n° **8**-C1
▶ London 124 mi – King's Lynn 34 mi – Norwich 22 mi

⌂ **Byfords**   ⌂ 🛏 ⚹ 🍴 🅿

TOWNHOUSE · MODERN Grade II listed, 15C flint house. Stunning bedrooms come with feature beds, underfloor heating and plenty of extras. Numerous characterful rooms incorporate a deli, a café and a restaurant. Light meals are served during the day and more substantial dishes in the evening; it's a real hit with the locals.

17 rooms ☷ – ♦£ 120/130 ♦♦£ 155/205
Shirehall Plain ⊠ *NR25 6BG* – ℘ *(01263) 711 400* – *www.byfords.org.uk*

🛏 **Tollgate Inn**   ⇦ 🛏 🅿

TRADITIONAL CUISINE · PUB The warm welcome and cheery, attentive staff at this village inn really set it apart. The menu keeps things simple, as befits a pub, with hearty, flavoursome dishes including steaks, fish of the day and a range of homemade pies. Cosy bedrooms have a homely style and charming personal touches.

Carte £ 17/39

5 rooms ☷ – ♦£ 70/120 ♦♦£ 80/120
Ham Grn ⊠ *BA14 6PX* – ℘ *(01225) 782 326* – *www.tollgateinn.co.uk* – *Closed Sunday dinner*

HOLYPORT

Windsor and Maidenhead – Regional map n° **6**-C3
▶ London 30 mi – Birmingham 107 mi – Bristol 93 mi – Croydon 37 mi

🛏 **Belgian Arms**   🍺 🛏 ⚹ 🅿

BRITISH TRADITIONAL · PUB Pretty 17C inn tucked away just off the village green, next to a pond fringed by willow trees. Gutsy pub dishes include tempting bar snacks and heartwarming desserts. It's a real locals' local, so there's always plenty going on.

Carte £ 26/36

Holyport St ⊠ *SL6 2JR* – ℘ *(01628) 634 468* – *www.thebelgianarms.com*
– *Closed Monday*

HONITON

Devon – Pop. 11 483 – Regional map n° **1**-D2
▶ London 186 mi – Exeter 17 mi – Southampton 93 mi – Taunton 18 mi

🛏 **Holt**

REGIONAL · PUB A rustic, family-run pub, where their passion for food is almost palpable. The regularly changing menu features regional and homemade produce, with meats and fish smoked and cured on-site; ales are from their nearby family brewery.

Carte £ 26/34

178 High St ⊠ *EX14 1LA* – ℘ *(01404) 47 707* – *www.theholt-honiton.com*
– *Closed 25-26 December, 1 January, Sunday and Monday*

🛏 **Railway**   ⇦ 🛏 ⚹ 🅿

MEDITERRANEAN · INN Smart, modern pub with a horseshoe bar, an open kitchen and a decked terrace. Authentic, affordable Mediterranean cooking features homemade pastas, brick-fired pizzas and well-cooked steaks. An eclectic wine list and an olive oil top-up service add to the fun, and comfortable bedrooms complete the picture.

Carte £ 25/37

5 rooms ☷ – ♦£ 75/95 ♦♦£ 85/105
Queen St ⊠ *EX14 1HE* – ℘ *(01404) 47 976* – *www.therailwayhoniton.co.uk*
– *Closed 25-26 December, Sunday and Monday*

at Gittisham Southwest: 3 mi by A30 – ⊠ Honiton

🏠 Combe House   ⚜ ⅌ ≤ 🏠 🏛 🅿

COUNTRY HOUSE · HISTORIC A hugely impressive Elizabethan mansion, set down a long drive and boasting wonderful country views. Characterful guest areas display original features and the imposing Great Hall is a feature. Menus showcase produce from the superb gardens. In 2016 it is set to become part of the stylish Pig hotel group.

17 rooms � – †£ 190/440 ††£ 220/460 – 4 suites

⊠ EX14 3AD – ℰ (01404) 540 400 – www.combehousedevon.com – Closed 2 weeks January

HOOK

Hampshire – ⊠ Basingstoke – Pop. 7 934 – Regional map n° **4**-B1

▶ London 47 mi – Oxford 39 mi – Reading 13 mi – Southampton 31 mi

🏠 Tylney Hall   ⚜ ⅌ 🏠 ⅂ 🖾 ⚫ 🏛 🛁 ⅍ ♿ 🏛 🅿

LUXURY · CLASSIC Impressively restored 19C mansion with a well-appointed spa and several sumptuous lounges. Country house style bedrooms boast good facilities – one even has a private conservatory. The formal panelled restaurant features classic menus and an evening pianist. The delightful gardens were designed by Jekyll.

112 rooms ⊠ – †£ 250/530 ††£ 250/530 – 15 suites

Rotherwick ⊠ RG27 9AZ – Northwest : 2.5 mi by A 30 and Newnham Rd on Ridge Ln – ℰ (01256) 764 881 – www.tylneyhall.com

🍴 Hogget   🏛 ♿ 🅿

TRADITIONAL CUISINE · FRIENDLY Brightly painted pub with a heated terrace, located at the junction of the A30 and A287. Accessible menus offer wholesome, honest cooking which shows respect for local ingredients; dishes are sensibly priced and service is cheery.

Carte £ 19/35

London Rd ⊠ RG27 9JJ – (at the junction of A 30 and A 287) – ℰ (01256) 763 009 – www.thehogget.co.uk – Closed 25-26 December

HOPE

Derbyshire – ⊠ Sheffield – Regional map n° **9**-A1

▶ London 180 mi – Derby 50 mi – Manchester 31 mi – Sheffield 15 mi

🏠 Losehill House   ⚜ ⅌ ≤ 🏠 🏛 🖾 ⅍ ⅌ ⅋ 🏛 🅿

TRADITIONAL · PERSONALISED Peacefully located former walkers' hostel affording wonderful views up to Win Hill; in summer it's a popular wedding venue. It has an airy open-plan lounge-bar and bright modern bedrooms. Unwind in the spa or in the hot tub on the terrace. The formally laid restaurant offers classic dishes with a modern edge.

23 rooms ⊠ – †£ 125/195 ††£ 165/225

Lose Hill Ln, Edale Rd ⊠ S33 6AF – North : 1 mi by Edale Rd – ℰ (01433) 621 219 – www.losehillhouse.co.uk

🏠 Underleigh House   ⅌ ≤ 🏠 ⅋ 🅿

TRADITIONAL · PERSONALISED Former Derbyshire longhouse and shippon with far-reaching views; the gregarious owner offers a friendly welcome. Traditional bedrooms, some opening onto the garden. Communal breakfasts include homemade preserves, bread and muesli.

5 rooms ⊠ – †£ 75/105 ††£ 95/125

Losehill Ln, Hope Valley ⊠ S33 6AF – North : 1 mi by Edale Rd – ℰ (01433) 621 372 – www.underleighhouse.co.uk – Closed Christmas-New Year and January

HOPTON HEATH

Shropshire – Regional map n° **10**-A2

▶ London 162 mi – Birmingham 66 mi – Leeds 152 mi – Sheffield 131 mi

🏠 Hopton House   🦢 ⪦ 🦮 ♿ 🅿

COUNTRY HOUSE · STYLISH An unassuming former granary backed by a wild flower meadow and the Shropshire Hills. Stylish bedrooms come with sofas and double-ended baths. One room has a balcony; one has a terrace – and they all come with a freshly baked cake.

3 rooms 🍽 – 🛏£ 90 🛏🛏£ 115/130

✉ SY7 0QD – on Clun rd – ☎ (01547) 530 885 – www.shropshirebreakfast.co.uk

HORLEY

Surrey – Pop. 22 693 – Regional map n° **4**-D2

▶ London 27 mi – Brighton 26 mi – Royal Tunbridge Wells 22 mi

🏨 Langshott Manor   🏠 🦢 🦮 🍽 🅿

HISTORIC · STYLISH Characterful 16C manor house set amidst roses, vines and ponds. The traditional exterior contrasts with contemporary furnishings; many of the bedrooms have fireplaces or four-posters and one has a balcony. Afternoon tea is a feature.

22 rooms – 🛏£ 99/259 🛏🛏£ 99/259 – 🍽 £ 17 – 1 suite

Langshott ✉ RH6 9LN – North : 0.5 mi by A 23 turning right at Chequers H. onto Ladbroke Rd – ☎ (01293) 786 680 – www.alexanderhotels.com

Mulberry – See restaurant listing

XxX Mulberry   🦮 🍴 🅿

BRITISH MODERN · FORMAL Smart hotel dining room within a Part-Elizabethan manor house, which uses many herbs, fruits and vegetables from the gardens. It offers everything from breakfast to two tasting dinner menus. Dishes are modern and well-presented.

Menu £ 29/50

Langshott Manor Hotel, Langshott ✉ RH6 9LN – North : 0.5 mi by A 23 turning right at Chequers H. onto Ladbroke Rd – ☎ (01293) 786 680
– www.langshottmanor.com

HORNCASTLE

Lincolnshire – Pop. 6 815 – Regional map n° **9**-C1

▶ London 143 mi – Lincoln 22 mi – Nottingham 62 mi

XX Magpies   ⪦ ♿ 🆎

BRITISH TRADITIONAL · FAMILY Three adjoining 18C cottages; now a cosy, family-run restaurant which hosts regular gourmet and wine dinners. Hearty, classically based dishes are attractively presented; don't miss the tasty homemade canapés and breads. Modern bedrooms have bold floral feature walls and impressive bathrooms.

Menu £ 25/47

3 rooms 🍽 – 🛏£ 70/80 🛏🛏£ 110/130

71-75 East St ✉ LN9 6AA – ☎ (01507) 527 004 – www.magpiesrestaurant.co.uk
– Closed 26-30 December, 1-7 January, Saturday lunch, Monday and Tuesday

HORNDON ON THE HILL

Thurrock – Pop. 1 596 – Regional map n° **7**-C3

▶ London 25 mi – Chelmsford 22 mi – Maidstone 34 mi – Southend-on-Sea 16 mi

🏠 Bell Inn   ⪦ 🍴 🅿

BRITISH TRADITIONAL · INN A characterful 15C coaching inn, run by the same family for over 70 years; look out for the hot cross buns hanging from the bar. Cooking uses quality produce to create classically based dishes with a modern touch. Pub bedrooms are traditional in style, while those in Hill House are thoroughly modern.

Carte £ 22/39

27 rooms 🍽 – 🛏£ 65/140 🛏🛏£ 65/140

High Rd ✉ SS17 8LD – ☎ (01375) 642 463 – www.bell-inn.co.uk – Closed
25-26 December and bank holidays

HORNING

Norfolk – Regional map n° **8**-D1

▶ London 121 mi – Great Yarmouth 16 mi – Norwich 11 mi

✗ Bure River Cottage

FISH AND SEAFOOD · **FRIENDLY** Friendly restaurant tucked away in a lovely riverside village that's famed for its boating. Informal, L-shaped room with modern tables and chairs. Blackboard menu features fresh, carefully cooked fish and shellfish; much from Lowestoft.

Carte £ 20/45

27 Lower St ⊠ NR12 8AA – ℰ (01692) 631 421 (booking advisable)
– www.burerivercottagerestaurant.co.uk – dinner only – Closed
25 December-13 February, Sunday and Monday

HORNINGSEA – Cambridgeshire ➜ See Cambridge

HORNINGSHAM – Wiltshire ➜ See Warminster

HORN'S CROSS

Devon – ⊠ Bideford – Regional map n° **1**-C1

▶ London 222 mi – Barnstaple 15 mi – Exeter 46 mi

⌂ Roundhouse ⚘ ⊞ ⇆

TRADITIONAL · **COSY** Spacious, welcoming guesthouse on the site of a 13C corn mill, with donkeys in the paddock, neat gardens and comfortable, homely guest areas. Immaculately kept bedrooms: ask for the round room (the largest) on the first floor.

3 rooms ⊡ – ♦£ 50 ♦♦£ 65

⊠ EX39 5DN – West : 1 mi on A 39 – ℰ (01237) 451 687
– www.the-round-house.co.uk

HORRINGER – Suffolk ➜ See Bury St Edmunds

HORSHAM

West Sussex – Pop. 48 041 – Regional map n° **4**-D2

▶ London 39 mi – Brighton 23 mi – Guildford 20 mi – Lewes 25 mi

✗ Restaurant Tristan (Tristan Mason)

⌘ BRITISH MODERN · **RUSTIC** 16C property with a ground floor coffee shop and a heavily beamed upstairs restaurant. Well-presented, classic dishes are delivered with a modern touch; ingredients are excellent and flavours, distinct and well-matched. Service is enthusiastic and friendly and the atmosphere, refreshingly relaxed.

➜ Duck egg 64°C, brill, white asparagus, morels. Lamb, kid, goat. Rhubarb soufflé, crème fraîche, liquorice, hibiscus.

Menu £ 25/80

Stans Way, East St ⊠ RH12 1HU – ℰ (01403) 255 688
– www.restauranttristan.co.uk – Closed 2 weeks late July-early August,
25-26 December, first week January, Sunday and Monday

at Rowhook Northwest: 4 mi by A264 and A281 off A29 – ⊠ Horsham

⌂ Chequers Inn ⚘ ⌂ ⊞

CLASSIC CUISINE · **COSY** Part-15C inn with a charming open-fired, stone-floored bar and an unusual dining room extension. The chef-owner grows, forages for or shoots the majority of his produce. Classical menus.

Carte £ 25/40

⊠ RH12 3PY – ℰ (01403) 790 480 – www.thechequersrowhook.com – Closed
25 December and Sunday dinner

HORSTED KEYNES

West Sussex – Pop. 1 180 – Regional map n° **4**-D2

▶ London 40 mi – Brighton 23 mi – Guildford 48 mi – Canterbury 75 mi

⌂ **Crown Inn** ⟷ ⌂ ⌂ **P**

CLASSIC CUISINE · PUB With its beams and feature inglenook, the front bar of this pub is full of character, while the smart dining room houses a grand piano, played on Friday nights. Classical dishes form the core of the menu, with more ambitious, seasonal specials. Simple bedrooms have views of the green; one is a four-poster.

Carte £ 25/45

4 rooms ⌂ – ♦£ 80/90 ♦♦£ 90/110

The Green ✉ *RH17 7AW* – ✆ *(01825) 791 609*
– www.thecrown-horstedkeynes.co.uk – Closed Sunday dinner and Monday January-June

HOUGH-ON-THE-HILL – Lincolnshire → See Grantham

HOVERINGHAM

Nottinghamshire – Pop. 359 – Regional map n° **9**-B2
▶ London 135 mi – Birmingham 77 mi – Leeds 74 mi – Sheffield 57 mi

⌂ **Reindeer Inn** **P**

BRITISH TRADITIONAL · PUB Characterful country inn set next to a cricket pitch, with old beams, an open fire and a cosy, relaxed atmosphere. Well-priced menus offer mainly classical dishes. It's popular with the locals.

Menu £ 11 (weekday lunch) – Carte £ 17/22

Main St ✉ *NG14 7JR* – ✆ *(01159) 663 629* – *www.thereindeerinn.com*
– Closed Monday lunch, Wednesday, Thursday and Sunday dinner

HOVINGHAM

North Yorkshire – ✉ York – Regional map n° **13**-C2
▶ London 235 mi – Leeds 47 mi – Middlesbrough 36 mi – York 25 mi

⌂ **Worsley Arms**

INN · HOMELY Characterful inn with cosy lounges and a large walled garden; dating back to 1841 and located in a delightful estate village. Homely bedrooms are split between the main building and a row of cottages on the green. Classic menus are served in the rustic bar at lunch and in the more formal dining room at dinner.

20 rooms ⌂ – ♦£ 110/115 ♦♦£ 132/152

High St ✉ *YO62 4LA* – ✆ *(01653) 628 234* – *www.worsleyarms.co.uk*

HUCCOMBE

Devon – Regional map n° **1**-C3
▶ London 217 mi – Bristol 121 mi – Cardiff 152 mi – Plymouth 30 mi

⌂ **Huccombe House**

FAMILY · PERSONALISED Converted Victorian school – the owner herself once went to school here! Pleasant lounge with high beamed ceilings and huge windows affording countryside views. Large bedrooms with sleigh beds made up with Egyptian cotton linen. Aga-cooked breakfasts at the communal table or on the patio.

3 rooms ⌂ – ♦£ 80 ♦♦£ 95

✉ *TQ7 2EP* – ✆ *(01548) 580 669* – *www.southdevonbandb.co.uk*

HUDDERSFIELD

West Yorkshire – Pop. 162 949 – Regional map n° **13**-B3
▶ London 191 mi – Bradford 11 mi – Leeds 15 mi – Manchester 25 mi

XX **Eric's**

MODERN CUISINE · NEIGHBOURHOOD Contemporary neighbourhood restaurant offering seasonal menus of appealing modern dishes packed with bold, distinct flavours. Great value lunch and early evening menu. On selected Saturdays they host brunch or afternoon tea events.

Menu £16 (weekday lunch)/25 – Carte £35/50

73-75 Lidgets St, Lindley ⊠ HD3 3JP – Northwest : 3.25 mi by A 629 and Birchencliffe Hill Rd. – ℰ (01484) 646 416 (booking advisable)
– www.ericsrestaurant.co.uk – Closed Monday except December and Sunday dinner

HULLBRIDGE

Essex – Pop. 6 097 – Regional map n° **7**-C2_3
▶ London 40 mi – Southend on Sea 10 mi – Chelmsford 13 mi

X **Anchor** ⟨ 佘 AK P

MODERN CUISINE · BRASSERIE A large, busy, open-plan restaurant with modern décor, a sleek bar and a superb terrace; sit here or in the Orangery for views of the River Crouch. The à la carte offers a wide range of tasty seasonal British dishes and there's an excellent value set price weekday menu too. Summer barbecues. Friendly service.

Menu £17 (weekdays) – Carte £25/40

Ferry Rd ⊠ SS5 6ND – ℰ (01702) 230 777 – www.theanchorhullbridge.co.uk
– Closed 25 December

HUMSHAUGH

Northumberland – Regional map n° **14**-A2
▶ London 290 mi – Birmingham 220 mi – Glasgow 132 mi

Carraw ⟨ 🕿 � P

FAMILY · PERSONALISED Converted farmhouse and barn on the foundations of Hadrian's Wall, with a bright pine-furnished breakfast room and an open-fired lounge which opens onto a terrace. Some bedrooms have exposed stone and beams; others are more modern.

8 rooms ⌷ – ♦£55/68 ♦♦£59/100

Carraw Farm, Military Rd ⊠ NE46 4DB – West : 5 mi on B 6318 – ℰ (01434) 689 857 – www.carraw.co.uk

HUNSDON

Hertfordshire – Regional map n° **7**-B2
▶ London 26 mi – Bishop's Stortford 8 mi – Harlow 7 mi

🍴 **Fox and Hounds** ⅾ 佘 P

BRITISH TRADITIONAL · PUB Sizeable pub with a rustic interior, a large garden and a terrace. Concise menus offer tasty, unfussy dishes that display a clear understanding of flavours. Pasta is are homemade, they smoke their own fish, and desserts are not to be missed; in summer, be sure to pay a visit to the popular outside seafood bar.

Menu £14 (weekdays) – Carte £25/42

2 High St ⊠ SG12 8NH – ℰ (01279) 843 999 – www.foxandhounds-hunsdon.co.uk
– Closed 25-26 December, Sunday dinner and Monday

HUNSTANTON

Norfolk – Pop. 8 704 – Regional map n° **8**-B1
▶ London 120 mi – Cambridge 60 mi – Norwich 45 mi

⌂ Lodge ⚘ P

HOLIDAY HOTEL · PERSONALISED After a long day at the beach head for this laid-back hotel and one of its modern, well-equipped, immaculately kept bedrooms. Dine in the large bar with its TV and pool table or head through to the more formal residents' dining room; the chef is Italian, so opt for a dish from his homeland.

16 rooms ⊑ – †£ 75/85 ††£ 120/130
Old Hunstanton Rd ⊠ PE36 6HX – Northeast : 1.5 mi on A 149 – ℰ (01485) 532 896 – www.thelodgehunstanton.co.uk

No. 33 🆕 ⇔ P

LUXURY · DESIGN A Victorian house with an unusual façade, set in a peaceful street. Designer touches feature throughout, from the cosy open-fired lounge to the boutique bedrooms with their creative feature walls; some even have baths in the room.

5 rooms – †£ 70/120 ††£ 80/170
33 Northgate ⊠ PE36 6AP – ℰ (01485) 524 352 – www.33hunstanton.co.uk

XX The Neptune (Kevin Mangeolles) ⇔ P

☸ **MODERN CUISINE · FRIENDLY** Very personally run, attractive, red-brick former pub. New England style interior with a rattan-furnished bar and large nautical photographs in the dining room. The constantly evolving menu relies on the latest local produce to arrive at the door. Presentation is modern; service is relaxed and efficient. Comfy bedrooms have Nespresso machines and thoughtful extras.
→ Brancaster lobster salad, star anise mousse and pea purée. Saddle and braised haunch of hare with cep and celeriac tart. Poached savarin sponge with compressed strawberries, lemon curd and strawberry sorbet.
Menu £ 55/72

5 rooms ⊑ – †£ 90/110 ††£ 150/160
85 Old Hunstanton Rd, Old Hunstanton ⊠ PE36 6HZ – Northeast : 1.5 mi on A 149 – ℰ (01485) 532 122 – www.theneptune.co.uk – dinner only and Sunday lunch – Closed 3 weeks January, 2 weeks November, 26 December and Monday

at Thornham Northeast: 4.5 mi on A149

▭ Orange Tree ⇔ ⇔ ⌂ P

MODERN CUISINE · INN You're guaranteed a warm welcome at this 17C inn; even your dog will be offered a snack in the laid-back bar. An array of menus offer everything from pub classics to globally-influenced restaurant dishes, via some vegetarian choices and daily specials. Contemporary restaurant and compact, modern bedrooms.
Carte £ 24/44 **s**

10 rooms ⊑ – †£ 65/140 ††£ 85/180
High St ⊠ PE36 6LY – ℰ (01485) 512 213 – www.theorangetreethornham.co.uk

HUNSTRETE
Bath and North East Somerset – Regional map n° **2**-C2
▶ London 124 mi – Bath 10 mi – Bournemouth 75 mi – Exeter 77 mi

▭ The Pig ⚘ 🐾 ⇔ ⇔ ⌂ 🕾 P

COUNTRY HOUSE · PERSONALISED Nestled in the Mendip Hills, with deer roaming around the parkland, this Grade II listed house is all about getting back to nature. It has a relaxed, friendly atmosphere and extremely comfortable bedrooms which feature handmade beds and fine linens; some are in converted sheds in the walled vegetable garden.

29 rooms – †£ 149/275 ††£ 149/275 – ⊑ £ 15 – 1 suite
Hunstrete House ⊠ BS39 4NS – ℰ (01761) 490 490 – www.thepighotel.com
The Pig – See restaurant listing

XX **The Pig**

TRADITIONAL CUISINE · BRASSERIE This rustic hotel conservatory takes things back to nature with pots of fresh herbs placed on wooden tables and chimney pots filled with flowering shrubs. The extremely knowledgeable team serve dishes which showcase ingredients from their extensive gardens, along with produce sourced from within 25 miles.

Carte £ 22/45

The Pig Hotel, Hunstrete House ⊠ BS39 4NS – ℰ (01761) 490 490 (booking advisable) – www.thepighotel.com

HUNTINGDON

Cambridgeshire – Pop. 23 937 – Regional map n° **8**-A2
▶ London 69 mi – Bedford 21 mi – Cambridge 16 mi

Old Bridge

TOWNHOUSE · STYLISH Attractive 18C former bank next to the River Ouse; its bright, contemporary décor cleverly blended with the property's original features. Individually styled, up-to-date bedrooms; some with four-poster beds. Cosy oak-panelled bar, conservatory restaurant with a lovely terrace and a superbly stocked wine shop.

24 rooms ☑ – †£ 90/125 ††£ 120/230

1 High St ⊠ PE29 3TQ – ℰ (01480) 424 300 – www.huntsbridge.com

Abbots Ripton North: 6.5 mi by B1514 and A141 on B1090

Abbot's Elm

MODERN CUISINE · FRIENDLY A modern reconstruction of an attractive 17C pub, with a spacious open-plan layout, homely touches and a vaulted, oak-beamed roof. Extensive menus offer hearty, flavoursome cooking; the wine list is a labour of love and the cosy, comfy bedrooms come with fluffy bathrobes and complimentary mineral water.

Menu £ 14 (weekday lunch)/23 – Carte £ 20/39

3 rooms ☑ – †£ 60/70 ††£ 75/85

Moat Ln ⊠ PE28 2PA – ℰ (01487) 773 773 – www.theabbotselm.co.uk – Closed Sunday dinner

at Hemingford Grey Southeast: 5 mi by A1198 off A14 – ⊠ Huntingdon

The Cock

TRADITIONAL CUISINE · PUB A homely 17C country pub with a split-level bar and a spacious dining room; run by an experienced team. Tried-and-tested British cooking, with extensive daily fish specials and more than 100 types of sausage; good value lunches.

Menu £ 13 (weekday lunch) – Carte £ 22/39

47 High St ⊠ PE28 9BJ – ℰ (01480) 463 609 (booking essential)
– www.cambscuisine.com

HURSTBOURNE TARRANT

Hampshire – ⊠ Andover – Pop. 676 – Regional map n° **4**-B1
▶ London 77 mi – Bristol 77 mi – Oxford 38 mi – Southampton 33 mi

Esseborne Manor

TRADITIONAL · CLASSIC Set in attractive grounds, this Victorian country house is a popular wedding venue. Smart, classically decorated bedrooms are split between the house, a cottage and the courtyard; some have whirlpool baths, two have four-posters and one leads out into the herb garden. The restaurant serves modern classics.

18 rooms ☑ – †£ 92/110 ††£ 112/125

⊠ SP11 0ER – Northeast : 1.5 mi on A 343 – ℰ (01264) 736 444
– www.esseborne-manor.co.uk

HURSTPIERPOINT

Pop. 12 730 – Regional map n° **4**-D2

▶ London 45 mi – Croydon 35 mi – Barnet 87 mi – Ealing 69 mi

✗ **Fig Tree**

BRITISH TRADITIONAL · COSY Attractive Victorian house in a pretty high street, personally run by a young couple: she looks after diners while he cooks. Carefully priced menus showcase local, seasonal ingredients. Loyal local following.

Menu £ 19 (lunch)/23 – Carte £ 27/38

120 High St ⊠ BN6 9PX – ✆ (01273) 832 183 – www.figtreerestaurant.co.uk
– Closed 2 weeks January, Tuesday lunch, Sunday dinner and Monday

HURWORTH-ON-TEES – Darlington → See Darlington

HUTTON-LE-HOLE

North Yorkshire – Pop. 162 – Regional map n° **13**-C1

▶ London 244 mi – Scarborough 27 mi – York 33 mi

🏠 **Burnley House**

TRADITIONAL · CLASSIC A cosy, welcoming guesthouse at the entrance to this picture postcard village on the edge of the moors. Small sitting room with a stone floor, coir carpet and wood-burning stove. Snug, bright bedrooms and a pretty garden.

7 rooms ☲ – ♦£ 56/88 ♦♦£ 88

⊠ YO62 6UA – ✆ (01751) 417 548 – www.burnleyhouse.co.uk

HUTTON MAGNA – Durham → See Barnard Castle

ICKLESHAM

East Sussex – Regional map n° **5**-C3

▶ London 66 mi – Brighton 42 mi – Hastings 7 mi

🏠 **Manor Farm Oast**

🐾 🛏 ⚘ 🅿

FAMILY · HOMELY Restored, extended oast house built in 1860 and surrounded by orchards and farmland. Original features remain both inside and out. The welcoming beamed lounge has an open fire; homely bedrooms feature large beds – one is completely round.

3 rooms ☲ – ♦£ 95/105 ♦♦£ 105

Windmill Ln ⊠ TN36 4WL – South : 0.5 mi – ✆ (01424) 813 787
– www.manorfarmoast.co.uk – Closed January and New Year

IDEN GREEN

Kent – Regional map n° **5**-B2

▶ London 55 mi – Croydon 49 mi – Barnet 81 mi – Ealing 85 mi

🏠 **Waters End Farm**

FAMILY · PERSONALISED Characterful part-timbered, part-brick house, in 43 peaceful acres. Bedrooms, in converted barns, boast heavy wood furniture and modern facilities. Eat beside the huge house mural in the breakfast room or out on the terrace in summer.

5 rooms ☲ – ♦£ 110/135 ♦♦£ 110/135

Standen St ⊠ TN17 4LA – Southeast : 1.25 mi – ✆ (01580) 850 731
– www.watersendfarm.co.uk – Closed September-April

ILFRACOMBE

Devon – Pop. 11 184 – Regional map n° **1**-C1

▶ London 218 mi – Barnstaple 13 mi – Exeter 53 mi

⌂ Hamptons   🌿 🅿

TRADITIONAL · STYLISH Imposing Victorian villa with individual, bohemian style. Open-plan lounge and breakfast room with honesty bar and DVDs. Well-equipped, individually styled bedrooms are designed by the friendly owner; those to the front boast rooftop views.

6 rooms ⌂ – 🛏£ 65/100 🛏🛏£ 75/125
Excelsior Villas, Torrs Pk. ✉ *EX34 8AZ –* 𝒞 *(01271) 864 246*
– www.thehamptonshotel.com

🏠 Westwood   ≤ 🌿 🅿

FAMILY · DESIGN Perched on the hillside overlooking the rooftops, this appealingly styled Victorian house offers warm décor and an eclectic mix of modern and retro furniture. Spacious bedrooms boast bold feature wallpaper; those to the front are the best.

5 rooms ⌂ – 🛏£ 75/125 🛏🛏£ 85/125
Torrs Pk ✉ *EX34 8AZ –* 𝒞 *(01271) 867 443 – www.west-wood.co.uk*

🏠 Olive Branch   🌿

TOWNHOUSE · HOMELY Centrally located 19C townhouse run by willing-to-please owners. Bedrooms have a pleasant period feel and some have great views over the town. Breakfast is a treat, courtesy of tasty homemade breads and meat from the local butcher's.

5 rooms – 🛏£ 45/85 🛏🛏£ 89/105
56 Fore St ✉ *EX34 9DJ –* 𝒞 *(01271) 879 005 – www.olivebranchguesthouse.co.uk*
– Closed 3 November-6 March

✕✕ Quay   ≤ 🆑

BRITISH MODERN · DESIGN Long-standing restaurant on the harbourside; one of the first floor rooms overlooks the sea. It's owned by local lad Damien Hirst, who designed everything from the uniform to the crockery. Menus focus on local fish and Devon beef.

Carte £ 23/44
11 The Quay ✉ *EX34 9EQ –* 𝒞 *(01271) 868 090 – www.11thequay.co.uk – Closed 4-17 January*

✕ Thomas Carr @ The Olive Room   🍴

BRITISH MODERN · RUSTIC A simple, homely restaurant beneath a B&B, run by an experienced local chef who trained under Nathan Outlaw. Ultra-fresh seafood is the focus, with dishes only confirmed once the day boat deliveries come in. Cooking is skilled.

Carte £ 27/40
56 Fore St ✉ *EX34 9DJ –* 𝒞 *(01271) 867 831 (booking essential)*
– www.thomascarrchef.co.uk – dinner only – Closed January and Monday

✕ La Gendarmerie

MODERN CUISINE · RUSTIC Once a police station, now a simple little restaurant with exposed stone walls and an intimate feel; personally run by a husband and wife team. Concise, daily changing menu showcases market produce in precise, skilfully executed combinations.

Menu £ 25/39
63 Fore St ✉ *EX34 9ED –* 𝒞 *(01271) 865 984 (booking advisable)*
– www.lagendarmerie.co.uk – dinner only – Closed November,
Tuesday-Wednesday October-March and Monday

ILKLEY

West Yorkshire – Pop. 14 809 – Regional map n° **13**-B2
▶ London 210 mi – Bradford 13 mi – Harrogate 17 mi – Leeds 16 mi

XXX Box Tree

BRITISH MODERN · ELEGANT An iconic restaurant set in two charming sandstone cottages, with a plush, antique-furnished lounge and two luxurious dining rooms; it celebrated 50 years in 2012. Cooking is refined and skilful, with a classical French base, and dishes are light and delicate. Only the best ingredients are used.

→ Cornish crab and haddock brandade with crispy hen's egg. Whole roasted squab pigeon, confit leg, Savoy cabbage and butternut squash. Yorkshire rhubarb soufflé, rhubarb compote and vanilla ice cream.

Menu £ 40/60

37 Church St ⊠ LS29 9DR – on A 65 – 𝒞 (01943) 608 484
– www.theboxtree.co.uk – dinner only and lunch Friday-Sunday – Closed
26-30 December, 1-8 January, Sunday dinner and Monday

ILMINGTON

Warwickshire – Regional map n° **10**-C3
▶ London 91 mi – Birmingham 31 mi – Oxford 34 mi – Stratford-upon-Avon 9 mi

Folly Farm Cottage

TRADITIONAL · COSY Characterful barn conversion with lovely gardens. The cosy breakfast room has floral fabrics and a cottagey feel; try the Folly Challenge! Two of the traditional beamed bedrooms have four-posters and all three come with homemade cake.

3 rooms ☑ – †£ 55/65 ††£ 64/88
Back St ⊠ CV36 4LJ – 𝒞 (01608) 682 425 – www.follyfarm.co.uk

INGHAM

Norfolk – Pop. 376 – Regional map n° **8**-D1
▶ London 139 mi – Norwich 25 mi – Ipswich 65 mi – Lowestoft 30 mi

Ingham Swan

BRITISH MODERN · PUB This cosy, attractive, 14C pub sits in the shadow of an 11C church and features a thatched roof and a rustic beamed interior, with four smart, modern bedrooms in a converted outbuilding. Dishes can be quite complex, using plenty of ingredients, albeit in classic combinations, and formal service comes from a keen young team. Popular wine dinners and cookery classes.

Menu £ 17 (weekday lunch)/28 **s** – Carte £ 29/49 **s**

4 rooms ☑ – †£ 85/155 ††£ 95/195
Sea Palling Rd ⊠ NR12 9AB – 𝒞 (01692) 581 099 (booking essential at dinner)
– www.theinghamswan.co.uk – Closed 25-26 December

INGLETON

North Yorkshire – Pop. 1 641 – Regional map n° **13**-A2
▶ London 266 mi – Kendal 21 mi – Lancaster 18 mi – Leeds 53 mi

Riverside Lodge

TRADITIONAL · COSY 19C doctor's house with a homely interior and a snooker table and sauna hidden in the basement. Spacious, pine-furnished bedrooms have modern bathrooms. The conservatory dining room offers views over the Dales and the river. Breakfast features homemade preserves and muesli, along with a fish special.

8 rooms ☑ – †£ 46/50 ††£ 62/70
24 Main St ⊠ LA6 3HJ – 𝒞 (015242) 41 359 – www.riversideingleton.co.uk
– Closed Christmas-New Year

IPSWICH

Suffolk – Pop. 144 957 – Regional map n° **8**-C3
▶ London 77 mi – Redbridge 64 mi – Romford 59 mi – Norwich 45 mi

IPSWICH

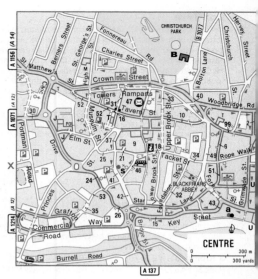

CENTRE

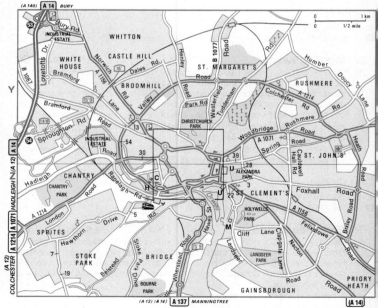

🏠 Salthouse Harbour ✿ ≪ 🖫 ఉ 🅿

BUSINESS · STYLISH Stylish former salt warehouse – its trendy lobby-lounge boasts floor to ceiling windows and great marina views. Modern boutique bedrooms have well-appointed bathrooms; some feature chaise longues, copper slipper baths or balconies.

70 rooms ⌦ – †£ 135/185 ††£ 150/195

Town plan: X-a – *1 Neptune Quay* ⊠ *IP4 1AX* – *𝒞 (01473) 226 789*
– *www.salthouseharbour.co.uk*

Eaterie – See restaurant listing

🏠 Kesgrave Hall ✿ ⛬ 🏠 ఉ 🔊 🅿

HISTORIC · MODERN An impressive house built in 1812, with a delightful terrace overlooking large lawned gardens to a 38 acre wood. Stylish lounges have a relaxed, urban-chic feel. Luxurious bedrooms boast quality furnishings, modern facilities and stylish bathrooms. The busy brasserie offers a European menu.

23 rooms ⌦ – †£ 130/280 ††£ 130/280

Hall Rd ⊠ *IP5 2PU* – *East : 4.75 mi by A 1214 on Bealings rd* – *𝒞 (01473) 333 471*
– *www.kesgravehall.com*

XX Trongs 🅰🅲

CHINESE · FRIENDLY Brightly painted restaurant filled with flowers and candles. The owners are from Hanoi: the parents and one son cook – his brother runs front of house. The extensive menu specialises in vibrant dishes from northern China; try the spring rolls.

Carte £ 21/46

Town plan: X-s – *23 St Nicholas St* ⊠ *IP1 1TW* – *𝒞 (01473) 256 833* – Closed
3 weeks August and Sunday

X Eaterie ≪ 🏠 🅿

MODERN CUISINE · TRENDY Modern hotel brasserie in an old salt warehouse, with a zinc-topped bar, gold pillars, modern art and padded booths. Tasty brasserie dishes and numerous specials focus largely on seafood. Eat on the terrace, overlooking the marina.

Menu £ 18 (lunch) – Carte dinner £ 25/40

Town plan: X-a – *Salthouse Harbour Hotel, 1 Neptune Quay* ⊠ *IP4 1AX*
– *𝒞 (01473) 226 789* – *www.salthouseharbour.co.uk*

at Chelmondiston Southeast : 6 mi by A 137 on B 1456

X Red Lion 🆕 🏠 ఉ ✿ 🅿

TRADITIONAL CUISINE · BISTRO Smartly refurbished former pub with a few comfy chairs in the bar and two dining rooms furnished with dark wood tables and Lloyd Loom chairs. Menus offer a broad range of dishes and daily specials. The bubbly owner leads the service.

Carte £ 20/31

Main St ⊠ *IP9 1DX* – *𝒞 (01473) 780 400* – *www.chelmondistonredlion.co.uk*
– *Closed Sunday dinner and Monday*

at Hintlesham West: 5 mi by A1214 on A1071 – Plan: Y – ⊠ Ipswich

🏠 Hintlesham Hall ✿ 🗲 ≪ ⛬ 🖫 ✿ 🔊 🅿

COUNTRY HOUSE · CLASSIC Impressive Georgian manor house with 16C roots; the original ornate plasterwork and gold leaf inlaid cornicing remain. Bedrooms in the main house are grand; the courtyard rooms are cosy – some have terraces. Dine in the impressive 'Salon' or wood-panelled 'Parlour'; fresh herbs come from the garden.

32 rooms – †£ 85/225 ††£ 85/395 – ⌦ £ 19 – 3 suites
⊠ *IP8 3NS* – *𝒞 (01473) 652 334* – *www.hintleshamhall.com*

IRBY
Merseyside – Regional map n° **11**-A3
▶ London 212 mi – Liverpool 12 mi – Manchester 46 mi – Stoke-on-Trent 56 mi

✗✗ Da Piero
ITALIAN · FAMILY The passionate owners of Da Piero extend a very warm welcome to one and all. The wide-ranging menu takes its influences from Sicily where the chef grew up, and from Northern Italy, the birthplace of his mother. Portions are hearty.
Carte £ 21/43
5-7 Mill Hill Rd ✉ CH61 4UB – 𝒞 (0151) 648 73 73 (booking essential)
– www.dapiero.co.uk – dinner only – Closed 1 week January, Sunday and Monday

IRONBRIDGE
Telford and Wrekin – Pop. 1 560 – Regional map n° **10**-B2
▶ London 135 mi – Birmingham 36 mi – Shrewsbury 18 mi

🏠 Library House
TOWNHOUSE · PERSONALISED Attractive former library, just a stone's throw from the famous bridge. It has a farmhouse-style breakfast room and a homely lounge where books sit on the old library shelves. Tastefully furnished bedrooms are named after poets.
4 rooms ⌂ – ♦£ 75/90 ♦♦£ 95/110
11 Severn Bank ✉ TF8 7AN – 𝒞 (01952) 432 299 – www.libraryhouse.com

✗✗ Restaurant Severn
BRITISH TRADITIONAL · COSY Traditional little restaurant with a loyal following; enter down a narrow side passage into a cosy low-beamed room. Classic dishes rely on seasonal local produce. It's run by a couple: she cooks starters and desserts; he cooks the mains.
Menu £ 26/30
33 High St. ✉ TF8 7AG – 𝒞 (01952) 432 233 (booking essential)
– www.restaurantsevern.co.uk – dinner only – Closed 1 week January, 1 week August, Sunday, Monday and Tuesday

at Coalport Southeast: 2 mi by B4373

🍴 Woodbridge Inn
BRITISH TRADITIONAL · INDIVIDUAL Spacious, modernised pub in a superb spot on the banks of the River Severn. Inside, it's airy and open, yet with nooks and crannies galore. Menus list all the usual suspects but it's worth going off-piste occasionally.
Carte £ 22/45
✉ TF8 7JF – 𝒞 (01952) 882 054 – www.woodbridge-coalport.co.uk

IRTHINGTON
Cumbria – Regional map n° **12**-B1
▶ London 314 mi – Newcastle upon Tyne 54 mi – Sunderland 67 mi – Carlisle 8 mi

🍴 Golden Fleece

BRITISH TRADITIONAL · COSY Located just off the A689 and handy for Carlisle Airport, Hadrian's Wall and Gretna Green. Dishes like twice-baked 3 cheese soufflé and pan-roasted Cumbrian lamb sit alongside tasty pub classics, juicy mature steaks and 'proper' puddings on something-for-everyone menus. Very comfortable bedrooms.
Carte £ 23/45
8 rooms ⌂ – ♦£ 70/80 ♦♦£ 85/100
Ruleholme ✉ CA6 4NF – Southeast : 1.5 mi by A 689 – 𝒞 (01228) 573 686
– www.thegoldenfleececumbria.co.uk – Closed 1-7 January

ISLEHAM

Cambridgeshire – Pop. 2 228 – Regional map n° **8**-B2

▶ London 73 mi – Cambridge 20 mi – Norwich 49 mi

✗ Merry Monk ⓝ   🛜 ⟷ 🅿

BRITISH TRADITIONAL · NEIGHBOURHOOD Originally 17C cottages, with time spent as a pub, this is now a quirky, rustic restaurant with beamed ceilings and farmhouse kitchen style décor. Hearty, flavoursome dishes use local produce and are given a personal twist by the chef.

Menu £ 24 – Carte £ 26/44

30 West St ✉ CB7 5SB – ☎ (01638) 780 900 – www.merry-monk.co.uk – Closed 1 week February, 25-26 December and Monday-Tuesday

ISLE OF MAN – I.O.M. ➜ See Man (Isle of)

ITTERINGHAM

Norfolk – ✉ Aylsham – Regional map n° **8**-C1

▶ London 126 mi – Cromer 11 mi – Norwich 17 mi

🍴 Walpole Arms   � 🛜 🅿

BRITISH TRADITIONAL · PUB Pretty 18C inn in a sleepy little village; its surprisingly modern interior designed in keeping with the building's age. Menus champion local, seasonal ingredients, with produce from their farm; rare breed beef is a speciality.

Carte £ 22/42

The Common ✉ NR11 7AR – ☎ (01263) 587 258 – www.thewalpolearms.co.uk – Closed 25 December and Sunday dinner in winter

IXWORTH – Suffolk ➜ See Bury St Edmunds

KEGWORTH

Leicestershire – Pop. 3 601 – Regional map n° **9**-B2

▶ London 123 mi – Leicester 18 mi – Loughborough 6 mi – Nottingham 13 mi

🏠 Kegworth House   � 🍽 🅿

TOWNHOUSE · CLASSIC Charming, family-run, Georgian townhouse with many original features and a pleasant walled garden. Individually furnished bedrooms; Room 11, with its exposed beams and four-poster, is one of the best. Extensive buffet breakfasts.

11 rooms ⌂ – ♦£ 87/150 ♦♦£ 107/210

42 High St ✉ DE74 2DA – ☎ (01509) 672 575 – www.kegworthhouse.co.uk – Closed Christmas and New Year

KELVEDON

Essex – Pop. 4 717 – Regional map n° **7**-C2

▶ London 56 mi – Colchester 11 mi – Chelmsford 14 mi

✗ George & Dragon   🛜 🅿

BRITISH MODERN · MINIMALIST Bright and welcoming former pub with a sleek, contemporary style encompassing topiary planters, marble tiled floors, antique mirrors and art deco pictures. Simple, well-priced menu with locally caught fish specials. Pretty terrace.

Carte £ 24/34

Coggleshall Rd ✉ CO5 9PL – Northwest : 2 mi on B 1024 – ☎ (01376) 561 797 – www.georgeanddragonkelvedon.co.uk – Closed 25 December-2 January, Sunday and Monday

KENDAL

Cumbria – Pop. 28 586 – Regional map n° **12**-B2

▶ London 270 mi – Bradford 64 mi – Burnley 63 mi – Carlisle 49 mi

Beech House

TOWNHOUSE · PERSONALISED Pretty, three-storey Georgian house set just out of town. Modern, open-plan lounge with comfy sofas and communal breakfast tables. Bright, airy, pine-furnished bedrooms with up-to-date bathrooms. Welcoming owners.

5 rooms ⌂ – †£ 60/75 ††£ 80/110

40 Greenside ✉ LA9 4LD – (by All Hallows Ln) – 𝒞 (01539) 720 385
– www.beechhouse-kendal.co.uk – Closed 1 week Christmas

XX Castle Dairy

BRITISH MODERN · INDIVIDUAL This delightful Grade I listed building dates back to 1402 and there's a cobbled Roman road running through its centre. It's run by college apprentices, under the eye of an experienced chef. Cooking is skilled, modern and flavoursome.

Menu £ 25/45 – Carte £ 24/36

Wildman St ✉ LA9 6EN – 𝒞 (01539) 733 946 – www.castledairy.co.uk – Closed 25-30 December, Sunday and Monday

X Newmoon

MEDITERRANEAN · NEIGHBOURHOOD Smart, high street restaurant with ground floor bar, intimate, beamed dining room and a loyal local following. The owner's Turkish heritage is reflected in the menu, which has a strong Mediterranean base; dishes are fresh and colourful.

Menu £ 13 (lunch) – Carte £ 22/31

129 Highgate ✉ LA9 4EN – 𝒞 (01539) 729 254 (booking advisable)
– www.newmoonrestaurant.co.uk – Closed 1-4 January, 25-26 December, Sunday and Monday

X Sawadee Thai

THAI · NEIGHBOURHOOD The staff, dressed in authentic Thai silks, provide a very warm welcome at this smart neighbourhood restaurant. The appealing menu offers flavoursome dishes ranging from Tom Yam soup to Som Tam Thai salad and Geng Ba Jungle curry.

Menu £ 20 – Carte £ 13/32

54 Stramongate ✉ LA9 4BD – 𝒞 (01539) 722 944
– www.thairestaurantkendal.co.uk – dinner only – Closed 24-31 December and Monday

at Crosthwaite West: 5.25 mi by All Hallows Ln – ✉ Kendal

Punch Bowl Inn

BRITISH TRADITIONAL · INN Charming 17C inn set in the picturesque Lyth Valley, boasting antiques, cosy fires and exposed wood beams; dine either in the rustic bar or the more formal restaurant. Cooking has a classical base but also features some modern touches; dishes display a degree of complexity that you wouldn't usually find in a pub. Luxury bedrooms boast quality linens and roll-top baths.

Carte £ 24/37

9 rooms ⌂ – †£ 95/125 ††£ 105/305

✉ LA8 8HR – 𝒞 (01539) 568 237 – www.the-punchbowl.co.uk

KENILWORTH

Warwickshire – Pop. 22 413 – Regional map n° **10**-C2
▶ London 102 mi – Birmingham 19 mi – Coventry 5 mi – Leicester 32 mi

Victoria Lodge

FAMILY · COSY This red-brick house makes the perfect base for exploring Shakespeare country. Some of the comfy bedrooms have balconies and one has a terrace overlooking the garden. There's fresh milk and water in a fridge on the landing.

10 rooms ⌂ – †£ 55/85 ††£ 75/95

180 Warwick Rd ✉ CV8 1HU – 𝒞 (01926) 512 020
– www.victorialodgekenilworth.co.uk – Closed 2 weeks Christmas-New Year

X **Number 11**   ⅋ AC ▢

MEATS · NEIGHBOURHOOD A rustic, ranch-style restaurant with exposed brick-work, slate flooring and quirky cowhide banquettes. Enjoy dishes like salt-baked beetroot or fried duck egg with black pudding to start, followed by a freshly made burger or a juicy steak.

Menu £ 17 (weekdays) – Carte £ 20/27

11 Warwick Rd ⊠ CV8 1HD – ℰ (01926) 863 311 – www.number11restaurant.com
– Closed 24-25 December and Sunday

🄳 **Cross at Kenilworth** (Adam Bennett)   🌡 🛱 ⅋ AC ⅋ ⇔ P

❀❀ CLASSIC CUISINE · ELEGANT Smartly furnished pub with eager, welcoming staff. Skilfully executed, classical cooking uses prime seasonal ingredients, and dishes not only look impressive but taste good too. Sit in the back room to watch the kitchen in action. The bright and airy room next door used to be a classroom.

→ Beef tartar, wasabi, radish salad and quinoa. Loin of venison with haggis, potato & bacon terrine, cranberries, kale and Laphroaig sauce. Floating islands.

Menu £ 25 (lunch)/65 – Carte £ 36/57

16 New St ⊠ CV8 2EZ – ℰ (01926) 853 840 – www.thecrosskenilworth.co.uk
– Closed Sunday dinner and bank holidays

KENTISBURY

Devon – Regional map n° **1**-C1

▶ London 220 mi – Exeter 58 mi – Barnstaple 10 mi

🏠 **Kentisbury Grange**   ⌂ 🌡 ⅋ P

COUNTRY HOUSE · DESIGN This Victorian country house may have a Grade II listing but it's been smartly decked out with designer fabrics and furnishings; albeit in the colours of the original stained glass windows. Go for a chic, freestanding Garden Room.

16 rooms (dinner included) ⌁ – ♦£ 125/245 ♦♦£ 125/245

⊠ *EX31 4NL – Southeast : 1 mi by B 3229 on A39 – ℰ (01271) 882 295*
– www.kentisburygrange.co.uk

Coach House by Michael Caines – See restaurant listing

XX **Coach House by Michael Caines**   🛱 ⅋ P

MODERN CUISINE · ELEGANT This large hotel restaurant has a funky lounge under the eaves and an elegant dining room featuring booths and plush blue velvet chairs. The experienced chef prepares flavoursome modern dishes of local meats and south coast fish.

Menu £ 15 – Carte approx. £ 38

Kentisbury Grange Hotel, ⊠ EX31 4NL – Southeast : 1 mi by B 3229 on A39
– ℰ (01271) 882 295 – www.kentisburygrange.co.uk

KENTON – Devon → See Exeter

KERNE BRIDGE – Herefordshire → See Ross-on-Wye

KERRIDGE

Cheshire East – Regional map n° **11**-B3

▶ London 179 mi – Manchester 24 mi – Macclesfield 4 mi

🄳 **Lord Clyde** Ⓝ   🛱 P

MODERN CUISINE · PUB A small, keenly run village pub with a simple, rustic interior. The cooking is a complete contrast, offering extremely creative, eye-catching modern dishes which use a wide range of complex techniques. The tasting menus are popular.

Carte £ 28/46

36 Clarke Ln ⊠ SK10 5AH – ℰ (01625) 562 123 – www.thelordclyde.co.uk – Closed Sunday dinner and Monday lunch

KESSINGLAND

Suffolk – Pop. 4 327 – Regional map n° **8**-D2

▶ London 126 mi – Norwich 28 mi – Ipswich 40 mi – Colchester 66 mi

🏚 Old Rectory   � ⚙ P

TRADITIONAL · PERSONALISED 1834 rectory with beautiful gardens, just a short walk from the beach. It retains plenty of original character, with individually furnished bedrooms boasting antique furniture and feature beds. Bay-windowed Room 1 is the most spacious.

3 rooms ⌷ – †£ 74/97 ††£ 104/112

157 Church Rd ⊠ NR33 7SQ – ℰ (01502) 742 188 – www.theoldrectorybandb.com

KESWICK

Cumbria – Pop. 4 984 – Regional map n° **12**-A2

▶ London 294 mi – Carlisle 31 mi – Kendal 30 mi

🏠 Lairbeck   🐾 🚍 ⚙ P

TRADITIONAL · PERSONALISED An attractive Victorian house in the suburbs – its mature garden boasting a huge Sequoia Redwood. Inside it has an original barley-twist staircase and a galleried landing. Bedrooms come in a mix of styles; some have lovely views.

14 rooms ⌷ – †£ 49/98 ††£ 118/160

Town plan: X-a – *Vicarage Hill ⊠ CA12 5QB – ℰ (017687) 73 373*
– www.lairbeckhotel-keswick.co.uk – Closed Christmas-New Year

🏚 Howe Keld   🕭 ⚙

TOWNHOUSE · CONTEMPORARY A comfortable, well-run guest house with boutique styling and strong eco-credentials. Contemporary bedrooms feature reclaimed wood furnishings. Good breakfasts with homemade granola, Cumbrian air-dried meats and home-baked bread.

12 rooms ⌷ – †£ 55/95 ††£ 100/150

Town plan: Z-s – *5-7 The Heads ⊠ CA12 5ES – ℰ (017687) 72 417*
– www.howekeld.co.uk

XX Morrel's   ⊡

BRITISH MODERN · BRASSERIE Popular local eatery with scrubbed wood flooring, etched glass dividers and a buzzy atmosphere. Seasonally changing dishes have subtle Mediterranean influences; some come in two sizes. Good value menus.

Menu £ 22 – Carte £ 22/35

Town plan: Z-x – *34 Lake Rd ⊠ CA12 5DQ – ℰ (017687) 72 666*
– www.morrels.co.uk – dinner only – Closed 24-26 December, 4-17 January and Monday

at Braithwaite West: 2 mi by A66 – Plan: X – on B5292 – ⊠ Keswick

XX Cottage in the Wood   ⇔ 🐾 ⬚ 🚍 🍴 P

BRITISH MODERN · ROMANTIC A keenly run restaurant in a superb forest setting, with a lovely terrace and great views over the fells and valley below. Lunch offers robust dishes to satisfy walkers and dinner is more modern; many ingredients are foraged from the surrounding forest. Bedrooms are contemporary; some have whirlpool baths.

Menu £ 25/65 **s**

10 rooms ⌷ – †£ 88/96 ††£ 110/205

Magic Hill, Whinlatter Forest ⊠ CA12 5TW – Northwest : 1.75 mi on B 5292
– ℰ (017687) 78 409 (bookings essential for non-residents)
– www.thecottageinthewood.co.uk – Closed 3-22 January, Sunday, Monday and Tuesday lunch

KESWICK

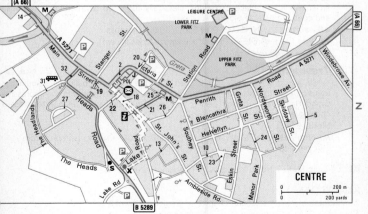

at Portinscale West: 1.5 mi by A66 – ⊠ Keswick

⌂ Swinside Lodge   ☆ ⅋ ≼ ⌂ ⅋ P

TRADITIONAL · PERSONALISED Whitewashed Georgian house in a countryside location, boasting lovely views over the fells. Local info in reception. Two small, traditional country house lounges filled with books and antiques, including an old jukebox. Comfortable bedrooms with homemade biscuits. Formal dining room has a house party atmosphere and offers a set 4 course menu.

7 rooms (dinner included) ☲ – **†**£ 98/129 **††**£ 138/228

Town plan: X-c – *Newlands* ⊠ CA12 5UE – *South : 1.5 mi on Grange Rd – 𝒞 (017687) 72 948 – www.swinsidelodge-hotel.co.uk – Restricted opening January and December*

KETTERING

Northamptonshire – Pop. 56 226 – Regional map n° **9**-C3
▶ London 88 mi – Birmingham 54 mi – Northampton 24 mi

⌂ Barton Hall 🆕   ☆ ⌂ ⊡ ⅆ ⅋ ⅏ P

BUSINESS · CONTEMPORARY A modernised period house on the outskirts of town; its original features include a flagged hall and a superb 17C orangery. Stylish, bright, well-equipped bedrooms are perfect for the business traveller. Relaxed dining from a menu of brasserie classics; the terrace overlooks 10 acres of gardens.

29 rooms ☲ – **†**£ 110/230 **††**£ 120/240

Barton Rd ⊠ NN15 6SG – *Southeast : 1.75 mi on A 6003 – 𝒞 (01536) 515 505 – www.bartonhall.com*

at Rushton Northwest : 3.5 mi by A 14 and Rushton Rd

⌂ Rushton Hall 🆕   ☆ ⅋ ⌂ ⌐ 🖼 ⊕ 🎞 ⅃ ⅋ ⊡ ⅆ ⅋ ⅏ P

HISTORIC · ELEGANT An imposing 15C house with stunning architecture, in 28 acres of countryside. The Grand Hall features huge stained glass windows and an impressive fireplace. Luxurious, classically furnished bedrooms in the house and converted stable block.

46 rooms ☲ – **†**£ 160/170 **††**£ 160/390 – 3 suites

⊠ NN14 1RR – 𝒞 (01536) 713 001 – www.rushtonhall.com

Tresham – See restaurant listing

XxX Tresham 🆕   ⌂ P

MODERN CUISINE · ELEGANT Named after the man who built the magnificent mansion in which this grand restaurant resides; enjoy an aperitif in the impressive Grand Hall. Ornate plaster ceiling and wood panelled walls. Elaborate modern cooking and formal service.

Menu £ 55

Rushton Hall Hotel, ⊠ NN14 1RR – 𝒞 (01536) 713 001 – www.rushtonhall.com – dinner only

KETTLESING – North Yorkshire ➜ See Harrogate

KEYSTON

Cambridgeshire – ⊠ Huntingdon – Pop. 257 – Regional map n° **8**-A2
▶ London 75 mi – Cambridge 29 mi – Northampton 24 mi

🍴 Pheasant   ⅋⅋ ⌂ P

BRITISH TRADITIONAL · PUB Hidden away in a sleepy hamlet, this is a big pub with enormous character; think exposed beams, hunting scenes, John Bull wallpaper and a stuffed albino pheasant. Wide-ranging seasonal menu includes a 'classic' section; excellent value set menu. Warm, attentive staff and delightful rear terrace.

Menu £ 15 (lunch and early dinner) – Carte £ 24/39

Village Loop Rd ⊠ PE28 0RE – 𝒞 (01832) 710 241 *(booking essential) – www.thepheasant-keyston.co.uk – Closed 2-15 January, Sunday dinner and Monday*

KIBWORTH BEAUCHAMP

Leicestershire – ✉ Leicester – Pop. 3 550 – Regional map n° **9**-B2
▶ London 85 mi – Birmingham 49 mi – Leicester 6 mi

✗ Lighthouse

🕓 **FISH AND SEAFOOD · NEIGHBOURHOOD** Personally run restaurant with a re-laxed atmosphere and a crisp white interior decorated with coastal pictures and other nautical knick-knacks. The appealing menu has its emphasis firmly on fresh seafood, offering everything from fish and chips to lobster; many dishes come in both 'small' and 'large' sizes.

Menu £15 (weekdays) – Carte £22/35

9 Station St ✉ LE8 0LN – ℰ (0116) 279 62 60 (booking essential)
– www.lighthousekibworth.co.uk – dinner only
– Closed Sunday, Monday and bank holidays

KIBWORTH HARCOURT

Leicestershire – Regional map n° **9**-B2
▶ London 101 mi – Leicester 9 mi – Birmingham 50 mi

✗ Boboli

ITALIAN · NEIGHBOURHOOD Buzzy, laid-back Italian restaurant with a sunny terrace; formerly a pub, it has a central bar and dining on 3 levels. Extensive se-lection of seasonally inspired dishes; flavours are bold and portions, large. Satis-fyingly affordable wines.

Menu £14 (lunch) – Carte £14/43

88 Main St ✉ LE8 0NQ – ℰ (0116) 279 33 03
– www.bobolirestaurant.co.uk – Closed 25-26 December and 1 January

KILPECK

Herefordshire – Regional map n° **10**-A3
▶ London 132 mi – Birmingham 71 mi – Liverpool 123 mi – Cardiff 47 mi

🍴 Kilpeck Inn

TRADITIONAL CUISINE · INDIVIDUAL A popular pub which narrowly escaped being turned into private housing thanks to the villagers' valiantly fought 'Save Our Pub' campaign. Its spacious interior and bedrooms are smart, modern and characterful, with impressive green credentials. Menus offer locally sourced meats and old fashioned puddings.

Menu £13 (weekday lunch) – Carte £18/30

4 rooms 🖙 – ♦£70/80 ♦♦£80/115

✉ HR2 9DN – ℰ (01981) 570 464 – www.kilpeckinn.com
– Closed 25 December

KINGHAM

Oxfordshire – Pop. 547 – Regional map n° **6**-A1
▶ London 81 mi – Gloucester 32 mi – Oxford 25 mi – Cardiff 91 mi

🏠 Mill House

TRADITIONAL · CLASSIC Smartly converted flour mill owned by a couple from the village; set in 10 acres of well-maintained gardens which lead down to a brook – opt for a bedroom with a terrace overlooking the lawns. Have a drink in the bright wood-furnished bar or on the terrace, before heading to dinner in the formal restaurant.

21 rooms 🖙 – ♦£107/152 ♦♦£120/165

✉ OX7 6UH – ℰ (01608) 658 188 – www.millhousehotel.co.uk

Moat End

FAMILY · COSY Stone-built barn conversion with ponies, hens and countryside views. Cosy sitting room with impressive wood-burning stove. Simple, neatly kept bedrooms. Communal breakfasts include fresh eggs, and bacon and sausages from a local butcher.

3 rooms ☲ – †£ 65/80 ††£ 78/90

The Moat ✉ OX7 6XZ – by West St – ℰ (01608) 658 090 – www.moatend.co.uk
– Closed Christmas and New Year

The Wild Rabbit

BRITISH TRADITIONAL · BRASSERIE A charming stone inn owned by the Bamford family, of Daylesford fame: its understated Cotswold makeover means flagged floors, log fires, leather sofas and expanses of wood and stone. Rustic cooking is British at heart and full of flavour. Bedrooms are named after woodland animals and feature a preponderance of natural products; 'Rabbit' is naturally the best.

Carte £ 35/54

13 rooms ☲ – †£ 105/285 ††£ 180/300

Church St ✉ OX7 6YA – ℰ (01608) 658 389 (booking advisable)
– www.thewildrabbit.co.uk – Closed first 2 weeks January

Kingham Plough

BRITISH MODERN · PUB Rustic, laid-back pub and restaurant located on the green in an unspoilt Cotswold village. It's run by a friendly team and an experienced chef-owner. The snack menu offers tasty classics, while the seasonal à la carte evolves as new ingredients arrive. Comfy bedrooms await: numbers 2 and 4 are the best.

Carte £ 28/40

6 rooms ☲ – †£ 110/150 ††£ 145/195

The Green ✉ OX7 6YD – ℰ (01608) 658 327 – www.thekinghamplough.co.uk
– Closed 25 December

Our selection of hotels, guesthouses and restaurants change every year, so change your MICHELIN Guide every year!

KING'S LYNN

Norfolk – Pop. 46 093 – Regional map n° **8**-B1

▶ London 103 mi – Cambridge 45 mi – Leicester 75 mi – Norwich 44 mi

Bank House

TOWNHOUSE · STYLISH Grade II listed townhouse by the river – this is the place where Barclays Bank was founded! Cosy bedrooms come in various shapes and sizes: all have good facilities and excellent bathrooms; some have pleasant views. Dine from a modern European menu in the bar, the charming billiard room or the brasserie.

11 rooms ☲ – †£ 80/110 ††£ 110/150

King's Staithe Sq ✉ PE30 1RD – ℰ (01553) 660 492 – www.thebankhouse.co.uk

Market Bistro

BRITISH MODERN · BISTRO 17C beams and a fireplace remain but this relaxed bistro is more up-to-date than its exterior suggests. Fresh, unfussy cooking uses passionately sourced local produce and modern techniques. The chef's wife looks after the service.

Menu £ 16 (weekday lunch) – Carte £ 23/41

11 Saturday Market Pl ✉ PE30 5DQ – ℰ (01553) 771 483 – www.marketbistro.co.uk
– Closed 25-26 December, Sunday dinner and Monday

at Grimston East: 6.25 mi by A148

🏨 Congham Hall 🏠 🐾 ⟨ 📶 🖥 📶 💆 ⓓ 🅿

COUNTRY HOUSE · ELEGANT Part-Georgian country house in 30 acres of peaceful grounds. Guest areas include a snug bar and a spacious drawing room with a subtle modern style. Opt for a lovely Garden Room by the spa, overlooking the flower or herb gardens.

26 rooms – ♦£ 95/125 ♦♦£ 125/250 – ☲ £ 15 – 2 suites
Lynn Rd. ✉ *PE32 1AH* – ✆ *(01485) 600 250* – *www.conghamhallhotel.co.uk*
Congham Hall – See restaurant listing

XXX Congham Hall ⟨ 📶 🖥 📶 💆 ⓘⓞ 🅿

MODERN CUISINE · INTIMATE Start with a drink in the elegant hotel bar, then head for the spacious dining room with its super terrace and garden views. Appealing menus have something to please everyone, from good old classics to more modern fare.

Carte £ 29/43
Congham Hall Hotel, Lynn Rd. ✉ *PE32 1AH* – ✆ *(01485) 600 250*
– www.conghamhallhotel.co.uk

KINGS MILLS → See Channel Islands (Guernsey)

KINGSBRIDGE

Devon – Pop. 6 116 – Regional map n° **1**-C3
▶ London 236 mi – Exeter 36 mi – Plymouth 24 mi – Torquay 21 mi

🏨 Buckland-Tout-Saints 🏠 🐾 ⟨ 📶 🖥 💆 🅿

HISTORIC · CLASSIC Appealing Queen Anne mansion set in large, peaceful grounds. Traditional, antique-furnished interior with wood-panelling in many rooms. Bedrooms vary in shape and size; some have a classic country house feel and others are more contemporary. Choice of two dining rooms offering accomplished dishes.

16 rooms ☲ – ♦£ 97/149 ♦♦£ 125/199 – 2 suites
Goveton ✉ *TQ7 2DS* – *Northeast : 3 mi by A 381* – ✆ *(01548) 853 055*
– www.tout-saints.co.uk

KINGSTON BAGPUIZE – Oxfordshire → See Oxford

KINGSTON-UPON-HULL

Kingston upon Hull – Pop. 284 321 – Regional map n° **13**-D2
▶ London 183 mi – Leeds 61 mi – Nottingham 94 mi – Sheffield 68 mi

XX 1884 Dock Street Kitchen ⓝ ⟨ 📶

BRITISH MODERN · FASHIONABLE A red-brick former ropery by the marina: built in 1884, it is now a stylish brasserie with a smart leather-furnished bar, an open kitchen and a buzzing feel. Appealing menus of modernised British classics, with a popular grill section.

Menu £ 18/22 – Carte £ 36/56
Humber Dock St, Marina Hull ✉ *HU1 1TB* – ✆ *(01482) 222 260*
– www.1884dockstreetkitchen.co.uk – Closed first week January, December 26-30, Sunday dinner and Monday

KINGSWEAR – Devon → See Dartmouth

KINTBURY

West Berkshire – Pop. 2 086 – Regional map n° **6**-B3
▶ London 65 mi – Birmingham 108 mi – Leicester 107 mi – Ealing 60 mi

🏠 Dundas Arms ⇔ 🛏 🏠 **P**

BRITISH TRADITIONAL · COSY Enjoy pub classics and a pint of real ale in the garden of this 18C inn; set in a wonderful location between the River Kennet and the Kennet and Avon Canal. More adventurous dinner menu. Stylish, comfy bedrooms are fittingly named after birds or fish; the latter have their own private riverside terraces.

Carte £ 25/38

8 rooms 🖵 – 🛉£ 85/125 🛉🛉£ 90/160

53 Station Rd ✉ RG17 9UT – 𝒞 (01488) 658 263 – www.dundasarms.co.uk

KIRKBY LONSDALE

Cumbria – Pop. 1 843 – Regional map n° **12**-B3

▶ London 259 mi – Carlisle 62 mi – Kendal 13 mi – Lancaster 17 mi

🏠🏠 Royal 🏠

TRADITIONAL · CONTEMPORARY Well-run Georgian hotel overlooking a characterful town square. The décor is a mix of modern and shabby-chic, and the owner has a keen eye for detail. Bedrooms are spacious; some have free-standing baths in the room. Snug, open-fired lounge and an all-day brasserie serving classics and wood-fired pizzas.

14 rooms 🖵 – 🛉£ 63/125 🛉🛉£ 85/180

Main St ✉ LA6 2AE – 𝒞 (01524) 271 966 – www.royalhotelkirkbylonsdale.co.uk

🏠 Plato's 🏠

TOWNHOUSE · PERSONALISED Georgian-style townhouse once home to Plato Harrison wine merchants. Tastefully decorated bedrooms blend modern furnishings with period charm and come with thoughtful extras. The all-day coffee-shop-cum-café offers an extensive range of modern, international dishes ranging from tapas to tasting boards.

10 rooms 🖵 – 🛉£ 70/110 🛉🛉£ 88/162

2 Mill Brow ✉ LA6 2AT – 𝒞 (01524) 274 180 – www.platoskirkbylonsdale.co.uk

🏠 Sun Inn ⇔ 🕅

BRITISH TRADITIONAL · PUB 17C inn with a characterful beamed bar and a smartly furnished restaurant which comes into its own in the evening. Menus are concise; bar snacks are served throughout the day and dinner is a serious affair. Smart modern bedrooms boast quality linens and thoughtful extras – the breakfasts are delicious.

Menu £ 23/35

11 rooms 🖵 – 🛉£ 80/123 🛉🛉£ 110/138

6 Market St ✉ LA6 2AU – 𝒞 (015242) 71 965 – www.sun-inn.info

at Lupton Northwest: 4.75 mi on A65

🏠 Plough ⇔ 🏠 👤 **P**

BRITISH TRADITIONAL · PUB A homely former coaching inn with exposed beams, comfy sofas and open fires, set on the main road from the Lake District to North Yorkshire. Sit the characterful bar or more formal restaurant and choose from an appealing list of traditional dishes. Smart, individually styled bedrooms boast roll-top baths.

Carte £ 22/36

6 rooms 🖵 – 🛉£ 85/115 🛉🛉£ 100/205

Cow Brow ✉ LA6 1PJ – 𝒞 (015395) 67 700 – www.theploughatlupton.co.uk

KIRKBY STEPHEN

Cumbria – Pop. 1 522 – Regional map n° **12**-B2

▶ London 296 mi – Carlisle 46 mi – Darlington 37 mi – Kendal 28 mi

⌂ Augill Castle
FAMILY · CLASSIC A carefully restored, castellated folly filled with period furniture and antiques. There are three interconnecting sitting rooms with vast open fires and a dining room with an ornate plaster ceiling; traditional dishes are taken at a communal table. Many of the bedrooms have four-posters or roll-top baths.

15 rooms 🖃 – ♦£ 180/240 ♦♦£ 180/240

✉ CA17 4DE – *Northeast : 4.25 mi by A 685* – ✆ (01768) 341 937
– *www.stayinacastle.com*

KIRKBY THORE
Cumbria – Pop. 758 – Regional map n° **12**-B2
▶ London 275 mi – Preston 68 mi – Sunderland 68 mi – Newcastle upon Tyne 68 mi

✗ Bridge
TRADITIONAL CUISINE · BISTRO A remodelled roadside pub with a bright extension and a bistro feel, which is keenly run by a husband and wife team. Cooking has a likeable simplicity, with the odd Asian touch, and there's a tempting display of cakes on the counter.

Menu £ 14 (weekday lunch)/16 – Carte £ 22/39

✉ CA10 1UZ – *on A66* – ✆ (01768) 362 766 – *www.thebridgebistro.co.uk* – *Closed Sunday dinner*

KIRKBYMOORSIDE
North Yorkshire – Pop. 2 751 – Regional map n° **13**-C1
▶ London 244 mi – Leeds 61 mi – Scarborough 26 mi – York 33 mi

⌂ Brickfields Farm
TRADITIONAL · PERSONALISED Red-brick former farmhouse set in 16 acres. Modern bedrooms have lovely bathrooms; some open onto terraces and one features a 17C four-poster marriage bed. Enjoy local meats and homemade preserves in the conservatory breakfast room.

8 rooms 🖃 – ♦£ 75/100 ♦♦£ 100/130

Kirby Mills ✉ YO62 6NS – *East : 0.75 mi by A 170 on Kirby Mills Industrial Estate rd* – ✆ (01751) 433 074 – *www.brickfieldsfarm.co.uk*

Cornmill
HISTORIC · RUSTIC Charming 18C cornmill with a pleasant courtyard and gardens; look for the mill race running beneath the glass panel in the characterful breakfast room. The cosy lounge and elegant bedrooms are set in the old farmhouse and stables.

5 rooms 🖃 – ♦£ 58/80 ♦♦£ 85/110

Kirby Mills ✉ YO62 6NP – *East : 0.5 mi by A 170* – ✆ (01751) 432 000
– *www.kirbymills.co.uk*

KIRKWHELPINGTON
Northumberland – ✉ Morpeth – Pop. 353 – Regional map n° **14**-A2
▶ London 305 mi – Carlisle 46 mi – Newcastle upon Tyne 20 mi

Shieldhall
HISTORIC · COSY Early 17C farmhouse and outbuildings, where Capability Brown's uncle once lived. Mix of rustic and country house guest areas; library-lounge has garden views. Individually styled bedrooms, with furniture handmade by the owner. Beamed, flag-floored dining room for classical British dishes and Aga-cooked breakfasts.

4 rooms 🖃 – ♦£ 60/80 ♦♦£ 80/96

Wallington ✉ NE61 4AQ – *Southeast : 2.5 mi by A 696 on B 6342* – ✆ (01830) 540 387 – *www.shieldhallguesthouse.co.uk* – *Closed November-February*

KIRTLINGTON

Oxfordshire – Regional map n° **6**-B2
▶ London 70 mi – Bicester 11 mi – Oxford 16 mi

⌂ Dashwood   ✿ ♿ 🅿

TRADITIONAL · MODERN Grade II listed former pub and barn, built in classic Cotswold stone; popular with visitors to Bicester Village. Clean, fresh, uncluttered bedrooms are decorated in a contemporary style; Room 1 is the best, with air con and a spacious bathroom. Modern European menu served in informal, ground floor restaurant.

12 rooms – ♦£ 90/135 ♦♦£ 110/135 – ⌷ £ 12
South Green, Heyford Rd ⊠ OX5 3HJ – ℰ (01869) 352 707
– www.thedashwood.co.uk – Closed 25 December-4 January

KNARESBOROUGH

North Yorkshire – Pop. 15 484 – Regional map n° **13**-B2
▶ London 217 mi – Bradford 21 mi – Harrogate 3 mi – Leeds 18 mi

⌂ Newton House   🅿

TOWNHOUSE · FUNCTIONAL Listed Georgian townhouse with a spacious lounge, an honesty bar and traditional bedrooms complete with books, sweets and mini-bars. Breakfast is a highlight, with Aga-baked garden fruits, homemade granola and rare breed meats.

12 rooms ⌷ – ♦£ 55/95 ♦♦£ 95/125
5-7 York Pl ⊠ HG5 0AD – ℰ (01423) 863 539
– www.newtonhouseyorkshire.com

at Ferrensby Northeast: 3 mi on A6055

XX General Tarleton Inn   ⇦ 🏠 ♻ 🅿

BRITISH TRADITIONAL · INN 18C coaching inn with a chic cocktail bar, a smart restaurant, a wicker-furnished conservatory and a large terrace. Menus offer a good range of hearty, classical dishes with a seasonal Yorkshire base. Bedrooms feature solid oak furnishings and come with home-baked biscuits; ask for one of the newer rooms.

Menu £ 15 (lunch and early dinner) – Carte £ 24/44
13 rooms ⌷ – ♦£ 75/95 ♦♦£ 129/150
Boroughbridge Rd ⊠ HG5 0PZ – ℰ (01423) 340 284
– www.generaltarleton.co.uk

KNOWSTONE

Devon – ⊠ South Molton – Regional map n° **1**-C1
▶ London 183 mi – Bristol 78 mi – Cardiff 109 mi – Plymouth 78 mi

🍴 Masons Arms (Mark Dodson)   ⇦ 🏠 🅿
✿

FRENCH CLASSIC · PUB Pretty 13C inn, in a secluded Exmoor village, with a cosy bar and a bright dining room featuring a celestial ceiling mural. The experienced owners offer attractively presented, sophisticated French and British classics. Ingredients are top class and flavours are pronounced and assured. Service is charming.

➔ Black treacle cured salmon, grapefruit and pomegranate vinaigrette. Breast and cannelloni of guinea fowl, sweet potato terrine and morel cream sauce. Trio of raspberry desserts.

Menu £ 25 (lunch) – Carte £ 37/50
⊠ EX36 4RY – ℰ (01398) 341 231 *(booking essential)*
– www.masonsarmsdevon.co.uk – Closed first week January, 1 week
mid-February, 10 days August-September, Sunday dinner and Monday

KNUTSFORD

Cheshire East – Pop. 13 191 – Regional map n° **11**-B3

▶ London 187 mi – Chester 25 mi – Liverpool 33 mi – Manchester 18 mi

✗✗ Belle Epoque Brasserie   🛋 🍴 ⇔

INTERNATIONAL · BRASSERIE Long-standing restaurant with striking exterior features and an impressive art nouveau interior; look out for the lovely mosaic floor. Relaxed brasserie-style dining, featuring British classics, grills and a few more modern dishes. Bedrooms are stylish and contemporary.

Menu £ 15 (lunch and early dinner) – Carte £ 27/42

7 rooms ⌷ – †£ 95 ††£ 110/115

60 King St ✉ WA16 6DT – ℰ (01565) 633 060 – www.thebelleepoque.com
– Closed Sunday dinner

at Mobberley Northeast: 2.5 mi by A537 on B5085 – ✉ Knutsford

🏠 Hinton   🛋 🌿 🅿

TRADITIONAL · PERSONALISED Welcoming creamwashed guesthouse on the main road through the village, with a homely, comfortable lounge and bright, well-kept bedrooms offering good facilities. Linen-clad breakfast room, or eat in the conservatory, overlooking the garden.

6 rooms ⌷ – †£ 48/52 ††£ 68/72

Town Ln ✉ WA16 7HH – on B 5085 – ℰ (01565) 873 484 – www.thehinton.co.uk

🍴 Church Inn ⓝ   🛋 🍴 🅿

TRADITIONAL CUISINE · COSY 18C brick pub beside the bowling green, offering lovely views of the 12C church from its terrace. Regularly changing menus reflect the seasons, with light dishes in summer and hearty stews in winter. Hand-pumped local beers feature.

Carte £ 21/40

Church Ln ✉ WA16 7RD – ℰ (01565) 873 178 – www.churchinnmobberley.co.uk

at Lower Peover Southwest: 3.25 mi by A50 on B5081

🍴 Bells of Peover   🛋 🍴 🅿

MEDITERRANEAN · PUB 16C coaching inn set down a narrow cobbled lane; its regulars once included Generals Eisenhower and Patton. It has a cosy bar, three tastefully decorated dining rooms and a smart terrace. Italian, Greek and Turkish dishes feature.

Menu £ 17 (weekdays) – Carte £ 23/39

The Cobbles ✉ WA16 9PZ – ℰ (01565) 722 269 – www.thebellsofpeover.com

LA PULENTE → See Channel Islands (Jersey)

LA HAULE → See Channel Islands (Jersey)

LALEHAM

Surrey – Regional map n° **4**-C1

▶ London 20 mi – Bristol 110 mi – Cardiff 143 mi – Southampton 63 mi

🍴 Three Horseshoes   🛋 🍴 🅿

TRADITIONAL CUISINE · INDIVIDUAL A pub with 17C origins but 21C sensibilities; take a seat in one of several smart rooms or in the pretty walled garden. The menu's got something for everyone from sandwiches and salads to meaty main courses, pub classics and sharing plates.

Menu £ 24/28 – Carte £ 23/49

25 Shepperton Rd ✉ TW18 1SE – ℰ (01784) 455 014
– www.3horseshoeslaleham.co.uk – Closed 26 December

LAMESLEY

Tyne and Wear – Regional map n° **14**-B2

▶ London 273 mi – Sheffield 130 mi – Nottingham 153 mi – York 85 mi

Stables Lodge ⏚ ⌖ P

TRADITIONAL · PERSONALISED Converted stone barn and outbuildings with a comfy, characterful style. Rustic, open-plan guest areas feature warm fabrics and colours. Spacious, cosy bedrooms have modern facilities; the two in the former barn each have a hot tub.

4 rooms ⌂ – ♦£ 69/95 ♦♦£ 89/169

South Farm ⌗ *NE11 0ET* – *ℰ (0191) 492 17 56* – *www.thestableslodge.co.uk*

LANCASTER

Lancashire – Pop. 48 085 – Regional map n° **11**-A1

▶ London 252 mi – Blackpool 26 mi – Bradford 62 mi – Burnley 44 mi

Ashton ⏡ ⏚ P

TRADITIONAL · MODERN Georgian house surrounded by lawned gardens; personally run by a friendly owner. Good-sized bedrooms are decorated in bold colours and feature a blend of modern and antique furniture. Eat in the small, informal dining room; home-cooked comfort food makes good use of local produce.

5 rooms ⌂ – ♦£ 100/125 ♦♦£ 125/175

Wyresdale Rd ⌗ *LA1 3JJ* – *Southeast : 1.25 mi by A 6 on Clitheroe rd* – *ℰ (01524) 68 460* – *www.theashtonlancaster.com*

LANGAR

Nottinghamshire – Regional map n° **9**-B2

▶ London 132 mi – Boston 45 mi – Leicester 25 mi – Lincoln 37 mi

Langar Hall ⏡ ⏞ ⋖ ⏚ ⌖ P

TRADITIONAL · HISTORIC Characterful Georgian manor surrounded by over 20 acres of pastoral land and ponds; its antique-furnished bedrooms named after those who've featured in the house's history. Dine by candlelight in the elegant, pillared dining room; classically based cooking features veg from the kitchen garden and local game.

12 rooms ⌂ – ♦£ 100/140 ♦♦£ 110/199 – 1 suite

⌗ *NG13 9HG* – *ℰ (01949) 860 559* – *www.langarhall.co.uk*

LANGHO – Lancashire ➜ See Blackburn

LANGTHWAITE – North Yorkshire ➜ See Reeth

LAPWORTH

Warwickshire – Pop. 2 100 – Regional map n° **10**-C2

▶ London 108 mi – Birmingham 23 mi – Leicester 47 mi – Coventry 19 mi

Boot Inn ⏚ ⌖ P

BRITISH TRADITIONAL · PUB A big, buzzy pub boasting a large terrace, a traditional quarry-floored bar and a modern restaurant. Dishes range from sandwiches, picnic boards and sharing plates to more sophisticated specials. You can eat in a tepee in the summer!

Menu £ 15 (lunch and early dinner) – Carte £ 22/41

Old Warwick Rd ⌗ *B94 6JU* – *ℰ (01564) 782 464 (booking essential)* – *www.bootinnlapworth.co.uk*

LAVENHAM

Suffolk – ✉ Sudbury – Pop. 1 413 – Regional map n° **8**-C3
▶ London 66 mi – Cambridge 39 mi – Colchester 22 mi – Ipswich 19 mi

🏨 Swan

HISTORIC · STYLISH Characterful 15C coaching inn with delightful lounges and a superbly atmospheric bar. Beamed, individually decorated bedrooms have a subtle contemporary style. Eat in the smart brasserie or from a modern menu under a timbered roof and a minstrels' gallery – with piano accompaniment at weekends.

45 rooms 🍽 – †£ 140/260 ††£ 185/400 – 1 suite
High St ✉ CO10 9QA – ℰ (01787) 247 477 – www.theswanatlavenham.co.uk
Brasserie – See restaurant listing

XXX Great House

FRENCH CLASSIC · ELEGANT Passionately run restaurant on the main square of an attractive town; its impressive Georgian façade concealing a timbered house with 14C origins. Choose between two dining rooms and a smart enclosed terrace. Concise menus offer ambitious dishes with worldwide influences and a French heart. Stylish, contemporary décor blends well with the old beams in the bedrooms.

Menu £ 25/35 – Carte £ 30/55
3 rooms – †£ 105/225 ††£ 105/225 – 🍽 £ 12 – 2 suites
Market Pl ✉ CO10 9QZ – ℰ (01787) 247 431 – www.greathouse.co.uk
– Closed 3 weeks January, 2 weeks summer, Sunday dinner, Monday and lunch Tuesday

XX Brasserie

MODERN CUISINE · RUSTIC Smart hotel restaurant which blends modern furnishings with traditional elements of the historic inn in which it resides. In winter, sit by the fire; in summer, sit on the terrace overlooking the gardens. Classic bistro menu.

Carte £ 23/40
Swan Hotel, High St ✉ CO10 9QA – ℰ (01787) 247 477
– www.theswanatlavenham.co.uk

🍺 Six Bells

TRADITIONAL · PUB Charming Grade II listed pub opposite the village church. Three characterful dining areas include an oak-panelled room with a parquet floor. Flavoursome dishes are well-proportioned and there's a comprehensive range of craft beers.

Carte £ 22/33
The Street, Preston St Mary ✉ C10 9NG – Northeast: 2.75 mi by A1141
– ℰ (01787) 247 440 – www.thesixbellspreston.com
– Closed Monday and lunch Tuesday and Wednesday

LEDBURY

Herefordshire – Pop. 8 862 – Regional map n° **10**-B3
▶ London 119 mi – Birmingham 53 mi – Bristol 58 mi

🏨 Feathers

HISTORIC · COSY Family-run, 16C black and white timbered coaching inn. Comfy bedrooms are a clever blend of old and new: those in the main inn are the most characterful, while the 'Superior' rooms are the most contemporary. Dine from modern seasonal menus in linen-clad Quills or beneath hop hung beams in informal Fuggles.

22 rooms 🍽 – †£ 99/145 ††£ 145/245
High St ✉ HR8 1DS – ℰ (01531) 635 266 – www.feathers-ledbury.co.uk

at Trumpet Northwest: 3.25 mi on A438 – ⊠ Ledbury

XX **Verzon** ⇔ ≼ 🏠 🛱 ᕦ 🅿

BRITISH TRADITIONAL · FORMAL Smartly restored Georgian manor house with a surprisingly stylish interior and a laid-back vibe. The chic restaurant offers a menu of precisely prepared, classic British dishes which show respect for fine local ingredients. Seductive modern bedrooms are named after cider apples; most have country views.

Menu £ 18/25 – Carte £ 27/75

8 rooms � – ♦£ 80/90 ♦♦£ 90/150

Hereford Rd ⊠ HR8 2PZ – ℰ (01531) 670 381 – www.verzonhouse.com

LEEDS

Kent – Regional map n° **5**-C2

▶ London 41 mi – Ealing 53 mi – Stratford 41 mi – Bromley 33 mi

🏠 **Leeds Castle** ✿ 🐾 ≼ 🏠 🖼 ᕦ 🌣 🖄 🅿

CASTLE · PERSONALISED This unique accommodation is in the grounds of 900 year old Leeds Castle. Stay in smart, modern bedrooms in the old 1920s staff accommodation blocks or a more historic room in the Maiden's Tower (an old Tudor bakehouse beside the castle). The timbered café morphs into a candlelit restaurant in the evening.

17 rooms ⊉ – ♦£ 75/90 ♦♦£ 120/150

⊠ ME17 1PL – ℰ (01622) 767 823 – www.leeds-castle.co.uk – Closed 24-26 December

GOOD TIPS!

This former mill town is now known as the 'Knightsbridge of the North' so it comes as no surprise to find restaurants located in retail spaces: from Crafthouse and Angelica in the Trinity shopping centre to the brasserie on the Fourth Floor at Harvey Nichols and the Michelin-starred Man Behind the Curtain on the top floor of fashion store Flannels.

LEEDS

West Yorkshire – Pop. 751 485 – Regional map n° **13**-B2
▶ London 204 mi – Liverpool 75 mi – Manchester 43 mi – Newcastle upon Tyne 95 mi

Hotels

🏨 **Malmaison**

BUSINESS · DESIGN Chic, boutique hotel in the former offices of the city's tram and bus department; hence the name of the stylish suite, 'Depot'. Generously sized bedrooms have warm colour schemes and good comforts. Smart, intimate guest areas include a relaxing bar and a modern take on a brasserie.

100 rooms – ♦£ 139/159 ♦♦£ 139/159 – ☲ £ 15 – 1 suite
Town plan: GZ-n – *1 Swinegate* ⊠ *LS1 4AG* – ℰ *(0113) 398 10 00*
– *www.malmaison.com*

🏨 **DoubleTree by Hilton**

BUSINESS · DESIGN Modern business hotel overlooking the canal basin. Photos of the city's industrial landmarks hang on white walls; well-equipped bedrooms boast iMac TVs and panoramic city views. Relax on the quayside terrace or in the 13th floor sky lounge. The chic restaurant serves modern cuisine.

333 rooms – ♦£ 69/249 ♦♦£ 69/249 – ☲ £ 17
Town plan: FZ-c – *2 Wharf Approach, Granary Wharf* ⊠ *LS1 4BR* – ℰ *(0113) 241 10 00* – *www.doubletree.com*

🏨 **Quebecs**

BUSINESS · ELEGANT Interesting 19C building – formerly a Liberal Club; its original features include wood-panelling, a curvaceous oak staircase and stained glass windows depicting districts of Leeds. Bedrooms blend the classic with the contemporary.

44 rooms – ♦£ 75/295 ♦♦£ 75/295 – ☲ £ 16
Town plan: FZ-a – *9 Quebec St* ⊠ *LS1 2HA* – ℰ *(0113) 244 89 89*
– *www.quebecshotel.co.uk* – Closed 23-27 December

525

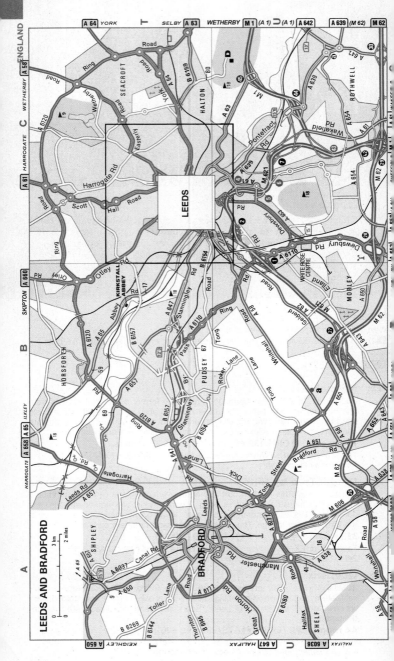

LEEDS AND BRADFORD

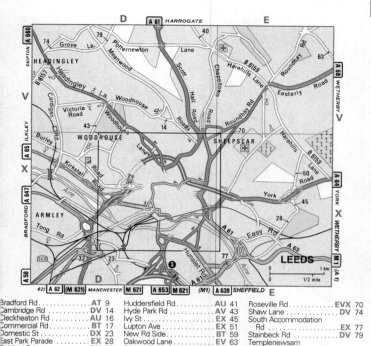

42 The Calls

BUSINESS · CONTEMPORARY Converted 18C grain mill on the banks of the River Aire. Many of the well-equipped bedrooms come complete with original beams, steel girders or industrial machinery; go for a room with a river view. Breakfasts are comprehensive.

41 rooms – ♥£ 85/150 ♥♥£ 95/195 – ☲ £ 16

Town plan: GZ-z – 42 The Calls ☒ LS2 7EW – ✆ (0113) 244 00 99
– www.42thecalls.co.uk – Closed 3 days Christmas
Brasserie Forty 4 – See restaurant listing

Restaurants

XX The Man Behind the Curtain 🆕 (Michael O'Hare)

MODERN CUISINE · FASHIONABLE A unique, very individually styled restaurant with a minimalist interior and bold graffiti artwork, set on the top floor of a privately owned fashion store. Accomplished, highly skilled cooking uses very original, creative combinations – and the artful presentation is equally striking.
➜ Hand-dived scallop, chorizo oil, grains. Pork jowl, oysters, cinders. Praline, passion fruit, meringue.

Menu £ 38/65 – set menu only

Town plan: GZ-c – 3rd Floor, Flannels, 68-78 Vicar Ln ☒ LS1 7JH – ✆ (0113) 243 23 76 (booking advisable) – www.themanbehindthecurtain.co.uk – Closed 19-31 December, Sunday-Tuesday and lunch Wednesday-Thursday

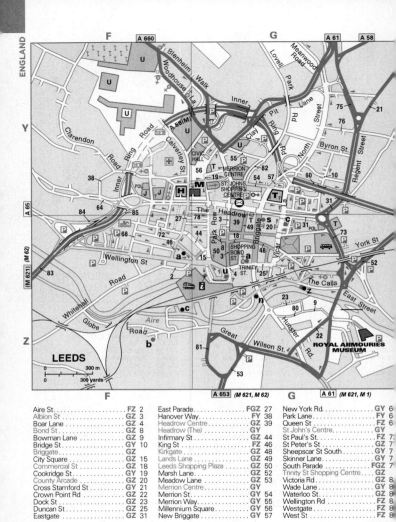

LEEDS

0 ___ 300 m
0 ___ 300 yards

XX Fourth Floor at Harvey Nichols 🍴 🛋 AC

BRITISH MODERN · BRASSERIE Bright, stylish dining room with rooftop views, metal fretwork screens and a Scandic feel; located on the top floor of a chic store. Watch the chefs prepare tasty, modern, globally influenced dishes. Pleasant service is from a smart team.

Menu £ 20 (lunch and early dinner)
– Carte £ 26/44

Town plan: GZ-s – *107-111 Briggate* ✉ *LS1 6AZ*
– 𝒞 *(0113) 204 80 00 (booking essential at lunch)*
– *www.harveynichols.com* – *Closed 25 December, 1 January,*
Easter Sunday and dinner Sunday-Monday

✗✗ Crafthouse

€ 🍴 ⅙ AK 🐕 ⟷

MODERN CUISINE · DESIGN Located in the Trinity shopping centre, with a wrap-around terrace and rooftop views. It has a bright, modern feel; the open kitchen and marble counter take centre stage. Menus offer European classics and meats from the Josper grill.

Menu £ 23 (lunch and early dinner) – Carte £ 26/71

Town plan: GZ-a – *Trinity Leeds (5th Floor), 70 Boar Ln* ✉ *LS1 6HW*
– ✆ *(0113) 897 0444* – *www.crafthouse-restaurant.co.uk*
– *Closed 25 December*

✗✗ Brasserie Forty 4

🍴 AK ⟷

INTERNATIONAL · BRASSERIE Contemporary hotel brasserie and a bright, stylish bar, set in an old 18C warehouse. Tables are spread amongst steel girders; sit by the window for a river view. Straightforward, up-to-date cooking displays European influences.

Menu £ 20 (lunch and early dinner) – Carte £ 24/38

Town plan: GZ-z – *42 The Calls Hotel, 44 The Calls* ✉ *LS2 7EW*
– ✆ *(0113) 234 32 32* – *www.brasserie44.com*
– *Closed Sunday, Monday and bank holidays*

✗✗ Angelica

🍷 € 🍴 AK ⤵

MODERN CUISINE · BRASSERIE Set above its sister 'Crafthouse' and also boasting a superb terrace and skyline views. The large bar is the focal point and cocktails are a speciality. Cooking is simple, modern and global – and, pleasingly, they're open all day.

Carte £ 16/42

Town plan: GZ-a – *Trinity Leeds (6th Floor), 70 Boar Ln* ✉ *LS1 6HW*
– ✆ *(0113) 897 0099* – *www.angelica-restaurant.co.uk*
– *Closed 25 December*

✗ Foundry

🍴 AK

TRADITIONAL CUISINE · WINE BAR Simply styled bistro-cum-wine bar on the site of the legendary steel foundry, with a vaulted ceiling, ornate bar and laid-back feel. Wine box ends and 'squashed' bottles feature. Classic dishes include plenty of specials.

Menu £ 14 (weekday lunch) – Carte £ 21/38

Town plan: FZ-b – *1 Saw Mill Yard, The Round Foundry* ✉ *LS11 5WH*
– ✆ *(0113) 245 03 90* – *www.thefoundrywinebar.co.uk*
– *Closed first week January, last week August, 25-26 December, Saturday lunch, Sunday and Monday*

✗ Tharavadu

🍽

INDIAN · EXOTIC A simple-looking restaurant with seascape murals. The extensive menu offers superbly spiced, colourful Keralan specialities and refined street food – the dosas are a hit. Service is bright and friendly and dishes arrive swiftly.

Carte £ 20/40

Town plan: GZ-u – *7-8 Mill Hill* ✉ *LS1 5DQ*
– ✆ *(0113) 244 0500 (booking essential)* – *www.tharavadurestaurants.com*
– *Closed 24-25 December and Sunday*

🍺 Cross Keys

🍴

BRITISH TRADITIONAL · FRIENDLY Traditional brick-built pub: a watering hole for foundry workers in the 19C. Cosy and welcoming with beams, flagged floors and wood-burning stoves. It gets busy, so book ahead. Hearty, straightforward, British cooking; popular Sunday lunch.

Carte £ 21/36

Town plan: FZ-b – *107 Water Ln, The Round Foundry* ✉ *LS11 5WD*
– ✆ *(0113) 243 37 11 (booking essential)* – *www.the-crosskeys.com*
– *Closed 25-26 December and 1 January*

529

🏨🏨 **Leicester Marriott**　　　　　　❀ 🔲 🏠 ⅃🖧 🖃 ⅃ 🔟 🕸 🕸 ☐

BUSINESS · MODERN Purpose-built hotel on a suburban business park. Stylish open-plan guest areas include an atrium lounge and informal café. Uniform bedrooms boast a good level of facilities. Smart executive lounge and excellent leisure club. East meets West in the restaurant; choose from the buffet or an eclectic à la carte.

227 rooms – 🛉£ 139/159 🛉🛉£ 159/169 – ☑ £ 16 – 1 suite
Town plan: AY-z – *Smith Way, Grove Park, Enderby* ✉ *LE19 1SW*
– ✆ *(0116) 282 01 00 – www.leicestermarriott.co.uk*

LEICESTER

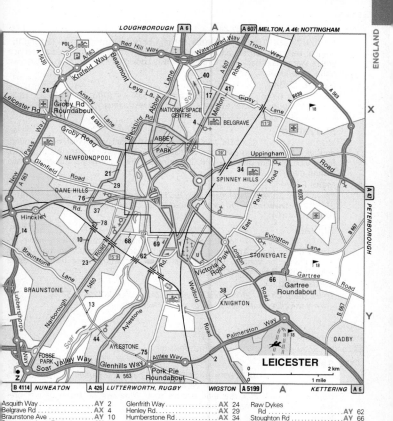

🏨 **Hotel Maiyango** ☆ 🏱 & 🕭 ⚡ ⚙

BUSINESS · STYLISH Privately owned city centre hotel in a 150 year old shoe factory. Stylish interior with a trendy bar opening onto a terrace overlooking the rooftops. Spacious, individually designed bedrooms boast bespoke wood furniture and a colonial feel.

14 rooms – 🛏£ 79/139 – 🛏🛏£ 79/139 – 🍽£ 8 – 1 suite

Town plan: BY-a – *13-21 St Nicholas Pl* ⊠ *LE1 4LD* – 𝒞 *(0116) 251 88 98*
– *www.maiyango.com* – *Closed 25-26 December*

Maiyango – See restaurant listing

✕✕ **Chutney Ivy** & 🕭 🕙 🕸

INDIAN · FASHIONABLE Keenly run former warehouse with a smart industrial feel; its floor-to-ceiling windows open onto the pavement. Mix of modern and classic dishes, with influences from Hyderabad, Goa and Bengal. Watch the chefs in the open kitchen.

Menu £ 17 (weekdays)/30 – Carte £ 15/33

Town plan: CY-x – *41 Halford St* ⊠ *LE1 1TR* – 𝒞 *(0116) 251 1889*
– *www.chutneyivy.com* – *Closed 25-26 December,1 January, Saturday lunch and Sunday*

X **Boot Room**

BRITISH TRADITIONAL · FRIENDLY Set in a brick-built former shoe factory; the original cast iron girders and pillars still remain. Simple styling, friendly service and a warm, laid-back feel. Unfussy British cooking with European influences; good value lunches.

Carte £ 22/34

Town plan: BY-x – *27-29 Millstone Ln* ✉ *LE1 5JN* – ℰ *(0116) 262 25 55* – *www.thebootroomeaterie.co.uk* – *Closed 2 weeks January, 2 weeks summer, Sunday and Monday*

X **Maiyango**

MODERN CUISINE · EXOTIC A glass-fronted restaurant in a stylish hotel. Round, dark wood booths and silk drapes create an Oriental feel and there's a relaxed, funky vibe. Modern dishes feature Indian spices and have global influences. Two tasting menus available.

Menu £ 18/45

Town plan: BY-a – *Hotel Maiyango, 13-21 St Nicholas Pl* ✉ *LE1 4LD* – ℰ *(0116) 251 88 98* – *www.maiyango.com* – *Closed 25-26 December and lunch Sunday-Tuesday*

X **Shivalli**

INDIAN VEGETARIAN · SIMPLE Simple, part-panelled restaurant with Indian artefacts on the walls. Appealing South Indian, vegetarian menu with most dishes also suitable for vegans. Tasty, authentic cooking with honest flavours. Good value thalis and buffet lunches.

Carte £ 11/21

Town plan: CY-a – *21 Welford Rd* ✉ *LE2 7AD* – ℰ *(0116) 255 01 37* – *www.shivallirestaurant.com* – *Closed 25 December*

LEIGH-ON-SEA

Southend-on-Sea – Regional map n° **7**-C3

▶ London 37 mi – Basildon 9 mi – Chelmsford 18 mi

XX **Sandbank**

INTERNATIONAL · NEIGHBOURHOOD Former bank in a parade of shops; now a spacious restaurant with a high ceiling, a classic black and white theme and a tropical fish tank in a dramatic feature wall. Wide-ranging menu of well-presented dishes with clear flavours.

Menu £ 20 (weekdays) – Carte £ 30/42

1470 London Rd ✉ *SS9 2UR* – ℰ *(01702) 719 000* – *www.sandbankrestaurant.co.uk* – *Closed Sunday dinner and Monday*

LEINTWARDINE

Herefordshire – ✉ Craven Arms – Regional map n° **10**-A2

▶ London 156 mi – Birmingham 55 mi – Hereford 24 mi – Worcester 40 mi

🍴 **The Lion**

BRITISH TRADITIONAL · CLASSIC 18C inn on the banks of the River Teme, next to an attractive medieval bridge. It's relaxed and stylish with a proper bar and a slightly smarter dining room with river views. Dishes are nicely presented and local produce plays a big part. Smart bedrooms have up-to-date facilities; some have river views.

Menu £ 30 (dinner) – Carte £ 24/44

8 rooms ✍ – ♦£ 80/85 ♦♦£ 100/120

✉ *SY7 0JZ* – ℰ *(01547) 540 203* – *www.thelionleintwardine.co.uk* – *Closed 25 December*

LEVISHAM – North Yorkshire ➜ See Pickering

LEWDOWN

Devon – Regional map n° **1**-C2

▶ London 238 mi – Exeter 37 mi – Plymouth 29 mi

🏠 Lewtrenchard Manor

🏠 🐾 🛏 ⚓ 🕙 🅿

HISTORIC · STYLISH Hugely impressive Grade II listed Jacobean manor house in mature grounds. The characterful antique-furnished interior features huge fireplaces, ornate oak panelling, intricately designed ceilings and mullioned windows. Bedrooms are spacious and well-equipped; those in the coach house are the most modern.

14 rooms ⌂ – †£ 140/200 ††£ 175/245 – 1 suite
✉ EX20 4PN – South : 0.75 mi by Lewtrenchard rd – ☎ (01566) 783 222
– www.lewtrenchard.co.uk
Lewtrenchard Manor – See restaurant listing

XX Lewtrenchard Manor

🛏 ⇔ 🅿

BRITISH MODERN · FORMAL Intimate wood-panelled dining room in a Jacobean manor house. Cooking is contrastingly modern yet refreshingly unadorned; flavoursome garden produce features. For a more unique experience book 'Purple Carrot' (the chef's table).

Menu £ 20/50
Lewtrenchard Manor Hotel, ✉ EX20 4PN – South : 0.75 mi by Lewtrenchard rd
– ☎ (01566) 783 222 (booking essential) – www.lewtrenchard.co.uk

LEWES

East Sussex – Pop. 17 297 – Regional map n° **5**-A3
▶ London 53 mi – Brighton 8 mi – Hastings 29 mi – Maidstone 43 mi

🏠 Shelleys

🏠 🛏 🎐 🔊 🅿

TOWNHOUSE · ELEGANT Formerly an inn and before that, a private house dating back to 1577, owned by the great poet's family. Spacious, classically styled bedrooms include a four-poster room and a suite overlooking the lovely gardens. The intimate dining room, with its elegant chandeliers, offers views over the lawns.

19 rooms ⌂ – †£ 130/160 ††£ 160/190 – 1 suite
High St ✉ BN7 1XS – ☎ (01273) 472 361 – www.the-shelleys.co.uk

X Real Eating Company

🎐 🔊 🆎

BRITISH TRADITIONAL · RUSTIC Buzzy all-day restaurant offering cakes throughout the day in the café and an extensive menu of seasonal local produce in the rustic dining room. Cooking is honest and unfussy and features plenty of hearty British favourites.

Carte £ 21/34
18 Cliffe High St ✉ BN7 2AJ – ☎ (01273) 402 650 – www.real-eating.co.uk
– Closed 25 December

at East Chiltington Northwest: 5.5 mi by A275 and B2116 off Novington Lane – ✉ Lewes

🍴 Jolly Sportsman

🐜 🛏 🎐 🆎 🅿

BRITISH TRADITIONAL · RUSTIC An olive green, clapperboard pub, popular with the locals. Choose from interesting bar bites, good value set menus, a rustic, British-based à la carte and blackboard specials; many of the herbs and fruits are from their own polytunnel.

Menu £ 16/22 (weekdays) – Carte £ 26/36
Chapel Ln ✉ BN7 3BA – ☎ (01273) 890 400 (booking essential)
– www.thejollysportsman.com – Closed 25 December

LEYBURN

North Yorkshire – Pop. 2 183 – Regional map n° **13**-B1
▶ London 251 mi – Darlington 25 mi – Kendal 43 mi – Leeds 53 mi

⌂ Clyde House

TRADITIONAL · PERSONALISED 18C former coaching inn on the main market square, run by an experienced owner and immaculately kept throughout. Small, cosy sitting room and cottagey breakfast room. Smart, comfortable bedrooms with good quality soft furnishings, hair dryers and bathrobes. Extensive buffet and 'full Yorkshire' breakfasts.

5 rooms ⌤ – ∮£ 50/60 ∮∮£ 85/95
5 Railway St ⌧ DL8 5AY – ℰ (01969) 623 941
– www.clydehouse.com – Closed 8-21 January

✗ Saddle Room ⓝ

BRITISH TRADITIONAL · BISTRO Located within an area of parkland close to the 'Forbidden Corner', is this converted stable decked out with equine paraphernalia – ask for a table in a stall! Unfussy, classical menus are offered from breakfast through to dinner.

Carte £ 32/50

Tupgill Park, Coverdale ⌧ DL8 4TJ – Southwest : 2.5 mi by Coverham rd
– ℰ (01969) 640 596 – www.thesaddleroom.co.uk
– Closed Sunday dinner

⌂ Sandpiper Inn

BRITISH TRADITIONAL · PUB A friendly Yorkshire welcome is extended at this characterful, stone-built, part-16C pub just off the main square. Subtle, refined cooking offers a modern take on the classics and the skilled kitchen prides itself on the provenance of its ingredients. Two country-chic style bedrooms offer excellent comforts.

Carte £ 29/42 **s**

2 rooms ⌤ – ∮£ 80/90 ∮∮£ 90/100
Market Pl ⌧ DL8 5AT – ℰ (01969) 622 206
– www.sandpiperinn.co.uk – Closed Tuesday in winter and Monday

LICHFIELD

Staffordshire – Pop. 32 877 – Regional map n° **10**-C2
▶ London 128 mi – Birmingham 16 mi – Derby 23 mi

⌂ Swinfen Hall ⓝ

COUNTRY HOUSE · HISTORIC Grade II listed Georgian mansion with an impressive façade, set in 100 acres. Original features abound, including a stucco ceiling in the magnificent foyer. Individually styled bedrooms; extras include fruit and freshly baked shortbread.

17 rooms ⌤ – ∮£ 190/350 ∮∮£ 210/375 – 1 suite
⌧ WS14 9RE – Southeast : 2.75 mi by A 5206 on A 38
– ℰ (01543) 481 494 – www.swinfenhallhotel.co.uk
– Restricted opening between Christmas and New Year
Four Seasons – See restaurant listing

⌂ Netherstowe House

COUNTRY HOUSE · HOMELY Extensively restored 19C country house; professionally run by a family team. Period lounges and luxurious bedrooms come with antique furnishings and original fireplaces; modern apartments complete with kitchenettes are located in the grounds. The elegant, formal restaurant offers ambitious modern cooking; the atmospheric cellar brasserie specialises in local steaks.

17 rooms (dinner included) ⌤ – ∮£ 185/215 ∮∮£ 185/215 – 8 suites
Netherstowe Ln ⌧ WS13 6AY – Northeast : 1.75 mi following signs for A 51 and A 38, off Eastern Ave
– ℰ (01543) 254 270 – www.netherstowehouse.com

⌂ St Johns House &⊘ P

TOWNHOUSE · CONTEMPORARY Impressive Regency townhouse fronted by large columns. Enter through a beautiful tiled hallway into a contemporary drawing room with ornate cornicing and chandeliers. Individually styled bedrooms have a modern, understated feel.

9 rooms ☞ – †£ 70/75 ††£ 95/125
*28 St John St ⊠ WS13 6PB – ℰ (01543) 252 080
– www.stjohnshouse.co.uk – Closed 25-30 December*

XX Four Seasons Ⓝ &◎ P

BRITISH MODERN · CLASSIC An impressive classical dining room with original wood panelling and a superbly ornate ceiling, set within the grand surroundings of Swinfen Hall. Elaborate modern cooking uses meat from the estate and veg and herbs from the walled garden.

Menu £ 36/52
*Swinfen Hall Hotel, ⊠ WS14 9RE – Southeast : 2.75 mi by A 5206 on A 38
– ℰ (01543) 481 494 – www.swinfenhallhotel.co.uk – Closed Sunday dinner and Monday*

X Wine House &

TRADITIONAL CUISINE · INDIVIDUAL Smart red-brick restaurant with a loyal local following. There's an open-fired bar at one end and a dining room at the other; it takes its name from the impressive glass wine cellar. Classically based menus have the occasional modern twist.

Menu £ 14 (lunch) – Carte £ 25/44
*27 Bird St ⊠ WS13 6PW – ℰ (01543) 419 999
– www.thewinehouselichfield.co.uk – Closed Sunday dinner and Monday*

at Wall South: 2.75 mi by A5127

▯ The Trooper &⇦⇪& P

TRADITIONAL CUISINE · FRIENDLY Feast like a Roman general after battle on mature steaks including local rump, Kobe beef and rare breed steaks which go up to 20oz. Tasty pizzas cooked to order in a wood-fired oven. Grab a seat on the terrace when the weather allows.

Menu £ 12 (weekday lunch)/20 – Carte £ 20/41
*Watling St ⊠ WS14 0AN – ℰ (01543) 480 413
– www.thetrooperwall.co.uk*

LICKFOLD – West Sussex → See Petworth

LIFTON

Devon – Pop. 1 180 – Regional map n° **1**-C2
▶ London 238 mi – Bude 24 mi – Exeter 37 mi – Launceston 4 mi

⌂ Arundell Arms 🌳 &⇦🛏⇪♨ P

TRADITIONAL · COSY Family-run roadside coaching inn with cosy, traditional bedrooms and access to 20 miles of private fishing on the River Tamar and its tributaries. The characterful lounge and bar serve a brasserie menu, while the restaurant – which overlooks the terrace and gardens – offers classical fare.

25 rooms ☞ – †£ 95/115 ††£ 150/180
*Fore St ⊠ PL16 0AA – ℰ (01566) 784 666
– www.arundellarms.com*

LINCOLN

Lincolnshire – Pop. 100 160 – Regional map n° **9**-C1
▶ London 140 mi – Leeds 73 mi – Nottingham 38 mi

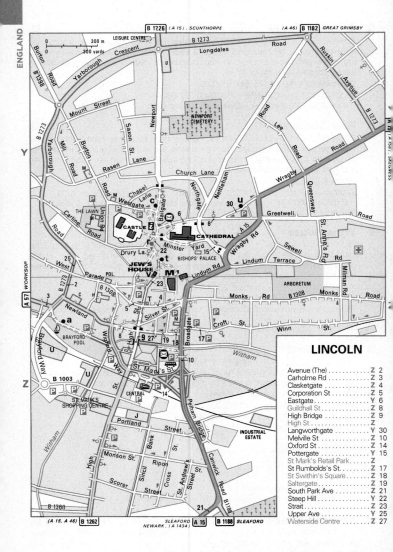

LINCOLN

🏨 **DoubleTree by Hilton Lincoln** ✿ ⇗ ⅙ ⊡ ঙ AC ⅛ P

CHAIN HOTEL · MODERN Modern corporate hotel with state-of-the-art conference rooms, set on the site of the old City of Lincoln Electrical works. Minimalist bedrooms have sleek, contemporary lines; suites overlook the marina. The smart brasserie has floor to ceiling windows and a modern menu with British influences.

115 rooms – ♦£ 79/150 ♦♦£ 89/160 – ⌧ £ 10 – 8 suites
Town plan: Z-a – *Brayford Wharf North* ⊠ *LN1 1YW*
– ✆ *(01522) 565 180* – *www.lincoln.doubletree.com*

536

The Rest

TOWNHOUSE · STYLISH With direct access to the bedrooms from the street, guests can come and go freely at this laid-back hotel. Breakfast is served in the coffee shop-cum-bar. Chic bedrooms feature bespoke furnishings and bathrooms with heated floors.

10 rooms ⌓ – ♦£ 89/199 ♦♦£ 89/199
Town plan: Y-t – *55A Steep Hill* ⊠ *LN2 1LR* – ℰ *(01522) 247 888*
– *www.theresthotellincoln.co.uk*

Bail House

TOWNHOUSE · PERSONALISED Part-14C baronial hall with a Georgian façade and Victorian additions. Modern facilities mix with original features in the characterful bedrooms: one has an exposed Roman wall. Breakfast is served in the neighbouring restaurant.

10 rooms – ♦£ 79/195 ♦♦£ 79/195 – ⌓£ 7
Town plan: Y-c – *34 Bailgate* ⊠ *LN1 3AP* – ℰ *(01522) 541 000*
– *www.bailhouse.co.uk*

St Clements Lodge

TOWNHOUSE · PERSONALISED Cosy, Edwardian-style house close to the cathedral and castle (where you can view the Magna Carta). Cheerful owners offer good old-fashioned hospitality. Spacious, well-equipped bedrooms have pine furnishings and a homely feel.

3 rooms ⌓ – ♦£ 65/70 ♦♦£ 80/85
Town plan: Y-u – *21 Langworthgate* ⊠ *LN2 4AD* – ℰ *(01522) 521 532*
– *www.stclementslodge.co.uk*

Jews House

MODERN CUISINE · COSY At the bottom of a steep cobbled hill is this cosy stone house dating from 1150; reputedly Europe's oldest surviving dwelling. Bold, ambitious dishes display an eclectic mix of influences – the tasting menu is a hit. Service is charming.

Menu £ 20 (lunch) – Carte £ 31/44
Town plan: Y-v – *15 The Strait* ⊠ *LN2 1JD* – ℰ *(01522) 524 851*
– *www.jewshouserestaurant.co.uk – Closed 2 weeks January, 2 weeks July, 1 week November, Sunday, Monday and lunch Tuesday*

Wig & Mitre

BRITISH TRADITIONAL · PUB Well-established pub with a cosy bar, period dining rooms and an airy beamed restaurant. Menus offer classical dishes with the odd Mediterranean or Asian influence, alongside daily specials, hearty breakfasts and over 20 wines by the glass.

Menu £ 18 (weekdays) – Carte £ 20/28
Town plan: Y-r – *30-32 Steep Hill* ⊠ *LN2 1LU* – ℰ *(01522) 535 190*
– *www.wigandmitre.com – Closed 25 December*

LISKEARD

Cornwall – Pop. 9 237 – Regional map n° **1**-B2
▶ London 261 mi – Exeter 59 mi – Plymouth 19 mi – Truro 37 mi

Pencubitt Country House

TRADITIONAL · PERSONALISED Sympathetically restored Victorian property with delightful views over the gardens and countryside – take it all in from the veranda or the balcony in bedroom 3. Look out too for the original windows and staircase in the lovely hall. They offer home-cooked dinners, cream teas and picnics, by arrangement.

9 rooms ⌓ – ♦£ 50/60 ♦♦£ 70/110
Station Rd ⊠ *PL14 4EB – South : 0.5 mi by B 3254 on Lamellion rd* – ℰ *(01579) 342 694 – www.pencubitt.com – Closed January and February*

LISS

Hampshire – Pop. 6 248 – Regional map n° **4**-C2

▶ London 53 mi – Bristol 104 mi – Cardiff 137 mi – Plymouth 184 mi

XX **Madhuban Tandoori**

INDIAN · FRIENDLY Smartly furnished restaurant owned by three enthusiastic brothers. The focus is on fresh north Indian dishes; most of which can be prepared to the desired heat – the menu provides a useful glossary of terms. They also sell their sauces.

Carte £ 15/27

94 Station Rd ⊠ GU33 7AQ – ℰ (01730) 893 363
– www.madhubanrestaurant.co.uk – Closed 25-26 December and Friday lunch

LITTLE BEDWYN – Wiltshire → See Marlborough

LITTLE COXWELL

Oxfordshire – Pop. 132 – Regional map n° **6**-A2

▶ London 79 mi – Sheffield 158 mi – Derby 120 mi – York 202 mi

🍴 **Eagle Tavern**

BRITISH TRADITIONAL · TRADITIONAL This welcoming pub was built in 1901 for the farmers of this sleepy hamlet and, although it might look a little different now, a convivial atmosphere still reigns. The self-taught chef cooks the kind of food he likes to eat, including dishes from his homeland, Slovakia. Spacious bedrooms are spotlessly kept.

Menu £ 20 (weekday lunch) – Carte £ 26/35

6 rooms � – ♦£ 60/70 ♦♦£ 80/90
⊠ SN7 7LW – ℰ (01367) 241 879 – www.eagletavern.co.uk – Closed Sunday dinner and Monday

LITTLE ECCLESTON

Lancashire – Regional map n° **11**-A2

▶ London 238 mi – Liverpool - 55 mi – Leeds 83 mi – Manchester 51 mi

🍴 **Cartford Inn**

TRADITIONAL CUISINE · PUB 17C coaching inn next to the Pilling Marshes, with a series of cosy little rooms; one overlooking the river. Cooking is in the tried-and-tested vein, offering proper pub classics, with signature dishes under the heading of 'Cartford Favourites'. Choose between quirky or French farmhouse style bedrooms.

Carte £ 21/36

15 rooms ⟲ – ♦£ 70/140 ♦♦£ 130/220
Cartford Ln ⊠ PR3 0YP – ℰ (01995) 670 166 – www.thecartfordinn.co.uk – Closed 25 December and Monday lunch except bank holidays

LITTLE LANGFORD – Wiltshire → See Salisbury

LITTLE MARLOW – Buckinghamshire → See Marlow

LITTLE PETHERICK – Cornwall → See Padstow

LITTLE THETFORD – Cambridgeshire → See Ely

LITTLE WILBRAHAM – Cambridgeshire → See Cambridge

LITTLETON – Hants. → See Winchester

LITTLEHAMPTON

West Sussex – Pop. 55 706 – Regional map n° **4**-C3

▶ London 64 mi – Brighton 18 mi – Portsmouth 31 mi

Bailiffscourt H. & Spa

COUNTRY HOUSE · HISTORIC Charming, reconstructed medieval manor in immaculately kept gardens. Bedrooms are split between the main house and the outbuildings; the newer rooms are in the grounds and are more suited to families. Beautiful spa facility. Classic country house cooking served in the formal dining room.

39 rooms ☑ – †£ 189/369 ††£ 219/399

Climping St, Climping ⊠ BN17 5RW – West : 2.75 mi by A 259 – ℰ (01903) 723 511 – www.hshotels.co.uk

LIVERPOOL

Merseyside – Pop. 552 267 – Regional map n° **11-A3**

▶ London 219 mi – Birmingham 103 mi – Leeds 75 mi – Manchester 35 mi

Aloft Liverpool ⓝ

HISTORIC · STYLISH Relaxed hotel in the Grade II listed Royal Insurance building in the centre of the city. It features stunning original panelling, stained glass and ornate plasterwork, alongside colourful contemporary décor and the latest mod cons. An open lounge with a pool table leads to the New York style restaurant.

116 rooms – †£ 60/250 ††£ 85/250 – ☑ £ 10

Town plan: 3CY-s – 1 North John St ⊠ L2 5QW – ℰ (0151) 294 4050 – www.aloftliverpool.com

Hilton

BUSINESS · MODERN Spacious, light-filled hotel in a waterfront location, with the latest in modern styling and facilities, including excellent conference spaces and a well-equipped gym. Bedrooms benefit from floor to ceiling windows. Unwind in the trendy cocktail bar, then choose from an accessible menu of international dishes.

215 rooms ☑ – †£ 109/249 ††£ 139/279 – 11 suites

Town plan: 3CZ-x – 3 Thomas Steers Way ⊠ L1 8LW – ℰ (0151) 708 42 00 – www.hilton.co.uk/liverpool

Malmaison

BUSINESS · STYLISH Contemporary hotel with a striking stone and black glass façade, overlooking the marina. Chic bedrooms are decorated in sensuous purple or orange tones and boast sunken baths; two are football-themed suites. Sexy, sophisticated bar and an industrial-style brasserie with pop art and a stylish chef's table.

130 rooms – †£ 69/250 ††£ 69/250 – ☑ £ 16 – 2 suites

Town plan: 3CY-n – 7 William Jessop Way, Princes Dock ⊠ L3 1QZ – ℰ (0151) 229 50 00 – www.malmaison.com

Hope Street

TOWNHOUSE · DESIGN Minimalist, boutique hotel in two interlinking buildings: bedrooms in the former carriage works have a slightly rustic edge, while those in the old police station are more modern. The top floor suites offer stunning city skyline views.

89 rooms ☑ – †£ 92/200 ††£ 104/212

Town plan: 4EZ-a – 40 Hope St ⊠ L1 9DA – ℰ (0151) 709 30 00 – www.hopestreethotel.co.uk

London Carriage Works – See restaurant listing

Hard Days Night

LUXURY · DESIGN Unique Beatles themed hotel – their story recounted in artwork from doorstep to rooftop – with contemporary bedrooms featuring original works, and suites styled around Lennon and McCartney. Blakes, named after the designer of the Sgt. Pepper album cover, features a modern brasserie menu.

110 rooms – †£ 95/270 ††£ 95/290 – 2 suites

Town plan: 3CY-b – Central Buildings, North John St ⊠ L2 6RR – ℰ (0151) 236 19 64 – www.harddaysnighthotel.com – Closed 25 December

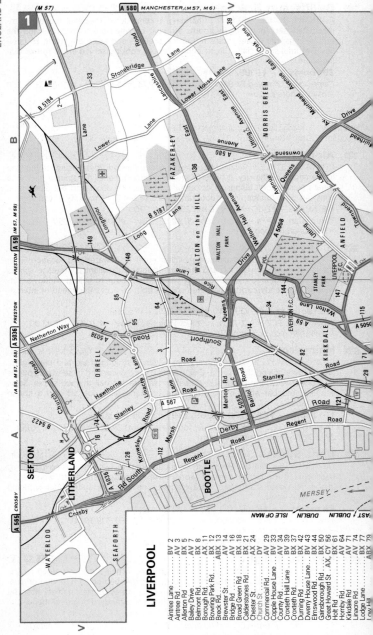

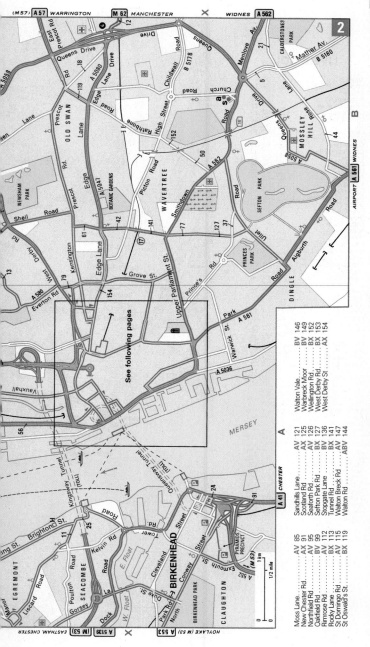

(M 57) **A 57** WARRINGTON | **M 62** MANCHESTER | WIDNES **A 562**

2

East Prescot Rd
Queens Drive
Queens Drive Rd
Prescot Lane Drive
OLD SWAN
Prescot Rd
Edge Lane Drive
Edge Lane
Prescot Rd
Kensington
Edge Lane
Everton Rd
West Derby Rd
NEWSHAM PARK
Sheil Road
Childwall Road
Queens Drive
Church Road
Rathbone Road
High Street
Picton Road
WAVERTREE
Smithdown Road
BOTANIC GARDENS
Grove St.
Upper Parliament St.
Prince's Rd
PRINCES PARK
SEFTON PARK
Ullet Road
Aigburth Road
MOSSLEY HILL
CALDERSTONES PARK
Mather Av.
Menlove Av.
Queens Drive
B 5178
B 5180
A 562
A 5058

Vauxhall

See following pages

MERSEY

Park St.
Warwick St.
A 5036
A 561
DINGLE
A 580
A 5047
A 5080

AIRPORT **A 561** WIDNES

B

A 41 CHESTER

Kingsway Tunnel (toll)
Queensway Tunnel (toll)
Brighton St.
King St.
Kelvin Rd
Tower Rd
Cleveland Street
Conway Street
Exmouth St.
BIRKENHEAD
PYRAMIDS PRECINCT
BIRKENHEAD PARK
CLAUGHTON
Park Rd North
Duke St.
Dock Rd
W. Float
E. Float
SEACOMBE
EGREMONT
Liscard
Poulton Road
Gorsey La
Manor Rd

HOYLAKE (M 53) **A 553** | **A 41** | **A 5139** | EASTHAM, CHESTER

A

0   1/2 mile
0   1 km

541

LIVERPOOL

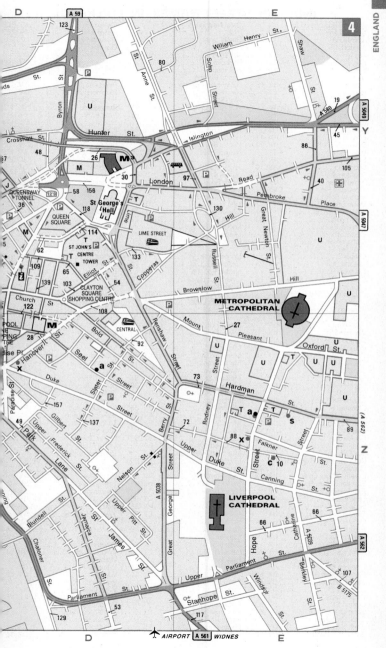

INDEX OF STREET NAMES IN LIVERPOOL

🏠 Hotel Indigo

BUSINESS · STYLISH Smart, modern hotel on the site of a former cotton trading hall and seaman's mission; characterised by its use of vibrant colours. Compact bedrooms have powerful walk-in showers. Staff are smart and cheery. All-day snacks in the lounge; classic dishes in the brightly decorated restaurant.

151 rooms – ♦£ 69/189 ♦♦£ 79/219 – ⬜ £ 14

Town plan: 3CY-a – *10 Chapel St* ⬚ *L3 9AG*

– ✆ *(0151) 559 0111* – *www.hotelindigoliverpool.com*

🏠 Hampton by Hilton

CHAIN HOTEL · FUNCTIONAL Smart, well-priced hotel, a 10min walk from the city centre, offering good modern comforts. It's worth paying a little extra for the 6th floor rooms, which have great views across the river. Buffet breakfasts. Hands-on staff.

151 rooms ⬜ – ♦£ 66/200 ♦♦£ 66/200

Town plan: 4DZ-s – *Kings Dock Mill, 7 Hurst St* ⬚ *L1 8DA*

– ✆ *(0871) 902 16 18* – *www.liverpoolcitycentre.hamptonbyhilton.com*

🏠 The Nadler

HISTORIC · FUNCTIONAL Something a little different, this converted 19C mill has rooms ranging from small singles to spacious duplex suites; one with a decked courtyard. All have modern bathrooms and kitchenettes. Pre-order breakfast to be delivered to your room.

106 rooms – ♦£ 49/159 ♦♦£ 59/169 – ⬜ £ 6

Town plan: 4DZ-a – *29 Seel St* ⬚ *L1 4AU* – ✆ *(0151) 705 2626*

– *www.thenadler.com/liverpool*

🏠 Racquet Club

TOWNHOUSE · HOMELY Ornate Victorian building, formerly a Shipping Agency office and then a gentleman's club, boasting a grand façade and a bohemian style. Bedrooms differ greatly both in layout and décor but most feature antique furniture and eclectic art. Airy restaurant; wide-ranging menu of British dishes.

8 rooms – ♦£ 80/100 ♦♦£ 80/100 – ⬜ £ 12

Town plan: 3CY-e – *Hargreaves Buildings, 5 Chapel St* ⬚ *L3 9AG*

– ✆ *(0151) 236 66 76* – *www.racquetclub.org*

– *Closed first week January, 25 December and bank holidays*

🏠 2 Blackburne Terrace

LUXURY · ELEGANT A delightful Georgian house with plenty of personality. Individually styled bedrooms come with top quality beds, free-standing baths and extras such as fresh fruit and cut flowers. Modern art features in the large sitting room.

4 rooms ⬜ – ♦£ 130/180 ♦♦£ 130/220

Town plan: 4EZ-c – *2 Blackburne Terr* ⬚ *L8 7PJ*

– ✆ *(0151) 702 48 40* – *www.2blackburneterrace.com*

– *Closed mid December- early January*

✕✕✕ The Art School ⓝ

BRITISH MODERN · ELEGANT Bright red chairs contrast with crisp white tablecloths at this elegant restaurant, where a huge glass roof floods the room with light. The experienced local chef carefully prepares a bewildering array of colourful modern dishes.

Menu £ 23/89

Town plan: 4EZ-s – *1 Sugnall St* ⬚ *L7 7DX* – ✆ *(0151) 230 8600*

– *www.theartschoolrestaurant.co.uk* – *Closed 25-26 December, 1 January, Sunday and Monday*

XxX Panoramic 34   ≤ ₺ AC

BRITISH MODERN · FASHIONABLE On the 34th floor of the city's highest sky-scraper you'll find this elegant restaurant with under-lit tables and fabulous 360° views. Ambitious dishes arrive swiftly and are attractively presented; the lunch menu offers good value.

Menu £ 22 (lunch) – Carte £ 35/46

Town plan: 3CY-r – *West Tower (34th floor), Brook St* ⊠ *L3 9PJ*
– ✆ *(0151) 236 55 34* – *www.panoramic34.com*
– *Closed 25-26 December, 1 January and Monday*

XX London Carriage Works   ₺ AC ⊕

MODERN CUISINE · FASHIONABLE Start with a drink in the hotel's lounge-bar, then head to the spacious modern restaurant divided by large shards of glass. The set menu represents the best value, while the à la carte steps things up a gear; both rely on local produce.

Menu £ 20 (lunch and early dinner) – Carte £ 27/54

Town plan: 4EZ-a – *Hope Street Hotel, 40 Hope St* ⊠ *L1 9DA*
– ✆ *(0151) 705 22 22* – *www.thelondoncarriageworks.co.uk*

XX 60 Hope Street   AC ⇔

REGIONAL · BRASSERIE An attractive Grade II listed Georgian house concealing a well-established modern brasserie with battleship grey walls and a smart base-ment wine bar. Menus feature interesting regional dishes; the set selection pro-vides good value.

Menu £ 20 – Carte £ 31/50

Town plan: 4EZ-x – *60 Hope St* ⊠ *L1 9BZ* – ✆ *(0151) 707 60 60*
– *www.60hopestreet.com* – *Closed 26 December and 1 January*

XX Spire   AC

BRITISH MODERN · BISTRO Simple neighbourhood restaurant set in the Penny Lane area of the city. Good value, understated menus offer regional and modern European dishes. Flavoursome cooking and friendly service.

Menu £ 13 (lunch) – Carte £ 24/41

Town plan: 2BX-a – *1 Church Rd* ⊠ *L15 9EA* – ✆ *(0151) 734 50 40*
– *www.spirerestaurant.co.uk* – *Closed 1-7 January and lunch Saturday-Monday*

X Hanover Street Social   ₸ AC ⊑ ⊞

BRITISH MODERN · RUSTIC Lively restaurant near the old docks, with a smart, rustic interior featuring a metal-topped cocktail bar and exposed bricks and air ducts. All-day menus offer something for everyone, from small plates and grills to charcuterie and oysters.

Menu £ 11 (weekday lunch)/20 – Carte £ 18/35

Town plan: 4DZ-x – *Casartelli Building, 16-20 Hanover St* ⊠ *L1 4AA*
– ✆ *(0151) 709 87 84* – *www.hanoverstreetsocial.co.uk*
– *Closed 25 December*

X Neon Jamón   ⊞ ⇔

SPANISH · TAPAS BAR In the bustling Penny Lane, you'll find this equally buzzy, informal tapas bar. Service is friendly and obliging, and dishes are carefully pre-pared and full of flavour. Sit at the counter or a table backed by bare brick walls.

Carte £ 12/20

Town plan: 2BX-s – *12 Smithdown Pl* ⊠ *L15 9EH*
– ✆ *(0151) 734 38 40 (bookings not accepted)* – *www.neonjamon.com*

LONDON STANSTED AIRPORT

Essex – ⊠ Stansted Mountfitchet – Regional map n° **7**-B2
▶ London 37 mi – Cambridge 29 mi – Chelmsford 18 mi – Colchester 29 mi

Radisson Blu H. London Stansted Airport

BUSINESS · DESIGN Spacious modern hotel with great facilities, just a stone's throw from the terminal. Smart, well-equipped bedrooms come in 3 colour schemes. The vast atrium is dominated by a 40ft glass tower, where 'Angels' fly up to your wine. Have snacks in the Tower Bar, Italian fare in Filini or American steakhouse dishes in the Grill Bar. They also do takeaway breakfast snacks.

494 rooms – ♦£ 109/199 ♦♦£ 119/209 – ☐ £ 10 – 6 suites
Waltham Close ✉ CM24 1PP – ☎ (01279) 661 012
– www.stansted.radissonblu.com

LONG ASHTON – North Somerset → See Bristol

LONG COMPTON

Warwickshire – ✉ Shipston-On-Stour – Pop. 705 – Regional map n° **10**-C3
▶ London 81 mi – Birmingham 53 mi – Liverpool 147 mi – Bristol 72 mi

Red Lion

BRITISH TRADITIONAL · FRIENDLY 18C former coaching inn with flag floors, log fires and a warm, modern feel. Seasonal menu of tasty, home-cooked pub classics, with more adventurous daily specials. Keen service. Good-sized garden and children's play area. Stylish bedrooms have a contemporary, country-chic feel and a good level of facilities.

Menu £ 14 (lunch and early dinner) – Carte £ 25/34
5 rooms ☐ – ♦£ 60 ♦♦£ 90/140
Main St ✉ CV36 5JS – ☎ (01608) 684 221 – www.redlion-longcompton.co.uk

LONG CRENDON

Buckinghamshire – ✉ Aylesbury – Pop. 2 335 – Regional map n° **6**-C2
▶ London 50 mi – Aylesbury 11 mi – Oxford 15 mi – Birmingham 82 mi

Angel

BRITISH TRADITIONAL · ROMANTIC Sweet former pub with low ceilings and plenty of character. Large, leather-furnished bar and a collection of intimate dining rooms leading to an airy conservatory. Traditional, unfussy, British-based dishes are accompanied by a well-chosen wine list. Bedrooms are cosy and individually decorated.

Menu £ 11 (weekday lunch) – Carte £ 27/52
4 rooms ☐ – ♦£ 75 ♦♦£ 110
47 Bicester Rd ✉ HP18 9EE – ☎ (01844) 208 268 – www.angelrestaurant.co.uk
– Closed 25 December, 1 January and Sunday dinner

Mole & Chicken

INTERNATIONAL · RURALLY A charming pub built in 1831 as part of a local farm workers' estate, with low wonky ceilings, open fires and a large garden offering commanding country views. The menu features classic British dishes and heartwarming puddings. Staff are friendly and there are five cosy bedrooms in the adjoining house.

Carte £ 24/37
5 rooms ☐ – ♦£ 85 ♦♦£ 110
Easington ✉ HP18 8EY – North 0.5 mi by Dorton rd – ☎ (01844) 208 387
– www.themoleandchicken.co.uk – Closed 25 December

LONG MELFORD

Suffolk – Pop. 2 898 – Regional map n° **8**-C3
▶ London 62 mi – Cambridge 34 mi – Colchester 18 mi – Ipswich 24 mi

🏨 Black Lion

TRADITIONAL · PERSONALISED Whitewashed Georgian inn overlooking the green, with a cosy, classical interior. Bedrooms are individually decorated in rich colours and named after wines. After dinner, sink into a deep sofa by the open fire in the panelled bar.

10 rooms 🖙 – 🛉£ 102/136 🛉🛉£ 125/175 – 1 suite
Church Walk, The Green ⊠ *CO10 9DN* – 𝒞 *(01787) 312 356*
– www.blacklionhotel.net
Black Lion – See restaurant listing

XX Scutchers

TRADITIONAL CUISINE · RUSTIC This converted medieval hall house is now a smart, personally run restaurant. Cooking is skilful, classical and full of flavour; everything from the bread to the sorbet is homemade. The wine list features some top class producers.

Carte £ 30/50
Westgate St ⊠ *CO10 9DP* – *on A 1092* – 𝒞 *(01787) 310 200* – *www.scutchers.com*
– Closed 2 weeks Christmas and Sunday-Wednesday

XX Black Lion

MODERN CUISINE · ROMANTIC First you must choose which of the three intimate rooms to dine in at this Georgian inn; then there's the huge array of menus to decide between. Cooking is rooted in the traditional British vein and dishes are full of flavour.

Menu £ 16 (weekdays) – Carte £ 29/38
Black Lion Hotel, Church Walk, The Green ⊠ *CO10 9DN* – 𝒞 *(01787) 312 356*
(booking advisable) – www.blacklionhotel.net

LONG SUTTON

Somerset – ⊠ Langport – Regional map n° **2**-B3
▶ London 131 mi – Bristol 39 mi – Cardiff 83 mi – Bournemouth 64 mi

🏠 Devonshire Arms

REGIONAL · INN Spacious Grade II listed hunting lodge set on the village green. The interior is contemporary, with a relaxing, open-plan bar and formal dining room. Locally sourced produce is used in seasonal European dishes. Comfortable bedrooms boast excellent quality linen and toiletries.

Carte £ 26/41
9 rooms 🖙 – 🛉£ 85/140 🛉🛉£ 100/145
⊠ *TA10 9LP* – 𝒞 *(01458) 241 271* – *www.thedevonshirearms.com* – *Closed 25-26 December*

LONG WHATTON

Leicestershire – Pop. 1 124 – Regional map n° **9**-B2
▶ London 120 mi – Birmingham 43 mi – Liverpool 101 mi – Leeds 84 mi

🏠 Royal Oak

BRITISH TRADITIONAL · PUB A smartly modernised pub in a sleepy village not far from East Midlands Airport. Menus offer plenty of choice, from sharing platters and pub favourites to ambitious main courses; some with Indian or Italian influences. Well-equipped, up-to-date bedrooms are in an adjacent block; one has a whirlpool bath.

Menu £ 16 (weekday dinner) – Carte £ 22/40
7 rooms 🖙 – 🛉£ 75/99 🛉🛉£ 75/99
The Green ⊠ *LE12 5BD* – 𝒞 *(01509) 843 694*
– www.theroyaloaklongwhatton.co.uk

LONGHORSLEY – Northumberland → See Morpeth

LONGPARISH
Hampshire – Regional map n° **4**-B2
▶ London 67 mi – Bristol 86 mi – Cardiff 119 mi – Plymouth 152 mi

🏷 Plough Inn
BRITISH MODERN · PUB An appealing country inn where the focus is firmly on the food. Skilful cooking has a classic heart and a modern edge. The bar menus offer pub classics and steaks to share, while the à la carte features more refined, elaborate dishes.
Carte £ 28/41
✉ SP11 6PB – ✆ (01264) 720 358 – www.theploughinn.info – Closed Sunday dinner and Monday

LONGSTOCK
Hampshire – ✉ Stockbridge – Regional map n° **4**-B2
▶ London 74 mi – Bristol 77 mi – Cardiff 110 mi – Plymouth 148 mi

🏷 Peat Spade Inn
BRITISH TRADITIONAL · PUB Charming 19C inn set in the heart of the Test Valley, with period furnishings, warming fires, welcoming candlelight and a country pursuits theme. Menus offer generous, classically based dishes with bold flavours and a refined style. Stylish bedrooms are split between the inn and annexe; the residents' lounge overlooks the garden and its sunken fire-pit.
Menu £ 23 – Carte £ 32/42
8 rooms ⌂ – †£ 110/145 ††£ 110/145
Village St ✉ SO20 6DR – ✆ (01264) 810 612 (booking advisable) – www.peatspadeinn.co.uk – Closed 25 December

LONGTOWN
Cumbria – Regional map n° **12**-A1
▶ London 326 mi – Carlisle 9 mi – Newcastle upon Tyne 61 mi

🏠 Bessiestown Farm
TRADITIONAL · PERSONALISED Converted farmhouse with spacious, comfortable bedrooms, set on a 150 acre sheep farm close to the English-Scottish border. The light, airy conservatory overlooks a windswept garden. Homemade bread and preserves feature at breakfast. 2 course dinners by arrangement in the bright dining room.
5 rooms ⌂ – †£ 57 ††£ 90
Catlowdy ✉ CA6 5QP – Northeast : 8 mi by Netherby St on B 6318 – ✆ (01228) 577 219 – www.bessiestown.co.uk – Closed 25 December

LOOE
Cornwall – Pop. 5 112 – Regional map n° **1**-B2
▶ London 264 mi – Plymouth 23 mi – Truro 39 mi

🏠 Barclay House
HOLIDAY HOTEL · PERSONALISED Imposing, whitewashed Victorian house in an elevated position; sit on the terrace and take in the view. Guest areas mix the traditional and the modern. Room 7 has an attractive estuary vista and Room 9 boasts a balcony and a whirlpool bath.
12 rooms ⌂ – †£ 55/90 ††£ 80/170 – 1 suite
St Martins Rd, East Looe ✉ PL13 1LP – East : 0.5 mi by A 387 on B 3253 – ✆ (01503) 262 929 – www.barclayhouse.co.uk
Barclay House – See restaurant listing

🏠 Beach House

FAMILY · HOMELY Detached house in a fantastic location, looking out to sea. Personally run, with immaculately kept bedrooms; Fistral, with its balcony and sea views, is the best. In-house beauty therapist; treatments by appointment.

5 rooms ☑ – ♥£60/100 ♥♥£80/130

Marine Dr, Hannafore ☒ PL13 2DH – Southwest : 0.75 mi by Quay Rd – ℰ (01503) 262 598 – www.thebeachhouselooe.co.uk – Closed Christmas

XX Barclay House

MODERN CUISINE · DESIGN Modern restaurant in a hillside hotel; its impressive terrace offering extensive views of the estuary. Seasonal dishes feature seafood from the day boats. Choose from the à la carte or a 6 course tasting menu with matching wine flights.

Menu £ 32/39

Barclay House Hotel, St Martins Rd, East Looe ☒ PL13 1LP – East : 0.5 mi by A 387 on B 3253 – ℰ (01503) 262 929 – www.barclayhouse.co.uk – dinner only – Closed Sunday

LORTON

Cumbria – Regional map n° **12**-A2

▶ London 302 mi – Carlisle 33 mi – Lancaster 71 mi

🏠 New House Farm

TRADITIONAL · COSY Part-17C former farmhouse complete with several beamed, open-fired lounges, a hot tub boasting fell views and a tea room in the old cow byres. Richly furnished bedrooms have king or super king sized beds and some feature double jacuzzis; the annexe rooms are the best. Meals are cooked on the Aga.

5 rooms ☑ – ♥£50/70 ♥♥£100/180

☒ CA13 9UU – South : 1.25 mi on B 5289 – ℰ (0784) 115 98 18 – www.newhouse-farm.co.uk

LOSTWITHIEL

Cornwall – Pop. 2 659 – Regional map n° **1**-B2

▶ London 244 mi – Bristol 148 mi – Cardiff 179 mi – Plymouth 32 mi

XX Asquiths

MODERN CUISINE · INTIMATE Smartly converted shop with exposed stone walls hung with modern Cornish art, funky lampshades and contemporary styling. Confidently executed dishes feature some original flavour combinations. The atmosphere is relaxed and intimate.

Carte £ 27/34

19 North St ☒ PL22 0EF – ℰ (01208) 871 714 – www.asquithsrestaurant.co.uk – dinner only – Closed first 2 weeks January, Sunday and Monday

LOUGHBOROUGH

Leicestershire – Pop. 59 932 – Regional map n° **9**-B2

▶ London 117 mi – Birmingham 41 mi – Leicester 11 mi

XX John's House ⑭ (John Duffin)

🕸 **MODERN CUISINE · RUSTIC** A 16C farmhouse where the eponymous and talented John was born and now cooks; his family also own the surrounding farm with its shop, café, petting farm and motor museum. Produce from the surrounding fields is used to create original, interesting dishes which show a real understanding of textures and flavours.

→ Ravioli of egg yolk, chestnuts and truffle. Fillet of cod, crab, cauliflower, lemon and roast chicken jus. Carrot sorbet with yoghurt, liquorice and mint.

Menu £ 24 (weekday lunch)/70

Stonehurst Farm, 139 Loughborough Rd, Mountsorrel ☒ LE12 7AR – Southeast : 4.5 mi by A 6 – ℰ (01509) 415 569 (booking essential at dinner) – www.johnshouse.co.uk – Closed Sunday and Monday

X **Blacksmiths Arms** Ⓝ   🕭 🅿

TRADITIONAL CUISINE · FRIENDLY A former pub and, before that, a black-smith's forge, built in 1753; now a stylish eatery with a sunny terrace, friendly service and a laid-back feel. Menus include all the favourites and cooking is straight-forward, fresh and tasty.

Carte £ 19/40

North St, Barrow-upon-Soar ⊠ LE12 8PP – Southeast : 3 mi by A 6 – ℰ (01509) 413 100 – www.blacksmiths1753.co.uk – Closed Sunday dinner and Monday

LOUTH

Lincolnshire – Pop. 16 419 – Regional map n° **9**-D1

▶ London 156 mi – Boston 34 mi – Grimsby 17 mi – Lincoln 26 mi

🏠 **Brackenborough**   🌳 🍴 🛉 🐾 🅿

BUSINESS · STYLISH Contemporary hotel with a relaxed feel and a warm, personal style. Spacious, individually designed bedrooms have bold feature walls, Egyptian cotton linen and the latest mod cons; executive rooms come with ja-cuzzi baths. The bistro and conservatory lounge-bar serve grills and classics with a modern twist.

24 rooms ⌂ – **†**£ 97/122 **††**£ 112/135

Cordeaux Corner, Brackenborough ⊠ LN11 0SZ – North : 2 mi by A 16 – ℰ (01507) 609 169 – www.oakridgehotels.co.uk

LOVINGTON

Somerset – Regional map n° **2**-C2

▶ London 126 mi – Bristol 30 mi – Taunton 33 mi

X **Pilgrims**   🍴 🅿

BRITISH MODERN · RUSTIC Cosy, hugely characterful restaurant with low-beamed ceilings, flagged floors and a roaring fire; run by a passionate husband and wife team. Well-prepared, classical dishes are made with quality local pro-duce. Comfortable, contemporary bedrooms, luxurious bathrooms and substantial breakfasts.

Carte £ 26/43

5 rooms ⌂ – **†**£ 70/120 **††**£ 80/120

⊠ BA7 7PT – ℰ (01963) 240 597 – www.thepilgrimsatlovington.co.uk – dinner only and lunch Friday-Saturday – Closed January, Sunday and Monday

LOW FELL

Tyne and Wear – Regional map n° **14**-B2

▶ London 272 mi – Newcastle upon Tyne 5 mi – Durham 15 mi

🏠 **Eslington Villa**   🌳 🍴 🐾 🅿

TRADITIONAL · PERSONALISED Comprising two red-brick Victorian houses in the city suburbs. It's well-run by its hand-on owners and has a relaxed atmo-sphere and a surprisingly large rear garden. Individually styled bedrooms have a contemporary edge. Dine from a traditional menu with modern twists in the din-ing room or conservatory.

18 rooms ⌂ – **†**£ 80/85 **††**£ 95/100

8 Station Rd ⊠ NE9 6DR – West : 0.75 mi by Belle Vue Bank, turning left at T junction, right at roundabout then taking first turn right – ℰ (0191) 487 60 17 – www.eslingtonvilla.co.uk – Closed 25-26 December and 1 January

LOW ROW – North Yorkshire → See Reeth

LOWER BEEDING

West Sussex – Regional map n° **4**-D2

▶ London 40 mi – Brighton 20 mi – Guildford 25 mi – Southampton 67 mi

⌂⌂⌂ South Lodge   🛜 🐾 ≼ 🛌 🖼 ⅃₅ ⌘ 🖵 ⅄ 🏊 🅿

LUXURY · HISTORIC Intricate carved fireplaces and ornate ceilings are on display in this Victorian mansion, which affords superb South Downs views from its 93 acres. Bedrooms are beautifully appointed; those in the wing are larger with feature bathrooms.

84 rooms 🖵 – 🛉£ 195/350 🛉🛉£ 195/350 – 4 suites

Brighton Rd ⊠ RH13 6PS – South : 1.5 mi by B 2110 on A 281 – ℰ (01403) 891 711
– www.southlodgehotel.co.uk – Closed 1-14 January

   ❀ **The Pass • Camellia** – See restaurant listing

XX The Pass   🛌 ⅄ 🅿

❀ **CREATIVE · DESIGN** A unique hotel restaurant where every table is the chef's table! High level chairs and banquettes are arranged around a glass-walled kitchen, and TVs screening live kitchen action are mounted on the walls. Expect beautifully presented, intricate modern dishes in balanced, well-thought-out combinations.
→ Mushroom, chocolate and finger lime. Pork with pear and pesto. Honeycomb, soy, bee pollen.

Menu £ 28/95 – set menu only

South Lodge Hotel, Brighton Rd ⊠ RH13 6PS – South : 1.5 mi by B 2110 on A 281
– ℰ (01403) 891 711 (number of covers limited, pre-book)
– www.southlodgehotel.co.uk – Closed first 2 weeks January, Monday and
Tuesday

XX Camellia   ≼ 🛌 🛋 🅿

MODERN CUISINE · ELEGANT Named after the tree which covers the front of the house, Camellia occupies three wood-panelled rooms with grand fireplaces and chandeliers. Refined modern dishes are light but boldly flavoured, and use produce from the walled garden.

Menu £ 20/38 – Carte £ 44/66

South Lodge Hotel, Brighton Rd ⊠ RH13 6PS – South : 1.5 mi by B 2110 on A 281
– ℰ (01403) 891 711 – www.exclusivehotels.co.uk – Closed 1-14 January

ᛒ Crabtree   🛌 🛋 ⅄ 🅿

TRADITIONAL CUISINE · PUB A family-run affair with a cosy, lived-in feel, warming fires and cheery, helpful staff. Traditional English dishes come with a touch of refinement and plenty of flavour, and the wine list is well-priced and full of helpful information.

Carte £ 18/37

Brighton Rd ⊠ RH13 6PT – South : 1.5 mi by B 2110 on A 281 – ℰ (01403) 892 666
– www.crabtreesussex.com – Closed Sunday dinner

> **On a budget? Take advantage of lunchtime prices.**

LOWESTOFT

Suffolk – Pop. 70 945 – Regional map n° **8**-D2
▶ London 116 mi – Ipswich 43 mi – Norwich 30 mi

🏨 Britten House   ⇐ 🛋 🕸 🅿

HOLIDAY HOTEL · CLASSIC Fine brick-built Victorian house overlooking the promenade; the birthplace of Benjamin Britten in 1913. Classically furnished bedrooms are named after composers; choose Mozart or Elgar, both of which have sea views.

10 rooms ⬓ – ♥£ 60/75 ♥♥£ 75/95

21 Kirkley Cliff Rd ⊠ *NR33 0DB –* ℰ *(01502) 573 950 – www.brittenhouse.co.uk*

LUDLOW

Shropshire – Pop. 10 515 – Regional map n° **10**-B2
▶ London 162 mi – Birmingham 39 mi – Hereford 24 mi

🏨 Fishmore Hall   ✿ 🕭 ⇐ 🛋 🖾 🛎 🕭 🅿

COUNTRY HOUSE · STYLISH Whitewashed Georgian mansion in half an acre of mature gardens, just out of town. Original features mix with modern fittings to create a boutique country house feel. Smart bedrooms have bold wallpapers, stylish bathrooms and good views.

15 rooms ⬓ – ♥£ 110/210 ♥♥£ 150/250

Fishmore Rd ⊠ *SY8 3DP – North : 1.5 mi by B 4361 and Kidderminster rd on Fishmore Rd –* ℰ *(01584) 875 148 – www.fishmorehall.co.uk*

Forelles – See restaurant listing

🏨 Overton Grange   ✿ 🕭 ⇐ 🛋 🖾 🏠 🛎 🅿

TRADITIONAL · CLASSIC Well-maintained Edwardian country house where subtle modern touches sit alongside original features. Well-equipped bedrooms and smart bathrooms. Good-sized pool, sauna and 2 treatment rooms. Dining rooms offer immaculately laid tables and countryside views; cooking has a refined French base.

14 rooms ⬓ – ♥£ 99/149 ♥♥£ 129/199

Old Hereford Rd ⊠ *SY8 4AD – South : 1.75 mi on B 4361 –* ℰ *(01584) 873 500 – www.overtongrangehotel.com – Closed 28 December-9 January*

🏨 Dinham Hall   ✿ 🛋 🕸 🛎 🅿

TOWNHOUSE · CLASSIC 18C former schoolhouse with a pretty walled garden, set overlooking the castle. Cosy guest areas are filled with antiques and ornaments. Comfy, traditionally styled bedrooms display original features and come with good mod cons. The bistro-style conservatory serves classic British dishes given a modern twist.

13 rooms ⬓ – ♥£ 99/199 ♥♥£ 129/249

Town plan: Z-b – *Dinham* ⊠ *SY8 1EJ –* ℰ *(01584) 876 464 – www.dinhamhall.com*

✕✕ Mr Underhill's at Dinham Weir (Chris Bradley)   ⊞ ⇐ ⇐ 🛋
❀ MODERN CUISINE · INTIMATE Smart, comfortable restaurant   ⤳ 🛖 🅿

in a stunning location by the weir. Traditionally based menus showcase superlative ingredients in skilfully and accurately prepared dishes, where natural flavours take the lead. Be sure to start your meal with drinks on the pretty terrace. Stylish bedrooms are all 'spa' suites and boast steam showers and garden views.

➜ Hake with ras el hanout crumb, chorizo and broad beans. Fillet of venison with beetroot and venison cannelloni, caper and raisin jus. Caramelised lemon tart with orange and thyme ice cream.

Menu £ 70 – set menu only

4 rooms ⬓ – ♥£ 195/325 ♥♥£ 225/360

Town plan: Z-f – *Dinham* ⊠ *SY8 1EH –* ℰ *(01584) 874 431 (booking essential) – www.mr-underhills.co.uk – dinner only – Closed 2 weeks June, 2 weeks October, Christmas, New Year, Monday and Tuesday*

LUDLOW

✗✗ **Forelles**   ≤ ⇔ 🏡 & ⑩ 🅿

MODERN CUISINE · DESIGN Attractive conservatory restaurant named after the pear tree outside, with lovely views over the hotel gardens. Attractively presented dishes use local produce and modern techniques, and feature good flavour and texture combinations.

Menu £ 49

Fishmore Hall Hotel, Fishmore Rd ⊠ SY8 3DP
- *North : 1.5 mi by B 4361 and Kidderminster rd on Fishmore Rd*
- *✆ (01584) 875 148 - www.fishmorehall.co.uk*
- *Closed Sunday dinner, Monday and lunch Tuesday*

XX Old Downton Lodge N

MODERN CUISINE · RURAL Supremely characterful farm buildings, dating from medieval to Georgian times and set on the 5,500 acre Downton Estate. Cooking is modern and original; choose from a 5 or 7 course menu in the 13C barn. Bedrooms combine period features with modern amenities; 7 and 8, with their antique four-posters, are best.

Menu £ 45/55 – set menu only

10 rooms ☲ – ♦£ 125/250 ♦♦£ 125/250

Downton on the Rock ✉ SY8 2HU – West : 7.5 mi by A 49, off A 4113
– ℰ (01568) 771 826 (booking essential) – www.olddowntonlodge.com – dinner only – Closed 24-27 December, February, Sunday and Monday

X French Pantry

FRENCH · COSY Pretty little café-cum-bistro on a paved side street, selling produce and wines imported from Parisian markets. Authentic French dishes are crafted from local and Gallic ingredients. Cooking is rustic, hearty and full of flavour.

Menu £ 26 (dinner) – Carte lunch £ 25/33

Town plan: Z-r – *15 Tower St. ✉ SY8 1RL*
– ℰ (01584) 879 133 (booking essential) – www.thefrenchpantry.co.uk
– Closed 1-5 January and Sunday

X Green Café

BRITISH MODERN · SIMPLE A modest little eatery with a delightful waterside terrace, set in a charming 14C watermill on the banks of the River Teme. The concise lunch menu offers unfussy daily dishes which showcase British ingredients in simple, flavoursome combinations. Outside of lunch hours they serve coffee and cake.

Carte £ 15/24

Town plan: Z-f – *Mill on the Green ✉ SY8 1EG*
– ℰ (01584) 879 872 (booking advisable) – www.thegreencafe.co.uk – lunch only
– Closed 23 December-13 February and Monday

Ⓘ Charlton Arms

BRITISH TRADITIONAL · FRIENDLY Claude Bosi is arguably the man who put Ludlow on the map and this pub in a commanding position on the banks of the River Teme is owned by his brother Cedric and Cedric's wife, Amy. Menus have something for everyone and dishes are good value and full of flavour. Up-to-date bedrooms; most have river outlooks.

Carte £ 20/34

9 rooms ☲ – ♦£ 80/100 ♦♦£ 90/120

Town plan: Z-x – *Ludford Bridge ✉ SY8 1PJ*
– ℰ (01584) 872 813 – www.thecharltonarms.co.uk
– Closed 25-26 December

at Cleestanton Northeast: 5.5 mi by A4117 and B4364

⌂ Timberstone

COUNTRY HOUSE · PERSONALISED This pair of cosy 17C cottages offer a wonderfully peaceful atmosphere and lovely rural views. Beamed bedrooms come with stylish modern bathrooms; one room even has its own balcony. Dine around the large farmhouse table – there's always a good selection, which includes many organic or home-grown options.

4 rooms ☲ – ♦£ 60 ♦♦£ 95

✉ SY8 3EL – ℰ (01584) 823 519 – www.timberstoneludlow.co.uk

LUND

East Riding of Yorkshire – Regional map n° **13**-C2
▣ London 213 mi – Leeds 61 mi – Sheffield 64 mi – Bradford 67 mi

🍴 **Wellington Inn** 🛋 ♿ 🅿

BRITISH TRADITIONAL · FRIENDLY Well-run pub with beamed, open-fired bars and more formal, linen-laid dining rooms. Experienced kitchen uses quality ingredients in dishes that are generous, both in flavour and portion. Efficient service. Good selection of Yorkshire beers.

Carte £ 30/40

19 The Green ✉ YO25 9TE – ℰ (01377) 217 294 – www.thewellingtoninn.co.uk – Closed 25 December, 1 January and Monday

LUPTON – Cumbria ➜ See Kirkby Lonsdale

LURGASHALL

West Sussex – Regional map n° **4**-C2

▶ London 49 mi – Bristol 124 mi – Cardiff 157 mi – Plymouth 197 mi

🏠 **Barn at Roundhurst** ♤ 🍃 � 🦉 🅿

HISTORIC · ELEGANT Beautifully restored, mid-17C threshing barn, on a 250 acre organic farm in the South Downs. The spacious lounge features fresh flowers, sculptures and modern art. Meals use eggs and meats from the farm, along with other local ingredients. Bedrooms, in the old outbuildings, are stylish and modern, and come with homemade biscuits, iPod docks and luxurious bathrooms.

6 rooms 🍵 – 🛏£ 120/200 🛏🛏£ 130/200

Lower Roundhurst Farm, Jobson's Ln ✉ GU27 3BY – Northwest : 3 mi by Haslemere rd – ℰ (01428) 642 535 – www.thebarnatroundhurst.com

🍴 **Noah's Ark Inn** 🚪 🛋 🅿

TRADITIONAL CUISINE · COSY Quintessentially English pub in a picturesque location right on the village green, overlooking the cricket pitch. Gloriously rustic interior with an inglenook and exposed beams. Wide-ranging menus; tasty, generously proportioned dishes.

Carte £ 25/37

The Green ✉ GU28 9ET – ℰ (01428) 707 346 – www.noahsarkinn.co.uk

Is breakfast included? If it is, the cup symbol 🍵 appears after the number of rooms.

LUTON

Luton – Pop. 211 228 – Regional map n° **7**-A2

▶ London 35 mi – Cambridge 36 mi – Ipswich 93 mi – Oxford 45 mi

🏰 **Luton Hoo**

GRAND LUXURY · HISTORIC Stunning 18C house in over 1,000 acres of gardens; some designed by Capability Brown. The main mansion boasts an impressive hallway, numerous beautifully furnished drawing rooms and classical, luxurious bedrooms. The marble-filled Wernher restaurant offers sophisticated modern cuisine. The old stable block houses the smart spa and the casual, contemporary brasserie.

135 rooms 🍵 – 🛏£ 185/340 🛏🛏£ 185/340 – 9 suites

The Mansion House ✉ LU1 3TQ – Southeast : 2.5 mi by A 505 on A 1081 – ℰ (01582) 734 437 – www.lutonhoo.com

LYDDINGTON – Rutland ➜ See Uppingham

LYDFORD

Devon – ✉ Okehampton – Pop. 1 734 – Regional map n° **1**-C2

▶ London 234 mi – Exeter 33 mi – Plymouth 25 mi

🍴 Dartmoor Inn

BRITISH MODERN · PUB Rustic pub with a shabby-chic style. Low ceilings add a cosy feel, while artwork provides a modern touch. Classic dishes are satisfying and full of flavour and there is an emphasis on local produce; Devon Ruby Red beef and dishes from the charcoal grill are the specialities. Spacious, elegant bedrooms.

Menu £ 13 (weekdays) – Carte £ 19/41

3 rooms ⌁ – †£ 85/100 ††£ 100/160

Moorside ✉ *EX20 4AY – East : 1 mi on A 386 –* ✆ *(01822) 820 221*
– www.dartmoorinn.com – Closed Sunday dinner and Monday

LYME REGIS

Dorset – Pop. 4 712 – Regional map n° **2**-B3
▶ London 160 mi – Dorchester 25 mi – Exeter 31 mi – Taunton 27 mi

🏨 Alexandra

FAMILY · MODERN 18C dower house with superb views over the Cobb and out to sea. There's a small terrace and a lookout tower (for hire) in the lovely gardens. The lounges and bedrooms are contemporary; No.12 has a large bay window to take in the views. Modern menus are served in the formal restaurant and conservatory.

26 rooms ⌁ – †£ 93 ††£ 185/250

Pound St ✉ *DT7 3HZ –* ✆ *(01297) 442 010 – www.hotelalexandra.co.uk*
– Closed 3-29 January

🏨 Hix Townhouse

TOWNHOUSE · STYLISH Georgian townhouse with stylishly understated bedrooms designed around various themes, including hunting and sailing; two rooms have lounges and two have terraces. There's a communal kitchen and breakfast is delivered in a hamper.

8 rooms ⌁ – †£ 125/165 ††£ 125/165

1 Pound St ✉ *D17 3HZ –* ✆ *(01297) 442 499 – www.hixtownhouse.co.uk*
– Closed January

✕ Hix Oyster & Fish House

FISH AND SEAFOOD · RUSTIC Modern, Scandic-style restaurant with a chef's table, a terrace and breathtaking views over Lyme Bay and the Cobb. Menus focus on the latest catch brought in by the day boats and dishes have a likeable simplicity. Service is charming.

Menu £ 17 (weekdays) – Carte £ 25/45

Lister Gdns, Cobb Rd ✉ *DT7 3JP –* ✆ *(01297) 446 910 (booking essential)*
– www.hixoysterandfishhouse.co.uk – Closed 3-29 January, 25-26 December, Monday and dinner Sunday November-March

LYMINGTON

Hampshire – Pop. 15 218 – Regional map n° **4**-A3
▶ London 103 mi – Bournemouth 18 mi – Southampton 19 mi – Winchester 32 mi

🏨 Stanwell House

TRADITIONAL · PERSONALISED Attractive 18C house in the town centre, run by a friendly owner. Tastefully designed bedrooms are comfy and well-equipped; those in the original house are the most characterful and those in the extension are more contemporary. Dine in the smart seafood restaurant, the rustic bistro or the trendy wine bar.

29 rooms ⌁ – †£ 99/145 ††£ 109/145 – 1 suite

14-15 High St ✉ *SO41 9AA –* ✆ *(01590) 677 123*
– www.stanwellhouse.com

🏠 Mill at Gordleton

TRADITIONAL · CLASSIC Charming, part-17C creeper-clad water mill with delightful terraces and colourful gardens. The comfy country house interior shows an eye for detail and bedrooms are extremely cosy. Have snacks in the bar or more substantial modern dishes in the restaurant; in summer, take afternoon tea by the river.

8 rooms 🖙 – †£ 135/275 ††£ 150/275 – 2 suites

Silver St, Hordle ⊠ SO41 6DJ – Northwest : 3.5 mi by A 337 off Sway Rd
– ℰ (01590) 682 219 – www.themillatgordleton.co.uk – Closed 25 December

XX Elderflower

MODERN CUISINE · FAMILY Their motto is 'quintessentially British, with a sprinkling of French', and that's just what you'll find at this proudly run restaurant. Cooking is playful and imaginative, with elderflower always featuring somewhere on the menu. Bedrooms are simply appointed and the quay is just a stone's throw away.

Menu £ 42 – Carte £ 30/47

3 rooms 🖙 – †£ 69/79 ††£ 89/99

4-5 Quay St ⊠ SO41 3AS – ℰ (01590) 676 908 – www.elderflowerrestaurant.co.uk
– Closed 24 January-7 February, Sunday dinner and Monday

at Downton West: 3 mi on A337⊠ Lymington

🏠 Olde Barn

FAMILY · CLASSIC This attractively converted 17C barn houses a traditional lounge and a communal breakfast room. Homely, cottage-style bedrooms are spotlessly kept – they are located in a smart red-brick building which was once the dairy.

3 rooms 🖙 – †£ 50/70 ††£ 50/75

Christchurch Rd ⊠ SO41 0LA – East : 0.5 mi on A 337 – ℰ (01590) 644 939
– www.theoldebarn.co.uk

LYMM

Warrington – Pop. 11 608 – Regional map n° **11**-B3
▶ London 190 mi – Liverpool 26 mi – Leeds 62 mi – Sheffield 68 mi

🍴 Church Green

BRITISH MODERN · PUB Double gable-fronted Victorian pub beside Lymm Dam, with a smart interior, an attractive terrace and a kitchen garden. Appealing menu includes 'pub classics' and 'steak house' sections: choose a cut, then add sauce, garnish and extras.

Carte £ 26/51

Higher Ln ⊠ WA13 0AP – on A 56 – ℰ (01925) 752 068 (booking essential)
– www.thechurchgreen.co.uk – Closed 25 December

LYNDHURST

Hampshire – Pop. 2 347 – Regional map n° **4**-A2
▶ London 95 mi – Bournemouth 20 mi – Southampton 10 mi – Winchester 23 mi

🏠 Lime Wood

BUSINESS · STYLISH Impressive Georgian mansion with a stunning spa topped by a herb garden roof. Stylish guest lounges have quality fabrics and furnishings; one is set around a courtyard and features a retractable glass roof. Beautifully furnished bedrooms boast luxurious marble-tiled bathrooms, and many have New Forest views.

32 rooms – †£ 315/950 ††£ 315/950 – 🖙 £ 19 – 14 suites

Beaulieu Rd ⊠ SO43 7FZ – Southeast : 1 mi by A 35 on B 3056 – ℰ (023)
8028 7177 – www.limewoodhotel.co.uk

Hartnett Holder & Co – See restaurant listing

✕✕ Hartnett Holder & Co

ITALIAN · INDIVIDUAL Elegant restaurant in an impressive Georgian mansion, offering views out over the delightful grounds. A central bar divides the room into several different dining areas; sit on the sofas, at the bar counter or in leather tub chairs. The tempting, Italian-based menu features home-smoked charcuterie.

Menu £ 20 (lunch)/55 – Carte £ 25/53

Lime Wood Hotel, Beaulieu Rd ⊠ SO43 7FZ – Southeast : 1 mi by A 35 on B 3056
– 𝒞 (023) 8028 7177 – www.limewood.co.uk

LYNMOUTH – Devon ➜ See Lynton

LYNTON
Devon – Pop. 1 157 – Regional map n° **1**-C1
▶ London 206 mi – Exeter 59 mi – Taunton 44 mi

⌂ Hewitt's - Villa Spaldi

HISTORIC · CLASSIC Splendid cliffside Arts and Crafts house in mature gardens. Antique-furnished bedrooms have up-to-date facilities, sea views and smart modern bathrooms. Informal weekday meals in wood-panelled bar; fine dining on Friday and Saturday evenings. High tea, with its homemade scones and excellent tea selection, is a must and the terrace is a delightful spot for breakfast.

8 rooms ⌂ – ♦£ 70/90 ♦♦£ 100/180
North Walk ⊠ EX35 6HJ – 𝒞 (01598) 752 293 – www.hewittshotel.com
– Closed October-March

⌂ St Vincent

TRADITIONAL · PERSONALISED Whitewashed, Grade II listed Georgian House in the village centre, 200m from the coastal path. Lovely fire-lit lounge with an honesty bar and well-kept, uncluttered bedrooms with smart bathrooms. Simple home-cooked meals use local produce where possible and tea and cakes are served outside when it's sunny.

7 rooms ⌂ – ♦£ 43/70 ♦♦£ 75/85
Market St, Castle Hill ⊠ EX35 6JA – 𝒞 (01598) 752 720
– www.st-vincent-hotel.co.uk

⌂ Castle Hill

FAMILY · PERSONALISED Stone-built house on the main street of this popular tourist village. Spacious, simply decorated bedrooms; 3 of the 7 have their own sitting area. Lounge with plenty of local info and a large fish tank. Friendly owners.

7 rooms ⌂ – ♦£ 50/75 ♦♦£ 70/95
Castle Hill ⊠ EX35 6JA – 𝒞 (01598) 752 291 – www.castlehill.biz

at Lynmouth East: 1 mi

⌂ Shelley's

TRADITIONAL · COSY A bright, keenly run hotel overlooking the sea; the eponymous poet honeymooned here in 1812. Traditionally styled guest areas include a homely lounge and a formally laid breakfast room with coastal views. Good-sized bedrooms.

11 rooms ⌂ – ♦£ 85/125 ♦♦£ 85/125
8 Watersmeet Rd ⊠ EX35 6EP – 𝒞 (01598) 753 219 – www.shelleyshotel.co.uk
– Closed November-February

at Martinhoe West: 4.25 mi via Coast rd (toll) – ⊠ Barnstaple

⌂ Old Rectory

TRADITIONAL · STYLISH Built in the 19C for a rector of Martinhoe's 11C church, this quiet country retreat is in a charming spot, with a well-tended 3 acre garden and a cascading brook. Fresh, bright bedrooms are modern, yet retain period touches: Heddon and Paddock are two of the best. Comfortable dining room; simple home-cooking.

11 rooms (dinner included) ⌂ – ♦£ 165/210 ♦♦£ 220/270
⊠ EX31 4QT – 𝒞 (01598) 763 368 – www.oldrectoryhotel.co.uk
– Closed November-March

LYTHAM ST ANNE'S

Lancashire – Pop. 42 953 – Regional map n° **11**-A2

▶ London 237 mi – Blackpool 7 mi – Liverpool 44 mi – Preston 13 mi

🏨 Rooms

TOWNHOUSE · DESIGN Mid-Victorian terrace on the approach road into this delightful estuary town. Striking, contemporary bedrooms come with good mod cons. Room One (on the top floor) is the largest, with a stone bath as part of the room. Bounteous breakfasts.

5 rooms ⌂ – ♦£ 90/100 ♦♦£ 110/140

35 Church Rd, Lytham ✉ FY8 5LL – ℰ (01253) 736 000
– www.theroomslytham.com

at St Anne's

🏨 Grand

FAMILY · DESIGN Keenly run by an experienced local hotelier: the most architecturally pleasing building on the promenade. Contemporary interior with Victorian stained glass windows and a grand staircase still in situ. Stylish, modern bedrooms.

76 rooms ⌂ – ♦£ 80/250 ♦♦£ 80/250

South Promenade ✉ FY8 1NB – ℰ (01253) 643 424 – www.the-grand.co.uk
– Closed 23-27 December

Cafe Grand – See restaurant listing

XX Cafe Grand

INTERNATIONAL · TRENDY Contemporary hotel restaurant with a fun, friendly atmosphere and a circular bar counter off to one side. Menus offer an interesting mix of Mediterranean dishes and modern-classics, including tapas and dishes 'a la plancha'.

Carte £ 27/48

Grand Hotel, South Promenade ✉ FY8 1NB – ℰ (01253) 643 409
– www.the-grand.co.uk – Closed 23-27 December

MADINGLEY – Cambridgeshire ➡ See Cambridge

MAENPORTH BEACH – Cornwall ➡ See Falmouth

MAIDENCOMBE – Torbay ➡ See Torquay

MAIDENHEAD

Windsor and Maidenhead – Pop. 63 580 – Regional map n° **6**-C3

▶ London 33 mi – Oxford 32 mi – Reading 13 mi

🏨 Fredrick's

BUSINESS · CLASSIC It's hard to imagine that this smart red-brick hotel – with its stylish spa – was once an inn. It's classically styled, with a marble reception, a clubby bar and a formal restaurant serving modern French dishes. Bedrooms have panelled walls and bespoke wooden furnishings, and most overlook the gardens.

36 rooms ⌂ – ♦£ 109/179 ♦♦£ 129/249 – 1 suite

Town plan: X-c *– Shoppenhangers Rd ✉ SL6 2PZ – ℰ (01628) 581 000*
– www.fredricks-hotel.co.uk

XX Boulters Riverside Brasserie

BRITISH MODERN · BRASSERIE Stylish modern eatery beside a lock, on a small island in the Thames. Full-length windows open onto the terrace and it boasts excellent river views. Hearty yet refined brasserie classics use quality produce.

Menu £ 16 (lunch) – Carte £ 26/43

Town plan: V-x *– Boulters Lock Island ✉ SL6 8PE – ℰ (01628) 621 291*
– www.boultersrestaurant.co.uk – Closed 27-30 December and Sunday dinner

MAIDENHEAD

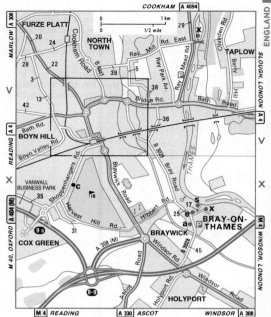

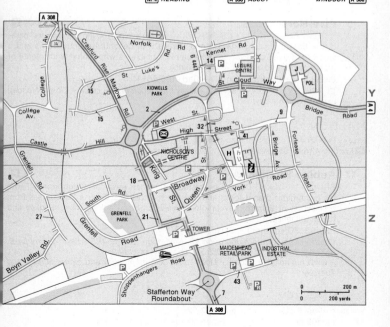

🏠 **Crown** 🖨 🅿

🍴 **REGIONAL · RUSTIC** Local drinkers fill the small bar, which leads to two intimate, open-fired dining rooms. The experienced chef-owner takes his cooking very seriously – the pub is closed on Mondays so he can visit his suppliers personally. Cooking is diverse; the appealing, flavoursome dishes are chalked on the board daily.

Carte £22/33

Burchett's Green ⊠ SL6 6QZ – West : 4 mi by A 4, A 404 and Burchett's Green Rd – ✆ (01628) 824 079 – www.thecrownburchettsgreen.com – Closed first 2 weeks August, Christmas, Sunday dinner,Wednesday lunch and Monday-Tuesday

MAIDEN NEWTON

Dorset – Regional map n° **2**-C3

▶ London 144 mi – Bristol 93 mi – Cardiff 113 mi – Southampton 66 mi

✗✗ **Le Petit Canard**

BRITISH TRADITIONAL · COSY This double-fronted former shop has a welcoming feel, with its cosy beamed interior and flickering candlelight. Run by a husband and wife team, it offers a seasonal menu of classic dishes; tasty duck and homemade bread feature.

Menu £29/34

Dorchester Rd ⊠ DT2 0BE – ✆ (01300) 320 536 – www.le-petit-canard.co.uk – dinner only and Sunday lunch – Closed 2 weeks January, Sunday dinner, alternate Sunday lunch and Monday

MAIDENSGROVE

Oxfordshire – ⊠ Henley-On-Thames – Pop. 1 572 – Regional map n° **6**-C3

▶ London 43 mi – Oxford 23 mi – Reading 15 mi

🏠 **Five Horseshoes** 🖨 🎱 🅿

BRITISH TRADITIONAL · NEIGHBOURHOOD Charming 17C inn – a walkers' paradise – boasting a large garden and terrace with delightful country views and a wood-fired oven used for bespoke pizzas. Cooking is wholesome, with plenty of meaty dishes and a good value set lunch.

Menu £13 (weekday lunch) – Carte £23/44

⊠ RG9 6EX – ✆ (01491) 641 282 – www.thefivehorseshoes.co.uk – Closed Monday except bank holidays

MALDON

Essex – Pop. 21 462 – Regional map n° **6**-C2

▶ London 42 mi – Chelmsford 9 mi – Colchester 17 mi

✗✗ **Rubino Kitchen** 🗔 🅿

BRITISH MODERN · COSY Tiny restaurant hidden away on Chigborough Farm; it's much older than it looks and has a rustic cosiness. Choose 2-5 courses from a selection of 9 fresh, flavoursome, weekly dishes. Cooking mixes English and Italian influences.

Menu £30 (dinner) – Carte £16/43

Chigborough Farm, Chigborough Rd, Heybridge ⊠ CM9 4RE – East : 2.5 mi by B 1022 off B 1026 – ✆ (01621) 855 579 (booking essential) – www.rubinokitchen.co.uk – Light Lunch Closed Monday and dinner Sunday and Tuesday

MALMESBURY

Wiltshire – Pop. 6 318 – Regional map n° **2**-C2

▶ London 108 mi – Bristol 28 mi – Gloucester 24 mi – Swindon 19 mi

Whatley Manor

LUXURY · CONTEMPORARY Charming Cotswold stone country house in 12 acres of beautiful formal gardens. Guest areas include a delightful wood-panelled sitting room, a stunning spa, a top class business centre and a private cinema. Luxurious, individually decorated bedrooms have a chic, contemporary feel and sumptuous bathrooms.

23 rooms ☐ – ♦£ 315/895 ♦♦£ 315/895 – 8 suites
Easton Grey ✉ *SN16 ORB – West : 2.25 mi on B 4040 – ℰ (01666) 822 888
– www.whatleymanor.com*
❀❀ **The Dining Room • Le Mazot** – See restaurant listing

Old Bell

HISTORIC · CLASSIC Characterful creeper-clad property beside a beautiful abbey; built in 1220 and reputedly the oldest hotel in England. The cosy beamed interior has parquet floors, open fires and smart feature bedrooms; the uniform annexe rooms are simpler.

34 rooms ☐ – ♦£ 90/99 ♦♦£ 115/275
Abbey Row ✉ *SN16 OBW – ℰ (01666) 822 344 – www.oldbellhotel.com*
Old Bell – See restaurant listing

The Dining Room

❀❀ **MODERN CUISINE · ELEGANT** Sophisticated country house restaurant overlooking the kitchen garden. Original modern dishes demonstrate the technical skill of the chefs, who have an excellent appreciation of ingredients and a superb understanding of combinations. Clearly defined flavours are complemented by interesting, top quality wines.
➔ Breast and leg of quail with Morteau sausage. Turbot with oyster and lime cannelloni, cucumber jelly and champagne caviar sauce. White chocolate sphere with pistachio kirsch mousse and cherry compote.

Menu £ 110 **s** – set menu only
Whatley Manor Hotel, Easton Grey ✉ *SN16 ORB – West : 2.25 mi on B 4040
– ℰ (01666) 822 888 (booking essential) – www.whatleymanor.com – dinner only
– Closed Monday and Tuesday*

Old Bell

MODERN CUISINE · ELEGANT Elegant, formal dining room in a charming 13C hotel, with old portraits and mirrors hung on modern aubergine walls. Menus offer ambitious modern dishes with a classical base. Start with a drink in the contemporary lounge-bar.

Carte £ 27/44
Old Bell Hotel, Abbey Row ✉ *SN16 OBW – ℰ (01666) 822 344 (booking essential
at dinner) – www.oldbellhotel.com*

Le Mazot

MODERN CUISINE · RUSTIC The less formal dining option at a delightful country hotel. With a comfy laid-back feel, wood panelling and carvings, it brings to mind a traditional Swiss chalet. Dishes have a modern edge and feature the occasional Swiss speciality.

Menu £ 19 (weekday lunch) – Carte £ 30/50 **s**
Whatley Manor Hotel, Easton Grey ✉ *SN16 ORB – West : 2.25 mi on B 4040
– ℰ (01666) 822 888 – www.whatleymanor.com*

at Crudwell North: 4 mi on A429 – ✉ Malmesbury

The Rectory

COUNTRY HOUSE · CONTEMPORARY Classical 18C former rectory with high ceilings, period features and a laid-back feel. Stylish fabrics and contemporary furnishings in the lounge and bar. Bedrooms boast bold feature walls, iPod docks, Roberts radios and some antiques. Oak-panelled dining room offers carefully cooked modern dishes.

12 rooms ☐ – ♦£ 95/205 ♦♦£ 105/205
 ✉ *SN16 9EP – ℰ (01666) 577 194 – www.therectoryhotel.com*

🍴 **Potting Shed Pub**   🛋 🏠 ⇔ 🅿

REGIONAL · COSY Spacious, light-filled pub with contemporary décor, exposed beams and a relaxing feel. Monthly changing menus offer wholesome, satisfying dishes, with vegetables and herbs from their garden.

Carte £ 24/33

The Street ✉ SN16 9EW – ✆ (01666) 577 833
– www.thepottingshedpub.com

MALPAS

Cheshire West and Chester – Pop. 3 684 – Regional map n° **11**-A3
▶ London 177 mi – Birmingham 60 mi – Chester 15 mi – Shrewsbury 26 mi

🏠 **Tilston Lodge**   🛏 🌳 🅿

TRADITIONAL · PERSONALISED Victorian hunting lodge with colourful gardens and welcoming owners. Classical bedrooms feature objets d'art and offer country views; two have four-posters. Spacious lounge and breakfast room. Juices are made from their home-grown apples.

3 rooms 🖾 – ♦£ 55/60 ♦♦£ 90/110

Tilston ✉ SY14 7DR – Northwest : 3 mi on Tilston Rd
– ✆ (01829) 250 223

MALTBY

Stockton-on-Tees – Regional map n° **14**-B3
▶ London 251 mi – Liverpool 141 mi – Leeds 69 mi – Sheffield 101 mi

🍴 **Chadwicks Inn**   🛋 🏠 🍽 🅿
🐾

BRITISH TRADITIONAL · NEIGHBOURHOOD This pub dates back over 200 years and was a favourite haunt of the Spitfire pilots before their missions. The à la carte menu features ambitious, intricate dishes and is supplemented by a good value set selection. The live acoustic evenings are popular, as are the wine and tapas evenings.

Menu £ 14 (weekday lunch)/28 – Carte £ 31/43

High Ln ✉ TS8 0BG – ✆ (01642) 590 300 (booking advisable)
– www.chadwicksinnmaltby.co.uk – Closed 26 December, 1 January and Monday except bank holidays

MALTON

North Yorkshire – Pop. 4 888 – Regional map n° **13**-C2
▶ London 234 mi – Pickering 9 mi – Scarborough 23 mi

🏠 **Talbot**   🏠 🛏 ⅃ 🅿

HISTORIC · CLASSIC Early 17C hunting lodge owned by the Fitzwilliam Estate, featuring an impressive wooden staircase and country house style guest areas filled with family artefacts and portraits. Traditional bedrooms have smart marble bathrooms.

26 rooms 🖾 – ♦£ 125/325 ♦♦£ 125/325 – 2 suites

Yorkersgate ✉ YO17 7AJ – ✆ (01653) 639 096 – www.talbotmalton.co.uk
Wentworth – See restaurant listing

XX **Wentworth**   🛏 ⅃ 🅿

BRITISH MODERN · FORMAL Grand country house restaurant with an elegant chandelier, heavy drapes and fine paintings. Good quality local and estate ingredients feature in carefully prepared, classically based dishes. Service is amiable, from a charming team.

Carte £ 32/43

Talbot Hotel, Yorkersgate ✉ YO17 7AJ – ✆ (01653) 639 096 (booking advisable)
– www.talbotmalton.co.uk

🍴 New Malton

BRITISH TRADITIONAL · PUB 18C stone pub with open fires, reclaimed furniture and photos of old town scenes. A good-sized menu offers hearty pub classics with the odd more adventurous dish thrown in; cooking is unfussy and flavour-some with an appealing Northern bias.

Carte £ 19/39

2-4 Market Pl ✉ YO17 7LX – ℰ (01653) 693 998 – www.thenewmalton.co.uk
– Closed 25-26 December and 1 January

at Burythorpe South: 4.25 mi by Pocklington rd

🏠 Burythorpe House   ✿ 🌳 🛏 ↻ ℀ ℀ 🅿

COUNTRY HOUSE · COSY Victorian country house set in 1.5 acres. Lovely large drawing room with open fire and oil paintings. Spacious, uniquely furnished bed-rooms come with a host of extras; some are classically styled, others, more mod-ern. Traditional cooking served in oak-panelled dining rooms.

14 rooms ☑ – ✝£ 85/185 ✝✝£ 95/205

✉ YO179LB – ℰ (01653) 658 200 – www.burythorpehouse.co.uk

MALVERN WELLS – Worcestershire ➜ See Great Malvern

MAN (Isle of)

I.O.M. – Pop. 80 058 – Regional map n° **11**-B1

Ballasalla

🍴 Abbey   🛏 🛋 ↻ 🅿

BRITISH MODERN · FRIENDLY An appealing former pub that was once a judge's house and a jam factory. Inside it's a cosy mix of the old and new; outside, a de-lightful terrace overlooks the abbey gardens. Careful modern British cooking showcases homemade produce.

Menu £ 40 – Carte £ 18/56

Rushen Abbey, Mill Rd ✉ IM9 3DB – ℰ (01624) 822 393
– www.theabbeyrestaurant.co.im – Closed Monday October-April

Douglas

🏨 Claremont   ✿ ⇐ 🖻 ℀ 🛁

BUSINESS · FUNCTIONAL Smart, modern hotel made up of several Victorian seaside properties. Bedrooms have good quality dark wood furnishings, Hungar-ian duck feather pillows, superb wet rooms, and state-of-the-art TV and audio equipment. The large brasserie-style restaurant serves modern dishes, which are presented by a cheery team.

56 rooms ☑ – ✝£ 70/150 ✝✝£ 90/240

18-22 Loch Promenade ✉ IM1 2LX – ℰ (01624) 617 068 – www.claremont.im

🏨 Regency   ✿ ⇐ 🖻 ℀ 🛁

TRADITIONAL · PERSONALISED Restored Victorian townhouse featuring wood panelling, stained glass and a substantial collection of seascape watercolours. Bedrooms are well-equipped for business travellers and mobile phones and iPads are available on loan.

38 rooms ☑ – ✝£ 85/140 ✝✝£ 110/170 – 4 suites

Queens Promenade ✉ IM2 4NN – ℰ (01624) 680 680 – www.regency.im
Stephen Dedman - A Restaurant – See restaurant listing

🏨 Penta   🖻 ℀

BUSINESS · FUNCTIONAL Good value hotel with bay views and a complimentary shuttle bus to the financial district from 8-9.30am. Large, functional bedrooms are well-maintained. Guests have access to all of the Regency's facilities, includ-ing the restaurant.

23 rooms ☑ – ✝£ 50/100 ✝✝£ 62/120

Queens Promenade ✉ IM9 4NE – ℰ (01624) 680 680 – www.regency.im

⌂ Inglewood

TOWNHOUSE · FUNCTIONAL Modern hotel at the quieter end of the promenade; the front-facing rooms enjoy views over the bay. Spacious bedrooms have chunky, contemporary furnishings, leather armchairs and modern shower rooms. Well-stocked residents' bar.

16 rooms ⌑ – ♦£ 55/85 ♦♦£ 65/125

26 Palace Terr, Queens Promenade ✉ IM2 4NF – ℰ (01624) 674 734
– www.inglewoodhotel-isleofman.com – Closed 4 -15 November and Christmas-New Year

XXX Stephen Dedman - A Restaurant

TRADITIONAL CUISINE · INTIMATE Traditional oak-panelled hotel restaurant displaying a collection of original island pictures. The menu of the day is rooted in the classics, while the à la carte offers original modern dishes which arrive artistically presented.

Carte £ 33/57

Regency Hotel, Queens Promenade ✉ IM2 4NN – ℰ (01624) 680 680
– www.regency.im – dinner only

XX Portofino

INTERNATIONAL · DESIGN This proudly run restaurant is on the ground floor of a chic apartment block on the harbour's edge. Menus offer classical international dishes with lots of Italian choices and verbally presented specials. Tables are smartly laid.

Menu £ 12 (weekdays) – Carte £ 25/50

Quay West ✉ IM1 5AG – ℰ (01624) 617 755 – www.portofino.im – Closed 25 December, Saturday lunch and Sunday

XX Macfarlane's

BRITISH MODERN · COSY Small restaurant in the heart of town, run by a personable couple. Sit in high-sided booths or on tall banquettes. Unfussy menus rely on fresh local produce; the blackboard specials have fresh fish and shellfish to the fore.

Menu £ 15 (weekday lunch)/28 – Carte £ 27/50

24 Duke St ✉ IM1 2AY – ℰ (01624) 624 777 (booking essential)
– www.macfarlanes.im – dinner only and lunch Thursday-Friday – Closed 2 weeks early August, 1 week spring, 1 week Christmas-New Year, Sunday and Monday

X Tanroagan

FISH AND SEAFOOD · BISTRO Friendly restaurant off the quayside, with seafaring décor and a cosy feel. Fish from the island's day boats are simply cooked, making the most of their natural flavours. Portions are hearty; bread, desserts and ice creams are homemade.

Menu £ 15 (weekday lunch) – Carte £ 21/57

9 Ridgeway St ✉ IM1 1EW – ℰ (01624) 612 355 – www.tanroagan.co.uk – Closed 25-26 December and Sunday

Port Erin

⌂ Rowany Cottier

TRADITIONAL · CLASSIC Large, purpose-built house set close to Bradda Glen. Pleasant guest areas have views over Port Erin and the Calf of Man. Bedrooms are simple and well-kept. Locally sourced breakfasts feature homemade bread.

5 rooms ⌑ – ♦£ 50/70 ♦♦£ 84/90

Spaldrick ✉ IM9 6PE – ℰ (01624) 832 287 – www.rowanycottier.com – Closed November-March

Ramsey

⌂ River House

TRADITIONAL · PERSONALISED Attractive Georgian country house in an idyllic riverside setting; its bright, spacious interior filled with antique furnishings and objets d'art. Traditional bedrooms come with floral fabrics, knick-knacks and large baths.

4 rooms ⌑ – ♦£ 70/110 ♦♦£ 95/140

✉ IM8 3DA – North : 0.25 mi by A 9 turning left immediately after bridge
– ℰ (01624) 816 412 – www.theriverhouse-iom.com

GOOD TIPS!

The Manchester dining scene has exploded in recent years and now offers a vibrancy and diversity unrivalled outside of London. Sample tasty, authentic sushi in Umezushi: a tiny Japanese restaurant hidden under the railway arches, or enjoy the best of British at Damson restaurant, part of the Salford Quays – symbol of this cool city's continued regeneration.

© P. Frilet/hemis.fr

MANCHESTER

Greater Manchester – Pop. 510 746 – Regional map n° **11**-B2

▶ London 202 mi – Birmingham 86 mi – Glasgow 221 mi – Leeds 43 mi

Plans pages 568, 569, 570

Hotels

🏨 **Lowry**

LUXURY · DESIGN Modern and hugely spacious, with excellent facilities, an impressive spa and a minimalist feel: art displays and exhibitions feature throughout. Stylish bedrooms with oversized windows; some have river views. The airy first floor restaurant serves a wide-ranging menu.

165 rooms – ♦£ 119/739 ♦♦£ 119/739 – ☲ £ 22 – 7 suites

Town plan: CY-n – *50 Dearmans Pl, Chapel Wharf, Salford* ✉ *M3 5LH* – ℰ *(0161) 827 40 00* – *www.thelowryhotel.com*

🏨 **Radisson Blu Edwardian**

BUSINESS · STYLISH This 14 floor hotel cleverly incorporates the façade of the former Free Trade Hall and has a great pool and spa. Bedrooms are contemporary – some have part-covered verandas; the Valentino Suite is the best and offers superb views. Sultry 'Opus One' is popular for afternoon tea, cocktails and seasonal modern dinners. Informal 'Steak and Lobster' serves an all-day menu.

263 rooms ☲ – ♦£ 110/360 ♦♦£ 110/360 – 4 suites

Town plan: CZ-a – *Free Trade Hall, Peter St* ✉ *M2 5GP* – ℰ *(0161) 835 9929* – *www.radissonblu-edwardian.com*

LEEDS **M 60** A **A 56** (M 60, M 66) BURY **A 665**

MANCHESTER

1 km

1 mile

BURY

PRESTWICH

HEATON PARK

HEATON PARK

18

M 666

M 60

(M 61)

PRESTWICH

Scholes Lane

POL

A 6044

Sheepfoot

BOWKER VALE

Middleton

PRESTON **A 6**

Hilton Lane

New Road

Bury Road

Manchester Road

16

97

A 580

Chorley Road

A 572

A 6

Manchester Road

Worsley Road

Partington

Station Road

Bolton Road

Hospital Rd

Agecroft A 6044

PENDLEBURY

LIVERPOOL (M 60, M 62)

East Lancashire Road

SALFORD

A 6

Cromwell Road

A 576

Great Cheetham Street West

Great Clowes St.

55

A 6

20

A 5185

Claremont Rd

Old Road

Weaste Lane

Langworthy Rd

A 5186

Broad St.

105

15

M 602

A 57 **M 602**

32 ECCLES

LADYWELL

WEST ONE Eccles RETAIL PARK

WEASTE New

LANGWORTHY Road

Broadway

ANCHORAGE

3

35

S

A 6042

U

M

A 5063

Albion Way

M 602

A 57

87

WARRINGTON, (M 62)

Centenary Way

TRAFFORD PARK

A 576

Village Way

Way

A 5081

Trafford Road

MEDIA CITY UK

LOWRY CENTRE Tr.

SALFORD QUAYS

HARBOUR CITY

a

Jt Wharf Rd

EXCHANGE QUAY

POMONA

Regent Rd

Trafford Rd

Ordsall

CORNBROOK

39

48

A 56

A 57 (M)

Chorton Road

X

Barton

Park

B 5211

Dock Road

Mosley Road

Wharfside Way

M

h

M.U.F.C.

WHITE CITY RETAIL PARK

TRAFFORD BAR

Seymour Grove

Upper Chorlton Road

81

M 60

9

TRAFFORD

Barton

Stretford

Park Rd

A 5067

Talbot Rd

STRETFORD

OLD TRAFFORD

FIRSWOOD

Manchester Road

ALEXAN PA

LIVERPOOL, (M 61, M62)

Stretford Road

Urmston La

Sandy Lane

Chester Rd

66

STRETFORD

A 5145

Edge

LONGFORD PARK

CHORLTON-CUM-HARDY

A 6010

8

URMSTON

Eccles By-Pass

7

CHESTER RD

Wilbraham

Lane

High

Lane

A 5145

Z

ST WERBURGH'S ROAD

Mauldeth Road

A 6144

CHESTER, (M 6) **A 56**

M 60 STOCKPORT A

BIRMINGHAM, AIRPORT, (M 60, M 56, M 6)

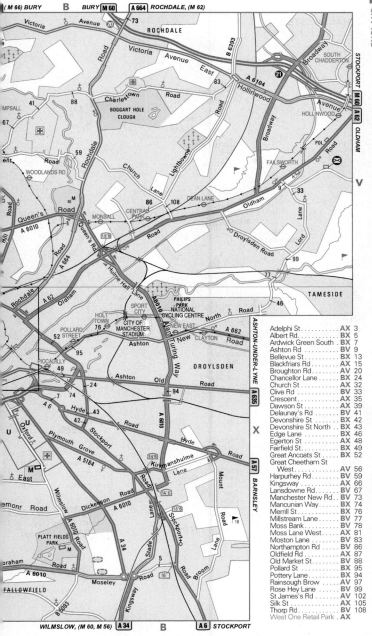

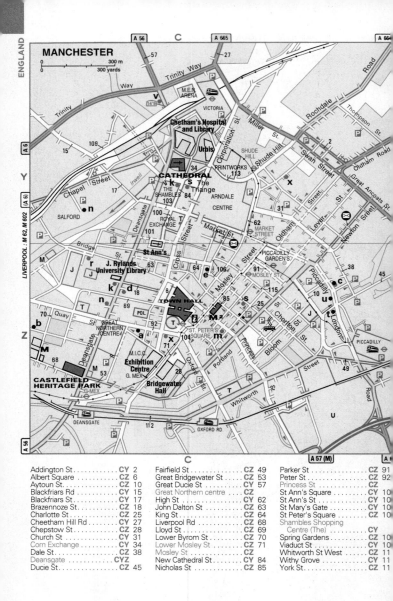

MANCHESTER

🏨 Malmaison   ✿ 🎢 🕹 💺 📶 ⏣ ✗ 🛁

LUXURY · STYLISH Old cotton warehouse and dolls hospital joined by a striking granite extension. Stylish bedrooms: some in dark, masculine shades; others in more subtle pastel hues. Uniquely designed suites include Man Utd and Man City themes. Smoak offers a menu inspired by American steakhouses.

167 rooms – ♂£ 99/199 ♂♂£ 99/199 – 🖵 £ 16 – 1 suite

Town plan: CZ-u – Piccadilly ✉ M1 3AQ – ✆ (0161) 278 10 00
– www.malmaison-manchester.com

🏨 Abode   ✿ 💺 🕹 📶 ✗ 🛁

BUSINESS · STYLISH This late Victorian former cotton merchant's HQ still has its iron columns and girders in situ. It has a boutique ambience with open-plan guest areas, modern bedrooms and stylish bathrooms; the 5th floor bedrooms are all suites.

61 rooms – ♂£ 79/250 ♂♂£ 79/250 – 🖵 £ 12

Town plan: CZ-c – 107 Piccadilly ✉ M1 2DB – ✆ (0161) 247 77 44
– www.abodehotels.co.uk

Michael Caines – See restaurant listing

🏨 Hotel Gotham 🅽   ✿ 💺 🕹 📶

LUXURY · ELEGANT This Grade II listed former bank has something of a Manhattan-style exterior, hence its name. Stylish modern bedrooms have black and white prints of Manchester and New York on the walls and some have projected 'wonderwalls' instead of windows. The delightful all-day dining room serves English classics.

60 rooms – ♂£ 129/350 ♂♂£ 129/350

Town plan: CZ-e – 100 King St ✉ M2 4WU – ✆ (0161) 357 5555
– www.hotelgotham.co.uk

🏨 Hotel Football 🅽   ✿ 💺 🕹 📶 ✗ 🅿

BUSINESS · MODERN Set in the shadow of Old Trafford; half of the stylish, well-equipped bedrooms have stadium views. Watch home and away games on huge plasma screens in the vast sport bar or, for an event, hire the 12th floor football pitch with a retractable roof. The modern bistro offers an all-purpose menu.

133 rooms 🖵 – ♂£ 89/315 ♂♂£ 99/325

Town plan: AX-h – 99 Sir Matt Busby Way ✉ M16 0SZ – ✆ (0161) 751 0430
– www.hotelfootball.com

🏨 Great John Street   🕹 💺 🕹 📶 ✗ 🛁 🚗

HISTORIC · CONTEMPORARY This stylish, boutique hotel was once a wonderful Victorian schoolhouse; you can hold a meeting in the old Headmaster's study! All of the bedrooms are duplex suites with roll-top baths. Relax on the roof terrace with its cocktail bar and hot-tub. There's no restaurant but they do offer room service.

30 rooms – ♂£ 108/402 ♂♂£ 108/402 – 🖵 £ 18

Town plan: CZ-b – Great John St ✉ M3 4FD – ✆ (0161) 831 3211
– www.greatjohnstreet.co.uk

🏨 Ainscow 🅽   ✿ 🛆 🕹 💺 🕹 🅿

BUSINESS · FUNCTIONAL Smart hotel set in an old brewery, in an up-and-coming part of town: the original building and an extension make for a pleasing mix of old and new. Bedrooms are state-of-the-art and many of the fabrics and furnishings are locally made; some of the duplex rooms have spiral staircases. Menus cover all bases.

71 rooms – ♂£ 109/199 ♂♂£ 109/199 – 🖵 £ 15

Town plan: AX-s – Trinty Way ✉ M3 5HY – ✆ (0161) 827 1650
– www.theainscow.com

🏨 DoubleTree by Hilton Manchester Piccadilly   ☆ 🛴 ⬚ ⬚   🆎 💱 ♨ 🚗

BUSINESS · MODERN Contemporary glass building with a spacious, airy interior and local art on display. Modern bedrooms boast pale hues, iMac computers and excellent entertainment facilities; showers only except top floor suites. Smart, stylish restaurant with an appealing, wide-ranging, modern menu.

285 rooms – ♦£ 79/225 ♦♦£ 79/225 – ⌂ £ 18 – 1 suite

Town plan: CZ-t – *One Piccadilly Pl, 1 Auburn St* ⊠ *M1 3DG* – ℰ *(0161) 242 10 00* – *www.manchesterpiccadilly.doubletree.com*

Restaurants

✖✖✖ The French by Simon Rogan   🆎

CREATIVE · ELEGANT Iconic restaurant with original ornate detailing, crystal chandeliers and an unusual carpet. Creative modern cooking showcases British ingredients, including some from Simon Rogan's own farm. Service is well-paced and knowledgeable.

Menu £ 50 (weekday lunch)/85 – set menu only

Town plan: CZ-x – *Midland Hotel. Peter St.* ⊠ *M60 2DS* – ℰ *(0161) 236 3333 (booking essential)* – *www.the-french.co.uk* – *Closed Sunday, Monday and lunch Tuesday*

✖✖✖ Wings   🏡 🆎

CHINESE · ELEGANT Well-run restaurant off a busy square. The narrow room features comfy booths, terracotta army replicas, Hong Kong skyline murals and celebrity-signed plates. Extensive menus offer authentic Cantonese dim sum; sea bass is a speciality.

Carte £ 20/61

Town plan: CZ-d – *1 Lincoln Sq* ⊠ *M2 5LN* – ℰ *(0161) 834 90 00 (booking essential at dinner)* – *www.wingsrestaurant.co.uk*

✖✖ Manchester House   🍷 🏡 ⬚ 🆎 🎦 ⬚

MODERN CUISINE · ELEGANT Step out the lift into this cool, industrial style restaurant with floor to ceiling windows. The passionate chef prepares inventive, playful dishes which feature lots of different ingredients; they serve only a tasting menu Sat eve.

Menu £ 28 (weekday lunch)/95 – Carte £ 52/67

Town plan: CZ-r – *Tower 12, 18-22 Bridge St* ⊠ *M3 3BZ* – ℰ *(0161) 835 25 57 (booking advisable)* – *www.manchesterhouse.uk.com* – *Closed 2 weeks January, 2 weeks August, 25-26 December, Sunday and Monday*

✖✖ 63 Degrees   ⬚ 🆎

FRENCH · INDIVIDUAL Family-run restaurant where iron pillars and bare bricks are juxtaposed with pretty French lampshades and patterned wallpapers. The experienced French chef prepares accomplished, classic dishes using ingredients from his homeland.

Menu £ 18 (weekdays)/25 – Carte £ 31/62

Town plan: CY-x – *104 High Street* ⊠ *M4 1HQ* – ℰ *(0161) 832 5438* – *www.63degrees.co.uk* – *Closed Monday*

✖✖ Michael Caines   🆎 🍽 ⬚

MODERN CUISINE · FASHIONABLE A lively modern restaurant in the basement of a stylish hotel, with subdued lighting and a sophisticated style. Contemporary cooking is largely British with some Mediterranean influences. The tasting menu also has wine suggestions.

Menu £ 23/60 – Carte £ 36/53

Town plan: CZ-c – *Abode Hotel, 107 Piccadilly* ⊠ *M1 2DB* – ℰ *(0161) 200 56 78* – *www.michaelcaines.co.uk* – *Closed Sunday and Monday*

XX Mr Cooper's

MODERN CUISINE · BRASSERIE This unique restaurant is inspired by Thomas Cooper's house and gardens, which stood here until 1819. Start with drinks in the 'library', then dine in the indoor 'garden'. Dishes are modern and flavoursome with global influences.

Menu £ 20 (weekday lunch)/24 – Carte £ 26/41

Town plan: CZ-x – *Midland Hotel, Peter St* ✉ *M60 2DS*
– ℰ *(0161) 932 4128* – *www.mrcoopershouseandgarden.co.uk*

XX Australasia

MODERN CUISINE · TRENDY Fun, fashionable basement restaurant on the site of the old Manchester Evening News; come for cocktails, small plates, sushi, designer styling, DJs and a clubby vibe. Vibrant dishes have European/Pacific Rim/Asian influences. Helpful staff.

Menu £ 45 (weekday lunch) – Carte £ 25/78

Town plan: CZ-k – *1 The Avenue, Spinningfields* ✉ *M3 3AP*
– ℰ *(0161) 831 0288* – *www.australasia.uk.com*
– *Closed 25-26 December and 1 January*

XX Yang Sing

CHINESE · FASHIONABLE Family-run Chinese restaurant spread over 4 floors of an imposing Victorian building, with a '1930s Shanghai' basement room, a classic ground floor and private rooms above. Authentic Cantonese cooking features tasty dim sum at lunch.

Menu £ 12 (weekday lunch)/18 – Carte £ 19/72

Town plan: CZ-m – *34 Princess St* ✉ *M1 4JY*
– ℰ *(0161) 236 22 00* – *www.yang-sing.com*
– *Closed 25 December*

XX San Carlo Bottega

ITALIAN · TAPAS BAR Take time out from shopping at Selfridges to relax in the elegant cocktail bar or long, brasserie-like dining room, which offers views across to the Cathedral. Tasty cicchetti dishes use fine Italian produce and arrive as they're ready.

Carte £ 20/30

Town plan: CY-s – *Selfridges (2nd floor), 1 Exchange Square Central* ✉ *M3 1BD*
– ℰ *(0161) 838 05 71* – *www.sancarlobottega.co.uk*
– *Closed 25 December*

X Second Floor Brasserie at Harvey Nichols

BRITISH MODERN · DESIGN Relaxed bar and brasserie with colour-changing lighting and a buzzy atmosphere; it's popular with shoppers and they don't take bookings at lunch, so arrive in good time. Brunch is followed by a selection of modern British dishes.

Carte £ 21/49

Town plan: CY-k – *21 New Cathedral St* ✉ *M1 1AD*
– ℰ *(0161) 828 88 98* – *www.harveynichols.com*
– *Closed 25 December, 1 January, Easter Sunday and dinner Sunday-Monday*

X Hawksmoor Manchester

MEATS · BISTRO A large former probate office with plenty of charm and character. Have a bespoke beer and snacks at the bar or head through to the high-ceilinged dining room. The bovine-based menu offers steaks for one or to share, from 500g-1kg.

Menu £ 29 – Carte £ 35/45

Town plan: CZ-n – *184-186 Deansgate* ✉ *M3 3WB*
– ℰ *(0161) 836 6980* – *www.thehawksmoor.com*

✗ Umezushi   ⅏ 🍴 ⅏

JAPANESE · NEIGHBOURHOOD A lovely little Japanese restaurant hidden under the railway arches, with a corrugated barrel ceiling, five light wood tables and counter seating for six. Tasty, unfussy dishes use good quality produce and arrive in no time.

Menu £ 30/42 – Carte £ 14/60

Town plan: CY-v – *4 Mirabel St* ✉ *M3 1PJ* – ℰ *(0161) 832 18 52*
– www.umezushi.co.uk – Closed Christmas-New Year, Monday and the last Sunday of every month

✗ Yuzu   🅰🅲

JAPANESE · SIMPLE Climb the steps to the upper floor of this converted Victorian warehouse, where you'll find an open kitchen, a counter and four communal tables. The Japanese cooking is fresh, authentic and healthy; the dumplings are delicious.

Carte £ 10/21

Town plan: CZ-s – *39 Faulkner St* ✉ *M1 4EE* – ℰ *(0161) 236 41 59 (bookings advisable at lunch) – www.yuzumanchester.co.uk – Closed Sunday and Monday*

at West Didsbury South : 4.75 mi by A 5103 – Plan: AX – ✉ Manchester

✗ Rose Garden ℕ

TRADITIONAL CUISINE · INDIVIDUAL This stylish little restaurant is a family project, with siblings and parents all involved, from the design and installation to the day-to-day running. Tasty modern dishes use top ingredients and there's a good value set menu Sun-Weds.

Menu £ 21 (weekdays) – Carte £ 29/38

218 Burton Rd ✉ *M20 2LW* – ℰ *(0161) 478 07 47*
– www.therosegardendidsbury.com – dinner only – Closed 25-26 December and 1 January

at Didsbury South: 5.5 mi by A5103 – Plan: AX – on A5145 – ✉ Manchester

🏨 Didsbury House   ⅃ 🅿

LUXURY · STYLISH Whitewashed Victorian villa – now a boutique townhouse – where original features include an impressive stained glass window. Bedrooms are stylish and well-appointed; some are duplex suites. There's no designated restaurant area but you can dine from an accessible menu in the bar, the lounges or your room.

27 rooms – ♟£ 73/120 ♟♟£ 73/120 – ⌧ £ 16 – 2 suites
Didsbury Pk ✉ *M20 5LJ* – *South : 1.5 mi on A 5145* – ℰ *(0161) 448 22 00*
– www.didsburyhouse.com

🏠 Eleven Didsbury Park   🚪 🅿

LUXURY · STYLISH Chic, comfortable townhouse in a pleasant residential setting. Contemporary bedrooms have warm décor and good facilities; many come with a bath tub beside the bed. Have breakfast in a simply furnished room overlooking the delightful garden. The informal all-day menu is available as room service only.

20 rooms – ♟£ 88/144 ♟♟£ 88/144 – ⌧ £ 16 – 1 suite
11 Didsbury Pk ✉ *M20 5LH* – *South : 1.5 mi by A 5145* – ℰ *(0161) 448 77 11*
– www.elevendidsburypark.com

at Salford Quays Southwest: 2.25 mi by A56 off A5063 – ✉ Manchester

✗✗ Damson   🍽 ⅏ ⅃ 🅰🅲 ⅏

MODERN CUISINE · FASHIONABLE Enter into the futuristic MediaCityUK – home of the BBC – and head for this smart first floor restaurant on the quay. The elaborate à la carte menu offers refined, modern dishes and the full-length windows afford great water views.

Menu £ 20/40 – Carte £ 37/48

Town plan: AX-a – *Orange Building, Media City* ✉ *M50 2HF* – ℰ *(0161) 751 70 20*
– www.damsonrestaurant.co.uk – Closed Sunday dinner

at Chorlton-Cum-Hardy Southwest: 4 mi by A5103 – Plan: AX – on A6010
– ✉ Manchester

🏠 Abbey Lodge

TOWNHOUSE · PERSONALISED Red-brick Edwardian house in the city suburbs; a 'wishing table' provides a splash of colour on the stairwell. Warm, homely bedrooms offer good facilities; Rooms 3 and 4 are the largest. Continental-style buffet in your room.

5 rooms ⌂ – ♦£ 50/70 ♦♦£ 75/95

Town plan: AX-z – *501 Wilbraham Rd* ✉ *M21 0UJ* – *℘ (0161) 862 92 66*
– *www.abbey-lodge.co.uk*

MANSFIELD

Nottinghamshire – Pop. 77 551 – Regional map n° **9**-B1
▶ London 143 mi – Chesterfield 12 mi – Worksop 14 mi

XX No.4 Wood Street

BRITISH TRADITIONAL · RUSTIC Modern restaurant on the first floor of a converted warehouse. Exposed stone walls and chunky wood furniture give it a rustic feel. Classical cooking has clearly defined flavours. Start with a speciality gin in the spacious lounge.

Carte £ 21/38

4 Wood St ✉ *NG18 1QA* – *℘ (01623) 424 824 (booking advisable)*
– *www.4woodstreet.co.uk* – *Closed Sunday dinner, Monday and Tuesday*

MARAZION

Cornwall – ✉ Penzance – Pop. 1 294 – Regional map n° **1**-A3
▶ London 318 mi – Penzance 3 mi – Truro 26 mi

🏠 Mount Haven

HOLIDAY HOTEL · PERSONALISED Small hotel overlooking St Michael's Bay, with a spacious bar and a lounge featuring Indian fabrics and artefacts. Contemporary bedrooms come with good modern amenities and most have a balcony and a view. Bright, attractive dining room offers elaborate modern dishes with ambitious flavour combinations.

18 rooms ⌂ – ♦£ 90/160 ♦♦£ 120/250

Turnpike Rd ✉ *TR17 0DQ* – *East : 0.25 mi* – *℘ (01736) 710 249*
– *www.mounthaven.co.uk* – *Closed 20 December-10 February*

X Ben's Cornish Kitchen

TRADITIONAL CUISINE · SIMPLE Rustic family-run eatery; sit upstairs for views over the rooftops to St Michael's Mount. Unfussy lunches are followed by sophisticated dinners, which feature some interesting flavour combinations. They offer 25 wines by the glass.

Menu £ 20 (lunch) – Carte dinner £ 25/38

West End ✉ *TR17 0EL* – *℘ (01736) 719 200* – *www.benscornishkitchen.com*
– *Closed 25-26 December, 1 January, Monday lunch and Sunday*

at Perranuthnoe Southeast: 1.75 mi by A394 – ✉ Penzance

🏠 Ednovean Farm

FAMILY · PERSONALISED 17C granite barn in a tranquil spot overlooking the bay and surrounded by 22 acres of sub-tropical gardens and paddocks. Individually styled bedrooms and locally produced toiletries; the Blue Room has a French bed, a roll-top bath and a terrace. Have a range-cooked breakfast at the oak table or a continental selection in your room. Complimentary sherry in the hall.

3 rooms ⌂ – ♦£ 100/134 ♦♦£ 110/140

✉ *TR20 9LZ* – *℘ (01736) 711 883* – *www.ednoveanfarm.co.uk* – *Closed Christmas*

🏠 **Victoria Inn** ⓝ ⇦ 🛋 **P**

CLASSIC CUISINE · PUB A well-established, bright pink pub, in a small village close to the sea; the owners are locals returned home. Menus stick mainly to the classics and fish, landed at nearby Newlyn, is in abundance. Be sure to save room for one of the tasty puddings! Cosy, unfussy bedrooms have a seaside feel.

Carte £ 25/35

2 rooms – 🛉£ 50 🛉🛉£ 75

✉ TR20 9NP – ✆ (01736) 710 309 – www.victoriapz.uk

– Closed 25 December and 1st January

MARGATE

Kent – Pop. 61 223 – Regional map n° **5**-D1

▶ London 74 mi – Canterbury 17 mi – Dover 21 mi – Maidstone 43 mi

🏨 **Sands** 🌣 ⇐ 🖃 🕭 🎬 ⚡ **P**

HISTORIC · STYLISH Set between the high street and the sea – a smartly refurbished hotel, with extremely stylish bedrooms. Have a cocktail in the white leather furnished lounge-bar overlooking the beach before watching the sun go down from the roof terrace. The brasserie serves modern British dishes and also shares the view.

20 rooms ☟ – 🛉£ 120/200 🛉🛉£ 120/200

16 Marine Dr ✉ CT9 1DH – (entrance on High St)

– ✆ (01843) 228 228 – www.sandshotelmargate.co.uk

🏠 **Crescent Victoria** ⓝ 🌣 ⇐

TOWNHOUSE · STYLISH Classic Georgian terraced house with pleasant views over the Winter Gardens and Margate Sands. Most of the bedrooms share the outlook and all are boldly decorated and come with quality linens and very comfortable beds. The modern cellar restaurant has a suntrap terrace and serves an all-encompassing menu.

14 rooms ☟ – 🛉£ 55/90 🛉🛉£ 90/130

25-26 Ford Cres ✉ CT9 1HX – ✆ (01843) 230 375

– www.crescentvictoria.co.uk

🏠 **Reading Rooms** ⚡

TOWNHOUSE · STYLISH Passionately run guesthouse with stripped plaster, worn woodwork and a unique shabby-chic style. Eclectic bedrooms – one per floor – boast distressed furniture, super-comfy beds and huge bathrooms. Extensive breakfasts served in your room.

3 rooms ☟ – 🛉£ 95/150 🛉🛉£ 95/180

31 Hawley Sq ✉ CT9 1PH – ✆ (01843) 225 166

– www.thereadingroomsmargate.co.uk

✗ **Ambrette Margate** 🕭 🍴 **P**

INDIAN · COSY Quirky restaurant with modest surroundings. The concise menu showcases Kentish produce in an original modern style; freshly prepared dishes offer well-balanced flavours and subtle Indian spicing – you won't find any curries here!

Menu £ 21 (lunch)/65 – Carte £ 25/40

44 King St ✉ CT9 1QE – ✆ (01843) 231 504

– www.theambrette.co.uk – Closed Monday in winter

MARKET DRAYTON

Shropshire – Pop. 11 773 – Regional map n° **10**-B1

▶ London 159 mi – Nantwich 13 mi – Shrewsbury 21 mi

ENGLAND

🏛 Goldstone Hall

TRADITIONAL · CLASSIC Attractive red-brick house with numerous extensions, surrounded by 5 acres of peaceful grounds. Lovely panelled drawing room and characterful beamed seating area with small bar. Classically styled bedrooms have plenty of space and pleasant country views. Modern menus feature kitchen garden produce.

12 rooms 🖙 – 🛉£ 90/110 🛉🛉£ 150/180

Goldstone ⊠ *TF9 2NA – South : 4.5 mi by A 529 – ℰ (01630) 661 202 – www.goldstonehall.com – Closed 26 December*

MARKET RASEN
Lincolnshire – Pop. 4 773 – Regional map n° **9**-C1
▶ London 158 mi – Nottingham 54 mi – Kingston upon Hull 37 mi – Sheffield 53 mi

🛏 Advocate Arms

BRITISH TRADITIONAL · INN Former hotel close to the market square, with an original revolving door and a smart, modern interior divided by etched glass walls. Lunch sticks to good old pub classics and at dinner, mature local steaks are a speciality; they also serve breakfast and afternoon tea. Bedrooms are spacious and well-equipped.

Menu £ 19 (weekdays) – Carte £ 20/43

10 rooms – 🛉£ 50/90 🛉🛉£ 50/130 – 🖙 £ 8

2 Queen St ⊠ *LN8 3EH – ℰ (01673) 842 364 – www.advocatearms.co.uk – Closed Sunday dinner except in December*

MARLBOROUGH
Wiltshire – Pop. 8 092 – Regional map n° **2**-D2
▶ London 84 mi – Bristol 47 mi – Southampton 40 mi – Swindon 12 mi

🍴 Coles

BRITISH MODERN · NEIGHBOURHOOD Cosy, buzzy bistro with a loyal local following. Two rooms feature an eclectic range of memorabilia – including architects' plans and vineyard maps. The menu is equally as diverse, with dishes ranging from fishcakes to monkfish 'ossobuco'.

Menu £ 16 (lunch) – Carte £ 21/42

27 Kingsbury Hill ⊠ *SN8 1JA – ℰ (01672) 515 004 – www.colesrestaurant.co.uk – Closed 25 December, Sunday and bank holidays except Good Friday*

at Little Bedwyn East: 9.5 mi by A4 ⊠ Marlborough

🍴🍴 Harrow at Little Bedwyn (Roger Jones)
❀ **MODERN CUISINE · FORMAL** Former pub with smartly laid tables and an intimate atmosphere. Flavourful, seasonal cooking is presented in a modern style, whilst still retaining a classical base; produce is top quality and fish plays an important role. The wine list is comprehensive and they also hold regular wine evenings.

→ Scallop carpaccio with caviar rocks and land & sea asparagus. Breast of English grey leg partridge, bon bons and its jus. Sweetcorn parfait, popcorn, caramel ice cream and toffee crisps.

Menu £ 40/75

⊠ *SN8 3JP – ℰ (01672) 870 871 – www.theharrowatlittlebedwyn.com – Closed 25 December-4 January and Sunday-Tuesday*

at West Overton West: 4 mi on A4

🛏 Bell

BRITISH MODERN · PUB A simple, friendly pub, rescued from oblivion by a local couple, who hired an experienced pair to run it. The menu mixes pub classics with Mediterranean-influenced dishes; presentation is modern but not at the expense of flavour.

Carte £ 24/45

Bath Rd ⊠ *SN8 1QD – ℰ (01672) 861 099 – www.thebellwestoverton.co.uk – Closed Sunday dinner and Monday except bank holidays*

at East Kennett West: 5.25 mi by A4

🏠 Old Forge   🚗 🅿

TRADITIONAL · COSY Take in pleasant country views from the family room, where the village blacksmith's once stood, or head out to the field in front to relax beside the riverbank. Bedrooms are comfortable and up-to-date; one has a small kitchenette.

4 rooms ⌂ – ♦£ 65/75 ♦♦£ 75/85

✉ SN8 4EY – ℰ (01672) 861 686 – www.theoldforge-avebury.co.uk – Closed 25-26 December

MARLDON

Devon – Pop. 1 906 – Regional map n° **1**-C2

▶ London 193 mi – Plymouth 30 mi – Torbay 3 mi – Exeter 23 mi

🍴 Church House Inn   🚗 🛗 🅿

MEDITERRANEAN · PUB Charming, well-run inn with wooden beams, open fires and original Georgian windows. Extensive choice on blackboard menus, with classically based dishes and some Mediterranean influences. Exotic theme nights and friendly, helpful service.

Carte £ 23/36

Village Rd ✉ TQ3 1SL – ℰ (01803) 558 279 – www.churchhousemarldon.com – Closed 25 December and dinner 26 December

MARLOW

Buckinghamshire – Pop. 14 823 – Regional map n° **6**-C3

▶ London 35 mi – Aylesbury 22 mi – Oxford 29 mi – Reading 14 mi

🏰 Danesfield House   🏦 🐾 ⬅ 🚗 🖼 🖥 ♨ ♨ 🍴 🎞 🧖 🛠 🅿

LUXURY · CLASSIC Stunning house built in Italian Renaissance style and affording breathtaking views of the Thames and the Chilterns. Bedrooms at the back are the best; most are traditional and some have four-poster beds. Unwind in the characterful guest areas or the smart spa, then dine in the intimate formal restaurant or charming orangery – the latter has a great garden outlook.

86 rooms ⌂ – ♦£ 139/264 ♦♦£ 179/264

Henley Rd ✉ SL7 2EY – Southwest : 2.5 mi on A 4155 – ℰ (01628) 891 010 – www.danesfieldhouse.co.uk

🏰 Compleat Angler   🏦 ⬅ 🚗 ♨ 🎞 🖼 🛠 🅿

TRADITIONAL · CLASSIC Well-kept hotel in an idyllic spot on the Thames, with views of the weir and the chain bridge. Comfy, corporate-style bedrooms blend classic furnishings with contemporary fabrics: some have balconies – go for a Feature Room. The restaurants offer modern British and South Indian cooking overlooking the river.

64 rooms ⌂ – ♦£ 150/300 ♦♦£ 170/320 – 3 suites

Marlow Bridge, Bisham Rd ✉ SL7 1RG – ℰ (0844) 879 9128 – www.macdonald-hotels.co.uk/compleatangler

Sindhu – See restaurant listing

✗✗ Vanilla Pod   🛗 🖼 🍽 ⇔

FRENCH · INTIMATE An intimate, well-established restaurant in T. S. Eliot's former home, featuring a plush interior and smartly laid tables. The chef works alone, cooking ambitious dishes with classical French foundations and original touches.

Menu £ 20/45 **s**

31 West St ✉ SL7 2LS – ℰ (01628) 898 101 (booking essential) – www.thevanillapod.co.uk – Closed 24 December-8 January, Sunday, Monday and bank holidays

ENGLAND

XX Sindhu ⇐ 🗚 ⑩ 🅿

INDIAN · INTIMATE Traditional stained glass and dark wood blend with bold modern fabrics in this glitzy waterside restaurant within a smart hotel. Authentic South Indian cooking is confidently spiced and features specialities from the tandoor oven.

Menu £ 19 (weekday lunch)/48 – Carte £ 34/60
Compleat Angler Hotel, Marlow Bridge, Bisham Rd ⊠ SL7 1RG
– 𝒞 (01628) 405 405 – www.sindhurestaurant.co.uk

🍴 Hand and Flowers (Tom Kerridge) ⇔ 🅿

🕸🕸 BRITISH MODERN · FRIENDLY A pretty little pub with low beams, flagged floors and a characterful lounge bar for pre and post-dinner drinks. Classic dishes display assured flavours, with quality ingredients marrying perfectly to turn the simple into the sublime. A lucky few get to dine without booking at the metal-topped bar counter. Bedrooms are beautifully furnished; some have outdoor jacuzzis.
➔ Potato "risotto" with baked potato stock, wild garlic and roast cep. Slow-cooked duck breast with Savoy cabbage, duck fat chips and gravy. Bitter orange soufflé with sweet toast crumb, cardamom ice cream and citrus syrup.

Menu £ 15 (weekday lunch) – Carte £ 46/68
8 rooms ⌑ – †£ 140/190 ††£ 140/190
126 West St. ⊠ SL7 2BP – 𝒞 (01628) 482 277 (booking essential)
– www.thehandandflowers.co.uk

🍴 The Coach 🗋 🍴

🕸 BRITISH MODERN · FRIENDLY Tom Kerridge's second pub offers a casual modern approach to dining. There are no starters or main courses, just flavoursome 'Meat' and 'No Meat' dishes that arrive as they're ready and are designed for sharing. Rotisserie dishes are a speciality and they also serve tasty breakfasts and coffee and cake.

Carte £ 15/36
3 West St ⊠ SL7 2LS (bookings not accepted)
– www.thecoachmarlow.co.uk – Closed 25 December

🍴 Royal Oak 🚗 🏡 🅿

BRITISH MODERN · PUB Part-17C, country-chic pub with a herb garden, a petanque pitch and a pleasant terrace. Set close to the M40 and M4, it's an ideal London-getaway. Cooking is British-led; wash down an ox cheek pasty with a pint of local Rebellion ale.

Carte £ 22/39
Frieth Rd, Bovingdon Green ⊠ SL7 2JF – West : 1.25 mi by A 4155
– 𝒞 (01628) 488 611 – www.royaloakmarlow.co.uk
– Closed 25-26 December

at Little Marlow East: 3 mi on A4155

🍴 Queens Head 🚗 🅿

BRITISH TRADITIONAL · FRIENDLY A charming 16C pub with a keen owner and friendly staff; popular with walkers. The light lunch menu offers sandwiches and pub classics; the regularly changing à la carte features produce from local farms, forages and shoots.

Menu £ 30 – Carte £ 23/37
Pound Ln ⊠ SL7 3SR – 𝒞 (01628) 482 927
– www.marlowslittlesecret.co.uk – Closed 25-26 December

MARPLE
Greater Manchester – Pop. 18 241 – Regional map n° **11**-B3
▶ London 190 mi – Chesterfield 35 mi – Manchester 11 mi

⌂ **Springfield** 🛏 ⌀ 🅿

TRADITIONAL · CLASSIC Personally run, part-Victorian house with sympathetic extensions and pleasant rural views. Bright breakfast room; individually styled bedrooms. Useful for visits to the Peak District.

8 rooms ☕ – 🛏£ 50/65 🛏🛏£ 65/85
99 Station Rd ⊠ SK6 6PA – ℰ (0161) 449 07 21
– www.springfieldhotelmarple.co.uk

MARSDEN
West Yorkshire – ⊠ Huddersfield – Pop. 3 499 – Regional map n° **13**-A3
▶ London 195 mi – Leeds 22 mi – Manchester 18 mi – Sheffield 30 mi

🍴 **Olive Branch** ⇔ 🛏 🏠 🅿

INTERNATIONAL · COSY Characterful drovers' inn with stone floors, rustic walls, a secluded garden and pleasant views from its terrace. The classical, French-influenced menu is supplemented by fish specials and there's a good choice of wines by the glass. Bedrooms are modern, cosy and individually themed.
Carte £ 23/45

3 rooms ☕ – 🛏£ 60/85 🛏🛏£ 80/180
Manchester Rd ⊠ HD7 6LU – ℰ (01484) 844 487 – www.olivebranch.uk.com
– dinner only – Closed Monday

MARTINHOE – Devon → See Lynton

MARTON
Shropshire – Regional map n° **10**-A2
▶ London 181 mi – Leeds 133 mi – Sheffield 132 mi – Manchester 95 mi

🍴 **Sun Inn** 🏠 🅿

TRADITIONAL CUISINE · PUB Welcoming country pub on the English-Welsh border, with a cosy bar and a brightly painted restaurant. The concise menu offers satisfying and comforting home-cooked dishes which include some great fish specials.
Carte £ 23/35

⊠ SY21 8JP – ℰ (01938) 561 211 – www.suninn.org.uk – Closed Sunday dinner, Monday and lunch Tuesday

MARTON CUM GRAFTON
North Yorkshire – Regional map n° **13**-B2
▶ London 206 mi – Birmingham 136 mi – Liverpool 103 mi – Leeds 28 mi

🍴 **Punch Bowl Inn** 🛏 🏠 ⇔ 🅿

BRITISH MODERN · RUSTIC Delightful inn, part-dating from the 14C; arrive early in summer to bag a seat on the terrace. All-encompassing, seasonal menu includes a seafood platter and a 'Yorkshire board', with excellent fish and chips and rib-eye steak to die for.
Carte £ 23/41

⊠ YO51 9QY – ℰ (01423) 322 519 – www.thepunchbowlmartoncumgrafton.com

MASHAM
North Yorkshire – ⊠ Ripon – Pop. 1 205 – Regional map n° **13**-B1
▶ London 231 mi – Leeds 38 mi – Middlesbrough 37 mi – York 32 mi

🏰 **Swinton Park** 🎾 ॐ ⇐ 🛏 🦢 🎬 ⊡ 🛗 🧖 🅿

HISTORIC · CLASSIC 17C castle with Georgian and Victorian additions, set on a 22,000 acre estate. The grand interior features open fires, ornate plasterwork, oil portraits and antiques. Try your hand at shooting, fishing, riding, falconry or cooking.

31 rooms ☕ – 🛏£ 195/460 🛏🛏£ 195/460 – 4 suites
Swinton ⊠ HG4 4JH – Southwest : 1 mi – ℰ (01765) 680 900
– www.swintonpark.com
Samuels – See restaurant listing

Bank Villa

TOWNHOUSE · CLASSIC Stone-built Georgian villa with a lovely stepped garden; the welcoming owners look after their guests well. Relax in one of two cosy lounges or the conservatory. Comfy bedrooms have modern feature walls; those in the eaves are the most characterful. Unfussy dinners. Homemade yoghurt features at breakfast.

5 rooms ☐ – †£ 50/65 ††£ 55/110

The Avenue ✉ HG4 4DB – *on A 6108* – ✆ *(01765) 689 605* – *www.bankvilla.com*

Samuels

BRITISH MODERN · FORMAL Beautiful rococo-style dining room with an ornate gilt ceiling and park views; set within a castle. Well-spaced tables are adorned with lilies. Complex modern cooking uses produce from the huge kitchen gardens and local suppliers.

Menu £ 28/65

Swinton Park Hotel, Swinton ✉ HG4 4JH – *Southwest : 1 mi* – ✆ *(01765) 680 900* – *www.swintonpark.com* – *dinner only and lunch Saturday-Sunday*

Vennell's

BRITISH TRADITIONAL · DESIGN This endearing, personally run restaurant has stylish purple walls, boldly patterned chairs and a striking feature wall – at weekends, sit downstairs amongst the local art for a more intimate experience. Seasonal menus offer 4 choices per course; cooking is well-judged, flavourful and has a modern edge.

Menu £ 28 **s**

7 Silver St ✉ HG4 4DX – ✆ *(01765) 689 000 (booking essential)* – *www.vennellsrestaurant.co.uk* – *dinner only and Sunday lunch* – *Closed first 2 weeks January, 1 week Easter, 1 week August, Sunday dinner and Monday*

MATFIELD

Regional map n° **5**-B2

▶ London 43 mi – Maidstone 15 mi – Royal Tunbridge Wells 6 mi

Wheelwrights Arms

BRITISH TRADITIONAL · RUSTIC 17C former Kentish farmhouse: outside it's all clapperboard and colourful flower baskets; inside it's rustic with low beamed ceilings crammed with hanging hops. Expect an abundance of local, seasonal produce in classic dishes.

Carte £ 24/42

The Green ✉ TN12 7JX – ✆ *(01892) 722 129* – *Closed Sunday dinner and Monday*

MATLOCK

Derbyshire – Pop. 14 956 – Regional map n° **9**-B1

▶ London 150 mi – Sheffield 23 mi – Derby 19 mi

Stones

BRITISH MODERN · NEIGHBOURHOOD Negotiate the steep steps down to this small riverside restaurant and head for the front room with its floor to ceiling windows. Unfussy, modern British dishes are attractively presented and display the odd Mediterranean touch.

Menu £ 18 (weekday lunch)/49

1C Dale Rd ✉ DE4 3LT – ✆ *(01629) 56 061 (booking advisable)* – *www.stones-restaurant.co.uk* – *Closed 25 December-2 January, Sunday, Monday and lunch Tuesday*

MAUNBY

North Yorkshire – Regional map n° **13**-B1

▶ London 358 mi – Northallerton 10 mi – Middlesbrough 46 mi

Buck Inn 🛜 ⟷ 🅿

BRITISH MODERN · PUB Well run pub with a characterful beamed bar and light and airy dining rooms. Creative, modern dishes are well-constructed and tasty. The weekday lunch and early dinner 'Market Menu' offers particularly good bang for your buck.

Menu £17 (lunch and early dinner) – Carte £24/64

✉ YO7 4HD – ℰ (01845) 587 777 – www.thebuckinnmaunby.co.uk – Closed 26 December, 1 January, Sunday dinner and Monday

MAWGAN PORTH – Cornwall ➡ See Newquay

MELLOR – Lancashire ➡ See Blackburn

MELLOR

Greater Manchester – Regional map n° **11**-B3
▶ London 185 mi – Bristol 163 mi – Cardiff 184 mi – Plymouth 277 mi

Oddfellows 🛜 🅿

BRITISH TRADITIONAL · PUB Oddies – as it is known locally – has a light, un-cluttered feel, with wood burning stoves adding an element of cosiness. The appealing, daily changing menu offers tasty, locally sourced 'British food with a modern twist'.

Carte £17/38

Moor End Rd ✉ SK6 5PT – ℰ (0161) 449 7826 – www.oddfellowsmellor.com – Closed Monday except bank holidays

MELLS

Somerset – Pop. 2 222 – Regional map n° **2**-C2
▶ London 117 mi – Bath 16 mi – Frome 3 mi

Talbot Inn ⟷ 🛜

BRITISH MODERN · RUSTIC Characterful 15C coaching inn with a cobbled courtyard, a cosy sitting room with an open fire, a snug bar offering real ales and an elegant Grill Room to keep carnivores happy at weekends. Delightful bedrooms are well-priced and understated in style. Food is seasonal, modern and full of flavour; and staff may be casually attired, but their manner is anything but.

Carte £21/36

8 rooms 🖵 – ♥£95/150 ♥♥£95/190

Selwood St ✉ BA11 3PN – ℰ (01373) 812 254 – www.talbotinn.com

MELPLASH

Dorset – Regional map n° **2**-B3
▶ London 147 mi – Yeovil 17 mi – Bridport 4 mi

Half Moon ⓝ 🛒 🛜 🅿

BRITISH TRADITIONAL · COSY Grade II listed village pub dating from the 17C, complete with a thatched roof, oak beams, cosy open fires and a friendly, welcoming team. Appealing British menus range from a traditional ploughman's to crispy rabbit croquettes.

Carte £21/33

✉ DT6 3UD – ℰ (01308) 488 321 – www.halfmoonmelplash.co.uk – Closed Sunday dinner and Monday except bank holidays

MELTON MOWBRAY

Leicestershire – Pop. 27 158 – Regional map n° **9**-B2
▶ London 113 mi – Leicester 15 mi – Northampton 45 mi – Nottingham 18 mi

🏨 Stapleford Park

HISTORIC · PERSONALISED Beautiful stately home in 500 acres of landscaped grounds, with grand drawing rooms, a lovely leather-furnished bar, exceedingly comfortable bedrooms and marble bathrooms. The extensive leisure facilities are a replica of those at Buckingham Palace! Ornate rococo dining room; mix of classic and modern dishes.

55 rooms ⌑ – ♦£ 180 ♦♦£ 240/490 – 3 suites
✉ LE14 2EF – East : 5 mi by B 676 on Stapleford rd – ☏ (01572) 787 000
– www.staplefordpark.com

MERE
Cheshire East – Regional map n° **11**-B3
▶ London 185 mi – Bristol 152 mi – Cardiff 173 mi – Plymouth 266 mi

🏨 Mere

COUNTRY HOUSE · CONTEMPORARY Red-brick house set in 150 acres, complete with a lake and a championship golf course. Spacious guest areas include numerous meeting rooms and a smart spa. Contemporary bedrooms offer the latest mod cons. Snacks in the spa and golf club; bistro-style menu in the glass-roofed courtyard restaurant.

81 rooms ⌑ – ♦£ 115/405 ♦♦£ 125/415 – 10 suites
Chester Rd ✉ WA16 6LJ – on A 556 – ☏ (01565) 830 155 – www.themereresort.co.uk

MEVAGISSEY
Cornwall – Pop. 2 117 – Regional map n° **1**-B3
▶ London 287 mi – Newquay 21 mi – Plymouth 44 mi – Truro 20 mi

🏠 Trevalsa Court

HOLIDAY HOTEL · STYLISH Charming Arts and Crafts style house which combines dark wood panelling and stone fireplaces with bright modern art and bold soft furnishings. Most of the well-appointed bedrooms have coastal views. The oak-panelled dining room looks onto the lovely terrace and garden and dishes showcase local produce.

14 rooms ⌑ – ♦£ 70/105 ♦♦£ 115/250
School Hill ✉ PL26 6TH – East : 0.5 mi – ☏ (01726) 842 468
– www.trevalsa-hotel.co.uk – Closed January and December

🏠 Pebble House 🆕

TOWNHOUSE · STYLISH This impressive three-storey property looks out over the bay to Chapel Point and all but one of its stylish, luxurious bedrooms share the view. Guests are welcomed with champagne and in summer they serve afternoon tea on the terrace. Breakfasts are extensive and the keen owners are very hands-on.

6 rooms ⌑ – ♦£ 120/210 ♦♦£ 120/210
Polkirt Hill ✉ PL26 6UX – South : 0.5 mi on Porthmellon rd – ☏ (01726) 844 466
– www.pebblehousecornwall.co.uk – Closed late November-Christmas

MICKLETON – Gloucestershire ➔ See Chipping Campden

MID LAVANT – West Sussex ➔ See Chichester

MIDDLESBROUGH
Middlesbrough – Pop. 174 700 – Regional map n° **14**-B3
▶ London 246 mi – Leeds 66 mi – Newcastle upon Tyne 41 mi

✗ Brasserie Hudson Quay

BRITISH TRADITIONAL · BRASSERIE Be sure to grab a window seat so that you can look out over Hudson Quay's old docks. Lunch offers snacks and a good value menu that's popular with local office workers, while dinner offers sharing plates and brasserie classics.

Menu £ 15 (weekday lunch) – Carte £ 21/45
Windward Way ✉ TS2 1QG – East : 0.5 mi by A 66 – ☏ (01642) 261 166
– www.brasseriehudsonquay.com

MIDDLETON-IN-TEESDALE
Durham – Pop. 934 – Regional map n° **14**-A3
▶ London 260 mi – Carlisle 91 mi – Leeds 124 mi – Middlesbrough 70 mi

🏠 Grove Lodge   ⚑ ← ⌕ 🅿 ⇥
COUNTRY HOUSE · COSY Old Victorian shooting lodge, perched on a hillside overlooking the valley; a place to relax and escape from technology. Traditional lounges are furnished with antiques and heavy fabrics. Neat, up-to-date bedrooms; some have private bathrooms. Home-cooked dinners are served in the formally laid dining room.

6 rooms 🖵 – †£ 55 ††£ 82

*Hude ⊠ DL12 0QW – Northwest : 0.5 mi on B 6277 – ℰ (01833) 640 798
– www.grovelodgeteesdale.co.uk*

MIDDLETON TYAS
North Yorkshire – Pop. 581 – Regional map n° **13**-B1
▶ London 235 mi – York 47 mi – Darlington 10 mi

XX The Coach House at Middleton Lodge 🄽   ⇦ ⌕ 🏠 ⅙ ⇧
BRITISH MODERN · DESIGN Stylishly converted coach house to a   🅿
Georgian mansion, where the owner grew up. The dining area is in the former stables and the bar is where the coaches once parked. Concise, constantly evolving menus feature produce from within 40 miles. Contemporary bedrooms come with roll-top baths and Roberts radios.

Carte £ 24/42

14 rooms 🖵 – †£ 135/195 ††£ 155/210

*Kneeton Ln ⊠ DL10 6NJ – Nortwest : 1 mi on Barton rd – ℰ (01325) 377 977
– www.middletonlodge.co.uk/coachhouse*

MIDHURST
West Sussex – Pop. 4 914 – Regional map n° **4**-C2
▶ London 57 mi – Brighton 38 mi – Chichester 12 mi – Southampton 41 mi

🏨 Spread Eagle   ⚑ 🏠 🔲 ⊕ 🎠 ⅙ ▵ 🅿
HISTORIC · RUSTIC Part-15C coaching inn retaining plenty of its original character and decked out with antiques, tapestries and gleaming brass – although there's also a modern, well-equipped spa. Bedrooms are traditional. Dine next to an inglenook fireplace under wooden beams and look out for the Christmas puddings too!

39 rooms 🖵 – †£ 89/329 ††£ 109/349 – 2 suites

South St ⊠ GU29 9NH – ℰ (01730) 816 911 – www.hshotels.co.uk

🏠 Church House 🄽   ⇦ ⌘
TOWNHOUSE · HOMELY An enthusiastically run townhouse; the main part dates from 1383 and features low beams and oak pillars. Bedrooms are quirky and luxurious; the best are 'Silver', with its slipper bath and 'Gaudi', with its vaulted ceiling and sleigh bed.

5 rooms 🖵 – †£ 95/140 ††£ 160/180

*Church Hill ⊠ GU29 9NX – ℰ (01730) 812 990 – www.churchhousemidhurst.com
– Closed Christmas*

at Henley North: 4.5 mi by A286

🏮 Duke of Cumberland Arms   ⇦ 🏠 🅿
MODERN CUISINE · COSY A hidden gem, with a delightfully low-beamed interior featuring a huge fireplace and flag floors; tiered gardens have babbling brooks, trout ponds and views over the Downs. Appealing, daily changing menu of carefully prepared, seasonal dishes; 2 courses at lunch and 3 at dinner. Charming service.

Carte £ 29/51

*⊠ GU27 3HQ – ℰ (01428) 652 280 – www.dukeofcumberland.com – Closed
25-26 December and dinner Sunday-Monday*

at Bepton Southwest: 2.5 mi by A286 on Bepton rd – ✉ Midhurst

🏛 Park House

COUNTRY HOUSE · STYLISH Family-run country house with a light modern style and smart spa and leisure facilities. Spacious, homely bedrooms are split between this and South Downs Cottage; they come in neutral hues and most have views of the well-tended gardens and golf course. The stylish conservatory restaurant serves modern menus.

21 rooms ⌑ – †£ 162/324 ††£ 162/324 – 1 suite

✉ GU29 0JB – ✆ (01730) 819 000 – www.parkhousehotel.com – *Closed 24-26 December*

at Redford Northwest: 4 mi by A272 then following signs for Redford

🏠 Redford Cottage

RURAL · HOMELY Hospitable owners welcome you to this charming 16C cottage, set in 3 acres of delightful gardens. Cosy beamed lounge with wood burner; traditionally furnished bedrooms. Aga-cooked breakfasts use local ingredients, with many homemade items.

3 rooms ⌑ – †£ 70 ††£ 95

✉ GU29 0QF – ✆ (01428) 741 242 – *Closed 23-27 December*

MILFIELD

Northumberland – Regional map n° **14**-A1

▶ London 336 mi – Glasgow 118 mi – Edinburgh 72 mi – Aberdeen 204 mi

🏨 Red Lion Inn

BRITISH TRADITIONAL · NEIGHBOURHOOD Set close to the Scottish border, this former coaching inn really is the heart of the village. It has a traditional look and feel, matched by a classical menu which makes good use of the larders of Scotland and England – and you definitely won't leave hungry! Bedrooms are homely; some are in wooden lodges.

Carte £ 16/28

5 rooms ⌑ – †£ 40 ††£ 75

Main Rd ✉ NE71 6JD – ✆ (01668) 216 224 *(booking advisable)* – www.redlionmilfield.co.uk – *Closed 1 January and 25 December*

MILFORD-ON-SEA

Hampshire – ✉ Lymington – Pop. 4 348 – Regional map n° **4**-A3

▶ London 109 mi – Bournemouth 15 mi – Southampton 24 mi – Winchester 37 mi

✗ Verveine

FISH AND SEAFOOD · FRIENDLY Bright, New England style restaurant fronted by a fishmonger's. Breads are baked twice-daily, veg is from the raised beds and smoking takes place on-site. The focus is on wonderfully fresh fish and cooking is accurate and original.

Menu £ 17 (lunch) – Carte £ 34/53

98 High St ✉ SO41 0QE – ✆ (01590) 642 176 – www.verveine.co.uk – *Closed Sunday and Monday*

MILSTEAD

Kent – Pop. 264 – Regional map n° **5**-C1

▶ London 46 mi – Maidstone 29 mi – Canterbury 19 mi

🏨 Red Lion

FRENCH CLASSIC · PUB Simple, cosy country pub, personally run by an experienced couple. Ever-changing blackboard menu offers French-influenced country cooking. Dishes are honest, wholesome and richly flavoured.

Carte £ 22/41

Rawling St ✉ ME9 0RT – ✆ (01795) 830 279 *(booking advisable)* – www.theredlionmilstead.co.uk – *Closed Sunday and Monday*

MILTON ABBOT – Devon ➜ See Tavistock

MILTON KEYNES

Milton Keynes – Pop. 171 750 – Regional map n° **6**-C1

▶ London 56 mi – Bedford 16 mi – Birmingham 72 mi – Northampton 18 mi

XX Brasserie Blanc

FRENCH CLASSIC · BRASSERIE Bustling French brasserie and a small shop, set within a striking modern building and accessed via a revolving 1930s mahogany door. Friendly team and a lively, buzzy atmosphere. Menus focus on tasty, wholesome, classic brasserie dishes.

Menu £12 – Carte £20/39

Town plan: EZ-c – *Chelsea House, 301 Avebury Blvd* ✉ *MK9 2GA* – *℘ (01908) 546 590 (booking essential)* – *www.brasserieblanc.com* – *Closed 1 January*

X Jamie's Italian

ITALIAN · FAMILY Busy, buzzy restaurant with a laid-back, family-friendly feel. The passionate team serve flavoursome, rustic Italian dishes; all of the pasta is made on-site. For a quieter time, head for the upstairs floor, which opens at the weekend.

Menu £20/40 – Carte £20/49

Town plan: EY-a – *3-5 Silbury Arcade* ✉ *MK9 3AG* – *℘ (01908) 769 011 (booking advisable)* – *www.jamiesitalian.com* – *Closed 26-26 December and Easter Sunday*

MINEHEAD

Somerset – Pop. 11 981 – Regional map n° **2**-A2

▶ London 187 mi – Bristol 64 mi – Exeter 43 mi – Taunton 25 mi

⌂ Channel House

TRADITIONAL · CLASSIC Passionately run, detached Edwardian house in an elevated position, with the sea just visible through its mature gardens. Comfy lounge and a cosy bar. Immaculately kept bedrooms have a modern edge; Rooms 7 and 8 are the most comfortable. Traditional, daily changing dinner menu and comprehensive breakfasts.

8 rooms ☲ – ♦£85/103 ♦♦£130/166
Church Path ✉ *TA24 5QG* – *off Northfield Dr* – *℘ (01643) 703 229*
– *www.channelhouse.co.uk* – *Closed November-February*

⌂ Old Stables

TOWNHOUSE · STYLISH Once the stables of the Northfield Hotel; now a delightful guesthouse with a stylish yet homely feel, just minutes from the sea. The owner's monochrome photos hang on white walls. Try the homemade cakes and preserves at breakfast.

3 rooms ☲ – ♦£60/70 ♦♦£80/90
Northfield Rd ✉ *TA24 5QH* – *℘ (07435) 964 882*
– *www.theoldstablesminehead.co.uk*

⌂ Glendower House

TRADITIONAL · CLASSIC Well-run guesthouse, a few minutes' walk from the seafront. Traditionally furnished lounge. Individually decorated, immaculately kept bedrooms; those upstairs at the front are larger. Good breakfasts, with ingredients from local farms.

11 rooms ☲ – ♦£42/66 ♦♦£60/84
30-32 Tregonwell Rd ✉ *TA24 5DU* – *℘ (01643) 707 144*
– *www.glendower-house.co.uk* – *Closed January*

MINSTER

Kent – Regional map n° **5**-D1

▶ London 73 mi – Canterbury 14 mi – Dover 21 mi – Brighton 103 mi

XX **Corner House** ⇦ 🎏 🖥 **P**

BRITISH TRADITIONAL · **NEIGHBOURHOOD** Pass the stone bar inset with a cart wheel, and the small lounge and terrace, to the characterful dining room with its low beamed ceiling and quarry tiled floor. Classic recipes use good quality produce; the dishes for two are a hit. Bedrooms have smart feature walls and modern facilities.

Menu £ 13 (weekday lunch)/22 – Carte approx. £ 30

2 rooms – ♦£ 90 ♦♦£ 90 – ☟ £ 8

42 Station Rd ✉ CT12 4BZ – 𝒞 (01843) 823 000
– www.thecornerhouseminster.co.uk

MINSTER LOVELL

Oxfordshire – Pop. 1 236 – Regional map n° **6**-A2
▶ London 74 mi – Birmingham 87 mi – Bristol 67 mi – Sheffield 151 mi

🏠 **Minster Mill** ⇦ 🍸 🏋 ℁ �└ **P**

BUSINESS · **FUNCTIONAL** Charming 17C Cotswold stone mill on the riverbank, with admirable eco-credentials. The open-fired lounge has a minstrels' gallery. Smart, well-appointed bedrooms come with robes and Sloe gin and the best boast riverside terraces. Meals are taken at the Old Swan, their sister establishment.

60 rooms ☟ – ♦£ 149/405 ♦♦£ 169/425

✉ OX29 ORN – 𝒞 (01993) 774 441 – www.oldswanandminstermill.com

🍴 **Old Swan** ⇦ 🍴 🎏 **P**

TRADITIONAL CUISINE · **SIMPLE** Smart inn with parquet floors, roaring open fires and garden games. Large herb plots contribute to unfussy pub classics; tasty daily specials feature fish from the Brixham day boats. Bedrooms boast period furnishings and mod cons, and some have feature bathrooms.

Carte £ 26/41

16 rooms ☟ – ♦£ 149/405 ♦♦£ 169/425

✉ OX29 ORN – 𝒞 (01993) 774 441 – www.oldswanandminstermill.com

MISTLEY

Essex – Pop. 1 696 – Regional map n° **7**-D2
▶ London 69 mi – Colchester 11 mi – Ipswich 14 mi

X **Mistley Thorn** ⇦ 🖥 **P**

INTERNATIONAL · **FRIENDLY** A bright, modern restaurant with an informal feel, in a historic coastal town. The appealing menu offers something for everyone, with seafood a speciality and plenty of local mussels and oysters. Smart bedrooms offer up-to-date facilities; some have river views. There's also a homeware/wine shop and cookery school.

Menu £ 13 (weekdays) – Carte £ 20/39

11 rooms ☟ – ♦£ 85/110 ♦♦£ 100/185

High St ✉ CO11 1HE – 𝒞 (01206) 392 821 – www.mistleythorn.co.uk – Closed 25 December

MITTON – Lancashire ➜ See Whalley

MOBBERLEY – Cheshire East ➜ See Knutsford

MONKTON COMBE – Bath and North East Somerset ➜ See Bath

MONKTON FARLEIGH

Wiltshire – Pop. 460 – Regional map n° **2**-C2
▶ London 112 mi – Exeter 103 mi – Cheltenham 58 mi

HORIZONTAL ROADS

Bletcham Way (H10) . . . . **CX**
Chaffron Way (H7) . . . . . . **BX, CV**
Childs Way (H6) . . . . **BX, CV**
Dansteed Way (H4) . . . . **ABV**
Groveway (H9) . . . . **CVX**
Millers Way (H2). . . . . **AV**
Monks Way (H3) . . . . **ABV**
Portway (H5) . . . . **BCV**
Ridgeway (H1) . . . . **AV**
Standing Way (H8) . . . . **BX, CV**

MILTON KEYNES

Buckingham Rd . . . . **BX**
London Rd. . . . . **CUV**
Manor Rd . . . . **CX**
Marsh End Rd . . . . **CU**
Newport Rd . . . . **BV**
Northampton Rd . . . . **AU**
Stoke Rd. . . . . **CX**
Stratford Rd . . . . **AV**
Whaddon Way . . . . **BX**
Wolverton Rd. . . . . **BU**

VERTICAL ROADS

Brickhill St (V10) . . . . **BU, CX**
Fulmer St (V3) . . . . **ABX**
Grafton St (V6) . . . . **BVX**
Great Monks St (V5) . . . . **AV**
Marlborough St (V8) . . . . . . **BV, CX**
Overstreet (V9) . . . . **BV**
Saxon St (V7) . . . . **BVX**
Snelshall St (V1) . . . . **BX**
Tattenhoe St (V2). . . . . **ABX**
Tongwell St (V11) . . . . **CVX**
Watling St (V4) . . . . **AV, BX**

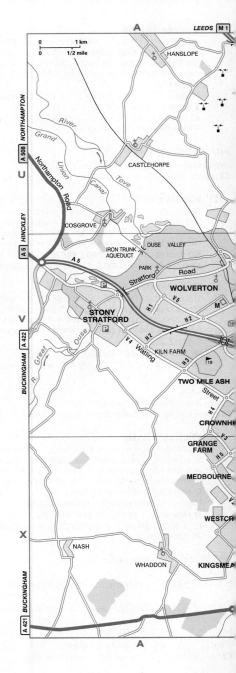

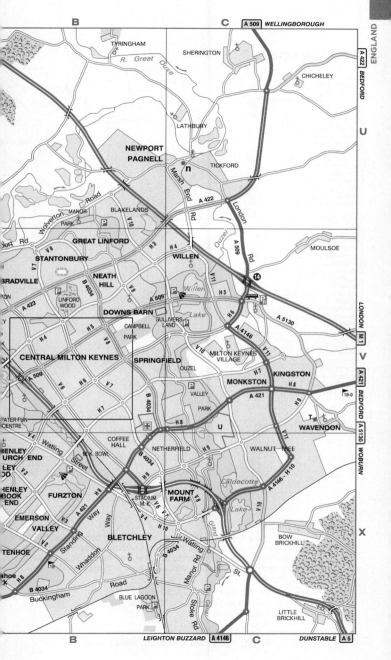

MILTON KEYNES

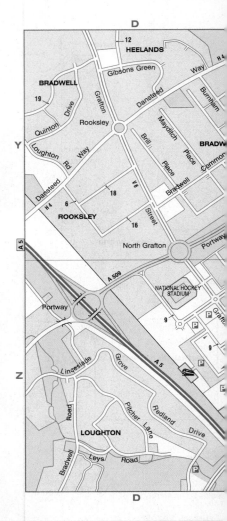

Muddy Duck

TRADITIONAL · PUB Reputedly Wiltshire's most haunted pub and dating from the 17C. Appealing menus offer classic British dishes with the occasional Asian flavour. Smart bedrooms; those in the converted barn feature their own separate snug with a wood burning stove. Switched-on staff are in tune with their guests' needs.

Carte £ 18/42

5 rooms ⌤ – ♦£ 120/250 ♦♦£ 120/250

42 Monkton Farleigh ⊠ *BA15 2QN –* ℰ *(01225) 858 705*
– www.themuddyduckbath.co.uk

The symbol ॐ guarantees a peaceful night's sleep.

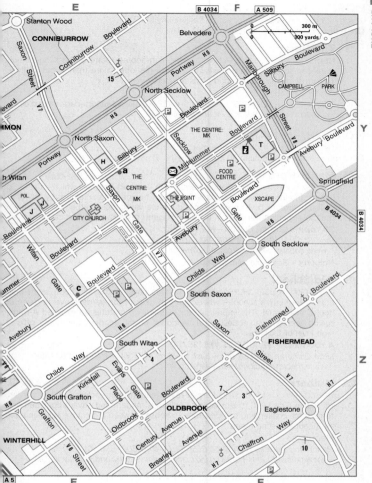

MORECAMBE

Lancashire – Pop. 33 432 – Regional map n° **11**-A1

▶ London 247 mi – Preston 27 mi – Blackpool 39 mi – Blackburn 34 mi

🏠 **Midland**   ⇘ ≼ 🍴 🚗 🔳 ₺ 🏋 🅿

BUSINESS · ART DECO Iconic 1933 hotel set in a stunning location, with views of Morecambe Bay and the mountains. Art deco styling – original features include a listed staircase. Variously sized, contemporary bedrooms. Modern restaurant offers a superb outlook and plenty of Lancashire produce. Afternoon tea in the conservatory.

44 rooms ⌧ – ♦£ 106/240 ♦♦£ 116/250 – 2 suites – ♦♦£ 250/380
Marine Road West ⌧ *LA4 4BU* – *☎ (01524) 424 000*
– www.englishlakes.co.uk

MORETONHAMPSTEAD

Devon – ⊠ Newton Abbot – Pop. 1 339 – Regional map n° **1**-C2
▶ London 213 mi – Exeter 13 mi – Plymouth 30 mi

ⁱ⊡ **The Horse**   ⛲ &

MEDITERRANEAN · PUB Pub with rustic, flag-floored rooms and a sunny, Mediterranean-style courtyard. Tasty, unfussy dishes offer more than a hint of Italy. Thin crust pizzas are baked in a custom-built oven.

Carte £ 21/38

*7 George St ⊠ TQ13 8PG – 𝒞 (01647) 440 242 – www.thehorsedartmoor.co.uk
– Closed 25 December and Monday lunch*

MORETON-IN-MARSH

Gloucestershire – Pop. 3 493 – Regional map n° **2**-D1
▶ London 86 mi – Birmingham 40 mi – Gloucester 31 mi – Oxford 29 mi

🏛 **Manor House**   ⛲ 🛏 🖥 & 🧖 🅿

INN · STYLISH Part-16C manor house with a smart interior which mixes old beams and inglenook fireplaces with modern fabrics and contemporary art. Chic, stylish bedrooms boast bold décor and feature walls; those in the main house are the most characterful. Dine in the sophisticated restaurant or classical brasserie.

35 rooms ⌂ – †£ 110/190 ††£ 170/210 – 1 suite

*High St ⊠ GL56 0LJ – 𝒞 (01608) 650 501
– www.cotswold-inns-hotels.co.uk/manor*

Mulberry – See restaurant listing

🏠 **Old School**   🛏 🛇 🅿

COUNTRY HOUSE · PERSONALISED Change pace at this laid-back, stone-built hotel – formerly a school – where you can relax in the gardens over a game of boules or croquet. The impressive upstairs lounge features an exposed A-frame ceiling and original ecclesiastical windows; bright, modern bedrooms offer a high level of facilities.

4 rooms ⌂ – †£ 100/125 ††£ 125/145

*Little Compton ⊠ GL56 0SL – East : 3.75 mi on A 44 – 𝒞 (01608) 674 588
– www.theoldschoolbedandbreakfast.com*

✗✗✗ **Mulberry**   🛏 & 🏧 🅿

BRITISH MODERN · DESIGN Formal restaurant with an enclosed walled garden, set within a part-16C manor house. Cooking is modern and adventurous and features some challenging combinations – choose between a 4 course set menu and an 8 course tasting menu.

Menu £ 43

*Manor House Hotel, High St ⊠ GL56 0LJ – 𝒞 (01608) 650 501
– www.cotswold-inns-hotels.co.uk/manor – dinner only and Sunday lunch*

at Bourton-on-the-Hill West: 2 mi on A44 – ⊠ Moreton-In-Marsh

ⁱ⊡ **Horse & Groom**   ⟷ 🛏 ⛲ 🅿

TRADITIONAL CUISINE · PUB Listed Cotswold stone property in a pretty village set high on the hillside; it's run by two brothers, who grew up working in their parents' pub. Study the daily changing blackboard menu then order at the bar. Unfussy dishes are good value, fresh and flavoursome. Individually decorated bedrooms are stylish and contemporary – and breakfast is well worth getting up for.

Carte £ 22/37

5 rooms ⌂ – †£ 80 ††£ 96/170

*⊠ GL56 9AQ – 𝒞 (01386) 700 413 (booking essential) – www.horseandgroom.info
– Closed 25, 31 December and Sunday dinner except bank holidays*

MORPETH

Northumberland – Pop. 14 403 – Regional map n° **14**-B2
▶ London 301 mi – Edinburgh 93 mi – Newcastle upon Tyne 15 mi

at Eshott North: 8.5 mi by A1 – ✉ Morpeth

🏠 Eshott Hall   ✿ ⌘ 🛏 ☆ ♨ P

COUNTRY HOUSE · STYLISH Attractive Georgian manor house in a quiet, rural location – yet only 5min from the A1. Classically stylish guest areas. Smart, modern bedrooms boast warm fabrics, antique furniture and good facilities. Formal dining room offers contemporary menus; local produce includes fruit and veg from the kitchen garden.

16 rooms ☟ – ♦£ 105/175 ♦♦£ 150/230

✉ NE65 9EN – ☎ (01670) 787 454 – www.eshotthall.co.uk

at Longhorsley Northwest: 6.5 mi by A192 on A697 – ✉ Morpeth

🏠 Thistleyhaugh Farm   ✿ ⌘ 🛏 ♨ P

FAMILY · COSY Attractive Georgian farmhouse, set off the beaten track on a 750 acre organic farm, with the River Coquet flowing through its grounds. Cosy, open-fired lounge and antique-filled dining room. Spacious, comfortable bedrooms – most have luxurious bathrooms with feature baths. Communal dinners; home-cooking features beef and lamb from the farm. Charming owners.

5 rooms ☟ – ♦£ 70/90 ♦♦£ 100

✉ NE65 8RG – Northwest : 3.75 mi by A 697 and Todburn rd taking first right turn – ☎ (01665) 570 629 – www.thistleyhaugh.co.uk – Closed Christmas-1 February

MORSTON – Norfolk → See Blakeney

MOULTON

Suffolk – Regional map n° **8**-B2

▶ London 64 mi – Ipswich 42 mi – Cambridge 14 mi

🍴 Packhorse Inn   ⇦ 🛏 P

MODERN CUISINE · ELEGANT Smart modern pub set in a pretty village and named after its famous 15C packhorse bridge. 'Packhorse Favourites' like Suffolk rib-eye and chips are offered alongside more adventurous, artily presented dishes. Bedrooms are ultra-stylish with quality furnishings, roll top baths and welcome extras.

Menu £ 18 (weekday lunch) – Carte £ 29/41

8 rooms ☟ – ♦£ 85/175 ♦♦£ 100/175

Bridge St ✉ CB8 8SP – ☎ (01638) 751 818 – www.thepackhorseinn.com

MOUSEHOLE

Cornwall – ✉ Penzance – Regional map n° **1**-A3

▶ London 321 mi – Penzance 3 mi – Truro 29 mi

🗙 2 Fore Street   🖼

FISH AND SEAFOOD · FRIENDLY Friendly, harbourside café-cum-bistro with a delightful terrace and garden. All-day menus offer everything from coffee and cake to a full meal, with brunch a feature at weekends. Tasty, unfussy dishes are guided by the day's catch.

Carte £ 25/32

2 Fore St ✉ TR19 6PF – ☎ (01736) 731 164 (booking essential at dinner) – www.2forestreet.co.uk – Closed January and Monday in winter

🗙 Old Coastguard   ⇦ ⋖ 🛏 🌳 & P

MEDITERRANEAN · BISTRO Old coastguard's cottage in a small fishing village, with a laid-back, open-plan interior, a sub-tropical garden and views towards St Clement's Isle. Well-presented brasserie dishes display a Mediterranean edge; great wine selection. Individually styled bedrooms – some with balconies, most with sea views.

Menu £ 24 – Carte £ 24/32 **s**

14 rooms ☟ – ♦£ 100/180 ♦♦£ 130/220

The Parade ✉ TR19 6PR – ☎ (01736) 731 222 – www.oldcoastguardhotel.co.uk – Closed 25 December and early January

MULLION

Cornwall – ⊠ Helston – Pop. 1 955 – Regional map n° **1**-A3
▶ London 287 mi – Birmingham 282 mi – Croydon 295 mi – Barnet 300 mi

🏠 **Polurrian Bay**   ⚘ ⋖ 🍴 🛋 ⅁ 🖾 🖆 ⚒ & ⚓ 🏊 🅿

HOLIDAY HOTEL · CONTEMPORARY Imposing Victorian hotel with 12 acres of grounds, in a commanding clifftop position. Spacious, modern interior is geared towards families, with a crèche, games room and cinema. Most of the bright bedrooms boast views across Mount's Bay. Unfussy menus showcase seasonal, local produce.

41 rooms ⊡ – ♦£ 95/550 ♦♦£ 99/550
⊠ TR12 7EN – ℰ (01326) 240 421 – www.polurrianhotel.com

MURCOTT

Oxfordshire – ⊠ Kidlington – Pop. 1 293 – Regional map n° **6**-B2
▶ London 70 mi – Oxford 14 mi – Witney 20 mi

🍴 **Nut Tree** (Mike North)   🛏 🍴 🅿
❀

BRITISH TRADITIONAL · RUSTIC Characterful thatched pub with a cosy bar and a smart restaurant. The appealing menus change constantly, relying on the latest seasonal ingredients to arrive at the door, and produce is organic, free range or wild wherever possible; they even rear rare breed pigs. Combinations are classical and satisfying.
➜ Griddled asparagus with broad beans, peas, aged parmesan and lemon vinaigrette. Braised shin of Charolais beef, seared foie gras, root vegetable purée and Pinot Noir sauce. Black cherry soufflé with Earl Grey tea sorbet.
Menu £ 18 (weekdays)/60 – Carte £ 36/58
Town plan: 10-B2 – Main St ⊠ OX5 2RE – ℰ (01865) 331 253
– www.nuttreeinn.co.uk – Closed 27 December-11 January, Sunday dinner and Monday except bank holidays

NAILSWORTH

Gloucestershire – Pop. 7 728 – Regional map n° **2**-C1
▶ London 110 mi – Bristol 30 mi – Swindon 28 mi

✗✗ **Wild Garlic**   ⇌ 🆎

BRITISH MODERN · INDIVIDUAL An attractive little restaurant in the heart of a market town. Two smart, contemporary, semi-panelled rooms feature bright food-themed photos and have a rustic feel. Monthly menus reflect the latest local ingredients available; there's also a popular tasting menu. Stylish, modern bedrooms are well-equipped.
Carte £ 26/42
3 rooms ⊡ – ♦£ 85/125 ♦♦£ 95/125
3 Cossack Sq ⊠ GL6 0DB – ℰ (01453) 832 615 – www.wild-garlic.co.uk – Closed first 2 weeks January and Sunday dinner-Tuesday

✗ **mark@street**

BRITISH MODERN · BISTRO Small, friendly restaurant on a narrow street. Simple lunch menus are supplemented by brunch at the weekends. Candlelit dinners offer well-balanced, classical dishes presented in a modern way; the vegetables are from their allotment.
Carte approx. £ 32
Market St ⊠ GL6 0BX – ℰ (01453) 839 251 – www.marketstreetnailsworth.co.uk – Closed 2 weeks January, 1 week September, Sunday dinner and Monday

NANTWICH

Cheshire East – Pop. 17 226 – Regional map n° **11**-A3
▶ London 176 mi – Chester 20 mi – Liverpool 45 mi – Manchester 40 mi

🏛️ **Rookery Hall** 🏠 🌿 ≼ 🛏 🍸 🍴 🖥 🕙 🏋 🎿 🅿

BUSINESS · MODERN 19C property set in pleasant grounds, with considerable extensions and a smart, impressive spa. The main building offers characterful, country house bedrooms; more modern rooms are located in the purpose-built rear wing. The formal, two-roomed, wood-panelled dining room overlooks the gardens.

70 rooms ☟ – †£ 147/209 ††£ 157/219 – 2 suites
Worleston ✉ CW5 6DQ – North : 2.5 mi by A 51 on B 5074 – ℰ (0845) 072 75 33
– www.handpicked.co.uk/hotels/rookery-hall

NAWTON → See Helmsley

NETHER BURROW

Lancashire – ✉ Kirkby Lonsdale – Regional map n° **11**-B1
📍 London 257 mi – Liverpool 73 mi – Leeds 101 mi – Manchester 68 mi

🍴 **Highwayman** 🍴 ≼ 🅿

REGIONAL · PUB Sizeable 18C coaching inn with open-fired, stone-floored bar and lovely terrace. A rustic, no-nonsense approach to food makes for well-crafted, flavourful dishes. Produce is local and seasonal, with Lancashire hotpot a perennial favourite.

Menu £ 13/21 (weekdays) – Carte £ 19/39
✉ LA6 2RJ – ℰ (01524) 273 338 – www.highwaymaninn.co.uk
– Closed 25 December

NETHER WESTCOTE – Gloucestershire → See Stow-on-the-Wold

NETLEY MARSH – Hampshire → See Southampton

NEW MILTON

Hampshire – Pop. 19 969 – Regional map n° **4**-A3
📍 London 106 mi – Bournemouth 12 mi – Southampton 21 mi – Winchester 34 mi

🏛️ **Chewton Glen** 🏠 🌿 ≼ 🛏 🔲 🏊 🖥 🕙 🏋 🍴 🖥 🖼 🎿 🅿

GRAND LUXURY · CLASSIC Professionally run country house with an impressive spa, set in 130 acres of New Forest parkland – try a host of outdoor pursuits, including croquet, archery and clay pigeon shooting. Luxurious bedrooms range from classic to contemporary; opt for one with a balcony or terrace, or try a unique Treehouse suite.

70 rooms – †£ 325/1595 ††£ 325/1595 – ☟ £ 26 – 15 suites
Christchurch Rd ✉ BH25 6QS – West : 2 mi by A 337 and Ringwood Rd on
Chewton Farm Rd – ℰ (01425) 275 341 – www.chewtonglen.com
Dining Room – See restaurant listing

XxX **Dining Room** 🏛️ ≼ 🛏 🍴 🖼 ⇔ 🅿

MODERN CUISINE · ELEGANT Stylish hotel restaurant comprising 5 impressive rooms, including one with wines displayed in illuminated cases. The seasonally inspired à la carte offers everything from fish and chips to oysters or caviar; from Friday-Sunday they also offer specials from the trolley. Some of the produce is from the garden.

Menu £ 27 (weekday lunch) **s** – Carte £ 47/85 **s**
Chewton Glen Hotel, Christchurch Rd ✉ BH25 6QS – West : 2 mi by A 337 and
Ringwood Rd on Chewton Farm Rd – ℰ (01425) 275 341 – www.chewtonglen.com

NEW ROMNEY

Kent – Regional map n° **5**-C2
📍 London 71 mi – Brighton 60 mi – Folkestone 17 mi – Maidstone 36 mi

Romney Bay House ⛵ 🦢 ⬚ 📞 🍽 🅿

HISTORIC · ART DECO Built by Sir Clough Williams-Ellis in the 1920s, for actress Hedda Hopper, and accessed via a private coast road. Open-fired drawing room with honesty bar; first floor lounge has a telescope and lovely views out to sea. Homely bedrooms. Conservatory dining room offers a daily, seafood-based menu.

10 rooms ⌧ – ∮£ 75/95 ∮∮£ 95/160

Coast Rd, Littlestone ⊠ TN28 8QY – East : 2.25 mi by B 2071 – ℰ (01797) 364 747
– www.romneybayhousehotel.co.uk – Closed 1 week Christmas and first week January

NEWARK-ON-TRENT

Nottinghamshire – Pop. 37 084 – Regional map n° **9**-C1
▶ London 127 mi – Lincoln 16 mi – Nottingham 20 mi – Sheffield 42 mi

Grange ⛵ 📞 🍽 🅿

TOWNHOUSE · PERSONALISED Personally run hotel with a small terrace and award-winning gardens. The main house has mock Tudor gables, a Victorian-style bar and lounge, and a smart restaurant decorated with antique plates and cutlery. Individually styled bedrooms are split between this and a second house, and offer good comforts.

19 rooms ⌧ – ∮£ 79/110 ∮∮£ 95/165

73 London Rd ⊠ NG24 1RZ – South : 0.5 mi on Grantham rd (B 6326) – ℰ (01636) 703 399 – www.grangenewark.co.uk – Closed 22 December-6 January

at Norwell North: 7.25 mi by A1

Willoughby House

HISTORIC · PERSONALISED A three-storey red-brick farmhouse and converted stables, with a chic, stylish interior, a small open-fired lounge and a deep red breakfast room. Bedrooms feature good quality furnishings and antiques, along with contemporary artwork and homemade flapjacks. The owner has a keen eye for detail.

3 rooms ⌧ – ∮£ 60/75 ∮∮£ 85/105

Main St ⊠ NG23 6JN – ℰ (01636) 636 266 – www.willoughbyhousebandb.co.uk

NEWBIGGIN – Cumbria ➔ See Penrith

NEWBOTTLE

Tyne and Wear – Regional map n° **14**-B2
▶ London 268 mi – Newcastle upon Tyne 14 mi – Sunderland 6 mi

Hideaway at Herrington Hill 🆕 🦢 ⬚ 📞 🅿

FAMILY · HOMELY The charming owners really look after their guests at this spacious former shooting lodge, built in 1838 for the Earl of Durham. Bedrooms blend period features and modern amenities. The Garden Room is largest, with views of the grounds.

4 rooms ⌧ – ∮£ 90 ∮∮£ 90/180

High Ln ⊠ DH4 4NH – West : 1 mi – ℰ (07730) 957 795
– www.hideawayatherringtonhill.com – Closed first 2 weeks in January

NEWBURY

West Berkshire – Pop. 38 762 – Regional map n° **6**-B3
▶ London 67 mi – Reading 17 mi – Bristol 66 mi – Oxford 28 mi

The Vineyard ⛵ 📞 🔲 🎵 🛗 🖼 🍽 ♨ 🅿

BUSINESS · CLASSIC Extended former hunting lodge with over 1,000 pieces of art and a striking fire and water feature. Some bedrooms have a country house style, while others are more contemporary; all boast smart marble bathrooms. The owner also has a vineyard in California, hence the stunning wine vault and the wine-themed bar.

49 rooms – ∮£ 155/660 ∮∮£ 205/660 – ⌧ £ 21 – 32 suites

Town plan: AV-b – *Stockcross ⊠ RG20 8JU – Northwest : 2 mi by A 4 on B 4000 – ℰ (01635) 528 770 – www.the-vineyard.co.uk*

The Vineyard – See restaurant listing

NEWBURY

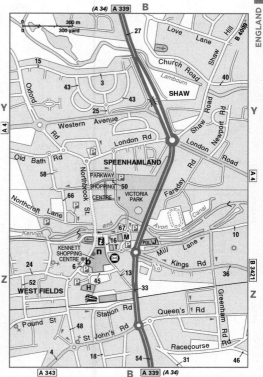

🏨 **Donnington Valley H. & Spa**   ❀ 👗 🖼 🔲 ⑨⑩ 🎵 🏃 ⬆ ⛎ AC 🏊 P

BUSINESS · FUNCTIONAL Modern business-orientated hotel on the town out-skirts, with large grounds and a golf course. Guest areas are spacious and styl-ishly furnished and there's a well-equipped gym and spa. Smart bedrooms offer a high level of facilities.

111 rooms ⌂ – ♦£ 89/177 ♦♦£ 89/192

Town plan: AV-a – *Old Oxford Rd, Donnington* ✉ *RG14 3AG*
– *North : 1.75 mi by A 4 off B 4494*
– ✆ *(01635) 551 199*
– *www.donningtonvalley.co.uk*

Winepress – See restaurant listing

𝒳𝒳 **The Vineyard**   🎎 👗 ⭐ AC ▶ P

MODERN CUISINE · FORMAL Smart hotel restaurant split over two levels. Choose 3-5 dishes from the main menu or try the tasting menu with matching wines; some from their own Californian vineyard. Accomplished, classical cooking is attractively presented.

Menu £ 29/75

Town plan: AV-b – *Vineyard Hotel, Stockcross* ✉ *RG20 8JU*
– *Northwest : 2 mi by A 4 on B 4000*
– ✆ *(01635) 528 770*
– *www.the-vineyard.co.uk*

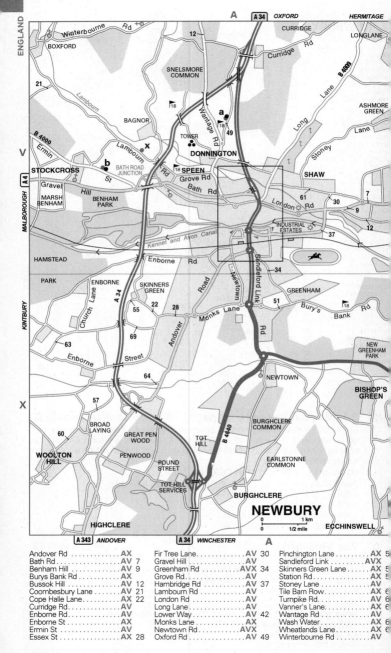

XX **Winepress**   🕸 🖴 AC P

BRITISH TRADITIONAL · BRASSERIE A split-level restaurant with an unusual pyramid roof, set within a business-led hotel. Lunch offers an accessible menu popular with local workers, while dinner offers more substantial classical dishes. The wine list is impressive.

Menu £ 23/28 **s** – Carte £ 30/49 **s**

Town plan: AV-a – *Donnington Valley Hotel & Spa, Old Oxford Rd, Donnington*
✉ *RG14 3AG – North : 1.75 mi by A 4 off B 4494 –* 𝒞 *(01635) 551 199*
– www.donningtonvalley.co.uk

X **Woodspeen** ⓝ (John Campbell)   🖴 🏡 ⅄ P
❀ MODERN CUISINE · FASHIONABLE Despite being set in an old pub, this smart neighbourhood eatery has more of a bistro feel, courtesy of its Scandic styling and bright, modern thatched extension. Mouth-watering seasonal dishes feature local and garden produce; flavour is paramount and dishes have a comforting, modern classic style.

→ Ham hock and black pudding terrine with piccalilli. Venison pavé and faggot, bacon, cabbage and creamed potatoes. Caramel rice pudding, pickled apple and cinnamon doughnuts.

Menu £ 24 (weekday lunch) – Carte £ 30/46

Town plan: AV-x – *Lambourn Rd, Bagnor* ✉ *RG20 8BN – Northwest : 2 mi by A4 and Station Rd - signed Watermill Theatre. –* 𝒞 *(01635) 265 070*
– www.thewoodspeen.com – Closed Monday and dinner Sunday

X **Brebis**   ⅄ AC ⬦

FRENCH CLASSIC · BISTRO Simplicity is key at this stylish little eatery. The floors are made from reclaimed wood, the service is friendly and the cooking keeps things straightforward. Tasty, carefully prepared French country dishes use good ingredients.

Menu £ 19 (lunch) – Carte £ 28/41

Town plan: BZ-b – *16 Bartholomew St* ✉ *RG14 5LL –* 𝒞 *(01635) 40 527*
– www.brebis.co.uk – Closed 25 December-1 January, 24-30 August and Sunday-Tuesday

🍴 **The Newbury**   🏡 AC

BRITISH TRADITIONAL · INDIVIDUAL Relaxed, trendy high street pub behind a traditional façade. Dishes range from pub classics to more adventurous offerings. There's brunch at weekends, an experienced team in charge and a lively buzz when it's busy.

Menu £ 20/45 – Carte £ 24/77

Town plan: BZ-n – *137 Bartholomew St* ✉ *RG14 5HB –* 𝒞 *(01635) 49 000*
– www.thenewburypub.co.uk

NEWBY BRIDGE

Cumbria – ✉ Ulverston – Regional map n° **12**-A3
🚗 London 270 mi – Kendal 16 mi – Lancaster 27 mi

🏨 **Lakeside**   ⅄ ≤ 🖴 🔽 🔲 ⊕ 🛁 🎱 🔁 🌾 🎿 P

TRADITIONAL · CLASSIC Superbly situated hotel on the water's edge. Extremely comfy guest areas have a traditional style. Bedrooms are smart and modern – some have four-poster beds and great views. Relax in the spa and leisure club, then dine in the stylish modern brasserie or more traditional dining room; and be sure to find time for afternoon tea in the conservatory, overlooking the lake.

74 rooms ⌑ – � £ 140/320 ♟♟ £ 159/380 – 7 suites

Lakeside ✉ *LA12 8AT – Northeast : 1 mi on Hawkshead rd –* 𝒞 *(015395) 30 001*
– www.lakesidehotel.co.uk – Closed 3-22 January

John Ruskin's Brasserie – See restaurant listing

🏨 Swan   ☆ 🛏 🗂 🖼 📶 🛎 🛗 🖵 ⛱ 🧖 🏕 🅰 🛜 ⚙ 🅿

INN · CONTEMPORARY Vibrant, extended coaching inn overlooking Newby Bridge; set in 10 acres, with gardens and a playground. Chic bedrooms feature bold wallpapers; the family suites come with dolls houses and PlayStations. Dine from the same accessible menu in the Swan Inn, the smart River Room or on the waterside terrace.

51 rooms ☑ – 🛏£ 99/199 🛏🛏£ 99/199

✉ *LA12 8NB – ℰ (015395) 31 681 – www.swanhotel.com*

🏠 Knoll   ☆ 🛏 ⚙ 🅿

TRADITIONAL · STYLISH Keenly run, slate-built Edwardian house opposite the lake, with a smart interior that blends classic and modern styles. Comfy, leather-furnished lounge. Good-sized bedrooms with bold décor and modern bathrooms; 'The Retreat' has a private entrance and hot tub. Simple dining room displays heart-themed art.

9 rooms ☑ – 🛏£ 75/115 🛏🛏£ 95/220

Lakeside ✉ *LA12 8AU – Northeast : 1.25 mi on Hawkshead rd*
– ℰ (015395) 31 347 – www.theknoll-lakeside.co.uk
– Closed 22-27, 31 December and 1 January

✗✗ John Ruskin's Brasserie   🛏 🅿

INTERNATIONAL · BRASSERIE This stylish brasserie resides within in a superbly situated hotel on Lake Windermere's shore. The menu offers old favourites and brasserie classics. Have a drink in the conservatory or on the terrace to fully appreciate the view.

Menu £ 29/39

Lakeside Hotel, Lakeside ✉ *LA12 8AT – Northeast : 1 mi on Hawkshead rd*
– ℰ (015395) 30 001 – www.lakesidehotel.co.uk – dinner only
– Closed 3-22 January

NEWCASTLE INTERNATIONAL AIRPORT – Tyne and Wear ➜ See
Newcastle Upon Tyne

NEWCASTLE UPON TYNE
Tyne and Wear – Pop. 268 064 – Regional map n° **14**-B2
▶ London 276 mi – Edinburgh 105 mi – Leeds 95 mi

🏨 Jesmond Dene House   ☆ 🦮 🛏 🖵 🛗 ⚙ 🅰 🅿

LUXURY · MODERN Stone-built Arts and Crafts house in a peaceful city dene; originally owned by the Armstrong family. Characterful guest areas with wood panelling, local art and striking original fireplaces. Individually furnished bedrooms have bold feature walls, modern facilities and smart bathrooms with underfloor heating.

40 rooms ☑ – 🛏£ 146/251 🛏🛏£ 172/382

Town plan: BV-x – *Jesmond Dene Rd* ✉ *NE2 2EY – Northeast : 1.5 mi by B 1318 off A 189 – ℰ (0191) 212 30 00 – www.jesmonddenehouse.co.uk*
Jesmond Dene House – See restaurant listing

🏨 Hotel du Vin   ☆ 🖵 🛗 🅰 ⚙ 🅿

BUSINESS · STYLISH Extended red-brick building overlooking the river – formerly home to the Tyne Tees Steam Shipping Company. Characterful lounge with gas fire and zinc-topped bar. Chic, stylish, wine-themed bedrooms; some boast feature baths or terraces. Classical brasserie features a glass-fronted wine tasting room.

42 rooms – 🛏£ 99/395 🛏🛏£ 99/395 – ☑ £ 17

Town plan: BX-a – *Allan House, City Rd* ✉ *NE1 2BE – ℰ (0191) 229 22 00*
– www.hotelduvin.com/newcastle

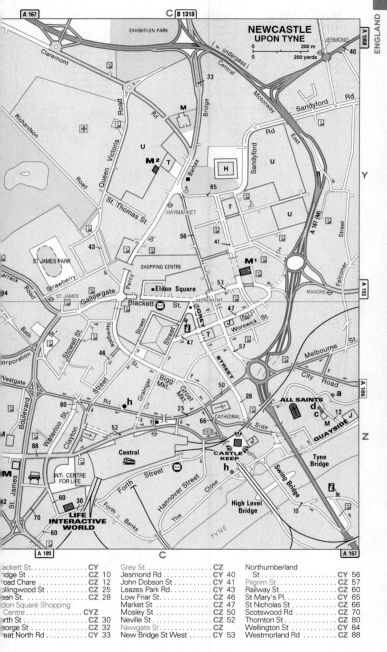

NEWCASTLE UPON TYNE

NEWCASTLE-UPON-TYNE

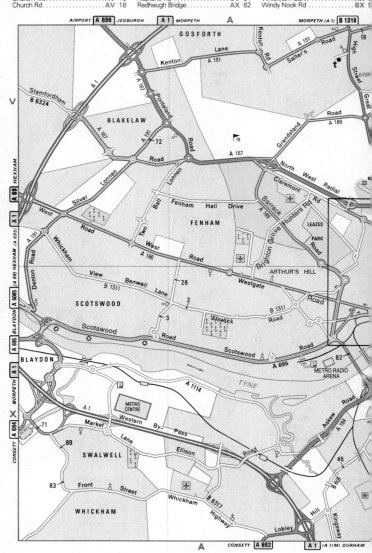

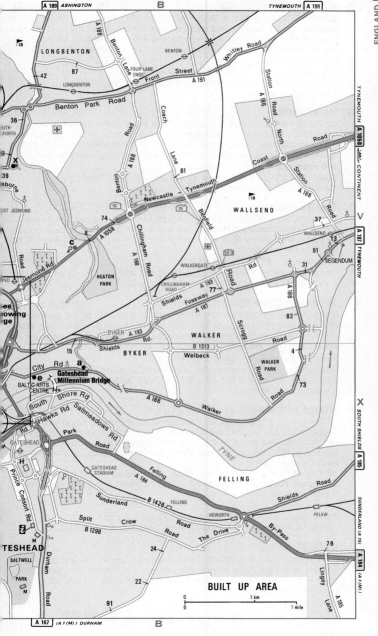

A 189 ASHINGTON   B   TYNEMOUTH A 191

LONGBENTON

BENTON

FOUR LANE
ENDS

Front   Street
A 191

LONGBENTON

Whitley Road

Station
Road
A 186

Benton Park   Road

Coast   Road   A 1058   CONTINENT

Coach

Lane

Newcastle   Tynemouth

WALLSEND

Station
Road
A 186

WALLSEND

A 187   TYNEMOUTH

Benton

Road

A 188

Chillingham   Road

A 188

Benfield

Road

SEGENDUM

HEATON
PARK

WALKERGATE

Jesmond Rd.

CHILLINGHAM
ROAD

A 193

Road   Rd

Shields   Fossway

A 187

Scrogg

Road

A 186

BYKER   A 193

Shields   Rd.

WALKER

Road

Welbeck   B 1313

WALKER
PARK

Walker   Road

City   Rd   a

Gateshead
Millennium Bridge

BALTIC ARTS
CENTRE   e

South   Shore Rd

A 186   Walker   Road

Hawks Rd   Saltmeadows Rd

Park   Road

GATESHEAD   TYNE

GATESHEAD
STADIUM

Felling
A 184   FELLING   Road

Shields   Road

SOUTH SHIELDS A 185

Prince   Consort Rd

Sunderland   B 1426   FELLING   HEWORTH   By-Pass   PELAW

SUNDERLAND (A 19)

TESHEAD   Split   Crow   Road   The   Drive

SALTWELL   B 1296   Road

PARK   Durham   76   A 184 (A 1 M)

24   Lingey

22   Lane   A 195

BUILT UP AREA

0   1 km
0   1 mile

91

A 167 (A 1(M)) DURHAM   B

Malmaison ✿ ☆ ㈜ ⊡ & 🅰 ♨ 🅿

BUSINESS · STYLISH The eye-catching former Co-Operative building on the quayside. Stylish, modern, well-equipped bedrooms; those at the front overlook the river and one suite has a four-poster bed and twin bathtubs. Brasserie classics and American style grills in the contemporary restaurant, with views to the Millennium Bridge.

122 rooms ⌷ – 🛏£ 105/209 🛏🛏£ 119/209
Town plan: BX-e – *104 Quayside* ✉ *NE1 3DX* – ✆ *(0191) 245 5000*
– *www.malmaison.com*

Hotel Indigo ✿ ㈜ ⊡ & 🅰 ⌁ 🅿

BUSINESS · MODERN Stylish city centre hotel in the former Eagle Star Insurance office block. Good-sized, well-equipped bedrooms; those on the top floor have their own balconies. Smart, leather-furnished Marco Pierre White restaurant offers classic British dishes with plenty of comfort food, including steaks and grills.

148 rooms ⌷ – 🛏£ 79/139 🛏🛏£ 89/149
Town plan: CZ-h – *2-8 Fenkle St* ✉ *NE1 5XU* – ✆ *(0191) 300 9222*
– *www.hotelindigonewcastle.co.uk*

⌂ The Townhouse

TOWNHOUSE · STYLISH End of terrace Victorian house in a residential area. All-day café serves breakfast, snacks, cakes and the like. Smart, stylish bedrooms offer bold, contemporary décor and extra touches such as iPod docks; Room 10 has a bath in the bedroom.

10 rooms ⌷ – 🛏£ 85/95 🛏🛏£ 95/135
Town plan: AV-t – *1 West Ave, Gosforth* ✉ *NE3 4ES* – *North : 2.5 mi by B 1318*
– ✆ *(0191) 285 6812* – *www.thetownhousehotel.co.uk*

XxX Jesmond Dene House � 🎠 & 🅰 🅿

BRITISH MODERN · DESIGN Smart, understated restaurant on the ground floor of an Arts and Crafts house hotel in a tranquil city dene. Sit in the bright extension for views over the gardens. Classic dishes may have a French heart but are crafted from local produce.

Menu £ 22 (lunch) **s** – Carte £ 27/60
Town plan: BV-x – *Jesmond Dene House Hotel, Jesmond Dene Rd* ✉ *NE2 2EY*
– *Northeast : 1.5 mi by B 1318 off A 189* – ✆ *(0191) 212 30 00*
– *www.jesmonddenehouse.co.uk*

XX House of Tides (Kenny Atkinson) & 🕼
❀

MODERN CUISINE · INDIVIDUAL Characterful 16C merchant's house with original flagged floors and exposed bricks. Accomplished, creative, very attractively presented dishes give a nod to the north – the chef-owner is a local. Choose between a market selection and two tasting menus; on Saturday evening, only a 6 course menu is served.

➜ King crab, pink grapefruit, sourdough, apple blossoms and sea fennel. Beef with pease pudding, heritage carrots, smoked bacon and cumin. Strawberries, dandelion and burdock.

Menu £ 29/65
Town plan: CZ-h – *28-30 The Close* ✉ *NE1 3RF* – ✆ *(0191) 230 37 20*
– *www.houseoftides.co.uk* – *Closed 2 weeks Christmas-New Year and Sunday*

XX Café 21 & 🅰 🕼 ⇆

BRITISH MODERN · BRASSERIE Stylish, open-plan brasserie where subtle greys contrast with bold floral fabrics. Eye-catching zinc-topped bar, smart dining room and efficient service. Appealing British and French classics, with a good value set lunch menu.

Menu £ 18/22 (lunch) – Carte £ 31/55
Town plan: CZ-a – *Trinity Gardens* ✉ *NE1 2HH* – ✆ *(0191) 222 07 55*
– *www.cafetwentyone.co.uk* – *Closed 25-26 December, 1 January and Easter Monday*

XX Peace & Loaf

MODERN CUISINE • NEIGHBOURHOOD Found in a smart suburban parade, this fashionable restaurant and bar is set over three levels and has a lively atmosphere. Attractively presented modern dishes are ambitious, complex and employ many different cooking techniques.

Menu £ 13 (lunch and early dinner) – Carte £ 29/47

Town plan: BV-c – *217 Jesmond Rd, Jesmond ✉ NE2 1LA – ✆ (0191) 281 52 22 – www.peaceandloaf.co.uk – Closed 25-26 December , 1 January and Sunday dinner*

X Caffé Vivo

ITALIAN • BRASSERIE In a converted quayside warehouse – also home to a theatre. Zinc ducting and steel pillars give it an industrial feel, while hams, salamis and oils add a touch of the Mediterranean. Simple, satisfying cooking of classic Italian dishes.

Menu £ 20 – Carte £ 21/39

Town plan: CZ-d – *29 Broad Chare ✉ NE1 3DQ – ✆ (0191) 232 13 31 – www.caffevivo.co.uk – Closed Sunday and bank holidays*

Broad Chare

BRITISH TRADITIONAL • PUB Owned by Terry Laybourne and next to its sister operation, Caffé Vivo. Sit in the snug ground floor bar or upstairs dining room. Choose from a snack menu of 'Geordie Tapas', an appealing 'on toast' selection, hearty daily specials and tasty nursery puddings. Over 40 ales, including some which are custom-made.

Carte £ 21/36

Town plan: CZ-c – *25 Broad Chare ✉ NE1 3DQ – ✆ (0191) 211 2144 (booking advisable) – www.thebroadchare.co.uk – Closed 25-26 December and Sunday dinner*

at Newcastle International Airport Northwest: 6.75 mi by A167 off A696 – Plan: AV – ✉ Newcastle Upon Tyne

DoubleTree by Hilton Newcastle International Airport

CHAIN HOTEL • CONTEMPORARY A modern, V-shaped building: the closest hotel to the airport. Contemporary bedrooms and compact, well-equipped bathrooms are geared towards the modern business traveller; ask for a room with a runway view. Traditional pub menu in the bar; the restaurant with a terrace serves Mediterranean-influenced dishes.

179 rooms – †£ 99/260 ††£ 109/270

Woolsington ✉ NE13 8BZ – ✆ (01661) 824 266 – www.doubletree-newcastle.com

at Ponteland Northwest: 8.25 mi by A167 on A696 – Plan: AV – ✉ Newcastle Upon Tyne

XX Haveli (N)

INDIAN • FASHIONABLE Haveli means 'grand house' and this neighbourhood restaurant is certainly very smart. Influences come from all over India; try one of the chef's signature curries. Staff combine personality with professionalism.

Menu £ 15 (weekdays)/30 – Carte £ 16/33

3-5 Broadway, Darras Hall ✉ NE20 9PW Ponteland – Southwest : 1.5 mi by B 6323 off Darras Hall Estate rd – ✆ (01661) 872 727 – www.haveliponteland.com – dinner only

NEWHAVEN

Derbyshire – Regional map n° **9**-A1

▶ London 159 mi – Leeds 84 mi – Manchester 38 mi – Derby 22 mi

🏠 The Smithy   🐾 🐎 ♿ 🅿 🚗

FAMILY · PERSONALISED Friendly owners keep the blacksmith theme alive at this cosy guesthouse. Tools and the old forge are found in the rustic breakfast room; while the bedrooms come with wrought-iron beds and are named Anvil, Swage, Bellows and Forge.

4 rooms 🍽 – 🛏£ 50 🛏£ 95

✉ SK17 0DT – South : 1 mi on A 515 – ☎ (01298) 84 548
– www.thesmithybedandbreakfast.co.uk

NEWLYN
Cornwall – Pop. 3 536 – Regional map n° **1**-A3
▶ London 288 mi – Camborne 16 mi – Saint Austell 44 mi – Falmouth 29 mi

🍴 Tolcarne Inn   🏠 🅿

FISH AND SEAFOOD · TRADITIONAL Unassuming family-run pub beside the sea wall. Inside it's narrow and cosy, with 18C beams, a wood burning stove and a long bar. The experienced chef offers appealing, flavoursome dishes which centre around fresh, locally landed fish and shellfish. They host jazz nights every first and third Sunday.

Carte £ 23/38

Tolcarne Pl ✉ TR18 5PR – ☎ (01736) 363 074 – www.tolcarneinn.co.uk

NEWNHAM BRIDGE
Worcestershire – Regional map n° **10**-B2
▶ London 145 mi – Birmingham 36 mi – Worcester 20 mi

🍴 Talbot Inn   🛋 🏠 ♿ 🅿

TRADITIONAL CUISINE · INN Red-brick 19C inn, originally built as a hunting lodge and once popular with hop pickers here for the harvest. Menus offer something for everyone; locally shot game in season is a speciality. Staff are friendly and efficient. Bedrooms provide contemporary comforts; ask for a room at the back.

Carte £ 20/50

7 rooms 🍽 – 🛏£ 65/85 🛏£ 85/115

✉ WR15 8JF – ☎ (01584) 781 941 – www.talbotinnnewnhambridge.co.uk

NEWQUAY
Cornwall – Pop. 20 189 – Regional map n° **1**-A2
▶ London 291 mi – Exeter 83 mi – Penzance 34 mi – Plymouth 48 mi

at Watergate Bay Northeast: 3 mi by A3059 on B3276 – ✉ Newquay

🏨 Watergate Bay   🏡 ← 🖥 ⊛ 🛁 ♿ 🏄 🧖 🅿

HOLIDAY HOTEL · CONTEMPORARY Long-standing seaside hotel where fresh, contemporary bedrooms range from standards to family suites; some have free-standing baths with sea outlooks. The beautiful infinity pool and hot tub share the view and there's direct beach access, beach changing rooms and even a surf-board store. Dine in the bar, the laid-back sandy-floored café or the smart modern bistro.

69 rooms 🍽 – 🛏£ 109/304 🛏£ 145/405

On The Beach ✉ TR8 4AA – ☎ (01637) 860 543 – www.watergatebay.co.uk

✕✕ Fifteen Cornwall   🍷 ← ♿ 🖥 ⇄

ITALIAN · TRENDY Lively beachfront restaurant with fabulous bay views; a social enterprise where the profits go to their registered charity, who train disengaged adults to become chefs. Unfussy Italian menus have a Cornish twist and feature homemade pastas and steaks from the Josper grill. They open for breakfast too.

Menu £ 32 (lunch) – Carte £ 30/62

On The Beach ✉ TR8 4AA – ☎ (01637) 861 000 (booking essential)
– www.fifteencornwall.co.uk

at Mawgan Porth Northeast: 6 mi by A3059 on B3276

🏨 **Scarlet**　　　　　　　　　🏕 🐾 🍴 🛋 🖼 ⓦ 🗓 👤 🅿

LUXURY · STYLISH Eco-centric, adults only hotel set high on a cliff and boasting stunning coastal views. Modern bar and lounges, and a great spa offering extensive treatments. Bedrooms range from 'Just Right' to 'Indulgent' and have unusual open-plan bathrooms and a cool, Scandic style – every room has a terrace and sea view.

37 rooms 🛏 – ♦£ 190/460 ♦♦£ 210/480

Tredragon Rd ⊠ *TR8 4DQ* – ℰ *(01637) 861 800* – *www.scarlethotel.co.uk* – *Closed 3-29 January*

Scarlet – See restaurant listing

🏨 **Bedruthan**　　　　🏕 🍴 🛋 🖼 ⓦ 🏋 🍽 🗓 👤 🚴 🐾 🍸 🅿

HOLIDAY HOTEL · CONTEMPORARY Unassuming hotel set in an elevated position overlooking the shore and boasting direct access to the beach. The interior is surprisingly contemporary and bedrooms are bright. Facilities and activities are family-orientated but the cocktail bar and lounge are set aside for adults. Interesting modern menus in Herring and accessible, family-focused dining in Wild Café.

89 rooms 🛏 – ♦£ 79/120 ♦♦£ 139/268 – 10 suites

⊠ *TR8 4BU* – *Northeast : 0.5 mi on B 3276* – ℰ *(01637) 860 860*
– *www.bedruthan.com* – *Closed Christmas-February*

✕✕ **Scarlet**　　　　　　　　　　　　　🍴 🏕 👤 🅿

BRITISH MODERN · DESIGN Contemporary hotel restaurant with huge windows offering stunning coastal views; start with a drink on the lovely terrace or in the chic bar. Concise daily menus promote small local suppliers; cooking is light, modern and seasonal.

Menu £ 23 (lunch)/44 – Carte £ 28/46

Scarlet Hotel, Tredragon Rd ⊠ *TR8 4DQ* – ℰ *(01637) 861 800 (bookings essential for non-residents)* – *www.scarlethotel.co.uk* – *Closed 3-29 January*

NEWTON LONGVILLE

Buckinghamshire – Pop. 1 846 – Regional map n° **6**-C1
▶ London 52 mi – Birmingham 77 mi – Bristol 110 mi – Sheffield 126 mi

🍺 **Crooked Billet**　　　　　　　　　　🍴 🏕 🍽 🅿

REGIONAL · NEIGHBOURHOOD Delightful 17C thatched pub with an inviting, firelit bar. Choose between traditional bar snacks or the more modern dishes on the à la carte menu, which include tasty meat and fish sharing platters. Attentive, personable service.

Carte £ 25/48

2 Westbrook End ⊠ *MK17 0DF* – ℰ *(01908) 373 936*
– *www.thecrookedbilletmiltonkeynes.co.uk*

NEWTON-ON-OUSE – North Yorkshire ➔ See York

NOMANSLAND

Hampshire – Regional map n° **2**-D3
▶ London 96 mi – Bournemouth 26 mi – Salisbury 13 mi – Southampton 14 mi

✕✕ **Les Mirabelles**　　　　　　　　　　🍸 🏕 🅰

FRENCH CLASSIC · FRIENDLY This bright, modern restaurant overlooks the common and is enthusiastically run by a welcoming Frenchman. The well-balanced menu features unfussy, classic Gallic dishes and the superb wine selection lists over 3,000 bins!

Menu £ 20 (weekdays) – Carte £ 28/43

Forest Edge Rd ⊠ *SP5 2BN* – ℰ *(01794) 390 205* – *www.lesmirabelles.co.uk*
– *Closed 22 December-13 January, 1 week May, 1 week September, Sunday and Monday*

NORTH BOVEY

Devon – ⊠ Newton Abbot – Pop. 254 – Regional map n° **1**-C2
▶ London 197 mi – Plymouth 41 mi – Torbay 23 mi – Exeter 15 mi

🏨 Bovey Castle

HISTORIC · STYLISH An impressive manor house on an extensive country estate, beautifully set within Dartmoor National Park. It has a relaxed, homely feel; bedrooms have contemporary touches but still retain their classic edge. The restaurant has a modern menu of local seasonal produce and the brasserie offers British classics.

64 rooms – ♦£ 139/199 ♦♦£ 159/279 – ☲£ 20 – 4 suites
⊠ TQ13 8RE – Northwest : 2 mi by Postbridge rd, bearing left at fork just out of village – ℰ (01647) 445 000 – www.boveycastle.com

🏠 Gate House

RURAL · COSY Charming 15C medieval hall house in the heart of an attractive village, boasting a characterful thatched roof, a large oak door and a lovely country garden with a small pool. Homely lounge, cosy low-beamed breakfast room and simple, spotlessly kept bedrooms, some with moor views. Charming owners.

3 rooms ☲ – ♦£ 55 ♦♦£ 90/92
⊠ TQ13 8RB – just off village green, past "Ring of Bells" public house – ℰ (01647) 440 479 – www.gatehouseondartmoor.com – Closed 24-26 December

NORTH CHARLTON – Northumberland ➜ See Alnwick

NORTH KILWORTH

Leicestershire – Regional map n° **9**-B3
▶ London 95 mi – Leicester 20 mi – Market Harborough 9 mi

🏨 Kilworth House

LUXURY · CLASSIC Impressively restored and extended Victorian mansion in 38 acres of tranquil grounds, which feature a popular open-air theatre. Spacious, classical, high-ceilinged drawing rooms. Immaculately kept bedrooms with luxurious bathrooms; the largest are in the main house. Traditional menus in ornate Wordsworth and light, brasserie-style dishes in the stunning Orangery.

44 rooms ☲ – ♦£ 130/330 ♦♦£ 130/330 – 3 suites
Lutterworth Rd ⊠ LE17 6JE – West : 0.5 mi on A 4304 – ℰ (01858) 880 058 – www.kilworthhouse.co.uk

NORTH LOPHAM

Norfolk – Regional map n° **8**-C2
▶ London 98 mi – Norwich 34 mi – Ipswich 31 mi – Bury Saint Edmunds 20 mi

🏠 Church Farm House

FAMILY · PERSONALISED Characterful thatched farmhouse in the shadow of the village church, with lovely gardens and a terrace for summer breakfasts. The comfy conservatory and spacious beamed lounge are filled with antiques and musical curios; bedrooms are traditional. The charming owners prepare homely meals of local produce.

3 rooms ☲ – ♦£ 55/75 ♦♦£ 110
Church Rd ⊠ IP22 2LP – ℰ (01379) 687 270 – www.churchfarmhouse.org – Closed January-mid February

NORTH SHIELDS

Tyne and Wear – Pop. 39 042 – Regional map n° **14**-B2
▶ London 288 mi – Newcastle upon Tyne 9 mi – Sunderland 14 mi – Middlesbrough 39 mi

✗ Irvins Brasserie

MODERN CUISINE · BRASSERIE Busy, informal restaurant in an old industrial building on the historic fish quay; brick walls and exposed pipes feature. The experienced chef has worked in a variety of places – menus are appealing and eclectic, with personal twists.

Menu £ 16 (lunch) – Carte £ 19/36
The Richard Irvin Building, Union Quay ⊠ NE30 1HJ
– ☏ (0191) 296 32 38 – www.irvinsbrasserie.co.uk
– Closed Monday and Tuesday

✗ River Cafe on the Tyne

BRITISH TRADITIONAL · BISTRO Laid-back restaurant run by a friendly local team, set above a pub in the North Shields fish quay. The daily changing à la carte offers unfussy, bistro-style dishes of fresh local produce, including fish from the market on the quayside. The 3 course set lunch and early dinner menu is a steal.

Menu £ 8 (lunch and early dinner)/15 – Carte £ 19/32
51 Bell St, Fish Quay ⊠ NE30 1HF – ☏ (0191) 296 61 68 (booking advisable)
– www.rivercafeonthetyne.co.uk – Closed 25-26 December, 1-2 January, Monday, Sunday dinner and Tuesday lunch

🍴 Staith House

BRITISH TRADITIONAL · PUB There's a pleasing no-frills feel to this cosy quayside pub with its portholes and nautical charts. Bypass classics like burger and chips in favour of fish or shellfish straight from the sea; cooking is robust, tasty and well-priced.

Menu £ 12 (weekday lunch) – Carte £ 20/40
57 Low Lights ⊠ NE30 1JA – ☏ (0191) 270 8441 (booking essential at dinner)
– www.thestaithhouse.co.uk – Closed 25-26 December and 1-2 January

NORTH WALSHAM
Norfolk – Pop. 12 463 – Regional map n° **8**-D1
▶ London 133 mi – Norwich 15 mi – Ipswich 61 mi – Lowestoft 34 mi

🏠 Beechwood

TOWNHOUSE · CLASSIC Attractive, creeper-clad, part-Georgian property, where the keen owners offer a warm welcome. The cosy interior displays original features and a host of memorabilia. Period bedrooms vary in size and comfort – many have feature beds and some have terraces onto the lovely gardens. A '10 Mile Menu' offers local ingredients in modern dishes with influences from the Med.

21 rooms ⌂ – ♦£ 90 ♦♦£ 100/175
20 Cromer Rd ⊠ NR28 0HD – ☏ (01692) 403 231
– www.beechwood-hotel.co.uk

NORTHAW
Hertfordshire – Regional map n° **7**-B2
▶ London 22 mi – St Albans 13 mi – Welwyn Garden City 10 mi

🍴 Sun at Northaw

BRITISH TRADITIONAL · PUB A restored, whitewashed, part-16C inn which sits by the village green; passionately run and contemporary in style, it's deceptively spacious, with a traditional edge. Hearty, unfussy, flavoursome cooking uses seasonal East of England produce, and beers and ciders are equally local. Friendly service.

Carte £ 25/44
1 Judges Hill ⊠ EN6 4NL – ☏ (01707) 655 507 – www.thesunatnorthaw.co.uk
– Closed Sunday dinner and Monday except bank holidays when closed Tuesday

NORTHLEACH
Gloucestershire – Pop. 1 854 – Regional map n° **2**-D1
▶ London 87 mi – Birmingham 73 mi – Bristol 54 mi – Coventry 47 mi

🍴 **Wheatsheaf Inn** ⇔ 🛱 ⇔ 🅿
BRITISH TRADITIONAL · INN Smart, 17C coaching inn with a pretty tiered terrace and two traditional dining rooms, either side of the stone-floored, open-
fired bar. The same menu is available throughout, offering classical dishes and
something to suit every taste. Stylish, contemporary bedrooms have quirky
touches and feature interesting French flea market finds; some have baths in
the rooms.
Menu £ 15 (weekday lunch) – Carte £ 24/60
14 rooms 🖙 – ♦£ 120/140 ♦♦£ 120/140
West End ✉ *GL50 3EZ* – ✆ *(01451) 860 244*
– www.cotswoldswheatsheaf.com

NORTHMOOR
Oxfordshire – Regional map n° **6**-B2
▶ London 111 mi – Oxford 23 mi – Gloucester 73 mi

🍴 **Red Lion**   🖴 🅿
BRITISH TRADITIONAL · FRIENDLY Extremely welcoming pub owned by the villagers and run by an experienced young couple and a friendly team. Low beams,
open fires and fresh flowers abound and the menu is a great mix of pub classics
and more modern daily specials.
Carte £ 19/36
Standlake Rd ✉ *OX29 5SX* – ✆ *(01865) 300 301*
*– www.theredlionnorthmoor.com – Closed third week January, Sunday dinner and
Monday*

NORTON DISNEY
Lincolnshire – Regional map n° **9**-C1
▶ London 134 mi – Nottingham 30 mi – Lincoln 13 mi

🏠 **Brills Farm** 🌣 ⇐ 🖴 🅿
FAMILY · PERSONALISED Charming Georgian farmhouse in a commanding hilltop position on a 2,000 acre working farm. Elegant country bedrooms have period wallpapers, goose down duvets and lovely rural views. Tasty Aga-cooked
dinners are served by arrangement (min. 6 people) at an antique table; the bacon
is from their farm.
3 rooms 🖙 – ♦£ 56 ♦♦£ 92
Brills Hill ✉ *LN6 9JN – West : 2 mi on Newark Rd*
– ✆ (01636) 892 311 – www.brillsfarm-bedandbreakfast.co.uk
– Closed Christmas-New Year

NORTON ST PHILIP
Somerset – ✉ Bath – Pop. 556 – Regional map n° **2**-C2
▶ London 113 mi – Bristol 22 mi – Southampton 55 mi – Swindon 40 mi

🏠 **The Plaine** 🅿
HISTORIC · COSY Charming 17C stone cottages in a delightful village, on the site
of the original market place. Snug, beamed interior with an airy breakfast room.
Simple bedrooms feature fresh, colour-themed linens. Bubbly owner.
3 rooms 🖙 – ♦£ 45/90 ♦♦£ 65/130
✉ *BA2 7LT* – ✆ *(01373) 834 723 – www.theplaine.co.uk*

NORWELL – Nottinghamshire → See Newark-on-Trent

NORWICH

Norfolk – Pop. 186 682 – Regional map n° **8**-D2

▶ London 109 mi – Kingston-upon-Hull 148 mi – Leicester 117 mi

St Giles House

TOWNHOUSE · CLASSIC Stylish, centrally located hotel with an impressive façade, columns and wood panelling. Luxurious 'Deluxe' front suites; the rear bedrooms are quieter and more contemporary. The open-plan lounge, bar and dining
room has a pleasant terrace and serves modern brasserie classics.

24 rooms ⌷ – ♦£ 120/210 ♦♦£ 130/220 – 3 suites

Town plan: YZ-a – 41-45 St Giles St ✉ NR2 1JR – ✆ (01603) 275 180
– www.stgileshousehotel.com

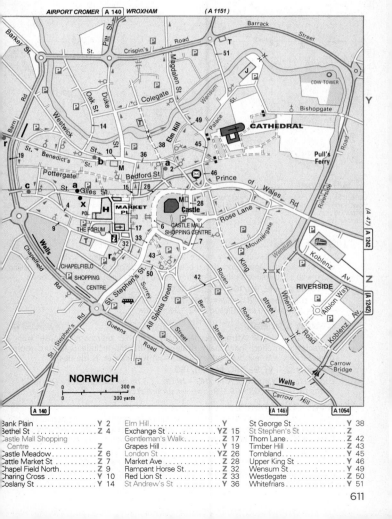

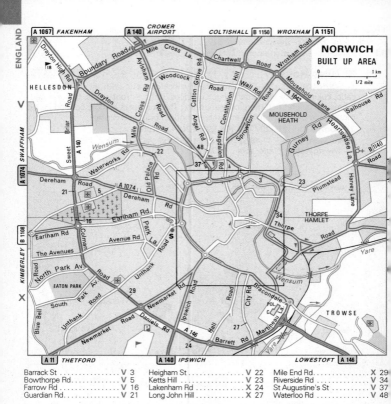

| A 1067 | FAKENHAM | A 140 | CROMER AIRPORT | COLTISHALL | B 1150 | WROXHAM | A 1151 |

NORWICH
BUILT UP AREA

0 _____ 1 km
0 _____ 1/2 mile

38 St Giles   ⚲ P

TOWNHOUSE · STYLISH City centre townhouse where boutique styling blends with original features. Elegant, uncluttered bedrooms boast high ceilings and wood panelling, along with silk curtains, handmade mattresses and quality linen. Excellent breakfasts.

7 rooms ⌂ – 🛉£ 90/100 🛉🛉£ 130/160

Town plan: Z-x – *38 St Giles St* ✉ *NR2 1LL* – ℰ *(01603) 662 944*
– www.38stgiles.co.uk – Closed 24-27 December

Catton Old Hall   🖧 ⚲ P

HISTORIC · CLASSIC Attractive, personally run, 17C merchant's house with a characterful interior. Individually designed bedrooms include 5 feature rooms; Anna Sewell, with exposed rafters and a vast four-poster, is the best.

7 rooms ⌂ – 🛉£ 99/150 🛉🛉£ 99/150

Lodge Ln, Old Catton ✉ *NR6 7HG – North : 3.5 mi by Catton Grove Rd off St Faiths Rd* – ℰ *(01603) 419 379 – www.catton-hall.co.uk*

XX Roger Hickman's   🅰🅺

MODERN CUISINE · FORMAL Personally run restaurant in a historic part of the city, with soft hues, modern art and romantic corners. Service is attentive yet unobtrusive. Cooking is modern, intricate and displays respect for ingredients' natural flavours.

Menu £ 25/60

Town plan: Z-c – *79 Upper St Giles St* ✉ *NR2 1AB* – ℰ *(01603) 633 522*
– www.rogerhickmansrestaurant.com – Closed 1 week August, 1 week Christmas, Sunday and Monday

XX Bishop's

BRITISH TRADITIONAL · ROMANTIC Intimate restaurant of only eight tables, in a 15C building with a country-chic décor of floral prints, oval mirrors, crystal chandeliers and silk curtains. Simply presented, traditional dishes. Efficient service.

Menu £ 15/34

Town plan: Y-a – *8-10 St Andrew's Hill* ⊠ *NR2 1AD* – ✆ *(01603) 767 321 (booking essential)* – *www.bishopsrestaurant.co.uk* – *Closed Sunday and Monday*

X Benedicts

MODERN · BISTRO Benedicts is a modern bistro which takes its name from the street in which it's located. Original modern cooking shows respect for the good quality Norfolk ingredients and the flavoursome dishes have a clean, simple style.

Menu £ 20/36

Town plan: Y-b – *9 St Benedicts* ⊠ *NR2 4PE* – ✆ *(01603) 926 080* – *www.restaurantbenedicts.com* – *Closed 24 December - 7 January, Sunday and Monday*

ⅼ Georgian Townhouse

TRADITIONAL CUISINE · NEIGHBOURHOOD Laid-back pub with a flexible menu: choose small plates to start or to share; dishes 'for the table' for 2 or 4; or something for yourself 'from the store'. Fruit and veg is home-grown and they home-smoke cheese and spit-roast and flame-grill meats. Bold, retro-style bedrooms have fridges and coffee machines.

Carte £ 23/42

7 rooms ⌂ – ♦£ 85/120 ♦♦£ 95/130

Town plan: X-s – *30-34 Unthank Rd* ⊠ *NR2 2RB* – ✆ *(01603) 615 655* – *www.thegeorgiantownhousenorwich.com*

ⅼ Reindeer

TRADITIONAL CUISINE · PUB Rustic neighbourhood pub with a keen local following. Plenty of space is kept aside for drinkers, who have 10 real ales to choose from. Straightforward, proudly British cooking employs lesser-used cuts and offers plenty of sharing dishes.

Carte £ 20/42

Town plan: Y-r – *10 Dereham Rd* ⊠ *NR2 4AY* – ✆ *(01603) 612 995* – *www.thereindeerpub.co.uk* – *Closed 25-26 December and Monday*

at Stoke Holy Cross *South: 5.75 mi by A140 – Plan: X –* ⊠ *Norwich*

XX Stoke Mill

TRADITIONAL CUISINE · INDIVIDUAL Characterful 700 year old mill spanning the River Tas; the adjoining building is where the Colman family started making mustard in 1814. Confidently prepared, classically based dishes use good ingredients and flavours are distinct.

Menu £ 20 (weekday lunch)/43 – Carte £ 28/46

Mill Rd ⊠ *NR14 8PA* – ✆ *(01508) 493 337* – *www.stokemill.co.uk* – *Closed Saturday lunch and Sunday dinner*

ⅼ Wildebeest

BRITISH MODERN · RUSTIC Unusually decorated pub with African rugs, wooden wild animals and tree trunk tables. An array of menus offer modern British and European flavours. Wednesday steak nights feature cuts from their own herd of cattle. Smart, polite service.

Menu £ 15/19 (weekdays) – Carte £ 28/42

82-86 Norwich Rd ⊠ *NR14 8QJ* – ✆ *(01508) 492 497 (booking essential)* – *www.animalinns.co.uk*

NOSS MAYO

Devon – Regional map n° **1-C3**

▶ London 217 mi – Plymouth 11 mi – Torbay 32 mi – Exeter 45 mi

🍴 **Ship Inn**   🛋 🅿

BRITISH TRADITIONAL · PUB Large, busy, well-run pub with characterful, nautical décor and wonderful waterside views from its peaceful spot on the Yealm Estuary. Appealing menu of unfussy pub classics. Bright, friendly service. Keep an eye on the tide!

Carte £ 25/30

✉ PL8 1EW – ℰ (01752) 872 387 – www.nossmayo.com

NOTTINGHAM

Nottingham – Pop. 289 301 – Regional map n° **9**-B2

▶ London 135 mi – Birmingham 50 mi – Leeds 74 mi – Leicester 27 mi

🏨 **Hart's**   🌳 ≼ 🛋 🖥 ᘐ 🛠 🅿

BUSINESS · DESIGN Sophisticated, boutique-style hotel built on the ramparts of a medieval castle. Compact bedrooms have modern bathrooms and a high level of facilities; some open onto garden terraces. The small bar-lounge doubles as a breakfast room.

32 rooms – 🛏 £ 129/179 🛏🛏 £ 129/179 – ⊡ £ 14 – 2 suites

Town plan: CZ-e – Standard Hill, Park Row ✉ NG1 6FN

– ℰ (0115) 988 19 00 – www.hartsnottingham.co.uk

Hart's – See restaurant listing

🍴🍴🍴 **Restaurant Sat Bains**   ➜ 🛋 🅰🅲 ⑰ ⇔ 🅿

❀❀ CREATIVE · INTIMATE Smart restaurant with an intimate atmosphere and slick service; incongruously located near a flyover. 7 and 10 course tasting menus feature refined, highly original dishes with distinct, carefully balanced flavours. Book a table in the 6-seater 'Nucleus' dining room to best see the kitchen's creativity. Bedrooms are modern and individually styled; some have feature beds.

➜ Scallop curry. Goosnargh duck, carrot and bitter chocolate. Lemon, marshmallow, basil and fennel.

Menu £ 85/125 – set menu only

8 rooms ⊡ – 🛏 £ 140 🛏🛏 £ 140 – 4 suites

Town plan: AZ-n – Trentside, Lenton Ln ✉ NG7 2SA

– ℰ (0115) 986 65 66 (booking essential) – www.restaurantsatbains.com

– Closed 2 weeks August, 2 weeks late December-early January, 1 week April, Sunday-Tuesday

🍴🍴 **Hart's**   🛋 ᘐ 🅰🅲 🐾 ⇔

BRITISH MODERN · FASHIONABLE Contemporary restaurant in the A&E department of the old city hospital; ask to sit in one of the central booths. British brasserie dishes feature on the daily menu and cooking is flavourful and well-priced. Service is polite.

Menu £ 19/24 (weekdays) – Carte £ 30/48

Town plan: CZ-e – Hart's Hotel, Standard Ct., Park Row ✉ NG1 6GN

– ℰ (0115) 988 19 00 – www.hartsnottingham.co.uk

– Closed 1 January and dinner 25-26 December

🍴🍴 **World Service**   🍷 🛋 ⇔

INTERNATIONAL · FORMAL Hidden in the extension of a Georgian property and accessed via an Indonesian-inspired courtyard garden. It has a clubby, colonial feel, with panelled walls and cases of archaeological artefacts. Appealing dishes have global influences.

Menu £ 15/25 (weekdays) – Carte £ 27/51

Town plan: CZ-n – Newdigate House, Castlegate ✉ NG1 6AF

– ℰ (0115) 847 55 87 – www.worldservicerestaurant.com

– Closed 1 January and Sunday dinner

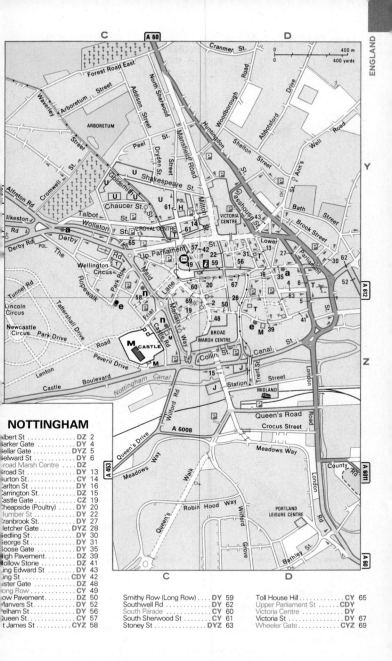

ENGLAND

NOTTINGHAM

NOTTINGHAM
BUILT UP AREA

See following page

ARNOLD

CARLTON

WOLLATON PARK

BEESTON

WEST
BRIDGFORD

EDWALTON

XX MemSaab

INDIAN · EXOTIC Professionally run restaurant with eye-catching artwork and a wooden 'Gateway of India'. Original, authentic cooking has a distinct North Indian influence. Spicing is well judged and dishes from the charcoal grill are a highlight.

Carte £ 19/37

Town plan: CY-n – 12-14 Maid Marian Way ⊠ NG1 6HS – ℰ (0115) 957 0009 – www.mem-saab.co.uk – dinner only – Closed 25 December

Ibérico World Tapas 🅰🅲 📷

MEDITERRANEAN · FASHIONABLE Lively, well-run restaurant hidden away in the basement of the former city jail and law courts, with a vaulted ceiling, colourful Moorish tiles and ornate fretwork. Tapas menu with 'Spanish' and 'World' sections; skilful cooking is full of flavour. Friendly staff offer good recommendations.

Menu £13 (weekdays) **s** – Carte £12/20 **s**

Town plan: DZ-e – *The Shire Hall, High Pavement* ✉ NG1 1HN – ✆ *(0115) 941 04 10 (booking essential at dinner)* – www.ibericotapas.com – *Closed 1-5 January and Sunday*

Larder on Goosegate 📷

BRITISH TRADITIONAL · RUSTIC Appealing restaurant with a shabby-chic feel, on the first floor of a listed Victorian building; sit in the window for a view of the street below. Unfussy dishes are skilfully cooked, good value and very tasty; the steaks are a hit.

Menu £16 (lunch and early dinner) – Carte £22/35

Town plan: DY-a – *1st Floor, 16-22 Goosegate* ✉ NG1 1FE – ✆ *(0115) 950 01 11* – www.thelarderongoosegate.co.uk – *dinner only and lunch Friday-Sunday* – *Closed Sunday and Monday*

Lime ♿ 🅰🅲

INDIAN · NEIGHBOURHOOD Bright, modern Indian restaurant away from the city centre; personally run by the cheery owner. Flavoursome food with distinctive spicing. Non-alcoholic bar, and no corkage fee if you bring your own wine or beer.

Carte £15/30

4 Upminster Dr, Nuthall ✉ NG16 1PT – *Northwest : 5.25 mi by A 610, A 6002 off Mornington Crescent* – ✆ *(0115) 975 0005* – www.lime-restaurant.co.uk – *dinner only* – *Closed 25 December*

at West Bridgford Southeast: 1.75 mi by A60 – Plan: DZ – ✉ Nottingham

escabeche 🍴 🅰🅲 🖥 📷

MEDITERRANEAN · FRIENDLY Informal, modern, Mediterranean-inspired restaurant with a sunny front terrace. The broad main menu lists vibrant, well-presented tapas dishes, offering a great variety of flavours. Excellent value set menu.

Menu £10 (lunch and early dinner) **s** – Carte £13/26

Town plan: BZ-x – *27 Bridgford Rd* ✉ NG2 6AU – ✆ *(0115) 981 7010* – www.escabeche.co.uk – *Closed 25-26 December and 1 January*

at Plumtree Southeast: 5.75 mi by A60 – Plan: BZ – off A606 – ✉ Nottingham

Perkins 🍴 🅰🅲 🅿

BRITISH MODERN · FRIENDLY Formerly a Victorian railway station, now a bright family-run brasserie; find a spot in the conservatory overlooking the railway line. Menus evolve daily and the modern British cooking features home-smoked fish, game and cheeses.

Menu £14/20 (weekdays) – Carte £26/38

Old Railway Station, Station Rd ✉ NG12 5NA – ✆ *(0115) 937 36 95 (booking advisable)* – www.perkinsrestaurant.co.uk – *Closed Sunday dinner*

at Ruddington South : 5.5 mi on A 60 – ✉ Nottinghamshire

Ruddington Arms ⓝ 🍴 ♿ 🅿

TRADITIONAL CUISINE · NEIGHBOURHOOD This dramatically refurbished, faux industrial style pub is found in a sleepy village. Flavoursome dishes cater for one and all, with everything from pub classics to more adventurous offerings. Tasty marmalades and chutneys are for sale.

Carte £23/38

56 Wilford Rd ✉ NG11 6EQ – ✆ *(0115) 984 16 28* – www.theruddingtonarms.com

ENGLAND

at Stapleford Southwest: 5.5 mi by A52 – Plan: AZ – ⊠ Nottingham

XX **Crème** 🖾

BRITISH MODERN · NEIGHBOURHOOD Well-run neighbourhood restaurant with a spacious, comfortable lounge area and a stylish, modern, formally laid dining room. Seasonally changing, modern British menu; well-presented dishes are served by friendly staff.

Carte £ 22/35

12 Toton Ln ⊠ NG9 7HA – 𝒞 (0115) 939 74 22 (booking advisable)
– www.cremerestaurant.co.uk – Closed 25-26 and 31 December, Saturday lunch, Sunday dinner and Monday

at Sherwood Business Park Northwest: 10 mi by A611 – Plan: AY – off A608
– ⊠ Nottingham

🏨 **Dakota** ✿ ⅃₅ 🖵 ሌ ⅄ Ⅶ ⅍ 🅿

BUSINESS · STYLISH An eye-catching black glass cube in the heart of a business park by the M1. Spacious modern bedrooms have good facilities and walk-in showers; executive rooms have super king sized beds and extras such as bathrobes and chocolates. The roomy, laid-back restaurant offers an international grill-style menu.

92 rooms – ♦£ 89/119 ♦♦£ 89/119 – ⋤ £ 14
Lake View Dr ⊠ NG15 0EA – 𝒞 (01623) 727 670 – www.dakotanottingham.co.uk

OAKHAM

Rutland – Pop. 10 922 – Regional map n° **9**-C2
▶ London 103 mi – Leicester 26 mi – Northampton 35 mi

🏨 **Barnsdale Lodge** ✿ ⊆ 🛏 ⇕ ሌ ⅍ 🅿

BUSINESS · CLASSIC A collection of interconnecting former farm buildings in neat lawned gardens. Characterful guest areas include a lounge with York stone flooring. Country style bedrooms have good facilities and bathrooms with remote-controlled showers. A menu of classic dishes is served in the dining room and conservatory.

45 rooms ⋤ – ♦£ 80/95 ♦♦£ 95/150
The Avenue, Rutland Water ⊠ LE15 8AH – East : 2.5 mi on A 606 – 𝒞 (01572) 724 678 – www.barnsdalelodge.co.uk

at Hambleton East: 3 mi by A606 – ⊠ Oakham

🏨 **Hambleton Hall** ✿ ⅀ ⇐ ⊆ ⊐ ⅍ 🖵 🅿

LUXURY · CLASSIC Beautiful Victorian manor house in a peaceful location, with mature grounds sloping down to Rutland Water. Classical country house drawing rooms boast heavy drapes, open fires and antiques. Good-sized bedrooms are designed by the owner herself and come with a host of thoughtful extras. Service is engaging.

16 rooms ⋤ – ♦£ 195/265 ♦♦£ 220/540 – 1 suite
⊠ LE15 8TH – 𝒞 (01572) 756 991 – www.hambletonhall.com
❀ **Hambleton Hall** – See restaurant listing

XXX **Hambleton Hall** ⅍ ⇐ ⊆ 🅿

❀ CLASSIC CUISINE · FORMAL A traditional dining room in a lovely Victorian manor house, boasting superb views over Rutland Water. Accomplished cooking marries together a host of top quality seasonal ingredients. Gallic dishes are classically based but display the occasional modern touch; the delicious bread is from their artisan bakery.

➔ Lasagne of morels with wild garlic. Loin of Belton Estate fallow venison with tamarillo and red cabbage coleslaw. Passion fruit soufflé with passion fruit & banana sorbet.

Menu £ 33/68

Hambleton Hall Hotel, ⊠ LE15 8TH – 𝒞 (01572) 756 991 – www.hambletonhall.com

🏠 Finch's Arms

BRITISH TRADITIONAL · PUB Quaint stone inn with a characterful bar, two very stylish dining rooms and a delightful terrace overlooking Rutland Water. Assured, seasonal dishes rely on local produce; desserts are satisfyingly old school and afternoon tea is also an option. Modern bedrooms complete the picture.

Menu £ 17 (weekday lunch) – Carte £ 21/40

10 rooms ⌂ – ♦£ 80/110 ♦♦£ 100/130

Oakham Rd ⌂ LE15 8TL – ℰ (01572) 756 575 – www.finchsarms.co.uk

OARE – Kent ➜ See Faversham

OBORNE – Dorset ➜ See Sherborne

OFFCHURCH – Warwickshire ➜ See Royal Leamington Spa

OLD BASING

Hampshire – Regional map n° **4**-B1

▶ London 50 mi – Bristol 84 mi – Cardiff 117 mi – Plymouth 169 mi

🏠 Crown

TRADITIONAL CUISINE · PUB Popular with locals and with a likeable simplicity to its menus. Choices range from simple snacks to flavoursome, classic dishes like roast chicken. Everything is homemade, from the bread to the fudge that comes with your coffee.

Carte dinner £ 22/38

The Street ⌂ RG24 7BW – ℰ (01256) 321 424 – www.thecrownoldbasing.com – Closed 1 January and Sunday dinner

OLD BURGHCLERE

Hampshire – ⌂ Newbury – Regional map n° **4**-B1

▶ London 77 mi – Bristol 76 mi – Newbury 10 mi – Reading 27 mi

XX Dew Pond

FRENCH CLASSIC · CLASSIC Long-standing, part-16C farmhouse with well-tended gardens leading down to a dew pond. Cooking is classic French and the dining rooms display local art for sale. Have an aperitif on the terrace, overlooking the real Watership Down.

Menu £ 36

⌂ RG20 9LH – ℰ (01635) 278 408 – www.dewpond.co.uk – dinner only – Closed 2 weeks Christmas-New Year, Sunday and Monday

OLDHAM

Greater Manchester – Pop. 96 555 – Regional map n° **11**-B2

▶ London 212 mi – Leeds 36 mi – Manchester 7 mi – Sheffield 38 mi

🏠 White Hart Inn

BRITISH MODERN · CLASSIC Extended stone inn overlooking Saddleworth Moor, with exposed beams and open fires. An array of menus includes a good value lunch and early evening selection, a 'brasserie' menu of classics and a 'restaurant' menu which shifts things up a gear. Individually styled bedrooms are named after noteworthy locals.

Menu £ 14 (weekdays)/40 – Carte £ 25/45

12 rooms ⌂ – ♦£ 120 ♦♦£ 165

51 Stockport Rd, Lydgate ⌂ OL4 4JJ – ℰ (01457) 872 566 – www.thewhitehart.co.uk – Closed 1 January and 26 December

OLDSTEAD

North Yorkshire – Regional map n° **13**-C2

▶ London 235 mi – Leeds 54 mi – Sheffield 86 mi

XX Black Swan

😊 **BRITISH MODERN · FAMILY** The Black Swan is owned by a family who've farmed in the area for generations. Enjoy an aperitif in the characterful bar, then head to the smart upstairs restaurant. Ambitious modern menus are driven by the produce grown in the garden; cooking is highly skilled and dishes are carefully presented. Antique-furnished bedrooms have luxurious bathrooms and private patios.

→ Brill, shallot, hazelnut and bean sprouts. Lamb, radish, nasturtium and turnip. Strawberry, sweet woodruff and apple marigold.

Menu £ 55/80 – set menu only

9 rooms 🖙 – 🛉£ 120/300 🛉🛉£ 120/300

✉ YO61 4BL – 𝒞 (01347) 868 387 (bookings essential for non-residents) – www.blackswanoldstead.co.uk – dinner only and lunch Saturday-Sunday

OMBERSLEY

Worcestershire – Pop. 623 – Regional map n° **10**-B3
▶ London 128 mi – Birmingham 25 mi – Coventry 41 mi

XX Venture In

BRITISH TRADITIONAL · COSY Black and white timbered house with 15C origins, exposed beams and a large inglenook fireplace. The concise menu is supplemented by specials. Cooking is classically based but has modern overtones; the chef-owner adds personal twists.

Menu £ 26/46

Main St ✉ WR9 0EW – 𝒞 (01905) 620 552 – www.theventurein.co.uk – Closed 2 weeks August, 1 week March, 1 week June, 1 week Christmas, Monday and dinner Sunday

ORFORD

Suffolk – ✉ Woodbridge – Pop. 1 153 – Regional map n° **8**-D3
▶ London 103 mi – Ipswich 22 mi – Norwich 52 mi

🏠 Crown and Castle

INN · STYLISH Beside a castle in a sleepy village; a refreshingly well-run Tudor-style house, where the service is relaxed yet professional. Most of the modern, individually designed bedrooms are in chalets in the grounds – all have good quality furnishings; many have seating areas, terraces and distant sea views.

21 rooms 🖙 – 🛉£ 120/200 🛉🛉£ 135/215 – 1 suite

✉ IP12 2LJ – 𝒞 (01394) 450 205 – www.crownandcastle.co.uk

Trinity – See restaurant listing

XX Trinity

BRITISH MODERN · RUSTIC Have a drink in the hotel's funky bar before heading through to the relaxed dining room with red banquettes and eclectic art. Simple yet precise cooking relies on quality, seasonal ingredients. Service is friendly and efficient.

Carte £ 28/42

Crown and Castle Hotel, ✉ IP12 2LJ – 𝒞 (01394) 450 205 (booking essential at dinner) – www.crownandcastle.co.uk – Closed lunch 31 December

OSMOTHERLEY

North Yorkshire – ✉ Northallerton – Pop. 668 – Regional map n° **13**-B1
▶ London 245 mi – Darlington 25 mi – Leeds 49 mi – Middlesbrough 20 mi

🏠 Golden Lion

BRITISH TRADITIONAL · PUB 18C stone inn set in a historic village in the North York Moors; make for the atmospheric bar which offers over 80 different whiskies. Cooking is traditional and satisfying, with filling dishes on the main menu and more ambitious weekly specials. Modern bedrooms have heavy oak furnishings and good facilities.

Carte £ 22/35

7 rooms 🖙 – 🛉£ 75 🛉🛉£ 95/100

6 West End ✉ DL6 3AA – 𝒞 (01609) 883 526 – www.goldenlionosmotherley.co.uk – Closed 25 December, lunch Monday and Tuesday except bank holidays

OSWESTRY

Shropshire – Pop. 16 660 – Regional map n° **10**-A1

London 182 mi – Birmingham 66 mi – Chester 28 mi

XX **Sebastians**

TRADITIONAL CUISINE · COSY Housed in three characterful 17C cottages, Sebastians is a long-standing restaurant with an open fire, lots of beams and bags of charm. Cooking uses good ingredients and is classically based, and you'll be well looked after by the team. Many of the cosy, characterful bedrooms are set around a courtyard.

Menu £ 23 (weekdays)/45

6 rooms – †£ 65 ††£ 75 – ☒ £ 12

45 Willow St ☒ SY11 1AQ – ℰ (01691) 655 444 – www.sebastians-hotel.co.uk – dinner only – Closed 25-26 December, 1 January, Sunday and Monday

XX **Townhouse** ⓝ

BRITISH MODERN · FRIENDLY Contemporary restaurant in a Georgian townhouse. There's a flamboyant cocktail bar, a sunny terrace and an airy dining room featuring glitzy chandeliers. Classical cooking has a modern edge and dishes are attractively presented.

Menu £ 13/20 – Carte £ 27/52

35 Willow St ☒ SY11 1AQ – ℰ (01691) 659 499 – www.townhouseoswestry.com – Closed Sunday dinner and Monday

at Rhydycroesau West: 3.5 mi on B4580 – ☒ Oswestry

🏠 **Pen-Y-Dyffryn**

TRADITIONAL · COSY Early Victorian rectory in a peaceful countryside setting, with a pretty garden and lovely views. Classical guest areas feature antique furnishings; bedrooms have good facilities and contemporary fabrics – coach house rooms have their own terrace. Daily menus use local and organic produce.

12 rooms ☒ – †£ 97 ††£ 132/194

☒ SY10 7JD – ℰ (01691) 653 700 – www.peny.co.uk – Closed 14 December-15 January

OTTERBOURNE

Hampshire – Pop. 1 246 – Regional map n° **4**-B2

London 72 mi – Birmingham 134 mi – Bristol 96 mi – Cardiff 129 mi

🍴 **White Horse**

TRADITIONAL CUISINE · PUB Smart pub with designer décor, vintage adverts and leather sofas; one side is for drinkers; the other, for diners. Wide-ranging menu with lovely local cheeses, artisan bread, Sunday roasts and afternoon teas. Friendly service.

Carte £ 23/33

Main Rd ☒ SO21 2EQ – ℰ (01962) 712 830 – www.whitehorseotterbourne.co.uk

OUSTON

Durham – Regional map n° **14**-B2

London 197 mi – Cardiff 141 mi – Swansea 177 mi – Gloucester 241 mi

🏡 **Low Urpeth Farm**

FAMILY · PERSONALISED A stone-built Victorian farmhouse on a working arable farm: a very welcoming place, full of warmth and run with pride. Cakes and biscuits are served on arrival in the traditional, antique-furnished lounge; breakfast features homemade bread and preserves, and the spacious, comfy bedrooms have country views.

3 rooms ☒ – †£ 55/60 ††£ 80/85

☒ DH2 1BD – North : 1 mi on Kibblesworth rd – ℰ (0191) 410 2901 – www.lowurpeth.co.uk – Closed Christmas and New Year

GOOD TIPS!

England's oldest university city has a rich architectural heritage and this is reflected in our hotel selection, with Malmaison, for example, offering the opportunity to sleep in a former prison cell. A global restaurant scene sees Chinese, Lebanese, British, Italian and Thai restaurants all featured, with a couple of Bib Gourmands and plenty of pubs too.

© M. Carassale/Sime/Photononstop

OXFORD

Oxfordshire – Pop. 159 994 – Regional map n° **6**-B2

London 59 mi – Birmingham 63 mi – Brighton 105 mi – Bristol 73 mi

Hotels

Randolph

HISTORIC • CLASSIC This grand old lady exudes immense charm and character, and comes complete with an intricate wrought iron staircase and plush modern bedrooms. Have a cocktail in the magnificent bar or afternoon tea in the drawing room beneath Sir Osbert Lancaster oils. The impressive formal dining room offers classic menus.

151 rooms – £ 179/389 £ 189/399 – 9 suites

Town plan: BY-n – *Beaumont St.* ✉ *OX1 2LN* – *(0844) 879 91 32*
– *www.macdonaldhotels.co.uk/randolph* – *Restricted opening at Christmas*

Malmaison

BUSINESS • STYLISH Unique hotel in the 13C castle prison, where a pleasant roof-top terrace contrasts with a moody interior. The most characterful bedrooms are in the old A Wing cells; feature rooms are in the Governor's House and House of Correction. The basement brasserie serves an accessible menu, with steaks a speciality.

95 rooms – £ 120/240 £ 120/240 – £ 14 – 3 suites

Town plan: BZ-a – *Oxford Castle, 3 New Rd* ✉ *OX1 1AY* – *(01865) 268 400*
– *www.malmaison.com*

Old Bank

LUXURY • MODERN Warm, welcoming hotel in the heart of the city: once the area's first bank. It has a smart neo-classical façade and plenty of style. Elegant bedrooms have modern furnishings and eclectic artwork – those higher up boast great views.

42 rooms – £ 145/320 £ 145/320 – £ 15 – 1 suite

Town plan: BZ-s – *92-94 High St* ✉ *OX1 4BJ* – *(01865) 799 599*
– *www.oldbank-hotel.co.uk*

Quod – See restaurant listing

Garsington Rd	**AZ** 7
Henley Ave	**AZ** 10
Marsh Lane	**AY** 19
Oxford Rd	**AZ** 27
Oxpens Rd	**AZ** 28
Rose Hill	**AZ** 37
St Clements St	**AZ** 38
West Way	**AZ** 44
Windmill Rd	**AY** 45

🏠 Old Parsonage

TOWNHOUSE · PERSONALISED This ivy-clad sandstone parsonage sits in the historic town centre and dates from the 1660s. Enter into the original house via a pretty terrace; inside it's chic and modern – bold greys and purples feature in the bedrooms, along with the latest mod cons. Appealing menus offer classic British comfort food.

35 rooms – 🛏£ 189/335 🛏🛏£ 189/335 – ☲ £ 20
Town plan: BY-p – *1 Banbury Rd* ✉ *OX2 6NN* – ☏ *(01865) 310 210*
– *www.oldparsonage-hotel.co.uk*

623

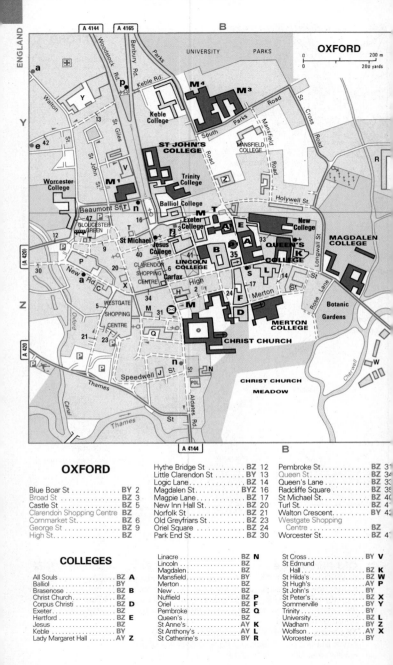

OXFORD

COLLEGES

⌂ Remont

BUSINESS · MODERN Spacious, stylish hotel on the outskirts of the city. Immaculately kept modern bedrooms are well-equipped and have plenty of personality; some have super king sized beds. The light, contemporary breakfast room overlooks the garden.

25 rooms ☑ – ♦£ 89/143 ♦♦£ 89/143

Town plan: AY-c – *367 Banbury Rd.* ✉ *OX2 7PL* – ℰ *(01865) 311 020*
– *www.remont-oxford.co.uk* – *Closed 2 weeks Christmas*

⌂ Burlington House   ♿ ⌦ P

TOWNHOUSE · STYLISH Handsome former merchant's house dating from 1889. Smart lounge with guest info overlooks a Japanese courtyard garden. Individually styled, modern bedrooms feature vivid wallpaper. Homemade bread and fresh fruit and juices at breakfast.

12 rooms ☑ – ♦£ 70/91 ♦♦£ 91/145

Town plan: AY-a – *374 Banbury Rd* ✉ *OX2 7PP* – ℰ *(01865) 513 513*
– *www.burlington-house.co.uk* – *Closed 21 December-2 January*

Restaurants

✗✗ Oxford Kitchen   ☕ 🅰️🅲

BRITISH MODERN · MINIMALIST Bright, modern neighbourhood restaurant hidden in a parade of shops in trendy Summertown. Menus list appealing, original dishes with a modern British base and cooking is refined and flavoursome. Come at the weekend for brunch.

Menu £ 19 (weekdays)/49 – Carte £ 29/52

Town plan: AY-e – *215 Banbury Rd, Summertown* ✉ *OX2 7HQ*
– ℰ *(01865) 511 149* – *www.theoxfordkitchen.co.uk*
– *Closed 2-15 January and Sunday dinner*

✗✗ Quod

INTERNATIONAL · BRASSERIE Buzzy brasserie in an old banking hall (now a stylish hotel). It's open from early 'til late and has a lovely terrace to the rear. Modern menus offer a mix of Italian and European dishes, along with twice-daily blackboard specials.

Menu £ 16 (lunch and early dinner) – Carte £ 22/52

Town plan: BZ-s – *Old Bank Hotel, 92-94 High St* ✉ *OX1 4BJ*
– ℰ *(01865) 799 599* – *www.oldbank-hotel.co.uk*

✗ Oli's Thai   🔟

THAI · FRIENDLY This lovely little restaurant is set off the beaten track, in an up-and-coming residential area. Start with a drink on the patio then make for the cool, relaxed restaurant; if you haven't booked, try for a seat at the counter. The concise menu offers fresh, meticulously prepared, vibrantly flavoured dishes.

Carte £ 15/25

Town plan: AZ-r – *38 Magdalen Rd* ✉ *OX4 1RB* – ℰ *(01865) 790 223 (booking essential)* – *www.olisthai.com* – *Closed Tuesday lunch, Sunday and Monday*

✗ Branca

ITALIAN · BISTRO Bustling restaurant with a spacious, modern interior and French doors opening onto a courtyard terrace. The menu is a roll call of Italian classics; portions are generous and lunch deals, good value. Friendly young staff; adjoining deli.

Menu £ 13 (lunch and early dinner) – Carte £ 19/34

Town plan: BY-a – *111 Walton St.* ✉ *OX2 6AJ*
– ℰ *(01865) 556 111* – *www.branca.co.uk*
– *Closed 24-25 December*

✗ Fishers

AC

FISH AND SEAFOOD · BISTRO Friendly, well-established seafood restaurant with a buzzy atmosphere and a pleasant nautical style; peep through the porthole in the kitchen door to watch the chefs preparing the simple, honest, daily fish and shellfish dishes.

Carte £ 20/36

Town plan: AZ-a – *36-37 St Clements* ✉ *OX4 1AB*
– ✆ *(01865) 243 003 – www.fishers-restaurant.com*
– *dinner only and lunch Saturday-Sunday*
– *Closed 25-26 December and 1 January*

✗ Shanghai 30's

CHINESE · ELEGANT Delightful, colonial-style restaurant in a characterful 15C building; the rooms are listed and feature wood panelling and ornate plaster ceilings. Menus offer a wide range of authentic Chinese dishes; don't miss the fiery Sichuan section.

Menu £ 12/23 – Carte £ 16/53

Town plan: BZ-n – *82 St Aldates* ✉ *OX1 1RA*
– ✆ *(01865) 242 230 – www.shanghai30s.com*
– *Closed 21 December-11 January and Monday lunch*

✗ Al Shami

&

LEBANESE · NEIGHBOURHOOD Smart, established neighbourhood restaurant serving well-priced, tasty Middle Eastern food. Beautiful, ornate ceiling in rear dining room. Lengthy menu offers wide range of authentic Lebanese dishes.

Menu £ 15/22 – Carte £ 12/19

Town plan: BY-e – *25 Walton Cres* ✉ *OX1 2JG*
– ✆ *(01865) 310 066 – www.al-shami.co.uk*

🍴 Magdalen Arms

BRITISH TRADITIONAL · PUB Buzzy battleship-grey pub boasting quirky old standard lamps, an eclectic collection of 1920s posters, board games and a bar billiards table. The experienced chef uses local ingredients to create flavoursome, good value dishes. Be sure to try the delicious fresh juices and homemade lemonade.

Carte £ 24/33

Town plan: AZ-s – *243 Iffley Rd* ✉ *OX4 1SJ*
– ✆ *(01865) 243 159 – www.magdalenarms.co.uk*
– *Closed 24-26 December, 1 January, Monday lunch and bank holidays*

🍴 The Anchor

BRITISH TRADITIONAL · PUB Not your typical pub, with subtle art deco styling and black and white dining room floor tiles. The main menu offers largely British classics with some Mediterranean influences as well as morning coffee and cakes and weekend brunches.

Carte £ 19/67

Town plan: AY-u – *2 Hayfield Rd* ✉ *OX2 6TT*
– ✆ *(01865) 510 282 – www.theanchoroxford.com*

🍴 Rickety Press

BRITISH MODERN · RUSTIC Professionally run by three friends; a shabby-chic pub in a residential area, with a cosy bar, a conservatory and a large room filled with wooden pews. Pub classics include the ever-popular Rickety burger with rosemary-salted chips.

Carte £ 15/33

Town plan: AY-r – *67 Cranham St* ✉ *OX2 6DE*
– ✆ *(01865) 424 581 – www.thericketypress.com*
– *Closed 25-27 December*

ᵀᴰ Black Boy

INTERNATIONAL · NEIGHBOURHOOD This sizeable pub serves unfussy, sensibly priced pub classics with a French edge; be sure to start with the tasty homemade bread. Alternatively, opt for cocktails and mix and match tapas at the bar. The Sunday roasts are popular.

Carte £ 25/41

Town plan: AY-v - *91 Old High St, Headington* ✉ *OX3 9HT*
- *𝒞 (01865) 741 137 - www.theblackboy.uk.com*
- *Closed 26 December and 1 January*

at Sandford-on-Thames Southeast: 5 mi by A4158 – ✉ Oxford

🏠 Oxford Thames Four Pillars

BUSINESS · FUNCTIONAL Extended sandstone cottages and a tithe barn set in 30 acres of peaceful parkland leading to the Thames. The bright College Hall bedrooms are the best; some have garden views and balconies. Great outlook over the river and gardens from the formal restaurant, which serves traditional dishes with a modern edge.

104 rooms - 🛏£ 130/300 🛏🛏£ 150/400 - ⌾ £ 13
Town plan: AZ-v - *Henley Rd* ✉ *OX4 4GX*
- *𝒞 (01865) 334 444 - www.oxfordthameshotel.co.uk*

at Toot Baldon Southeast: 5.5 mi by B480 – Plan: AZ – ✉ Oxford

ᵀᴰ Mole Inn

REGIONAL · PUB Popular pub with a pleasant terrace, beautiful gardens and a warm, welcoming atmosphere. The appealing menu caters for all tastes and appetites; sourcing is taken seriously and dishes disappear from the menu as ingredients are used up.

Menu £ 18 – Carte £ 28/34

✉ *OX44 9NG - 𝒞 (01865) 340 001 (booking advisable)*
- *www.themoleinn.com - Closed 25 December*

at Great Milton Southeast: 12 mi by A40 off A329 – Plan: AZ – ✉ Oxford

🏠 Belmond Le Manoir aux Quat' Saisons

GRAND LUXURY · PERSONALISED Majestic, part-15C country house offering the ultimate in guest services. Bedrooms are extremely comfortable – those in the Garden Wing are the most luxurious and have subtle themes. Relax by an open fire in the sumptuous sitting rooms or out on the delightful terrace overlooking the pristine gardens.

32 rooms ⌾ - 🛏£ 555/1790 🛏🛏£ 555/805 – 16 suites
Church Rd ✉ *OX44 7PD - 𝒞 (01844) 278 881*
- *www.belmond.com*

🏵🏵 **Belmond Le Manoir aux Quat' Saisons** – See restaurant listing

XxxX Belmond Le Manoir aux Quat' Saisons (Raymond Blanc)

🏵🏵 **FRENCH · LUXURY** Elegant beamed restaurant in a truly luxurious hotel; head for the large conservatory overlooking the lovely gardens. French-inspired cooking uses seasonal garden produce and dishes are prepared with skill, clarity and a lightness of touch. Choose from the monthly à la carte or one of two superb tasting menus.

→ Agnolotti of goat's cheese, honey and olives. Braised fillet of Cornish turbot with oyster, cucumber and wasabi. Trio of Grand Cru chocolate desserts.

Menu £ 82/159 – Carte £ 122/128
Church Rd ✉ *OX44 7PD - 𝒞 (01844) 278 881 (booking essential)*
- *www.belmond.com*

at Kingston Bagpuize Southwest: 11.5 mi by A420 – Plan: AZ – ⊠ Oxford

🏠 Fallowfields ⇗ ⇗ P

TRADITIONAL · RURAL 18C manor house in 12 acres of gardens and parkland; they keep an array of animals, from chickens and ducks to pigs and cows. Spacious bedrooms come in a mix of traditional and more modern styles; the rear rooms have the best views.

10 rooms ⌑ – †£ 115/135 ††£ 140/180

Faringdon Rd. ⊠ OX13 5BH – ℰ (01865) 820 416 – www.fallowfields.com

Fallowfields – See restaurant listing

XX Fallowfields ⇗ ⇗ ⑩ P

MODERN CUISINE · INTIMATE Light, airy restaurant in an 18C manor house, overlooking the croquet lawn and the paddocks. Elaborate modern cooking showcases produce from their garden, orchard and livestock. Every dish on the menu has a suggested wine pairing.

Menu £ 35 (lunch) – Carte £ 39/66

Fallowfields Hotel, Faringdon Rd. ⊠ OX13 5BH – ℰ (01865) 820 416 (bookings advisable at dinner) – www.fallowfields.com

at Fyfield Southwest: 9.5 mi by A420 – Plan: AZ – ⊠ Abingdon

⑩ White Hart ⇗ ⇗ P

BRITISH TRADITIONAL · PUB An intriguing 15C chantry house with a cosy open-fired bar, a minstrels' gallery and an impressive vaulted, flag-floored dining room – not forgetting a pleasant terrace. The diverse range of dishes is guided by produce from the vegetable plot; save room for one of the excellent desserts.

Menu £ 17 (weekday lunch) – Carte £ 25/42

Main Rd ⊠ OX13 5LW – ℰ (01865) 390 585 – www.whitehart-fyfield.com – Closed Monday except bank holidays

OXHILL

Warwickshire – Pop. 303 – Regional map n° **10**-C3

▶ London 90 mi – Banbury 11 mi – Birmingham 37 mi

🏠 Oxbourne House ⌆ ⇗ ⇗ ⑫ ⑰ P ⇥

FAMILY · HOMELY Large brick house in a quiet village, with a lovely mature garden and a tennis court. Elegant, antique-furnished lounge features a wood burning stove. Comfy, immaculately kept bedrooms offer good facilities and extras; one is split-level.

3 rooms ⌑ – †£ 60/75 ††£ 80/100

⊠ CV35 0RA – ℰ (01295) 688 202 – www.oxbournehouse.com

PADSTOW

Cornwall – Pop. 2 449 – Regional map n° **1**-B2

▶ London 288 mi – Exeter 78 mi – Plymouth 45 mi – Truro 23 mi

🏠 Metropole ⇗ ⇗ ⇗ ⌂ ⑲ P

HOLIDAY HOTEL · CLASSIC Grand 19C hotel perched on a cliff above the old railway station, just a short walk from town. Characterful, well-appointed guest areas. Bedrooms are a mix of traditional and contemporary styles; No.6 boasts great harbour and estuary views. Simply prepared lunches; more elaborate dinners.

58 rooms ⌑ – †£ 65/120 ††£ 69/259

Town plan: BY-a – *Station Rd ⊠ PL28 8DB – ℰ (01841) 532 486 – www.the-metropole.co.uk*

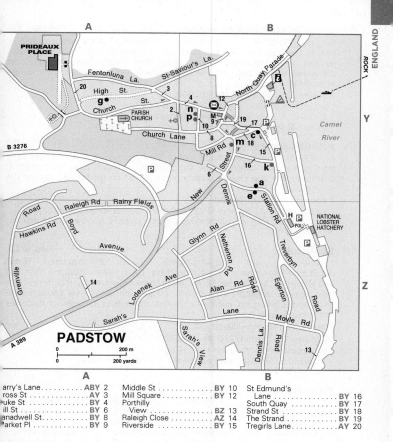

ENGLAND

PRIDEAUX PLACE

ROCK

A   B

Fentonluna La.   St-Saviour's La.

North Quay Parade

20 High St.

3

Church St.

g

Church

PARISH CHURCH

4 **12**

2

n **p**

M

10 **9**

19 **17**

Church Lane

8

m **c**

Mill Rd

18

15

16

k

6

New Street

Dennis Street

e **a**

Station Rd

H

POL

NATIONAL LOBSTER HATCHERY

Road

Raleigh Rd   Rainy Fields

Hawkins Rd   Boyd

Grenville

Avenue

Glynn Rd

Nelheton Rd

Lodenek Ave

Alan Rd

Road

Treverbyn

Egerton Road

Road

14

Sarah's

Sarah's View

Lane

Moyle Rd

Dennis La.

Road

13

B 3276

B 3276

A 389

PADSTOW

Camel River

Y

Z

0   200 m
0   200 yards

🏠 Old Custom House Inn

🏠 ≤ ⚲

INN · COSY Well-run, slate hotel; formerly a grain store and an exciseman's house. Relax in the beauty studio or the ice cream parlour. Nautically themed bedrooms feature good mod cons – some have roll-top baths or harbour/estuary views. Traditional bar and open-plan seafood restaurant; watch the chefs at work.

21 rooms ☟ – ♦£ 140/195 ♦♦£ 140/195

Town plan: BY-c – *South Quay* ✉ *PL28 8BL* – ℰ *(01841) 532 359*
– *www.oldcustomhousepadstow.co.uk*

🏠 Treverbyn House

≤ 🚗 ⚲ **P** 🚪

TOWNHOUSE · PERSONALISED Charming Edwardian house built for a wine merchant and run by a delightful owner. Comfy bedrooms feature interesting furniture from local sale rooms; one has a huge roll-top bath and all have harbour views – the Turret Room is the best. Have breakfast in your bedroom, the dining room or the garden.

3 rooms ☟ – ♦£ 100 ♦♦£ 130

Town plan: BY-e – *Station Rd* ✉ *PL28 8DA* – ℰ *(01841) 532 855*
– *www.treverbynhouse.com* – *Closed November-March*

Woodlands Country House

LUXURY · PERSONALISED Characterful Victorian house with a great coastal out-look to the rear. Tastefully furnished lounge, breakfast room and honesty bar; pictures, books and objets d'art abound. Comfy, homely bedrooms; 'Beach' is the largest and the best. The homemade muesli and hot specials are a feature at breakfast.

8 rooms ⌂ – †£75/89 ††£106/158

Treator ⊠ PL28 8RU – West : 1.25 mi on B 3276
– ℰ (01841) 532 426 – www.woodlands-padstow.co.uk
– Closed 20 December-1 February

Althea Library

FAMILY · RUSTIC Grade II listed former Sunday school and library, just 5min from the harbour. Homely lounge and breakfast room; pine-furnished bedrooms. In summer, the Aga-cooked breakfasts are served on the terrace, next to the pond and water feature.

3 rooms ⌂ – †£80 ††£98

Town plan: AY-g *– 27 High St ⊠ PL28 8BB – (access via 64 Church St.)*
– ℰ (01841) 532 717 – www.althealibrary.co.uk – Closed 1 January-1 March and
30 April-3rd May

XxX Seafood

FISH AND SEAFOOD · ROMANTIC Stylish, laid-back, local institution – dominated by a large stainless steel topped bar. Daily menus showcase fresh fish and shellfish. Classic dishes sit alongside those influenced by Rick Stein's travels; perhaps Singapore chilli crab or Madras fish curry. New England style bedrooms boast good quality furnishings; some have terraces or balconies and estuary views.

Menu £40 (lunch) – Carte £42/78

16 rooms ⌂ – †£154/270 ††£154/270

Town plan: BY-k *– Riverside ⊠ PL28 8BY*
– ℰ (01841) 532 700 (booking essential) – www.rickstein.com
– Closed 25-26 December

X Paul Ainsworth at No.6

❀ **MODERN CUISINE · COSY** A delightful Georgian townhouse on a harbour back-water, run by a friendly, enthusiastic team. There's a relaxed air throughout – the intimate ground floor is buzzier than the refined upstairs room. Seasonal modern cooking displays originality and the occasional playful element, and textures and flavours are bold yet refined. Try the 'Fairground Tale' for dessert. Bed-rooms were being added as we went to print.

➜ Smoked haddock, pearl barley, parsley, lemon and aged parmesan. Cornish hogget, Merguez roll, yeast-glazed celery root and spring garlic. A trifle 'Cornish', rhubarb & custard(c.1596), and saffron.

Menu £26 (lunch) – Carte £53/79

Town plan: BY-n *– 6 Middle St ⊠ PL28 8AP*
– ℰ (01841) 532 093 – www.number6inpadstow.co.uk
– Closed 10 January-4 February, 23-26 December, 1 May, Sunday and Monday

X St Petroc's

FISH AND SEAFOOD · BISTRO An attractive house on a steep hill, with an oak-furnished bistro and terraces to both the front and back. The menu offers a mix of simply prepared classics, with an emphasis on seafood and grills. Smart, well-appointed bedrooms are split between the house and an annexe – where you'll also find a small lounge and a peaceful library.

Menu £25 (lunch) – Carte £29/43

14 rooms ⌂ – †£160/250 ††£160/250

Town plan: BY-m *– 4 New St ⊠ PL28 8EA*
– ℰ (01841) 532 700 (booking essential) – www.rickstein.com
– Closed 24-26 December

Ⅹ Rick Stein's Café ⇔ 🏠 🖵

INTERNATIONAL · BISTRO Deceptively large café hidden behind a tiny shop front on a side street. Concise, seasonally changing menu of tasty, unfussy cooking with influences from Thailand, Morocco and the Med. Homemade bread and great value set menus. Comfy, simply furnished bedrooms; breakfast in the café or small courtyard garden.

Menu £ 24 – Carte £ 24/33

3 rooms ⌸ – ♥£ 113/154 ♥♥£ 113/154

Town plan: BY-p – *10 Middle St* ✉ *PL28 8AP* – *ℰ (01841) 532 700 (booking essential at dinner)* – *www.rickstein.com* – *Closed 24-26 December and 1 May*

at St Merryn West: 2.5 mi by A389 on B3276 – ✉ Padstow

🍴 Cornish Arms ⇔ 🏠 🅿

TRADITIONAL CUISINE · PUB Popular with locals – one of them was Rick Stein, who liked it so much, he now leases it! Nicely priced menu of pub classics, with seafood specials, Sunday roasts and nursery puddings. Cosy, beamed bar; light, airy dining room.

Carte £ 17/38

Churchtown ✉ *PL28 8ND* – *ℰ (01841) 532 700 (bookings not accepted)* – *www.rickstein.com/eat-with-us/the-cornish-arms/* – *Closed 25 December*

at Constantine Bay West: 4 mi by B3276 – ✉ Padstow

🏨 Treglos 🏠 ⑆ ⇔ ☒ ⊡ ⅙ 🚗

FAMILY · CLASSIC Long-standing, family-owned hotel, with tiered lawns leading down to the beach. Guest areas are spacious and well-kept and there's a lovely pool and spa. Classically styled bedrooms exhibit modern touches and many have balconies and sea views. Dress smartly for dinner in the traditional, formal restaurant.

42 rooms ⌸ – ♥£ 70/115 ♥♥£ 140/230 – 4 suites

✉ *PL28 8JH* – *ℰ (01841) 520 727* – *www.tregloshotel.com* – *Closed December-February*

at Little Petherick South: 3 mi on A389 – ✉ Wadebridge

🏠 Molesworth Manor ⇔ 🏠 ⅍ 🅿

COUNTRY HOUSE · PERSONALISED Part 16C and 17C former rectory set in mature gardens and run by affable owners. Elegant drawing room with honesty bar; spacious bedrooms boast period features, roll top baths and large walk in showers. Homemade preserves at breakfast.

9 rooms ⌸ – ♥£ 80/128 ♥♥£ 118/128

✉ *PL27 7QT* – *ℰ (01841) 540 292* – *www.molesworthmanor.co.uk* – *Closed November-January*

PATELEY BRIDGE

North Yorkshire – ✉ Harrogate – Pop. 1 432 – Regional map n° **13**-B2
▶ London 225 mi – Leeds 28 mi – York 32 mi

ⅩⅩⅩ Yorke Arms (Frances Atkins) 🏵 ⇔ ⅍ ⑆ 🏠 ⟲ 🅿

😊 MODERN CUISINE · FRIENDLY Charming, part-17C former shooting lodge overlooking the village green and run in a friendly, professional manner. Traditional, antique-furnished restaurant with a beamed ceiling and open fires. Measured and accomplished classical cooking demonstrates a good understanding of flavours; presentation is contemporary. Bedrooms have a subtle modern style and good comforts.

➔ Rabbit with broad beans, buckwheat, asparagus, quail's egg and dill pesto. Skrei cod with seaweed and lime crumb, mussels, scallop and lobster thermidor. Dark 80% chocolate mousse with raspberry, pistachio and chocolate & nut bar.

Menu £ 40 (weekday lunch)/85 – Carte £ 45/65

16 rooms ⌸ – ♥£ 250/275 ♥♥£ 345/430 – 4 suites

Ramsgill-in-Nidderdale ✉ *HG3 5RL* – *Northwest : 5 mi by Low Wath Rd* – *ℰ (01423) 755 243* – *www.yorke-arms.co.uk* – *Closed Sunday dinner to non-residents and Monday*

PATRICK BROMPTON
North Yorkshire – ⊠ Bedale – Regional map n° **13**-B1
▶ London 242 mi – Newcastle upon Tyne 58 mi – York 43 mi

⌂ Elmfield House ॐ ⇔ ⤳ ⅏ 🅿

TRADITIONAL · FUNCTIONAL Spacious guesthouse in a peaceful farmland setting, complete with livery stables, a fishing lake and a 14 acre forest. Bedrooms are warm and welcoming – two have four-poster beds. Relax in the vast conservatory or cottagey lounge.

4 rooms ⌂ – ♦£ 70/78 ♦♦£ 82/89

*Arrathorne ⊠ DL8 1NE – Northwest : 2.25 mi by A 684 on Richmond rd
– ℰ (01677) 450 558 – www.elmfieldhouse.co.uk*

⌂ Mill Close Farm ॐ ⇔ ⅏ 🅿

TRADITIONAL · COSY Modernised farmhouse with a walled garden and a summerhouse. Bedrooms blend contemporary furnishings with traditional features and have an uncluttered, homely feel; two boast whirlpool baths.

3 rooms ⌂ – ♦£ 50/65 ♦♦£ 85/100

⊠ *DL8 1JY – Northeast : 1.25 mi by Hackforth rd. – ℰ (01677) 450 257
– www.millclose.co.uk – Closed January and December*

PATTISWICK – Essex ➜ See Coggeshall

PENSHURST
Kent – Pop. 708 – Regional map n° **5**-B2
▶ London 40 mi – Royal Tunbridge Wells 7 mi – Maidstone 22 mi

⌂ Leicester Arms ⇔ ⇔ 🅿

BRITISH TRADITIONAL · INN Sympathetically refurbished 16C former coaching inn offering an evolving menu of rustic and satisfying pub classics. Sit in the garden room: a large bright space with a lovely rural view. Bedrooms are furnished in a contemporary style; ask for Room 8, which is the biggest, with the best outlook.

Carte £ 17/53

13 rooms ⌂ – ♦£ 75/105 ♦♦£ 85/135

High St ⊠ TN11 8BT – ℰ (01892) 871 617 – www.theleicesterarmshotel.com

PENN
Buckinghamshire – Pop. 3 779 – Regional map n° **6**-D2
▶ London 31 mi – High Wycombe 4 mi – Oxford 36 mi

⌂ Old Queens Head ⇔ ⌺ 🅿

BRITISH TRADITIONAL · PUB Smart country pub purchased in 1666 by one of the King's physicians; find a spot on the paved terrace or take in the view from the dining room. Big, hearty dishes are the order of the day; come on a Saturday for a laid-back brunch.

Carte £ 23/37

*Hammersley Ln ⊠ HP10 8EY – ℰ (01494) 813 371
– www.oldqueensheadpenn.co.uk – Closed 25-26 December*

PENRITH
Cumbria – Pop. 15 181 – Regional map n° **12**-B2
▶ London 290 mi – Carlisle 24 mi – Kendal 31 mi – Lancaster 48 mi

⌂ Brooklands ⅏

TRADITIONAL · PERSONALISED This Victorian terraced house is located close to the town centre and is run by warm, welcoming owners. It has a traditional, antique-furnished hall and a smart breakfast room with marble-topped tables. Homely bedrooms come with fridges and robes; one has a locally crafted four-poster bed.

6 rooms ⌂ – ♦£ 40/70 ♦♦£ 80/90

*2 Portland Pl ⊠ CA11 7QN – ℰ (01768) 863 395 – www.brooklandsguesthouse.com
– Closed Christmas and New Year*

at Temple Sowerby East: 6.75 mi by A66 – ✉ Penrith

Temple Sowerby House

COUNTRY HOUSE · CLASSIC Attractive, red-brick Georgian mansion with spacious, classically styled guest areas. Traditional country house bedrooms boast antique furnishings and contemporary facilities. Enthusiastic owners. Ambitious, modern menus of local, seasonal produce served overlooking enclosed, lawned gardens.

12 rooms ☑ – †£ 99/115 ††£ 145/170

✉ CA10 1RZ – ✆ (01768) 361 578 – www.templesowerby.com – Closed Christmas

at Clifton Southeast: 3 mi on A6

George and Dragon

TRADITIONAL CUISINE · INN Whitewashed coaching inn with a characterful 18C bar and modern, brasserie-style restaurant. Appealing dishes feature vegetables from the garden, game from the moors and organic meats from the Lowther Estate farms. Modern bedrooms showcase furniture and paintings from the family's collection.

Menu £ 15 (weekdays) – Carte £ 27/40

11 rooms ☑ – †£ 85/119 ††£ 95/155

✉ CA10 2ER – ✆ (01768) 865 381 – www.georgeanddragonclifton.co.uk – Closed 26 December

at Askham South: 6 mi by A6

Askham Hall

COUNTRY HOUSE · HISTORIC A fine, family-run castle on the edge of the Lowther Estate, dating from the 1300s and now stylishly and sympathetically refurbished. Spacious rooms are packed with period family furnishings. A 3 course menu reflects the seasons and features meat from the farm and vegetables from the superb kitchen garden.

15 rooms ☑ – †£ 138/308 ††£ 150/320

✉ CA10 2PF – ✆ (01931) 712 350 – www.askhamhall.co.uk – Closed Christmas and 3 January-mid February

at Newbiggin West: 3.5 mi by A66 – ✉ Penrith

Old School

TRADITIONAL · PERSONALISED Grey-stone Victorian schoolhouse in a small village. Compact, traditionally styled guest areas. Classical bedrooms are named after the colour of their décor – red, green and blue – the latter is the largest and has the best outlook. Home-cooked meals eaten at a communal oak table.

3 rooms ☑ – †£ 40/45 ††£ 80/90

✉ CA11 0HT – ✆ (01768) 483 709 – www.theold-school.com
– Closed 21 December-1 January

PENZANCE

Cornwall – Pop. 16 336 – Regional map n° **1**-A3

▶ London 319 mi – Exeter 113 mi – Plymouth 77 mi – Taunton 155 mi

Hotel Penzance

TOWNHOUSE · FUNCTIONAL Two adjoining Edwardian merchants' houses in a residential street, overlooking the bay. Relax in a period lounge or out on the terrace beside the pool. Bedrooms range from classic to modern in their styling and are well-equipped.

25 rooms ☑ – †£ 114 ††£ 165/220

Town plan: Y-c – Britons Hill ✉ TR18 3AE – ✆ (01736) 363 117
– www.hotelpenzance.com – Closed 2-12 January

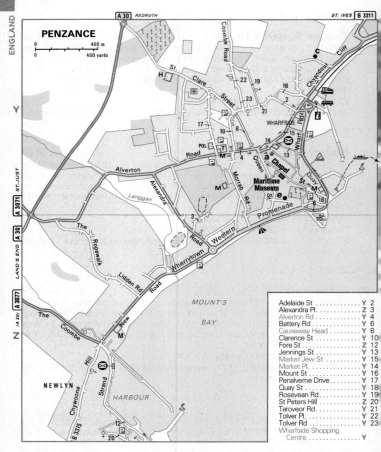

🏠 Chy-An-Mor   ⬳ 🛏 🥗 🅿

TOWNHOUSE · PERSONALISED This fine Georgian townhouse overlooks the promenade; fittingly, its name means 'House of the Sea'. Bedrooms have lovely soft furnishings
– two have 6ft cast iron beds. In the evening, twinkling garden lights welcome you home
and at breakfast they offer homemade muffins, Scotch pancakes and granola sundaes.

9 rooms ⌘ – 🛏£ 46 🛏🛏£ 82/95

Town plan: Y-e – *15 Regent Terr* ⌧ *TR18 4DW* – *ℰ (01736) 363 441*
– www.chyanmor.co.uk – Closed November-March

XX Harris's

TRADITIONAL CUISINE · CLASSIC Long-standing, split-level restaurant with
a spiral staircase and an unusual Welsh black metal plate ceiling; run by a keen
husband and wife. Classical cooking uses seasonal Cornish produce; try the
steamed lobster when it's in season.

Carte £ 32/49

Town plan: Y-a – *46 New St* ⌧ *TR18 2LZ* – *ℰ (01736) 364 408*
*– www.harrissrestaurant.co.uk – Closed 3 weeks winter, 25-26 December, Sunday
and Monday except Monday dinner June-September*

at Gulval Northeast: 1.25 mi by A30

🍺 Coldstreamer

TRADITIONAL CUISINE · PUB Dating from 1895, this striking pub sits opposite the church in the heart of Gulval. Its large bar is adorned with Coldstream Guards memorabilia; it has a bright dining room and fresh, well-appointed bedrooms. Concise menus feature local, seasonal produce in unfussy, traditional dishes. Good value lunches.

Carte £ 20/34

3 rooms ⛲ – 🛉£ 50/85 🛉🛉£ 65/85

✉ TR18 3BB – 𝒞 (01736) 362 072 – www.coldstreamer-penzance.co.uk – Closed 26 December

PERRANUTHNOE – Cornwall ➜ See Marazion

PERSHORE
Worcestershire – Pop. 7 125 – Regional map n° **10**-C3
▶ London 106 mi – Birmingham 33 mi – Worcester 8 mi

🏠 Barn

TRADITIONAL · COSY A hugely characterful series of outbuildings in a hillside location, run by a charming owner. There's a homely beamed lounge and three warmly decorated, well-equipped bedrooms: two share the lovely view and the third has a sauna. Communal breakfasts feature apple juice from the fruit trees in the garden.

3 rooms ⛲ – 🛉£ 60 🛉🛉£ 90/95

Pensham Hill House, Pensham ✉ WR10 3HA – Southeast : 1 mi by B 4084
– 𝒞 (01386) 555 270 – www.pensham-barn.co.uk

XX Belle House   🚹 AC

BRITISH TRADITIONAL · TRADITIONAL A pleasantly restored Georgian house in the centre of town, offering classically based cooking with modern touches; be sure to try the homemade bread. The well-stocked 'traiteur' selling freshly prepared takeaway dishes is a hit.

Menu £ 24/35 **s**

Bridge St ✉ WR10 1AJ – 𝒞 (01386) 555 055 – www.belle-house.co.uk – Closed first 2 weeks January, 25-30 December, Sunday and Monday

at Eckington Southwest: 4 mi by A4104 on B4080

🏠 Eckington Manor

TRADITIONAL · STYLISH A series of characterful, converted barns and a 13C manor house, set on a 300 acre farm. The charming owner runs it with pride and welcomes guests with homemade cake. Bedrooms are stylish; some have a freestanding bath in the room and all have eye-catching bathrooms with underfloor heating. The restaurant offers country views and unfussy dishes of local ingredients.

17 rooms ⛲ – 🛉£ 79/149 🛉🛉£ 129/249

Manor Farm, Hammock Rd ✉ WR10 3BH – (via Drakes Bridge Rd) – 𝒞 (01386) 751 600 – www.eckingtonmanor.co.uk

PETERBOROUGH
Peterborough – Pop. 161 707 – Regional map n° **8**-A2
▶ London 85 mi – Cambridge 35 mi – Leicester 41 mi – Lincoln 51 mi

XX Clarkes

BRITISH MODERN · FORMAL Contemporary restaurant on a paved square in the heart of the city. It's a spacious, formally run place; enjoy a drink in the smart bar or, in summer, make for the pleasant private courtyard. Cooking is complex, modern and seasonal.

Menu £ 20/40

Town plan: Y-x – 10 Queen St ✉ PE1 1PA – 𝒞 (01733) 892 681
– www.clarkespeterborough.co.uk – Closed first week January, dinner 25-26 December and Sunday-Monday

PETERBOROUGH

🍴 **Beehive**   😊 ⅍ AK 🔄

BRITISH MODERN · PUB Set just off the city centre ring road, with a smart modern interior, a zinc-topped bar and a mix of high stools, armchairs and banquettes. Dishes are well-presented, flavoursome and satisfying; the house pâté with chutney is a must-try.

Carte £ 20/30

Town plan: Z-x – *62 Albert Pl* ✉ *PE1 1DD* – *℘ (01733) 310 600*
– *www.beehivepub.co.uk* – *Closed 1 January and Sunday dinner*

at Glinton North: 5 mi off A15

🍴 **Blue Bell**   😊 ⅍ P

BRITISH TRADITIONAL · PUB Welcoming 18C pub in a pretty village. A colourful flower display greets you at the front and there's a pleasant terrace hidden at the back. Lunch offers pub favourites while dinner has a more ambitious edge; save room for dessert!

Carte £ 22/35

10 High St ✉ *PE6 7LS* – *℘ (01733) 252 285* – *www.thebluebellglinton.co.uk*
– *Closed Sunday dinner*

PETERSFIELD
Hampshire – Pop. 14 974 – Regional map n° **4**-C2
▶ London 60 mi – Brighton 45 mi – Portsmouth 21 mi – Southampton 34 mi

🏠 **Langrish House**   😊 🐾 ⪡ 🚪 🕍 P

FAMILY · PERSONALISED Mid-17C house surrounded by 15 acres of lovely gardens and grounds, and run by charming owners. Spacious country house lounges include one in the old Civil War cellars. Traditional bedrooms are individually themed and have good modern facilities. The tiny formal dining room offers contemporary cuisine.

13 rooms ⊇ – ♦£ 98/108 ♦♦£ 119/188

Langrish ✉ *GU32 1RN – West : 3.5 mi by A 272* – *℘ (01730) 266 941*
– *www.langrishhouse.co.uk* – *Closed 27 December-12 January*

XxX **JSW** (Jake Watkins)   🍸 🔄 😊 ⅍ 🕪 🔄 P
❀

BRITISH MODERN · RUSTIC 17C former coaching inn, in the centre of a pleasant town. The spacious, elegant beamed restaurant leads through to a wood-furnished terrace. Technically accomplished cooking is refined and flavoursome and relies on top quality ingredients. Choose between 3 and 9 courses from a huge array of menus. Staff are eager to please and bedrooms are modern with good facilities.

➜ Scallops with celeriac purée, mushrooms and nasturtium. Lamb 'Spag Boll', slow cooked tomato and basil cress. Milk chocolate ganache, popcorn, burnt butter sauce and lime.

Menu £ 40/50 **s**

4 rooms ⊇ – ♦£ 80/105 ♦♦£ 95/120

20 Dragon St ✉ *GU31 4JJ* – *℘ (01730) 262 030* – *www.jswrestaurant.com*
– *Closed 2 weeks January, 2 weeks April-May, 2 weeks August and Sunday dinner-Tuesday*

X **Annie Jones**   😊 🕮

MODERN CUISINE · BISTRO Relaxed neighbourhood restaurant on a busy street. Start with a drink on the terrace then make for the tapas bar to sample authentic, tasty small plates. The adjoining bistro has a bohemian feel and serves Mediterranean cuisine.

Menu £ 28 (lunch)/40 **s**

10 Lavant St ✉ *GU32 3EW* – *℘ (01730) 262 728* – *www.anniejones.co.uk*
– *Closed 25-26 December, 1 January, Sunday dinner, Monday and lunch Tuesday*

PETWORTH

West Sussex – Pop. 2 544 – Regional map n° **4**-C2

▶ London 54 mi – Brighton 31 mi – Portsmouth 33 mi

⌂ **Old Railway Station**   🚗 � ⚘ P

HISTORIC · PERSONALISED The perfect place for train enthusiasts: 8 of the 10 bedrooms are sited in genuine Pullman carriages; wonderfully restored, with impressive marquetry and sited at what was the platform of the station house. Check in at the ticket booth.

10 rooms 🖙 – 🛉£ 68/120 🛉🛉£ 90/198

✉ GU28 0JF – South : 1.5 mi by A 285 – 𝒞 (01798) 342 346
– www.old-station.co.uk – Closed 23-26 December

XX **Leconfield**   🏠 🅰 ⟳

BRITISH MODERN · ELEGANT Attractive, red-brick 19C building; inside it resembles a stylish brasserie – tastefully furnished, with a formal restaurant, a timbered first floor dining room and a cobbled courtyard terrace. Concise menu of refined, classic dishes.

Menu £ 25 (weekdays)/29 – Carte £ 40/54

New St ✉ GU28 0AS – 𝒞 (01798) 345 111 – www.theleconfield.co.uk – Closed Sunday dinner and Monday

at Tillington West: 1 mi on A272

🍴 **Horse Guards Inn**   ⟳ 🚗 🏠

REGIONAL · RUSTIC In an elevated spot in the heart of a quiet village sits this pretty mid-17C inn, which is as charming on the inside as it is out. Local seafood stands out and some of the vegetables come from their own patch. Young, friendly service. Simple, rustic bedrooms, with a family room in the cottage next door.

Carte £ 21/37

3 rooms 🖙 – 🛉£ 100/135 🛉🛉£ 100/150

Upperton Rd ✉ GU28 9AF – 𝒞 (01798) 342 332 – www.thehorseguardsinn.co.uk
– Closed 25 December

at Halfway Bridge West: 3 mi on A272 – ✉ Petworth

🍴 **Halfway Bridge**   ⟳ 🚗 🏠 🖳 P

TRADITIONAL CUISINE · COSY Charming 17C brick and flint pub; the open-fired bar is a great place to sit. Dishes are classically based but presented in a modern style – influences could come from Morocco, France or Italy, and puddings are nursery-style with a twist. The country-chic bedrooms are in the nearby converted stables.

Carte £ 29/51

7 rooms 🖙 – 🛉£ 85/105 🛉🛉£ 140/230

✉ GU28 9BP – 𝒞 (01798) 861 281 – www.halfwaybridge.co.uk

at Lickfold Northwest : 6 mi by A 272 – ✉ Petworth

🍴 **Lickfold Inn** ⓝ   🚗 ⅃ P

BRITISH MODERN · INN A pretty Grade II listed brick and tile pub with a characterful bar and a formal upstairs restaurant. Innovative, modern, highly seasonal dishes are accompanied by a degree of theatre. Terse dish descriptions and earthenware pottery give proceedings a Scandic feel; staff are friendly and eager to please.

Menu £ 25 (weekday lunch) – Carte £ 38/48

Highstead Ln ✉ GU28 9EY – 𝒞 (01789) 532 535 (booking essential)
– www.thelickfoldinn.co.uk – Closed Sunday dinner and Monday except bank holidays

PICKERING

North Yorkshire – Pop. 6 588 – Regional map n° **13**-C1

▶ London 237 mi – Middlesbrough 43 mi – Scarborough 19 mi – York 25 mi

🏠 White Swan Inn   ☆ 🅿

HISTORIC · COSY Well-run former coaching inn, with its cosy bar and lounges decorated in modern hues. Appealing bedrooms boast good mod cons and smart bathrooms; those in the outbuildings have heated stone floors and one even has a bath in the lounge. The brasserie-style restaurant specialises in meats and grills.

21 rooms ⌂ – 🛉£ 89/139 🛉🛉£ 99/169 – 2 suites
Market Pl ⌧ YO18 7AA – ℰ (01751) 472 288
– www.white-swan.co.uk

🏠 17 Burgate   🚗 🅿

TOWNHOUSE · STYLISH Substantial 17C townhouse with colourful gardens, run by a charming, experienced couple. The lounge features a large inglenook fireplace and a comprehensive honesty bar; the breakfast room has Mackintosh-style chairs and offers a menu of local produce. Spacious modern bedrooms are individually styled.

5 rooms ⌂ – 🛉£ 75/95 🛉🛉£ 85/108
17 Burgate ⌧ YO18 7AU – ℰ (01751) 473 463
– www.17burgate.co.uk – Restricted opening in spring and winter

🏠 Bramwood   🚗 🛇 🅿

TOWNHOUSE · COSY Friendly Georgian townhouse with a cosy, homely interior and pretty gardens complete with a pergola. Have breakfast in the large kitchen beside the china-filled dressers or in smarter dining room. Bedrooms are comfy and cottagey.

8 rooms ⌂ – 🛉£ 43/48 🛉🛉£ 68/82
19 Hall Garth ⌧ YO18 7AW – ℰ (01751) 474 066
– www.bramwoodguesthouse.co.uk – Closed Christmas

at Levisham Northeast: 6.5 mi by A169 – ⌧ Pickering

🏠 Moorlands Country House   ☆ 🛇 ⪕ 🚗 🛇 🅿

TRADITIONAL · PERSONALISED 19C restored vicarage in the heart of the national park, boasting superb views down the valley. Spacious, well-maintained interior with a classically decorated lounge and flowery wallpapers. Comfortable bedrooms boast rich colour schemes; one has a four-poster bed. Traditional three course dinners. Menu changes daily.

4 rooms ⌂ – 🛉£ 120/140 🛉🛉£ 150/170
⌧ YO18 7NL – ℰ (01751) 460 229 – www.moorlandslevisham.co.uk
– Closed November-April, minimum 2 night stay

at Sinnington Northwest: 4 mi by A170 – ⌧ York

🍴 Fox and Hounds   🔄 🚗 🅿

BRITISH TRADITIONAL · PUB Pretty 18C inn in a sleepy hamlet, with spacious, homely, individually decorated bedrooms: well-located for visiting the moors. Formal dining room, residents lounge and cosy bar with exposed beams and hanging hop bines. Big portions of proper, hearty, Yorkshire cooking. Service is a strength.
Carte £ 24/48

10 rooms ⌂ – 🛉£ 59/84 🛉🛉£ 60/170
· *Main St ⌧ YO62 6SQ – ℰ (01751) 431 577*
– www.thefoxandhoundsinn.co.uk – Closed 25-27 December

PICKHILL

North Yorkshire – ⌧ Thirsk – Pop. 401 – Regional map n° **13**-B1
▶ London 229 mi – Leeds 41 mi – Middlesbrough 30 mi – York 34 mi

🍴 **Nags Head Country Inn** ⇐ 👪 🏠 🅿

TRADITIONAL CUISINE · FRIENDLY Quirky pub close to the A1, with a rustic open-fired bar filled with framed ties, and a dining area hung with hunting prints. Blackboard menus list all the classics, accompanied by seasonal veg; game season is the best time to visit, as the owner likes to shoot. Cosy bedrooms are set in the pub and an annexe.

Carte £ 14/34

12 rooms ⌂ – ╪£ 50/78 ╪╪£ 80/97

✉ YO7 4JG – ℰ (01845) 567 391 – www.nagsheadpickhill.co.uk – Closed 25 December

PIFF'S ELM – Gloucestershire → See Cheltenham

PILSLEY
Derbyshire – Regional map n° **9**-A1
▶ London 161 mi – Manchester 37 mi – Sheffield 22 mi – Nottingham 20 mi

🍴 **Devonshire Arms** ⇐ 🏠 & 🅿

BRITISH TRADITIONAL · INN Traditional pub dishes get a makeover on the menu sourced from the Chatsworth Estate; servings are generous and dishes, satisfyingly filling. The stylish, contemporary bedrooms were designed by the Duchess of Devonshire. Stock up in the nearby Chatsworth Farm shop before going home.

Carte £ 20/31

13 rooms – ╪£ 89/169 ╪╪£ 89/169 – ⌂ £ 12

✉ DE45 1UL – ℰ (01246) 583 258 (booking advisable)
– www.devonshirepilsley.co.uk

PLUMTREE – Nottinghamshire → See Nottingham

PLYMOUTH
Plymouth – Pop. 234 982 – Regional map n° **1**-C2
▶ London 242 mi – Bristol 124 mi – Southampton 161 mi

Plans pages 641, 642

XX **Greedy Goose** ❶ 🏠

BRITISH MODERN · ELEGANT Smart restaurant housed in a delightful building dating from 1482 and named after the children's book 'Chocolate Mousse for Greedy Goose'. Cooking is modern and flavoursome and the local beef is superb. Sit in the 'quad' in summer.

Menu £ 20 – Carte £ 24/50

Town plan: BZ-n – Prysten House, Finewell St ✉ PL1 2AE – ℰ (01752) 252 001
– www.thegreedygoose.co.uk – Closed Christmas, Sunday and Monday

XX **Rhodes @ The Dome** 🍷 ⇐ & 🕸

BRITISH TRADITIONAL · BRASSERIE Contemporary restaurant with a stunning panoramic view over Plymouth Sound; start off with a cocktail beneath the vast cupola. The menu offers unfussy, fairly priced brasserie classics; from a burger to a smoked salmon croque monsieur.

Menu £ 25 (lunch and early dinner) – Carte £ 23/47

Town plan: BZ-d – Hoe Rd ✉ PL1 2NZ – ℰ (01752) 266 600
– www.rhodesatthedome.co.uk

XX **Barbican Kitchen** & 🅰🅲 🕸 ⇄

INTERNATIONAL · DESIGN Informal eatery set in the Plymouth Gin Distillery, comprising two long, narrow rooms with vibrant pink chairs and green banquettes. Brasserie menus offer a good selection of simply cooked dishes, with classic comfort food to the fore.

Menu £ 16 (weekdays) – Carte £ 25/46 s

Town plan: BZ-u – Black Friars Distillery, 60 Southside St ✉ PL1 2LQ – ℰ (01752) 604 448 (booking advisable) – www.barbicankitchen.com – Closed 25-26 December, dinner 31 December and Sunday

PLYMOUTH

641

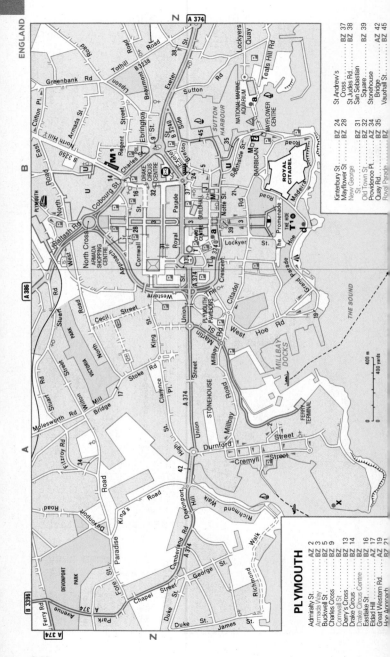

ENGLAND

PLYMOUTH

XX Chloe's

FRENCH · FRIENDLY Friendly neighbourhood restaurant with a small paved terrace, an airy, open-plan interior and a nightly pianist. Cooking is hearty and satisfying, featuring good old French classics; the lunch and early evening menus are good value.

Menu £19 (lunch and early dinner) – Carte £26/53

Town plan: BZ-a – *Gill Akaster House, Princess St* ⊠ *PL1 2EX* – *&* (01752) 201 523 – www.chloesrestaurant.co.uk – Closed 25 December-4 January and Sunday

X River Cottage Canteen & Deli

REGIONAL · BISTRO Large, buzzy restaurant in an impressive spot on the old dockside; inside, thick stone walls and reclaimed wood give it a rustic feel. Appealing menus offer gutsy, satisfying dishes and produce is seasonal, wild and organic. Most ingredients come from within 50 miles; buy some to take home from the deli.

Carte £19/30

Town plan: AZ-x – *No 1 Brew House, Royal William Yard* ⊠ *PL1 3QQ* – *&* (01752) 252 702 (booking essential) – www.rivercottage.net/canteens/plymouth – Closed 25-26 December and Sunday dinner

X Rockfish

FISH AND SEAFOOD · RUSTIC This buzzy quayside shack is ideal for those in 'holiday mode'. The rustic interior features reclaimed wood, hull-shaped banquettes and seaside snaps. Simply prepared seafood sits on greaseproof paper, atop stainless steel plates.

Carte £16/33

Town plan: BZ-r – *Sutton Harbour, Cox Side, 3 Rope Walk* ⊠ *PL4 OLB* – *&* (01752) 255 974 – www.therockfish.co.uk – Closed 25 December

at Plympton St Maurice East: 6 mi by A374 on B3416 – Plan: BY – ⊠ Plymouth

🏠 St Elizabeth's House

TRADITIONAL · MODERN Family-run boutique hotel – a former convent – with a stylish lounge and a pewter-topped bar. Good-sized bedrooms offer up-to-date facilities – their stark décor given splashes of colour by eye-catching fabrics. The smart dining room overlooks the garden; classical cooking displays Mediterranean influences.

15 rooms ⊊ – ♦£89/129 ♦♦£99/139 – 1 suite
Longbrook St ⊠ *PL7 1NJ* – *&* (01752) 344 840 – www.stelizabeths.co.uk – Closed 24-26 December

PLYMPTON ST MAURICE Devon – Plymouth ➜ See Plymouth

POLPERRO

Cornwall – ⊠ Looe – Regional map n° **1**-B2
▶ London 238 mi – Birmingham 223 mi – Bristol 142 mi – Cardiff 173 mi

🏠 Trenderway Farm

RURAL · RURAL 16C farmhouse and outbuildings in 206 acres of working farmland. Well-appointed bedrooms in a mix of styles; some with seating areas and kitchenettes. Cream tea on arrival; Aga-cooked breakfasts.

7 rooms ⊊ – ♦£95/175 ♦♦£95/175
⊠ *PL13 2LY* – *Northeast : 2 mi by A 387* – *&* (01503) 272 214
– www.trenderwayfarm.co.uk

PONTELAND – Northumberland ➜ See Newcastle upon Tyne

POOLE see Bournemouth plan

Poole – Pop. 154 718 – Regional map n° **2**-C3
▶ London 116 mi – Bournemouth 4 mi – Dorchester 23 mi – Southampton 36 mi

Plan : see Bournemouth

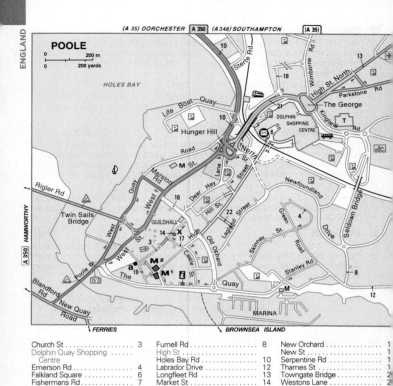

🏨 Hotel du Vin   ✿ & 🆔 🛁 🅿

TOWNHOUSE · MODERN A strikingly extended Queen Anne property in the old town. Smart guest areas have eye-catching wine-themed murals; stylish, modern bedrooms are named after wine or champagne houses – one boasts an 8ft bed and twin roll-top baths. Local produce features in classic French dishes and there's a 300 bin wine list.

38 rooms ⌷ – ♦£ 180/250 ♦♦£ 190/270

Town plan: -a – *7-11 Thames St.* ✉ *BH15 1JN* – ✆ *(0844) 748 92 65 – www.hotelduvin.com*

🏨 Harbour Heights   ✿ ≼ 🛏 🖶 🆔 ⅋ 🛁 🅿

HOLIDAY HOTEL · MINIMALIST 1920s whitewashed hotel, perched on the hillside, overlooking Poole Bay and Brownsea Island; the modern lounge-bar boasts a superb three-tiered terrace which makes the most of the view. Contemporary bedrooms come with good mod cons and smart bathrooms. The open-plan restaurant serves a modern menu.

38 rooms ⌷ – ♦£ 70/240 ♦♦£ 80/250

Town plan: BX-n – *Haven Rd, Sandbanks* ✉ *BH13 7LW* – *Southeast : 3 mi by A 35 and B 3369* – ✆ *(01202) 707 272* – *www.harbourheights.com*

ENGLAND

XX Isabel's

INTERNATIONAL · NEIGHBOURHOOD Lovingly run restaurant in a former chemist's shop, where the old shelving is still in situ. Grab a booth in the characterful red dining room or make for the basement room which opens onto the garden. Hearty French dishes feature.

Menu £ 25/35 – Carte £ 29/40

Town plan: BX-a – *32 Station Rd, Lower Parkstone* ✉ *BH14 8UD* – *☏ (01202) 747 885 (booking essential)* – *www.isabelsrestaurant.co.uk* – *dinner only* – *Closed 25-26 December, 1-2 January, Sunday and Monday*

XX Guildhall Tavern

FISH AND SEAFOOD · BISTRO Proudly run restaurant opposite the Guildhall, with a bright, cheery interior and a nautical theme. Tasty, classical French dishes are generously proportioned and largely seafood-based. They also host monthly gourmet evenings.

Menu £ 20 (weekday lunch) – Carte £ 30/52

Town plan: -x – *15 Market St* ✉ *BH15 1NB* – *☏ (01202) 671 717 (booking advisable)* – *www.guildhalltavern.co.uk* – *Closed 25 December-6 January, 2 weeks April, 2 weeks July, Sunday and Monday*

POOLEY BRIDGE

Cumbria – Regional map n° **12**-B2

▶ London 294 mi – Carlisle 25 mi – Keswick 16 mi

🏠 Sharrow Bay Country House

TRADITIONAL · CLASSIC Long-standing, celebrated Victorian villa in mature gardens and woodland; beautifully located on the shore of Lake Ullswater. It has a traditional country house style throughout, with extremely charming drawing rooms and a great sense of tranquillity. Comfortable bedrooms have a classic, cottagey feel.

17 rooms ⌑ – 🛏£ 150/520 🛏🛏£ 150/520

Ullswater ✉ *CA10 2LZ – South : 2 mi on Howtown Rd* – *☏ (017684) 86 301* – *www.sharrowbay.co.uk*

Sharrow Bay Country House – See restaurant listing

XXX Sharrow Bay Country House

CLASSIC CUISINE · ELEGANT Two delightful dining rooms in a beautifully located, traditional country house; 'Lakeside' has superb views over Lake Ullswater. Service is formal and dishes are as classic as they come; don't miss the 'icky sticky toffee pudding'.

Menu £ 27 (weekday lunch)/65

Sharrow Bay Country House Hotel, Ullswater ✉ *CA10 2LZ – South : 2 mi on Howtown Rd* – *☏ (017684) 86 301 (booking essential)* – *www.sharrowbay.co.uk*

at Watermillock Southwest 2.5 mi by B5320 on A592 – ✉ *Penrith*

🏠 Rampsbeck Country House

TRADITIONAL · CLASSIC 18C country house in mature grounds, affording lovely views over Ullswater and the fells. Spacious guest areas feature heavy fabrics and antique furniture; modern country house bedrooms have good facilities and marble bathrooms.

19 rooms ⌑ – 🛏£ 110/135 🛏🛏£ 170/350 – 1 suite

✉ *CA11 0LP – on A 592 – ☏ (017684) 86 442* – *www.rampsbeck.co.uk*

Rampsbeck Country House – See restaurant listing

XX Rampsbeck Country House ⟨ 🛋 🅿

BRITISH MODERN · FORMAL Elegant hotel restaurant with good-sized tables and beautiful lake and fell views. The oft-changing menu showcases local produce; cooking is modern and follows the seasons. Take your canapés and coffee in one of the drawing rooms.

Menu £ 32/69 **s**

Rampsbeck Country House Hotel, ⊠ CA11 0LP – on A 592
– ℰ (017684) 86 442 (booking essential) – www.rampsbeck.co.uk

PORLOCK

Somerset – ⊠ Minehead – Pop. 1 395 – Regional map n° **2**-A2
▶ London 190 mi – Bristol 67 mi – Exeter 46 mi – Taunton 28 mi

🏠 Oaks ✿ ⟨ 🛋 🕸 🅿

TRADITIONAL · CLASSIC Imposing Edwardian house boasting great views over the weir and Porlock Bay. Antique-filled entrance hall with a beautiful parquet floor. Cake on arrival in snug lounge. Large, comfy bedrooms come with fresh fruit bowls, good mod cons and smart bathrooms. Dining room offers classical daily menu and views from every table.

7 rooms ☲ – †£ 110/130 ††£ 160/185

⊠ TA24 8ES – ℰ (01643) 862 265 – www.oakshotel.co.uk
– Closed November-March

🏠 Cross Lane House ✿ 🛋 🕸 🅿

HISTORIC · STYLISH A very stylishly restored farmhouse and outbuildings dating from 1584. Inside it cleverly blends the old with the new, and great attention has been paid to detail. Cake is served on arrival and afternoon tea is a feature. The intimate formal restaurant offers a concise menu of modern dishes.

4 rooms ☲ – †£ 110/140 ††£ 140/190

Allerford ⊠ TA24 8HW – East : 1.25 mi on A 39
– ℰ (01643) 863 276 – www.crosslanehouse.com
– Closed 3 January-12 February and 1 week mid-November

> Take note of the classification: you should not expect the same level of service in a X or 🏠 as in a XXXXX or 🏨🏨.

PORT ERIN – Port Erin → See Man (Isle of)

PORT ISAAC

Cornwall – Regional map n° **1**-B2
▶ London 264 mi – Plymouth 50 mi – Newquay 24 mi

XX Restaurant Nathan Outlaw 🅽 (Nathan Outlaw) ⟨ 🕸🅾

🏵🏵 **FISH AND SEAFOOD · INTIMATE** A smart yet casual restaurant in a great headland location – the views from the first floor dining room are stunning. No-choice set menus focus on ultra-fresh fish and shellfish landed at the nearby harbour. Classical combinations are very carefully crafted, keeping the focus firmly on the main ingredient.

→ Lemon sole, oyster and seaweed. Turbot with watercress, cauliflower, bacon and razor clams. Rhubarb, strawberry, vanilla and yoghurt.

Menu £ 49/99 – set menu only

6 New Rd ⊠ PL29 3SB – ℰ (01208) 880 896 (booking essential)
– www.nathan-outlaw.com – dinner only and lunch Friday-Saturday
– Closed January and Sunday-Tuesday

✗ Outlaw's Fish Kitchen

⮷ **FISH AND SEAFOOD · INTIMATE** This intimate 15C building has low ceilings and wonky walls and is found in the heart of this famous harbourside fishing village. The day boats guide the menu, which offers a delicious mix of old favourites and appealing small plates – 3 or 4 dishes should suffice. Cornish gins, beers and wines also feature.

→ Gin-cured salmon with rye bread and horseradish yoghurt. Red wine braised cuttlefish with bean and samphire stew. White chocolate cream, caramelised banana and butterscotch.

Menu £ 40 (dinner) – Carte £ 12/29

1 Middle St ✉ PL29 3RH – ✆ (01208) 881 183 (booking essential at dinner) – www.outlaws.co.uk/fishkitchen – Closed January, Sunday and Monday October-May

PORT SUNLIGHT
Merseyside – Regional map n° **11**-A3
▶ London 206 mi – Liverpool 6 mi – Bolton 42 mi – St Helens 20 mi

⌂ Leverhulme

HISTORIC · STYLISH Attractive Edwardian building – originally the cottage hospital for a charming conservation village; now a boutique hotel where art deco features blend with contemporary styling. Well-equipped bedrooms and modern bathrooms. The restaurant serves tapas-style dishes; ingredients are sourced from within 28 miles.

23 rooms ⌂ – ♦£ 114/490 ♦♦£ 150/510

Lodge Ln, Central Rd ✉ CH62 5EZ – ✆ (0151) 644 66 55 – www.leverhulmehotel.co.uk

PORTHLEVEN
Cornwall – Pop. 3 059 – Regional map n° **1**-A3
▶ London 284 mi – Helston 3 mi – Penzance 12 mi

✗✗ Kota

⮷ **ASIAN INFLUENCES · RUSTIC** Welcoming 18C harbourside granary; its name meaning 'shellfish' in Maori. Cottagey interior with thick stone walls, a tiled floor and a mix of wood furnishings. Menus offer a mix of unfussy and more elaborate dishes, and display subtle Asian influences courtesy of the owner's Chinese and Malaysian background; many of the ingredients are foraged. Simple bedrooms.

Menu £ 18 – Carte £ 19/42

2 rooms ⌂ – ♦£ 50/95 ♦♦£ 60/95

Harbour Head ✉ TR13 9JA – ✆ (01326) 562 407 – www.kotarestaurant.co.uk – dinner only – Closed 1 January-10 February, 25-26 December, Sunday and Monday

✗✗ Rick Stein Fish and Shellfish ⓝ

FISH AND SEAFOOD · FASHIONABLE This old harbourside clay store has been transformed into a smart restaurant with floor to ceiling windows and a first floor terrace. Top quality seafood small plates are inspired by Rick Stein's travels and sharing is encouraged.

Carte £ 29/38

Mount Pleasant Rd ✉ TR13 9JS – ✆ (01326) 565 636 – www.rickstein.com – Closed 25 December, Sunday dinner and Monday in winter

✗ Square ⓝ

⮷ **MODERN CUISINE · SIMPLE** Small harbourside bistro: in summer, bag a table on the terrace; in winter, cosy up and watch the waves crash on the harbour wall. Coffee and cakes are followed by snacks and sharing platters, with more structure at dinner. Well-prepared modern classics have punchy flavours; go for the freshly landed seafood.

Menu £ 14/21 – Carte £ 24/35

7 Fore St ✉ TR13 9HQ – ✆ (01326) 573 911 – www.thesquareatporthleven.co.uk – Closed Sunday in winter

PORTINSCALE – Cumbria ➜ See Keswick

PORTLOE
Cornwall – Regional map n° **1**-B3
▶ London 296 mi – Plymouth 51 mi – Truro 15 mi

⌂ Lugger   🏦 🅿
HOLIDAY HOTEL · HOMELY This 17C smugglers' inn sits in a picturesque fishing village and affords dramatic views over the rugged bay. It's snug and cosy throughout, with open fires, low ceilings and friendly, personal service. Have a drink on the terrace and dinner in the elegant dining room, which serves seafood fresh from the bay.

23 rooms ☲ – ♥£ 65/175 ♥♥£ 99/255
✉ TR2 5RD – ☎ (01872) 501 322 – www.luggerhotel.co.uk

PORTSCATHO
Cornwall – ✉ Truro – Regional map n° **1**-B3
▶ London 298 mi – Plymouth 55 mi – Truro 16 mi

⌂ Driftwood   🏦 🍸 ≼ 🛋 🏊 🅿
COUNTRY HOUSE · PERSONALISED Charming clifftop hotel looking out over mature grounds, which stretch down to the shore and a private beach. Stylish contemporary guest areas are decorated with pieces of driftwood. Smart bedrooms – in the main house and annexed cottages – have a good level of modern facilities; some have decked terraces.

15 rooms ☲ – ♥£ 148/175 ♥♥£ 175/285
Rosevine ✉ *TR2 5EW – North : 2 mi by A 3078 –* ☎ *(01872) 580 644*
– www.driftwoodhotel.co.uk – Closed 8 December-5 February
    ✿ **Driftwood** – See restaurant listing

⌂ Rosevine   🏦 ≼ 🛋 🏡 🖥 ⚡ 🐾 🅿
HOLIDAY HOTEL · ELEGANT Dramatically refurbished country house overlooking the sea, with modern guest areas and stylish bedrooms with kitchenettes. They cater strongly for families: children have their own lounge, they offer family high tea, and the large grounds have a pool and play area. The all-day brasserie uses local produce.

15 suites – ♥♥£ 150/395 – ☲ £ 12
Rosevine ✉ *TR2 5EW – North : 2 mi by A 3078 –* ☎ *(01872) 580 206*
– www.rosevine.co.uk – Closed mid November-early December and January

✕✕ Driftwood   ≼ 🛋 🅿
✿ **MODERN CUISINE · INDIVIDUAL** Bright, New England style restaurant in an attractive house in a peaceful clifftop setting; it's delightfully run by a friendly, efficient team and boasts superb views out to sea. Unfussy, modern, seasonally pertinent dishes display technical adroitness and feature excellent flavour and texture combinations.
➜ Ballotine of lemon sole, shiitake mushroom, soy, sesame, radish and pak choi. Roast monkfish, with pomme purée, wild garlic, hazelnut pesto, cured lardo and morels. Driftwood chocolate bar, salted peanuts, honeycomb and milk sorbet.
Menu £ 58/95
Driftwood Hotel, Rosevine ✉ *TR2 5EW – North : 2 mi by A 3078 –* ☎ *(01872) 580 644 (booking essential) – www.driftwoodhotel.co.uk – dinner only – Closed 8 December-5 February*

PORTSMOUTH and SOUTHSEA
Portsmouth – Pop. 238 137 – Regional map n° **4**-B3
▶ London 78 mi – Brighton 48 mi – Salisbury 44 mi – Southampton 21 mi

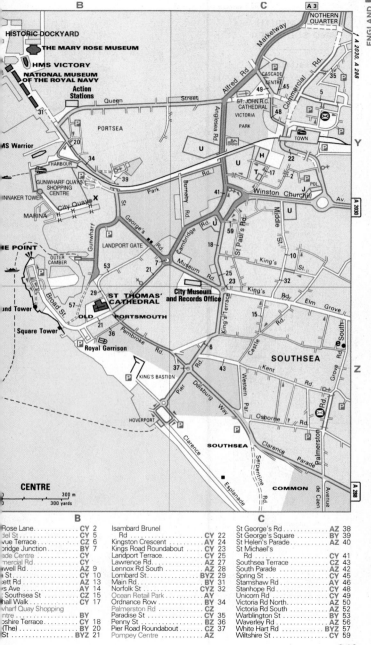

HISTORIC DOCKYARD

THE MARY ROSE MUSEUM

HMS VICTORY

NATIONAL MUSEUM OF THE ROYAL NAVY

Action Stations

MS Warrior

INNAKER TOWER

MARINA

E POINT

und Tower

Square Tower

Queen Street

PORTSEA

HARBOUR

GUNWHARF QUAYS SHOPPING CENTRE

City Quay

OUTER CAMBER

LANDPORT GATE

ST THOMAS' CATHEDRAL

OLD PORTSMOUTH

Royal Garrison

KING'S BASTION

HOVERPORT

Markettway

Alfred Rd.

CASCADE CENTRE

ST. JOHN R.C. CATHEDRAL

VICTORIA PARK

TOWN

Winston Churchill

Av.

City Museum and Records Office

SOUTHSEA

Kent Rd.

SOUTHSEA

COMMON

CENTRE

300 m

300 yards

PORTSMOUTH AND SOUTHSEA

For names of numbered streets,
see following page.

650

Clarence

TOWNHOUSE · PERSONALISED Immaculately kept, bay windowed house, just a short walk from the sea. Bedrooms come in various sizes and feature contemporary décor, superb modern bathrooms and pleasing extra touches; some have a TV inset in the bathroom wall.

8 rooms ⌂ – ♦£ 99/159 ♦♦£ 99/245

Town plan: AZ-c – *Clarence Rd, Southsea* ⊠ *PO5 2LQ* – *ℰ (023) 9200 9777 – www.theclarencehotel.co.uk*

Retreat

FAMILY · STYLISH Grade II listed Arts and Crafts house run by very friendly owners. It was built for the local mayor in 1889 and still has its original floors and stained glass windows. Rooms are spacious and understated and the place has a relaxed air.

4 rooms ⌂ – ♦£ 90 ♦♦£ 110

Town plan: CZ-e – *35 Grove Rd South, Southsea* ⊠ *PO5 3QS* – *ℰ (023) 9235 3701 – www.theretreatguesthouse.co.uk*

XX Restaurant 27

BRITISH MODERN · NEIGHBOURHOOD This long-standing, elegant restaurant is professionally and passionately run by its owner-chef. Contemporary cooking has a slightly Scandic style; attractively presented dishes taste as good as they look and are full of flavour.

Menu £ 50

Town plan: AZ-x – *27a South Par, Southsea* ⊠ *PO5 2JF* – *ℰ (023) 9287 6272 (booking advisable) – www.restaurant27.com – dinner only and Sunday lunch – Closed 25-26 December, Sunday dinner, Monday and Tuesday*

XX Brasserie Blanc

FRENCH CLASSIC · BRASSERIE Large bustling brasserie on the ground floor of the 'Lipstick' tower, complete with a bar, a small shop and a terrace. Watch the chefs prepare unfussy French classics in the open kitchen: the set menu is particularly good value.

Menu £ 12/17 – Carte £ 21/40

Town plan: BY-x – *1 Gunwharf Quays* ⊠ *PO1 3FR* – *ℰ (023) 9289 1320 – www.brasserieblanc.com*

POSTBRIDGE

Devon – Regional map n° **1**-C2

▶ London 207 mi – Exeter 21 mi – Plymouth 21 mi

Lydgate House

TRADITIONAL · COSY Personally run whitewashed house, set in a secluded spot high on the moors and accessed via a narrow track. Homely, cosy lounge and conservatory restaurant offering home-cooked local produce. Bedrooms are named after birds; many offer lovely views over the 36 acre grounds and the East Dart River.

7 rooms ⌂ – ♦£ 50/61 ♦♦£ 95/132

⊠ *PL20 6TJ* – *ℰ (01822) 880 209 – www.lydgatehouse.co.uk – Closed January*

PRESTBURY

Cheshire East – Pop. 3 269 – Regional map n° **11**-B3

▶ London 184 mi – Liverpool 43 mi – Manchester 17 mi – Stoke-on-Trent 25 mi

White House Manor

TOWNHOUSE · PERSONALISED Attractive Georgian house with a mature lawned garden and a sheltered terrace. Nicely furnished lounge boasts an honesty bar. Beautifully appointed bedrooms display quality furnishings; Crystal has a four-poster and a feature bathroom.

12 rooms – ♦£ 85/130 ♦♦£ 120/150 – ⌂ £ 12

New Rd ⊠ *SK10 4HP* – *ℰ (01625) 829 376 – www.thewhitehousemanor.co.uk – Closed 24-26 December*

PRESTON CANDOVER

Hampshire – Regional map n° **4**-B2

▶ London 59 mi – Croydon 67 mi – Barnet 72 mi – Ealing 54 mi

🍴 **Purefoy Arms**   ☐ P

🐸 **MEDITERRANEAN · PUB** Dating from the 1860s, this once crumbling pub was thoughtfully restored and is run by a charming, young but experienced couple. There are hints of Spain on the menu, especially in the bar nibbles; prices are very competitive and the focus is on flavour.

Menu £ 18 (weekday lunch) – Carte £ 22/43

Alresford Rd ✉ RG25 2EJ – ℰ (01256) 389 777 – www.thepurefoyarms.co.uk
– Closed 26 December, 1 January, Sunday dinner and Monday

PULHAM MARKET

Norfolk – ✉ Diss – Pop. 722 – Regional map n° **8**-C2

▶ London 106 mi – Cambridge 58 mi – Ipswich 29 mi – Norwich 16 mi

🏠 **Old Bakery**   ⇔ ⊗ P

FAMILY · CLASSIC Pretty 16C former bakery just off the green. The characterful interior features exposed beams and inglenooks. There's a homely lounge and breakfast room and good-sized bedrooms with modern facilities. Don't miss the 'Baker's Breakfast'.

5 rooms ⊵ – ♦£ 60/85 ♦♦£ 80/100

Church Walk ✉ IP21 4SL – ℰ (01379) 676 492 – www.theoldbakery.net – Closed Christmas-New Year

PURTON

Wiltshire – ✉ Swindon – Pop. 3 328 – Regional map n° **2**-D2

▶ London 94 mi – Bristol 41 mi – Gloucester 31 mi – Oxford 38 mi

🏠 **Pear Tree at Purton**   ☆ ⇔ ⚒ P

COUNTRY HOUSE · CLASSIC Heavily extended, personally run, 16C vicarage in 7 acres of grounds, which include mature gardens and a vineyard used for making their own wine. Comfortably and traditionally furnished throughout; some bedrooms have balconies or terraces. Conservatory offers a classical menu and garden views.

17 rooms ⊵ – ♦£ 109/149 ♦♦£ 109/149 – 2 suites

Church End ✉ SN5 4ED – South : 0.5 mi by Church St on Lydiard Millicent rd
– ℰ (01793) 772 100 – www.peartreepurton.co.uk – Closed 26 December

RAINHAM

Medway – Regional map n° **5**-C1

▶ London 14 mi – Basildon 16 mi – Dartford 9 mi

🍴 **Barn**   AC P

TRADITIONAL CUISINE · RUSTIC Black and white timbered barn transported from Essex and reconstructed on this site. It's heavily beamed throughout, with a rustic dining room and an upstairs lounge. The enthusiastic owner offers a menu of elaborate modern dishes.

Menu £ 25 (weekdays) **s** – Carte £ 31/42 **s**

507 Lower Rainham Rd ✉ ME8 7TN – North : 1.75 mi by Station Rd – ℰ (01634) 361 363 – www.thebarnrestaurant.co.uk – dinner only and Sunday lunch
– Closed 25-26 December, 1 January, Sunday dinner, Monday and bank holidays

RAMSBOTTOM

Greater Manchester – Pop. 17 872 – Regional map n° **11**-B2

▶ London 223 mi – Blackpool 39 mi – Burnley 12 mi – Leeds 46 mi

XX Sanmini's

SOUTH-INDIAN · FAMILY Charming little restaurant in a Victorian gatehouse. Neatly presented south Indian dishes have gentle spicing and are made from scratch; the family are doctors, so the cooking's healthy too. They also offer their own label beer.

Menu £ 25 (weekdays)/35 – Carte £ 17/31

7 Carrbank Lodge, Ramsbottom Ln ⊠ BL0 9DJ – ℰ (01706) 821 831 (booking essential) – www.sanminis.com – dinner only and lunch Saturday-Sunday – Closed Monday-Tuesday, Thursday and Sunday dinner

X Hearth of the Ram

TRADITIONAL CUISINE · RUSTIC Rustic former pub with characterful original features, a friendly team and a laid-back feel. The experienced chef offers a good value menu – choose from enticing pies and platters during the day and more sophisticated dishes in the evening. Cooking is classically based but has a light, modern touch.

Carte £ 17/41

13 Peel Brow ⊠ BL0 0AA – ℰ (01706) 828 681 – www.hearthoftheram.com

X Levanter ◯

SPANISH · SIMPLE Joe has a passion for all things Spanish – he's even a trained flamenco guitarist – so, unsurprisingly, his sweet little tapas bar has an authentic feel. The menu is dictated by market produce; try some freshly sliced Iberico ham.

Carte £ 20/25

10 Square St ⊠ BL0 9BE – ℰ (01706) 551 530 (bookings not accepted) – www.levanterfinefoods.co.uk – Closed Monday, Tuesday and Wednesday lunch

RAMSBURY

Wiltshire – Pop. 1 540 – Regional map n° **2**-D2
◘ London 73 mi – Bristol 53 mi – Cardiff 86 mi – Plymouth 172 mi

ⁱⁿ Bell

MODERN CUISINE · INN Charming 16C pub with stylish, well-appointed bedrooms. Dine on pub favourites among hop-covered beams in the open-fired bar or sit on smart tartan banquettes in the crisply laid dining room and choose from more ambitious, accomplished dishes. You'll find the locals at the back in 'Café Bella'.

Carte £ 24/40

9 rooms ⌂ – ♦£ 110 ♦♦£ 130/150
The Square ⊠ SN8 2PE – ℰ (01672) 520 230 – www.thebellramsbury.com – Closed 25 December

RAMSEY – Ramsey → See Man (Isle of)

RAMSHOLT

Suffolk – Regional map n° **8**-D3
◘ London 96 mi – Norwich 54 mi – Ipswich 17 mi – Colchester 38 mi

ⁱⁿ Ramsholt Arms

BRITISH TRADITIONAL · SIMPLE Honest, well-priced pub food and Suffolk ales in a great location. This striking inn is set against the spectacular backdrop of the River Deben; particularly magnificent at sunset and on summer days. Plenty of room on the terrace.

Carte £ 17/29

Dock Rd ⊠ IP12 3AB – ℰ (01394) 411 209 – www.theramsholtarms.com – Closed January and Monday-Thursday dinner November-February

RAVENSTONEDALE

Cumbria – Pop. 886 – Regional map n° **12**-B2
◘ London 272 mi – Bristol 247 mi – Cardiff 268 mi – Plymouth 361 mi

🏠 King's Head ⟵ ⌂

TRADITIONAL CUISINE · INN Whitewashed inn consisting of four 17C cottages; its smart interior featuring polished timbers, a flagged floor and a wood-burning stove. Well-prepared, appealingly presented, tasty dishes; eat in the garden, with a view of the babbling beck. Comfortable, elegant bedrooms.

Carte £ 19/37

6 rooms ⌂ – � £ 70/75 ♦♦ £ 85/98

✉ CA17 4NH – ✆ (01539) 623 050 – www.kings-head.com – Closed 25 December

READING

Reading – Pop. 218 705 – Regional map n° **6**-C3

▶ London 43 mi – Oxford 29 mi – Bristol 78 mi

🏨 The Forbury ❀ 🗓 ⟨ 🎱 🖨 🅿

TOWNHOUSE · STYLISH An impressive former civic hall overlooking Forbury Square Gardens; now a smart townhouse hotel where contemporary designs meet with original features. Luxurious bedrooms come with Nespresso machines, fridges and Bang & Olufsen electronics. The chic basement bar and restaurant offer modern menus.

23 rooms ⌂ – ♦ £ 138/300 ♦♦ £ 138/300

Town plan: Y-c – 26 The Forbury ✉ RG1 3EJ – ✆ (0118) 952 77 70
– www.theforburyhotel.co.uk

🏨 Holiday Inn ❀ 🗓 🏋 ⅃↓ 🖨 ⟨ 🆚 🎱 ⟰

BUSINESS · MODERN Conveniently located for the M4, with spacious open-plan guest areas, smart function facilities and a well-equipped leisure club. Stylish, uniform bedrooms come with good facilities and compact, up-to-date bathrooms. Have snacks in the comfy lounge or classic dishes in the formal split-level restaurant.

174 rooms – ♦ £ 55/199 ♦♦ £ 55/199 – ⌂ £ 15

Wharfedale Rd, Winnersh Triangle ✉ RG41 5TS – Southeast : 4.5 mi by A 4 and A 3290 off Winnerish rd – ✆ (0118) 944 04 44 – www.hireadinghotel.com

🏨 Malmaison ❀ 🖨 ⟨ 🆚 🎱

BUSINESS · CONTEMPORARY This is the oldest operating railway hotel in the world! Stylish lounges have rich contemporary décor and the bedrooms are dark and moody with good facilities and quirky touches; one even has its own train set. The dimly lit brasserie features exposed brick and pipework and is hung with railway photos.

75 rooms – ♦ £ 85/225 ♦♦ £ 85/225 – ⌂ £ 16

Town plan: Y-e – Great Western House, 18-20 Station Rd ✉ RG1 1JX – ✆ (0118) 956 23 00 – www.malmaison.com

✕✕ Forbury's ❀ ⌂ ⟨ 🆚 ⟺

MODERN CUISINE · FORMAL In a city centre square near the law courts, with a pleasant terrace, a leather-furnished bar-lounge and a smart, spacious dining room decorated with wine paraphernalia. Menus offer French-inspired dishes. Popular monthly wine events.

Menu £ 20/26 – Carte £ 32/58

Town plan: Y-a – 1 Forbury Sq ✉ RG1 3BB – ✆ (0118) 957 40 44
– www.forburys.co.uk – Closed 1-6 January

✕ London Street Brasserie ⌂ ⟨

TRADITIONAL CUISINE · BRASSERIE Bright, 200 year old building which was once a post office; the two decked terraces and some of the first floor tables overlook the River Kennet. The extensive menu offers something for everyone and dishes are stout and satisfying.

Menu £ 17 (lunch and early dinner) – Carte £ 29/51

Town plan: Z-c – 2-4 London St ✉ RG1 4PN – ✆ (0118) 950 50 36 (booking essential) – www.londonstbrasserie.co.uk – Closed 25 December

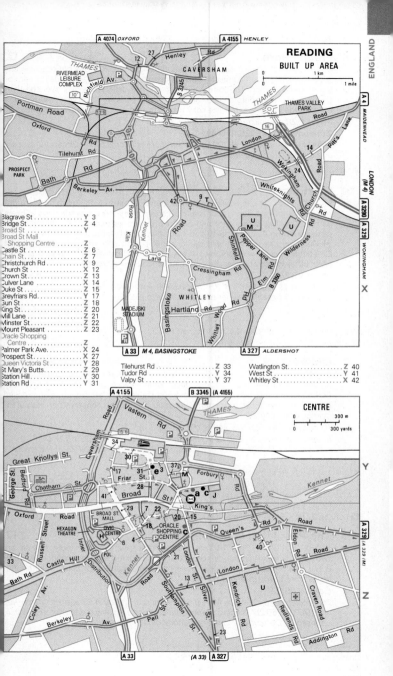

A 4074 OXFORD   A 4155 HENLEY

THAMES

RIVERMEAD LEISURE COMPLEX

Henley Rd

CAVERSHAM

Richfield Av.

Portman Road

Oxford

Rd

Tilehurst Rd

Rd

PROSPECT PARK

Bath

Berkeley Av.

THAMES

THAMES VALLEY PARK

Road

London

Wokingham

Whiteknights

Pitt's Lane

MAIDENHEAD
LONDON (M 4)
A 4
A 329(M)
A 329 WOKINGHAM

X

Rose

Kennet

Kiln

Lane

Cressingham Rd

WHITLEY

Hartland Rd

Basingstoke

Shinfield

Pepper Lane

Elm Rd

Wilderness

Church Rd

U

M

U

B 3350

Whitley

Wood

Rd

MADEJSKI STADIUM

A 33 M 4, BASINGSTOKE   A 327 ALDERSHOT

CENTRE

A 4155   B 3345 (A 4155)

Vastern Rd

THAMES

Caversham

Road

Great Knollys St.

George St

Bedford

Chatham St

Friar

Broad

Oxford Road

BROAD ST MALL

HEXAGON THEATRE

CIVIC CENTRE

POL

Russell Street

Bath Rd

Castle Hill

Coley

Av.

Berkeley

Av.

Pell

Distribution

Road

Southampton

Inner

Kennet

St Mary's Butts

King's

St

Forbury

M

ORACLE SHOPPING CENTRE

Queen's

Rd

London

Road

London

Silver

St.

Kendrick

Rd

Eldon

Rd

Road

Redlands

Craven Road

Addington Rd

U

A 329
A 329 (M)

Y

Z

A 33   (A 33) A 327

at Sonning-on-Thames Northeast: 4.25 mi by A4 on B4446

XxX **French Horn** ⇦ ⪍ 🛏 ⅊ 📺 ⇔ P

BRITISH TRADITIONAL · ELEGANT Beautifully located, 200 year old coaching inn, set on a bank of the Thames fringed by weeping willows; on sunny days head for the splendid terrace. The formal dining room has delightful views over the river and gardens and offers a classical menu of dishes from yesteryear – a gueridon trolley adds to the theatre. The cosy bedrooms are also traditionally appointed.

Menu £ 28 (weekdays) – Carte £ 39/70 **s**

21 rooms ⌷ – ♦£ 125/170 ♦♦£ 160/215 – 4 suites

✉ RG4 6TN – ℰ (0118) 969 22 04 – www.thefrenchhorn.co.uk – Closed 1-2 January and dinner 25-26 December

at Shinfield South: 4.25 mi on A327 – Plan: X – ✉ Reading

XxX **L'Ortolan** 🛏 🎁 ⇔ P

❀ FRENCH · FORMAL Beautiful, red-brick former vicarage with stylish, modern décor, several private dining rooms and a conservatory-lounge overlooking a lovely garden. Cooking is confident and passionate, with well-crafted, classically based dishes showing flair, originality and some playful, artistic touches.

➜ Hen's egg ravioli with wild garlic, confit potato and white truffle. Breast of Gressingham duck with pommes Anna, orange and ginger jus. Mandarin cheesecake, bitter chocolate ganache and mint chocolate ice cream.

Menu £ 32/65

Church Ln ✉ RG2 9BY – ℰ (0118) 988 8500 – www.lortolan.com
– Closed 25 December-3 January, Sunday and Monday

REDDITCH

Worcestershire – Pop. 81 919 – Regional map n° **10**-C2
▶ London 111 mi – Birmingham 15 mi

⌂ **Old Rectory** ⛲ 🌿 🛏 🎿 P

TRADITIONAL · PERSONALISED Part-Elizabethan, part-Georgian former rectory in well-tended gardens. Spacious guest areas have a cosy, country house feel. Bedrooms are split between the house and stables; the latter, with their exposed beams, are the most characterful. Dine in the bright conservatory restaurant overlooking the garden.

10 rooms – ♦£ 69/143 ♦♦£ 69/150 – ⌷ £ 13

Ipsley Lane, Ipsley ✉ B98 0AP – Southeast : 2.5 mi by A 4023 off B 4497
– ℰ (01527) 523 000 – www.theoldrectory-hotel.co.uk – Closed 25-31 December

REDFORD – West Sussex ➜ See Midhurst

REDHILL

Surrey – Pop. 34 498 – Regional map n° **4**-D2
▶ London 22 mi – Brighton 31 mi – Guildford 20 mi – Maidstone 34 mi

⅋ **The Pendleton in St Johns** ⅋ P

CLASSIC CUISINE · DESIGN The buzzing atmosphere and friendly service are two reasons why this pub is so popular and booking is recommended. Another is the food: generous, flavourful portions of seasonal French classics, with influences from S. America and the Med.

Carte £ 25/39

26 Pendleton Rd, St Johns ✉ RH1 6QF – South : 1 mi by A 23 and Pendleton Rd
– ℰ (01737) 760 212 (bookings advisable at dinner) – www.thependleton.co.uk
– Closed 25 December-2 January, Sunday dinner, Monday and Tuesday

REEPHAM

Lincolnshire – Pop. 2 405 – Regional map n° **9**-C1
▶ London 148 mi – Lincoln 7 mi – Grimsby 39 mi

X **Dial House**

TRADITIONAL CUISINE · SIMPLE Attractive Georgian house in a pretty village; all of its furniture, fabrics and antiques are for sale. Dine in the endearing Garden Room or in the Aga Room, where you can watch them making pancakes. Cooking is simple, fresh and tasty. 7 charming bedrooms are set to open in late 2015.

Carte £ 19/29

7 Market Pl ⊠ NR10 4JJ – ℰ (01603) 879 900 – www.thedialhouse.org.uk – lunch only and dinner Friday-Saturday

REETH

North Yorkshire – ⊠ Richmond – Pop. 724 – Regional map n° **13**-B1

▶ London 253 mi – Leeds 53 mi – Middlesbrough 36 mi – Newcastle upon Tyne 61 mi

🏠 **Burgoyne**

TRADITIONAL · CLASSIC A late Georgian house with a cosy, comforting feel, set in a lovely spot overlooking the village green and the Yorkshire Dales. The two lounges are filled with antiques and vases of flowers. Bedrooms are individually styled and traditionally appointed. The elegant dining room offers an all-encompassing menu.

10 rooms ⊇ – †£ 93/203 ††£ 110/220 – 1 suite

On The Green ⊠ DL11 6SN – ℰ (01748) 884 292 – www.theburgoyne.co.uk – Restricted opening in January

at Low Row West: 4 mi on B6270

🍴 **Punch Bowl Inn**

TRADITIONAL CUISINE · PUB Set deep in the heart of Swaledale, this traditional 17C stone-built inn is a popular stop-off point for walkers, who refuel on classic dishes like local lamb shank or beef and red wine casserole. Supremely comfortable bedrooms have a fresh, modern style and great views; superior rooms are more spacious.

Carte £ 20/33

11 rooms ⊇ – †£ 81/107 ††£ 95/130

⊠ DL11 6PF – ℰ (01748) 886 233 – www.pbinn.co.uk – Closed 25 December

at Langthwaite Northwest: 3.25 mi on Langthwaite rd – ⊠ Reeth

🍴 **Charles Bathurst Inn**

TRADITIONAL CUISINE · PUB Characterful 18C hostelry, set in a peaceful hillside village and offering commanding rural views. Lunchtime sees hearty British pub classics, while more elaborate dishes follow in the evening, with plenty of fish and game in season. Local beers include Black Sheep Ale. Bedrooms are spacious and comfortable.

Carte £ 20/43

19 rooms ⊇ – †£ 65/120 ††£ 85/135

⊠ DL11 6EN – ℰ (0333) 700 07 79 – www.cbinn.co.uk – Closed 25 December

REIGATE

Surrey – Pop. 22 123 – Regional map n° **4**-D2

▶ London 26 mi – Brighton 33 mi – Guildford 20 mi – Maidstone 38 mi

XX **Tony Tobin @ The Dining Room**

CLASSIC CUISINE · ELEGANT Chic, contemporary restaurant with a comfortable atmosphere and professional staff. Cooking demonstrates the chef's classical background whilst also incorporating some international influences. Most plump for the 5 course tasting menu.

Menu £ 25 (weekdays) – Carte £ 46/54

59a High St (1st Floor) ⊠ RH2 9AE – ℰ (01737) 226 650 – www.tonytobinrestaurants.co.uk – Closed 23 December-4 January, Saturday lunch, Sunday dinner and bank holidays

X **Barbe** 　　　　　　　　　　　　　　　　　AC

FRENCH CLASSIC · NEIGHBOURHOOD A long-standing French bistro with a cheery owner and a huge local following. Two main dining areas are strewn with Gallic memorabilia. Simply laid, tightly packed tables. Classical, bi-monthly menu.
Menu £ 20/35

71 Bell St ⊠ RH2 7AN – ℰ (01737) 241 966 – www.labarbe.co.uk – Closed 26-28 December, 1 January, Saturday lunch, Sunday dinner and bank holiday Mondays

RETFORD

Nottinghamshire – Pop. 22 023 – Regional map n° **9**-B1
▶ London 148 mi – Lincoln 23 mi – Nottingham 31 mi – Sheffield 27 mi

Barns 　　　　　　　　　　　　　　　　　⬠ ⇔ ⅌ P

TRADITIONAL · PERSONALISED 18C barn with a pleasant garden and a traditionally styled interior. The oak-beamed breakfast room is furnished with old dressers and Regency-style tables and chairs. Country bedrooms have good rural outlooks; one has a four-poster.

6 rooms ⊇ – ✝£ 39/75 ✝✝£ 64/75

Morton Farm, Babworth ⊠ DN22 8HA – Southwest : 2.25 mi by A 620 on B 6420 – ℰ (01777) 706 336 – www.thebarns.co.uk – Closed Christmas-New Year

RHYDYCROESAU – Shropshire → See Oswestry

RIBCHESTER

Lancashire – Pop. 888 – Regional map n° **11**-B2
▶ London 229 mi – Blackburn 7 mi – Manchester 41 mi

XxX **Angels** 　　　　　　　　　　　　　　　　　⚱ P

MODERN CUISINE · INTIMATE Smartly converted roadside pub with a cocktail bar and comfy lounge seating. Two formally dressed dining rooms, with a grand piano played on Friday evenings. Classic dishes with a modern edge; tasty, well-balanced and good value.

Menu £ 15 (weekdays)/45 – Carte £ 34/50

Fleet Street Ln ⊠ PR3 3ZA – Northwest : 1.5 mi by B 6245 (Longridge Rd) – ℰ (01254) 820 212 – www.angelsribchester.co.uk – dinner only and Sunday lunch – Closed Monday

RICHMOND

North Yorkshire – Pop. 8 413 – Regional map n° **13**-B1
▶ London 243 mi – Leeds 53 mi – Middlesbrough 26 mi – Newcastle upon Tyne 44 mi

Easby Hall 　　　　　　　　　　　　　⬠ < ⇔ P ⊟

COUNTRY HOUSE · HOMELY The views of the church, the abbey ruins and the hills are as stunning as this part-18C hall itself. There are two gardens, a kitchen garden, an orchard and a paddock – and even stables for your horse! Inside it's elegant and luxurious. Tea and scones or cocktails are served on arrival, depending on the time.

3 rooms ⊇ – ✝£ 150 ✝✝£ 180

Easby ⊠ DL10 7EU – Southeast : 2.5 mi by A 6108 off B 6271 – ℰ (01748) 826 060 – www.easbyhall.com

Millgate House 　　　　　　　　　　　　< ⇔ P ⊟

TOWNHOUSE · PERSONALISED Traditional Georgian guesthouse with a beautiful garden leading down to the river and a wonderful collection of silverware, grandfather clocks and antiques on display. Most rooms offer commanding views over the waterfall and castle.

4 rooms ⊇ – ✝£ 92/145 ✝✝£ 110/145

3 Millgate ⊠ DL10 4JN – ℰ (01748) 823 571 – www.millgatehouse.com

✗✗ Frenchgate   🗢 🍴 🛖 P

MODERN CUISINE · SIMPLE Part-dating from the 17C, with two open-fired lounges filled with vivid art, a simply furnished dining room and a lovely terrace and walled garden. Modern, ambitious dishes. Immaculately kept, well-equipped bedrooms; breakfast features local bacon and sausages, and preserves made from berries picked nearby.

Menu £14/39

9 rooms 🖵 – 🛉£88/198 🛉🛉£118/250

59-61 Frenchgate ✉ DL10 7AE – ☎ (01748) 822 087 – www.thefrenchgate.co.uk

✗ Richmond Grill + Brasserie

MEATS · BRASSERIE This modern brasserie provides a complete contrast to the cobbled marketplace in which it stands. Bold wallpaper, lime green banquettes and grey chairs feature. Menus offer grills, sharing plates and modern takes on brasserie classics.

Menu £15 (weekdays) – Carte £21/76

2-3 Trinity Sq. Market Pl. ✉ DL10 4HY – ☎ (01748) 822 602 – www.rgandb.co.uk – Closed Sunday and Monday

RIMPTON

Somerset – Pop. 235 – Regional map n° **2**-C3

▶ London 126 mi – Bath 50 mi – Bournemouth 44 mi – Exeter 57 mi

🍴 White Post   🗢 🛖 🛓 P

CLASSIC CUISINE · PUB On the Dorset/Somerset border, with stunning views of the West Country. Plenty of pub classics alongside more imaginative creations and quirky touches like piggy nibbles and the Sunday roast board: surely every carnivore's dream dish? Bedrooms are simply furnished: ask for Dorset, which has the best views.

Menu £15/45 – Carte £23/41

3 rooms 🖵 – 🛉£80 🛉🛉£95

✉ BA22 8AR – ☎ (01935) 851 525 – www.thewhitepost.com – Closed 1-14 January and Sunday dinner

RINGWOOD

Hampshire – Pop. 13 943 – Regional map n° **4**-A2

▶ London 102 mi – Bournemouth 11 mi – Salisbury 17 mi – Southampton 20 mi

🏨 Moortown Lodge   P

BUSINESS · PERSONALISED Welcoming Georgian hunting lodge built in 1760, set on a busy road at the edge of the forest. The large main room has fireside sofas and neatly laid breakfast tables. Well-kept bedrooms offer good comforts; some have feature beds.

7 rooms 🖵 – 🛉£75/86 🛉🛉£86/96

244 Christchurch Rd ✉ BH24 3AS – South : 1 mi on B 3347 – ☎ (01425) 471 404 – www.moortownlodge.co.uk

RIPLEY

North Yorkshire – ✉ Harrogate – Pop. 193 – Regional map n° **13**-B2

▶ London 213 mi – Bradford 21 mi – Leeds 18 mi – Newcastle upon Tyne 79 mi

🏨 Boar's Head   🏊 🍴 🗢 ✗ P

HISTORIC · CLASSIC 18C creeper-clad coaching inn, set in an estate-owned village and reputedly furnished from the nearby castle's attics. Family portraits and knick-knacks fill the lounges. Comfy bedrooms are found in the inn, the courtyard and an adjacent house. The all-encompassing menu is served in various different rooms.

25 rooms 🖵 – 🛉£85/105 🛉🛉£100/125

✉ HG3 3AY – ☎ (01423) 771 888 – www.boarsheadripley.co.uk

RIPLEY
Surrey – Pop. 2 041 – Regional map n° **4**-C1
▶ London 24 mi – Croydon 22 mi – Barnet 46 mi – Ealing 28 mi

Broadway Barn
TOWNHOUSE · DESIGN This charming red-brick building was formerly an antique shop. Inside it's smart and modern with spacious guest areas; bedrooms show good attention to detail and come with thoughtful extras.
4 rooms � – ♦£ 99 ♦♦£ 99
High St ✉ *GU23 6AQ –* ☏ *(01483) 223 200 – www.broadwaybarn.com*

Drake's (Steve Drake)
MODERN CUISINE · INTIMATE A red-brick Georgian building with a large double-sided clock above the door and a drinks terrace overlooking a beautiful garden to the rear. The panelled bar leads to an elegant modern dining room. At dinner, choose between two set menus; creative, accomplished, very visual cooking pushes the boundaries.
➜ Charred salmon, rhubarb emulsion, radish and sorrel. Suckling pig, piquillo pepper, pickled parsnip and sage butter. Raspberry panna cotta, Piura chocolate and hazelnut milk sorbet.
Menu £ 30/60
The Clock House, High St ✉ *GU23 6AQ –* ☏ *(01483) 224 777*
– www.drakesrestaurant.co.uk – Closed 2 weeks August, 1 week January, 1 week Christmas, Tuesday lunch, Sunday and Monday

Anchor
CLASSIC CUISINE · RUSTIC A smart yet rustic pub with polished slate floors and on-trend grey walls; it is nowhere near water but it is near a famous 19C cycle route, which explains the bicycle theme. Classic dishes are carefully executed and bursting with flavour.
Carte £ 24/42
High St ✉ *GU23 6AE –* ☏ *(01483) 211 866 – www.ripleyanchor.co.uk – Closed Monday*

RIPON
North Yorkshire – Pop. 16 363 – Regional map n° **13**-B2
▶ London 222 mi – Leeds 26 mi – Middlesbrough 35 mi – York 23 mi

Old Deanery
TOWNHOUSE · PERSONALISED Attractive former deanery opposite Ripon Cathedral. Inside, modern furnishings blend with older features; climb the 18C oak staircase to the comfy, up-to-date bedrooms – some have beams, Victorian-style baths and cathedral views. Light supper sharing boards are served in the bar.
10 rooms ☐ – ♦£ 85/110 ♦♦£ 105/150
Minster Rd ✉ *HG4 1QS –* ☏ *(01765) 600 003 – www.theolddeanery.co.uk – Closed 25 December*

at Aldfield Southwest: 3.75 mi by B6265 – ✉ Ripon

Bay Tree Farm
TRADITIONAL · COSY 18C sandstone barn on a working beef farm, with a smartly furnished farmhouse interior and country views. The open-fired lounge is hung with farm implements and opens onto the garden. The welcoming owners always make time to talk.
6 rooms ☐ – ♦£ 50/80 ♦♦£ 90/100
✉ *HG4 3BE –* ☏ *(01765) 620 394 – www.baytreefarm.co.uk*

ROADE
Northamptonshire – Pop. 2 312 – Regional map n° **9**-B3
▶ London 66 mi – Coventry 36 mi – Leicester 42 mi – Northampton 5 mi

XX **Roade House**

TRADITIONAL CUISINE · FRIENDLY Longstanding, personally run, former village pub and schoolhouse, with an open-fired lounge and a simple, linen-laid dining room. The set lunch and à la carte dinner menus offer classical French cooking with the occasional Mediterranean influence. Pleasant bedrooms are furnished in pine.

Menu £ 21 (weekday lunch) – Carte £ 27/42

10 rooms 🖙 – 🛉£ 75/90 🛉🛉£ 75/90

16 High St ⊠ NN7 2NW – ℰ (01604) 863 372 – www.roadehousehotel.co.uk
– Closed 26-30 December, Sunday dinner and bank holiday Mondays

ROCHDALE

Greater Manchester – Pop. 107 926 – Regional map n° **11**-B2

▶ London 224 mi – Blackpool 40 mi – Burnley 11 mi – Leeds 45 mi

XX **Peacock Room at The Crimble**

TRADITIONAL CUISINE · FORMAL A winding drive leads up to this landmark Victorian house. Bypass the pub and head for the restaurant, where you'll find a large mirror-ceilinged room with vast chandeliers. Constantly evolving modern menus rely on local produce.

Menu £ 14 (weekdays)/22 – Carte £ 26/44

Crimble Ln, Bamford ⊠ OL11 4AD – West : 2 mi on B 6222
– ℰ (01706) 368 591 – www.thedeckersgroup.com
– Closed Monday, Tuesday and lunch Saturday

XX **Nutters**

BRITISH MODERN · FRIENDLY Enthusiastically run restaurant in a beautiful old manor house – and a popular spot for afternoon tea. Appealing menus list modern British dishes with international influences. Can't decide? Go for the 6 course 'Surprise' menu.

Menu £ 17 (weekday lunch) – Carte £ 26/40

Edenfield Rd, Norden ⊠ OL12 7TT – West : 3.5 mi on A 680
– ℰ (01706) 650 167 – www.nuttersrestaurant.com
– Closed 29-30 December, 5-6 January and Monday

ROCK

Cornwall – ⊠ Wadebridge – Pop. 4 593 – Regional map n° **1**-B2

▶ London 266 mi – Newquay 24 mi – Tintagel 14 mi – Truro 32 mi

🏠 **St Enodoc**

FAMILY · PERSONALISED Beautifully located hotel boasting stunning bay views. There's a strong New England feel throughout, courtesy of striped sofas and pastel coloured woodwork. Most of the contemporary, well-appointed bedrooms have a sea outlook.

20 rooms 🖙 – 🛉£ 175/265 🛉🛉£ 195/425

⊠ PL27 6LA – ℰ (01208) 863 394 – www.enodoc-hotel.co.uk

Outlaw's – See restaurant listing

XX **Dining Room**

BRITISH TRADITIONAL · NEIGHBOURHOOD Immaculately kept, understated restaurant with modern seascapes on the walls; run by a friendly, family-led team. Flavoursome, classically based cooking features local seasonal produce. Everything is homemade, including the butter.

Carte £ 36/45

Pavilion Buildings, Rock Rd ⊠ PL27 6JS – ℰ (01208) 862 622 (booking essential)
– www.thediningroomrock.co.uk – dinner only
– Closed 2 weeks January-February, 2 weeks November, Monday except bank holidays and Tuesday

✗ Outlaw's ⟨ 🏠 🅿

FISH AND SEAFOOD · BRASSERIE All-day brasserie and bar with views over the Camel Estuary and doors which open out onto a lovely rear terrace. Menus feature simply executed steak and seafood dishes, along with some lighter offerings; local ingredients are key.

Menu £ 25/45

St Enodoc Hotel, ✉ PL27 6LA – 𝒞 (01208) 862 737 – www.nathan-outlaw.com – Closed 20 December-29 January

🍴 Mariners ⓝ ⟨ 🏠 🛅 🖵

TRADITIONAL CUISINE · PUB Two of Cornwall's top ambassadors – Sharp's Brewery and Nathan Outlaw – have come together to run this pub. Satisfying dishes feature local seafood and top quality meats. Sit on the terrace for stunning views of the Camel Estuary.

Carte £ 21/47

Slipway ✉ PL27 6LD – 𝒞 (01208) 863 679 – www.marinersrock.com – Closed 25 December

at Trebetherick North: 1 mi by Trewint Lane

🏨 St Moritz ⟨ 🏠 🛅 🅿

HOLIDAY HOTEL · CONTEMPORARY Art deco style hotel with a leisure club, indoor and outdoor swimming pools and a 6 room spa. Contemporary bedrooms have a minimalistic style and spacious bathrooms. Suites have an open plan lounge, a kitchen and balconies with estuary views. Modern brasserie serves a simple, flavoursome menu of unfussy dishes. Informal, poolside restaurant, Sea Side.

30 rooms 🖵 – †£ 90/278 ††£ 120/370 – 15 suites

✉ *PL27 6SD – 𝒞 (01208) 862 242 – www.stmoritzhotel.co.uk*

ROCKBEARE – Devon ➜ See Exeter

ROECLIFFE – North Yorkshire ➜ See Boroughbridge

ROMALDKIRK – Durham ➜ See Barnard Castle

ROMSEY

Hampshire – Pop. 16 998 – Regional map n° **4**-A2

▶ London 82 mi – Bournemouth 28 mi – Salisbury 16 mi – Southampton 8 mi

🏨 White Horse ⟨ 🏠

HISTORIC · FUNCTIONAL Smartly refurbished coaching inn; one of only 12 in the country to have continuously served as a hotel since the 14C – maybe even earlier! Guest areas feature beams, exposed brick and inglenook fireplaces. Well-equipped modern bedrooms include two duplex suites. The extensive brasserie menu suits all tastes.

31 rooms 🖵 – †£ 95/110 ††£ 145/270

Market Pl ✉ SO51 8ZJ – 𝒞 (01794) 512 431 – www.thewhitehorseromsey.com

🏠 Ranvilles Farm House ⟨ 🅿 📠

TRADITIONAL · CLASSIC Attractive, part-16C farmhouse in colourful grounds. The spacious beamed interior has a cottagey, country house feel and period pieces feature throughout – the comfy lounge boasts an antique breakfast table. Bedrooms are homely.

5 rooms 🖵 – †£ 35/50 ††£ 78/85

Ower ✉ SO51 6AA – Southwest : 2 mi on A 3090 (southbound carriageway) – 𝒞 (023) 8081 4481 – www.ranvilles.com – Closed 25 December

Three Tuns

BRITISH MODERN · PUB A delightful pub, dating back to the 1720s; with its rustic beamed bar and panelled dining room, it oozes charm. The well-priced 'proper' pub menu proudly lists local suppliers and dishes might include ham hock terrine or pot roast partridge. Service comes from a young, very hospitable team.

Carte £ 24/30

58 Middlebridge St ⊠ SO51 8HL – ℰ (01794) 512 639 – www.the3tunsromsey.co.uk – Closed 25-26 December

ROSS-ON-WYE

Herefordshire – Pop. 10 582 – Regional map n° **10**-B3

▶ London 118 mi – Gloucester 15 mi – Birmingham 61 mi

Wilton Court

HISTORIC · COSY Attractive, part-Elizabethan house out of the town centre, on the banks of the River Wye. Traditionally styled, comfortable bedrooms have good facilities; those to the front have a river view. Tasty breakfasts with home-made preserves. Choice of two dining rooms; classic menus utilise local produce.

11 rooms ⊡ – ♦£ 100/155 ♦♦£ 135/185

Wilton Ln, Wilton ⊠ HR9 6AQ – West : 0.75 mi by B 4260 – ℰ (01989) 562 569 – www.wiltoncourthotel.com – Closed 2-22 January

Bridge House

TOWNHOUSE · STYLISH You get a lot more than you bargained for at this 18C townhouse: original features combine with chic, stylish furnishings; there's a superb view of the town and the River Wye; and the ruins of Castle Wilton border the grounds.

6 rooms ⊡ – ♦£ 85/95 ♦♦£ 95/125

Wilton ⊠ HR9 6AA – West : 0.75 mi by B 4260 – ℰ (01989) 562 655 – www.bridgehouserossonwye.co.uk

at Walford South: 3 mi on B4234

Mill Race

BRITISH TRADITIONAL · PUB It might not look like a village pub but inside there's an atmosphere of relaxed contentment. Simple cooking showcases produce from their estate and farm and lets ingredients speak for themselves; dishes have recommended wine matches.

Carte £ 20/38

⊠ HR9 5QS – ℰ (01989) 562 891 – www.millrace.info

at Kerne Bridge South: 3.75 mi on B4234 – ⊠ Ross-On-Wye

Lumleys

TRADITIONAL · COSY Double-fronted brick house with colourful gardens; formerly the village pub, now a cosy, characterful guesthouse run with love and care. It has cluttered, homely bedrooms, a comfy first floor lounge and a drying room for walkers.

3 rooms ⊡ – ♦£ 65/75 ♦♦£ 70/80

⊠ HR9 5QT – ℰ (01600) 890 040 – www.thelumleys.co.uk

at Upton Bishop Northeast: 3 mi by A40 on B4221

Moody Cow

BRITISH TRADITIONAL · FRIENDLY A traditional country pub serving classic dishes to match the surroundings. What the food may lack in originality, it makes up for with quality ingredients, careful cooking and distinct flavours. Friendly owners run the place with a passion.

Carte £ 24/42

⊠ HR9 7TT – ℰ (01989) 780 470 – www.moodycowpub.co.uk – Closed 4-19 January, Sunday dinner and Monday

ROTHBURY

Northumberland – ✉ Morpeth – Pop. 2 326 – Regional map n° **14**-A2
▶ London 311 mi – Edinburgh 84 mi – Newcastle upon Tyne 29 mi

Thropton Demesne Farmhouse   ⌂ ⪡ ⌂ ⏚ P ⇌

TRADITIONAL · COSY Extended stone farmhouse with lovely valley views.
Comfy lounge and conservatory; bright, well-kept bedrooms with good facilities
– one has a private bathroom. Artwork is by the chatty owner. Homemade bread
and marmalade at breakfast.
3 rooms � – ♦£ 85/90 ♦♦£ 85/90
Thropton ✉ *NE65 7LT – West : 2.5 mi on B 6341*
– ℰ (01669) 620 196 – www.throptondemesne.co.uk
– Closed January

ROWDE – Wiltshire ➜ See Devizes

ROWHOOK – West Sussex ➜ See Horsham

ROWSLEY

Derbyshire – ✉ Matlock – Pop. 451 – Regional map n° **9**-A1
▶ London 157 mi – Derby 23 mi – Manchester 40 mi – Nottingham 30 mi

Peacock   ⌂ ⏚ ⌖ ⏛ P

TRADITIONAL · PERSONALISED Characterful 17C Dower House of the Duchess
of Rutland, with gardens leading down to the river. There's a snug open-fired sitting room and a characterful bar with stone walls, wood-panelling and a large
peacock mural. Bedrooms mix antique furnishings with modern facilities and service is top notch.
15 rooms ☲ – ♦£ 110/240 ♦♦£ 180/280
Bakewell Rd ✉ *DE4 2EB – ℰ (01629) 733 518 – www.thepeacockatrowsley.com*
– Closed first 2 weeks January and 24-26 December
Peacock – See restaurant listing

East Lodge   ⌂ ⌖ ⏚ ⌂ ⏛ P

TRADITIONAL · PERSONALISED 17C hunting lodge surrounded by 10 acres of
landscaped gardens and ponds. Guest areas are elegant and well-appointed.
Many of the bedrooms have great views; the two 'Luxury' rooms come with
four-poster beds and TVs in the bathrooms. The elegant formal dining room
serves classic dishes with a modern touch.
12 rooms ☲ – ♦£ 120/295 ♦♦£ 120/295
Main St ✉ *DE4 2EF – ℰ (01629) 734 474 – www.eastlodge.com*

XX Peacock   ⏚ ⌂ ⏛ P

MODERN CUISINE · FORMAL Elegant hotel restaurant where old mullioned stone
windows, oak Mousey Thompson furnishings and antique oil paintings are juxtaposed with modern lighting and contemporary art. Classic dishes at lunch are followed by more complex, elaborate combinations comprising lots of ingredients in
the evening.
Menu £ 18 (lunch) – Carte dinner £ 33/56
Peacock Hotel, Bakewell Rd ✉ *DE4 2EB*
– ℰ (01629) 733 518 – www.thepeacockatrowsley.com
– Closed first 2 weeks January, 24-26 December and Sunday dinner

ROYAL LEAMINGTON SPA

Warwickshire – Pop. 55 733 – Regional map n° **10**-D3
▶ London 99 mi – Birmingham 23 mi – Coventry 9 mi – Leicester 33 mi

ROYAL LEAMINGTON SPA

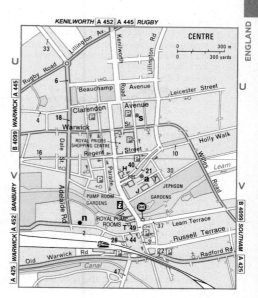

🏨 Mallory Court

LUXURY · CLASSIC Part-Edwardian house in Lutyens' style, with lovely gardens. Classic lounges display fine antiques and quality furnishings. Fresh flowers and fruit feature in the bedrooms; those in the main house are in keeping with the building's age.

31 rooms ☒ – ♦£ 125/425 ♦♦£ 149/525

Harbury Ln, Bishop's Tachbrook ☒ CV33 9QB
– South : 2.25 mi by B 4087 (Tachbrook Rd)
– ☎ (01926) 330 214 – www.mallory.co.uk
Dining Room at Mallory · Brasserie at Mallory – See restaurant listing

🏠 Adams

TOWNHOUSE · CLASSIC Attractive, double-fronted Regency house run by passionate owners. Classically styled bedrooms come with extra touches; those to the rear are smaller but quieter. The smart, bay-windowed lounge has a small bar and ornate cornicing.

12 rooms ☒ – ♦£ 79/93 ♦♦£ 85/105

Town plan: V-n – *22 Avenue Rd ☒ CV31 3PQ*
– ☎ (01926) 450 742 – www.adams-hotel.co.uk
– Closed 23 December-2 January

XxX Dining Room at Mallory

BRITISH MODERN · FORMAL Elegant wood-panelled dining room hidden within a lovely country house and looking out over its delightful grounds. Herbs, vegetables and soft fruits come from the kitchen garden. Cooking is modern; the simplest dishes are the best.

Menu £ 33 (lunch) – Carte dinner £ 49/71

Mallory Court Hotel, Harbury Ln, Bishop's Tachbrook ☒ CV33 9QB
– South : 2.25 mi by B 4087 (Tachbrook Rd)
– ☎ (01926) 330 214 (booking essential) – www.mallory.co.uk
– Closed Saturday lunch

XX Restaurant 23

MODERN CUISINE · FORMAL Smart restaurant with a chic cocktail bar and a stylish, elegant dining room, which is intimately candlelit at dinner. Modern cooking has classical European tendencies and is attractively presented. Top quality ingredients are the focus.

Menu £ 25/45

Town plan: V-a – 34 Hamilton Terr ⊠ CV32 4LY
– 𝒞 (01926) 422 422 (booking advisable) – www.restaurant23.co.uk
– Closed 25-26 December, 1 January, Sunday and Monday

XX Brasserie at Mallory

MODERN CUISINE · BRASSERIE Smart brasserie in a charming country house. The bar-lounge has striking black art deco features and the airy conservatory dining room looks out over the pretty walled garden. Wide-ranging modern British menus follow the seasons.

Menu £ 20 (weekday lunch) – Carte £ 26/44

Mallory Court Hotel, Harbury Ln, Bishop's Tachbrook ⊠ CV33 9QB
– South : 2.25 mi by B 4087 (Tachbrook Rd)
– 𝒞 (01926) 453 939 (booking essential) – www.mallory.co.uk
– Closed Sunday dinner

X Oscar's

FRENCH CLASSIC · BISTRO Friendly French bistro with two rustic rooms downstairs and a third above; the walls busy with pictures. There's a buzzy atmosphere, especially on the good value 'Auberge' nights, and the classic Gallic dishes are truly satisfying.

Menu £ 17 (weekday lunch) – Carte £ 27/41

Town plan: U-s – 39 Chandos St ⊠ CV32 4RL
– 𝒞 (01926) 452 807 (booking essential) – www.oscarsfrenchbistro.co.uk
– Closed Sunday and Monday

at Weston under Wetherley Northeast: 4.5 mi by A445 on B4453 – ⊠ Royal Leamington Spa

🏠 Wethele Manor

TRADITIONAL · CLASSIC 16C farmhouse on a 250 acre arable farm with a pond, an orchard and alpacas! Some of the classical bedrooms have four-posters; the family rooms are duplex. The lounge is in the old milking parlour and the timbered breakfast room has a well.

11 rooms ⊡ – ♦£ 65/100 ♦♦£ 75/120
⊠ CV33 9BZ – 𝒞 (01926) 831 772 – www.wethelemanor.com
– Closed 25-26 December

at Offchurch East: 3.5 mi by A425

🍺 Stag

MODERN CUISINE · FRIENDLY An attractive 16C thatched pub with a modern interior, where bold decorative features stand out against white walls. Generous seasonal dishes come in classical combinations; the sharing plates and Aubrey Allen steaks are a hit.

Carte £ 23/40

Welsh Rd ⊠ CV33 9AQ – 𝒞 (01926) 425 801 – www.thestagatoffchurch.com

ROYAL TUNBRIDGE WELLS

Kent – Pop. 57 772 – Regional map n° 5-B2
▶ London 36 mi – Brighton 33 mi – Folkestone 46 mi – Hastings 27 mi

ROYAL TUNBRIDGE WELLS

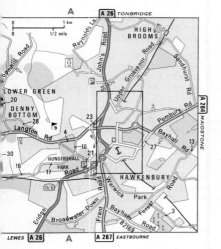

⛟ Hotel du Vin ☂ 🛏 ⬆ ♨ 🅿

BUSINESS · CLASSIC Attractive Georgian property in the town centre, boasting southerly views over Calverley Park. It's wine-themed throughout, with a well-stocked clubby bar, two comfy lounges and contemporary bedrooms; some have emperor-sized beds and baths in the rooms. The rustic bistro and terrace serve French cuisine.

34 rooms – 🛏£115/500 🛏🛏£115/500 – ⬜£17

Town plan: **B-c** – *Crescent Rd* ✉ TN1 2LY – ☎ (08447) 489 266
– www.hotelduvin.com

⛟ Tunbridge Wells ◑ ☂ ♨

TOWNHOUSE · ELEGANT This long-standing hotel sits at the centre of the Pantiles, a Georgian colonnade which leads to the famous well. Bedrooms are modern and stylish; most have French antique walnut beds with Hypnos mattresses. Dine informally in the Eating House, which has a subtle French feel, or out on the terrace in summer.

20 rooms ⬜ – 🛏£75/85 🛏🛏£109/195

Town plan: **B-w** – *58 The Pantiles* ✉ TN2 5TD – ☎ (01892) 530 501
– www.thetunbridgewellshotel.com

⛟ Danehurst ✗ 🅿

TRADITIONAL · PERSONALISED Quiet Edwardian house with a terrace and koi carp pond, set in a residential area and run by charming owners. It has top quality furnishings and displays good attention to detail. Tasty homemade bread and jam feature at breakfast.

4 rooms ⬜ – 🛏£100/149 🛏🛏£109/175

Town plan: **A-e** – *41 Lower Green Rd, Rusthall* ✉ TN4 8TW – West : 1.75 mi by A
264 – ☎ (01892) 527 739 – www.danehurst.net – Closed 20 December-2 January

XxX Thackeray's

BRITISH MODERN · FORMAL Grade II listed clapperboard house; the oldest in town and once home to the eponymous author. It has two stylish dining rooms and a delightful terrace; original features include lovely oak flooring. Exacting, skilful cooking has clear, well-defined flavours: classical dishes display modern elements.

→ Butter-poached Cardigan Bay lobster with cannelloni of lobster mousse. Fillet of Old Spot pork with shoulder ravioli, sauerkraut and crackling. Raspberry soufflé, raspberry sorbet and Tahitian vanilla sauce.

Menu £ 20/30 (weekday dinner) – Carte £ 49/58

Town plan: B-n – *85 London Rd* ⊠ *TN1 1EA* – *ℰ (01892) 511 921*
– *www.thackerays-restaurant.co.uk* – *Closed Sunday dinner and Monday*

Black Pig ⓝ

BRITISH MODERN · FRIENDLY The black façade may feel quite austere but inside it's quite the opposite, courtesy of a friendly team, a laid-back vibe and rustic shabby-chic styling. Dishes are gutsy and full-flavoured and there's even a 'PIG Heaven' section.

Carte £ 24/37

Town plan: B-b – *18 Grove Hill Rd* ⊠ *TN1 1RZ* – *ℰ (01892) 523 030*
– *www.theblackpig.net* – *Closed 26 December and 1 January*

at Speldhurst Northwest: 3.5 mi by A26 – Plan: A

George & Dragon

BRITISH TRADITIONAL · PUB Hugely characterful Wealden Hall house dating back to 1212 and boasting an impressive beamed ceiling and an unusual Queen's post. Generous cooking uses local, organic produce, offering pub classics alongside more elaborate dishes.

Carte £ 21/46

Speldhurst Hill ⊠ *TN3 0NN* – *ℰ (01892) 863 125* – *www.speldhurst.com*

ROZEL BAY – Saint Martin → See Channel Islands (Jersey)

RUDDINGTON – Nottinghamshire → See Nottingham

RUGBY

Warwickshire – Pop. 70 628 – Regional map n° **10**-D2
▶ London 88 mi – Birmingham 33 mi – Northampton 20 mi

XX Ferguson's ⓝ

MODERN CUISINE · INDIVIDUAL Have light bites on the terrace or head into the airy contemporary interior, where glass and light wood feature. Understated menu descriptions give little away – cooking is carefully prepared and ambitious with modern overtones.

Menu £ 16/25 – Carte £ 25/44

7A Eastfield Pl ⊠ *CV21 3AT* – *ℰ (01788) 550 222* – *www.fergusonsrugby.co.uk*
– *Closed 25-26 December, 1 January, Sunday dinner and Monday*

RUNSWICK BAY

North Yorkshire – ⊠ Whitby – Regional map n° **13**-C1
▶ London 285 mi – Middlesbrough 24 mi – Whitby 9 mi

ⓐ Cliffemount

TRADITIONAL · PERSONALISED Perched on the clifftop, with amazing views down to the bay – watch the sun rise and set from the delightful garden. Simply furnished bedrooms share the view and some have balconies or patios. Snacks served in the bar; classical dishes featuring local meats and seafood in the dining room.

20 rooms ⌗ – ♦£ 65/160 ♦♦£ 110/195
⊠ *TS13 5HU* – *ℰ (01947) 840 103* – *www.cliffemounthotel.co.uk*

RUSHLAKE GREEN

East Sussex – ✉ Heathfield – Regional map n° **5**-B2
▶ London 54 mi – Brighton 26 mi – Eastbourne 13 mi

🏠 Stone House

HISTORIC · PERSONALISED Beautiful gardens lead up to this charming part-15C house, set in 1,000 acres of tranquil grounds. It's been in the family for 500 years and is very personally run. The traditional country house interior features original staircases, wood-panelling and antiques; some of the individually decorated bedrooms have four-poster beds. Classic menus use kitchen garden produce.

7 rooms ⌂ – ♦ 115/150 ♦♦ 150/290 – 1 suite

✉ TN21 9QJ – *(Northeast corner of the green)* – ☏ *(01435) 830 553* – *www.stonehousesussex.co.uk* – *Closed 23 December-2 January and 15 February-7 March*

RUSHTON – Northamptonshire ➡ See Kettering

RYE

East Sussex – Pop. 3 708 – Regional map n° **5**-C2
▶ London 61 mi – Brighton 49 mi – Folkestone 27 mi – Maidstone 33 mi

🏠 George in Rye

INN · DESIGN Charming, centrally located former coaching inn offering an attractive blend of the old and the new. Characterful beamed bar and cosy, wood-panelled lounge. Individually styled bedrooms with bold, modern colour schemes. Grill-based menu with steaks the highlight.

34 rooms ⌂ – ♦£ 135/325 ♦♦£ 135/325

98 High St. ✉ *TN31 7JT* – ☏ *(01797) 222 114* – *www.thegeorgeinrye.com*

🏠 Mermaid Inn

INN · HISTORIC One of England's oldest coaching inns, offering immense charm and character, from its heavy beams and carved wooden fireplaces to its tapestries, false stairways and priests' holes. Formal dining features mainly local fish and game. The owner has been looking after guests here for over three decades.

31 rooms ⌂ – ♦£ 90/220 ♦♦£ 150/220

Mermaid St. ✉ *TN31 7EY* – ☏ *(01797) 223 065* – *www.mermaidinn.com*

🏠 Jeake's House

TOWNHOUSE · PERSONALISED Three 17C houses joined together over time, set down a cobbled lane. A former wool store and Quaker meeting place, it is set apart by its substantial charm. Characterful beamed rooms are warmly decorated and filled with antiques.

11 rooms ⌂ – ♦£ 75/79 ♦♦£ 90/140

Mermaid St. ✉ *TN31 7ET* – ☏ *(01797) 222 828* – *www.jeakeshouse.com*

🏠 Willow Tree House

TOWNHOUSE · COSY 300 year old boathouse on the main road into town. Comfy bedrooms are decorated in warm colours and are tastefully furnished; those at the top have exposed beams. Substantial breakfasts are served in a conservatory-style room.

6 rooms ⌂ – ♦£ 90/104 ♦♦£ 90/135

113 Winchelsea Rd. ✉ *TN31 7EL* – *South : 0.5 mi on A 259* – ☏ *(01797) 227 820* – *www.willow-tree-house.com* – *Closed 20-30 October and 24-30 December*

✗ Webbe's at The Fish Café

FISH AND SEAFOOD · BISTRO Relaxed café in a former antiques warehouse and teddy bear factory, with terracotta-coloured brick walls, a small counter and a cookery school above. Extensive menus offer simply prepared seafood from the Rye and Hastings day boats.

Menu £ 15 (weekday lunch) – Carte £ 26/35

17 Tower St. ✉ *TN31 7AT* – ☏ *(01797) 222 226* – *www.webbesrestaurants.co.uk* – *Closed 24 December-10 January*

X **Tuscan Kitchen**

ITALIAN · RUSTIC Centrally located, with dark wood tables, studded leather chairs, Italian memorabilia and even a stuffed wild boar. Rustic, classical cooking with everything homemade. The olive oil comes from the family farm in Tuscany.

Carte £ 20/45

8 Lion St ⊠ TN31 7LB – ℰ (01797) 223 269 (booking advisable)
– www.tuscankitchenrye.co.uk – dinner only and lunch Friday and Sunday
– Closed Monday and Tuesday

X **Ambrette** 🕭

INDIAN · CLASSIC Set in a historic building in the heart of town and sister to the Margate and Canterbury restaurants of the same name. Skilful modern cooking showcases a concise selection of subtly flavoured interpretations of classic Indian dishes.

Menu £ 21 (lunch) – Carte dinner £ 26/41

6 High St ⊠ TN31 7JE – ℰ (01797) 222 043 – www.theambrette.co.uk – Closed Monday

🍴 **Ship Inn** ⇦ 🛏

BRITISH TRADITIONAL · PUB 16C former warehouse on the quayside; now a laid-back pub with quirky styling incorporating stuffed boars heads, fairy lights and retro posters. Concise daily menu of flavoursome pub favourites with a modern twist; steak is a popular choice. Compact bedrooms have eye-catching feature walls and bold styling.

Carte £ 24/39

10 rooms ⌷ – ♦£ 100 ♦♦£ 125
The Strand ⊠ TN31 7DB – ℰ (01797) 222 233 – www.theshipinnrye.co.uk

at Camber Southeast: 4.25 mi by A259 – ⊠ Rye

🏠 **Gallivant** ☆ 🅰 ♨ 🅿

TRADITIONAL · RUSTIC Laid-back hotel opposite Camber Sands, run by a friendly team. Relax in the shabby chic lounge or on the terrace. Bedrooms come in blues and whites, with distressed wood furniture and modern facilities; some have decked terraces.

20 rooms ⌷ – ♦£ 95/250 ♦♦£ 95/250
New Lydd Rd. ⊠ TN31 7RB – ℰ (01797) 225 057 – www.thegallivant.co.uk
Beach Bistro – See restaurant listing

X **Beach Bistro** 🛏 🅰 🅿

BRITISH MODERN · BISTRO Informal hotel bistro with distressed wood furniture, white and blue hues and a pleasant covered terrace. Appealing all-day menus keep local seafood to the fore; refreshingly, the good value two-choice set menu is always available.

Menu £ 13 (weekday lunch) – Carte £ 24/44

Gallivant Hotel, New Lydd Rd. ⊠ TN31 7RB – ℰ (01797) 225 057
– www.thegallivant.co.uk

RYHALL

Rutland – Pop. 1 459 – Regional map n° **9**-C2
▶ London 94 mi – Leicester 35 mi – Nottingham 45 mi

XX **Wicked Witch** 🚘 ♿ 🅿

MODERN CUISINE · FASHIONABLE Formerly a pub, now a smart restaurant with a relaxed formality. Seasonal menus follow the décor's lead, offering modern dishes with an emphasis on presentation. Combinations are original and recipes have wide-ranging influences.

Menu £ 15/26

Bridge St ⊠ PE9 4HH – ℰ (01780) 763 649
– www.thewickedwitchexperience.co.uk – Closed Sunday dinner and Monday

ST ALBANS

Hertfordshire – Pop. 82 146 – Regional map n° **7**-A2

▶ London 27 mi – Cambridge 41 mi – Luton 10 mi

🏠 St Michael's Manor

TOWNHOUSE · PERSONALISED Part-16C William and Mary manor house with well-kept gardens and lake views. Characterful guest areas display contemporary touches. Bedrooms are well-appointed; those in the Garden Wing are the most modern and some have terraces.

30 rooms ⌂ – ♦£ 110/115 ♦♦£ 150/340 – 1 suite

Town plan: AY-d – *St Michael's Village, Fishpool St* ⊠ *AL3 4RY* – ✆ *(01727) 864 444 – www.stmichaelsmanor.com*

Lake – See restaurant listing

XX Thompson @ Darcy's

MODERN CUISINE · INTIMATE Come on a Sunday for 'lobster and steak' night or any day of the week for refined, tasty dishes with a modern edge. Three contemporary dining rooms feature bold artwork from the local gallery. Try the lesser-known wines by the glass.

Menu £ 23 (weekdays) – Carte £ 37/59

Town plan: BY-t – *2 Hatfield Rd* ⊠ *AL1 3RP* – ✆ *(01727) 730 777 – www.thompsonatdarcys.co.uk*

XX Lake

MODERN CUISINE · ELEGANT Spacious, airy orangery in a family owned manor house, which looks out over well-tended gardens and a lake. Daily changing dishes feature contemporary twists; the Lake Menu is good value. Formal service comes from a chatty team.

Menu £ 18 (weekdays) – Carte £ 28/46

Town plan: AY-d – *St Michael's Manor Hotel, St Michael's Village, Fishpool St* ⊠ *AL3 4RY* – ✆ *(01727) 864 444 – www.lakerestaurant.co.uk*

ST ANNE'S – Lancashire ➜ See Lytham St Anne's

ST AUBIN ➜ See Channel Islands (Jersey)

ST AUSTELL

Cornwall – Pop. 23 864 – Regional map n° **1**-B2

▶ London 281 mi – Newquay 16 mi – Plymouth 38 mi – Truro 14 mi

🏠 Anchorage House

FAMILY · HOMELY Modern guesthouse owned by an ex-Canadian Naval Commander. Afternoon tea is served in the comfy lounge. Charming, antique-filled bedrooms boast modern fabrics, state-of-the-art bathrooms and plenty of extras. Facilities include an indoor pool, a gym, a sauna and a chill-out lounge. The conservatory dining room offers simple, home-cooked dishes. The owners are lovely.

5 rooms ⌂ – ♦£ 70/80 ♦♦£ 105/140

Nettles Corner, Boscundle ⊠ *PL25 3RH* – *East : 2.75 mi by A 390* – ✆ *(01726) 814 071 – www.anchoragehouse.co.uk – Closed 15 November-15 March*

🏠 Grange

TOWNHOUSE · STYLISH A cheery owner welcomes you to this small but perfectly formed guesthouse. Bedrooms are bright and modern yet have a cosy, homely feel; one has a four-poster bed and a roll-top bath. The extensive breakfast menu features items from the local butcher's; dinners, by arrangement, feature old favourites.

3 rooms ⌂ – ♦£ 55/89 ♦♦£ 65/130

19 Southbourne Rd ⊠ *PL25 4RU* – ✆ *(01726) 73 351 – www.accommodationstaustell.co.uk – Closed Christmas*

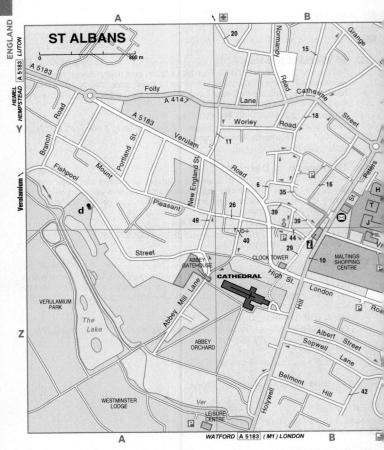

ST ALBANS

at **Carlyon Bay** East: 2.5 mi by A3601 – ⊠ St Austell

🏠 **Carlyon Bay**   🌿 ⬳ 🛌 🖥 🏊 🎿 🐾 ✕ 🏡 🚴 ✗ 🚗 🅿

HOLIDAY HOTEL · CLASSIC Imposing 1920s hotel boasting original art deco features and superb bay views. Large, traditionally furnished guest areas. Modern bedrooms feature lightly hued fabrics: rear rooms are bright; front rooms have views. Aptly named Bay View serves unfussy classics. Taste offers grills and seafood, using the best Cornish produce.

86 rooms (dinner included) ⌕ – 🛏£ 110/185 🛏🛏£ 220/450
⊠ PL25 3RD – ☎ (01726) 812 304 – www.carlyonbay.com

✕✕ **Brett@Austell's**

MODERN CUISINE · NEIGHBOURHOOD Keenly run neighbourhood restaurant with a brightly lit, mirror-filled interior. Modern, seasonal menus showcase local produce in elaborate, confidently executed dishes with original touches. Watch the chefs in the open-plan kitchen.

Menu £ 28 – Carte £ 31/44

10 Beach Rd ⊠ PL25 3PH – ☎ (01726) 813 888 – www.austells.co.uk – *dinner only and Sunday lunch – Closed first 2 weeks January and Monday*

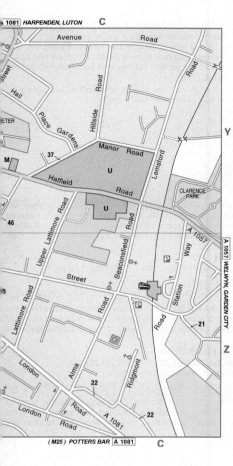

Abbey Mill Lane	**AZ**
Albert St.	**BZ**
Alma Rd.	**CZ**
Avenue Rd	**CY**
Beaconsfield Rd	**CYZ**
Belmont Hill.	**BZ**
Branch Rd	**AY**
Bricket Rd	**BCYZ** 5
Britton Ave	**BY** 6
Carlisle Ave.	**BCY** 8
Catherine St	**BY**
Chequer St	**BZ** 10
Church Crescent	**ABY** 11
Cottonmill Lane	**BCZ** 13
Dalton St	**BY** 15
Drovers Way	**BY** 16
Etna Rd	**BY** 18
Fishpool St	**AYZ**
Folly Ave	**BY** 20
Folly Lane	**ABY**
Grange St	**BY**
Grimston Rd	**CZ** 21
Grosvenor Rd	**CZ** 22
Hall Pl. Gardens	**CY**
Hatfield Rd	**CY**
High St.	**BZ**
Hillside Rd	**CY**
Holywell Hill.	**BZ**
Lattimore Rd	**CZ**
Lemsford Rd.	**CY**
London Rd	**BCZ**
Lower Dagnall St	**BYZ** 26
Maltings Shopping Centre	**BZ**
Manor Rd	**CY**
Market Pl.	**BZ** 29
Marlborough Rd	**CZ** 28
Mount Pleasant.	**AY**
New England St	**AY**
Normandy Rd	**BY**
Old London Rd	**CZ**
Portland St.	**AY**
Ridgemont Rd.	**CZ**
Russell Ave	**BY** 35
St Peter's Rd.	**CY** 37
St Peter's St.	**BCY**
Sopwell Lane	**BZ**
Spencer St	**BY** 39
Spicer St College	**BYZ** 40
Station Way.	**CZ**
Thorpe Rd	**BZ** 42
Upper Dagnall St	**BYZ** 44
Upper Lattimore Rd	**CYZ**
Upper Marlborough Rd	**CYZ** 46
Verulam Rd	**ABY**
Victoria St	**BCZ**
Watson's Walk	**CZ** 48
Welclose St	**AYZ** 49
Worley Rd	**BY**

ST BLAZEY

Cornwall – Pop. 9 958 – Regional map n° **1**-B2

▶ London 276 mi – Newquay 21 mi – Plymouth 33 mi – Truro 19 mi

🏠 **Penarwyn House**   🛏 🕸 🅿

TRADITIONAL · CLASSIC Whitewashed former gentleman's residence, surrounded by mature gardens and run by welcoming owners. Spacious lounge, clubby snooker room and formal breakfast room. Bedrooms boast modern facilities, antique furniture and art deco touches.

3 rooms ☲ – †£ 70/105 ††£ 80/160

✉ PL24 2DS – *South : 0.75 mi by A 390 turning left at Doubletrees School*
– ℰ (01726) 814 224 – www.penarwyn.co.uk – *Closed 1 week Christmas*

ST EWE

Cornwall – Regional map n° **1**-B3

▶ London 258 mi – Bristol 161 mi – Cardiff 192 mi – Plymouth 46 mi

Lower Barn ⛲ 🐾 🛏 ♿ 🐕 🅿

FAMILY · STYLISH The gregarious owner extends a warm welcome at this stylishly converted 18C granite barn; formerly part of the Heligan Estate, set in 2 acres. Modern, brightly furnished bedrooms have a South American feel and a hot tub on the decking overlooks the garden. Set menu of home-cooked dishes.

6 rooms ⌂ – 🛌£ 50/75 🛌🛌£ 80/145

Bosue ✉ PL26 6ET – North : 1.25 mi by Crosswyn rd, St Austell rd and signed off St Mawes rd – ☎ *(01726) 844 881 – www.lowerbarns.co.uk*

ST HELENS ➜ See Wight (Isle of)

ST HELIER ➜ See Channel Islands (Jersey)

ST IVES
Cornwall – Pop. 9 966 – Regional map n° 1-A3
▶ London 319 mi – Penzance 10 mi – Truro 25 mi

No 27 🛏 🐾 🅿

HOLIDAY HOTEL · PERSONALISED Unusually for St Ives, this smartly restored Georgian house has its own car park and a sun terrace... even more unusually, it has its own beach! Take in a view of the bay from the airy breakfast room. Bedrooms are modern and appealing.

9 rooms ⌂ – 🛌£ 70/130 🛌🛌£ 90/150

Town plan: Y-n – 27 The Terrace ✉ TR26 2BP – ☎ *(01736) 797 450 – www.27theterrace.co.uk*

Blue Hayes ⬅ 🛏 🐾 🅿

HISTORIC · PERSONALISED Built in 1922 for Professor Whitnall, a surgeon friend of Edward III. Comfortable bedrooms: one with French doors onto a roof terrace; another with four-poster and balcony. Single course dinner available. Breakfast on the terrace in summer.

6 rooms ⌂ – 🛌£ 120/208 🛌🛌£ 190/260

Town plan: Y-u – Trelyon Ave ✉ TR26 2AD – ☎ *(01736) 797 129 – www.bluehayes.co.uk – Closed November-February*

Primrose Valley ⬅ 🐾 🅿

HOLIDAY HOTEL · PERSONALISED Navigate the steep road up to this terraced Edwardian villa, where you'll find individually furnished bedrooms with good mod cons – Room 3 has a terrace with views over the lovely beach. Extensive breakfasts feature organic produce.

10 rooms ⌂ – 🛌£ 80/195 🛌🛌£ 115/220

Town plan: Y-r – Porthminster Beach ✉ TR26 2ED – ☎ *(01736) 794 939 – www.primroseonline.co.uk – Closed December and January*

Trevose Harbour House 🐾 🅿

TOWNHOUSE · STYLISH The owners have decorated this elegant hotel themselves, so you'll find lots of knick-knacks and some unusual, personal touches. It's simple but stylish, with a mix of period and modern furnishings. The breakfasts are top notch.

6 rooms ⌂ – 🛌£ 100/255 🛌🛌£ 150/265

Town plan: Y-t – 22 The Warren ✉ TR26 2EA – ☎ *(01736) 793 267 – www.trevosehouse.co.uk – Closed mid December-March*

No.1 St Ives 🛏 🐾 🅿

TOWNHOUSE · MODERN Chic guesthouse which was once a post office (the owner was the postmistress!) The minimalist sitting room is filled with books and DVDs; bedrooms are stylish – two have sea views. The lovely garden is home to a monkey puzzle tree.

4 rooms ⌂ – 🛌£ 75/100 🛌🛌£ 129/149

Town plan: Y-x – 1 Fern Glen ✉ TR26 1QP – (on The Stennack) – ☎ *(01736) 799 047 – www.no1stives.co.uk*

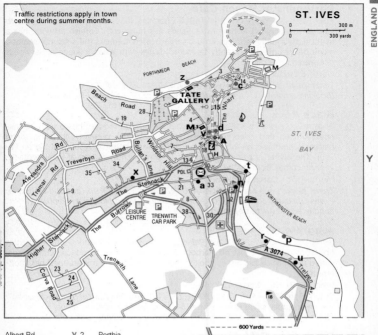

Traffic restrictions apply in town centre during summer months.

ST. IVES

PORTHMEOR BEACH

TATE GALLERY

ST. IVES BAY

PORTHMINSTER BEACH

LEISURE CENTRE

TRENWITH CAR PARK

CARBIS BAY

Albert Rd	**Y** 2	Porthia		
Back Rd West	**Y** 3	Crescent	**Y** 24	
Barnoon Hill	**Y** 4	Porthia Rd	**Y** 25	
Bedford Rd	**Y** 7	Porthmeor		
Bishop's Rd	**Y** 8	Hill	**Y** 28	
Carnellis Rd	**Y** 9	Porthrepta Rd	**Z** 29	
Chapel St	**Y** 13	Talland Rd	**Y** 30	
Fish St	**Y** 14	Tregenna		
Fore St	**Y** 15	Terrace	**Y** 33	
High St	**Y** 18	Trelawney Rd	**Y** 34	
Orange Lane	**Y** 19	Trerice Rd	**Y** 35	
Parc Owles	**Z** 20	Trewidden Rd	**Y** 38	
Park Ave	**Y** 21	Wheal		
Penwith Rd	**Y** 23	Whidden	**Z** 40	

600 Yards

Pannier Lane

Trelyon Av.

A 3074

Trenwith Lane

(A 30) **A 3074** HAYLE (A 3074)

🏠 11 Sea View Terrace

⇐ 🌿 **P**

TOWNHOUSE · CONTEMPORARY Three-storey Edwardian villa with a small terrace, a cosy bay-windowed lounge and a compact rear breakfast room. Spacious, contemporary bedrooms; one has a south-facing sun-terrace and two have great views over the harbour and bay.

3 rooms ⌂ – 🛏£ 75/100 🛏🛏£ 100/140

Town plan: Y-a – *11 Sea View Terr* ✉ *TR26 2DH* – 𝒞 *(01736) 798 440*
– www.11stives.co.uk – Closed November-February

✗✗ Alba

⇐ **AC**

BRITISH MODERN · ROMANTIC Former lifeboat station in a great harbourside location; sit upstairs by the window. Both the set and à la carte menus are offered throughout the day. Dishes are European in base with a modern slant – go for one of the fish specials.

Carte £ 20/45

Town plan: Y-d – *Old Lifeboat House, The Wharf* ✉ *TR26 1LF* – 𝒞 *(01736)*
797 222 – www.thealbarestaurant.com – dinner only – Closed 25-26 December

✗ Porthminster Beach Café ← ⌂

FISH AND SEAFOOD · FASHIONABLE Charming 1930s beach house in a superb location overlooking Porthminster Sands. It's hung with Cornish artwork, has a nautical style and leads out onto a large heated terrace. The seasonal seafood menu offers unfussy, vibrantly flavoured dishes with Asian influences. Service is relaxed and friendly.

Carte £ 29/51

Town plan: Y-p – *Porthminster Beach ⊠ TR26 2EB – ℰ (01736) 795 352 (booking advisable) – www.porthminstercafe.co.uk – Closed 1-13 January*

✗ Black Rock ⟐
🕸

FISH AND SEAFOOD · NEIGHBOURHOOD A relaxed modern bistro with a semi-open kitchen and a contemporary art display. The regularly changing menu places its emphasis on local seafood and cooking is gutsy, rustic and big on flavour. The owner is a third generation fisherman and has lots of local contacts; venison comes from the nearby estate.

Menu £ 17 – Carte £ 24/36

Town plan: Y-v – *Market Pl ⊠ TR26 1RZ – ℰ (01736) 791 911 (booking advisable) – www.theblackrockstives.co.uk – dinner only – Closed November-February, Sunday and restricted opening in winter*

✗ seagrass

BRITISH MODERN · FRIENDLY Personally run with a reassuring efficiency, this first floor restaurant just off Harbour Beach puts Cornish produce centre stage, with a menu of classic dishes cooked in a modern style. Marble-topped bar; modern décor.

Menu £ 17/20 – Carte £ 27/48

Town plan: Y-c – *Fish St ⊠ TR26 1LT – ℰ (01736) 793 763 (booking advisable) – www.seagrass-stives.com – dinner only – Closed 1-2 January, dinner 25 December, Sunday and Monday November-April except bank holidays*

✗ Porthmeor Café Bar ← ⌂ 🖵 ▤

MEDITERRANEAN · SIMPLE Simple beachfront café; a very popular spot, as all of the tables have a view. Service is friendly and the atmosphere, laid-back. They offer breakfast, fresh cakes, Mediterranean small plates and a few more substantial dishes too. No lunch bookings.

Carte £ 19/30

Town plan: Y-z – *Porthmeor Beach ⊠ TR26 1JZ – ℰ (01736) 793 366 (booking essential at dinner) – www.porthmeor-beach.co.uk – Closed November-March*

at Carbis Bay South: 1.75 mi on A3074 – ⊠ St Ives

🏨 Boskerris ⚑ ← 🖴 ⅋ 🅿

FAMILY · CONTEMPORARY Contemporary hotel with panoramic views of Carbis Bay and the coastline. Contemporary lounge-bar with French styling and doors onto the terrace. Uncluttered bedrooms have a cool, modern style; some have roll-top baths and iPod docks. Enthusiastic young owners. Concise menu of good, honest home-cooking.

15 rooms ⌑ – ♦£ 113/207 ♦♦£ 150/275

Town plan: Z-x – *Boskerris Rd ⊠ TR26 2NQ – ℰ (01736) 795 295 – www.boskerrishotel.co.uk – Closed mid-November-March*

🏨 Beachcroft ← 🖴 ⅋ 🅿

LUXURY · PERSONALISED Set in an elevated position, with stunning views across the bay. Contemporary interior with subtle 1920s touches. Comfy, understated bedrooms have bespoke furnishings and luxurious bathrooms. Have your breakfast on the delightful terrace.

5 rooms ⌑ – ♦£ 140/160 ♦♦£ 140/160

Town plan: Z-a – *Valley Rd ⊠ TR26 2QS – ℰ (01736) 794 442 – www.beachcroftstives.co.uk – Closed November-March except New Year*

🏠 Headland House   ← 🛏 ⚲ 🅿

TOWNHOUSE · CONTEMPORARY Substantial house built in 1901, with a decked terrace, an attractive garden and a lovely conservatory breakfast room. Contemporary, New England style décor; cake is served every afternoon in the lounge. The sea is at the end of the road.

9 rooms 🖙 – ♦£ 85/150 ♦♦£ 95/160

Town plan: Z-b – *Headland Rd* ✉ *TR26 2NS* – ℰ *(01736) 796 647* – *www.headlandhousehotel.co.uk* – *Closed October-February*

at Halsetown Southwest: 1.5 mi on B3311

🍴 Halsetown Inn   🏡 🅿

🍷 **MEDITERRANEAN · FRIENDLY** Relaxed, slightly quirky pub, a short drive from St Ives; there are various little areas to sit in, as well as a lovely suntrap of a terrace. Tasty seasonal cooking, with strong Asian influences; Wednesday theme nights include Chinese or Thai. Excellent value set lunch menu and warm, friendly staff.

Menu £ 15 (weekday lunch) – Carte £ 21/34

✉ *TR26 3NA* – ℰ *(01736) 795 583* – *www.halsetowninn.co.uk* – *Closed January and Sunday dinner*

ST KEVERNE

Cornwall – Pop. 939 – Regional map n° **1**-A3
▶ London 302 mi – Penzance 26 mi – Truro 28 mi

🏠 Old Temperance House   ⚲ 🚲

🏛 **TOWNHOUSE · CONTEMPORARY** This pretty pink-washed cottage framed by olive trees was once a 15C temperance house. The interior is contemporary and immaculately kept. Bright bedrooms are named after alcoholic drinks and display thoughtful touches. Fresh fruit and produce from the local butcher features at breakfast.

4 rooms 🖙 – ♦£ 59 ♦♦£ 85

The Square ✉ *TR12 6NA* – ℰ *(01326) 280 986* – *www.oldtemperancehouse.co.uk*

X Greenhouse

REGIONAL · RUSTIC Simple eatery in a sleepy little village, where they sell their own bread and meringues. Daily blackboard menus are centred around local, organic and gluten free produce; cooking is unfussy and flavoursome. Seafood is a feature.

Carte £ 21/35

6 High St. ✉ *TR12 6NN* – ℰ *(01326) 280 800 (booking advisable)* – *www.tgor.co.uk* – *dinner only and occasional Sunday lunch* – *Closed last 3 weeks January*

ST KEW

Cornwall – Regional map n° **1**-B2
▶ London 265 mi – Newquay 20 mi – Liskeard 24 mi

🍴 St Kew Inn   🛏 🏡 🅿

BRITISH TRADITIONAL · PUB Characterful country pub in quintessentially English location. Wide-ranging menu of fresh, tasty dishes and St Austell beer in wooden casks. Attractive garden with picnic tables and heaters.

Carte £ 25/35

✉ *PL30 3HB* – ℰ *(01208) 841 259* – *www.stkewinn.co.uk*

ST MARTIN → See Channel Islands (Guernsey)

ST MARY'S → See Scilly (Isles of)

ST MAWES

Cornwall – ✉ Truro – Regional map n° **1**-B3
▶ London 299 mi – Plymouth 56 mi – Truro 18 mi

🏠 Hotel Tresanton

TOWNHOUSE · STYLISH Collection of old fishermen's cottages and a former yacht club. Elegant, nautically themed guest areas include an intimate bar and a movie room. Understated bedrooms, some in cottages, have a high level of facilities and superb sea views. Lovely split-level terrace shares the outlook. Delightful team.

30 rooms � – ♦£ 190/270 ♦♦£ 210/300 – 4 suites
27 Lower Castle Rd ⊠ TR2 5DR – ℰ (01326) 270 055 – www.tresanton.com – Closed 2 weeks January

Restaurant Tresanton – See restaurant listing

🏠 Idle Rocks

HOLIDAY HOTEL · PERSONALISED Boutique hotel on the water's edge, with fabulous views over the harbour and the estuary. The décor is personalised and local art is displayed throughout. Cosy, contemporary bedrooms have pleasing subtle touches and are well-equipped. The relaxed restaurant has bay views, a modern menu and a superb terrace.

20 rooms ⊔ – ♦£ 150/350 ♦♦£ 150/350
Harbourside ⊠ TR2 5AN – ℰ (01326) 270 270 – www.idlerocks.com – Closed 5-29 January

🏡 Nearwater

FAMILY · PERSONALISED Modern, purpose-built guesthouse with small lawned garden, set on the main road of a popular coastal town. Open-plan lounge and breakfast room with real fires and subtle nautical theme. Smart, New England style bedrooms offer good mod cons.

3 rooms ⊔ – ♦£ 81/108 ♦♦£ 90/120
Polvarth Rd. ⊠ TR2 5AY – East : 0.5 mi on A 3078 – ℰ (01326) 279 278 – www.nearwaterstmawes.co.uk – Closed Christmas

XX Restaurant Tresanton

BRITISH MODERN · FASHIONABLE Appealing hotel restaurant boasting a large terrace and superb bay views; popular for its Sunday BBQs and live jazz band. Bright interior with nautical theme and attractive mosaic flooring. Daily menus offer unfussy dishes crafted from quality local produce; seafood is a feature. Polite, efficient service.

Carte £ 33/58

Hotel Tresanton, 27 Lower Castle Rd ⊠ TR2 5DR – ℰ (01326) 270 055 (booking essential) – www.tresanton.com – Closed 2 weeks January

X Watch House

MEDITERRANEAN · SIMPLE Old Customs and Excise watch house on the quayside, with a nautically styled interior, friendly service and harbour views. Light lunches and substantial dinners; unfussy cooking follows a Mediterranean theme – try the tasty fish specials.

Menu £ 25 – Carte £ 26/46

1 The Square ⊠ TR2 5DJ – ℰ (01326) 270 038 – www.watchhousestmawes.co.uk – Closed 25-26 December and Sunday dinner-Tuesday except Easter-September

ST MELLION
Cornwall – Regional map n° **1**-C2
▶ London 225 mi – Bristol 129 mi – Cardiff 160 mi – Plymouth 13 mi

🏡 Pentillie Castle

COUNTRY HOUSE · HISTORIC 17C house – later transformed into a castle – set in 2,000 acres overlooking the river. Classical guest areas include a dining room with a crystal chandelier; traditional menus require a minimum of 6 guests. Spacious, elegant bedrooms with antique furnishings, luxurious bathrooms and some great views.

9 rooms ⊔ – ♦£ 120/265 ♦♦£ 120/265
⊠ PL12 6QD – Southeast : 1 mi by A 388 on Cargreen rd – ℰ (01579) 350 044 – www.pentillie.co.uk

ST MERRYN – Cornwall → See Padstow

ST OSYTH

Essex – Pop. 2 118 – Regional map n° **7**-D2

▶ London 83 mi – Colchester 12 mi – Clacton-on-Sea 5 mi

🏠 **Park Hall**   ♨ 🏕 ⌚ 🕭 **P**

HISTORIC · PERSONALISED Charming 14C former monastery with a homely feel, surrounded by 400 acres of arable farmland. Characterful bedrooms come with good extras, and antiques and ornaments abound. Seek out the hidden seating areas in the large gardens.

4 rooms ☷ – ♦£ 75/110 ♦♦£ 120/190

Bypass Rd ⊠ CO16 8HG – East : 1.5 mi on B 1027
– ℰ (01255) 820 922 – www.parkhall.info

ST PETER PORT → See Channel Islands (Guernsey)

ST SAVIOUR → See Channel Islands (Jersey)

ST SAVIOUR → See Channel Islands (Guernsey)

SALCOMBE

Devon – Pop. 1 893 – Regional map n° **1**-C3

▶ London 243 mi – Exeter 43 mi – Plymouth 27 mi – Torquay 28 mi

🏨 **Salcombe Harbour**   ♀ ⪤ ▧ 🌐 🍸 🛋 ☐ 🕭 🛎 🚗 **P**

HOLIDAY HOTEL · CONTEMPORARY Take in views of the estuary from this contemporary seaside hotel, with its sleek, nautical edge. Stylish bedrooms come with Nespresso machines and tablets; many also have balconies. For relaxation there's a chic spa and even a cinema! The restaurant offers modern menus, with local seafood a feature.

50 rooms ☷ – ♦£ 215/465 ♦♦£ 215/465 – 1 suite

Town plan: Z-s – *Cliff Rd ⊠ TQ8 8JH – ℰ (01548) 844 444*
– www.salcombe-harbour-hotel.co.uk

🏨 **South Sands**   ♀ ⪤ 🕭 **P**

FAMILY · STYLISH Stylish hotel by the water's edge, with a subtle New England theme running throughout and South Sands views. Small, modern bar and lounges. Smart bedrooms have heavy wood furnishings and good facilities; opt for one with a balcony.

27 rooms ☷ – ♦£ 195/395 ♦♦£ 195/395 – 5 suites

Town plan: Z-x – *Bolt Head ⊠ TQ8 8LL – Southwest : 1.25 mi*
– ℰ (01548) 845 900 – www.southsands.com

Beachside – See restaurant listing

XX **Beachside**   ⪤ 🍸 🕭 🄰 **P**

FISH AND SEAFOOD · FASHIONABLE Large, airy, hotel restaurant with full-length windows opening onto a delightful decked terrace overlooking the bay. Modern, daily changing menus offer a good mix of unfussy, flavoursome dishes, with plenty of fresh seafood options.

Menu £ 20 (weekday lunch)/30 – Carte £ 32/60

Town plan: Z-x – *South Sands Hotel, Bolt Head ⊠ TQ8 8LL – Southwest : 1.25 mi*
– ℰ (01548) 845 900 (booking advisable) – www.southsands.com

🐦 **Follow our inspectors @MichelinGuideUK**

SALCOMBE

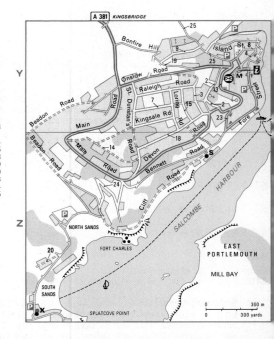

at Soar Mill Cove Southwest: 4.25 mi by A381 – Plan: Y – via Malborough village – ⊠ Salcombe

🏨 Soar Mill Cove
🌂 🐾 🏄 🛋 🏠 🖼 🎐 ✕ 🅿

FAMILY · PERSONALISED Family-run hotel built from local slate and stone; delightfully set above a secluded cove. Relax in the modern lounge or smart bar. Spacious bedrooms come in bright, contemporary styles; half have private patios and sea views. Blue-hued restaurant offers a modern menu and a lovely outlook from every table.

22 rooms ⌑ – †£ 99/186 ††£ 99/249
⊠ TQ7 3DS – ✆ (01548) 561 566
– www.soarmillcove.co.uk
– Closed 1 January-14 February

SALE

Greater Manchester – ⊠ Manchester – Pop. 134 022 – Regional map n° **11**-B3
▶ London 212 mi – Liverpool 36 mi – Manchester 6 mi – Sheffield 43 mi

🏠 Cornerstones
🛋 ✕ 🅿

TOWNHOUSE · PERSONALISED Substantial red-brick Victorian house with neat garden, in leafy suburban location. Slightly wacky interior with bohemian-style lounge and breakfast room. Bedrooms range from retro to modern.

9 rooms – †£ 45/48 ††£ 60/65 – ⌑ £ 7
230 Washway Rd ⊠ M33 4RA – (on A 56)
– ✆ (0161) 283 69 09
– www.cornerstonesguesthouse.com
– Closed Christmas-New Year

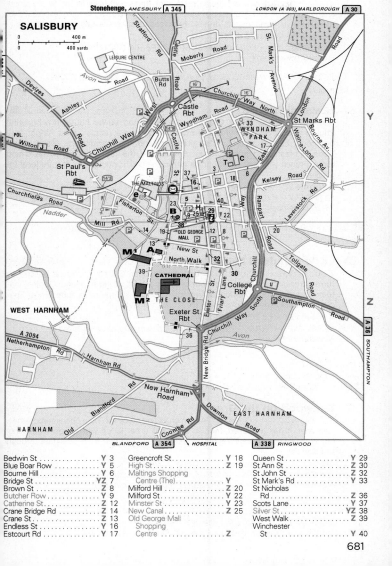

SALFORD QUAYS – Gtr Manchester → See Manchester

SALISBURY
Wiltshire – Pop. 44 748 – Regional map n° **2**-D3
▶ London 91 mi – Bournemouth 28 mi – Bristol 53 mi – Southampton 23 mi

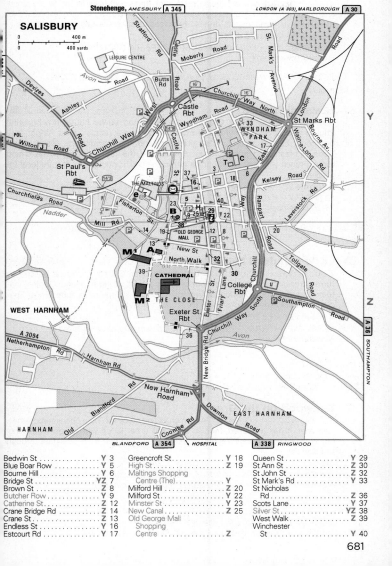

⌂ Cricket Field House

FAMILY · HOMELY Family-run hotel overlooking the local cricket pitch. They offer a host of hot and cold dishes in the conservatory breakfast room. Comfy bedrooms are set around an internal courtyard; there's a min. 2 night weekend stay Apr-Oct.

9 rooms ⌂ – ♦£ 75/150 ♦♦£ 85/150

*Wilton Rd ⌂ SP2 9NS – West : 1.25 mi on A 36 – 𝒞 (01722) 322 595
– www.cricketfieldhouse.co.uk – Closed 15 December-1 January*

✗✗ Anokaa

INDIAN · DESIGN A smart Indian restaurant that's a little different, with colour-changing lights and interesting water features. Originality is also expressed in the extensive menu: expect dishes like spiced crushed scallops or duck jaalsha.

Menu £ 15 – Carte £ 19/48

Town plan: Y-e – *60 Fisherton St ⌂ SP2 7RB – 𝒞 (01722) 414 142
– www.anokaa.com*

at Teffont Evias West: 10.25 mi by A36 – Plan: Y – and A30 on B3089
– ⌂ Salisbury

⌂ Howard's House

COUNTRY HOUSE · COSY Charming Grade II listed dower house in a beautiful English village; the eponymous 'Howard' was once a regular guest. Bright, airy bedrooms have a smart, understated feel and offer garden or village views. Good old-fashioned hospitality is provided by the family team. In the dining room, French windows open onto a terrace; sophisticated dishes feature local ingredients.

9 rooms ⌂ – ♦£ 120 ♦♦£ 190/210

⌂ SP3 5RJ – 𝒞 (01722) 716 392 – www.howardshousehotel.co.uk – Closed 23-26 December

at Little Langford Northwest: 8 mi by A36 – Plan: Y – and Great Wishford
rd ⌂ Salisbury

🏠 Little Langford Farmhouse

TRADITIONAL · PERSONALISED Unusual Victorian Gothic farmhouse boasting a turret, crenellations and lancet windows; set amidst rolling farmland. Original features include a fine tile-floored entranceway and stripped oak furnishings. Spacious, double aspect bedrooms have a classical style.

3 rooms ⌂ – ♦£ 70/75 ♦♦£ 90/95

⌂ SP3 4NP – 𝒞 (01722) 790 205 – www.littlelangford.co.uk – Closed November-March

SALTWOOD

Kent – Regional map n° **5**-D2
▶ London 65 mi – Maidstone 30 mi – Margate 37 mi

✗ Saltwood on the Green ⓝ

BRITISH MODERN · FRIENDLY A former village store run by a charismatic American chef. It has a relaxed, modish style and a bar laden with cakes. Appealing, highly original dishes are flavourful and healthy. It's open from breakfast through to cocktails.

Menu £ 18 (weekday lunch) – Carte £ 24/34

*The Green ⌂ CT21 4PS – 𝒞 (01303) 237 800 – www.saltwoodrestaurant.co.uk
– Closed 1 week September, Christmas and Sunday dinner-Tuesday*

SANCTON

East Riding of Yorkshire – Pop. 286 – Regional map n° **13**-C2
▶ London 194 mi – Croydon 205 mi – Ealing 193 mi – Wandsworth 199 mi

ENGLAND

🍴 **Star** 🛋 & 🕙 🅿

MODERN CUISINE · FRIENDLY A personally run pub in a small village, with a cosy bar and two smart dining rooms. Homemade nibbles and hearty, boldly flavoured dishes, with regional suppliers proudly listed on a blackboard. Staff are young, local and full of smiles.

Menu £17 (weekday lunch) – Carte £24/44

King St ✉ YO43 4QP – ℰ (01430) 827 269 – www.thestaratsancton.co.uk – Closed Monday

SANDBACH

Cheshire East – Pop. 17 976 – Regional map n° **11**-B3

▶ London 177 mi – Liverpool 44 mi – Manchester 28 mi – Stoke-on-Trent 16 mi

🍴 **Old Hall** 🛋 ⇔ 🅿

TRADITIONAL CUISINE · PUB Total restoration of this 17C black and white former manor house has created a smart new look, whilst retaining original features like oak panelling and timber beams. The daily menu focuses on keenly priced pub classics.

Carte £19/43

High St ✉ CW11 1AL – ℰ (01270) 758 170 – www.oldhall-sandbach.co.uk

SANDFORD-ON-THAMES – Oxfordshire → See Oxford

SANDIACRE

Derbyshire – Pop. 9 600 – Regional map n° **9**-B2

▶ London 123 mi – Birmingham 46 mi – Leeds 75 mi – Sheffield 45 mi

XX **La Rock** & 🄰🄺

BRITISH MODERN · RUSTIC Charming, personally run restaurant with an airy feel – it was once a butcher's. Exposed brick walls and antler chandeliers feature. Cooking combines classical flavours with modern techniques; home-grown fruits are well utilised.

Menu £27 (weekday lunch) – Carte £34/48

4 Bridge St ✉ NG10 5QT – ℰ (0115) 939 9833 – www.larockrestaurant.co.uk – Closed 26 December-mid January, 2 weeks summer, Monday, Tuesday and lunch Wednesday

SANDIWAY

Cheshire West and Chester – ✉ Northwich – Pop. 4 430 – Regional map n° **11**-A3

▶ London 191 mi – Liverpool 34 mi – Manchester 22 mi – Stoke-on-Trent 26 mi

🏨 **Nunsmere Hall** ⚑ 🛏 🖭 & 🛎 🅿

LUXURY · CLASSIC Built in 1904 for Sir Aubrey Brocklebank, chairman of Cunard Line shipping. Attractive gardens and lovely terrace; several sumptuous lounges and a maritime-themed bar. Spacious, individually furnished bedrooms, some with modern touches.

36 rooms 🖙 – †£105/250 ††£115/320

Tarporley Rd ✉ CW8 2ES – Southwest : 1.5 mi A 556 on A 49 – ℰ (01606) 889 100 – www.nunsmere.co.uk

Crystal – See restaurant listing

XxX **Crystal** 🛏 🛋 & 🅿

TRADITIONAL CUISINE · FORMAL Long, narrow hotel dining room with traditional styling and views over the terrace and garden. Simply prepared, classically based dishes have strong, gutsy flavours; be sure to try the homemade bread to start and chocolates to finish.

Menu £17/35

Nunsmere Hall Hotel, Tarporley Rd ✉ CW8 2ES – Southwest : 1.5 mi by A 556 on A 49 – ℰ (01606) 889 100 (booking essential) – www.nunsmere.co.uk

SANDSEND – North Yorkshire → See Whitby

SANDWICH
Kent – Pop. 4 398 – Regional map n° **5**-D2
▶ London 72 mi – Canterbury 13 mi – Dover 12 mi

🏠 Bell at Sandwich

HISTORIC · DESIGN Substantial Victorian property with a cool modern interior, located next to the River Stour. Kick-back in the bar, in one of the lounges or on the terrace. Stylish modern bedrooms come in cool pastel shades and some overlook the river. Dine from accessible menus in the restaurant or brasserie.

37 rooms ⊇ – 👤£ 75/100 👥£ 90/125
The Quay ✉ *CT13 9EF* – ☎ *(01304) 613 388* – *www.bellhotelsandwich.co.uk*

SANDYPARK – Devon → See Chagford

SAPPERTON – Gloucestershire → See Cirencester

SAWDON – North Yorkshire → See Scarborough

SAWLEY
Lancashire – Pop. 237 – Regional map n° **11**-B2
▶ London 242 mi – Blackpool 39 mi – Leeds 44 mi – Liverpool 54 mi

🍽 Spread Eagle

TRADITIONAL CUISINE · DESIGN Stylishly made-over, but still very much at the heart of the community. Gutsy, flavourful cooking, with a menu of pub favourites available in two sizes; plus platters, tapas-style nibbles and daily changing specials. Comfortable bedrooms feature smart, modern bathrooms.

Carte £ 18/32

7 rooms ⊇ – 👤£ 85 👥£ 110/140
✉ *BB7 4NH* – ☎ *(01200) 441 202* – *www.spreadeaglesawley.co.uk*

SAXILBY
Lincolnshire – Pop. 3 992 – Regional map n° **9**-C1
▶ London 145 mi – Lincoln 7 mi – Newark-on-Trent 22 mi

🏠 Canal View

FAMILY · HOMELY Guests are welcomed to this pleasant guesthouse with a cup of tea and a slice of homemade cake. Neat bedrooms come with fridges, goose feather duvets and Egyptian cotton linen. As the name suggests, it has a view over the canal.

3 rooms ⊇ – 👤£ 50/60 👥£ 70/80
Lincoln Rd ✉ *LN1 2NF* – *on A 57* – ☎ *(01522) 704 475* – *www.canal-view.co.uk*

SCARBOROUGH
North Yorkshire – Pop. 61 749 – Regional map n° **13**-D1
▶ London 253 mi – Kingston-upon-Hull 47 mi – Leeds 67 mi – Middlesbrough 52 mi

🏠 Crown Spa

TRADITIONAL · FUNCTIONAL 19C landmark hotel, in a prime position on the headland of a Victorian seaside town. Contemporary guest areas, superb leisure facilities and state-of-the-art meeting rooms. Smart bedrooms feature bespoke furnishings and the latest mod cons. Informal, bistro-style dining is split over four different rooms.

115 rooms – 👤£ 48/250 👥£ 75/250 – ⊇ £ 15 – 2 suites
Town plan: Z-n – *8-10 Esplanade* ✉ *YO11 2AG* – ☎ *(01723) 357 400*
– *www.crownspahotel.com*

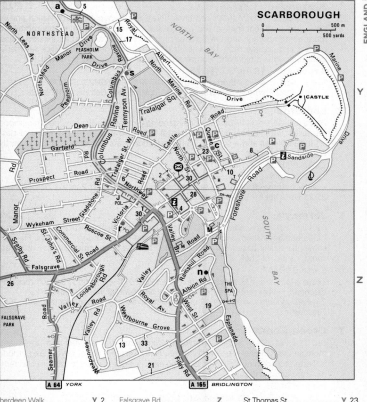

ENGLAND

CASTLE

NORTH BAY

SOUTH BAY

A 64 YORK

A 165 BRIDLINGTON

🏠 Ox Pasture Hall

♨ ⅋ ⇐ 🛏 🏌 🕭 🅿

TRADITIONAL · COSY This charming creeper-clad farmhouse in set in 17 acres of landscaped grounds and is a popular venue for weddings. Guest areas are stylish and contemporary. Bedrooms are well-equipped – those in the courtyard wing are the most modern and afford the best views. Dine from a modern menu in the formal restaurant or choose from hearty, unfussy dishes in the bistro.

32 rooms – ♦£ 90/125 ♦♦£ 110/450 – ☕ £ 13

Lady Edith's Dr, Raincliffe Woods ✉ *YO12 5TD* – *West : 3.25 mi by A 171 following signs for Raincliffe Woods* – *ℰ (01723) 365 295* – *www.oxpasturehallhotel.com*

Enjoy good food without spending a fortune! Look out for the Bib Gourmand ⊛ symbol to find restaurants offering good food at great prices!

⌂ Alexander

🏨 **TOWNHOUSE · COSY** 1930s red-brick house at the popular North Beach end of town. The well-kept lounge and cocktail bar are traditional styled; bedrooms are more contemporary and have a clean, uncluttered style – extras include robes, biscuits and seaside rock. The linen-laid dining room offers a 3 choice set menu; local seafood is a highlight. Homemade shortbread is served on arrival.

8 rooms 🖙 – ♦£ 48/60 ♦♦£ 76/92

Town plan: Y-a – *33 Burniston Rd* ✉ *YO12 6PG* – ✆ *(01723) 363 178*
– www.alexanderhotelscarborough.co.uk – Closed mid October-mid March

✗✗ Lanterna

ITALIAN · NEIGHBOURHOOD Long-standing, passionately run neighbourhood restaurant with homely décor and a loyal local following. Extensive menu of classic Italian dishes and a sizeable truffle selection – but go for one of the expertly cooked fish specials.

Carte £ 31/97

Town plan: Y-c – *33 Queen St* ✉ *YO11 1HQ* – ✆ *(01723) 363 616*
– www.lanterna-ristorante.co.uk – dinner only – Closed last 2 weeks October, 25-26 December, 1 January and Sunday

✗ Jeremy's

BRITISH MODERN · NEIGHBOURHOOD This smart, buzzy bistro started life as a 1930s butcher's shop, and the original wall and floor tiling still remains. Flavoursome, classically based dishes have Asian touches and come courtesy of an assured, confident chef.

Carte £ 29/47

Town plan: Y-s – *33 Victoria Park Ave* ✉ *YO12 7TR* – ✆ *(01723) 363 871 (booking essential) – www.jeremys.co – dinner only and Sunday lunch – Closed first 2 weeks January, 1 week May, 1 week October, Sunday dinner, Monday and Tuesday*

✗ Green Room

BRITISH MODERN · SIMPLE Traditional family-run bistro – the son cooks and mum serves. Original modern dishes are well-executed, full of flavour and include a 'Taste of Yorkshire' selection. Cooking explores different taste, texture and temperature combinations.

Menu £ 14/35

Town plan: Z-r – *138 Victoria Rd* ✉ *YO11 1SL* – ✆ *(01723) 501 801*
– www.thegreenroomrestaurant.com – dinner only – Closed Sunday and Monday

at Sawdon Southwest: 10 mi by A170 – Plan: Z – ✉ Scarborough

☼ Anvil Inn

BRITISH TRADITIONAL · PUB Charming former smithy, with its bellows, tools, forge and anvil still in situ. Classical cooking uses regional produce and features the odd international influence; Sunday lunch is a hit. The intimate restaurant has just 7 tables.

Carte £ 24/35

Main St ✉ *YO13 9DY* – ✆ *(01723) 859 896 – www.theanvilinnsawdon.co.uk*
– dinner only and Saturday-Sunday lunch – Closed 25-26 December, 1 January, Monday and Tuesday

SCAWTON – North Yorkshire → See Helmsley

SCILLY (Isles of)
Cornwall – Regional map n° **1**-A3
▶ London 295 mi – Camborne 23 mi – Saint Austell 52 mi – Falmouth 36 mi

Bryher

Cornwall – Pop. 78

686

⌂ Hell Bay

HOLIDAY HOTEL · STYLISH Several charming, New England style buildings arranged around a central courtyard, with a contemporary, nautical-style interior displaying an impressive collection of modern art. Immaculately kept bedrooms come with plenty of thoughtful extras. Fabulous coastal location allows for far-reaching views.

25 rooms (dinner included) ⌨ – †£ 150/400 ††£ 240/640 – 14 suites
✉ TR23 0PR – ℰ (01720) 422 947 – www.hellbay.co.uk – Closed November-February

Hell Bay – See restaurant listing

⌂ Bank Cottage

HOLIDAY HOTEL · PERSONALISED Friendly guesthouse with a well-tended, subtropical garden, a koi carp pond and even a rowing boat. Lounge boasts an honesty bar and artefacts from shipwrecks. Bedrooms are simple and compact – one has a roof terrace. Free use of kitchen.

4 rooms ⌨ – †£ 60 ††£ 116/120
✉ TR23 0PR – ℰ (01720) 422 612 – www.bank-cottage.com – Closed November-April

✗✗ Hell Bay

MODERN CUISINE · FRIENDLY Hotel restaurant with a relaxed 'boat house' feel. Light, Mediterranean-influenced lunches in the bar, courtyard or terrace. Dinner steps things up a gear, with unfussy, modern dishes displaying fresh ingredients and clear flavours.

Menu £ 43 (dinner) – Carte lunch £ 23/37
Hell Bay Hotel, ✉ TR23 0PR – ℰ (01720) 422 947 (booking essential) – www.hellbay.co.uk – Closed November-February

St Martin's

Cornwall – Pop. 113 – Regional map n° **1**-A3

⌂ Karma St Martin's Ⓝ

HOLIDAY HOTEL · PERSONALISED The owner of Karma Resorts spent time on the Isles of Scilly when he was young and its sandy white beaches and clear blue waters fit the group's ethos perfectly. The hotel resembles a row of cottages and has a bright, calming feel; Indonesian-style furniture is a feature. The modern menu is all-encompassing.

30 rooms – †£ 132/169 ††£ 175/225 – 4 suites
Lower Town ✉ TR25 0QW – ℰ (01720) 422 368 – www.karmaroyalgroup.com – Closed November-March

St Mary's

Cornwall – Pop. 1 607

⌂ Star Castle

CASTLE · HISTORIC Elizabethan castle in the shape of an 8-pointed star. Well-appointed, classical bedrooms and brighter garden suites – some with harbour or island views. 17C staircase leads from the stone ramparts to the charming Dungeon bar. Fabulous fireplace and kitchen garden produce in the Dining Room. Seafood menus in the Conservatory.

38 rooms ⌨ – †£ 80/153 ††£ 160/360 – 4 suites
The Garrison ✉ TR21 0JA – ℰ (01720) 422 317 – www.star-castle.co.uk – Closed 2 January-10 February

⌂ Atlantic

INN · FUNCTIONAL Former Customs Office in a charming bay setting, affording lovely views across the harbour. Bedrooms – accessed through twisty passages – are well-equipped, and many share the view. Comfortable lounge and small bar. Wicker-furnished restaurant offers an accessible menu.

21 rooms ⌨ – †£ 110 ††£ 160/230
Hugh St, Hugh Town ✉ TR21 0PL – ℰ (01720) 422 417 – www.atlantichotelscilly.co.uk – Closed November-February

⌂ Evergreen Cottage

FAMILY · COSY 300 year old captain's cottage with colourful window boxes, set in the heart of town. The interior is cosy, with a small, low-ceilinged lounge and breakfast room. The modest oak-furnished bedrooms are compact but spotlessly kept.

5 rooms ☲ – ♦£ 42/65 ♦♦£ 80/84

Parade, Hugh Town ⊠ TR21 0LP – ℰ (01720) 422 711
– www.evergreencottageguesthouse.co.uk – Closed 1 week February and Christmas-New Year

Tresco

Cornwall – Pop. 167

⌂ Sea Garden Cottages

HOLIDAY HOTEL · CONTEMPORARY A smart aparthotel divided into New England style 'cottages'. Each has an open-plan kitchen and lounge with a terrace; the first floor bedroom opens onto a balcony offering stunning views over Old Grimsby Quay and Blockhouse Point.

16 rooms ☲ – ♦£ 240/315 ♦♦£ 320/420

Old Grimsby ⊠ TR24 0QQ – ℰ (01720) 422 849 – www.tresco.co.uk – Closed mid November-mid February

Ruin Beach Café – See restaurant listing

⌂ New Inn

INN · COSY Stone-built inn boasting a large terrace, an appealing outdoor pool and pleasant coastal views. Bedrooms are bright, fresh and very comfy. Regular live music events attract guests from near and far. The hugely characterful bar and restaurant offer accessible menus.

16 rooms ☲ – ♦£ 70/150 ♦♦£ 140/300

New Grimsby ⊠ TR24 0QQ – ℰ (01720) 422 849 – www.tresco.co.uk

✗ Ruin Beach Café ⓝ

MEDITERRANEAN · RUSTIC Relaxed beachside restaurant in an old smugglers cottage – part of an aparthotel. The rustic room is decorated with striking Cornish art and opens onto a terrace with superb St Martin views. Colourful Mediterranean dishes have big, bold flavours; seafood and pizzas from the wood-burning oven are a hit.

Carte £ 26/40

Sea Garden Cottages Hotel, Old Grimsby ⊠ TR24 0QQ – ℰ (01720) 424 849 (booking essential) – www.tresco.co.uk – Closed mid November-mid February

SCUNTHORPE

North Lincolnshire – Pop. 79 977 – Regional map n° **13**-C3
▶ London 167 mi – Leeds 54 mi – Lincoln 30 mi – Sheffield 45 mi

⌂ San Pietro

TOWNHOUSE · DESIGN A 19C listed windmill and former pub on the main road. Modern, comfortable bedrooms have a slightly kitsch feel. Enjoy an aperitif or a cocktail in the chic lounge bar with its cream banquettes. The stylish restaurant offers set price menus with some Mediterranean influences; desserts are a highlight.

14 rooms ☲ – ♦£ 99/199 ♦♦£ 99/199

11 High St East ⊠ DN15 6UH – ℰ (01724) 277 774 – www.sanpietro.uk.com

SEAHAM

Durham – Pop. 22 373 – Regional map n° **14**-B2
▶ London 284 mi – Newcastle upon Tyne 17 mi – Leeds 84 mi

🏨 Seaham Hall

LUXURY · CONTEMPORARY An imposing, part-18C mansion which combines grand original features with striking modern styling. Bedrooms are spacious and contemporary, and come with luxurious touches such as Nespresso machines. There's a chic lounge; a grill restaurant complete with velour booths and a zinc-topped bar; and a stylish Asian restaurant set within the impressively equipped spa.

20 rooms ☕ – ♦£175/295 ♦♦£175/295 – 4 suites
Lord Byron's Walk ✉ SR7 7AG – North : 1.5 mi by B 1287 – ℰ (0191) 516 14 00
– www.seaham-hall.com

SEAHOUSES
Northumberland – Regional map n° **14**-B1
▶ London 328 mi – Edinburgh 80 mi – Newcastle upon Tyne 46 mi

🏠 Olde Ship

TRADITIONAL · COSY A long-standing, stone-built, family-run inn in a popular seaside town; full to bursting with nautical memorabilia. This cosy former farmhouse offers comfy, individually designed bedrooms; those in the annexe are bigger, with better views but less character. Formal dining room serves simple, traditional menu.

18 rooms ☕ – ♦£47/94 ♦♦£94/130
9 Main St ✉ NE68 7RD – ℰ (01665) 720 200 – www.seahouses.co.uk – Closed
December-February

🏨 St Cuthbert's House

           ♿ ⅍ P

HISTORIC · STYLISH Former Georgian Presbyterian chapel, with comfortable modern bedrooms, a homely lounge and a wood-furnished breakfast room; large arched windows and many original features remain. The friendly, welcoming owners often host music nights.

6 rooms ☕ – ♦£90/120 ♦♦£90/120
192 Main St ✉ NE68 7UB – Southwest : 0.5 mi by Beadnell rd on North
Sunderland rd – ℰ (01665) 720 456 – www.stcuthbertshouse.com – Restricted
opening in winter

SEASALTER – Kent → See Whitstable

SEAVIEW – Isle of Wight → See Wight (Isle of)

SEDGEFORD
Norfolk – Pop. 613 – Regional map n° **8**-B1
▶ London 121 mi – Norwich 42 mi – Hunstanton 5 mi

🏨 Magazine Wood 🅝

               ♨ ≼ 🚗 P

LUXURY · CONTEMPORARY Stylish guesthouse on a family farm beside the Peddars Way. Luxuriously appointed bedrooms come with dining areas, continental breakfasts and terraces overlooking the fields; you can order a newspaper or a cooked breakfast online.

3 rooms ☕ – ♦£105/139 ♦♦£105/139
Peddars Way ✉ PE36 5LW – East : 0.75 mi on B 1454 – ℰ (01485) 570 422
– www.magazinewood.co.uk – Closed Christmas (minimum two night stay at
weekends)

SEER GREEN – Buckinghamshire → See Beaconsfield

SENNEN COVE
Cornwall – Pop. 410 – Regional map n° **1**-A3
▶ London 316 mi – Truro 37 mi – Exeter 119 mi

X **Ben Tunnicliffe Sennen Cove** 🅝   ⇐ 🏠 🕭 🖵 🅿

CLASSIC CUISINE · SIMPLE Just along from Land's End, you'll find this modern brick and glass eatery, superbly located overlooking a lovely sandy cove. Tasty unfussy dishes showcase fresh local ingredients, including seafood from the nearby day boats.

Carte £ 23/36

Sennen Cove ✉ TR19 7BT – 𝒞 (01736) 871 191 (bookings advisable at dinner) – www.benatsennen.com – Closed January

SHAFTESBURY

Dorset – Pop. 7 314 – Regional map n° **2**-C3

▶ London 115 mi – Bournemouth 31 mi – Bristol 47 mi – Dorchester 29 mi

🏠 **Grosvenor Arms**   ⇑ 🕭 🛌

INN · STYLISH A modern take on a classic coaching inn, with a Georgian-style façade and a stylish interior. Understated bedrooms have a boutique feel and come with espresso machines. Kick-back with a drink on the delightful courtyard terrace.

16 rooms ☲ – ♦£ 130 ♦♦£ 130

High St ✉ SP7 8JA – 𝒞 (01747) 850 580 – www.thegrosvenorarms.co.uk

Grosvenor Arms – See restaurant listing

🏠 **Fleur de Lys**   ⇑ 🕭 ⁒ 🅿

TRADITIONAL · CLASSIC Keenly run, ivy-clad stone house in a lovely market town. Comfortable, well-kept bedrooms are named after grape varieties; each comes with its own laptop. Cosy lounge features a mahogany bar. Dine from traditional menus in the L-shaped restaurant or on the wood-furnished terrace.

8 rooms ☲ – ♦£ 85/110 ♦♦£ 100/170

Bleke St ✉ SP7 8AW – 𝒞 (01747) 853 717 – www.lafleurdelys.co.uk – Closed 2 weeks January

🏠 **Retreat**   🕭 ⁒ 🅿

TRADITIONAL · CLASSIC Pretty Georgian house on a narrow street in a delightful market town; built for a local doctor on the old site of a school for poor boys. Wood-furnished breakfast room and immaculately kept bedrooms with good facilities. Charming owner.

9 rooms ☲ – ♦£ 75/90 ♦♦£ 90/95

47 Bell St ✉ SP7 8AE – 𝒞 (01747) 850 372 – www.the-retreat.co.uk – Closed 28 December-31 January

XX **Grosvenor Arms**   🏠 🕭 🍴 ⇔

MODERN CUISINE · FRIENDLY Bright, contemporary brasserie in an updated coaching inn. Service is relaxed and attentive and the cooking is modern and refreshing. There's a selection of nibbles and tapas, homemade pizzas and clean, unfussy dishes in two sizes.

Carte £ 21/43

High St ✉ SP7 8JA – 𝒞 (01747) 850 580 – www.thegrosvenorarms.co.uk

SHALDON

Devon – Pop. 1 762 – Regional map n° **1**-D2

▶ London 188 mi – Exeter 16 mi – Torquay 7 mi – Paignton 13 mi

X **ODE**

BRITISH MODERN · NEIGHBOURHOOD Proudly run neighbourhood restaurant in a glass-fronted Georgian house on a narrow village street. It has a strong sustainable and organic ethos, sourcing recycled glassware, biodynamic wines and produce from small local suppliers and foragers. Simple dishes are precisely prepared and attractively presented.

Menu £ 35/40

21 Fore St ✉ TQ14 0DE – 𝒞 (01626) 873 977 (booking essential) – www.odetruefood.com – dinner only – Closed October, 25-26 December, Sunday-Tuesday and bank holidays

SHALFLEET → See Wight (Isle of)

SHANKLIN – Isle of Wight → See Wight (Isle of)

SHEFFIELD
South Yorkshire – Pop. 518 090 – Regional map n° **13**-B3
▶ London 174 mi – Leeds 36 mi – Liverpool 80 mi – Manchester 41 mi

Leopold
BUSINESS · PERSONALISED Evidence of this hotel's past can be seen in the boys grammar school photos hung throughout and in the Victorian wood-panelling in its meeting rooms. Contemporary bedrooms have fridges and iPod docks; some overlook the rear courtyard.
90 rooms – ♛£ 79/149 ♛♛£ 79/149 – ☑ £ 13 – 14 suites
Town plan: CZ-a – 2 Leopold St ✉ S1 2GZ – ℰ (0114) 252 40 00
– www.leopoldhotelssheffield.com – Closed 23-27 December

Halifax Hall 🆕
HISTORIC · MODERN Set just out of town is this converted Victorian mansion which, in a previous life, provided student accommodation. Good-sized, modern bedrooms feature bold décor; the suites are the largest and also have a lounge area. The restaurant offers classic dishes and has a terrace overlooking the gardens.
38 rooms ☑ – ♛£ 75/115 ♛♛£ 85/135
Town plan: AZ-h – Endcliffe Vale Rd ✉ S10 3ER
– ℰ (0114) 222 8810 – www.halifaxhall.co.uk

Hampton by Hilton 🆕
BUSINESS · MODERN The former South Yorkshire Police HQ in the city centre: inside it's now smart, modern and bright – perfect for the business traveller. Bedrooms vary in shape and size but are all simply decorated, with up-to-date facilities.
142 rooms ☑ – ♛£ 60/80 ♛♛£ 69/119
West Bar Green ✉ S1 2DA – ℰ (0114) 399 09 99 – www.hamptonhilton.com

Old Vicarage
MODERN CUISINE · FAMILY Long-standing restaurant with a loyal following, set in a former Victorian vicarage; dine in the traditional front room or the fairy light festooned conservatory. Set price menus offer classic dishes presented in a modern style.
Menu £ 40/75
Ridgeway Moor ✉ S12 3XW – Southeast : 6.75 mi by A 6135 (signed Hyde Park) and B 6054 on Marsh Lane rd.
– ℰ (0114) 247 58 14 – www.theoldvicarage.co.uk
– Closed 26 December-4 January, last week July, first week August, Saturday lunch, Sunday, Monday and Tuesday after bank holidays

Rafters
BRITISH MODERN · CLASSIC Two experienced local lads run this long-standing restaurant, which is a favourite spot for celebrating special occasions. Cooking respects the natural flavours of good quality ingredients and dishes are attractively presented.
Menu £ 39/58
220 Oakbrook Rd, Nether Green ✉ S11 7ED – West : 2.5 mi by A 57 and Fulwood rd, turning left onto Hangingwater Rd
– ℰ (0114) 230 48 19 – www.raftersrestaurant.co.uk
– dinner only and Sunday lunch
– Closed 1-10 January and 22-28 August

691

SHEFFIELD

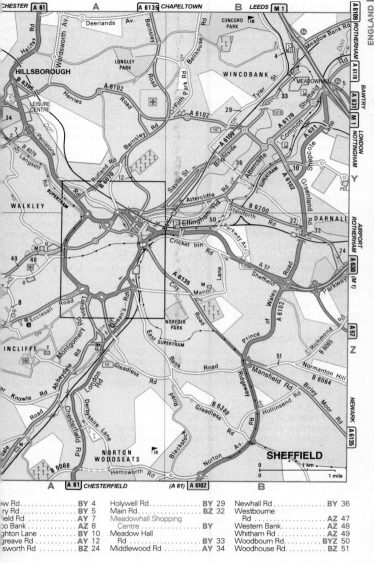

X Nonnas

ITALIAN · NEIGHBOURHOOD Long-standing Italian restaurant with a lively atmosphere. The extensive menu offers old favourites, from antipasti and sharing dishes to tasty homemade pastas and stews. You can also stop by for coffee and homemade cake in the bar.

Carte £ 23/35

Town plan: AZ-e – *535-541 Ecclesall Rd* ⊠ *S11 8PR* – *𝒞 (0114) 268 61 66*
– *www.nonnas.co.uk* – *Closed 25 December and 1 January*

X Milestone

MODERN CUISINE · NEIGHBOURHOOD Spacious 18C former pub set over two floors, in a regenerated area of the city. An array of regularly changing, seasonal menus offer modern, boldly flavoured dishes; presentation mixes the traditional and the contemporary.

Menu £ 15/17 – Carte £ 15/31

Town plan: CY-e – *84 Green Ln* ⊠ *S3 8SE* – *𝒞 (0114) 272 83 27*
– *www.the-milestone.co.uk* – *Closed 25-26 December and 1 January*

ID Wig & Pen

MODERN CUISINE · PUB Sister to the Milestone, but nearer to the heart of the city; its busy bar a magnet for office workers on their way home. A 'brunch' menu is served during the day, with hearty, satisfying pub dishes on offer in the evening.

Carte £ 14/25

Town plan: CY-x – *44 Campo Ln* ⊠ *S1 2EG* – *𝒞 (0114) 272 21 50*
– *www.the-wigandpen.co.uk* – *Closed 25-26 December and 1 January*

SHELLEY

West Yorkshire – Regional map n° **13**-B3
▶ London 185 mi – Leeds 22 mi – Manchester 37 mi – Sheffield 22 mi

XX Three Acres

BRITISH TRADITIONAL · RUSTIC Traditional stone inn on top of the moors, with a maze of charmingly cluttered low-beamed dining rooms. Choose from a large, traditional menu which features plenty of steak and rotisserie dishes. Bedrooms are warmly decorated; those in the adjacent cottages are the most modern and also the most peaceful.

Carte £ 30/41

17 rooms � – ♥£ 50/80 ♥♥£ 50/100

Roydhouse ⊠ *HD8 8LR* – *Northeast : 1.5 mi on Flockton rd* – *𝒞 (01484) 602 606*
(booking essential) – *www.3acres.com* – *Closed 25-26 December and 1 January*

SHEPTON MALLET

Somerset – Pop. 10 369 – Regional map n° **2**-C2
▶ London 127 mi – Bristol 20 mi – Southampton 63 mi – Taunton 31 mi

🏠 Charlton House

LUXURY · CONTEMPORARY Fine 17C house previously owned by Mulberry and now by Duncan Bannatyne: influences from both are evident. Smart boutique styling, with a touch of informality; individually furnished bedrooms feature luxurious bathrooms. Superb spa. Carefully prepared, modern European dishes served in conservatory.

28 rooms � – ♥£ 100/400 ♥♥£ 100/400

⊠ *BA4 4PR* – *East : 1 mi on A 361* – *𝒞 (08442) 483 830* – *www.bannatyne.co.uk*

SHERBORNE

Dorset – Pop. 9 523 – Regional map n° **2**-C3
▶ London 128 mi – Bournemouth 39 mi – Dorchester 19 mi – Salisbury 36 mi

The Green

BRITISH MODERN • BISTRO Pretty Grade II listed stone property at the top of the hill, with a traditional bistro style, an inglenook fireplace and ecclesiastical panelling. Concise à la carte and a good value set lunch; classical, confident, satisfying cooking.

Menu £ 20 (weekdays) – Carte £ 28/47

3 The Green ✉ DT9 3HY – ✆ (01935) 813 821 – www.greenrestaurant.co.uk – Closed 25-26 December, Sunday and Monday

at Oborne Northeast: 2 mi by A30 – ✉ Sherborne

Grange

TRADITIONAL • PERSONALISED Family-run, stone-built country house in pretty village; dating back 200 years. Comfy guest areas overlook attractive mature gardens. Spacious bedrooms boast good facilities; some have balconies or patios. Menus showcase the latest local, seasonal ingredients.

18 rooms – †£ 90/120 ††£ 99/180

✉ DT9 4LA – ✆ (01935) 813 463 – www.thegrangeatoborne.co.uk

SHERE – Surrey ➜ See Guildford

SHERINGHAM

Norfolk – Pop. 7 367 – Regional map n° **8**-C1

London 136 mi – Cromer 5 mi – Norwich 27 mi

Ashbourne House

TOWNHOUSE • PERSONALISED Well-appointed guesthouse in an elevated position; its large, landscaped garden has access to the clifftop. Two of the homely, comfortable bedrooms have coastal views. Local bacon and sausages feature at breakfast, which is taken beside an impressive fireplace in the wood-panelled breakfast room.

4 rooms – †£ 55/60 ††£ 75/80

1 Nelson Rd ✉ NR26 8BT – ✆ (01263) 821 555 – www.ashbournehousesheringham.co.uk – Closed 21 December-3 January

SHERWOOD BUSINESS PARK – Nottinghamshire ➜ See Nottingham

SHILTON

Warwickshire – ✉ Coventry – Regional map n° **10**-D2

London 97 mi – Bristol 99 mi – Cardiff 131 mi – Plymouth 213 mi

Barnacle Hall

HISTORIC • HOMELY Welcoming farmhouse in mature gardens, on a 170 acre arable farm. Traditional, beamed interior with a comfy, fire-lit lounge and 16C origins; spacious bedrooms offer pleasant country views. Hearty, home-cooked, communal breakfasts.

3 rooms – †£ 45/55 ††£ 75/85

Shilton Ln., Barnacle ✉ CV7 9LH – Northwest : 1 mi by B 4029 – ✆ (024) 7661 2629 – www.barnaclehall.co.uk – Closed 24 December-2 January

SHILTON – Oxfordshire ➜ See Burford

SHINFIELD – Wokingham ➜ See Reading

SHIPLAKE – Oxfordshire ➜ See Henley-on-Thames

SHIRLEY – Derbyshire ➜ See Ashbourne

SHOTTLE

Derbyshire – Regional map n° **9**-B2

London 140 mi – Sheffield 33 mi – Derby 13 mi

⌂ **Dannah Farm Country House**

TRADITIONAL · PERSONALISED 18C stone farmhouse on 154 acre working farm owned by the Chatsworth Estate; its outbuildings converted into spacious, well-equipped bedrooms. Many rooms have spa baths and the Granary and Studio Suites have hot tubs and terraces.

8 rooms ⌷ – ♦£ 95/185 ♦♦£ 185/305

Bowmans Ln. ⌧ DE56 2DR – North : 0.25 mi by Alport rd – ℰ (01773) 550 273 – www.dannah.co.uk – Closed 24-26 December

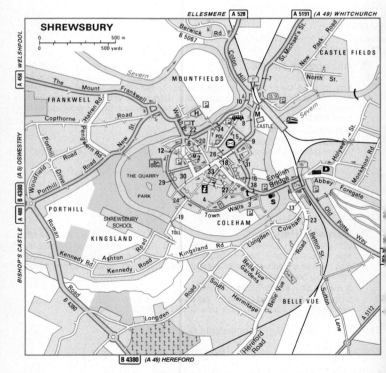

SHREWSBURY

Shropshire – Pop. 71 715 – Regional map n° **10**-B2

▶ London 164 mi – Birmingham 48 mi – Chester 43 mi – Derby 67 mi

🏠 Lion and Pheasant   ✿ ✾ P

HISTORIC · CONTEMPORARY A collection of adjoining 16C and 18C townhouses on a famous medieval street. Inside it's modern, quirky and understated. Chic bedrooms – designed by the owner's daughter – have a French boutique feel; the rear rooms are quieter.

22 rooms ☑ – †£ 89/104 ††£ 104/224
Town plan: -s – 49-50 Wyle Cop ✉ SY1 1XJ
– ℰ (01743) 770 345 – www.lionandpheasant.co.uk
– Closed 25-26 December
Lion and Pheasant – See restaurant listing

✗✗ Henry Tudor House   AC ⇔

BRITISH MODERN · INDIVIDUAL This impressive 15C timbered building is one of the oldest in town. Inside it's been subtly modernised and features a chic bar and a conservatory with birdcage chandeliers. Classic dishes have modern twists and the odd Asian touch.

Menu £ 13 (weekday lunch)/35 – Carte dinner £ 22/36
Town plan: -t – Barracks Passage, Wyle Cop ✉ SY1 1XA
– ℰ (01743) 361 666 – www.henrytudorhouse.com
– Closed 25-26 December and 1 January

✗ Lion and Pheasant   🏡 P

BRITISH MODERN · FASHIONABLE Head through the hotel's café-bar and up the stairs to this cosy beamed restaurant. Carefully prepared dishes rely on quality ingredients and have a subtle modern touch. Another more formally set room is also opened at weekends.

Carte £ 24/49
Town plan: -s – Lion and Pheasant Hotel, 49-50 Wyle Cop ✉ SY1 1XJ
– ℰ (01743) 770 345 – www.lionandpheasant.co.uk
– Closed 25-26 December

at Grinshill North: 7.5 mi by A49 – ✉ Shrewsbury

🛏 Inn at Grinshill   ⇔ 🍴 🏡 P

BRITISH TRADITIONAL · INN Family-owned and very personally run, this inn stands in the middle of a pretty Shropshire village and its food revolves around the seasons. A cosy bar plays host to walkers and locals while the contemporary restaurant has a view to the kitchen. Six pretty bedrooms are individually decorated and comfortable.

Carte £ 22/36 **s**
6 rooms ☑ – †£ 70/90 ††£ 90/120
The High St ✉ SY4 3BL – ℰ (01939) 220 410 – www.theinnatgrinshill.co.uk
– Closed first week January, Sunday dinner, Monday and Tuesday

at Upton Magna East : 6 mi by A 5064 off B 4380

🛏 The Haughmond ❶   ⇔ 🏡 P

TRADITIONAL CUISINE · PUB A stylish dining pub complete with a 'Village Shop', smart modern bedrooms and a recurring stag theme. Lunchtime sees a good value selection of pub classics, the evening menus are more ambitious and at weekends they open Basil's – an 18-seater restaurant offering a sophisticated 5 course set menu.

Carte £ 21/34
5 rooms ☑ – †£ 68/90 ††£ 85/120
✉ SY4 4TZ – ℰ (01743) 709 918 – www.thehaughmond.co.uk
– Closed 25 December and 1 January

at Condover South: 5 mi by A49

🏠 Grove Farm House   🖨 ⅌ **P**

COUNTRY HOUSE · HOMELY The friendly owners of this 18C farmhouse have opened up their family home. Bedrooms are pleasantly furnished and come with well-equipped bathrooms and country views. Extensive breakfasts showcase local and homemade choices.

4 rooms ☲ – 🛉£ 60/65 🛉🛉£ 85/90

⊠ SY5 7BH – South : 0.75 mi on Dorrington rd
– ℰ (01743) 718 544 – www.grovefarmhouse.com

SHREWTON

Wiltshire – Pop. 1 723 – Regional map n° **2**-D2
▶ London 91 mi – Bristol 53 mi – Southampton 52 mi – Reading 69 mi

🏠 Rollestone Manor   ⌂ 🖨 ⅌ **P**

COUNTRY HOUSE · PERSONALISED Grade II listed house on a main road just outside the village, on a part-working farm; once the home of Jane Seymour's family. Good-sized, antique-furnished bedrooms offer modern facilities; one even has a bath in the room, set on top of a plinth. The contemporary restaurant serves modern classics.

7 rooms ☲ – 🛉£ 80/90 🛉🛉£ 90/105

⊠ SP3 4HF – Southeast : 0.5 mi on A 360
– ℰ (01980) 620 216 – www.rollestonemanor.com
– Closed 24-26 December

SHURDINGTON – Gloucestershire ➡ See Cheltenham

SIBFORD GOWER

Oxfordshire – Regional map n° **6**-B1
▶ London 82 mi – Oxford 28 mi – Cheltenham 40 mi

🍴 Wykham Arms   🖨 🏕 **P**

BRITISH TRADITIONAL · PUB 17C thatched pub with sand-coloured stone walls, set down narrow country lanes in a small village. Menus feature local produce and range from bar snacks and light bites to the full 3 courses. There's a good range of wines by the glass.

Carte £ 21/33

Temple Mill Rd ⊠ OX15 5RX
– ℰ (01295) 788 808 – www.wykhamarms.co.uk
– Closed Monday except bank holidays

SIDFORD – Devon ➡ See Sidmouth

SIDLESHAM

West Sussex – Regional map n° **4**-C3
▶ London 84 mi – Bristol 137 mi – Cardiff 170 mi – Plymouth 187 mi

🏠 Landseer House   ⌕ ≼ 🖨 **P**

LUXURY · ELEGANT Tastefully furnished guesthouse, with numerous antiques and pleasant views of the surrounding wetlands. Contemporary bedrooms; go for Room 1 – the most luxurious. Those in the garden have their own terraces and kitchens.

6 rooms ☲ – 🛉£ 85/175 🛉🛉£ 95/185

Cow Ln ⊠ PO20 7LN – South : 1.5 mi by B 2145 and Keynor Ln
– ℰ (01243) 641 525 – www.landseerhouse.co.uk

🗓 **Crab & Lobster**   ⇦ 🛋 **P**

FISH AND SEAFOOD · PUB Historic inn, in a wonderful setting on a nature reserve, with pretty gardens and a light, relaxed feel. Seasonal menu focuses on seafood. Very comfy bedrooms have a modern, minimalist style; one has its own garden and an open-fired stove.

Menu £ 23 (weekday lunch) – Carte £ 30/53

5 rooms ⌕ – ♦£ 90/100 ♦♦£ 160/280

Mill Ln ✉ *PO20 7NB*

– ℰ *(01243) 641 233 (booking advisable)*

– *www.crab-lobster.co.uk*

SIDMOUTH

Devon – Pop. 12 569 – Regional map n° **1**-D2

▶ London 176 mi – Exeter 14 mi – Taunton 27 mi – Weymouth 45 mi

🏠 **Riviera**   ✧ ≼ 🛋 ☉ 🛁 **P**

TRADITIONAL · PERSONALISED Long-standing, family-run hotel with characterful Regency façade. Superbly kept classical guest areas; fresh flowers and friendly staff abound. Smart bedrooms in rich blues and gold, some with a view. Traditional menus have a modern edge. Cream teas a speciality.

26 rooms (dinner included) ⌕ – ♦£ 109/188 ♦♦£ 218/422

The Esplanade ✉ *EX10 8AY*

– ℰ *(01395) 515 201* – *www.hotelriviera.co.uk*

– *Closed 2 January-12 February*

at Sidford North: 2 mi – ✉ Sidmouth

XX **Salty Monk**   ⇦ 🛋 🛋 🛁 **P**

REGIONAL · INTIMATE Smart, proudly run restaurant in an old 16C salt house, featuring striking purple woodwork and a pleasant blend of the old and new. The Abbots Den offers a casual brasserie menu, while the Garden Room serves more elaborate modern dishes. Bedrooms have good extras and there's a gym and hot tub in the garden.

Menu £ 45 (dinner) – Carte £ 24/50

6 rooms ⌕ – ♦£ 85/120 ♦♦£ 135/190

Church St ✉ *EX10 9QP* – *on A 3052*

– ℰ *(01395) 513 174 (booking essential)*

– *www.saltymonk.co.uk*

– *dinner only and lunch Thursday-Sunday*

– *Closed January, 2 weeks November and Monday*

SINNINGTON – North Yorkshire → See Pickering

SISSINGHURST

Kent – Regional map n° **5**-B2

▶ London 50 mi – Maidstone 13 mi – Ashford 18 mi

🗓 **The Milk House**   ⇦ 🛋 🛋 ⴵ **P**

BRITISH TRADITIONAL · FASHIONABLE Set on a road originally known as Milk Street: turn right into the bar with its soft sofas, huge fire and Grazing Menu; turn left into the dining room for a seasonal menu of modern British dishes. Pub Classics and Children's menus available in either area. Upstairs bedrooms are smart and contemporary.

Carte £ 19/42

4 rooms ⌕ – ♦£ 100/120 ♦♦£ 100/120

The Street ✉ *TN17 2JG*

– ℰ *(01580) 720 200* – *www.themilkhouse.co.uk*

SITTINGBOURNE

Kent – Pop. 48 948 – Regional map n° **5**-C1

London 44 mi – Canterbury 18 mi – Maidstone 15 mi – Sheerness 9 mi

Hempstead House

COUNTRY HOUSE · PERSONALISED Privately run red-brick Victorian house in pleasant landscaped gardens. Classical bedrooms are found in the main house; more contemporary rooms are set above the luxurious spa. The wood-panelled lounges are cosy and characterful.

34 rooms – †£ 89/119 ††£ 120/170

London Rd, Bapchild ✉ ME9 9PP – East : 2 mi on A 2 – ✆ (01795) 428 020 – www.hempsteadhouse.co.uk

Lakes – See restaurant listing

XX Lakes

BRITISH TRADITIONAL · FORMAL Set in the conservatory of a well-run Victorian hotel, this formal restaurant features Georgian columns, crystal chandeliers and smartly laid tables. Menus are classical. Start with a drink in the homely sitting rooms.

Menu £ 20/30 – Carte £ 31/43

Hempstead House Hotel, London Rd, Bapchild ✉ ME9 9PP – East : 2 mi on A 2 – ✆ (01795) 428 020 – www.hempsteadhouse.co.uk – residents only Sunday dinner

SIX MILE BOTTOM

Cambridgeshire – Regional map n° **8**-B3

London 59 mi – Birmingham 106 mi – Norwich 55 mi – Cambridge 9 mi

Paddocks House

COUNTRY HOUSE · PERSONALISED Black, grey and silver décor gives this stylish hotel a masculine feel, and horse-themed prints are a reminder that Newmarket is nearby. Spacious bedrooms boast excellent quality linens and all but one have a bath in the room; No.12 even has its own cinema! The intimate dining room offers modern classics.

13 rooms – †£ 169/199 ††£ 169/199 – 1 suite

London Rd ✉ CB8 0UE – ✆ (01638) 593 222 – www.thehousecollection.com

SLALEY – Northumberland → See Hexham

SLAPTON

Devon – Regional map n° **1**-C3

London 223 mi – Plymouth 30 mi – Torbay 26 mi – Exeter 50 mi

Tower Inn

TRADITIONAL CUISINE · INN Charming pub overlooked by the ruins of a chantry tower (leave your car in the village and walk the narrow lane). Menus differ between services and offer pub food with a twist: maybe fish and chips in vodka batter at lunch or sea bass with crab dumplings in the evening. Simple bedrooms await.

Carte £ 21/35

3 rooms – †£ 65/75 ††£ 75/95

Church Rd ✉ TQ7 2PN – ✆ (01548) 580 216 – www.thetowerinn.com – Closed first 2 weeks January and Sunday dinner in winter

SNAPE

Suffolk – Pop. 1 509 – Regional map n° **8**-D3

London 113 mi – Ipswich 19 mi – Norwich 50 mi

Crown Inn

REGIONAL · FRIENDLY The affable owners of this characterful 15C former smugglers' inn grow fruit and vegetables and raise various animals, which provide much of the meat for their constantly evolving menus; the rosettes in the bar come from showing their Gloucester Old Spot pigs. Rustic bedrooms have beams and sloping floors.

Carte £ 20/38

2 rooms – †£ 70/90 ††£ 70/90

Bridge Rd ✉ IP17 1SL – ✆ (01728) 688 324 – www.snape-crown.co.uk

SNETTISHAM
Norfolk – Pop. 2 570 – Regional map n° **8**-B1
▶ London 113 mi – King's Lynn 13 mi – Norwich 44 mi

🏠 **Rose and Crown**　　　　　　　　　　　　　⇔ 🛏 🏠 P

TRADITIONAL CUISINE · PUB 14C pub featuring a warren of rooms with uneven floors and low beamed ceilings. Gutsy cooking uses locally sourced produce, with globally influenced dishes alongside trusty pub classics. Impressive children's adventure fort. Modern bedrooms are decorated in sunny colours, and offer a good level of facilities.

Carte £ 21/36

16 rooms 😊 – 🛉£ 90/130 🛉🛉£ 110/175
Old Church Rd ✉ PE31 7LX – ✆ (01485) 541 382
– www.roseandcrownsnettisham.co.uk

SOAR MILL COVE – Devon → See Salcombe

SOMERTON
Somerset – Pop. 4 133 – Regional map n° **2**-B2
▶ London 138 mi – Bristol 32 mi – Taunton 17 mi

🏠 **Lynch Country House**　　　　　　　　　　　　🛏 P

COUNTRY HOUSE · PERSONALISED Personally run Regency house with mature grounds that incorporate some unusual plants and a lake frequented by a variety of wildfowl. Traditional country house interior with a conservatory breakfast room and individually decorated bedrooms.

9 rooms 😊 – 🛉£ 70/95 🛉🛉£ 80/115
4 Behind Berry ✉ TA11 7PD – ✆ (01458) 272 316
– www.thelynchcountryhouse.co.uk

🏠 **White Hart**　　　　　　　　　　　　⇔ 🛏 🏠 ♿

MEDITERRANEAN · RUSTIC A 16C inn on the village's main market square; its beautiful parquet-floored entrance leads to six characterful rooms, including 'the barn' where you can watch the chefs at work. Seasonal food centres around the wood burning oven. Cosy, modern bedrooms; Room 3, with a bath centre stage, is the best.

Carte £ 24/38

8 rooms 😊 – 🛉£ 85/130 🛉🛉£ 85/130
Market Pl ✉ TA11 7LX – ✆ (01458) 272 273 – www.whitehartsomerton.com
– Closed 25 December, dinner 26 December and 1 January

SONNING-ON-THAMES – Wokingham → See Reading

SOUTH BRENT
Devon – Pop. 2 559 – Regional map n° **2**-C2
▶ London 201 mi – Exeter 29 mi – Plymouth 17 mi

🏠 **Glazebrook House** 🆕　　　　　　　　🔆 🌱 🛏 P

COUNTRY HOUSE · PERSONALISED A stunning 150 year old property set in 4 acres of peaceful grounds. It's been delightfully refurbished and features a lovely teak parquet floor and an eclectic mix of décor. Beautifully appointed, boutique bedrooms are named after characters from 'Alice in Wonderland'. Menus offer seasonal British dishes.

8 rooms 😊 – 🛉£ 119/159 🛉🛉£ 139/249
✉ TQ10 9JE – Southwest : 0.5 mi by Exeter Rd – ✆ (01364) 73 322
– www.glazebrookhouse.com – Closed 3 weeks January

SOUTH DALTON – East Riding of Yorkshire → See Beverley

SOUTH FERRIBY
North Lincolnshire – Pop. 651 – Regional map n° **13**-C2
▶ London 180 mi – Kingston upon Hull 13 mi – Lincoln 39 mi

🏠 Hope & Anchor ❶   ⬅ 🛋 ⭐ 🅿

BRITISH TRADITIONAL · PUB Rustic, nautically-themed pub with Humber views. Well-priced, tasty British dishes showcase fish from Grimsby, fruit and veg from their smallholding and meats from the Lake District – which are aged in a glass-fronted drying cabinet.

Carte £ 22/28

Sluice Rd ✉ DN18 6JQ – ℰ (01652) 635 334 (booking advisable)
– www.thehopeandanchorpub.co.uk – Closed Sunday dinner, Monday except Bank Holidays and lunch Tuesday

SOUTH MOLTON

Devon – Pop. 5 108 – Regional map n° **2**-C1
▶ London 197 mi – Barnstaple 11 mi – Bristol 81 mi

🏡 Ashley House ❶   🛋 🅿

HISTORIC · HOMELY You'll be warmly welcomed into this snug guesthouse, set next to the village green. It dates from 1879 and is named after the majestic ash tree out the front. Bedrooms are homely; dramatic photos of the local area hang on the walls.

3 rooms ⌂ – ♦£ 75/85 ♦♦£ 95/105
3 Paradise Lawn ✉ EX36 3DJ – ℰ (01769) 573 444
– www.ashleyhousebedandbreakfast.com

SOUTH POOL

Devon – Regional map n° **1**-C3
▶ London 218 mi – Plymouth 26 mi – Torbay 25 mi – Exeter 46 mi

🏠 Millbrook Inn   🛋

TRADITIONAL CUISINE · PUB Characterful, passionately run, shabby-chic pub squeezed between the houses on a narrow village street. Choice of cosy, low-beamed interior or two terraces. Cooking is traditional and hearty with Mediterranean influences.

Menu £ 12 (weekday lunch) – Carte £ 26/46
✉ TQ7 2RW – ℰ (01548) 531 581 – www.millbrookinnsouthpool.co.uk

SOUTH RAUCEBY

Lincolnshire – Pop. 335 – Regional map n° **9**-C2
▶ London 131 mi – Nottingham 40 mi – Leicester 54 mi

🏠 Bustard Inn   🛋 ⭐ 🅿

MODERN CUISINE · PUB Grade II listed inn set in a peaceful hamlet, with a light and airy flag-floored bar and a spacious, beamed restaurant. Good value lunch menu and a more ambitious à la carte offering modern English dishes. Satisfying desserts.

Menu £ 17 (weekday lunch)/25 – Carte £ 23/48
44 Main St ✉ NG34 8QG – ℰ (01529) 488 250 – www.thebustardinn.co.uk
– Closed 1 January, Sunday dinner and Monday except bank holidays

SOUTHAMPTON

Southampton – Pop. 253 651 – Regional map n° **4**-B2
▶ London 87 mi – Bristol 79 mi – Plymouth 161 mi

🏠 Pig in the Wall   🆎 🅿

TOWNHOUSE · PERSONALISED Delightfully run, early 19C property that's been lovingly restored. The rustic lounge-cum-deli serves superb breakfasts and light meals; for something more substantial they will chauffeur you to their sister restaurant. Smart, boutique bedrooms come with antiques, super-comfy beds and Egyptian cotton linen.

12 rooms – ♦£ 129/185 ♦♦£ 129/185 – ⌂ £ 10
Town plan: AZ-a – *8 Western Esplanade ✉ SO14 2AZ – ℰ (023) 8063 6900*
– www.thepighotel.co.uk

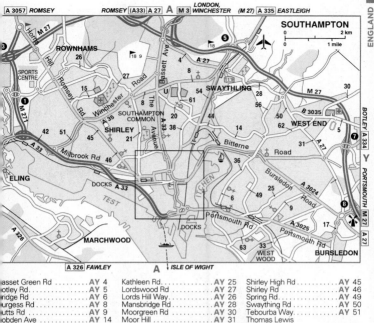

SOUTHAMPTON

ROWNHAMS

SPORTS CENTRE

SWAYTHLING

M 27

B 3035

WEST END

SOUTHAMPTON COMMON

SHIRLEY

BOTLEY A 334

PORTSMOUTH M 27   A 27

Bitterne

Road

ITCHEN

Bursledon

Road

A 3024

ELING

DOCKS A 33

TEST

Portsmouth Rd

DOCKS

Portsmouth Rd

A 3025

MARCHWOOD

WEST WOOD

BURSLEDON

A 326 *FAWLEY*   **A**   ↓ *ISLE OF WIGHT*

🍴 White Star Tavern, Dining and Rooms   ⇦ 🍷 🛏 ⚠ 🅰

BRITISH MODERN · PUB Eye-catching black pub with vast windows and a smart pavement terrace, set in the lively maritime district. Choice of all day tapas-style small plates or modern British à la carte of meaty dishes. Smart, modern bedrooms boast good facilities and extra touches.

Carte £ 19/44

16 rooms – 🛏£ 105/145 🛏🛏£ 105/145 – ☒ £ 9

Town plan: AZ-x - *28 Oxford St* ⊠ *SO14 3DJ*

– *℘ (023) 8082 1990* – *www.whitestartavern.co.uk*

– *Closed 25-26 December*

at Netley Marsh West: 6.5 mi by A33 off A336

🏠 Hotel TerraVina   🔆 ⇦ ⌂ ⚠ 🌿 ♨ 🅿

BUSINESS · STYLISH Neat and friendly Victorian red-brick house with wood-clad extensions, in a peaceful New Forest location. Comfy lounge and good-sized bar. Brown and orange hues create a relaxed Mediterranean feel. Bedrooms boast superb bedding, good facilities and thoughtful extras; some have roof terraces.

11 rooms – 🛏£ 155/165 🛏🛏£ 165/265

174 Woodlands Rd ⊠ *SO40 7GL*

– *℘ (023) 8029 3784* – *www.hotelterravina.co.uk*

Restaurant TerraVina – See restaurant listing

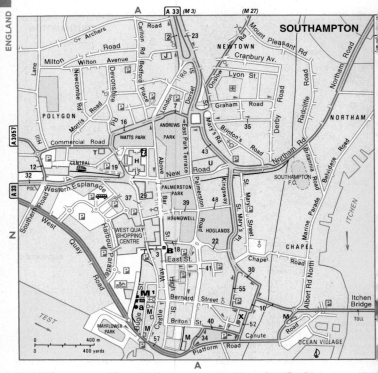

A 33 (M 3)   (M 27)

SOUTHAMPTON

XX **Restaurant TerraVina**   🕮 🛏 🛋 ⅃ AC P

MODERN CUISINE · BRASSERIE Modern hotel restaurant with an open-plan
kitchen, a glass-fronted wine cave and a large covered terrace. Lunch sticks to
the classics, while dinner introduces some imaginative modern dishes and a 6
course tasting menu. Service is attentive and the sommelier offers some original
and well-judged wine pairings.

Menu £ 24 (weekday lunch) – Carte £ 37/53

*Hotel TerraVina, 174 Woodlands Rd ⊠ SO40 7GL – 𝒞 (023) 8029 3784
– www.hotelterravina.co.uk*

SOUTHBOURNE – Bournemouth → See Bournemouth

SOUTHPORT

Merseyside – Pop. 91 703 – Regional map n° **11**-A2

▶ London 221 mi – Liverpool 25 mi – Manchester 38 mi – Preston 19 mi

Vincent

BUSINESS · DESIGN Striking glass, steel and stone hotel beside the gardens and bandstand. Stylish, boutique interior with chic bar, fitness room and spa. Sleek, modern bedrooms come in dark colours, boasting Nespresso machines and deep Japanese soaking tubs.

59 rooms – ♦£ 93/148 ♦♦£ 93/148 – ☲£ 10 – 2 suites
98 Lord St. ⊠ PR8 1JR – ☏ (01704) 883 800 – www.thevincenthotel.com
V-Café – See restaurant listing

✗ V-Café

ASIAN INFLUENCES · BRASSERIE Relaxed café in a striking modern hotel, its glass façade overlooking the street. Open all-day and offering everything from sushi at the counter to 3 courses of globally influenced dishes.

Carte £ 24/44
*Vincent Hotel, 98 Lord St. ⊠ PR8 1JR – ☏ (01704) 883 800
– www.thevincenthotel.com*

✗ Bistrot Vérité

FRENCH CLASSIC · FRIENDLY Simple neighbourhood bistro with panelled walls and candles; sit on the red banquette which runs down one side. Gutsy, traditional French cooking, with desserts a speciality. Friendly, efficient service.

Carte £ 22/42
7 Liverpool Rd, Birkdale ⊠ PR8 4AR – South : 1.5 mi by A 565 – ☏ (01704) 564 199 (booking essential) – www.bistrotverite.co.uk – Closed 1 week summer, 1 week winter, 25-26 December, 1 January, Sunday and Monday

SOUTHROP

Gloucestershire – Regional map n° **2**-D1
▶ London 87 mi – Birmingham 77 mi – Bristol 60 mi – Sheffield 146 mi

ᛁᗄ Swan

BRITISH TRADITIONAL · NEIGHBOURHOOD Delightful Virginia creeper clad inn set in a quintessential Cotswold village in the Leach Valley. With its characterful low-beamed rooms and charming service, it's popular with locals and visitors alike. Dishes are mainly British-based and feature garden produce; try the delicious homemade bread.

Carte £ 25/51
⊠ GL7 3NU – ☏ (01367) 850 205 – www.theswanatsouthrop.co.uk – Closed 25 December

SOUTHWOLD

Suffolk – Pop. 1 098 – Regional map n° **8**-D2
▶ London 108 mi – Great Yarmouth 24 mi – Ipswich 35 mi – Norwich 34 mi

 Swan

HISTORIC · DESIGN Attractive 17C coaching inn set in the town centre, close to the brewery. The cosy lounge and bar display subtle modern touches. Bedrooms are a mix: some are traditional, some are boldly coloured and some are charming. The grand dining room is hung with portraits and chandeliers and has a modern European menu.

42 rooms ☲ – ♦£ 115/125 ♦♦£ 185/255 – 2 suites
Market Pl. ⊠ IP18 6EG – ☏ (01502) 722 186 – www.adnams.co.uk

ᛁᗄ Crown

BRITISH TRADITIONAL · INN 17C Georgian-fronted former coaching inn with appealing, relaxed style, buzzing atmosphere and nautically-themed locals bar. Modern, seasonal menu served in all areas. Contemporary, individually styled bedrooms; those at the rear are the quietest.

Carte £ 23/38
14 rooms ☲ – ♦£ 135/185 ♦♦£ 185/235
90 High St ⊠ IP18 6DP – ☏ (01502) 722 275 – www.adnams.co.uk/hotels

SOWERBY BRIDGE
West Yorkshire – ⊠ Halifax – Pop. 4 601 – Regional map n° **13**-A2
▶ London 211 mi – Bradford 10 mi – Burnley 35 mi – Manchester 32 mi

XX **Gimbals**
MODERN CUISINE · BISTRO Personally and passionately run restaurant on the high street of a former mill town; look out for the eye-catching illuminated window display. Modern monthly menus have subtle Mediterranean influences and the desserts are a real highlight.
Menu £ 20/25 – Carte £ 24/40
76 Wharf St ⊠ HX6 2AF – ℰ (01422) 839 329 – www.gimbals.co.uk – dinner only – Closed 25-27 December, 1-2 January, Sunday and Monday

SPARKWELL
Devon – Regional map n° **1**-C2
▶ London 210 mi – Bristol 114 mi – Cardiff 145 mi – Plymouth 10 mi

🏠 **Treby Arms** (Anton Piotrowski)   🌿 ㄆ 🄿
❀ MODERN CUISINE · COSY A row of whitewashed cottages converted into a pub, hidden in a tiny hamlet but very busy, so book ahead. Carefully prepared, visually appealing and boldly flavoured modern dishes often feature a playful twist to surprise and delight. The 6 or 8 course 'taster' menus best demonstrate the chef's talent.
→ Brixham crab with blow-torched cucumber, avocado purée and cucumber consommé. West Country beef, flank cigar, roast sirloin, braised brisket, horseradish and creamed cabbage. Treby's Gone Carrots with orange sorbet.
Menu £ 25 (weekday lunch)/70 – Carte £ 27/52
⊠ PL7 5DD – ℰ (01752) 837 363 (booking essential) – www.thetrebyarms.co.uk – Closed 25-26 December, 1 January and Monday

SPARSHOLT – Hampshire → See Winchester

SPARSHOLT
Oxfordshire – Regional map n° **6**-A3
▶ London 77 mi – Oxford 21 mi – Swindon 17 mi

🏠 **Star Inn** 🅝   ⇦ 🌿 🄿
MODERN CUISINE · FRIENDLY Lovingly restored, flint-walled inn at the very heart of village life. Have a drink on the squashy sofas by the wood-burning stove then dine overlooking the garden. Carefully prepared, appealing dishes range from comforting to adventurous and game features highly. Comfy bedrooms are located in the barn behind.
Menu £ 16 (weekdays) – Carte £ 26/47
8 rooms ⌣ – †£ 75/95 ††£ 95/135
Watery Ln ⊠ OX12 9PL – ℰ (01235) 751 873 – www.thestarsparsholt.co.uk – Closed 4-11 January

SPELDHURST – Kent → See Royal Tunbridge Wells

SPRIGG'S ALLEY – Oxfordshire → See Chinnor

ST BRELADE'S BAY → See Channel Islands (Jersey)

STADDLEBRIDGE
North Yorkshire – Regional map n° **13**-B1
▶ London 236 mi – Leeds 48 mi – York 34 mi

ENGLAND

XX **Cleveland Tontine** ⇦ ⇩ P

BRITISH TRADITIONAL · BISTRO This established basement bistro is something of a local institution. Start with a drink in the champagne and cocktail bar then make for the characterful bistro or airy conservatory. Quirky modern bedrooms boast bold wallpapers and free-standing baths. Yorkshire meets France on the classically based menus.

Menu £ 17 (lunch and early dinner) - Carte £ 27/57

7 rooms �a - ♦£ 115/175 ♦♦£ 130/190

✉ DL6 3JB - On southbound carriageway of A 19 - ℰ (01609) 882 671 (booking essential) - www.theclevelandtontine.co.uk

STADHAMPTON

Oxfordshire - Pop. 702 - Regional map n° **6**-B2

▶ London 53 mi - Aylesbury 18 mi - Oxford 10 mi

🏡 **Crazy Bear** ✿ ⇔ ⅏ ⅍ P

LUXURY · MODERN Wacky converted pub with a London bus reception, a characterful bar, a smart glasshouse and even a Zen garden. Sumptuous, quirky bedrooms are spread about the place; some have padded walls and infinity baths. Eat in 'Thai' or flamboyant 'English', with its mirrored walls and classic British and French dishes.

16 rooms �a - ♦£ 199 ♦♦£ 199/399

Bear Ln ✉ OX44 7UR - Off Wallingford rd - ℰ (01865) 890 714
- www.crazybeargroup.co.uk

Thai - See restaurant listing

XX **Thai** ⇔ ⇧ ⇦ P

THAI · INTIMATE Cosy hotel restaurant in an intimate basement room, with ornate silk hangings and 8 tables topped with polished brass. Flavoursome, authentic dishes are skilfully prepared by a Thai chef; the 10 and 12 plate sharing menus are popular.

Menu £ 30 - Carte £ 19/45

Crazy Bear Hotel, Bear Ln ✉ OX44 7UR - Off Wallingford rd - ℰ (01865) 890 714
(booking essential) - www.crazybeargroup.co.uk

STAFFORD

Staffordshire - Pop. 68 472 - Regional map n° **10**-C1

▶ London 142 mi - Birmingham 26 mi - Stoke-on-Trent 17 mi

🏡 **Moat House** ✿ ⇔ ⅏ & AK ⅍ ⅍ P

BUSINESS · CLASSIC The original 15C farmhouse is now a classically styled pub and the sympathetically added extensions house a modern orangery restaurant and attractively furnished contemporary bedrooms. As its name suggests, it's surrounded by a moat; there's also a duck pond to the front and a canal to the rear.

41 rooms �a - ♦£ 79/148 ♦♦£ 99/168 - 1 suite

Lower Penkridge Rd, Acton Trussell ✉ ST17 0RJ - South : 3.75 mi by A 449
- ℰ (01785) 712 217 - www.moathouse.co.uk - Closed 25 December

Orangery - See restaurant listing

🏡 **The Swan** ✿ ⅏ & ⅍ P

INN · CONTEMPORARY This 17C coaching inn is found among some impressive old buildings, including a neighbouring Jacobean townhouse. Inside it's stylish and contemporary with up-to-date bedrooms. The brasserie offers a large menu of modern classics and there's also a coffee shop and two bars which share a pleasant terrace.

31 rooms �a - ♦£ 50/98 ♦♦£ 65/118

46 Greengate St ✉ ST16 2JA - ℰ (01785) 258 142 - www.theswanstafford.co.uk
- Closed 24-25 December

XXX Pillar

MODERN CUISINE · DESIGN Red-brick former post office with a modern ground floor bistro, an intimate cocktail bar and a trendy club. Smart, formal first floor dining room features eye-catching lampshades and an open kitchen. Classic cooking has a modern touch.

Carte £ 21/43

The Post House, 35 Greengate St, (1st floor) ⊠ *ST16 2HZ*
– ℰ (01785) 231 450 – www.pillarrestaurant.co.uk – dinner only
– Closed Sunday

XX Orangery

BRITISH MODERN · ELEGANT Head to this attractive hotel conservatory for views over the leafy garden to barges passing by on the canal. Cooking is in a modern British vein and dishes are accomplished and well-judged. On Saturdays they offer a 'Gourmet' menu.

Menu £ 21 (lunch and early dinner) – Carte £ 32/49

Moat House Hotel, Lower Penkridge Rd, Acton Trussell ⊠ *ST17 0RJ*
– South: 3.75 mi by A 449 – ℰ (01785) 712 217 – www.moathouse.co.uk
– Closed 25 December

STALISFIELD

Kent – Regional map n° **5**-C2
▶ London 51 mi – Bristol 169 mi – Cardiff 202 mi – Plymouth 261 mi

▷ Plough

BRITISH TRADITIONAL · RUSTIC Rurally set, 15C pub with thick walls, exposed beams, farming implements and hop bines. The usual suspects on the bar snack menu; more ambitious dishes on the à la carte. Nursery puddings and an impressive range of Kentish real ales.

Menu £ 17 (weekday lunch)/20 (weekday dinner) – Carte £ 22/33

⊠ *ME13 0HY – ℰ (01795) 890 256 – www.theploughinnstalisfield.co.uk*
– Closed Monday except bank holidays

STAMFORD

Lincolnshire – Pop. 22 574 – Regional map n° **9**-C2
▶ London 92 mi – Leicester 31 mi – Lincoln 50 mi – Nottingham 45 mi

🏠 George of Stamford

INN · COSY This characterful coaching inn dates back over 500 years and, despite its bedrooms having a surprisingly contemporary feel, still offers good old-fashioned hospitality. There are plenty of places to relax, with various bars, lounges and a walled garden. Dine in the laid-back Garden Room or more formal restaurant – both spill out into the lovely courtyard in summer.

47 rooms � – ♦£ 100 ♦♦£ 195/260 – 1 suite
71 St Martins ⊠ *PE9 2LB – ℰ (01780) 750 750*
– www.georgehotelofstamford.com
The Oak Panelled Restaurant – See restaurant listing

🏠 William Cecil

COUNTRY HOUSE · HISTORIC Extended 17C cream-stone rectory, named after the 1st Baron Burghley, with access through the garden to the estate. Contemporary, shabby-chic, panelled interior. Colonial-style bedrooms feature wood carvings and pastoral scene wallpaper. The restaurant has intimate, Regency-style booths and a classical menu.

27 rooms ⊆ – ♦£ 95/325 ♦♦£ 110/375 – 1 suite
High St, St Martins ⊠ *PE9 2LJ – ℰ (01780) 750 070*
– www.thewilliamcecil.co.uk

🏨 Crown   ☆ 🏡 🍴 P

HISTORIC · STYLISH Former coaching inn set in historic market town. Main house bedrooms have a funky, boutique style; those in the Town House are larger with a more classical feel. Dine in the modern cocktail bar, in one of the cosy lounges or in the quieter rear dining room.

28 rooms � – †£ 85/165 ††† £ 95/185

All Saints Pl. ✉ *PE9 2AG –* 𝒞 *(01780) 763 136*
– www.thecrownhotelstamford.co.uk

XxX The Oak Panelled Restaurant   🕸 🍴 🏡 P

BRITISH TRADITIONAL · INN Smart dress is required in this lovely oak-panelled dining room, which is found at the heart of an equally charming 16C coaching inn. Classical menus are largely British based with a few international influences. 'Carving', 'cheese' and 'sweet' trolleys all feature and the wine list is top notch.

Menu £ 27 (weekday lunch) – Carte £ 40/64

George of Stamford Hotel, 71 St Martins ✉ *PE9 2LB –* 𝒞 *(01780) 750 750*
– www.georgehotelofstamford.com

X No 3 The Yard ⓝ   🏡 ႕

TRADITIONAL CUISINE · BISTRO This relaxed, friendly restaurant is spread over two rustic cottages. The wide-ranging menu offers everything from fish & chips to roast local partridge. Dine in the courtyard, in the conservatory or under the vaulted, beamed ceiling.

Menu £ 20 – Carte £ 24/34

3 Ironmonger St ✉ *PE9 1PL –* 𝒞 *(01780) 756 080 – www.no3theyard.co.uk*
– Closed Sunday dinner and Monday

🍴 Bull & Swan   ⇐ 🏡

BRITISH TRADITIONAL · INN Stone-built former hall house converted to an inn during the 1600s and still the only pub south of the river. Characterful beamed bar and smarter dining room. Menu ranges from sharing slates to regional classics and locally sourced steaks. Stylish bedrooms are named after members of a historic drinking club.

Carte £ 22/44

9 rooms � – †£ 70/150 ††† £ 80/160

St Martins ✉ *PE9 2LJ –* 𝒞 *(01780) 766 412 – www.thebullandswan.co.uk*

STANFORD DINGLEY

West Berkshire – Pop. 179 – Regional map n° **6**-B3
✈ London 52 mi – Sheffield 168 mi – Nottingham 130 mi – Bristol 69 mi

🍴 Bull Inn   ⇐ 🍴 🏡 P

BRITISH TRADITIONAL · RUSTIC Locals and their dogs gather in the rustic bar of this beamed 15C inn, while the garden plays host to alfresco diners, chickens and the annual village dog show. The experienced chef-owner offers a wide range of tasty dishes; 'beer tapas' allows you to sample local ales and bedrooms are cosy and great value.

Carte £ 22/50

5 rooms – †£ 60 ††† £ 60 – � £ 12

Cock Ln ✉ *RG7 6LS –* 𝒞 *(01189) 744 582 – www.thebullinnstanforddingley.co.uk*
– Closed Sunday dinner

STANHOE

Norfolk – Pop. 289 – Regional map n° **8**-C1
✈ London 124 mi – Norwich 36 mi – Kings Lynn 18 mi

🍴 Duck Inn   ⇐ 🍴 🏡 P

TRADITIONAL CUISINE · INN Local ales and bar bites like scotch quail's egg in the buzzy, slate-floored bar. Three dining rooms with a rustic, relaxed feel for open sandwiches, fresh fish dishes and thick, juicy local steaks. Fairy lights and ducks in the picket fence fringed garden. Bedrooms are cosy and well-kept.

Carte £ 18/45

2 rooms � – †£ 75/90 ††† £ 95/135

Burnham Rd ✉ *PE31 8QD –* 𝒞 *(01485) 518 330 – www.duckinn.co.uk*

STANNINGTON

Northumberland – Regional map n° **14**-B2

▶ London 288 mi – Morpeth 7 mi – Newcastle upon Tyne 9 mi

🏠 St Mary's Inn Ⓝ   ⇔ 🛜 ૐ 🅿

TRADITIONAL CUISINE · PUB Spacious pub in the striking red-brick offices o
the old St Mary's Hospital. The experienced owners offer hearty dishes that peo
ple will know and love; meat and fish are cooked on the lumpwood charcoal gri
and afternoon tea is a hit. Bright, airy bedrooms feature ultra-modern bathroom
and local art.

Carte £ 20/38

11 rooms 🖙 – ♦£ 70/130 ♦♦£ 80/140
St Mary's Ln, St Mary's Park ✉ *NE61 6BL – West : 2.5 mi by Saltwick rd*
– ℰ (01670) 293 293 – www.stmarysinn.co.uk

STANSTED MOUNTFITCHET

Essex – Pop. 6 669 – Regional map n° **7**-B2

▶ London 39 mi – Chelmsford 23 mi – Cambridge 29 mi

🏠 Chimneys   🅿

TOWNHOUSE · COSY Charming 17C house with low-beamed ceilings and cos
guest areas. Pine-furnished bedrooms have a modern cottagey style and come
with homely touches. Tasty breakfasts include Manx kippers and smoked had
dock with poached eggs.

4 rooms 🖙 – ♦£ 58 ♦♦£ 85
44 Lower St ✉ *CM24 8LR – on B 1351 – ℰ (01279) 813 388*
– www.chimneysguesthouse.co.uk

✗✗ Linden House Ⓝ   ⇔ 🛜

BRITISH MODERN · RUSTIC This part-timbered former antique shop is now
rustic restaurant and bar characterised by dark wood, leather and a shabby-chic
masculine feel. Concise menus list country classics, including terrines, fish on the
bone and steaks. Bedrooms mix classic and modern elements; most come with
bath in the room.

Menu £ 15 (weekdays) – Carte £ 27/49

9 rooms 🖙 – ♦£ 109/154 ♦♦£ 119/174
1-3 Silver St ✉ *CM24 8HA – ℰ (01279) 813 003 – www.lindenhousestansted.co.uk*
– Closed Sunday dinner

STANTON

Suffolk – Pop. 2 073 – Regional map n° **8**-C2

▶ London 88 mi – Cambridge 38 mi – Ipswich 40 mi – King's Lynn 38 mi

✗ Leaping Hare   🖴 🛜 🅿

BRITISH MODERN · RUSTIC This beautiful 17C timber-framed barn sits at the
centre of a 7 acre vineyard. Carefully judged cooking relies on well-sourced, sea
sonal ingredients; many from their own farm. Sit on the lovely terrace and try the
interesting all-day light bites, or something from the accomplished, daily chang
ing menu.

Menu £ 19/28 – Carte £ 29/39

Wyken Vineyards ✉ *IP31 2DW – South : 1.25 mi by Wyken Rd – ℰ (01359) 250 28.*
(booking essential) – www.wykenvineyards.co.uk – lunch only and dinner
Friday-Saturday – Closed 25 December-5 January

STAPLEFORD – Nottinghamshire ➜ See Nottingham

STATHERN

Leicestershire – ✉ Melton Mowbray – Regional map n° **9**-B2

▶ London 119 mi – Birmingham 69 mi – Sheffield 62 mi – Leicester 24 mi

🕙 **Red Lion Inn**   🚐 🛆 **P**

TRADITIONAL CUISINE · RUSTIC Large, creamwashed village pub serving straightforward pub classics alongside well-presented restaurant-style dishes. Produce is sourced from their kitchen garden and local suppliers; service is friendly and attentive.

Menu £ 15 (weekdays) – Carte £ 24/45

2 Red Lion St ⊠ LE14 4HS – ℰ (01949) 860 868 (booking essential)
– www.theredlioninn.co.uk – Closed Sunday dinner and Monday

STAVERTON → See Daventry

STILTON
Cambridgeshire – ⊠ Peterborough – Pop. 2 455 – Regional map n° **8**-A2
▶ London 76 mi – Cambridge 30 mi – Northampton 43 mi – Peterborough 6 mi

🏠 **Bell Inn**   🖤 🚐 ⅙ 🕉 🛋 **P**

INN · COSY Historic coaching inn with a characterful beamed lounge and bar; run by a hospitable, hands-on owner. Comfy bedrooms have a traditional feel – some feature original beams or four-posters and those in the old smithy overlook the garden. The first floor restaurant offers a seasonal, classically based menu.

22 rooms ⌸ – ♦£ 82/125 ♦♦£ 110/145

Great North Rd ⊠ PE7 3RA – ℰ (01733) 241 066 – www.thebellstilton.co.uk
– Closed 25 December

STOCKBRIDGE
Hampshire – Pop. 570 – Regional map n° **4**-B2
▶ London 75 mi – Salisbury 14 mi – Southampton 19 mi – Winchester 9 mi

🕙 **Greyhound on the Test**   🖙 🚐 🍸 🛆 🖵 **P**

BRITISH MODERN · PUB Eye-catching pub with mustard-coloured walls, a red tiled roof and over a mile of River Test fishing rights to the rear. Low beams and wood burning stoves abound, and elegant décor gives it a French bistro feel. Menus offer an appealing range of well-presented, classically based, refined brasserie-style dishes. Homely bedrooms have large showers and quality bedding.

Menu £ 14 (weekday lunch) – Carte £ 24/49

10 rooms ⌸ – ♦£ 85/95 ♦♦£ 130/230

31 High St ⊠ SO20 6EY – ℰ (01264) 810 833 (booking advisable)
– www.thegreyhoundonthetest.co.uk – Closed 25 December

STOCKPORT
Greater Manchester – Pop. 105 878 – Regional map n° **11**-B3
▶ London 201 mi – Liverpool 42 mi – Leeds 50 mi – Sheffield 52 mi

XX **Damson**   🛆 AC

BRITISH MODERN · NEIGHBOURHOOD Smart, modern, glass-fronted restaurant on a corner site, with a pavement terrace, damson walls, velvet chairs and rustic tables. Appealing menu of traditional dishes with modern touches. Attentive, formal service.

Menu £ 17 – Carte £ 27/50

113 Heaton Moor Rd ⊠ SK4 4HY – Northwest : 2.25 mi by A 6, Heaton Rd, A 5145 and Bank Hall Rd – ℰ (0161) 432 46 66 – www.damsonrestaurant.co.uk – Closed 26 December, 1 January, lunch Monday and Saturday

X **brassicagrill** 🆕

🐜 BRITISH MODERN · NEIGHBOURHOOD The walls of this neighbourhood restaurant are filled with old lithographs of brassica plants and tea lights twinkle on the tables in the evening. Cooking is honest, flavoursome and good value; be sure to try the 'stout' ice cream. The team have worked together for many years and it shows.

Menu £ 17 – Carte £ 17/38

27 Shaw Rd ⊠ SK4 4AG – ℰ (0161) 442 67 30 – www.brassicagrill.com – Closed 25-26 December, Monday and Sunday dinner

STOCKSFIELD

Northumberland – Regional map n° **14**-A2

▶ London 279 mi – Liverpool 156 mi – Glasgow 140 mi – Manchester 146 mi

Locksley   🐾 🛝 🖙 🕹 🅿

FAMILY · HOMELY A welcoming house with lovely gardens and a fish pond – set in a peaceful location and ideal for discovering the Tyne Valley. There's homely lounge and an open-plan kitchen/breakfast room. Spacious bedrooms have superb bathrooms.

3 rooms 🖙 – ♦£ 40/45 ♦♦£ 70/80

45 Meadowfield Rd ⊠ NE43 7PY – Southeast : 2 mi by A 695 and New Ridley Road – ℰ (01661) 844 778 – www.locksleybedandbreakfast.co.uk – Closed 31 December

STOKE BY NAYLAND

Suffolk – Regional map n° **8**-C3

▶ London 70 mi – Bury St Edmunds 24 mi – Cambridge 54 mi – Colchester 11 mi

Crown   🐾 🖙 🛝 🕹 🅿

REGIONAL · PUB Smart, relaxed pub in a great spot overlooking the Box and Stour river valleys. Globally influenced menus feature produce from local farms and estates, with seafood from the east coast. Well-priced wine list with over 25 wines by the glass. Large, luxurious, superbly equipped bedrooms with king or super king sized beds; some have French windows and terraces.

Menu £ 15 (weekday lunch) – Carte £ 19/43

11 rooms 🖙 – ♦£ 95/150 ♦♦£ 135/245

⊠ CO6 4SE – ℰ (01206) 262 001 – www.crowninn.net – Closed 25-26 December

STOKE D'ABERNON

Surrey – Regional map n° **4**-D1

▶ London 21 mi – Brighton 49 mi – Guildford 13 mi

Old Plough   🛝 🕹 Ⓜ 🅿

TRADITIONAL CUISINE · FASHIONABLE The fourth venture for this small pub group has a smart yet satisfyingly pubby feel. Sit in a comfy chair in the open-fired bar or at a chunky wood table in the restaurant, and choose from sharing plates or more sophisticated dishes.

Carte £ 22/42

2 Station Rd ⊠ KT11 3BN – ℰ (01932) 862 244 – www.oldploughcobham.co.uk – Closed 26 December

STOKE HOLY CROSS – Norfolk → See Norwich

STOKE POGES

Buckinghamshire – Pop. 3 962 – Regional map n° **6**-D3

▶ London 23 mi – Bristol 99 mi – Croydon 44 mi

Stoke Park   🛝 🐾 🖙 🕹 🛝 📖 🎭 ⛳ 💆 🎾 🌳 🏊 🅿

LUXURY · CLASSIC Grade I listed Palladian property – once home to the Penn family, who created England's first country club. Extensive sporting activities, impressive spa and characterful guest areas. Mix of chic and luxurious 'Feature' bedrooms.

49 rooms – ♦£ 170/325 ♦♦£ 170/590 – 🖙 £ 22 – 1 suite

Park Rd ⊠ SL2 4PG – Southwest : 0.75 mi on B 416 – ℰ (01753) 717 171 – www.stokepark.com – Closed 3-6 January

Humphry's – See restaurant listing

🏚 **Stoke Place**   ✿ 🏠 🦢 🕭 ⚅ 🎿 P

HISTORIC · MODERN 17C Queen Anne mansion, set by a large lake and surrounded by delightful gardens and parkland. Quirky guest areas display bold
wallpapers and original furnishings. Uniquely styled bedrooms are spread about
the house and grounds.

39 rooms 🖃 – †£ 105/250 ††£ 195/390

*Stoke Green ✉ SL2 4HT – South : 0.5 mi by B 416 – 𝒞 (01753) 534 790
– www.stokeplace.co.uk*

Seasons – See restaurant listing

XxxX **Humphry's**   ⇐ 🏠 P

BRITISH MODERN · ELEGANT Impressive hotel dining room named after 18C
landscape gardener Humphry Repton, who designed the surrounding gardens;
the lake and parkland views are superb. Classically based dishes are presented
in a modern style. Service is professional.

Menu £ 29/68

*Stoke Park Hotel, Park Rd ✉ SL2 4PG – 𝒞 (01753) 717 171 (booking essential)
– www.humphrysrestaurant.co.uk – Closed 3-6 January, 25-26 December, Monday
and lunch Tuesday*

XX **Seasons** Ⓝ   🏠 P

MODERN CUISINE · ELEGANT Smart hotel dining room overlooking a lake and
gardens designed by Capability Brown. Modern menus rely on good quality local
ingredients and many dishes uses herbs, vegetables or fruit from the kitchen garden. Service is attentive.

Menu £ 24/45

*Stoke Green ✉ SL2 4HT – South : 0.5 mi by B 416 – 𝒞 (01753) 534 790
– www.stokeplace.co.uk – Closed Sunday dinner and Monday*

STOKE-ON-TRENT

Stoke-on-Trent – Pop. 270 726 – Regional map n° **10**-C1

🖪 London 162 – Birmingham 46 – Leicester 59 – Liverpool 58

STONE

Staffordshire – Pop. 16 385 – Regional map n° **10**-C1

🖪 London 151 mi – Birmingham 37 mi – Stoke-on-Trent 10 mi

XX **Cullens**   🅰🅲

MODERN CUISINE · CLASSIC Cullens is run by an experienced young couple and
is simply but comfortably furnished in a classic style. Fresh ingredients are carefully cooked in a subtle modern manner. Dishes are attractively presented and
lunch is a steal.

Menu £ 19/60

*16-18 Radford St ✉ ST15 8DA – 𝒞 (01785) 818 925 – www.cullensrestaurant.co.uk
– Closed 4-13 January*

STONE IN OXNEY

Kent – Regional map n° **5**-C2

🖪 London 73 mi – Barnet 89 mi – Ealing 85 mi – Brent 86 mi

🍴 **Crown Inn**   ⇐ 🏠 ⚅ P

BRITISH TRADITIONAL · INN A self-taught chef offers tasty comfort food in this
rural pub, with chutneys and preserves for sale at the bar, and pizzas from the
oven on summer weekends. Not-to-be-missed puddings include homemade ice
cream. Smartly decorated bedrooms come with modern shower rooms and a
continental breakfast.

Carte £ 23/32

2 rooms 🖃 – †£ 105/125 ††£ 105/125

*✉ TN30 7JN – 𝒞 (01233) 758 302 – www.thecrowninnstoneinoxney.co.uk – Closed
January and Sunday dinner-Wednesday*

STOKE-ON-TRENT NEWCASTLE-UNDER-LYME

STON EASTON

Somerset – Pop. 579 – Regional map n° **2**-C2

▶ London 131 mi – Bath 12 mi – Bristol 11 mi – Wells 7 mi

Ston Easton Park

GRAND LUXURY · ELEGANT Striking aristocratic Palladian mansion in 36 acres of delightful grounds designed by Humphry Repton. Fine rooms of epic proportions are filled with antiques, curios and impressive floral arrangements. Many of the stylish, uniquely designed bedrooms have coronet or four-poster beds; one is set in a cottage.

22 rooms ☑ – ♦£ 149/399 ♦♦£ 149/399 – 2 suites

✉ BA3 4DF – ☏ (01761) 241 631 – www.stoneaston.co.uk

Sorrel – See restaurant listing

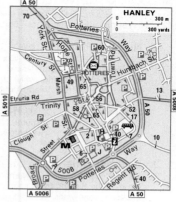

XXX Sorrel

≤ & P

BRITISH MODERN · ELEGANT Set in a striking Palladian mansion and surrounded by extensive formal gardens, this elegant, formal restaurant has high ceilings, panelled walls and crisp white linen on the tables. Classical menus showcase luxurious ingredients and produce from the Victorian kitchen garden. Service is professional.

Menu £ 23/50

Ston Easton Park Hotel, ⊠ BA3 4DF – ℰ (01761) 241 631 (bookings essential for non-residents) – www.stoneaston.co.uk

STONOR – Oxfordshire → See Henley-on-Thames

STOWMARKET

Suffolk – Pop. 19 280 – Regional map n° **8**-C3

▶ London 95 mi – Ipswich 14 mi – Colchester 35 mi – Clacton-on-Sea 40 mi

X Buxhall Coach House

🚗 🕾 ⇔ P

ITALIAN · COSY A realisation of a family dream: a homely, farmhouse-style restaurant run by a welcoming mother-daughter team. Pass the large, open-plan kitchen with its Aga, to the cosy dining room. Daily menus offer flavoursome Northern Italian dishes; good quality ingredients are cooked simply and with plenty of care.

Carte £ 30/52

Buxhall Vale, Buxhall ⊠ IP14 3DH – West : 3 mi by B 1115 and Rattlesden rd – ℰ (01449) 736 032 (booking advisable) – www.buxhallcoachhouse.com – Closed February, Sunday dinner, Monday and Tuesday

STOW-ON-THE-WOLD

Gloucestershire – Pop. 2 042 – Regional map n° **2**-D1

▶ London 86 mi – Gloucester 27 mi – Birmingham 44 mi – Oxford 30 mi

Number Four at Stow

BUSINESS · CONTEMPORARY Contemporary, open-plan hotel; so named as it's the fourth this experienced family own. The comfy lounge boasts bold brushed velvet seating, while the bright, compact bedrooms feature smart leather headboards, cream furniture and modern facilities. The comfortable brasserie offers a classical menu.

18 rooms ☲ – †£ 100/150 ††£ 120/180 – 3 suites

Fosseway ⊠ GL54 1JX – South : 1.25 mi by A 429 on A 424
– ℰ (01451) 830 297 – www.hotelnumberfour.co.uk
– Closed 23-31 December

Number Nine

FAMILY · COSY Expect a warm welcome at this ivy-clad, 18C stone house, close to the historic town square. The cosy lounge and breakfast room boast exposed stone walls, open fireplaces and dark wood beams. A winding staircase leads up to the pleasant wood-furnished bedrooms, which come with plenty of extras.

3 rooms ☲ – †£ 45/60 ††£ 70/85

9 Park St ⊠ GL54 1AQ – ℰ (01451) 870 333 – www.number-nine.info

XX Old Butchers ⓝ

CLASSIC CUISINE · FRIENDLY An old butcher's shop with quirky décor, colourful chairs and ice bucket and colander lampshades. The menu offers plenty of choice from old favourites to dishes with a Mediterranean slant. The 'bin end' wine list is worth a look.

Carte £ 26/39

7 Park St ⊠ GL54 1AQ – ℰ (01451) 831 700 – www.theoldbutchers.com

at Lower Oddington East: 3 mi by A436 – ⊠ Stow-On-The-Wold

Fox Inn

BRITISH TRADITIONAL · PUB Creeper-clad, quintessentially English pub at the heart of a peaceful Cotswold village, with beamed ceilings, solid stone walls, flagged floors and plenty of cosy nooks and crannies. The menu focuses on carefully prepared, tasty British classics and the comfortable bedrooms are individually furnished.

Carte £ 20/30

3 rooms ☲ – †£ 85/100 ††£ 85/100

⊠ GL56 0UR – ℰ (01451) 870 555 (booking essential)
– www.foxinn.net – Closed dinner Sunday and Monday

at Daylesford East: 3.5 mi by A436 – ⊠ Stow-On-The-Wold

X Café at Daylesford Organic

BRITISH MODERN · INDIVIDUAL Stylish café attached to a farm shop; its rustic interior boasting an open charcoal grill and a wood-fired oven. Throughout the day, tuck into light dishes and small plates; at night, candle-lit suppers step things up a gear. Everything is organic, with much of the produce coming from the farm. Stay overnight in one of their rustic cottages and unwind in the lovely spa.

Carte £ 23/43

4 rooms – †£ 330 ††£ 330/990 – ☲ £ 20

⊠ GL56 0YG – ℰ (01608) 731 700 (bookings not accepted)
– www.daylesford.com – lunch only and dinner Friday-Saturday
– Closed 25-26 December and 1 January

at Bledington Southeast: 4 mi by A436 on B4450

🖭 Kings Head Inn

BRITISH TRADITIONAL · INN Charming 16C former cider house on a picturesque village green, bisected by a stream filled with bobbing ducks. Appealing bar snacks include pheasant in a basket; pub classics and some interesting modern dishes on the à la carte. Large bar with a vast inglenook fireplace. Cosy bedrooms.
Carte £ 21/45

12 rooms ☲ – ♦£ 75/105 ♦♦£ 95/135

The Green ⊠ OX7 6XQ – ℰ (01608) 658 365 – www.kingsheadinn.net – Closed 25-26 December

at Nether Westcote Southeast: 4.75 mi by A429 and A424

🖭 Feathered Nest

MODERN CUISINE · INN Smart pub with a laid-back bar, a rustic snug, a casual conservatory and a formal dining room. Sit on quirky horse saddle stools and sample unfussy dishes from the daily blackboard or head through to elegant antique tables for more complex offerings; the wine list features over 200 bins. Comfy bedrooms boast antiques, quality linens and roll-top baths. The views are superb.
Menu £ 24 (weekday lunch) – Carte £ 40/58

4 rooms ☲ – ♦£ 160/210 ♦♦£ 190/240

⊠ OX7 6SD – ℰ (01993) 833 030 – www.thefeatherednestinn.co.uk – Closed 25 December, Sunday dinner and Monday except bank holidays

at Lower Swell West: 1.25 mi on B4068 ⊠ Stow-On-The-Wold

🏠 Rectory Farmhouse

TRADITIONAL · COSY Charming 17C stone-built farmhouse; to the rear, a terrace overlooks the lovely enclosed garden with its pond and water feature. Relax in the characterful beamed lounge; the cottage bedrooms have good facilities and extras. Aga-cooked breakfasts are taken in the country kitchen, conservatory or garden.

3 rooms ☲ – ♦£ 85/95 ♦♦£ 104/110

⊠ GL54 1LH – By Rectory Barns Rd – ℰ (01451) 832 351
– www.rectoryfarmhouse.yolasite.com – Closed Christmas-New Year

STRATFORD-UPON-AVON

Warwickshire – Pop. 27 830 – Regional map n° **10**-C3
▶ London 96 mi – Birmingham 23 mi – Coventry 18 mi – Leicester 44 mi

🏨 Welcombe H. Spa and Golf Club

LUXURY · CLASSIC Imposing Jacobean-style house built in 1866, featuring a golf course and a superb spa and leisure club. Well-proportioned, wood panelled guest areas with marble fireplaces. Grand, well-equipped bedrooms; the best are in the main house. The bar and restaurant overlook an impressive parterre and water feature.

85 rooms ☲ – ♦£ 99/250 ♦♦£ 99/500 – 5 suites

*Warwick Rd ⊠ CV37 0NR – Northeast : 1.5 mi on A 439 – ℰ (01789) 295 252
– www.menzieshotels.co.uk*

🏨 Ettington Park

HISTORIC · CLASSIC Impressive neo-Gothic mansion surrounded by lovely gardens. Characterful guest areas have vaulted ceilings and ornate rococo plasterwork. Feature bedrooms boast original fireplaces and four-posters; other rooms are more contemporary. The Oak Room – named after its ornate panelling – offers a modern menu.

48 rooms ☲ – ♦£ 105/250 ♦♦£ 115/260

*Alderminster ⊠ CV37 8BU – Southeast : 6.5 mi on A 3400 – ℰ (01789) 450 123
– www.handpickedhotels.co.uk/ettingtonpark*

ENGLAND

STRATFORD-
UPON-AVON

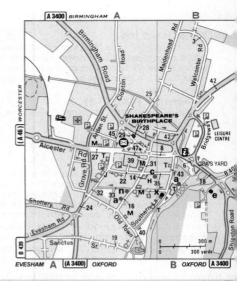

🏠 Arden ✿ 🕭 🎬 ⅏ 🖴 🅿

BUSINESS · MODERN Set in a great location opposite the RSC theatre, with a split-level terrace overlooking the river. There's a smart bar-lounge and a second plush lounge for afternoon tea. Twisty corridors lead to stylish modern bedrooms in vibrant contemporary colour schemes; one has a roll-top bath in the room.
45 rooms ☟ – ♦£125/258 ♦♦£150/415
Town plan: B-x – *Waterside* ✉ *CV37 6BA* – ℰ *(01789) 298 682*
– *www.theardenhotelstratford.com*
Waterside Brasserie – See restaurant listing

🏠 White Sails 🛏 🎬 ⅏ 🅿

LUXURY · STYLISH Detached Edwardian house; look out for the 'Sail' signs. Leather-furnished lounge with local info, a Nespresso machine and a decanter of sherry. Smart bedrooms with superb bathrooms and good extras. Comprehensive buffet breakfasts.
4 rooms ☟ – ♦£90/115 ♦♦£105/130
85 Evesham Rd ✉ *CV37 9BE* – *Southwest : 1 mi on B 439* – ℰ *(01789) 550 469*
– *www.white-sails.co.uk* – *Closed Christmas-New Year*

🏠 Cherry Trees 🛏 ⅏ 🅿

TOWNHOUSE · PERSONALISED Hidden away close to the river, beside the Butterfly Farm. Spacious bedrooms come with good extras; two have small conservatories and overlook the attractively landscaped garden. Homemade bread and granola feature at breakfast.
3 rooms ☟ – ♦£95/110 ♦♦£110/135
Town plan: B-e – *Swan's Nest Ln* ✉ *CV37 7LS* – ℰ *(01789) 292 989*
– *www.cherrytrees-stratford.co.uk* – *Closed November-mid February*

XX Waterside Brasserie 🕭 🕭 🎬 🅿

INTERNATIONAL · BRASSERIE Contemporary hotel brasserie with purple chairs and doors that open onto a landscaped terrace overlooking the river. Light bites at lunch are followed by well-presented British brasserie classics at dinner; the set menu is good value.
Menu £19/25 – Carte £34/50
Town plan: B-x – *Arden Hotel, Waterside* ✉ *CV37 6BA* – ℰ *(01789) 298 682*
– *www.theardenhotelstratford.com*

XX **Rooftop**   ≤ 🏤 ⅙ 🕸

TRADITIONAL CUISINE · DESIGN Curvaceous open-plan restaurant with a lovely terrace, set on top of the Royal Shakespeare Theatre and boasting great views over the canal basin, river and gardens. Menus offer brasserie classics with some European influences.

Menu £ 20 (lunch) – Carte lunch £ 21/31

Town plan: B-a – *Royal Shakespeare Theatre, Waterside* ⊠ *CV37 6BB* – *𝒞 (01789) 403 449* – *www.rsc.org.uk/eat* – *Closed 25 December and Sunday dinner*

XX **No 9 Church St.**   🕸 ⇔

BRITISH MODERN · BISTRO A friendly, cosy restaurant in a 400 year old townhouse a little off the main streets. The experienced chef-owner offers flavoursome British cooking with an original modern twist. Dishes are attractive and use lots of ingredients.

Menu £ 18 (lunch and early dinner) – Carte dinner £ 25/47 **s**

Town plan: A-a – *9 Church St* ⊠ *CV37 6HB* – *𝒞 (01789) 415 522* – *www.no9churchst.com* – *Closed 25 December-3 January, Sunday and bank holidays*

X **Church Street Town House**   ⇔ ⅙ 🕮 🕸

BRITISH TRADITIONAL · FRIENDLY Handsome part-17C property opposite Shakespeare's old school. The bright, bold interior is made up of a number of adjoining rooms. Appealing menus have Mediterranean influences and offer good value lunch and pre-theatre choices. Drinkers are also welcome. Funky, richly-coloured bedrooms have silver furnishings.

Menu £ 15 (lunch and early dinner) – Carte £ 25/38

12 rooms ⌑ – ♦£ 100/190 ♦♦£ 110/200

Town plan: A-n – *16 Church St* ⊠ *CV37 6HB* – *𝒞 (01789) 262 222* – *www.churchstreettownhouse.com* – *Closed 25 December*

X **Lambs**   🕸

TRADITIONAL CUISINE · RUSTIC Attractive 16C house with an interesting history; dine on one of several intimate levels, surrounded by characterful beams and original features. The classic bistro menu lists simply, carefully prepared favourites and daily fish specials.

Menu £ 14 – Carte £ 22/37

Town plan: B-c – *12 Sheep St* ⊠ *CV37 6EF* – *𝒞 (01789) 292 554* – *www.lambsrestaurant.co.uk* – *Closed 25-26 December and lunch Monday except bank holidays*

at Alveston East: 2 mi by B4086 – Plan: B – ⊠ Stratford-Upon-Avon

X **Baraset Barn**   🏤 🅰🅲 ⇔ 🅿

TRADITIONAL CUISINE · RUSTIC With original features, contemporary furnishings and large terraces, this modernised barn offers something for everyone. The good-sized menu also caters for one and all, offering a mix of pub classics and Mediterranean dishes.

Menu £ 14 (weekdays) – Carte £ 24/55

1 Pimlico Ln ⊠ *CV37 7RJ* – *off B 4086* – *𝒞 (01789) 295 510* – *www.barasetbarn.co.uk* – *Closed 1 January and Sunday dinner*

STRETE – Devon ➜ See Dartmouth

STRETTON

Rutland – Regional map n° **9**-C2

🔳 London 100 mi – Leicester 33 mi – Nottingham 37 mi

Jackson Stops Inn 🚪 🛜 🅿

BRITISH TRADITIONAL · RUSTIC A lovely stone and thatch pub comprising several different seating areas, including a small open-fired bar, a cosy barn and several beamed rooms. Choose from the list of classics and pub favourites; the sharing boards are a hit.

Carte £ 15/30

Rookery La ⊠ LE15 7RA – ℰ (01780) 410 237 – www.thejacksonstops.com
– Closed Monday except bank holidays and Sunday dinner

STROUD

Gloucestershire – Pop. 32 670 – Regional map n° **2**-C1
▶ London 113 mi – Bristol 30 mi – Gloucester 9 mi

🏠 The Bear of Rodborough 🍴 ≼ 🚪 🛁 🅿

INN · RUSTIC There's plenty of character to this 17C coaching inn, which stands on Rodborough Common and affords pleasant country views. The cosy beamed lounge and bar provide an atmospheric setting for a casual meal, while the library offers more formal modern cooking. Bedrooms are stylish and contemporary.

45 rooms ⊑ – ♥£ 80/95 ♥♥£ 85/150

Rodborough Common ⊠ GL5 5DE – Southeast : 2 mi by A 419 on Butterow Hill rd
– ℰ (01453) 878 522 – www.cotswold-inns-hotels.co.uk

Bisley House 🛜

TRADITIONAL CUISINE · FRIENDLY Stroud's oldest pub has been given a new lease of life and now sports a bright, modern look, with tiled floors, white walls – and not a beam or a horse brass in sight! The menu changes almost daily and cooking is simple, fresh and tasty.

Carte £ 21/31

Middle St ⊠ GL5 1DZ – ℰ (01453) 751 328 – www.bisleyhousecafe.co.uk – Closed
Monday

STUDLAND

Dorset – Pop. 299 – Regional map n° **2**-C3
▶ London 135 mi – Bournemouth 25 mi – Southampton 53 mi – Weymouth 29 mi

🏠 Pig on the Beach 🍴 ⌗ ≼ 🚪 🛁 🅿

COUNTRY HOUSE · STYLISH Delightful country house with commanding coastal views and lovely gardens leading down to the sea – the wonderful kitchen garden informs the traditional menu. The hotel has a relaxed, shabby-chic style and its furnishings are a pleasing mix of the old and the new. For something a little different, stay in an old shepherd's hut or dovecote. Staff are extremely welcoming.

23 rooms – ♥£ 135/269 ♥♥£ 150/310 – ⊑ £ 15

Manor Rd ⊠ BH19 3AU – ℰ (01929) 450 288 – www.thepighotel.com

✗ Shell Bay ≼ 🛜

FISH AND SEAFOOD · BISTRO Simply furnished seafood restaurant with a decked terrace; superbly set on the waterfront and boasting views over the water to Brownsea Island – all tables have a view. The daily menu mixes the classical with the more adventurous.

Carte £ 25/42

Ferry Rd ⊠ BH19 3BA – North : 3 mi or via car ferry from Sandbanks – ℰ (01929
450 363 (booking essential) – www.shellbay.net – Closed October-February

SUMMERHOUSE – Darlington ➜ See Darlington

SUNBURY ON THAMES

Surrey – Pop. 27 415 – Regional map n° **4**-C1
▶ London 16 mi – Croydon 38 mi – Barnet 44 mi – Ealing 10 mi

Plan : see Greater London (South-West) 5

XX **Indian Zest** 🍴

INDIAN · NEIGHBOURHOOD Pleasant restaurant with two small terraces, in a building dating back over 450 years. Pretty interior with black and white photos of Colonial India and a fine array of polo mallets. Large, interesting dishes originate from all over India.

Menu £ 11 (lunch)/36 – Carte £ 19/31

Town plan: BY-z – *21 Thames St* ⊠ *TW16 5QF* – ℰ *(01932) 765 000*
– www.indianzest.co.uk – Closed dinner 25 December and lunch 26 December

SUNNINGDALE

Windsor and Maidenhead – Regional map n° **6**-D3
▶ London 33 mi – Croydon 39 mi – Barnet 46 mi – Ealing 22 mi

XXX **Bluebells** 🚗 🍴 ⅙ 🎬 ⇔ 🅿

MODERN CUISINE · INTIMATE The smart façade of this professionally run restaurant is matched by a sophisticated interior, where white leather furnishings stand out against dark green walls. Beautifully presented dishes are crafted using modern techniques.

Menu £ 15/29 (lunch) – Carte dinner £ 35/69

Shrubbs Hill, London Rd ⊠ *SL5 0LE* – *Northeast : 0.75 mi on A 30* – ℰ *(01344) 622 722 – www.bluebells-restaurant.com – Closed 1-12 January, 25-26 December, Sunday dinner and Monday*

SUNNISIDE

Tyne and Wear – Regional map n° **14**-B2
▶ London 283 mi – Newcastle upon Tyne 6 mi – Sunderland 16 mi – Middlesbrough 41 mi

🏠 **Hedley Hall** 🐾 🚗 🐕 🅿

TRADITIONAL · COSY Stone-built former farmhouse in a quiet location close to the Beamish Open Air Museum. Formal, linen-laid breakfast room and a comfy lounge with a large conservatory extension. Good-sized bedrooms offer pleasant countryside views.

4 rooms ⊡ – ✦£ 65/75 ✦✦£ 95

Hedley Ln ⊠ *NE16 5EH* – *South : 2 mi by A 6076* – ℰ *(01207) 231 835*
– www.hedleyhall.com – Closed Christmas-New Year

SUTTON

Central Bedfordshire – Pop. 299 – Regional map n° **7**-B1
▶ London 47 mi – Cambridge 35 mi – Huntingdon 22 mi

🍴 **John O'Gaunt Inn** 🚗 🍴 🅿

TRADITIONAL CUISINE · COSY Well-run by experienced owners, this is a cosy, honest village inn with a fire-warmed bar, a smart dining room and delightful gardens overlooking wheat fields. The tried-and-tested menu includes some tasty 'Crumps Butchers' steaks.

Carte £ 24/42

30 High St ⊠ *SG19 2NE* – ℰ *(01767) 260 377 – www.johnogauntsutton.co.uk*
– Closed Monday except bank holidays and Sunday dinner

SUTTON COLDFIELD

West Midlands – Pop. 109 015 – Regional map n° **10**-C2
▶ London 124 mi – Birmingham 8 mi – Coventry 29 mi
Plan : see Birmingham

🏨 **The Belfry** 🏌 🚗 🎬 📺 ⚙ 🐕 𝟣ₐ 🍴 🔁 ⅙ 🎬 🧖 🏋 🅿

LUXURY · CONTEMPORARY Home to the PGA, The Belfry comes with three championship golf courses, a superb golf academy and even bespoke light fittings made from clubs. Bedrooms are contemporary and there's an impressive spa and fitness facility. The stylish restaurant offers steaks and grills, while the clubhouse has a pubby style.

319 rooms ⊡ – ✦£ 110/210 ✦✦£ 110/210 – 15 suites

Lichfield Rd, Wishaw ⊠ *B76 9PR* – *East : 6 mi by A 453 on A 446* – ℰ *(0844) 980 0600 – www.thebelfry.com*

🏚 New Hall

HISTORIC · ELEGANT Despite its name, this is one of the oldest inhabited moated houses in England, dating back to the 13C. Mature, topiary-filled grounds give way to a characterful interior of wood panelling and stained glass; bedrooms are luxurious. Refined, elaborate dishes are offered in the elegant dining room.

59 rooms ⌚ – 🛏£124/181 🛏🛏£134/191 – 5 suites

Town plan: 2DT-x – *Walmley Rd ⊠ B76 1QX – Southeast : 2.5 mi by A 5127 off Wylde Green Rd – ℰ (0845) 072 75 77 – www.handpickedhotels.co.uk/newhall*

SUTTON COURTENAY

Oxfordshire – Pop. 2 421 – Regional map n° **6**-B2

▶ London 72 mi – Bristol 77 mi – Coventry 70 mi

🍴 Fish

TRADITIONAL CUISINE · FRIENDLY A taste of France in Oxfordshire: expect French pictures, French music and charming Gallic service. Robust country cooking offers both French and British classics; ask for wine recommendations. Sit in the lovely garden or conservatory.

Menu £18 (weekdays) – Carte £27/48

4 Appleford Rd ⊠ OX14 4NQ – ℰ (01235) 848 242
– www.thefishatsuttoncourtenay.co.uk – Closed January, Monday except bank holidays and Sunday dinner

SUTTON GAULT – Cambridgeshire ➜ See Ely

SUTTON-ON-THE-FOREST

North Yorkshire – Pop. 539 – Regional map n° **13**-C2

▶ London 230 mi – Kingston-upon-Hull 50 mi – Leeds 52 mi – Scarborough 40 mi

🍴 Rose & Crown

BRITISH TRADITIONAL · PUB Welcoming pub in a beautiful village. Dine in the rustic bar, the bohemian restaurant or the airy conservatory. Menus offer plenty of choice, from pub classics to creative modern dishes. There's a superb terrace and garden to the rear.

Menu £19 (weekday lunch) s – Carte £25/40 s

Main St ⊠ YO61 1DP – ℰ (01347) 811 333 – www.theroseandcrownyork.co.uk
– Closed Monday except bank holidays

SWAFFHAM

Norfolk – Pop. 6 734 – Regional map n° **8**-C2

▶ London 97 mi – Cambridge 46 mi – King's Lynn 16 mi – Norwich 27 mi

🏚 Strattons

TOWNHOUSE · PERSONALISED Laid-back, eco-friendly hotel, in an eye-catching 17C villa with Victorian additions. Quirky, individually styled bedrooms are spread about the place; some are duplex or have terraces or courtyards. The rustic basement restaurant serves modern British dishes; on quieter days, breakfast is taken in their deli.

14 rooms ⌚ – 🛏£92/230 🛏🛏£116/250

4 Ash Cl. ⊠ PE37 7NH – ℰ (01760) 723 845 – www.strattonshotel.com – Closed 21-27 December

SWAY

Hampshire – Pop. 2 421 – Regional map n° **4**-A3

▶ London 96 mi – Bournemouth 15 mi – Lymington 5 mi

🏛 **Manor at Sway** ⒩ 🏞 🛏 🅿

FAMILY · PERSONALISED The Manor is set in the centre of a busy New Forest village and comes with a delightful rear garden where a mature Cedar of Lebanon takes centre stage. Inside it's bold and bright, with cosy modern bedrooms and Hypnos beds. The showy dining room has flock wallpaper, black tables and a French-inspired menu.

15 rooms ⌂ – †£ 90 ††£ 100

Station Rd ✉ SO41 1QE – 𝒞 (01590) 682 754 – www.themanoratsway.com

SWETTENHAM

Cheshire East – Pop. 248 – Regional map n° **11**-B3

▶ London 177 mi – Birmingham 63 mi – Liverpool 43 mi – Leeds 79 mi

🏠 **Swettenham Arms** 🛏 🏞 🅿

BRITISH TRADITIONAL · INN Traditional pub with a beaten copper bar, open fires, horse brasses and a lavender meadow. Seasonal menus provide plenty of choice, from sharing platters and pub classics to carefully prepared, well-presented restaurant-style dishes.

Carte £ 23/49

✉ CW12 2LF – 𝒞 (01477) 571 284 – www.swettenhamarms.co.uk – Closed dinner 25 December

SWINBROOK – Oxfordshire → See Burford

TALATON

Devon – Regional map n° **1**-D2

▶ London 165 mi – Bristol 76 mi – Exeter 14 mi

🏛 **Larkbeare Grange** 🐾 🛏 🍴 🅿

FAMILY · PERSONALISED A friendly, experienced couple run this well-kept house. Start the day with homemade yoghurt and preserves, and end it in the cosy lounge beside the wood-burner. Bedrooms feature stripped pine furnishings and floral fabrics.

4 rooms ⌂ – †£ 90/125 ††£ 115/175

Larkbeare ✉ EX5 2RY – South : 1.5 mi by Fairmile rd – 𝒞 (01404) 822 069 – www.larkbeare.net

TANGMERE – West Sussex → See Chichester

TAPLOW

Buckinghamshire – Pop. 518 – Regional map n° **6**-C3

▶ London 33 mi – Maidenhead 2 mi – Oxford 36 mi – Reading 12 mi

🏛🏛 **Cliveden House** 🏞 🐾 ⟨ 🛏 ⟩ ⟳ 📺 ◉ ♨ 🛋 📠 ♨ 🅿

HISTORIC · CLASSIC Stunning Grade I listed, 19C stately home in a superb location, boasting views over the formal parterre and National Trust gardens towards the Thames. The opulent interior boasts sumptuous antique-filled lounges and luxuriously appointed bedrooms. Unwind in the smart spa then take a picnic or afternoon tea hamper and kick-back in style on one of their vintage launches.

44 rooms ⌂ – †£ 495/750 ††£ 495/750 – 9 suites

✉ SL6 0JF – North : 2 mi by Berry Hill – 𝒞 (01628) 668 561
– www.clivedenhouse.co.uk

André Garrett at Cliveden House – See restaurant listing

XxX **André Garrett at Cliveden House** ⟨⟨ ⟨ 🛏 🍴 ◌ 🅿

MODERN CUISINE · LUXURY A grand hotel dining room with views over the parterre garden. Classic recipes are brought up-to-date in refined, well-presented dishes where local and seasonal produce feature highly. These are accompanied by a superb wine list.

Menu £ 32/70

Cliveden House Hotel, ✉ SL6 0JF – North : 2 mi by Berry Hill – 𝒞 (01628) 607 100 – www.clivedenhouse.co.uk/restaurant

TARRANT LAUNCESTON – Dorset → See Blandford Forum

TARR STEPS
Somerset – Regional map n° **2**-A2
▶ London 191 mi – Taunton 31 mi – Tiverton 20 mi

🏠 Tarr Farm Inn   ⇔ 🍴 ☂ P
BRITISH TRADITIONAL · RUSTIC Cosy, beamed pub in an idyllic riverside spot, overlooking a 1000 BC, stone-slab clapper bridge. If it's sunny, head for the garden for afternoon tea; if not, make for the narrow bar or cosy restaurant for everything from potted shrimps and sharing boards to Devon Ruby steak. Comfy, well-equipped bedrooms.
Carte £ 22/37

9 rooms ☲ – †£ 75/90 ††£ 100/150
✉ TA22 9PY – ℰ (01643) 851 507 – www.tarrfarm.co.uk – Closed 1-13 February

TATTENHALL
Cheshire West and Chester – Pop. 1 950 – Regional map n° **11**-A3
▶ London 200 mi – Birmingham 71 mi – Chester 10 mi – Liverpool 29 mi

🏡 Higher Huxley Hall   🦮 ⇇ 🍴 ⚅ P
FAMILY · HOMELY Attractive, part-13C farmhouse boasting an original Elizabethan staircase and field and castle views. Classical, open-fired lounge and linen-laid breakfast room. Homely bedrooms with good facilities.
4 rooms ☲ – †£ 65/85 ††£ 90/105
Red Lane ✉ CH3 9BZ – North : 2.25 mi on Huxley rd – ℰ (01829) 781 100
– www.huxleyhall.co.uk – Closed Christmas

at Higher Burwardsley Southeast: 1 mi – ✉ Tattenhall

🏠 Pheasant Inn   ⇔ 🦮 ⇇ 🍴 ☂ P
BRITISH TRADITIONAL · PUB Well-run, modern pub set atop a sandstone escarpment, with views across the Cheshire Plains. The menu focuses on simple pub classics, with no-nonsense cooking and clear, gutsy flavours. Spacious beamed bedrooms in the main building; more modern rooms with views in the barn. Staff are keen to please.
Carte £ 20/37

12 rooms ☲ – †£ 85/135 ††£ 95/150
✉ CH3 9PF – ℰ (01829) 770 434 – www.thepheasantinn.co.uk

TAUNTON
Somerset – Pop. 60 479 – Regional map n° **2**-B3
▶ London 168 mi – Bournemouth 69 mi – Bristol 50 mi – Exeter 37 mi

🏰 Castle   🏠 🍴 🖵 🛎 P
CASTLE · CLASSIC Part-12C, wisteria-clad Norman castle with impressive gardens, a keep and two wells. It's been run by the Chapman family for three generations and retains a fittingly traditional style. Well-kept, individually decorated bedrooms. Castle Bow serves modern dishes; relaxed Brazz offers brasserie classics.
44 rooms ☲ – †£ 92/115 ††£ 150/180
Town plan: V-a – Castle Grn ✉ TA1 1NF – ℰ (01823) 272 671
– www.the-castle-hotel.com
Castle Bow Bar & Grill – See restaurant listing

XX Castle Bow Bar & Grill   🍴 🆎 P
MODERN CUISINE · FRIENDLY Elegant, art deco style restaurant in the old snooker room of a Norman castle. Regularly changing menus showcase top quality regional produce. Well-balanced dishes are classically based yet refined, and feature some playful modern touches.
Carte £ 28/49

Town plan: V-a – Castle Hotel, Castle Grn ✉ TA1 1NF – ℰ (01823) 328 328
(booking advisable) – www.castlebow.com – dinner only – Closed Sunday,
Monday and Tuesday

TAUNTON

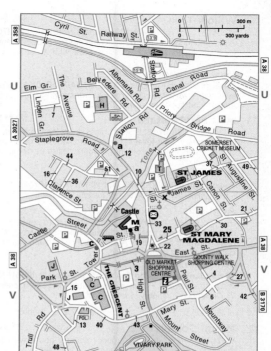

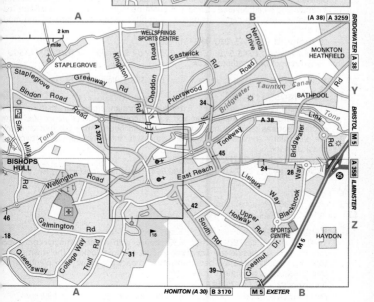

725

✗✗ **Willow Tree** 🛱 ⇔

MODERN CUISINE · INTIMATE Intimate restaurant in a 17C townhouse, featuring exposed beams and a large inglenook fireplace. Daily menus evolve with the seasons and blend a robust classical base with artful, innovative ideas. Service is friendly and efficient.

Menu £ 28 (weekdays)/33

Town plan: V-c – *3 Tower Ln ⊠ TA1 4AR* – *𝒞 (01823) 352 835 (booking essential)* – *www.thewillowtreerestaurant.com* – *dinner only* – *Closed January, August, Sunday, Monday and Thursday*

✗✗ **Mint and Mustard** ৬ 🄰🄲

INDIAN · FASHIONABLE Smart glass doors lead to a teak-furnished lounge and a contemporary, split-level restaurant in shades of green and mustard. Thalis and curries at lunch; highly original, modern dishes at dinner. The Keralan specialities are a highlight.

Carte £ 16/32

Town plan: U-a – *10 Station Rd ⊠ TA1 1NH* – *𝒞 (01823) 330 770* – *www.mintandmustard.com* – *Closed 25-26 December and 1 January*

✗ **Augustus** 🛱

BRITISH MODERN · BISTRO Simple little bistro set in a small courtyard and run by an experienced chef. Good-sized menu of hearty, unfussy dishes which mix French, British and some Asian influences – supplemented by blackboard specials. Bright and breezy service.

Carte £ 20/38

Town plan: V-x – *3 The Courtyard, St James St. ⊠ TA1 1JR* – *𝒞 (01823) 324 354 (booking essential)* – *www.augustustaunton.co.uk* – *Closed 23 December-2 January, Sunday and Monday*

at Henlade East: 3.5 mi on A358 – Plan: BZ – ⊠ Taunton

🏠 **Mount Somerset** ✿ 🐾 ⪬ 🛋 🕸 🌿 ⊡ 🛁 🅿

HISTORIC · STYLISH Fine Regency country house with well-tended formal gardens and lovely views. Contemporary décor blends with period features including a copula and a cantilevered staircase. Elegant bedrooms come with excellent feature bathrooms. The capacious dining room offers a mix of traditional and modern dishes.

19 rooms � – ♦£ 145/210 ♦♦£ 195/320

Lower Henlade ⊠ TA3 5NB – *South : 0.75 mi by Stoke Rd* – *𝒞 (01823) 442 500* – *www.mountsomersethotel.co.uk*

at Hatch Beauchamp Southeast: 6 mi by A358 – Plan: BZ – ⊠ Taunton

🏠 **Farthings** ✿ ⪬ 🕼 🅿

TRADITIONAL · PERSONALISED Extended Georgian house in mature, well tended gardens, with a small bar and a cosy, country house style lounge; many original features remain. Charming, antique-filled bedrooms – the master rooms are particularly comfortable. Two-roomed restaurant offers constantly evolving classical menu.

12 rooms � – ♦£ 75/155 ♦♦£ 85/175

Village Rd ⊠ TA3 6SG – *𝒞 (01823) 480 664* – *www.farthingshotel.co.uk*

TAVISTOCK

Devon – Pop. 12 280 – Regional map n° **1**-C2
▶ London 239 mi – Exeter 38 mi – Plymouth 16 mi

🏠 **Rockmount** 🅿

TOWNHOUSE · CONTEMPORARY 1920s house with a contrastingly contemporary interior, set beside the Tavistock viaduct and overlooking the town's roof tops. Individually furnished bedrooms are compact but come with plenty of extras. Breakfast is brought to your room.

5 rooms � – ♦£ 59/75 ♦♦£ 65/115

Drake Rd ⊠ PL19 0AX – *𝒞 (01822) 611 039* – *www.rockmount-tavistock.com*

🍴 **Cornish Arms**   🏡 ⚹

🍸 TRADITIONAL CUISINE · COSY It might have been refurbished but the Cornish Arms is still a pleasingly traditional pub and its quarry-tiled bar is invariably filled with regulars playing darts and watching football. The ambitious, talented chef prepares a range of tasty classic and modern dishes, and attractive, sophisticated desserts.

Carte £ 22/40

15 West St ⊠ PL19 8AN – 𝒞 (01822) 612 145 – www.thecornisharmstavistock.co.uk
– Closed dinner 24 December

at Gulworthy West: 3 mi on A390 – ⊠ Tavistock

🍴🍴 **Horn of Plenty**   ⇄ 🦆 ⪕ 🏡 🏠 AC ⟷ 🅿

MODERN CUISINE · ELEGANT Extremely friendly restaurant in an attractive creeper-clad country house, which offers lovely moor and valley views; ask for a window table. The modern menu has wide-ranging influences – the tasting menu best showcases the chef's talent. Bedrooms are bright and modern and many have balconies or terraces.

Menu £ 20/65

16 rooms ⌑ – ∮£ 100/235 ∮∮£ 110/245

Gulworthy ⊠ PL19 8JD – Northwest : 1 mi by B 3362 – 𝒞 (01822) 832 528
– www.thehornofplenty.co.uk

at Milton Abbot Northwest: 6 mi on B3362 – ⊠ Tavistock

🏠 **Hotel Endsleigh**   🌳 🦆 ⪕ 🏡 🔵 🅿

HISTORIC · CLASSIC Restored Regency lodge in an idyllic rural setting; spacious guest areas offer wonderful countryside views and have a warm, classical style with a contemporary edge. Comfortable, antique-furnished bedrooms boast an understated elegance; choose one overlooking the magnificent gardens.

17 rooms ⌑ – ∮£ 171/360 ∮∮£ 190/400 – 3 suites

⊠ PL19 0PQ – Southwest : 1 mi – 𝒞 (01822) 870 000
– www.hotelendsleigh.com

Restaurant Endsleigh – See restaurant listing

🍴🍴 **Restaurant Endsleigh**   ⪕ 🏡 🏠 ⚹ 🅿

MODERN CUISINE · INTIMATE Elegant, wood-panelled restaurant in a peacefully located hotel; ask for a window table for superb countryside views. Classic cooking with a modern edge; dishes are neatly presented and flavoursome, with local produce to the fore. Attentive service, with a pleasant degree of informality.

Menu £ 26/44

Hotel Endsleigh, ⊠ PL19 0PQ – Southwest : 1 mi
– 𝒞 (01822) 870 000 (bookings essential for non-residents)
– www.hotelendsleigh.com

at Chillaton Northwest: 6.25 mi by Chillaton rd – ⊠ Tavistock

🏠 **Tor Cottage**   🦆 ⪕ 🏡 ⌇ 🐾 🅿

TRADITIONAL · CLASSIC Remotely set cottage in 28 hillside acres, with peaceful gardens and a lovely outdoor pool. Bedrooms, most in converted outhouses, boast small kitchenettes and wood burning stoves. Breakfast is taken on the terrace or in the conservatory. Charming owner.

5 rooms ⌑ – ∮£ 98 ∮∮£ 150/155

⊠ PL16 0JE – Southwest : 0.75 mi by Tavistock rd, turning right at bridle path
– 𝒞 (01822) 860 248 – www.torcottage.co.uk
– Closed mid-December-1 February (minimum 2 night stay)

TEFFONT EVIAS – Wiltshire → See Salisbury

TEMPLE SOWERBY – Cumbria ➡ See Penrith

TENTERDEN
Kent – Pop. 7 118 – Regional map n° **9**-C2
▶ London 57 mi – Folkestone 26 mi – Hastings 21 mi – Maidstone 19 mi

XX **Swan Wine Kitchen**   🏠 🎦 ⇔ P

BRITISH MODERN · FRIENDLY This rustic modern restaurant sits above the shop in the Chapel Down vineyard and boasts a lovely rooftop terrace with views over the vines; naturally, wines from the vineyard feature. Cooking is refined, precise and full of flavour. The midweek menu is good value and they also serve afternoon tea.

Menu £ 20 – Carte £ 27/37
*Chapel Down Winery, Small Hythe Rd ⊠ TN30 7NG – 𝒫 (01580) 761 616
– www.illbemother.co.uk – Closed dinner Sunday-Wednesday*

> Prices quoted after the symbol ♦ refer to the lowest rate for a single room in low season, followed by the highest rate in high season. The same principle applies to the symbol ♦♦ for a double room.

TETBURY
Gloucestershire – Pop. 5 250 – Regional map n° **2**-C1
▶ London 113 mi – Bristol 27 mi – Gloucester 19 mi

🏨 **Calcot Manor**   📶 🐾 🛏 🍴 🖥 📶 🏠 📗 ✕ 🏃 🏊 ♨ P

FAMILY · CONTEMPORARY Impressive collection of converted farm buildings in a peaceful country setting, comprising ancient barns, old stables and a characterful farmhouse. Comfy lounges and stylish bedrooms have good mod cons; the out buildings house a crèche, conference rooms and a superb spa complex. The laid back conservatory offers classical dishes and there's a popular pub in the grounds.

35 rooms ⊆ – ♦£ 225/450 ♦♦£ 250/500 – 1 suite
*Calcot ⊠ GL8 8YJ – West : 3.5 mi on A 4135 – 𝒫 (01666) 890 391
– www.calcotmanor.co.uk*
🍴 Gumstool Inn – See restaurant listing

🏠 **The Close**   📶 🛏 ♨ P

TOWNHOUSE · CONTEMPORARY The rear garden and courtyard of this 16C townhouse provide the perfect spot on a warm summer's day. Bold colours and contemporary furnishings blend well with the building's period features; look out for the superb cupola ceiling in the bar. Choose from a list of classics in the brasserie or a selection of refined, modern dishes in the more sophisticated restaurant.

18 rooms ⊆ – ♦£ 130/170 ♦♦£ 160/250
Long St ⊠ GL8 8AQ – 𝒫 (01666) 502 272 – www.cotswold-inns-hotels.co.uk

🍴 **Gumstool Inn**   🛏 🏠 P

TRADITIONAL CUISINE · RUSTIC Set in the grounds of 700 year old Calcot Manor; an attractive outbuilding which cleverly blends classic country style with a more modern edge. Wide-ranging British menus showcase the latest meat and fish to arrive at the door. A flexible format offers snacks, two sizes of starter and hearty main courses.

Carte £ 21/41
Calcot Manor Hotel, Calcot ⊠ GL8 8YJ – West : 3.5 mi on A 4135 – 𝒫 (01666) 890 391 – www.calcotmanor.co.uk

TEWKESBURY

Gloucestershire – Pop. 19 778 – Regional map n° **2**-C1

▶ London 108 mi – Birmingham 39 mi – Gloucester 11 mi

at Corse Lawn Southwest: 6 mi by A38 and A438 on B4211 – ✉ Gloucester

🏠 Corse Lawn House   ⚑ ⇱ 🖼 ✕ 🔱 🅿

COUNTRY HOUSE · CLASSIC Elegant Grade II listed Queen Anne house, just off the
village green and fronted by a pond. The traditionally appointed interior features open
fires and antiques; some of the spacious bedrooms have four-poster or half-tester beds.
Dine from classical menus in the formal restaurant or characterful bistro-bar.

18 rooms 🖙 – ♦£ 75/95 ♦♦£ 120/160 – 3 suites

✉ GL19 4LZ – 𝒞 (01452) 780 771 – www.corselawn.com – *Closed 24-26 December*

THORNBURY

South Gloucestershire – ✉ Bristol – Pop. 11 687 – Regional map n° **2**-C1

▶ London 128 mi – Bristol 12 mi – Gloucester 23 mi – Swindon 43 mi

🏠 Thornbury Castle   ⚑ 🐾 ⇱ 🖕 🔱 🅿

HISTORIC · CLASSIC Impressive 16C castle with a vineyard, hidden away in a surprisingly tranquil spot in the centre of town. The luxurious library has a high ceiling
and an open fire. Baronial bedrooms feature old wooden beams and four-posters.

26 rooms 🖙 – ♦£ 185/255 ♦♦£ 195/265 – 3 suites

Castle St ✉ BS35 1HH – 𝒞 (01454) 281 182 – www.thornburycastle.co.uk

Tower – See restaurant listing

✕✕ Tower   ⇱ 🅿

MODERN CUISINE · ELEGANT Sited in a tower within the main 16C part of
Thornbury Castle; a small, partly wood-panelled, circular room decorated in
deep red, with coats of arms and an impressive fireplace. Elegantly laid tables;
elaborate, modern dishes.

Menu £ 15 (weekday lunch)/50

Thornbury Castle Hotel, Castle St ✉ BS35 1HH – 𝒞 (01454) 281 182
– www.thornburycastle.co.uk

THORNHAM – Norfolk ➜ See Hunstanton

THORNTON – Lancashire ➜ See Blackpool

THORNTON HOUGH

Merseyside – ✉ Wirral – Regional map n° **11**-A3

▶ London 215 mi – Birkenhead 12 mi – Chester 17 mi – Liverpool 12 mi

🏠 Thornton Hall   ⚑ ⇱ 🖼 ⑳ 🐾 🛏 🖕 ✕ 🔱 🅿

BUSINESS · CLASSIC Extended manor house on the Wirral Peninsula. Wood panelling and stained glass feature in the main house, along with some luxurious
bedrooms – the remainder are more contemporary, with balconies or terraces.
Impressively equipped spa.

62 rooms – ♦£ 75/250 ♦♦£ 85/250 – 🖙 £ 15 – 1 suite

Neston Rd ✉ CH63 1JF – On B 5136 – 𝒞 (0151) 336 3938
– www.thorntonhallhotel.com

Lawns – See restaurant listing

🏠 Mere Brook House   ⇱ 🖕 ✕ 🔱 🅿

FAMILY · PERSONALISED Restored Victorian house with colourful gardens and
beehives which provide their honey. Bedrooms mix modern fabrics with traditional furnishings; stay in the original house or the newer cottage which has its
own lounge and pantry kitchen.

8 rooms 🖙 – ♦£ 75/120 ♦♦£ 90/130

Thornton Common Rd ✉ CH63 OLU – East : 1.5 mi by B 5136 – 𝒞 (07713) 189 949
– www.merebrookhouse.co.uk – *Closed 20 December-2 January*

XX Lawns   🍴 ♿ 🕥 ⇔ 🅿

MODERN CUISINE · ELEGANT Grand hotel restaurant with oak-panelled walls, overlooking the lawns; formerly the house's billiard room. Chandeliers hang from the embossed leather ceiling. Elaborate modern cooking shows respect for local ingredients. Friendly service.

Menu £ 25 (weekday lunch) – Carte £ 40/56

Thornton Hall Hotel, Neston Rd ⊠ CH63 1JF – On B 5136 – ℰ (0151) 336 3938 (bookings essential for non-residents) – www.lawnsrestaurant.com – Closed Sunday and Monday

THORPE MARKET

Norfolk – ⊠ North Walsham – Regional map n° **8**-D1

▶ London 134 mi – Norwich 20 mi – Ipswich 63 mi – Lowestoft 39 mi

🍴 Gunton Arms   ⇔ ⋖ 🍴 🛖 ⇔ 🅿

BRITISH MODERN · INDIVIDUAL Charming pub overlooking the 1,000 acre Gunton Estate deer park. Enjoy a tasty homemade snack over a game of either pool or darts in the flag-floored bar, or make for a gnarled wood table by the fireplace in the Elk Room. Dishes are fiercely seasonal; some – such as the Aberdeen Angus steaks – are cooked over the fire. Elegant bedrooms have a stylish, country house feel.

Carte £ 22/40

8 rooms ⌂ – †£ 85/99 ††£ 130/185

Gunton Park ⊠ NR11 8TZ – South : 1 mi on A 149 – ℰ (01263) 832 010 (booking advisable) – www.theguntonarms.co.uk – Closed 25 December

THUNDER BRIDGE

West Yorkshire – Regional map n° **13**-B3

▶ London 299 mi – Leeds 35 mi – Huddersfield 10 mi

🍴 Woodman Inn Ⓝ   ⇔ 🛖 ⇔ 🅿

BRITISH TRADITIONAL · INN Dark stone pub in a lovely wooded South Pennine valley, run by a local father and son. Menus strike a great balance between pub and restaurant style dishes; start with the Yorkshire tapas sharing plate and end with a comforting pudding. Smart, modern country bedrooms include a 3 level suite.

Carte £ 24/44

13 rooms ⌂ – †£ 50/96 ††£ 75/160

⊠ HD8 0PX – ℰ (01484) 605 778 – www.woodman-inn.com

THURLESTONE

Devon – Regional map n° **1**-C3

▶ London 214 mi – Plymouth 21 mi – Torbay 23 mi – Exeter 43 mi

🏨 Thurlestone   ☆ ⇙ ⋖ 🍴 🖼 ⟰ 🔲 ⊛ 🕸 🎣 ✗ 🖽 ♿ 🚶 ⚓ 🅿

HOLIDAY HOTEL · CLASSIC Long-standing, family-friendly hotel with a subtle contemporary style, superb sea views and plenty of activities. Have afternoon tea in the comfy drawing room or relax on the terrace overlooking the manicured grounds. Ask for a room with a view; some even come with children's beds. Refined, traditional dishes in Margaret Amelia and pub fare in the cosy Village Inn.

65 rooms ⌂ – †£ 78/140 ††£ 205/280 – 6 suites

⊠ TQ7 3NN – ℰ (01548) 560 382 – www.thurlestone.co.uk – Closed 3-16 January

THURSFORD GREEN

Norfolk – Regional map n° **8**-C1

▶ London 120 mi – Fakenham 7 mi – Norwich 29 mi

🏠 Holly Lodge   ⌂ ⅌ 🛋 ⌘ 🅿

TRADITIONAL · STYLISH Remotely set 18C house with delightful gardens and a nice pond. Individually themed bedrooms are located in the old stable block and boast exposed beams, feature beds and numerous extra touches. Communal breakfasts, in the smart conservatory, use local and homemade produce. Home-cooked dinners offer a daily changing set menu.

3 rooms ☑ – ♦£70/100 ♦♦£90/120

The Street ⊠ NR21 0AS – ℰ (01328) 878 465 – www.hollylodgeguesthouse.co.uk

THURSLEY

Surrey – Regional map n° **4**-C2

◗ London 40 mi – Birmingham 144 mi – Bristol 115 mi – Ealing 43 mi

🍴 Three Horseshoes   🛋 🏡 🅿

TRADITIONAL CUISINE · CLASSIC No doubting this pub is at the heart of the community – the locals clubbed together to save it from developers. Hearty, traditional meals are high on flavour yet low on price. Real fires and fresh flowers give the place a homely feel.

Carte £23/50

Dye House Rd ⊠ GU8 6QD – ℰ (01252) 703 268
– www.threehorseshoesthursley.com – Closed Sunday dinner

TICEHURST

East Sussex – ⊠ Wadhurst – Pop. 1 705 – Regional map n° **5**-B2

◗ London 49 mi – Brighton 44 mi – Folkestone 38 mi – Hastings 15 mi

🍴 Bell   ⇦ 🛋 🏡 ⇧ 🅿

BRITISH TRADITIONAL · INDIVIDUAL With top hats as lampshades, tubas in the loos and a dining room called 'the stable with a table', 'quirky' is this 16C coaching inn's middle name. Seasonal menus offer proper, tasty pub food, and rustic bedrooms – each with their own silver birch tree – share the pub's idiosyncratic charm.

Carte £24/38

11 rooms ☑ – ♦£95/145 ♦♦£95/145

High St ⊠ TN5 7AS – ℰ (01580) 200 234 (booking advisable)
– www.thebellinticehurst.com

TICKTON – East Riding of Yorkshire → See Beverley

TILFORD

Surrey – Regional map n° **4**-C2

◗ London 43 mi – Bristol 101 mi – Cardiff 134 mi – Bournemouth 70 mi

🍴 Duke of Cambridge   🛋 🏡 🅿

TRADITIONAL CUISINE · COSY 18C pub in the heart of the forest, with a rustic, flag-floored bar, a cosy snug and an appealing heated terrace covered by an impressive oak-beamed roof. Menu offers everything from deli boards and pub classics to more adventurous dishes.

Carte £21/36

Tilford Rd ⊠ GU10 2DD – ℰ (01252) 792 236 – www.dukeofcambridgetilford.co.uk
– Closed 25 December

TILLINGTON – West Sussex → See Petworth

TISBURY

Wiltshire – Pop. 2 178 – Regional map n° **2**-C3

◗ London 103 mi – Bristol 45 mi – Cardiff 87 mi – Torbay 98 mi

🏠 **Beckford Arms** ⇦ 🖨 🛜 ⇔ 🅿

TRADITIONAL CUISINE · FRIENDLY Charming 18C inn with a beamed dining room, a rustic bar and a lovely country house sitting room – where films are screened on Sundays. There's a delightful terrace and garden with hammocks, a petanque pitch and even a dog bath. Tasty, unfussy classics and country-style dishes. Tasteful bedrooms provide thoughtful comforts. Smart duplex suites, a 3min drive away.

Carte £ 24/38

10 rooms ☲ – ♦£ 95/120 ♦♦£ 95/120

Fonthill Gifford ⊠ SP3 6PX – Northwest : 2 mi by Greenwich Rd – ℰ (01747) 870 385 (booking essential) – www.beckfordarms.com – Closed 25 December

TITCHWELL
Norfolk – Pop. 99 – Regional map n° **8**-C1
▶ London 128 mi – King's Lynn 25 mi – Boston 56 mi – Wisbech 36 mi

🏡 **Titchwell Manor** ☆ 🖨 � & 🅿

COUNTRY HOUSE · STYLISH This attractive brick farmhouse has a stylish interior, where bare floorboards and seaside photos feature. Bedrooms in the grounds are modern, colourful and originally styled; those in the main house are slightly more conservative.

27 rooms ☲ – ♦£ 60/140 ♦♦£ 95/275

⊠ PE31 8BB – ℰ (01485) 210 221 – www.titchwellmanor.com

The Conservatory – See restaurant listing

🏠 **Briarfields** ☆ 🖨 & 🅿

HOLIDAY HOTEL · MODERN In winter, sink into a sofa by the cosy fire; in summer, relax on the deck overlooking the salt marshes and the sea, or in the secluded courtyard, beside the pond. Bedrooms are modern and immaculately kept; some have patio doors.

23 rooms ☲ – ♦£ 80/85 ♦♦£ 115/145

Main Street ⊠ PE31 8BB – ℰ (01485) 210 742 – www.briarfieldshotelnorfolk.co.uk

XX **The Conservatory** 🖨 🛜 & 🆎 🅿

MODERN CUISINE · FASHIONABLE An appealing hotel restaurant offering plenty of choice. The trendy 'Eating Rooms' area offers sea views and comfort food. The smart 'Conservatory' area offers two more ambitious, accomplished menus of interesting modern dishes.

Carte £ 26/35 s

Titchwell Manor Hotel, ⊠ PE31 8BB – ℰ (01485) 210 221
– www.titchwellmanor.com

TITLEY
Herefordshire – ⊠ Kington – Regional map n° **10**-A3
▶ London 176 mi – Plymouth 196 mi – Torbay 175 mi – Exeter 159 mi

🏠 **Stagg Inn** ⇦ 🖨 🛜 🕼 🅿

BRITISH MODERN · PUB Deep in the rural heart of Herefordshire, at the meeting point of two drover's roads, sits this characterful, part-medieval, part-Victorian pub. Seasonal menus offer tried-and-tested combinations; save room for one of the generous desserts. The cosy pub bedrooms can be noisy; opt for one in the former vicarage.

Carte £ 31/45

6 rooms ☲ – ♦£ 80/120 ♦♦£ 100/150

⊠ HR5 3RL – ℰ (01544) 230 221 (booking essential) – www.thestagg.co.uk
– Closed 2 weeks January-February, first 2 weeks November,
25-26 December, Monday and Tuesday

TOLLARD ROYAL
Wiltshire – Regional map n° **2**-C3
▶ London 118 mi – Bristol 63 mi – Southampton 40 mi – Portsmouth 59 mi

🏠 **King John Inn** ⇔ 🛏 🏡 🅿️

REGIONAL · PUB Creeper-clad Victorian pub in a pretty village, with a smart, spacious, open-plan interior. Daily changing, classically based menus, with game a speciality. Contemporary bedrooms mix modern facilities with antique furniture; some are in the coach house opposite.

Menu £ 20 (weekday lunch) – Carte £ 30/45

8 rooms ⊊ – 🛏£ 80/95 🛏🛏£ 90/170

✉ SP5 5PS – ℰ (01725) 516 207 – www.kingjohninn.co.uk – Closed 25 December

TOOT BALDON – Oxfordshire → See Oxford

TOPSHAM

Devon – ✉ Exeter – Pop. 3 730 – Regional map n° **1**-D2

▶ London 175 mi – Torbay 26 mi – Exeter 4 mi – Torquay 24 mi

XX **Salutation Inn** ⇔ 🏡 ⅁ 🗗 ⇔

MODERN CUISINE · DESIGN 1720s coaching inn with a surprisingly contemporary interior. The glass-covered courtyard serves breakfast, light lunches and after-noon tea, while the stylish dining room offers nicely balanced 4, 6 and 8 course weekly set menus of well-judged modern cooking. Bedrooms are similarly up-to-date and understated.

Menu £ 40/60

6 rooms ⊊ – 🛏£ 120/140 🛏🛏£ 200/240

68 Fore St ✉ EX3 0HL – ℰ (01392) 873 060 (booking essential at dinner)
– www.salutationtopsham.co.uk

XX **La Petite Maison**

FRENCH CLASSIC · NEIGHBOURHOOD Cosy two-roomed restaurant in a charm-ing riverside village, with bright décor and eye-catching Peter Blake art. Season-ally evolving menus feature meat from the village butcher's and cheese from the nearby shop. Friendly, welcoming owners.

Menu £ 30 (weekdays)/40

35 Fore St ✉ EX3 0HR – ℰ (01392) 873 660 (booking essential at lunch)
– www.lapetitemaison.co.uk – Closed 2 weeks autumn, 1 week
April, 24-30 December, Sunday and Monday

TORQUAY

Torbay – Pop. 49 094 – Regional map n° **1**-C-D2

▶ London 223 mi – Exeter 23 mi – Plymouth 32 mi

🏠 **Marstan** 🛏 ⅀ 🌀 🅿️

TOWNHOUSE · PERSONALISED Keenly run Victorian villa in a quiet part of town, with an opulent lounge, a pool, a hot tub and a lovely suntrap terrace. Comfy bedrooms have antique furnishings and good facilities. Substantial breakfasts in-clude homemade granola.

9 rooms ⊊ – 🛏£ 59/115 🛏🛏£ 79/160

Town plan: CX-a – Meadfoot Sea Rd ✉ TQ1 2LQ – ℰ (01803) 292 823
– www.marstanhotel.co.uk – Closed November-18 March except
23 December-2 January

🏠 **Somerville** 🛏 🌀 🅿️

TRADITIONAL · PERSONALISED Comfortable hotel, an easy walk down the hill into town. Open-plan lounge and breakfast room filled with ornaments. Modern, slightly kitsch bedrooms with antique French furniture and good mod cons; Room 12 has direct access to the garden.

9 rooms ⊊ – 🛏£ 55/145 🛏🛏£ 75/155

Town plan: CX-u – 515 Babbacombe Rd. ✉ TQ1 1HJ – ℰ (01803) 294 755
– www.somervillehotel.co.uk – Closed 15 November-8 December

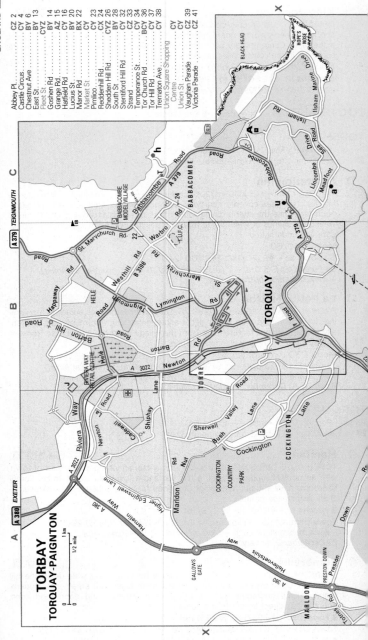

TORBAY
TORQUAY-PAIGNTON

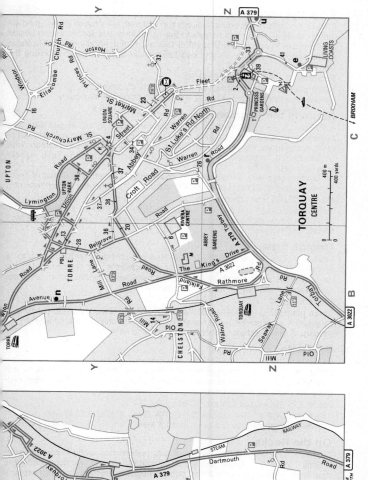

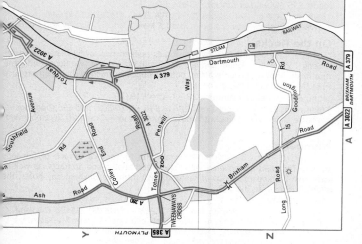

Kingston House

FAMILY · HOMELY This enthusiastically run Victorian guesthouse shows good attention to detail, with fresh flowers in the hall, homemade scones served beside the fireplace on arrival, and thoughtful touches such as locally made chocolates in the modern bedrooms. Sit on Lloyd Loom chairs at breakfast, overlooking the courtyard.

5 rooms ☉ – ∮£ 70/85 ∮∮£ 80/95

Town plan: BY-n – *75 Avenue Rd* ✉ *TQ2 5LL* – ℰ *(01803) 212 760*
– www.kingstonhousetorquay.co.uk – Closed 20 December-6 January

✗✗ Room in the Elephant (Simon Hulstone)

MODERN CUISINE · INDIVIDUAL First floor restaurant in an elegant Georgian terrace overlooking Torbay, with a Colonial-style cocktail bar and a simply decorated dining room. The tasting menu offers appealing, classical combinations with no unnecessary elaboration. Ingredients are top notch – most come from their 94 acre farm near Brixham.
→ Brixham crab with shiitake and soy dashi, crispy chicken skin. Breast of Crediton duck, turnip purée, onion fondant and lemon thyme. Elderflower tart.
Menu £ 55/65 – set menu only
Town plan: CZ-e – *3-4 Beacon Terr* ✉ *TQ1 2BH* – *(1st Floor)* – ℰ *(01803) 200 044* – *www.elephantrestaurant.co.uk – dinner only – Closed October-Easter, Sunday and Monday*

✗✗ Orange Tree

FRENCH CLASSIC · NEIGHBOURHOOD Modern, split-level restaurant with a homely feel, set down a narrow town centre backstreet. The seasonally evolving menu is made up of classically based, French-influenced dishes, which are carefully prepared and rely on fresh, local produce.
Carte £ 27/44
Town plan: CZ-u – *14-16 Parkhill Rd* ✉ *TQ1 2AL* – ℰ *(01803) 213 936 (booking essential)* – *www.orangetreerestaurant.co.uk – dinner only – Closed 2 weeks January, 2 weeks October-November, Sunday and Monday*

✗ Brasserie

MODERN CUISINE · BRASSERIE An airy brasserie under the 'Room in the Elephant', displaying an intriguing mix of nautical colours and Indian artefacts. Appealing modern menus revolve around the seasons and use their own farm produce. The wine list is good value.
Menu £ 15 (weekday lunch) – Carte £ 27/44
Town plan: CZ-e – *3-4 Beacon Terr* ✉ *TQ1 2BH* – ℰ *(01803) 200 044* – *www.elephantrestaurant.co.uk – Closed 3 weeks January, Sunday and Monday*

✗ On the Rocks

BRITISH MODERN · BISTRO Two local lads opened this lovely restaurant overlooking Torbay. It's modern and laid-back, with dining over two floors and furniture made from reclaimed scaffold boards. Appealing menus champion produce from the bay and the fields above.
Menu £ 13 (weekday lunch)/28 – Carte £ 19/39
Town plan: CZ-r – *1 Abbey Cres.* ✉ *TQ2 5HB* – ℰ *(01803) 203 666 (bookings advisable at dinner)* – *www.ontherocks-torquay.co.uk – Closed 26 December and 1 January*

✗ Number 7

FISH AND SEAFOOD · BISTRO Personally run bistro in a terrace of Regency houses. The walls are covered with fish-related photos and artefacts, as well as extensive blackboard menus of seafood fresh from the Brixham day boats; the simplest dishes are the best.
Carte £ 23/44
Town plan: CZ-e – *7 Beacon Terr.* ✉ *TQ1 2BH* – ℰ *(01803) 295 055 (booking advisable)* – *www.no7-fish.com – dinner only and lunch Wednesday-Saturday – Closed 2 weeks February, 1 week November, Christmas-New Year, Monday November-May and Sunday October-June*

at Maidencombe North: 3.5 mi by A379 – Plan: BX – ⊠ Torquay

🏤 **Orestone Manor** 🏵 🐾 ⇐ 🏨 🛋 ⚒ 🏌 🅿

TRADITIONAL · PERSONALISED Characterful house set amongst thick shrubbery and mature trees. It has a Colonial feel courtesy of dark wood furnishings and Oriental and African artefacts. Most of the individually designed bedrooms have sea or country views. Menus are classical – dine in the restaurant, the conservatory or on the terrace.

12 rooms ⊊ – †£ 110/150 ††£ 150/190

Rockhouse Ln ⊠ TQ1 4SX – ℰ (01803) 328 098 – www.orestonemanor.com – Closed 3-30 January

at Babbacombe Northeast: 2 mi on A379

🏩 **Cary Arms** ⇐ ⇐ 🏠 🅿

CLASSIC CUISINE · INN Set in an idyllic location and built into the rocks, with terraces down to the shore. The stone and slate-floored bar serves traditional pub dishes. There's a nautically styled residents lounge and modern, boutique-chic bedrooms in a New England style, with roll-top baths looking out to sea.
Carte £ 22/39

12 rooms ⊊ – †£ 156/316 ††£ 195/395

Town plan: CX-h – *Babbacombe Beach ⊠ TQ1 3LX – East : 0.25 mi by Beach Rd. – ℰ (01803) 327 110 – www.caryarms.co.uk*

TOTNES

Devon – Pop. 8 076 – Regional map n° **1**-C2

▶ London 224 mi – Exeter 24 mi – Plymouth 23 mi – Torquay 9 mi

🏤 **Royal Seven Stars** 🏵 🎴 🅿

HISTORIC · PERSONALISED Centrally located, 17C coaching inn; the characterful glass-roofed, flag-floored reception was once the carriage entrance. Smart colonial-style lounge. Well-equipped, individually designed bedrooms mix the old and the new; some have jacuzzi baths. Snacks in the bars or on the terrace; brasserie dishes in TQ9.

21 rooms ⊊ – †£ 91/120 ††£ 125/156

The Plains ⊠ TQ9 5DD – ℰ (01803) 862 125 – www.royalsevenstars.co.uk

TOWCESTER

Northamptonshire – Pop. 9 057 – Regional map n° **9**-B3

▶ London 70 mi – Birmingham 50 mi – Northampton 9 mi – Oxford 36 mi

XX **Vine House** ⇐ 🏨 🅿

MODERN CUISINE · INTIMATE A pair of pretty stone cottages in this tranquil village; dating from the 17C and home to a passionately run restaurant decorated with foodie photos. Daily changing, fixed price menu of accomplished modern dishes, deftly made using good quality ingredients. Cosy beamed bedrooms are named after grape vines.
Menu £ 33

6 rooms ⊊ – †£ 69/85 ††£ 95/110

100 High St, Paulerspury ⊠ NN12 7NA – Southeast : 4 mi by A 5 – ℰ (01327) 811 267 (booking advisable) – www.vinehousehotel.com – Closed 1 week January, Sunday and lunch Monday

TREBETHERICK – Cornwall ➜ See Rock

TREBURLEY

Cornwall – Pop. 252 – Regional map n° **1**-B2

▶ London 359 mi – Truro 83 mi – Plymouth 35 mi

🏩 **Springer Spaniel** ⓞ 🏠 🅿

MODERN CUISINE · PUB Unassuming-looking roadside pub in a small hamlet, where three cosy rooms are filled with scrubbed wooden tables. It might feel like your village local but when it comes to the food, expect bold flavours and colourful combinations.
Menu £ 20 (weekdays) – Carte £ 24/36

⊠ PL15 9NS – ℰ (01579) 370 424 – www.thespringerspaniel.org.uk – Closed Monday

TREGONY

Cornwall – Pop. 768 – Regional map n° **1**-B3

▶ London 416 mi – Truro 14 mi – Plymouth 78 mi

Hay Barton ⓝ   🛏 ✗ ⅙ 🅿 ⊟

COUNTRY HOUSE · COSY The owner has lived in this warm, cosy farmhouse since the 1960s and still keeps some cattle. Country-style bedrooms come with Roberts radios and plenty to read; two have antique bath tubs. Cornish produce features at breakfast.

3 rooms ☟ – †£ 65/70 ††£ 85/90

✉ TR2 5TF – *South : 1 mi on A 3078* – ℰ *(01872) 530 288* – *www.haybarton.com*

TRELOWARREN – Cornwall ➡ See Helston

TRENT

Dorset – Regional map n° **2**-C3

▶ London 128 mi – Southampton 67 mi – Bristol 39 mi – Bournemouth 46 mi

🍽 Rose & Crown   ⇔ 🛏 🏠 ⅙ 🖵 🅿

MODERN CUISINE · RUSTIC Pretty 14C part-thatched pub with plenty of rustic charm courtesy of an open-fired lounge and a bar complete with a grandfather clock. On sunny days head for the conservatory or the lovely garden. Menus showcase West Country produce.

Carte £ 21/37

3 rooms ☟ – †£ 75/105 ††£ 85/120

✉ DT9 4SL – ℰ *(01935) 850 776* – *www.roseandcrowntrent.co.uk*

TRESCO ➡ See Scilly (Isles of)

TRISCOMBE

Somerset – Regional map n° **2**-B2

▶ London 163 mi – Bristol 50 mi – Swansea 116 mi – Exeter 42 mi

🍽 Blue Ball Inn   ⇔ 🛏 🏠 ⅙ 🅿

MODERN CUISINE · RUSTIC Characterful former barn in the Quantock Hills; rustic and cosy with exposed rafters and open fires. Lunchtime sandwiches and pub classics provide fuel for passing walkers; dinner sees well-presented, original, modern dishes. Lovely tiered garden and stylish, comfortable bedrooms in a pretty thatched cottage.

Carte £ 20/38

3 rooms ☟ – †£ 65/95 ††£ 75/105

✉ TA4 3HE – ℰ *(01984) 618 242* – *www.blueballinn.info* – *Closed 25 December, dinner 1 January and Sunday dinner*

TRUMPET – Herefordshire ➡ See Ledbury

TRURO

Cornwall – Pop. 20 332 – Regional map n° **1**-B3

▶ London 295 mi – Exeter 87 mi – Penzance 26 mi – Plymouth 52 mi

🏨 Mannings   ⚡ ⅙ ⅙ 🅿

BUSINESS · MODERN Imposing hotel located in the city centre, close to the cathedral. Boutique bedrooms are bright, modern and stylish; spacious apartment-style rooms, in the neighbouring mews, boast over-sized beds and galley kitchens. Chic cocktail bar. Stylish restaurant offers eclectic, all-day menu.

42 rooms ☟ – †£ 65/129 ††£ 85/129

Lemon St ✉ *TR1 2QB* – ℰ *(01872) 270 345* – *www.manningshotels.co.uk* – *Closed Christmas*

XX **Tabb's**

BRITISH MODERN · NEIGHBOURHOOD A series of lilac-painted rooms with matching chairs, in a small former pub. The appealing menu lists refined, classically based dishes where good quality produce shines through. Tasty tapas-style lunches offer three dishes for £12.

Menu £25 – Carte £31/39

85 Kenwyn St ⊠ TR1 3BZ – ℰ (01872) 262 110 – www.tabbs.co.uk – Closed 1 week January, 1 week October, Saturday lunch, Sunday dinner and Monday

X **Saffron**

TRADITIONAL CUISINE · RUSTIC Smart rustic restaurant in the city's heart, run by a charming owner. There's a snug bar to the front, a lovely open room behind and pots of fresh flowers throughout. A blackboard lists what's in season, which is reflected on the menu.

Menu £16 (lunch) – Carte £25/38

5 Quay St ⊠ TR1 2HB – ℰ (01872) 263 771 – www.saffronrestauranttruro.co.uk – Closed 25-26 December, Monday dinner January-April, Sunday and bank holidays

TUDDENHAM

Suffolk – Pop. 400 – Regional map n° **8**-B2

▶ London 76 mi – Birmingham 120 mi – Sheffield 152 mi – Croydon 96 mi

XX **Tuddenham Mill** ⇔ 🖙 ⇔ 🅿

BRITISH CREATIVE · FORMAL Delightful 18C watermill overlooking the millpond; the old workings are still in situ in the stylish bar and there's a beamed restaurant with black furnishings above. Cooking features quality seasonal produce in unusual, innovative combinations. Some of the trendy bedrooms are in attractive outbuildings.

Menu £20 (weekday lunch)/25 – Carte dinner £31/45

15 rooms � – ♦£185/395 ♦♦£185/395

High St ⊠ IP28 6SQ – ℰ (01638) 713 552 – www.tuddenhammill.co.uk

TURNERS HILL

West Sussex – Pop. 885 – Regional map n° **4**-D2

▶ London 33 mi – Brighton 24 mi – Crawley 7 mi

🏨🏨 **Alexander House** 🏡 🖄 🖙 🖾 ⑩ 🕏 🖄 ✗ 🖃 🕹 ❄ 🖾 🅿

COUNTRY HOUSE · ELEGANT A stunning 18C country house once owned by Percy Shelley's family. Well-equipped, spacious bedrooms; some with four-poster beds. The contemporary Cedar Lodge Suites feature mood lighting and balconies or terraces. Superb spa with 21 treatment rooms and a Grecian pool. Dine in the brasserie or in formal AG's.

58 rooms – ♦£145/245 ♦♦£145/245 – ⊐ £20 – 3 suites

East St ⊠ RH10 4QD – East : 1 mi on B 2110 – ℰ (01342) 714 914 – www.alexanderhouse.co.uk

AG's – See restaurant listing

XXX **AG's** 🖙 🕹 🅿

MODERN CUISINE · FORMAL Have drinks in the smart champagne bar before dinner in the formal two-roomed restaurant of this fabulous 18C country house. Presentation and flavour combinations are modern and original and cooking follows the seasons closely.

Menu £65

Alexander House Hotel, East St ⊠ RH10 4QD – East : 1 mi on B 2110 – ℰ (01342) 714 914 (booking essential) – www.alexanderhouse.co.uk – dinner only and Sunday lunch

TWO BRIDGES

Devon – ✉ Yelverton – Regional map n° **1**-C2

▶ London 226 mi – Exeter 25 mi – Plymouth 17 mi

🏠 Prince Hall
⌂ ⅀ ≤ 🛏 🐾 🅿

TRADITIONAL · COSY Remote former hunting lodge with a welcoming, shabby-chic interior and wide-ranging views. Dogs are welcome throughout, except for in the bright restaurant, where you'll find vibrantly flavoured dishes with Mediterranean influences. Homely bedrooms display subtle modern touches; some overlook the moor.

8 rooms ⅀ – **†**£ 140/220 **††**£ 160/240

✉ PL20 6SA – East : 1 mi on B 3357 – ℰ (01822) 890 403 – www.princehall.co.uk

TYNEMOUTH

Tyne and Wear – Pop. 67 519 – Regional map n° **14**-B2

▶ London 290 mi – Newcastle upon Tyne 8 mi – Sunderland 7 mi

🏠 Grand
⌂ ≤ 🖭 ⅀ 🔋

TRADITIONAL · CLASSIC A Victorian hotel with superb sea views: the Duchess of Northumberland's one-time holiday home. Original features include an impressive staircase. Bedrooms are either traditionally styled and spacious or smaller and more modern; 222 has a four-poster and jacuzzi. Classical dining room with a menu to match.

46 rooms ⅀ – **†**£ 76/189 **††**£ 76/199

14 Grand Par. ✉ NE30 4ER – ℰ (0191) 293 6666 – www.grandhotel-uk.com

🏠 Martineau
🛏 ⅀

TOWNHOUSE · STYLISH Attractive 18C red-brick house named after Harriet Martineau. Cosy, individually furnished bedrooms come with thoughtful extras; two offer pleasant Tyne views. Superb communal breakfasts or a pre-ordered hamper in your room.

4 rooms ⅀ – **†**£ 75/85 **††**£ 95/100

57 Front St ✉ NE30 4BX – ℰ (0191) 257 90 38 – www.martineau-house.co.uk
– Closed 24-26 December

UCKFIELD

East Sussex – Pop. 15 213 – Regional map n° **5**-A2

▶ London 45 mi – Brighton 17 mi – Eastbourne 20 mi – Maidstone 34 mi

🏠 Horsted Place
⌂ ⅀ ≤ 🛏 🖭 🏡 ⅂ 🖭 ⅀ 🔋 🅿

HISTORIC · CLASSIC Impressive country house in Victorian Gothic style. The tiled entrance hall leads to an impressive main gallery, where ornate sitting rooms are furnished with fine antiques. Individually styled bedrooms are well-equipped; most have great views over the parkland. The formal dining room offers a classical menu.

20 rooms ⅀ – **†**£ 145/375 **††**£ 145/375 – 5 suites

Little Horsted ✉ TN22 5TS – South : 2.5 mi by B 2102 and A 22 on A 26
– ℰ (01825) 750 581 – www.horstedplace.co.uk – Closed first week January

UFFORD

Suffolk – Regional map n° **8**-D3

▶ London 91 mi – Bristol 221 mi – Bournemouth 211 mi – Poole 215 mi

🍴 Ufford Crown
🛏 🏡 🅿

BRITISH TRADITIONAL · FRIENDLY Welcoming former coaching inn run by an enthusiastic husband and wife team. The daily menu of hearty, honest cooking includes a great grill section featuring rib of Ketley beef for 3 to share. Portions are generous and service is keen.

Carte £ 22/40

High St ✉ IP13 6EL – ℰ (01394) 461 030 – www.theuffordcrown.com – Closed Tuesday

UPPER SLAUGHTER – Gloucestershire ➜ See Bourton-on-the-Water

UPPER SOUTH WRAXALL
Wiltshire – Regional map n° **2**-C2

▣ London 201 mi – Birmingham 326 mi – Liverpool 419 mi – Leeds 393 mi

⅏ **Longs Arms**   🖴 🛱 ⅃ 🅿

ⓐ   **BRITISH TRADITIONAL · PUB** Handsome, bay-windowed, Bath stone pub opposite a medieval church in a sleepy village. Traditional British dishes are full-flavoured, hearty and satisfying; everything is homemade and they smoke their own meats and fish. Dine in the characterful area in front of the bar. Warm, friendly service.

Carte £ 17/45

✉ BA15 2SB – ℰ (01225) 864 450 (booking essential) – www.thelongsarms.com
– Closed 3 weeks January-February, Sunday dinner and Monday

UPPINGHAM
Rutland – Pop. 4 745 – Regional map n° **9**-C2

▣ London 101 mi – Leicester 19 mi – Northampton 28 mi – Nottingham 35 mi

✕✕ **Lake Isle**   😋 ⇦ 🛱 AC ⇦ 🅿

CLASSIC CUISINE · FRIENDLY Characterful 18C town centre property accessed via a narrow passageway and very personally run by experienced owners. It has a cosy lounge and a heavy wood-furnished dining room. Light lunches are followed by much more elaborate modern dinners. Bedrooms come with good extras and some have whirlpool baths.

Carte £ 26/42

12 rooms ⌂ – ♦£ 58/68 ♦♦£ 85/110

16 High St East ✉ LE15 9PZ – ℰ (01572) 822 951 – www.lakeisle.co.uk – Closed Sunday dinner and Monday lunch

at Lyddington South: 2 mi by A6003 – ✉ Uppingham

⅏ **Marquess of Exeter**   ⇦ 🖴 🛱 ⅃ ⇦ 🅿

BRITISH TRADITIONAL · PUB Attractive 16C thatched pub with a cosy bar, characterful exposed beams, inglenook fireplaces and a rustic dining room. The daily changing menu offers tasty, classical combinations of local, home-grown and home-reared produce. Comfortable bedrooms are located across the car park.

Menu £ 13 (weekday lunch) – Carte £ 24/44

17 rooms ⌂ – ♦£ 80/105 ♦♦£ 100/135

52 Main St ✉ LE15 9LT – ℰ (01572) 8224 77/822212 – www.marquessexeter.co.uk
– Closed 25 December

⅏ **Old White Hart**   ⇦ 🖴 🛱 ⅃ 🅿

TRADITIONAL CUISINE · PUB This pub offers all you'd expect from a traditional 17C coaching inn – and a lot more besides. It's got the chocolate box village setting, the open fires and the seasonal menu of hearty, classic dishes; but also gives you a relaxing ambience, charming service, a 10-piste petanque pitch and stylish bedrooms.

Carte £ 24/32

10 rooms ⌂ – ♦£ 70 ♦♦£ 95/105

51 Main St ✉ LE15 9LR – ℰ (01572) 821 703 – www.oldwhitehart.co.uk
– Closed 25 December and Sunday dinner in winter

UPTON BISHOP – Herefordshire ➜ See Ross-on-Wye

UPTON MAGNA – Shropshire ➜ See Shrewsbury

VENTNOR – Isle of Wight ➜ See Wight (Isle of)

VERYAN
Cornwall – ✉ Truro – Pop. 877 – Regional map n° **1**-B3

▣ London 291 mi – St Austell 13 mi – Truro 13 mi

🏨 Nare 　🐾 🐕 ⇐ 🛏 ⤒ 🖼 🛁 🖫 ✕ 🅿

COUNTRY HOUSE · CLASSIC Personally run, classic country house with a stunning bay outlook; take it in from the pool or hot tub. Most bedrooms have views and some have patios or balconies. Have afternoon tea in the drawing room, evening canapés in the bar, then choose from a traditional daily menu or more modern fare in Quarterdeck.

37 rooms 🖵 – 🛏£ 147/192 🛏🛏£ 284/534 – 7 suites
Carne Beach ✉ *TR2 5PF – Southwest : 1.25 mi – ℰ (01872) 501 111*
– www.narehotel.co.uk
Quarterdeck – See restaurant listing

✕ Quarterdeck 　⇐ 🛏 AC 🅿

BRITISH TRADITIONAL · FRIENDLY Informal restaurant in a classic country house, with large black and white prints on the walls and a nautical theme. The menu offers a range of dishes, from omelette Arnold Bennett to lobster – the local Fowey Oysters are a hit.

Carte £ 27/44
Nare Hotel, Carne Beach ✉ *TR2 5PF – Southwest : 1.25 mi – ℰ (01872) 500 000*
(bookings essential for non-residents) – www.narehotel.co.uk – Closed
25 December and 31 January

VIRGINSTOW
Devon – Regional map n° **1**-C2
▶ London 227 mi – Bideford 25 mi – Exeter 41 mi – Launceston 11 mi

🏠 Percy's 　🐾 🐕 ⇐ 🛏 🏡 ✕ 🅿

TRADITIONAL · COSY Stone house in 130 acres of fields and woodland. The owners grow veg, breed racehorses, rear pigs and sheep, and sell wool, skins and produce. Spacious, comfy bedrooms in the former barn – some have jacuzzi baths. Set menu of traditional dishes in the formal dining room; ingredients are from the estate.

7 rooms 🖵 – 🛏£ 125/215 🛏🛏£ 140/230
Coombeshead Estate ✉ *EX21 5EA – Southwest : 1.75 mi on Tower Hill rd*
– ℰ (01409) 211 236 – www.percys.co.uk

WADDESDON
Buckinghamshire – ✉ Aylesbury – Pop. 1 797 – Regional map n° **6**-C2
▶ London 51 mi – Aylesbury 5 mi – Northampton 32 mi – Oxford 31 mi

✕✕ Five Arrows 　⇐ 🛏 🏡 ⇄ 🅿

BRITISH TRADITIONAL · INDIVIDUAL Half-timbered house on the Rothschild Estate, with Elizabethan chimney stacks, attractive gabling and mullioned windows. Bedrooms in the main house feature antiques and original pieces from Waddesdon Manor; those in the courtyard are more modern. Local game is a highlight in the traditional restaurant.

Menu £ 15 (weekday lunch) – Carte £ 29/41
16 rooms 🖵 – 🛏£ 75/100 🛏🛏£ 105/155
High St ✉ *HP18 0JE – ℰ (01296) 651 727 – www.waddesdon.org.uk/fivearrows*

WADEBRIDGE
Cornwall – Pop. 6 599 – Regional map n° **1**-B2
▶ London 245 mi – Truro 26 mi – Newquay 19 mi

🍴 Ship Inn 🆕 　🏡

TRADITIONAL CUISINE · COSY This 16C inn is one of the oldest public houses in town and has a real community feel. The menu offers something for everyone, mixing pub classics with more modern dishes. Choose a seat in one of the three cosy, low-beamed rooms.

Carte £ 20/34
Gonvena Hill ✉ *PL27 6DF – ℰ (01208) 813 845 – www.shipinnwadebridge.com*
– Closed Sunday dinner in winter.

WALBERSWICK

Suffolk – Pop. 380 – Regional map n° **8**-D2

▶ London 115 mi – Norwich 31 mi – Ipswich 31 mi – Lowestoft 16 mi

⑲ Anchor

REGIONAL · PUB Welcoming, relaxing pub in an Arts and Crafts building; its sizeable garden features a wood-fired oven and seaward views. Global flavours feature alongside British classics; try some home-baked bread. Excellent beers and wines. Impressive breakfasts. Choose a wood-clad chalet in the garden.

Carte £ 24/40

10 rooms ☒ – **†**£ 85/155 **††**£ 110/155

Main St ✉ *IP18 6UA* – *℘ (01502) 722 112* – *www.anchoratwalberswick.com*
– Closed 25 December

WALFORD – Herefordshire → See Ross-on-Wye

WALKDEN

Greater Manchester – Pop. 21 194 – Regional map n° **11**-B2

▶ London 205 mi – Birmingham 91 mi – Liverpool 30 mi – Sheffield 62 mi

XX Grenache

BRITISH MODERN · FRIENDLY A smart neighbourhood restaurant with a friendly, laid-back feel. The passionate chef cooks seasonal, modern dishes with clean, clear flavours and a young team provide attentive, professional service. 7 course tasting menu available.

Menu £ 20 (lunch)/25 (weekday dinner) – Carte £ 32/46

15 Bridgewater Rd ✉ *M28 3JE* – *℘ (0161) 799 8181*
– www.grenacherestaurant.co.uk – Closed Sunday dinner, Monday, Tuesday and Wednesday lunch

WALL – Staffordshire → See Lichfield

WAREHAM

Dorset – Pop. 5 496 – Regional map n° **2**-C3

▶ London 123 mi – Bournemouth 13 mi – Weymouth 19 mi

⌂ Priory

TRADITIONAL · COSY Delightfully located part-16C priory, which is proudly and personally run. Have afternoon tea on the terrace, overlooking the beautiful manicured gardens and on towards the river – here, peace and tranquility reign. The country house inspired bedrooms are charming; those in the 'Boathouse' are the most luxurious. Dress smartly for dinner in the formal candlelit cellar.

17 rooms ☒ – **†**£ 180/308 **††**£ 225/385 – 2 suites

Church Grn ✉ *BH20 4ND* – *℘ (01929) 551 666* – *www.theprioryhotel.co.uk*

⌂ Gold Court House

TOWNHOUSE · CLASSIC Charmingly run Georgian house in a small square off the high street; which stands on the foundations of a 13C goldsmith's house. It has a fire-lit lounge, a lovely breakfast room with garden views and traditional, restful bedrooms.

3 rooms ☒ – **†**£ 60 **††**£ 85

St John's Hill ✉ *BH20 4LZ* – *℘ (01929) 553 320* – *www.goldcourthouse.co.uk*
– Closed 25 December-2 January

WAREN MILL – Northumberland → See Bamburgh

WARKWORTH

Northumberland – Regional map n° **14**-B2

▶ London 316 mi – Alnwick 7 mi – Morpeth 24 mi

🏠 Roxbro House

TOWNHOUSE · STYLISH 'Elegant' and 'opulent' are suitable adjectives to describe these two houses in the shadow of Warkworth Castle, where boutique bedrooms mix modern facilities with antique furniture. Choose between two comfy lounges – one with an honesty bar; tasty breakfasts are served in a conservatory-style room.

6 rooms � – ♦£ 65/75 ♦♦£ 95/120
5 Castle Terr ⊠ NE65 0UP – ℰ (01665) 711 416 – www.roxbrohouse.co.uk – Closed 24-28 December

WARMINGHAM
Cheshire East – Regional map n° **11**-B3
▶ London 174 mi – Birmingham 61 mi – Manchester 33 mi – Bristol 143 mi

🏠 Bear's Paw

BRITISH TRADITIONAL · INDIVIDUAL Handsome 19C inn with a spacious, wood-panelled bar and a huge array of local ales. The menu will please all appetites, with everything from nibbles, salads and deli boards to European dishes, pub favourites and steaks you can cook yourself on a hot stone. Stylish, good value bedrooms.

Carte £ 19/37
17 rooms � – ♦£ 105/135 ♦♦£ 115/145
School Ln ⊠ CW11 3QN – ℰ (01270) 526 317 – www.thebearspaw.co.uk

WARMINSTER
Wiltshire – Pop. 17 490 – Regional map n° **2**-C2
▶ London 111 mi – Bristol 29 mi – Exeter 74 mi – Southampton 47 mi

🏠 Bishopstrow H. and Spa

COUNTRY HOUSE · STYLISH It may look like a typical Georgian country house but both the drawing rooms and the bedrooms have a stylish, modern edge. There's a well-equipped spa and a stunning glass conservatory which overlooks the terrace to the manicured gardens. The elegant restaurant serves classic dishes with a modern edge.

32 rooms � – ♦£ 120/195 ♦♦£ 155/230 – 4 suites
*Boreham Rd ⊠ BA12 9HH – Southeast : 1.5 mi on B 3414 – ℰ (01985) 212 312
– www.bishopstrow.co.uk*

🏠 Weymouth Arms

BRITISH TRADITIONAL · NEIGHBOURHOOD Grade II listed building with plenty of history. It's immensely characterful, with original wood panelling, antiques and lithographs, as well as two fireplaces originally intended for nearby Longleat House. Cooking is fresh and fittingly traditional. Cosy bedrooms have charming original fittings.

Carte £ 19/40
6 rooms – ♦£ 65/75 ♦♦£ 75/85 – � £ 7
*12 Emwell St ⊠ BA12 8JA – ℰ (01985) 216 995 – www.weymoutharms.co.uk
– Closed Monday-Wednesday lunch*

at Heytesbury Southeast: 3.75 mi by B3414 – ⊠ Warminster

🏠 Resting Post

FAMILY · HOMELY This attractive 17C listed cottage is the village's former post office; look out for the mail box on the wall outside. Neat, cosy bedrooms feature up-to-date bathrooms. Traditional English breakfasts are taken in the original shop.

3 rooms � – ♦£ 55/70 ♦♦£ 70/90
67 High St ⊠ BA12 0ED – ℰ (01985) 840 204 – www.therestingpost.co.uk

ⓘ Angel Inn

TRADITIONAL CUISINE · COSY Pretty, family-run, 16C pub with open fires and beams; it boasts a typically English feel, emphasised by the locals and their dogs. Flavoursome dishes come in generous portions and make use of fresh, regional produce.
Carte £ 23/36
High St ⊠ BA12 0ED – ℰ (01985) 840 330 – www.theangelatheytesbury.co.uk
– Closed Sunday dinner

at Crockerton South: 2 mi by A350

ⓘ Bath Arms ⇔ 🛏 🏠 🕭 🄿

BRITISH TRADITIONAL · RUSTIC Down-to-earth pub; once part of the Longleat Estate. Daily changing menu features classic pub dishes, snacks and grills, along with a selection of daily specials; try the legendary 'sticky' beef with braised red cabbage. Two ultra-spacious, contemporary bedrooms, amusingly named 'Left' and 'Right'.
Carte £ 19/36
2 rooms ⌗ – ♦£ 80/110 ♦♦£ 80/110
Clay St ⊠ BA12 8AJ – on Shearwater rd – ℰ (01985) 212 262
– www.batharmscrockerton.co.uk – Closed dinner 25-26 December

at Horningsham Southwest: 5 mi by A362 – ⊠ Wiltshire

ⓘ Bath Arms ⇔ 🛏 🏠 🄿

TRADITIONAL CUISINE · INN Charming pub within the Longleat estate, with open fire in bar, grand dining room and delightful terrace. Appealing menus offer something for everyone; produce is locally sourced, much of it from the estate. Quirky, comfortable, individually themed bedrooms.
Carte £ 23/41
17 rooms ⌗ – ♦£ 95/215 ♦♦£ 95/215
Longleat ⊠ BA12 7LY – ℰ (01985) 844 308 – www.batharms.co.uk

WARTLING – East Sussex → See Herstmonceux

WARWICK

Warwickshire – Pop. 31 345 – Regional map n° **10**-C3
▶ London 96 mi – Birmingham 20 mi – Coventry 11 mi – Leicester 34 mi

🏠 Park Cottage

HISTORIC · CLASSIC 15C cross-wing house with wattle and daub walls; originally set within the grounds of Warwick Castle and belonging to the Earl (the 300 year old yew tree was once used to make longbows). Spacious bedrooms come with lots of extras.
8 rooms ⌗ – ♦£ 59/75 ♦♦£ 79/95
Town plan: Y-e *– 113 West St ⊠ CV34 6AH – ℰ (01926) 410 319*
– www.parkcottagewarwick.co.uk – Closed 23-31 December

✗ Tailors

MODERN CUISINE · INTIMATE As well as a tailor's, this intimate restaurant was once a fishmonger's, a butcher's and a casino! It's run by two ambitious chefs, who offer good value modern lunches, and elaborate dinners which feature unusual flavour combinations.
Menu £ 17 (lunch)/40
Town plan: Y-a *– 22 Market Pl ⊠ CV34 4SL*
– ℰ (01926) 410 590 – www.tailorsrestaurant.co.uk
– Closed Christmas, Sunday and Monday

WARWICK-ROYAL LEAMINGTON SPA

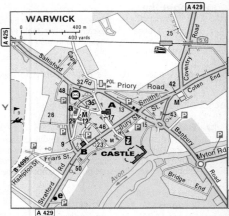

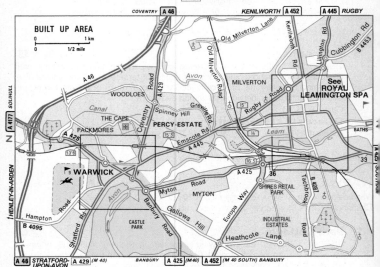

WATCHET

Somerset – Pop. 3 581 – Regional map n° **2**-B2

▶ London 174 mi – Bristol 60 mi – Exeter 49 mi – Cardiff 86 mi

🏠 **Swain House**

TOWNHOUSE · PERSONALISED In the characterful high street of this coastal town, you'll find this super smart guesthouse with spacious bedrooms and a sleek yet cosy feel. Parts of famous paintings make up feature walls and all have roll-top baths and rain showers.

4 rooms ☲ – 🛉£ 115 🛉🛉£ 135

48 Swain St ⌧ TA23 0AG – ℰ (01984) 631 038
– www.swain-house.com

WATERGATE BAY – Cornwall → See Newquay

WATERMILLOCK – Cumbria → See Pooley Bridge

WATFORD

Hertfordshire – Pop. 131 982 – Regional map n° **7**-A2

London 20 mi – Hertford 36 mi – Luton 32 mi

Plan : see Greater London (North-West) 2

Grove

BUSINESS · MODERN An impressive Grade II listed country house in 300 acres, with elegant lounges and smart, contemporary bedrooms - some with balconies. There's a superb spa and an outdoor pool, as well as tennis, croquet, golf and volleyball facilities. Fine dining in Colette's; casual meals in Stables; buffet in Glasshouse.

214 rooms ☑ – ♥£ 275/350 ♥♥£ 300/375 – 6 suites

Chandler's Cross ✉ *WD3 4TG – Northwest : 2 mi on A 411* – *℘ (01923) 807 807* – *www.thegrove.co.uk*

Colette's • Stables – See restaurant listing

Colette's

MODERN CUISINE · DESIGN A sleek, contemporary hotel restaurant with high ceilings and large windows overlooking the grounds. Complex modern dishes feature imaginative combinations; choose between set 5 and 8 course menus.

Menu £ 75/85 – set menu only

Grove Hotel, Chandler's Cross ✉ *WD3 4TG – Northwest : 2 mi on A 411* – *℘ (01923) 296 015 – www.thegrove.co.uk – dinner only – Closed Sunday-Monday except Sunday dinner on bank holidays*

Stables

INTERNATIONAL · RUSTIC Informal, New England style restaurant in the clubhouse of an impressive Grade II listed country house. It boasts its own sports bar, has pleasant views over the golf course and offers a gutsy British menu with plenty of grills.

Carte £ 27/44

Grove Hotel, Chandler's Cross ✉ *WD3 4TG – Northwest : 2 mi on A 411* – *℘ (01923) 296 010 – www.thegrove.co.uk*

WATLINGTON

Oxfordshire – Pop. 2 139 – Regional map n° **6**-C2

London 45 mi – Birmingham 89 mi – Bristol 88 mi – Sheffield 153 mi

Fat Fox Inn

BRITISH TRADITIONAL · COSY In the heart of a busy market village; a 19C pub run with honesty and integrity by experienced owners. The menu reflects what they themselves like to eat, covering all bases from potted mackerel to pheasant pie. Fight the cats for a seat by the wood burning range, then settle in to one of the cosy bedrooms.

Carte £ 20/35

9 rooms ☑ – ♥£ 65/109 ♥♥£ 75/119

13 Shireburn St ✉ *OX49 5BU – ℘ (01491) 613 040 – www.thefatfoxinn.co.uk* – *Closed dinner 25 December and 1 January*

WATTON

Norfolk – Pop. 7 435 – Regional map n° **8**-C2

London 95 mi – Norwich 22 mi – Swaffham 10 mi

XX Café at Brovey Lair

FISH AND SEAFOOD · INTIMATE Dining here has more of a dinner party atmosphere than a restaurant feel. The spacious conservatory has an open kitchen with stool seating and a teppan-yaki grill. The no-choice set menu revolves around seafood and Asian flavours. Well-appointed bedrooms are situated beside the pool in lovely gardens.

Menu £ 53 – set menu only

3 rooms ⌓ – ♦£ 100/135 ♦♦£ 120/150

Carbrooke Rd., Ovington ⊠ IP25 6SD – Northeast : 1.75 mi by A 1075 – ℰ (01953) 882 706 – www.broveylair.com – Closed 25 December and 1 January

WEDMORE

Somerset – Pop. 1 409 – Regional map n° **2**-B2

▶ London 155 mi – Bristol 23 mi – Cardiff 67 mi – Plymouth 100 mi

⌂ Swan

BRITISH TRADITIONAL · INN Spacious 18C coaching inn with a buzzy bar, a comfy restaurant and an open-plan kitchen with an appealing display of freshly baked breads linking the two. Good quality British ingredients match the seasons and daily changing dishes are unfussy and flavoursome. Stylish bedrooms complete the picture.

Carte £ 23/39

7 rooms ⌓ – ♦£ 85 ♦♦£ 85/125

Cheddar Rd ⊠ BS28 4EQ – ℰ (01934) 710 337 (booking essential) – www.theswanwedmore.com – Closed 25 December

WELBURN

North Yorkshire – Regional map n° **13**-C2

▶ London 225 mi – Leeds 40 mi – York 14 mi

⌂ Crown and Cushion

MEATS · FRIENDLY Well run 18C pub two miles from Castle Howard. The menu champions local meats and the kitchen's pride and joy is its charcoal-fired rotisserie. Dishes are hearty; sandwiches are doorstops and puddings are of the nursery variety.

Menu £ 7 – Carte £ 26/40

⊠ YO60 7DZ – ℰ (01653) 618 777 – www.thecrownandcushionwelburn.com

WELLAND – Worcestershire → See Great Malvern

WELLINGHAM

Norfolk – Regional map n° **8**-C1

▶ London 120 mi – King's Lynn 29 mi – Norwich 28 mi

⌂ Manor House Farm

TRADITIONAL · CLASSIC Attractive, wisteria-clad farmhouse with large gardens, set by a church in a beautifully peaceful spot. Spacious, airy bedrooms are located in the former stables. Home-grown and home-reared produce is served at breakfast.

3 rooms ⌓ – ♦£ 65/80 ♦♦£ 110/140

⊠ PE32 2TH – ℰ (01328) 838 227 – www.manor-house-farm.co.uk

WELLS

Somerset – Pop. 10 536 – Regional map n° **2**-C2

▶ London 132 mi – Bristol 20 mi – Southampton 68 mi – Taunton 28 mi

🏨 Swan

INN · STYLISH 15C former coaching inn with a good outlook onto the famous cathedral; its charming interior has subtle, contemporary touches, particularly in the lounge and bar. Comfortable, stylish, well-equipped bedrooms and opulent 'Cathedral Suite'. Formal, wood-panelled restaurant serves classic dishes.

48 rooms ⬜ – ♦£ 90/137 ♦♦£ 104/500 – 1 suite

11 Sadler St ⬚ *BA5 2RX* – *℘ (01749) 836 300* – *www.swanhotelwells.co.uk*

🏠 Beryl

COUNTRY HOUSE · CLASSIC Fine 19C country house in mature gardens, overlooking the town and run by a charming owner. Delightful, antique-filled drawing room. Individually styled bedrooms: some have four-posters; 'Master and Butterfly' is the best.

13 rooms ⬜ – ♦£ 75/160 ♦♦£ 100/160

⬚ *BA5 3JP* – *East : 1.25 mi by B 3139 off Hawkers Lane* – *℘ (01749) 678 738* – *www.beryl-wells.co.uk* – *Closed 23-30 December*

🏡 Stoberry House

TRADITIONAL · HOMELY 18C coach house with a delightful walled garden, overlooking Glastonbury Tor. Large lounge with a baby grand piano and antique furniture. Breakfast is an event, with 7 homemade breads, a porridge menu and lots of cooked dishes. Immaculately kept bedrooms come with fresh flowers, chocolates and a pillow menu.

5 rooms ⬜ – ♦£ 65/110 ♦♦£ 85/145

Stoberry Park ⬚ *BA5 3LD* – *Northeast : 0.5 mi by A 39 on College Rd* – *℘ (01749) 672 906* – *www.stoberryhouse.co.uk*

✗ Old Spot

BRITISH MODERN · BISTRO Simple, understated restaurant with an airy feel. Framed menus hang on plain walls and it affords stunning cathedral views from the rear. Well-executed dishes rely on flavoursome English produce but have a classical French and Italian base. Preparation is unfussy and some lesser-used ingredients feature.

Menu £ 13/23 (lunch) – Carte dinner £ 26/41

12 Sadler St ⬚ *BA5 2SE* – *℘ (01749) 689 099* – *www.theoldspot.co.uk* – *Closed 1 week Christmas, Monday, Sunday dinner and Tuesday lunch*

at Easton Northwest: 3 mi on A371 – ⬚ Wells

🏡 Beaconsfield Farm

COUNTRY HOUSE · COSY A former farmhouse hidden away in the foothills of the Mendip Hills and run by a personable owner. The lounge and bedrooms have a modern feel, while the breakfast room, which overlooks the colourful garden, is more traditional.

3 rooms ⬜ – ♦£ 70/85 ♦♦£ 75/95

⬚ *BA5 1DU* – *℘ (01749) 870 308* – *www.beaconsfieldfarm.co.uk* – *Closed 25 October-24 March*

WELLS-NEXT-THE-SEA

Norfolk – Pop. 2 165 – Regional map n° **8**-C1
▶ London 122 mi – Cromer 22 mi – Norwich 38 mi

🏠 Crown

INN · STYLISH Characterful 16C former coaching inn located in the centre of town, overlooking the green. Individually styled bedrooms blend classical furniture with more modern décor and facilities. Dine from an accessible menu in the charming bar, orangery or dining room.

12 rooms ⬜ – ♦£ 80/135 ♦♦£ 100/195

The Buttlands ⬚ *NR23 1EX* – *℘ (01328) 710 209* – *www.flyingkiwiinns.co.uk*

🏠 Machrimore ⌲ ⌖ 🅿 ⊟

TRADITIONAL · CLASSIC Cross the delightful gardens with their illuminated water features to this collection of converted farm outbuildings. Bedrooms are well-equipped and come with quality furniture and private patios. Photos of old Wells feature throughout.

4 rooms ⌲ – ♦£ 70 ♦♦£ 88/92

Burnt St ✉ NR23 1HS – on A 149 – ☎ (01328) 711 653
– www.machrimore.co.uk

at Wighton Southeast: 2.5 mi by A149

🏠 Meadowview ⌲ ⌖ 🅿

FAMILY · MODERN Set in the centre of a peaceful village, this smart, modern guesthouse is the perfect place to unwind, as its neat garden boasts a hot tub and a comfy seating area overlooking a meadow. Breakfast is cooked on the Aga in the country kitchen.

5 rooms ⌲ – ♦£ 90/100 ♦♦£ 100/110

53 High St ✉ NR23 1PF – ☎ (01328) 821 527
– www.meadow-view.net

WELWYN

Hertfordshire – Pop. 3 497 – Regional map n° **7**-B2
▶ London 31 mi – Bedford 31 mi – Cambridge 31 mi

🏠 Tewin Bury Farm ⌂ ⌲ & 🆔 ⌖ 🄰 🅿

BUSINESS · STYLISH A collection of converted farm buildings on a 400 acre working farm, next to a nature reserve. Rustic interior with comfy oak-furnished bedrooms in various wings. The function room is in an impressive tithe barn beside the old mill race.

36 rooms ⌲ – ♦£ 124/144 ♦♦£ 139/159

✉ AL6 0JB – Southeast : 3.5 mi by A 1000 on B 1000 – ☎ (01438) 717 793
– www.tewinbury.co.uk
Williams' – See restaurant listing

✗ Williams' ⌲ ⌖ & 🆔 ⬚ 🅿

BRITISH MODERN · RUSTIC A characterful, rustic hotel restaurant in an old timber chicken shed on a working farm; black and white photos of farm life adorn the walls. Fresh, well-executed, modern dishes are pleasing to the eye as well as the taste buds.

Menu £ 24 (weekday lunch) – Carte £ 27/40

Tewin Bury Farm Hotel, ✉ AL6 0JB – Southeast : 3.5 mi by A 1000 on B 1000
– ☎ (01438) 717 793 – www.tewinbury.co.uk

at Ayot Green Southwest: 2.5 mi by B 197

🍴 Waggoners ⌲ ⌂ 🅿

FRENCH · PUB A delightful 17C pub on the edge of the Brocket Hall Estate, with a welcoming owner, a charming young team and a pleasant, buzzy atmosphere. Choose from unfussy pub dishes or a more ambitious French-based à la carte.

Menu £ 15 (weekday lunch)/30 – Carte £ 24/41

Brickwall Close ✉ AL6 9AA – ☎ (01707) 324 241 (booking advisable)
– www.thewaggoners.co.uk – Closed Sunday dinner

WENTBRIDGE

West Yorkshire – ✉ Pontefract – Regional map n° **13**-B3
▶ London 183 mi – Leeds 19 mi – Nottingham 55 mi – Sheffield 28 mi

🏠 Wentbridge House 🍃 🛏 ⊡ ♿ ⛱ **P**

COUNTRY HOUSE · STYLISH Personally run, bay-windowed house, dating back to the 19C and surrounded by 20 acres of immaculate gardens. Bedrooms are a mix of characterful, wood-panelled period styles and spacious modern designs with up-to-date facilities. Classical menu in formal restaurant; smart brasserie serves more modern dishes.

41 rooms ⊒ – ♦£ 85/105 ♦♦£ 115/135
Old Great North Rd. ⊠ *WF8 3JJ* – *ℰ (01977) 620 444*
– www.wentbridgehouse.co.uk

WEST ASHLING - West Sussex → See Chicester

WEST BAGBOROUGH
Somerset – Regional map n° **2**-B2
▶ London 161 mi – Bristol 57 mi – Cardiff 88 mi – Plymouth 82 mi

🍸 Rising Sun Inn ⇦ 🏠 ♿

BRITISH TRADITIONAL · INDIVIDUAL Traditional-looking pub in the Quantock Hills, with several little rooms, a pleasing mix of old tables and chairs, smart slate floors and bright modern art. Menus offer plenty of choice, from typical pub-style light bites to more hearty classics. Two contemporary bedrooms offer great views.
Carte £ 22/38

2 rooms ⊒ – ♦£ 65 ♦♦£ 95
⊠ *TA4 3EF* – *ℰ (01823) 432 575* – *www.risingsuninn.info* – *Closed 25 December*

WEST BRIDGFORD - Nottinghamshire → See Nottingham

WEST CLANDON - Surrey → See Guildford

WEST END
Surrey – ⊠ Guildford – Pop. 4 135 – Regional map n° **4**-C1
▶ London 37 mi – Bracknell 7 mi – Camberley 5 mi – Guildford 8 mi

🍸 The Inn West End 💱 ⇦ 🛏 🏠 ♿ **P**

TRADITIONAL CUISINE · PUB A big-hearted, recently refurbished pub offering genuine hospitality and a lively atmosphere. Wide-ranging menus offer generously proportioned, seasonal dishes with robust flavours and original touches. The wine shop specialises in European wines. Smart boutique bedrooms complete the picture.
Menu £ 13/28 – Carte £ 26/45

12 rooms ⊒ – ♦£ 125/150 ♦♦£ 125/150
42 Guildford Rd ⊠ *GU24 9PW* – *on A 322* – *ℰ (01276) 858 652*
– www.the-inn.co.uk

WEST HATCH
Wiltshire – Regional map n° **2**-C3
▶ London 104 mi – Swindon 88 mi – Salisbury 28 mi

✗ Pythouse Kitchen Garden Shop and Café 🛏 🏠 ♿ 🖵 **P**

BRITISH TRADITIONAL · SIMPLE Simple, rustic café in a former potting shed, serving breakfast, coffee, lunch and afternoon tea; order in the well-stocked shop. Tasty, unfussy cooking uses seasonal produce from the charming 18C walled garden. Save room for some cake!
Carte £ 20/28

⊠ *SP3 6PA* – *ℰ (01747) 870 444 (booking advisable)*
– www.pythousekitchengarden.co.uk – *lunch only and dinner Friday-Saturday*
– Closed 25-26 December, 1 January and Tuesday

WEST HOATHLY
West Sussex – Pop. 709 – Regional map n° **4**-D2
▶ London 36 mi – Bristol 141 mi – Croydon 26 mi – Barnet 78 mi

🏠 Cat Inn

BRITISH TRADITIONAL · COSY Popular with the locals and very much a village pub, with beamed ceilings, pewter tankards, open fires and plenty of cosy corners. Carefully executed, good value cooking focuses on tasty pub classics like locally smoked ham, egg and chips or steak, mushroom and ale pie. Service is friendly and efficient – and four tastefully decorated bedrooms complete the picture.

Carte £ 26/39

4 rooms ☐ – †£ 85/120 ††£ 120/160

Queen's Sq ⊠ RH19 4PP – ℰ (01342) 810 369 – www.catinn.co.uk
– Closed 25 December and Sunday dinner

WEST KIRBY

Merseyside – Regional map n° **11**-A3
▶ London 219 mi – Chester 19 mi – Liverpool 12 mi

🏠 Peel Hey

TRADITIONAL · PERSONALISED Personally run, detached 19C house with attractive bedrooms; those to the rear are quieter, with countryside views. Comfortable conservatory and pleasant lawned garden. Simple evening meals and Sunday lunch.

10 rooms – †£ 55/75 ††£ 75/95 – ☐ £ 10

Frankby Rd, Frankby ⊠ CH48 1PP – ℰ (0151) 677 90 77 – www.peelhey.com

WEST LULWORTH

Dorset – ⊠ Wareham – Regional map n° **2**-C3
▶ London 129 mi – Bournemouth 21 mi – Dorchester 17 mi – Weymouth 19 mi

🏠 Bishop's Cottage

FAMILY · PERSONALISED Attractive cottage part-dating from the 17C, set on the hillside in a pretty village and looking over the Jurassic Coast. Sizeable, very contemporary bedrooms with stylish bathrooms. Rustic bar with a wood-burning stove. Pre-book dinner in the dining room, which doubles as a vegetarian café during the day.

8 rooms ☐ – †£ 70/120 ††£ 75/180

Lulworth Cove ⊠ BH20 5RQ – ℰ (01929) 400 552 – www.bishopscottage.co.uk

WEST MALLING

Kent – Pop. 2 266 – Regional map n° **5**-B1
▶ London 35 mi – Maidstone 7 mi – Royal Tunbridge Wells 14 mi

X Swan

MODERN CUISINE · FASHIONABLE Informal 15C former coaching inn where original beams blend with stylish, contemporary furnishings. The nicely appointed bar and lounge are upstairs. Modern European menus offer flavoursome combinations; side dishes are required.

Menu £ 17 (weekdays) – Carte £ 26/41

35 Swan St. ⊠ ME19 6JU – ℰ (01732) 521 910 (booking essential)
– www.theswanwestmalling.co.uk – Closed 1 January

WEST MEON

Hampshire – Regional map n° **4**-B2
▶ London 74 mi – Southampton 27 mi – Portsmouth 21 mi – Basingstoke 32 mi

🏠 Thomas Lord

TRADITIONAL CUISINE · PUB Smartly refurbished, early 19C pub named after the founder of Lord's Cricket Ground. The atmosphere is warm and welcoming, there's a lovely garden where they grow herbs and veg, and the menu perfectly balances the classics with some more adventurous offerings. They host music evenings twice a month.

Menu £ 16 (weekdays) – Carte £ 23/40

High St ⊠ GU32 1LN – ℰ (01730) 829 444 – www.thomaslord.co.uk – Closed 25 December

WEST OVERTON – Wiltshire → See Marlborough

WEST TANFIELD
North Yorkshire – ✉ Ripon – Pop. 293 – Regional map n° **13**-B2
▶ London 237 mi – Darlington 29 mi – Leeds 32 mi – Middlesbrough 39 mi

⌂ Old Coach House
TRADITIONAL · ELEGANT Smart 18C coach house nestled between the dales and the moors. Bedrooms differ in size but all have a bright modern style and are furnished by local craftsmen. The breakfast room overlooks the fountain in the courtyard garden.
8 rooms ☲ – **♦**£ 70/100 **♦♦**£ 80/110
2 Stable Cottage, North Stainley ✉ HG4 3HT – Southeast : 1 mi on A 6108
– ℰ (07912) 632 296 – www.oldcoachhouse.info

WEST WITTERING
West Sussex – Pop. 875 – Regional map n° **4**-C3
▶ London 87 mi – Southampton 38 mi – Brighton and Hove 41 mi

✗ Beach House
TRADITIONAL CUISINE · FRIENDLY It might be 10 minutes' from the beach but the Beach House definitely has a seaside feel, with its large veranda, shuttered windows and scrubbed wooden tables. Tasty breakfasts, coffee and cakes morph into fresh, bistro-style dishes later in the day. Bedrooms are simple and modern, with comfy beds.
Carte £ 19/39
7 rooms ☲ – **♦**£ 70/80 **♦♦**£ 100/120
Rookwood Rd ✉ PO20 8LT – ℰ (01243) 514 800 (booking advisable)
– www.beachhse.co.uk – Closed 3 weeks January and Monday-Tuesday November-May

WEST WITTON
North Yorkshire – ✉ Leyburn – Regional map n° **13**-B1
▶ London 241 mi – Kendal 39 mi – Leeds 60 mi – Newcastle upon Tyne 65 mi

⌂ Wensleydale Heifer
TRADITIONAL · PERSONALISED Pretty, whitewashed former pub on the main street of the village. Quirky, themed bedrooms boast quality linen and the latest mod cons. Characterful lounge has a roaring fire. Dine in the fish bar or at clothed tables in the beamed restaurant; cooking has a strong seafood base.
13 rooms ☲ – **♦**£ 90/240 **♦♦**£ 120/240
✉ DL8 4LS – ℰ (01969) 622 322 – www.wensleydaleheifer.co.uk

WEST DIDSBURY – Greater Manchester → See Manchester

WESTON-SUB-EDGE – Gloucestershire → See Chipping Campden

WESTON UNDER WETHERLEY – Warwickshire → See Royal Leamington Spa

WESTONBIRT
Gloucestershire – Regional map n° **2**-C1
▶ London 104 mi – Bristol 24 mi – Cardiff 57 mi – Plymouth 144 mi

⌂ Hare & Hounds
COUNTRY HOUSE · CONTEMPORARY Attractive former farmhouse with lovely gardens, set between Highgrove House and the National Arboretum. The country house style interior features several lounges and a small library; bedrooms blend modern fabrics with period furniture – half are located in the old outbuildings. Formal Beaufort offers classical dishes with a modern edge, while Jack Hare's serves a pub-style menu and real ales.
42 rooms ☲ – **♦**£ 100/110 **♦♦**£ 160/200 – 3 suites
✉ GL8 8QL – on A 433 – ℰ (01666) 881 000 – www.cotswold-inns-hotels.co.uk

WESTFIELD

East Sussex – Pop. 1 509 – Regional map n° **5**-B3

▶ London 66 mi – Brighton 38 mi – Folkestone 45 mi – Maidstone 30 mi

XX Wild Mushroom   🖨 **P**

FRENCH CLASSIC · **ELEGANT** Keenly run restaurant in a 17C farmhouse, with a contemporary dining room and an intimate lounge-bar in the conservatory. Good value French menus feature well-presented, tried-and-tested combinations; a tasting menu is available.

Menu £ 25 (lunch) – Carte dinner £ 30/41

Woodgate House, Westfield Ln. ✉ TN35 4SB – Southwest : 0.5 mi on A 28 – 𝒞 (01424) 751 137 (booking essential) – www.webbesrestaurants.co.uk – Closed 1 week October, 1-10 January, 25-26 December, Sunday dinner, Monday and Tuesday

WESTLETON

Suffolk – ✉ Saxmundham – Pop. 349 – Regional map n° **8**-D2

▶ London 97 mi – Cambridge 72 mi – Ipswich 28 mi – Norwich 31 mi

🏠 Westleton Crown   ⇆ 🖨 🏡 🕼 **P**

BRITISH MODERN · **INN** Good-looking, 17C former coaching inn with an appealing terrace and garden, set in a pretty little village. Welcoming beamed bar with open fires; more modern conservatory. Seasonal menu, with special diets well-catered for. Uncluttered bedrooms are named after birds found on the adjacent RSPB nature reserve.

Carte £ 26/40

34 rooms ⌂ – ♦£ 90/100 ♦♦£ 125/215

The Street ✉ IP17 3AD – 𝒞 (01728) 648 777 – www.westletoncrown.co.uk

WESTON-SUPER-MARE

North Somerset – Pop. 83 641 – Regional map n° **2**-B2

▶ London 147 mi – Bristol 24 mi – Taunton 32 mi

XX Duets   AC

BRITISH TRADITIONAL · **INDIVIDUAL** A husband and wife team duet here, with him in the kitchen and her out front; there's also always a duet dish on the menu. Carefully prepared classical dishes follow the seasons. It's more modern inside than the exterior suggests.

Menu £ 19/31

Town plan: BY-a *– 103 Upper Bristol Rd. ✉ BS22 8ND – 𝒞 (01934) 413 428 (booking essential at lunch) – www.duets.co.uk – Closed 1 week spring, 1 week summer, 1 week winter, Sunday dinner, Monday and Tuesday*

XX Cove   ⇐ 🏡 🗄

BRITISH TRADITIONAL · **DESIGN** Stylish, modern restaurant on the promenade; every table has bay views. Light bites at lunch. More formal dinner menu offers carefully cooked European dishes with modern touches. Open for breakfast every day. Keen, helpful service.

Menu £ 15 (lunch)/20 – Carte £ 20/32

Town plan: AY-e *– Birnbeck Rd ✉ BS23 2BX – 𝒞 (01934) 418 217 – www.the-cove.co.uk – Closed 25 December, Monday and Tuesday October-April*

X Mint and Mustard 🆕   AC

INDIAN · **NEIGHBOURHOOD** Modern, friendly restaurant with eye-catching Indian art. The extensive menu includes tandoori dishes from the north, biryanis from Hyderabad and fish dishes from Kerala, where the owner grew up. Herbs and spices are well-balanced.

Carte £ 14/29

Town plan: BZ-c *– 45 Oxford St ✉ BS23 1TN – 𝒞 (01934) 626 363 – www.mintandmustard.com – Closed 25 December*

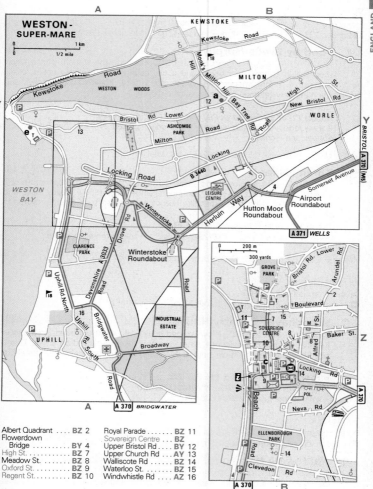

WEYBRIDGE

Surrey – Pop. 29 837 – Regional map n° **4**-C1

▶ London 23 mi – Crawley 27 mi – Guildford 17 mi – Reading 33 mi

🏠 **Brooklands**　　　🕭 ⑳ 🎐 ⅃⅋ ⊡ ₺ AK 🏖 🏊 🅿

BUSINESS · MODERN Contemporary hotel with an art deco feel, situated next to Mercedes Benz World, on what was once Brooklands racetrack. Stylish, good-sized bedrooms. Great spa with outdoor hot tub. Chic, brasserie-style bar/restaurant serving well-presented modern dishes; head to the far end for a more intimate atmosphere.

131 rooms – ♟£ 139/275 ♟♟£ 139/275 – ☕ £ 17 – 7 suites
Brooklands Dr ✉ *KT13 OSL – Southwest : 1.5 mi by B 374 and A 318 – 𝒞 (01932) 335 700 – www.brooklandshotelsurrey.com*

755

WHALLEY

Lancashire – ⊠ Blackburn – Pop. 3 230 – Regional map n° **11**-B2

▶ London 233 mi – Blackpool 32 mi – Burnley 12 mi – Manchester 28 mi

✗ Food by Breda Murphy

TRADITIONAL CUISINE · **NEIGHBOURHOOD** Opposite the station, with a smart shop selling gadgets and books and a deli counter for takeaway meals, cakes and coffee. Bright, modern restaurant offers tasty, home-cooked lunches and charming service; open for dinner once a month.

Carte £ 23/34

Abbots Ct, 41 Station Rd ⊠ BB7 9RH – ℰ (01254) 823 446
– www.foodbybredamurphy.com – lunch only – Closed 24 December-7 January,
Sunday and Monday

at Mitton Northwest: 2.5 mi on B6246 – ⊠ Whalley

⊓ Three Fishes

REGIONAL · **PUB** 'Regional' and 'local' are the buzzwords at this behemoth of a country pub. Expect shrimps from Morecambe Bay, Ribble Valley beef and Fleetwood fish, with specialities like hotpot and cheese soufflé firmly rooted in the region.

Menu £ 15 (weekdays) – Carte £ 19/39

Mitton Rd ⊠ BB7 9PQ – ℰ (01254) 826 888 – www.thethreefishes.com

WHEPSTEAD – Suffolk ➜ See Bury St Edmunds

WHIMPLE

Devon – Regional map n° **1**-D2

▶ London 166 mi – Bristol 81 mi – Cardiff 112 mi – Plymouth 52 mi

⌂ Woodhayes Country House

HISTORIC · **STYLISH** 18C yellow-washed house with mature grounds, in a peaceful village. Small comfy lounge, where tea and cake are served on arrival. Good-sized bedrooms with simple, neutral décor and modern facilities. Order breakfast the night before.

6 rooms ☲ – ♦£ 85/165 ♦♦£ 85/165

Woodhayes Ln ⊠ EX5 2TQ – ℰ (01404) 823 120
– www.woodhayescountryhouse.co.uk

WHITBY

North Yorkshire – Pop. 13 213 – Regional map n° **13**-C1

▶ London 257 mi – Middlesbrough 31 mi – Scarborough 21 mi – York 45 mi

⌂⌂⌂ Raithwaite Hall

LUXURY · **FUNCTIONAL** Modern resort hotel in 80 acres of delightful parkland complete with a carp lake. Bedrooms are stylish and well-equipped; some have small terraces and some are duplex suites. Brace serves modern menus of fine local produce, while informal Hunters offers brasserie-style dishes. Kick-back in the smart spa.

81 rooms ☲ – ♦£ 114/274 ♦♦£ 125/285 – 18 suites

Sandsend Rd ⊠ YO21 3ST – West : 2 mi on A 197 – ℰ (01947) 661 661
– www.raithwaiteestate.com

⌂⌂ Bagdale Hall

HISTORIC · **CLASSIC** Charming Tudor manor house built in 1516, featuring carved wood fireplaces, mullioned windows and antique furnishings. Period bedrooms – some with four-posters – and smart bathrooms; more modern rooms in a rear wing. Spacious dining room with 19C Delft tiles from Holland and a traditional menu.

16 rooms ☲ – ♦£ 60/200 ♦♦£ 90/240

1 Bagdale ⊠ YO21 1QL – ℰ (01947) 602 958 – www.bagdale.co.uk

🏠 Dillons of Whitby

TOWNHOUSE · DESIGN Charming Victorian townhouse built for a sea captain, set opposite the beautiful Pannett Park. Immaculately kept bedrooms are individually themed and feature Egyptian cotton linens. Extensive breakfasts are something of an event.

5 rooms ☑ – **♦**£ 70/85 **♦♦**£ 80/120

14 Chubb Hill Rd ⊠ YO21 1JU – ℰ (01947) 600 290 – www.dillonsofwhitby.co.uk

✗ Green's

FISH AND SEAFOOD · BISTRO Established eatery near the quay. Lively bistro atmosphere downstairs and a more formal room above. Menus feature grills and local seafood: blackboards name the skipper and his daily catch; the mussels are particularly good.

Menu £ 13 (weekday lunch) – Carte £ 23/40

13 Bridge St ⊠ YO22 4BG – ℰ (01947) 600 284 (booking essential) – www.greensofwhitby.com – Closed 25-26 December and 1 January

at Sandsend Northwest: 3 mi on A174 – ⊠ Whitby

✗✗ Estbek House

FISH AND SEAFOOD · FRIENDLY Personally run Regency house close to the beach, with a lovely front terrace and elegant dining room. Basement bar overlooks the kitchens and doubles as a breakfast room. Menus offer unfussy dishes of sustainable wild fish from local waters. Smart bedrooms come with stylish bathrooms.

Carte £ 35/70

5 rooms ☑ – **♦**£ 90/165 **♦♦**£ 125/200

East Row ⊠ YO21 3SU – ℰ (01947) 893 424 – www.estbekhouse.co.uk – dinner only – Closed January-9 February

WHITEHAVEN

Cumbria – Pop. 23 986 – Regional map n° **12**-A2

▶ London 332 mi – Carlisle 39 mi – Keswick 28 mi – Penrith 47 mi

✗✗ Zest

BRITISH MODERN · FRIENDLY An unassuming exterior conceals a stylish red-hued room with spotted chairs, stripy booths and a lively atmosphere. The extensive modern menu has an Asian edge and they are known for their excellent selection of Cumbrian steaks.

Carte £ 18/38

Low Rd ⊠ CA28 9HS – South : 0.5 mi on B 5345 (St Bees) – ℰ (01946) 692 848 – www.zestwhitehaven.com – dinner only – Closed 25 December, 1 January and Sunday-Tuesday

WHITE WALTHAM

Windsor and Maidenhead – Pop. 349 – Regional map n° **6**-C3

▶ London 54 mi – Maidenhead 10 mi – Reading 16 mi

🏠 Beehive ⓝ

CLASSIC CUISINE · PUB Chef Dominic Chapman now has his own place – this traditional pub overlooking the village cricket pitch. The classically based, seasonal menu changes daily and the eye-catching dishes are full of flavour, with a staunch sense of Britishness.

Carte £ 24/37

Waltham Rd ⊠ SL6 3SH – ℰ (01628) 822 877 – thebeehivewhitewaltham.com – Closed Sunday dinner

WHITEWELL

Lancashire – ⊠ Clitheroe – Pop. 5 617 – Regional map n° **11**-B2

▶ London 281 mi – Lancaster 31 mi – Leeds 55 mi – Manchester 41 mi

🛏 Inn at Whitewell 　　　　　　　🛥 ≼ 🛁 🞧 🏕 ♿ ☺ 🅿

BRITISH TRADITIONAL · INN 14C creeper-clad inn, high on the banks of the River Hodder, with stunning valley views. Characterful bar and more formal restaurant. Classic menus of regionally inspired dishes. Spacious bedrooms; some traditional in style, with four-posters and antique baths.

Carte £ 30/41

23 rooms 🕿 – ♦£ 92/204 ♦♦£ 128/253
Forest of Bowland ⊠ *BB7 3AT* – *ℰ (01200) 448 222* – *www.innatwhitewell.com*

WHITSTABLE

Kent – Pop. 32 100 – Regional map n° **5**-C1
▶ London 68 mi – Dover 24 mi – Maidstone 37 mi – Margate 12 mi

🏠 Crescent Turner 🆕 　　　　　　　　🌂 ≼ 🛁 🞧 🅿

COUNTRY HOUSE · STYLISH Smart rural retreat named after the artist, who painted the local landscapes. Their strapline is 'British, Boutique and Unique' and with its bold furnishings, it's exactly that. Take in sea views from the terrace, have a drink in the inviting lounge or head to the conservatory for a modern British dish.

17 rooms 🕿 – ♦£ 75 ♦♦£ 135/200
Wraik Hill ⊠ *CT5 3BY* – *Southwest : 2.75mi by B 2205 off A 290* – *ℰ (01227) 263 506* – *www.crescentturner.co.uk*

✗✗ East Coast Dining Room 　　　　　　　　　🏕 ♿ 🅰

BRITISH MODERN · NEIGHBOURHOOD Find a spot on the terrace or head inside, where you'll find reupholstered chairs from the 1960s and 70s, along with pictures of designer chairs. Concise, modern British menus offer fresh, flavoursome dishes; fish is a strength.

Menu £ 13 (weekday lunch)/22 – Carte £ 25/40
101 Tankerton Rd ⊠ *CT5 2AJ* – *East : 1 mi on B 2205* – *ℰ (01227) 281 180* – *www.eastcoastdiningroom.co.uk* – *Closed 25 December, 1 January, Sunday dinner, Monday and Tuesday*

✗ JoJo's 　　　　　　　　　　　　　　　　🏕 🞧

MEDITERRANEAN · BISTRO Unusually converted from a supermarket, this buzzy coffee shop, deli and restaurant offers good views over the Thames Estuary. The self-taught chef offers a large menu of Mediterranean and meze-style dishes and sharing boards.

Carte £ 12/33
2 Herne Bay Rd ⊠ *CT5 2LQ* – *East : 1.75 mi by B 2205* – *ℰ (01227) 274 591* – *www.jojosrestaurant.co.uk* – *Closed Sunday dinner-Wednesday*

✗ Whitstable Oyster Company 　　　　　　　　　　≼ 🏕

FISH AND SEAFOOD · RUSTIC An old seafront oyster warehouse with a rough rustic interior and a great informal atmosphere. Blackboards list simply prepared seafood dishes; from Sept-Dec try oysters from their own beds – the staircase leads to the seedling pool.

Carte £ 30/58
Royal Native Oyster Stores, Horsebridge ⊠ *CT5 1BU* – *ℰ (01227) 276 856 (booking essential)* – *www.whitstableoystercompany.com* – *Closed 25-26 December and lunch Monday-Thursday November-January*

🛏 Pearson's Arms 　　　　　　　　　　　　　　　≼ 🅰

BRITISH TRADITIONAL · PUB Characterful refurbished pub in a great spot, with the Thames Estuary stretched out in front. Busy ground floor bar for nibbles like jellied eels; top floor dining room serves reassuringly familiar dishes, with Kentish produce to the fore.

Menu £ 11 (weekday lunch) – Carte £ 25/41
The Horsebridge, Sea Wall ⊠ *CT5 1BT* – *ℰ (01227) 773 133* – *www.pearsonsarmsbyrichardphillips.co.uk*

at Seasalter Southwest: 2 mi by B2205 – ⊠ Whitstable

🕸 **The Sportsman** (Steve Harris)

REGIONAL · **PUB** An unassuming-looking pub serving excellent food: dishes feature four or five complementary ingredients; flavours are well-judged and presentation is original. The full tasting menu must be booked in advance but the 5 course option can be ordered on arrival.

→ Grilled slip sole and seaweed butter. Roast saddle of Monkshill Farm lamb with mint sauce. Apple soufflé with salted caramel ice cream.

Menu £ 45/65 – Carte £ 37/44

Faversham Rd ⊠ CT5 4BP – Southwest : 2 mi following coast rd – ℰ (01227) 273 370 (booking advisable) – www.thesportsmanseasalter.co.uk – Closed 25-26 December, 1 January, Sunday dinner and Monday

WHITTLESFORD
Cambridgeshire – Regional map n° **8**-B3

▶ London 50 mi – Cambridge 11 mi – Peterborough 46 mi

🕸 **Tickell Arms**

BRITISH TRADITIONAL · **PUB** Large pub with an orangery-style extension overlooking a pond. Fish is delivered 6 days a week; on Tuesdays diners can select their own cuts for 'Steak and Chop' night; and on Sundays they leave freshly roasted potatoes on the bar.

Menu £ 19 (weekday lunch) – Carte £ 24/38

1 North Rd ⊠ CB22 4NZ – ℰ (01223) 833 025
– www.cambscuisine.com/the-tickell-whittlesford

WIGHT (Isle of)
Isle of Wight – Pop. 138 500 – Regional map n° **4**-A/B 3

Godshill

🕸 **Taverners**

BRITISH TRADITIONAL · **PUB** Passionately run roadside pub featuring its own deli selling homemade produce including bread, sauces and pies. Menus offer a mix of traditional and more adventurous dishes and use seasonal, local island ingredients.

Carte £ 19/28

High St ⊠ PO38 3HZ – ℰ (01983) 840 707 – www.thetavernersgodshill.co.uk
– Closed first 3 weeks January

Gurnard

X **Little Gloster**

MODERN CUISINE · **INDIVIDUAL** Set in a great spot among the beach huts, with lovely views over The Solent. Have a cocktail on the terrace beside the croquet lawn or head inside to the large table by the kitchen or the relaxed, shabby chic dining room. Unfussy, flavoursome cooking uses island produce. Bedrooms have a fresh nautical theme.

Carte £ 25/71

3 rooms ⊑ – †£ 100/220 ††£ 110/230

31 Marsh Rd ⊠ PO31 8JQ – ℰ (01983) 298 776 – www.thelittlegloster.com – Closed 1 January-early February, Tuesday in low season, Sunday dinner and Monday

St Helens

X **Dans Kitchen**

TRADITIONAL CUISINE · **FRIENDLY** Old corner shop in a lovely location overlooking the village green. Simple wood furnishings, scatter cushions and nautical pictures feature. Traditional, hearty dishes showcase island produce; blackboard specials include the daily catch.

Menu £ 14 (lunch) – Carte £ 27/45

Lower Green Rd ⊠ PO33 1TS – ℰ (01983) 872 303 – www.danskitcheniow.co.uk
– Closed 3 weeks January, 1 week June, 1 week October, Sunday, Monday and Tuesday lunch

Seaview

🏠 Priory Bay
☆ 🦢 🛏 ⌨ ✗ 🅿

TRADITIONAL · CLASSIC Peacefully located medieval priory with a romantic, shabby-chic interior and a relaxed vibe; wander down the woodland path and you arrive at their private beach. Bedrooms have good facilities and range in style from classical country house to nautical. The formal 'Island Room' boasts impressive 1810 murals, while bistro-style 'Priory Oyster' opens onto a terrace.

18 rooms 🖙 – ♦£ 90/225 ♦♦£ 160/300 – 2 suites

*Priory Dr ⊠ PO34 5BU – Southeast : 1.5 mi by B 3330 – ℰ (01983) 613 146
– www.priorybay.co.uk*

🏠 Seaview
☆ 🖙 ⊡ 🚻

TRADITIONAL · PERSONALISED Long-standing hotel covered in foliage; its interesting nautical-themed interior filled with old photos, seafaring maps and model ships. Comfy bedrooms come in various styles; some are in 'The Old Bank' and 'The Modern' annexes.

29 rooms 🖙 – ♦£ 75/140 ♦♦£ 95/160 – 3 suites

High St ⊠ PO34 5EX – ℰ (01983) 612 711 – www.seaviewhotel.co.uk – Closed 24-27 December

🍴 **The Restaurant** – See restaurant listing

XX The Restaurant 🆕
🍴 🚻

BRITISH MODERN · FRIENDLY The seafaring décor gives a clue as to their focus here – fish is a speciality; indeed, the crab ramekin has become something of an institution. Meat and veg come from the hotel's own farm and dishes are well-prepared, modern and tasty. The bar snacks are equally tempting, if more classic in style.

Menu £ 23/28

*Seaview Hotel, High St ⊠ PO34 5EX – ℰ (01983) 612 711 (booking essential)
– www.seaviewhotel.co.uk – Closed 24-27 December and Sunday dinner September-May*

Shalfleet

🍴 New Inn
🛖 🅿

TRADITIONAL CUISINE · PUB Characterful pub on the main Newport to Yarmouth road, with inglenook fireplaces, slate floors and simple, scrubbed wood tables. Proper pub dishes are proudly made with island produce; lots of locally caught fish and seafood.

Carte £ 17/54

Mill Rd ⊠ PO30 4NS – ℰ (01983) 531 314 – www.thenew-inn.co.uk

Shanklin

▶ Newport 9 mi

🏠 Rylstone Manor
☆ 🦢 🛏 ✗ 🅿

FAMILY · CLASSIC This attractive part-Victorian house sits in the historic gardens and was originally a gift from the Queen to one of her physicians. The classical interior has a warm, cosy feel and combines antique furnishings with modern facilities. Carefully prepared dishes are served in the formally laid dining room.

9 rooms 🖙 – ♦£ 68/120 ♦♦£ 135/165

*Rylstone Gdns ⊠ PO37 6RG – ℰ (01983) 862 806 – www.rylstone-manor.co.uk
– Closed 28 November-10 February*

🏠 Foxhills
🛏 ✗ 🅿

TRADITIONAL · HOMELY Large, honey-stone house on a tree-lined avenue into town, with a spacious Victorian-style lounge, a bright modern breakfast room and immaculately kept contemporary bedrooms. They also have a jacuzzi and a beauty treatment room.

8 rooms 🖙 – ♦£ 65/98 ♦♦£ 98/108

*30 Victoria Ave ⊠ PO37 6LS – ℰ (01983) 862 329 – www.foxhillsofshanklin.co.uk
– Closed November-February*

X **Fine Nammet**

BRITISH MODERN · SIMPLE The old tiles out front are from its fishmonger days and the name is island slang for 'hearty meal'. 80% of the ingredients they use come from the island and the veg is picked daily – just 30mins before it arrives at the door!

Menu £ 24 (dinner) – Carte £ 27/45

35 High St ⊠ PO37 6JJ – ℰ (01983) 300 335 – www.finenammet.co.uk – Closed 25 December-2 February and Sunday

Ventnor

▶ Newport 10 mi

ⓐ **Royal**

TRADITIONAL · CONTEMPORARY A sympathetically restored classic Victorian house with mature lawned gardens and a heated outdoor pool. The interior mixes bygone elegance with hints of modernity. Traditionally styled bedrooms have good facilities and some offer lovely sea views. A modern menu is served in the formal dining room.

52 rooms ⊡ – ♦£ 95/195 ♦♦£ 190/290

Belgrave Rd ⊠ PO38 1JJ – ℰ (01983) 852 186 – www.royalhoteliow.co.uk – Closed 2 weeks January

ⓐ **Hillside**

VILLA · PERSONALISED Set high above the town, this wonderful thatched Georgian house has a beautiful terrace and superb sea views. The Danish owner has fused period furnishings with clean-lined Scandinavian styling, and displays over 350 pieces of CoBrA and Scandinavian art. Everything is immaculate and the linens are top quality. Frequently changing menus use local and garden produce.

14 rooms ⊡ – ♦£ 68/133 ♦♦£ 146/196

151 Mitchell Ave ⊠ PO38 1DR – ℰ (01983) 852 271 – www.hillsideventnor.co.uk

X **Bistro**

TRADITIONAL CUISINE · DESIGN Pleasant café-cum-bistro decorated with vivid artwork. Delightful breakfast dishes, like Eggs benedict, morph into coffee and cake, then again into tasty bistro classics. Produce comes from the island and the Hillside hotel garden.

Menu £ 20 – Carte £ 16/37

30 Pier St ⊠ PO38 1SX – ℰ (01983) 853 334 – www.hillsideventnor.co.uk/bistro

Yarmouth

▶ Newport 10 mi

ⓐ **George**

TRADITIONAL · CLASSIC Smart 17C townhouse that blends subtle modern touches with characterful period features. Bedrooms vary in shape and style: one has a large wet room and opens onto the garden; another has a sizeable balcony and excellent Solent views. Eat in the cool, elegant restaurant or modern conservatory.

17 rooms ⊡ – ♦£ 110/315 ♦♦£ 130/375 – 1 suite

Quay St ⊠ PO41 0PE – ℰ (01983) 760 331 – www.thegeorge.co.uk

Isla's Conservatory – See restaurant listing

XX **Isla's Conservatory**

MODERN CUISINE · BRASSERIE Hidden at the back of the George hotel is this modern conservatory with a lovely garden leading down to the water's edge. Flexible brasserie-style menus offer tasty nibbles and a choice of dish size; ingredients are local and organic.

Carte £ 28/48

George Hotel, Quay St ⊠ PO41 0PE – ℰ (01983) 760 331 – www.thegeorge.co.uk

Wootton Bridge

ENGLAND

🏨 Lakeside Park   ❀ ⪤ 🛏 🖼 🕸 🛁 ⊡ ⛓ 🎿 𝆑 ⚓ 🅿

BUSINESS · MODERN Unassuming, purpose-built hotel with a bright modern interior and a smart spa offering health and beauty treatments. Some of the stylish, well-equipped bedrooms have patios overlooking the lake. The airy multi-level brasserie and bar-lounge has a large decked terrace and lovely water views.

44 rooms 🛏 – ♦£140/165 ♦♦£140/165

High St. ✉ PO33 4LJ – ℰ (01983) 882 266 – www.lakesideparkhotel.com – Closed 1-11 January

---

WIGHTON – Norfolk → See Wells-Next-The-Sea

WILLIAN

Hertfordshire – Pop. 326 – Regional map n° **7**-B2

▶ London 38 mi – Croydon 48 mi – Barnet 24 mi – Ealing 37 mi

🍴 Fox   ⪤ 🛏 🅿

BRITISH MODERN · FRIENDLY A popular, bright and airy pub with a sheltered terrace, set right in the heart of the village. Dishes are modern and there's a good choice of seafood and game in season; if you can't decide, try 'The Fox Slate' for two.

Carte £20/38

✉ SG6 2AE – ℰ (01462) 480 233 – www.foxatwillian.co.uk

WILMINGTON

Kent – Regional map n° **5**-B1

▶ London 17 mi – Royal Tunbridge Wells 28 mi – Maidstone 24 mi

🏨 Rowhill Grange   ❀ ⪤ 🖼 🕸 🛁 🎿 ⊡ ⛓ 𝆑 ⚓ 🅿

COUNTRY HOUSE · MODERN Early 19C house in 15 acres of pretty gardens, with smart modern bedrooms in dark, bold hues. The fantastic spa has 9 treatment rooms, a large gym and a superb swimming pool, along with a separate infinity pool with a waterfall. RG's Grill serves fresh seasonal dishes – try the mixed grill.

38 rooms 🛏 – ♦£129/209 ♦♦£139/209 – 1 suite

✉ DA2 7QH – Southwest : 2 mi on Hextable rd (B 258) – ℰ (01322) 615 136 – www.rowhillgrange.com

WIMBORNE MINSTER

Dorset – Pop. 15 174 – Regional map n° **2**-C3

▶ London 112 mi – Bournemouth 10 mi – Dorchester 23 mi – Salisbury 27 mi

✗ Tickled Pig   🕸 🛁 🗄

BRITISH MODERN · BISTRO Charmingly run shop conversion in the heart of a pretty market town. Modern, country style interior with a laid-back feel and a lovely rear terrace. Daily brown paper menus feature home-grown veg and home-reared pork; their mantra is 'taking food back to its roots'. Cooking is vibrant, flavourful and unfussy.

Menu £20 – Carte £16/36

26 West Borough ✉ BH21 1NF – ℰ (01202) 886 778 – www.thetickledpig.co.uk – Closed 25-26 December and 1 January

WINCHCOMBE

Gloucestershire – Pop. 4 538 – Regional map n° **2**-D1

▶ London 100 mi – Birmingham 43 mi – Gloucester 26 mi – Oxford 43 mi

XX **5 North St** (Marcus Ashenford)
❀ BRITISH MODERN · COSY Established neighbourhood restaurant that's very personally run by a husband and wife team. Low-beamed ceilings and burgundy walls provide an intimate feel. Menus change with the seasons and feature regional ingredients in classic combinations. Assured, well-crafted dishes are guaranteed to be full of flavour.
→ Roast halibut with crab, quinoa, smoked chestnut pasta and sweet & sour peppers. Suckling pig, scallop, black pudding, pumpkin purée and sage jus. Bay leaf and rice pudding panna cotta with lemon meringue and caramelised pineapple.
Menu £ 29/52
5 North St ⊠ GL54 5LH – ℰ (01242) 604 566 – www.5northstreetrestaurant.co.uk
– Closed 2 weeks January, 1 week August, Monday, Tuesday lunch and Sunday dinner

XX **Wesley House** ⇦
TRADITIONAL CUISINE · RUSTIC Characterful 15C house with lots of beams, a cosy open-fired bar and a smart rear dining room and conservatory. Cooking is classical and flavourful, and service is relaxed and cheery; simpler meals are served in their next door wine bar. The cosy bedrooms have a comfortingly traditional feel.
Menu £ 15/30 – Carte £ 30/42
5 rooms ⌑ – ♦£ 70/110 ♦♦£ 80/110
High St ⊠ GL54 5LJ – ℰ (01242) 602 366 – www.wesleyhouse.co.uk – Closed
26 December, Sunday dinner and Monday

🍴 **Lion Inn** ⇦ 🛏 🌲
BRITISH TRADITIONAL · RUSTIC Located in the heart of this historic town, close to Sudeley Castle; a 15C Cotswold stone inn with chic, country style décor and a pleasant terrace and garden. Menus are guided by the latest seasonal produce available. Stylish, contemporary bedrooms come with biscuits and board games instead of TVs.
Carte £ 22/42
7 rooms ⌑ – ♦£ 110/185 ♦♦£ 110/185
North St ⊠ GL54 5PS – ℰ (01242) 603 300 (booking advisable)
– www.thelionwinchcombe.co.uk

at Gretton Northwest: 2 mi by B4632 and B4078

🍴 **Royal Oak** ⇐ 🛏 🌲 ※ 🅿
BRITISH TRADITIONAL · RUSTIC In summer, head for the large garden, with its chickens, kids' play area, tennis court and passing steam trains; in winter, sit in one of two snug dining rooms or in the conservatory. Local produce features in honest, traditional dishes.
Carte £ 20/53
⊠ GL54 5EP – ℰ (01242) 604 999 – www.royaloakgretton.co.uk

WINCHELSEA
East Sussex – Regional map n° **5**-C3
▶ London 64 mi – Brighton 46 mi – Folkestone 30 mi

🏠 **Strand House** 🛏 🅿
HISTORIC · PERSONALISED Part-timbered, low-beamed house dating from the 14 and 15C; mind your head! The cosy open-fired sitting room and main house bedrooms are hugely characterful – some have four-posters; three more spacious, modern rooms in the garden annexe. A 4 course dinner party is offered to guests on Saturdays.
13 rooms ⌑ – ♦£ 55/125 ♦♦£ 70/180
Tanyard's Ln. ⊠ TN36 4JT – East : 0.25 mi on A 259 – ℰ (01797) 226 276
– www.thestrandhouse.co.uk – Closed 1-14 January

WINCHESTER

Hampshire – Pop. 45 184 – Regional map n° **4**-B2

▶ London 72 mi – Bristol 76 mi – Oxford 52 mi – Southampton 12 mi

🏠 Winchester

BUSINESS · FUNCTIONAL Stylishly refurbished business hotel within walking distance of the town centre. Bright, fresh interior with modern bedrooms, a well-equipped gym and small pool. Open-plan foyer leads to the bar and restaurant, the latter serving a mix of grills and international favourites.

96 rooms ☑ – †£ 80/170 ††£ 80/170
Town plan: A-w – *Worthy Ln* ✉ SO23 7AB – ℰ *(01962) 709 988*
– *www.thewinchesterhotel.co.uk*

🏠 Hotel du Vin

TOWNHOUSE · MODERN Attractive Georgian house dating from 1715, and the first ever Hotel du Vin. Wine-themed bedrooms, split between the house and garden, are stylish and well-equipped; some have baths in the room. The characterful split-level bistro offers unfussy French cooking and – as hoped – an excellent wine selection.

24 rooms ☑ – †£ 159/239 ††£ 179/249
Town plan: B-c – *14 Southgate St* ✉ SO23 9EF – ℰ *(01962) 841 414*
– *www.hotelduvin.com*

🏠 Giffard House

TOWNHOUSE · PERSONALISED Imposing Victorian house in a quiet road. Spacious, classically styled guest areas include a comfy drawing room, modern bar and formal breakfast room. Individually styled bedrooms boast quality furnishings and good facilities.

13 rooms ☑ – †£ 78/128 ††£ 103/140
Town plan: B-s – *50 Christchurch Rd* ✉ SO23 9SU – ℰ *(01962) 852 628*
– *www.giffardhotelwinchester.co.uk* – *Closed 24 December-2 January*

🏠 29 Christchurch Road

TOWNHOUSE · PERSONALISED Spacious, Regency-style guesthouse with a pretty walled garden, set in an attractive residential area close to town. It's immaculately kept throughout, from the homely bedrooms to the fire-lit lounge and elegant breakfast room.

3 rooms ☑ – †£ 65/85 ††£ 90/100
Town plan: B-v – *29 Christchurch Rd.* ✉ SO23 9SU – ℰ *(01962) 868 661*
– *www.bedbreakfastwinchester.co.uk*

🏠 Black Hole ⓝ

TOWNHOUSE · PERSONALISED This three-storey guesthouse is fashioned on an 18C prison – the Black Hole of Calcutta – and comes with heavy prison doors, framed prints of history's villains and themed wallpapers. The top floor terrace has city rooftop views.

10 rooms ☑ – †£ 100 ††£ 100
Town plan: B-h – *Wharf Hill* ✉ SO23 9NP – ℰ *(01962) 807 010*
– *www.blackholebb.co.uk*

XX Rick Stein ⓝ

FISH AND SEAFOOD · ELEGANT Winchester's high street is the location of the first outpost of the Stein empire outside Cornwall: a smart restaurant with a large open kitchen. Simply cooked fresh fish and seafood, with some Asian influences; good value set lunch.

Menu £ 25 (lunch) – Carte £ 36/62
Town plan: B-e – *7-8 High St* ✉ SO23 9JX – ℰ *(01962) 353 535*
– *www.rickstein.com* – *Closed 25 December*

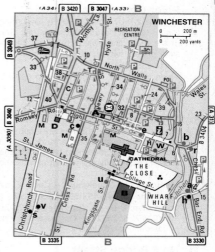

XX Chesil Rectory

BRITISH TRADITIONAL · INTIMATE Timbered 15C house on edge of the town centre; its characterful interior taking in beamed ceilings and a large inglenook fireplace. Appealing menu of classically based dishes.

Menu £ 20 (lunch and early dinner) – Carte £ 27/42

Town plan: B-r – *Chesil St.* ⊠ *SO23 0HU*
– *☎ (01962) 851 555 – www.chesilrectory.co.uk*
– *Closed 25-26 December and 1 January*

X Black Rat

❀ **MODERN CUISINE · RUSTIC** This unassuming building conceals a quirky, bohe-mian-style interior with a small bar, a lounge and a two-roomed restaurant. Refined, classically based cooking displays Mediterranean influences and mod-ern twists. The four wicker-roofed booths on the rear terrace are an unusual feature.

→ Rabbit ravioli with wild garlic purée, raw carrot, snails and watercress. Pork tenderloin, rolled head meat, parsnips in praline, crispy pig's ear and hazelnut jus. Cardamom panna cotta with roasted and poached plums.

Menu £ 26 (lunch) – Carte £ 38/46

Town plan: B-a – *88 Chesil St.* ⊠ *SO23 0HX*
– *☎ (01962) 844 465 – www.theblackrat.co.uk*
– *dinner only and lunch Saturday-Sunday*
– *Closed 2 weeks December-January, 1 week spring and 1 week autumn*

**Your discoveries and comments help us improve the guide.
Please let us know about your experiences - good or bad!**

☆ River Cottage Canteen ❶   🐾 ⒶⒸ

BRITISH TRADITIONAL · RUSTIC Delightfully located in a listed, 200 year old former silk mill close to the high street. Seasonal regional produce is at the core of the menu and dishes are hearty and rustic, with some sharing boards and small plates. Helpful staff.

Carte £ 22/32

Town plan: B-w – *Abbey Mill, Abbey Mill Gardens* ⊠ *SO23 9GH*
– *𝒞 (01962) 457 747 (booking essential) – www.rivercottage.net*
– *Closed 25-26 December, Sunday dinner and Monday*

⊨ Wykeham Arms   🐾 🛏 ⇔

MODERN CUISINE · PUB Red-brick pub decorated with all manner of bric-a-brac, including over a thousand tankards. Elaborate dishes showcase modern cooking techniques; for something a bit simpler, choose a dish from the 'home comforts' section. Individually styled bedrooms: some above the pub and some in an annexe over the road.

Menu £ 16/35 (weekdays) – Carte £ 23/42
14 rooms 🖙 – ♦£ 45/159 ♦♦£ 99/169
Town plan: B-u – *75 Kingsgate St* ⊠ *SO23 9PE*
– *𝒞 (01962) 853 834 (booking essential) – www.wykehamarmswinchester.co.uk*
– *Closed dinner 25 December*

⊨ No.5 Bridge Street   🐾 🍷 🛏 🖥 📖 ⇔

MODERN CUISINE · TRENDY Roadside pub with a fashionable, modern feel; head to the dining room at the back for table service and a view of the open kitchen. Sections on the Mediterranean-influenced menu include 'small plates' and 'British charcuterie and cheese'. Simply styled, comfortable bedrooms – those at the front hear the traffic.

Carte £ 21/41
6 rooms 🖙 – ♦£ 99/135 ♦♦£ 124/146
Town plan: B-b – *5 Bridge St* ⊠ *SO23 OHN*
– *𝒞 (01962) 863 838 – www.no5bridgestreet.co.uk*
– *Closed 25 December*

at Littleton Northwest: 2.5 mi by B3049 – Plan: A – ⊠ Winchester

⊨ Running Horse   🐾 🍴 🛏 & 🖥 🅿

TRADITIONAL CUISINE · FRIENDLY A smart, grey-painted pub with a straw-roofed cabana at the front (heated, very cosy and it can be booked!) The menu is concise and constantly evolving and dishes are fuss-free and big on flavour. Service is pleasingly unpretentious and the simple bedrooms are arranged around the garden, motel-style.

Carte £ 22/35
15 rooms 🖙 – ♦£ 80/130 ♦♦£ 80/130
88 Main Rd ⊠ *SO22 6QS* – *𝒞 (01962) 880 218 – www.runninghorseinn.co.uk*
– *Closed dinner 25 December*

at Sparsholt Northwest: 3.5 mi by B3049 – Plan: A – ⊠ Winchester

🏚 Lainston House   ☆ 🐾 ⇐ 🍴 🍷 🛏 ☆ ⚓ 🅿

TRADITIONAL · CLASSIC Impressive 17C William and Mary manor house with attractive gardens and a striking avenue of lime trees. Guest areas include a clubby wood-panelled bar and a modern drawing room; spacious bedrooms vary from classical to contemporary and boast good facilities. Relax over a game of tennis, croquet or boules.

50 rooms – ♦£ 195/245 ♦♦£ 195/245 – 🖙 £ 21 – 3 suites
Woodman Ln ⊠ *SO21 2LT* – *𝒞 (01962) 776 088 – www.lainstonhouse.com*
Avenue – See restaurant listing

XxX **Avenue**

MODERN CUISINE · FORMAL Set within an impressive 17C country house and named after the mile-long avenue of lime trees it overlooks. Cooking is modern, innovative and complex, and features plenty of produce from the kitchen garden; opt for a tasting menu.

Menu £ 33/55

Lainston House Hotel, Woodman Ln ⊠ *SO21 2LT* – ℰ *(01962) 776 088*
– *www.lainstonhouse.com* – *Closed Saturday lunch in winter*

WINDERMERE

Cumbria – Pop. 5 243 – Regional map n° **12**-A2
▶ London 274 mi – Blackpool 55 mi – Carlisle 46 mi – Kendal 10 mi

⛫ **Holbeck Ghyll**

TRADITIONAL · CLASSIC Charming, stone-built Victorian hunting lodge, set in 15 acres and boasting stunning views over the lake and mountains. Traditional guest areas feature antiques and warming open fires. Well-equipped bedrooms range from classical to contemporary in style; Miss Potter, complete with a hot tub, is the best.

31 rooms ⊑ – †£ 120/375 ††£ 170/425 – 4 suites
Holbeck Ln ⊠ *LA23 1LU* – *Northwest : 3.25 mi by A 591* – ℰ *(015394) 32 375*
– *www.holbeckghyll.com* – *Closed first 2 weeks January*
Holbeck Ghyll – See restaurant listing

⛫ **Miller Howe**

COUNTRY HOUSE · CLASSIC Superbly situated Victorian villa in mature gardens, looking down the lake to the mountains. Arts and Crafts furnishings feature in the guest areas; take in the fabulous view from the conservatory. Comfy, classical bedrooms have a contemporary edge. Traditional menus are served in the split-level dining room.

15 rooms ⊑ – †£ 110/145 ††£ 200/290 – 2 suites
Town plan: Y-s – *Rayrigg Rd* ⊠ *LA23 1EY* – ℰ *(015394) 42 536*
– *www.millerhowe.com*

⛫ **Windermere Suites**

LUXURY · DESIGN Spacious Edwardian house with a seductive interior. Funky, sexy bedrooms boast bold modern décor, iPod docks and walk-in wardrobes. Huge bathrooms feature TVs and colour-changing lights. Breakfast is served in your room.

8 rooms ⊑ – †£ 180/295 ††£ 180/295
Town plan: Y-e – *New Rd* ⊠ *LA23 2LA* – ℰ *(015394) 47 672*
– *www.windermeresuites.co.uk* – *Closed 24-25 December*

⛫ **Cedar Manor**

TRADITIONAL · STYLISH Victorian house with ecclesiastical influences – built by a former minister, with a cedar tree in the garden. Contemporary country house bedrooms display locally made furniture; some have spa baths or views and the Coach House suite has a private terrace. Appealing menus of local produce.

10 rooms ⊑ – †£ 105/370 ††£ 135/385
Town plan: Y-m – *Ambleside Rd* ⊠ *LA23 1AX* – ℰ *(015394) 43 192*
– *www.cedarmanor.co.uk* – *Closed 5-21 January and 13-26 December*

⛫ **Jerichos**

TOWNHOUSE · CONTEMPORARY Victorian slate house in the town centre, with a contrastingly contemporary interior. The lounge is decorated in silver and the smart modern bedrooms have bold feature walls and good facilities; first floor rooms are the largest.

10 rooms ⊑ – †£ 75 ††£ 105/135
Town plan: Y-z – *College Rd* ⊠ *LA23 1BX* – ℰ *(015394) 42 522*
– *www.jerichos.co.uk*

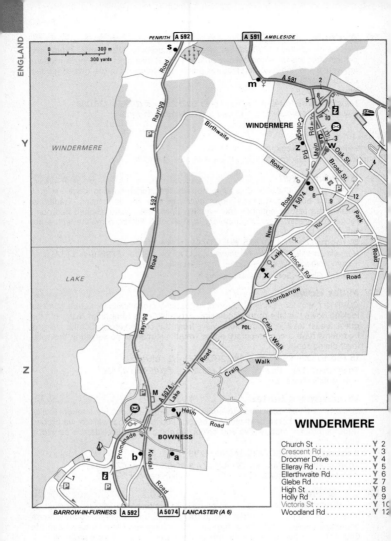

WINDERMERE

Howbeck

令 ⅋ **P**

TOWNHOUSE · STYLISH Smart slate house close to the town centre, with a comfy leather-furnished lounge. Ask for one of the stylish newer bedrooms – some have four-posters or jacuzzi baths; the 'Retreat Suite' with its private entrance, spa bath and patio is the best. The restaurant serves a light dinner menu of old favourites.

11 rooms ☲ – ♥£ 82/105 ♥♥£ 125/215
Town plan: Y-e – *New Rd* ✉ *LA23 2LA*
– ℰ *(015394) 44 739*
– www.howbeck.co.uk

Fir Trees

TRADITIONAL · PERSONALISED Reputedly built as a vicarage in 1888, this welcoming guesthouse boasts many original features, including a lovely tile-floored hallway, a pitch pine staircase and ornate woodwork. Simple, comfortable bedrooms are well-maintained.

9 rooms ☑ – ♦£ 55/60 ♦♦£ 72/76

Town plan: Z-x – *Lake Rd* ⊠ *LA23 2EQ* – *℘ (015394) 42 272*
– *www.fir-trees.co.uk*

✗✗ Holbeck Ghyll

CLASSIC CUISINE · ROMANTIC Two-roomed restaurant in a traditional stone-built hunting lodge; its wood-panelled front room offers superb views. At lunch, dine from a flexible à la carte menu; at dinner, choose between a set and a 7 course 'gourmet' menu. Seasonal dishes use good quality local produce and are classically based.

Menu £ 68/88 (dinner) – Carte lunch £ 45/70

Holbeck Ghyll Hotel, Holbeck Ln ⊠ *LA23 1LU – Northwest : 3.25 mi by A 591*
– ℘ (015394) 32 375 (booking advisable) – www.holbeckghyll.com – Closed first 2 weeks January

✗ Wild & Co

BRITISH TRADITIONAL · BISTRO Passionately run modern restaurant offering well-proportioned yet refined comfort food. Cumbrian produce features in flavoursome homemade dishes. As well as lunch and dinner, they serve brunch, coffee and cake and afternoon tea.

Carte £ 22/40

Town plan: Z-b – *31-33 Crescent Rd* ⊠ *LA23 1BL – ℘ (015394) 43 877*
– *www.wildandco.co.uk – Closed 2 weeks January and Tuesday*

✗ Francine's

FRENCH · NEIGHBOURHOOD Intimate neighbourhood restaurant with a homely feel; local art hangs on the walls and the service is friendly. Wide-ranging menus offer straightforward classical cooking with French influences; the chef is passionate about game.

Menu £ 14/20 – Carte £ 21/56

Town plan: Y-c – *27 Main Rd* ⊠ *LA23 1DX – ℘ (015394) 44 088 (booking essential at dinner) – www.francinesrestaurantwindermere.co.uk – Closed last 2 weeks January, first week December, 25-26 December, 1 January and Monday*

at Bowness-on-Windermere *South: 1 mi - Plan: Z* - ⊠ *Windermere*

Gilpin H. & Lake House

LUXURY · PERSONALISED Delightful country house hotel run by a charming, experienced family. Bedrooms range from contemporary country doubles to spacious garden suites with outdoor hot tubs. There are even more peaceful, luxurious suites a mile down the road beside a tarn – stay here for exclusive use of the smart spa.

26 rooms (dinner included) ☑ – ♦£ 195/524 ♦♦£ 255/535

Crook Rd ⊠ *LA23 3NE – Southeast : 2.5 mi by A 5074 on B 5284 – ℘ (015394) 88 818 (booking essential) – www.thegilpin.co.uk*

Gilpin H. & Lake House – See restaurant listing

Linthwaite House

TRADITIONAL · STYLISH Set in a peaceful spot overlooking the lake and fells and surrounded by 14 acres of beautiful grounds. Guest areas are cosy and stylish and the service is polished and personable. Smart modern bedrooms feature mood lighting; some come with terraces and hot tubs and number 31 has a retractable glass roof.

30 rooms ☑ – ♦£ 115/200 ♦♦£ 128/214

Crook Rd ⊠ *LA23 3JA – South : 0.75 mi by A 5074 on B 5284 – ℘ (015394) 88 600 – www.linthwaite.com*

Linthwaite House – See restaurant listing

Laura Ashley-Belsfield ⓝ 🌤 ⪕ 🛏 🖥 🛗 🖨 ⑤ ⅍ 🅿

COUNTRY HOUSE · STYLISH A Victorian mansion built in Italianate style, perched overlooking Lake Windermere. An eye-catching glass and steel reception opens into four elegant lounges, where contemporary décor marries with original features. Every piece of furniture, every fabric and every ornament is made by Laura Ashley. Dine from classic menus in the all-day brasserie or formal restaurant.

62 rooms – ♠£ 179/249 ♠♠£ 199/399 – 6 suites

Town plan: Z-b – *Kendal Rd* ✉ LA23 3EL – 𝒞 (015394) 42 448 – www.lauraashleyhotels/thebelsfield

Lindeth Howe 🌤 🐧 ⪕ 🛏 🖥 🦢 🛗 ⑤ ⅍ 🅿

TRADITIONAL · CLASSIC An attractive country house once bought by Beatrix Potter for her mother, with a clubby bar, a homely lounge and pleasant views from the drawing room. Bedrooms are traditional: the top floor rooms have the best views; the suites are more contemporary. The large, classical restaurant has menus to match.

34 rooms ⚌ – ♠£ 95/350 ♠♠£ 180/350 – 2 suites

Lindeth Dr. Longtail Hill ✉ LA23 3JF – South : 1.25 mi by A 5074 on B 5284 – 𝒞 (015394) 45 759 – www.lindeth-howe.co.uk – Closed 3-16 January

Ryebeck 🌤 🐧 🛏 ⑤ 🅿

FAMILY · ELEGANT Have afternoon tea on the terrace, looking over the gardens and down to the famous lake. Some of the bright, airy bedrooms share the view and some come with patios or Juliet balconies. Kick-back in one of the cosy lounges then head to the dining room to sample fresh local meats and tasty Cumbrian produce.

26 rooms – ♠£ 69/199 ♠♠£ 109/220

Lyth Valley Rd ✉ LA23 3JP – South : 0.75 mi on A 5074 – 𝒞 (015394) 88 195 – www.ryebeck.com – Closed 1 week in January

Angel Inn 🌤 🛏 🍴 🅰 ⅍ 🅿

INN · MODERN A cosy creamwashed inn just off the main street, with a large open-fired lounge and comfortable, contemporary bedrooms – two are in an annexed 18C cottage with lake views. Dine on classic pub dishes or sharing plates in the welcoming bar or minimalistic dining room, or head for the terraced garden in summer.

13 rooms ⚌ – ♠£ 65/150 ♠♠£ 75/220

Town plan: Z-v – *Helm Rd* ✉ LA23 3BU – 𝒞 (015394) 44 080 – www.theangelinnbowness.com – Closed 24-25 December

Dome House 🐧 ⪕ 🖥 ⅍ 🅿

FAMILY · CONTEMPORARY Futuristic-looking house with a grass-covered domed roof and superb lake views – the owner designed it himself and it was featured on 'Grand Designs'. Modern, minimalist bedrooms have balconies; one has a wooden bath in the room.

5 rooms ⚌ – ♠£ 190/280 ♠♠£ 190/280

Town plan: Z-a – *Brantfell Rd* ✉ LA23 3AE – 𝒞 (015394) 47 244 – www.domehouselakedistrict.co.uk

Fair Rigg ⪕ ⅍ 🅿

TRADITIONAL · HOMELY Late 19C house run by cheery owners, set in a conservation area and affording distant lake and hill views. Spacious, immaculately kept bedrooms come with up-to-date facilities. Enjoy Cumbrian sausages and bacon at breakfast.

6 rooms ⚌ – ♠£ 55/65 ♠♠£ 74/94

Ferry View ✉ LA23 3JB – South : 0.5 mi on A 5074 – 𝒞 (015394) 43 941 – www.fairrigg.co.uk – Closed January-March

XxX Gilpin H. & Lake House

MODERN CUISINE · FAMILY A series of intimate, individually styled dining rooms in a charming country house hotel; the Garden Room is perhaps the most pleasant. Start with an aperitif in the comfy lounge or the funky bar. Modern, very attractively presented dishes provide a fitting sense of occasion. Service is excellent.

Menu £ 35/58

Gilpin Hotel & Lake House, Crook Rd ⊠ LA23 3NE
– Southeast : 2.5 mi by A 5074 on B 5284
– ℰ (015394) 88 818 (booking essential) – www.thegilpin.co.uk

XxX Linthwaite House

MODERN CUISINE · ROMANTIC Contemporary country house restaurant – sit in the intimate Mirror Room with its romantic booths or in the airy, bay-windowed former billiard room. Constantly evolving menus showcase Lakeland produce; cooking is modern and complex.

Menu £ 20/52

Linthwaite House Hotel, Crook Rd ⊠ LA23 3JA
– South : 0.75 mi by A 5074 on B 5284
– ℰ (015394) 88 600 – www.linthwaite.com
– Residents only Christmas and New Year

at Winster South: 4 mi on A5074 – ⊠ Windermere

⥮ Brown Horse Inn

BRITISH TRADITIONAL · PUB Shabby-chic coaching inn with a lovely split-level terrace. Seasonal menus feature unfussy, generous dishes and more adventurous specials. Much of the produce is from their fields out the back and they brew their own beers too. Bedrooms are a mix of classic and boutique styles; some have terraces.

Carte £ 18/52

9 rooms � – †£ 55/110 ††£ 80/150
⊠ LA23 3NR – On A 5074 – ℰ (015394) 43 443
– www.thebrownhorseinn.co.uk

WINDSOR

Windsor and Maidenhead – Pop. 31 225 – Regional map n° **6**-D3
⏵ London 28 mi – Reading 19 mi – Southampton 59 mi

🏠 Macdonald Windsor

BUSINESS · STYLISH Opened in 2010 in a former department store opposite the Guildhall. Pass by the attractive open-plan guest areas up to contemporary bedrooms with a high level of facilities and bold, masculine hues. Meeting rooms are small but state-of-the-art. The modern brasserie specialises in steaks from the Josper grill.

120 rooms – †£ 130/295 ††£ 130/295 – � £ 19
Town plan: Z-r – *23 High St. ⊠ SL4 1LH – ℰ (01753) 483 100*
– www.macdonald-hotels.co.uk/windsor

🏠 Sir Christopher Wren's House

HISTORIC · CONTEMPORARY Impressive house on the riverbank, built by Wren in 1676 as his family home. Characterful guest areas have high ceilings, panelled walls and bold modern furnishings. Some of the stylish bedrooms are beamed and some have balconies and river views. The modern restaurant has a lovely Thames outlook.

98 rooms – †£ 110/190 ††£ 130/280 – ⊠ £ 16 – 3 suites
Town plan: Z-e – *Thames St ⊠ SL4 1PX – ℰ (01753) 442 400*
– www.sarova.com

WINDSOR

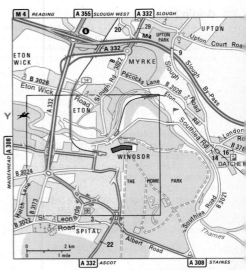

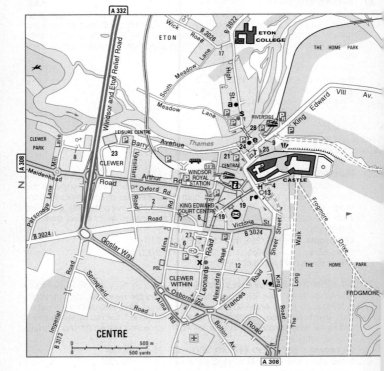

CENTRE

772

🏠 Royal Adelaide

TOWNHOUSE · CONTEMPORARY Comprising three adjoining Georgian townhouses with a powder blue and white façade, set close to the 'Long Walk' and built for Queen Adelaide. It's bright and comfortable throughout; feel like royalty by choosing one of the four-poster bedrooms. The accessible brasserie menu also offers a few Moroccan dishes.

43 rooms ☱ – †£ 69/105 ††£ 89/155

Town plan: Z-v – *46 Kings Rd* ✉ *SL4 2AG* – ✆ *(01753) 863 916*
– *www.theroyaladelaide.com*

🏠 Christopher

INN · CONTEMPORARY 18C brick-built coaching inn close to Eton College; cross the footbridge over the Thames to reach the castle. Contemporary bedrooms are spread about the main building and a mews; guest areas have an informal feel. The brightly coloured bistro offers international menus with subtle North African influences.

34 rooms – †£ 100/130 ††£ 120/160 – ☱ £ 14

Town plan: Z-a – *110 High St, Eton* ✉ *SL4 6AN* – ✆ *(01753) 852 359*
– *www.thechristopher.co.uk*

✗ Gilbey's

TRADITIONAL CUISINE · BISTRO Opened by the Gilbey family in 1975, as the first wine bar outside London. It's relaxed and friendly, with an airy conservatory and terrace. Carefully cooked French and British dishes are accompanied by an interesting wine selection.

Menu £ 21 – Carte £ 31/51

Town plan: Z-s – *82-83 High St* ✉ *SL4 6AF* – ✆ *(01753) 854 921*
– *www.gilbeygroup.com* – *Closed 23-29 December and Monday lunch*

✗ Windsor Grill

MEATS · BISTRO By day, this rustic Victorian property operates as a café, offering light bites and pub-style favourites. At night, it becomes a restaurant, specialising in steaks and grills; the mixed grill for 3-4 must be ordered 24hrs ahead.

Menu £ 16 (weekday dinner) – Carte £ 24/56

Town plan: Z-x – *65 St Leonards Rd* ✉ *SL4 3BX* – ✆ *(01753) 859 658*
– *www.windsorgrill.co.uk* – *Closed 25 December-5 January, Sunday and bank holiday Mondays*

🍴 Greene Oak 🆕

MODERN CUISINE · DESIGN Set close to the racecourse is this 'country pub and eating house', with its smart sun-trap terrace. Refined modern dishes show a good level of technical skill; textures and flavours are well-balanced; and portions are satisfying.

Menu £ 19 (weekday lunch) – Carte £ 25/34

Oakley Green ✉ *SL4 5UW* – *West : 3 mi by A 308 on B 3024* – ✆ *(01753) 864 294*
– *www.thegreeneoak.co.uk* – *Closed Sunday dinner*

WINFORTON

Herefordshire – Regional map n° **10**-A3
🗺 London 175 mi – Plymouth 188 mi – Torbay 167 mi – Exeter 151 mi

🏠 Winforton Court

HISTORIC · RUSTIC Hugely characterful part-timbered house with 16C origins: once home to 'Hanging Judge Jeffries'. The charming owner welcomes you with tea by the fire. Bedrooms have a warm, rustic style and lots of extras; two have four-poster beds.

3 rooms ☱ – †£ 73/83 ††£ 88/108

✉ *HR3 6EA* – ✆ *(01544) 328 498* – *www.winfortoncourt.co.uk* – *Closed 23-27 December*

WINSFORD

Somerset – ⊠ Minehead – Pop. 270 – Regional map n° **2**-A2

▶ London 194 mi – Exeter 31 mi – Minehead 10 mi – Taunton 32 mi

🏠 **Royal Oak Inn** ⇔ 🛏 🏡 🅿

BRITISH TRADITIONAL · RUSTIC Delightful 12C farmhouse and dairy, beside a ford in a charming little village. Sit in the dining room or the rustic bar with its wood-furnished dining area and enjoy well-executed British classics and tasty desserts. Spacious country bedrooms come with huge bathrooms; most have four-poster beds.

Carte £ 20/33

10 rooms ⊑ – ♦£ 65/75 ♦♦£ 100/140

Halse Ln ⊠ TA24 7JE – ℰ (01643) 851 455 – www.royaloakexmoor.co.uk

WINSLEY – Wiltshire ➜ See Bradford-on-Avon

WINSTER – Cumbria ➜ See Windermere

WINSTER

Derbyshire – Pop. 1 787 – Regional map n° **9**-A1

▶ London 153 mi – Derby 25 mi – Matlock 4 mi

🏘 **Old Shoulder of Mutton** ⓝ 🛏 ⌧

LUXURY · RUSTIC This old village pub closed in 1916 but its name and character have been kept and it's been transformed into a stylish, cosy guesthouse. Beams and handmade furniture abound and local produce features at breakfast. (Min 2 nights stay).

3 rooms ⊑ – ♦£ 100/135 ♦♦£ 115/150

West Bank ⊠ DE4 2DQ – ℰ(01629) 650 005 – www.oldshoulderofmutton.co.uk – Closed December-February

WINSTON

Durham – Regional map n° **14**-A3

▶ London 244 mi – Darlington 10 mi – York 56 mi

🏠 **Bridgewater Arms** 🏡 🅿

FISH AND SEAFOOD · COSY The former village school, this traditional pub attracts many regulars thanks to its food. The chef is known for his fish and seafood, and dishes are unashamedly classic, accurately executed and extremely satisfying.

Carte £ 22/65

⊠ DL2 3RN – ℰ (01325) 730 302 – www.thebridgewaterarms.com – Closed 25-26 December, 1 January, Sunday and Monday

WINTERBOURNE STEEPLETON – Dorset ➜ See Dorchester

WINTERINGHAM

North Lincolnshire – ⊠ Scunthorpe – Pop. 1 000 – Regional map n° **13**-C3

▶ London 176 mi – Kingston-upon-Hull 16 mi – Sheffield 67 mi

🏛 **Winteringham Fields** ⇔ ⌂ 🅿

MODERN CUISINE · FORMAL Characterful 16C house in a remote rural location, featuring an elegant dining room and several private rooms. The chef adopts a complex, modern approach to cooking, offering a set price or tasting menu at lunch and a daily 'Menu Surprise' of up to 11 courses at dinner; many of the ingredients come from their smallholding. Comfy bedrooms are furnished with antiques

Menu £ 40/79

15 rooms ⊑ – ♦£ 115/175 ♦♦£ 155/250

1 Silver St ⊠ DN15 9ND – ℰ (01724) 733 096 (booking essential) – www.winteringhamfields.co.uk – Closed 1 week April, 3 weeks August, 2 weeks December-January, Sunday and Monday

WISWELL

Lancashire – Regional map n° **11**-B2

▶ London 232 mi – Liverpool 49 mi – Manchester 28 mi

⏁ **Freemasons**   🕷 🛋 & ♔

BRITISH MODERN · PUB A delightful pub, hidden away on a narrow lane, with flagged floors, low beams and open fires downstairs, and elegant, antique-furnished, country house style dining rooms upstairs. The interesting menu features modern versions of traditional pub dishes and cooking is refined and skilful. Charming service.

Menu £ 16 (lunch and early dinner) – Carte £ 35/60

8 Vicarage Fold ✉ *BB7 9DF –* ℰ *(01254) 822 218 – www.freemasonsatwiswell.com – Closed 2-14 January and Monday-Tuesday except bank holidays*

WITHAM ON THE HILL

Lincolnshire – Pop. 260 – Regional map n° **9**-C2

▶ London 99 mi – Lincoln 42 mi – Leicester 40 mi

⏁ **Six Bells** ⓝ   ⇦ 🛋 & 🕼 🅿

TRADITIONAL CUISINE · FRIENDLY This pub's spacious courtyard is an obvious draw and the bright, stylish interior keeps things cheery whatever the weather. Choose hand-crafted pizzas cooked in the wood-burning oven in the bar or something more sophisticated from the main menu. Bedrooms are very stylishly appointed; Hayloft is the best.

Carte £ 19/35

3 rooms ⌷ – 🛉£ 60/65 🛉🛉£ 80/120

✉ *PE10 0JH –* ℰ *(01778) 590 360 – www.sixbellswitham.co.uk – Closed 31 December-1 January, Sunday dinner and Monday in winter*

WITHERNWICK

East Riding of Yorkshire – Regional map n° **13**-D2

▶ London 201 mi – Kingston Upon Hull 13 mi – Bridlington 24 mi

⏁ **Falcon Inn** ⓝ   🛋 🅿

BRITISH MODERN · NEIGHBOURHOOD Traditional-looking pub where the regulars gather on pew seating with pints of locally brewed beer and homemade crackling. The menu may be concise but it has plenty of appeal: substantial, flavour-packed dishes are made from scratch.

Menu £ 22 (weekdays) – Carte £ 25/44

Main St ✉ *HU11 4TA –* ℰ *(01964) 527 925 – www.thefalconatwithernwick.co.uk – dinner only and Sunday lunch – Closed Monday and Tuesday*

WIVETON – Norfolk → See Blakeney

WOBURN

✉ Milton Keynes – Pop. 1 534 – Regional map n° **7**-A2

▶ London 49 mi – Bedford 13 mi – Luton 13 mi – Northampton 24 mi

⏁ **The Woburn**   🏡 & 🕉 🛝 🅿

HISTORIC · CLASSIC The Woburn Estate comprises a 3,000 acre deer park, an abbey and this 18C coaching inn. Charming guest areas include a cosy original bar and brasserie-style Olivier's. This was where afternoon tea was popularised in the 1840s. The best of the bedrooms are the themed suites and the 300yr old beamed Cottages.

55 rooms ⌷ – 🛉£ 145/292 🛉🛉£ 177/292 – 1 suite

George St ✉ *MK17 9PX –* ℰ *(01525) 290 441 – www.thewoburnhotel.co.uk*

ENGLAND

XXX **Paris House** (Phil Fanning)   🛋 🛋 🕙 ⬧ 🅿

❀ FRENCH MODERN · FORMAL Striking black & white timbered house; built in Paris and reassembled in this charming location, where deer wander freely. 6, 8 and 10 course tasting menus feature classic recipes given an imaginative modern makeover; dishes are boldly flavoured and artistically presented. Service is slick and unobtrusive.

➔ Hamachi with braised dulse, red miso sorbet and olive oil caviar. Anjou pigeon with almond, turnip and black figs. Marinated pineapple with Thai green curry, lychee and coconut.

Menu £39/99

Woburn Park ⊠ MK17 9QP
– Southeast : 2.25 mi on A 4012
– ℰ (01525) 290 692 (booking essential)
– www.parishouse.co.uk
– Closed dinner 24 December-6 January and Sunday dinner-Tuesday

WOKING

Surrey – Pop. 105 367 – Regional map n° **4**-C1
▶ London 31 mi – Croydon 25 mi – Barnet 44 mi – Ealing 26 mi

XX **London House**   🛋 🅰🅒 🅿

BRITISH MODERN · INTIMATE Friendly neighbourhood restaurant in a 17C red brick former post office, where oil lamps create an element of intimacy. The classically trained French chef offers well-presented, satisfying dishes with interesting modern touches.

Menu £37

134 High St, Old Woking ⊠ GU22 9JN
– Southeast : 2 mi by A 320 on A 247
– ℰ (01483) 750 610 (booking advisable)
– www.londonhouseoldwoking.co.uk
– dinner only
– Closed 3-18 August, 1-12 January, Sunday and Monday

🍴 **Red Lion**   🛋 🛋 🅰🅒 🅿

TRADITIONAL CUISINE · NEIGHBOURHOOD Sit on a sofa in the open-fired bar or amongst Brooklands racing memorabilia in the rustic beamed dining room; or head out to the terrace and landscaped garden. Dishes range from pub classics to some more unusual combinations.

Carte £21/40

High St, Horsell ⊠ GU21 4SS
– Northwest : 1.5 mi by A 324
– ℰ (01483) 768 497 (booking advisable)
– www.redlionhorsell.co.uk
– Closed 26 December

WOLD NEWTON

East Riding of Yorkshire – Regional map n° **13**-D2
▶ London 229 mi – Bridlington 25 mi – Scarborough 13 mi

🏠 **Wold Cottage**   ⬥ ⬱ 🛋 ⬧ 🅿

COUNTRY HOUSE · ELEGANT A fine Georgian manor house and outbuildings in 300 acres of peaceful farmland, which guests are encouraged to explore. Personal items abound in the elegant, tastefully furnished interior. Sizeable bedrooms boast luxurious soft furnishings and antiques; some have four-poster – the courtyard rooms are simpler.

6 rooms � – ♦£75/90 ♦♦£100/130

⊠ YO25 3HL – South : 0.5 mi on Thwing rd
– ℰ (01262) 470 696 – www.woldcottage.com

WOLVERHAMPTON
Staffordshire – Pop. 210 319 – Regional map n° **10**-C2
▶ London 132 mi – Birmingham 15 mi

XX Bilash   AC ✿ ♿

INDIAN · FAMILY This smart contemporary restaurant is well-established and has several generations of the same family involved. Appealing, original menus offer South Indian and Bangladeshi dishes, crafted only from local and home-made produce.
Menu £ 10/20 – Carte £ 25/49
Town plan: B-c – No 2 Cheapside ⌧ WV1 1TU – ℰ (01902) 427 762
– www.thebilash.co.uk – Closed 25-27 December and Sunday

WOMBLETON – North Yorkshire → See Helmsley

WOOBURN COMMON – Buckinghamshire → See Beaconsfield

WOODBRIDGE
Suffolk – Pop. 11 341 – Regional map n° **8**-D3
▶ London 81 mi – Great Yarmouth 45 mi – Ipswich 8 mi – Norwich 47 mi

🏚️ Seckford Hall   ✿ ⌘ ⌂ ⌐ 🖻 🖾 🛏 & 🛎 🅿

HISTORIC · DESIGN This part-Tudor country house in attractive gardens was reputedly once visited by Elizabeth I – she would hardly recognise it now, with its bold champagne bar, stylish sitting rooms and creatively designed modern bedrooms. The laid-back brasserie features dark wood tables and an updated menu.
32 rooms – ♦£ 65/100 ♦♦£ 90/350 – ⌧ £ 12 – 7 suites
⌧ IP13 6NU – Southwest : 1.25 mi by A 12 – ℰ (01394) 385 678
– www.seckford.co.uk

X Riverside   ⌂ AC

MODERN CUISINE · FRIENDLY A restaurant, cinema and theatre in one – where several of the menu prices include entrance to a film. It's light and airy, with floor to ceiling windows, a terrace and a marble-topped counter displaying freshly baked bread.
Carte £ 24/37
Quayside ⌧ IP12 1BH – ℰ (01394) 382 174 (booking advisable)
– www.theriverside.co.uk – Closed 25-26 December, 1 January and Sunday dinner

🍴 Crown   ⌐ ⌂ ♿ 🅿

REGIONAL · TRENDY A modern dining pub in the town centre, with a smart granite-floored bar and four different dining areas. Seasonal menus of well-presented, modern classics, with plenty of shellfish; the set menu is particularly good value. Polite, friendly service. Minimalist, very cosy bedrooms boast good facilities.
Menu £ 15 (weekdays) – Carte £ 25/46
10 rooms ⌧ – ♦£ 90/140 ♦♦£ 100/170
Thoroughfare ⌧ IP12 1AD – ℰ (01394) 384 242
– www.thecrownatwoodbridge.co.uk

WOODSTOCK
Oxfordshire – Pop. 2 389 – Regional map n° **6**-B2
▶ London 65 mi – Gloucester 47 mi – Oxford 8 mi

🏚️ Bear   ✿ & 🅿

HISTORIC · CLASSIC Characterful 13C coaching inn with exposed stone walls, charming oak beams, welcoming open fires and a cosy first floor lounge. Extremely comfy, well-equipped bedrooms are spread about the house and courtyard; pay the extra for an executive. The formal restaurant serves a menu of classically based dishes.
54 rooms ⌧ – ♦£ 114/274 ♦♦£ 129/309
Park St ⌧ OX20 1SZ – ℰ (01993) 811 124 – www.macdonaldhotels.co.uk/bear

Cleveland St. .... **B** 7	Market St. .... **B** 14	Salop St .... **B**
Darlington St .... **B**	Princess St. .... **B** 15	School St .... **B**
Garrick St .... **B** 8	Queen Square .... **B** 17	Victoria St............. **B**
Lichfield St .... **B** 12	Railway Drive .... **B** 20	Wulfrun
Mander Centre .... **B**	St Johns Retail Park ...... **B**	Centre .... **B**

🏠 **Feathers**   🍴 ⓩ ♿

TOWNHOUSE · STYLISH Stylish 17C house boasting individually styled bedrooms with boutique twists: some have feature walls; others, bold fabrics and modern art. The bar-lounge and walled terrace offer a casual menu and a fabulous gin selection. The formal dining room serves classically based dishes with a creative original edge.

21 rooms ⓩ – 🛏£139/399 🛏🛏£159/419 – 5 suites
Market St ✉ *OX20 1SX* – ☎ *(01993) 812 291* – *www.feathers.co.uk*

⌂ Kings Arms

TRADITIONAL · MODERN Keenly run, contemporary hotel in the heart of a busy market town. Its immaculately kept interior displays a good eye for detail; cosy up and enjoy a drink in the open-fired bar. Sleek, stylish bedrooms are named after English kings.

15 rooms ☕ – ♦£ 85 ♦♦£ 150/160
19 Market St ✉ OX20 1SU – ℰ (01993) 813 636
– www.kingshotelwoodstock.co.uk
Kings Arms – See restaurant listing

✗ Kings Arms

BRITISH MODERN · BISTRO Spacious hotel restaurant with a large glass atrium, a striking black and white tiled floor and a welcoming open fire. Robust, flavoursome British dishes come with modern twists. They offer a good value set lunch and early evening menu.

Menu £ 15 (lunch and early dinner)
– Carte £ 23/35
19 Market St ✉ OX20 1SU – ℰ (01993) 813 636
– www.kingshotelwoodstock.co.uk

⅊ Crown

MEDITERRANEAN · FRIENDLY It might have 18C origins but inside it has a bright, airy, almost greenhouse-style dining room with an attractive Belgian tiled floor. Fresh, light cooking takes its influences from the Med and makes good use of the wood-fired oven.

Carte £ 18/26
31 High St ✉ OX20 1TE – ℰ (01993) 813 339
– www.thecrownwoodstock.com

WOOLACOMBE

Devon – Pop. 840 – Regional map n° **2**-C1
London 237 mi – Exeter 55 mi – Barnstaple 15 mi

✗ NC@EX34

BRITISH MODERN · INTIMATE Homely, constantly evolving restaurant seating 10 diners at three tables and 6 at the kitchen counter. Choose 5 or 7 courses from the daily set menu; skilful modern cooking uses seasonal Devon produce. Opt for the wine pairings.

Menu £ 55 – set menu only
South St ✉ EX34 7BB
– ℰ (01271) 871 187 (booking essential)
– www.noelcorston.com – dinner only
– Closed November-Easter and Sunday-Tuesday

WOOLER

Northumberland – Pop. 1 983 – Regional map n° **14**-A1
London 330 mi – Alnwick 17 mi – Berwick-on-Tweed 17 mi

⌂ Firwood

TRADITIONAL · COSY Bay-windowed dower house in a peaceful setting, with a beautiful tiled hall, a comfy lounge and lovely countryside views. Spacious bedrooms are furnished in a simple period style. The friendly owners are a font of local knowledge.

3 rooms ☕ – ♦£ 60 ♦♦£ 90
Middleton Hall ✉ NE71 6RD – South : 1.75 mi by Earle rd on Middleton Hall rd
– ℰ (01668) 283 699 – www.firwoodhouse.co.uk
– Closed 1 December-13 February

WOOLHOPE

Herefordshire – Regional map n° **10**-B3

▶ London 138 mi – Birmingham 70 mi

�🍴 **Butchers Arms**   🔥 🏠 **P**

TRADITIONAL CUISINE · RUSTIC Unfussy, classical cooking, with game in season, plenty of offal, tasty home-baked bread and hearty, reasonably priced dishes. The décor is traditional too, with a welcoming log fire, wattle walls and low-slung beams.

Carte £ 24/36

✉ HR1 4RF – ✆ (01432) 860 281

– www.butchersarmswoolhope.com

– Closed Sunday dinner in winter and Monday except bank holidays

WOOTTON

Oxfordshire – Regional map n° **6**-B2

▶ London 61 mi – Birmingham 81 mi – Bristol 68 mi – Croydon 71 mi

⛲ **Killingworth Castle**   ⟵ 🔥 🏠 **P**

BRITISH TRADITIONAL · RUSTIC A welcoming roadside inn dating from the 16C, set just outside the village centre. The chatty staff know what they're doing and food is great value, especially the dish of the day. Interesting menus champion local produce; here they bake their own breads, butcher their own meats and brew their own beers. Retire to one of the spacious bedrooms feeling suitably fortified.

Menu £ 19 (weekday lunch) – Carte £ 23/37

8 rooms ☑ – ♦£ 102/126 ♦♦£ 112/136

Glympton Rd ✉ OX20 1EJ – ✆ (01993) 811 401

– www.thekillingworthcastle.com

– Closed 25 December

WOOTTON BRIDGE → See Wight (Isle of)

WORCESTER

Worcestershire – Pop. 100 153 – Regional map n° **10**-B3

▶ London 124 mi – Birmingham 26 mi – Bristol 61 mi – Cardiff 74 mi

✕ **Bindles**   🍷 🏠 ♿ 🆎 ⟵

BRITISH TRADITIONAL · BRASSERIE Modern, boldly decorated brasserie, set on a busy junction and run by a friendly team. The large menu offers everything from light bites and deli boards to pasta and steaks; the busy downstairs bar is well-known for its cocktails.

Carte £ 22/47

Town plan: -c – 55 Sidbury ✉ WR1 2HU

– ✆ (01905) 611 120 – www.bindles.co.uk

– Closed Sunday dinner

🍴 **Old Rectifying House** ❶   🍷 🏠 ♿

BRITISH TRADITIONAL · PUB You'll find shabby-chic décor, easy-going staff and a cocktail list in this striking mock-Tudor building overlooking Worcester Bridge and the River Avon. Most dishes have a British slant, but there's the odd international influence too.

Carte £ 24/43

Town plan: -a – North Par. ✉ WR1 3NN

– ✆ (01905) 619 622

– www.theoldrec.co.uk

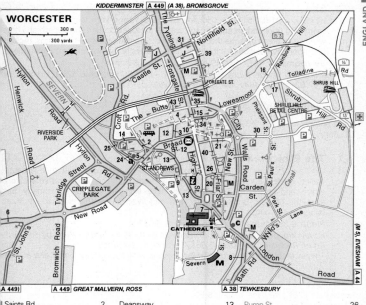

WORKSOP

Nottinghamshire – Pop. 41 820 – Regional map n° **9**-B1

London 160 mi – Sheffield 20 mi – Nottingham 37 mi – Rotherham 17 mi

Browns

TRADITIONAL · COSY Cross the ford to this keenly run, cosy cottage, which dates back to 1730. Lovely garden with mature fruit trees. Bedrooms are in the old cow shed; all have four-posters and open onto a large decked terrace. Appealing breakfast menu.

3 rooms ⌷ – †£ 59/69 ††£ 87/97

Old Orchard Cottage, Holbeck Ln, Holbeck. ⌂ *S80 3NF*
– Southwest : 4.5 mi by A 60
– ℰ (01909) 720 659 – www.brownsholbeck.co.uk
– Closed 24 December-2 January

WORTH – Kent → See Deal

WREA GREEN

Lancashire – ⌂ Kirkham – Pop. 1 373 – Regional map n° **11**-A2

London 185 mi – Bristol 226 mi – Cardiff 246 mi – Plymouth 340 mi

🏠 **Spa**   ☈ ⌇ 🛏 ⌇ 🖥 💿 🛁 ♨ 🎾 🖲 ⚡ 🅰 💱 ⚓ 🅿

HEALTH HOTEL · STYLISH Holiday park and village with lodges, shops, bars, swimming pool and an equestrian centre – all based around this superb spa hotel which specialises in 'aqua thermal journeys'. Spacious, modern bedrooms; those on first floor have balconies. Light brasserie lunches and more formal evening meals

39 rooms ⌑ – ♦£148/219 ♦♦£198/500 – 8 suites

Ribby Hall Village, Ribby Rd ⊠ *PR4 2PR – East : 0.5 mi on B 5259 (Kirkham Rd)*
– ☏(01772) 674 484 – www.ribbyhall.co.uk/spa-hotel

WRINGTON

North Somerset – Pop. 1 918 – Regional map n° **2**-B2
▶ London 130 mi – Birmingham 99 mi – Bristol 12 mi – Leicester 130 mi

🍴 **The Ethicurean**   ⬅ 🛏 🖨 🅰 🖵 🅿

BRITISH MODERN · SIMPLE Two converted glasshouses within a beautiful walled garden. It's rustic, informal and a break from the norm, and strives to be ethical and epicurean. The daily menu uses excellent ingredients – many, fresh from the garden. Burger nights Tues and Weds; Thurs-Sat sees a set 3 or course menu only.

Menu £28 (dinner) – Carte lunch £19/37

Barley Wood Walled Garden, Long Ln ⊠ *BS40 5SA – East : 1.25 mi by School Rd on Redhill rd – ☏(01934) 863 713 (booking essential)*
– www.theethicurean.com – Closed 2 weeks January, Sunday dinner and Monday

WROTHAM

Kent – Pop. 1 767 – Regional map n° **5**-B1
▶ London 27 mi – Sevenoaks 9 mi – Maidstone 12 mi

🏨 **The Bull**   ⬌ ⬦ 🅿

BRITISH TRADITIONAL · RUSTIC First impressions of this 14C inn might make you drive on past, but that would be a mistake. The interior is not the most characterful, but the food is mighty tasty: enjoy traditional British dishes as well as game in season, Spanish pork steaks and USA hanger steaks. Bedrooms are smart and up-to-date.

Carte £28/42

11 rooms ⌑ – ♦£69/149 ♦♦£79/159

Bull Ln. ⊠ *TN15 7RF – ☏(01732) 789 800 – www.thebullhotel.com – Closed 1 January*

WYMESWOLD

Leicestershire – Regional map n° **9**-B2
▶ London 120 mi – Birmingham 47 mi – Liverpool 109 mi – Leeds 91 mi

🍴 **hammer & pincers**   🖨 🅿

TRADITIONAL CUISINE · RUSTIC Formerly the village forge (the old water pump can still be seen at the back), then a pub, and now a rustic restaurant. Menus mix classic British and Italian influences; the 8 course grazing menu is more modern and creative.

Menu £20 (lunch and early dinner) – Carte dinner £24/45

5 East Rd ⊠ *LE12 6ST – ☏(01509) 880 735 – www.hammerandpincers.co.uk*
– Closed 25 December, Sunday dinner and Monday

WYMONDHAM

Leicestershire – Pop. 600 – Regional map n° **9**-C2
▶ London 107 mi – Birmingham 70 mi – Liverpool 138 mi – Leeds 100 mi

🍴 Berkeley Arms 🪑 ♿ ⇄ 🅿️

BRITISH TRADITIONAL · PUB Attractive 16C village pub run by an experienced local couple; turn left for the low-beamed bar or right for the dining room. Appealing, gutsy dishes rely on seasonal local produce and are constantly evolving; alongside British favourites you'll find the likes of mallard with poached pears. Service is relaxed.

Menu £ 15 (weekday lunch)/19 – Carte £ 24/42

59 Main St ✉ LE14 2AG – ℰ (01572) 787 587 (booking essential)
– www.theberkeleyarms.co.uk – Closed first 2 weeks January, 2 weeks summer, Sunday dinner and Monday

WYNYARD

Stockton-on-Tees – Regional map n° **14**-B3
▶ London 250 mi – Leeds 72 mi – Bradford 74 mi – Sunderland 24 mi

🏰 Wynyard Hall 🏡 🌿 ← 🍸 🛏 🕸 🖥 ♿ ⁇ 🚣 🅿️

COUNTRY HOUSE · ELEGANT Impressive Georgian mansion built for the Marquis of Londonderry; its smart spa overlooks a lake. Traditional bedrooms in the main house and more modern lodges spread about the vast grounds. Classical guest areas feature stained glass, open fires and antiques. The formal dining room offers modern classics.

22 rooms ☲ – ♦£ 175/195 ♦♦£ 175/235 – 3 suites

✉ TS22 5NF – ℰ (01740) 644 811 – www.wynyardhall.co.uk

YARM

Stockton-on-Tees – Pop. 19 184 – Regional map n° **14**-B3
▶ London 239 mi – Leeds 61 mi – Bradford 63 mi – Sunderland 34 mi

🏰 Judges Country House 🏡 🌿 🍸 🕸 ⁇ 🚣 🅿️

LUXURY · CLASSIC Victorian former judge's house with wood panelling, antiques and ornaments, set in well-kept gardens. Traditional country house bedrooms offer a high level of facilities, bright modern bathrooms and extra touches such as fresh fruit, flowers and even a goldfish! Welcoming atmosphere; pleasant service.

21 rooms ☲ – ♦£ 110/215 ♦♦£ 145/235

Kirklevington Hall, Kirklevington ✉ TS15 9LW – South : 1.5 mi on A 67 – ℰ (01642) 789 000 – www.judgeshotel.co.uk

Judges Country House – See restaurant listing

✕✕✕ Judges Country House 🍸 ⇄ 🅿️

MODERN CUISINE · TRADITIONAL Formal, two-roomed restaurant on the ground floor of a traditional country house hotel; the conservatory extension has a lovely outlook over the lawns. Modern, well-prepared dishes are simple and straightforward, yet full of flavour.

Menu £ 36/59

Judges Country House, Kirklevington Hall, Kirklevington ✉ TS15 9LW – South : 1.5 mi on A 67 – ℰ (01642) 789 000 – www.judgeshotel.co.uk

✕ Muse 🍷 🪑 ♿ 🆎 🖵

INTERNATIONAL · BRASSERIE Smart, modern continental café: bright and busy, with a pavement terrace in the summer. Extensive menu offers international brasserie dishes from lunchtime salads to pasta and grills; very good value set price menu of simpler dishes.

Menu £ 14 (lunch and early dinner) – Carte £ 20/48

104b High St ✉ TS15 9AU – ℰ (01642) 788 558 (booking advisable)
– www.museyarm.com – Closed 25 December, 1 January and Sunday dinner

YARMOUTH – Isle of Wight ➔ See Wight (Isle of)

YATTENDON

West Berkshire – ✉ Newbury – Pop. 288 – Regional map n° **6**-B3
▶ London 54 mi – Bristol 68 mi – Newbury 9 mi

🍴 Royal Oak ⇦ 🍴 🏠 ⟡

BRITISH TRADITIONAL · INN A red-brick pub bursting with country charm, in picture postcard village close to the M4; you'll find a heavily beamed bar with roaring fire at its hub. Menus offer honest British dishes and traditional puddings. Country house style bedrooms are named after guns; Heym is the most comfortable.

Menu £ 14 (weekday lunch) – Carte £ 27/45
10 rooms �'' – ♦£ 95/130 ♦♦£ 95/130
The Square ✉ RG18 0UF – ℰ (01635) 201 325 (booking advisable)
– www.royaloakyattendon.co.uk

at Frilsham South: 1 mi by Frilsham rd on Bucklebury rd – ✉ Yattendon

🍴 Pot Kiln 🏵 🍴 🏠 🅿

BRITISH TRADITIONAL · COSY A pretty pub in prime game country. Rustic, flavoursome British dishes arrive in unashamedly gutsy portions. The chef-owner stalks or gathers much of the produce himself and fish comes from local rivers.

Carte £ 30/43
✉ RG18 0XX – ℰ (01635) 201 366 – www.potkiln.org – Closed 25 December and
Tuesday

YEOVIL

Somerset – Pop. 45 784 – Regional map n° **2**-B3
▶ London 130 mi – Bristol 42 mi – Cardiff 86 mi – Southampton 77 mi

🏨 Lanes 🍴 🍴 🏠 🦢 ⅓ 🎱 🅿

BUSINESS · MODERN 18C former rectory with modern extensions, set in pleasant walled grounds. Airy interior boasts modern meeting rooms, a laid-back lounge and a large bar. Relax in the smart leisure suite or on the croquet lawn. Stylish bedrooms come with up-to-date bathrooms. Modern bistro dishes in the striking dining room.

30 rooms �'' – ♦£ 110/160 ♦♦£ 150/200
West Coker ✉ BA22 9AJ – Southwest : 3 mi on A 30 – ℰ (01935) 862 555
– www.laneshotel.net

at Barwick South: 2 mi by A30 off A37 – ✉ Yeovil

✕✕ Little Barwick House ⇦ 🍴 🍴 🎱 🅿

BRITISH MODERN · INTIMATE Attractive Georgian dower house on the outskirts of town, run by a hospitable husband and wife team. Relax on deep sofas before heading into the elegant dining room with its huge window and heavy drapes. Cooking is classical, satisfying and full of flavour – a carefully chosen wine list accompanies. Charming, comfortably furnished bedrooms, each with its own character.

Menu £ 27/48
6 rooms �'' – ♦£ 75/140 ♦♦£ 100/170
✉ BA22 9TD – ℰ (01935) 423 902 (booking essential)
– www.littlebarwickhouse.co.uk – Closed 26 December-27 January, dinner Sunday,
Monday and lunch Tuesday

YORK

York – Pop. 198 900 – Regional map n° **13**-C2

▶ London 213 mi – Newcastle upon Tyne 90 mi – Scarborough 41 mi – Leeds 28 mi

Hotels

🏨🏨 Grand H. & Spa York   ⚘ 🔲 🕸 🏋 🖵 🛗 🏧 🛜 🅿

BUSINESS · CONTEMPORARY Original features blend with contemporary décor in the former offices of the North Eastern Railway Company. Spacious, modern bedrooms are individually designed and well-equipped; and there's an impressive spa and leisure facility in the cellar. The formal, two-roomed restaurant serves ambitious modern dishes.

107 rooms – 🛏£ 123/320 🛏🛏£ 123/320 – ☒ £ 20 – 13 suites
Town plan: CY-v – Station Rise ✉ YO1 6HT – ☎ (01904) 380 038
– www.thegrandyork.co.uk

🏨🏨 Middlethorpe Hall   ⚘ ⬅ 🍴 🔲 🕸 🏋 🖵 🛗 🛜 🅿

HISTORIC · CLASSIC A fine William and Mary House dating from 1699, set in 20 acres of impressive gardens and parkland. The elegant sitting room features French-style furnishings, oil paintings and fresh flower arrangements. Traditional, antique-furnished bedrooms are split between the house and courtyard. Classic cooking uses luxury ingredients, along with produce from the kitchen garden.

29 rooms ☒ – 🛏£ 129/159 🛏🛏£ 199/279 – 9 suites
Bishopthorpe Rd ✉ YO23 2GB – South : 1.75 mi – ☎ (01904) 641 241
– www.middlethorpe.com

If you are looking for particularly pleasant accommodation, book a hotel shown in red: 🏠...🏨🏨 .

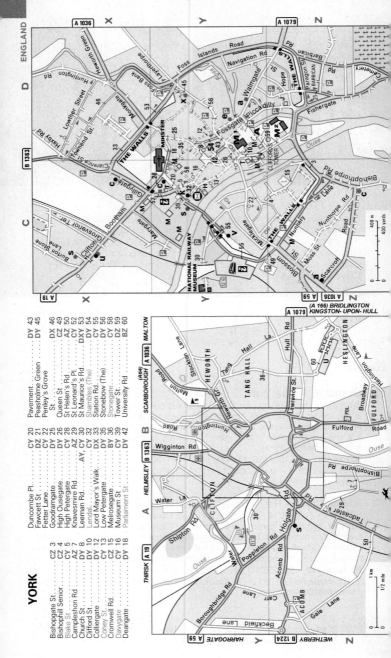

🏠 Grange
☆ 🕯 **P**

TOWNHOUSE · CLASSIC Well-run, classical, Grade II listed hotel; floral decorations, by the owner, and horse racing memorabilia abound. Choose between traditional bedrooms – some with four-posters – or more contemporary rooms with TVs in the bathrooms. Informal Brasserie serves a classic menu specialising in steaks from the grill.

36 rooms ☲ – ♦£ 89/144 ♦♦£ 99/254 – 1 suite
Town plan: CX-u – *1 Clifton* ✉ *YO30 6AA* – ☎ *(01904) 644 744*
– *www.grangehotel.co.uk*

🏠 Hotel du Vin
☆ 🕯 🖵 🕭 ㋛ 🕭 **P**

TOWNHOUSE · DESIGN Large Georgian manor house in a residential area just outside the city centre. Stylish interior with two snug lounges and a glass-roofed courtyard for afternoon tea. Well-equipped, contemporary bedrooms feature Nespresso machines. Chic champagne bar; imaginative wine list in the popular French bistro.

44 rooms – ♦£ 159/320 ♦♦£ 159/320 – ☲ £ 15
Town plan: CZ-a – *89 The Mount* ✉ *YO24 1AX* – ☎ *(01904) 557 350*
– *www.hotelduvin.com*

🏠 York Pavilion
☆ 🕭 ㋛ 🕭 **P**

BUSINESS · CLASSIC This well-run Georgian property sits on the edge of the city and is a popular spot for weddings. Bedrooms in the main house are the most characterful; many of those in the extension have balconies. The French café style bar has a jazz theme and the informal brasserie serves steaks and grills.

62 rooms ☲ – ♦£ 82/132 ♦♦£ 89/140
45 Main St, Fulford ✉ *YO10 4PJ* – *South : 1.5 mi on A 19* – ☎ *(01904) 622 099*
– *www.yorkpavilionhotel.com*

🏠 Dean Court
☆ 🖵 ㋛ 🕭 **P**

TOWNHOUSE · FUNCTIONAL Built in 1865 next to York Minster, to house the visiting clerics. Bedrooms mix modern and classical styles; the smartest also have the best views. Guest areas include a contemporary lounge-bar serving all-day snacks and a restaurant with an ambitious modern menu; the rib of beef for two is popular.

37 rooms ☲ – ♦£ 150 ♦♦£ 170/200
Town plan: CY-c – *Duncombe Pl* ✉ *YO1 7EF* – ☎ *(01904) 625 082*
– *www.deancourt-york.co.uk*

🏠 Judge's Lodgings ⓝ
☆ 🕭 ㋛

HISTORIC · CONTEMPORARY Built for a doctor in 1706 and later used by judges sitting at the nearby court. Rooms in the main building have high ceilings and antique furnishings; the terrace rooms are more modern with smart shower rooms. It also has a wonderfully characterful barrel-ceilinged bar and a stylish brasserie and terrace.

23 rooms ☲ – ♦£ 100/130 ♦♦£ 110/190
Town plan: CY-k – *9 Lendal* ✉ *YO1 8AQ* – ☎ *(01904) 638 733*
– *www.judgeslodgingsyork.co.uk*

🏠 Bishops ⓝ
㋛ **P**

TRADITIONAL · PERSONALISED This centrally located Victorian guesthouse is run by a welcoming couple (he was once a professional footballer for Sunderland). Well-kept bedrooms vary in shape and size; some have four-posters. Local produce is served at breakfast.

11 rooms ☲ – ♦£ 45/55 ♦♦£ 70/140
Town plan: AZ-s – *135 Holgate Rd* ✉ *YO24 4DF* – ☎ *(01904) 628 000*
– *www.bishopsyork.co.uk* – *Closed 1 week Christmas*

🏛 **Hazelwood**   🕸 **P**

TOWNHOUSE · FUNCTIONAL A pair of Victorian townhouses by the ancient city walls, in the Gillygate conservation area. It has a cosy basement lounge, a spacious Shaker-style breakfast room and well-kept, traditional bedrooms – some with four-poster beds.

12 rooms ⊊ – †£ 80/115 ††£ 90/145

Town plan: CX-c – 24-25 Portland St ⊠ YO31 7EH – ℰ (01904) 626 548 – www.thehazelwoodyork.com – Restricted opening at Christmas

Restaurants

XX **Star Inn The City**   🏡 & 🗚 ⌸ ⇔

BRITISH MODERN · DESIGN Busy, buzzy, all-day brasserie in an old brick engine house in Museum Gardens, affording views over the river. Well-judged dishes showcase top Yorkshire produce and are modern yet gutsy. The chargrilled meats are a highlight.

Menu £ 22 (weekday lunch) – Carte £ 27/58

Town plan: CY-s – Lendal Engine House, Museum St ⊠ YO1 7DR – ℰ (01904) 619 208 – www.starinnthecity.co.uk

XX **Melton's**   🗚 ⇔

BRITISH MODERN · NEIGHBOURHOOD Long-standing, split-level restaurant with simply laid tables and a large mural. Cooking is firmly rooted in the classics, with everything made to order and Yorkshire produce to the fore. Good value 'early bird' menu and speciality nights.

Menu £ 23 (lunch and early dinner) – Carte £ 29/40

Town plan: CZ-c – 7 Scarcroft Rd ⊠ YO23 1ND – ℰ (01904) 634 341 (booking essential) – www.meltonsrestaurant.co.uk – Closed 3 weeks Christmas, Sunday and Monday

XX **The Park** ⓝ   🗚 **P**

MODERN CUISINE · NEIGHBOURHOOD Adam Jackson has moved his restaurant to a quiet residential suburb of York; it's set within a hotel and is run by a chatty, knowledgeable team. The seasonal 6 course menu features complex, eye-catching dishes comprising many flavours.

Menu £ 48 – set menu only

Town plan: CX-s – Marmadukes Hotel, 4-5 St Peters Grove, Bootham ⊠ YO30 6AQ – ℰ (01904) 540 903 – www.theparkrestaurant.co.uk – dinner only – Closed 24-26 December, 2 weeks January, 2 weeks summer, Sunday and Monday

X **Le Cochon Aveugle** ⓝ

FRENCH · BISTRO A rustic bistro with chequer-board flooring, contemporary art and an antique dresser overflowing with top quality spirits. It's a tiny place with just 7 tables but that's part of the charm. The 6 course menu features refined modern versions of French bistro classics. Service is charming and well-paced.

Menu £ 35 – set menu only

Town plan: DY-a – 37 Walmgate ⊠ YO1 9TX – ℰ (01904) 640 222 (booking essential) – www.lecochonaveugleyork.com – dinner only – Closed 3 weeks January and Sunday-Monday

X **Le Langhe**   🏵 🏡 ⇔

ⓐ ITALIAN · NEIGHBOURHOOD Well-established eatery consisting of an upmarket deli – selling imported Italian produce and a great array of wines – and a small dining room and terrace. They offer an extensive selection of fresh, unfussy Italian dishes and some well-priced fine wines. The formal upstairs dining room is open Fri and Sat.

Menu £ 25/39 – Carte £ 18/36

Town plan: DY-x – Peasholme Grn ⊠ YO1 7PW – ℰ (01904) 622 584 (booking advisable) – www.lelanghe.co.uk – lunch only and dinner Friday-Saturday – Closed first 2 weeks January, Easter Sunday, 25-27 December, Monday and Tuesday

ENGLAND

X **Blue Bicycle**

INTERNATIONAL · RUSTIC Characterful Mediterranean bistro overlooking the river, with a cosy bar and a spiral staircase leading down to intimate booths. It has a buzzy atmosphere and an almost burlesque feel. Menus offer modern classics. Smart, studio-style bedrooms are in a mews and breakfast ingredients are provided in the kitchen.

Carte £ 31/47

6 rooms ⌂ – †£175 ††£175

Town plan: DY-e – *34 Fossgate ✉ YO1 9TA – ℰ (01904) 673 990 (booking essential) – www.thebluebicycle.com – dinner only and lunch Thursday-Sunday and December – Closed 24-27 December, 1-6 January and lunch 28 December*

at Newton-on-Ouse Northwest: 8 mi by A19 – Plan: AY

🍴 **Dawnay Arms**

BRITISH MODERN · PUB A handsome pub with stone floors, low beams, open fires and all manner of bric-a-brac; its delightful dining room has views over the terrace and garden to the river. Gutsy, well executed, British-inspired dishes, with plenty of local game.

Menu £ 16 (weekday lunch) – Carte £ 24/49

✉ *YO30 2BR – ℰ (01347) 848 345 – www.thedawnayatnewton.co.uk – Closed 1 January, Sunday dinner and Monday except bank holidays*

ZENNOR

Cornwall – Regional map n° **1**-A3

▶ London 289 mi – Camborne 17 mi – Saint Austell 45 mi – Falmouth 33 mi

🍴 **Gurnard's Head**

REGIONAL · INN Remotely located, dog-friendly pub, with stone floors, shabby-chic décor, blazing fires and a relaxed, cosy feel. Menus rely on regional and foraged produce, and the wine list offers some interesting choices by the glass. Good value set lunch. Compact bedrooms feature good quality linen and colourful throws.

Menu £ 19 (weekday lunch) – Carte £ 26/32

7 rooms ⌂ – †£ 88/133 ††£ 103/175

Treen ✉ TR26 3DE – West : 1.5 mi on B 3306 – ℰ (01736) 796 928 (booking advisable) – www.gurnardshead.co.uk – Closed 24-25 December and 4 days early December

SCOTLAND

Scotland may be small, but its variety is immense.
The vivacity of Glasgow can seem a thousand miles from
the vast peatland wilderness of Caithness; the arty vibe
of Georgian Edinburgh a world away from the remote and
tranquil Ardnamurchan peninsula. Wide golden sands
trim the Atlantic at South Harris, and the coastline of the
Highlands boasts empty islands and turquoise waters.
Meantime, Fife's coast draws golf fans to St Andrews and
the more secretive delights of East Neuk, an area
of fishing villages and stone harbours. Wherever you travel,
a sense of a dramatic history prevails in the shape
of castles, cathedrals and rugged lochside monuments to
the heroes of old.

Food and drink embraces the traditional too, typified by
Speyside's famous Malt Whisky Trail. And what better
than Highland game, fresh fish from the Tweed or haggis,
neeps and tatties to complement a grand Scottish hike?
The country's glorious natural larder yields such jewels
as Spring lamb from the Borders, Perthshire venison,
fresh fish and shellfish from the Western Highlands and
Aberdeen Angus beef.

- Michelin Road map n° 501,
  502 and 713
- Michelin Green Guide:
  Great Britain

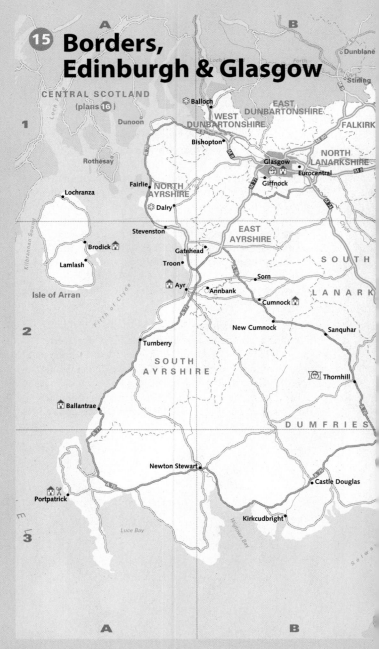

Borders, Edinburgh & Glasgow

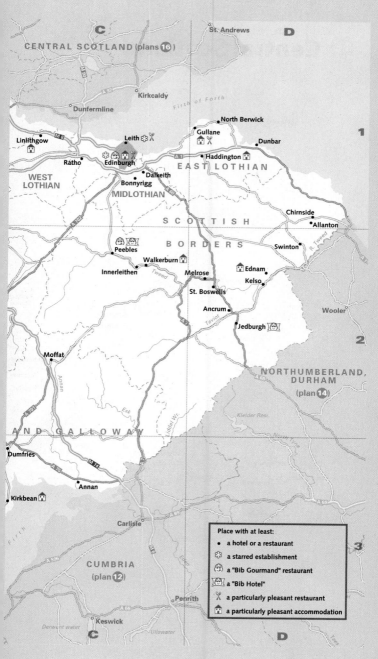

16 Central Scotland

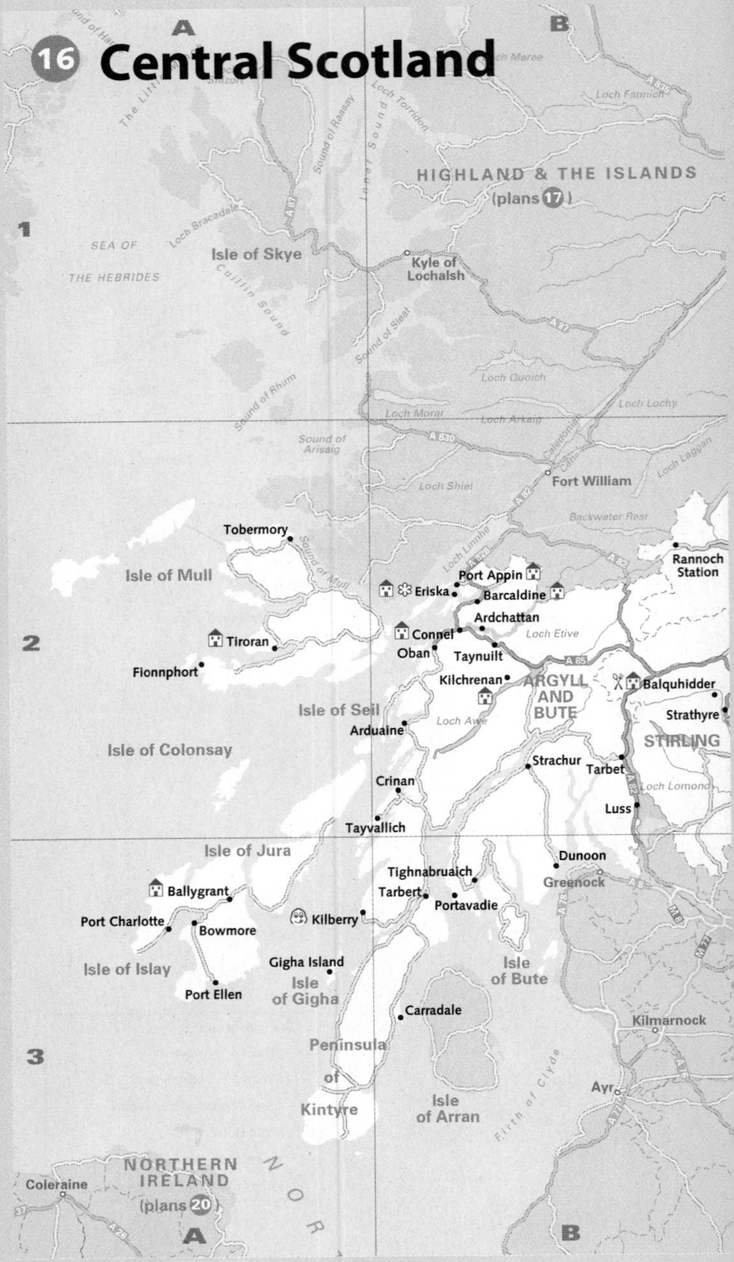

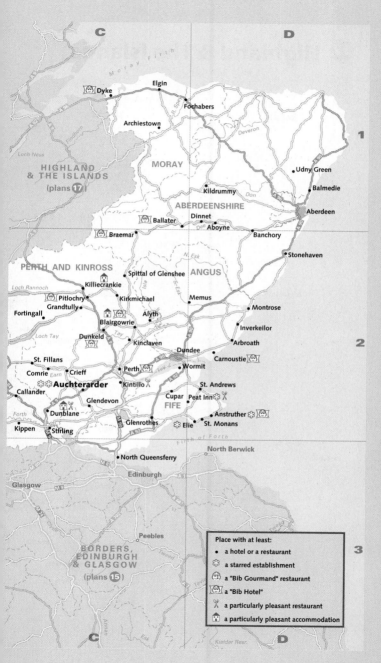

Galson

Back

Isle of Lewis
and Harris

Uig

Stornoway

1

*Isle of Lewis
and Harris*

THE MINCH

West Loch Tarbert

OUTER HEBRIDES

WESTERN ISLES

Ardhasaig

Tarbert

Scarista

Borve

Scalpay

Gruinard
Bay

Sound of Harris

Poolewe

Loch

Isles of Uist

Flodigarry

Loch Torridon

Loch Snizort

Waternish

Bernisdale

Torridon

Colbost

Edinbane

Shieldaig

2

Isles of Uist

Dunvegan

Struan

Portree

Applecross

Sound of Monach

Sound of Barra

The Little Minch

Sound of Raasay

Inner Sound

Plockton

SEA OF
THE HEBRIDES

Loch Bracadale

Isle of Skye

Broadford

Sleat

Ratagan

Cuillin Sound

Elgol

Duisdalemore

Teangue

Sound of Sleat

North Bay

Castlebay

Isle of Barra

INNER HEBRIDES

Arisaig

Loch Morar

Glenfinnan

A 830

Sound of Rhum

Sound of
Arisaig

Loch Shiel

Loch

Onich

3

Strontian

Duror

Kingairloch

Lochaline

*Isle
of Mull*

Loch Linnhe

Oban

A

B

Firth of Lorn

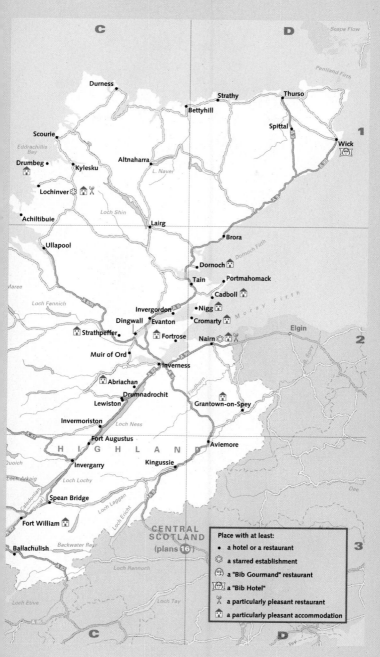

Place with at least:

● a hotel or a restaurant

✿ a starred establishment

🏠 a "Bib Gourmand" restaurant

🏨 a "Bib Hotel"

X a particularly pleasant restaurant

🏠 a particularly pleasant accommodation

Shetland & Orkney 18

1   **1**

Unst

Yell

St. Magnus Bay

Muckle
Roe

Papa Stour   Whalsay

Mainland

Veensgarth   Bressay

Foula   **Lerwick**

SHETLAND
ISLANDS

2   **2**

Westray *The North* North Ronaldsay
Pierowall • *Sound*

Westray Firth

      Sanday

    Eday
Mainland **Dounby** Stronsay
 🏠 **Harray** *Stronsay Firth*

      Shapinsay
Stromness **Kirkwall** • ORKNEY
   Scapa Flow ISLANDS
Hoy   •**Deerness** 🏠
St Margaret's Hope • •**Burray**
    South Ronaldsay

Pentland Firth

3 Thurso   **3**

    Wick

HIGHLAND
& THE ISLANDS
(plans 17)

Place with at least:

•	a hotel or a restaurant
🏵	a starred establishment
🏠	a "Bib Gourmand" restaurant
🏠	a "Bib Hotel"
✗	a particularly pleasant restaurant
🏠	a particularly pleasant accommodation

A   B

FOOD NOT TO BE MISSED

STARRED RESTAURANTS

© *Michelin*

OUR TOP PICKS

BIB GOURMANDS 😊
Good quality, good value cooking

A SENSE OF GOLFING HISTORY

CHARMING GUESTHOUSES

KNOWN FOR THEIR WELCOME

SOMETHING A LITTLE DIFFERENT

© Michelin

© *Michelin*

HIDEAWAYS

ABERDEEN

Aberdeen City – Pop. 195 021 – Regional map n° **16**-D1

▶ Edinburgh 126 mi – London 528 mi – Dundee 65 mi – Dunfermline 112 mi

Marcliffe H. and Spa ⓝ

BUSINESS · PERSONALISED Modern country house in 11 acres of mature grounds. Spacious, individually designed bedrooms are comfortable and well-equipped; meeting rooms have the latest facilities. The cosy bar offers an amazing array of malt whiskies and the dining room serves a traditional menu, with mature Scottish steaks a feature.

42 rooms ⊆ – ♦£ 170/220 ♦♦£ 170/220 – 2 suites

Town plan: X-r – *North Deeside Rd* ⊠ *AB15 9YA* – ℰ *(01224) 861 000*
– *www.marcliffe.com*

The Chester

TOWNHOUSE · STYLISH This smart boutique townhouse fits perfectly in this wealthy residential area. Sleek, contemporary bedrooms come with the latest mod cons (including Apple TV), and show a keen eye for detail. The cocktail bar and restaurant are set over three levels; seafood and grills from the Josper oven are a highlight.

54 rooms ⊆ – ♦£ 165/195 ♦♦£ 185/215 – 2 suites

Town plan: X-v – *59-63 Queens Rd* ⊠ *AB15 4YP* – ℰ *(01224) 327 777*
– *www.chester-hotel.com*

Malmaison

BUSINESS · DESIGN In a smart city suburb and built around a period property; now the height of urban chic. Black, slate-floored reception adorned with bagpipes and kilts; stylish bar with a whisky cellar. Funky, modern bedrooms have atmospheric lighting. High-ceilinged brasserie serves modern dishes, with steaks a speciality.

79 rooms ⊆ – ♦£ 79/259 ♦♦♦£ 99/279

Town plan: X-e – *49-53 Queens Rd* ⊠ *AB15 4YP* – ℰ *(01224) 327 370*
– *www.malmaison.com*

bauhaus

BUSINESS · MINIMALIST Modern hotel just off the main street, its functional, minimalist style in keeping with the Bauhaus school of design. Trendy lounge; stylish, colour-coded bedrooms with sharp, clean lines and uncluttered feel – 'Gropius' and 'Kandinsky' are the best. First-floor restaurant offers a menu of modern classics.

39 rooms ⊆ – ♦£ 65/115 ♦♦£ 85/210 – 1 suite

Town plan: Z-r – *52-60 Langstane Pl.* ⊠ *AB11 6EN* – ℰ *(01224) 212 122*
– *www.thebauhaus.co.uk*

Atholl

TOWNHOUSE · CLASSIC Extended baronial-style hotel in a leafy suburb: a good choice for the business traveller. Warm and friendly, with an up-to-date interior. Bedrooms are well-kept and bright; those on the top floor are the largest and some have cityscape views. Comfortable dining room serves tried-and-tested Scottish classics.

34 rooms ⊆ – ♦£ 70/120 ♦♦£ 100/170

Town plan: X-s – *54 King's Gate* ⊠ *AB15 4YN* – ℰ *(01224) 323 505*
– *www.atholl-aberdeen.co.uk* – *Closed 1 January*

XX Fusion

MODERN CUISINE · FASHIONABLE Modernised granite townhouse featuring an airy bar with lime green furniture and a more intimate mezzanine restaurant. Choose between a concise set menu & a 5 course tasting selection.

Menu £ 30

Town plan: Z-c – *10 North Silver St* ⊠ *AB10 1RL* – ℰ *(01224) 652 959*
– *www.fusionbarbistro.com* – *(dinner only and Saturday lunch)*
– *Closed 1-5 January, Sunday and Monday*

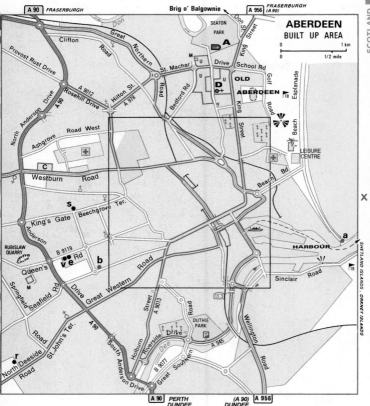

ABERDEEN
BUILT UP AREA

XX **Silver Darling** ⇐ ⇔

FISH AND SEAFOOD · FRIENDLY Attractively set at the port entrance, on the top floor of the castellated former customs house. Floor to ceiling windows make the most of the superb view. Neatly presented, classical dishes; excellent quality seafood is a highlight.

Menu £ 20 (weekday lunch)
– Carte £ 33/68

Town plan: X-a – Pocra Quay, North Pier ⊠ AB11 5DQ
– ✆ (01224) 576 229 – www.thesilverdarling.co.uk
– Closed 2 weeks Christmas-New Year, Saturday lunch and Sunday

X **Rock & Oyster**

FISH AND SEAFOOD · NEIGHBOURHOOD Simple, modern seafood restaurant with seascapes on the walls and chatty, genuine service. Flavoursome cooking mixes the modern and the classic – the lunch-cum-pre-theatre menu is good value. All wines are available by the glass.

Menu £ 24 (lunch) – Carte £ 33/50

Town plan: Z-s – 27-29 Union Ter ⊠ AB10 1NN
– ✆ (01224) 622 555 – www.rock-oyster.com
– Closed Sunday and Monday

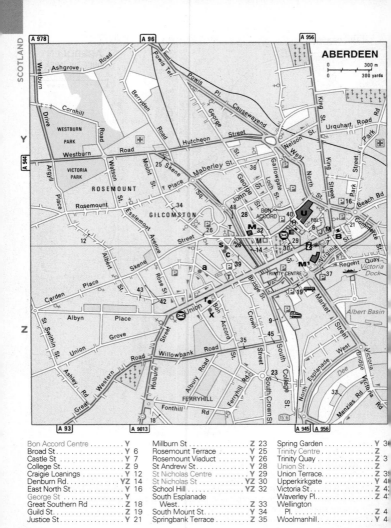

ABERDEEN

0   300 m
0   300 yards

✗ Rendezvous at Nargile

⌂ AC 📶

TURKISH · NEIGHBOURHOOD Bright neighbourhood restaurant run by a cheerful team. All-day menus are great for sharing. Well-spiced dishes have Middle Eastern flavours – particularly Turkish; the meze and banquet meals are a highlight and the baklava are homemade.

Menu £ 16 (early dinner) – Carte £ 26/37

Town plan: X-b – *106-108 Forest Ave* ✉ *AB15 4UP*
– ℰ *(01224) 323 700* – *www.rendezvousatnargile.co.uk*
– *Closed 25-26 December and 1-2 January*

✗ Yatai   🖐 AC 🎏

JAPANESE · SIMPLE Atmospheric Japanese restaurant in the style of a laid-back izakaya. The ground floor has a wooden counter and a robata grill; upstairs is airy and intimate. Menus offer tasty, authentic dishes – the sushi, sashimi and maki are highlights.

Carte £ 20/49

Town plan: Z-x – *53 Langstane Pl* ⊠ *AB11 6EN* – 𝒞 *(01224) 592 355 (booking advisable)* – *www.yatai.co.uk* – *Closed 25 December-5 January and Monday*

✗ Yorokobi by CJ   AC

JAPANESE · INTIMATE Popular Japanese restaurant with a name meaning 'joyous bliss'; C is for chef and J is for Jang, who takes on that role. Flavourful, authentic, good value Japanese and Korean dishes; try one of the sizzling platters or a Korean pot dish.

Carte £ 17/49

Town plan: Z-a – *51 Huntly St* ⊠ *AB10 1TH* – 𝒞 *(01224) 566 002 (booking advisable)* – *www.yorokobibycj.co.uk* – *dinner only and lunch Friday-Saturday* – *Closed 2 weeks summer, 2 weeks Christmas-New Year, Sunday and Monday*

ABOYNE

Aberdeenshire – Pop. 2 602 – Regional map n° **16**-D1
▶ Edinburgh 131 mi – Aberdeen 30 mi – Dundee 68 mi

🍴 Boat Inn

TRADITIONAL CUISINE · FRIENDLY Concise menu of traditional bar meals with the occasional international dish; portions are generous and there are freshly baked cakes for sale on the counter. Bright front room; cosy back bar and a smart private dining room called the Pine Loft. Spacious bedrooms come with their own kitchenettes.

Menu £ 10 (weekday lunch) – Carte £ 18/31

8 rooms ⊑ – ♦£ 75/110 ♦♦£ 85/135

Charleston Rd ⊠ *AB34 5EL* – 𝒞 *(01339) 886 137* – *www.theboatinnaboyne.co.uk* – *Closed 25 December and 1-2 January*

ABRIACHAN

Highland – Pop. 120 – Regional map n° **17**-C2
▶ Edinburgh 167 mi – London 567 mi – Dundee 148 mi – Dunfermline 153 mi

🏠 Loch Ness Lodge

LUXURY · STYLISH Passionately run modern country house, set in 18 acres of immaculately kept grounds overlooking Loch Ness. A classic-contemporary style features throughout. Spacious bedrooms have a high level of facilities and come with extras such as sherry and Penhaligon toiletries. Afternoon tea is served on arrival.

7 rooms ⊑ – ♦£ 90/260 ♦♦£ 165/330

Brachla ⊠ *IV3 8LA* – on A 82 – 𝒞 *(01456) 459 469* – *www.loch-ness-lodge.com* – *Closed November-March*

ACHILTIBUIE

Highland – Regional map n° **17**-C1
▶ Edinburgh 243 mi – Inverness 84 mi – Ullapool 25 mi

🏠 Summer Isles

FAMILY · HOMELY Remotely located hotel with magnificent views over the eponymous islands. Bedrooms are split between the main house and various outbuildings; the duplex 'Boat House' suite has a spiral staircase, and quirky 'Chaplin' comes with a cast-iron bath, a bowler hat and a cane! Modern menus include a 6 course 'Signature' selection, which best shows the kitchen's talents.

13 rooms ⊑ – ♦£ 79/170 ♦♦£ 99/190 – 3 suites

⊠ *IV26 2YG* – 𝒞 *(01854) 622 282* – *www.summerisleshotel.com* – *Closed November-March*

Summer Isles (Bar) – See restaurant listing

🍴 **Summer Isles (Bar)** 🛋 **P**

FISH AND SEAFOOD · PUB 19C former crofters' bar with two snug rooms, a large garden and a small terrace with glorious views. Concise, daily menus have a strong seafood base. Baguettes, salads and platters are replaced by blackboard specials in the evening.

Carte £ 23/47

Summer Isles Hotel, ⊠ IV26 2YG – 𝒞 (01854) 622 282
– www.summerisleshotel.com – Closed November-March

ALLANTON

The Scottish Borders – Regional map n° **15**-D1
▶ Edinburgh 52 mi – Dumfries 92 mi – Glasgow 98 mi

🍴 **Allanton Inn** ⓝ ⇦ 🛏

BRITISH MODERN · FRIENDLY Striking stone inn in a conservation village. It's warm and welcoming, with a rustic bar, a cosy restaurant and bright, simply furnished bedrooms. Thoughtfully prepared modern dishes are crafted from local farm meats and Eyemouth fish. The regional cheeses are a hit, as is the pretty garden with country views.

Carte £ 22/38

6 rooms ⌕ – ♦£ 70/85 ♦♦£ 75/95
⊠ TD11 3JZ – 𝒞 (01890) 818 260 – www.allantoninn.co.uk

ALTNAHARRA

Highland – ⊠ Lairg – Regional map n° **17**-C1
▶ Edinburgh 223 mi – London 627 mi – Inverness 68 mi

🏠 **Altnaharra** 🕊 🐾 ⇐ 🛋 **P**

COUNTRY HOUSE · COSY Remotely situated, extended drovers' inn dating back to the 1600s. The interior is homely and bedrooms are of a good size, with tartan décor. The small locals bar serves soup and sandwiches at lunch and the open-fired restaurant offers a classical menu at dinner. The nearby estate offers fishing and stalking.

14 rooms ⌕ – ♦£ 65/85 ♦♦£ 99/150
⊠ IV27 4UE – 𝒞 (01549) 411 222 – www.altnaharra.com – Closed
November-January

ALYTH

Perth and Kinross – Pop. 2 403 – Regional map n° **16**-C2
▶ Edinburgh 63 mi – Aberdeen 69 mi – Dundee 16 mi – Perth 21 mi

🏠 **Tigh Na Leigh** 🕊 🛏 **P**

LUXURY · MODERN An imposing Victorian house run in a relaxed yet professional manner. The interior is surprisingly modern – guest areas are inviting and contemporary bedrooms boast feature beds and great bathrooms with spa baths. The kitchen garden informs the unfussy modern menu; enjoy the lovely garden view while dining.

5 rooms ⌕ – ♦£ 58/81 ♦♦£ 108/130
22-24 Airlie St ⊠ PH11 8AJ – 𝒞 (01828) 632 372 – www.tighnaleigh.co.uk
– Closed 2 December-1 March

ANCRUM

The Scottish Borders – Regional map n° **15**-D2
▶ Edinburgh 44 mi – Glasgow 87 mi – Carlisle 55 mi – Perth 92 mi

🍴 **Ancrum Cross Keys** 🛏 🛋 ⅙

BRITISH MODERN · PUB What sets this place apart is the food – this is not everyday pub grub but carefully crafted, tasty cooking with a refined edge. Sit in the larger of the dining rooms to watch the chef at work. Local ales and locals in the rustic bar.

Carte £ 23/37

The Green ⊠ TD8 6XH – 𝒞 (01835) 830 242 – www.ancrumcrosskeys.com
– Closed Monday, Tuesday and lunch Wednesday

ANNAN

Dumfries and Galloway – Pop. 8 960 – Regional map n° **15**-C3

▶ Edinburgh 79 mi – London 321 mi – Glasgow 84 mi – Liverpool 141 mi

XX Del Amitri   AC

MODERN CUISINE · ELEGANT Above a fish and chip shop on the main street. Dark walls provide an intimate feel and tables are elegantly laid. Interesting, intricate dishes are skilfully prepared and packed with local produce: the chef has close ties with his suppliers.

Carte £ 24/34

95a High St ✉ DG12 6DJ – 𝒞 (01461) 201 999 – www.del-amitri.co.uk – dinner only and Sunday lunch – Closed 2-12 November, 1-10 January, Sunday dinner and Monday

ANNBANK

South Ayrshire – Pop. 912 – Regional map n° **15**-B2

▶ Edinburgh 84 mi – Ayr 6 mi – Glasgow 36 mi

🏠 Enterkine House   ✿ 🐾 ≼ 🛏 🍴 🎿 🄿

HISTORIC · CLASSIC Country house surrounded by 350 acres of countryside; originally built for the MacKay family in the 1930s and now a popular wedding venue. Spacious, individually furnished bedrooms; most with estate views. The Bothy is a honeymooners' cottage in the garden. Bright restaurant serves modern dishes.

14 rooms ☲ – †£ 45/95 ††£ 95/150 – 1 suite

✉ KA6 5AL – Southeast : 0.5 mi on B 742 (Coylton rd) – 𝒞 (01292) 520 580 – www.enterkine.com

ANSTRUTHER

Fife – Pop. 3 446 – Regional map n° **16**-D2

▶ Edinburgh 46 mi – Dundee 23 mi – Glasgow 77 mi

🏠 Spindrift   ✿ 🐾 🄿

TRADITIONAL · COSY A detached Victorian house on the edge of the village, originally owned by a tea clipper captain. The comfy lounge features an honesty bar. Some of the cosy, individually furnished bedrooms have distant sea views; the wood-panelled Captain's Cabin on the top floor is the most characterful. Cooking relies on local produce, with seafood from East Neuk to the fore.

8 rooms ☲ – †£ 45/65 ††£ 66/100

Pittenweem Rd ✉ KY10 3DT – 𝒞 (01333) 310 573 – www.thespindrift.co.uk – Closed January and 24-26 December

XX The Cellar 🆕 (Billy Boyter)

❀ **MODERN CUISINE · RUSTIC** Previously a smokehouse and a cooperage – now an iconic restaurant with exposed beams, stone walls and a cosy, characterful feel; pleasingly run by a local lad. Delicious, deftly prepared dishes are light, well-balanced and have subtle modern influences. Service is friendly and the atmosphere is relaxed.

➜ Scallops with chicken wing, cauliflower and curry oil. Hogget with anchovy & parsley gnocchi, cockles and cabbage. Valrhona chocolate crémeux, banana, pecan and lime.

Menu £ 25/43

24 East Green ✉ KY10 3AA – 𝒞 (01333) 310 378 (booking essential) – www.thecellaranstruther.co.uk – Closed Closed January-1st week February, last week September, 25-26 December, Wednesday February-March and Sunday-Wednesday lunch

APPLECROSS

Highland – Regional map n° **17**-B2

▶ Edinburgh 233 mi – Inverness 80 mi – Fort William 104 mi

✗ Applecross Walled Garden 🍴 🏠 ♿ 🅿

TRADITIONAL CUISINE · FRIENDLY Set in a former potting shed in a 17C walled garden – where much of the produce is grown. A small counter displays home-made cakes. Light lunches are followed by more original dishes with clearly defined natural flavours at dinner.

Carte £ 19/38

✉ IV54 8ND – North : 0.5 mi – 𝒞 (01520) 744 440 – www.applecrossgarden.co.uk – Closed November-February

🛏 Applecross Inn ⟵ ≼ 🍴 🏠 ♿ 🅿

FISH AND SEAFOOD · INN Unpretentious inn with friendly service and a bustling atmosphere; take the scenic route over the hair-raising, single-track Bealach na Ba, with its stunning views and hairpin bends to reach it. Dine on the freshest of seafood, often caught within sight of the door. Simple bedrooms have marvellous sea views.

Carte £ 20/35

7 rooms 🖵 – †£ 80/85 ††£ 120/130

Shore St ✉ IV54 8LR – 𝒞 (01520) 744 262 (booking essential) – www.applecross.uk.com – Closed 25 December and 1 January

ARBROATH

Angus – Pop. 23 902 – Regional map n° **16**-D2
▶ Edinburgh 72 mi – Dundee 17 mi – Montrose 12 mi

🏨 Old Vicarage 🍴 ⚘ 🅿 🚭

TRADITIONAL · PERSONALISED Detached 19C house with curios and antiques filling every room – look out for the lovely grandfather clock. Immaculately kept bedrooms have a Victorian feel; some have abbey views. Glorious buffet breakfasts include smokies from the quay.

3 rooms 🖵 – †£ 65/75 ††£ 85/90

2 Seaton Rd ✉ DD11 5DX – Northeast : 0.75 mi by A 92 and Hayshead Rd – 𝒞 (01241) 430 475 – www.theoldvicaragebandb.co.uk

ARCHIESTOWN

Moray – Regional map n° **16**-C1
▶ Edinburgh 194 mi – Aberdeen 62 mi – Inverness 49 mi

🏠 Archiestown ⚘ 🍴 🔌 🏠 ⚘ 🅿

TRADITIONAL · CLASSIC Welcoming hotel overlooking the square in a planned Victorian village; ideal for fishermen and visitors to the Whisky Trail. Spacious, comfy sitting rooms with open fires. Classical bedrooms; many have country views. Intimate restaurant with a feature wall serves a traditional menu with Scottish touches.

11 rooms 🖵 – †£ 75/100 ††£ 180/200

The Square ✉ AB38 7QL – 𝒞 (01340) 810 218 – www.archiestownhotel.co.uk – Closed 2 January-10 February and 23-29 December

ARDCHATTAN

Argyll and Bute – Regional map n° **16**-B2
▶ Edinburgh 123 mi – London 494 mi – Glasgow 98 mi – Belfast 146 mi

🏨 Blarcreen House ⚘ 🐾 ≼ 🍴 ⚘ 🅿

RURAL · HOMELY Friendly Victorian former farmhouse set in a tranquil location down a single track and boasting superb views over Loch Etive. Homely lounge and comfy bedrooms: two with four-posters and double-aspects; all with robes, fridges and fresh milk. Lovely dining room offers a daily menu of home-cooked dishes.

3 rooms 🖵 – †£ 90/110 ††£ 110/130

✉ PA37 1RG – East : 1 mi past Ardchattan Priory and gardens on Bonawe rd – 𝒞 (01631) 750 272 – www.blarcreenhouse.com – Closed Christmas and New Year

ARDHASAIG – Western Isles → See Lewis and Harris (Isle of)

ARDUAINE

Argyll and Bute – ⊠ Oban – Regional map n° **16**-B2

▶ Edinburgh 141 mi – Glasgow 105 mi – Paisley 98 mi – Greenock 105 mi

🏰 Loch Melfort   ✿ ⅏ ⋞ ⌂ 🅿

TRADITIONAL · CLASSIC Large hotel next to the beautiful Arduaine Gardens, affording superb views out over the bay and Sound of Jura. Modern lounges with tartan/nautical themes. Bigger bedrooms in the main house; great outlook from private terraces in the wing. Simple, largely seafood menu in Chartroom II; more formal Asknish Bay.

25 rooms ☑ – †£105/176 ††£150/272

⊠ PA34 4XG – ℰ (01852) 200 233 – www.lochmelfort.co.uk
– Closed December-January except Christmas-New Year and mid-week November-March

Asknish Bay – See restaurant listing

XX Asknish Bay   ⋞ ⌂ 🅿

FISH AND SEAFOOD · FORMAL Formal hotel restaurant in a beautiful setting, with panoramic views of the bay. Menus focus on the freshest seafood available, with Loch Fyne langoustines, Islay scallops and Gigha halibut; carnivores are also well-catered for.

Menu £ 40 – Carte £ 34/49

Loch Melfort Hotel, ⊠ PA34 4XG – ℰ (01852) 200 233 – www.lochmelfort.co.uk
– dinner only – Closed December-January except Christmas-New Year and mid-week November-March

ARISAIG

Highland – Regional map n° **17**-B3

▶ Edinburgh 178 mi – Fort William 36 mi – Oban 80 mi

🏰 Arisaig House 🆕   ✿ ⅏ ⋞ ⌂ ✕ 🅿

COUNTRY HOUSE · PERSONALISED Attractive Victorian country house surrounded by mature grounds which lead down to the sea. Bedrooms retain their traditional feel and the building's original features are enhanced by a fine collection of artwork. Classic menus use ingredients from the kitchen garden, nearby estates and local waters.

14 rooms ☑ – †£85/125 ††£160/225

Beasdale ⊠ PH39 4NR – East : 2.5 mi by A 830 – ℰ (01687) 450 730
– www.arisaighouse.co.uk – Closed November-April

ARRAN (Isle of)

North Ayrshire – Pop. 4 629 – Regional map n° **15**-A2

▶ Edinburgh 83 mi – London 414 mi – Glasgow 37 mi – Liverpool 234 mi

Brodick

🏨 Auchrannie   ✿ ⌂ 🖃 ⊕ 🏊 ♨ 🎱 ♿ 🕱 ⚲ 🅿

TRADITIONAL · CLASSIC Mini resort hotel set in 96 acres and offering a good range of family orientated leisure facilities. Built in 1869, the old dower house boasts well-equipped, classical and contemporary bedrooms; family rooms are located in the resort house. Smart conservatory restaurant offers fine dining menu; Brambles serves seafood and grills; all-day Cruize is ideal for families.

64 rooms ☑ – †£60/149 ††£89/169 – 2 suites

⊠ KA27 8BZ – Northwest : 0.75 mi by Shore Rd. – ℰ (01770) 302 234
– www.auchrannie.co.uk

🏠 Kilmichael Country House ☆ 🐾 ← 🚗 P

COUNTRY HOUSE · CLASSIC Sympathetically restored 17C house – reputedly the oldest house on the Isle of Arran – delightfully located in a peaceful glen and surrounded by mountains. Comfy, antique-furnished bedrooms; those in the converted stable block offer a little more comfort and privacy. Four course set menu of accomplished cooking served in the classically decorated dining room.

8 rooms ☲ – ∮£ 75/98 ∮∮£ 163/205
Glen Cloy ⊠ KA27 8BY – West : 1 mi by Shore Rd, taking left turn opposite Golf Club – ℰ (01770) 302 219 – www.kilmichael.com
– Closed November-Easter

🏠 Douglas ☆ ← 🚗 🖬 ❹ �, P

TOWNHOUSE · STYLISH Stylish, modern hotel with attractive pink granite façade, set just past the ferry terminal. Spacious, light-filled bedrooms are decorated in a contemporary style; most have a sea view and room 202 has a large roof terrace. Informal, pubby bar. Smart bistro offers classical French dishes with a modern twist.

22 rooms ☲ – ∮£ 85/115 ∮∮£ 129/199
⊠ KA27 8AW – ℰ (01770) 302 968 – www.thedouglashotel.co.uk

Lamlash

🏠 Glenisle ☆ ← 🚗 🖬 �, P

TRADITIONAL · COSY Attractive whitewashed Victorian property, formerly an inn, boasting views over the bay to Holy Island. Open-plan bar-lounge and small snug. Bright, airy bedrooms come in natural hues; one covers the whole top floor and has a roll-top bath. Rustic dining room with terrace offers fresh, simple, homely cooking.

13 rooms ☲ – ∮£ 90/94 ∮∮£ 124/215
Shore Rd. ⊠ KA27 8LY – ℰ (01770) 600 559 – www.glenislehotel.com

Lochranza

🏠 Apple Lodge ☆ ← 🚗 �, P 🛏

TRADITIONAL · CLASSIC Former manse with attractive gardens, in a quiet hamlet surrounded by mountains. Traditionally decorated, comfortable and personally run, with many regular guests. Bedrooms have pleasant views; Apple Cottage is a self-contained garden suite. 3 course menu of classic, home-cooked dishes served by candlelight.

4 rooms ☲ – ∮£ 50 ∮∮£ 78/90
⊠ KA27 8HJ – ℰ (01770) 830 229 – www.applelodgearran.co.uk
– Closed 15 December-15 January

AUCHTERARDER

Perth and Kinross – Pop. 4 206 – Regional map n° **16**-C2
▶ Edinburgh 55 mi – London 438 mi – Aberdeen 102 mi – Glasgow 46 mi

🏨 Gleneagles ☆ ← 🚗 🝔 🖬 🗔 ❹ 🎠 🐾 ✕ ❹ �, ⚶ 🖳 P

GRAND LUXURY · ART DECO World-famous resort hotel with a renowned championship golf course, majestic art deco styling, an elegant interior and luxurious bedrooms. Excellent leisure facilities include a state-of-the-art spa, a popular equestrian centre and a gun-dog school. Strathearn offers a classical menu and superb estate views. All-day Deseo serves Mediterranean-influenced dishes and tapas.

232 rooms ☲ – ∮£ 265/465 ∮∮£ 265/465 – 16 suites
⊠ PH3 1NF – Southwest : 2 mi by A 824 on A 823 – ℰ (01764) 662 231
– www.gleneagles.com
❀❀ **Andrew Fairlie at Gleneagles** – See restaurant listing

⌂ Cairn

✿ ⌂ ⚙ ♨ P

COUNTRY HOUSE · DESIGN Glitzy lodge with pleasant gardens and a monochrome theme. There's a piano in the hall and an elegant bar with white tub chairs. Stylish modern bedrooms feature black ash furnishings and coffee machines. The chic restaurant has studded leather walls, twisty chandeliers and sumptuous leather seating.

14 rooms ☐ – ♦£ 69/205 ♦♦£ 99/255

Orchill Rd ⊠ PH3 1LX – West : 0.5 mi by Townhead Rd and Western Rd
– ☏ (01764) 662 634 – www.cairnlodge.co.uk

XxxX Andrew Fairlie at Gleneagles

& ⓀⒶ ⌂ P

❀❀ **FRENCH CREATIVE · LUXURY** Elegant restaurant hung with portraits of its famous chef. The à la carte focuses on refined French classics, with home-smoked lobster a signature dish, while the 8 course dégustation menu showcases their top picks 'en miniature'. Much of the produce is from their walled garden. Accomplished, carefully balanced cooking is coupled with professional, good-humoured service.

➜ Home-smoked lobster, lime and herb butter. Roast loin of roe deer with pearl barley risotto, smoked venison bon bon and port jus. Milk chocolate mousse, dark chocolate crémeux and lime sorbet.

Menu £ 95/125

Gleneagles Hotel, ⊠ PH3 1NF – Southwest : 2 mi by A 824 on A 823 – ☏ (01764)
694 267 – www.andrewfairlie.co.uk – dinner only – Closed 3-28 January,
25-26 December and Sunday

AVIEMORE

Highland – Pop. 3 147 – Regional map n° **17**-D3
◪ Edinburgh 129 mi – Inverness 29 mi – Perth 85 mi

⌂ Old Minister's Guest House

⌂ ⚙ P

TRADITIONAL · PERSONALISED A 19C stone-built manse with unusual carved wood animals out the front and pretty gardens leading down to the river. The smart lounge has deep sofas and an honesty bar and the stylish bedrooms are spacious and well-appointed.

5 rooms ☐ – ♦£ 105/120 ♦♦£ 115/145

Rothiemurchus ⊠ PH22 1QH – Southeast : 1 mi on B 970 – ☏ (01479) 812 181
– www.theoldministershouse.co.uk

AYR

South Ayrshire – Pop. 46 849 – Regional map n° **15**-A2
◪ Edinburgh 82 mi – London 395 mi – Glasgow 36 mi

⌂ Western House

✿ ⌂ 🖥 & ♨ P

LUXURY · STYLISH Attractive country house designed by Lutyens and set on the Ayr racecourse. Tastefully styled bedrooms are named after racecourses; those in the original house are the largest and most luxurious. Wood-panelled lounge-bar. Restaurant offers appealing menu of British classics based around Ayrshire ingredients.

49 rooms ☐ – ♦£ 80/190 ♦♦£ 80/190

Town plan: BZ-w *– Ayr Racecourse, Craigie Rd ⊠ KA8 0HA – ☏ (01292)*
294 990 – www.westernhousehotel.co.uk

⌂ No.26 The Crescent

⚙

TOWNHOUSE · PERSONALISED Well-run Victorian terraced house, displaying a pleasing mix of traditional features – such as original fireplaces – and smart, modern décor. Comfortable throughout, with individually furnished bedrooms; the best one has a four-poster. Cosy breakfast room; the smoked haddock with poached eggs is a speciality.

5 rooms ☐ – ♦£ 53/85 ♦♦£ 77/97

Town plan: BZ-c *– 26 Bellevue Cres ⊠ KA7 2DR – ☏ (01292) 287 329*
– www.26crescent.co.uk – Closed 22-26 December

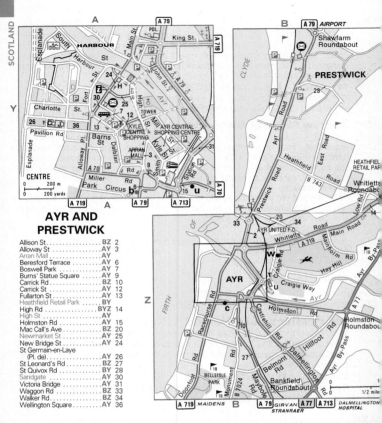

AYR AND PRESTWICK

Coila

TRADITIONAL · CLASSIC Comfortable, traditionally furnished Victorian house on the edge of town, proudly decorated with the owners' personal ornaments and family photos. Homely sitting room and well-kept bedrooms; those to the rear are quieter.

4 rooms ☑ – ♦£ 50/80 ♦♦£ 65/90

Town plan: AY-u – *10 Holmston Rd ⊠ KA7 3BB – ℰ (01292) 262 642 – www.coila.co.uk*

BACK – Western Isles → See Lewis and Harris (Isle of)

BALLACHULISH

Highland – Pop. 666 – Regional map n° **17**-C3

▶ Edinburgh 117 mi – Inverness 80 mi – Kyle of Lochalsh 90 mi – Oban 38 mi

Ardno House

TRADITIONAL · PERSONALISED Spotlessly kept modern guesthouse in an elevated position, with a fine view of Loch Linnhe and the Ardgour Hills. Spacious pine-furnished bedrooms are named after Scottish clans and tartans; those at the front have the best outlooks.

4 rooms ☑ – ♦£ 40/68 ♦♦£ 74/84

Lettermore, Glencoe ⊠ PH49 4JD – West : 3.5 mi by A 82 on A 828 – ℰ (01855) 811 830 – www.ardnohouse.co.uk – Closed November-February

BALLANTRAE

South Ayrshire – ✉ Girvan – Pop. 672 – Regional map n° **15**-A2
▶ Edinburgh 115 mi – Ayr 33 mi – Stranraer 18 mi

🏰🏰🏰 Glenapp Castle   🐦 🦆 ⤚ 🛏 🍴 ⚅ P

CASTLE · CLASSIC A long wooded drive leads to this stunning baronial castle with beautifully manicured gardens and Ailsa Craig views; it's personally run and the service is charming. The grand antique-filled interior has oak-panelled hallways, luxurious, impressively proportioned lounges and handsomely appointed bedrooms. The elegant dining room showcases local and garden ingredients.

17 rooms (dinner included) ⌧ – 🛉£ 280/460 🛉🛉£ 435/610 – 3 suites
✉ KA26 0NZ – South : 1 mi by A 77 taking first right turn after bridge – ☎ (01465) 831 212 – www.glenappcastle.com – Closed 3 January-25 March and 23-27 December

🏠 Cosses Country House   🐦 🦆 🛏 P

TRADITIONAL · COSY A 17C shooting lodge with lovely gardens, in an idyllic rural location. Immaculately kept bedrooms and suites – two in the old stables and byre – boast iPod docks, fresh flowers and underfloor heated bathrooms. Homemade cake is served on arrival in the kitchen, dining room or garden, and the 4 course, single-choice set dinners showcase local and garden produce.

3 rooms ⌧ – 🛉£ 85/130 🛉🛉£ 110/130
✉ KA26 0LR – East : 2.25 mi by A 77 (South) taking first turn left after bridge – ☎ (01465) 831 363 – www.cossescountryhouse.com – Restricted opening in winter

 Enjoy good food without spending a fortune! Look out for the Bib Gourmand 🐷 symbol to find restaurants offering good food at great prices!

BALLATER

Aberdeenshire – Pop. 1 533 – Regional map n° **16**-C1
▶ Edinburgh 111 mi – Aberdeen 41 mi – Inverness 70 mi – Perth 67 mi

🏠 Auld Kirk   P

HISTORIC · PERSONALISED Striking granite building – a church from 1870-1938; the bar-lounge still has the original stained glass windows. Bright, modern bedrooms with bold furnishings. Comprehensive breakfasts; the 'spirit of ecstasy' sculpture is a talking point!

7 rooms ⌧ – 🛉£ 70/105 🛉🛉£ 110/140
Braemar Rd ✉ AB35 5RQ – ☎ (013397) 55 762 – www.theauldkirk.com – Closed Christmas

🏠 Moorside House   🛏 ⚅ P

TRADITIONAL · CLASSIC Traditional 19C former manse with a large garden, simple, homely bedrooms and a comfortable lounge filled with books about the local area. Original Victorian features include ornate cornicing and an attractive pine staircase. Hearty breakfasts feature homemade bread, muffins, muesli and preserves.

9 rooms ⌧ – 🛉£ 50 🛉🛉£ 60/70
26 Braemar Rd ✉ AB35 5RL – ☎ (013397) 55 492 – www.moorsidehouse.co.uk – Closed October-Easter

BALLOCH

West Dunbartonshire – ✉ Alexandria – Regional map n° **15**-B1
▶ Edinburgh 72 mi – Glasgow 20 mi – Stirling 30 mi

SCOTLAND

815

🏨 Cameron House

SPA HOTEL · CONTEMPORARY An extensive Victorian house and lodges set in 250 acres on the shore of Loch Lomond. Excellent leisure facilities include a spa, a golf course, a launch and a seaplane. Bedrooms are modern and moody, aside from the Whisky Suites which are more traditional. There are several dining options, including the informal Claret Jug bar and masculine grill restaurant Camerons.

132 rooms ⊡ – ♦£129/400 ♦♦£129/400 – 12 suites
Loch Lomond ✉ G83 8QZ – Northwest : 1.5 mi by A 811 on A 82 – ℰ (01389) 755 565 – www.cameronhouse.co.uk

❀ **Martin Wishart at Loch Lomond • Boat House** – See restaurant listing

XxX Martin Wishart at Loch Lomond

❀ **MODERN CUISINE · FORMAL** Smart restaurant in a lochside resort hotel, offering superb water and mountain views. Seasonal modern menus showcase Scottish ingredients in well-judged, creative combinations. Cooking is accomplished and dishes are attractively presented. The tasting menus include a 6 course vegetarian option.

➜ Orkney scallops with beurre noisette, caramelised cauliflower and sea vegetables. Salt-baked Anjou pigeon with turnips, beetroot and mushroom purée. Lemon mousse and coconut parfait with Valrhona chocolate and lime.

Menu £32/75
Cameron House Hotel, Loch Lomond ✉ G83 8QZ – Northwest : 1.5 mi by A 811 on A 82 – ℰ (01389) 722 504 (booking essential) – www.mwlochlomond.co.uk – Closed 1-14 January, Monday, Tuesday and lunch Wednesday

XX Boat House

MEDITERRANEAN · BISTRO Relaxed, buzzy restaurant in the grounds of Cameron House. The décor has a New England feel and its doors open out onto a jetty; bag a spot on the terrace if you can. Unfussy Mediterranean dishes include fresh Loch Fyne seafood.

Carte £22/47
Cameron House Hotel, Loch Lomond ✉ G83 8QZ – Northwest : 1.5 mi by A 811 on A 82 – ℰ (01389) 722 585 – www.cameronhouse.co.uk

BALLYGRANT – Argyll and Bute ➜ See Islay (Isle of)

BALMEDIE

Aberdeenshire – Pop. 2 534 – Regional map n° **16**-D1
▶ Edinburgh 137 mi – Aberdeen 7 mi – Peterhead 24 mi

🏨 Trump International Golf Links Scotland 🅝

LUXURY · PERSONALISED Intimate hotel with a Championship links golf course, set on a 2,200 acre estate. The hotel is split between an 18C stone house and a lodge and features plush fabrics and opulent furnishings. Large bedrooms have arabesque furnishings and offer all you could want. The intimate restaurant serves a modern menu.

19 rooms – ♦£225/265 ♦♦£250/290
MacLeod House and Lodge, Menie Estate ✉ AB23 8YE – ℰ (01358) 743 300 – www.trumpgolfscotland.com – Closed 1-14 January

🍺 Cock and Bull

BRITISH TRADITIONAL · RUSTIC Quirky pub with a profusion of knick-knacks; dine in the cosy, open-fired lounge, the formal dining room or the airy conservatory. Menus offer a mix of pub classics and well-presented, restaurant style dishes. Some of the contemporary bedrooms are in a nearby annexe; there's a complimentary shuttle service.

Carte £21/36
4 rooms – ♦£90/120 ♦♦£90/120 – ⊡£10
Ellon Rd, Blairton ✉ AB23 8XY – North : 1 mi on A 90 – ℰ (01358) 743 249 – www.thecockandbull.co.uk

BALQUHIDDER

Stirling – Regional map n° **16**-B2

▶ Edinburgh 70 mi – Stirling 29 mi – Perth 42 mi

⌂ Monachyle Mhor ⚕ ⌘ ⪡ 🛏 & P

TRADITIONAL · PERSONALISED A former farmhouse, located in a beautiful, very remote glen. Contemporary furnishings blend with original features in the reception, lounge and cosy bar. Smart, modern bedrooms boast slate-tiled bathrooms with underfloor heating; those in the main house afford great views over the Braes of Balquhidder.

14 rooms ⌘ – 🛇£195/265 🛇🛇£195/265

✉ FK19 8PQ – West : 3.75 mi – ☎ (01877) 384 622 – www.mhor.net
– Closed 5-25 January

Monachyle Mhor – See restaurant listing

✗✗ Monachyle Mhor ⪡ 🛏 🏠 & P

MODERN CUISINE · **INDIVIDUAL** In the rurally set hotel of the same name is this candlelit conservatory restaurant with a warm, relaxing ambience and views of the glen. The set price menu features produce reared on the family farm and grown in the kitchen garden; cooking is modern and accomplished, with lots of natural flavours.

Menu £30/57

Monachyle Mhor Hotel, ✉ FK19 8PQ – West : 3.75 mi – ☎ (01877) 384 622
(booking essential) – www.mhor.net – Closed 5-25 January

✗ Mhor 84 ⪢ 🏠 & P

TRADITIONAL CUISINE · INDIVIDUAL Food is served all day, every day at this café-style restaurant, where shelves bursting with cakes and meringues from their bakery greet you. Fresh, regional ingredients feature in unfussy dishes; things step up a gear on the daily changing evening menu. Cosy, simply furnished bedrooms complete the picture.

Carte £16/36

7 rooms – 🛇£80 🛇🛇£80 – ⌘£9

Kingshouse ✉ FK19 8NY – East: 2 mi at junction with A 84 – ☎ (01877) 384 646
– www.mhor.net

BANCHORY

Aberdeenshire – Pop. 7 278 – Regional map n° **16**-D2

▶ Edinburgh 118 mi – Aberdeen 17 mi – Dundee 55 mi – Inverness 94 mi

⌂ Raemoir House ⚕ ⌘ ⪡ 🛏 🛁 P

COUNTRY HOUSE · CLASSIC Impressive Scottish country house in an idyllic rural spot. Original features include an intricately carved counter in the bar and pitch pine panelling in the drawing room. Classical bedrooms have been subtly modernised. Elegant dining room serves a daily menu of classically based dishes with a modern twist.

18 rooms ⌘ – 🛇£115 🛇🛇£165/305

✉ AB31 4ED – North : 2.5 mi by A 980 – ☎ (01330) 824 884 – www.raemoir.com

⌂ Tor-Na-Coille ⚕ 🛏 🖃 🛁 P

HISTORIC · PERSONALISED Well-run mansion dating from 1873 and surrounded by mature grounds. The décor blends the modern with the classic and original cornicing, fireplaces and staircases feature. Bedrooms boast stylish wallpapers and bright, bold furnishings. The intimate restaurant showcases Scottish produce in modern dishes.

25 rooms ⌘ – 🛇£100/115 🛇🛇£125/200

Inchmarlo Rd ✉ AB31 4AB – West : 0.5 mi on A 93 – ☎ (01330) 822 242
– www.tornacoille.com

✗ Cowshed   占 🅿

MODERN CUISINE · MINIMALIST Impressive modern building with a cavernous dining room and countryside views. Simple, good value lunches, followed by more ambitious evening menus; meat and game is from the surrounding estates. Cookery classes available.

Carte £ 21/46

Raemoir Rd ⊠ AB31 5QB – North : 1.5 mi on A 980 – 𝒞 (01330) 820 813 (booking advisable) – www.cowshedrestaurant.co.uk – Closed 1-7 January, Sunday dinner-Tuesday lunch

BARCALDINE

Argyll and Bute – Regional map n° **16**-B2

▶ Edinburgh 124 mi – London 495 mi – Glasgow 98 mi – Leeds 317 mi

🏠 Ardtorna   👒 ← 🖢 ⅋ 🅿

LUXURY · CONTEMPORARY Ultra-modern guesthouse in a stunning spot, with lovely views of the lochs and mountains, and amazing sunsets. Immaculate bedrooms have well-stocked fridges and plenty of space in which to relax; perhaps with a complimentary glass of Baileys or whisky. The charming owners offer archery lessons.

4 rooms ⊇ – †£ 99/180 ††£ 99/190

Mill Farm ⊠ PA37 1SE – Southwest : 1.5 mi on A 828 – 𝒞 (01631) 720 125 – www.ardtorna.co.uk

BARRA (Isle of)

Western Isles – ⊠ Castlebay – Regional map n° **17**-A3

▶ Edinburgh 126 mi – London 497 mi – Glasgow 101 mi – Liverpool 317 mi

Castlebay

🏠 Castlebay   🍴 ← 占 ⑩ 🅿

TRADITIONAL · FUNCTIONAL Homely hotel boasting excellent castle and island views – the hub of the island community. Bedrooms are a mix of styles: the newer rooms feature subtle tartan fabrics and 'MacNeil' has harbour views. There's a cosy lounge, a busy locals bar and a linen-clad dining room serving seafood specials.

15 rooms ⊇ – †£ 55/175 ††£ 85/185

⊠ HS9 5XD – 𝒞 (01871) 810 223 – www.castlebayhotel.com – Closed 21 December-6 January

🏠 Grianamul   ← 🖢 ⅋ 🅿

TRADITIONAL · COSY Pale yellow dormer bungalow at the heart of a small hamlet – a homely place run by caring owners. There's a comfortable lounge and sunny breakfast room where huge, satisfying breakfasts are served. Bedrooms are bright and spacious.

3 rooms ⊇ – †£ 45 ††£ 70

⊠ HS9 5XD – 𝒞 (01871) 810 416 – www.isleofbarraaccommodation.com – Closed October-March

North Bay

🏠 Heathbank   🍴 ← 🖢 🛋 ⅋ 🅿

TRADITIONAL · FUNCTIONAL Former Presbyterian Church, now a smart, modern, well-run hotel that's popular with locals and visitors alike. A bright, airy bar forms the hotel's hub and, along with the dining room, serves straightforward, local seafood orientated menus. Good-sized bedrooms are light, airy and up-to-date.

5 rooms ⊇ – †£ 67 ††£ 108

⊠ HS9 5YQ – 𝒞 (01871) 890 266 – www.barrahotel.co.uk – Closed November-March

BERNISDALE – Highland → See Skye (Isle of)

BETTYHILL

Highland – Regional map n° **17**-C1
▶ Edinburgh 246 mi - London 647 mi - Glasgow 260 mi

✗ Côte du Nord ⓟ ⊠

CREATIVE · INDIVIDUAL Intimate restaurant of just 3 tables; converted from an old school house by a local doctor-cum-self-taught-chef. Modern, innovative cooking; the 10-12 course menu features local and foraged ingredients and salt from reduced seawater.

Menu £ 39 – set menu only
The School House, Kirtomy ⊠ KW14 7TB – East : 4 mi by A 836
– ☎ (01641) 521 773 (booking essential) – www.cotedunord.co.uk – dinner only
– Closed October-March, Sunday-Tuesday and Thursday

BISHOPTON

Renfrewshire – Regional map n° **15**-B1
▶ Edinburgh 59 mi - Dumbarton 9 mi - Glasgow 13 mi

Mar Hall ⓟ

HISTORIC · STYLISH Impressive Gothic mansion – a former hospital – on the banks of the Clyde; popular for weddings and with good links to Glasgow city and the airport. Well-equipped spa and championship golf course. Spacious, contemporary bedrooms; 'Deluxe' have river views. Enjoy afternoon tea in the cavernous Grand Hall. Cristal offers a classic French menu; Italian fare in Il Posto.

53 rooms ⊇ – †£ 185/245 ††£ 185/245 – 10 suites
Earl of Mar Dr ⊠ PA7 5NW – Northeast : 1 mi on B 815
– ☎ (0141) 812 99 99 – www.marhall.com

BLAIRGOWRIE

Perth and Kinross – Pop. 8 954 – Regional map n° **16**-C2
▶ Edinburgh 60 mi - Dundee 19 mi - Perth 16 mi

Kinloch House ⓟ

FAMILY · PERSONALISED Imposing ivy-clad country house in a tranquil, elevated setting, with beautiful walled gardens to the rear and 25 acres of grounds. Smart oak-panelled hall and a vast array of welcoming guest areas complete with log fires and antiques. Classical bedrooms are well-appointed and immaculately maintained.

15 rooms ⊇ – †£ 150/180 ††£ 185/200 – 1 suite
⊠ PH10 6SG – West : 3 mi on A 923
– ☎ (01250) 884 237 – www.kinlochhouse.com
– Closed 12-29 December
Kinloch House – See restaurant listing

Gilmore House ⓟ

TRADITIONAL · COSY Proudly run, stone-built house with a pretty, flower-filled entrance. Antlers, deer heads and old lithographs fill the walls. The first floor lounge has a good outlook; complimentary sherry and whisky are left out for a traditional nightcap. Immaculately kept modern bedrooms and plentiful breakfasts.

3 rooms ⊇ – †£ 55 ††£ 75/85
Perth Rd ⊠ PH10 6EJ – Southwest : 0.5 mi on A 93
– ☎ (01250) 872 791 – www.gilmorehouse.co.uk

XXX **Kinloch House** ≤ 🖢 **P**

TRADITIONAL CUISINE · FORMAL Formal hotel dining room with twinkling chandeliers and smartly dressed tables. Start with drinks in the clubby bar or cosy, open-fired sitting room. The latest local, seasonal produce informs the daily menu – maybe West Coast crab or Perthshire venison. Dishes are well-crafted, traditional and flavoursome.

Menu £ 26/55

Kinloch House Hotel, ✉ PH10 6SG – West : 3 mi on A 923
– ℰ (01250) 884 237 – www.kinlochhouse.com
– Closed 12-29 December

🍴 **Dalmore Inn** 🖢 🛱 **P**

TRADITIONAL CUISINE · PUB Traditional-looking pub with a surprisingly stylish interior, where brightly coloured walls are juxtaposed with old stonework. Good value cooking is unfussy and full of flavour; everything is freshly prepared using Scottish produce.

Menu £ 10 (lunch)/20 – Carte £ 22/37

Perth Rd ✉ PH10 6QB – Southwest : 1.5 mi on A 93
– ℰ (01250) 871 088 – www.dalmoreinn.com
– Closed 25 December and 1-2 January

BONNYRIGG

Midlothian – Pop. 15 677 – Regional map n° **15**-C1
▶ Edinburgh 8 mi – Galashiels 27 mi – Glasgow 50 mi

🏰 **Dalhousie Castle** ⓝ 🎣 🦢 🖢 🐾 🏊 **P**

CASTLE · CLASSIC Stunning crenellated castle with 13C origins – the oldest inhabited castle in Scotland. Guest areas display many original features. The best bedrooms are themed and come with four-poster or canopied beds. Dine from a modern menu under a barrel-vaulted ceiling in atmospheric Dungeon or enjoy brasserie dishes in the Orangery while looking out over the extensive grounds.

36 rooms ☲ – **♥♥**£ 125/340 – 2 suites
✉ EH19 3JB – Southeast : 1.25 mi on B 704
– ℰ (01875) 820 153 – www.dalhousiecastle.co.uk

BORVE – Western Isles → See Lewis and Harris (Isle of)

BOWMORE – Argyll and Bute → See Islay (Isle of)

BRAEMAR

Aberdeenshire – Pop. 500 – Regional map n° **16**-C2
▶ Edinburgh 85 mi – Aberdeen 58 mi – Dundee 51 mi – Perth 51 mi

🏠 **Callater Lodge** 🖢 🕸 **P**

FAMILY · COSY A Victorian granite house on the village outskirts, with colourful, uplifting décor. Cosy up in an armchair by the fire then head past the old British Rail posters in the hallway to the immaculately kept bedrooms. Local wood features in the bright bathrooms and regional ingredients are used at breakfast.

6 rooms ☲ – **♥**£ 50 **♥♥**£ 85/90
9 Glenshee Rd ✉ AB35 5YQ
– ℰ (013397) 41 275 – www.callaterlodge.co.uk
– Closed 1 week Christmas

BROADFORD – Highland → See Skye (Isle of)

BRODICK – North Ayrshire → See Arran (Isle of)

BRORA

Highland – Pop. 1 282 – Regional map n° **17**-D2

▶ Edinburgh 234 mi – Inverness 78 mi – Wick 49 mi

🏠 Royal Marine

TRADITIONAL · COSY Cream-washed Arts and Crafts house, set next to a top golf course. Leather-furnished lounges and a wood-floored bar. Smart, modern, country house bedrooms with warm fabrics and a good level of facilities. Formal linen-laid restaurant offers traditional Scottish menus.

21 rooms 🖂 – 🛉£ 90/135 🛉🛉£ 110/220

Golf Rd ✉ *KW9 6QS*
– ☎ (01408) 621 252 – www.royalmarinebrora.com

BUNCHREW – Highland ➜ See Inverness

BURRAY – Orkney Islands ➜ See Orkney Islands (Mainland)

CADBOLL – Highland ➜ See Tain

CALLANDER

Stirling – Pop. 3 077 – Regional map n° **16**-C2

▶ Edinburgh 52 mi – Glasgow 43 mi – Oban 71 mi – Perth 41 mi

🏰 Roman Camp

COUNTRY HOUSE · CLASSIC Pretty pink house – a former 17C hunting lodge – set by the river among well-tended gardens. Traditional bedrooms with a subtle contemporary edge and smart, marble-tiled bathrooms. Characterful panelled library and chapel. Charming service.

15 rooms 🖂 – 🛉£ 110/160 🛉🛉£ 160/230 – 3 suites

Main St ✉ *FK17 8BG*
– ☎ (01877) 330 003 – www.romancamphotel.co.uk
Roman Camp – See restaurant listing

🏠 Westerton

TOWNHOUSE · PERSONALISED Homely stone house run by delightful owners, with a colourful garden sweeping down to the river – take it all in from the pleasant terrace. Spotlessly kept bedrooms have wrought iron beds and good mod cons; some have mountain views.

3 rooms 🖂 – 🛉£ 80/125 🛉🛉£ 85/130

Leny Rd ✉ *FK17 8AJ*
– ☎ (01877) 330 147 – www.westertonhouse.co.uk
– Closed November-Easter

XXX Roman Camp

MODERN CUISINE · ELEGANT Enjoy drinks and canapés in the characterful lounge or library of this charming riverside hotel, before dinner in the formal restaurant. Ambitious, modern, well-presented cooking; choose the tasting menu for the best value.

Menu £ 29/55 – Carte £ 48/73

Roman Camp Hotel, Main St ✉ *FK17 8BG – ☎ (01877) 330 003 (bookings essential for non-residents) – www.romancamphotel.co.uk*

X Mhor Fish

FISH AND SEAFOOD · FRIENDLY A high street eatery: on one side of it, there's a classic take-away chippy; on the other, a funky, modern, all-day café. The tasty chips are cooked in beef dripping and the pies and bread are from their nearby bakery.

Carte £ 11/36

75-77 Main St ✉ *FK17 8DX – ☎ (01877) 330 213 – www.mhor.net*
– Closed 25-26 December, 1 January and Monday in winter except bank holidays

CARNOUSTIE

Angus – Pop. 11 394 – Regional map n° **16**-D2

▶ Edinburgh 46 mi – London 438 mi – Glasgow 46 mi – Aberdeen 102 mi

Old Manor

TRADITIONAL · CLASSIC Sizeable house built in 1765 – formerly a manse – commanding great views over patchwork fields to the sea beyond. Comfortable lounge and a good-sized breakfast room. Spotlessly kept bedrooms come with quality bedding, biscuits and chocolates; 'Balmoral' and 'Dunotter' boast superb outlooks.

5 rooms ⌂ – †£ 70 ††£ 90

Panbride ⊠ DD7 6JP – Northeast : 1.25 mi by A 930 on Panbride Rd – ℰ (01241) 854 804 – www.oldmanorcarnoustie.com – Closed November-March

CARRADALE – Argyll and Bute → See Kintyre (Peninsula)

CASTLE DOUGLAS

Dumfries and Galloway – Pop. 4 174 – Regional map n° **15**-B3

▶ Edinburgh 98 mi – Ayr 49 mi – Dumfries 18 mi – Stranraer 57 mi

Douglas House

TOWNHOUSE · HOMELY An attractive 19C townhouse, run by experienced owners. Comfy, individually decorated bedrooms have a modern edge. The lounge-cum-breakfast-room is light and airy; breakfast offers plenty of choice and features only local produce.

4 rooms ⌂ – †£ 40 ††£ 77/82

63 Queen St ⊠ DG7 1HS – ℰ (01556) 503 262 – www.douglas-house.com

CASTLEBAY – Western Isles → See Barra (Isle of)

CHIRNSIDE

The Scottish Borders – ⊠ Duns – Pop. 1 459 – Regional map n° **15**-D1

▶ Edinburgh 52 mi – Berwick-upon-Tweed 8 mi – Glasgow 95 mi
– Newcastle upon Tyne 70 mi

Chirnside Hall

CASTLE · CLASSIC Sizeable 1834 country house with a lovely revolving door and beautiful views over the Cheviots. Grand lounges have original cornicing and huge fireplaces. Bedrooms are cosy and classical; some have four-poster beds. Local, seasonal dishes in traditional dining room.

10 rooms ⌂ – †£ 100/195 ††£ 150/195

*⊠ TD11 3LD – East : 1.75 mi on A 6105 – ℰ (01890) 818 219
– www.chirnsidehallhotel.com – Closed March*

COLBOST – Highland → See Skye (Isle of)

COMRIE

Perth and Kinross – Pop. 1 927 – Regional map n° **16**-C2

▶ Edinburgh 66 mi – Glasgow 56 mi – Oban 70 mi – Perth 24 mi

Royal

TRADITIONAL · PERSONALISED Charming coaching inn dating back to the 18C and set at the heart of a riverside town. Cosy bar and lovely open-fired library with squashy sofas. Well-appointed bedrooms; some with four-posters and antiques. Relaxed, personable service.

11 rooms ⌂ – †£ 90/110 ††£ 150/190

Melville Sq ⊠ PH6 2DN – ℰ (01764) 679 200 – www.royalhotel.co.uk – Closed 25-26 December

Royal – See restaurant listing

XX **Royal**

TRADITIONAL CUISINE · **COSY** Intimate dining room and a bright conservatory, set within a stylishly decorated coaching inn. Concise menu of classically based dishes with modern touches. Produce is seasonal and locally sourced; the mussels and steaks are superb.

Carte £ 20/37

Royal Hotel, Melville Sq ⊠ PH6 2DN – ℰ (01764) 679 200 – www.royalhotel.co.uk – Closed 25-26 December

CONNEL

Argyll and Bute – ⊠ Oban – Regional map n° **16**-B2

▶ Edinburgh 118 mi – Glasgow 88 mi – Inverness 113 mi – Oban 5 mi

🏠 **Ards House**

TRADITIONAL · **PERSONALISED** Attractive house with an equally welcoming, hospitable owner. The large, homely lounge is packed with books and antiques. Cosy, personally decorated bedrooms show good attention to detail; small bathrooms boast locally made toiletries. Excellent breakfasts with fresh fruit and delicious roasted coffee.

4 rooms ⌂ – †£ 65/95 ††£ 85/98

⊠ PA37 1PT – on A 85 – ℰ (01631) 710 255 – www.ardshouse.com – Closed Christmas-New Year

CRIEFF

Perth and Kinross – Pop. 7 368 – Regional map n° **16**-C2

▶ Edinburgh 60 mi – Glasgow 50 mi – Oban 76 mi – Perth 18 mi

🏠 **Merlindale**

TRADITIONAL · **CLASSIC** Spacious manor house with a comfy lounge, a well-stocked library and a dark wood furnished room for family-style breakfasts. Immaculate bedrooms have classic furnishings, floral drapes and large bathrooms; some boast roll-top baths.

3 rooms ⌂ – †£ 70/90 ††£ 85/100

Perth Rd ⊠ PH7 3EQ – on A 85 – ℰ (01764) 655 205 – www.merlindale.co.uk – Closed mid-December-February

XX **Yann's at Glenearn House**

FRENCH CLASSIC · **BISTRO** Busy restaurant in a Victorian house, with a delightful lounge and a large bistro-style dining room hung with French prints. Gallic cooking makes good use of Scottish produce and Savoyard sharing dishes are a speciality. Comfy, cosy bedrooms have good facilities and a relaxed, bohemian style. Pleasant team.

Carte £ 22/33

4 rooms ⌂ – †£ 75 ††£ 95/100

Perth Rd ⊠ PH7 3EQ – on A 85 – ℰ (01764) 650 111 – www.yannsatglenearnhouse.com – dinner only and lunch Friday-Sunday – Closed 2 weeks October and 25-26 December

at Muthill South: 3 mi by A822

X **Barley Bree**

CLASSIC CUISINE · **RUSTIC** Intimate coaching inn at the centre of a busy village, with a spacious fire-lit sitting room and a dining room hung with angling memorabilia. Classical cooking utilises local ingredients and arrives in a modern manner. Service is friendly and bedrooms are comfortable and well-thought-out.

Carte £ 37/46 **s**

6 rooms ⌂ – †£ 70/85 ††£ 110/150

6 Willoughby St ⊠ PH5 2AB – ℰ (01764) 681 451 (booking advisable) – www.barleybree.com – Closed Christmas-New Year, Monday and Tuesday

CRINAN

Argyll and Bute – ⊠ Lochgilphead – Regional map n° **16**-B2
▶ Edinburgh 137 mi – Glasgow 91 mi – Oban 36 mi

🏚 Crinan ☆ ⪵ 🍴 🔃 🅿

TRADITIONAL · PERSONALISED Built in the 19C to accommodate the Laird of Jura's business associates. Some of the simply furnished bedrooms have balconies and lovely Sound views. The small coffee shop sells homemade cakes, the 3rd floor bar has a superb terrace, and the large wood-panelled bar-restaurant offers an appealing seafood menu.

20 rooms ☡ – 🛉£ 65/150 🛉🛉£ 95/260

⊠ PA31 8SR
– ☏ (01546) 830 261
– www.crinanhotel.com
– Closed January and Christmas
Westward – See restaurant listing

✗✗ Westward ⪵ 🍴 🅿

FISH AND SEAFOOD · FORMAL Set within a welcoming, family-run hotel and boasting lovely views out over the Sound of Jura. Concise, seafood-based menus rely on local and island produce; langoustines are landed daily from Loch Crinan, right beside the hotel.

Menu £ 35

Crinan Hotel, ⊠ PA31 8SR
– ☏ (01546) 830 261
– www.crinanhotel.com
– dinner only
– Closed January and Christmas

CROMARTY

Highland – Pop. 726 – Regional map n° **17**-D2
▶ Edinburgh 177 mi – Inverness 23 mi – Fort William 88 mi

🏠 Factor's House 🆕 ☆ ⅋ 🍴 ⅋ 🅿

LUXURY · STYLISH This late Georgian house is very passionately run by a charming owner. It sits in a peaceful spot on the edge of an attractive town and offers pleasant sea views from its mature gardens. Bedrooms have a subtle contemporary style and good extras. Breakfast and dinner are taken around a farmhouse table; the latter is four courses and features accomplished home cooking.

3 rooms – 🛉£ 90/110 🛉🛉£ 110/130

Denny Rd ⊠ IV11 8YT
– ☏ (01381) 600 394
– www.thefactorshouse.com
– Closed Christmas-New Year

✗ Sutor Creek Cafe 🆕

TRADITIONAL CUISINE · FRIENDLY A great little eatery hidden away by the harbour in a well-preserved coastal town. Wonderfully seasonal cooking features seafood from the local boats and pizzas from the wood-fired oven. It's run by a friendly, experienced couple.

Carte £ 17/45

21 Bank St ⊠ IV11 8YE
– ☏ (01381) 600 855 (booking essential)
– www.sutorcreek.co.uk
– Closed January, Monday-Wednesday lunch September-April

CULLODEN – Highland → See Inverness

CULNAKNOCK – Highland → See Skye (Isle of)

CUMNOCK

East Ayrshire – Pop. 9 039 – Regional map n° **15**-B2

▶ Edinburgh 85 mi – Glasgow 38 mi – Dumfries 44 mi – Carlisle 88 mi

⌂ Dumfries House Lodge

COUNTRY HOUSE · HOMELY This old factor's house and adjoining steading – set at the entrance to the 2,000 acre Dumfries Estate – is now a stylish country house hotel. There are two cosy lounges and a billiard room, and some of the furniture is from the original manor house. Bedrooms are designed by the Duchess of Cornwall's sister.

22 rooms ⌧ – ♦£ 85 ♦♦£ 110

Dumfries House ⌧ KA18 2NJ – West : 1.5 mi on A 70
– ℰ (01290) 429 920 – www.dumfrieshouselodge.co.uk
– Closed 23-27 December and 31-December-3 January

CUPAR

Fife – Pop. 9 339 – Regional map n° **16**-C2

▶ Edinburgh 45 mi – Dundee 15 mi – Perth 23 mi

⌂ Ferrymuir Stables

LUXURY · CONTEMPORARY The old stables of Ferrymuir House date from 1800 – but you'd never tell. The hub of the house is a light, spacious orangery overlooking the stable yard. Modern bedrooms come with designer furnishings, smart wet rooms and Netbooks.

3 rooms ⌧ – ♦£ 55/75 ♦♦£ 98/120

Beechgrove Rise ⌧ KY15 5DT – West : 1 mi by Bonnygate (A91) and West Park Rd off Westfield Rd
– ℰ (01334) 657 579 – www.ferrymuirstables.co.uk

XX Ostlers Close

TRADITIONAL CUISINE · INTIMATE Cosy, cottagey little restaurant hidden away down a narrow alley. It's been personally run since 1981 and service is warm and chatty. Classic cooking features local ingredients, including mushrooms foraged for by the owner-chef.

Carte £ 38/49

25 Bonnygate ⌧ KY15 4BU – ℰ (01334) 655 574
– www.ostlersclose.co.uk – dinner only and Saturday lunch
– Closed 2 weeks April, 25-26 December, 1-2 January, Sunday and Monday

CURRIE – City of Edinburgh ➜ See Edinburgh

DALKEITH

Midlothian – Pop. 12 342 – Regional map n° **15**-C1

▶ Edinburgh 6 mi – London 374 mi – Glasgow 51 mi – Manchester 208 mi

⌂ Sun Inn

TRADITIONAL CUISINE · PUB 17C former blacksmith's with two large, open-fired rooms; their wood and stone-faced walls hung with modern black and white photos. Extensive menus feature good quality local produce; lunch keeps things simple but appealing. Smart bedrooms boast handmade furniture and Egyptian cotton linen.

Menu £ 11 (weekdays)/18 – Carte £ 21/42

5 rooms ⌧ – ♦£ 75/100 ♦♦£ 95/150

Lothian Bridge ⌧ EH22 4TR – Southwest : 2 mi by A 6094 and B 6392 on A 7
– ℰ (0131) 663 24 56 – www.thesuninnedinburgh.co.uk
– Closed 26 December and 1 January

DALRY

North Ayrshire – Regional map n° **15**-A1

▶ Edinburgh 70 mi – Ayr 21 mi – Glasgow 25 mi

⌂ Lochwood Farm Steading   🐾 ⩽ 🛏 🖋 🅿

COUNTRY HOUSE · PERSONALISED Remote farmhouse on a 100 acre working dairy farm, boasting impressive panoramic views. Luxuriously appointed bedrooms are split between an old barn and a wooden house – two have private hot tubs. Breakfast is served by candlelight!

5 rooms 🖵 – ╪£ 60 ╪╪£ 80/140

Saltcoats ✉ KA21 6NG – Southwest : 5 mi by A 737 and Saltcoats rd
– 𝒞 (01294) 552 529 – www.lochwoodfarm.co.uk
– Closed Christmas-New Year

XX Braidwoods (Keith Braidwood)   🅿

❀   **CLASSIC CUISINE · COSY** Former crofter's cottage hidden away in the countryside; personally run by experienced owners. Cosy and charming, with just a handful of tables in each of its two rooms. Concise menu of confident, classical cooking uses quality seasonal ingredients; dishes have clear flavours. Great value lunch.

➜ Warm Arbroath smokie and hot-smoked timbale with horseradish butter glazed leeks. Roast turbot with new season asparagus and Potencross lobster jus. Chilled caramelised rice pudding with warm Agen prunes in Armagnac.

Menu £ 28/46

Drumastle Mill Cottage ✉ KA24 4LN – Southwest : 1.5 mi by A 737 on Saltcoats rd
– 𝒞 (01294) 833 544 (booking essential) – www.braidwoods.co.uk
– Closed 25 December-29 January, 2 weeks September, Sunday dinner, Monday, Tuesday lunch and Sunday from May-mid September

DEERNESS ➜ See Orkney Islands (Mainland)

DINGWALL

Highland – Pop. 5 491 – Regional map n° **17**-C2

▶ Edinburgh 172 mi – Inverness 14 mi – Glasgow 182 mi – Aberdeen 115 mi

XX Café India Brasserie   🆔

INDIAN · NEIGHBOURHOOD Well-run Indian restaurant close to the town centre. Small lounge and several dining areas separated by etched glass screens. Good range of authentic, regional dishes, with tasty Thalis, set menus for 2+ and good value two course lunches.

Menu £ 9 (weekday lunch) – Carte £ 15/32

Lockhart House, Tulloch St ✉ IV15 9JZ – 𝒞 (01349) 862 552
– www.cafeindiadingwall.co.uk – Closed 25 December

DINNET

Aberdeenshire – Regional map n° **16**-D1

▶ Edinburgh 114 mi – London 517 mi – Glasgow 134 mi – Bradford 325 mi

⌂ Glendavan House   🐾 🛏 🖋 🅿

FAMILY · HOMELY Set in 9 lochside acres, this former shooting lodge is somewhere to 'get away from it all'. Two of the three bedrooms are very large suites; all are tastefully furnished with antiques and memorabilia. Delicious communal breakfasts.

3 rooms 🖵 – ╪£ 95/125 ╪╪£ 120/160

✉ AB34 5LU – Northwest : 3 mi by A 97 on B 9119
– 𝒞 (01339) 881 610 – www.glendavanhouse.com

DORNOCH

Highland – Pop. 1 208 – Regional map n° **17**-D2

▶ Edinburgh 219 mi – Inverness 63 mi – Wick 65 mi

🏨 Links House

LUXURY · CONTEMPORARY This restored 19C manse sits opposite the first tee of the Royal Dornoch Golf Club. Enjoy a dram from the honesty bar in the pine-panelled library or have tea and cake in the antique-furnished sitting room. Some of the beautifully furnished bedrooms feature bespoke tweed fabrics. The elegant orangery boasts an impressive stone fireplace and an elaborate 4 course menu.

8 rooms ☲ – ♦£ 280/380 ♦♦£ 280/380

Golf Rd ✉ IV25 3LW – ✆ (01862) 810 279 – www.linkshousedornoch.com – Closed 5 January-1 March

🏨 Highfield House

FAMILY · MODERN Welcoming guesthouse with immaculately kept gardens and a pleasant summer house. Spacious guest areas consist of a conservatory style lounge and a smart breakfast room. Comfy bedrooms have good facilities.

4 rooms ☲ – ♦£ 68/100 ♦♦£ 90/100

Evelix Rd ✉ IV25 3HR – ✆ (01862) 810 909 – www.highfieldhouse.co.uk – Closed January-February

🏨 2 Quail

TOWNHOUSE · HOMELY A bijou terraced house, built in 1898 for a sea captain. Intimate bedrooms are furnished with antiques, in a Victorian style; one has a wrought iron bedstead. The small open-fired library-lounge boasts a large array of vintage books.

3 rooms ☲ – ♦£ 80/120 ♦♦£ 80/120

Castle St ✉ IV25 3SN – ✆ (01862) 811 811 – www.2quail.com – Closed 2 weeks February-March and Christmas

DOUNBY → See Orkney Islands (Mainland)

DRUMBEG

Highland – Regional map n° **17**-C1

▶ Edinburgh 262 mi – Inverness 105 mi – Ullapool 48 mi

🏨 Blar na Leisg at Drumbeg House

FAMILY · MODERN This remotely set Edwardian house affords lovely loch views. The large open-fired sitting room is filled with a vast array of books; and impressive modern art and Bauhaus-style furnishings feature throughout. Bedrooms are spacious and luxuriously appointed. Highland beef and game birds are a speciality at dinner, which is served in a smart, contemporary dining room.

5 rooms ☲ – ♦£ 80/138 ♦♦£ 150/160

✉ IV27 4NW – Take first right on entering village from Kylesku direction – ✆ (01571) 833 325 – www.blarnaleisg.com

DRUMNADROCHIT

Highland – ✉ Milton – Pop. 1 101 – Regional map n° **17**-C2

▶ Edinburgh 172 mi – Inverness 16 mi – Kyle of Lochalsh 66 mi

🏨 Drumbuie Farm

TRADITIONAL · CLASSIC Friendly guesthouse above Loch Ness, on a 120 acre sheep and cattle farm. It's warm and welcoming, from the traditional lounge to the pine-furnished bedrooms; two of which have body jet showers. Take in the view from the breakfast room.

3 rooms ☲ – ♦£ 44 ♦♦£ 68/70

Drumbuie ✉ IV63 6XP – East : 0.75 mi by A 82 – ✆ (01456) 450 634 – www.loch-ness-farm.co.uk – Closed December-January

DUISDALEMORE – Highland → See Skye (Isle of)

DUMFRIES
Dumfries and Galloway – Pop. 32 914 – Regional map n° **15**-C3
▶ Edinburgh 80 mi – Ayr 59 mi – Carlisle 34 mi – Glasgow 79 mi

Hazeldean House

TOWNHOUSE · PERSONALISED Victorian villa built in 1898, with a lovely garden, a curio-filled lounge and a conservatory breakfast room. Victorian-themed bedrooms – three with four-posters; the basement room has a nautical cabin style.

6 rooms ⌂ – ♦£ 35/45 ♦♦£ 60/65
Town plan: B-u – 4 Moffat Rd ⌂ DG1 1NJ – ✆ (01387) 266 178
– www.hazeldeanhouse.com

DUMFRIES

Aldermanhill Rd	B	2
Bank St	A	3
Buccleuch St	A	4
Cardoness St	B	5
Cassalands	A	6
Castle Douglas Rd	A	8
Castle St	A	7
Catherine St	B	9
Corberry Ave	A	10
Cornwall Mount Rd	B	12
Cuckoo Bridge Retail Park	A	
Friars Vennel	A	13
Galloway St	A	14
Glebe St	B	15
Great King St	A	16
Hermitage Drive	A	17
High St	A	18
Loreburn Centre	A	20
Loreburn St	A	21
Nith St	AB	22
Queensberry St	A	24
Queen St	B	23
Rae St	B	26
St Mary's St	B	27
St Michael St	B	28
St Michael's Bridge Rd	A	30
Shakespeare St	B	31
Union St	A	32
Whitesands	A	34

Hamilton House

TOWNHOUSE · PERSONALISED Converted Victorian townhouse next to a bowls club, with a large conservatory lounge and neat breakfast tables overlooking the tennis courts. Large bedrooms come with power showers and combine the classical with the contemporary.

7 rooms ☑ – ♦£ 40/50 ♦♦£ 60/65
Town plan: B-c – *12 Moffat Rd ⊠ DG1 1NJ*
– *☎ (01387) 266 606 – www.hamiltonhousedumfries.co.uk*
– *Closed 24 December-3 January*

DUNBAR

East Lothian – Pop. 8 486 – Regional map n° **15**-D1
▶ Edinburgh 30 mi – London 369 mi – Glasgow 76 mi – Leeds 190 mi

✗ Creel

TRADITIONAL CUISINE · BISTRO An unassuming, cosy former pub with a wood panelled ceiling and walls. The experienced chef creates good value, full-flavoured dishes, with fresh fish and shellfish from the adjacent harbour. Friendly service.
Menu £ 17 (lunch)/28
The Harbour, 25 Lamer St ⊠ EH42 1HG
– *☎ (01368) 863 279 (booking essential) – www.creelrestaurant.co.uk*
– *Closed Sunday dinner-Wednesday lunch*

DUNBLANE

Stirling – Pop. 8 811 – Regional map n° **16**-C2
▶ Edinburgh 42 mi – Glasgow 33 mi – Perth 29 mi

Cromlix

COUNTRY HOUSE · MODERN This grand country house, owned by Andy Murray, has elegantly appointed sitting rooms, a whisky room, a chapel and a superb games room, as well as a smart tennis court in its 30 acre grounds. Luxurious, antique-furnished bedrooms feature modern touches while also respecting the original style of the house.

16 rooms ☑ – ♦£ 160/595 ♦♦£ 250/450 – 5 suites
Kinbuck ⊠ FK15 9JT – North : 3.5 mi on B 8033
– *☎ (01786) 822 125 – www.cromlix.com*
Chez Roux – See restaurant listing

Doubletree by Hilton Dunblane Hydro

HOLIDAY HOTEL · CONTEMPORARY A 'grand old lady' originally built in the 1800s; rejuvenated and given a modern, corporate style. Set in ten acres, it boasts extensive conference facilities, a family-orientated spa and smart, up-to-date bedrooms.

200 rooms ☑ – ♦£ 89/169 ♦♦£ 99/250 – 4 suites
Perth Rd ⊠ FK15 OHG – North : 0.75 mi on B 8033
– *☎ (01786) 826 600 – www.doubletreedunblane.com*
Kailyard by Nick Nairn – See restaurant listing

✗✗ Chez Roux ⓝ

FRENCH · BRASSERIE Light and spacious conservatory restaurant in a magnificent country house hotel. Smart, yet relaxed, it's a hit with locals and tourists alike thanks to the enthusiastic service and good value, flavoursome cooking. Classic French dishes might include soufflé Suissesse, chateaubriand or tarte au citron.
Menu £ 32 – Carte £ 33/49
Cromlix Hotel, Kinbuck ⊠ FK15 9JT – North : 3.5 mi on B 8033
– *☎ (01786) 822 125 – www.cromlix.com*

XX **Kailyard by Nick Nairn**   🛏 ⅙ 🅿

MODERN CUISINE · BRASSERIE Large, contemporary restaurant set within a characterful, grand hotel; its name means 'small Scottish vegetable garden'. Menus focus on well-prepared modern classics with some Nick Nairn signature dishes.
Menu £ 30

Doubletree by Hilton Dunblane Hydro Hotel, Perth Rd ⊠ FK15 OHG – North : 0.75 mi on B 8033 – ℰ (01786) 822 551 (bookings essential for non-residents) – www.doubletreedunblane.com/the_kailyard – dinner only and Sunday lunch

DUNDEE

Dundee City – Pop. 147 285 – Regional map n° **16**-C2
▶ Edinburgh 63 mi – London 458 mi – Glasgow 76 mi – Newcastle upon Tyne 163 mi

🏨 **Apex City Quay**   ☆ ≤ 🔲 🌐 🕸 ⅙ 🔲 ⅙ 🏊 🅿

BUSINESS · MODERN Modern waterfront hotel with good business facilities and an atmospheric spa; located in an up-and-coming area. Well-proportioned, contemporary bedrooms boast king-sized beds and oversized windows that look out towards the city or marina. Vast bar-lounge and spacious brasserie with an accessible menu.
151 rooms – †£ 72/250 ††£ 72/250 – � £ 10 – 2 suites
Town plan: Y-a – *1 West Victoria Dock Rd ⊠ DD1 3JP – ℰ (01382) 202 404 – www.apexhotels.co.uk*

🏨 **Malmaison**   ☆ 🔲 ⅙ 🆎 🏊

CHAIN HOTEL · STYLISH The best feature of this lovingly restored hotel is the wrought iron cantilevered staircase topped by a domed ceiling. Contemporary bedrooms come in striking bold colours and have a masculine feel. The all-day bar serves cocktails and nibbles and there's a DJ at weekends; the brasserie offers a grill menu.
91 rooms – †£ 75/315 ††£ 75/315 – ⊠ £ 16
Town plan: Y-s – *44 Whitehall Cres ⊠ DD1 4AY – ℰ (0844) 693 0661 – www.malmaison.com*

🏨 **Doubletree by Hilton Dundee**   ☆ 🛏 🔲 🕸 ⅙ ⅙ 🏊 🅿

CHAIN HOTEL · FUNCTIONAL Charming granite country house – formerly a private residence – dating from 1870 and surrounded by smart landscaped gardens. Sizeable modern bedrooms have good facilities; there's also a small gym and a 24hr business centre. The elegant L-shaped conservatory restaurant keeps Scottish ingredients to the fore.
95 rooms – †£ 89/99 ††£ 89/99 – ⊠ £ 14 – 2 suites
Kingsway West ⊠ DD2 5JT – West : 5.5 mi by A 85 at junction with A 90 – ℰ (01382) 641 122 – www.doubletree@.hilton.com

🏨 **Balmuirfield House** ❶   🛏 🅿

COUNTRY HOUSE · HOMELY A double-fronted stone dower house built in 1904; Dighty Water runs past the bottom of the garden. Inside it's spacious and homely, with a cosy open-fired lounge. Two of the bedrooms have four-posters and one has an antique bath.
4 rooms ⊠ – †£ 50/70 ††£ 80/95
Harestane Rd ⊠ DD3 0NU – North : 3.5 mi by A 929, A 90, Claverhouse rd and Old Glamis rd. – ℰ (01382) 819 655 – www.balmuirfieldhouse.com

XX **Castlehill** ❶   ⅙

MODERN CUISINE · INTIMATE Smart designer restaurant close to the waterfront; its décor celebrates the history of the city. Modern dishes feature some innovative flavour combinations and have playful touches – the concise evening menu is the most imaginative.
Menu £ 18/36
Town plan: Y-c – *22 Exchange St ⊠ DD1 3DL – ℰ (01382) 220 008 – www.castlehillrestaurant.co.uk – Closed Sunday and Monday*

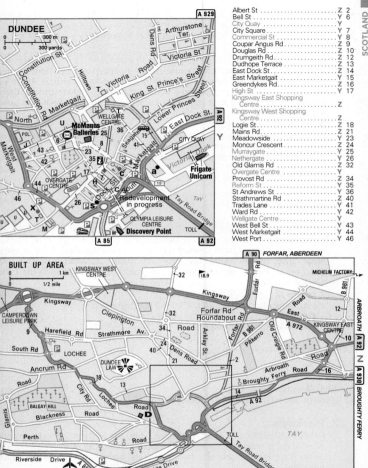

DUNDEE

XX Playwright

🍷 AC 🐕

BRITISH MODERN · FASHIONABLE Smart, modern bar and restaurant in an imposing 19C grey-stone building beside the Rep Theatre. Seasonal menus offer modern interpretations of classical dishes and everything from the bread to ice cream is made in-house. Great value lunch.

Menu £13 (lunch)/20
– Carte £40/50

Town plan: Y-x – *11 Tay Sq, South Tay St.* ✉ *DD1 1PB*
– ✆ *(01382) 223 113*
– *www.theplaywright.co.uk*
– *Closed 25-26 December, 1-3 January and Sunday*

DUNKELD

Perth and Kinross - Pop. 1 005 - Regional map n° **16**-C2
Edinburgh 58 mi - Aberdeen 88 mi - Inverness 98 mi - Perth 14 mi

Letter Farm

FAMILY • RUSTIC A traditional farmhouse on a family-run stock farm, nestle between Butterstone Loch and the Loch of Lowes Nature Reserve. There's a welcoming open-fired lounge and a homely communal breakfast room. Comfortable, immaculately kept bedrooms come with king-sized beds and good extras touches.

3 rooms - £ 55 £ 90

Loch of the Lowes ✉ PH8 0HH - Northeast : 3 mi by A 923 on Loch of Lowes rd - (01350) 724 254 - www.letterfarmdunkeld.co.uk - Closed late November-early May

DUNOON

Argyll and Bute - Pop. 8 454 - Regional map n° **16**-B3
Edinburgh 73 mi - Glasgow 27 mi - Oban 77 mi

Dhailling Lodge

TRADITIONAL • PERSONALISED A well-kept and proudly run Victorian villa se on the main seafront, with pleasant gardens and nice bay views from its gues areas. Snug, homely lounge and cosy, individually decorated bedrooms with good extras. Classic menu of unfussy pies, roasts and fish served in the tradi tional dining room.

7 rooms - £ 40/60 £ 76/81

155 Alexandra Par ✉ PA23 8AW - North : 0.75 mi on A 815 - (01369) 701 253 - www.dhaillinglodge.com - Closed December-February

DUNVEGAN - Highland

➜ See Skye (Isle of)

DURNESS

Highland - Regional map n° **17**-C1
Edinburgh 266 mi - Thurso 78 mi - Ullapool 71 mi

Mackay's

FAMILY • MODERN This smart grey stone house sits at the most north-westerly point of the mainland. It has a light, airy lounge and a cosy open-fired snug. The owner is a textile designer and this shows in the bedrooms, which have a stylish rustic feel.

7 rooms - £ 110 £ 129/139

✉ IV27 4PN - (01971) 511 202 - www.visitdurness.com - May-September

DUROR

Highland - Regional map n° **17**-B3
Edinburgh 131 mi - Ballachulish 7 mi - Oban 26 mi

Bealach House

TRADITIONAL • PERSONALISED Superbly set, former crofter's house with an impressive 1.5 mile driveway lined with mature, deer-filled forest: the scenery is breathtaking. Snug conservatory and cosy bedrooms; homely guest areas are hung with Lowry tapestries. Classical, daily changing menu.

3 rooms - £ 70/80 £ 90/110

Salachan Glen ✉ PA38 4BW - Southeast : 4.5 mi by A 828 - (01631) 740 298 - www.bealachhouse.co.uk - Closed November-February

DYKE

Moray – Regional map n° **16**-C1

▶ Edinburgh 163 mi – London 564 mi – Aberdeen 81 mi – Glasgow 177 mi

🏠 Old Kirk ⌖ ⟲ 🖨 🐾 🅿

📷 **HISTORIC · DESIGN** A peacefully set, converted 1856 church, surrounded by grain fields. Airy interior, with a cosy library and a comfortable, open-fired lounge displaying an original stained glass window. Charming, individually decorated bedrooms boast original stonework and arched windows; one has a carved four-poster.

3 rooms ⌷ – ♦£ 85/95 ♦♦£ 85/95

✉ IV36 2TL – Northeast : 0.5 mi – ℰ (01309) 641 414 – www.oldkirk.co.uk

EDDLESTON – The Scottish Borders ➜ See Peebles

EDINBANE – Highland ➜ See Skye (Isle of)

EDINBURGH

City of Edinburgh – Pop. 459 366 – Regional map n° **15**-C1
▶ London 397 mi – Glasgow 46 mi – Newcastle upon Tyne 120 mi – Aberdeen 126 mi

Hotels

Balmoral

🏨 **Balmoral**   ⚐ 🔲 📶 🏊 ⅃₆ 🖃 ⅃₆ AC 🍴 🧖 🚗

GRAND LUXURY · CLASSIC Renowned Edwardian hotel which provides for the modern traveller whilst retaining its old-fashioned charm. Bedrooms are classical with a subtle contemporary edge; JK Rowling completed the final Harry Potter book in the top suite! Live harp music accompanies afternoon tea in the Palm Court and 'Scotch' offers over 460 malts. Dine on modern dishes or brasserie classics.

188 rooms – 🛉£ 190/595 🛉🛉£ 190/595 – 🍽 £ 21 – 20 suites
Town plan: EY-n – *1 Princes St* ✉ *EH2 2EQ* – ℰ *(0131) 556 24 14*
– *www.roccofortehotels.com*
✿ **Number One** – See restaurant listing

Sheraton Grand H. & Spa

🏨 **Sheraton Grand H. & Spa**   ⚐ 🔲 📶 🏊 ⅃₆ 🖃 ⅃₆ AC 🍴 🧖 🅿

GRAND LUXURY · MODERN Spacious modern hotel with castle views from some rooms. Sleek, stylish bedrooms boast strong comforts, the latest mod cons and smart bathrooms with mood lighting. An impressive four-storey glass cube houses the stunning spa.

269 rooms – 🛉£ 195/595 🛉🛉£ 195/595 – 🍽 £ 15 – 12 suites
Town plan: CDZ-v – *1 Festival Sq* ✉ *EH3 9SR* – ℰ *(0131) 229 91 31*
– *www.sheratonedinburgh.co.uk*
One Square – See restaurant listing

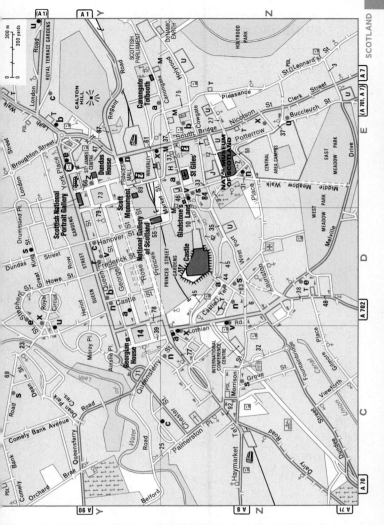

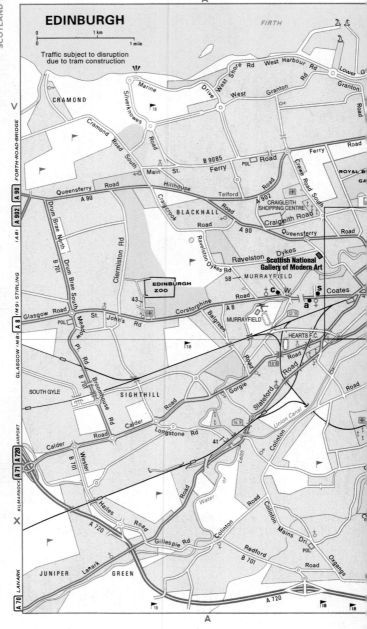

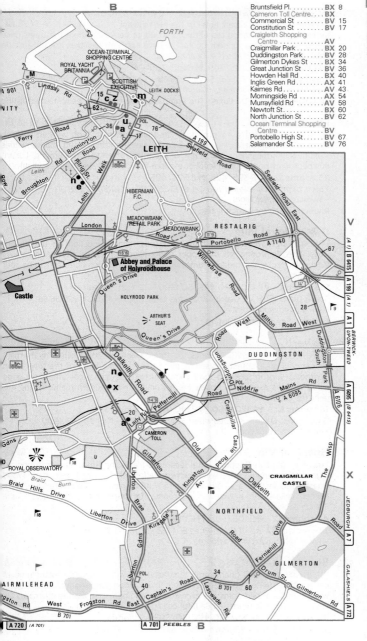

Waldorf Astoria Edinburgh The Caledonian

HISTORIC · DESIGN Smart hotel in the old railway terminus: have afternoon tea in the forecourt where the trains once pulled in. Sumptuous modern bedrooms have excellent facilities; ask for a castle view. They have the UK's first Guerlain spa.

241 rooms – †£ 195/749 ††£ 215/769 – 6 suites
Town plan: CZ-x – *Princes St* ⊠ *EH1 2AB* – *℘ (0131) 222 8888*
– *www.waldorfastoriaedinburgh.com*
⊛ **Galvin Brasserie De Luxe • The Pompadour by Galvin** – See restaurant listing

Prestonfield

LUXURY · STYLISH 17C country house in a pleasant rural spot, with an opulent dimly lit interior displaying warm colours, fine furnishings and old tapestries – it's hugely atmospheric and is one of the most romantic hotels around. Luxurious bedrooms boast a high level of modern facilities and service is excellent.

23 rooms – †£ 325/425 ††£ 325/425 – 5 suites
Town plan: BX-r – *Priestfield Rd* ⊠ *EH16 5UT* – *℘ (0131) 225 78 00*
– *www.prestonfield.com*
Rhubarb – See restaurant listing

G & V Royal Mile

LUXURY · DESIGN A striking hotel in a great central location on the historic Royal Mile. Bedrooms on the upper floors have impressive city skyline views. Bold colour schemes, modern furnishings and clever design features can be seen throughout.

136 rooms – †£ 150/390 ††£ 150/390 – ⊏ £ 21 – 7 suites
Town plan: EZ-v – *1 George IV Bridge* ⊠ *EH1 1AD* – *℘ (0131) 220 66 66*
– *www.gandvhotel.com*
Cucina – See restaurant listing

Howard

TOWNHOUSE · CLASSIC A series of three Georgian townhouses with many characterful original features still in situ; situated in the heart of the New Town. Bedrooms vary in size and have classic furnishings and a contemporary edge; every room is assigned a butler. Formal dining from modern menus in the elegant restaurant.

18 rooms – †£ 120/450 ††£ 140/450 – 3 suites
Town plan: DY-s – *34 Great King St* ⊠ *EH3 6QH* – *℘ (0131) 557 35 00*
– *www.thehoward.com*

Hotel du Vin

LUXURY · DESIGN Boutique hotel located close to the Royal Mile, featuring unique modern murals and wine-themed bedrooms furnished with dark wood. Guest areas include a whisky snug and a mezzanine bar complete with glass-fronted cellars and a wine tasting room. The traditional bistro offers classic French cooking.

47 rooms – †£ 105/305 ††£ 115/330
Town plan: EZ-n – *11 Bristo Pl* ⊠ *EH1 1EZ* – *℘ (0131) 247 49 00*
– *www.hotelduvin.com/edinburgh*

Scotsman

BUSINESS · CLASSIC Characterful Victorian hotel within the old Scotsman newspaper offices. Period guest areas feature lovely wood panelling and stained glass, while traditional bedrooms are accessed via an impressive marble staircase. The stunning brasserie boasts a beautiful ceiling and a minstrels' gallery.

69 rooms – †£ 115/380 ††£ 130/395 – 2 suites
Town plan: EY-x – *20 North Bridge* ⊠ *EH3 1TR* – *℘ (0131) 556 55 65*
– *www.thescotsmanhotel.co.uk*

Tigerlily

TOWNHOUSE · DESIGN Classical Georgian townhouse concealing a funky, boutique interior. Large, individually designed bedrooms are luxurious, boasting seductive lighting, quality furnishings and superb wet rooms. The busy open-plan bar and dining room have similarly stylish modern décor and offer a worldwide menu.

33 rooms ⌂ - †£100/260 ††£100/260

Town plan: DY-a - *125 George St* ✉ *EH2 4JN* - ✆ *(0131) 225 50 05*
- *www.tigerlilyedinburgh.co.uk* - *Closed 25 December*

Glasshouse

BUSINESS · MODERN A striking combination of a 150 year old church and sleek glass, topped by an impressive two acre roof garden. Stylish bedrooms feature floor to ceiling windows and lots of wood and leather; the suites open onto a sweeping balcony. Contemporary Scottish fare served in smart Observatory restaurant.

77 rooms - †£120/455 ††£120/455 - ⌂ £19

Town plan: EY-b - *2 Greenside Pl* ✉ *EH1 3AA* - ✆ *(0131) 525 82 00*
- *www.theglasshousehotel.co.uk*

Chester Residence

TOWNHOUSE · STYLISH A series of smart Georgian townhouses in a quiet street. The luxurious, individually furnished suites come with kitchens and state-of-the-art facilities include video entry and integrated sound systems; the Mews apartments are the best.

23 suites - ††£145/365 - ⌂ £12

Town plan: CZ-c - *9 Rothesay Pl* ✉ *EH3 7SL* - ✆ *(0131) 226 2075*
- *www.chester-residence.com* - *Closed 23-26 December*

Nira Caledonia

TOWNHOUSE · STYLISH Two luxurious townhouses with romantic interiors and stunningly restored staircases. Bedrooms boast top class furnishings and are decorated in gold, black and silver colour schemes; some have jacuzzis in the rooms. The sleek, modern dining room – in the main house – offers meats cooked on the Josper grill.

28 rooms ⌂ - †£100/205 ††£140/325

Town plan: DY-u - *6 and 10 Gloucester Pl* ✉ *EH3 6EF* - ✆ *(0131) 225 27 20*
- *www.niracaledonia.com*

Rutland

TOWNHOUSE · DESIGN Boutique hotel occupying a commanding position at the top of Princes Street. Stylish modern bedrooms have bold décor, bluetooth media hubs and slate-floored shower rooms. The restaurant is a contemporary take on a steakhouse and the smart cocktail bar shares its cellar with the Edinburgh Gin Distillery.

11 rooms ⌂ - †£110/190 ††£120/220

Town plan: CZ-a - *1-3 Rutland St* ✉ *EH1 2AE* - ✆ *(0131) 229 34 02*
- *www.therutlandhotel.com* - *Closed 25 December*

Hotel Indigo

TOWNHOUSE · CONTEMPORARY Hotel Indigo comprises five interconnecting Georgian townhouses (one was previously a famous tea and coffee merchant's) and has a stylish, contemporary feel. Bedrooms have bold feature walls and good amenities; those to the front are the largest. The simple bistro serves an accessible all-day menu.

60 rooms ⌂ - †£119/349 ††£119/349

Town plan: EY-e - *51-59 York Pl* ✉ *EH1 3JD* - ✆ *(0131) 556 5577*
- *www.hiedinburgh.co.uk*

🏠 The Dunstane ✿ ✧ P

TOWNHOUSE · CONTEMPORARY An impressive house which used to be a training centre for the Royal Bank of Scotland. Guest areas retain original Victorian features and the smart modern bedrooms have designer touches; some are located across a busy road. Small restaurant with a stylish cocktail bar; the menu champions local produce.

38 rooms ⌨ – †£ 79/139 ††£ 89/249
Town plan: AV-s – *4 West Coates* ✉ EH12 5JQ
– ✆ *(0131) 337 61 69* – www.thedunstane.co.uk

🏠 Kildonan Lodge ✿ ✧ P

TOWNHOUSE · CLASSIC Large detached Victorian house on the main road into the city. Cosy drawing room with an open fire and an honesty bar. Comfy, traditionally furnished bedrooms: some have four-posters or jacuzzis; those in the basement are more contemporary. Appealing, classical dishes with Italian influences.

12 rooms ⌨ – †£ 75/159 ††£ 79/220
Town plan: BX-a – *27 Craigmillar Pk.* ✉ EH16 5PE
– ✆ *(0131) 667 27 93* – www.kildonanlodgehotel.co.uk
– *Closed 25-26 December*

🏠 Six Brunton Place   🛏 ✧

TOWNHOUSE · CONTEMPORARY This late Georgian townhouse – run by a charming owner – was once home to Frederick Ritchie, who designed the One O'Clock Gun and Time Ball. Inside you'll find flagged floors, columns, marble fireplaces and a cantilevered stone staircase; these contrast with contemporary furnishings and vibrant modern art.

4 rooms ⌨ – †£ 89/179 ††£ 109/199
Town plan: EY-u – *6 Brunton Place* ✉ EH7 5EG
– ✆ *(0131) 622 00 42* – www.sixbruntonplace.com

🏠 94 DR ✧ P

TOWNHOUSE · STYLISH Charming owners welcome you to this very stylish and individual hotel in a Victorian terraced house. Retro lounge with honesty bar; breakfast conservatory with decked terrace. Well-equipped bedrooms named after Islay whisky distilleries.

6 rooms ⌨ – †£ 80/125 ††£ 85/220
Town plan: BX-n – *94 Dalkeith Rd* ✉ EH16 5AF
– ✆ *(0131) 662 92 65* – www.94dr.com
– *Closed 4-18 January and 25-26 December*

🏠 23 Mayfield 🛏 ✧ P

TRADITIONAL · CLASSIC Lovingly restored Victorian house with a very welcoming, helpful owner and an outdoor hot-tub. Spacious lounge has an honesty bar and a collection of old and rare books. Sumptuous bedrooms come with coordinated soft furnishings, some mahogany features and luxurious bathrooms. Extravagant breakfast choices.

8 rooms ⌨ – †£ 75/130 ††£ 80/190
Town plan: BX-x – *23 Mayfield Gdns* ✉ EH9 2BX
– ✆ *(0131) 667 5806* – www.23mayfield.co.uk

🏠 Millers64 ✧

TOWNHOUSE · STYLISH A modernised Victorian terraced house in an up and coming part of the city. Smart, spacious bedrooms boast good quality linens; those on the first floor are the best. Complimentary drinks in the lounge. Communal breakfasts.

3 rooms ⌨ – †£ 85/95 ††£ 95/150
Town plan: BV-e – *64 Pilrig St* ✉ EH6 5AS
– ✆ *(0131) 454 3666* – www.millers64.co.uk

🏡 Kew House 🍽 🅿

TOWNHOUSE · PERSONALISED A warm, welcoming stone house with a neat lounge and a wood-furnished breakfast room; very personally run by its charming owners. Modern, immaculately kept bedrooms come with chocolates, a decanter of sherry and fresh flowers.

7 rooms � – †£ 82/99 ††£ 99/185

Town plan: AV-a – *1 Kew Terr, Murrayfield* ⊠ *EH12 5JE*
– ✆ *(0131) 313 07 00 – www.kewhouse.com*
– *Closed 4-31 January and 25-26 December*

🏡 Ardmor House

TOWNHOUSE · PERSONALISED Comfy, laid-back guesthouse on a residential street; the owner has good local knowledge. Variously sized bedrooms boast bright décor, original plaster ceilings and granite fireplaces. Homemade cakes and preserves feature at breakfast.

5 rooms ⊠ – †£ 65/95 ††£ 95/170

Town plan: BV-n – *74 Pilrig St* ⊠ *EH6 5AS* – ✆ *(0131) 554 4944*
– *www.ardmorhouse.com*

Restaurants

XxX Number One 🍸 ⚗ 🖭 ⅋

❀ **MODERN CUISINE · FORMAL** A stylish, long-standing restaurant with a chic cocktail bar, set in the basement of a grand hotel. Richly upholstered banquettes and red lacquered walls give it a plush, luxurious feel. Cooking is modern and intricate and prime Scottish ingredients are key. Service is professional and has personality.

➜ Balvenie-smoked salmon with lemon butter, quail's egg and caviar. Fillet of Orkney beef with baba ganoush and braised oxtail. Valrhona chocolate tart, praline and white chocolate.

Menu £ 70

Town plan: EY-n – *Balmoral Hotel, 1 Princes St* ⊠ *EH2 2EQ*
– ✆ *(0131) 557 67 27 – www.restaurantnumberone.com – dinner only*
– *Closed 2 weeks mid-January*

XxX 21212 (Paul Kitching) 🖭 ⅋

❀ **CREATIVE · ELEGANT** Stunningly refurbished Georgian townhouse designed by William Playfair. The glass-fronted kitchen is the focal point of the stylish, high-ceilinged dining room. Cooking is skilful, innovative and features quirky combinations; '21212' reflects the number of dishes per course at lunch – at dinner it's '31313'. Some of the luxurious bedrooms overlook the Firth of Forth.

➜ Lamb curry, chilli, coriander, currants and courgettes. Oriental sea bass, chestnuts, soy and beansprouts. Peach, apricot, coconut, crème anglaise and nutmeg.

Menu £ 32/69 **s**

4 rooms ⊠ – †£ 115/325 ††£ 115/325

Town plan: EY-c – *3 Royal Terr* ⊠ *EH7 5AB*
– ✆ *(0131) 523 1030 (booking essential) – www.21212restaurant.co.uk*
– *Closed 10 days January, 10 days summer Sunday and Monday*

XxX Rhubarb 🖭 🅿

MODERN CUISINE · ELEGANT Two sumptuous, richly decorated dining rooms set within a romantic 17C country house; so named as this was the first place in Scotland where rhubarb was grown. The concise menu lists modern dishes with some innovative touches and is accompanied by an interesting wine list, with a great selection by the glass.

Menu £ 20/35 – Carte £ 38/72

Town plan: BX-r – *Prestonfield Hotel, Priestfield Rd* ⊠ *EH16 5UT*
– ✆ *(0131) 225 13 33 – www.prestonfield.com*

SCOTLAND

XXX The Pompadour by Galvin   🔥 🎨 🕸 🅿

FRENCH · FORMAL A grand, first floor hotel restaurant which opened in the 1920s and is modelled on a French salon. Classic Gallic dishes showcase Scottish produce, using techniques introduced by Escoffier, and are executed with a lightness of touch.

Carte £ 43/67

Town plan: CZ-x – Waldorf Astoria Edinburgh The Caledonian, Princes St ⊠ EH1 2AB – ℰ (0131) 222 8975 – www.galvinrestaurants.com – dinner only – Closed first two weeks January, 26 December, dinner 25 December, Sunday and Monday

XX Castle Terrace   🔥 🎨 🕸

MODERN CUISINE · INTIMATE Set in the shadow of the castle, an understated restaurant with a gilded ceiling. Ambitious cooking uses seasonal local produce and follows a 'nature to plate' philosophy. The accompanying wine list offers a great selection.

Menu £ 29/75 – Carte £ 50/74

Town plan: DZ-a – 33-35 Castle Terr ⊠ EH1 2EL – ℰ (0131) 229 12 22 – www.castleterracerestaurant.com – Closed Christmas, New Year, Sunday and Monday

XX Mark Greenaway   🍸 ✿

MODERN CUISINE · FORMAL Smart restaurant located in an old Georgian bank – they store their wine in the old vault. The well-travelled chef employs interesting texture and flavour combinations. Dishes are modern, ambitious and attractively presented.

Menu £ 22 (lunch and early dinner)/66 – Carte £ 39/54

Town plan: DY-b – 69 North Castle St ⊠ EH2 3LJ – ℰ (0131) 226 1155 (booking advisable) – www.markgreenaway.com – Closed 25-26 December, 1-2 January, Sunday and Monday

XX The Honours   🎨 🍸

CLASSIC CUISINE · BRASSERIE Bustling brasserie with a smart, stylish interior and a pleasingly informal atmosphere. Classical brasserie menus have French leanings but always offer some Scottish dishes too; meats cooked on the Josper grill are popular.

Menu £ 19 (lunch and early dinner) – Carte £ 36/64

Town plan: DY-n – 58A North Castle St ⊠ EH2 3LU – ℰ (0131) 220 2513 – www.thehonours.co.uk – Closed 25-26 December, 1-3 January, Sunday and Monday

XX Cucina   🍴 🔥 🎨 🍸

ITALIAN · DESIGN A buzzy mezzanine restaurant in a chic hotel, featuring red and blue glass-topped tables and striking kaleidoscope-effect blocks on the walls. Italian dishes follow the seasons – some are classically based and others are more modern.

Menu £ 19 – Carte £ 23/50

Town plan: EZ-v – G & V Royal Mile Hotel, 1 George IV Bridge ⊠ EH1 1AD – ℰ (0131) 220 66 66 – www.gandvhotel.com

XX Galvin Brasserie De Luxe   🎨 🅿

🖤   FRENCH · BRASSERIE Accurately described by its name: a simply styled restaurant which looks like a brasserie of old but with the addition of a smart shellfish counter and formal service. There's an appealing daily menu of French classics and a concise, good value set selection; dishes are refined, flavoursome and a good size.

Menu £ 20 – Carte £ 26/42

Town plan: CZ-x – Waldorf Astoria Edinburgh The Caledonian, Princes St ⊠ EH1 2AB – ℰ (0131) 222 8988 – www.galvinrestaurants.com

SCOTLAND

XX **One Square** 🛱 ᜵ 🖾 ⇔ 🅿

TRADITIONAL CUISINE · CLASSIC So named because it covers one side of the square, this smart hotel restaurant offers casual dining from an all-encompassing menu, accompanied by views towards Edinburgh Castle. Its stylish bar also stocks over 50 varieties of gin.

Menu £ 16 (lunch) – Carte £ 30/53

Town plan: CDZ-v – *Sheraton Grand Hotel & Spa, 1 Festival Sq* ⊠ EH3 9SR
– ℰ (0131) 221 64 22 – www.onesquareedinburgh.co.uk

XX **Ondine** ᜵ 🖾 ᜵

FISH AND SEAFOOD · BRASSERIE Smart, lively restaurant dominated by an impressive horseshoe bar and a crustacean counter. Classic menus showcase prime Scottish seafood in tasty, straightforward dishes which let the ingredients shine. Service is well-structured.

Menu £ 20 (lunch and early dinner) – Carte £ 33/74

Town plan: EZ-s – *2 George IV Bridge (1st floor)* ⊠ EH1 1AD
– ℰ (0131) 226 18 88 – www.ondinerestaurant.co.uk
– Closed 1 week early January and 24-26 December

XX **Forth Floor at Harvey Nichols** 🍸 ⩽ 🛱 ᜵ 🖾 🕅

MODERN CUISINE · FASHIONABLE A buzzy fourth floor eatery and terrace offering wonderful rooftop views. Dine on accomplished modern dishes in the restaurant or on old favourites in the all-day bistro. Arrive early and start with a drink in the smart cocktail bar.

Menu £ 33 (lunch and early dinner) – Carte £ 35/49

Town plan: EY-z – *30-34 St Andrew Sq* ⊠ EH2 2AD
– ℰ (0131) 524 83 50 – www.harveynichols.com
– Closed 25 December, 1 January and dinner Sunday-Monday

XX **Angels with Bagpipes** 🛱

MODERN CUISINE · BISTRO Small, stylish restaurant named after the wooden sculpture in St Giles Cathedral, opposite. Dishes are more elaborate than the menu implies; modern interpretations of Scottish classics could include 'haggis, neeps and tattiesgine'.

Menu £ 15 (lunch) – Carte £ 29/49

Town plan: EZ-a – *343 High St, Royal Mile* ⊠ EH1 1PW
– ℰ (0131) 220 1111 – www.angelswithbagpipes.co.uk
– Closed 4-19 January and 24-26 December

X **Timberyard** 🛱 ᜵ 🕅 ⇔

MODERN CUISINE · RUSTIC Trendy warehouse restaurant; its spacious, rustic interior incorporating wooden floors and wood-burning stoves. Scandic-influenced menu offers 'bites', 'small' and 'large' sizes, with some home-smoked dishes and an emphasis on distinct, punchy flavours. Cocktails are made with vegetable purées and foraged herbs.

Menu £ 27 (lunch and early dinner) – Carte £ 44/51

Town plan: DZ-s – *10 Lady Lawson St* ⊠ EH3 9DS
– ℰ (0131) 221 1222 (booking essential at dinner) – www.timberyard.co
– Closed Christmas, 1 week April, 1 week October, Sunday and Monday

X **Aizle** 🆕 🕅

MODERN CUISINE · SIMPLE Modest little suburban restaurant whose name means 'ember' or 'spark'. Well-balanced, skilfully prepared dishes are, in effect, a surprise, as the set menu is presented as a long list of ingredients – the month's 'harvest'.

Menu £ 45 – set menu only

Town plan: EZ-z – *107-109 St Leonard's St* ⊠ EH8 9QY
– ℰ (0131) 662 9349 – www.aizle.co.uk – dinner only
– Closed 4-19 July, 25-31 December, Monday and Tuesday

X Passorn

THAI · FRIENDLY The staff are super-friendly at this extremely popula neighbourhood restaurant, whose name means 'Angel'. Authentic menu feature Thai classics and old family recipes; the seafood dishes are a high light and presentation is first class. Spices and other ingredients are flown in from Thailand.

Menu £16 (weekday lunch)
– Carte £23/36

Town plan: DZ-e – 23-23a Brougham Pl ⊠ EH3 9JU
– ℰ (0131) 229 1537 (booking essential)
– www.passornthai.com
– Closed 25-26 December, 1-2 January, Sunday and Monday lunch

X Dogs

TRADITIONAL CUISINE · BISTRO Cosy, slightly bohemian-style eatery on the first floor of a classic Georgian mid-terrace, with two high-ceilinged, shabby chic dining rooms and an appealing bar. Robust, good value comfort food is crafted from local, seasonal produce; dishes such as cock-a-leekie soup and devilled ox livers feature.

Carte £14/21

Town plan: DY-c – 110 Hanover St (1st Floor) ⊠ EH2 1DR
– ℰ (0131) 220 1208
– www.thedogsonline.co.uk
– Closed 25 December and 1 January

X The Atelier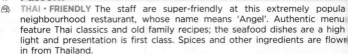

MEDITERRANEAN · BISTRO Attractive little restaurant with bright orange chairs and a stone feature wall. The chef is Polish but his dishes have French and Italian influences; fresh ingredients are prepared with care and cooking has a subtle modern slant.

Menu £20 (lunch)
– Carte £24/46

Town plan: CZ-s – 159 Morrison St ⊠ EH3 8AG
– ℰ (0131) 629 13 44
– www.theatelierrestaurant.co.uk
– Closed 2-3 weeks January and 25-26 December

X Edinburgh Larder Bistro

REGIONAL · BISTRO Sustainability and provenance are key here: the chef is forager and fisherman, the tables are crafted from scaffold boards, old lobster creels act as lampshades, and the daily menu features carefully prepared sea sonal dishes.

Menu £15 (weekday lunch)
– Carte £24/36

Town plan: CZ-n – 1a Alva St ⊠ EH2 4PH
– ℰ (0131) 225 4599
– www.edinburghlarder.co.uk
– Closed 3-8 January, Sunday and Monday

X Blackfriars

REGIONAL · NEIGHBOURHOOD Hidden behind the castle is this intimate, nature themed, neighbourhood restaurant, which is well run by its experienced owners Produce is seasonal and dishes take their influences from around the world; the local game is a must-try.

Menu £19 (lunch)
– Carte dinner £25/40

Town plan: EZ-b – 57-61 Blackfriars St ⊠ EH1 1NB
– ℰ (0131) 558 8684
– www.blackfriarsedinburgh.co.uk
– Closed 25-26 December, 1 January, Monday and Tuesday except August

X Purslane

MODERN CUISINE · NEIGHBOURHOOD Set in a residential area, in the basement of a terraced Georgian house; an intimate restaurant of just 7 tables, with wallpaper featuring a pine tree motif. The chef carefully prepares modern dishes using well-practiced techniques.

Menu £ 18/30

Town plan: DY-e – *33a St Stephen St* ⊠ *EH3 5AH* – ℰ *(0131) 226 3500 (booking essential)* – *www.purslanerestaurant.co.uk* – *Closed 25-26 December, 1 January and Monday*

X Gardener's Cottage

TRADITIONAL CUISINE · INDIVIDUAL This quirky little eatery was once home to a royal gardener. Two cosy, simply furnished rooms have long communal tables. Lunch is light and dinner offers a 7 course, no-choice set menu; much of the produce is from the kitchen garden.

Menu £ 35 (dinner) – Carte lunch £ 16/24

Town plan: EY-c – *1 Royal Terrace Gardens* ⊠ *EH7 5DX* – ℰ *(0131) 558 1221 (bookings advisable at dinner)* – *www.thegardenerscottage.co* – *Closed Tuesday and Wednesday*

X Field

MODERN CUISINE · SIMPLE A rustic restaurant run by two young owners, comprising just 8 tables – which are overlooked by a huge canvas of a prized cow. The appealing menu changes slightly each day, offering original modern cooking with a playful element.

Menu £ 15 (lunch and early dinner) – Carte £ 22/28

Town plan: EZ-x – *41 West Nicholson St* ⊠ *EH8 9DB* – ℰ *(0131) 667 7010* – *www.fieldrestaurant.co.uk* – *Closed Monday*

X Bon Vivant

TRADITIONAL CUISINE · WINE BAR A relaxed wine bar in the city backstreets, with a dimly lit interior, tightly packed tables and a cheery, welcoming team. The appealing, twice daily menu has an eclectic mix of influences; start with some of the bite-sized nibbles.

Carte £ 17/30

Town plan: DY-v – *55 Thistle St* ⊠ *EH2 1DY* – ℰ *(0131) 225 3275* – *www.bonvivantedinburgh.co.uk* – *Closed 25-26 December and 1 January*

X Kanpai

JAPANESE · SIMPLE Uncluttered, modern Japanese restaurant with a smart sushi bar and cheerful service. Colourful, elaborate dishes have clean, well-defined flavours; the menu is designed to help novices feel confident and experts feel at home.

Carte £ 15/38

Town plan: DZ-n – *8-10 Grindlay St* ⊠ *EH3 9AS* – ℰ *(0131) 228 1602* – *www.kanpaisushi.co.uk* – *Closed Monday*

X Kim's Mini Meals

KOREAN · SIMPLE A delightfully quirky little eatery filled with bric-a-brac and offering good value, authentic Korean home cooking. Classic dishes like bulgogi, dolsot and jjigae come with your choice of meat or vegetables as the main ingredient.

Carte approx. £ 17

Town plan: EZ-u – *5 Buccleuch St* ⊠ *EH8 9JN* – ℰ *(0131) 629 79 51 (booking essential at dinner)* – *www.kimsminimeals.com*

X Bia Bistrot

CLASSIC CUISINE · NEIGHBOURHOOD A simple, good value neighbourhood bistro with a buzzy vibe. Unfussy, flavoursome dishes range in their influences due to the friendly owners' Irish-Scottish and French-Spanish heritages; they are husband and wife and cook together.

Menu £ 10 (lunch and early dinner)/26 – Carte £ 19/33

Town plan: AX-a – *19 Colinton Rd* ⊠ *EH10 5DP* – ℰ *(0131) 452 84 53* – *www.biabistrot.co.uk* – *Closed first week January, 1 week July, Sunday and Monday*

✕ Café St Honoré

FRENCH CLASSIC · BISTRO Long-standing French bistro, tucked away down a side street. The interior is cosy, with wooden marquetry, mirrors on the walls and tightly packed tables. Traditional Gallic menus use Scottish produce and they even smoke their own salmon.

Menu £16/19 – Carte £30/41

Town plan: DY-r – *34 North West Thistle Street Ln.* ⊠ *EH2 1EA* – ℰ *(0131) 226 22 11 (booking essential)* – *www.cafesthonore.com* – *Closed 24-26 December and 1-2 January*

✕ Wedgwood   AC 🕅

MODERN CUISINE · FRIENDLY Atmospheric bistro hidden away at the bottom of the Royal Mile. Well-presented dishes showcase produce foraged from the surrounding countryside and feature some original, modern combinations. It's personally run by a friendly team.

Menu £17 (lunch) – Carte £30/49

Town plan: EY-a – *267 Canongate* ⊠ *EH8 8BQ* – ℰ *(0131) 558 87 37* – *www.wedgwoodtherestaurant.co.uk* – *Closed 2-22 January and 25-26 December*

🕼 The Scran & Scallie   & AC

BRITISH TRADITIONAL · NEIGHBOURHOOD A more casual venture from Tom Kitchin and Dominic Jack, with a wood furnished bar and a dining room which blends rustic and contemporary décor. Extensive menus follow a 'Nature to Plate' philosophy and focus on the classical and the local.

Menu £15 (weekday lunch) – Carte £20/43

Town plan: CY-s – *1 Comely Bank Rd, Stockbridge* ⊠ *EH4 1DT* – ℰ *(0131) 332 6281 (booking advisable)* – *www.scranandscallie.com* – *Closed 25 December*

at Leith

🏠 Malmaison   ⌂ Ⅼ⅄ 🖵 & ⅘ 🅿

BUSINESS · STYLISH Impressive former seamen's mission located on the quayside; the first of the Malmaison hotels. The décor is a mix of bold stripes and contrasting black and white themes. Comfy, well-equipped bedrooms; one with a four-poster and a tartan roll-top bath. Intimate bar and a popular French brasserie and terrace.

100 rooms – 🛏£89/300 🛏🛏£89/300 – ☕£14

Town plan: BV-m – *1 Tower Pl* ⊠ *EH6 7BZ* – ℰ *(0844) 693 0652* – *www.malmaison.com*

✕✕✕ Martin Wishart   & AC 🕅

❀ **MODERN CUISINE · FORMAL** Elegant modern restaurant with immaculately set tables and attentive, professional service. Three 6 course menus – Tasting, Seafood and Vegetarian – and a concise à la carte. Fine ingredients are used in well-judged, flavourful combinations. Dishes display a classical base and elaborate, original touches.

→ Scallops with Jerusalem artichoke, sweet potato, hazelnut and truffle velouté. Roe deer with braised lettuce, carrot, date and BBQ winter onion. Valrhona dark chocolate and passion fruit délice, banana and yuzu sorbet, cocoa tuille.

Menu £29 (weekday lunch)/75

Town plan: BV-u – *54 The Shore* ⊠ *EH6 6RA* – ℰ *(0131) 553 35 57 (booking essential)* – *www.martin-wishart.co.uk* – *Closed 31 December-19 January, 25-26 December, Sunday and Monday*

Is breakfast included? If it is, the cup symbol ☕ appears after the number of rooms.

XX **Kitchin** (Tom Kitchin)   ♿ 🅰️ 🍸 ⇔

CLASSIC CUISINE · DESIGN Set in a smart, converted whisky warehouse. 'From nature to plate' is the eponymous chef-owner's motto and the use of natural features like bark wall coverings, alongside the more traditional Harris tweed, reflect his passion for using the freshest and best quality Scottish ingredients. Refined, generously proportioned classic French dishes are packed with vivid flavours.

➜ Local shellfish and sea vegetables with shellfish consommé. Boudin of Inverurie ox tongue, braised shin, bone marrow, potato and Vallum Farm carrots. Yoghurt panna cotta with apple sorbet and local sea buckthorn.

Menu £ 30/75 – Carte £ 53/87

Town plan: BV-z – *78 Commercial Quay* ✉ *EH6 6LX*
– ☏ *(0131) 555 17 55 (booking essential) – www.thekitchin.com*
– *Closed Christmas, New Year, Sunday and Monday*

XX **Plumed Horse**

MODERN CUISINE · NEIGHBOURHOOD A cosy, personally run restaurant with an ornate ceiling, colourful local art and an intimate feel. Well-crafted classical cooking has strong, bold flavours and makes good use of Scottish ingredients; the lunch menu is good value.

Menu £ 26/59

Town plan: BV-a – *50-54 Henderson St* ✉ *EH6 6DE*
– ☏ *(0131) 554 55 56 – www.plumedhorse.co.uk*
– *Closed 2 weeks summer, 1 week Easter, Christmas-early January, Sunday and Monday*

XX **Bistro Provence**   ♿

FRENCH CLASSIC · BISTRO This converted warehouse brings a taste of France to the cobbled quayside of Leith. It's very personally run by a gregarious owner and a welcoming team, and offers an appealing range of unfussy dishes with Provençal leanings.

Menu £ 10/36

Town plan: BV-c – *88 Commercial St* ✉ *EH6 6LX*
– ☏ *(0131) 344 4295 – www.bistroprovence.co.uk*
– *Closed 4-14 January and Monday*

at Currie Southwest: 5 mi on A70 – ✉ City Of Edinburgh

🏠 **Violet Bank House**   🚪 ⅋ 🅿️

FAMILY · COSY 200 year old cottage in a conservation zone, with gardens running down to the river. Homely bedrooms have a host of thoughtful extras. Impressive breakfasts feature everything from pancakes to cheese and herb scones with poached eggs.

3 rooms ☑ – †£ 60/120 ††£ 100/140
167 Lanark Rd West ✉ *EH14 5NZ*
– ☏ *(0131) 451 51 03 – www.violetbankhouse.co.uk*
– *Closed November -March*

at Kirknewton Southwest: 7 mi by A71 – Plan: AX – ✉ Edinburgh

🏨 **Dalmahoy H. & Country Club**   ⛲ ⅋ ⇐ 🚪 🖥️ 🖥️ ♨ 🛁 ⅋ 🍽️ 🖥️ ⚡ ⅋

CHAIN HOTEL · CONTEMPORARY An extended Georgian mansion boasting a championship golf course and extensive leisure facilities. Country house style guest areas and well-equipped bedrooms; the best, in the main house, are a blend of the old and the new. Traditional, formal dining and good views over the 1,000 acre grounds in Pentland; laid-back all-day menus in bright, modern Zest.

215 rooms ☑ – †£ 95/195 ††£ 95/195 – 5 suites
✉ *EH27 8EB – Northwest : 2 mi on A 71*
– ☏ *(0131) 333 18 45 – www.marriottdalmahoy.co.uk*

at Ingliston West: 7 mi on A8

🏨 Norton House   ✿ ⇦ ☒ ☻ ⋔ ♨ ☳ ⊡ ⚐ ⛨ 🅿

COUNTRY HOUSE · CONTEMPORARY 19C country house in mature grounds close to the airport. Bedrooms in the main house are classical; the executive rooms in the extension are stylish and modern. An impressive oak staircase and country house lounges contrast with a state-of-the-art spa. Dine in the intimate restaurant or relaxed brasserie.

83 rooms ☲ – �£ 89/295 ♗♗£ 99/295 – 2 suites

✉ EH28 8LX – 𝒞 (0131) 333 12 75 – www.handpicked.co.uk

Ushers – See restaurant listing

𝕏𝕏 Ushers   ⇦ ⅙ 🆔 🅿

MODERN CUISINE · INTIMATE Intimate hotel restaurant named after former owners of the house. Elaborate cooking uses top quality seasonal ingredients. Choose from the tasting menu or a concise, weekly à la carte. Techniques are modern and combinations, original.

Carte £ 38/58

Norton House Hotel, ✉ EH28 8LX – 𝒞 (0131) 333 12 75 (booking essential)
– www.handpicked.co.uk – dinner only – Closed January-February and Sunday-Tuesday

EDNAM – The Scottish Borders ➔ See Kelso

ELGIN

Moray – Pop. 23 128 – Regional map n° **16**-C1

▶ Edinburgh 198 mi – Aberdeen 68 mi – Fraserburgh 61 mi – Inverness 39 mi

🏨 Mansion House   ✿ ⇦ ☒ ⋔ ♨ ⚐ ⛨ 🅿

CASTLE · HISTORIC Grand Victorian country house in pleasant gardens. Beautiful Georgian-style drawing room with a grand piano, and a snooker table in the 'wee bar'. Luxurious bedrooms – some with sleigh beds, four-posters or river views. Classically furnished, formal dining room offers an eclectic mix of dishes.

26 rooms ☲ – ♗£ 107/134 ♗♗£ 164/212

The Haugh ✉ IV30 1AW – via Haugh Rd – 𝒞 (01343) 548 811
– www.mansionhousehotel.co.uk – Closed 25 December

🏠 Pines   ⇦ 🅿

TOWNHOUSE · CLASSIC Charming Victorian villa featuring original tiled floors and stained glass windows. Homely lounge and comfortable, traditionally styled bedrooms; Room 4 is the best with its antique four-poster bed. Highland products at breakfast.

6 rooms ☲ – ♗£ 50/60 ♗♗£ 66/70

East Rd ✉ IV30 1XG – East : 0.5 mi on A 96 – 𝒞 (01343) 552 495
– www.thepinesguesthouse.com

ELIE

Fife – Pop. 942 – Regional map n° **16**-D2

▶ Edinburgh 44 mi – Dundee 24 mi – St Andrews 13 mi

𝕏𝕏 Sangster's (Bruce Sangster)

❀ **CLASSIC CUISINE · COSY** Sweet little restaurant in a sleepy coastal hamlet, slickly run by a husband and wife team. The well-respected chef uses Fife's natural larder and willingly embraces new ideas. Appealing, flavoursome dishes are well-proportioned, carefully executed and have modern overtones: the simplest dishes are the best.

➔ Truffled Ragstone goat's cheese mousse with gingerbread and beetroot meringues. Roast saddle of red deer with celeriac & potato gratin and braised lentils. Caramel cream with poached kumquats, orange sorbet and honeycomb.

Menu £ 42/48

51 High St ✉ KY9 1BZ – 𝒞 (01333) 331 001 (booking essential)
– www.sangsters.co.uk – dinner only and Sunday lunch – Closed January-mid February, 1 week November, 25-26 December, Sunday dinner, Monday and Tuesday November-March

ERISKA (Isle of)

Argyll and Bute – ⊠ Oban – Regional map n° **16**-B2
▶ Edinburgh 127 mi – Glasgow 104 mi – Oban 12 mi

🏰 **Isle of Eriska** ☆ 🐾 ≤ 🍴 🔲 🗓 🌐 🛋 🎿 👙 ♨ 🅿

GRAND LUXURY · PERSONALISED 19C baronial mansion in an idyllic spot on a private island, boasting fantastic views over Lismore and the mountains; unusually, it's family run. Open-fired guest areas display modern touches and the spa and leisure facilities are superb. Bedrooms are bright, stylish and well-equipped; some feature hot tubs.

23 rooms � – ♦£ 180/410 ♦♦£ 350/500 – 7 suites
Benderloch ⊠ *PA37 1SD* – ⌀ *(01631) 720 371* – *www.eriska-hotel.co.uk* – *Closed 3-20 January*

🌼 **Isle of Eriska** – See restaurant listing

XXX **Isle of Eriska** ≤ 🍴 🅰🅲 🅿

🌼 **MODERN CUISINE · ELEGANT** Set in a country house on a private island, this modern dining room and conservatory offer enviable views. The concise daily menu has top Scottish produce to the fore and leaves plenty to the imagination; cooking is original and creative but still gives a nod to the classics. Textures and tastes are spot on.

➜ Braised ox cheek, parsley porridge, onion and cep. Isle of Gigha halibut with BBQ leek, samphire and pine vinegar sauce. Muscovado parfait with poached rhubarb, white chocolate curd and oats.

Menu £ 55

Isle of Eriska H., Benderloch ⊠ *PA37 1SD* – ⌀ *(01631) 720 371 (bookings essential for non-residents)* – *www.eriska-hotel.co.uk* – *dinner only* – *Closed 3-20 January*

EUROCENTRAL

North Lanarkshire – Regional map n° **15**-B1
▶ Edinburgh 34 mi – London 397 mi – Glasgow 12 mi – Paisley 20 mi

🏰 **Dakota** ☆ 🛋 🖵 ⚖ 🅰🅲 👙 🅿

BUSINESS · STYLISH Sleek black hotel visible from the M8: perfect for the image-conscious business traveller. Spacious bedrooms offer free wi-fi, king-sized beds and smart, modern shower rooms. Classic dishes served in the open-plan Grill restaurant, which is decorated with huge, blown-up pictures from 'The Eagle' comic.

92 rooms ⊆ – ♦£ 99/199 ♦♦£ 109/254
1-3 Parklands Ave ⊠ *ML1 4WQ* – ⌀ *(01698) 835 440* – *www.dakotahotels.co.uk*

EVANTON

Highland – Regional map n° **17**-C2
▶ Edinburgh 171 mi – Inverness 17 mi – Dingwall 7 mi

🏠 **Kiltearn House** 🆕 🐾 ≤ 🍴 🐾 🅿

COUNTRY HOUSE · CONTEMPORARY This large sandstone former manse sits in a quiet spot, yet is only a few minutes from the A9. It has a classical sitting room and a conservatory breakfast room; bedrooms are more modern – two have views over Cromarty Firth.

5 rooms ⊆ – ♦£ 72/130 ♦♦£ 96/230
⊠ *IV16 9UY* – *South : 1 mi by B 817 on Kiltearn Burial Ground rd* – ⌀ *(01349) 830 617* – *www.kiltearn.co.uk* – *Closed 25 December*

FAIRLIE

North Ayrshire – Pop. 1 424 – Regional map n° **15**-A1
▶ Edinburgh 79 mi – London 434 mi – Glasgow 34 mi

✕ Catch at Fins   🚫 P

FISH AND SEAFOOD · RUSTIC Seafood is the order of the day – with crab, lobster and mackerel from Largs – but there's also beech-smoked produce from the next door smokery. Sit in the cosy bothy or spacious conservatory and bring a bottle from the farm shop.
Carte £ 23/36

Fencebay Fisheries, Fencefoot Farm ⊠ KA29 0EG – South : 1.5 mi on A 78 – ℰ (01475) 568 989 (booking essential) – www.fencebay.com – Closed 26 December, 1-2 January, Sunday dinner-Wednesday

FIONNPHORT – Argyll and Bute → See Mull (Isle of)

FLODIGARRY – Highland → See Skye (Isle of)

FOCHABERS
Moray – Pop. 1 728 – Regional map n° **16**-C1
▶ Edinburgh 175 mi – London 580 mi – Aberdeen 56 mi – Inverness 48 mi

🏠 Trochelhill Country House   🌿 🚲 ✗ ✗ P

COUNTRY HOUSE · CLASSIC Whitewashed Victorian house; well-run by friendly owners who serve tea and cake on arrival. Spacious bedrooms feature modern bathrooms with walk-in showers; 2 have roll-top baths. Breakfast includes haggis, black pudding and homemade bread.
3 rooms 🖙 – 🛏£ 70 🛏🛏£ 110

⊠ IV32 7LN – West : 2.75 mi by A 96 off B 9015 – ℰ (01343) 821 267 – www.trochelhill.co.uk

FORT AUGUSTUS
Highland – Pop. 621 – Regional map n° **17**-C3
▶ Edinburgh 158 mi – Inverness 34 mi – Fort William 32 mi

🏠 The Lovat   ✿ 🚲 🖥 🚲 P

TRADITIONAL · STYLISH A professionally run Victorian house which has been given a bold, stylish makeover. Bedrooms are a mix of the classic – with feature beds and antique furnishings – and the contemporary, with vibrant colours and feature wallpapers.
28 rooms 🖙 – 🛏£ 75/252 🛏🛏£ 83/263

⊠ PH32 4DU – ℰ (01456) 459 250 – www.thelovat.com
Station Road • Brasserie – See restaurant listing

✕✕ Station Road ⓝ   🚲 🚲 P

MODERN CUISINE · FORMAL Light, spacious hotel dining room with views up the Great Glen and a formal feel. It's only open for dinner and offers a 5 course no-choice set menu. Elaborate modern cooking features adventurous texture and flavour combinations.
Menu £ 50 – set menu only

The Lovat Hotel, ⊠ PH32 4DU – ℰ (01456) 459 250 (booking essential) – www.thelovat.com – dinner only – Closed November-Easter and Sunday-Tuesday

✕ Brasserie ⓝ   🚲 🏵 🚲

MODERN CUISINE · BRASSERIE Modern brasserie at the side of a hotel, with a large lawned garden and picnic benches; it offers informal yet surprisingly sophisticated dining. Classically based dishes are given a modern makeover and feature good ingredients.
Carte £ 26/45

The Lovat Hotel, ⊠ PH32 4DU – ℰ (01456) 459 250 – www.thelovat.com

FORT WILLIAM
Highland – Pop. 5 883 – Regional map n° **17**-C3
▶ Edinburgh 133 mi – Glasgow 104 mi – Inverness 68 mi – Oban 50 mi

🏰 Inverlochy Castle

GRAND LUXURY · CLASSIC Striking castellated house in beautiful grounds, boasting stunning views over the loch to Glenfinnan. The classical country house interior comprises sumptuous open-fired lounges and a grand hall with an impressive ceiling mural. Elegant bedrooms offer the height of luxury; mod cons include mirrored TVs.

18 rooms ☟ – †£ 295/425 ††£ 450/695 – 4 suites

Torlundy PH33 6SN – Northeast : 3 mi on A 82 – ℰ (01397) 702 177
– www.inverlochycastlehotel.com

Inverlochy Castle – See restaurant listing

🏠 Grange

TOWNHOUSE · PERSONALISED Delightful Victorian house with an attractive garden and immaculate interior, set in a quiet residential area. The beautiful lounge displays fine fabrics and the lovely breakfast room boasts Queen Anne style chairs. Bedrooms are extremely well appointed, with smart bathrooms.

3 rooms ☟ – †£ 140 ††£ 150

Grange Rd. ✉ PH33 6JF – South : 0.75 mi by A 82 and Ashburn Lane
– ℰ (01397) 705 516 – www.thegrange-scotland.co.uk
– Closed November-mid March

🏠 Ashburn House

TRADITIONAL · PERSONALISED Attractive Victorian guesthouse overlooking the loch and mountains. Bedrooms are bright and modern; Room 1 is the largest and has the best views. On arrival, tea and homemade shortbread are served in the comfy conservatory lounge.

6 rooms ☟ – †£ 50/55 ††£ 100/120

18 Achintore Rd. ✉ PH33 6RQ – South : 0.5 mi on A 82 – ℰ (01397) 706 000
– www.highland5star.co.uk

🏠 The Gantocks

TRADITIONAL · COSY Whitewashed bungalow with loch views; run by experienced owners. Spacious, modern bedrooms boast king-sized beds, large baths and nice toiletries. Unusual offerings and water views at breakfast.

3 rooms ☟ – †£ 110/120 ††£ 130/140

Achintore Rd. ✉ PE33 6RN – South : 1 mi on A 82
– ℰ (01397) 702 050 – www.fortwilliam5star.co.uk
– Closed December-February

XxxX Inverlochy Castle

TRADITIONAL CUISINE · LUXURY Set within a striking castle in the shadow of Ben Nevis and offering stunning loch views. Three smart, candlelit dining rooms are filled with period sideboards and polished silver. Traditional dishes feature quality Scottish produce.

Menu £ 38/67

Torlundy ✉ PH33 6SN – Northeast : 3 mi on A 82 – ℰ (01397) 702 177 (booking essential) – www.inverlochycastlehotel.com

X Lime Tree An Ealdhain

MODERN CUISINE · RUSTIC Attractive 19C manse – now an informally run restaurant and art gallery displaying the owner's landscape pieces. The appealingly rustic dining room has exposed beams and an open kitchen and cooking is fresh and modern. Bedrooms are simply furnished and well-priced – ask for one with a view of Loch Linnhe.

Carte £ 26/48

9 rooms ☟ – †£ 70/120 ††£ 80/130

Achintore Rd ✉ PH33 6RQ – ℰ (01397) 701 806 – www.limetreefortwilliam.co.uk
– dinner only – Closed November and 24-26 December

✗ Crannog

FISH AND SEAFOOD · COSY Popular restaurant with a bright red roof and a colourful boat-like interior; set on the pier above Loch Linnhe – try to get a table by the window. Fresh local fish and shellfish are simply prepared. The 2 course lunch is good value.

Menu £15 (lunch) – Carte £28/36

Town Pier ⊠ PH33 6DB – ℰ (01397) 705 589 (booking essential)
– www.crannog.net – Closed 25-26 December and 1 January

FORTINGALL

Perth and Kinross – Regional map n° **16**-C2
▶ Edinburgh 84 mi – Perth 40 mi – Pitlochry 23 mi

⌂ Fortingall

TRADITIONAL · STYLISH Stylish Arts and Crafts house on a tranquil private estate, boasting lovely country views. The interior is delightful, with its snug open-fired bar and cosy sitting rooms filled with Scottish country knick-knacks. Bedrooms are modern but in keeping with the building's age. Dining is formal and classical.

10 rooms ⊊ – †£80/90 ††£180

⊠ PH15 2NQ – ℰ (01887) 830 367 – www.fortingall.com

FORTROSE

Highland – Pop. 1 367 – Regional map n° **17**-C2
▶ Edinburgh 166 mi – London 571 mi – Inverness 12 mi – Elgin 48 mi

⌂ Water's Edge

LUXURY · STYLISH Smart, personally run guesthouse with attractive garden and stunning views over the Moray Firth. Immaculately kept guest areas include a small lounge and an adjoining antique-furnished breakfast room. Classically stylish first floor bedrooms open out onto a roof terrace – keep an eye out for the dolphins!

3 rooms ⊊ – †£150/160 ††£150/160

Canonbury Ter ⊠ IV10 8TT – on A 832 – ℰ (01381) 621 202
– www.watersedge.uk.com – Closed mid October-April

GALSON – Western Isles ➜ See Lewis and Harris (Isle of)

GATEHEAD

East Ayrshire – ⊠ East Ayrshire – Regional map n° **15**-B2
▶ Edinburgh 72 mi – Glasgow 25 mi – Kilmarnock 5 mi

ℙ Cochrane Inn

TRADITIONAL CUISINE · PUB This ivy-covered pub is surprisingly bright and modern inside, with its copper lampshades, coal-effect gas fires and striking contemporary art. It offers a good range of tasty, generously priced dishes; the Express Menu is a steal.

Menu £15 (lunch and early dinner) – Carte £20/37

45 Main Rd ⊠ KA2 0AP – ℰ (01563) 570 122 – www.costley-hotels.co.uk

GATTONSIDE – The Scottish Borders ➜ See Melrose

GIFFNOCK

East Renfrewshire – Pop. 12 156 – Regional map n° **15**-B1
▶ Glasgow 7 mi – Edinburgh 46 mi – London 404 mi

X **Catch** Ⓝ &. AK

FISH AND CHIPS · **SIMPLE** Modern fish and chip shop with exposed brick walls and nautical styling; sit in a booth to take in all the action from the large open kitchen. Fresh, sustainably sourced fish comes in crisp batter, accompanied by twice-cooked chips.

Carte £ 15/29

186 Fenwick Rd ⊠ *G46 6XF* – *℘ (0141) 638 9169 (bookings advisable at dinner)*
– www.catchfishandchips.co.uk – Closed Monday

GIGHA (Isle of)

Argyll and Bute – Regional map n° **16**-A3
▶ Edinburgh 168 mi – Oban 74 mi – Dunoon 100 mi

X **The Boathouse** 🛱 P

FISH AND SEAFOOD · **RUSTIC** This 300 year old boathouse is set on a small community-owned island, overlooking the water. Whitewashed stone walls and beamed ceilings enhance the rustic feel. Menus cater for all, centring around fresh seafood and local meats.

Carte £ 21/43

Ardminish Bay ⊠ *PA41 7AA* – *℘ (01583) 505 123 – www.boathousegigha.co.uk*
– Closed November-Easter

GOOD TIPS!

This former industrial powerhouse has been reborn as a cultural and commercial hub, with a lively dining scene to boot. History is all around: witness the Grand Central Hotel, to which the world's first long-distance television pictures were transmitted by John Logie Baird. Modernity comes in the form of creative, cutting-edge restaurants like Cail Bruich.

GLASGOW

Glasgow City – Pop. 590 507 – Regional map n° **15**-B1
▶ Edinburgh 46 mi – London 399 mi

Hotels

🏠🏠 Hotel du Vin at One Devonshire Gardens 🏠🏠 ⚜ 🕭 🖐

TOWNHOUSE · STYLISH Collection of adjoining townhouses boasting original 19C stained glass, wood panelling and a labyrinth of corridors. Furnished in dark opulent shades but with a modern, country house air. Luxurious bedrooms; one with a small gym and sauna.

49 rooms – ♦£ 109/300 ♦♦£ 109/300 – ☷ £ 18 – 4 suites
Town plan: AV-a – *1 Devonshire Gdns* ⊠ *G12 0UX* – *𝒞 (0844) 736 42 56*
– *www.hotelduvin.com*
Bistro – See restaurant listing

🏠🏠 Blythswood Square 🏠 ⊕ 🕭 🖐 🕭 🕭 🕭 🖐

HISTORIC · DESIGN Stunning property on a delightful Georgian square; once the Scottish RAC HQ. Modern décor contrasts with original fittings. Dark, moody bedrooms have marble bathrooms; the Penthouse Suite features a bed adapted from a snooker table.

100 rooms ☷ – ♦£ 120/400 ♦♦£ 120/400 – 1 suite
Town plan: CY-n – *11 Blythswood Sq* ⊠ *G2 4AD* – *𝒞 (0141) 248 88 88*
– *www.blythswoodsquare.com*
Blythswood Square – See restaurant listing

Symbols shown in red 🏠🏠 XxX indicate particularly charming establishments.

INDEX OF STREET NAMES IN GLASGOW

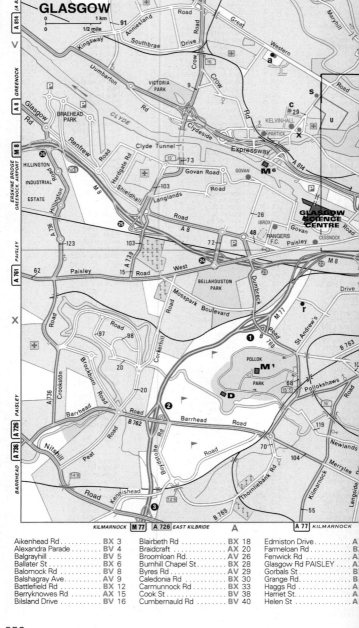

GLASGOW

DUMBARTON, CRIANLARICH A 82 A 739 (A 81) A

A 82 (A 82)
A 814
A 8 GREENOCK
M 8 ERSKINE BRIDGE GREENOCK, AIRPORT
A 761 PAISLEY
A 736 PAISLEY
A 726 BARRHEAD

0 1 km
0 1/2 mile

91

Anniesland Road

Kingsway Southbrae Drive

Dumbarton Road

Crow Road

VICTORIA PARK

CLYDE

BRAEHEAD PARK

Glasgow Rd

Renfrew Road

Hardgate Rd

Shieldhall

HILLINGTON INDUSTRIAL ESTATE

Hillington Road

M 8

123

62

Paisley 15 A 739 Road West

Road

Crookston

Brockburn Road

Barrhead Road B 762

Nitshill Peat Road

Kennishead Road

Clyde Tunnel

Govan Road GOVAN

Langlands Road

Road A 8

103

103

72

Mosspark Boulevard

BELLAHOUSTON PARK

Corkerhill Road

20

20

Barrhead Road

Boydstone Rd

Road

KILMARNOCK M 77 A 726 EAST KILBRIDE A

Great Western Road

Maryhill

a

Road

KELVINHALL PARTICK

Clydeside Expressway

A 814

M 6

GLASGOW SCIENCE CENTRE

IBROX Govan Road

RANGERS F.C. Paisley

48

26

Dumbreck Road

M 77

St Andrew's Road B 768

POLLOK PARK M 1 D

68 15.3

Pollokshaws Road

119

70

104

Newlands

Merrylee

Thornliebank Rd

Kilmarnock Road

55

B 769 A 77 KILMARNOCK

Drive

B 763

Langside

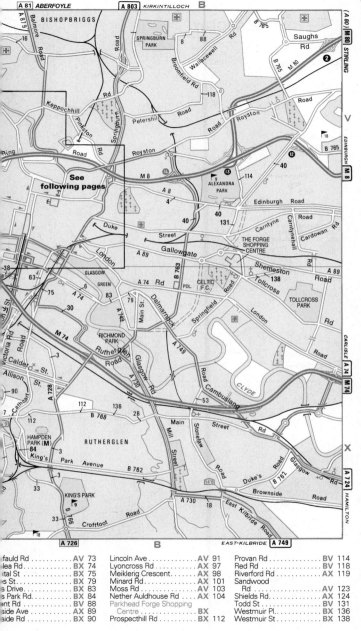

A 81 *ABERFOYLE*   A 803 *KIRKINTILLOCH*   **B**

BISHOPBRIGGS

SPRINGBURN PARK

Keppochhill   Rd

**See
following pages**

GLASGOW

GLASGOW
GREEN

RICHMOND
PARK

Ruther Glen   Road

M 74

HAMPDEN
PARK (M)

RUTHERGLEN

King's   Park   Avenue   B 762

KING'S PARK

Crofttoot   Road

A 726   B   EAST-KILBRIDE   A 749

ALEXANDRA
PARK

Edinburgh Road

THE FORGE SHOPPING
CENTRE

CELTIC
F.C.

TOLLCROSS
PARK

CLYDE

Cambuslang

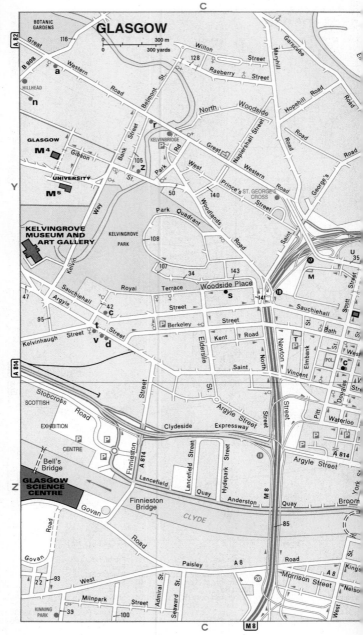

GLASGOW

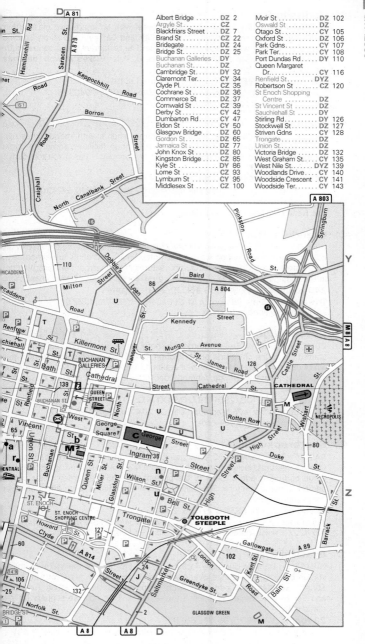

859

🏨 Radisson Blu

☆ ▧ 🏠 ⬚ ☺ ♿ ▣ 🏊 ▣

BUSINESS · MODERN Stylish commercial hotel with an impressive glass atrium. Bedrooms come in three styles – Modern, City, and Gallery – and all are spacious and contemporary with a Scandinavian edge. The restaurant has a central buffet breakfast area and an all-encompassing menu; Peter Blake's artwork decorates the walls.

247 rooms 🖵 – ♦£ 99/305 ♦♦£ 99/325 – 1 suite
Town plan: DZ-d – *301 Argyle St.* ✉ *G2 8DL* – ✆ *(0141) 204 33 33*
– *www.radissonblu.co.uk/hotel-glasgow*

🏨 Malmaison

☆ ⬚ ♿ 🏊

BUSINESS · STYLISH Impressive-looking former church with moody, masculine décor. Stylish, boldly coloured bedrooms offer good facilities; some are duplex suites. The Big Yin Suite – named after Billy Connolly – has a roll-top bath in the room.

72 rooms 🖵 – ♦£ 99/185 ♦♦£ 109/195 – 8 suites
Town plan: CY-c – *278 West George St* ✉ *G2 4LL* – ✆ *(0141) 572 10 00*
– *www.malmaison.com*
The Honours – See restaurant listing

🏨 Grand Central

☆ ⬚ ♿ 🏊 🏊

HISTORIC · MODERN Renowned hotel built into the main station; the first TV signal broadcast from London was to this hotel. Smart bedrooms are aimed at the corporate market. Original plasterwork features in the ballroom and marble floors in the champagne bar. The contemporary restaurant boasts Murano chandeliers.

240 rooms 🖵 – ♦£ 99/369 ♦♦£ 99/369 – 3 suites
Town plan: DZ-a – *99 Gordon St* ✉ *G1 3SF* – ✆ *(0141) 240 37 00*
– *www.grandcentralhotel.co.uk*

🏨 Hotel Indigo

☆ 🏊 ⬚ ♿ ▣ 🏊

BUSINESS · DESIGN Stylish, corporate hotel in a grand 19C building which started life as the city's first power station. Bright colour schemes and bold murals of city sights feature in the well-equipped bedrooms; each floor has a different colour theme. The huge, vibrantly decorated restaurant offers a classic brasserie menu.

94 rooms – ♦£ 100/250 ♦♦£ 120/300 – 🖵 £ 17
Town plan: CZ-v – *75 Waterloo St* ✉ *G2 7DA* – ✆ *(0141) 226 77 00*
– *www.hotelindigoglasgow.com*

🏨 Sherbrooke Castle

☆ 🛏 🏊 🏊 ▣

CASTLE · FUNCTIONAL 19C pink granite castle, in an attractive leafy suburb. Original features include an impressive staircase and stained glass windows. Large bedrooms add a touch of the present day and the garden suites provide additional home comforts. The panelled, open-fired dining room offers an all-encompassing menu.

18 rooms 🖵 – ♦£ 85/150 ♦♦£ 95/245 – 1 suite
Town plan: AX-r – *11 Sherbrooke Ave, Pollokshields* ✉ *G41 4PG* – ✆ *(0141) 427 42 27* – *www.sherbrookecastlehotel.com* – *Closed 1 January*

🏨 Grasshoppers

BUSINESS · DESIGN Unusually located, on the 6th floor of the Victorian railway station building; the lounge overlooks what is the largest glass roof in Europe. Stylish, well-designed bedrooms with bespoke Scandinavian-style furnishing and Scottish art. Smart, compact shower rooms. Three course suppers for residents only.

29 rooms 🖵 – ♦£ 75/95 ♦♦£ 85/115
Town plan: DZ-r – *Caledonian Chambers (6th Floor), 87 Union St* ✉ *G1 3TA* – ✆ *(0141) 222 2666* – *www.grasshoppersglasgow.com* – *Closed 3 days Christmas*

15 Glasgow 🛏 🕸 🅿

TOWNHOUSE · STYLISH Delightful Victorian townhouse on a quiet square, run by a charming, professional owner. Original features include mosaic floors and ornate cornicing. Extremely spacious, luxurious bedrooms have top quality furnishings and underfloor heating in the bathrooms. Cooked breakfast trays are delivered to your door.

5 rooms ☕ - ♥£ 99/135 ♥♥£ 99/145

Town plan: CY-s – *15 Woodside Pl.* ✉ *G3 7QL* – ☏ *(0141) 332 12 63* – *www.15glasgow.com* – *Closed 25 December and 3 January*

Restaurants

XXX Brian Maule at Chardon d'Or 🗚 🍷 🐝 ⇔

MODERN CUISINE · FORMAL Georgian townhouse in the city's heart, with original pillars, ornate carved ceilings and white walls hung with vibrant modern art. Classical cooking with a modern edge; luxurious ingredients and large portions. Friendly, efficient service.

Menu £ 22 (lunch and early dinner) – Carte £ 36/53

Town plan: CY-b – *176 West Regent St.* ✉ *G2 4RL* – ☏ *(0141) 248 38 01* – *www.brianmaule.com* – *Closed 25 December, 1 January, Sunday and bank holidays*

XXX Bistro 🐝 ₺

MODERN CUISINE · ELEGANT Elegant oak-panelled restaurant in a luxurious hotel. The three rooms are dark, moody and richly appointed, and there's a lovely lounge and whisky snug. Choose from well-prepared classics or more ambitious offerings on the degustation menu.

Menu £ 22 (lunch and early dinner) – Carte £ 31/74

Town plan: AV-a – *Hotel du Vin at One Devonshire Gardens, 1 Devonshire Gdns* ✉ *G12 OUX* – ☏ *(0844) 736 42 56* – *www.hotelduvin.com*

XX The Honours 🆕 ₺ 🗚 🖵

MODERN CUISINE · CLASSIC Intimate brasserie named after the Scottish Crown Jewels and set in the crypt of an old Greek Orthodox Church. Sit on leather banquettes under a vaulted ceiling and beside gilded columns. Classic brasserie dishes have a modern edge.

Menu £ 19 (lunch and early dinner) – Carte £ 33/57

Town plan: CY-c – *Malmaison Hotel, 278 West George St* ✉ *G2 4LL* – ☏ *(0141) 572 10 01* – *www.thehonours.co.uk*

XX Cail Bruich 🗚 🍷

MODERN CUISINE · INTIMATE High ceilinged restaurant with red leather banquettes and low hanging copper lamps. Menus range from a market selection to tasting options; cooking is modern and creative, with BBQ dishes a specialty. Its name means 'to eat well'.

Menu £ 21 (lunch and early dinner)/25 – Carte £ 32/53

Town plan: CY-a – *725 Great Western Rd.* ✉ *G12 8QX* – ☏ *(0141) 334 62 65* *(booking advisable)* – *www.cailbruich.co.uk* – *Closed 25-26 December, 1-2 January and lunch Monday and Tuesday*

XX Gamba 🐝

FISH AND SEAFOOD · BRASSERIE Tucked away in a basement but well-known by the locals. Appealing seafood menu of unfussy, classical dishes with the odd Asian influence; lemon sole is a speciality. Cosy bar-lounge and contemporary dining room hung with fish prints.

Menu £ 19 (lunch and early dinner) – Carte £ 26/53

Town plan: DZ-x – *225a West George St.* ✉ *G2 2ND* – ☏ *(0141) 572 08 99* – *www.gamba.co.uk* – *Closed 25 December and first 2 weeks January*

XX La Parmigiana 🔊 🕸

ITALIAN · NEIGHBOURHOOD Unashamedly classic in terms of its décor and its dishes, this well-regarded, professionally run Italian restaurant celebrated its 35th birthday in 2013. Red walls, white linen and efficient service. Refined cooking delivers bold flavours.

Menu £ 17 (lunch) – Carte £ 29/50

Town plan: CY-r – 447 Great Western Rd, Kelvinbridge ⊠ G12 8HH
– ℰ (0141) 334 06 86 (booking essential) – www.laparmigiana.co.uk
– Closed 25-26 December, 1 January and Sunday dinner

XX Ubiquitous Chip 🕸 ᖴ 🔊 🕸

MODERN CUISINE · BISTRO An iconic establishment on a cobbled street. The restaurant – with its ponds, fountains and greenery – offers modern classics which showcase local ingredients, while the mezzanine-level brasserie serves tasty Scottish favourites.

Menu £ 20 (lunch and early dinner) – Carte £ 29/64

Town plan: CY-n – 12 Ashton Ln ⊠ G12 8SJ
– ℰ (0141) 334 5007 (bookings advisable at dinner) – www.ubiquitouschip.co.uk
– Closed 25 December and 1 January

XX Blythswood Square 🍷 ᖴ 🔊 🕸

MODERN CUISINE · FASHIONABLE Stylish hotel restaurant in the ballroom of the old RAC building; chic in black and white, with a zinc-topped bar and Harris Tweed banquettes. Classic menu with meats from the Josper grill. Desserts showcase the kitchen's ambitious side.

Menu £ 22 (lunch and early dinner) – Carte £ 28/58

Town plan: CY-n – Blythswood Square Hotel, 11 Blythswood Sq ⊠ G2 4AD
– ℰ (0141) 248 88 88 – www.blythswoodsquare.com

XX Two Fat Ladies in the City ᖴ 🕸

TRADITIONAL CUISINE · CLASSIC Intimate restaurant which resembles an old-fashioned brasserie, courtesy of its wooden floor, banquettes and mirrors. Classically based dishes are straightforward in style, with a modern edge, and fresh Scottish seafood is a feature.

Menu £ 16 (lunch and early dinner) – Carte £ 30/56

Town plan: CY-e – 118a Blythswood St ⊠ G2 4EG
– ℰ (0141) 847 00 88 – www.twofatladiesrestaurant.com

XX Urban 🍷 🔊 🕸 ⇔

BRITISH TRADITIONAL · BRASSERIE Formerly the Bank of England's HQ. The grand dining room has booths, vibrant artwork and an impressive illuminated glass and wrought iron ceiling. Classic British dishes feature, along with live music every Friday and Saturday evening.

Menu £ 16 (lunch and early dinner) – Carte £ 22/63

Town plan: DZ-b – 23-25 St Vincent Pl. ⊠ G1 2DT
– ℰ (0141) 248 56 36 – www.urbanbrasserie.co.uk
– Closed 25 December and 1 January

X The Gannet ᖴ 🔊 🕸

🏵 BRITISH MODERN · RUSTIC You may well feel like a gannet after a visit to this appealingly rustic restaurant, where the tasty menus are constantly evolving. Classic dishes are presented in a modern style and are brought to the table by a charming team. Exposed stone, untreated wood and corrugated iron feature throughout.

Menu £ 25 (lunch and early dinner) – Carte £ 23/36

Town plan: CY-t – 1155 Argyle St ⊠ G3 8TB
– ℰ (0141) 204 20 81 – www.thegannetglasgow.com
– Closed first week January, 20-28 July, 25-26 December, Sunday dinner and Monday

✗ Ox and Finch 🏧 🛏 🍷 ⇔

🅐 BRITISH MODERN · DESIGN A bright, breezy team run this likeable rustic restaurant, with its tile-backed open kitchen and wines displayed in a huge metal cage. The Scottish and European small plates will tempt one and all: cooking centres around old favourites but with added modern twists, and the flavours really shine through.

Carte £ 15/25

Town plan: CY-c – 920 Sauchiehall St ✉ G3 7TF
– ✆ (0141) 339 8627 – www.oxandfinch.com
– Closed 25 December

✗ Porter & Rye 🆕 🍷 � 🏧 🛏

MEATS · TRENDY Small, well-run loft style operation where wooden floors and exposed bricks blend with steel balustrades and glass screens. Menus offer creative modern small plates and a good range of aged Scottish steaks, from onglet to porterhouse.

Carte £ 22/85

Town plan: CY-v – 1131 Argyle St ✉ G3 8ND
– ✆ (0141) 572 1212 (booking advisable) – www.porterandrye.com
– Closed 25 December and 1 January

✗ Stravaigin 🏡 � 🏧 🖵

🅐 INTERNATIONAL · SIMPLE Well-run eatery with a relaxed shabby-chic style, a bustling café bar and plenty of nooks and crannies. Interesting menus uphold the motto 'think global, eat local', with dishes ranging from carefully prepared Scottish favourites to tasty Asian-inspired fare. Monthly 'theme' nights range from haggis to tapas.

Carte £ 23/37

Town plan: CY-z – 28 Gibson St, ✉ G12 8NX
– ✆ (0141) 334 26 65 (booking essential at dinner) – www.stravaigin.co.uk
– Closed 25 December and 1 January

✗ Two Fat Ladies West End 🍷

FISH AND SEAFOOD · NEIGHBOURHOOD Quirky neighbourhood restaurant – the first in the Fat Ladies group – with red velour banquettes, bold blue and gold décor, and a semi open plan kitchen in the window. Cooking is simple and to the point, focusing on classical fish dishes.

Menu £ 18 (lunch and early dinner) – Carte £ 27/48

Town plan: AV-x – 88 Dumbarton Rd ✉ G11 6NX
– ✆ (0141) 339 1944 – www.twofatladiesrestaurant.com
– Closed 25-26 December and 1-2 January

✗ Dhabba 🛏 🏧 🕦

INDIAN · EXOTIC Stylish, modern restaurant in the heart of the Merchant City; its walls decorated with huge photos of Indian street scenes. Menus focus on northern India, with interesting breads and lots of tandoor dishes – the speciality is 'dum pukht'.

Menu £ 10 (weekday lunch) – Carte £ 20/38

Town plan: DZ-u – 44 Candleriggs ✉ G1 1LE
– ✆ (0141) 553 12 49 – www.thedhabba.com
– Closed 25 December and 1 January

✗ Hanoi Bike Shop 🛏 🏧

VIETNAMESE · SIMPLE Relaxed Vietnamese café; head to the lighter upstairs room with its fine array of lanterns. Simple menu of classic Vietnamese dishes including street food like rice paper summer rolls. Charming, knowledgeable staff offer recommendations.

Carte £ 20/27

Town plan: AV-s – 8 Ruthven Ln ✉ G12 9BG – (off Byres Road)
– ✆ (0141) 334 7165 – www.thehanoibikeshop.co.uk
– Closed 25 December and 1 January

✗ **Dakhin** ♿ ⑩

SOUTH-INDIAN · SIMPLE It's all about the cooking at this modest, brightly decorated restaurant: authentic, southern Indian dishes might include seafood from Kerala, lamb curry from Tamil Nadu, and their speciality, dosas – available with a variety of fillings.

Menu £10 (weekday lunch) – Carte £18/35

Town plan: DZ-n – 89 Candleriggs ⊠ G1 1NP
- ℰ (0141) 553 25 85 – www.dakhin.com
- Closed 25 December and 1 January

✗ **Cafezique** Ⓝ ♿ 🖭 🖵

MODERN CUISINE · BISTRO Behind the old Hargan's Dairy sign is a buzzy shabby-chic eatery with stone walls, original wood floors and striking monotone screen prints. All-day breakfasts and Mediterranean light bites are followed by vibrant dishes in two sizes.

Carte £21/28

Town plan: AV-c – 66 Hyndland St ⊠ G11 5PT
- ℰ (0141) 339 7180 – www.delizique.co.uk
- Closed 25-26 December and 1 January

🍴 **The Finnieston** 🍷 🏡 ♿

FISH AND SEAFOOD · FRIENDLY Small, cosy pub specialising in Scottish seafood and gin cocktails; with an intriguing ceiling, a welcoming fire and lots of booths. Dishes are light, tasty and neatly presented, relying on just a few ingredients so that flavours are clear.

Carte £19/51

Town plan: CY-d – 1125 Argyle St ⊠ G3 8ND
- ℰ (0141) 222 28 84 – www.thefinniestonbar.com
- Closed 25-26 December and 1 January

🍴 **Salisbury** Ⓝ 🖭

BRITISH MODERN · NEIGHBOURHOOD A bijou pub on the south side of the city. Its interior is modern and cosy; the staff are friendly; and the monthly menu has an eclectic mix of Scottish and international flavours. Local seafood is given an original modern twist.

Carte £19/43

Town plan: AX-s – 72 Nithsdale Rd ⊠ G41 2AN
- ℰ (0141) 423 0084 – www.salisburybar.com
- Closed 25 December and 1 January

GLENDEVON
Perth and Kinross – Regional map n° **16**-C2
▶ Edinburgh 37 mi – London 434 mi – Glasgow 43 mi – Aberdeen 109 mi

🍴 **Tormaukin Inn** ⇦ 🍷 🏡 🅿

TRADITIONAL CUISINE · RUSTIC Characterful inn run by a truly welcoming team. Eat in the dark beamed bar or the airy dining room. Well-priced, carefully executed dishes are traditionally based; for something a little different, choose one of the daily specials. Cosy bedrooms are spread between the inn, a chalet and a stable block.

Carte £19/49

13 rooms ⌑ – ♦£50/70 ♦♦£50/80
⊠ FK14 7JY – ℰ (01259) 781 252 – www.tormaukinhotel.co.uk
- Closed 25 December

GLENFINNAN
Highland – ⊠ Highland – Regional map n° **17**-B3
▶ Edinburgh 150 mi – Inverness 85 mi – Oban 66 mi

🏠 Prince's House   ☆ ⅍ 🅿

COUNTRY HOUSE · CLASSIC This 17C coaching inn – named after Bonnie Prince Charlie – once served the 'Road to the Isles'. It's still fiercely traditional, with its pitch pine ceilinged lounge-bar and comfy, cosy bedrooms. Dine from a daily menu of classical dishes, surrounded by an eclectic array of the owner's art.

9 rooms 🖵 – ♦£ 75/90 ♦♦£ 150/180

✉ PH37 4LT – ✆ (01397) 722 246 – www.glenfinnan.co.uk – Closed November-mid March except 27 December-2 January

GLENROTHES

Fife – Pop. 39 277 – Regional map n° **16**-C2

▶ Edinburgh 33 mi – Dundee 25 mi – Stirling 36 mi

🏠 Balbirnie House   ☆ ⅏ 🆓 🖾 🕹 🅿

COUNTRY HOUSE · CLASSIC Stunning Palladian mansion with formal gardens and extensive parkland. Large, well-furnished, country house drawing rooms; period features abound. Luxurious, comfortable bedrooms come in varying sizes. Elegant glass-roofed Orangery serves classics with a twist. Basement Bistro offers French favourites.

31 rooms 🖵 – ♦£ 115/145 ♦♦£ 190/300 – 1 suite

Balbirnie Park, Markinch ✉ KY7 6NE – Northeast : 1.75 mi by A 911 and A 92 on B 9130 – ✆ (01592) 610 066 – www.balbirnie.co.uk

GRANDTULLY

Perth and Kinross – Pop. 750 – Regional map n° **16**-C2

▶ Edinburgh 70 mi – London 475 mi – Glasgow 84 mi – Dundee 51 mi

🍴 Inn on the Tay   ⇔ 🆓 🕍 🕹 🅿

TRADITIONAL CUISINE · FRIENDLY A smart modern inn on the banks of the Tay. There's a snug bar and a large dining room with superb views over the water. Burgers and gourmet sandwiches fill the lunch menu, while in the evening, satisfying tried-and-tested classics feature. The owners are cheery and welcoming and the bedrooms, comfy and cosy.

Menu £ 12/35 – Carte £ 20/36

6 rooms 🖵 – ♦£ 55/75 ♦♦£ 110/150

✉ PH9 0PL – ✆ (01887) 840 760 – www.theinnonthetay.co.uk

GRANTOWN-ON-SPEY

Highland – Pop. 2 428 – Regional map n° **17**-D2

▶ Edinburgh 143 mi – Inverness 34 mi – Perth 99 mi

🏠 Culdearn House   ☆ 🆓 ⅍ 🅿

HISTORIC · ELEGANT Granite house built in 1860 by Lord Seafield for one of his four daughters; its small garden is home to a family of red squirrels. The elegant, open-fired lounge and spacious bedrooms are furnished in a period style. Formal dining room offers a classical daily menu which features quality Scottish ingredients.

6 rooms (dinner included) 🖵 – ♦£ 90/110 ♦♦£ 200/296

Woodlands Terr ✉ PH26 3JU – ✆ (01479) 872 106 – www.culdearn.com

🏠 Dulaig   🆓 ⅍ 🅿

TRADITIONAL · CLASSIC Small, detached, personally run guesthouse, built in 1910 and tastefully furnished with original Arts and Crafts pieces. Modern fabrics and an uncluttered feel in the comfortable bedrooms. Tea and homemade cake on arrival. Communal breakfasts include home-baked bread and muffins.

3 rooms 🖵 – ♦£ 120/140 ♦♦£ 160/180

Seafield Ave ✉ PH26 3JF – ✆ (01479) 872 065 – www.thedulaig.com – Closed 19 December-8 January

GULLANE

East Lothian – Pop. 2 568 – Regional map n° **15**-C1

▶ Edinburgh 20 mi – London 384 mi

Greywalls

🐾 🐕 ⚔ 🛏 🎿 🍽 ♨ 🏊 **P**

COUNTRY HOUSE · CLASSIC A long-standing, classic Edwardian country house by Lutyens, in a superb location adjoining the famous Muirfield golf course and overlooking the Firth of Forth. Classically styled, antique-furnished bedrooms and a cosy library. Assured, professional service. Delightful formal gardens designed by Jekyll.

23 rooms ⌿ – ♦£ 85/125 ♦♦£ 255/335

Duncur Rd, Muirfield ✉ *EH31 2EG – Northeast : 0.75 mi by A 198 –* ✆ *(01620) 842 144 – www.greywalls.co.uk*

Chez Roux – See restaurant listing

XX La Potinière

♿ **P**

TRADITIONAL CUISINE · COSY Sweet little restaurant with white walls and striking red curtains. Concise, regularly changing menus of carefully prepared, classical dishes; lunch is good value and their homemade bread is renowned. The two owners share the cooking.

Menu £ 20/45

Main St ✉ *EH31 2AA –* ✆ *(01620) 843 214 (booking essential) – www.lapotiniere.co.uk – Closed January, 25-26 December, Sunday dinner October-April, Monday, Tuesday and bank holidays*

XX Chez Roux

⚔ 🛏 ♻ **P**

FRENCH · INTIMATE A formal restaurant set in a classic country house hotel; enjoy an aperitif in the lounge or in the delightful Jekyll-designed gardens before dining with a superb view over the Muirfield golf course. Classical French menus have a Roux signature style and feature tried-and-tested classics with a modern edge.

Menu £ 30/32 – Carte £ 34/51

Greywalls Hotel, Duncur Rd, Muirfield ✉ *EH31 2EG – Northeast : 0.75 mi by A 198 –* ✆ *(01620) 842 144 (bookings essential for non-residents) – www.greywalls.co.uk*

HADDINGTON

East Lothian – Pop. 9 064 – Regional map n° **15**-D1

▶ Edinburgh 17 mi – Hawick 53 mi – Newcastle upon Tyne 101 mi

Letham House ⓝ

🐕 🛏 🍽 **P**

COUNTRY HOUSE · CLASSIC A classically proportioned former laird's house dating from 1645 and lovingly restored by the current owners. Luxurious bedrooms feature antique furniture, beautiful fabrics and modern, well-equipped bathrooms. Dine with your fellow guests: 3 courses of seasonal local produce are tailored to requirements.

6 rooms ⌿ – ♦£ 95/120 ♦♦£ 140/195

✉ *EH41 3SS – West : 1.25 mi on B 6471 –* ✆ *(01620) 820 055 – www.lethamhouse.com*

HARRAY → See Orkney Islands (Mainland)

HARRIS – Highland → See Lewis and Harris (Isle of)

INGLISTON – City of Edinburgh → See Edinburgh

INNERLEITHEN

The Scottish Borders – Pop. 3 031 – Regional map n° **15**-C2

▶ Edinburgh 31 mi – Dumfries 57 mi – Glasgow 60 mi

⌂ Caddon View ☆ 🛏 🅿

TOWNHOUSE · STYLISH Substantial Victorian house with a large garden and a cosy open-fired lounge; run by a hospitable couple. Individually decorated bedrooms have modern touches – 'Yarrow' is the most spacious and 'Moorfoot' has the best view. The bright, airy dining room offers a daily set menu of produce from the Tweed Valley.

8 rooms ☲ – **†**£ 52/80 **††**£ 70/110

14 Pirn Rd. ⊠ EH44 6HH – ℰ (01896) 830 208 – www.caddonview.co.uk – Closed 25-26 December

INVERGARRY

Highland – ⊠ Inverness – Regional map n° **17**-C3

▶ Edinburgh 159 mi – Fort William 25 mi – Inverness 43 mi – Kyle of Lochalsh 50 mi

⛫ Glengarry Castle ☆ 🐾 ⟨ 🛏 🔄 ⌘ 🅿

COUNTRY HOUSE · HISTORIC Family-run Victorian house built in a baronial style and named after the ruined castle in its 60 acre grounds. Two large, open-fired sitting rooms are filled with stuffed wild animals. Classical bedrooms are individually designed; some come with four-poster beds. Dine formally, from a 4 course Scottish menu.

26 rooms ☲ – **†**£ 75/180 **††**£ 120/220

⊠ PH35 4HW – South : 0.75 mi on A 82 – ℰ (01809) 501 254 – www.glengarry.net – Closed 3 November-19 March

⌂ Invergarry ☆ 🛏 ⌘ 🅿

INN · COSY Welcoming hotel designed in the style of a traditional inn. Bedrooms in the eaves are cosy and quirky, while the first floor rooms are more luxurious. Relax in the tiny open-fired lounge or in one of the characterful bar rooms amongst mountain memorabilia; cooking focuses on fresh Highland produce.

12 rooms ☲ – **†**£ 60/75 **††**£ 85/140

⊠ PH35 4HJ – On A 87 – ℰ (01809) 501 206 – www.invergarryhotel.co.uk

INVERGORDON

Highland – Regional map n° **17**-C2

▶ Edinburgh 178 mi – Elgin 60 mi – Inverness 24 mi

✕ Birch Tree ♿ 🅿

BRITISH MODERN · SIMPLE Friendly little restaurant located within a rural riding school. The good value, set price lunch menu is followed by a more ambitious à la carte and a popular steak menu. Cooking is classically based and relies on Scottish ingredients.

Menu £ 18/30 – Carte £ 23/37

Delney Riding Centre ⊠ IV18 0NP – Northeast : 3.75 mi by A 9 – ℰ (01349) 853 549 (booking essential) – www.the-birch-tree.com – Closed Sunday dinner, Monday and Tuesday

INVERKEILOR

Angus – ⊠ Arbroath – Pop. 902 – Regional map n° **16**-D2

▶ Edinburgh 85 mi – Aberdeen 32 mi – Dundee 22 mi

✕✕ Gordon's ⌔ 🛏 🅿

MODERN CUISINE · INTIMATE Long-standing, passionately run restaurant with stone walls, open fires and exposed beams. The wife oversees the service and the husband and son are in the kitchen. The concise menu lists carefully prepared classic dishes which use local seasonal produce. Bedrooms are smart, modern and well-kept.

Menu £ 34/55

5 rooms ☲ – **†**£ 110 **††**£ 130

32 Main St ⊠ DD11 5RN – ℰ (01241) 830 364 (booking essential) – www.gordonsrestaurant.co.uk – Closed 2 weeks January and lunch by arrangement Monday-Saturday

INVERMORISTON

Highland – Regional map n° **17**-C2

▶ Edinburgh 164 mi – Inverness 28 mi – Fort William 38 mi

Tigh na Bruach $\Leftarrow \Leftarrow \Leftarrow \heartsuit \heartsuit$ P

FAMILY · CLASSIC Superbly set on the lochside; its name meaning 'House on the Bank'. Traditional breakfast room. Comfy bedrooms with doors opening onto private terraces, which boast stunning views over neatly tended gardens to Loch Ness and the mountains.

3 rooms �־ – †£ 83/105 ††£ 110/140

✉ IV63 7YE – Southwest : 0.5 mi on A 82

– ☏ (01320) 351 349 – www.tighnabruach.com

– Restricted opening in winter

INVERNESS

Highland – Pop. 48 201 – Regional map n° **17**-C2

▶ Edinburgh 156 mi – Aberdeen 107 mi – Dundee 134 mi

Rocpool Reserve $\heartsuit$ P

BUSINESS · DESIGN Stylish boutique hotel with a chic lounge and a sexy split-level bar. Minimalist bedrooms come with emperor-sized beds and are graded 'Hip', 'Chic', 'Decadent' and 'Extra Decadent'; some have iPod docks, terraces, hot tubs or saunas.

11 rooms �־ – †£ 160/395 ††£ 195/395

Town plan: Z-r – 14 Culduthel Rd ✉ IV2 4AG

– ☏ (01463) 240 089 – www.rocpool.com

Chez Roux – See restaurant listing

Glenmoriston Town House $\heartsuit \heartsuit \triangle$ P

BUSINESS · CONTEMPORARY Two stylish Victorian townhouses next to the river. Bedrooms in the main hotel are contemporary and minimalistic; those in the annexe have solid wooden beds and wicker chairs. Start with drinks in the chic cocktail bar; then choose a modern dish in formal 'Abstract' or a brasserie classic in 'Contrast'.

31 rooms �־ – †£ 70/170 ††£ 75/250

Town plan: Z-x – 20 Ness Bank ✉ IV2 4SF

– ☏ (01463) 223 777 – www.glenmoristontownhouse.com

– Closed 8-9 January

Abstract – See restaurant listing

Trafford Bank $\Leftarrow \heartsuit$ P

HISTORIC · PERSONALISED 19C house with a modern, bohemian style. Original features include a tiled entrance and cast iron banister. Bedrooms come with iPod docks and decanters of sherry. Breakfast arrives on local china and includes haggis and tattie scones.

5 rooms �־ – †£ 75/100 ††£ 94/132

96 Fairfield Rd ✉ IV3 5LL – West : 0.75 mi by A 82 and Harrowden Rd

– ☏ (01463) 241 414 – www.traffordbankguesthouse.co.uk

– Closed mid-December-mid-February

Ballifeary Guest House $\heartsuit$ P

TRADITIONAL · HOMELY Pleasant house set away from the town centre, with a homely sitting room and comfortable, immaculately kept bedrooms. Smart breakfast room set with crisp linen and polished glassware; local produce includes salmon, kippers and cheeses.

7 rooms �־ – †£ 45/70 ††£ 76/85

Town plan: Z-n – 10 Ballifeary Rd ✉ IV3 5PJ – ☏ (01463) 235 572

– www.ballifearyguesthouse.co.uk – Closed 24-28 December

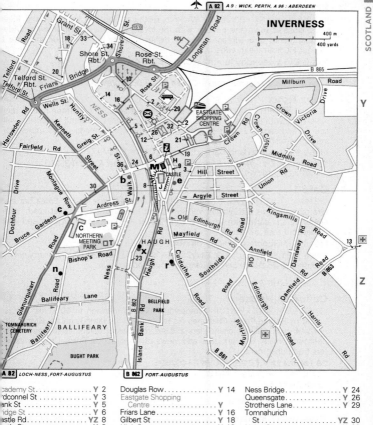

INVERNESS

A 9 : WICK, PERTH, A 96 : ABERDEEN

A 82

B 865

A 82 LOCH-NESS, FORT-AUGUSTUS

B 862 FORT-AUGUSTUS

Moyness House

TRADITIONAL · CLASSIC Detached Victorian villa framed by neatly clipped hedges. Period lounge with lots of local info; immaculately kept breakfast room. Variously sized bedrooms come with thoughtful extras, including ear plugs; the first floor rooms are the best.

6 rooms ☲ – †£65/70 ††£73/86

Town plan: Z-c – 6 Bruce Gdns ⊠ IV3 5EN – ℰ (01463) 233 836
– www.moyness.co.uk – Closed 24-26 December

Abstract

MODERN CUISINE · MINIMALIST Intimate hotel restaurant with abstract ink pictures hung on dark panelled walls and a contemporary, minimalist style. Elaborate modern menus feature ambitious flavour combinations and there's a pianist Friday and Saturday nights.

Menu £45

Town plan: Z-x – Glenmoriston Town House Hotel, 20 Ness Bank ⊠ IV2 4SF
– ℰ (01463) 223 777 – www.abstractrestaurant.com – Closed Sunday-Monday

XX **Rocpool**

BRITISH MODERN · FRIENDLY Well-run restaurant on the banks of the River Ness; close to town and popular with the locals. Modern, modish interior. Wide-ranging menus offer vibrant, colourful dishes that are full of flavour and have a distinct Mediterranean edge.

Menu £ 16 (weekday lunch) – Carte £ 24/44

Town plan: Y-b – *1 Ness Walk* ⊠ *IV3 5NE* – *℘ (01463) 717 274*
– www.rocpoolrestaurant.com – Closed 25-26 December, 1-3 January and Sunday

XX **Chez Roux**

FRENCH · MINIMALIST Smart modern restaurant consisting of three rooms; their walls hung with photos of the Roux brothers' early days. Polished tables are well-spaced and service is professional. The French-inspired menu offers robust, flavoursome dishes.

Menu £ 30 (lunch and early dinner) – Carte £ 30/47

Town plan: Z-r – *Rocpool Reserve Hotel, 14 Culduthel Rd* ⊠ *IV2 4AG*
– ℘ (01463) 240 089 – www.rocpool.com

X **Café 1**

BRITISH MODERN · BISTRO Bustling bistro opposite the castle. Small bar and two dining rooms with walnut veneer topped tables. Good value set lunch; more elaborate à la carte with an Asian and Mediterranean edge. Pork, beef and lamb come from their own croft.

Menu £ 13 (lunch and early dinner) – Carte £ 20/43

Town plan: Y-e – *Castle St* ⊠ *IV2 3EA* – *℘ (01463) 226 200 – www.cafe1.net*
– Closed 25-26 December, 1-2 January and Sunday

at Culloden East: 3 mi by A96 – Plan: Y – ⊠ Inverness

🏠 **Culloden House**

COUNTRY HOUSE · HISTORIC Imposing Palladian mansion in 40 acres; requisitioned by Bonnie Prince Charlie as his HQ prior to the famous battle. Grand interior with high ceilings, chandeliers and Adam's plaster reliefs. Well-proportioned bedrooms; many with antiques and views of the grounds. Formal restaurant offers traditional menus.

28 rooms ⊇ – ♦£ 95/250 ♦♦£ 140/395 – 3 suites
⊠ *IV2 7BZ* – *℘ (01463) 790 461 – www.cullodenhouse.co.uk – Closed 25-26 December*

at Bunchrew West: 3 mi on A862 – Plan: Y – ⊠ Inverness

🏠 **Bunchrew House**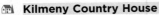

HISTORIC · CLASSIC Impressive 17C Scottish mansion, in a beautiful spot on the shore of Beauly Firth. Clubby, cosy, open-fired bar and intimate, wood-panelled drawing room. Good-sized, traditionally styled bedrooms; one with a four-poster, another with estuary views. Classical restaurant, with a menu to match and garden views.

16 rooms ⊇ – ♦£ 130/250 ♦♦£ 140/260
⊠ *IV3 8TA* – *℘ (01463) 234 917 – www.bunchrewhousehotel.com*

ISLAY

Argyll and Bute – Regional map n° **16**-A3
▶ Edinburgh 164 mi – London 518 mi – Greenock 117 mi – Irvine 132 mi

Ballygrant

🏠 **Kilmeny Country House**

TRADITIONAL · HOMELY Delightful house in 350 acres of working farmland. Large lounge with a mock open fire and a fine array of books about Islay. Superb bedrooms have beautiful feature beds, lovely tartans, tweeds and woollens woven on the island, and thoughtful extras. Welcoming owner.

5 rooms ⊇ – ♦£ 90/100 ♦♦£ 110/162
⊠ *PA45 7QW – Southwest : 0.5 mi on A 846 – ℘ (01496) 840 668*
– www.kilmeny.co.uk – Closed Christmas-New Year

Bowmore

XX Harbour Inn

REGIONAL · BRASSERIE Traditional restaurant with a pleasant bar and chunky wooden tea tables covered in deep blue cloths. Classical cooking uses fresh local seafood and island meats. Bedrooms are brightly decorated. Two cosy residents' lounges afford fantastic bay and island views.

Menu £ 35 (dinner) – Carte £ 30/47

7 rooms – ♦£ 85/130 ♦♦£ 105/170

The Square ✉ PA43 7JR – ☎ (01496) 810 330 – www.harbour-inn.com – Closed 21 December-12 January

Port Charlotte

⌂ Port Charlotte

TRADITIONAL · PERSONALISED Waterside hotel packed full of modern art. Large lounge with a wood burning stove and a cosy bar hung with old island photos. Bedrooms display traditional furniture and modern colour schemes; most have a sea view. Good mix of meat and fish dishes in the restaurant.

10 rooms – ♦£ 125 ♦♦£ 205

Main St ✉ PA48 7TU – ☎ (01496) 850 360 – www.portcharlottehotel.co.uk – Closed 24-26 December

Port Ellen

⌂ Glenegedale House

TRADITIONAL · PERSONALISED Well-run hotel by the airport, with views over the Mull of Oa and out to sea. Immaculately kept, individually styled bedrooms feature designer fabrics. The two sitting rooms come with open fires, antiques and an array of curios.

6 rooms – ♦£ 70/100 ♦♦£ 120/140

✉ PA42 7AS – Northwest : 4.75 mi on A 846 – ☎ (01496) 300 400 – www.glenegedalehouse.co.uk – Closed Christmas-New Year

JEDBURGH

The Scottish Borders – Pop. 4 030 – Regional map n° **15**-D2

▶ Edinburgh 48 mi – Carlisle 54 mi – Newcastle upon Tyne 57 mi

⌂ Willow Court

TOWNHOUSE · STYLISH Contemporary guesthouse looking out over the town's rooftops. Comfortable ground floor bedrooms offer a light, stylish space and come with iPod docks, DVD players and smart modern bathrooms. Communal breakfasts feature eggs from their own hens. Take time for yourself in the conservatory or out on the patio.

3 rooms – ♦£ 75/80 ♦♦£ 80/89

The Friars ✉ TD8 6BN – ☎ (01835) 863 702 – www.willowcourtjedburgh.co.uk

KELSO

The Scottish Borders – Pop. 5 639 – Regional map n° **15**-D2

▶ Edinburgh 44 mi – Hawick 21 mi – Newcastle upon Tyne 68 mi

⌂ Roxburghe

HISTORIC · ELEGANT Characterful Jacobean-style mansion owned by the Duke of Roxburghe, set in extensive parkland and boasting a fly fishing school and a golf course. Plush guest areas display antiques and heirlooms. The 'Feature' bedrooms are luxurious; rooms in the courtyard are more modern. Chez Roux offers formal fine dining.

22 rooms – ♦£ 150/365 ♦♦£ 225/365 – 2 suites

Heiton ✉ TD5 8JZ – Southwest : 3.5 mi by A 698 – ☎ (01573) 450 331 – www.roxburghe-hotel.com

🏠 Ednam House

🐟 ⟨ 🚗 ⟩ 🏊 ℗

HISTORIC · CLASSIC Long-standing, fishing-orientated hotel, superbly sited on the banks of the Tweed. Its grand drawing rooms and classically styled bedrooms boast a timeless elegance and a genteel air. The bar features a mural of the river, while the dining room overlooks it; much of the produce is home-grown.

32 rooms 🛏 – †£ 80/115 ††£ 128/180

Bridge St ⊠ TD5 7HT – ℰ (01573) 224 168 – www.ednamhouse.com

at Ednam North: 2.25 mi on B6461⊠ Kelso

🏠 Edenwater House

🐟 ⟨ ⟨ 🚗 ℗

LUXURY · CLASSIC This delightful house is run by an equally charming couple. Relax in the lovely garden beside the stream or in one of the antique-filled lounges, before heading up to one of the tastefully furnished, individually styled bedrooms. The dining room overlooks a meadow and offers a traditional menu Thursday-Saturday, with wine-themed suppers in the cellar on Wednesdays.

4 rooms 🛏 – †£ 70/85 ††£ 95/120

⊠ TD5 7QL – Off Stichill rd – ℰ (01573) 224 070 – www.edenwaterhouse.co.uk – Closed 1 January-12 March

KILBERRY – Argyll and Bute ➜ See Kintyre (Peninsula)

KILCHRENAN

Argyll and Bute – ⊠ Taynuilt – Regional map n° **16**-B2
▶ Edinburgh 117 mi – Glasgow 87 mi – Oban 18 mi

🏠 Ardanaiseig

🐟 ⟨ ⟨ 🚗 ⟩ 🍴 ℗

COUNTRY HOUSE · PERSONALISED Stunningly located, laid-back country house boasting a vast azalea-filled estate and lovely views down the loch. The large sitting room features impressive columns; bedrooms come in a mix of styles – the Boat Shed is the best. The elegant dining room offers modern dishes and water views.

19 rooms – †£ 185/330 ††£ 185/330 – 🛏 £ 17 – 1 suite

⊠ PA35 1HE – Northeast : 4 mi – ℰ (01866) 833 333 – www.ardanaiseig.com

🏠 Roineabhal

⟨ 🚗 ⟨ ℗

RURAL · COSY Rustic stone and log house with a riverside garden – built by its charming owners, who provide tea and homemade biscuits on arrival. Relaxing lounge with an open fire. Immaculate bedrooms; two up a spiral staircase. The guest bathroom has a roll-top bath. Local produce is served in the homely breakfast room.

3 rooms 🛏 – †£ 83 ††£ 110

⊠ PA35 1HD – ℰ (01866) 833 207 – www.roineabhal.com – Closed Christmas-New Year

KILDRUMMY

Aberdeenshire – Regional map n° **16**-D1
▶ Edinburgh 137 mi – Aberdeen 35 mi

🏠 Kildrummy Inn 🆕

⟨ ℗

BRITISH TRADITIONAL · COSY 19C coaching inn with a dining room, a conservatory and a lovely open-fired bar where you can cosy up in an armchair and sample the local whiskies. Set menus offer modern main courses and more classical desserts. Cosy, contemporary bedrooms offer all you could want. They also have 4 miles of fishing rights.

Carte £ 30/35

4 rooms 🛏 – †£ 89 ††£ 99

⊠ AB33 8QS – North : 0.5 mi on A 97 – ℰ (01975) 571 227 – www.kildrummyinn.co.uk – dinner only and Sunday lunch – Closed January and Tuesday

KILLIECRANKIE – Perth and Kinross → See Pitlochry

KINCLAVEN
Perth and Kinross – ⊠ Stanley – Pop. 394 – Regional map n° **16**-C2
▶ Edinburgh 55 mi – London 456 mi – Belfast 127 mi – Dundee 21 mi

🏠 **Ballathie House**
COUNTRY HOUSE · CLASSIC Mid-19C shooting lodge located on a peaceful estate of several hundred acres, on the banks of the River Tay. Bedrooms in the main house are the most characterful; the Riverside Rooms are more contemporary. The dining room has delightful river views and offers a concise menu of seasonal, regional produce.
41 rooms ⌂ – †£ 80/135 ††£ 150/190 – 3 suites
Stanley ⊠ PH1 4QN – ℰ (01250) 883 268 – www.ballathiehousehotel.com

KINGAIRLOCH
Highland – Regional map n° **17**-B3
▶ Edinburgh 139 mi – Fort William 25 mi – Oban 52 mi

X **Boathouse**
REGIONAL · BRASSERIE Smartly converted Victorian boathouse on the shore of Loch a'Choire, in the heart of the 14,000 acre Kingairloch Estate. Appealing dishes use venison from the estate and langoustines from Loch Linnhe, along with seasonal herbs and veg from the kitchen garden. Head straight for the terrace in warmer weather.
Carte £ 22/36
Ardgour ⊠ PH33 7AE – ℰ (01967) 411 232 (booking advisable)
– www.kingairloch.co.uk – Closed November-March and Sunday
dinner-Wednesday

KINGUSSIE
Highland – Pop. 1 476 – Regional map n° **17**-C3
▶ Edinburgh 117 mi – Inverness 41 mi – Perth 73 mi

🏠 **Hermitage**
HISTORIC · PERSONALISED Traditional 1833 property built from stone and slate. It has a warm, cosy lounge and comfy bedrooms; one has a super-king-sized bed and a wet room. The spacious garden offers great views of the Cairngorms and the Ruthven Barracks.
5 rooms ⌂ – †£ 52/92 ††£ 62/92
Spey St ⊠ PH21 1HN – ℰ (01540) 662 137 – www.thehermitage-scotland.com
– Closed 20 December-4 January

XX **Cross at Kingussie**
BRITISH MODERN · RURALLY 19C tweed mill in four acres of wooded grounds. Enjoy drinks on the terrace or in the first floor lounge then head to the smart dining room with its low beams, antiques and ornaments. Cooking is modern British/Scottish and is attractively presented. Pleasant, pine-furnished bedrooms have thoughtful extras.
Menu £ 25/55
8 rooms ⌂ – †£ 90/180 ††£ 110/180
Tweed Mill Brae, Ardbroilach Rd ⊠ PH21 1LB – ℰ (01540) 661 166 (booking
essential) – www.thecross.co.uk – Closed January and Christmas

KINTILLO – Perth and Kinross → See Perth

KINTYRE (Peninsula)
Argyll and Bute – Regional map n° **16**-B3
▶ Edinburgh 165 mi – London 515 mi – Dundee 164 mi – Paisley 111 mi

Carradale

🏠 Dunvalanree

TRADITIONAL · HISTORIC 1930s Arts and Crafts house with gardens and a terrace overlooking the beach and the Sound. Characterful interior with many original features. Unfussy, individually furnished bedrooms – one in Mackintosh style; some with views. Homely cooking has a traditional, seafood base.

5 rooms ⌷ – ♦£ 75 ♦♦£ 100/135

Port Righ Bay ⊠ PA28 6SE – ℰ (01583) 431 226 – www.dunvalanree.com – Closed Christmas

Kilberry

✗ Kilberry Inn

REGIONAL · INN Remotely set, rustic country inn with wooden beams, stone walls, open fires and a mix of bare and linen-laid tables. Classic dishes are crafted from carefully sourced local produce; meat and fish are smoked in-house. Comfy modern bedrooms are named after nearby islands; one has an outdoor hot tub.

Carte £ 23/37

5 rooms (dinner included) ⌷ – ♦£ 130 ♦♦£ 215

⊠ PA29 6YD – ℰ (01880) 770 223 (booking essential at dinner) – www.kilberryinn.com – dinner only and lunch Thursday-Sunday – Closed January-mid March, Christmas and Monday

Tarbert

🏠 Anchor

TOWNHOUSE · MODERN Smart, blue, mid-terraced house; once a church and later, a cinema. Modern interior with bright bedrooms, king-sized beds and small bathrooms; half of the rooms have views over the harbour. Informal, all-day bar-cum-restaurant offers good old favourites and tasty seafood specials.

12 rooms ⌷ – ♦£ 80/120 ♦♦£ 80/120

Harbour St ⊠ PA29 6UB – ℰ (01880) 820 577 – www.lochfyne-scotland.co.uk – Closed 4-17 January

KIPPEN

Stirling – Pop. 1 026 – Regional map n° **16**-C2

▶ Edinburgh 50 mi – Glasgow 41 mi – Stirling 10 mi

🍴 The Inn at Kippen

TRADITIONAL CUISINE · FRIENDLY Bigger than it looks from the outside; bright and subtly modernised on the inside, with simply furnished, contemporary bedrooms upstairs. The owners are keen to respect Scottish traditions and take full advantage of the bounteous local larder; dishes are attractively presented in an elaborate, modern style.

Carte £ 16/45

4 rooms ⌷ – ♦£ 65/95 ♦♦£ 75/125

Fore Rd ⊠ FK8 3DT – ℰ (01786) 870 500 – www.theinnatkippen.co.uk

KIRKBEAN

Dumfries and Galloway – Regional map n° **15**-C3

▶ Edinburgh 92 mi – Dumfries 13 mi – Kirkcudbright 29 mi

🏠 Cavens

LUXURY · PERSONALISED Attractive 18C country house in 20 acres of mature grounds. Relax in the cosy, book-filled Green Room or the elegant drawing room with its grand piano. Luxurious 'Estate' bedrooms boast views over the Solway Firth, while the comfy 'Country' rooms have a simpler style. The linen-clad dining room offers an unfussy daily menu of local produce; complimentary afternoon tea.

7 rooms ⌷ – ♦£ 80/150 ♦♦£ 90/220

⊠ DG2 8AA – ℰ (01387) 880 234 – www.cavens.com – Closed January-February

KIRKCUDBRIGHT

Dumfries and Galloway – Pop. 3 352 – Regional map n° **15**-B3

▶ Edinburgh 105 mi – London 369 mi – Glasgow 90 mi – Liverpool 185 mi

Selkirk Arms

TRADITIONAL · PERSONALISED Well-run 18C coaching inn, where Robert Burns reputedly wrote the Selkirk Grace. Bedrooms are spacious and comfortable – some are in the courtyard. Light lunches are served in the busy bar, which displays paintings of local scenes.

16 rooms ☑ – ♦£ 70/110 ♦♦£ 87/140 – 2 suites

High St ⊠ *DG6 4JG* – *℘ (01557) 330 402* – *www.selkirkarmshotel.co.uk* – *Closed 24-26 December*

Artistas – See restaurant listing

Gladstone House

TOWNHOUSE · COSY Attractive 18C former merchant's house with friendly owners. Comfy, antique-furnished lounge. Simple, pastel-hued bedrooms with seating areas by the windows and views over the rooftops. 3 course dinner of local produce, tailored around guests' preferences.

3 rooms ☑ – ♦£ 65 ♦♦£ 80

48 High St ⊠ *DG6 4JX* – *℘ (01557) 331 734* – *www.kirkcudbrightgladstone.com* – *Closed 2 weeks January-February and Christmas*

Glenholme Country House

COUNTRY HOUSE · HOMELY Take in mountain views from this stone house's spacious garden. Inside, it has a cosy, eye-catching style and there's a large book and music library in place of TVs. Bedrooms are themed around Victorian political figures. The dining room features Chinese furnishings and meals are tailored to guests' tastes.

4 rooms ☑ – ♦£ 90/100 ♦♦£ 100/125

Tongland Rd ⊠ *DG6 4UU* – *Northeast : 1 mi on A 711* – *℘ (01557) 339 422* – *www.glenholmecountryhouse.com* – *Closed Christmas-New Year*

✗ Artistas

BRITISH MODERN · FRIENDLY Relaxed, brasserie-style restaurant in a traditional coaching inn. Extensive menus mix classic and modern dishes. They are very passionate about using local produce; the Kirkcudbright scallops and Galloway Beef are worth a try.

Carte £ 21/36

Selkirk Arms Hotel, High St ⊠ *DG6 4JG* – *℘ (01557) 330 402* – *www.selkirkarmshotel.co.uk* – *dinner only and Sunday lunch* – *Closed 24-26 December except lunch 25 December*

KIRKMICHAEL

Perth and Kinross – Regional map n° **16**-C2

▶ Edinburgh 73 mi – Aberdeen 85 mi – Inverness 102 mi – Perth 29 mi

Strathardle Inn ⓝ

TRADITIONAL CUISINE · PUB 18C drovers' inn opposite the river. Regulars and their dogs gather in the cosy bar and those after a hearty meal head for the dining room. Lunch focuses on pub favourites, while dinner offers grills and roasts; some Scottish dishes always feature too. Modern bedrooms make a great base for exploring the area.

Carte £ 18/33

8 rooms ☑ – ♦£ 50/60 ♦♦£ 85/95

⊠ *PH10 7NS* – *On A 924* – *℘ (01250) 881 224* – *www.strathardleinn.co.uk*

KIRKNEWTON – West Lothian ➡ See Edinburgh

KYLESKU

Highland – Regional map n° **17**-C1

▶ Edinburgh 256 mi – Inverness 100 mi – Ullapool 34 mi

Kylesku

REGIONAL · PUB Breathtaking views of Loch Glendhu and the mountains make this 17C coaching inn an essential stop-off point. Fresh seafood is the way to go, with langoustines and mussels landed 200 yards away. Relax on the waterside terrace then make for one of the cosy bedrooms; two have balconies with panoramic views.

Carte £ 17/46

11 rooms ☲ - †£ 67/95 ††£ 100/140

✉ IV27 4HW – ℰ (01971) 502 231 – www.kyleskuhotel.co.uk – Closed November-February

LAIRG

Highland – Pop. 857 – Regional map n° **17**-C2

▶ Edinburgh 218 mi – Inverness 61 mi – Wick 72 mi

Park House

TRADITIONAL · HOMELY A traditional property built in 1925, with views over Loch Shin. The owners offer fishing and field sports and the walls are hung with rods and hunting prints. Relax in the cosy lounge then retire to one of the homely bedrooms.

4 rooms ☲ - †£ 65 ††£ 95

✉ IV27 4AU – ℰ (01549) 402 208 – www.parkhousesporting.com – Closed Christmas-New Year

LEITH – City of Edinburgh ➜ See Edinburgh

LERWICK ➜ See Shetland Islands (Mainland)

© image source/hemis.fr

LEWIS and HARRIS (Isle of)
Western Isles – Regional map n° **17**-A1

LEWIS
Western Isles – Regional map n° **17**-A1
▶ Edinburgh 210 mi – London 611 mi – Dundee 192 mi

Back

🏠 **Broad Bay House**　　　　　　　　　< 🛏 ᵭ ∽ 🄿

LUXURY · STYLISH Delightful guesthouse with a decked terrace and a garden leading down to the beach. Luxurious interior features an open-plan, Scandinavian-style lounge and a dining area with panoramic views. Modern, oak-furnished bedrooms come with super king sized beds, sliding doors onto private terraces and great extras.

4 rooms ☲ – 🛉£ 139 🛉🛉£ 179

✉ HS2 0LQ – *Northeast : 1 mi on B 895*
– ☎ *(01851) 820 990 – www.broadbayhouse.co.uk*
– *Closed October-April*

Galson

🏠 **Galson Farm**　　　　　　　　🛩 ⌔ < 🛏 ⅙ 🄿

TRADITIONAL · CLASSIC Welcoming guesthouse in a wonderfully remote location, boasting views out across the Atlantic. Traditional, homely guest areas and cosy bedrooms. The owner also operates the village post office from just inside the porch. Freshly prepared, home-cooked meals.

4 rooms ☲ – 🛉£ 53 🛉🛉£ 90/104

South Galson ✉ HS2 0SH
– ☎ *(01851) 850 492 – www.galsonfarm.co.uk*

Stornoway

🏠 **Braighe House**　　　　　　　　　　< 🛏 ⅙ 🄿

TRADITIONAL · PERSONALISED Smart dormer bungalow with a neat garden and a relaxed, modern interior. Immaculately kept bedrooms come with mineral water and chocolates; 'Deluxe' rooms have sleigh beds and sea outlooks. Complimentary port. Diverse, appealing breakfasts.

4 rooms ☲ – 🛉£ 115/130 🛉🛉£ 130/149

20 Braighe Rd ✉ HS2 0BQ – *Southeast : 3 mi on A 866*
– ☎ *(01851) 705 287 – www.braighehouse.co.uk*
– *Closed October-March*

SCOTLAND

Uig

XX Auberge Carnish

TRADITIONAL CUISINE · FRIENDLY Modern, timber-clad building with decking all around, set in an idyllic position above the sweeping sands of Uig Bay. Lewis produce features in satisfying, classically based dishes with a twist; daily specials are usually seafood-based. Spacious, minimalist bedrooms have stylish bathrooms and stunning views.

Menu £ 36

4 rooms ⌂ – †£ 99/125 ††£ 130/149

5 Carnish ✉ HS2 9EX – Southwest : 3.25 mi – ✆ (01851) 672 459 (booking essential) – www.aubergecarnish.co.uk – dinner only – Closed December-mid February

HARRIS

Western Isles – Regional map n° **17**-A1

▶ Edinburgh 261 mi – London 638 mi – Dundee 242 mi

Ardhasaig

XX Ardhasaig House

REGIONAL · FRIENDLY Purpose-built house that's been in the family for over 100 years. Modern, airy bar-lounge; flag-floored dining room with antique tables and dramatic bay and mountain views. Set menu offers local meats and seafood. Cosy bedrooms; the one in the stone lodge is the best.

Menu £ 59

6 rooms ⌂ – †£ 60/80 ††£ 120/200

✉ HS3 3AJ – ✆ (01859) 502 500 (booking essential) – www.ardhasaig.co.uk – dinner only – Closed November, January and February

Borve

🏠 Pairc an t-Srath

FAMILY · PERSONALISED Welcoming guesthouse on a working croft, with views out over the Sound of Taransay. Comfy, open-fired lounge has a chaise longue; the intimate dining room offers delicious home-cooked meals and wonderful vistas. Extremely friendly owners serve tea and homemade cake on arrival. Immaculate bedrooms feature smart oak furniture and brightly coloured Harris Tweed fabrics.

4 rooms ⌂ – †£ 52/84 ††£ 104/108

✉ HS3 3HT – ✆ (01859) 550 386 – www.paircant-srath.co.uk – Closed 2 weeks October-November and Christmas-New Year

Scalpay

🏠 Hirta House

TRADITIONAL · HOMELY Simple, characterful guesthouse in a small fishing village. Loch and mountain views from the lounge and conservatory. One traditional four-poster bedroom; two more modern rooms – one with a round bed. Nautically themed breakfast room.

3 rooms ⌂ – †£ 65 ††£ 75/85

✉ HS4 3XZ – ✆ (01859) 540 394 – www.hirtahouse.co.uk

Scarista

🏠 Scarista House

TRADITIONAL · CLASSIC 19C former manse boasting amazing bay and mountain views. Caring owners; cosy, homely interior with open-fired library and drawing room. Traditional bedrooms, those at the rear are best. Classically inspired menu features garden produce.

6 rooms ⌂ – †£ 125/155 ††£ 185/240

✉ HS3 3HX – ✆ (01859) 550 238 – www.scaristahouse.com – Closed 21 December-31 January and restricted opening in winter

SCOTLAND

Tarbert

🏠 Ceol na Mara

TRADITIONAL · CLASSIC Former crofter's cottage – one of only three on the island with three storeys. Spacious, homely interior. Various well-kept lounges and good-sized, comfy bedrooms. Stunning lochside location.

4 rooms 🍴 – †£ 90/120 ††£ 90/120

7 Direcleit ⊠ HS3 3DP – South : 1 mi by A 859 – ℰ (01859) 502 464
– www.ceolnamara.com

LEWISTON

Highland – Regional map n° **17**-C2
▶ Edinburgh 172 mi – London 553 mi – Dundee 153 mi

🍴 Loch Ness Inn

TRADITIONAL CUISINE · PUB There are two parts to this pub: the small Brewery Bar, home to locals and walkers fresh from the Great Glen Way; and the open-plan Lewiston restaurant with its wood burning stove and bright timbered beams. Hearty, robust, flavoursome dishes champion Scottish produce. Bedrooms are spacious and comfortable.

Carte £ 20/36

12 rooms 🍴 – †£ 55/89 ††£ 55/115

⊠ *IV63 6UW – ℰ (01456) 450 991 – www.staylochness.co.uk*

LINLITHGOW

West Lothian – Pop. 13 462 – Regional map n° **15**-C1
▶ Edinburgh 19 mi – Glasgow 35 mi – Perth 45 mi

🏠 Arden House

LUXURY · MODERN Purpose built guesthouse bordering a 105 acre sheep farm. Tea and cake on arrival. Spacious, tastefully styled bedrooms boast modern, slate-floored bathrooms and plenty of extras like fresh flowers and magazines. Tasty, wide-ranging breakfasts are a highlight. Welcoming owner pays great attention to detail.

3 rooms 🍴 – †£ 78/128 ††£ 90/128

Belsyde ⊠ EH49 6QE – Southwest : 2.25 mi on A 706 – ℰ (01506) 670 172
– www.ardencountryhouse.com – Closed 25-26 December and restricted opening in winter

XxX Champany Inn

MEATS · INTIMATE Set in a collection of whitewashed cottages – the traditional restaurant was once a flour mill, hence its unusual shape. The focus is on meat and wine, with 21-day aged Aberdeen Angus beef a speciality. There's also a well-stocked wine shop, a more laid-back 'Chop and Ale House' and 16 tartan-themed bedrooms.

Menu £ 26/43 – Carte £ 50/75

16 rooms 🍴 – †£ 99/119 ††£ 99/129

Champany ⊠ EH49 7LU – ℰ (01506) 834 532 – www.champany.com – Closed 25-26 December, 1-2 January, Saturday lunch and Sunday

XX Livingston's

MODERN CUISINE · INTIMATE This long-standing family-owned restaurant is run by a friendly, efficient team. Two conservatory-style dining rooms overlook a garden filled with wildlife. Cooking is traditional but there's a modern edge to the presentation.

Menu £ 25/43 (dinner) – Carte lunch £ 24/33

52 High St ⊠ EH49 7AE – ℰ (01506) 846 565 – www.livingstons-restaurant.co.uk
– Closed 2 weeks January, 1 week June, 1 week October, Sunday dinner and Monday

LOANS – South Ayrshire ➜ See Troon

LOCHALINE
Highland – Regional map n° **17**-B3
▶ Edinburgh 162 mi – Craignure 6 mi – Oban 7 mi

✗ Whitehouse　　　　　　　　　　　　　🅿
TRADITIONAL CUISINE · FAMILY Understated wood-panelled restaurant in a remote headland village, run by keen, hands-on owners. The constantly evolving blackboard menu showcases local seafood, game and garden produce. Cooking is pleasingly unfussy and flavoursome.
Menu £ 19 (lunch) – Carte £ 28/54
✉ PA80 5XT – ℰ (01967) 421 777 – www.thewhitehouserestaurant.co.uk – Closed November-Easter, Sunday and Monday

LOCHINVER
Highland – ✉ Lairg – Pop. 470 – Regional map n° **17**-C1
▶ Edinburgh 251 mi – Inverness 95 mi – Wick 105 mi

🏨 Inver Lodge　　　　　　　　　　✿ ⩽ 🛏 🤍 🎵 🅿
TRADITIONAL · PERSONALISED Superbly located on a hillside, overlooking a quiet fishing village. Smart bedrooms have good mod cons and great bay and island views. Relax in the open-fired lounge or billiard room – or try one of their whiskies in the elegant bar.
21 rooms ⥱ – †£ 150/180 ††£ 225/530
Iolaire Rd ✉ IV27 4LU – ℰ (01571) 844 496 – www.inverlodge.com – Closed November-April
Chez Roux – See restaurant listing

🏨 Ruddyglow Park Country House　　　⩥ ⩽ 🛏 🤍 🐾 🅿
TRADITIONAL · CLASSIC Creamwashed house in a superb location, boasting fantastic loch and mountain views. Spacious guest areas are filled with antiques, paintings and silverware. A high level of facilities and extras feature in classically styled bedrooms; the room in the modern log cabin offers extra privacy.
3 rooms ⥱ – †£ 100/130 ††£ 130/200
Loch Assynt ✉ IV27 4HB – Northeast : 6.75 mi on A 837 – ℰ (01571) 822 216 – www.ruddyglowpark.com – Closed December-February

✗✗ Albannach (Colin Craig and Lesley Crosfield)　⇔ ⩥ ⩽ 🛏 🅿
❀ **TRADITIONAL CUISINE · COSY** Substantial 19C Scottish house in a remote location, boasting exceptional bay and mountain views from the conservatory, terrace and garden. Traditional 5 course dinners rely on top quality local produce, with seafood from the harbour below and Scottish beef the specialities. Contemporary bedrooms are spread about the building; one boasts a private terrace and a hot tub.
➜ Lochinver langoustines with ginger. Highland hogget with croft kale, turnip and red wine & blackcurrant sauce. Hot citrus soufflé with bitter chocolate and brambles.
Menu £ 70 – set menu only
5 rooms (dinner included) ⥱ – †£ 180/225 ††£ 260/385
Baddidarroch ✉ IV27 4LP – West : 1 mi by Baddidarroch rd – ℰ (01571) 844 407 (bookings essential for non-residents) – www.thealbannach.co.uk – dinner only – Closed 3 January-mid March and Monday-Wednesday November-December except for festive fortnight

✗✗ Chez Roux　　　　　　　　　　　⩽ 🛏 🎬 🅿
FRENCH · FORMAL Romantic restaurant hung with photos of the eponymous brothers, where well-spaced tables take in fantastic bay and mountain views. Regularly changing, classical French menus make use of the wealth of produce on their doorstep.
Menu £ 45 – bar lunch Monday-Saturday
Inver Lodge Hotel, Iolaire Rd ✉ IV27 4LU – ℰ (01571) 844 496 (bookings essential for non-residents) – www.inverlodge.com – Closed November-April

⟨◻⟩ **Caberfeidh** ⓝ   ⪤ 🏠 🍽

FISH AND SEAFOOD · COSY An informal lochside sister to the Albannach restaurant, which follows the same ethos of championing fresh local produce. Constantly evolving menus have a seafood slant. The majority of dishes are generously proportioned 'small plates'.

Carte £ 16/26

Main St ⊠ IV27 4JY – ℰ (01571) 844 321 – www.caberfeidhlochinver.co.uk – Closed 25 December, 1 January and Monday-Wednesday lunch

LOCHRANZA – North Ayrshire ➜ See Arran (Isle of)

LUSS
Argyll and Bute – Pop. 402 – Regional map n° **16**-B2
▶ Edinburgh 89 mi – Glasgow 26 mi – Oban 65 mi

🏠 **Loch Lomond Arms**   ⪢ 🍴 🏠 ⅋ ⬇ 🚗 **P**

INN · COSY Retaining the warmth and character of an old inn, this hotel offers individual, contemporary bedrooms. 'Lomond' and 'Colquhoun' are the most luxurious: the former has a four-poster bed; the latter, superb views. Wide-ranging menu: dine in the open-fired bar, the relaxed dining room or the more formal library.

14 rooms 🖙 – ♥£ 90/110 ♥♥£ 120/140

Main Rd ⊠ G83 8NY – ℰ (01436) 860 420 – www.lochlomondarmshotel.com

MELROSE
The Scottish Borders – Pop. 2 307 – Regional map n° **15**-D2
▶ Edinburgh 38 mi – London 347 mi – Glasgow 84 mi – Aberdeen 170 mi

🏠 **Burts**   ⪢ 🍴 🏠 **P**

INN · RUSTIC Characterful coaching inn on the main square; run by the same family for two generations. Appealing bedrooms blend contemporary furnishings with original features. Cosy bar serves old classics; formal dining room offers a mix of modern and traditional dishes.

20 rooms 🖙 – ♥£ 74/100 ♥♥£ 115/150

Market Sq. ⊠ TD6 9PL – ℰ (01896) 822 285 – www.burtshotel.co.uk – Closed 6-12 January and 26 December

🏠 **Townhouse**   ⪢ 🏠 ⅋ 🚗 **P**

TOWNHOUSE · STYLISH The former home of Catherine Spence and a contemporary sibling to Burts. Stylish bedrooms are decorated in black and purple and display bold feature walls; some are shower only. Dine in the trendy all-day café-cum-bar or head for the dining room and courtyard which offers top Border ingredients.

11 rooms 🖙 – ♥£ 90/95 ♥♥£ 132/149

Market Sq. ⊠ TD6 9PQ – ℰ (01896) 822 645 – www.thetownhousemelrose.co.uk – Closed 12-20 January and 25-26 December

at Gattonside North: 2 mi by B6374 on B6360 – ⊠ Melrose

🏠 **Fauhope House**   ⪩ ⪤ 🍴 ⅋ **P**

HISTORIC · PERSONALISED Charming 19C house by the Tweed, overlooking Melrose – its delightful gardens stretching for 15 acres. Quirky interior displays an eclectic mix of art and antiques. Bedrooms are all very different; some boast stylish bold colour schemes.

3 rooms 🖙 – ♥£ 80/90 ♥♥£ 110/145

⊠ TD6 9LU – East : 0.25 mi by B 6360 taking unmarked lane to the right of Monkswood Rd at edge of village – ℰ (01896) 823 184 – www.fauhopehouse.com

MEMUS
Angus – Regional map n° **16**-D2
▶ Edinburgh 76 mi – London 478 mi – Dundee 21 mi

🏠 **Drovers Inn**   🛏 🛋 **P**

CLASSIC CUISINE · COSY Attractive Highland inn in an extremely remote spot, with a delightful beamed interior and an open-fired bar. The wide-ranging menu is good value for money and showcases local, seasonal produce; game and vegetables come from the estate.

Carte £ 26/39

✉ DD8 3TY – ☎ (01307) 860 322 – www.the-drovers.com
– Closed 25-26 December

MOFFAT

Dumfries and Galloway – Pop. 2 582 – Regional map n° **15**-C2
▶ Edinburgh 61 mi – Carlisle 43 mi – Dumfries 22 mi – Glasgow 60 mi

🏠 **Hartfell House**   🕊 🛏 ⚙ **P**

TOWNHOUSE · CLASSIC Keenly run house built in 1866 and located in a peaceful crescent. Original features include parquet floors and ornate cornicing. Bedrooms are spacious and traditional and the comfy first floor drawing room has a southerly aspect.

7 rooms 🖃 – ♦£ 40/45 ♦♦£ 65/75

Hartfell Cres. ✉ DG10 9AL – ☎ (01683) 220 153 – www.hartfellhouse.co.uk
– Closed 1 week autumn, 1 week January and Christmas
Lime Tree – See restaurant listing

🏠 **Bridge House**   🕊 🛏 ⚙ **P**

TRADITIONAL · CLASSIC Large Victorian house on a quiet residential road, run by experienced owners and affording beautiful valley views. Relax in deep sofas in the comfortable lounge. Bedrooms are individually decorated; those to the front are the biggest. The dining room displays lovely cornicing and offers traditional fare.

7 rooms 🖃 – ♦£ 55 ♦♦£ 70/100

Well Rd ✉ DG10 9JT – East : 0.75 mi by Selkirk rd (A 708) taking left hand turn before bridge – ☎ (01683) 220 558 – www.bridgehousemoffat.co.uk
– Closed 25 December-February

XX **Brodies**   🕭 AC 🕪

REGIONAL · TRADITIONAL Large, laid-back, modern eatery that caters for all appetites – serving snacks, light lunches, afternoon tea, more substantial dinners and all-day brunch on Sundays. Cooking has a traditional base and features fresh local ingredients.

Menu £ 15 (early dinner) – Carte £ 20/34

1-2 Altrive Pl, Holm St ✉ DG10 9EB
– ☎ (01683) 222 870 – www.brodiesofmoffat.co.uk
– Closed 25-27 December

XX **Lime Tree**   **P**

TRADITIONAL CUISINE · COSY Small hotel restaurant with a feature fireplace, attractive marquetry and a large bay window looking down the valley. Good value, weekly changing menus feature well-judged, attractively presented classics that are full of flavour.

Menu £ 24/29

Hartfell House Hotel, Hartfell Cres. ✉ DG10 9AL
– ☎ (01683) 220 153 (booking essential) – www.hartfellhouse.co.uk – dinner only
– Closed 1 week autumn, 1 week October, Christmas, Sunday and Monday

MONTROSE

Angus – Pop. 11 955 – Regional map n° **16**-D2
▶ Edinburgh 92 mi – Aberdeen 39 mi – Dundee 29 mi

🏠 36 The Mall

TRADITIONAL · PERSONALISED Large, immaculately kept former manse, run by warm, welcoming owners. Homely, characterful interior with tastefully styled, high-ceilinged bedrooms and a lovely conservatory overlooking the lawned garden. Good buffet selection and cooked choices in the communal breakfast room.

3 rooms ☐ – ♦£ 55/70 ♦♦£ 70/85

36 The Mall ✉ DD10 8SS – North : 0.5 mi by A 92 at junction with North Esk Road – ℰ (01674) 673 646 – www.36themall.co.uk

MUIR OF ORD

Highland – Pop. 2 555 – Regional map n° **17**-C2
▶ Edinburgh 173 mi – Inverness 10 mi – Wick 121 mi

🏠 Dower House

TRADITIONAL · CLASSIC Personally run, part-17C house with charming mature gardens. Characterful guest areas include an antique-furnished dining room and a small, open-fired lounge with fresh flowers and shelves crammed with books. Comfy bedrooms; one with a bay window overlooking the garden. Traditional, daily set menu.

4 rooms ☐ – ♦£ 90/120 ♦♦£ 140/160

Highfield ✉ IV6 7XN – North : 1 mi on A 862 – ℰ (01463) 870 090 – www.thedowerhouse.co.uk – Closed November-March

MULL (Isle of)

Argyll and Bute – Pop. 2 800 – Regional map n° **16**-A2
▶ Edinburgh 141 mi – London 512 mi – Belfast 163 mi – Dundee 136 mi

Fionnphort

✕✕ Ninth Wave

FISH AND SEAFOOD · EXOTIC This stylish modern restaurant started life as a crofter's bothy, over 200 years ago. Local seafood plays a key role, with crab and lobster caught every day. The fruit, vegetables and herbs are from their organic kitchen garden.

Menu £ 46/64

Bruach Mhor ✉ PA66 6BL – East : 0.75 mi by A 849 – ℰ (01681) 700 757 (booking essential) – www.ninthwaverestaurant.co.uk – dinner only – Closed November-April, Monday and Tuesday

Tiroran

🏠 Tiroran House

LUXURY · PERSONALISED Stunning 19C whitewashed house with a welcoming owner, set in 17 acres of parkland that run down to the water's edge. Charming, antique-filled interior with two open-fired lounges and immaculate, highly individual bedrooms. The dining room is split into a conservatory and a darker, more clubby area, and offers concise, daily changing menus.

11 rooms ☐ – ♦£ 100/160 ♦♦£ 175/220

✉ PA69 6ES – ℰ (01681) 705 232 – www.tiroran.com

Tobermory

🏠 Tobermory

TRADITIONAL · PERSONALISED Converted fishermen's cottages in a colourful quayside terrace, not far from the local distillery. Watch the sun go down over the sea while planning your next activity. Quirky bedrooms vary in size but most have pleasant harbour views.

16 rooms ☐ – ♦£ 35/128 ♦♦£ 40/128

53 Main St ✉ PA75 6NT – ℰ (01688) 302 091 – www.thetobermoryhotel.com – March-October

🏠 Sonas House

FAMILY · DESIGN Set in an elevated position above Tobermory, with views over the Sound of Mull. Choose a bedroom in the main house or in the annexe studio; all come with a host of extras and superb views. The lovely swimming pool is open year-round.

3 rooms ⊊ – 🛏£ 70/100 🛏🛏£ 90/125

The Fairways ✉ PA75 6PS – North : 0.5 mi by Black Brae and Erray Rd following signs for the golf club – ☎ (01688) 302 304 – www.sonashouse.co.uk – Closed November-February

🏠 Brockville

TRADITIONAL · PERSONALISED Welcoming guesthouse with a warm, homely feel; run by a friendly owner with plenty of local knowledge. Extremely spacious bedrooms offer good modern facilities and everything you could want. The communal breakfast room boasts pleasant sea views; menus change daily and feature plenty of fresh fruits.

3 rooms ⊊ – 🛏£ 90/100 🛏🛏£ 100/120

Raeric Rd ✉ PA75 6RS – by Back Brae and Erray Rd – ☎ (01688) 302 741 – www.brockville-tobermory.co.uk

XX Highland Cottage

TRADITIONAL CUISINE · FAMILY Long-standing, personally run restaurant in an intimate cottage, where family antiques and knick-knacks abound. Classical linen-laid dining room and a homely lounge. Traditional daily menu with a seafood base features plenty of local produce. Bedrooms are snug and individually styled.

Menu £ 40

6 rooms ⊊ – 🛏£ 110/165 🛏🛏£ 135/165

Breadalbane St ✉ PA75 6PD – via B 8073 – ☎ (01688) 302 030 (bookings essential for non-residents) – www.highlandcottage.co.uk – dinner only – Closed 15 October-1 April

MUTHILL – Perth and Kinross → See Crieff

NAIRN
Highland – Pop. 9 773 – Regional map n° **17**-D2
▶ Edinburgh 172 mi – Aberdeen 91 mi – Inverness 16 mi

🏨 Golf View

TRADITIONAL · FUNCTIONAL Set on the coast, between two golf courses, with pleasant gardens and Moray Firth vistas. Large lounge, clubby bar and smart spa. Spacious bedrooms have Stag-style furnishings; one has a whirlpool bath and views from its four-poster bed. Traditional menus in the part-panelled dining room and airy brasserie.

42 rooms ⊊ – 🛏£ 110/160 🛏🛏£ 145/180 – 1 suite

63 Seabank Rd ✉ IV12 4HD – ☎ (01667) 452 301 – www.crerarhotels.com

🏠 Boath House

HISTORIC · PERSONALISED An elegant 1825 neo-classical mansion framed by Corinthian columns. Inside it cleverly blends contemporary furnishings and original features; most of the modern art is for sale. Bedrooms are elegant and intimate – one has 'his and hers' roll-top baths and some have views over the 20 acre grounds and the lake.

8 rooms ⊊ – 🛏£ 190/260 🛏🛏£ 260/365

Auldearn ✉ IV12 5TE – East : 2 mi on A 96 – ☎ (01667) 454 896 – www.boath-house.com

 Boath House – See restaurant listing

🏠 Cawdor House   🛏 ⌀

TOWNHOUSE · PERSONALISED 19C former manse where the friendly owners are a font of local knowledge. The cosy lounge has a marble fireplace and bedrooms are clean and uncluttered; original features blend with contemporary styling throughout. They serve local bacon and sausages at breakfast and offer set dinners by arrangement.

7 rooms 🖙 - 🛉£ 53/75 🛉🛉£ 80/96

7 Cawdor St ⊠ IV12 4QD - 𝒞 (01667) 455 855 - www.cawdorhousenairn.co.uk
- Closed 21 December-14 January

XX Boath House   ≤ 🛏 ⇔ 🅿

❀ **MODERN CUISINE · INTIMATE** An elegant oval dining room in an early 19C mansion. Well-balanced modern menus showcase the chef's skill and understanding. Cooking is accomplished, with vivid presentation and interesting flavours – much of the produce is from their garden and orchard. Sit at bespoke oak tables and take in the lake view.

→ Scallop, leek and celeriac. Roe deer with artichoke and salsify. Rhubarb, almond and ginger.

Menu £ 30/70 **s**

Boath House Hotel, Auldearn ⊠ IV12 5TE - East : 2 mi on A 96 - 𝒞 (01667)
454 896 (booking essential) - www.boath-house.com

NEW CUMNOCK

East Ayrshire - Pop. 2 860 - Regional map n° **15**-B2
▶ Edinburgh 66 mi - London 378 mi - Glasgow 42 mi - Hamilton 36 mi

🏠🏠 Lochside House

BUSINESS · CONTEMPORARY The Marquis of Bute's 19C shooting lodge is impressively located on a loch shore and surrounded by acres of countryside. The lodges with private hot tubs and saunas offer the ultimate experience. Unwind in the intimate spa then eat in the stylish restaurant with its international menu and panoramic views.

39 rooms 🖙 - 🛉£ 55/220 🛉🛉£ 80/260 - 4 suites

⊠ KA18 4PN - Northwest : 1.5 mi on A 76 - 𝒞 (01290) 333 000
- www.lochside-hotel.com

NEWTON STEWART

Dumfries and Galloway - Pop. 4 092 - Regional map n° **15**-B3
▶ Edinburgh 131 mi - Dumfries 51 mi - Glasgow 87 mi - Stranraer 24 mi

🏠🏠 Kirroughtree House   🏠 🦮 ≤ 🛏 ⊡ 🅿

HISTORIC · CLASSIC An impressive 1719 mansion in mature gardens, overlooking the woods and the bay. The interior is grand, with a vast open-fired hall and an impressive staircase leading up to traditionally styled bedrooms. The concise dinner menu sees good quality produce served in classic combinations.

17 rooms 🖙 - 🛉£ 90/140 🛉🛉£ 90/150 - 2 suites

⊠ DG8 6AN - Northeast : 1.5 mi by A 75 on A 712 - 𝒞 (01671) 402 141
- www.kirroughtreehouse.co.uk - Closed 2 January-1 February

NIGG → See Tain

NORTH BAY - Western Isles → See Barra (Isle of)

NORTH BERWICK

East Lothian - Pop. 6 605 - Regional map n° **15**-D1
▶ Edinburgh 141 mi - London 512 mi - Belfast 163 mi - Dundee 136 mi

⌂ Glebe House

FAMILY · HOMELY Spacious, welcoming Georgian house with attractive walled gardens and views over the town and sea. It's beautifully furnished inside, with good quality fabrics and antiques. Classically styled bedrooms have lots of extra touches.

3 rooms ⌂ – ♦£ 85/90 ♦♦£ 120/130

Law Rd ⊠ EH39 4PL – ℰ (01620) 89 2608 – www.glebehouse-nb.co.uk
– Closed Christmas-New Year and restricted opening in winter

NORTH QUEENSFERRY

Fife – Pop. 1 076 – Regional map n° **16**-C3

▶ Edinburgh 13 mi – London 416 mi – Glasgow 47 mi – Aberdeen 116 mi

✕ Wee Restaurant

TRADITIONAL CUISINE · BISTRO Simple, quarry-floored restaurant in the shadow of the Forth Rail Bridge. Fresh Scottish ingredients are served in neatly presented, classical combinations. Lunch represents the best value.

Menu £ 23/36 **s**

17 Main St ⊠ KY11 1JT – ℰ (01383) 616 263 – www.theweerestaurant.co.uk
– Closed 25-26 December, 1-2 January and Monday

NORTH UIST – Western Isles → See Uist (Isles of)

OBAN

Argyll and Bute – Pop. 8 574 – Regional map n° **16**-B2

▶ Edinburgh 123 mi – Dundee 116 mi – Glasgow 93 mi – Inverness 118 mi

⌂ Manor House

TRADITIONAL · CLASSIC 18C dower house; formerly part of the Argyll Estate. The country house style interior offers traditional comforts, and the spacious lounge and rustic bar boast delightful bay and harbour views. Individually styled bedrooms. Concise daily menu served in the formal dining room.

11 rooms ⌂ – ♦£ 110/185 ♦♦£ 120/235

Gallanach Rd. ⊠ PA34 4LS – ℰ (01631) 562 087 – www.manorhouseoban.com
– Closed 25-26 December

⌂ Glenburnie House

TOWNHOUSE · PERSONALISED Bay-windowed house on the main esplanade affording great bay and island views. Period features include a delightful staircase and etched glass widows; antiques abound. Comfy, good-sized bedrooms.

12 rooms ⌂ – ♦£ 55/65 ♦♦£ 80/120

Corran Esplanade ⊠ PA34 5AQ – ℰ (01631) 562 089 – www.glenburnie.co.uk
– Closed December-February

✕✕ Coast

BRITISH MODERN · BRASSERIE Busy high street restaurant in a former bank with a high ceiling, a stripped wooden floor and khaki fabric strips on the walls. Unfussy, modern cooking with good seasoning; local produce is key. 'Light bite' lunches are a steal.

Menu £ 15 (lunch and early dinner) – Carte £ 21/42

104 George St ⊠ PA34 5NT – ℰ (01631) 569 900 – www.coastoban.co.uk
– Closed 25-26 December, January, Sunday-Monday October-March and Sunday lunch

✕ Ee-usk

FISH AND SEAFOOD · DESIGN Long-standing seafood restaurant run by experienced owners, located on the harbourfront and offering great views over the bay from its floor to ceiling windows. Extensive menus focus on simply prepared fresh local fish and shellfish.

Carte £ 19/57

The North Pier ⊠ PA34 5QD – ℰ (01631) 565 666 – www.eeusk.com
– Closed 3 weeks January and 25-26 December

ONICH

Highland – ✉ Fort William – Regional map n° **17**-B3
▶ Edinburgh 123 mi – Glasgow 93 mi – Inverness 79 mi – Oban 39 mi

X **Lochleven Seafood Café** ≤ 🏠 & AC P

FISH AND SEAFOOD · **NEIGHBOURHOOD** Simple little restaurant in a stunning lochside spot, looking towards the Glencoe Mountains. Fresh fish and shellfish come from the west coast of Scotland and the seafood platter is a speciality. In winter they host themed evenings.

Carte £ 19/57 **s**

Lochleven ✉ PH33 6SA – Southeast : 6.5 mi by A 82 on B 863 – ☎ (01855) 821 048 (bookings advisable at dinner) – www.lochlevenseafoodcafe.co.uk – Closed November-March

© C. Meier/doc-stock GmbH RM/age fotostock

ORKNEY ISLANDS

Orkney Islands – Pop. 21 349

ISLE OF WESTRAY

Orkney Islands – Regional map n° **18**-A2

▶ Edinburgh 289 mi – London 690 mi – Dundee 270 mi

Pierowall

No 1 Broughton

FAMILY • COSY 19C pink-washed house on the waterside, with views over Pierowall Bay and out to Papa Westray. Take in the view from the conservatory or relax in the sauna (on request). Bedrooms are homely. They also offer dry stone walling courses!

5 rooms – †£ 50 ††£ 60/70

✉ KW17 2DA – ✆ (01857) 677 726 – www.no1broughton.co.uk – Closed 24-25 December

MAINLAND

Orkney Islands – Regional map n° **18**-A3

▶ Edinburgh 277 mi – London 677 mi – Dundee 258 mi

Burray

Sands

FAMILY • MODERN Converted 19C herring packing store in a small hamlet overlooking the Scapa Flow. Pleasant bedrooms boast smart bathrooms. The bar has a pool table and a dartboard and offers a traditional menu. The dining room serves more refined dishes, featuring island produce and lots of shellfish.

8 rooms – †£ 65/80 ††£ 80/100

✉ KW17 2SS – ✆ (01856) 731 298 – www.thesandshotel.co.uk – Closed 1-3 January and 25-26 December

Deerness

Northfield

FAMILY • MODERN Follow the bumpy lane towards the water and you'll receive a warm welcome from the charming owner and her ducks. Despite being a modern build it has plenty of charm courtesy of lovely oak timbers and wonderful views across the Stronsay Firth; two of the bedrooms have views from the bed. The owner sells locally crafted items. Light suppers are offered by arrangement.

4 rooms – †£ 65/95 ††£ 90/95

✉ KW17 2QL – North : 2 mi turning left by village shop – ✆ (01856) 741 353 – www.orkneybedandbreakfast.com

Dounby

🏠 Ashleigh

FAMILY · MODERN A purpose-built house in a tranquil spot at the heart of the island's countryside; take time to sit and appreciate the loch and mountain views. Good-sized bedrooms have modern facilities. Hearty breakfasts include Orkney breads.

4 rooms – ♥£ 40/43 ♥♥£ 74/78

Howaback Rd ⊠ KW17 2JA – South : 0.75 mi by A 986 – ℰ (01856) 771 378 – www.ashleigh-orkney.com – Closed 20 December-20 January

Harray

🏠 Merkister

FAMILY · CLASSIC This family-run lochside hotel affords wonderful water and mountain views. Bedrooms are comfortable and well-kept; the best are set outside and have their own terraces and gardens. The modern bar with slate-tiled walls serves pub classics, while the dining room offers Orkney-based produce and a scenic backdrop.

16 rooms ⌷ – ♥£ 55/95 ♥♥£ 90/230

⊠ KW17 2LF – Off A 986 – ℰ (01856) 771 366 – www.merkister.com – Closed 23 December-4 January

🏠 Holland House

FAMILY · COSY This delightful converted manse is run by a welcoming owner and offers commanding views from every room. The open-fired lounge is packed with local art and handmade furniture, and the conservatory overlooks the colourful garden. Spotless bedrooms come with a host of extras and show great attention to detail.

3 rooms ⌷ – ♥£ 52/60 ♥♥£ 104

⊠ KW17 2LQ – On St Michael's Church rd – ℰ (01856) 771 400 – www.hollandhouseorkney.co.uk – Closed 7 December-12 January and restricted opening in winter

Kirkwall

🏠 Ayre

BUSINESS · FUNCTIONAL A well-run property close to the harbour. Formerly three Victorian houses, it's now a traditionally styled hotel with comfortable bedrooms – the newer rooms in the extension are the biggest and best. The spacious bar is popular with locals and the dining room offers a sizeable menu of Orcadian produce.

51 rooms ⌷ – ♥£ 76/95 ♥♥£ 100/135

Ayre Rd. ⊠ KW15 1QX – ℰ (01856) 873 001 – www.ayrehotel.co.uk – Closed 25 December and 1 January

🏠 Lynnfield

FAMILY · PERSONALISED 18C manse which was extended during the war to become an officers' mess. Bedrooms have period Orcadian furnishings and ultra-modern bathrooms. It's close to the Highland Park Distillery and has a wonderful collection of over 360 whiskies.

10 rooms ⌷ – ♥£ 90/110 ♥♥£ 100/170 – 3 suites

Holm Rd ⊠ KW15 1SU – South : 1 mi on A 961 – ℰ (01856) 872 505 – www.lynnfieldhotel.com – Closed 1-7 January and 25-26 December

Lynnfield – See restaurant listing

🏠 Avalon House

FAMILY · MODERN Modern guesthouse in a pleasant residential area; it has a nice coastal outlook and makes a great base for exploring. Good-sized modern bedrooms are furnished in oak. Island produce is served at breakfast – go for the Orkney kippers.

5 rooms ⌷ – ♥£ 55/60 ♥♥£ 70/80

Carness Rd ⊠ KW15 1UE – Northeast : 1.5 mi by Shore St. – ℰ (01856) 876 665 – www.avalon-house.co.uk – Closed Christmas-New Year

✗✗ **Foveran** ⇦ ⊗ ≼ ⌂ ⌂ & 🅿

TRADITIONAL CUISINE · FRIENDLY Sit by the large floor to ceiling window or out on the terrace to take in superb panoramic views over the Scapa Flow and the south islands. Traditional menus feature North Ronaldsay lamb, Orkney beef and plenty of fresh seafood from local waters. Homely, well-kept bedrooms have a slight New England edge.

Carte £ 21/48

8 rooms � – ♦£ 75/95 ♦♦£ 110/116

St Ola ⊠ KW15 1SF – Southwest : 3 mi on A 964 – ℰ (01856) 872 389
– www.thefoveran.com – dinner only – Restricted opening October-April

✗✗ **Lynnfield** ⓝ ≼ ⌂ & 🅿

MODERN CUISINE · TRADITIONAL Traditional hotel dining room decorated with whisky memorabilia. Lunch is fairly classical, while dinner offers more interesting modern dishes which champion the very best Orcadian produce – including some foraged ingredients.

Menu £ 15/55 – Carte £ 24/45 – bar lunch

Lynnfield Hotel, Holm Rd ⊠ KW15 1SU – South : 1 mi on A 961 – ℰ (01856) 872 505
(booking advisable) – www.lynnfieldhotel.com – Closed 1-10 January and 25-26 December

St Margaret's Hope

✗✗ **Creel** ⇦ ≼ 🅿

FISH AND SEAFOOD · TRADITIONAL Set in an idyllic harbourside location in a small fishing village, with views out across the bay; the experienced owners have been here for over 30 years. The concise daily menu utilises top Orcadian produce and boldly flavoured dishes have a refined, modern edge. Colour co-ordinated bedrooms share the view.

Menu £ 40

3 rooms ⊻ – ♦£ 75/85 ♦♦£ 110/130

Front Rd ⊠ KW17 2SL – ℰ (01856) 831 311 – www.thecreel.co.uk – dinner only
– Closed October-April, Sunday and Monday

Stromness

✗ **Hamnavoe**

TRADITIONAL CUISINE · NEIGHBOURHOOD Homely restaurant in a backstreet of a sleepy harbourside town; its name means 'Safe Haven' and it has the feel of an old family parlour. Unfussy home cooking utilises fresh market produce and dishes are hearty and full of flavour.

Carte £ 27/38

35 Graham Pl ⊠ KW16 3BY – off Victoria St – ℰ (01856) 850 606 (booking essential) – dinner only – Closed Monday and restricted opening in winter

---

PEAT INN
Fife – Regional map n° **16**-D2
▶ Edinburgh 44 mi – Dundee 16 mi – Stirling 50 mi

✗✗✗ **The Peat Inn** (Geoffrey Smeddle)

✿ CLASSIC CUISINE · FORMAL Whitewashed former pub; now a contemporary restaurant run by a charming team. The smart lounge still has its original open log fireplace; ask for a table overlooking the floodlit gardens. Accomplished, classical cooking has subtle modern touches and local ingredients are to the fore. Stylish, split-level bedrooms have plenty of extras and breakfast is served in your room.
→ St. Andrew's Bay lobster in seaweed butter sauce. Hay-baked leg of lamb for two, with potato and Anster cheese gratin. Ganache of Scottish 'bean to bar' chocolate, coffee mousse and caramel ice cream.

Menu £ 19/45 – Carte £ 35/59

8 rooms ⊻ – ♦£ 175/205 ♦♦£ 195/225

⊠ KY15 5LH – ℰ (01334) 840 206 (booking essential) – www.thepeatinn.co.uk
– Closed 1 week January, Christmas, Sunday and Monday

PEEBLES

The Scottish Borders – Pop. 8 376 – Regional map n° **15**-C2

▶ Edinburgh 24 mi – London 382 mi – Glasgow 53 mi – Aberdeen 151 mi

Cringletie House

COUNTRY HOUSE · HISTORIC A handsome, early Victorian shooting lodge with a baronial feel, set in acres of gardens and parkland. Smart bedrooms – named after border towns – have views of the gardens. Dine under a stunning 1902 ceiling fresco; good quality local produce includes herbs and veg from the walled garden.

15 rooms ☑ – †£135/180 ††£150/195 – 2 suites

Edinburgh Rd ⊠ EH45 8PL – North : 3 mi on A 703 – ℰ (01721) 722 510 – www.cringletie.com – Closed 2-22 January

Rowanbrae

TOWNHOUSE · PERSONALISED Snug Victorian villa with a pretty terrace and a surprisingly spacious interior; in a peaceful cul-de-sac close to town. The long-standing owners provide a warm welcome and a homely atmosphere reigns. Bedrooms are cosy and well-kept, and original cornicing and old pine woodwork feature throughout.

3 rooms ☑ – †£45 ††£70

103 Northgate ⊠ EH45 8BU – ℰ (01721) 721 630 – www.aboutscotland.co./peebles/rowanbrae – Closed December-February

✗ Restaurant at Kailzie Gardens

TRADITIONAL CUISINE · FRIENDLY Rustic eatery in the old stables of a large estate, surrounded by semi-formal gardens, a fishery and an osprey viewing centre. Brunch, homemade cakes and afternoon tea are accompanied by a concise selection of Scandic open sandwiches and classic dishes from 12pm. Seasonal dinners are served once a month.

Carte £14/37

Kailzie Estate ⊠ EH45 9HT – East : 2 mi on B 7062 – ℰ (01721) 722 807 (booking advisable) – www.kailzie.com – lunch only – Closed 1-14 January, Monday and Tuesday October-March

✗ Osso

MODERN CUISINE · FRIENDLY By day, this is a bustling coffee shop serving a bewildering array of light snacks and daily specials; come evening, it transforms into a more sophisticated restaurant offering a great value, regularly changing menu of well-presented, flavoursome dishes. Service is friendly and attentive, whatever the time.

Carte £21/40

Innerleithen Rd ⊠ EH45 8BA – ℰ (01721) 724 477 – www.ossorestaurant.com – Closed 1 January, 25 December, dinner Tuesday and Wednesday in winter except December and dinner Sunday and Monday

at Eddleston North: 4.5 mi on A703

✗✗ The Horseshoe

MODERN CUISINE · INN Once a roadside inn; now a smart, columned restaurant with elegant tableware and formal service. Sophisticated menus offer ambitious, well-presented dishes which take their influences from across Europe. Chic, modern bedrooms are located in the old village schoolhouse and come with pleasing extras.

Menu £25 (lunch) – Carte £30/44

8 rooms ☑ – †£80/130 ††£120/160

Edinburgh Rd ⊠ EH45 8QP – ℰ (01721) 730 225 – www.horseshoeinn.co.uk – Closed first 2 weeks January, last 2 weeks September, Monday and Tuesday

PERTH

Perth and Kinross – Pop. 46 970 – Regional map n° **16**-C2

▶ Edinburgh 44 mi – Aberdeen 86 mi – Dundee 22 mi – Dunfermline 29 mi

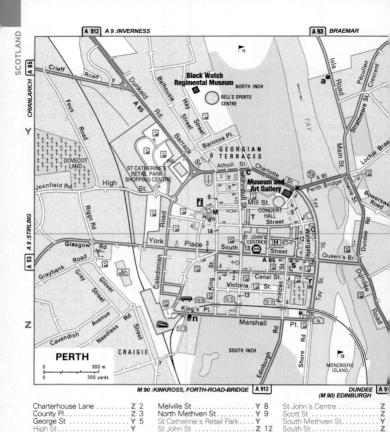

PERTH

0 — 300 m
0 — 300 yards

🏨 Parklands

BUSINESS · MODERN Located close to the railway station, a personally run, extended Georgian house with a contemporary interior. Spacious modern bedrooms have good facilities and sizeable bathrooms; those to the front have pleasant views over the park. Modern menu in the intimate 63@Parklands; informal dining in No.1 The Bank.

15 rooms ☲ – †£ 95/170 ††£ 120/200

Town plan: **Z-n** – *2 St Leonard's Bank* ⊠ *PH2 8EB* – ℰ *(01738) 622 451*
– *www.theparklandshotel.com* – *Closed 26 December-5 January*

63@Parklands – See restaurant listing

🏨 Taythorpe

TRADITIONAL · COSY Modern, stone-built house run by a bubbly owner; superbly located close to Scone Palace, the city and the racecourse. Large, cosy sitting room hung with homely pictures and salmon fishing maps; pleasant communal breakfast room where tasty Scottish dishes are served. Appealing, immaculately kept bedrooms.

3 rooms ☲ – †£ 50 ††£ 80

Town plan: **Y-a** – *Isla Rd* ⊠ *PH2 7HQ* – *North : 1 mi on A 93* – ℰ *(01738) 447 994*
– *www.taythorpe.co.uk* – *Closed 21 December-4 January*

XX **63 Tay Street**

BRITISH MODERN · INTIMATE Well-established riverside restaurant run by an attentive team. Ambitious dishes feature an array of flavours and textures; the mid-week pre-theatre menus represent good value and the impressive wine list features over 250 bins.

Menu £ 20 (weekdays)/55

Town plan: Z-r – 63 Tay St ⊠ PH2 8NN – ℰ (01738) 441 451
– www.63taystreet.co.uk – Closed 1-4 January, 5-11 July, 26-31 December, Sunday, Monday and lunch Tuesday-Wednesday

XX **Deans**

TRADITIONAL CUISINE · FRIENDLY Bottle-green restaurant close to the theatre and the concert hall. All-encompassing menus feature passionately prepared, classically based dishes with an ambitious edge. The smart lounge serves cocktails and sharing platters.

Menu £ 18 (weekday lunch)/20 – Carte £ 20/36

Town plan: Y-c – 77-79 Kinnoull St ⊠ PH1 5EZ – ℰ (01738) 643 377
– www.letseatperth.co.uk – Closed second and third weeks January, 1 week November, Sunday dinner and Monday

XX **63@Parklands**

BRITISH MODERN · INTIMATE Intimate conservatory restaurant with a relaxed lounge, set within a privately run hotel. The gourmet-style 5 course menu offers one or two choices per course and changes weekly; cooking is modern and features some interesting combinations.

Menu £ 40

Town plan: Z-n – Parklands Hotel, 2 St Leonard's Bank ⊠ PH2 8EB – ℰ (01738) 622 451 – www.63atparklands.com – dinner only – Closed 26 December-5 January, Tuesday and Wednesday

X **Pig Halle**

FRENCH · SIMPLE Lively bistro; its square, marble-floored room tightly packed with tables and dominated by a mirror stencilled with a Paris Metro map. Menus list Gallic favourites. The adjoining deli serves wood-fired pizzas and tasty pastries.

Menu £ 15 – Carte £ 15/39

Town plan: Z-s – 38 South St ⊠ PH2 8PG – ℰ (01738) 248 784
– www.pighalle.co.uk – Closed 26 December and 1 January

X **Post Box**

CLASSIC CUISINE · BRASSERIE Striking building with bright red doors: formerly the first Post Office in Perth. Classic lunches are followed by an evening menu with a more modern edge. The stone walled cellar bar hosts live jazz and blues on Fridays and Saturdays.

Menu £ 16 (lunch) – Carte £ 27/40

Town plan: Y-x – 80 George St ⊠ PH1 5LB – ℰ (01738) 248 971
– www.thepostboxperth.co.uk – Closed first 2 weeks January and Monday

at Kintillo Southeast: 4.5 mi off A912

X **Roost**

BRITISH MODERN · INTIMATE A converted brick hen house in the heart of the village, with a smart modern interior and hen references in its décor. Service is engaging and eager to please. The experienced chef prepares refined, classical dishes with some restrained modern touches; meats are local and veg is from the garden.

Menu £ 24 (weekday lunch) – Carte £ 27/31

Forgandenny Rd ⊠ PH2 9AZ – ℰ (01738) 812 111 – www.theroostrestaurant.co.uk
– Closed 1-16 January, 25-26 December, Monday and dinner Sunday, Tuesday and Wednesday

PIEROWALL → See Orkney Islands (Isle of Westray)

PITLOCHRY

Perth and Kinross – Pop. 2 776 – Regional map n° **16**-C2

▶ Edinburgh 71 mi – Inverness 85 mi – Perth 27 mi

🏨 Fonab Castle

HISTORIC · CONTEMPORARY This 19C baronial-style castle offers superb views over the loch to the hills beyond. Bedrooms have a subtle traditional feel and smart bathrooms; the 'Woodland' rooms are more modern and have terraces or balconies. Dine from a tasting menu in intimate Sandemans or on modern classics in the Brasserie.

26 rooms ⌂ – ♦£ 260/320 ♦♦£ 280/340 – 4 suites
Town plan: A-z – Foss Rd ⌂ PH16 5ND – ☎ (01796) 470 140
– www.fonabcastlehotel.com
Brasserie • Sandemans on the Loch – See restaurant listing

🏨 Green Park

TRADITIONAL · CLASSIC Long-standing, family-run hotel on the shore of Loch Faskally; many of its guests return year after year. Well-appointed lounges offer stunning loch and countryside views. Bedrooms vary in style; the largest and most modern are in the newer wing. A traditional dinner is included in the price of the room.

51 rooms (dinner included) ⌂ – ♦£ 91/114 ♦♦£ 182/228
Town plan: A-a – Clunie Bridge Rd ⌂ PH16 5JY – ☎ (01796) 473 248
– www.thegreenpark.co.uk – Closed 17-27 December

🏨 East Haugh House

TRADITIONAL · PERSONALISED 17C turreted stone house in two acres of gardens; originally part of the Atholl Estate. Cosy, traditionally appointed bedrooms are named after fishing flies and are split between the house, a former bothy and the old gatehouse.

14 rooms ⌂ – ♦£ 129/199 ♦♦£ 129/199
⌂ PH16 5TE – Southeast : 1.75 mi off A 924 (Perth Rd) – ☎ (01796) 473 121
– www.easthaugh.co.uk – Closed 1 week Christmas
Two Sisters – See restaurant listing

🏨 Craigmhor Lodge and Courtyard

COUNTRY HOUSE · MODERN Spacious, cosy house just out of town, with an airy breakfast room where local fruits, bacon and sausages are served. Well-kept modern bedrooms are set in the courtyard – some have balconies. Supper hampers can be delivered to your room.

12 rooms ⌂ – ♦£ 65/90 ♦♦£ 79/115
Town plan: B-a – 27 West Moulin Rd ⌂ PH16 5EF – ☎ (01796) 472 123
– www.craigmhorlodge.co.uk – Closed Christmas

🏠 Craigatin House and Courtyard

TOWNHOUSE · MODERN Built in 1822 as a doctor's house; now a stylish boutique hotel. The stunning open-plan lounge and breakfast room centres around a wood burning stove and overlooks the garden. Contemporary, minimalist bedrooms – some in the old stables.

14 rooms ⌂ – ♦£ 85/107 ♦♦£ 95/127
Town plan: A-e – 165 Atholl Rd ⌂ PH16 5QL – ☎ (01796) 472 478
– www.craigatinhouse.co.uk – Closed Christmas

🏠 Beinn Bhracaigh

TOWNHOUSE · MODERN An extended stone house built in 1880 and run by passionate owners. The spacious, immaculately kept interior has good comforts and most rooms boast lovely views of the Tummel Valley. Breakfast includes French toast and pancakes.

13 rooms ⌂ – ♦£ 59/119 ♦♦£ 69/129
Town plan: B-n – 14 Higher Oakfield ⌂ PH16 5HT – ☎ (01796) 470 355
– www.beinnbhracaigh.com – Closed 20 December-4 February

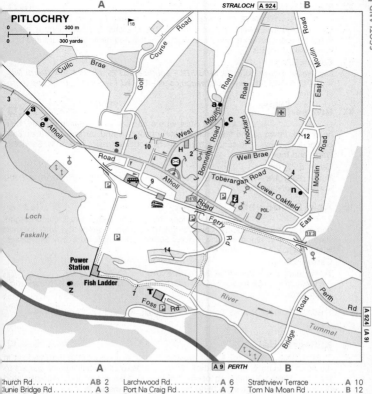

PITLOCHRY

STRALOCH A 924

0 ____ 300 m
0 ____ 300 yards

A 9 PERTH

Dunmurray Lodge

TOWNHOUSE · STYLISH Imposing 19C former doctor's surgery, set close to the town and boasting views across to the mountains. Cosy, open-fired lounge and snug, well-equipped bedrooms with co-ordinating décor; the best outlooks are from the front. Bright breakfast room – choose from a huge array of very locally sourced produce.

4 rooms ⌂ - ♦£60 ♦♦£75/90

Town plan: B-c – *72 Bonnethill Rd* ⊠ *PH16 5ED*
– ℰ *(01796) 473 624* – *www.dunmurray.co.uk*
– *Closed mid November-mid March*

Sandemans on the Loch N

MODERN CUISINE · INTIMATE Despite its name, this intimate hotel restaurant – of just 8 tables – does not overlook the loch. Choose between two well-balanced set menus; cooking is clean and precise and showcases top Scottish ingredients, from mountain to coast.

Menu £50/70 – set menu only

Town plan: A-z – *Fonab Castle Hotel, Foss Rd* ⊠ *PH16 5ND*
– ℰ *(01796) 470 140* – *www.fonabcastlehotel.com* – *dinner only*
– *closed Sunday-Tuesday*

XX Two Sisters   ⬛

REGIONAL · INTIMATE Charming fishermen's bar and a bright, laid-back restaurant, located in a lovely 17C stone house. The seasonal Scottish menu is served in both areas; cooking is clean and exact, with fish and game to the fore and tasty home-baked breads.

Carte £ 22/44

East Haugh House Hotel, ⊠ PH16 5TE – Southeast : 1.75 mi off A 924 (Perth Rd) – ℰ (01796) 473 121 – www.easthaugh.co.uk – Closed 1 week Christmas and lunch in winter

XX Brasserie   🍸 ⋖ 🏠 & 🅰 🅿

MODERN CUISINE · BRASSERIE Start with a cocktail in the 'Bar in the Air', then head back down to the fashionable hotel restaurant and terrace with their panoramic loch views. The concise menu offers modern classics and grills. Service is warm and friendly.

Carte £ 27/54

Town plan: A-z – Fonab Castle Hotel, Foss Rd ⊠ PH16 5ND – ℰ (01796) 470 140 – www.fonabcastlehotel.com

🍴 Auld Smiddy Inn   🏠 🏠 &

TRADITIONAL CUISINE · PUB Old blacksmith's forge with a small, colourful garden and a large terrace and courtyard. It has a likeable simplicity, with polished slate floors and wood burning stoves. Summer menus feature fish and salads; winter menus, hearty classics.

Carte £ 20/42

Town plan: A-s – 154 Atholl Rd ⊠ PH16 5AG – ℰ (01796) 472 356 – www.auldsmiddyinn.co.uk – Closed last week January-first week February and 25-26 December

at Killiecrankie Northwest: 4 mi by A924 – Plan: A – and B8019 on B8079 – ⊠ Pitlochry

🏠 Killiecrankie   🌣 🦢 ⋖ 🏠 🅿

TRADITIONAL · CLASSIC A whitewashed former vicarage built in 1840 and set in 4.5 acres of mature, rhododendron-filled grounds, with a small kitchen garden to the rear. There's a charming open-fired lounge, a snug bar and well-appointed bedrooms which offer everything you might want, including a hot water bottle. Choose between light suppers and traditional dinners. Service is excellent.

10 rooms ⊡ – ♦£ 90/160 ♦♦£ 180/200

⊠ PH16 5LG – ℰ (01796) 473 220 – www.killiecrankiehotel.co.uk – Closed 3 January-18 March

PLOCKTON

Highland – Regional map n° **17**-B2

▶ Edinburgh 210 mi – Inverness 88 mi – Fort William 77 mi

🍴 Plockton Hotel   ⬅ ⋖ 🏠 🏠 &

TRADITIONAL CUISINE · INN A one-time ships' chandlery with a distinctive black exterior and stunning views over Loch Carron to the mountains beyond. Cooking is honest and hearty with a strong Scottish influence, so expect haggis and whisky or herring in oatmeal – and don't miss the Plockton prawns. Simple, comfortable bedrooms.

Carte £ 18/40

15 rooms ⊡ – ♦£ 45/95 ♦♦£ 90/140

41 Harbour St ⊠ IV52 8TN – ℰ (01599) 544 274 – www.plocktonhotel.co.uk

POOLEWE

Highland – Regional map n° **17**-B2

▶ Edinburgh 230 mi – London 635 mi – Inverness 76 mi – Elgin 112 mi

🏠 Pool House

FAMILY · PERSONALISED A unique, family-run Victorian house by the water's edge, with a quirky whisky bar in the old billiard room. Bedrooms are all large suites – each individually themed with incredible attention to detail; the Ashanti room features a 19C marriage bed. The formal restaurant offers a classic seasonal menu.

4 rooms ⌑ – †£ 250 ††£ 275/375

✉ IV22 2LD – 𝒞 (01445) 781 272 – www.pool-house.co.uk – *Closed mid November-mid March*

PORT APPIN

Argyll and Bute – ✉ Appin – Regional map n° **16**-B2

▶ Edinburgh 136 mi – Ballachulish 20 mi – Oban 24 mi

🏠 Airds

LUXURY · PERSONALISED Characterful former ferryman's cottage fronted by colourful planters and offering lovely loch and mountain views. Two sumptuous, open-fired sitting rooms are furnished with antiques and bedrooms provide good comforts. The intimate dining room offers excellent water views and has a classical menu with a modern edge; a 7 course tasting menu is available at dinner.

11 rooms ⌑ – †£ 240/470 ††£ 295/525

✉ PA38 4DF – 𝒞 (01631) 730 236 – www.airds-hotel.com – *Closed 1-12 December and Monday-Tuesday November-January*

PORT CHARLOTTE – Argyll and Bute ➔ See Islay (Isle of)

PORT ELLEN – Argyll and Bute ➔ See Islay (Isle of)

PORTMAHOMACK

Highland – Regional map n° **17**-D2

▶ Edinburgh 194 mi – Dornoch 21 mi – Tain 12 mi

✗✗ Oystercatcher

FISH AND SEAFOOD · BISTRO Set in a lovely spot in a tiny fishing village, with lobster pots hanging outside. One formal and one rustic room, with walls crammed with memorabilia. Menus offer fresh seafood in some unusual combinations; the boats that land the fish can be seen by the jetty. Modest bedrooms; nearly 20 choices at breakfast.

Menu £ 37 (dinner) **s** – Carte lunch £ 20/42 **s**

3 rooms ⌑ – †£ 54/82 ††£ 85/115

Main St ✉ IV20 1YB – 𝒞 (01862) 871 560 *(booking essential)*
– www.the-oystercatcher.co.uk – *Closed November-February, Sunday dinner, Wednesday lunch, Monday and Tuesday*

PORTPATRICK

Dumfries and Galloway – ✉ Stranraer – Pop. 534 – Regional map n° **15**-A3

▶ Edinburgh 141 mi – Ayr 60 mi – Dumfries 80 mi – Stranraer 9 mi

🏠 Knockinaam Lodge

TRADITIONAL · PERSONALISED Charming country house, superbly set in its own private cove, with the sea at the bottom of the garden. Classical guest areas include a wood-panelled bar and open-fired sitting rooms; a relaxed atmosphere pervades. Traditional, antique-furnished bedrooms; 'Churchill' boasts its original 100 year old bath.

10 rooms (dinner included) ⌑ – †£ 175/325 ††£ 290/440

✉ DG9 9AD – *Southeast : 5 mi by A 77 off B 7042* – 𝒞 (01776) 810 471
– www.knockinaamlodge.com

Knockinaam Lodge – See restaurant listing

XX **Knockinaam Lodge** 🐘 ≤ ⛶ P

CLASSIC CUISINE · FORMAL A traditionally furnished, smartly dressed dining room with delightful sea views, in a charming country house, idyllically set in its own private cove. The set four course menu evolves with the seasons and offers good quality produce – often from their own gardens – cooked in classic combinations.

Menu £ 40/68 – set menu only

Knockinaam Lodge Hotel, ✉ DG9 9AD – Southeast : 5 mi by A 77 off B 7042 – ✆ (01776) 810 471 (booking essential) – www.knockinaamlodge.com

PORTAVADIE

Argyll and Bute – Regional map n° **16**-B3

▶ Edinburgh 107 mi – Dunoon 28 mi – Oban 55 mi

🏠 **Portavadie** ⛱ 🦌 ≤ ⌁ 📶 🛏 ⛶ 🍽 ⛴ P

RURAL · DESIGN This peaceful lochside complex consists of a marina, self-catering apartments and a small hotel. Good-sized bedrooms have a modern Scandic style and pleasant views; some have balconies or kitchenettes. There's also an informal dining room with a leather-furnished lounge and a brasserie in another building.

16 rooms ⌷ – †£ 60/110 ††£ 60/110

Portavadie Marina ✉ PA21 2DA – ✆ (01700) 811 075 – www.portavadiemarina.com

PORTREE – Highland → See Skye (Isle of)

RANNOCH STATION

Perth and Kinross – Regional map n° **16**-B2

▶ Edinburgh 108 mi – Kinloch Rannoch 17 mi – Pitlochry 36 mi

🏠 **Moor of Rannoch** ⛱ 🦌 ≤ ⛶ P

FAMILY · COSY This 19C hotel is perched high on the moor and is the ultimate in hiking getaways. The views are delightful, the whole place has a serene feel and wildlife is in abundance. Bedrooms are cosy and the open-fired guest areas come with jigsaws instead of TVs. Rustic home cooking utilises Scottish ingredients.

5 rooms ⌷ – †£ 95 ††£ 120

✉ PH17 2QA – ✆ (01882) 633 238 – www.moorofrannoch.co.uk – Closed November-mid February

RATAGAN

Highland – Regional map n° **17**-B2

▶ Edinburgh 186 mi – Inverness 65 mi – Fort William 65 mi

🏠 **Grants at Craigellachie** ⛱ ⛶ P

TRADITIONAL · FUNCTIONAL Set in an idyllic spot beside Loch Duich and named after the eponymous local gamekeeper. Compact, pine-furnished bedrooms in the main house; the larger annexe rooms are more comfortable but don't have water views. Small conservatory restaurant with a Mediterranean-influenced menu. Good malt whisky selection.

4 rooms ⌷ – †£ 68/120 ††£ 105/185

✉ IV40 8HP – ✆ (01599) 511 331 – www.housebytheloch.co.uk – Restricted opening October-Easter

RATHO

City of Edinburgh – Pop. 1 634 – Regional map n° **15**-C1

▶ Edinburgh 10 mi – Glasgow 40 mi – Dunfermline 15 mi

🅿 **Bridge Inn** ⓝ   ⇔ 🕮 🏠 ⅃ & 🅿

MODERN CUISINE · PUB Friendly pub on the tow path between Edinburgh and the Falkirk Wheel. Fruit and veg come from their walled garden, pork comes from their saddleback pigs and the eggs, from their chickens and ducks. All of the cosy bedrooms have water views. For a treat, book a cruise on their restaurant barge.

Carte £ 19/43

4 rooms ☲ – ♦£ 65/105 ♦♦£ 80/120

27 Baird Rd ⊠ EH28 8RU
– ℰ (0131) 333 13 20 – www.bridgeinn.com
– Closed 25 December

ST ANDREWS

Fife – Pop. 16 870 – Regional map n° **16**-D2
▸ Edinburgh 51 mi – Dundee 14 mi – Stirling 51 mi

🏨 **Old Course H. Golf Resort & Spa**   ⌂ ← ▣ ▨ ⑩ ⅏ ⅃ ⋄ & ⅍

LUXURY · CLASSIC Vast resort hotel with an impressive spa,   ⅗ ⅍ 🅿
set on a world-famous golf course overlooking the bay. Luxurious guest areas have a subtle Scottish theme and bedrooms are chic, sumptuous and well-equipped; those in the wing are the most modern.

144 rooms ☲ – ♦£ 190/400 ♦♦£ 220/450 – 15 suites

Town plan: A-b – *Old Station Rd ⊠ KY16 9SP*
– ℰ (01334) 474 371 – www.oldcoursehotel.co.uk
Road Hole · Sands Grill – See restaurant listing

🏨 **Fairmont St Andrews**   ⌂ ← ⇔ ▣ ▨ ⑩ ⅏ ⅃ ⋄ & ⅍ ⅗ 🅿

BUSINESS · CONTEMPORARY Modern, purpose-built property in 520 acres, with extensive conference and leisure facilities, including two golf courses, a superb spa and a wellness centre. Spacious guest areas have a subtle Scottish theme. Well-appointed bedrooms feature tartan and driftwood; 'Deluxe' are worth it for the view. La Cucina serves Italian fare; the Clubhouse offers steaks and seafood.

209 rooms ☲ – ♦£ 129/290 ♦♦£ 129/290 – 12 suites

⊠ *KY16 8PN – Southeast : 3.5 mi on A 917*
– ℰ (01334) 837 000 – www.fairmont.com/standrews

🏨 **Rusacks** ⓝ   ⌂ ← ⅃ & ⅍

LUXURY · STYLISH The oldest hotel in St Andrews sits in a commanding position overlooking the 18th green of the Old Course. Original 1846 columns feature in the lobby and a huge array of paintings pay homage to golfing greats. Bedrooms are stylish; choose one with a view. Dine in the pub or the formal restaurant.

70 rooms ☲ – ♦£ 235/300 ♦♦£ 250/315 – 4 suites

Town plan: A-s – *Pilmour Links ⊠ KY16 9JQ*
– ℰ (0844) 879 9136 – www.macdonaldhotels.co.uk
Rocca – See restaurant listing

🏨 **Hotel du Vin**   ⌂ ← ⅃ & ⅍

BUSINESS · MODERN This stylish, moodily lit hotel sits overlooking West Sands Beach, close to the famous 'Old Course'. Smart bedrooms are named after wines and whisky houses and come with Egyptian cotton linen and monsoon showers. The elegant bistro serves French classics and the bar is a hit with locals and visitors alike.

36 rooms ☲ – ♦£ 105/280 ♦♦£ 115/300

Town plan: A-d – *40 The Scores ⊠ KY16 9AS*
– ℰ (0844) 748 92 69 – www.hotelduvin.com

ST ANDREWS

[Map of St Andrews with labelled streets, showing NORTH SEA, Royal and Ancient Golf Club, St Salvator's College, Castle, Deans Court, Cathedral, St Mary of the Rock, Harbour, Holy Trinity, Blackfriars Chapel, St Mary's College, St Leonard's, Botanic Garden; scale 200 m / 200 yards; route references LEUCHARS, CUPAR TAY ROAD BRIDGE, A 91, A 915 KIRKCALDY, B 939, A 917 CRAIL, ANSTRUTHER]

🏛 Rufflets Country House

❀ 🐾 🛏 🍴 🅿

COUNTRY HOUSE · STYLISH This country house hotel is surrounded by well-tended gardens and has been owned by the same family since 1952. Inside it's a mix of the old and the new, with original Arts and Crafts features sitting alongside stylish, contemporary bedrooms. Menus offer modern interpretations of classic dishes.

24 rooms ⊑ – ❙£ 120/205 ❙❙£ 175/415 – 2 suites
Strathkinness Low Rd ⊠ KY16 9TX – West : 1.5 mi on B 939
– ℰ (01334) 472 594 – www.rufflets.co.uk
– Closed 3-21 January

🏠 Five Pilmour Place

✄

TOWNHOUSE · STYLISH Victorian terraced house with a surprisingly stylish interior. There's a bright, clubby lounge and a locker room with underfloor heating. Bedrooms have bold feature walls and smart walk-in showers; Room 3 also has a claw-foot bath.

7 rooms ⊑ – ❙£ 69/79 ❙❙£ 95/160
Town plan: A-x – *5 Pilmour Pl. ⊠ KY16 9HZ*
– ℰ (01334) 478 665 – www.5pilmourplace.com
– Closed 18 December-31 January

🏠 Fairways

✄

TOWNHOUSE · STYLISH This tall Victorian building is the closest guesthouse to the Old Course – ask for Room 3 and sit on the balcony overlooking the 18th hole. Bedrooms are contemporary and of a good size. Nothing is too much trouble for the owners.

3 rooms ⊑ – ❙£ 65/80 ❙❙£ 80/130
Town plan: A-z – *8a Golf Pl. ⊠ KY16 9JA*
– ℰ (01334) 479 513 – www.fairwaysofstandrews.co.uk

Six Murray Park

TOWNHOUSE · STYLISH Victorian terraced townhouse with a leather-furnished breakfast room, a golf club storage area and lots of golfing memorabilia. Compact, modern bedrooms come with bold feature walls, coffee machines and smart shower rooms.

9 rooms ⌑ – †£ 70/110 ††£ 110/150

Town plan: A-n – *6 Murray Pk.* ⊠ *KY16 9AW*
– *☏ (01334) 473 319 – www.sixmurraypark.co.uk*
– *Closed 1 December-15 February*

Road Hole

MODERN CUISINE · FORMAL Formal wood-panelled restaurant on the top floor of a smart golf resort, with stunning views of the 18th hole and the beach. Modern versions of classic dishes use local produce; watch the chefs in the open kitchen while you eat.

Menu £ 20 (lunch) – Carte £ 34/64

Town plan: A-b – *Old Course Hotel Golf Resort & Spa, Old Station Rd*
⊠ *KY16 9SP* – *☏ (01334) 474 371 – www.oldcoursehotel.co.uk*
– *Closed January, February, Monday, Tuesday and Wednesday lunch*

Rocca

MODERN CUISINE · DESIGN A formal hotel restaurant with designer wallpapers, richly coloured fabrics and great Old Course views. Interesting modern menus feature Scottish dishes with Italian twists and use artisan produce both from the region and from Tuscany.

Carte £ 36/55

Town plan: A-s – *Rusacks Hotel, Pilmour Links* ⊠ *KY16 9JQ*
– *☏ (01334) 472 549 (booking essential) – www.roccarestaurant.com – dinner only*
– *Closed Sunday December-March*

Sands Grill

MEATS · BRASSERIE An informal grill restaurant with smart wood panelling and a clubby feel – part of a stylish golf resort and spa. Classically based menus comprise mainly of seafood and steaks, with all meats cooked on the Josper grill.

Menu £ 20 **s** – Carte £ 24/51

Town plan: A-b – *Old Course Hotel Golf Resort & Spa, Old Station Rd*
⊠ *KY16 9SP* – *☏ (01334) 474 371 – www.oldcoursehotel.co.uk – dinner only*
– *Closed Wednesday October-March*

Adamson

MEATS · BRASSERIE A stylish modern brasserie and cocktail bar in a house owned by eminent photographer John Adamson in the 19C and the town's Post Office in the 20C. The wide-ranging menu of tasty dishes includes steaks from the Josper grill.

Menu £ 18 (lunch and early dinner) – Carte £ 18/49

Town plan: A-v – *127 South St* ⊠ *KY16 9UH*
– *☏ (01334) 479 191 – www.theadamson.com*
– *Closed 25-26 December and 1 January*

Seafood

FISH AND SEAFOOD · DESIGN This striking glass cube juts out over the sea and offers commanding bay views. The immaculate modern interior comes complete with an open kitchen where you can watch Fife coast seafood being prepared in elaborate combinations.

Menu £ 22/49

Town plan: A-c – *Bruce Embankment, The Scores* ⊠ *KY16 9AB*
– *☏ (01334) 479 475 – www.theseafoodrestaurant.com*
– *Closed 25-26 December and 1 January*

X **Grange Inn**

TRADITIONAL CUISINE · COSY A former pub, atop a hill, with great views over the bay. Have an aperitif beside the fire, then head for the stone-walled restaurant with its huge stag's head. The experienced chef serves a menu of tasty well-prepared classics.

Menu £15/38

Grange Rd ⊠ KY16 8LJ – Southeast : 1.75 mi by A 917
- *✆ (01334) 472 670 (booking essential) – www.thegrangeinn.com*
- *Closed 3 weeks January, Sunday dinner and Monday*

ST BOSWELLS

The Scottish Borders – ⊠ Melrose – Pop. 1 279 – Regional map n° **15**-D2
▶ Edinburgh 39 mi – Glasgow 79 mi – Hawick 17 mi – Newcastle upon Tyne 66 mi

🏠 **Buccleuch Arms**

INN · HOMELY A smart, long-standing coaching inn which offers popular golfing, fishing and shooting breaks. Cosy bedrooms have co-ordinated headboards and soft furnishings. After dinner, sink into a squashy sofa in the semi-panelled fire-lit bar.

19 rooms ⊊ – ♦£ 75/120 ♦♦£ 85/130

The Green ⊠ TD6 0EW
- *✆ (01835) 822 243 – www.buccleucharms.com*
- *Closed 24-25 December*

Blue Coo Bistrot – See restaurant listing

🏠 **Whitehouse**

TRADITIONAL · PERSONALISED Former dower house built in 1872 by the Duke of Sutherland, with a cosy, country house feel. Traditionally furnished bedrooms boast excellent views across the estate. Many people come for the on-site shooting and fishing; wild salmon and local game – including venison – feature at dinner.

3 rooms ⊊ – ♦£ 90/95 ♦♦£ 130/150

⊠ TD6 0ED – Northeast : 3 mi on B 6404
- *✆ (01573) 460 343 – www.whitehousecountryhouse.com*

🏠 **Clint Lodge**

TRADITIONAL · PERSONALISED Former shooting lodge with superb river and hill views. Characterful interior boasts antiques and fishing memorabilia. Traditionally decorated bedrooms; luxurious No. 4 and the south facing rooms are the best. Daily changing 5 course dinner served at a beautiful table.

5 rooms ⊊ – ♦£ 70/110 ♦♦£ 100/140

⊠ TD6 0DZ – North : 2.25 mi by B 6404 on B 6356
- *✆ (01835) 822 027 – www.clintlodge.co.uk*

X **Blue Coo Bistrot**

MEATS · RUSTIC The heart of the Buccleuch Arms is this relaxed, shabby chic bistrot comprising three different rooms. Accessible menus offer classics and grills, alongside afternoon tea and daily blackboard specials. Local fish and game feature.

Carte £ 20/44

at Buccleuch Arms Hotel, The Green ⊠ TD6 0EW
- *✆ (01835) 822 243 – www.buccleucharms.com*
- *Closed 24-25 December*

ST FILLANS

Perth and Kinross – Regional map n° **16**-C2
▶ Edinburgh 65 mi – Lochearnhead 8 mi – Perth 29 mi

⌂ Achray House

🕊 ⋞ 🛏 ⅋ P

TRADITIONAL · COSY Superbly located Edwardian villa offering stunning views over Loch Earn. Bright breakfast room and an inviting lounge with open fires and a polished Douglas Fir floor. Modern bedrooms have bespoke pine furnishings and contemporary bathrooms. Simple restaurant offers global dishes crafted from local produce.

8 rooms 🖙 – ♦£ 60/130 ♦♦£ 90/199

✉ PH6 2NF – ℰ (0560) 368 42 52 – www.achrayhouse.com – Closed 1-26 January, 5-22 December and Monday

ST MARGARET'S HOPE → See Orkney Islands (Mainland)

ST MONANS

Fife – Pop. 1 265 – Regional map n° **16**-D2

🗗 Edinburgh 47 mi – Dundee 26 mi – Perth 40 mi

✗✗ Craig Millar @ 16 West End

⋞ 🏠

MODERN CUISINE · FRIENDLY Unassuming former pub with an attractive interior, run by a charming team. There's a characterful lounge and a smart restaurant with a small terrace and great harbour views. The experienced chef offers refined, flavoursome dishes.

Menu £ 18/42

16 West End ✉ KY10 2BX – ℰ (01333) 730 327 (booking essential)
– www.16westend.com – Closed Monday-Tuesday and restricted opening October-March

SANQUHAR

Dumfries and Galloway – Pop. 2 021 – Regional map n° **15**-B2

🗗 Edinburgh 57 mi – London 362 mi – Dundee 113 mi – Paisley 56 mi

✗✗ Blackaddie House

⋞ 🛏 P

BRITISH TRADITIONAL · TRADITIONAL A stone-built former manse with 16C origins, set by the river. Lunch offers good value classics, while dinner is more elaborate and features original modern cooking; ingredients are luxurious and dishes are well-presented. Bedrooms are named after game birds – ask for 'Grouse', which has a four-poster bed.

Menu £ 36/55

7 rooms 🖙 – ♦£ 90/190 ♦♦£ 110/210

Blackaddie Rd ✉ DG4 6JJ – ℰ (01659) 50 270 (booking essential at lunch)
– www.blackaddiehotel.co.uk

SCALPAY – Western Isles → See Lewis and Harris (Isle of)

SCARISTA – Western Isles → See Lewis and Harris (Isle of)

SCOURIE

Highland – ✉ Lairg – Regional map n° **17**-C1

🗗 Edinburgh 245 mi – London 646 mi – Dundee 226 mi

⌂ Eddrachilles

🕊 🦐 ⋞ 🛏 ⅋ P

FAMILY · CLASSIC Remotely set, converted 18C manse, with views of the countryside, Badcall Bay and its islands. Snug bar and flag-floored breakfast room; cosy, well-kept bedrooms. Delightful outlook from the conservatory dining room, which offers a daily menu with a strong French slant. Meats are cured on-site.

11 rooms 🖙 – ♦£ 80 ♦♦£ 110

Badcall Bay ✉ IV27 4TH – South : 2.5 mi on A 894 – ℰ (01971) 502 080
– www.eddrachilles.com – Closed October-March

SCRABSTER – Highland → See Thurso

SHETLAND ISLANDS
Shetland Islands – Pop. 21 800 – Regional map n° **18**-B2

MAINLAND
Shetland Islands – Regional map n° **18**-B2
▶ Edinburgh 360 mi – London 543 mi – Dundee 86 mi

Lerwick

🏨 Kveldsro House ✿ ✣ 🅿
BUSINESS · PERSONALISED Spacious Georgian house hidden in the town centre; its name means 'evening peace'. There's a cosy sitting room with original ceiling mouldings and a comfy bar with views of the islands; bedrooms are traditionally styled. Menus offer mainly island produce; portions are hearty.

17 rooms ☲ – ♦£ 115 ♦♦£ 145
Greenfield Pl ✉ ZE1 0AQ – ℰ (01595) 692 195 – www.shetlandhotels.com – Closed 25-26 December and 1-2 January

Veensgarth

🏠 Herrislea House ✿ ◜ 🅿
TRADITIONAL · CLASSIC Large, family-run hotel set just out of town. Unusual African hunting theme with mounted antlers, animal heads and skins on display. Cosy, individually designed bedrooms; some with valley views. Fresh cooking uses local produce and meats from the family crofts.

9 rooms ☲ – ♦£ 90 ♦♦£ 130/150
✉ ZE2 9SB – ℰ (01595) 840 208 – www.herrisleahouse.co.uk – Closed 10 December-10 January

SHIELDAIG
Highland – ✉ Strathcarron – Regional map n° **17**-B2
▶ Edinburgh 226 mi – Inverness 68 mi – Fort William 123 mi

🏠 Tigh An Eilean ✾ ◁
TRADITIONAL · CLASSIC Personally run hotel in a charming lochside setting, with fine views over the Shieldaig Islands. Two small, cottagey lounges and well-kept, compact bedrooms – most with views. Linen-laid restaurant offers traditional, daily changing dishes; informal Coastal Kitchen serves a wide-ranging, all-day menu.

11 rooms ☲ – ♦£ 80/120 ♦♦£ 140/170
✉ IV54 8XN – ℰ (01520) 755 251 – www.tighaneilean.co.uk – Restricted opening in winter

SKYE (Isle of)
Highland – Pop. 10 008 – Regional map n° **17**-B2

Bernisdale

🏨 Spoons
LUXURY · DESIGN Luxurious, purpose-built guesthouse in an unspoilt hamlet with an airy, wood-floored lounge and a breakfast room overlooking the loch. Bedrooms are individually decorated in a crisp, modern style and provide every conceivable extra. Superb 3 course breakfasts, with eggs from the charming owners' chickens.

3 rooms ☲ – ♦£ 120/140 ♦♦£ 145/165
75 Aird Bernisdale ✉ IV51 9NU – ℰ (01470) 532 217 – www.thespoonsonskye.com – Closed mid-November-mid-March

Broadford

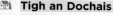 **Tigh an Dochais**

LUXURY · MODERN Striking house with award-winning architecture, overlooking Broadford Bay and the Applecross Peninsula. Comfy lounge has well-stocked bookshelves. Modern, minimalist bedrooms boast superb views and good facilities, including underfloor heating and plenty of extras. Communal, home-cooked meals by arrangement.

3 rooms �ిం – †£ 80/90 ††£ 95/110
13 Harrapool ⊠ IV49 9AQ – on A 87
– ✆ (01471) 820 022 – www.skyebedbreakfast.co.uk
– Closed November-February

Colbost

Hillstone Lodge

LUXURY · DESIGN With its superb outlook over Loch Dunvegan and plenty of stone, slate and wood on display, this striking modern house is at one with nature. Vibrant Scottish art covers the walls and stylish bedrooms have a minimalist feel. Local ingredients feature at breakfast and dinner (in winter only), often showcases island seafood. The owner is also qualified in 'sound massage'.

3 rooms ☞ – †£ 75/103 ††£ 110/138
⊠ IV55 8ZT – ✆ (01470) 511 434 – www.hillstonelodge.com
– Closed Christmas-New Year

XX **Three Chimneys & The House Over-By**

MODERN CUISINE · RUSTIC Immaculately kept crofter's cottage in a stunning lochside setting. Contemporary art hangs on exposed stone walls in the characterful low-beamed dining rooms. Modern Scottish menus showcase good regional ingredients and seafood from local waters is a highlight. Spacious, split-level bedrooms are stylishly understated and the residents' lounge has a great outlook.

Menu £ 38/65

6 rooms ☞ – †£ 218/345 ††£ 218/345
⊠ IV55 8ZT – ✆ (01470) 511 258 (booking essential) – www.threechimneys.co.uk
– dinner only and lunch April-October – Closed 1 December-23 January and Sunday lunch in winter

Duisdalemore

Duisdale House

TRADITIONAL · STYLISH Stylish, up-to-date hotel with lawned gardens, a hot tub and coastal views. Comfortable bedrooms boast bold décor, excellent bathrooms and a pleasing blend of contemporary and antique furniture. Modern cooking makes good use of local produce. Smart uniformed staff.

19 rooms ☞ – †£ 149/210 ††£ 158/338 – 1 suite
Sleat ⊠ IV43 8QW – on A 851 – ✆ (01471) 833 202 – www.duisdale.com

Dunvegan

Roskhill House

COUNTRY HOUSE · CONTEMPORARY Welcoming 19C croft house with a small garden, set in peaceful location close to the water. Formerly the old post office, the lounge boasts exposed stone, wooden beams and an open fire. Fresh, bright bedrooms have a contemporary edge and smart, modern bathrooms.

5 rooms ☞ – †£ 60/68 ††£ 80/96
Roskhill ⊠ IV55 8ZD – Southeast : 2.5 mi by A 863
– ✆ (01470) 521 317 – www.roskhillhouse.co.uk
– Closed 15 December-2 February

Edinbane

🏠 Greshornish House

🎐 🦢 ≼ 🛏 ❤️ 🅿️

TRADITIONAL · PERSONALISED Early 18C lochside house. Relax in the comfy panelled drawing room or in the old billiard room with its snooker table, piano, books and games. Country house style bedrooms – some with four-posters or loch views. Breakfast is in the conservatory; seasonal, island dinners are taken in the candlelit dining room.

6 rooms 🖅 – †£ 110/130 ††£ 140/190

✉ IV51 9PN – North : 3.75 mi by A 850 in direction of Dunvegan – ℰ (01470) 582 266 – www.greshornishhouse.com – Restricted opening in winter

🍴 Edinbane Inn

🅿️

TRADITIONAL CUISINE · COSY This traditional-looking former farmhouse is the perfect place to cosy up by the fire on a misty night. Choose a pub favourite or one of the appealing specials. Come on a Wednesday, Friday or Sunday for the popular music sessions.

Carte £ 22/37

✉ IV51 9PW – ℰ (01470) 582 414 – www.edinbaneinn.co.uk – Closed Monday-Friday October-March

Elgol

🍴 Coruisk House

⇦ ≼ 🅿️

TRADITIONAL CUISINE · SIMPLE This traditional croft house is very remotely set on the west of the island and offers superb views over the hills to the mountains. It's very personally run and seats just 16. Skye produce features in fresh, flavoursome daily dishes. Two simply furnished bedrooms share the stunning outlook.

Carte £ 28/43

2 rooms 🖅 – †£ 120/150 ††£ 120/150

✉ IV49 9BL – ℰ (01471) 866 330 (booking essential) – www.coruiskhouse.com – Closed November-February except 1 week New Year

Flodigarry

🏠 Flodigarry Country House

🎐 🦢 ≼ 🛏 🋨 🅿️

COUNTRY HOUSE · STYLISH This Victorian house was once Jacobite heroine Flora MacDonald's home. Lawned gardens lead down to the coast and it has excellent panoramic views; stylish designer décor features throughout. The bar is in the old billiard room and has its original ceiling windows. Cooking is modern and Scottish.

17 rooms 🖅 – †£ 180/260 ††£ 180/260

✉ IV51 9HZ – ℰ (01470) 552 203 – www.flodigarry.co.uk – Restricted opening in winter

Portree

🏠 Cuillin Hills

🎐 🦢 ≼ 🛏 ᪄ 🋨 🅿️

TRADITIONAL · CLASSIC Set in 15 acres of grounds, a 19C hunting lodge offering stunning views over Portree Bay towards the Cuillin Mountains; enjoy top Scottish produce in the restaurant, which shares the outlook. Bedrooms have good facilities – the best are to the front. The stylish open-plan bar serves over 100 malt whiskies.

28 rooms 🖅 – †£ 60/150 ††£ 80/300

✉ IV51 9QU – Northeast : 0.75 mi by A 855 – ℰ (01478) 612 003 – www.cuillinhills-hotel-skye.co.uk

🏠 Bosville

🎐 ≼

INN · STYLISH The Bosville sits in an elevated spot overlooking the harbour and the Cuillin Mountains; choose a bedroom at the front to best appreciate the view. Enjoy a dram by the fire in the lively red and black bar then head for the bistro-style dining room, which showcases the best of Skye's natural larder.

18 rooms 🖅 – †£ 95/225 ††£ 125/295

Bosville Terr ✉ IV51 9DG – ℰ (01478) 612 846 – www.bosvillehotel.co.uk – Closed Christmas

X **Scorrybreac**

MODERN CUISINE · BISTRO Simply furnished restaurant with distant mountain views and just 8 tables; named after the chef's parents' house, where he ran his first pop-up. Creative modern cooking uses meats from the hills and seafood from the harbour below.

Menu £ 33 (dinner) – Carte £ 23/26

7 Bosville Terr ⊠ IV51 9DG
– ✆ (01478) 612 069 (booking essential at dinner)
– www.scorrybreac.com – Closed Monday and Tuesday-Wednesday lunch

Sleat

🏠 **Kinloch Lodge**

COUNTRY HOUSE · CLASSIC With a loch in front and heather-strewn moorland behind, this 17C hunting lodge affords fantastic panoramic views. Inside, it has a traditional country house feel; comfy antique-filled lounges are hung with photos of the Macdonald clan and each of the contemporary bedrooms is themed around a different tartan.

19 rooms (dinner included) ⌺ – ♦£ 139/280 ♦♦£ 278/460 – 3 suites
⊠ IV43 8QY – ✆ (01471) 833 214
– www.kinloch-lodge.co.uk
❀ **Kinloch Lodge** – See restaurant listing

XXX **Kinloch Lodge**

❀ MODERN CUISINE · CLASSIC Elegant dining room in a 17C hunting lodge, offering stunning views across a loch. Dine beneath portraits of the Macdonald clan or watch the kitchen action from the chef's table. Cooking is classically based but has clever modern touches. Good service and a well-written wine list complete the picture.

➜ Slow-roast Moray pork cheek with seared scallops and pickled fennel. Fort Augustus venison, spinach, herb purée, chorizo and apple. Lemony tart 'brûlée', salted caramel popcorn ice cream and raspberry.

Menu £ 33/70 **s**

Kinloch Lodge Hotel, ⊠ IV43 8QY
– ✆ (01471) 833 214 (booking essential)
– www.kinloch-lodge.co.uk

Struan

🏠 **Ullinish Country Lodge**

TRADITIONAL · CLASSIC Personally run, 18C former hunting lodge in a windswept location, affording lovely loch and mountain views. The lounge is filled with ornaments and books about the area. Warmly decorated bedrooms boast good facilities and extras.

6 rooms ⌺ – ♦£ 125/160 ♦♦£ 190/260
⊠ IV56 8FD – West : 1.5 mi by A 863
– ✆ (01470) 572 214 – www.theisleofskye.co.uk
– Closed January, Christmas and New Year
Ullinish Country Lodge – See restaurant listing

XX **Ullinish Country Lodge**

MODERN CUISINE · CLASSIC Formal hotel dining room with a traditional masculine style and a house party atmosphere. The daily changing, 2-choice set menu uses good quality local ingredients; dishes are modern and inventive and combinations are well-judged.

Menu £ 55

Ullinish Country Lodge Hotel, ⊠ IV56 8FD – West : 1.5 mi by A 863
– ✆ (01470) 572 214 (bookings essential for non-residents)
– www.theisleofskye.co.uk – dinner only
– Closed January, Christmas and New Year

SCOTLAND

Teangue

⌂ **Toravaig House**　　　　　　　🕏 ⪕ 🛏 ⚒ 🎰 **P**

COUNTRY HOUSE · CONTEMPORARY Stylish whitewashed house with neat gardens, set on the road to the Mallaig ferry. Cosy, open-fired lounge with baby grand piano and heavy fabrics. Individually designed bedrooms boast quality materials and furnishings. Good service with extras. Two-roomed restaurant offers concise, classical menu of island produce.

9 rooms ⌷ – †£ 149/210　††£ 170/280

Knock Bay ⊠ IV44 8RE – on A 851 – 𝒞 (01471) 820 200 – www.skyehotel.co.uk

Waternish

✗ **Loch Bay Seafood**　　　　　　　　　　　　**P**

FISH AND SEAFOOD · BISTRO This pretty little cottage is set in a superb waterside spot and is fittingly decorated with seaside memorabilia. Set price menus list simply prepared, classically based dishes of locally sourced seafood. The service is charming.

Menu £ 35

*1 MacLeod Terr, Stein ⊠ IV55 8GA – 𝒞 (01470) 592 235 (booking essential)
– www.lochbay-seafood-restaurant.co.uk – dinner only and lunch
Wednesday-Thursday – Closed November-Easter, Sunday and Monday*

SLEAT – Highland ➜ See Skye (Isle of)

SORN

East Ayrshire – Regional map n° **15**-B2

▶ Edinburgh 67 mi – Ayr 15 mi – Glasgow 35 mi

🍴 **Sorn Inn**　　　　　　　　　　　　🛬 ⪕ **P**

BRITISH TRADITIONAL · PUB It's very much a family affair at this unassuming inn – the father checks you in and the son does the cooking. Sit in either the smart bar or larger dining room. The extensive menu includes a variety of British dishes plus some more elaborate international offerings. The neat, simple bedrooms are good value.

Menu £ 18 (weekdays) – Carte £ 19/32

4 rooms ⌷ – †£ 45/60　††£ 60/90

35 Main St ⊠ KA5 6HU – 𝒞 (01290) 551 305 – www.sorninn.com – Closed 10 days January and Monday

SPEAN BRIDGE

Highland – Regional map n° **17**-C3

▶ Edinburgh 143 mi – Fort William 10 mi – Glasgow 94 mi – Inverness 58 mi

⌂ **Corriegour Lodge**　　　　　　　🕏 ⪕ 🛏 ⚒ **P**

TRADITIONAL · COSY 19C hunting lodge with pretty gardens, set in a great loch side location – they even have their own private beach. Inside there's a homely curio-filled lounge and comfy bedrooms featuring top quality beds, linens and fabrics. Every dining table has a loch view; the classical 4 course menu features local meats.

11 rooms ⌷ – †£ 169/199　††£ 169/199

*Loch Lochy ⊠ PH34 4EA – North : 8.75 mi on A 82 – 𝒞 (01397) 712 685
– www.corriegour-lodge-hotel.com – Closed November-22 March*

⌂ **Old Pines**　　　　　　　　🕏 🐕 ⪕ 🛏 ⚒ **P**

RURAL · COSY A friendly couple run this log cabin style property, which blends well with the Highland scenery. Guest areas are comfy and homely. Feature walls add a splash of colour to the pine-furnished bedrooms and the slate-tiled bathrooms come with underfloor heating. Dining has a classic dinner party feel.

7 rooms ⌷ – †£ 60/80　††£ 90/120

*⊠ PH34 4EG – Northwest : 1.5 mi by A 82 on B 8004 – 𝒞 (01397) 712 324
– www.oldpines.co.uk – Closed November-Easter*

🏠 Distant Hills

TRADITIONAL · CLASSIC Welcoming guesthouse with friendly owners, who suggest walks and provide packed lunches. The French windows in the large lounge lead to stream-side seating. Bedrooms are modern and the breakfasts are wide-ranging.

7 rooms ☑ – **†**£ 67/83 **††**£ 82/100

*Roy Bridge Rd ⊠ PH34 4EU – East : 0.5 mi on A86 – ℰ (01397) 712 452
– www.distanthillsspeanbridge.co.uk – Closed 10 November-26 February*

🏠 Corriechoille Lodge

TRADITIONAL · PERSONALISED Charming, part-18C house in a remote location, boasting large gardens and views over the Grey Corries and Aonach Mor. Comfy lounge and spacious, pine-furnished bedrooms; two wooden bothy lodges provide more intimacy. Homely cooking; the fish is smoked on site.

4 rooms ☑ – **†**£ 48/53 **††**£ 76/86

*⊠ PH34 4EY – East : 2.75 mi on Corriechoille rd – ℰ (01397) 712 002
– www.corriechoille.com – Closed November-March*

✗✗ Russell's at Smiddy House

BRITISH TRADITIONAL · INTIMATE Friendly, passionately run restaurant in an appealing Highland village, with a smart ornament-filled lounge and two intimate dining rooms. Tasty dishes use locally sourced ingredients and old Scottish recipes take on a modern style. Cosy, well-equipped bedrooms come with comfy beds and fine linens.

Menu £ 33

4 rooms ☑ – **†**£ 85/115 **††**£ 90/125

*Roybridge Rd ⊠ PH34 4EU – ℰ (01397) 712 335 (booking essential)
– www.smiddyhouse.com – dinner only – restricted opening in winter – Closed Monday to non residents*

SPITTAL

Highland – Regional map n° **17**-D1
▶ Edinburgh 253 mi – London 654 mi – Dundee 234 mi

🏠 Auld Post Office

FAMILY · PERSONALISED Greatly extended former post office, set in a remote spot on a road that cuts across the moors. Homely lounge with a wood-burning stove. Cosy, well-furnished bedrooms open onto a colourful garden and have compact, modern shower rooms.

3 rooms ☑ – **†**£ 55/60 **††**£ 75/85

⊠ KW1 5XR – on A 9 – ℰ (01847) 841 391 – www.auldpostoffice.com

SPITTAL OF GLENSHEE

Perth and Kinross – ⊠ Blairgowrie – Regional map n° **16**-C2
▶ Edinburgh 79 mi – London 489 mi – Glasgow 98 mi – Livingston 81 mi

🏰 Dalmunzie Castle

HISTORIC · CLASSIC A traditional baronial style castle and Edwardian hunting lodge, on a stunning 6,500 acre estate encircled by mountains; the open hall has a large window looking towards the snow-capped peaks. Bedrooms are classical, the cosy bar stocks over 100 whiskies and the dining room offers pretty valley views.

17 rooms ☑ – **†**£ 95/300 **††**£ 125/375

⊠ PH10 7QG – ℰ (01250) 885 224 – www.dalmunzie.com – Closed 3 January-4 February and 1-23 December

STEVENSTON

North Ayrshire – Pop. 9 330 – Regional map n° **15**-A2
▶ Edinburgh 82 mi – Ayr 19 mi – Glasgow 36 mi

🏠 Ardeer Farm Steading

TRADITIONAL · CONTEMPORARY Converted, family-owned farm buildings on the edge of a 100 acre working farm. Large, leather-furnished lounge and breakfast room boast pleasant country views. Spacious, comfy, up-to-date bedrooms. Complimentary pick-up from the station.

4 rooms 🍽 – 🛏£ 38/40 🛏🛏£ 50/55

Ardeer Mains Farm ⊠ KA20 3DD – East : 0.75 mi by A 738 and B 752 taking fist left onto Kilwinning rd – 𝒞 (01294) 465 438 – www.ardeersteading.co.uk

STIRLING

Stirling – Pop. 36 142 – Regional map n° **16**-C2

▶ Edinburgh 37 mi – Glasgow 28 mi – Perth 34 mi

🏨 Colessio

BUSINESS · STYLISH This grand, Victorian building close to the castle was once the city's hospital, although you wouldn't know it from its stylish, modern interior. The chic, well-equipped bedrooms are very much designed for the business traveller. Meats cooked on the Josper grill form the backbone of the restaurant's menu.

38 rooms 🍽 – 🛏£ 89/179 🛏🛏£ 99/189

Town plan: B-c – *33 Spittal St. ⊠ FK8 1DX – 𝒞 (01786) 448 880 – www.hotelcolessio.com*

STIRLING

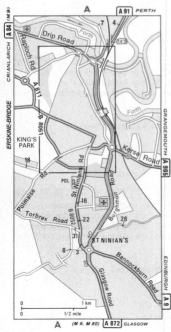

SCOTLAND

⌂ Park Lodge

TOWNHOUSE · CLASSIC Lovely part-Georgian, part-Victorian, creeper-clad house, with a mature garden and fruit trees to the rear. Warm, intimate bar and sitting room. Traditional, individually designed bedrooms; the four-poster room is particularly popular. Formal dining room has a beautiful ornate ceiling and traditional menu.

9 rooms ⌑ – ♦£ 80/85 ♦♦£ 90/95

Town plan: B-a – *32 Park Terr ⌂ FK8 2JS – ℰ (01786) 474 862
– www.parklodge.net – Closed 25-26 December and 1-2 January*

⌂ Victoria Square ⓝ

⌀ P

TOWNHOUSE · ELEGANT Many original features remain in this detached 1880s house overlooking Victoria Square – from the stained glass on the staircase to the impressive ornate cornicing in the sitting room. Spacious bedrooms; some with four-posters.

7 rooms ⌑ – ♦£ 68/85 ♦♦£ 83/140

Town plan: B-x – *12 Victoria Sq. ⌂ FK8 2QZ – ℰ (01786) 473 920
– www.victoriasquareguesthouse.com – Closed 1-15 January and 22-28 December*

⌂ West Plean House

TRADITIONAL · PERSONALISED An attractive house with a long history and a hospitable owner; next to a working farm. Beautiful tiled hall, classic country house lounge and warm, traditionally styled bedrooms. Eggs come from their hens and jams, from the kitchen garden.

4 rooms ⌑ – ♦£ 60 ♦♦£ 94

⌂ *FK7 8HA – South : 3.5 mi on A 872 (Denny rd) – ℰ (01786) 812 208
– www.westpleanhouse.com – Closed 15 December-15 January*

⌂ Number 10

⌂ ⌀

TOWNHOUSE · PERSONALISED Light-stone Victorian townhouse in a quiet street, with an attractive garden and a surprisingly spacious interior. Individually furnished bedrooms have good facilities. Linen-laid breakfast room features ornate coving; choose the porridge.

3 rooms ⌑ – ♦£ 35/60 ♦♦£ 50/75

Town plan: B-v – *10 Gladstone Pl ⌂ FK8 2NN – ℰ (01786) 472 681
– www.cameron-10.co.uk*

STONEHAVEN

Aberdeenshire – Pop. 11 431 – Regional map n° **16**-D2
▶ Edinburgh 111 mi – Glasgow 130 mi – Dundee 50 mi – Aberdeen 15 mi

⌂ Beachgate House

LUXURY · PERSONALISED Well-run guesthouse looking out over Stonehaven Bay. Super views from well-appointed, first floor lounge. Bedrooms are furnished in a luxurious, modern style. Breakfast includes fresh poached fish or a full Scottish with hen or duck eggs.

5 rooms ⌑ – ♦£ 80/95 ♦♦£ 95/125

Beachgate Ln ⌂ AB39 2BD – ℰ (01569) 763 155 – www.beachgate.co.uk

XX Tolbooth

FISH AND SEAFOOD · RUSTIC Stonehaven's oldest building, located on the harbourside: formerly a store, sheriff's courthouse and prison. Classic dishes have modern touches; the emphasis being on local seafood, with langoustines and crab the highlights. Choose table 3.

Menu £ 20 (weekday lunch)/27 – Carte £ 31/46

*Old Pier, Harbour ⌂ AB39 2JU – ℰ (01569) 762 287
– www.tolbooth-restaurant.co.uk – Closed 3 weeks January, 1 week October, 25-26 December and Monday. Sunday dinner and Tuesday October-April*

STORNOWAY – Western Isles ➡ See Lewis and Harris (Isle of)

STRACHUR

Argyll and Bute – Pop. 628 – Regional map n° **16**-B2

▶ Edinburgh 112 mi – Glasgow 66 mi – Inverness 162 mi – Perth 101 mi

🏠 Creggans Inn   ☆ ⇐ 🍴 🅿

INN · CLASSIC Well-established inn on the shores of Loch Fyne; the conservatory is a popular spot for a taking in the enviable view. Spacious, well-kept bedrooms with traditional décor in keeping with the building's age. The vast restaurant serves classical dishes, while the pubby bar offers an accessible menu of local produce, along with drinks and a game of pool.

14 rooms ⊑ – ♦£ 80/95 ♦♦£ 100/180 – 1 suite

✉ PA27 8BX

– ℰ (01369) 860 279 – www.creggans-inn.co.uk

– Closed 2 weeks January and Christmas

🍴 Inver Cottage   ⇐ 🍴 ⇔ 🅿

MODERN CUISINE · COSY A former crofter's cottage and boat store on the loch shore. There's a small bar – with some tables at the front for drinks – and a simple, airy restaurant behind. Menus use only local produce and have a modern Scandic style.

Menu £ 35 (dinner)

– Carte £ 14/32

Strathlaclan ✉ PA27 8BU

– Southwest : 6.5 mi by A 886 on B 8000

– ℰ (01369) 860 537 – www.inverrestaurant.co.uk

– Closed late December-March, Monday except bank holidays and Tuesday

STRATHPEFFER

Highland – Pop. 1 109 – Regional map n° **17**-C2

▶ Edinburgh 173 mi – Dundee 155 mi – Inverness 20 mi

🏠 Craigvar   🍴 ⅋ 🅿

TRADITIONAL · CLASSIC Proudly run by a charming owner, an attractive Georgian house overlooking the main square of a delightful spa village. Traditional guest areas include a comfy lounge and an antique-furnished breakfast room. Spacious bedrooms have a modern edge and plenty of personal touches. Good breakfast selection.

3 rooms ⊑ – ♦£ 60/65 ♦♦£ 95/100

The Square ✉ IV14 9DL

– ℰ (01997) 421 622 – www.craigvar.com

– Closed 23 December-12 January

STRATHY

Highland – Regional map n° **15**-D1

▶ Edinburgh 264 mi – Inverness 110 mi – Thurso 20 mi

🏠 Sharvedda 🆕   ⅋ ⇐ 🍴 ⅋ 🅿 ⇄

FAMILY · HOMELY You won't find a warmer welcome than at this remotely located guesthouse on a working croft. Homemade fudge and cake are served on arrival and breakfast is taken in the sunny conservatory, with its wild views over the Pentland Firth.

3 rooms ⊑ – ♦£ 50/55 ♦♦£ 76/80

Strathy Point ✉ KW14 7RY

– North : 1.5 mi on Strathy Point rd

– ℰ (01641) 541 311 – www.sharvedda.co.uk

– Closed 25-26 December

STRATHYRE
Stirling – ✉ Callander – Regional map n° **16**-B2
▶ Edinburgh 62 mi – Glasgow 53 mi – Perth 42 mi

XX **Creagan House**   ⇦ 🛏 **P**

TRADITIONAL CUISINE · COSY Long-standing, personally run restaurant in a 17C
farmhouse. Snug sitting rooms lead to a baronial-style dining room with a vast
fireplace and handmade local china. Traditional cooking uses Perthshire's natural
larder; the 'Smokie in a Pokie' is a speciality. Watch red squirrels from the comfy,
cosy bedrooms.

Menu £ 38

5 rooms ⌑ – †£ 90/100 ††£ 135/155

✉ FK18 8ND – On A 84 – ℰ (01877) 384 638 (booking essential)
– www.creaganhouse.co.uk – dinner only – Closed 26 October-17 March,
Wednesday and Thursday

STROMNESS → See Orkney Islands (Mainland)

STRONTIAN
Highland – Regional map n° **17**-B3
▶ Edinburgh 139 mi – Fort William 23 mi – Oban 66 mi

🏠 **Kilcamb Lodge**   🏕 🐾 ⇐ 🛏 🌙 **P**

COUNTRY HOUSE · RUSTIC Charming lochside hunting lodge with 19 acres of
gardens and woodland running down to a private shore. The traditional interior
has a modern edge but still boasts rich fabrics and log fires. Dine from classic
menus in the laid-back brasserie; seafood and game feature highly in the more
formal restaurant.

11 rooms (dinner included) ⌑ – †£ 90/110 ††£ 120/175

On A 861 ✉ PH36 4HY – ℰ (01967) 402 257 – www.kilcamblodge.co.uk
– Closed January and restricted opening in winter

🏠 **Rockpool House**   🏕 🐾 ⇐ 🛏 🌂 **P**

RURAL · MODERN Be at one with nature in this comfy guesthouse on the Ardnamurchan Peninsula. Take in the views of the loch and the mountains from both
the upstairs lounge and the modern, well-equipped bedrooms. Local meats and
fish feature on the menu and you can buy local and homemade gifts from their
craft shop.

3 rooms ⌑ – †£ 65/85 ††£ 85/110

Acharacle ✉ PH36 4HX – West : 7.5 mi on A 861 – ℰ (01967) 431 335
– www.rockpoolhouse.co.uk – Closed 10 days Christmas

STRUAN – Highland → See Skye (Isle of)

SWINTON
The Scottish Borders – ✉ Duns – Pop. 472 – Regional map n° **15**-D2
▶ Edinburgh 49 mi – London 351 mi – Newcastle upon Tyne 74 mi – Darlington 110 mi

🏠 **Wheatsheaf**   ⇦ 🛏 ♿ **P**

REGIONAL · INN Substantial stone inn overlooking the village green. The extensive dinner menu offers a mix of pub classics and some more ambitious dishes;
specials feature seafood from Eyemouth and meat comes from the surrounding
border farms and is smoked on-site. Bedrooms are spacious, cosy and well-
equipped.

Menu £ 13 (weekday lunch) – Carte £ 28/46

13 rooms ⌑ – †£ 89/109 ††£ 119/159

Main St ✉ TD11 3JJ – ℰ (01890) 860 257 (booking advisable)
– www.wheatsheaf-swinton.co.uk – closed Monday-Friday lunch January-March
– Closed 23 and 24 December

TAIN

Highland – Pop. 3 655 – Regional map n° **17**-D2
▶ Edinburgh 191 mi – Inverness 35 mi – Wick 91 mi

Golf View House
≼ ⬗ ⚲ **P**

TRADITIONAL · PERSONALISED Well-cared-for Victorian manse close to the golf
course, boasting a neat lawned garden and views over the mountains and out to
sea. The bright, fresh interior features modern, uncluttered bedrooms and a
homely lounge and breakfast room.

5 rooms ⌖ – †£ 45/65 ††£ 75/90
13 Knockbreck Rd ⌗ IV19 1BN – ℰ (01862) 892 856 – www.tainbedandbreakfast.co.uk

at Nigg Southeast: 7 mi by A9, B9175 and Pitcalnie Rd

Wemyss House
⚘ ⬗ ⬗ ⚲ **P**

FAMILY · STYLISH Remotely set guesthouse run by charming owners; sit in the
modern conservatory extension or on the terrace to enjoy views across the Cromarty Firth to the mountains. The bright, Scandic-style interior features bespoke
furniture from Stuart's on-site workshop and Christine often plays the grand piano in the cosy lounge. Freshly prepared dishes promote local ingredients.

3 rooms ⌖ – †£ 115/120 ††£ 115/120
*Bayfield ⌗ IV19 1QW – South : 1 mi past church – ℰ (01862) 851 212
– www.wemysshouse.com*

at Cadboll Southeast: 8.5 mi by A9 and B9165 (Portmahomack rd) off Hilton rd
– ⌗ Tain

Glenmorangie House
⚘ ⬗ ≼ ⬗ ⬗ ⚲ **P**

TRADITIONAL · CLASSIC Charming 17C house owned by the famous distillery.
Antiques, hand-crafted local furnishings and open peat fires feature; there's even
a small whisky tasting room. Luxuriously appointed bedrooms show good attention to detail; those in the courtyard cottages are suites. Communal dining from a
classical Scottish menu.

9 rooms (dinner included) ⌖ – †£ 235/250 ††£ 370/400
*Fearn ⌗ IV20 1XP – ℰ (01862) 871 671 – www.theglenmorangiehouse.com
– Closed January*

TARBERT – Argyll and Bute → See Kintyre (Peninsula)

TARBERT – Western Isles → See Lewis and Harris (Isle of)

TARBET

Argyll and Bute – ⌗ Arrochar – Regional map n° **16**-B2
▶ Edinburgh 88 mi – Glasgow 42 mi – Inverness 138 mi – Perth 78 mi

Lomond View Country House
≼ ⬗ ⚲ **P**

COUNTRY HOUSE · MODERN Purpose-built guesthouse whose Norwegian pine
furnished bedrooms come with tartan fabrics and spectacular loch and bay outlooks. The bright breakfast room, with its antique silverware and heirloom tea
sets, shares the super view.

3 rooms ⌖ – †£ 70/80 ††£ 90/100
⌗ G83 7DG – On A 82 – ℰ (01301) 702 477 – www.lomondview.co.uk

TAYNUILT

Argyll and Bute – Regional map n° **16**-B2
▶ Edinburgh 114 mi – Oban 12 mi – Fort William 46 mi

🏠 **Taynuilt** ⇦ P

BRITISH TRADITIONAL · CLASSIC Coleridge and Wordsworth enjoyed this inn's hospitality back in 1803; these days it is run with pride and passion by the McNulty family and cooking is the main focus. Menus offer tasty pub classics with a twist and they have their own bespoke lager on tap. Well-kept bedrooms are named after lochs.
Carte £ 20/45

9 rooms 🍽 – †£ 45/65 ††£ 75/150
✉ PA35 1JN – ℰ (01866) 822 437 – www.taynuilthotel.co.uk – *Restricted opening in January*

TAYVALLICH
Argyll and Bute – ✉ Lochgilphead – Regional map n° **16**-B2
▶ Edinburgh 148 mi – Glasgow 103 mi – Inverness 157 mi

🏠 **Tayvallich Inn** ⇐ 🏠 P

TRADITIONAL CUISINE · PUB Dine in the bar, the more formal dining room or on the decked terrace, with views over the bay. Menu focuses on locally caught fish and shellfish, but also lists classic pub dishes like steak and chips.
Carte £ 19/36

✉ PA31 8PL – ℰ (01546) 870 282 – www.tayvallichinn.com
– *Closed Monday November-March*

TEANGUE – Highland ➜ See Skye (Isle of)

THORNHILL
Dumfries and Galloway – Pop. 1 674 – Regional map n° **15**-B2
▶ Edinburgh 64 mi – Ayr 44 mi – Dumfries 15 mi – Glasgow 63 mi

🏠 **Buccleuch & Queensberry Arms** 🏠 🏠 & 🏠

TOWNHOUSE · STYLISH Smartly refurbished coaching inn, designed by the owner, who also runs an interiors shop. Boldly coloured bedrooms are named after various estates owned by the Duke of Buccleuch and come with eclectic artwork and superb bathrooms. Informal dining options range from bar snacks to a more adventurous à la carte

14 rooms 🍽 – †£ 70/150 ††£ 80/175
112 Drumlanrig St ✉ DG3 5LU – ℰ (01848) 323 101 – www.bqahotel.com

🏠 **Holmhill Country House** 🆕 🏠 🏠 ⇐ 🏠 🏠 P

COUNTRY HOUSE · PERSONALISED 18C country house, peacefully set beside the river, in 8 acres of woodland. It was given to Charles Douglas by the Duke of Buccleuch and the elegant sitting room is filled with his family photos. Spacious bedrooms feature Egyptian cotton linen and have great country views. Communal dinners must be pre-booked.

3 rooms 🍽 – †£ 70/80 ††£ 97/110
Holmhill ✉ DG3 4AB – West 0.5mi on A702
– ℰ (01848) 332 239 – www.holmhill.co.uk
– *Closed Christmas to New Year*

🏠 **Gillbank House** 🏠 P

TOWNHOUSE · PERSONALISED Red stone house built in 1895; originally the holiday home of the Jenner family of department store fame. A lovely stained glass front door leads to a spacious light-filled interior. The breakfast room has distant hill views and two of the large, simply furnished bedrooms have feature beds; all have wet rooms.

6 rooms 🍽 – †£ 65/85 ††£ 85
8 East Morton St ✉ DG3 5LZ – ℰ (01848) 330 597 – www.gillbank.co.uk

THURSO

Highland – Pop. 7 933 – Regional map n° **17**-D1
▶ Edinburgh 289 mi – Inverness 133 mi – Wick 21 mi

Forss House

TRADITIONAL · COSY Traditional Scottish hotel geared towards fishing; the have a 'rod room' and mounted fish sit beside deer heads on the walls. Bedroom are of a good size – those in 'River House' are the most private with great views The elegant dining room serves a classic Scottish menu – Scrabster seafood is speciality.

14 rooms ☑ – ♦£ 99/135 ♦♦£ 135/185
Forss ✉ KW14 7XY – West : 5.5 mi on A 836 – ℰ (01847) 861 201
– www.forsshousehotel.co.uk – Closed 24 December-4 January

Pennyland House

FAMILY · PERSONALISED Old farmhouse built in 1780; where the founder of th Boys' Brigade was born. Simple, stylishly furnished bedrooms with quality oa furnishings, golf course pictures and modern bathrooms. Open-plan lounge-cum dining room with harbour views.

6 rooms ☑ – ♦£ 60/70 ♦♦£ 80/90
✉ KW14 7JU – Northwest : 0.75 mi on A 9 – ℰ (01847) 891 194
– www.pennylandhouse.co.uk – Closed Christmas

Murray House

FAMILY · PERSONALISED Family-run Victorian house in a great central location There's a small lounge and breakfast room, and packed breakfasts and lunche are available. Bedrooms are bright and compact with modern shower rooms two are family-friendly.

5 rooms ☑ – ♦£ 35/40 ♦♦£ 60/80
1 Campbell St ✉ KW14 7HD – ℰ (01847) 895 759 – www.murrayhousebb.com
– Closed Christmas-New Year

at Scrabster Northwest: 2.25 mi on A9

✗ Captain's Galley

FISH AND SEAFOOD · RUSTIC Classic seafood restaurant on the pier, with vaulted stone dining room and an old chimney from its former ice house days The owner was once a fisherman so has excellent local contacts – he keep some produce in creels in the harbour.

Menu £ 54
The Harbour ✉ KW14 7UJ – ℰ (01847) 894 999 (booking essential)
– www.captainsgalley.co.uk – dinner only – Closed 25-26 December, 1-2 January, Sunday and Monday

TIGHNABRUAICH

Argyll and Bute – Regional map n° **16**-B3
▶ Edinburgh 113 mi – Glasgow 63 mi – Oban 66 mi

Royal An Lochan

FAMILY · PERSONALISED Spacious 19C hotel located in a peaceful village, over looking the Kyles of Bute. Comfortable bedrooms; some with excellent outlook. The characterful bar with its nautical theme serves a snack menu, while the for mal conservatory restaurant offers water views and seasonal seafood dishes.

11 rooms ☑ – ♦£ 75/150 ♦♦£ 75/150
Shore Rd ✉ PA21 2BE – ℰ (01700) 811 239 – www.theroyalanlochan.co.uk

TIRORAN – Argyll and Bute → See Mull (Isle of)

TOBERMORY – Argyll and Bute → See Mull (Isle of)

TORRIDON

Highland – ⊠ Achnasheen – Regional map n° **17**-B2
▶ Edinburgh 234 mi – Inverness 62 mi – Kyle of Lochalsh 44 mi

🏠 Torridon

🏠 🐕 ⪦ 🛋 🍴 🔄 ⏷ & 🅿

TRADITIONAL · CLASSIC A former hunting lodge built in 1887 by Lord Lovelace; set in 40 acres and offering superb loch and mountain views. The delightful interior features wood-panelling, ornate ceilings and a peat fire. Bedrooms are spacious and luxurious, with top quality furnishings and feature baths. The whisky bar has over 350 malts and the smart dining room offers a modern daily menu.

18 rooms ☺ – †£ 210/475 ††£ 195/460 – 2 suites

⊠ IV22 2EY – South : 1.5 mi on A 896 – ℰ (01445) 791 242 – www.thetorridon.com
– Closed January and Monday-Tuesday November-March

🍴 Torridon Inn

⪦ 🐕 🛋 🍴 🍴 & 🅿

TRADITIONAL CUISINE · INN Tranquil inn geared towards those who enjoy outdoor pursuits. The timbered bar features stags' antlers and an ice axe; the restaurant overlooks the gardens and loch. Satisfying walkers' favourites mix with more elaborate dishes. Simply furnished, modern bedrooms; the larger ones are ideal for families.

Carte £ 19/38 **s**

12 rooms ☺ – †£ 110 ††£ 110

⊠ IV22 2EY – South : 1.5 mi on A 896 – ℰ (01445) 791 242 – www.thetorridon.com
– Closed mid-December-January and Monday-Thursday November, February and
March

TROON

South Ayrshire – Pop. 14 752 – Regional map n° **15**-A2
▶ Edinburgh 77 mi – Ayr 7 mi – Glasgow 31 mi

🏠 Lochgreen House

🌲 🐕 🛋 ⏷ & 🍴 🏊 🅿

COUNTRY HOUSE · HOMELY Edwardian country house in a pleasant coastal spot, with sumptuous lounges and a Whisky Room stocked with an extensive range of malts. Bedrooms in the main house are cosy and traditional; those in the extension are more luxurious.

32 rooms ☺ – †£ 115/165 ††£ 175/195 – 1 suite

Monktonhill Rd, Southwood ⊠ KA10 7EN – Southeast : 2 mi on B 749 – ℰ (01292)
313 343 – www.costley-hotels.co.uk

Tapestry – See restaurant listing

XxX Tapestry

🛋 & 🗚 🅿

BRITISH MODERN · ELEGANT A cavernous country house dining room with exposed rafters, huge mirrors and chandeliers – but no tapestries! Interesting set menus feature refined, flavoursome modern dishes that use the best of Scottish produce. Service is formal.

Menu £ 17 (weekday lunch)/43 – Carte £ 33/56

Lochgreen House Hotel, Monktonhill Rd, Southwood ⊠ KA10 7EN – Southeast :
2 mi on B 749 – ℰ (01292) 313 343 – www.costley-hotels.co.uk

at Loans East: 2 mi on A759 – ⊠ Troon

🏠 Highgrove House

🌲 ⪦ 🛋 🏊 🅿

TRADITIONAL · DESIGN Hillside property with a stunning panoramic view of the coastline and the Isle of Arran. Comfortable, contemporary bedrooms; Room 1 is the best. Clubby dining room with floor to ceiling windows and a smart, friendly team; sit in one of the plush booths at the top. Classic menus focus on seafood and grills.

9 rooms ☺ – †£ 69 ††£ 110

Old Loans Rd ⊠ KA10 7HL – East : 0.25 mi on Dundonald rd – ℰ (01292) 312 511
– www.costley-hotels.co.uk

TURNBERRY

South Ayrshire – ⊠ Girvan – Regional map n° **15**-A2

▶ Edinburgh 97 mi – London 416 mi – Glasgow 51 mi – Carlisle 108 mi

---

🏨🏨 **Trump Turnberry**   🏦 ≼ 🛜 🖼 🗔 ⊕ 🏠 🖼 🗒 ⏳ 🛖 🛐 🅿

GRAND LUXURY · DESIGN Resort-style, Edwardian railway hotel boasting a smart spa and 3 golf courses – one a championship course. Bedrooms are luxurious and the suites have stunning coast and course views. The restaurant offers French classics; Duel in the Sun, in the clubhouse, serves dishes from the charcoal grill. The hotel is closing for major refurbishment from late 2015 to mid 2016.

149 rooms ⊇ – ♦£ 155/305 ♦♦£ 175/325 – 4 suites

⊠ KA26 9LT – On A 719 – ℰ (01655) 331 000 – www.trumpturnberry.com

1906 – See restaurant listing

XxX **1906**   ≼ 🛜 ⏳ 🅺 🅿

FRENCH CLASSIC · ELEGANT This smart hotel restaurant boasts lovely views out across the sea. Classical French menus feature dishes true to the spirit of Auguste Escoffier. The hotel and restaurant are closing for major refurbishment from late 2015 to mid 2016.

Carte £ 42/68

Trump Turnberry Hotel, ⊠ KA26 9LT – On A 719 – ℰ (01655) 331 000 – www.turnberryresort.co.uk – dinner only

---

UDNY GREEN

Aberdeenshire – Regional map n° **16**-D1

▶ Edinburgh 140 mi – London 543 mi – Dundee 80 mi

XX **Eat on the Green**   🛜 🅺 ⇔ 🅿

BRITISH MODERN · ELEGANT An attractive former inn overlooking the village green, with a cosy lounge and two traditionally furnished dining rooms. Well-presented modern dishes change with the seasons and feature vegetables and herbs from their smallholding.

Menu £ 24 (weekday lunch)/59 – Carte £ 38/50

⊠ AB41 7RS – ℰ (01651) 842 337 (booking essential) – www.eatonthegreen.co.uk – Closed Monday, Tuesday and Saturday lunch

---

UIG – Western Isles ➜ See Lewis and Harris (Isle of)

UIST (Isles of)

Western Isles – Pop. 3 510 – Regional map n° **17**-A2

NORTH UIST

Western Isles

Carinish

Western Isles

🏠 **Temple View**   🏦 ≼ 🛜 🅿

TRADITIONAL · FUNCTIONAL Victorian house with an uncluttered interior and a homely style. Small bar, sitting room and sun lounge. Simple, comfortable bedrooms: those to the rear have moor views; those at the front overlook the sea or the 13C ruins of Trinity Temple. Cosy dining room offers popular seafood specials.

10 rooms ⊇ – ♦£ 70/80 ♦♦£ 110/120

⊠ HS6 5EJ – ℰ (01876) 580 676 – www.templeviewhotel.co.uk – Closed Christmas

Langass

Western Isles

🏠 Langass Lodge

HISTORIC · CLASSIC Victorian former shooting lodge nestled in heather-strewn hills and boasting distant loch views. Characterful bedrooms in the main house; more modern, spacious rooms with good views in the wing. Eat in the comfy bar or linen-clad dining room from simple, seafood based menus.

11 rooms 🛏 – †£ 75/100 ††£ 95/149

✉ HS6 5HA – *℘ (01876) 580 285* – www.langasslodge.co.uk
– Closed 1 January, 24-25 and 31 December

Lochmaddy

Western Isles

🏠 Hamersay House

TRADITIONAL · FUNCTIONAL Stylish hotel with a sleek, boutique style, a well-equipped gym, a sauna, a steam room and bikes for hire. Chic, modern bedrooms offer good facilities. The forward-thinking owner continually reinvests. Smart bar and dining room; menus display plenty of seafood.

8 rooms 🛏 – †£ 90/95 ††£ 110/135

✉ HS6 5AE – *℘ (01876) 500 700* – www.hamersayhouse.co.uk – Closed November-March

ULLAPOOL

Highland – Pop. 1 541 – Regional map n° **17**-C2

▶ Edinburgh 215 mi – London 616 mi – Inverness 58 mi – Elgin 94 mi

🏠 Westlea House 🅽

FAMILY · CONTEMPORARY It might look like an ordinary house but inside, Westlea has been transformed into a stylish, boutique-style B&B. Individually decorated bedrooms feature bold modern artwork and have a funky feel; two have roll-top baths in the room.

5 rooms 🛏 – †£ 40/45 ††£ 80/100

2 Market St ✉ IV26 2XE – *℘ (01854) 612 594* – www.westlea-ullapool.co.uk

🏠 Point Cottage

FAMILY · COSY This cosy, compact former fisherman's cottage sits on the shore of Loch Broom. Bedrooms are modern, immaculately kept and have loch views – one room has views from the bed! Good quality continental breakfasts are served in your room.

3 rooms 🛏 – †£ 65/80 ††£ 65/80

22 West Shore St ✉ IV26 2UR – *℘ (01854) 613 015*
– www.pointcottagebandb.co.uk – Restricted opening in winter

VEENSGARTH → See Shetland Islands (Mainland)

WALKERBURN

The Scottish Borders – Pop. 700 – Regional map n° **15**-C2

▶ Edinburgh 30 mi – London 362 mi – Aberdeen 161 mi – Hartlepool 120 mi

🏠 Windlestraw

LUXURY · ELEGANT Attractive Arts and Crafts property built in 1906, boasting original fireplaces, old plaster ceilings and great valley views. Stylish, tastefully modernised bedrooms. Comfy bar, plush lounge and an attractive, wood-panelled dining room offering a daily changing menu.

6 rooms 🛏 – †£ 100/200 ††£ 150/170

✉ EH43 6AA – *On A 72* – *℘ (01896) 870 636* – www.windlestraw.co.uk – Closed 24-26 December and 31 December- 2 January

WATERNISH - Highland → See Skye (Isle of)

WESTRAY (Isle of) → See Orkney Islands

WICK
Highland - Pop. 7 155 - Regional map n° **17**-D1
▶ Edinburgh 282 mi - Inverness 126 mi

⌂ Clachan
FAMILY · PERSONALISED Smart detached house on the edge of town, a short drive from the Queen Mother's former holiday residence, the Castle of Mey. Stylish, well-kept bedrooms blend oak furnishings with tartan fabrics. Black and white photos of the town's herring fishing days decorate the cosy dining room. Extensive breakfasts.

3 rooms ⌕ - †£ 65/70 ††£ 80/85

13 Randolph Pl, South Rd ⌗ KW1 5NJ - South : 0.75 mi on A 99 - ℰ (01955) 605 384 - www.theclachan.co.uk - Closed 2 weeks Christmas-New Year

✗ Bord De L'Eau
FRENCH CLASSIC · BISTRO Long-standing riverside bistro with a simple dining room and a conservatory. Framed Eiffel Tower prints and French posters adorn the walls. Authentic, classic Gallic dishes feature plenty of local seafood.

Carte £ 25/40

2 Market St (Riverside) ⌗ KW1 4AR - ℰ (01955) 604 400 - Closed 25-26 December, 1-2 January, Sunday lunch and Monday

WORMIT
Fife - Regional map n° **16**-C2
▶ Edinburgh 53 mi - Aberdeen 70 mi - Dundee 5 mi

✗ View
TRADITIONAL CUISINE · FRIENDLY Unassuming former pub run by a husband and wife team, set in a small village and boasting superb views over the Tay Bridge to Dundee. Unfussy, classically based dishes include their ever-popular haggis fritters; lunch is good value.

Menu £ 23 (lunch) - Carte £ 27/43

Naughton Rd ⌗ DD6 8NE - ℰ (01382) 542 287 - www.view-restaurant.co.uk - Closed 25-26 December, 1-2 January and Monday

WALES

It may only be 170 miles from north to south, but Wales contains great swathes of beauty, such as the dark and craggy heights of Snowdonia's ninety mountain peaks, the rolling sandstone bluffs of the Brecon Beacons, and Pembrokeshire's tantalising golden beaches. Bottle-nosed dolphins love it here too, arriving each summer at New Quay in Cardigan Bay. Highlights abound: formidable Harlech Castle dominates its coast, Bala Lake has a railway that steams along its gentle shores, and a metropolitan vibe can be found in the capital, Cardiff, home to the Millennium stadium and the National Assembly.

Wales is a country which teems with great raw ingredients and modern-day chefs are employing these to their utmost potential; from succulent slices of Spring lamb farmed on the lush mountains and valleys, through to the humblest of cockles; from satisfying native Welsh Black cattle through to abundant Anglesey oysters, delicious Welsh cheeses and the edible seaweed found on the shores of the Gower and known as laverbread.

- Michelin Road map n° 503 and 713
- Michelin Green Guide: Great Britain

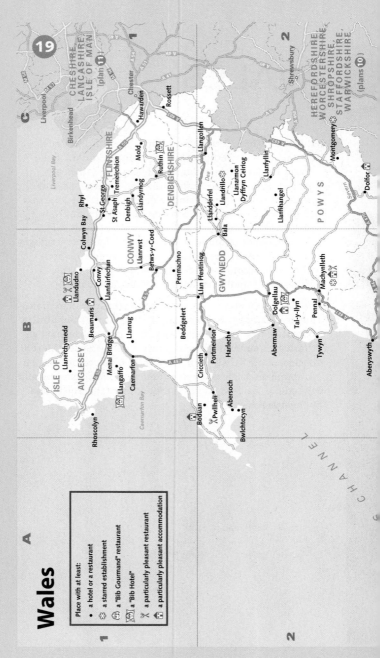

Wales

Place with at least:

- • a hotel or a restaurant
- ✿ a starred establishment
- ⓐ a "Bib Gourmand" restaurant
- ⓗ a "Bib Hotel"
- ✕ a particularly pleasant restaurant
- ⓝ a particularly pleasant accommodation

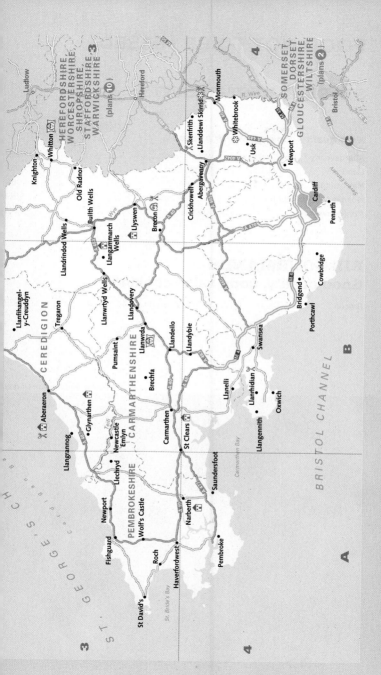

FOOD NOT TO BE MISSED

STARRED RESTAURANTS

❄️

High quality cooking, worth a stop!

BIB GOURMANDS 😋
Good quality, good value cooking

OUR TOP PICKS

GLORIOUSLY REMOTE

GOOD VALUE HOME FROM HOME

IT'S ALL ABOUT THE FOOD

MADE THEIR MARK

MORE THAN JUST THE VILLAGE PUB

© Michelin

© Michelin

QUINTESSENTIAL COUNTRY HOUSES

SPECIAL OCCASION

ABERAERON ABER AERON

Ceredigion – Pop. 1 422 – Regional map n° **19**-B3

▶ London 231 mi – Cardiff 104 mi – Birmingham 138 mi – Liverpool 124 mi

🏠 Ty Mawr Mansion Country House

TRADITIONAL · CLASSIC Grade II listed Georgian stone mansion in 12 acres of delightful grounds. Several well-appointed lounges with high ceilings; spacious bedrooms boast marble bathrooms and a good level of facilities. The small basement cinema offers dining packages and the smart restaurant serves bold widely-influenced dishes.

9 rooms ⌨ – †£ 90/120 ††£ 120/220 – 1 suite

Cilcennin ✉ SA48 8DB – East : 5 mi by A 482 – 𝒞 (01570) 470 033
– www.tymawrmansion.co.uk – Closed 27 December-20 January

🏠 3 Pen Cei ⩽ 🕸

TOWNHOUSE · STYLISH Vibrant blue house on the harbourfront; formerly the Packet Steam Company HQ. Stylish modern bedrooms are named after local rivers: those to the front overlook the water; Aeron has a free-standing bath and large walk-in shower. Good choice at breakfast, from fruit salad to smoked salmon and scrambled eggs.

5 rooms ⌨ – †£ 95/140 ††£ 105/150

3 Quay Par ✉ SA46 0BT – 𝒞 (01545) 571 147 – www.pencei.co.uk – Closed 25-26 December

🏠 Llys Aeron ⇦ 🕸 🅿

FAMILY · PERSONALISED Charmingly run Georgian guesthouse with a conservatory lounge and a breakfast room overlooking the pleasant walled garden. Bedrooms come in neutral colour schemes and have modern bathrooms. For breakfast, choose from extensive Aga-cooked options, as well as local honey and homemade granola and preserves.

3 rooms ⌨ – †£ 45/75 ††£ 75/110

Lampeter Rd ✉ SA46 0ED – on A 482 – 𝒞 (01545) 570 276 – www.llysaeron.co.uk
– Closed 15 December-31 January

🍴 Harbourmaster

BRITISH TRADITIONAL · INN Vibrant blue inn with a New England style bar, lounge, a modern dining room and lovely harbour views. Choose between the bar menu, a more substantial evening à la carte and daily specials. Smart bedrooms, split between the house and a nearby cottage, are brightly decorated and well-equipped; some have terraces.

Carte £ 30/47

13 rooms ⌨ – †£ 70/240 ††£ 120/250

Quay Par ✉ SA46 0BA – 𝒞 (01545) 570 755 – www.harbour-master.com – Closed dinner 24 December - 26 December

ABERGAVENNY Y-FENNI

Monmouthshire – Pop. 13 423 – Regional map n° **19**-C4

▶ London 163 mi – Cardiff 31 mi – Gloucester 43 mi – Newport 19 mi

🏠 Llansantffraed Court

HISTORIC · CLASSIC Attractive William and Mary country house, with an ornamental lake and a chapel in its 20 acre grounds. Have afternoon tea in the traditional lounge. Bedrooms come in dark-hues – the corner rooms have both mountain and valley views.

20 rooms ⌨ – †£ 105/135 ††£ 135/185

Llanvihangel Gobion ✉ NP7 9BA – Southeast : 6.5 mi by A 40 and B 4598 off on Raglan rd – 𝒞 (01873) 840 678 – www.llch.co.uk

The Court – See restaurant listing

Angel

🏛️ 📥 🛎️ 🅿️

HISTORIC · PERSONALISED Keenly run, family-owned, Georgian coaching inn and outbuildings. Characterful guest areas have a contemporary, shabby-chic feel. Mix of traditional and more contemporary bedrooms. Smart brasserie with oak furniture offers a classical menu with international influences. Afternoon tea in the Wedgewood Room.

34 rooms ⌁ – ♦£ 111/324 ♦♦£ 111/324 – 2 suites
15 Cross St ⊠ *NP7 5EN* – *℗ (01873) 857 121* – *www.angelabergavenny.com*
– Closed 25 December

XX The Court

🍴 🏡 🅿️

BRITISH MODERN · CLASSIC Contemporary country house restaurant, hung with large photos of local scenes. Dishes have a classical British base but are given a modern twist; fruit, veg and herbs are from the walled garden. The wines provide plenty of interest.

Menu £ 15 (lunch)/30 – Carte £ 27/45
Llansantffraed Court Hotel, Llanvihangel Gobion ⊠ *NP7 9BA – Southeast : 6.5 mi by A 40 and B 4598 off old Raglan rd* – *℗ (01873) 840 678 (booking essential)*
– www.llch.co.uk

X The Hardwick

🍴 ♿ 🅿️

REGIONAL · RURAL Smart modern pub conversion with a large bar, great mountain views and a trio of interconnecting dining rooms. Well thought-through dishes combine modern and classic elements and seasonal Welsh produce forms the backbone of the menu. Stylish modern bedrooms are set around a courtyard and have superb comforts.

Menu £ 26 – Carte £ 28/44
8 rooms – ♦£ 125/155 ♦♦£ 155/170
Old Raglan Rd ⊠ *NP7 9AA – Southeast :2 mi by A 40 on B 4598* – *℗ (01873) 854 220 – www.thehardwick.co.uk*

at Llanddewi Skirrid Northeast: 3.25 mi on B4521 – ⊠ Abergavenny

X Walnut Tree (Shaun Hill)

🍷 🏡 🅰️ 🅿️

❀

BRITISH MODERN · SIMPLE A reinvigorated, long-standing Welsh institution, set in a wooded valley and always bustling with regulars. Start with drinks in the flag-floored lounge-bar. Classic, seasonal dishes are well-priced and refreshingly simple, eschewing adornment and letting the ingredients speak for themselves.
➜ Veal sweetbreads with sauerkraut. Halibut with wild garlic and bubble & squeak. Somlói Galuska.

Menu £ 30 (weekday lunch) – Carte £ 33/51
⊠ *NP7 8AW* – *℗ (01873) 852 797 (booking essential)*
– www.thewalnuttreeinn.com – Closed 1 week Christmas, Sunday and Monday

at Cross Ash Northeast: 8.25 mi on B4521

XX 1861

🅿️

BRITISH TRADITIONAL · COSY Part-timbered Victorian pub named after the year it was built; now a cosy restaurant and lounge with contemporary furnishings. Classically based cooking has modern twists – much of the fruit and veg is grown by the owner's father.

Menu £ 22 (lunch)/35 – Carte £ 36/49
⊠ *NP7 8PB – West : 0.5 mi on B 4521* – *℗ (01873) 821 297 – www.18-61.co.uk*
– Closed first 2 weeks January, Sunday dinner and Monday

ABERSOCH

Gwynedd – ⊠ Pwllheli – Pop. 783 – Regional map n° **19**-B2
London 265 mi – Caernarfon 28 mi – Shrewsbury 101 mi

WALES

✕✕ Venetia　　　　　　　　　　　⇦ & P

ITALIAN · BRASSERIE Double-fronted house once owned by a sea captain, with a minimalist bar-lounge and a contemporary dining room with lime and aubergine seating. Classic Italian dishes are presented in a distinctly modern style. Friendly, efficient service. Chic, well-equipped bedrooms; one has a jacuzzi with a waterproof TV.

Carte £ 23/46

5 rooms � – ♥£ 65/133 ♥♥£ 80/148

Lon Sarn Bach ✉ *LL53 7EB*
– ℰ (01758) 713 354 – www.venetiawales.com – dinner only and Sunday lunch
– Closed 3 January-11 February, 22-27 December, Sunday lunch July-August and Sunday dinner September-June

at Bwlchtocyn South: 2 mi – ✉ Pwllheli

🏠 Porth Tocyn　　　　　🏕 🐾 ≤ 🛋 🍹 ⅋ 🚡 P

FAMILY · PERSONALISED High on the headland overlooking Cardigan Bay, a traditional hotel that's been in the family for three generations. Relax in the cosy lounges or explore the many leisure and children's facilities. Homely, modernised bedrooms; some with balconies or sea views. Menus offer interesting, soundly executed dishes.

17 rooms ⊻ – ♥£ 80/95 ♥♥£ 110/190

✉ *LL53 7BU* – ℰ *(01758) 713 303*
– www.porthtocynhotel.co.uk
– Closed early November-mid March

ABERYSTWYTH ABERESTUUTH

Ceredigion – Pop. 18 093 – Regional map n° **19**-B2
▶ London 238 mi – Chester 98 mi – Fishguard 58 mi – Shrewsbury 74 mi

🏠 Nanteos　　　　　　🏕 🐾 ≤ 🛋 🍹 & ⅋ 🛁 P

HISTORIC · STYLISH Impressive Georgian house in the shadow of the mountain, in a peaceful wooded valley. Original flag flooring and ornate coving feature; breakfast is in the characterful old kitchen. Stylish, boldly coloured bedrooms come with antiques, modern facilities and super bathrooms. Classic menus feature Welsh produce.

16 rooms ⊻ – ♥£ 125/180 ♥♥£ 180/300 – 2 suites

Rhydyfelin ✉ *SY23 4LU* – *Southeast : 4 mi by A 487 off A 4120*
– ℰ (01970) 600 522 – www.nanteos.com

🏠 Gwesty Cymru　　　　　　　🏕 ≤ 🏠 ⅋ 🞉

TOWNHOUSE · STYLISH Grade II listed Georgian townhouse on the seafront, with a brightly painted exterior and a terrace overlooking the bay. Thoughtfully designed modern bedrooms vary in size and décor – all are colour themed, with smart bathrooms. Small, stylish basement bar and dining room; ambitious, adventurous dishes.

8 rooms ⊻ – ♥£ 70/80 ♥♥£ 90/165

19 Marine Terr ✉ *SY23 2AZ*
– ℰ (01970) 612 252 – www.gwestycymru.com
– Closed 1-2 January and 23-31 December

ANGLESEY (Isle of) SIR YNYS MÔN

Isle of Anglesey – Pop. 68 900 – Regional map n° **19**-B1
▶ London 270 mi – Cardiff 205 mi – Liverpool 92 mi – Birkenhead 86 mi

Beaumaris

▶ London 253 mi – Birkenhead 74 mi – Holyhead 25 mi

WALES

🏠 Ye Olde Bull's Head Inn 🏵 🖭 🕭

INN · STYLISH Characterful 1670s coaching inn – look out for the old water clock and ducking stool in the bar. Bedrooms in the main house are named after Dickens characters and are traditional; those in the townhouse are more modern and colourful.

26 rooms ⌑ – ♥£ 88/143 ♥♥£ 93/160

Castle St ⊠ LL58 8AP – ℰ (01248) 810 329 – www.bullsheadinn.co.uk
– Closed 25-26 December and 1 January
Brasserie · Loft – See restaurant listing

🏠 Cleifiog ⇐ 🖙

TOWNHOUSE · PERSONALISED Delightful seafront guesthouse overlooking the mountains and the Menai Strait; run by a welcoming owner. Watercolours hang on wood-panelled walls in the cosy, antique-furnished lounge. Comfortable bedrooms have fine linens and large bathrooms. Excellent communal breakfasts feature tasty fresh juices.

3 rooms – ♥£ 60/90 ♥♥£ 90/120

Townsend ⊠ LL58 8BH – ℰ (01248) 811 507 – www.cleifiogbandb.co.uk
– Closed Christmas-early January

🏠 Churchbank 🖙 ⁒ 🅿

TOWNHOUSE · PERSONALISED Georgian guesthouse with a homely, antique-furnished interior and modern day comforts. Cosy bedrooms look out over the large walled garden and the church opposite; one has a private bathroom. Helpful, amiable owner and hearty breakfasts.

3 rooms ⌑ – ♥£ 65/70 ♥♥£ 80/90

28 Church St ⊠ LL58 8AB – ℰ (01248) 810 353
– www.bedandbreakfastanglesey.com

✗✗ Loft

BRITISH MODERN · ELEGANT Formal restaurant under the eaves of an old coaching inn, with a plush, open-fired lounge and an elegant candlelit dining room with exposed beams and immaculately laid tables. Creative modern cooking champions top Anglesey produce.

Menu £ 48

Ye Olde Bull's Head Inn, Castle St ⊠ LL58 8AP
– ℰ (01248) 810 329 – www.bullsheadinn.co.uk – dinner only
– Closed 25-26 December, 1 January, Sunday and Monday

✗ Brasserie 🕭

BRITISH MODERN · FASHIONABLE Set overlooking a courtyard, a large brasserie in the old stables of a 17C coaching inn, with a Welsh slate floor, oak tables, a fireplace built from local stone and a relaxed feel. Wide-ranging modern menus feature lots of specials.

Carte £ 22/36

Ye Olde Bull's Head Inn, Castle St ⊠ LL58 8AP
– ℰ (01248) 810 329 (bookings not accepted) – www.bullsheadinn.co.uk
– Closed 25-26 December and 1 January

Ianerchymedd

🏠 Llwydiarth Fawr 🐾 ⇐ 🖙 ⁒ ⁒ 🅿

FAMILY · HISTORIC Lovely Georgian house surrounded by 1,000 acres of farmland. Well-kept interior with an impressive hallway and an open-fired drawing room. Bedrooms are classically furnished, with smart wallpapers and colourful throws adding a modern edge.

4 rooms ⌑ – ♥£ 50/65 ♥♥£ 90

⊠ LL71 8DF – North : 1 mi on B 5111
– ℰ (01248) 470 321 – www.llwydiarthfawr.com

WALES

Llangaffo

🏠 Outbuildings

RURAL · PERSONALISED A tastefully converted former granary set close to prehistoric burial ground and offering fantastic views over Snowdonia. Stylish modern bedrooms come with local artwork and smart bathrooms; for a romantic hideaway, choose the 'Pink Hut' in the garden. Afternoon tea is served in the cosy open-fired lounge and a concise, seasonally led menu in the spacious dining room.

5 rooms ☑ – 🛉£ 75 🛉🛉£ 90

Bodowyr Farmhouse ⊠ LL60 6NH – Southeast : 1.5 mi by B 4419 turning left at crossroads and left again by post box.
– ☏ (01248) 430 132 – www.theoutbuildings.co.uk

Menai Bridge

🏰 Château Rhianfa

COUNTRY HOUSE · PERSONALISED Built in 1849 and a smaller copy of the Château de Chenonceau. Formal gardens lead down to the Menai Strait and boast fantastic views over Snowdonia. The striking Victorian interior displays original wood panelling, stained glass and turrets, which contrast with bold modern colour schemes. Formal dining.

19 rooms ☑ – 🛉£ 175/300 🛉🛉£ 175/300 – 1 suite

Glyn Garth ⊠ LL59 5NS – East : 1 mi on A 545
– ☏ (01248) 713 656 – www.chateaurhianfa.com

✗ Sosban & The Old Butchers

MODERN CUISINE · INTIMATE Brightly painted restaurant with smart awnings; one of the walls displays Welsh slate and hand-painted tiles from its butcher's shop days. A well-balanced, 6-8 course surprise menu offers boldly flavoured, carefully cooked dishes.

Menu £ 45 – surprise menu only
Trinity House, 1A High St ⊠ LL59 5EE
– ☏ (01248) 208 131 (booking essential) – www.sosbanandtheoldbutchers.com
– dinner only – Closed January-mid February, Christmas-New Year and Sunday-Wednesday

✗ Dylan's

MODERN CUISINE · FAMILY An old boat yard timber store; now a smart, busy two-storey eatery by the water's edge, overlooking Bangor. Extensive menus offer everything from homemade cakes and weekend brunch to sourdough pizzas. Find a spot on the terrace if you can.

Carte £ 20/69
St George's Rd ⊠ LL59 5DE
– ☏ (01248) 716 714 (booking advisable) – www.dylansrestaurant.co.uk
– Closed 25-26 December

Rhoscolyn

🍺 White Eagle

BRITISH TRADITIONAL · PUB Large pub with a cosy bar, a modern dining room, a decked terrace and stunning sea views. Monthly menus offer everything from sandwiches and pub classics to more sophisticated fare. Daily fish specials and regular themed weeks feature.

Carte £ 21/37
⊠ LL65 2NJ – ☏ (01407) 860 267 – www.white.eagle.co.uk
– Closed 25 December

BALA

Gwynedd – ⊠ Gwynedd – Pop. 1 974 – Regional map n° **19**-B2
▶ London 213 mi – Cardiff 160 mi – Chester 48 mi

🏠 Bryniau Golau

COUNTRY HOUSE · PERSONALISED Victorian tiling, plasterwork and fireplaces are proudly displayed in this elegant house. Spacious bedrooms overlook the lake and mountains: one has a four-poster bed; another, a bath which affords lake views. Their own honey features at breakfast, while dinner – served Fri and Sun – showcases local produce.

3 rooms � – 🛏£ 70/75 🛏🛏£ 110/120

Llangower ✉ LL23 7BT – South : 2 mi by A 494 and B 4931 off B 4403
– 𝒞 (01678) 521 782 – www.bryniau-golau.co.uk – Closed December-February

🏠 Abercelyn Country House

TRADITIONAL · PERSONALISED Attractive former rectory with a brook running through the pleasant garden. Period charm blends with modern touches and up-to-date facilities; bedrooms are warmly decorated and the lounge is cosy. The owner knows the mountains well.

3 rooms � – 🛏£ 50/70 🛏🛏£ 70/100

Llanycil ✉ LL23 7YF – Southwest : 1 mi on A 494 – 𝒞 (01678) 521 109
– www.abercelyn.co.uk – Closed November-January

BARMOUTH ABERMAW

Gwynedd – Pop. 2 315 – Regional map n° **19**-B2
▶ London 231 mi – Chester 74 mi – Dolgellau 10 mi – Shrewsbury 67 mi

✗ Bistro Bermo

TRADITIONAL CUISINE · BISTRO An intimate, personally run bistro with a lively atmosphere. The concise menu follows the seasons and the tasty dishes are neatly presented; go for the dry-aged Welsh Black rib-eye or one of the local fish specials listed on the blackboard.

Carte £ 25/40

6 Church St ✉ LL42 1EW – 𝒞 (01341) 281 284 (booking essential)
– www.bistrobarmouth.co.uk – dinner only – Closed Sunday, Monday and restricted opening in winter

BEAUMARIS → See Anglesey (Isle of)

BEDDGELERT BEDKELERD

Gwynedd – Pop. 535 – Regional map n° **19**-B1
▶ London 249 mi – Caernarfon 13 mi – Chester 73 mi

🏠 Sygun Fawr Country House

FAMILY · COSY A part-16C stone house; halfway up a mountain and boasting views over the valley. The charming interior features a snug sitting room, a spacious conservatory and good-sized bedrooms with a cosy, homely feel. The traditional dining room serves hearty, regional dishes; Mon and Weds they offer simpler suppers.

12 rooms � – 🛏£ 63 🛏🛏£ 85/110

✉ LL55 4NE – Northeast : 0.75 mi by A 498 – 𝒞 (01766) 890 258
– www.sygunfawr.co.uk – Closed 15 November-12 February

BETWS-Y-COED

Conwy – Pop. 255 – Regional map n° **19**-B1
▶ London 226 mi – Holyhead 44 mi – Shrewsbury 62 mi

🏠 Tan-y-Foel Country House

FAMILY · STYLISH Personally run, part-16C country house in 4 acres of grounds, affording stunning views over the Vale of Conwy and Snowdonia. The snug lounge and breakfast room display traditional features. Modern, individually styled bedrooms have smart bathrooms; the spacious loft room has a vaulted ceiling.

6 rooms � – 🛏£ 100/185 🛏🛏£ 100/185

✉ LL26 0RE – East : 2.5 mi by A 5, A 470 and Capel Garmon rd on Llanwrst rd
– 𝒞 (01690) 710 507 – www.tyfhotel.co.uk – Closed December and January

Pengwern

TRADITIONAL · PERSONALISED Cosy Victorian house with stunning mountain and valley views. Warm, well-proportioned bedrooms are named after famous artists and retain charming original features like the old fireplaces. Comfy lounge. Communal breakfasts.

3 rooms ☑ – ♦£ 55/67 ♦♦£ 70/82

Allt Dinas ⊠ LL24 0HF – Southeast : 1.5 mi on A 5 – ℰ (01690) 710 480
– www.snowdoniaaccommodation.co.uk – Closed 21 December-4 January

Bryn Bella

TRADITIONAL · COSY Comfy, well-kept guesthouse with a pleasant garden, valley views and every conceivable extra in the bedrooms. Keen, friendly owners provide reliable local info. Hearty cooked breakfasts feature fresh, tasty eggs from their rescued hens.

5 rooms ☑ – ♦£ 75/85 ♦♦£ 80/90

Lôn Muriau, Llanrwst Rd ⊠ LL24 0HD – Northeast : 1 mi by A 5 on A 470
– ℰ (01690) 710 627 – www.bryn-bella.co.uk

at Penmachno Southwest: 4.75 mi by A5 on B4406 – ⊠ Betws-Y-Coed

Penmachno Hall

TRADITIONAL · PERSONALISED A former rectory in a pleasant valley location with delightful views. Cosy lounge, eclectic art collection and lovely mature gardens. Boldly coloured bedrooms contain a host of thoughtful extras. Light supper by arrangement.

3 rooms ☑ – ♦£ 75/100 ♦♦£ 90/100

⊠ LL24 0PU – On Ty Mawr rd – ℰ (01690) 760 410 – www.penmachnohall.co.uk
– Closed Christmas-New Year

BODUAN – Gwynedd ➜ See Pwllheli

BRECHFA

Carmarthenshire – Regional map n° **19**-B3
▶ London 216 mi – Cardiff 71 mi – Birmingham 183 mi – Liverpool 164 mi

Ty Mawr Country

TRADITIONAL · RUSTIC 16C stone-built farmhouse, set in the centre of the village next to the river. It's personally run and boasts charm and character aplenty, with exposed bricks, wooden beams, open fires, a comfy lounge and pine-furnished bedrooms. The modern menu has Welsh twists and produce is homemade or from the valley.

6 rooms ☑ – ♦£ 75 ♦♦£ 115/130

⊠ SA32 7RA – ℰ (01267) 202 332 – www.wales-country-hotel.co.uk

BRECON

Powys – Pop. 8 250 – Regional map n° **19**-C3
▶ London 171 mi – Cardiff 40 mi – Carmarthen 31 mi – Gloucester 65 mi

Peterstone Court

HISTORIC · CLASSIC Large Georgian house with a lovely mountain backdrop. Two comfy, characterful lounges. Sizeable, traditional bedrooms in the main house; those in the old stables are duplex-style. Two-roomed restaurant has lovely views and a terrace overlooking the swimming pool; extensive, classical menus of local produce.

12 rooms ☑ – ♦£ 85/125 ♦♦£ 85/265

Brecon Rd, Llanhamlach ⊠ LD3 7YB – Southeast : 4 mi by B 4601 on A 40
– ℰ (01874) 665 387 – www.peterstone-court.com

🏠 Felin Glais

🎋 🍸 🚗 **P** 🚭

TRADITIONAL · COSY 17C stone barn and mill, set in a tranquil hamlet and run with pride. Spacious interior has a pleasant 'lived in' feel; cosy, homely bedrooms have toiletries and linen from Harrods. Large beamed lounge; dine here, at the communal table, or in the conservatory in summer. Lengthy menu – order two days ahead.

4 rooms ⌷ – 🛉£ 90/100 🛉🛉£ 90/100

Aberyscir ✉ LD3 9NP
– *West : 4 mi by Cradoc rd turning right immediately after bridge*
– 𝒞 (01874) 623 107 – www.felinglais.co.uk
– Closed 25 December

🛏 Felin Fach Griffin

🥓 🍸 🚗 ☂ **P**

🅐 **REGIONAL · INN** Located in picturesque countryside; a rather unique pub with bright paintwork, colourful artwork and an extremely laid-back atmosphere. The young serving team are friendly and have a good knowledge of what they're serving. Following the motto 'simple things, done well', dishes are straightforward, tasty and refined. Pleasant bedrooms come with comfy beds but no TVs.

Menu £ 21 (weekday lunch)/29
– Carte £ 30/36

7 rooms ⌷ – 🛉£ 108/135 🛉🛉£ 125/165

Felin Fach ✉ LD3 0UB – *Northeast : 4.75 mi by B 4602 off A 470*
– 𝒞 (01874) 620 111 – www.felinfachgriffin.co.uk
– Closed 25 December and early January

BRIDGEND PEN-Y-BONT

Bridgend – Pop. 46 757 – Regional map n° **19**-B4
▶ London 177 mi – Cardiff 20 mi – Swansea 23 mi

🏠 Great House

🎋 🚗 🎵 🕰 🥂 🛁 **P**

HISTORIC · COSY Welcoming 15C, Grade II listed property; the home of the Lord of the Manor of Laleston and reputedly a gift from Elizabeth I to the Earl of Leicester. Characterful bar and lounge. Individually styled bedrooms; those in the coach house are the most modern. Restaurant offers a seasonal menu of regional produce.

12 rooms ⌷ – 🛉£ 90/120 🛉🛉£ 135/160

High St, Laleston ✉ CF32 0HP – *West : 2 mi on A 473*
– 𝒞 (01656) 657 644 – www.great-house-laleston.co.uk
– Closed 24-27 December

BUILTH WELLS LLANFAIR-YM-MUALLT

Powys – Pop. 2 829 – Regional map n° **19**-C3
▶ London 191 mi – Cardiff 63 mi – Brecon 20 mi – Swansea 58 mi

🏠 Rhedyn

🎋 🍸 🍴 🚗 **P**

FAMILY · PERSONALISED Former forester's cottage with a small garden and pleasant country views, run by very welcoming owners. Tiny lounge with a bookcase full of local info and DVDs; cosy communal dining room where home-cooked, local market produce is served. Good-sized, modern bedrooms feature heavy wood furnishings, good facilities and quirky touches. Tea and cake are served on arrival.

3 rooms ⌷ – 🛉£ 85 🛉🛉£ 95

Cilmery ✉ LD2 3LH – *West : 4 mi on A 483*
– 𝒞 (01982) 551 944 – www.rhedynguesthouse.co.uk

BWLCHTOCYN – Gwynedd ➔ See Abersoch

CAERNARFON

Gwynedd – Pop. 9 493 – Regional map n° **19**-B1

▶ London 249 mi – Birkenhead 76 mi – Chester 68 mi – Holyhead 30 mi

---

⌂ **Plas Dinas**   ⌖ 🐾 ⚙ **P**

TRADITIONAL · CLASSIC The former family home of Lord Snowdon, set in large
gardens and filled with antiques, historical documents and family portraits. The
spacious drawing room has an open fire and a piano; smart bedrooms boast designer touches and immaculate bathrooms. Traditional 4 course dinners are
served on request.

9 rooms ⌖ – ♛£ 99/249 ♛♛£ 99/249

✉ LL54 7YF – South : 2.5 mi on A 487 – ℰ (01286) 830 214 – www.plasdinas.co.uk
– Closed Christmas

✗ **Blas** 🅝   🍴

MODERN CUISINE · SIMPLE Relaxed, friendly restaurant set into the old city
walls – which you can see in the upstairs room. It's open all day but menus are
the most ambitious and creative at dinner. Framed recipes and striking modern
art hang on the walls.

Carte £ 20/38

23-25 Hole in the Wall St ✉ LL55 1RF – ℰ (01286) 677 707
– www.blascaernarfon.co.uk – Closed 2 weeks January, 25-26 December,
1 January, Sunday dinner and Monday

---

at Seion Northeast: 5.5 mi by A4086 and B4366 on Seion rd – ✉ Gwynedd

---

⌂ **Ty'n Rhos Country House**   ⌖ ≤ ⚙ 🍴 **P**

FAMILY · PERSONALISED Personally run former farmhouse with a large conservatory and a cosy lounge with an inglenook fireplace. Comfortable, modern bedrooms; some have balconies or terraces and others, their own garden. The formal
restaurant offers pleasant views over Anglesey; classically based dishes are presented in modern ways.

19 rooms – ♛£ 72/85 ♛♛£ 90/175

✉ LL55 3AE – Southwest : 0.75 mi – ℰ (01248) 670 489 – www.tynrhos.co.uk

---

at Dolydd South: 3.5 mi by A487

⌂ **Y Goeden Eirin**   🐾 ≤ ⚙ 🍴 **P** 🔄

TRADITIONAL · RUSTIC Cosy stone cottage with interesting furniture, eclectic
artwork and a slightly bohemian feel. The bedroom in the main house has views
of both the mountains and the sea; bedrooms in the old outbuildings have slate
floors, stable doors and small kitchen areas. Tasty home-cooked breakfasts.

3 rooms ⌖ – ♛£ 65 ♛♛£ 90/100

✉ LL54 7EF – ℰ (01286) 830 942 – www.ygoedeneirin.co.uk – Closed
Christmas-New Year

---

at Llanrug East: 3 mi on A4086 – ✉ Caernarfon

⌂ **Seiont Manor**   ⌖ 🐾 ≤ ⚙ 🍴 🍳 ✂ 🔄 **P**

COUNTRY HOUSE · CONTEMPORARY Small manor house in a peaceful location;
follow the nature trails or fish on the river in the 150 acre grounds. Spacious
modern country bedrooms – some with Juliet balconies or terraces. Have after
noon tea in one of the lounges, a light meal in the conservatory or modern classics in the formal restaurant.

28 rooms – ♛£ 110/250 ♛♛£ 130/250

✉ LL55 2AQ – ℰ (01286) 673 366 – www.handpickedhotels.co.uk

GOOD TIPS!

Wales' capital combines a rich history with top-class sporting venues, big name shops and a lively cultural scene, and this is reflected in our selection, with restaurants like Park House, in a late 19C property built by the founder of modern Cardiff, the 2nd Marquess of Bute, alongside the ultra-modern, glass-fronted St. David's Hotel & Spa.

CARDIFF

Cardiff – Pop. 346 090 – Regional map n° **19**-C4

▶ London 155 mi – Birmingham 110 mi – Bristol 46 mi – Coventry 124 mi

Hotels

St David's H. & Spa

BUSINESS · MINIMALIST Modern, purpose-built hotel on the waterfront, affording lovely 360° views. Good-sized, minimalist bedrooms have a slightly funky feel; all boast balconies and bay outlooks. Smart spa features seawater pools and a dry floatation tank. Stylish restaurant with superb terrace views serves modern British dishes.

142 rooms – †£ 99/399 ††£ 99/399 – ☑ £ 19 – 12 suites

Town plan: CU-a – *Havannah St, Cardiff Bay* ⊠ CF10 5SD – ☎ (02920) 454 045 – *www.principal-hayley.com/thestdavids*

Hilton Cardiff

CHAIN HOTEL · MODERN Imposing former tax office in the city centre, with excellent views of the castle, law courts and city hall. Large atrium; well-equipped function rooms and leisure club. Spacious bedrooms are a touch functional – some have great outlooks. Conservatory-style restaurant offers a Mediterranean-influenced menu.

197 rooms ☑ – †£ 119/149 ††£ 129/159 – 4 suites

Town plan: BZ-x – *Kingsway* ⊠ CF10 3HH – ☎ (029) 2064 6300 – *www.placeshilton.com/cardiff*

Park Plaza

BUSINESS · MINIMALIST Formerly municipal offices, now a light, airy hotel with a stylish lounge, extensive conference facilities and a vast leisure centre boasting a smart, stainless steel pool and 8 treatment rooms. Stark, modern bedrooms have laptop safes and slate bathrooms. Informal brasserie serves international dishes.

129 rooms – †£ 89/349 ††£ 99/359 – ☑ £ 13

Town plan: BY-s – *Greyfriars Rd* ⊠ CF10 3AL – ☎ (029) 20 111 111 – *www.parkplazacardiff.com* – *Closed 25-26 December*

939

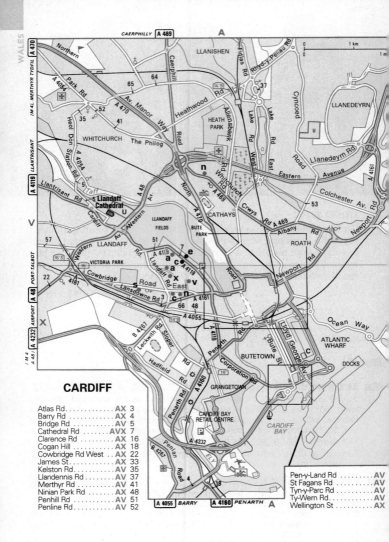

CARDIFF

🏨 Radisson Blu Cardiff

BUSINESS · MODERN Large glass building in a great central location. Spacious modern guest areas, excellent meeting facilities and a smart bar. Modern slightly minimalist bedrooms in three styles – Fresh, Fashion and Chic – all boast slate-tiled bathrooms and city views. The simple restaurant offers accessible Italian menus.

215 rooms ⌂ - †£ 70/400 ††£ 80/410

Town plan: BZ-a – *Meridian Gate, Bute Terr.* ✉ CF10 2FL
- ✆ (029) 2045 4777
- www.radissonblu.com/hotel-cardiff

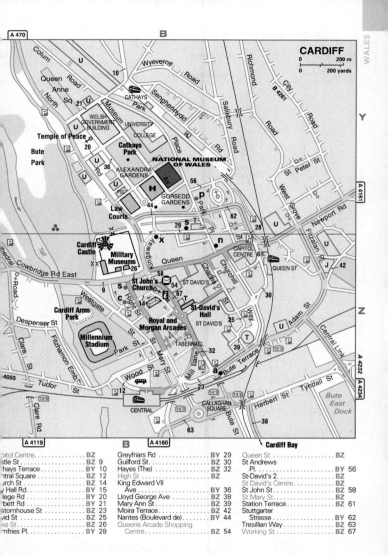

Parc

🛎️ 🔁 ♿ AC 📶 🧖

BUSINESS · MODERN Centrally located commercial hotel with striking décor; hidden behind a classic Victorian façade. Marble-tiled lobby and fashionable bar. Stylish, contemporary bedrooms feature bright white décor and offer good facilities; those to the rear are quieter. Accessible menus in the smart restaurant.

140 rooms ☕ – ♦£ 70/125 ♦♦£ 90/200 – 1 suite

Town plan: BZ-n – _Park Pl_ ✉ _CF10 3UD_
– ✆ _(029) 2038 3471_
– _www.thistle.com/theparchotel_

941

CARDIFF BAY

Britannia Quay . . . . CU 2
Bute Crescent . . . . CT 4
Clarence Embankment . . . CT 8
Dudley St . . . . CU 9
Hemingway Rd . . . . CT 12
Lloyd George Ave . . . . CT 14
Mermaid Quay Shopping Centre . . . . CU
Mount Stuart Square . . . . CT
Pomeroy St . . . . CT
Windsor Esplanade . . . . . CU

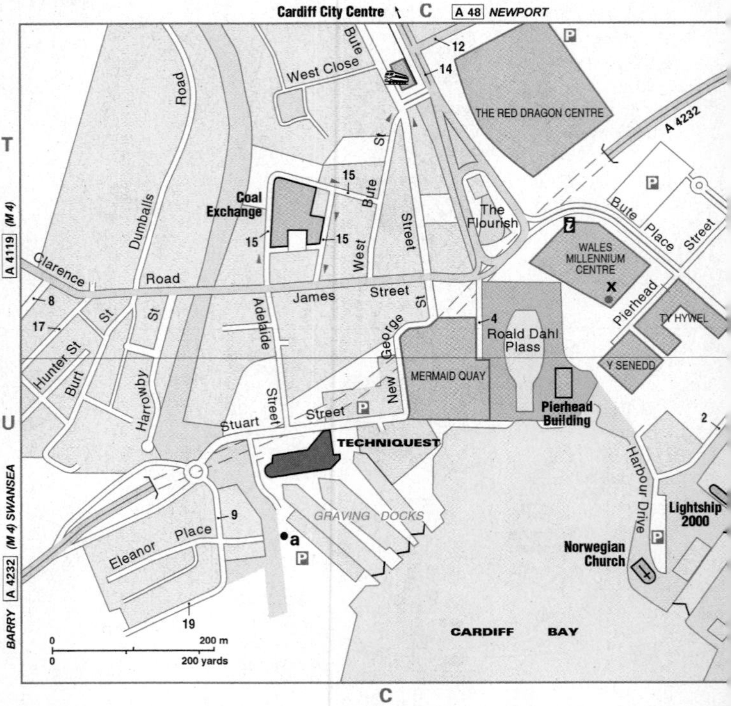

Cathedral 73

TOWNHOUSE • CONTEMPORARY Delightful Victorian terraced house on th edge of the city, with boutique furnishings, designer bedrooms and a chauffeu driven Rolls Royce. Afternoon tea is served in the spacious sitting room an breakfast, in the orangery.

10 rooms – £ 150/250 £ 150/400

Town plan: AV-c – *73 Cathedral Rd ✉ CF11 9HE – ✆ (029) 2023 5005 – www.cathedral73.com*

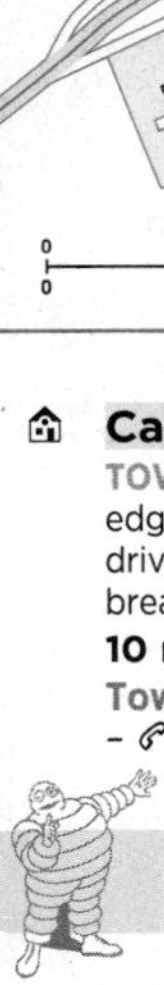

Follow our inspectors @MichelinGuideUK

Lincoln House

TOWNHOUSE • PERSONALISED Two lovingly restored Victorian houses on th main road into town: family owned and run, with a classic style and contempo rary touches. Bedrooms offer a high level of facilities; some feature four-poste and those to the rear are quieter.

23 rooms – £ 75/125 £ 95/125

Town plan: AV-e – *118-120 Cathedral Rd ✉ CF11 9LQ – ✆ (029) 2039 5558 – www.lincolnhotel.co.uk*

Restaurants

XXX **Park House**

MODERN CUISINE · ELEGANT Striking building designed by William Burgess in the late 1800s, overlooking Gorsedd Gardens. The oak-panelled dining room has a formal air. Menus are modern – each dish is matched with a wine from the impressive New World list.

Menu £ 25 (lunch) – Carte £ 48/62

Town plan: BY-p – *20 Park Pl.* ✉ *CF10 3DQ* – ℘ *(029) 2022 4343* – *www.parkhouserestaurant.co.uk* – *Closed 24-25 December, 1 January and Monday*

XX **Purple Poppadom**

INDIAN · DESIGN Smart Indian restaurant with bold purple décor. Classic combinations are cooked in a refined modern style and given a personal twist. The tasting menus provide plenty of interest and the seafood dishes are particularly popular.

Menu £ 15 (weekdays)/43 – Carte £ 20/35

Town plan: AX-n – *185a Cowbridge Rd East* ✉ *CF11 9AJ* – ℘ *(029) 2022 0026* – *www.purplepoppadom.com* – *Closed 25-26 December, 1 January and Monday*

X **'Bully's**

FRENCH · NEIGHBOURHOOD Welcoming neighbourhood bistro run by a passionate, hands-on owner. The simply furnished interior boasts a fascinating array of memorabilia. Classic cooking displays a strong Gallic edge; carefully prepared dishes use quality ingredients.

Menu £ 16 (weekday lunch)/20 – Carte £ 26/45

Town plan: AX-x – *5 Romilly Cres.* ✉ *CF11 9NP* – ℘ *(029) 2022 1905* – *www.bullysrestaurant.co.uk* – *Closed Christmas and Sunday dinner*

X **Arbennig**

REGIONAL · SIMPLE Homely neighbourhood bistro with a buzzy feel. Daily baked bread is made to match the dishes on the weekly changing menu. Cooking covers all bases, from soup to steak, and there's a great value set selection available at lunch.

Menu £ 16 (lunch) – Carte £ 22/40

Town plan: AX-a – *6-10 Romilly Cres.* ✉ *CF11 9NR* – ℘ *(029) 2034 1264* – *www.arbennig.co.uk* – *Closed Sunday dinner and Monday*

X **Potted Pig**

BRITISH TRADITIONAL · RUSTIC Atmospheric restaurant in a stripped back former bank vault, with brick walls, barrel ceilings and a utilitarian feel. Lesser-known products and cuts of meat are used in robust, tasty dishes. The gin cocktails are a speciality.

Carte £ 21/44

Town plan: BZ-s – *27 High St* ✉ *CF10 1PU* – ℘ *(02920) 22 4817* – *www.thepottedpig.com* – *Closed 23 December-3 January, Monday and Sunday dinner*

X **Mint & Mustard**

INDIAN · NEIGHBOURHOOD Well-run, welcoming neighbourhood restaurant with a modern, laid-back feel; ask for a table in the front room. The chef's training in Kerala is reflected in the extensive menu of original, authentic Indian dishes and well-balanced spicing.

Menu £ 35/50 – Carte £ 17/39

Town plan: AV-n – *134 Whitchurch Rd* ✉ *CF14 3LZ* – ℘ *(029) 2062 0333* *(booking essential at dinner) – www.mintandmustard.com – Closed 25-26 December and 1 January*

X **La Cuina**　　　　　　　　　　　　　　　　　AC 🍽

SPANISH · BISTRO A smart, well-stocked deli sells top quality imported Spanish produce and the rustic restaurant serves authentic Spanish dishes with strong Catalonian influences. Tapas is served at lunch and on Wednesday evenings.

Menu £15 (weekday lunch) – Carte £26/45

Town plan: AX-v – *11 Kings Rd* ⊠ *CF11 9BZ* – ℰ *(029) 2019 0265*
– www.lacuina.co.uk – Closed 25-27 December and Sunday-Tuesday

X **Ffresh**　　　　　　　　　　　　　　　　　🛱 👌 AC ☺

BRITISH TRADITIONAL · BRASSERIE Located within the striking, modern 'Wales Millennium Centre', overlooking the piazza and frequented by theatregoers. Large, airy interior with a relaxed atmosphere. Simple, classical cooking is founded on fresh Welsh ingredients.

Menu £17 (lunch and early dinner)/24 – Carte £23/38

Town plan: CT-x – *Wales Millennium Centre, Bute Plas, Cardiff Bay* ⊠ *CF10 5AL* – ℰ *(029) 2063 6465 – www.ffresh.org.uk – Closed 25 December, Mondays in low season and Sunday dinner*

X **Fish at 85**

FISH AND SEAFOOD · SIMPLE Simplicity is key at this unpretentious, pared down restaurant, where a large fish counter displays the latest catch from the day boats. Choose your fish, your cooking method and your accompaniments and let the chef do the rest.

Menu £16 (weekday lunch) – Carte £31/62

Town plan: AV-a – *85 Pontcanna St* ⊠ *CF11 9HS* – ℰ *(029) 2023 5666 (booking essential at dinner) – www.fishat85.co.uk – Closed Sunday and Monday*

X **Chez Francis** Ⓝ　　　　　　　　　　　　　　　　AC

FRENCH · SIMPLE Intimate eatery run by an experienced French owner. Dine at tightly packed tables in the narrow bistro or at barrels which act as the bar. All the classics are here from Bayonne ham to coq au vin, roast duck to tarte au citron.

Menu £13 (lunch) – Carte £25/40

Town plan: AX-c – *185 Cowbridge Rd East* ⊠ *CF11 9AJ* – ℰ *(029) 2022 4959 – www.chez-francis.co.uk – Closed Sunday and Monday*

X **Casanova** Ⓝ

ITALIAN · SIMPLE Long-standing restaurant near the stadium. Flavoursome country dishes are a perfect match for the rustic, osteria-style interior, and range from carpaccio of beef to homemade pasta with a rich ragu or roast mallard with polenta.

Menu £15/30

Town plan: BZ-c – *13 Quay St* ⊠ *CF10 1EA* – ℰ *(029) 2034 4044 – www.casanovacardiff.co.uk – Closed Sunday and bank holidays*

X **Chai St** Ⓝ　　　　　　　　　　　　　　　　　AC

INDIAN · EXOTIC Vibrantly decorated Indian restaurant with a mix of wooden seating; some tables you share. Simple menus focus on thalis, which come with meat, rice, vegetables, naan, poppadoms and raita. Dishes are well-spiced and good value.

Carte £13/18

Town plan: AX-s – *153 Cowbridge Rd East* ⊠ *CF11 9AH* – ℰ *(02920) 228 888 (bookings not accepted) – www.chaistreet.com – Closed 25-26 December and Easter*

CARMARTHEN

Carmarthenshire – Pop. 15 854 – Regional map n° **19**-B3
▶ London 219 mi – Fishguard 47 mi – Haverfordwest 32 mi – Swansea 27 mi

WALES

at Felingwm Uchaf Northeast: 8 mi by A40 on B4310 – ✉ Carmarthen

🏠 **Allt y Golau Uchaf**

TRADITIONAL · COSY Converted farmhouse dating from 1812, up a steep slope on a two acre smallholding. Well-kept, rustic interior; neat, pine-furnished bedrooms have a homely feel. Extensive breakfasts feature local meats and eggs from their own hens.

3 rooms 🖃 – 🛏£ 45 🛏🛏£ 75

✉ SA32 7BB – North : 0.5 mi on B 4310 – 𝒞 (01267) 290 455
– www.alltygolau.com – Closed 20 December-2 January

at Llanllawddog Northeast: 8 mi by A485

🏠 **Glangwili Mansion**

FAMILY · MODERN Part-17C mansion rebuilt in a Georgian style, set in a great location on the edge of the forest. The spacious interior features sleek tiled floors, contemporary artwork and bright, bold bedrooms with modern oak furnishings.

4 rooms 🖃 – 🛏£ 89/115 🛏🛏£ 115/140

✉ SA32 7JE – 𝒞 (01267) 253 735 – www.glangwilimansion.co.uk – Closed 24-25, 31 December and 1 January

at Nantgaredig East: 5 mi by A4300 on A4310 – ✉ Carmarthen

🍴 **Y Polyn**

BRITISH TRADITIONAL · PUB Small, rustic, unfussy pub on a busy country road; close to a stream and boasting pleasant views. Cooking is stout, filling and British at heart, offering satisfying soups, fresh salads, slow-cooked meats and classical puddings.

Menu £ 17 (weekday lunch)/35 – Carte lunch £ 28/36

✉ SA32 7LH – South : 1 mi on B 4310 – 𝒞 (01267) 290 000 (booking advisable) – www.ypolynrestaurant.co.uk – Closed Sunday dinner and Monday

COLWYN BAY BAE COLWYN

Conwy – Pop. 29 405 – Regional map n° **19**-B1
🚗 London 237 mi – Birkenhead 50 mi – Chester 42 mi – Holyhead 41 mi

🍴 **Pen-y-Bryn**

TRADITIONAL CUISINE · PUB Unassuming pub with a spacious, open-plan interior, a laid-back feel and impressive panoramic views over Colwyn Bay, especially from the garden and terrace. The extensive all-day menu ranges from pub classics to more adventurous fare.

Carte £ 20/32

Pen-y-Bryn Rd, Upper Colwyn Bay ✉ LL29 6DD – Southwest : 1 mi by B 5113 – 𝒞 (01492) 533 360 – www.penybryn-colwynbay.co.uk

at Rhos-on-Sea Northwest: 1 mi – ✉ Colwyn Bay

🏠 **Plas Rhos House**

TRADITIONAL · PERSONALISED Smartly refurbished 19C house with a pleasant terrace, on a small street overlooking the sea. Cosy lounge and bright, cheery breakfast room. Bedrooms have modern bathrooms and thoughtful extras such as chocolates and a decanter of sherry.

5 rooms 🖃 – 🛏£ 60/75 🛏🛏£ 80/105

53 Cayley Promenade ✉ LL28 4EP – 𝒞 (01492) 543 698 – www.plasrhos.co.uk – Closed November-Mid March

CONWY

Conwy – Pop. 3 873 – Regional map n° **19**-B1
🚗 London 241 mi – Caernarfon 22 mi – Chester 46 mi – Holyhead 37 mi

🏨 Castle   ☆ ♨ 🅿

INN · PERSONALISED Friendly, family-run former coaching inn whose distinctive granite and red-brick façade, added in the late 19C, gives it a Victorian appearance. Bedrooms vary in style; some have a country house feel, while others are more modern. Wide-ranging menu available in both the restaurant and the cosy bar-lounge.

27 rooms ⌂ – ♦£ 89/99 ♦♦£ 138/270 – 1 suite
High St ⊠ LL32 8DB – ℰ (01492) 582 800 – www.castlewales.co.uk

XX Signatures   ☆ ﴾ 🅰🅲 🅿

MODERN CUISINE · DESIGN Stylish, contemporary restaurant with elegantly laid tables and a well-versed team, in a holiday park close to the sea. Brasserie classics and snacks at lunch; more inventive, modern choices at dinner including chef's 'signature' dishes.

Menu £20 (weekday dinner)/26 – Carte £33/44
Aberconwy Resort and Spa ⊠ LL32 8GA – Northwest 1.5 mi by A 547 – ℰ (01492) 583 513 (booking advisable) – www.signaturesrestaurant.co.uk – dinner only – Closed Monday and Tuesday

🍴 Groes Inn   ⇔ ﴾ 🍴 🏡 🅿

TRADITIONAL CUISINE · INN The first licensed house in Wales, dating from 1573, in a great location in the foothills of Snowdonia. An appealing menu offers traditional dishes with the occasional international flavour. Spacious, comfy bedrooms - some with a balcony or terrace; ask for one at the rear with far-reaching rural views.

Carte £22/46
14 rooms ⌂ – ♦£ 100/200 ♦♦£ 125/225
⊠ LL32 8TN – South : 3 mi on B 5106 – ℰ (01492) 650 545 – www.groesinn.com – Closed Sunday dinner and Monday November-mid March

at Rowen South: 3.5 mi by B5106

🏨 Tir Y Coed   ☆ ♨ 🏡 🅿

COUNTRY HOUSE · PERSONALISED Late 19C house in a secluded valley at the foothills of Snowdonia. With mature gardens which are a haven for wildlife, this is an ideal spot for those who have come away to unwind. Cosy bedrooms feature smart, modern bathrooms. The intimate dining room offers a daily menu of tried-and-tested classics.

7 rooms (dinner included) ⌂ – ♦£ 120/170 ♦♦£ 135/185
⊠ LL32 8TP – ℰ (01492) 650 219 – www.tirycoed.com

COWBRIDGE Y BONT FAEN
The Vale of Glamorgan – Pop. 3 616 – Regional map n° **19**-B4
▶ London 170 mi – Cardiff 15 mi – Swansea 30 mi

XX Huddarts

TRADITIONAL CUISINE · COSY Honest restaurant in an ancient market town the husband cooks and the wife looks after the friendly service. Traditional décor with a stone fireplace and colourful tapestries. Carefully executed, classic dishes with good presentation.

Menu £21 (weekday lunch) – Carte £26/40
69 High St ⊠ CF71 7AF – ℰ (01446) 774 645 – Closed 1 week Christmas-New Year, 1 week summer, 1 week autumn, Sunday dinner and Monday

X Arboreal   🍴

MEDITERRANEAN · RUSTIC There's a lively Antipodean vibe at this all-day bar and café, where the chef uses local produce in dishes with a Mediterranean, Asian and North African edge. Bespoke, wood-fired pizzas feature highly and folk music accompanies.

Carte £23/38
68 Eastgate ⊠ CF71 7AB – ℰ (01446) 775 093 – www.arboreal.uk.com – Closed first 2 weeks January, Monday and Tuesday in winter

CRICCIETH

Gwynedd – Pop. 1 753 – Regional map n° **19**-B2

▶ London 249 mi – Caernarfon 17 mi – Shrewsbury 85 mi

🏰 Bron Eifion

COUNTRY HOUSE · CONTEMPORARY Characterful country house built in 1883 for a wealthy slate merchant; the feature staircase is constructed from Oregon pitch pine, which he brought back from the USA. Spacious modern bedrooms; some with carved wooden beds from the Middle East. Lovely garden views and an extensive menu in the restaurant.

18 rooms ⌑ – †£ 95/135 ††£ 145/225

✉ LL52 0SA – West : 1 mi on A 497 – ℰ (01766) 522 385 – www.broneifion.co.uk

CRICKHOWELL CRUCYWEL

Powys – Pop. 2 063 – Regional map n° **19**-C4

▶ London 169 mi – Abergavenny 6 mi – Brecon 14 mi – Cardiff 40 mi

🏰 Gliffaes Country House

HISTORIC · PERSONALISED Impressive semi-Italianate country house built in 1886, in 32 acres of delightful grounds on the Glanusk Estate. Take in the view from the well-appointed lounges, conservatories or delightful terrace. Bedrooms are individually styled – book one with a balcony. Welsh produce is showcased in the dining rooms.

23 rooms ⌑ – †£ 108/135 ††£ 122/275

✉ NP8 1RH – West : 3.75 mi by A 40 – ℰ (01874) 730 371
– www.gliffaeshotel.com – Closed 28 December-25 January

🏰 Bear

TRADITIONAL · COSY Well-known, family-run coaching inn filled with various charming rooms and dating from the 15C. Bedrooms are modern; the most characterful are in the main house and feature beams, four-posters and fireplaces; some have jacuzzis.

36 rooms ⌑ – †£ 80/135 ††£ 99/169 – 1 suite

High St ✉ NP8 1BW – ℰ (01873) 810 408 – www.bearhotel.co.uk – Closed 25 December

Bear – See restaurant listing

🏠 Glangrwyney Court

TRADITIONAL · PERSONALISED Passionately run country house with Georgian origins, featuring a large lounge and a high-ceilinged breakfast room. Fresh flowers and objets d'art cover every surface. Bedrooms boast rich fabrics, good facilities and country views.

8 rooms ⌑ – †£ 80/140 ††£ 115/145

✉ NP8 1ES – Southeast : 2 mi on A 40 – ℰ (01873) 811 288 – www.glancourt.co.uk
– Closed 24-26 December

🏠 Ty Gwyn

TOWNHOUSE · PERSONALISED Proudly run whitewashed guesthouse with a stream running through the pretty garden; take it all in from the conservatory breakfast room. Simple, traditional bedrooms. The owners have good local knowledge – one is a certified guide!

3 rooms ⌑ – †£ 50/60 ††£ 75/85

Brecon Rd ✉ NP8 1DG – ℰ (01873) 811 625 – www.tygwyn.com – Closed November-March

🍴 Bear

BRITISH TRADITIONAL · INN Well-maintained 15C coaching inn adorned with hanging baskets and full of nooks and crannies. The menu offers honest pub classics alongside more elaborate specials. Sit in the hugely characterful lounge-bar or more formal restaurant.

Carte £ 20/46

High St ✉ NP8 1BW – ℰ (01873) 810 408 (bookings not accepted)
– www.bearhotel.co.uk – Closed 25 December

CROSS ASH – Monmouthshire → See Abergavenny

CROSSGATES – Powys → See Llandrindod Wells

DEGANWY – Conwy → See Llandudno

DENBIGH
Denbighshire – Pop. 8 514 – Regional map n° **19**-C1
▶ London 215 mi – Cardiff 162 mi – Swansea 151 mi – Telford 70 mi

⌂ Castle House   ≤ 🚗 P
COUNTRY HOUSE · PERSONALISED By the ruins of the 16C cathedral, overlooking the Vale of Clwyd; its gardens incorporate the ancient town walls. Spacious bedrooms retain period character and the décor blends the old and new. Afternoon tea by the fire or in the garden.
4 rooms ⌂ – 🛏£ 85/170 🛏🛏£ 145/180
Bull Ln ⌂ *LL16 3LY –* ℰ *(01745) 816 860 – www.castlehousebandb.co.uk – Closed Christmas*

DINAS CROSS – Pembrokeshire → See Newport (Pembrokeshire)

DOLFOR
Powys – Regional map n° **19**-C2
▶ London 199 mi – Cardiff 93 mi – Oswestry 34 mi – Ludlow 39 mi

⌂ Old Vicarage   ⌂ ≤ 🚗 🍴 P
TRADITIONAL · PERSONALISED Extended 19C red-brick house – formerly a vicarage – with large gardens where they grow the produce used in their home-cooked meals. Classical, country house style lounge and dining room. Cosy bedrooms – named after local rivers – mix period furnishings with bright modern colours. Chutney, preserves and soaps are for sale and afternoon tea is served on arrival.
4 rooms ⌂ – 🛏£ 70/90 🛏🛏£ 95/150
⌂ *SY16 4BN – North : 1.5 mi by A 483 –* ℰ *(01686) 629 051*
– www.theoldvicaragedolfor.co.uk – Closed Christmas-New Year

DOLGELLAU
Gwynedd – Pop. 2 688 – Regional map n° **19**-B2
▶ London 221 mi – Birkenhead 72 mi – Chester 64 mi – Shrewsbury 57 mi

⌂ Penmaenuchaf Hall   ⌂ 🐾 ≤ 🚗 🍴 🍴 P
COUNTRY HOUSE · PERSONALISED Personally run Victorian house with wood panelling, ornate ceilings and original stained glass windows. Bedrooms blend the traditional and the modern; some have balconies overlooking the beautiful grounds, mountains and estuary. Classic dishes and a well-chosen wine list in formal conservatory dining room.
14 rooms ⌂ – 🛏£ 128/195 🛏🛏£ 185/288
Penmaenpool ⌂ *LL40 1YB – West : 1.75 mi on A 493 (Tywyn Rd) –* ℰ *(01341) 422 129 – www.penhall.co.uk – Closed 12-22 December and 4-17 January*

⌂ Ffynnon   🚗 P
TOWNHOUSE · STYLISH A spacious Victorian house which once operated as a cottage hospital. Original features and period furnishings abound, offset by stylish modern designs which pay great attention to detail. Keep your wine and snacks in the pantry and enjoy homemade crumpets or pancakes for breakfast. Outdoor hot tub.
6 rooms ⌂ – 🛏£ 100/205 🛏🛏£ 150/205
Love Ln, off Cader Rd ⌂ *LL40 1RR –* ℰ *(01341) 421 774*
– www.ffynnontownhouse.com – Closed Christmas

⌂ Y Meirionnydd

TOWNHOUSE · PERSONALISED Double-fronted house in the heart of a small town; Gwynedd was known as Meirionnydd up until the 1970s. Simple, modern, homely style with a small bar and a snug basement restaurant. Bedrooms are decorated in subtle hues and have very comfy beds. Hearty breakfasts and traditional dinners with a modern twist.

5 rooms ⌂ – **†**£ 65/79 **††**£ 75/125

Smithfield Sq ⌂ LL40 1ES – 𝒞 (01341) 422 544 – www.themeirionnydd.com – Closed 2 weeks January and 1 week Christmas

🏠 Tyddyn Mawr

FAMILY · COSY A peaceful haven on a secluded sheep farm; located at the foot of Cader Idris mountain and boasting stunning views. Immaculately kept bedrooms have handmade Welsh furnishings and plenty of extras; one has a balcony, another, a terrace. Great hospitality. 5 course breakfasts beside the impressive inglenook.

3 rooms ⌂ – **†**£ 65 **††**£ 86

Islawdref, Cader Rd ⌂ LL40 1TL – Southwest : 2.5 mi by Tywyn rd on Cader Idris rd – 𝒞 (01341) 422 331 – www.wales-guesthouse.co.uk – Closed December-January

at Llanelltyd Northwest: 2.25 mi by A470 on A496

✕✕ Mawddach

MODERN CUISINE · RUSTIC Stylish barn conversion run by two brothers and set on the family farm. Terrace and airy dining room offer superb views of the mountains and estuary. Unfussy Italian-influenced cooking features lamb from the farm and veg from the garden.

Carte £ 28/39

⌂ LL40 2TA – 𝒞 (01341) 421 752 – www.mawddach.com – Closed 2 weeks November, 1 week January, 1 week spring, Sunday dinner, Monday, Tuesday and Wednesday

> Prices quoted after the symbol **†** refer to the lowest rate for a single room in low season, followed by the highest rate in high season. The same principle applies to the symbol **††** for a double room.

DOLYDD – Gwynedd → See Caernarfon

FELINGWM UCHAF – Carmarthenshire → See Carmarthen

FISHGUARD

Pembrokeshire – Pop. 3 419 – Regional map n° **19**-A3

▶ London 265 mi – Cardiff 114 mi – Gloucester 176 mi – Holyhead 169 mi

🏠 Manor Town House

TOWNHOUSE · PERSONALISED Well-run, listed Georgian townhouse, boasting fabulous harbour views. Stylish, elegant lounges and individually designed, antique-furnished bedrooms; some in art deco and some in Victorian styles. Tasty breakfasts; charming owners.

6 rooms ⌂ – **†**£ 70/90 **††**£ 90/115

11 Main St ⌂ SA65 9HG – 𝒞 (01348) 873 260 – www.manortownhouse.com – Closed 24-26 December

GLYNARTHEN

Ceredigion – Regional map n° **19**-B3

▶ London 231 mi – Birmingham 152 mi – Bristol 131 mi – Leicester 185 mi

🏠 Penbontbren   🕭 🖫 & 🅿

COUNTRY HOUSE · CONTEMPORARY Converted farm buildings surrounded by an attractive landscaped garden and 35 acres of rolling countryside. Spacious, stylish bedrooms; each has a sitting room, a mini bar, a coffee machine and a patio. The smart breakfast room features exposed stone, bold wallpaper, Portmeirion china and an extensive menu.

5 rooms ⌂ – †£ 79/90 ††£ 110/120

Glynarthen ⌂ SA44 6PE – North : 1 mi taking first left at crossroads then next left onto unmarked lane – 𝒞 (01239) 810 248 – www.penbontbren.com – Closed Christmas

HARLECH

Gwynedd – Pop. 1 762 – Regional map n° **19**-B2
▶ London 241 mi – Chester 72 mi – Dolgellau 21 mi

✗✗ Castle Cottage   ⇦

CLASSIC CUISINE · COSY Sweet little cottage behind Harlech Castle, with a cosy yet surprisingly contemporary interior. Start with canapés and an aperitif in the lounge; the table is yours for the evening. Classical menus feature local produce and modern touches. Spacious bedrooms have smart bathrooms and stunning mountain views.

Menu £ 40

7 rooms ⌂ – †£ 85/125 ††£ 130/175

Pen Llech ⌂ LL46 2YL – by B 4573 – 𝒞 (01766) 780 479 (booking essential) – www.castlecottageharlech.co.uk – dinner only – Closed 3 weeks October-November and Sunday-Wednesday November-February

HAVERFORDWEST HWLFFORDD

Pembrokeshire – Pop. 14 596 – Regional map n° **19**-A3
▶ London 250 mi – Fishguard 15 mi – Swansea 57 mi

🏠 Lower Haythog Farm   🕭 🖫 ℁ 🅿

TRADITIONAL · COSY Welcoming guesthouse with mature gardens, part-dating from the 14C and set on a working dairy farm. Cosy bedrooms feature bespoke cherry wood furniture and organic toiletries. Pleasant lounge and conservatory Aga-cooked breakfasts.

4 rooms ⌂ – †£ 40/60 ††£ 75/85

Spittal ⌂ SA62 5QL – Northeast : 5 mi on B 4329 – 𝒞 (01437) 731 279 – www.lowerhaythogfarm.co.uk

🏠 Paddock   ✿ 🕭 🖫 ℁ 🅿

FAMILY · MODERN Contemporary guesthouse on a working dairy farm. Comfy lounge with books, board games and a wood-burning stove. Modern bedrooms feature chunky wood furniture and sleigh beds made up with Egyptian cotton. Home-cooked meals rely on local and market produce; eggs are from their own hens.

3 rooms ⌂ – †£ 60/65 ††£ 80/85

Lower Haythog, Spittal ⌂ SA62 5QL – Northeast : 5 mi on B 4329 – 𝒞 (01437) 731 531 – www.thepaddockwales.co.uk

HAWARDEN PENARLÂG

Flintshire – Pop. 1 858 – Regional map n° **19**-C1
▶ London 205 mi – Chester 9 mi – Liverpool 17 mi – Shrewsbury 45 mi

🍴 Glynne Arms   🏠 & ⇔ 🅿

MODERN CUISINE · PUB 200 year old coaching inn opposite Hawarden Castle owned by the descendants of PM William Gladstone. Choose between bar snacks, steaks from the estate or classically inspired dishes with a modern twist. Desserts are a highlight.

Carte £ 18/38

3 Glynne Way ⌂ CH3 3NS – 𝒞 (01244) 569 988 – www.theglynnearms.co.uk

HOWEY – Powys ➡ See Llandrindod Wells

KNIGHTON TREFYCLAWDD
Powys – Pop. 2 851 – Regional map n° **19**-C3

▶ London 162 mi – Birmingham 59 mi – Hereford 31 mi – Shrewsbury 35 mi

🏠 **Milebrook House**

TRADITIONAL · PERSONALISED Part-Georgian dower house surrounded by superb formal gardens filled with exotic plants; located in the Teme Valley and once home to explorer Wilfred Thesiger. Well-appointed lounges and spacious, comfortable bedrooms furnished in a country house style. Traditional restaurant showcases kitchen garden produce.

10 rooms ⌂ – †£ 87/93 ††£ 147

Ludlow Rd, Milebrook ✉ LD7 1LT – East : 2 mi on A 4113 – ✆ (01547) 528 632 – www.milebrookhouse.co.uk – Closed November-February, Sunday and Monday

LLANARMON DYFFRYN CEIRIOG
Wrexham – ✉ Llangollen (denbighshire) – Regional map n° **19**-C2

▶ London 196 mi – Chester 33 mi – Shrewsbury 32 mi

🏚 **Hand at Llanarmon**

TRADITIONAL CUISINE · INN Rustic, personally run inn with stone walls, open fires and ancient beams, which provides a warm welcome and wholesome meals to those travelling through the lush Ceiriog Valley. Generous portions of fresh, flavoursome cooking. Cosy bedrooms offer hill views and modern bathrooms; most have a roll-top bath.

Menu £ 18 (weekday lunch) – Carte £ 23/43

13 rooms ⌂ – †£ 50/74 ††£ 90/130

✉ LL20 7LD – ✆ (01691) 600 666 – www.thehandhotel.co.uk – Closed 25 December

LLANDDERFEL
Gwynedd – Pop. 4 500 – Regional map n° **19**-C2

▶ London 210 mi – Cardiff 157 mi – Birmingham 97 mi – Liverpool 72 mi

🏰 **Palé Hall**

HISTORIC · PERSONALISED Impressive Victorian house with lovely marquetry, fine oil paintings and a Scottish hunting lodge feel. Beautiful wood-panelled hall and traditional lounges; bedrooms boast period fireplaces and antique furniture. Classical menu in the elegant dining room. They even produce their own hydro-electricity here!

16 rooms ⌂ – †£ 90/155 ††£ 125/210 – 2 suites

Palé Estate ✉ LL23 7PS – ✆ (01678) 530 285 – www.palehall.co.uk – Closed January-mid February

LLANDDEWI SKIRRID – Monmouthshire ➡ See Abergavenny

LLANDEILO
Carmarthenshire – Pop. 1 731 – Regional map n° **19**-B3

▶ London 218 mi – Brecon 34 mi – Carmarthen 15 mi – Swansea 25 mi

🏠 **Plough Inn**

TRADITIONAL · PERSONALISED Powder blue inn with a contemporary interior and pleasant country views. Stylish, wood-furnished bedrooms feature good modern facilities; the best come with balconies and whirlpool baths. Small bar and gym. Various different rooms are used for informal lunches and more substantial dinners.

23 rooms ⌂ – †£ 75/100 ††£ 95/120

Rhosmaen ✉ SA19 6NP – Northeast : 1 mi on A 40 – ✆ (01558) 823 431 – www.ploughrhosmaen.com – Closed 26 December

LLANDOVERY

Carmarthenshire – Pop. 2 065 – Regional map n° **19**-B3

▶ London 207 mi – Cardiff 61 mi – Swansea 37 mi – Merthyr Tydfil 34 mi

⌂ **New White Lion** 🛜 ♿ 🎾 🅿

TOWNHOUSE · DESIGN Laid-back, Grade II listed former pub, in a small town – now a stylish hotel. Comfortable lounge with an honesty bar. Smart, individually designed bedrooms are named after folklore characters and boast contemporary fabrics and furnishings. Cosy designer restaurant, where menus feature seasonal local produce.

6 rooms 🖵 – †£ 120/160 ††£ 130/180

43 Stone St ⊠ SA20 0BZ – ℰ (01550) 720 685 – www.newwhitelion.com
– Closed 25-27 December

LLANDRILLO

Denbighshire – ⊠ Corwen – Pop. 1 048 – Regional map n° **19**-C2

▶ London 210 mi – Chester 40 mi – Dolgellau 26 mi – Shrewsbury 46 mi

✗✗ **Tyddyn Llan** (Bryan Webb) 🍴 ⇦ 🐌 🖴 🅿

❀ **CLASSIC CUISINE · ELEGANT** Attractive former shooting lodge in a pleasant valley location, surrounded by lovely gardens and run by a husband and wife team. Spacious country house lounges and a blue-hued, two-roomed restaurant. Hearty, satisfying cooking is based around the classics; tasting menus show the kitchen's talent to the full. Smart, elegant bedrooms offer a good level of facilities.

→ Grilled red mullet with aubergine purée, chilli and garlic oil. Cefnllan Farm duck breast, confit potato, duck faggot, cider and apples. Whinberry crème brûlée.

Menu £ 30/57 – Carte lunch £ 45/57

13 rooms 🖵 – †£ 130/160 ††£ 180/320

⊠ LL21 0ST – ℰ (01490) 440 264 (booking essential)
– www.tyddynllan.co.uk – dinner only and lunch Friday-Sunday
– Closed last 2 weeks January

LLANDRINDOD WELLS

Powys – Pop. 5 309 – Regional map n° **19**-C3

▶ London 204 mi – Brecon 29 mi – Carmarthen 60 mi – Shrewsbury 58 mi

🏨 **Metropole** 🛜 ⇦ 🖥 🎷 🖸 ♿ 🧖 🅿

BUSINESS · CLASSIC Large green hotel run for many years by the Baird-Murray family; popular with both leisure and business guests courtesy of its many lounges, conference rooms and leisure facilities. Spacious bedrooms offer good amenities; the tower rooms are popular. Smart brasserie with extensive classical menus; bright fine dining restaurant showcases local produce.

110 rooms 🖵 – †£ 75/105 ††£ 85/150 – 10 suites

Temple St ⊠ LD1 5DY – ℰ (01597) 823 700
– www.metropole.co.uk

at Crossgates Northeast: 3.5 mi on A483⊠ Llandrindod Wells

🏠 **Guidfa House** ⇦ 🎾 🅿

TRADITIONAL · COSY Georgian gentleman's residence with a pleasant garden, a smart breakfast room and a period lounge featuring an original cast iron ceiling rose. Bright, airy bedrooms; the best is in the coach house. Friendly owners serve tea on arrival.

6 rooms 🖵 – †£ 75/105 ††£ 95/125

⊠ LD1 6RF – ℰ (01597) 851 241 – www.guidfahouse.co.uk

at Howey South: 1.5 mi by A483 ⊠ Llandrindod Wells

Acorn Court

FAMILY · PERSONALISED Chalet-style house set in 40 acres, with views over rolling countryside towards a river and lake. Welcoming owner and a real family feel. Spacious, well-kept bedrooms come with good extras. Try the Welsh whisky porridge for breakfast.

3 rooms ⊊ – †£ 55/80 ††£ 78/90

Chapel Rd ⊠ LD1 5PB – Northeast : 0.5 mi
– ✆ (01597) 823 543 – www.acorncourt.co.uk
– Closed 23-31 December

LLANDUDNO

Conwy – Pop. 15 371 – Regional map n° **19**-B1

▶ London 243 mi – Birkenhead 55 mi – Chester 47 mi – Holyhead 43 mi

Bodysgallen Hall

LUXURY · HISTORIC Stunning, National Trust owned country house with a 13C tower, 200 acres of delightful gardens and parkland, and a superb outlook to the mountains beyond. Welcoming, open-fired hall and characterful wood-panelled lounge. Antique-furnished bedrooms: some set in cottages and some affording splendid Snowdon views.

31 rooms ⊊ – †£ 159/375 ††£ 179/425 – 21 suites

Royal Welsh Way ⊠ LL30 1RS – Southeast : 2 mi on A 470
– ✆ (01492) 584 466 – www.bodysgallen.com
Dining Room – See restaurant listing

 Empire

FAMILY · PERSONALISED Family-run hotel – a former Victorian shopping arcade – with a grand columned façade; its interior hung with chandeliers and Russell Flint prints. Smartly dressed bedrooms with sleek, modern bathrooms; rooms at No. 72 are the most spacious. Stoutly traditional set price menu served in elegant Watkins & Co.

58 rooms ⊊ – †£ 65/135 ††£ 110/150 – 1 suite

Town plan: A-e – *73 Church Walks ⊠ LL30 2HE*
– ✆ (01492) 860 555 – www.empirehotel.co.uk
– Closed 20-31 December

Osborne House

LUXURY · PERSONALISED Victoriana reigns in this smart townhouse overlooking the bay. Bedrooms are spacious open-plan suites with canopied beds and lounges; chandeliers cast a romantic glow and marble bathrooms come with double-ended roll-top baths. Breakfast is served in your room. The opulent restaurant serves a wide-ranging menu.

7 rooms ⊊ – †£ 125/185 ††£ 125/185

Town plan: A-c – *17 North Par ⊠ LL30 2LP – ✆ (01492) 860 330*
– www.osbornehouse.co.uk – Closed 18-31 December

St Tudno

TOWNHOUSE · CLASSIC Long-standing hotel opposite the old Victorian pier; Alice Liddell, who was immortalised in Alice in Wonderland, stayed here in 1861. The classic bar and lounge afford bay views. Bedrooms are traditional – some have whirlpool baths.

18 rooms ⊊ – †£ 70/90 ††£ 85/120 – 1 suite

Town plan: A-c – *North Par ⊠ LL30 2LP*
– ✆ (01492) 874 411 – www.st-tudno.co.uk
Terrace – See restaurant listing

LLANDUDNO

⌂ **Escape Boutique B&B**   ⟨ ⇔ ⅏ P

TOWNHOUSE · DESIGN Attractive Arts and Crafts house with stained glass windows, parquet floors and a chic, modern interior that sets it apart. Stylish lounge and spacious, contemporary bedrooms; those on the top floor have a stunning view of the bay.

9 rooms ⌷ – ♦£ 80/134 ♦♦£ 95/149

Town plan: A-n – 48 Church Walks ⌂ LL30 2HL – ℰ (01492) 877 776
– www.escapebandb.co.uk – Closed 1 week Christmas

⌂ **Space Boutique B&B**   ⌘ ⅏ P

TOWNHOUSE · STYLISH Three-storey Victorian house in a quiet residential area with a lovely lounge-style drinks terrace out the front. Contemporary bedrooms are named after Indian elements and feature striking headboards and brightly coloured fabrics. The funky restaurant offers traditional Punjabi dishes with a Kenyan twist.

10 rooms ⌷ – ♦£ 72/95 ♦♦£ 85/115

Town plan: A-s – 36 Church Walks ⌂ LL30 2HN – ℰ (01492) 818 198
– www.spaceboutique.co.uk – Closed 22 December-mid January and 1 week May-June

WALES

Abbey Lodge

TOWNHOUSE · PERSONALISED Welcoming terraced property – built in the early 1850s as a gentleman's residence and retaining its Victorian style. Individually decorated bedrooms with modern touches; all have baths. Cosy lounge and communal breakfasts from an extensive menu. Pleasant rear garden boasts views up to the Great Orme.

4 rooms – ♥£ 50 ♥♥£ 75/80

Town plan: A-x – *14 Abbey Rd* ⊠ *LL30 2EA* – ℰ *(01492) 878 042*
– *www.abbeylodgeuk.com* – *Closed November-March*

Sefton Court

TOWNHOUSE · MODERN Substantial Victorian house in an elevated position, affording good town views. Original features include pretty stained glass windows and interesting friezes. Contemporary bedrooms provide a pleasant contrast with their stylish wallpapers.

10 rooms ⊠ – ♥£ 50/70 ♥♥£ 74/80

Town plan: A-n – *49 Church Walks* ⊠ *LL30 2HL* – ℰ *(01492) 875 235*
– *www.seftoncourt-hotel.co.uk* – *Closed November-Easter*

XxX Dining Room

MODERN CUISINE · FORMAL Located within a beautiful country house which part-dates from the 13C, and overlooking its delightful gardens, is this grand, formal dining room with clothed tables and an inglenook fireplace. Well-judged, modern interpretations of classically based dishes; simpler offerings at lunch. Smart dress required.

Menu £ 25 (weekday lunch)/49

Bodysgallen Hall Hotel, Royal Welsh Way ⊠ *LL30 1RS* – *Southeast : 2 mi on A 470* – ℰ *(01492) 584 466 (booking essential)* – *www.bodysgallen.com* – *Closed Monday lunch November-April*

XX Terrace

MODERN CUISINE · INTIMATE A uniquely styled restaurant within a classical seaside hotel; murals of Lake Como run the length of the walls and the chandeliers are adorned with flowers. Menus offer a good range of traditionally based dishes with a modern edge.

Menu £ 12/20 – Carte £ 31/43 **s**

Town plan: A-c – *St Tudno Hotel, North Par* ⊠ *LL30 2LP* – ℰ *(01492) 874 411* – *www.st-tudno.co.uk*

at Deganwy South: 2.75 mi on A546 – Plan: A – ⊠ Llandudno

Quay H. & Spa

BUSINESS · MODERN Smart hotel in a modern marina development by the Conwy Estuary. Large guest areas have superb harbour and castle outlooks and there's an excellent spa; contemporary bedrooms include penthouses with balconies. The designer restaurant comes with a cosy bar, a large glass wine cave and a superb terrace.

74 rooms ⊠ – ♥£ 95/285 ♥♥£ 95/285 – 19 suites

Deganwy Quay ⊠ *LL31 9DJ* – ℰ *(01492) 564 100* – *www.quayhotel.co.uk*

LLANDYBIE

Carmarthenshire – Pop. 2 813 – Regional map n° **19**-B4

▶ London 204 mi – Birmingham 122 mi – Bristol 97 mi – Leicester 192 mi

XX Valans

INTERNATIONAL · FRIENDLY Simple little restaurant run by a local and his wife, with a bright red, white and black colour scheme. Fresh, unfussy dishes rely on local produce and offer classical flavour combinations. Good value light lunches; more elaborate dinners.

Menu £ 13 (weekdays)/23 – Carte £ 28/38

Primrose House, 29 High St ⊠ *SA18 3HX* – ℰ *(01269) 851 288 (booking advisable)* – *www.valans.co.uk* – *Closed 26 December-4 January, Sunday and Monday*

LLANDYRNOG

Denbighshire – Regional map n° **19**-C1

▶ London 211 mi – Cardiff 158 mi – Birmingham 98 mi – Liverpool 34 mi

🏠 Pentre Mawr   🏖 🦢 ⪜ 🛋 🍸 🍽 🅿

HISTORIC · CLASSIC Unusual guesthouse on a 200 acre estate, featuring characterful antique-filled guest areas and a modern conservatory. Bedrooms in the Georgian house are classical, those in the outbuildings are contemporary and there's also 6 luxurious African lodges with hot tubs. Traditional dinners are served Fri and Sat.

12 rooms 🖵 – 🛉£ 165/200 🛉🛉£ 165/200

✉ LL16 4LA – *North : 1.25 mi by B 5429 taking left hand fork after 0.75 mi* – ✆ *(01824) 790 732* – *www.pentremawrcountryhouse.co.uk* – *Closed Christmas, Monday and Tuesday*

LLANELLI

Carmarthenshire – Pop. 43 878 – Regional map n° **19**-B4

▶ London 202 mi – Cardiff 54 mi – Swansea 12 mi

XX Sosban   🍴 🖤 🅿

MODERN CUISINE · INDIVIDUAL Built in 1872 to house a pumping engine for the adjacent docks. Impressively restored interior with a relaxed lounge-bar and airy dining room with exposed stone walls. Large à la carte offers tasty, well-prepared dishes; good value lunches.

Menu £ 16 – Carte £ 22/44

The Pump House, North Dock ✉ SA15 2LF – ✆ *(01554) 270 020* – *www.sosbanrestaurant.com* – *Closed 25 December, 1 January and Sunday dinner*

LLANELLTYD – Gwynedd → See Dolgellau

LLANERCHYMEDD → See Anglesey (Isle of)

LLANFAIRFECHAN

Conwy – ✉ Conwy – Pop. 3 637 – Regional map n° **19**-B1

▶ London 247 mi – Cardiff 200 mi – Swansea 166 mi – Telford 107 mi

🏠 Grove   🛋 🖤 🅿 🛏

TRADITIONAL · COSY Originally built for an Edwardian cockle merchant, this house has been tastefully modernised, retaining its period features and showcasing the owners' collection of books, antiques and Welsh porcelain. Cosy bedrooms are named after rivers.

3 rooms 🖵 – 🛉£ 70/90 🛉🛉£ 70/90

Ffordd Aber ✉ LL33 OHR – *West : 0.75 m on Bangor rd* – ✆ *(01248) 369 111* – *www.thegrovenorthwales.co.uk*

LLAN FFESTINIOG

Gwynedd – Regional map n° **19**-B2

▶ London 234 mi – Bangor 35 mi – Wrexham 52 mi

🏠 Cae'r Blaidd Country House   🏖 🦢 ⪜ 🛋 🖤 🅿

TRADITIONAL · PERSONALISED It's all about mountain pursuits at this alpine-themed guesthouse: the welcoming owners are mountain guides; ice axes, crampons and skis fill the walls; and there's a climbing wall, a drying room and even equipment for hire in the basement. Dine on local produce while taking in the stunning panoramic view.

3 rooms 🖵 – 🛉£ 55 🛉🛉£ 90

✉ LL41 4PH – *North : 0.75 mi by A 470 on Blaenau Rd* – ✆ *(01766) 762 765* – *www.caerblaidd.com* – *Closed January*

LLANFIHANGEL – Powys → See Llanfyllin

LLANFIHANGEL-Y-CREUDDYN
Ceredigion – Regional map n° **19**-B3

London 235 mi – Cardiff 109 mi – Birmingham 121 mi – Liverpool 123 mi

🍴 Y Ffarmers
REGIONAL · RUSTIC Life in this remote, picturesque valley revolves around the passionately run village pub. Sit in the locals bar or the homely restaurant which opens onto the garden. Regional and valley produce features in satisfying, original dishes.

Menu £15 (weekday lunch) – Carte £20/32
✉ SY23 4LA – ☎ (01974) 261 275 – www.yffarmers.co.uk
– Closed first week January and Sunday dinner-Tuesday lunch

LLANFYLLIN
Powys – Pop. 1 105 – Regional map n° **19**-C2

London 188 mi – Chester 42 mi – Shrewsbury 24 mi – Welshpool 11 mi

🍴 Seeds
REGIONAL · RUSTIC Converted 16C red-brick cottages in a sleepy village; run with pride by a friendly husband and wife team. Cosy, pine-furnished room with an old range and a country kitchen feel. Unfussy, classical dishes and comforting homemade desserts.

Menu £24 (weekday dinner) – Carte lunch £21/33
5 Penybryn Cottages, High St ✉ SY22 5AP – ☎ (01691) 648 604
– Closed Wednesday in winter and Sunday-Tuesday

at Llanfihangel Southwest: 5 mi by A490 and B4393 on B4382 – ✉ Llanfyllin

🏠 Cyfie Farm
TRADITIONAL · PERSONALISED 17C longhouse and barn conversions, set in a great spot and boasting far-reaching views across the valley. Mix of bedrooms and self-catering cottages; some with beams and wood-burning stoves. Spacious lounges and communal dining, with porridge cooked overnight on the Aga and Cordon Bleu dinners.

3 rooms ⌑ – ♦£80/100 ♦♦£110/140
✉ SY22 5JE – South : 1.5 mi by B 4382 – ☎ (01691) 648 451 – www.cyfiefarm.co.uk
– Closed November-February

LLANGAFFO → See Anglesey (Isle of)

LLANGAMMARCH WELLS
Powys – Regional map n° **19**-B3

London 200 mi – Brecon 17 mi – Builth Wells 8 mi – Cardiff 58 mi

🏠 Lake Country House and Spa

TRADITIONAL · PERSONALISED Extended, part-timbered 19C country house in 50 acres of mature gardens and parkland, with a pond, a lake and a river. Comfortable lounges and well-appointed bedrooms with antiques and extras; some are set in the lodge. The impressive spa overlooks the river. Breakfast is in the orangery; the elegant restaurant is perfect for a classical, candlelit dinner.

32 rooms ⌑ – ♦£145/210 ♦♦£195/260 – 8 suites
✉ LD4 4BS – East : 0.75 mi – ☎ (01591) 620 202
– www.lakecountryhouse.co.uk

LLANGENNITH

Swansea – Regional map n° **19**-B4

▶ London 207 mi – Cardiff 61 mi – Swansea 17 mi – Newport 71 mi

🏠 Blas Gŵyr   ✿ ❀ P

FAMILY · PERSONALISED Converted farm buildings on the Gower Peninsula. Smart, well-equipped bedrooms are set around a courtyard and feature local fabrics and slate bathrooms with underfloor heating. The small stone-walled coffee shop cum dining room serves simple, often Tuscan-based dinners; cockles are popular at breakfast.

4 rooms ⌑ – †£ 100/115 ††£ 115/125

✉ SA3 1HU – ℰ (01792) 386 472 – www.blasgwyr.co.ok

LLANGOLLEN

Denbighshire – Pop. 3 466 – Regional map n° **32**-C2

▶ London 194 mi – Chester 23 mi – Holyhead 76 mi – Shrewsbury 30 mi

🏠 Geufron Hall ⓝ   ⮕ ⟨ ⮑ ❀ P

FAMILY · HOMELY A homely, welcoming house in a great location, with impressive views of the Vale of Llangollen. Bedrooms feature retro furnishings; Eglwseg with its private terrace is the best. Enjoy local produce at breakfast.

4 rooms ⌑ – †£ 50/75 ††£ 100/130

✉ LL20 8DY – North : 1 mi by A 539 and Wharf Hill off Dinbren Rd – ℰ (01978) 860 676 – www.geufronhall.co.uk – Closed 24-25 December

LLANGRANNOG

Ceredigion – Regional map n° **19**-B3

▶ London 241 mi – Cardiff 96 mi – Aberyswyth 30 mi – Carmarthen 28 mi

🏠 Grange   ⮕ ⮑ P ⮐

COUNTRY HOUSE · PERSONALISED Traditional Georgian manor house with a pretty breakfast room and individually decorated bedrooms which feature brass beds and cast iron slipper baths. On arrival, the hospitable owner welcomes you with a pot of tea beside the fire.

4 rooms ⌑ – †£ 40/50 ††£ 80/90

Pentregat ✉ SA44 6HW – Southeast : 3 mi by B 4321 on A 487 – ℰ (01239) 654 121 – www.grangecountryhouse.co.uk – Restricted opening in winter

LLANLLAWDDOG – Carmarthenshire ➜ See Carmarthen

LLANRHIDIAN

Swansea – Pop. 512 – Regional map n° **19**-B4

▶ London 198 mi – Cardiff 56 mi – Aberystwyth 83 mi

✕✕✕ Fairyhill   ❀ ⮌ ⮕ ⮑ ⌂ P

BRITISH MODERN · ELEGANT Attractive Georgian country house with a lake and well-manicured gardens; take it all in from the red and gold dining room or from the terrace. Modern menus rely on seasonal Gower produce. Spacious bedrooms blend the traditional and the contemporary and come with good facilities. Charming guest areas include a cosy bar and a contemporary lounge with a piano.

Menu £ 20 (weekday lunch)/45

8 rooms ⌑ – †£ 180/280 ††£ 200/300

Reynoldston ✉ SA3 1BS – West : 2.5 mi by Llangennith Rd – ℰ (01792) 390 139 – www.fairyhill.net – Closed 3 weeks January, 25-26 December, Monday and Tuesday in winter

LLANRUG – Gwynedd ➜ See Caernarfon

LLANRWST

Conwy – Pop. 3 323 – Regional map n° **19**-B1

▶ London 229 mi – Holyhead 51 mi – Chester 54 mi

🏠 Ffin y Parc Country House & Gallery

HISTORIC · PERSONALISED This Victorian slate house is an impressive art gallery, a comfy café and a likeable guesthouse all in one. The elegant, well-proportioned interior mixes the classic and the contemporary and has a slightly bohemian feel; bedrooms are bold and bathrooms are modern. Dinner is served on Fridays and Saturdays.

6 rooms 🖵 – ♥£ 130/195 ♥♥£ 145/210

Betwys Rd ✉ *LL26 0PT – South : 1.75 mi on A 470 –* ℰ *(01492) 642 070*
– www.ffinyparc.com – Closed January

LLANWRDA

Carmarthenshire – Pop. 287 – Regional map n° **19**-B3

▶ London 199 mi – Cardiff 65 mi – Swansea 33 mi – Newport 64 mi

🏠 Tŷ Llwyd Hir

FAMILY · PERSONALISED Follow the long track past the old farm buildings to reach this lovely slate guesthouse on the hillside, which overlooks the Black Mountains in the Brecon Beacons National Park. Smart, modern rooms mix the old and the new. The friendly owners keep three donkeys and the brood of hens supply the breakfast eggs.

3 rooms 🖵 – ♥£ 65 ♥♥£ 80/90

✉ *SA19 8AS – North : 2 mi by A 482 turning right at caravan park*
– ℰ *(01550) 777 362 – www.bandbwestwales.co.uk*
– Closed 22-26 December

LLANWRTYD WELLS

Powys – Pop. 630 – Regional map n° **19**-B3

▶ London 214 mi – Brecon 32 mi – Cardiff 68 mi – Carmarthen 39 mi

✕✕ Carlton Riverside

BRITISH TRADITIONAL · COSY Traditional stone building in the centre of the village, with two comfy lounges and a small bar filled with books and modern art. Well-spaced tables in the dining room, which overlooks the River Irfon. Concise menu utilises local produce; classic dishes have a modern touch. Neat, tidy, well-priced bedrooms.

Carte £ 28/42

4 rooms 🖵 – ♥£ 50 ♥♥£ 70/90

Irfon Cres ✉ *LD5 4SP –* ℰ *(01591) 610 248 – www.carltonriverside.com – dinner only – Closed 23-30 December, Sunday and Monday*

LLECHRYD

Ceredigion – Pop. 875 – Regional map n° **19**-A3

▶ London 238 mi – Cardiff 93 mi – Swansea 53 mi – Newport 102 mi

🏠 Hammet House

COUNTRY HOUSE · DESIGN Attractive Georgian house built for a former Sheriff of London, Sir Benjamin Hammet. It has contemporary monochrome styling, quirky furnishings and a relaxed, bohemian feel. Bedrooms boast locally hand-made beds, good facilities and views over the grounds. The smart restaurant offers appealing modern menus.

15 rooms 🖵 – ♥£ 95/200 ♥♥£ 120/220

✉ *SA43 2QA –* ℰ *(01239) 682 382 – www.hammethouse.co.uk*

LLYSWEN

Powys – ⊠ Brecon – Regional map n° **19**-C3

▶ London 188 mi – Brecon 8 mi – Cardiff 48 mi – Worcester 53 mi

🏤 Llangoed Hall   ☆ ॐ ≼ 🖙 ⬎ ※ ⚒ 🄿

HISTORIC · PERSONALISED Homely country house beside the River Wye, redesigned by Sir Clough Williams-Ellis in 1910 and restored by the late Sir Bernard Ashley. Delightful sitting rooms and sumptuous bedrooms feature rich fabrics, mullioned windows and antiques; the impressive art collection includes pieces by Whistler. Ambitious modern cooking is led by what's fresh in the kitchen garden.

23 rooms ⌂ – †£ 99/350 ††£ 125/500

⊠ LD3 0YP – Northwest : 1.25 mi on A 470 – ℰ (01874) 754 525
– www.llangoedhall.com

MACHYNLLETH

Powys – Pop. 2 235 – Regional map n° **19**-B2

▶ London 220 mi – Shrewsbury 56 mi – Welshpool 37 mi

🏤 Ynyshir Hall   ☆ ॐ ≼ 🖙 🄿

COUNTRY HOUSE · PERSONALISED Beautiful part-Georgian house set within a 1,000 acre RSPB reserve and run with pride and passion. Comfy lounges are decorated with the owner's eye-catching art. Sumptuous bedrooms have a chic, contemporary style yet retain their country house feel; the two most luxurious suites are situated in the grounds.

10 rooms ⌂ – †£ 215/950 ††£ 215/950 – 3 suites

Eglwysfach ⊠ SY20 8TA – Southwest : 6 mi on A 487 – ℰ (01654) 781 209
– www.ynyshirhall.co.uk – Closed first 2 weeks January

🕸 **Ynyshir Hall** – See restaurant listing

XXX Ynyshir Hall   ≼ 🖙 🄿

🕸 **CREATIVE · INTIMATE** Set within a plush hotel, an opulent restaurant with azure blue walls, striking artwork and a summery vibe. The talented chef uses superb local and foraged ingredients to create original dishes with wonderfully balanced flavours; some are finished at the table, which adds a sense of theatre.

→ Mackerel with pork belly, oyster and seaweed. Fallow deer, black bean and wild garlic. Rhubarb pudding with marjoram.

Menu £ 35/90

Ynyshir Hall Hotel, Eglwysfach ⊠ SY20 8TA – Southwest: 6 mi on A 487
– ℰ (01654) 781 209 (booking essential) – www.ynyshirhall.co.uk – Closed first
2 weeks January

MENAI BRIDGE → See Anglesey (Isle of)

MOLD YR WYDDGRUG

Flintshire – Pop. 10 058 – Regional map n° **19**-C1

▶ London 211 mi – Chester 12 mi – Liverpool 22 mi – Shrewsbury 45 mi

🍺 Tavern   🖙 🛦 🄿

CLASSIC CUISINE · PUB Modern-looking pub with leather chairs and a formal feel; in contrast, the cooking is hearty and comforting. Blackboard specials, particularly the market fish, prove popular. Regular themed gourmet dinners best show the chef's talent.

Carte £ 21/40

Mold Rd, Alltami ⊠ CH7 6LG – Northeast : 2.5 mi by A 5119 on A 494 – ℰ (01244)
550 485 – www.tavernrestaurant.co.uk – Closed 26 December and Monday

MONMOUTH TREFYNWY

Monmouthshire – Pop. 10 110 – Regional map n° **19**-C4

▶ London 135 mi – Abergavenny 19 mi – Cardiff 40 mi

X Stonemill

REGIONAL · RUSTIC Attractive 16C cider mill with exposed timbers and an old millstone at the centre of the characterful, rustic restaurant. Good value set menus are supplemented by a more ambitious evening à la carte. Dishes are hearty and classically based.

Menu £15 (weekday lunch)/22 – Carte £30/43

Rockfield ⊠ NP25 5SW – Northwest : 3.5 mi on B 4233 – ℰ (01600) 716 273 – www.thestonemill.co.uk – Closed 2 weeks January, 25-26 December, Sunday dinner and Monday

at Penallt South: 5 mi by B4293

⊙ The Inn at Penallt

BRITISH TRADITIONAL · INN Proudly and personally run pub. Its neutrally hued rooms are furnished with heavy wood; for the best views, make for the conservatory. Menus offer good-sized dishes with classical roots. Bread is baked daily and the ice creams are homemade. Bedrooms are cosy, neat and tidy with modern facilities.

Menu £17 (weekday lunch) – Carte £27/40

4 rooms ⊇ – †£55/65 ††£85

⊠ NP25 4SE – ℰ (01600) 772 765 – www.theinnatpenallt.co.uk – Closed 5-22 January, Sunday dinner and Monday except bank holidays

at Whitebrook South: 8.25 mi by A466 – ⊠ Monmouth

XX The Whitebrook

❀ **BRITISH MODERN · FRIENDLY** Both the bedrooms and the cooking are modern and understated at this rustic house, where the atmosphere is intimate, relaxed and friendly. Menus showcase top quality local and foraged ingredients; descriptions are concise and the elegantly presented dishes are more complex than they first appear. You'll find this whitewashed property off the beaten track, in a wooded valley.

➔ Wye Valley asparagus, hogweed, pine and Tintern mead. Huntsham Farm suckling pig, celeriac, pear and sorrel. Black cherries with cherry stone ice cream and hazelnuts.

Menu £29/67

8 rooms ⊇ – †£105/165 ††£130/190

⊠ NP25 4TX – ℰ (01600) 860 254 (booking essential) – www.thewhitebrook.co.uk – Closed first 2 weeks January and Monday

MONTGOMERY TREFALDWYN

Powys – Pop. 986 – Regional map n° **19**-C2

▣ London 194 mi – Birmingham 71 mi – Chester 53 mi – Shrewsbury 30 mi

XX The Checkers (Stéphane Borie)

❀ **CLASSIC CUISINE · FRIENDLY** Charming 18C coaching inn on the main square of a hilltop town, run by an enthusiastic Frenchman and his family. It has a characterful beamed lounge and a stylish two-roomed restaurant. Seasonal menus offer a mix of modern and classical French dishes that are executed with a deft touch, and flavours are sharply defined. Elegant bedrooms are furnished with antiques.

➔ Homemade boudin noir with pommes mousseline and Madeira jus. Roast fillet of monkfish, Cornish crab tortellini and bouillabaisse. Rhubarb crumble soufflé with vanilla ice cream.

Menu £75 – Carte £34/56 **s**

5 rooms ⊇ – †£115/150 ††£135/180

Broad St ⊠ SY15 6PN – ℰ (01686) 669 822 – www.thecheckersmontgomery.co.uk – dinner only and lunch Friday-Saturday – Closed 2 weeks January, 1 week late summer, 25-26 December, Sunday and Monday

MUMBLES (The) - Swansea ➔ See Swansea

NANTGAREDIG - Carmarthenshire ➔ See Carmarthen

NARBERTH
Pembrokeshire – Pop. 2 265 – Regional map n° **19**-A4
▶ London 234 mi – Cardiff 88 mi – Swansea 51 mi – Rhondda 79 mi

Grove
HISTORIC · STYLISH Set in 35 acres, in a charming rural location, the Grove comprises a 15C longhouse and an immaculately whitewashed property with Stuart and Victorian additions. Bedrooms blend boldly coloured walls and bright fabrics with more traditional furnishings – and spacious bathrooms boast underfloor heating and deep cast iron baths. Seasonal modern menus use garden produce.
24 rooms ☑ – †£ 180/340 ††£ 190/340 – 6 suites
Molleston ✉ SA67 8BX – South : 2 mi by A 478 on Herons Brook rd – ℰ (01834) 860 915 – www.thegrove-narberth.co.uk

Canaston Oaks
FAMILY · PERSONALISED Converted longhouse and outbuildings in 35 acres of gardens and grasslands leading down to the river. Set around a courtyard water feature, the wood-furnished bedrooms boast fridges and DVD players; some have jacuzzis, others, patios.
10 rooms ☑ – †£ 90/150 ††£ 100/170
Canaston Bridge ✉ SA67 8DE – West : 3 mi by B 4314 and A 40 on A 4075 – ℰ (01437) 541 254 – www.canastonoaks.co.uk

NEWCASTLE EMLYN
Carmarthenshire – Pop. 1 883 – Regional map n° **19**-B3
▶ London 232 mi – Birmingham 156 mi – Bristol 121 mi – Leicester 189 mi

Gwesty'r Emlyn
INN · CONTEMPORARY 300 year old coaching inn set in the centre of town and concealing a surprisingly modern interior. Guest areas include a stylish lounge, a snug bar, a small fitness room and a sauna; bedrooms are contemporary and well-equipped. The smart restaurant offers a classic menu centred around local produce.
29 rooms ☑ – †£ 80/95 ††£ 120/160 – 2 suites
Bridge St ✉ SA38 9DU – ℰ (01239) 710 317 – www.gwestyremlynhotel.co.uk

NEWPORT
Newport – Pop. 128 060 – Regional map n° **19**-C4
▶ London 145 mi – Bristol 31 mi – Cardiff 12 mi – Gloucester 48 mi

Celtic Manor Resort
BUSINESS · PERSONALISED Vast resort hotel in 1,400 acres, boasting 3 golf courses, an impressive pool and spa, two floors of function rooms and even a shopping arcade. Mix of classical and modern bedrooms, which range from standard to presidential suites. Modern fine dining in Terry M; grills in Rafters, in the clubhouse; buffet and carvery in Olive Tree; and a French bistro menu in Le Patio.
409 rooms ☑ – †£ 116/207 ††£ 195/244 – 19 suites
Coldra Woods ✉ NP18 1HQ – East : 3 mi on A 48 – ℰ (01633) 413 000 – www.celtic-manor.com
Terry M – See restaurant listing

XxX **Terry M**

BRITISH MODERN · **FORMAL** Named after the owner of the huge hotel in which it's set. Comfy lounge for aperitifs and canapés; bright, contemporary dining room with well-spaced tables and cream leather chairs. Menus are modern and ambitious, and service is formal.

Menu £ 30/50 **s**

Celtic Manor Resort Hotel, Coldra Woods ⊠ NP18 1HQ – East : 3 mi on A 48 – ℰ (01633) 413 000 – www.celtic-manor.com – Closed Monday, Tuesday and lunch Wednesday-Thursday

NEWPORT TREFDRAETH
Pembrokeshire – Pop. 1 162 – Regional map n° **19**-A3
▶ London 258 mi – Fishguard 7 mi

⌂ **Cnapan**

TOWNHOUSE · **FUNCTIONAL** Keenly run, part-Georgian house in a busy coastal village. The bar and lounge have a homely feel. Well-maintained, compact bedrooms have a clean, modern style and smart shower rooms; a shared bath is available. The candlelit restaurant opens onto a large garden and offers an extensive menu of home cooking.

5 rooms 😋 – ♦£ 65 ♦♦£ 95

East St ⊠ SA42 0SY – on A 487 – ℰ (01239) 820 575 – www.cnapan.co.uk – Closed January-mid-March and 25-26 December

XX **Llys Meddyg** ⇔ 🛏 🅿

MODERN CUISINE · **RUSTIC** Centrally located restaurant with a kitchen garden and a slightly bohemian style. Eat in the formal dining room or the characterful, laid-back cellar bar; the owner's father's art is displayed throughout. Cooking showcases local produce in ambitious, complex dishes. Modern bedrooms have a Scandinavian style.

Carte £ 27/40

8 rooms 😋 – ♦£ 75/120 ♦♦£ 120/160

East St ⊠ SA42 0SY – ℰ (01239) 820 008 – www.llysmeddyg.com – dinner only – Closed Monday and Tuesday

at Dinas Cross West: 3.25 mi on A487

🏠 **Y Garth** 🅿

FAMILY · **STYLISH** Welcoming pink-washed guesthouse in a small village. Comfy lounge with a conservatory extension where homemade cakes are served on arrival. Stylish bedrooms have bright, bold décor; 'Strumble Head' has views to the peninsula.

3 rooms 😋 – ♦£ 70/99 ♦♦£ 90/105

Cae Tabor ⊠ SA42 0XR – via un-named road opposite bus stop. – ℰ (01348) 811 777 – www.bedandbreakfast-pembrokeshire.co.uk – Closed 1 week Christmas

OLD RADNOR PENCRAIG
Powys – Pop. 400 – Regional map n° **19**-C3
▶ London 180 mi – Cardiff 81 mi – Birmingham 86 mi – Liverpool 121 mi

🍴 **Harp Inn**

TRADITIONAL CUISINE · **INN** This 15C stone inn welcomes drinkers and diners alike. The charming, flag-floored rooms boast open fires and beams hung with hop bines, and the terrace offers glorious views. 'Seasonality' and 'sustainability' are key, and menus are concise but original. Simple bedrooms come with wonderful views.

Carte £ 20/37

5 rooms 😋 – ♦£ 70/80 ♦♦£ 95/105

⊠ LD8 2RH – ℰ (01544) 350 655 – www.harpinnradnor.co.uk – Closed Monday except bank holidays and lunch Tuesday-Friday - Restricted opening in winter

OXWICH

Swansea – Regional map n° **19**-B4

▶ London 201 mi – Llanelli 20 mi – Swansea 14 mi

X **Coalhouse** Ⓝ   ☆ P

BRITISH TRADITIONAL · ROMANTIC Lovely 19C stone building at the heart of the Penrice Estate; it's set on a delightful beach, so the terrace is the place to be. Daily set menus feature local produce, including fish and lobsters from the bay; go for a seafood dish.

Menu £ 25 (lunch) – Carte £ 30/46

Oxwich Beach ✉ SA3 1LS

– 𝒞 (01792) 390 965 – www.thecoalhouserestaurant.co.uk

– Closed Monday-Tuesday April-June, September and restricted opening in winter

PEMBROKE PENFRO

Pembrokeshire – Pop. 7 552 – Regional map n° **19**-A4

▶ London 252 mi – Carmarthen 32 mi – Fishguard 26 mi

🏛 **Lamphey Court**   ☆ ⅋ ⌂ ▤ ⊛ ⋔ Ⅰⅰ ※ ⅍ P

HISTORIC · CLASSIC Impressive Georgian mansion, fronted by columns and surrounded by mature parkland. Typical country house feel throughout, from the classical lounge to the well-kept bedrooms with mahogany furnishings. Smart modern spa and leisure facilities. Dine in the informal orangery or traditional dining room.

39 rooms ⌂ – ♥£ 89/119 ♥♥£ 109/179

✉ SA71 5NT – East : 1.75 mi by A 4139

– 𝒞 (01646) 672 273 – www.lampheycourt.co.uk

PENALLT – Monmouthshire ➜ See Monmouth

PENARTH

The Vale of Glamorgan – Pop. 27 226 – Regional map n° **19**-C4

▶ London 152 mi – Birmingham 111 mi – Bristol 47 mi – Leicester 149 mi

XX **James Sommerin**   ⇦ ⇐ ⊡ ⅍ ⇔

MODERN CUISINE · FASHIONABLE A smart restaurant on the esplanade, affording panoramic views over the Severn Estuary. Choose the 5 course 'Beach', 7 course 'Cliff' or 3 course à la carte menu. Cooking is innovative and features unusual taste and texture combinations. Five of the comfy, relaxing bedrooms share the wonderful view.

Menu £ 32/65

9 rooms ⌂ – ♥£ 150/190 ♥♥£ 150/190

Esplanade ✉ CF64 3AU

– 𝒞 (029) 2070 6559 – www.jamessommerinrestaurant.co.uk

– Closed 26 December, 1-8 January and Monday

XX **Mint and Mustard** Ⓝ   🅰🅲

INDIAN · NEIGHBOURHOOD Appealing neighbourhood restaurant with smartly laid tables and colourful décor. The menu offers an extensive selection of vibrantly flavoured curries and Keralan-inspired dishes. Ingredients are sourced locally where possible.

Carte £ 33/45

46 Plassey St ✉ CF64 1EL

– 𝒞 (029) 2070 0500 (booking essential)

– www.mintandmustard.com

– dinner only

XX **Pier 64**

MODERN CUISINE · FASHIONABLE Modern, wood-clad, all-day restaurant, set on stilts in an enviable harbour location. Light, airy interior with a smart bar and huge windows giving every table a view. Accessible menu features plenty of seafood and 28 day dry-aged steaks.

Menu £ 13 (weekday lunch)/25 – Carte £ 27/80

Penarth Marina ⊠ *CF64 1TT* – ℰ *(029) 2000 0064* – *www.pier64.co.uk*
– *Closed Christmas and Sunday dinner*

🍴 **The Pilot**

BRITISH TRADITIONAL · PUB A neat dining pub that's part of the local community. Regulars gather in the front room; diners head to the rear. A good-sized blackboard menu mixes hearty, honest pub dishes with more adventurous offerings. Ingredients are laudably local.

Carte £ 19/34

67 Queens Rd ⊠ *CF64 1DJ* – ℰ *(029) 2071 0615*
– *www.knifeandforkfood.co.uk/pilot*

PENMACHNO – Conwy → See Betws-y-Coed

PENNAL

Gwynedd – Regional map n° **19**-B2
▶ London 225 mi – Cardiff 125 mi – Chester 80 mi

🍴 **Riverside**

TRADITIONAL CUISINE · PUB Enter under the 'Glan Yr Afron' (Riverside) sign, then make for the 'Cwtch' with its wood-burning stove. Despite its Grade II listing, it has a bright modern feel. Hearty, no-nonsense pub classics are full of flavour and keenly priced.

Menu £ 13 (weekdays) – Carte £ 18/36

⊠ *SY20 9DW* – ℰ *(01654) 791 285* – *www.riversidehotel-pennal.co.uk*
– *Closed 2 weeks January and Monday October-May*

PORTHCAWL

Bridgend – Pop. 15 672 – Regional map n° **19**-B4
▶ London 183 mi – Cardiff 28 mi – Swansea 18 mi

🏠 **Foam Edge**

TOWNHOUSE · PERSONALISED A smart, modern, semi-detached house – a family home – set next to the promenade, with great views over the Bristol Channel. Spacious, stylish bedrooms offer good facilities. Comfortable lounge and communal breakfasts.

3 rooms � – ♦£ 45/70 ♦♦£ 80/100

9 West Dr ⊠ *CF36 3LS* – ℰ *(01656) 782 866* – *www.foam-edge.co.uk*
– *Closed 25 December*

PORTMEIRION

Gwynedd – Regional map n° **19**-B2
▶ London 245 mi – Caernarfon 23 mi – Colwyn Bay 40 mi – Dolgellau 24 mi

🏛 **Portmeirion**

HISTORIC · ART DECO A unique, Italianate village built on a private peninsula and boasting wonderful estuary views – the life work of Sir Clough Williams-Ellis. There's an appealing 1930s hotel and snug, well-appointed bedrooms, which are spread about the village. The dining room has an art deco feel and a lovely parquet floor.

46 rooms ⊯ – ♦£ 84/194 ♦♦£ 99/209 – 22 suites

⊠ *LL48 6ER* – ℰ *(01766) 770 000* – *www.portmerion-village.com*
– *Closed 3-7 September and 15-27 November*

🏠 Castell Deudraeth   ☆ 🛏 🖳 💱 🛗 🅿

CASTLE · STYLISH Impressive crenellated manor house at the entrance to the Italianate village; its name means 'castle of two beaches'. Huge modern bedrooms have stylish bathrooms and kitchen areas. Enjoy cocktails by the fire then head to the Grill for brasserie classics and views of the well-tended walled garden.

11 rooms ⌘ – **†**£ 104/119 **††**£ 119/244 – 3 suites

✉ LL48 6EN – ☎ (01766) 772 400 – www.portmeirion-village.com

PUMSAINT
Carmarthenshire – Regional map n° **19**-B3
▶ London 227 mi – Cardiff 81 mi – Llandovery 12 mi

🏠 Dolaucothi Arms 🆕   ⇦ 🛏 🏡 🛗 🅿

BRITISH TRADITIONAL · RUSTIC 300 year old drovers' inn in the picturesque Cothi Valley; it's a cosy, rustic kind of a place and the garden looks out over the river, where they have 4 miles of fishing rights. One menu list pub classics, while the second is more adventurous. Bedrooms are comfy and cosy – ask if you want a TV.

Carte £ 15/29

3 rooms ⌘ – **†**£ 55 **††**£ 85

✉ SA19 8UW – ☎ (01558) 650 237 – www.thedolaucothiarms.co.uk – Closed 24-26 and 31 December, 1 January, Tuesday lunch, Monday except bank holidays and lunch midweek in winter

PWLLHELI
Gwynedd – Pop. 4 076 – Regional map n° **19**-B2
▶ London 261 mi – Aberystwyth 73 mi – Caernarfon 21 mi

✕✕ Plas Bodegroes   🏵 ⇦ 🦢 🛏 🅿

MODERN CUISINE · FORMAL A charming, Grade II listed Georgian house set in peaceful grounds; inside it's beautifully decorated and features an eclectic collection of modern Welsh art. There's a well-chosen wine list and the kitchen uses the best of the local larder to create classic dishes with a contemporary edge. Understated bedrooms are named after trees and have sleek, modern bathrooms.

Menu £ 25 (lunch)/49

10 rooms ⌘ – **†**£ 120/160 **††**£ 140/180

✉ LL53 5TH – Northwest : 1.75 mi on A 497 – ☎ (01758) 612 363 (booking essential) – www.bodegroes.co.uk – dinner only and Sunday lunch – Closed December-February, dinner Sunday except bank holidays and Monday

at Boduan Northwest: 3.75 mi on A497 ✉ Pwllheli

🏠 Old Rectory   🦢 🛏 💱 🅿

VILLA · PERSONALISED Lovely part-Georgian family home with well-tended gardens and a paddock. Comfy lounge features a carved wood fireplace; communal breakfasts at a large table include plenty of fresh fruits. Tastefully decorated, homely bedrooms overlook the garden and come with complimentary chocolates and sherry or sloe gin.

3 rooms ⌘ – **†**£ 80/90 **††**£ 95/115

✉ LL53 6DT – ☎ (01758) 721 519 – www.theoldrectory.net – Closed Christmas

RHOSCOLYN → See Anglesey (Isle of)

RHOS-ON-SEA – Conwy → See Colwyn Bay

RHYL
Denbighshire – Pop. 25 149 – Regional map n° **19**-C1
▶ London 228 mi – Cardiff 181 mi – Birmingham 114 mi – Wolverhampton 108 mi

XX Barratt's at Ty'n Rhyl ⇦ ⇛ 🅿

TRADITIONAL CUISINE · COSY Built in 1672 and retaining many original features, including a carved wooden fireplace reputed to have been the top of a bed owned by Catherine of Aragon! The characterful drawing rooms have a cosy, lived in feel; the dining room, by contrast, is light and airy. Classically based menu. Traditional bedrooms.

Menu £ 40

3 rooms 🖙 – †£ 80 ††£ 98

167 Vale Rd. ✉ LL18 2PH – South : 0.5 mi on A 525
– ✆ (01745) 344 138 (booking essential) – www.barrattsattynrhyl.co.uk
– dinner only and Sunday lunch

ROCH

Pembrokeshire – Pop. 463 – Regional map n° **19**-A3
▶ London 258 mi – Swansea 64 mi – Haverfordwest 8 mi

🏠 Roch Castle Ⓝ ⇛ 🅿

HISTORIC · DESIGN An intimate 12C castle set over 7 storeys, which has been fully refurbished by its architect owner. It's modern and stylish throughout, from the bedrooms with their quality linens to the fantastic Sun Room with its far-reaching views.

6 rooms – †£ 150/230 ††£ 150/230

✉ *SA62 6AQ – ✆ (01437) 729 900 – www.rochcastle.com*

ROSSETT

Wrexham – ✉ Wrexham – Pop. 2 007 – Regional map n° **19**-C1
▶ London 200 mi – Holyhead 86 mi – Chester 9 mi

X Machine House 🍴 🅿

REGIONAL · FRIENDLY Once an agricultural machinery repair shop, this 19C barn is cosier than its name implies. Flavoursome cooking has a modern touch and uses the best of local produce; try the crab or lobster, caught by the owner's father-in-law.

Menu 45 – Carte £ 18/42

Chester Rd ✉ LL12 0HW
– ✆ (01244) 571 678 (bookings advisable at dinner) – www.machinehouse.co.uk
– Closed 25-26 December, 1 January, Monday, Tuesday lunch and Sunday dinner

ROWEN – Conwy → See Conwy

RUTHIN RHUTHUN

Denbighshire – Pop. 5 461 – Regional map n° **19**-C1
▶ London 210 mi – Birkenhead 31 mi – Chester 23 mi – Liverpool 34 mi

🏠 Firgrove ⭐ ⇛ ⚅ 🅿

FAMILY · COSY Attractive stone-built cottage set in stunning gardens. Sit in the snug by the cosy inglenook fireplace in winter or in the delightful, plant-filled glasshouse in summer. Two comfortable four-poster bedrooms and a self-contained cottage offer pleasant valley views. The owners join guests for hearty, home-cooked dinners which showcase locally sourced farm produce.

3 rooms 🖙 – †£ 65/80 ††£ 90/110

Llanfwrog ✉ LL15 2LL – West : 1.25 mi by A 494 on B 5105
– ✆ (01824) 702 677 – www.firgrovecountryhouse.co.uk
– Closed November-February

XX **Manorhaus Ruthin**

MODERN CUISINE · DESIGN A lovely Georgian townhouse which retains its period character whilst also boasting a stylish, 'of-the-moment' feel. The formally laid conservatory serves classically based seasonal dishes, presented in a modern style. A cocktail bar, a basement cinema and cosy, cleverly designed bedrooms also feature.

Menu £ 30

8 rooms ☲ – †£ 83/123 ††£ 90/170

10 Well St ⊠ LL15 1AH – ℰ (01824) 704 830 (booking advisable)
– www.manorhaus.com – dinner only and lunch Saturday-Sunday by arrangement

X **On the Hill**

TRADITIONAL CUISINE · NEIGHBOURHOOD Immensely charming 16C house in a busy market town; a real family-run business. It has characterful sloping floors, exposed beams and a buzzy, bistro atmosphere. The accessible menu offers keenly priced, internationally influenced classics.

Menu £ 18 (lunch) – Carte £ 25/40

1 Upper Clwyd St ⊠ LL15 1HY – ℰ (01824) 707 736 (booking essential)
– www.onthehillrestaurant.co.uk – Closed 1-7 January, 25-26 December, 1 January and Monday

ST ASAPH

Denbighshire – Pop. 3 491 – Regional map n° **19**-C1
▶ London 223 mi – Cardiff 176 mi – Liverpool 46 mi – Manchester 69 mi

⌂ **Tan-yr-Onnen**

FAMILY · DESIGN Extended modern building with pleasant gardens; its name means 'house under the ash tree'. Spacious, tastefully furnished bedrooms; ground floor rooms have French windows and terraces; first floor rooms come with their own sitting rooms.

6 rooms ☲ – †£ 75/95 ††£ 95/135

Waen ⊠ LL17 0DU – East : 1.5 mi by A 55 and B 5429 on Trefnant rd – ℰ (01745) 583 821 – www.northwalesbreaks.co.uk – Closed 31 December and 1 January

ST CLEARS

Carmarthenshire – Pop. 1 989 – Regional map n° **19**-B3
▶ London 221 mi – Cardiff 76 mi – Swansea 37 mi – Llanelli 33 mi

⌂ **Coedllys Country House**

TRADITIONAL · PERSONALISED Lovely country house in a peaceful hillside location, complete with a sanctuary where they keep rescued animals – the hens provide the eggs at breakfast. Comfy, traditional guest areas and charming, antique-furnished bedrooms with good mod cons and binoculars for bird watchers. Welsh cakes served on arrival.

4 rooms ☲ – †£ 75/85 ††£ 90/110

Llangynin ⊠ SA33 4JY – Northwest : 3.5 mi by A 40 turning first left after 30 mph sign on entering village. – ℰ (01994) 231 455
– www.coedllyscountryhouse.co.uk – Closed 22-28 December

ST DAVIDS TYDDEWI

Pembrokeshire – ⊠ Haverfordwest – Pop. 1 959 – Regional map n° **19**-A3
▶ London 266 mi – Carmarthen 46 mi – Fishguard 16 mi

⌂ **Penrhiw** ⓝ

COUNTRY HOUSE · ELEGANT A fine house built from local red stone, set in 12 acres of gardens which offer great country views. The original stained glass door is delightful and the guest areas are impressive. Spacious, stylish bedrooms come in muted tones.

8 rooms – †£ 140/230 ††£ 140/230

⊠ SA62 6PG – Northwest : 0.5 mi by A 487 and Quickwell Hill Rd – ℰ (01437) 729 431 – www.penrhiwhotel.com

🏠 Ramsey House　　　　🕸 ⪦ 🛋 🕸 🅿

TRADITIONAL · STYLISH Unassuming house on the edge of the UK's smallest city. Stylish modern bedrooms have coastal views, bold décor and a boutique style; the smart shower rooms feature aromatherapy toiletries. A comfy lounge leads through to the wood-furnished dining room, where tasty, attractively presented dishes are served.

6 rooms 🛏 – †£ 70/120 ††£ 100/120

Lower Moor ⊠ SA62 6RP – Southwest : 0.5 mi on Porth Clais rd – ℰ (01437) 720 321 – www.ramseyhouse.co.uk – Closed January, December and restricted opening November and February

✗ Cwtch

BRITISH TRADITIONAL · RUSTIC Popular, laid-back restaurant; its name meaning 'hug'. The three rustic dining rooms boast stone walls, crammed bookshelves and log-filled alcoves. Classical British dishes arrive in generous portions and service is polite and friendly.

Menu £ 22/30

22 High St ⊠ SA62 6SD – ℰ (01437) 720 491 (booking advisable) – www.cwtchrestaurant.co.uk – dinner only – Closed 1 January-10 February and Monday-Tuesday November-March

ST GEORGE LLAN SAIN SIÔR

Conwy – Regional map n° **19**-C1

▶ London 227 mi – Cardiff 180 mi – Dublin 62 mi – Birmingham 113 mi

🏠 Kinmel Arms　　　　⪦ 🕸 🅿

TRADITIONAL CUISINE · INN Early 17C stone inn, hidden away in a hamlet by the entrance to Kinmel Hall, with a delightful open-fired bar and two spacious dining areas. Lunch offers pub favourites, while dinner is more complex; home-grown herbs and fruit feature. Stylish, contemporary bedrooms boast large kitchenettes for breakfast.

Menu £ 15 (weekday dinner)/35 – Carte £ 25/42

4 rooms 🛏 – †£ 115/165 ††£ 135/175

The Village ⊠ LL22 9BP – ℰ (01745) 832 207 – www.thekinmelarms.co.uk – Closed Sunday and Monday

SAUNDERSFOOT

Pembrokeshire – Pop. 2 767 – Regional map n° **19**-A4

▶ Cardiff 90 mi – Haverfordwest 18 mi – Swansea 51 mi

🏨 St Brides Spa　　🕸 ⪦ 🌐 🛀 🔲 ⅃ 🕸 🛁 🅿

LUXURY · PERSONALISED Nautically styled hotel overlooking the harbour and bay, featuring wood panelling and contemporary Welsh art. The stylish spa boasts an outdoor infinity pool. Well-appointed bedrooms come in cream and blue hues and have smart bathrooms.

46 rooms 🛏 – †£ 130/205 ††£ 160/310 – 6 suites

St Brides Hill ⊠ SA69 9NH – ℰ (01834) 812 304 – www.stbridesspahotel.com

Cliff – See restaurant listing

✗✗ Cliff　　　　⪦ 🕸 🛁 🎛 🅿

MODERN CUISINE · BRASSERIE Smart yet casual restaurant in a New England style hotel, boasting beautiful decked terraces and stunning views over the bay. Extensive lunch menu; dinner is more refined, offering modern British dishes with local produce to the fore.

Carte £ 29/45

St Brides Spa Hotel, St Brides Hill ⊠ SA69 9NH – ℰ (01834) 812 304 – www.stbridesspahotel.com

X **Coast**   ⩽ ⌂ P

MODERN CUISINE · MINIMALIST Striking modern restaurant; when the weather's right, head for the terrace with its stunning coastal views. Seafood dominates the menu, which ranges from nibbles to a tasting selection. Local produce features in creative dishes.

Carte £ 34/52

Coppet Hall Beach ⊠ *SA69 9AJ* – *℘ (01834) 810 800*
– www.coastsaundersfoot.co.uk – Closed 25 December, Sunday dinner,
Monday-Tuesday in winter

SEION – Gwynedd ➔ See Caernarfon

SKENFRITH

Monmouthshire – Regional map n° **19**-C4
▶ London 135 mi – Hereford 16 mi – Ross-on-Wye 11 mi

🍴 **Bell at Skenfrith**   🕸 ⩽ 🛏 🐾 ⌂ ⬦ P

CLASSIC CUISINE · PUB Well-run pub in a verdant valley, offering hearty, classical cooking with the occasional ambitious twist and using ingredients from the organic kitchen garden. There's an excellent choice of champagnes and cognacs, and service is warm and unobtrusive. Super-comfy bedrooms have an understated elegance.

Carte £ 20/35

11 rooms ⌷ – ♦£ 75/120 ♦♦£ 130/225
⊠ *NP7 8UH* – *℘ (01600) 750 235 (booking essential) – www.skenfrith.co.uk*

SWANSEA

Swansea – Pop. 179 485 – Regional map n° **19**-B4
▶ London 191 mi – Birmingham 136 mi – Bristol 82 mi – Cardiff 40 mi

🏠🏠 **Morgans**   ✿ 🖥 🕭 🎞 🍸 🛋 P

BUSINESS · PERSONALISED Impressive Edwardian building by the docks; once the harbour offices. Beautiful façade and charming interior with original plasterwork, stained glass and a soaring cupola. Modern bedrooms – those in the main house are the most spacious. The restaurant boasts an original hand-painted mural and a modern menu.

42 rooms ⌷ – ♦£ 90/250 ♦♦£ 110/250
Town plan: B-b – *Somerset Pl* ⊠ *SA1 1RR* – *℘ (01792) 484 848*
– www.morganshotel.co.uk

XX **Hanson at The Chelsea** ⓝ

BRITISH TRADITIONAL · FRIENDLY This rustic pub conversion is found in the city's heart, close to St Mary's Church. A blackboard announces the specials – which are formed around the latest produce available from the nearby market – and dishes are tasty and filling.

Carte £ 23/39

Town plan: B-a – *17 St Mary's St* ⊠ *SA1 3LH* – *℘ (01792) 464 068*
– www.hansonatthechelsea.co.uk – Closed Sunday and bank holiday Mondays

X **Slice**

BRITISH MODERN · INTIMATE Sweet former haberdashery in a residential area; the name reflecting its tapered shape. It's run by two friends who alternate weekly between cooking and serving. Precisely prepared, appealing modern dishes are packed with flavour.

Menu £ 26 (lunch)/35

Town plan: A-x – *73-75 Eversley Rd, Sketty* ⊠ *SA2 9DE* – *West : 2 mi by A 4118*
– ℘ (01792) 290 929 (booking essential) – www.sliceswansea.co.uk – dinner
only and Friday-Sunday lunch – Closed 1 week autumn, 1 week Christmas, Monday
and Tuesday

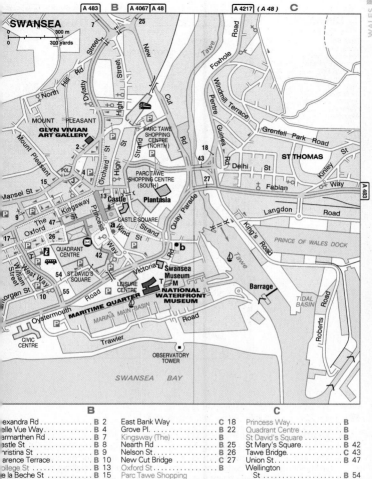

Map labels:

A 483 | B | A 4067 | A 48 | A 4217 | (A 48) | C

SWANSEA

300 m
300 yards

North | Hill | Rd | Dyfatty | Street | New | Street | Cut | Tawe | Foxhole | Windmill Terrace | Pentre | Guinea | Grenfell Park Road

MOUNT PLEASANT

GLYN VIVIAN
ART GALLERY

PARC TAWE
SHOPPING
CENTRE
(NORTH)

Mount Pleasant

POL

Mansel St

The
Oxford

QUADRANT
CENTRE

West Way

ST DAVID'S
SQUARE

Morgan St

CIVIC
CENTRE

PARC TAWE
SHOPPING CENTRE
(SOUTH)

Orchard | St | High | St | Strand | Rd | Quay Parade

Castle
Plantasia

CASTLE SQUARE

Kingsway | Princess | Wind | Strand | Rd | Victoria | Rd

Swansea
Museum

NATIONAL
WATERFRONT
MUSEUM

LEISURE
CENTRE

Oystermouth | Road

MARITIME QUARTER

MARINA MAIN BASIN

Trawler | Road

OBSERVATORY
TOWER

SWANSEA BAY

ST THOMAS

Delhi | St | Kinley | St | Fabian | Way | Langdon | Road

PRINCE OF WALES DOCK

King's | Road | Tawe

Barrage

TIDAL
BASIN

Roberts | Road

	B				C	
exandra Rd	B 2	East Bank Way	C 18	Princess Way		B	
elle Vue Way	B 4	Grove Pl.	B 22	Quadrant Centre		B	
armarthen Rd	B 7	Kingsway (The)	B	St David's Square		B	
astle St	B 8	Nearth Rd	B 25	St Mary's Square		B	42
hristina St	B 9	Nelson St	B 26	Tawe Bridge.		C	43
arence Terrace	B 10	New Cut Bridge	C 27	Union St		B	47
ollege St	B 13	Oxford St	B	Wellington			
e la Beche St	B 15	Parc Tawe Shopping		St		B	54
llwyn St	B 17	Centre	B	West Way		B	55

at The Mumbles Southwest: 5 mi by A4067 – Plan: A – ✉ Swansea

✗ Munch of Mumbles

BRITISH MODERN · SIMPLE It would be all too easy to walk past this simple bistro overlooking the bay – but you'd be missing out. Good value menus offer well-presented modern British dishes that are homemade and full of flavour. The BYO is only £1 a bottle!

Menu £16/30

650 Mumbles Rd ✉ SA3 4EA – ✆ (01792) 362 244 (booking advisable)
– www.munchofmumbles.com – Closed 1 week February, 1 week May,
3 weeks mid October, 25-26 December, 1 January, Monday, Tuesday and Sunday
dinner

SWANSEA

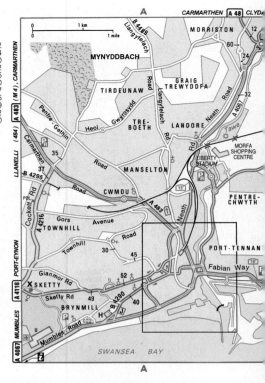

TAL-Y-LLYN

Gwynedd – ⊠ Tywyn – Regional map n° **19**-B2

▶ London 224 mi – Dolgellau 9 mi – Shrewsbury 60 mi

🏠 **Dolffanog Fawr**   ⇖ ⇐ ⇑ P

FAMILY · HOMELY This homely 18C farmhouse stands in the shadow of Cadair Idris, just up from a lake; kick-back in the hot tub to make the most of the terrific valley views. Modern bedrooms are furnished in solid oak. Breakfast could include Welsh cakes and dinner might feature local lamb or sea trout caught by the owner.

4 rooms ⊊ – ♥£ 50/120 ♥♥£ 100/120

⊠ LL36 9AJ – On B 4405 – 𝒞 (01654) 761 247 – www.dolffanogfawr.co.uk
– Closed November-March

> Our selection of hotels, guesthouses and restaurants change
> every year, so change your MICHELIN Guide every year!

TREDUNNOCK – Newport ➔ See Usk

TREGARON

Ceredigion – Regional map n° **19**-B3

▶ London 245 mi – Cardiff 100 mi – Aberystwyth 18 mi

WALES

🏠 Y Talbot

🔄 🛋 🏠 & 🖵 ⇄

TRADITIONAL CUISINE · CLASSIC Originally a drover's inn dating back to the 17C; the bar rooms are where the action is, and the best place to sit. Seasonal menus offer full-flavoured traditional dishes made with Welsh produce. Bedrooms are bright and modern: ask for one of the newest. Oh, and there's an elephant buried in the garden!

Carte £ 17/30

13 rooms ⌷ - ♦£ 60/100 ♦♦£ 80/130

✉ SY25 6JL - ℰ (01974) 298 208 - www.ytalbot.com - Closed 25 December

TREMEIRCHION

Denbighshire - ✉ St Asaph - Regional map n° **19**-C1

▶ London 225 mi - Chester 29 mi - Shrewsbury 59 mi

🏠 Bach-Y-Graig

🐾 🛋 🥐 🗀 🖻

TRADITIONAL · CLASSIC A welcoming, 16C red-brick farmhouse on a 200 acre, 5th generation working dairy farm. Decently sized, antique-furnished bedrooms boast countryside views. Traditional lounges and communal breakfasts at a large oak table.

3 rooms ⌷ - ♦£ 60 ♦♦£ 80

✉ LL17 0UH - Southwest : 2 mi by B 5429 off Denbigh rd - ℰ (01745) 730 627 - www.bachygraig.co.uk - Closed Christmas-New Year

TYWYN

Gwynedd - Regional map n° **19**-B2

▶ London 230 mi - Chester 85 mi - Aberystwyth 34 mi

🍴 Salt Marsh Kitchen 🆕

BRITISH TRADITIONAL · SIMPLE Sweet little café-cum-bistro run by a proud, hardworking owner. Scrubbed wooden tables and a blue floor give it a New England feel. Cooking is honest and generous; the owner is a keen fisherman and will advise you of what's best.

Carte £ 20/35

9 College Green ✉ LL36 9BS - ℰ (01654) 711 949 - www.saltmarshkitchen.co.uk - dinner only - Closed Monday-Thursday November-April

USK

Monmouthshire - Pop. 2 834 - Regional map n° **19**-C4

▶ London 144 mi - Bristol 30 mi - Cardiff 26 mi - Gloucester 39 mi

🏠 Glen-Yr-Afon House

🏠 🛋 🖃 & 🚲 🖻

TRADITIONAL · PERSONALISED Olive-green, extended Victorian villa just across the bridge from town. Comfortable, traditionally styled guest areas overlook the well-tended gardens. Mix of country house and more modern bedrooms; one is a four-poster. Wood-panelled, two-roomed restaurant serves traditional dishes made with Welsh produce.

28 rooms ⌷ - ♦£ 84/99 ♦♦£ 136/159

Pontypool Rd ✉ NP15 1SY - ℰ (01291) 672 302 - www.glen-yr-afon.co.uk - Closed 24-26 December

🏠 Three Salmons 🆕

🏠 🚲 🖻

TOWNHOUSE · HOMELY Characterful 300 year old coaching inn by the river. Bedrooms have creaky floorboards and a warm, cosy feel; ask about their fishing packages. Have snacks by the fire in the wood-panelled bar or head to the formal dining room for a larger seasonal menu which features local lamb, beef and of course, salmon.

10 rooms ⌷ - ♦£ 80/95 ♦♦£ 100/130

Bridge St ✉ NP15 1RY - ℰ (01291) 672 133 - www.threesalmons.co.uk

at Tredunnock South: 4.75 mi by Llangybi rd – ⊠ Newport

X **Newbridge on Usk**

BRITISH TRADITIONAL · BISTRO 200 year old inn by a bridge over the Rive
Usk; choose from several dining areas set over two levels or sit on the terrace
to have the snack menu. Classic British cooking has a modern twist; sharing
plates are popular and include a crumble dessert. The smart, comfortable bed
rooms are in a separate block.

Menu £ 20 (weekday lunch) – Carte £ 31/48

6 rooms ⌂ – ♦£ 75/100 ♦♦£ 85/135

⊠ NP15 1LY – East : 0.5 mi – ℰ (01633) 451000 – www.celtic-manor.com

WHITEBROOK – Monmouthshire → See Monmouth

WHITTON

Powys – Pop. 300 – Regional map n° **19**-C3

▶ London 185 mi – Cardiff 84 mi – Birmingham 84 mi – Liverpool 108 mi

🏠 **Pilleth Oaks**

FAMILY · CLASSIC Double-gabled country house set in 100 acres, overlooking
two lakes and the surrounding hills. The traditional, antique-filled interior feature
an elegant lounge and comfortable bedrooms; one has a balcony and grea
views. The welcoming owner offers tea on arrival and communal breakfasts at
smart oak table.

3 rooms ⌂ – ♦£ 45 ♦♦£ 80/85

⊠ LD7 1NP – Northwest : 1.25 mi on B 4356 – ℰ (01547) 560272
– www.pillethoaks.co.uk – Closed 25-26 December

WOLF'S CASTLE CAS-BLAIDD

Pembrokeshire – ⊠ Haverfordwest – Pop. 616 – Regional map n° **19**-A3

▶ London 258 mi – Fishguard 7 mi – Haverfordwest 8 mi

🏠 **Wolfscastle Country H.**

BUSINESS · PERSONALISED Former manor house that's been greatly expande
over the years; a popular place for weddings and conferences. Bedrooms ar
modern, well-equipped and have very comfy beds – some are four-posters. Ea
in the formal restaurant, in the bright and airy brasserie or on the terrace
Friendly, efficient service.

20 rooms ⌂ – ♦£ 75/105 ♦♦£ 110/145

⊠ SA62 5LZ – ℰ (01437) 741225 – www.wolfscastle.com – Closed
24-26 December

IRELAND

NORTHERN IRELAND

Think of Northern Ireland and you think of buzzing Belfast, with its impressive City Hall and Queen's University. But the rest of the Six Counties demand attention too. Forty thousand stone columns of the Giants Causeway step out into the Irish Sea, while inland, Antrim boasts nine scenic glens. County Down's rolling hills culminate in the alluring slopes of Slieve Donard in the magical Mourne Mountains, while Armagh's Orchard County is a riot of pink in springtime. Fermanagh's glassy, silent lakelands are a tranquil attraction, rivalled for their serenity by the heather-clad Sperrin Mountains, towering over Tyrone and Derry.

Rich, fertile land, vast waterways and a pride in traditional crafts like butchery and baking mean that Northern Ireland yields a wealth of high quality produce: tender, full-flavoured beef and lamb, and fish and shellfish from the lakes, rivers and sea, including salmon, oysters, mussels and crabs. You can't beat an eel from Lough Neagh – and the seaweed called Dulse is a local delicacy not to be missed.

- Michelin Road map n° 712, 713 and 501
- Michelin Green Guide: Ireland

FoodCollection/Photononstop

20 Northern Ireland

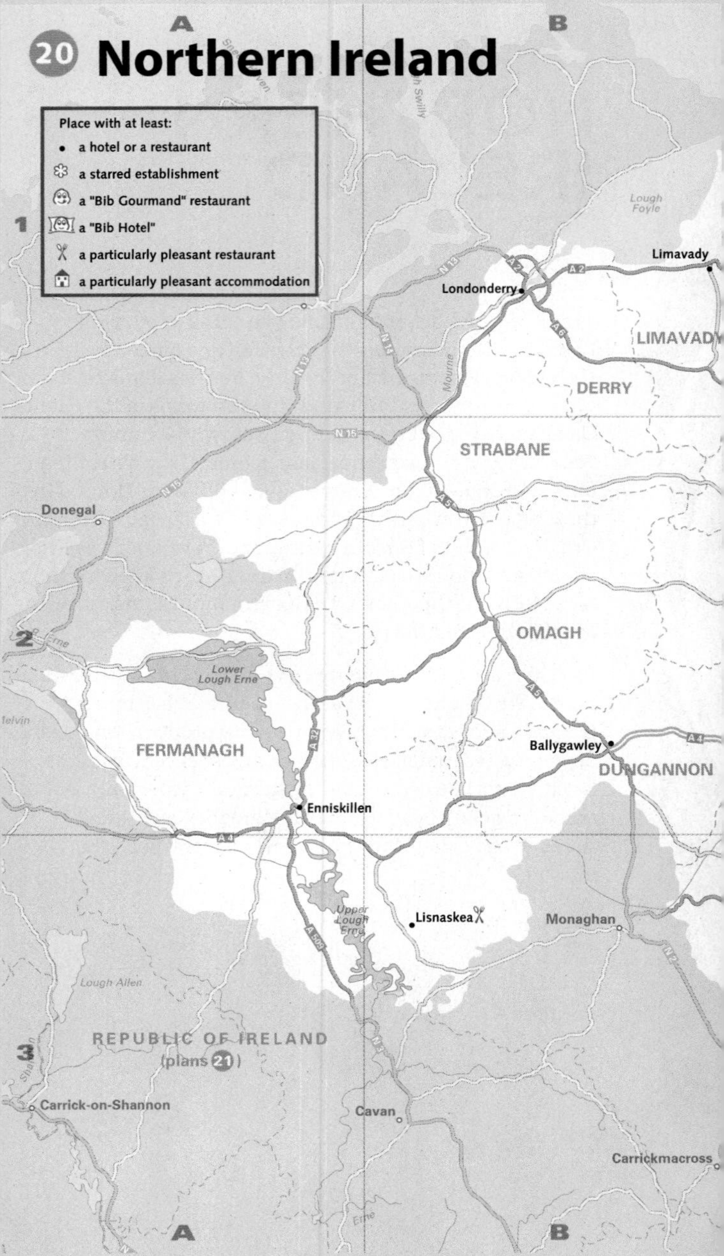

Place with at least:
- a hotel or a restaurant
- 🏵 a starred establishment
- 😊 a "Bib Gourmand" restaurant
- 🏠 a "Bib Hotel"
- ✗ a particularly pleasant restaurant
- 🏠 a particularly pleasant accommodation

Limavady

Londonderry

LIMAVADY

DERRY

STRABANE

Donegal

Lower Lough Erne

OMAGH

FERMANAGH

Ballygawley

DUNGANNON

Enniskillen

Upper Lough Erne

Lisnaskea ✗

Monaghan

Lough Allen

REPUBLIC OF IRELAND
(plans 21)

Carrick-on-Shannon

Cavan

Carrickmacross

FOOD NOT TO BE MISSED

STARRED RESTAURANTS

☘

High quality cooking, worth a stop!

BIB GOURMANDS ☺
Good quality, good value cooking

© *Michelin*

OUR TOP PICKS

A WARM WELCOME AWAITS

CITY HOTSPOTS

LIKEABLE LOCALS

SPA RETREATS

ANNAHILT EANACH EILTE – Lisburn → See Hillsborough

ARMAGH ARD MHACHA
Armagh – Regional map n° **20**-C3
▶ Belfast 39 mi – Dungannon 13 mi – Portadown 11 mi

✗ Moody Boar   🛋 ♿ ▯ 🅿
TRADITIONAL CUISINE · BISTRO Set in the stables of the former Primate of A..
Ireland's house and run by a young team. Characterful, rustic interior with
vaulted ceiling, a stone floor and booths in the old stalls. Wide choice of classic
dishes with personal touches.
Menu £ 20 (early dinner) – Carte £ 23/32
Palace Stables, Palace Demense ⊠ BT60 4EL – South : 0.5 mi off A 3 – ℰ (028)
3752 9678 – www.themoodyboar.com – Closed 25-26 December and Monday
dinner in winter

✗ Uluru Bar & Grill   ♿ 🆎 ▯
CLASSIC CUISINE · DESIGN Rustic designer restaurant overlooking the market
place. The chef spent time in Australia, so alongside comforting classics and
Asian-inspired dishes, you'll find meats such as kangaroo and ostrich, some
cooked on the Josper grill.
Menu £ 15 (weekday dinner)/17 – Carte £ 18/33
3-5 Market St ⊠ BT61 7BW – ℰ (028) 3751 8051 (booking essential)
– www.ulurubistro.com – Closed 25-26 December, 1 January, Monday and Sunday
lunch

BALLINTOY
Moyle – Regional map n° **20**-C1
▶ Belfast 59 mi – Ballycastle 8 mi – Londonderry 48 mi – Lisburn 67 mi

🏠 Whitepark House   � ⚑ 🅿
TRADITIONAL · CLASSIC Charming 18C house near the Giant's Causeway, deco
rated with lovely wall hangings, framed silks and other artefacts from the person
able owner's travels. Large, open-fired lounge where cakes are served on arrival
Bright, antique-furnished bedrooms have four-posters or half-testers and smart
modern bathrooms.
4 rooms ⛌ – ♦£ 80 ♦♦£ 120
150 Whitepark Rd ⊠ BT54 6NH – West : 1.5 mi on A 2 – ℰ (028) 2073 1482
– www.whiteparkhouse.com – Closed December and January

BALLYGAWLEY
Dungannon – Pop. 642 – Regional map n° **20**-B2
▶ Belfast 53 km – Dungannon 14 km – Londonderry 51 km

✗ Black Cat 🆕   ≼ 🛋 🆎 🅿
CLASSIC CUISINE · SIMPLE Friendly, rustic restaurant with a small lounge and
light-filled dining room which looks out across fields and a lake. Well-propor
tioned, classically based dishes keep the focus on their main ingredient; desserts
are a strength.
Menu £ 21 (weekdays) – Carte £ 22/40
32 Dungannon Rd ⊠ BT70 2JU – Northwest : 1 mi on A 4 – ℰ (028) 8556 7040
– www.theblackcatrestaurant.com – Closed Monday and Tuesday except bank
holiday Mondays

BALLYMENA AN BAILE MEÁNACH
Ballymena – Pop. 29 782 – Regional map n° **20**-C2
▶ Belfast 27 mi – Dundalk 78 mi – Larne 21 mi – Londonderry 51 mi

at Galgorm West: 3 mi on A42

🏛️ Galgorm Resort and Spa 🕊️ 🐾 🛜 🍸 📺 🌐 ⚴ 🖪 ⚿ 🛗 ☽ 🄿

LUXURY · STYLISH Victorian manor house with newer extensions, set in large grounds. Stylish interior with plenty of lounge space, a huge function capacity and an excellent leisure club with a superb outdoor spa pool. Modern bedrooms boast state-of-the-art facilities; some have balconies. Extensive all-day menus served in characterful Gillies; informal Fratelli offers Italian fare.

122 rooms ☑ – †£ 145/195 ††£ 145/285 – 1 suite
136 Fenaghy Rd ⊠ BT42 1EA – West : 1.5 mi on Cullybacky rd
– ℰ (028) 2588 1001 – www.galgorm.com
River Room – See restaurant listing

XxX River Room ≤ 🛜 & 🄰🄲 🄿

BRITISH MODERN · INTIMATE Formal, warmly decorated dining room set on the ground floor of a stylishly furnished, whitewashed Victorian manor house, with good views across the River Mein. Refined, classically based cooking and attentive service.

Carte £ 38/43
Galgorm Resort and Spa Hotel, 136 Fenaghy Rd ⊠ BT42 1EA – West : 1.5 mi on Cullybacky rd – ℰ (028) 2588 1001 – www.galgorm.com
– dinner only and Sunday lunch – Closed Monday and Tuesday

3ANGOR BEANNCHAR

North Down – Pop. 60 260 – Regional map n° **20**-D2
▶ Belfast 15 mi – Newtownards 5 mi

🏛️ Clandeboye Lodge 🕊️ 🛜 🖪 ☽ & ⚿ ☽ 🄿

BUSINESS · MODERN Well-run property on the site of a former estate school house. A popular wedding venue, it is surrounded by 4 acres of woodland and is well-placed for country and coast. Airy, open-plan guest areas and contemporary bedrooms with a high level of facilities. An accessible menu is served in the brasserie.

43 rooms ☑ – †£ 75/105 ††£ 90/145
10 Estate Rd, Clandeboye ⊠ BT19 1UR – Southwest : 3 mi by A 2 and Dundonald rd following signs for Blackwood Golf Centre
– ℰ (028) 9185 2500 – www.clandeboyelodge.com
– Closed 24-26 December

🏛️ Salty Dog 🕊️ 🕾

INN · PERSONALISED Welcoming hotel in a pair of bay-windowed, red-brick Victorian townhouses overlooking Bangor Marina and Belfast Lough. Contemporary bedrooms vary greatly in shape and size; go for one of the larger front rooms with a view. The bistro, with its terrace, serves a mix of classics and more ambitious dishes.

15 rooms ☑ – †£ 70/90 ††£ 85/120
10-12 Seacliff Rd ⊠ BT20 5EY – ℰ (028) 9127 0696
– www.saltydogbangor.com

🏛️ Cairn Bay Lodge ≤ 🛜 ⚿ 🄿

🏠 **FAMILY · COSY** Large, whitewashed Edwardian house just out of the town centre, overlooking the bay. Comfy guest areas feature unusual objets d'art and ornaments; spacious, individually styled bedrooms boast plenty of extras. The friendly owners leave homemade cake on the landing. Small beauty and therapy facility.

8 rooms ☑ – †£ 50/60 ††£ 80/99
278 Seacliffe Rd ⊠ BT20 5HS – East : 1.25 mi by Quay St
– ℰ (028) 9146 7636 – www.cairnbaylodge.com

Shelleven House

⌖ **P**

TRADITIONAL · CLASSIC Double-fronted, three-storey, Victorian end terrace, in a smart residential area near the marina. Open-plan lounge and breakfast room; excellent breakfasts. Well-kept bedrooms vary in shape and size; front rooms boast great coastal views.

10 rooms ⌁ – †£ 40/60 ††£ 75/90
59-61 Princetown Rd ✉ BT20 3TA – ℰ (028) 9127 1777 – www.shellevenhouse.com
– Closed 23-28 December

XX Boat House

⌂ **AC**

MODERN CUISINE · FRIENDLY This former lifeboat station is home to an intimate dining room with a harbourside terrace and is run by two experienced brothers. Ambitious modern dishes have the occasional Dutch twist. Be sure to try one of the specialist gins.

Menu £ 18 (lunch and early dinner) – Carte £ 25/54
Seacliff Rd ✉ BT20 5HA – ℰ (028) 9146 9253 – www.theboathouseni.co.uk
– Closed 1 January, Monday and Tuesday

GOOD TIPS!

Optimism abounds in the city, with industry, commerce, arts and tourism all playing a role. With it has come a vibrant and ever-expanding restaurant scene that offers something for everyone, from delis and fish bars to bistros and brasseries. The Cathedral Quarter is the new dining hub attracting the foodies, while Eipic and OX have brought Michelin Stars.

© R. Mattes/hemis.fr

BELFAST BÉAL FEIRSTE

Belfast – Pop. 267 742 – Regional map n° **20**-D2
🚹 Dublin 103 mi – Londonderry 70 mi

Hotels

🏠🏠🏠 Merchant

🏊 🌐 ⌨ 🖵 🔥 🅰 ♨ 🔋 🚗

LUXURY · STYLISH Former Ulster Bank HQ with an impressive Victorian façade. Plush, intimately styled bedrooms; those in the annexe have an art deco theme. Rooftop gym with an outdoor hot tub and a skyline view; relax afterwards in the swish cocktail bar. British dishes with a Mediterranean edge in the opulent former banking hall. Classic French brasserie dishes and live jazz in Berts.

62 rooms – 🛏£150/270 🛏🛏£160/280 – ♨£14 – 2 suites
Town plan: BX-x – *16 Skipper St* ✉ *BT1 2DZ* – *𝒞 (028) 9023 4888* – *www.themerchanthotel.com*

🏠🏠 Fitzwilliam

🏊 ⌨ 🔥 🖵 🔥 🅰 ♨ 🔋

BUSINESS · STYLISH Stylish hotel by the Grand Opera House. Smart modern bedrooms have striking colour schemes, contemporary furnishings and good facilities; the higher up you go, the better the grade. Informal dining in the bar and afternoon tea in the lobby.

130 rooms ♨ – 🛏£210/270 🛏🛏£220/280 – 1 suite
Town plan: BY-e – *Great Victoria St* ✉ *BT2 7BQ* – *𝒞 (028) 9044 2080* – *www.fitzwilliamhotelbelfast.com*
Fitzwilliam – See restaurant listing

On a budget? Take advantage of lunchtime prices.

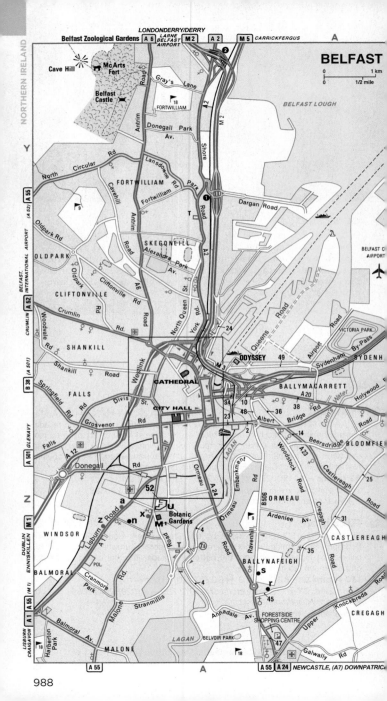

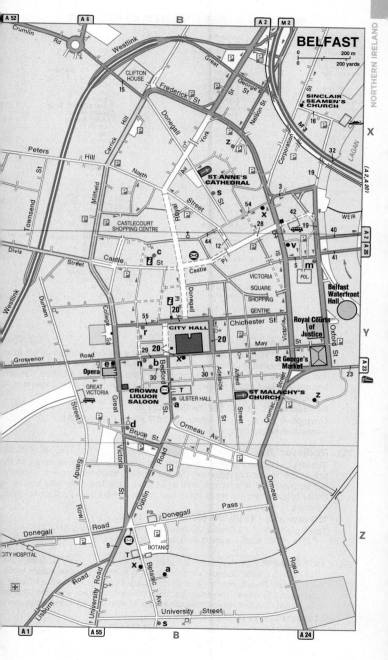

INDEX OF STREET NAMES IN BELFAST

Malmaison ⇧ Ⓕ🅱 🔁 ⎘

BUSINESS · STYLISH A converted Victorian seed warehouse with an ornate exterior; inside, original features blend with modern furnishings. The dark-hued reception leads to a snug bar and the stylish bedrooms offer good facilities: 'Samson' features a 7' bed and a snooker table. French menus in the New England styl brasserie.

64 rooms – †£ 99/189 ††£ 99/189 – ☲ £ 16

Town plan: BY-v – *34-38 Victoria St ⊠ BT1 3GH –* ℰ *(0844) 693 06 50*
– www.malmaison.com

Radisson Blu ⇧ ⇐ Ⓕ 🔁 🅰🅼 ⅏ 🅰 🅿

BUSINESS · MODERN Stylish hotel with spacious, open-plan guest areas; on the site of the former city gasworks. Smart, modern bedrooms come in Urban c Nordic styles and offer a high level of facilities, including underfloor heating i the bathrooms. Mediterranean-influenced menus in Filini, with its floor to ceiling windows.

120 rooms ☲ – †£ 99/179 ††£ 109/189 – 1 suite

Town plan: BY-z – *3 Cromac Pl, Cromac Wood, Ormeau Rd ⊠ BT7 2JB*
– ℰ *(028) 9043 4065 – www.radissonblu.co.uk/hotel-belfast*

Ten Square ⇧ Ⓕ 🔁 🅰🅼 ⅏ 🅰

BUSINESS · STYLISH Sizeable Victorian property in the city centre, hidden behin the City Hall. Stylish, modern bedrooms display bold feature walls and offer good level of facilities. The vibrant bar has a pavement terrace and entertainmer at weekends. The Grill Room offers something for everyone on its extensive menu

22 rooms – †£ 90/265 ††£ 90/265

Town plan: BY-x – *10 Donegall Sq South ⊠ BT1 5JD*
– ℰ *(028) 9024 1001 – www.tensquare.co.uk*
– Closed 24-25 December

🏠 Malone Lodge   ☆ ⊡ & ⅋ 🏛 🅿

BUSINESS · MODERN Well-run, privately owned townhouse, in a peaceful Victorian terrace. Smart, spacious bedrooms are spread over various annexes and range from corporate rooms to presidential suites and apartments. State-of-the-art function rooms include a large ballroom. Characterful bar and next door grill restaurant.

100 rooms ⌑ – †£ 75/239 ††£ 75/249 – 3 suites

Town plan: AZ-n – 60 Eglantine Ave ⊠ BT9 6DY – 𝒞 (028) 9038 8000
– www.malonelodgehotelbelfast.com

🏠 Crescent Townhouse   ☆ & ⅋ 🏛

BUSINESS · CLASSIC Regency-style townhouse run by a welcoming team. Snug first floor lounge hung with oils. Smart, spacious bedrooms - all are well-equipped and some boast four-posters and huge bathrooms. Classic bistro dishes with a modern twist in the restaurant; sharing plates and live music in the trendy bar.

17 rooms ⌑ – †£ 65/105 ††£ 75/125

Town plan: BZ-x – 13 Lower Cres ⊠ BT7 1NR – 𝒞 (028) 9032 3349
– www.crescenttownhouse.com – Closed 1 January, 5 April, 11-12 July and
24-26 December

🏠 Tara Lodge 🆕   ⊡ & ⅋ 🅿

TOWNHOUSE · FUNCTIONAL Small hotel close to the Botanic Gardens, not far from town. Smart contemporary bedrooms are split between two buildings; go for a 'Signature' room, which comes with bluetooth speakers, hair straighteners and a coffee machine.

34 rooms ⌑ – †£ 75/99 ††£ 89/119

Town plan: BZ-a – 36 Cromwell Rd ⊠ BT7 1JW – 𝒞 (028) 9059 9099
– www.taralodge.com – Closed 25-26 December

🏠 Ravenhill House   ⅋ 🅿

TRADITIONAL · CLASSIC Red-brick Victorian house set in the city suburbs. Bright, homely lounge and wood-furnished breakfast room; colourful bedrooms boast good facilities. Organic breakfasts feature homemade muesli and the wheat for the bread is home-milled.

5 rooms ⌑ – †£ 60/95 ††£ 90/110

Town plan: AZ-s – 690 Ravenhill Rd ⊠ BT6 0BZ – 𝒞 (028) 9020 7444
– www.ravenhillhouse.com – Closed 1-7 January, 7-15 July,
27 August-2 September and 20-31 December

🏠 Roseleigh House   ⅋ 🅿

FAMILY · CLASSIC Victorian bay-windowed house in a residential area by the Belvoir Park golf course; the friendly owner really makes guests feel welcome. Small lounge with lots of local info and a linen-laid breakfast room. Simple, well-kept bedrooms.

6 rooms ⌑ – †£ 50/60 ††£ 80/90

Town plan: AZ-r – 19 Rosetta Park ⊠ BT6 0DL – 𝒞 (028) 9064 4414
– www.roseleighhouse.co.uk – Closed Easter, 2 weeks July and Christmas

Restaurants

❀❀❀ Eipic   & 🄺 🄸♡ ⟷

❀ **MODERN CUISINE · ELEGANT** An elegant, intimate restaurant featuring a glass-fronted wine room and adjoined by a smart champagne bar. Top quality local ingredients feature on modern, seasonal menus and combinations are original and creative. Flavours are clearly defined and the occasional playful element features too.

→ Strangford crab, BBQ cabbage, radish and salted peanuts. Grilled halibut and langoustine with coastal greens and roast bone sauce. Chocolate caramel mousse with burnt white chocolate and sour cherries.

Menu £ 30/60

Town plan: BY-n – 28-40 Howard St ⊠ BT1 6PF – 𝒞 (028) 9033 1134 (booking essential) – www.michaeldeane.co.uk – dinner only and Friday lunch – Closed 6-31 July, 25-26 December, 1 January and Sunday-Tuesday

XX Saphyre

MODERN CUISINE · ELEGANT A former church houses this intimate, opulently styled restaurant, as well as an interior design showroom and boutique. Time-honoured flavour combinations are given a modern twist; make sure you save room for dessert.

Menu £ 26 (weekday lunch) – Carte £ 31/50

Town plan: AZ-a – 135 Lisburn Rd ⊠ BT9 7AG – ℰ (028) 9068 8606
– www.saphyrerestaurant.com – Closed Sunday, dinner Monday and Tuesday and bank holidays

XX Meat Locker

MEATS · BRASSERIE Sit on smart banquettes and look through the large window into the meat fridge, where cubes of pink Himalayan salt gradually dry age the beef. Try the Carlingford rock oysters, followed by a prime Irish cut, cooked on the Asador grill.

Menu £ 18 (lunch and early dinner) – Carte £ 23/60

Town plan: BY-n – 28-40 Howard St ⊠ BT1 6PF – ℰ (028) 9033 1134
– www.michaeldeane.co.uk – Closed 12-14 July, 25-26 December, Easter Sunday-Monday, 1 January and Sunday

XX James Street South

MODERN CUISINE · DESIGN A light and airy restaurant with a vibrant colour scheme, funky light pendants and a large bar for pre-dinner cocktails. Classic dishes use good quality seasonal produce and the cooking is hearty and masculine line with bold flavours.

Menu £ 17 – Carte £ 23/41

Town plan: BY-b – 21 James St South ⊠ BT2 7GA – ℰ (028) 9043 4310
– www.jamesstreetsouth.co.uk – Closed Easter Monday, 12-17 July, 25-26 December, 1 January and Sunday

XX Shu

BRITISH MODERN · DESIGN A well-established neighbourhood restaurant with modern look and a lively, vibrant atmosphere. Menus are guided by seasonality and the ambitious, modern British dishes have international influences. Good value set price menu.

Menu £ 14 (lunch)/31 – Carte £ 23/40

Town plan: AZ-z – 253 Lisburn Rd ⊠ BT9 7EN – ℰ (028) 9038 1655
– www.shu-restaurant.com – Closed 1 January, 11-13 July, 24-26 December and Sunday

XX Fitzwilliam

MODERN CUISINE · FASHIONABLE Bright, three-roomed restaurant on the first floor of a stylish hotel. If you're in a group choose one of the large communal tables; if you're a couple, opt for one of the intimate booths. Concise menus feature modern Irish dishes.

Menu £ 16 – Carte £ 25/42

Town plan: BY-e – Fitzwilliam Hotel, Great Victoria St ⊠ BT2 7BQ – ℰ (028) 9044 2080 (booking essential) – www.fitzwilliamhotelbelfast.com – dinner only

X OX (Stephen Toman)

❀ **BRITISH MODERN · BISTRO** Top quality seasonal produce guides the menus at this buzzy, rustic restaurant, where the cooking is flavoursome and precise, with modern Scandic influences. The welcoming minstrel's gallery is now a bar and the large windows offer views over the river; arrive early for an aperitif in their Wine Cave. Tasting menus only on Fri and Sat.

→ Finnebrogue venison, fermented kohlrabi, black garlic, mushroom. John Dory, ham hock, razor clam, vin jaune. Valrhona chocolate, blackberry, malt, salt caramel.

Menu £ 20 (weekday lunch)/45 – Carte £ 27/41

Town plan: BY-m – 1 Oxford St ⊠ BT1 3LA – ℰ (028) 9031 4121
– www.oxbelfast.com – Closed Christmas-early January, 2 weeks July, 1 week Easter, Sunday and Monday

Bar + Grill at James Street South

BRITISH MODERN · BRASSERIE Vibrant modern bistro that's popular with one and all. It's a simple place with red brick walls, a high ceiling and warehouse-style windows. Menus are classic brasserie style. The grill dishes are a hit and the succulent steaks are cooked on the Josper, served on boards and come with a choice of sauces.

Carte £ 18/42

Town plan: BY-b – *21 James St South* ⊠ *BT2 7GA* – ℰ *(028) 9560 0700 (booking advisable)* – *www.belfastbargrill.co.uk* – *Closed 1 January, 12 July and 25-26 December*

Deanes at Queens

BRITISH MODERN · BRASSERIE This bustling brasserie is part of Queen's University and is just a short walk from the city centre. Those after coffee and cake – or a cocktail – should make for the bar, while the terrace is a great spot on a sunny day. Refined modern dishes are full of flavour; the Mibrasa charcoal grill is a feature.

Menu £ 20 (weekdays) – Carte £ 22/38

Town plan: AZ-x – *1 College Gdns* ⊠ *BT9 6BQ* – ℰ *(028) 9038 2111* – *www.michaeldeane.co.uk* – *Closed 1 January, 5-6 April, 12 July, 25-26 December and Sunday dinner*

Home

BRITISH TRADITIONAL · RUSTIC A popular restaurant with a deli and café to the front offering sandwiches and cakes, and a simple, rustic dining room to the rear. As its name suggests, cooking is straightforward, focusing on tasty, refined versions of dishes that are often prepared at home. Service is attentive and has personality.

Menu £ 15 (weekday dinner)/19 – Carte £ 23/35

Town plan: BY-r – *22 Wellington Pl* ⊠ *BT1 6GE* – ℰ *(028) 9023 4946* – *www.homebelfast.co.uk* – *Closed 12 July and 25-26 December*

Ginger Bistro

TRADITIONAL CUISINE · BISTRO Rustic neighbourhood bistro close to the Grand Opera House. The two rooms feature bright modern artwork and bespoke fish-themed paintings. Good-sized menus feature simply cooked Irish ingredients and display some Asian influences.

Carte £ 20/39

Town plan: BYZ-d – *7-8 Hope St* ⊠ *BT2 5EE* – ℰ *(028) 9024 4421* – *www.gingerbistro.com* – *Closed Christmas, New Year, Easter, 5 days mid-July, Sunday, Monday and bank holidays*

Deanes Deli

BRITISH MODERN · BISTRO Glass-fronted city centre eatery. One side is a smart restaurant offering an appealing menu of classical dishes with some Asian and Mediterranean influences; the other side acts as a coffee shop by day and a buzzy tapas bar by night.

Menu £ 16 (dinner) – Carte £ 20/40

Town plan: BY-a – *42-44 Bedford St* ⊠ *BT2 7FF* – ℰ *(028) 9024 8800* – *www.michaeldeane.co.uk* – *Closed Easter, 1 January, 12 July, 25-26 December and Sunday*

Coppi

MEDITERRANEAN · BISTRO Set on the ground floor of a purpose built property in the Cathedral Quarter. It's big and buzzy, with rustic furnishings and leather booths, and staff are bright and friendly. Good value Italian dishes; start with a selection of cicchetti.

Menu £ 13/23 – Carte £ 19/31

Town plan: BX-z – *St Annes Sq* ⊠ *BT1 2LD* – ℰ *(028) 9031 1959* – *www.coppi.co.uk* – *Closed 25 December*

X **Love Fish**   & AK ⌷ ⇔

FISH AND SEAFOOD · ELEGANT If it comes from the sea, they'll serve it here! A glass ceiling makes it light and airy and the décor has a maritime feel. The à la carte offers three sizes of platter and everything from cod croquettes to lobster. Lunch is good value.

Carte £16/34

Town plan: BY-n – *28-40 Howard St* ✉ *BT1 6PF*
– ℰ *(028) 9033 1134 – www.michaeldeane.co.uk*
– *Closed 12-14 July, 25-26 December, Easter Sunday-Monday, 1 January and Sunday dinner*

X **Il Pirata**   & AK ⌷ ⍦

MEDITERRANEAN · RUSTIC Rustic restaurant with scrubbed wooden floors and an open kitchen. Mediterranean-influenced menus offer an extensive range of mainly Italian small plates; 3 or 4 dishes per person (plus dessert) should suffice. Bright, friendly service.

Carte £18/25

279-281 Upper Newtownards Rd ✉ *BT4 3JF* – *East : 3 mi by A 2 on A 20*
– ℰ *(028) 9067 3421 – www.ilpiratabelfast.com*

X **Hadskis**   ⌂ AK ⌷ ⇔

CLASSIC CUISINE · RUSTIC This modern conversion is in the up-and-coming Cathedral Quarter. The long, narrow room has an open kitchen, where you can watch the chefs use the latest market produce to prepare globally-influenced dishes and tasty small plates.

Carte £19/38

Town plan: BX-s – *33 Donegall St* ✉ *BT1 2NB*
– ℰ *(028) 9032 5444 – www.hadskis.co.uk*
– *Closed 25-26 December, 1 January and 12 July*

X **Mourne Seafood Bar**   AK ⇔

FISH AND SEAFOOD · BISTRO This popular seafood restaurant comes complete with a small shop and a cookery school. Blackboard menus offer a huge array of freshly prepared dishes; go for the classics, such as the Carlingford oysters, accompanied by a pint of stout.

Menu £25 – Carte £22/38

Town plan: BY-c – *34-36 Bank St* ✉ *BT1 1HL*
– ℰ *(02890) 248 544 (booking essential at dinner)*
– *www.mourneseafood.com*
– *Closed 24-26 December, 1 January, 17 March, Easter Sunday-Monday and dinner Sunday*

X **Molly's Yard**   ⌂ & ⍦ ⍨

BRITISH TRADITIONAL · BISTRO Split-level bistro in a former coach house and stables, with exposed brickwork and a pleasant courtyard. Simple lunches and more ambitious dinners with classical combinations given a personal twist. Fine selection of ales and stouts.

Menu £20/26 – Carte £23/38

Town plan: BZ-s – *1 College Green Mews, Botanic Ave* ✉ *BT7 1LW*
– ℰ *(028) 9032 2600 (booking essential)*
– *www.mollysyard.co.uk – Closed 11-12 July, 24-26 December, 1 January and Sunday*

BRYANSFORD – Down → See Newcastle

BUSHMILLS MUILEANN NA BUAISE

Moyle – ✉ Bushmills – Pop. 1 343 – Regional map n° **20**-C1
▶ Belfast 57 mi – Ballycastle 12 mi – Coleraine 10 mi

Bushmills Inn

TRADITIONAL · CLASSIC Proudly run, part-17C whitewashed inn that successfully blends the old with the new. The conference room features a state-of-the-art cinema. Up-to-date bedrooms are split between the original house and an extension. Have a drink beside the peat fire in the old whiskey bar before dining on classic dishes.

41 rooms ⌑ – ♦£ 98/278 ♦♦£ 128/398

9 Dunluce Rd ⊠ BT57 8QG – ℰ (028) 2073 3000 – www.bushmillsinn.com – Closed 24-25 December

Causeway Lodge

FAMILY · STYLISH Set inland from the Giant's Causeway, in a peaceful location. Guest areas come with polished wood floors, leather furnishings and artwork of local scenes. Spacious, boutique bedrooms have bold feature walls and a high level of facilities.

5 rooms ⌑ – ♦£ 85/110 ♦♦£ 90/140

52 Moycraig Rd, Dunseverick ⊠ BT57 8TB – East : 5 mi by A 2 and Drumnagee Rd – ℰ (028) 2073 0333 – www.causewaylodge.com

COLERAINE CÚIL RAITHIN

Coleraine – Pop. 24 455 – Regional map n° **20**-C1

▨ Belfast 53 mi – Ballymena 25 mi – Londonderry 31 mi – Omagh 65 mi

Greenhill House

TRADITIONAL · CLASSIC Long-standing guesthouse with mature gardens and a traditional country house style. Spacious open-fired lounge and linen-laid breakfast room; heavy drapes, antiques and ornaments feature. Chatty, welcoming owner.

4 rooms ⌑ – ♦£ 45 ♦♦£ 70

24 Greenhill Rd, Aghadowey ⊠ BT51 4EU – South : 9 mi by A 29 on B 66 – ℰ (028) 7086 8241 – www.greenhill-house.co.uk – Closed November-February

CRUMLIN CROMGHLINN

Antrim – Pop. 5 117 – Regional map n° **20**-C2

▨ Belfast 14 mi – Ballymena 20 mi

Ballyrobin

BUSINESS · STYLISH A smart, country style lodge – a former farmhouse – just a stone's throw from the airport and offering a week's free parking. Stylish, modern bedrooms. Menus offer a wide array of international dishes to be enjoyed in the traditional, characterful bar or the conservatory dining room.

20 rooms – ♦£ 52/101 ♦♦£ 52/101 – ⌑£ 9

144-146 Ballyrobin Rd, Aldergrove ⊠ BT29 4EG – North : 7 mi by A 52 and A 26 on A 57 – ℰ (028) 9442 2211 – www.ballyrobincountrylodge.com – Closed 25 December

Caldhame Lodge

FAMILY · PERSONALISED Purpose-built guesthouse near the airport, with a pleasant mix of lawns and paved terracing. Comfy guest areas include a conservatory breakfast room and a lounge filled with family photos. Good-sized, individually decorated bedrooms are immaculately kept and feature warm fabrics and iPod docking stations.

7 rooms ⌑ – ♦£ 40/48 ♦♦£ 70/78

102 Moira Rd, Nutts Corner ⊠ BT29 4HG – Southeast : 2 mi on A 26 – ℰ (028) 9442 3099 – www.caldhamelodge.co.uk

DERRY/LONDONDERRY → See Londonderry

DONAGHADEE DOMHNACH DAOI

Ards – Pop. 6 856 – Regional map n° **20**-D2

▨ Belfast 18 mi – Ballymena 44 mi

🏮 Pier 36

TRADITIONAL CUISINE · PUB Spacious family-run pub set on the quayside, opposite a lighthouse, overlooking the picturesque harbour. Extensive menus feature a mix of classic, modern and international influences, with good weekday deals and plenty of fresh, local seafood. Bright, modern bedrooms; some with great sea and harbour views.

Menu £17 (early dinner) – Carte £16/38

6 rooms ⌧ – †£50/75 ††£70/99

36 The Parade ⌧ BT21 0HE – ℰ (028) 9188 4466 – www.pier36.co.uk – Closed 25 December

DUNDRUM DÚN DROMA

Down – Pop. 1 522 – Regional map n° **20**-D3
▶ Belfast 29 mi – Downpatrick 9 mi – Newcastle 4 mi

🏠 Carriage House

TRADITIONAL · CLASSIC Sweet, lilac-washed terraced house with colourful window boxes. Homely lounge with books and local info. Simple, antique-furnished bedrooms; some affording pleasant bay views. Breakfast in the conservatory overlooking the pretty garden.

3 rooms ⌧ – †£60/80 ††£80/90

71 Main St ⌧ BT33 0LU – ℰ (028) 4375 1635 – www.carriagehousedundrum.com

X Buck's Head Inn

FISH AND SEAFOOD · NEIGHBOURHOOD Converted village pub. Have drinks in the lounge then head for the front room with its cosy booths and open fire, or the rear room which overlooks the garden. Unfussy, traditional lunches and more ambitious dinners; seafood is a strength.

Menu £30 (dinner) – Carte lunch £22/34

77-79 Main St ⌧ BT33 0LU – ℰ (028) 4375 1868 – Closed 24-25 December and Monday from October-March

X Mourne Seafood Bar

FISH AND SEAFOOD · RUSTIC Friendly, rustic restaurant on the main street of a busy coastal town. Simple, wood-furnished dining room with nautically themed artwork. Classic menus centre around seafood, with oysters and mussels from the owners' beds the specialities.

Carte £19/30

10 Main St ⌧ BT33 0LU – ℰ (028) 4375 1377 (booking essential)
– www.mourneseafood.com – Closed dinner 24 December, 25 December and Monday-Wednesday in winter

DUNGANNON DÚN GEANAINN

Dungannon – Pop. 14 380 – Regional map n° **20**-C2
▶ Belfast 42 mi – Ballymena 37 mi – Dundalk 47 mi – Londonderry 60 mi

🏠 Grange Lodge

TRADITIONAL · CLASSIC Attractive Georgian country house surrounded by mature, well-kept gardens, ideal for afternoon tea. Antique-furnished guest areas display fine sketches and lithographs. Snug, well-appointed bedrooms are immaculately kept and have good extras. The flower-filled dining room serves classically based Irish dishes.

5 rooms ⌧ – †£75/85 ††£85/95

7 Grange Rd, Moy ⌧ BT71 7EJ – Southeast : 3.5 mi by A 29 – ℰ (028) 8778 4212 – www.grangelodgecountryhouse.com – Closed 20 December-1 February

ENNISKILLEN INIS CEITHLEANN

Fermanagh – Pop. 13 757 – Regional map n° **20**-A2
▶ Belfast 84 mi – Londonderry 60 mi – Craigavon 62 mi – Portadown 59 mi

Lough Erne Resort

LUXURY · MODERN Vast, luxurious golf and leisure resort on a peninsula between two loughs. Bedrooms have a classical style and are extremely well-appointed; the suites and lodges are dotted about the grounds. Relax in the beautiful Thai spa or the huge pool with its stunning mosaic wall. Ambitious, contemporary dining and lough views in Catalina; steaks and grills in the clubhouse.

120 rooms ☑ – ♦£100/180 ♦♦£120/230 – 6 suites
Belleek Rd ⊠ BT93 7ED – Northwest : 4 mi by A 4 on A 46
– ℰ (028) 6632 3230 – www.lougherneresort.com

Manor House

TRADITIONAL · MODERN Impressive yellow-washed manor house overlooking Lough Erne and surrounded by mature grounds. Comfy, stylish guest areas mix the traditional and the contemporary. Bedrooms range from characterful in the main house to smart and modern in the extensions. The formal dining room offers classical cooking and there's a more casual all-day menu served in the old vaults.

79 rooms ☑ – ♦£70/125 ♦♦£80/325 – 2 suites
Killadeas ⊠ BT94 1NY – North : 7.5 mi by A 32 on B 82
– ℰ (028) 6862 2200 – www.manorhousecountryhotel.com
Belleek – See restaurant listing

XX Belleek 🅝

CLASSIC CUISINE · FORMAL Formal hotel dining room comprising three rooms – two with high ceilings and ornate plasterwork and the third in a glass-fronted cube which offers unrivalled views across the marina. Classic dishes are presented in a modern manner.

Menu £35
Manor House Hotel, Killadeas ⊠ BT94 1NY – North : 7.5 mi by A 32 on B 82
– ℰ (028) 6862 2200 – www.manorhousecountryhotel.com
– closed Monday-Friday lunch and Sunday dinner in winter

GALGORM Antrim – Ballymena → See Ballymena

HILLSBOROUGH CROMGHLINN

Lisburn – Pop. 3 738 – Regional map n° **20**-C2
◖ Belfast 12 mi – London 358 mi – Lisburn 4 mi – Craigavon 21 mi

Lisnacurran Country House 🅝

FAMILY · HOMELY Homely Edwardian house, where spacious rooms are furnished with antiques. Choose a bedroom in the main house, the former milking parlour or the old barn. Breakfasts are hearty – the homemade soda and potato bread is a must.

9 rooms ☑ – ♦£50/55 ♦♦£65/80
6 Listullycurran Rd, Dromore ⊠ BT25 1RB – Southwest : 3 mi on A 1
– ℰ (028) 9269 8710 – www.lisnacurrancountryhouse.co.uk

Parson's Nose

BRITISH TRADITIONAL · PUB Characterful Georgian property built by the first Marquis of Downshire. Rustic, open-fired bar; restaurant above overlooks a lake in the castle grounds. Unashamedly traditional menus and generous portions; the daily fish specials are a hit.

Menu £17 (weekdays)/24 – Carte £21/36
48 Lisburn St ⊠ BT26 6AB
– ℰ (028) 9268 3009 (booking advisable) – www.theparsonsnose.co.uk
– Closed 25 December

Plough Inn
🛜 ⏱

TRADITIONAL CUISINE · PUB Family-run, 18C coaching inn that's three establish
ments in one: a bar with an adjoining dining room; a café-cum-bistro; and a sea
food restaurant. Dishes range from light snacks and pub classics to more moder
international offerings.

Menu £ 13 – Carte £ 22/41

*3 The Square ⊠ BT26 6AG – ℰ (028) 9268 2985
– www.theploughhillsbrough.co.uk – Closed 25-26 December*

at Annahilt Southeast: 4 mi on B177 – ⊠ Hillsborough

Fortwilliam
🖨 🛇 D

TRADITIONAL · CLASSIC Attractive bay-windowed farmhouse with neat ga
dens, surrounded by 80 acres of land. Homely lounge and a country kitche
with an Aga. Traditional bedrooms have flowery fabrics, antiques and countr
views; two have private bathrooms.

3 rooms ⊊ – †£ 50 ††£ 75

*210 Ballynahinch Rd ⊠ BT26 6BH – Northwest : 0.25 mi on B 177 – ℰ (028)
9268 2255 – www.fortwilliamcountryhouse.com – Closed 24-27 December*

Pheasant
🛜 D

TRADITIONAL CUISINE · PUB Sizeable creamwashed pub with Gothic stylin
Guinness-themed artwork and a typically Irish feel. Internationally influenced m
nus showcase local, seasonal produce, with seafood a speciality in summer ar
game featuring highly in winter.

Menu £ 20 – Carte £ 20/35

*410 Upper Ballynahinch Rd ⊠ BT26 6NR – North : 1 mi on Lisburn rd – ℰ (028)
9263 8056 – www.thepheasantrestaurant.co.uk – Closed 12 July and 25 Decemb*

HOLYWOOD ARD MHIC NASCA
North Down – Pop. 12 131 – Regional map n° **20**-D2
▶ Belfast 7 mi – Bangor 6 mi

Culloden
🖨 🍽 ⬆ 🏞 ⊕ 🗗 🖅 🍷 🛇 ♨ D

BUSINESS · CLASSIC An extended Gothic mansion overlooking Belfast Loug
with well-maintained gardens full of modern sculptures, and a smart spa. Charm
ing, traditional, antique-furnished guest areas have open fires and fine ceilir
frescoes. Characterful bedrooms offer good facilities. Classical menus and goc
views in formal Mitre; wide range of traditional dishes in Cultra Inn.

102 rooms ⊊ – †£ 130/220 ††£ 165/300 – 2 suites

*142 Bangor Rd ⊠ BT18 0EX – East : 1.5 mi on A 2 – ℰ (028) 9042 1066
– www.hastingshotels.com*

Rayanne House
🖨 ⬆ ⊊ 🛇 D

TRADITIONAL · CLASSIC Keenly run, part-Victorian house in a residential are
Homely, antique-filled guest areas. Smart, country house bedrooms with a mod
ern edge; those to the front offer the best views. Ambitious, seasonal dishes
formal dining room; try the Titanic tasting menu – a version of the last me
served on the ship.

10 rooms ⊊ – †£ 80/95 ††£ 120/140

*60 Demesne Rd ⊠ BT18 9EX – by My Lady's Mile Rd – ℰ (028) 9042 5859
– www.rayannehouse.com*

Beech Hill
🛇 ⬆ D

TRADITIONAL · CLASSIC An antique-furnished guesthouse in a peaceful cou
tryside setting; personally run by the friendly owner. Comfortable lounge and tr
ditional, individually styled bedrooms with fresh flowers. Communal breakfasts.

3 rooms ⊊ – †£ 60/65 ††£ 100/110

*23 Ballymoney Rd, Craigantlet ⊠ BT23 4TG – Southeast : 4.5 mi by A 2 on
Craigantlet rd – ℰ (028) 9042 5892 – www.beech-hill.net*

✗✗ Fontana

🍴 **MODERN CUISINE · NEIGHBOURHOOD** A favourite with the locals is this smart, modern, first floor restaurant; accessed down a narrow town centre passageway and decorated with contemporary art. Menus offer British, Mediterranean and some Asian dishes, with local seafood a speciality. Good value set menus are available at both lunch and dinner.

Menu £ 23 – Carte £ 21/32

61A High St ⊠ BT18 9AE – 𝒞 (028) 9080 9908 – www.restaurantfontana.com
– Closed 25-26 December, 1-2 January, Saturday lunch, Sunday dinner and Monday

KILLINCHY

Ards – Regional map n° **20**-D2

▶ Belfast 16 mi – Newtownards 11 mi – Lisburn 17 mi – Bangor 16 mi

🍽 Balloo House 🆕

CLASSIC CUISINE · PUB Characterful former farmhouse with a smart dining pub feel. Lengthy menus offer a mix of hearty pub classics and dishes with more international leanings. Pies are popular, as is High Tea, which is served every day except Saturday.

Menu £ 14 (weekday lunch)/19 – Carte £ 20/37

1 Comber Rd ⊠ BT23 6PA – West : 0.75 mi on A 22
– 𝒞 (028) 9754 1210 (bookings advisable at dinner) – www.balloohouse.com
– Closed 25 December

LARNE LATHARNA

Larne – Pop. 18 323 – Regional map n° **20**-D2

▶ Belfast 23 mi – Ballymena 20 mi

🏠 Manor House

TRADITIONAL · CLASSIC Large Victorian house filled with family antiques. The lounge boasts an immense Chinese vase and gilded art, and the snug dining room features flocked walls. Cosy, immaculate bedrooms are reached via an original carved staircase.

8 rooms ⊑ – ♦£ 30/35 ♦♦£ 56/60

23 Olderfleet Rd, Harbour Highway ⊠ BT40 1AS
– 𝒞 (028) 2827 3305 – www.themanorguesthouse.com
– Closed 25-26 December

LIMAVADY LÉIM AN MHADAIDH

Limavady – Pop. 12 669 – Regional map n° **20**-B1

▶ Belfast 62 mi – Ballymena 39 mi – Coleraine 13 mi – Londonderry 17 mi

✗✗ Lime Tree

TRADITIONAL CUISINE · NEIGHBOURHOOD Keenly run neighbourhood restaurant; its traditional exterior concealing a modern room with purple velvet banquettes and colourful artwork. Unfussy, classical cooking features meats and veg from the village; try the homemade wheaten bread.

Menu £ 20 (weekday lunch) – Carte £ 25/38

60 Catherine St ⊠ BT49 9DB
– 𝒞 (028) 7776 4300 – www.limetreerest.com
– dinner only and lunch Thursday-Friday
– Closed 25-26 December, Sunday and Monday

LISBANE AN LIOS BÁN

Ards – ⊠ Comber – Regional map n° **20**-D2

▶ Belfast 14 mi – Newtownards 9 mi – Saintfield 7 mi

NORTHERN IRELAND

🏠 Anna's House 🦢 ⋖ 🛜 📶

FAMILY · MODERN An extended farmhouse with welcoming owners, cosy bed rooms and a superb lake and meadow outlook; take in the view from the contemporary lounge. The snug breakfast room has a wood burning stove and local organic produce features.

4 rooms ⌑ – ♦£50/65 ♦♦£80/100

Tullynagee, 35 Lisbarnett Rd. ⊠ BT23 6AW – Southeast : 0.5 mi – ℰ (028) 9754 1566 – www.annashouse.com – Closed Christmas-New Year

✗ Old Schoolhouse Inn ⇦ 🛜 🎐 🖨

🏵 **BRITISH MODERN · INDIVIDUAL** Just a stone's throw from Strangford Lough this stylish, sumptuous restaurant, which has been passed down from parents son. Modern dishes are skilfully prepared, full of flavour and use top notch ingredients – including plenty of local seafood and game. Satisfyingly, the chef isn't afraid to prepare some simpler dishes too. Homely bedrooms complete the picture.

Menu £14/24 – Carte £24/38

8 rooms ⌑ – ♦£55/70 ♦♦£80/90

100 Ballydrain Rd ⊠ BT23 6EA – Northeast : 1.5 mi by Quarry Rd on Ballydrain R – ℰ (028) 9754 1182 (booking essential) – www.theoldschoolhouseinn.com

🍴 Poacher's Pocket 🎐 🖨

BRITISH TRADITIONAL · PUB Modern-looking building in the centre of a small village; the best seats are in the two-tiered extension overlooking the internal courtyard. Wide-ranging menus offer rustic, hearty dishes; come at the weekend for a laid-back brunch.

Menu £14 (weekdays) – Carte £21/36

181 Killinchy Rd ⊠ BT23 5NE – ℰ (028) 9754 1589 – www.poacherspocketlisbane.com – Closed 25 December

LISNASKEA

Fermanagh – Pop. 2 880 – Regional map n° **20**-B3
▶ Belfast 82 mi – Dublin 91 mi – Londonderry 67 mi – Omagh 33 mi

✗✗ Watermill Lodge ⇦ ⋖ 🛜 🎐 🖨 ⒶⒶ

FRENCH CLASSIC · CLASSIC Charming red-brick cottage with a thatched roof, delightful terrace and superb water gardens flowing down to Lough Erne – where you can hire one of their fishing boats. Characterful, rustic interior with smart laid tables and a 25,000 litre aquarium; classical Gallic menu. Comfy, airy bedrooms have stone floors and heavy wood furnishings; some look over the water.

Menu £20/26 – Carte £33/57

7 rooms ⌑ – ♦£59 ♦♦£79/99

Kilmore Quay ⊠ BT92 0DT – Southwest: 3 mi by B 127 – ℰ (028) 6772 4369 (booking advisable) – www.watermillrestaurantfermanagh.com – dinner only an lunch Saturday and Sunday – Closed January

LONDONDERRY/DERRY

Derry – Pop. 85 016 – Regional map n° **20**-B1
▶ Belfast 70 mi – Dublin 146 mi – Omagh 34 mi

🏨 City 🛜 ⋖ 📺 🏊 💪 🍴 🖨

BUSINESS · MODERN Large, centrally located hotel overlooking the Peace Bridge on the River Foyle. Well-maintained, modern interior with a comfortable lounge and a well-equipped leisure centre. Smart bedrooms; those on the upper floors have great outlooks. Informal brasserie affords pleasant water views.

158 rooms ⌑ – ♦£72/152 ♦♦£79/159 – 8 suites

Queens Quay ⊠ BT48 7AS – ℰ (028) 7136 5800 – www.cityhotelderry.com – Closed 24-26 December

NORTHERN IRELAND

🏠 Beech Hill Country House

TRADITIONAL · CLASSIC Once a US marine camp, this 18C house is now a welcoming hotel and popular wedding venue. Characterful guest areas feature ornate coving and antiques. Country house bedrooms in the original building; others are more modern and spacious. Dine from traditional menus overlooking the lake and water wheel.

31 rooms ☑ – †£ 99/109 ††£ 129/235 – 2 suites

32 Ardmore Rd ⊠ BT47 3QP – Southeast : 3.5 mi by A 6
– ℰ (028) 7134 9279 – www.beech-hill.com
– Closed 24-25 December

🏠 Ramada H. Da Vinci's

BUSINESS · MODERN Located on the northern edge of the city, beside an extremely characterful pub dating from 1986 – now the hotel's bar. Photos of stars who've stayed here fill the corridors, modern bedrooms are the biggest in the city and there are plenty of stylish function spaces, along with an atmospheric brasserie.

70 rooms – †£ 56/129 ††£ 65/170 – ☑ £ 9

15 Culmore Rd ⊠ BT48 8JB – North : 1 mi on A 2 (Foyle Bridge rd)
– ℰ (028) 7127 9111 – www.davincishotel.com
– Closed 24-25 December

XX Browns In Town

BRITISH MODERN · BRASSERIE Just across the river from the original 'Browns', is this stylish, modern bigger sister. A bewildering array of menus offer everything you could want, from light snacks to hearty main courses of Irish meats and local vegetables.

Menu £ 22 (dinner) – Carte £ 26/41

Strand Rd ⊠ BT48 7DJ – ℰ (028) 7136 2889 – www.brownsrestaurant.com
– Closed 25-26 December and Sunday lunch

XX Browns

BRITISH MODERN · NEIGHBOURHOOD Smart neighbourhood restaurant with a plush lounge and an intimate dining room featuring monochrome photos and some banquette seating. Cooking is modern and technically adept, relying on local produce, home-baking and home-smoking.

Menu £ 22/40 – Carte £ 34/41

1 Bonds Hill, Waterside ⊠ BT47 6DW – East : 1 mi by A 2
– ℰ (028) 7134 5180 (booking advisable) – www.brownsrestaurant.com
– Closed Monday, Saturday lunch and Sunday dinner

MAGHERA MACHAIRE RÁTHA

Magherafelt – Pop. 3 886 – Regional map n° **20**-C2
📍 Belfast 40 mi – Ballymena 19 mi – Coleraine 21 mi – Londonderry 32 mi

🏠 Ardtara Country House

COUNTRY HOUSE · HOMELY Spacious, elegant 19C country house, originally built for a local linen manufacturer. It's set in 8 acres of mature grounds and has a calming, restful air; many period features remain. The intimate wood-panelled restaurant offers a menu of modern classics which feature ingredients foraged for by the chef.

9 rooms ☑ – †£ 79/99 ††£ 79/129

8 Gorteade Rd, Upperlands ⊠ BT46 5SA
– ℰ (028) 7964 4490 – www.ardtara.com
– Closed Monday in winter

MAGHERAFELT

Magherafelt – Pop. 8 881 – Regional map n° **20**-C2
📍 Belfast 76 mi – Dublin 117 mi – Londonderry 5 mi – Craigavon 75 mi

NORTHERN IRELAND

XX **Church Street** &. 🗚 🚭

BRITISH TRADITIONAL · NEIGHBOURHOOD Bustling eatery on the main stree
of a busy country town. The long, narrow room has a mix of bistro, pew an
high-backed seating, and there's a second smart room above. Unfussy, classica
dishes rely on good quality local produce.

Menu £ 12 (early dinner) – Carte £ 22/36

23 Church St ⊠ BT45 6AP – ℰ (028) 7932 8083 (booking advisable)
– www.churchstreetrestaurant.co.uk – dinner only and Sunday lunch – Closed
4-14 January, 4-14 July, Monday and Tuesday

MAGHERALIN

Craigavon – Pop. 1 403 – Regional map n° **20**-C2
▶ Belfast 20 mi – Downpatrick 32 mi – Londonderry 77 mi

🏡 **Newforge House** 🄽 ⇧ 🐾 🚒 ⅋ P

COUNTRY HOUSE · PERSONALISED A traditional Georgian building with an ol
linen mill behind and colourful gardens and a meadow in front. Bedrooms ar
named after former inhabitants of the house and are tastefully furnished with pe
riod pieces. Three course dinners are replaced by simpler suppers on Sunday
and Mondays.

6 rooms – ⚊£ 80/115 ⚊⚊£ 120/180

58 Newforge Rd ⊠ BT67 0QL – ℰ (028) 9261 1255 – www.newforgehouse.com
– Closed 20 December-1 February

MOUNTHILL

Antrim – Pop. 69 – Regional map n° **20**-D2
▶ Belfast 15 mi – Templepatrick 7 mi – Lar 5 mi

🍴 **Billy Andy's** ⇦ P

BRITISH TRADITIONAL · RUSTIC It used to be the village store as well as a pul
and although the groceries are gone, this place still seems to be all things to a
people. Cooking is filling, with a strong Irish accent. They offer a fine selection o
whiskies, there are four modern bedrooms and Saturday music sessions pack th
place out.

Menu £ 18/22 – Carte £ 21/36

4 rooms �), – ⚊£ 40/50 ⚊⚊£ 60/80

66 Browndod Rd ⊠ BT40 3DX – Northeast : 0.5 mi on Browndod Rd – ℰ (028)
2827 0648 – www.billyandys.com – Closed 25-26 December and lunch
Monday-Thursday

NEWCASTLE AN CAISLEÁN NUA

Down – Pop. 7 723 – Regional map n° **20**-D3
▶ Belfast 32 mi – Londonderry 101 mi

🏨 **Slieve Donard** ⇧ ⋖ 🚒 🗒 ☺ 🐾 ⒧ ℅ ⅋ 🅟

TRADITIONAL · CLASSIC Grand railway hotel built in 1897, set right beside th
beach and boasting excellent sea and mountain views. Guest areas are spaciou
and modern, bedrooms are stylish, and the superb leisure facilities include
smart spa with a pool overlooking the sea. There's casual all-day dining in th
lounge, an accessible menu in Percy French and classic dining in formal Oak.

181 rooms ⊡ – ⚊£ 110/230 ⚊⚊£ 130/280

Downs Rd ⊠ BT33 0AH – ℰ (028) 4372 1066 – www.hastingshotels.com

🏨 **Burrendale H. Country Club & Spa** ⇧ 🚒 🏠 🗒 ☺ 🐾 ℅ ℁

BUSINESS · CLASSIC Privately owned hotel between the &. ℁ P
Mourne Mountains and the Irish Sea, close to the Royal County Down golf cours
Well-equipped modern bedrooms. Good leisure facilities and a vast spa offering
comprehensive range of treatments. Large, open-plan bar and lounge, with infor
mal dining from extensive menus.

68 rooms ⊡ – ⚊£ 130/150 ⚊⚊£ 180/230 – 1 suite

51 Castlewellan Rd ⊠ BT33 0JY – North : 1 mi on A 50 – ℰ (028) 4372 2599
– www.burrendale.com

XX **Vanilla** &. AC

INTERNATIONAL · **NEIGHBOURHOOD** Contemporary restaurant; its black canopy standing out amongst the town centre shops. The long, narrow room is flanked by brushed velvet banquettes and polished tables. Attractively presented, internationally influenced modern dishes.

Menu £ 20 (weekdays) – Carte £ 28/40

67 Main St ⊠ BT33 0AE – ℰ (028) 4372 2268 – www.vanillarestaurant.co.uk
– Closed 25-27 December and 1 January and Wednesday dinner in winter

at Bryansford Northwest: 2.75 mi on B180

🏠 **Tollyrose Country House** ⇐ 🚗 ⅏ 🅿

FAMILY · **HOMELY** Purpose-built guesthouse beside the Tollymore Forest Park, at the foot of the Mourne Mountains. Simple, modern bedrooms come in neutral hues; those on the top floor have the best views. Lots of local info in the lounge. Friendly owners.

6 rooms ⊊ – †£ 45 ††£ 75

15 Hilltown Rd ⊠ BT33 0PX – Southwest : 0.5 mi on B 180 – ℰ (028) 4372 6077
– www.tollyrose.com

NEWTOWNABBEY

Newtownabbey – Pop. 61 713 – Regional map n° **20**-D2
▶ Belfast 7 mi – Templepatrick 12 mi – Carrickfurgus 13 mi

X **Sleepy Hollow** &. 🅿

MODERN CUISINE · **RURAL** This remote, passionately run restaurant is a real find, with its rustic rooms, large terrace, cosy hayloft bar and farm shop! Cooking is contrastingly modern, and the chef prides himself on using seasonal ingredients with a story.

Menu £ 20 – Carte £ 21/36

15 Klin Rd ⊠ BT36 4SU – Northwest : 1 mi by Ballyclare Rd and Ballycraig Rd
– ℰ (028) 9083 8672 – www.sleepyhollowrestaurant.com – Closed
25-26 December

NEWTOWNARDS BAILE NUA NA HARDA

Ards – Pop. 28 437 – Regional map n° **20**-D2
▶ Belfast 10 mi – Bangor 144 mi – Downpatrick 22 mi

🏠 **Edenvale House** ⌂ ⇐ 🚗 ⅏ 🅿

TRADITIONAL · **CLASSIC** Attractive Georgian farmhouse with a charming owner and pleasant lough and mountain views. It's traditionally decorated, with a comfy drawing room and a wicker-furnished sun room. Spacious, homely bedrooms boast good facilities.

3 rooms ⊊ – †£ 60 ††£ 110

130 Portaferry Rd ⊠ BT22 2AH – Southeast : 2.75 mi on A 20 – ℰ (028) 9181 4881
– www.edenvalehouse.com – Closed Christmas-New Year

PORTRUSH PORT ROIS

Coleraine – Pop. 6 640 – Regional map n° **20**-C1
▶ Belfast 58 mi – Coleraine 4 mi – Londonderry 35 mi

🏠 **Shola Coach House** 🆕 🚗 ⅏ 🅿

TOWNHOUSE · **HOMELY** This attractive stone coach house once belonged to the Victorian manor house next door. Inside it's light and airy, with a tasteful contemporary style and modern facilities. Bedrooms are spacious; one is in the colourful garden.

4 rooms – †£ 70 ††£ 90/110

110A Gateside Rd ⊠ BT56 8NP – East : 1.5 mi by Ballywillan Road – ℰ (028)
7082 5925 – www.sholabandb.com – Closed December and January

NORTHERN IRELAND

🏠 Beulah

TRADITIONAL · COSY Double-fronted, bay-windowed terraced house in a seaside town, run by a very charming, chatty owner with plenty of local knowledge. Comfy, spotlessly kept bedrooms have compact bathrooms. The homemade bread is a hit at breakfast.

9 rooms �? – 🛏£ 45 🛏🛏£ 65/70

16 Causeway St ⌧ BT56 8AB – ℰ (028) 7082 2413 – www.beulahguesthouse.com

PORTSTEWART PORT STIÓBHAIRD

Coleraine – Regional map n° **35**-C1

▶ Belfast 60 mi – Ballymena 32 mi – Coleraine 6 mi

🏠 Strandeen

FAMILY · CONTEMPORARY A great place to escape everyday life: the rooms are light and airy, the atmosphere is serene and the open-plan lounge takes in beach and mountain views. Organic breakfasts feature smoothies, chai porridge and bircher muesli.

5 rooms �? – 🛏£ 75/100 🛏🛏£ 110/120

63 Strand Rd ⌧ BT55 7LU – ℰ (028) 7083 3872 – www.strandeen.com – Closed January

𝗫 Harry's Shack

TRADITIONAL CUISINE · RUSTIC The location is superb, on a sandy National Trust beach, with views across to Inishowen. It's an appealingly simple place with wooden tables and classroom style chairs. Concise menus wisely let local ingredients speak for themselves.

Carte £ 23/32

118 Strand Rd ⌧ BT55 7PG – West : 1 mi by Strand Rd – ℰ (028) 7083 1783 – Closed Sunday evening and Monday

REPUBLIC OF IRELAND

They say that Ireland offers forty luminous shades of green, but it's not all wondrous hills and down-home pubs: witness the limestone-layered Burren, cut-through by meandering streams, lakes and labyrinthine caves; or the fabulous Cliffs of Moher, looming for mile after mile over the wild Atlantic waves. The cities burst with life: Dublin is one of Europe's coolest capitals, and free-spirited Cork enjoys a rich cultural heritage. Kilkenny mixes a medieval flavour with a strong artistic tradition, while the 'festival' city of Galway is enhanced by an easy, international vibe.

This is a country known for the quality and freshness of its produce, and farmers' markets and food halls yield an array of artisanal cheeses and freshly baked breads. Being an agricultural country, Ireland produces excellent home-reared meat and dairy products and a new breed of chefs are giving traditional dishes a clever modern twist. Seafood, particularly shellfish, is popular – nothing beats sitting on the quayside with a bowl of steaming mussels and the distinctive taste of a micro-brewery beer.

- Michelin Road map n° 712 and 713
- Michelin Green Guide: Ireland

21 Republic of Ireland

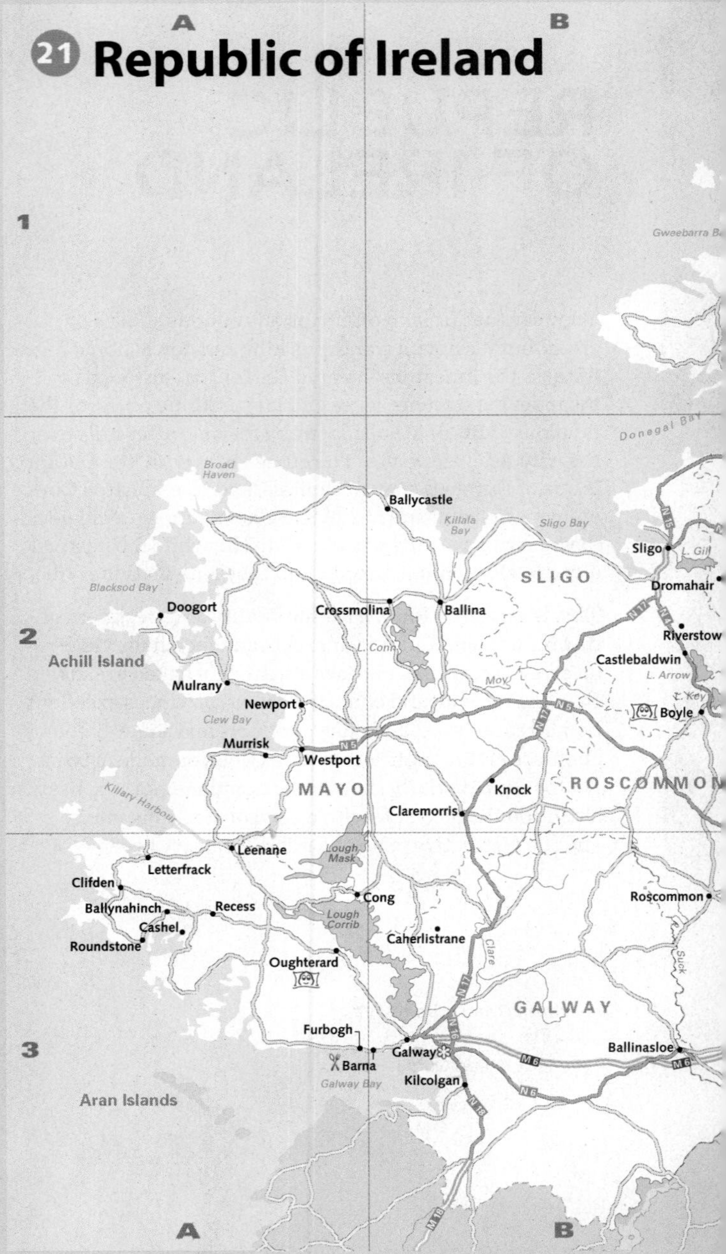

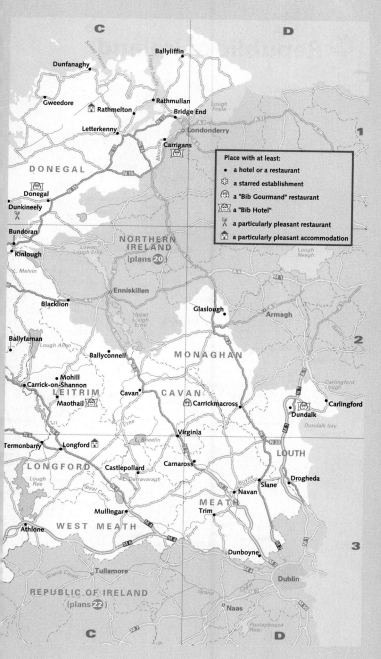

Clifden

Lough Mask

Lough Corrib

Galway

Galway Bay

Inishmore

Aran Islands

Ballyvaughan

Inishmaan

Fanore

Inisheer

New Quay

Doolin

Lisdoonvarna

Liscannor

Corrofin

Lahinch

Spanish Point

CLARE

Doonbeg

Killaloe

Newmarket on Fergus

Bunratty

Limerick

River Shannon

Mouth of the Shannon

Ballybunnion

Adare

Listowel

LIMERICK

Tralee Bay

Ballingarry

Castlegregory

Tralee

Ballydavid

Dingle

Cromane

Killorglin

Dingle Bay

Caragh Lake

Killarney

Kanturk

Mallow

Valencia Island

Cahersiveen

KERRY

Blackwater

CORK

Castlelyor

Portmagee

Kenmare

Lee

Blarney

Cork

Fota Islan

Carrigaline

Ballylickey

Crosshaven

Bantry

Bandon

Bandon

Durrus

Kilbrittain

Kinsale

Toormore

Clonakilty

Ounmamus Bay

Skibbereen

Crookhaven

Goleen

Castletownshend

Barrells Cross

Baltimore

Roaringwater Bay

C E L T I

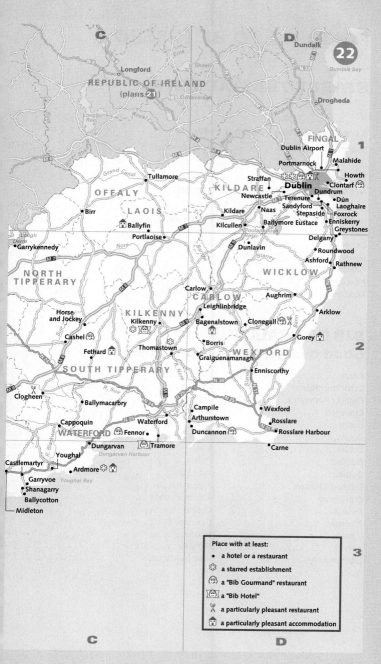

FOOD NO TO BE MISSED

STARRED RESTAURANTS

Excellent cooking, worth a detour!

High quality cooking, worth a stop!

BIB GOURMANDS
Good quality, good value cooking

OUR TOP PICKS

IMPRESSIVE FOR GOLF

LITTLE GEMS

© Pichet

NOTABLY NEIGHBOURHOOD

SERIOUS ABOUT FOOD

© Pichet

© deanes at Queens

SOME GRANDEUR

THE CLASSICS

ACHILL ISLAND ACAILL

Mayo – Regional map n° **21**-A2

▶ Dublin 288 km – Castlebar 54 km – Galway 144 km

Doogort DUMHA GOIRT

🏠 Gray's   🕏 🛏 🤏 🅿

FAMILY · CLASSIC Two adjoining whitewashed houses; one displaying an old clock face from its former life as a mission. Well-kept, modest bedrooms have small shower rooms and colourful throws and cushions. Striking artwork of local island scenes adorns the dining room walls. Simple dinners often feature the catch of the day.

14 rooms 🖙 – 🛉 € 46/56 🛉🛉 € 80/100

– 𝒞 (098) 43 244 – www.grays-guesthouse.ie

– Closed October-March

> Prices quoted after the symbol 🛉 refer to the lowest rate for a single room in low season, followed by the highest rate in high season. The same principle applies to the symbol 🛉🛉 for a double room.

ADARE ÁTH DARA

Limerick – Pop. 1 106 – Regional map n° **22**-B2

▶ Dublin 210 km – Killarney 95 km – Limerick 16 km

🏠🏠🏠 Dunraven Arms   🕏 🛏 🖾 🎐 🖼 ᵴ 🅿

TRADITIONAL · CLASSIC A charming extended former coaching inn dating from 1792, very personally run by the Murphy brothers. Classically furnished lounges and a wood-panelled bar. Smart, spacious bedrooms; some with four-poster beds and garden views.

86 rooms 🖙 – 🛉 € 120 🛉🛉 € 185

Main St – 𝒞 (061) 605 900 – www.dunravenhotel.com

Maigue – See restaurant listing

✗✗ 1826 🅽   🎐

MODERN CUISINE · RUSTIC This pretty little thatched cottage was built in 1826; inside it's cosy and characterful, with a wood burning stove and a rustic feel. Interesting, attractively presented dishes use well-sourced ingredients and have subtle modern touches. It's owned by an experienced young couple: he cooks and she serves.

Carte € 30/46

Main St – 𝒞 (061) 396 004 (booking essential)

– www.1826adare.ie – dinner only

– Closed Monday-Tuesday

✗✗ Wild Geese

TRADITIONAL CUISINE · COSY Long-standing restaurant located in a delightful terrace of thatched cottages, on the main street of a pretty village. The atmosphere is intimate and cosy, and the service, friendly. Traditional menus make good use of local produce.

Menu € 37

Rose Cottage – 𝒞 (061) 396 451 (booking essential) – www.wild-geese.com

– dinner only and Sunday lunch – Closed 2 weeks January, 24-26 December, Sunday dinner and Monday

XX Maigue 🛥 ⚐ AC P

TRADITIONAL CUISINE · FORMAL Named after the nearby river, this is a traditional hotel dining room with a formal feel and professional service. Menus focus on Irish produce and are firmly rooted in tradition; a trolley features, offering prime roast rib of beef.

Menu € 45 – Carte € 27/43 – bar lunch Monday-Saturday

Dunraven Arms Hotel, Main St – ℰ (061) 605 900 – www.dunravenhotel.com

ARAN ISLANDS OILEÁIN ÁRANN

Galway – Pop. 1 280 – Regional map n° **22**-B1

▶ Dublin 260 km – Galway 43 km – Limerick 145 km – Ennis 111 km

Inishmore

🏠 Óstán Árann 🎿 ⚐ 🛥 🏠 ⚐ ⚐ ⚐ P

TRADITIONAL · CLASSIC Comfortable, family-owned hotel with a great view of the harbour. Bustling bar with live music most nights in high season. Spacious, up-to-date bedrooms are decorated in bright colours. Traditional dishes in the wood-floored restaurant.

22 rooms ⚏ – † € 69/89 †† € 78/118

Kilronan – ℰ (099) 61 104 – www.aranislandshotel.com – Closed November-February

🏠 Pier House 🎿 ⚐ 🛥 🏠 ⚐ P

TRADITIONAL · CLASSIC Brightly painted hotel in great location overlooking Kilronan pier, not far from the ferry point and the village centre; take advantage of the outlook from the comfy lounge. Cosy bedrooms come with good mod cons and some share the view. The intimate restaurant offers a concise, accessible menu.

12 rooms ⚏ – † € 55/90 †† € 80/100

Kilronan – ℰ (099) 61 417 – www.pierhousearan.com – Closed November-February

🏠 Ard Einne Guesthouse 🎿 ⚐ ⚐ 🛥 ⚐ P

TRADITIONAL · COSY Close to the airport, an attractive chalet-style guesthouse set back on a hill and boasting superb views of Killeany Bay; relax in the comfy lounge while taking it all in. Uniformly decorated bedrooms have pine furnishings and afford great outlooks. Homely cooking with a menu featuring lots of island fish.

6 rooms ⚏ – † € 60/90 †† € 80/90

Killeany – ℰ (099) 61 126 – www.ardeinne.com – Closed November-February

Inishmaan

XX Inis Meáin Restaurant & Suites 🛥 ⚐ ⚐ 🛥 ⚐ P

REGIONAL · FRIENDLY Set on a beautiful island, this futuristic stone building is inspired by the surrounding landscapes and features limed walls, sage banquettes and panoramic views. Cooking is modern, tasty and satisfyingly straightforward, showcasing island ingredients including seafood caught in currachs and hand-gathered urchins. Minimalist bedrooms feature natural furnishings.

Menu € 65

5 rooms ⚏ – † € 230/460 †† € 230/460

– ℰ (086) 826 60 26 (booking essential) – www.inismeain.com – dinner only – closed Sunday – Closed October-March, 2 night minimum stay

Inisheer

🏠 South Aran House 🎿 ⚐ ⚐ ⚐

HOLIDAY HOTEL · FUNCTIONAL Simple guesthouse on the smallest of the Aran Islands, where traditional living still reigns. With its whitewashed walls and tiled floors, it has a slight Mediterranean feel; bedrooms are homely, with wrought iron beds and modern amenities. Their next door restaurant serves breakfast, snacks and hearty meals.

4 rooms ⚏ – † € 49 †† € 78

– ℰ (087) 340 56 87 – www.southaran.com – Restricted opening in winter

ARDMORE AIRD MHÓR

Waterford – Pop. 435 – Regional map n° **22**-C3
▶ Dublin 240 km – Waterford 71 km – Cork 60 km – Kilkenny 123 km

Cliff House

LUXURY · MODERN Stylish cliffside hotel with a superb bay outlook and lovely spa. Slate walls, Irish fabrics and bold colours feature throughout. Modern bedrooms have backlit glass artwork and smart bathrooms; some have balconies and all share the wonderful view. Choose from an extensive menu in the delightful bar and on the terrace; the restaurant serves more creative dishes.

39 rooms ⌑ – ♦ € 150/170 ♦♦ € 180/245 – 3 suites
Middle Rd – ℰ (024) 87 800 – www.thecliffhousehotel.com
– Closed 24-26 December
❀ **House** – See restaurant listing

XxX House

❀ **CREATIVE · DESIGN** Smart hotel restaurant where full length windows provide every table with an impressive coastal view. Local and garden produce feature in concise menus; cooking is technically strong and complex. Creative, original dishes combine good flavours and textures; be sure to try the signature maple smoked salmon.
➜ Bantry Bay organic salmon with pickled vegetables, horseradish and herbs. Fillet and sausage of Black Angus beef, spinach, Kilbeggan whiskey and beef tea. Organic chocolate with olive oil, apricot, sea salt and white coffee ice cream.
Menu € 75/95
Cliff House Hotel, Middle Rd – ℰ (024) 87 800 – www.thecliffhousehotel.com
– dinner only – Closed 24-26 December, Tuesday November-February and Sunday-Monday

ARKLOW

Wicklow – Pop. 1 277 – Regional map n° **22**-D2
▶ Dublin 71 km – Wexford 70 km – Wicklow 30 km

X Park Bistro 🆕

BRITISH TRADITIONAL · SIMPLE A modern bistro with forest-style wallpaper and a small enclosed terrace. The wide-ranging menu offers simply cooked, tasty Irish dishes, from a warming homemade chowder to steak or roast chicken. Buy some bread or scones to take home.
Menu € 26/35
Fenbyrne House, Castle Pk – ℰ (0402) 23 894 – www.theparkbistro.ie
– Closed Sunday dinner-Wednesday lunch

ARTHURSTOWN COLMÁN

Wexford – Pop. 135 – Regional map n° **22**-D2
▶ Dublin 166 km – Cork 159 km – Limerick 162 km – Waterford 42 km

Dunbrody Country House

COUNTRY HOUSE · ELEGANT Part-Georgian former hunting lodge; once owned by the Marquis of Donegal and now by celebrity chef, Kevin Dundon, who runs his cookery school here. Comfy lounge-bar with a marble-topped counter. Spacious bedrooms furnished in a period style.
16 rooms ⌑ – ♦ € 125/195 ♦♦ € 165/325 – 6 suites
– ℰ (051) 389 600 – www.dunbrodyhouse.com
– Closed 21-26 December and Monday-Tuesday except July-September
Harvest Room – See restaurant listing

XXX Harvest Room

BRITISH MODERN · ELEGANT Light, spacious, classically styled restaurant in keeping with the Georgian country house hotel in which it is sited; bright rugs and vividly coloured seats add a modern touch. Classic dishes feature produce from their own kitchen garden.

Menu € 55/65 – Carte € 35/42

Dunbrody Country House Hotel, – ℰ (051) 389 600 (booking essential)
– www.dunbrodyhouse.com – dinner only and Sunday lunch
– Closed 21-26 December and Monday-Tuesday except July-September

ASHFORD ÁTH NA FUINSEOG

Wicklow – Pop. 1 449 – Regional map n° **22**-D2
▶ Dublin 43 km – Rathdrum 17 km – Wicklow 6 km

⌂ Ballyknocken House

TRADITIONAL · PERSONALISED Part-Victorian house with neat gardens and an adjoining cookery school, located next to the family farm. Traditional lounge and good-sized bedrooms with antique furnishings, modern feature walls and bright fabrics; some have claw-foot baths. Traditional dishes of local produce at gingham-clothed tables.

7 rooms ☲ – † € 89/98 †† € 110/123

Glenealy – South : 4.75 km on L 1096 – ℰ (0404) 44 627 – www.ballyknocken.com
– Closed December-February

ATHLONE BAILE ÁTHA LUAIN

Westmeath – Pop. 15 558 – Regional map n° **21**-C3
▶ Dublin 120 km – Galway 92 km – Limerick 120 km – Roscommon 32 km

⌂⌂⌂ Sheraton Athlone

BUSINESS · DESIGN Modern hotel built around a smart shopping centre. The bedroom grade increases with the floor number – all have excellent mod cons and some offer super lough views; the best are in the 11-storey glass tower. Very smart leisure, spa and aquatics area. Eat in the restaurant, the laid-back café or the chic bar.

167 rooms ☲ – † € 89/305 †† € 98/530

Gleeson St – ℰ (090) 645 1000 – www.sheratonathlonehotel.com
– Closed 24-25 December

⌂ Shelmalier House

TRADITIONAL · PERSONALISED Well-run guesthouse with neat gardens, homely décor and strong green credentials. Relax in the sauna then head for one of the comfy bedrooms – Room 1 is the best. Extensive breakfasts often include a daily special such as pancakes.

7 rooms ☲ – † € 45 †† € 74

Retreat Rd., Cartrontroy – East : 2.5 km by Dublin rd (N 6, junction 9)
– ℰ (090) 647 22 45 – www.shelmalierhouse.com
– Closed December-February

X Thyme

REGIONAL · FRIENDLY Welcoming corner restaurant with candles in the windows; set next to the river and run by a chatty, personable team. Hearty, flavoursome dishes are a mix of the traditional and the modern. Local suppliers are listed on the menu.

Menu € 29 – Carte € 27/43

Custume Pl., Strand St – ℰ (090) 647 88 50
– www.thymerestaurant.ie – dinner only and Sunday lunch
– Closed 24-26 December, 1 January and Good Friday

REPUBLIC OF IRELAND

X **Left Bank Bistro**   AC

INTERNATIONAL · FRIENDLY Keenly run, airy bistro with rough floorboards brick walls and an open-plan kitchen. Extensive menus offer an eclectic mix c dishes, from light lunches and local fish specials to tasty Irish beef and eve Asian-inspired fare.

Menu €25 (weekday dinner) – Carte €31/46

Fry Pl – ℰ (090) 649 44 46 – www.leftbankbistro.com – Closed 1 week Christmas Sunday and Monday

X **Kin Khao**   AC

THAI · FRIENDLY Vivid yellow building with red window frames, hidden down side street near the castle. The upstairs restaurant is decorated with tapestrie and there's a good selection of authentic Thai dishes – try the owner's recom mendations.

Menu €10 (weekday lunch)/20 – Carte €28/37

Abbey Ln. – ℰ (090) 649 88 05 – www.kinkhaothai.ie – dinner only and lunch Wednesday-Friday and Sunday – Closed 25 and 31 December

at Glasson Northeast: 8 km on N55 – ✉ Athlone

🏨🏨 **Glasson Golf H. & Country Club**   ✿ ♨ ⟨ 🖶 🖼 🎄 🕅 ⬆ ⅙ AC
                                                        ✿ 🛠 P

BUSINESS · FUNCTIONAL Greatly extended period house with views over the golf course and Lough Ree; the owner was born here and severa family generations are now involved. Golfing memorabilia fills the walls. Bed rooms are spacious and modern; some have huge balconies and all have a view Classical menu served in the dining room.

65 rooms ⊡ – ♦ €75/120 ♦♦ €110/250

West : 2.75 km – ℰ (090) 648 51 20 – www.glassoncountryhouse.ie – Closed 24-25 December

🏨 **Wineport Lodge**   ✿ ♨ ⟨ 🖶 🎄 ⬆ ⅙ AC ✿ 🛠 P

LUXURY · STYLISH A superbly located hotel where the bedroom wing follow the line of the lough shore and each luxurious room boasts a balcony or a wa terside terrace (it's worth paying the extra for the Champagne Suite). The out door hot tubs make a great place to take in the view. Extensive menus utilis seasonal produce.

30 rooms ⊡ – ♦ €105/235 ♦♦ €120/300

Southwest : 1.5 km – ℰ (090) 643 90 10 – www.wineport.ie – Closed 23-26 December

🏠 **Glasson Stone Lodge**   ⟨ ✿ P ⇛

FAMILY · PERSONALISED Smart guesthouse built from local Irish limestone. Pin features strongly throughout; bedrooms boast thoughtful extras and locally mad furniture – Room 4 is the best. Breakfast includes homemade bread and frui from the garden.

6 rooms ⊡ – ♦ €55 ♦♦ €80

– ℰ (090) 648 50 04 – www.glassonstonelodge.com – Closed November-April

AUGHRIM EACHROIM

Wicklow – Pop. 1 364 – Regional map n° **22**-D2

▶ Dublin 74 km – Waterford 124 km – Wexford 96 km

🏨🏨 **Brooklodge H & Wells Spa**   ✿ ♨ ⟨ 🖶 🖼 🖥 ⓦ 🕅 ⅙ ✗ ⬆ ⅙ 🛠 P

SPA HOTEL · CLASSIC Sprawling hotel in 180 peaceful acres in the Wicklow Va ley. Flag-floored reception, comfy lounge, informal café and pub. Smart, moder bedrooms with large bathrooms; some in an annexe, along with the conferenc rooms. State-of-the-art spa.

86 rooms ⊡ – ♦ €100/140 ♦♦ €120/200 – 18 suites

Macreddin Village – North : 3.25 km – ℰ (0402) 36 444 – www.brooklodge.com – Closed 24-25 December

Strawberry Tree • Armento – See restaurant listing

✗✗✗ Strawberry Tree

BRITISH TRADITIONAL · ELEGANT Ireland's only certified organic restaurant. It's formal, with an intimate, atmospheric feel, and is set on a village-style hotel estate. Menus feature wild and organic ingredients sourced from local artisan suppliers.

Menu € 65/85 – Carte approx. € 59

Brooklodge Hotel, Macreddin Village – North : 3.25 km
– ℰ (0402) 36 444 – www.brooklodge.com – dinner only
– Closed 24-25 December

✗ Armento

ITALIAN · BISTRO Informal Italian restaurant set in a smart hotel on a secluded 180 acre estate. Southern Italian menus feature artisan produce imported from Armento and pizzas cooked in the wood-fired oven.

Menu € 35/40 – Carte approx. € 37

Brooklodge Hotel, Macreddin Village – North : 3.25 km
– ℰ (0402) 36 444 – www.brooklodge.com – dinner only
– Closed 24-25 December

BAGENALSTOWN MUINE BHEAG
Carlow – Pop. 2 775 – Regional map n° **22**-D2
▶ Dublin 101 km – Carlow 16 km – Kilkenny 21 km – Wexford 59 km

⌂ Kilgraney Country House

COUNTRY HOUSE · PERSONALISED Georgian country house which adopts a truly holistic approach. Period features blend with modern, minimalist furnishings and the mood is calm and peaceful. It boasts a small tea room, a craft gallery and a spa with a relaxation room, along with pleasant herb, vegetable, zodiac and monastic gardens.

7 rooms ☲ – ♦ € 120 ♦♦ € 170/240

South : 6.5 km by R 705 (Borris Rd)
– ℰ (059) 977 52 83 – www.kilgraneyhouse.com
– Closed November-February and Monday-Wednesday

BALLINA BÉAL AN ÁTHA
Mayo – Pop. 10 490 – Regional map n° **21**-B2
▶ Dublin 241 km – Galway 117 km – Roscommon 103 km – Sligo 59 km

⌂ Mount Falcon

HISTORIC · PERSONALISED Classic country house built in 1872, with golf, cycling, fishing and archery available in its 100 acre grounds. Characterful bedrooms in the main house; spacious, contemporary rooms in the extension. The Boathole Bar has a clubby feel.

32 rooms ☲ – ♦ € 140/180 ♦♦ € 160/200 – 1 suite

Foxford Rd – South : 6.25 km on N 26
– ℰ (096) 74 472 – www.mountfalcon.com
– Closed 24-26 December

Kitchen – See restaurant listing

⌂ Ice House

HOLIDAY HOTEL · MODERN A former ice vault for local fishermen; now a modern hotel offering great river and woodland views. Feature bedrooms have fireplaces and a traditional feel – the rest are modern and named after ice crystals; the spa suites are the largest. The restaurant opens onto a terrace with two hot tubs. Modern menus.

32 rooms ☲ – ♦ € 135/150 ♦♦ € 190

The Quay Village – Northeast : 2.5 km by N 59
– ℰ (096) 23 500 – www.theicehouse.ie
– Closed 24-26 December

REPUBLIC OF IRELAND

🏠 Belleek Castle 🕯 🦢 🤚 ⚛ 🅿

CASTLE · HOMELY An imposing house built on the site of an old medieval abbey and surrounded by 1,000 acres of mature park and woodland. An amazing array of characterful rooms come complete with open fires, ornate panelling, antiques and old armour.

10 rooms � – 🛉 € 80/120 🛉🛉 € 89/220

Northeast : 2.5 km by Castle Rd – ☎ (096) 22 400 – www.belleekcastle.com
– Closed 1 January-13 February

Belleek Castle – See restaurant listing

XX Belleek Castle 🅝 🤚 🕯 ⟷ 🅿

MODERN CUISINE · ELEGANT Start with a drink in the bar, which is fitted out with original pieces from a 16C Spanish galleon, then head through to the dramatic candlelit dining room. Seasonal modern dishes include fillet of beef flambéed on a sword at the table!

Menu € 30 (early dinner)/70

Belleek Castle Hotel, Northeast : 2.5 km by Castle Rd
– ☎ (096) 22 400 – www.belleekcastle.com – dinner only
– Closed 1 January-13 February

XX Kitchen 🅝 ⟵ 🤚 🅿

MODERN CUISINE · INTIMATE Set in the high-ceilinged former kitchens of the Mount Falcon hotel, with woodland views from the windows. Classic dishes have been brought up-to-date and use seasonal ingredients including veg, herbs and fruits from the kitchen garden.

Menu € 59

Mount Falcon Hotel, Foxford Rd – South : 6.25 km on N 26
– ☎ (096) 74 472 – www.mountfalcon.com – dinner only
– Closed 24-26 December

BALLINASLOE BÉAL ÁTHA NA SLUAIGHE

Galway – Pop. 6 449 – Regional map n° **21**-B3
▶ Dublin 146 km – Galway 66 km – Limerick 106 km – Roscommon 58 km

🏠 Moycarn Lodge and Marina 🕯 🤚 🖼 🖭 🕭 ⚛ 🅿

FAMILY · FUNCTIONAL Purpose-built hotel run by friendly owners; its pleasant gardens and terrace overlooking the river, where there's free berthing for guests. Light, airy bedrooms – five open onto a large shared balcony offering pleasant river views. The rustic bar and restaurant serve an accessible menu of traditional dishes.

15 rooms ⊆ – 🛉 € 39/49 🛉🛉 € 79/99

Shannonbridge Rd – Southeast : 2.5 km by N 6 off R 357
– ☎ (090) 964 50 50 – www.moycarnlodge.ie
– Closed 25 December

BALLINGARRY BAILE AN GHARRAÍ

Limerick – Pop. 527 – Regional map n° **22**-B2
▶ Dublin 227 km – Killarney 90 km – Limerick 29 km

🏠 Mustard Seed at Echo Lodge 🕯 🦢 🤚 🕭 🅿

TRADITIONAL · CLASSIC Surrounded by well-kept gardens is this former convent: personally run by its exuberant owner and filled with antique furniture, paintings, books, magazines and fresh flowers. Period-style bedrooms in the main house; those in the former school house are brighter and more modern. Dinner is an occasion – elaborate, boldly flavoured cooking shows respect for the produce.

16 rooms ⊆ – 🛉 € 120/175 🛉🛉 € 180/360

– ☎ (069) 68 508 – www.mustardseed.ie
– Closed late January-mid February and 24-26 December

BALLSBRIDGE DROICHEAD NA DOTHRA – Dublin ➜ See Dublin

BALLYBUNION BAILE AN BHUINNEÁNAIGH

Kerry – Pop. 1 354 – Regional map n° **22**-A2

▶ Dublin 283 km – Limerick 90 km – Tralee 42 km

⌂ **Teach de Broc Country House**

TRADITIONAL · MODERN A purpose-built house by the Ballybunion golf course, with a spacious, open-plan lounge and bar and eye-catching modern Irish art. Comfortable, good-sized bedrooms with smart bathrooms; ask for one at the front, which looks to the links. The simple bistro dining room serves a wide-ranging menu.

14 rooms ☑ – ♦ € 85/120 ♦♦ € 120/160

Link Rd – South : 2.5 km by Golf Club rd
– ℰ (068) 27 581 – www.ballybuniongolf.com
– Closed November-25 December and 7 January-February

⌂ **19th Lodge**

TOWNHOUSE · PERSONALISED Run by a welcoming couple, this guesthouse overlooks the fairways of the famed course and is filled with golfing memorabilia. Spacious bedrooms are named after golfers or courses; the best have whirlpool baths. Substantial breakfasts.

14 rooms ☑ – ♦ € 70/120 ♦♦ € 100/180

Links Rd – South : 2.75 km by Golf Club rd
– ℰ (068) 27 592 – www.ballybuniongolflodge.com
– Closed Christmas and restricted opening in winter

⌂ **Tides**

FAMILY · PERSONALISED Generously sized bedrooms, superb views and welcoming hosts are the draw at this purpose built guesthouse. Quiz David about the local area in the comfy lounge and, at breakfast, enjoy Doreen's pancakes amongst a host of other delights.

6 rooms ☑ – ♦ € 90 ♦♦ € 95/150

East : 1.75 km. by R 551 on R 553
– ℰ (086) 6000 665 – www.ballybunionbandb.ie
– Closed December-January

BALLYCASTLE BAILE AN CHAISIL

Mayo – Pop. 215 – Regional map n° **21**-B2

▶ Dublin 267 km – Galway 140 km – Sligo 88 km

⌂ **Stella Maris Country House**

COUNTRY HOUSE · PERSONALISED Former coastguard station and convent; now a homely hotel. Simple bedrooms display period furnishings and religious samplers that were left behind. The conservatory runs the length of the building and looks over the water. Snug, open-fired bar and a cosy dining room offering a daily menu of local ingredients.

11 rooms ☑ – ♦ € 125/150 ♦♦ € 190/225

Northwest : 3 km by R 314
– ℰ (096) 43 322 – www.stellamarisireland.com
– Closed October-April

BALLYCONNELL BÁAL ATHA CONAILL

Cavan – Pop. 1 061 – Regional map n° **21**-C2

▶ Dublin 143 km – Drogheda 122 km – Enniskillen 37 km

Slieve Russell ✿ ⌂ ▣ ◫ ☼ ♨ ♨ ⅃ ⌸ ✕ ⊡ ⅙ ✦ ⌸ ₚ

LUXURY · CLASSIC Well-run hotel with immaculate gardens, an impressive mock-Georgian façade and good facilities for families, golfers and businesspeople. Bedrooms overlook the grounds and are large and luxurious, with every mod con. The restaurants are named after Irish folk heroes – Conall Cearnach offers classical dishes and stylish Setanta serves a European menu.

222 rooms ☲ – ♦ € 87/153 ♦♦ € 125/248 – 15 suites
Southeast : 2.75 km on N 87 – 𝒞 (049) 952 64 44 – www.slieverussell.ie

BALLYCOTTON BAILE CHOITÍN

Cork – Pop. 476 – Regional map n° **22**-C3
▶ Dublin 265 km – Cork 43 km – Waterford 106 km

Bayview ✿ ≼ ⌂ ⊡ ⅙ ₚ

HOLIDAY HOTEL · PERSONALISED This hotel is set in an elevated position, with superb views over the bay, the harbour and the island opposite. Two cosy lounges; one on each floor. Spacious bedrooms with floral fabrics and sea views – many have Juliet balconies. Ambitious modern menus; ask for a seat in one of the bay windows.

35 rooms ☲ – ♦ € 70/96 ♦♦ € 120/160 – 2 suites
– 𝒞 (021) 464 67 46 – www.thebayviewhotel.com – Closed November-March

BALLYDAVID BAILE NA NGALL

Kerry – ⊠ Dingle – Regional map n° **22**-A2
▶ Dublin 362 km – Dingle 11 km – Tralee 58 km

Gorman's Clifftop House ⓝ ✿ ≼ ⌂ ⅙ ₚ

FAMILY · CLASSIC Purpose-built house in a wonderfully rural location, offering great views out across Ballydavid Head and the Three Sisters. It's family run and has a lovely homely feel. Bright, spacious bedrooms have good facilities; those to the front share the view. The small menu features home-cooked local produce.

8 rooms – ♦ € 85/105 ♦♦ € 110/150
*Slea Head Dr, Glashabeg – North : 2 km on Feomanagh rd. – 𝒞 (066) 915 51 62
– www.gormans-clifftophouse.com – Closed October-mid March*

BALLYFARNAN BÉAL ÁTHA FEARNÁIN

Roscommon – Pop. 205 – Regional map n° **21**-C2
▶ Dublin 111 km – Roscommon 42 km – Sligo 21 km – Longford 38 km

Kilronan Castle ✿ ⅋ ≼ ⌂ ♙ ◫ ☼ ♨ ⅃ ⊡ ⅙ ⋒ ✕ ⅙ ₚ

CASTLE · CLASSIC Impressively restored castle with characterful sitting rooms, a library and a palm court; wood panelling, antiques and oil paintings feature throughout. Smart leisure club and hydrotherapy centre. Opulent red and gold bedrooms offer a high level of comfort. The formal dining room serves a classical menu.

84 rooms ☲ – ♦ € 125/179 ♦♦ € 158/218
Southeast : 3.5 km on Keadew rd – 𝒞 (071) 961 80 00 – www.kilronancastle.ie

BALLYFIN

Laois – Pop. 633 – Regional map n° **22**-C1
▶ Dublin 69 km – Portlaoise 11 km – Cork 114 km – Limerick 67 km

Ballyfin ✿ ⅋ ≼ ⌂ ♙ ⌂ ◫ ⅃ ✕ ⊡ ⅙ ✕ ⌸ ₚ

GRAND LUXURY · HISTORIC An immaculate Regency mansion built in 1820 and set in 600 acres. Stunning interior with a drawing room decorated in gold leaf, a library featuring 7,000 old books and a cantilever staircase. Luxurious, elegant antique-furnished bedrooms boast marble bathrooms. Produce grown in the kitchen garden informs dishes served in the State dining room. Excellent service.

20 rooms (dinner included) ☲ – ♦ € 335/560 ♦♦ € 520/1420 – 3 suites
– 𝒞 (057) 875 58 66 – www.ballyfin.com – Closed January

BALLYLICKEY BÉAL ÁTHA LEICE

Cork – ⊠ Bantry – Regional map n° **22**-A3
▶ Dublin 347 km – Cork 88 km – Killarney 72 km

🏠 Seaview House

TRADITIONAL · CLASSIC Well-run Victorian house that upholds tradition in both its décor and its service. Pleasant drawing room, cosy bar and antique-furnished bedrooms; some with sea views. The attractive gardens lead down to the shore of the bay. A classical menu is served at elegant polished tables laid with silver tableware.

25 rooms ♀ – ♦ € 75/95 ♦♦ € 120/150

– ℰ (027) 50 073 – www.seaviewhousehotel.com – Closed mid November-mid March

We list three typical dishes for every Starred restaurant. These may not always be on the menu but you're sure to find similar, seasonal dishes - do try them.

BALLYLIFFIN BAILE LIFÍN

Donegal – Pop. 461 – Regional map n° **21**-C1
▶ Dublin 174 km – Lifford 46 km – Letterkenny 39 km

🏠 Ballyliffin Lodge

BUSINESS · MODERN Remote hotel with well-kept gardens, affording a superb outlook over the countryside to the beach. Bedrooms offer good facilities; ask for one facing the front. Relax in the lovely spa and pool, or enjoy afternoon tea with a view in the lounge. Informal, bistro-style dining, with international menus.

40 rooms ♀ – ♦ € 100/120 ♦♦ € 150/190

Shore Rd – ℰ (074) 937 82 00 – www.ballyliffinlodge.com – Closed 25 December

BALLYMACARBRY BAILE MHAC CAIRBRE

Waterford – ⊠ Clonmel – Pop. 132 – Regional map n° **22**-C2
▶ Dublin 190 km – Cork 79 km – Waterford 63 km

🏠 Hanora's Cottage

TRADITIONAL · HOMELY Dating back to 1891 and named after the owner's grandmother, to whom it once belonged. Relax on the terrace by the river or explore the nearby Comeragh Mountains. Spacious, brightly painted bedrooms have characterful furnishings and most boast whirlpool baths. The comfy dining room offers a classical menu.

10 rooms ♀ – ♦ € 99/125 ♦♦ € 99/125

Nire Valley – East : 6.5 km by Nire Drive rd on Nire Valley Lakes rd – ℰ (052) 613 61 34 – www.hanorascottage.com – Closed 1 week Christmas

🏠 Glasha Farmhouse

TRADITIONAL · CLASSIC Large farmhouse between the Knockmealdown and Comeragh Mountains. Guest areas include a cosy lounge, an airy conservatory and a pleasant patio. Bedrooms are comfortable and immaculately kept; some have jacuzzis. The welcoming owner has good local knowledge. Home-cooked meals, with picnic lunches available.

6 rooms ♀ – ♦ € 60 ♦♦ € 100

Northwest : 4 km by R 671 – ℰ (052) 613 61 08 – www.glashafarmhouse.com – Closed December

BALLYMORE EUSTACE AN BAILE MÓR

Kildare – Pop. 872 – Regional map n° **22**-D1
▶ Dublin 48 km – Naas 12 km – Drogheda 99 km

🛏 Ballymore Inn 🍴 & 🅰️ 🕦 🅿️

TRADITIONAL CUISINE · BRASSERIE Remote village pub with a small deli selling homemade breads, pickles, oils and the like. The owner promotes small artisan producers, so expect organic veg, meat from quality assured farms and farm-house cheeses. Portions are generous.

Menu € 25 (weekday lunch)/37 – Carte € 24/48

– ℰ (045) 864 585 – www.ballymoreinn.com

BALLYNAHINCH BAILE NA HINSE

Galway – ✉ Recess – Regional map n° **21**-A3
▶ Dublin 225 km – Galway 66 km – Westport 79 km

🏰 Ballynahinch Castle 🏕 🐾 ⬅ 🛋 🦌 🍴 & 🐾 🅿️

TRADITIONAL · CLASSIC Part-17C grey-stone castle and extensive grounds, set in an unrivalled riverside location. Log-fired entrance, well-appointed sitting rooms and modern country house style bedrooms with up-to-date facilities. The pub attracts the locals; the restaurant offers classical 4 course dinners and water views.

45 rooms ⌃ – 🛉 € 160/310 🛉🛉 € 180/500 – 3 suites

– ℰ (095) 31 006 – www.ballynahinch-castle.com
– Closed February and Christmas

BALLYVAUGHAN BAILE UÍ BHEACHÁIN

Clare – Pop. 258 – Regional map n° **22**-B1
▶ Dublin 240 km – Ennis 55 km – Galway 46 km

🏰 Gregans Castle 🏕 🐾 ⬅ 🛋 🅿️

FAMILY · STYLISH Well-run, part-18C country house with superb views of The Burren and Galway Bay. The open-fired hall leads to a cosy, rustic bar-lounge and an elegant sitting room. Bedrooms are furnished with antiques: two open onto the garden; one is in the old kitchen and features a panelled ceiling and a four-poster bed.

21 rooms ⌃ – 🛉 € 165/200 🛉🛉 € 225/265 – 4 suites

Southwest : 6 km on N 67
– ℰ (065) 707 70 05 – www.gregans.ie
– Closed November-11 February

Gregans Castle – See restaurant listing

🏠 Drumcreehy House ⬅ 🛋 🅿️

TRADITIONAL · STYLISH Brightly painted house overlooking Galway Bay. The interior is warm and welcoming, with rug-covered wood floors, peat fires and an honesty bar. The cosy bedrooms are named after flowers found on The Burren and feature bold colours and German stripped pine furnishings. Excellent continental buffet breakfasts.

12 rooms ⌃ – 🛉 € 60/70 🛉🛉 € 80/110

Northeast : 2 km on N 67
– ℰ (065) 707 73 77 – www.drumcreehyhouse.com
– Closed 25-26 December and restricted opening in winter

🏠 Ballyvaughan Lodge 🅿️

TRADITIONAL · PERSONALISED Welcoming guesthouse with a colourful flower display and a decked terrace. The vaulted, light-filled lounge features a locally made flower chandelier; bedrooms boast co-ordinating fabrics. Breakfast uses quality farmers' market produce.

11 rooms ⌃ – 🛉 € 45/60 🛉🛉 € 80/95

– ℰ (065) 707 72 92 – www.ballyvaughanlodge.com
– Closed 23-28 December

XX Gregans Castle

MODERN CUISINE · FAMILY Have an aperitif in the drawing room of this country house hotel before heading through to the restaurant (ask for a table close to the window, to take in views stretching as far as Galway Bay). Interesting modern dishes have clean, clear flavours and showcase the latest local produce. Service is attentive.

Menu € 70 **s**

Gregans Castle Hotel, Southwest : 6 km on N 67 – ℰ (065) 707 70 05 (booking advisable) – www.gregans.ie – dinner only – Closed November-11 February

BALTIMORE DÚN NA SÉAD
Cork – Pop. 347 – Regional map n° **22**-A3
▶ Dublin 344 km – Cork 95 km – Killarney 124 km

⌂ Casey's of Baltimore

FAMILY · FUNCTIONAL Extended 19C pub with a terracotta façade, well located near the seashore. Comfy lounge and simple pine-furnished bedrooms with good facilities. You're guaranteed a warm welcome from the family owners. The restaurant and beer garden overlook the bay; classical menus, and traditional music at the weekend.

14 rooms ⊡ – ♦ € 107 ♦♦ € 158/180

East : 0.75 km on R 595 – ℰ (028) 20 197 – www.caseysofbaltimore.com – Closed 20-26 December

⌂ Slipway

TRADITIONAL · COSY Laid-back guesthouse in a lovely spot. The open-fired lounge is hung with tapestries made by the charming owner and the breakfast room leads onto a veranda with stunning views over the bay. Modest, well-kept bedrooms feature fresh flowers.

4 rooms ⊡ – ♦ € 45/60 ♦♦ € 70/80

The Cove – Southwest : 0.75 km – ℰ (028) 20 134 – www.theslipway.com – Closed 15 September-1 May

BANDON DROICHEAD NA BANDAN
Cork – Pop. 1 917 – Regional map n° **22**-B3
▶ Dublin 181 km – Cork 20 km – Carrigaline 28 km – Cobh 33 km

⌑ Poacher's Inn

REGIONAL · PUB Cosy neighbourhood pub that's popular with the locals. There's a snug, a wood-panelled bar, and an upstairs restaurant which opens later in the week. West Cork seafood takes centre stage and you can buy homemade bread to take home.

Menu € 25 (weekday dinner)/32 – Carte € 27/44

Clonakilty Rd – Southwest : 1.5 km on N 71 – ℰ (023) 884 1159 – www.poachers.ie – Closed Monday-Tuesday

BANTRY BEANNTRAÍ **Cork**
Cork – Regional map n° **22**-A3
▶ Dublin 215 km – Cork 53 km – Killarney 49 km – Macroom 34 km

X O'Connors AC

FISH AND SEAFOOD · BISTRO Well-run harbourside restaurant, with a compact, bistro-style interior featuring model ships in the windows and modern art on the walls. The menu focuses on local seafood, mostly from the small fishing boats in the harbour.

Menu € 10 (lunch)/28 – Carte € 28/45

Wolf Tone Sq – ℰ (027) 55 664 (booking essential) – www.oconnorsbantry.com – Closed Tuesday and Wednesday November-April

BARNA BEARNA
Galway – Pop. 1 878 – Regional map n° **21**-B3
▶ Dublin 227 km – Galway 9 km

🏨 Twelve   ✿ 🖭 & 🎬 🛋 🅿

BUSINESS · MODERN An unassuming exterior hides a keenly run boutique hotel complete with a bakery, a pizza kitchen and a deli. Stylish, modern bedrooms have large gilt mirrors, mood lighting and designer 'seaweed' toiletries; some even boast cocktail bars! Innovative menus in Upstairs @ West; modern European dishes in The Pins.

48 rooms 🖙 – 🛉 € 89/150 🛉🛉 € 99/160 – 10 suites
Barna Crossroads – ℰ (091) 597 000 – www.thetwelvehotel.ie
Upstairs @ West – See restaurant listing

✗✗ Upstairs @ West   🎎 & 🎬 🅿

MODERN CUISINE · INTIMATE Stylish first floor restaurant in a smart boutique hotel, with a chic champagne bar, booth seating and a moody, intimate feel. Seasonal menus offer ambitious, innovative dishes, showcasing meats and seafood from the 'West' of Ireland.

Menu € 25 (weekdays) **s** – Carte € 33/58 **s**
Twelve Hotel, Barna Crossroads – ℰ (091) 597 000 – www.westrestaurant.ie
– dinner only – Closed Monday and Tuesday

✗ O'Grady's on the Pier   ≤ 🎬

FISH AND SEAFOOD · RUSTIC Smartly painted white and powder blue building on the water's edge, with views across Co. Clare and a charming interior with real fires and fresh flowers. Fish is from Galway or Kinsale; go for the daily catch, which could be classically presented or may have a modern twist. Cheerful, attentive service.

Carte € 29/50
– ℰ (091) 592 223 (booking essential) – www.ogradysonthepier.com – Closed 24-26 December

BARRELLS CROSS – Cork ➜ See Kinsale

BEAUFORT LIOS AN PHÚCA – Kerry ➜ See Killarney

BIRR BIORRA
Offaly – Pop. 4 428 – Regional map n° **22**-C1
▶ Dublin 140 km – Athlone 45 km – Kilkenny 79 km – Limerick 79 km

🏠 Maltings   ⅋ 🅿

TOWNHOUSE · RUSTIC Characterful stone house, once used to store malt in the production of Guinness. Enjoy homemade soda bread, scones and jams in the breakfast-room-cum-lounge, which overhangs the river and looks out towards the castle grounds.

6 rooms 🖙 – 🛉 € 45/50 🛉🛉 € 70/80
Castle St – ℰ (057) 912 13 45 – www.themaltingsbirr.com

BLACKLION AN BLAIC
Cavan – Pop. 229 – Regional map n° **20**-A3
▶ Dublin 194 km – Drogheda 170 km – Enniskillen 19 km

✗✗✗ MacNean House   ⇔ 🎬 ⑩

CREATIVE · ELEGANT Stylish restaurant in a smart townhouse, with a chic lounge, a plush dining room and a cookery school. Choose between a 4 course set selection or a 9 course tasting menu – cooking is ambitious and uses complex techniques, and dishes are attractively presented. Bedrooms are a mix of modern and country styles.

Menu € 72/87
19 rooms 🖙 – 🛉 € 96 🛉🛉 € 134/192
Main St – ℰ (071) 985 30 22 (booking essential) – www.macneanrestaurant.com
– dinner only and Sunday lunch – Closed January, Monday-Tuesday and Sunday dinner

BLACKROCK Dublin – Dún Laoghaire-Rathdown → See Dublin

BLARNEY AN BHLARNA
Cork – ✉ Cork – Pop. 2 437 – Regional map n° **22**-B3
▶ Dublin 268 km – Cork 9 km

🏠 Killarney House   ⛟ 🕸 🅿

FAMILY · PERSONALISED Well-kept, friendly guesthouse on the edge of town, with immaculate gardens, simple, spacious bedrooms, comfortable lounges and a wood-furnished breakfast room. The extensive breakfast menu includes a 'full Irish'.

6 rooms �' — ♥ € 43/50 ♥♥ € 60/69
*Station Rd – Northeast : 1.5 km on Carrignavar rd. – 𝒞 (021) 438 18 41
– www.killarneyhouseblarney.com – Closed November-December*

XX Square Table ⓝ

FRENCH · COSY Sweet restaurant with a warm, welcoming, neighbourhood feel. Menus offer French-influenced dishes crafted from Irish produce; the early evening menu is good value. It's proudly and enthusiastically run by twins Tricia and Martina.

Menu € 24 (dinner) – Carte € 20/44
*5 The Square – 𝒞 (021) 438 28 25 (booking essential at dinner)
– www.thesquaretable.ie – Closed Sunday dinner and Monday except bank holidays, Tuesday and lunch Wednesday October-April*

at Tower West: 3.25 km on R617 – ✉ Cork

🏠 Ashlee Lodge   🎐 🕭 🄰🄲 🕸 🅿

LUXURY · PERSONALISED Smart hotel with a cosy lounge featuring a wood burning stove, board games and an honesty bar. Comfortable bedrooms offer all you could want; some have whirlpool baths. Outdoor hot tub, sauna and in-room treatments. Extensive breakfasts.

10 rooms ☑ — ♥ € 75/95 ♥♥ € 99/140
Tower – 𝒞 (021) 438 53 46 – www.ashleelodge.com – Closed November-mid March

BORRIS
Carlow – Pop. 646 – Regional map n° **22**-D2
▶ Dublin 121 km – Carlow 36 km – Waterford 66 km

🏠 Step House   ⛷ ⋖ ⛟ 🕙 🄵 🕭 🕸 🕍 🅿

TOWNHOUSE · PERSONALISED Welcoming, family-run, Georgian townhouse in a small heritage village. Spacious, modern bedrooms; most have lovely mountain views and the penthouse boasts a terrace. The comfy bar, 1808, is named after the year the original hotel was built.

20 rooms ☑ — ♥ € 75/140 ♥♥ € 130/400 – 1 suite
Main St – 𝒞 (059) 977 32 09 – www.stephousehotel.ie – Closed 15 August and 25 December
Cellar – See restaurant listing

XX Cellar   ⛟ 🕭 🅿

BRITISH MODERN · ROMANTIC Atmospheric hotel restaurant with vaulted ceilings and archways; set in the kitchens of the old MacMurrough Kavanagh Estate dower house. Interesting modern menu of local and artisan ingredients.

Menu € 28/40 – bar lunch
Step House Hotel, Main St – 𝒞 (059) 977 32 09 – www.stephousehotel.ie – closed Monday-Tuesday – Closed 15 August and 25 December

REPUBLIC OF IRELAND

XX Clashganny House ⛟ P

CLASSIC CUISINE · INTIMATE Hidden away in a lovely valley, this early Victorian house is the setting for the realisation of one couple's dream. The modern restaurant is split over three rooms; appealing menus balance light options with more gutsy dishes.

Menu € 30

Clashganny – South : 5 km by R 702 and R 729 – 𝒞 *(059) 977 10 03*
– www.clashgannyhouse.com – dinner only and Sunday lunch
– Closed 24-27 December, Sunday dinner, Monday and Tuesday

BOYLE MAINISTIR NA BÚILLE

Roscommon – Pop. 1 459 – Regional map n° **21**-B2
▶ Dublin 168 km – Roscommon 43 km – Galway 103 km

🏠 Lough Key House ⛟ P

HISTORIC · CLASSIC Welcoming Georgian house with neat garden and mature grounds, located next to Lough Key Forest Park. Homely guest areas are filled with antiques and ornaments; bedrooms in the original house are the best, with their antique four-posters and warm fabrics. You're guaranteed a warm Irish welcome.

5 rooms ⌑ – ♦ € 49/59 ♦♦ € 89/98
Southeast : 3.75 km by R 294 on N 4 – 𝒞 *(071) 966 21 61*
– www.loughkeyhouse.com – Closed 2 January-16 March

🏠 Rosdarrig House ⛟ ⚘ P

FAMILY · PERSONALISED Neat house on the edge of town, close to the abbey; the friendly owners offer genuine Irish hospitality. Guest areas include two homely lounges and a linen-laid breakfast room. Simply furnished bedrooms overlook the colourful garden.

5 rooms ⌑ – ♦ € 35/40 ♦♦ € 65/75
Carrick Rd – East : 1.5 km on R 294 – 𝒞 *(071) 966 20 40 – www.rosdarrig.com*
– Closed November-March

BRIDGE END

Donegal – Pop. 497 – Regional map n° **21**-C1
▶ Dublin 158 km – Lifford 25 km – Belfast 78 km – Londonderry 5 km

XX Harrys P

REGIONAL · BISTRO Long-standing, passionately run restaurant with an open-plan interior and a modern bistro feel. Menus evolve with the seasons, offering flavoursome, classical dishes. Traceability is key, with much produce coming from their walled garden.

Menu € 16/18 – Carte € 16/37
– 𝒞 *(074) 936 85 44 – www.harrys.ie – Closed 24-26 December*

BUNDORAN BUN DOBHRÁIN

Donegal – Pop. 1 781 – Regional map n° **21**-C2
▶ Dublin 259 km – Donegal 27 km – Sligo 37 km

🏨 Fitzgerald's ⚐ ⪉ 🗐 ⚘ P

FAMILY · CLASSIC Family-owned hotel in a popular seaside town overlooking Donegal Bay. Characterful guest areas feature tiled floors, stained glass windows and a wood burning stove. Bedrooms are pastel coloured; those facing the sea are the ones to choose. Informal, split-level bistro offers extensive menus of comfort dishes.

16 rooms ⌑ – ♦ € 60/80 ♦♦ € 95/140
– 𝒞 *(071) 984 13 36 – www.fitzgeraldshotel.com – Restricted opening in winter*

BUNRATTY BUN RAITE

Clare – Regional map n° **22**-B2
▶ Dublin 207 km – Ennis 24 km – Limerick 13 km

⌂ **Bunratty Manor** ⏚ 🚗 🛏 👜 ❄ 🅿

FAMILY · PERSONALISED Smart hotel close to a castle and a folk park, in a busy tourist town. Comfy lounge has walls adorned with horse racing memorabilia. Good-sized, brightly decorated bedrooms display colourful fabrics. Traditional bar and restaurant with a courtyard offer a classical set menu and more imaginative à la carte.

20 rooms � – 🛉 € 79/89 🛉🛉 € 79/109

– ☎ (061) 707 984 – www.bunrattymanor.ie – Closed 23-28 December

CAHERLISTRANE CATHAIR LOISTREÁIN

Galway – Regional map n° **21**-B3

▶ Dublin 256 km – Ballina 74 km – Galway 42 km

⌂ **Lisdonagh House** ⏚ 🚲 ⇐ 🛏 👜 ❄ 🅿 �:

TRADITIONAL · CLASSIC Ivy-clad Georgian house with pleasant lough views. The traditional country house interior boasts eye-catching murals and open-fired lounges. Antique-furnished bedrooms have marble bathrooms; the first floor rooms are larger and brighter. The grand dining room offers 5 course dinners and simpler suppers.

9 rooms ⊑ – 🛉 € 120/180 🛉🛉 € 180/240

Northwest : 4 km by R 333 off Shrule rd – ☎ (093) 31 163 – www.lisdonagh.com – Closed November-April

CAHERSIVEEN CATHAIR SAIDHBHÍN

Kerry – Pop. 1 168 – Regional map n° **22**-A2

▶ Dublin 355 km – Killarney 64 km – Tralee 67 km

✕ **QC's** ⇐ 🛏 🅿

FISH AND SEAFOOD · PUB A cosy, atmospheric restaurant with a nautical theme. Seafood-orientated menus offer fresh, unfussy classics and more unusual daily specials; the family also own a local fish wholesalers. Stylish, spacious and well-equipped bedrooms are located just around the corner. Continental breakfast in your room.

Menu € 21 (dinner) – Carte € 23/54

6 rooms ⊑ – 🛉 € 75/95 🛉🛉 € 79/139

3 Main St – ☎ (066) 947 22 44 (booking advisable) – www.qcbar.com – Closed Monday-Wednesday in winter

🍴 **O'Neill's (The Point) Seafood Bar** ⇐ 🛏 🅰🅲 🅿

TRADITIONAL CUISINE · PUB In a great location beside Valentia Island ferry slipway, and run by the O'Neill family for over 150 years. Generous portions of locally landed seafood; salmon comes from a nearby smokehouse.

Carte € 27/35

Renard Point – Southwest : 4.5 km by N 70 – ☎ (066) 947 21 65 (bookings not accepted) – Closed mid November-mid March

CAMPILE CEANN POILL

Wexford – Pop. 411 – Regional map n° **22**-D2

▶ Dublin 154 km – Waterford 35 km – Wexford 37 km

⌂ **Kilmokea Country Manor** ⏚ 🚲 🚗 🛏 🖼 🎐 🗘 ❄ 🅿

HISTORIC · PERSONALISED Georgian rectory set in 20 acres, 7 of which are formal gardens open to the public. Small antique-furnished drawing room with oils and a piano. Bedrooms, some in the old coach house, are more contemporary. Conservatory tea rooms and smart restaurant with daily changing classical menu of organic garden produce.

6 rooms ⊑ – 🛉 € 75/95 🛉🛉 € 150/180

West : 8 km by R 733 and Great Island rd – ☎ (051) 388 109 – www.kilmokea.com – Closed January and December

CAPPOQUIN CEAPACH CHOINN

Waterford – Pop. 759 – Regional map n° **22**-C2

▶ Dublin 219 km – Cork 56 km – Waterford 64 km

XX **Richmond House** ⇦ 🖦 🕼 **P**

TRADITIONAL CUISINE · FORMAL Imposing Georgian house built in 1704 for the Earl of Cork and Burlington, and filled with family curios. Have a drink in the cosy lounge before heading to the cove-ceilinged dining room. Cooking is classically based; be sure to try the delicious local lamb. Cosy bedrooms are decorated in period styles.

Menu € 55

9 rooms 🖙 – ♦ € 60/80 ♦♦ € 110/150

Southeast : 0.75 km on N 72 – 𝒞 (058) 54 278 – www.richmondhouse.net – dinner only – Closed Christmas-New Year and Monday-Thursday January-February

CARAGH LAKE LOCH CÁRTHAÍ

Kerry – Regional map n° **22**-A2

▶ Dublin 341 km – Killarney 35 km – Tralee 40 km

🏠 **Ard-Na-Sidhe** ☆ ♨ ≼ 🖦 ➲ ᴭ ⅋ **P**

COUNTRY HOUSE · CLASSIC 1913 Arts and Crafts house set on the shores of Lough Caragh and surrounded by mountains. A subtle yet stylish modernisation has emphasised many original features such as oak-panelled walls and leaded windows. Bedrooms are smart and contemporary. The restaurant offers classic dishes with subtle modern twists.

18 rooms 🖙 – ♦ € 160/275 ♦♦ € 180/295

– 𝒞 (066) 976 91 05 – www.ardnasidhe.com – Closed October-April

🏠 **Carrig Country House** ☆ ♨ ≼ 🖦 ➲ ⅋ **P**

TRADITIONAL · CLASSIC Victorian former hunting lodge set down a wooded drive, located on the lough shore and surrounded by mountains. Cosy, country house interior with traditionally furnished guest areas. Individually decorated bedrooms boast antique furnishings. Beautiful views from the dining room; fresh country house cooking.

17 rooms 🖙 – ♦ € 130/175 ♦♦ € 150/350 – 1 suite

– 𝒞 (066) 976 91 00 – www.carrighouse.com – Closed November-February

CARLINGFORD CAIRLINN

Louth – Pop. 1 045 – Regional map n° **21**-D2

▶ Dublin 106 km – Dundalk 21 km

🏠 **Four Seasons** ☆ 🖦 🍴 ▣ 🕉 🅛🕉 ⊡ ⅒ ⅋ 🕉 **P**

BUSINESS · MODERN Purpose-built hotel on the edge of the village, with a lovely mountain backdrop. Large leisure centre; open-plan bar. Well-equipped bedrooms; 'Executives' are of a good size, with a separate bath and shower. Ask for a room with lough views. Informal bistro overlooks the garden with its wrought iron pergola.

58 rooms 🖙 – ♦ € 65/150 ♦♦ € 69/190

– 𝒞 (042) 937 35 30 – www.4seasonshotelcarlingford.ie

🏠 **Beaufort House** ♨ ≼ 🖦 ⅋ **P**

FAMILY · PERSONALISED Modern house in a lovely spot on the lough shore. The welcoming owners used to run a sailing school and the spacious lounge is filled with old maritime charts and memorabilia. Large, bright bedrooms have water or mountain views.

6 rooms 🖙 – ♦ € 70/120 ♦♦ € 90/120

– 𝒞 (042) 937 38 79 – www.beauforthouse.net

🏠 Carlingford House

TRADITIONAL · PERSONALISED Early Victorian house close to the old ruined abbey; the owner was born and has always lived here. Smart, understated bedrooms have good mod cons and are immaculately kept. Pleasant breakfast room; tasty locally smoked salmon and bacon.

5 rooms ☑ – 🛉 € 70/120 🛉🛉 € 100/120

– ℰ (042) 937 31 18 – www.carlingfordhouse.com – Closed 3 January-6 February and Christmas

✗✗ Bay Tree ⇔⇔

MODERN CUISINE · FRIENDLY Keenly run neighbourhood restaurant fronted by bay trees and decorated with branches and hessian. Attractively presented, well-balanced modern dishes feature herbs and salad from the garden and seafood from nearby Carlingford Lough. Service is polite and organised, and the bedrooms are warm and cosy.

Menu € 25 (weekdays)/35 – Carte € 30/49

7 rooms ☑ – 🛉 € 55/65 🛉🛉 € 80/90

Newry St – ℰ (042) 938 3848 (booking essential) – www.belvederehouse.ie
– dinner only and Sunday lunch – Closed 24-26 December, Monday and Tuesday

CARLOW CEATHARLACH
Carlow – Pop. 13 698 – Regional map n° **22**-D2
▶ Dublin 80 km – Kilkenny 37 km – Wexford 75 km

🏠 Barrowville Town House

TOWNHOUSE · ELEGANT Attractive Georgian house on the main road into town. Comfortable, characterful drawing room with heavy fabrics, period ornaments and a grand piano. Breakfast is in the conservatory, overlooking the pretty garden. Spacious, brightly decorated bedrooms offer a good level of comfort and modern facilities.

7 rooms ☑ – 🛉 € 40/70 🛉🛉 € 70/90

Kilkenny Rd – South : 0.75 km on N 9 – ℰ (059) 914 33 24 – www.barrowville.com
– Closed 24-26 December

CARNAROSS CARN NA ROS
Meath – ✉ Kells – Regional map n° **21**-D3
▶ Dublin 69 km – Cavan 43 km – Drogheda 48 km

✗✗ Forge ⇔⇔ 🅿

TRADITIONAL CUISINE · RUSTIC Stone-built former forge in rural Meath; its atmospheric interior features flagged floors and warm red décor. Two fairly priced menus offer hearty dishes made from local produce, with some of the veg and herbs taken from the garden.

Menu € 25/40

Pottlereagh – Northwest : 7 km by R 147 and N 3 on L 7112 – ℰ (046) 924 50 03
– www.theforgerestaurant.ie – dinner only and Sunday lunch – Closed 1 week
February, 1 week July, 24-26 December, 1 January, Sunday dinner, Monday and Tuesday

CARNE
Wexford – Regional map n° **22**-D3
▶ Dublin 169 km – Waterford 82 km – Wexford 21 km

🍴 Lobster Pot

FISH AND SEAFOOD · PUB Popular pub filled with a characterful array of memorabilia. Large menus feature tasty, home-style cooking. Fresh seafood dishes are a must-try, with oysters and lobster cooked to order being the specialities. No children after 7pm.

Carte € 27/59

Ballyfane – ℰ (053) 913 11 10 – www.lobsterpotwexford.ie – Closed
1 January-10 February, 24-26 December, Good Friday and Monday except bank holidays

CARRICKMACROSS CARRAIG MHACHAIRE ROIS
Monaghan – Pop. 1 978 – Regional map n° **21**-D2
▶ Dublin 92 km – Dundalk 22 km

🏠 Nuremore
COUNTRY HOUSE · PERSONALISED Long-standing Victorian house with extensive gardens and a golf course. Classical interior with a formal bar and a comfy lounge serving three-tiered afternoon tea. Good leisure facilities. Peaceful bedrooms; many have rural views.

72 rooms ☑ – ♦ € 90/320 ♦♦ € 110/420
South : 2.25 km by R 178 on old N 2 – ℰ (042) 966 14 38 – www.nuremore.com
Nuremore – See restaurant listing

🏠 Shirley Arms ⓝ
INN · MODERN An early 19C coaching inn, which forms part of the Shirley Estate and sits beside the Courthouse Square. Bedrooms are surprisingly modern; those in the original house are slightly more characterful. There's a welcoming bar, an informal bistro and, for private parties, a stylish bar-cum-nightclub.

25 rooms ☑ – ♦ € 75/95 ♦♦ € 110/200
Main St. – ℰ (042) 967 31 00 – www.shirleyarmshotel.ie – Closed 25-26 December and Good Friday

XxX Nuremore
MODERN CUISINE · FORMAL Traditional split-level dining room within a well-established Victorian hotel. Formally set, linen-laid tables are well-spaced and service is attentive. Menus showcase luxurious seasonal ingredients and dishes are stylishly presented.

Menu € 30
Nuremore Hotel, South : 2.25 km by R 178 on old N 2 – ℰ (042) 966 14 38 – www.nuremore.com – dinner only and Sunday lunch – closed Sunday dinner, Monday-Thursday

X Courthouse
REGIONAL · RUSTIC Relaxed, rustic restaurant featuring wooden floors, exposed ceiling rafters and bare brick; ask for table 20, by the window. Great value menus offer carefully prepared, flavourful dishes which are a lesson in self-restraint – their simplicity being a key part of their appeal. Friendly, efficient service.

Menu € 25 (weekday dinner)/28 – Carte € 27/43 **s**
1 Monaghan St – ℰ (042) 969 28 48 (pre-book at weekends) – www.courthouserestaurant.ie – Closed 1 week January, 25-26 December, Good Friday, Monday except bank holidays and Tuesday

CARRICK-ON-SHANNON CORA DROMA RÚISC
Leitrim – Pop. 3 980 – Regional map n° **21**-C2
▶ Dublin 156 km – Ballina 80 km – Galway 119 km – Roscommon 42 km

🏠 Landmark
BUSINESS · DESIGN Large, modern hotel next to the Shannon, with a water feature in reception and duck-themed pictures throughout; a popular venue for weddings. Bright, bold bedrooms with good facilities. Stylish cocktail lounge with a stunning contemporary design. Informal dining and pleasant river views in Boardwalk.

49 rooms ☑ – ♦ € 69/105 ♦♦ € 110/150
on N 4 – ℰ (071) 962 22 22 – www.thelandmarkhotel.com – Closed 25 December

🏠 Oarsman
TRADITIONAL CUISINE · PUB Traditional family-run pub set close the river and filled with pottery, bygone artefacts and fishing tackle; it's a real hit with the locals. Flavoursome cooking uses local produce. The upstairs restaurant opens late in the week.

Menu € 22 (weekdays)/35 – Carte € 26/48
Bridge St – ℰ (071) 962 1733 – www.theoarsman.com – Closed 25-26 December, Good Friday, Monday and Sunday October-April

CARRIGALINE CARRAIG UÍ LEIGHIN

Cork – Pop. 14 775 – Regional map n° **22**-B3

▶ Dublin 262 km – Cork 14 km – Kinsale 13 km

🏨 Carrigaline Court ❀ ▨ 🏠 🐬 🗐 �& 🎇 �̇ 🅿

CONFERENCE HOTEL · MODERN A busy, purpose-built hotel in the town centre; it features well-equipped events facilities and an excellent leisure centre complete with a 20m swimming pool. Spacious, modern bedrooms have queen-sized beds. Light meals are served in the atmospheric bar and an international menu in the bistro.

91 rooms 🖵 – 🛉 € 85/145 🛉🛉 € 95/155 – 2 suites
Cork Rd – 𝒞 (021) 485 21 00 – www.carrigcourt.com – Closed 23-26 December

CARRIGANS AN CARRAIGAIN

Donegal – Pop. 336 – Regional map n° **21**-C1

▶ Dublin 225 km – Donegal 66 km – Letterkenny 230 km – Sligo 124 km

🏠 Mount Royd 🖨 🎇 🅿 🛏

TRADITIONAL · PERSONALISED Traditional, creeper-clad house in a quiet village. It's immaculately kept throughout, from the snug lounge and pleasant breakfast room to the four cosy bedrooms – one of which opens onto a terrace overlooking the well-tended gardens and fountain. Tasty, locally smoked salmon features at breakfast.

4 rooms 🖵 – 🛉 € 40 🛉🛉 € 75/80
– 𝒞 (074) 914 01 63 – www.mountroyd.com – Closed 1 week Christmas and restricted opening in winter

CASHEL CAISEAL

South Tipperary – Pop. 2 275 – Regional map n° **22**-C2

▶ Dublin 162 km – Cork 96 km – Kilkenny 55 km – Limerick 58 km

🏨 Baileys of Cashel ❀ 🗐 �& 🖾 🎇 🅿

TOWNHOUSE · MODERN Extended Georgian townhouse, used as a grain store during the Irish famine. Small lounge with a library and spacious, contemporary bedrooms, furnished to a high standard. Popular cellar bar offers live music and traditional dishes. More contemporary restaurant serves modern European cooking.

20 rooms 🖵 – 🛉 € 65/80 🛉🛉 € 100/120
42 Main St – 𝒞 (062) 61 937 – www.baileyshotelcashel.com – Closed 23-28 December

🏠 Aulber House 🖨 �& 🎇 🅿

FAMILY · PERSONALISED Within walking distance of the Rock of Cashel and the 13C Cistercian abbey ruins. Well-kept gardens with a wooden gazebo. Comfy, open-fired lounge. Bespoke mahogany staircase leads to an open-plan landing; many rooms have king-sized beds.

11 rooms 🖵 – 🛉 € 60/80 🛉🛉 € 80/100
Deerpark, Golden Rd – West : 0.75 km on N 74 – 𝒞 (062) 63 713 – www.aulberhouse.com – Closed November-January

XX Chez Hans 🅿

TRADITIONAL CUISINE · INDIVIDUAL Longstanding family-owned restaurant in an imposing former Synod Hall built in 1861. Good value set price midweek menu and a more interesting à la carte of classic dishes at the weekend. Quality local ingredients are prepared with care.

Menu € 28 (weekdays) – Carte € 40/56
Rockside, Moor Ln. – 𝒞 (062) 61 177 (booking essential) – www.chezhans.net – dinner only – Closed last week January, 1 week Easter, 24-26 December, Sunday and Monday

REPUBLIC OF IRELAND

✗ Cafe Hans   AC ☐ 🛏

TRADITIONAL CUISINE · FRIENDLY Located just down the road from the Rock of Cashel; a vibrant, popular eatery set next to big sister 'Chez Hans' and run by the same family. Sit at closely set tables amongst an interesting collection of art. Tasty, unfussy lunchtime dishes are crafted from local ingredients. Arrive early as you can't book.

Menu € 12/20 – Carte € 24/37

Rockside, Moore Lane St – 𝒞 (062) 63 660 (bookings not accepted) – lunch only – Closed 2 weeks late January, 1 week October, 25 December, Sunday and Monday

CASHEL AN CAISEAL

Galway – Regional map n° **21**-A3
▶ Dublin 278 km – Galway 66 km

🏠 Cashel House   🐾 ⌷ 🚗 🔌 ☐

TRADITIONAL · CLASSIC Whitewashed country house built in 1840, surrounded by delightful gardens (gardening courses are available). Plenty of peaceful little seating areas; china and knick-knacks abound. The rear bedrooms are biggest – those higher up have better views. Formal dining room and elegant conservatory. Classical menus.

30 rooms ⌷ – ♦ € 75/210 ♦♦ € 150/230

– 𝒞 (095) 31 001 – www.cashel-house-hotel.com – Closed 1 January-mid February

CASTLEBALDWIN BÉAL ÁTHA NA GCARRAIGÍNÍ

Sligo – ✉ Boyle (roscommon) – Regional map n° **21**-B2
▶ Dublin 190 km – Longford 67 km – Sligo 24 km

🏠 Cromleach Lodge   🐾 ⌷ ⟨ 🚗 🔌 🌐 🎿 ☑ 🖫 ☐

FAMILY · STYLISH Remotely located hotel with superb views over Lough Arrow and the Carrowkeel Cairns. Bedrooms come in either a modern or classic style and some have balconies or terraces. Unwind in the comfy split-level lounge-bar or stylish spa.

57 rooms ⌷ – ♦ € 90/150 ♦♦ € 120/200

Ballindoon – Southeast : 5.5 km – 𝒞 (071) 916 51 55 – www.cromleach.com
Moira's – See restaurant listing

✗✗✗ Moira's   ⟨ 🚗 🖫 ☐

REGIONAL · ELEGANT Smart, modern hotel restaurant with a glass-fronted kitchen, brushed velvet booths, and lough and country views. Good-sized menus offer classically based dishes with personal twists; local growers and producers are credited on the menu.

Menu € 60 – Carte € 44/62

Cromleach Lodge Hotel, Ballindoon – Southeast : 5.5 km – 𝒞 (071) 916 51 55 – www.cromleach.com – dinner only and Sunday lunch

CASTLEGREGORY CAISLEÁN GHRIAIRE

Kerry – Pop. 243 – Regional map n° **22**-A2
▶ Dublin 330 km – Dingle 24 km – Killarney 54 km

🏠 Shores Country House   ⟨ 🚗 🛁 ☐

LUXURY · STYLISH Modern guesthouse, beautifully set in an elevated position between Stradbally Mountain and a spectacular beach. The friendly owner has added a touch of fun to the place. Stylish bedrooms, some with antique beds all with good attention to detail. Room 3 has a balcony. Plush breakfast room.

6 rooms ⌷ – ♦ € 50/90 ♦♦ € 90/140

Conor Pass Rd, Cappateige – Southwest : 6 km on R 560 – 𝒞 (066) 713 91 95 – www.shorescountryhouse.com – Closed 2 December-10 January

CASTLELYONS CAISLEÁN Ó LIATHÁIN

Cork – Pop. 292 – Regional map n° **22**-B2

▶ Dublin 219 km – Cork 30 km – Killarney 104 km – Limerick 64 km

🏠 **Ballyvolane House**   ⚘ 🐾 ⪢ 🍴 🔌 P

FAMILY · PERSONALISED Stately 18C Italianate mansion surrounded by lovely gardens, lakes and woodland; children can help feed the hens, collect the eggs, pet the donkeys or go on a tractor tour. Comfy guest areas and bedrooms match the period style of the house, and family antiques and memorabilia feature throughout. The walled garden and latest farm produce guide what's on the menu.

6 rooms ⌂ – 🛏 € 135 🛏🛏 € 200/240

Southeast : 5.5 km by Midleton rd on Britway rd – ☎ *(025) 36 349*
– www.ballyvolanehouse.ie – Closed 24 December-4 January and restricted opening in winter

CASTLEMARTYR BAILE NA MARTRA

Cork – Pop. 1 277 – Regional map n° **22**-C3

▶ Dublin 174 km – Cork 20 km – Waterford 58 km

🏰 **Castlemartyr**   ⚘ 🐾 ⪢ 🍴 🔒 📶 🖥 🌐 ♨ ♠ ♨ ⚏ 🏊 AC ⚒ P

GRAND LUXURY · MODERN Impressive 17C manor house in 220 acres of grounds, complete with castle ruins, lakes, a golf course and a stunning spa. Luxurious bedrooms have superb marble bathrooms. Look out for the superb original ceiling in the Knight's Bar. Franchini's offers an extensive Italian menu; the Bell Tower is more formal.

103 rooms ⌂ – 🛏 € 175/205 🛏🛏 € 190/220 – 28 suites
– ☎ *(021) 421 90 00 – www.castlemartyrresort.ie*
Bell Tower – See restaurant listing

XxX **Bell Tower**   🍴 ♿ AC P

CLASSIC CUISINE · LUXURY A bright, formally laid restaurant set on the ground floor of a 17C manor house, with traditional décor and plenty of windows overlooking the attractive gardens. Classic dishes with a modern twist from an experienced team.

Carte € 40/60 **s** – bar lunch

Castlemartyr Hotel, – ☎ *(021) 421 90 00 (bookings essential for non-residents) – www.castlemartyrresort.ie – dinner only – Closed Monday and Tuesday October-March*

CASTLEPOLLARD BAILE NA GCROS

Westmeath – Pop. 1 042 – Regional map n° **21**-C3

▶ Dublin 63 km – Mullingar 13 km – Tullamore 37 km – Édenderry 36 km

🏡 **Lough Bishop House**   ⚘ 🐾 🍴 🐴 P 🪑

TRADITIONAL · PERSONALISED Charming 18C farmhouse on a tranquil, south-facing hillside. The hospitable owners and their dogs greet you, and tea and cake are served on arrival in the cosy lounge. Simple bedrooms have neat shower rooms and no TVs. Communal dining – home-cooked dishes include meats and eggs from their own farm.

3 rooms ⌂ – 🛏 € 60/100 🛏🛏 € 120/180

Derrynagarra, Collinstown – South : 6 km by R 394 taking L 5738 opposite church and school after 4 km – ☎ *(044) 966 13 13 – www.loughbishophouse.com – Closed Christmas-New Year*

CASTLETOWNSHEND BAILE AN CHAISLEÁIN

Cork – Pop. 187 – Regional map n° **22**-B3

▶ Dublin 346 km – Cork 95 km – Killarney 116 km

REPUBLIC OF IRELAND

🍴 **Mary Ann's** 🏠

TRADITIONAL CUISINE · PUB Bold red pub set up a steep, narrow street in a sleepy village. Dine in the rustic bar, the linen-laid restaurant or the lovely garden; be sure to visit the art gallery. All-encompassing menus often feature seafood and several Asian dishes.

Carte € 26/51

Main St – ℰ (028) 36 146 – www.westcorkweek.com/maryanns – dinner only – Closed 10 January-3 February, 24-26 December and Monday-Tuesday November-March

CAVAN AN CABHÁN

Cavan – Pop. 3 649 – Regional map n° **21**-C2
▶ Dublin 114 km – Drogheda 93 km – Enniskillen 64 km

🏨 **Radisson Blu Farnham Estate** 🛜 ⟨ 🛏 🌿 📺 🎿 🗒 📶 🏖 🖥

LUXURY · DESIGN Set in extensive parkland and boasting 🖥 ⚙ 🏊 🖥 every conceivable outdoor activity and an impressive spa. Original Georgian features are combined with contemporary furnishings and the luxurious bedrooms offer superb views. Traditional menus feature local, seasonal ingredients and afternoon teas are a speciality.

158 rooms ☑ – ♦ € 105/250 ♦♦ € 115/300 – 4 suites
Farnham Estate – Northwest : 3.75 km on R 198 – ℰ (049) 437 77 00 – www.farnhamestate.com

🏨 **Cavan Crystal** 🛜 🗒 📶 🏖 🖥 🛏 ⚙ 🏊 🖥

BUSINESS · MODERN Modern hotel next to the Cavan Crystal factory, with an impressive atrium, a large, stylish lounge-bar and red and black bedrooms in a uniform design. It comes with good meeting and leisure facilities and is popular for spa breaks.

85 rooms ☑ – ♦ € 75/100 ♦♦ € 99/150
Dublin Rd – ℰ (049) 436 0600 – www.cavancrystalhotel.com
Opus One – See restaurant listing

XX **Opus One** 🆎 🖥

CREATIVE · FRIENDLY Contemporary restaurant hidden away on the first floor a smart hotel. Cooking uses good quality ingredients and modern techniques. Ambitious dishes feature unusual flavour and texture combinations and are attractively presented.

Menu € 25/35 – Carte € 20/50

Cavan Crystal Hotel, Dublin Rd – East : 2.5 km on R 212 – ℰ (049) 436 0600 – www.cavancrystalhotel.com – dinner only and Sunday lunch light lunch – Closed 26-28 December

at Cloverhill North: 12 km by N3 on N54 – ✉ Belturbet

XX **Olde Post Inn** 🛜 🛏 🆎 🍴 ⟲ 🖥

TRADITIONAL CUISINE · RUSTIC Enjoy a fireside aperitif in the characterful, flag floored bar or the wood-framed conservatory of this red-brick former post office. The well-established restaurant serves traditional cooking made with Irish produce, wherein classic flavour combinations are given a modern twist. Contemporary bedrooms.

Menu € 35/63 – Carte € 41/62

6 rooms ☑ – ♦ € 65/75 ♦♦ € 100/120
– ℰ (047) 55 555 – www.theoldepostinn.com – dinner only and Sunday lunch – Closed 24-27 December, Monday and Tuesday

CLAREMORRIS CLÁR CHLAINNE MHUIRIS

Mayo – Pop. 3 412 – Regional map n° **21**-B2
▶ Dublin 149 km – Castlebar 18 km – Galway 39 km – Newbridge 41 km

🏨 McWilliam Park

BUSINESS · CLASSIC Popular, purpose-built hotel, named after an 18C landowner and located on the outskirts of town, close to the airport. Spacious, modern bedrooms; pay the extra for a VIP upgrade. Numerous meeting and events rooms. Carvery offered in the bar; wide-ranging menu in the restaurant. Breakfasts are cooked to order.

103 rooms 🛏 – 🛉 € 95/125 🛉🛉 € 150/190 – 2 suites

Knock Rd – East : 2 km on N 60 – 𝒞 (094) 937 80 00 – www.mcwilliampark.ie

CLIFDEN AN CLOCHÁN

Galway – Pop. 2 056 – Regional map n° **21**-A3

▶ Dublin 291 km – Ballina 124 km – Galway 79 km

🏨 Clifden Station House

BUSINESS · MODERN Purpose-built hotel beside the old Galway-Clifden railway line, in a modern residential and leisure complex, with a residents-only kids club, gym and wellness centre. Spacious, uniform bedrooms have good facilities. Local seafood orientated menus in the restaurant. Classic pub dishes in the Signal Bar.

78 rooms 🛏 – 🛉 € 65/120 🛉🛉 € 80/160

– 𝒞 (095) 21 699 – www.clifdenstationhouse.com

– Closed 25 December

🏨 Ardagh

FAMILY · PERSONALISED Neat, modern hotel overlooking a small bay. Choice of three lounges. Pleasant bedrooms; many with bold fabrics and colourful headboards designed by the owner – some with sofas and armchairs from which to admire the views. Bright restaurant affords an excellent outlook; seafood is a speciality.

19 rooms 🛏 – 🛉 € 80/120 🛉🛉 € 100/200

Ballyconneely Rd – South : 3 km. on R 341 – 𝒞 (095) 21 384

– www.ardaghhotel.com – Closed November-Easter

🏠 Dolphin Beach Country House

TRADITIONAL · COSY Terracotta-coloured former farmhouse in a peaceful hillside location. The interior is styled like a Mediterranean villa, with bright décor and red stone tiles. Good-sized bedrooms display artwork by the friendly owner. Traditional home-cooked meals and wonderful bay views from the dining room.

9 rooms 🛏 – 🛉 € 55/85 🛉🛉 € 100/150

Lower Sky Rd – West : 5.5 km. by Sky Rd – 𝒞 (095) 21 204

– www.dolphinbeachhouse.com – Closed November-March

🏠 Quay House

FAMILY · PERSONALISED A former harbourmaster's house and monastery overlooking the bay. The relaxed bohemian-style interior is filled with antiques and wild animal memorabilia. Bedrooms are comfortable and spacious; those in the wing have kitchenettes.

14 rooms 🛏 – 🛉 € 90/110 🛉🛉 € 135/160

Beach Rd – 𝒞 (095) 21 369 – www.thequayhouse.com

– Closed November-mid March

🏠 Sea Mist House

TRADITIONAL · COSY Centrally located, stone-built house with pleasant gardens, a homely lounge and a bright conservatory breakfast area. Spacious, modern bedrooms boast colourful co-ordinating fabrics and fresh flowers; no TVs. Eclectic Irish art collection.

4 rooms 🛏 – 🛉 € 55/70 🛉🛉 € 90/120

– 𝒞 (095) 21 441 – www.seamisthouse.com

– Closed November-March

REPUBLIC OF IRELAND

🏠 Buttermilk Lodge

TRADITIONAL · COSY Immaculate guesthouse filled with bovine memorabilia. Homely, colour co-ordinated bedrooms; games, hot drinks and a real turf fire in the lounge. Friendly owners offer local info, packed lunches and walking tours. Extensive breakfasts.

11 rooms ⌁ – ♦ € 50/75 ♦♦ € 70/100

Westport Rd – ℰ (095) 21 951 – www.buttermilklodge.com
– Closed November-February

✗ Mitchells ⓝ

FISH AND SEAFOOD · FAMILY Long-standing, family-run restaurant which specialises in seafood. It's set over two floors and decorated with regional prints and seascapes. They offer a huge array of traditional dishes; local prawns, mussels and oysters feature.

Menu € 27 (dinner) – Carte € 29/47

Market St – ℰ (095) 21 867 – www.mithcellsofclifden.com – Closed November-mid March

CLOGHEEN AN CHLOICHÍN

South Tipperary – Pop. 491 – Regional map n° **22**-C2
▶ Dublin 122 km – Tipperary 23 km – Clonmel 21 km – Dungarvan 28 km

✗✗ Old Convent

MODERN CUISINE · FORMAL A very personally run restaurant in a former convent set on the edge of the village. The candlelit former chapel with its delightful original stained glass windows is where dinner is served. The set 8 course daily changing menu features original, modern dishes. Smart, comfortable bedrooms have good quality linens; help yourself to goodies from the pantry.

Menu € 65 – set menu only

7 rooms ⌁ – ♦ € 150 ♦♦ € 170/195

Mount Anglesby – Southeast : 0.5 km on R 668 (Lismore rd) – ℰ (052) 746 55 65 (booking essential) – www.theoldconvent.ie – dinner only
– Closed 21-26 December, 3 January-11 February and Sunday-Thursday September-May

CLONAKILTY CLOICH NA COILLTE

Cork – Pop. 4 000 – Regional map n° **22**-B3
▶ Dublin 310 km – Cork 51 km

🏨 Inchydoney Island Lodge and Spa

FAMILY · MODERN Superbly located on a remote headland and boasting stunning views over the beach and out to sea; all of the contemporary bedrooms have a balcony or terrace. The impressive spa boasts a seawater pool and 27 treatment rooms. Dine in the modern restaurant or in the nautically styled bistro-bar.

67 rooms ⌁ – ♦ € 158/250 ♦♦ € 158/250 – 4 suites

South : 5.25 km by N 71 following signs for Inchydoney Beach – ℰ (023) 883 31 4.
– www.inchydoneyisland.com – Closed 24-25 December

Gulfstream – See restaurant listing

✗✗ Gulfstream

MODERN CUISINE · FORMAL Contemporary New England style restaurant set on the first floor of a vast hotel and offering superb views over the beach and out to sea. Modern menus highlight produce from West Cork and feature plenty of fresh local seafood.

Carte € 50/66

Inchydoney Island Lodge and Spa Hotel, South : 5.25 km by N 71 following signs for Inchydoney Beach – ℰ (023) 883 31 43 – www.inchydoneyisland.com – dinner only and Sunday lunch – Closed 24-25 December

Deasy's ⌂ 🅿

TRADITIONAL CUISINE · COSY An appealing pub in a picturesque hamlet, offering lovely views out across the bay. Its gloriously dated interior is decorated with maritime memorabilia. Menus are dictated by the seasons and the latest catch from the local boats.

Menu € 26 (dinner)/32 – Carte € 31/47

Ring – Southeast : 3 km – 𝒞 (023) 883 57 41 – Closed 24-26 December, Good Friday, Sunday dinner, Monday, Tuesday and restricted opening in winter

CLONEGALL CLUAIN NA NGALL

Carlow – Pop. 245 – Regional map n° **22**-D2

▶ Dublin 73 km – Carlow 20 km – Kilkenny 39 km – Wexford 30 km

✗ Sha-Roe Bistro

BRITISH TRADITIONAL · FRIENDLY Rurally located restaurant with a good reputation, set in a pretty little cottage and run by an keen, friendly couple. Rustic lounge and a small dining room with an enormous inglenook and a kitchen table. Flavoursome, classical cooking of local produce; the cheese comes from the weekly farmers' market.

Carte € 32/42

Main St – 𝒞 (053) 937 56 36 (booking essential) – dinner only and Sunday lunch – Closed January, 1 week April, 1 week October, Sunday dinner, Monday and Tuesday

CLONTARF CLUAIN TARBH – Dublin → See Dublin

CLOVERHILL DROIM CAISIDE – Cavan → See Cavan

CONG CONGA

Mayo – Pop. 178 – Regional map n° **21**-A3

▶ Dublin 257 km – Ballina 79 km – Galway 45 km

Ashford Castle 🏰

CASTLE · HISTORIC Hugely impressive lochside castle surrounded by a moat and formal gardens; try your hand at archery, falconry and clay pigeon shooting in the large grounds. Handsome guest areas feature antiques and bedrooms are sumptuously appointed. Dine casually in Cullen's; elegant George V requires a jacket and tie.

82 rooms � – ♦ € 205/2480 ♦♦ € 225/2500 – 5 suites

– 𝒞 (094) 954 60 03 – www.ashfordcastle.com

Cullen's at the Cottage – See restaurant listing

The Lodge at Ashford Castle

COUNTRY HOUSE · STYLISH This extended Georgian house is younger sister to Ashford Castle and offers lovely views down to Lough Corrib. Most of the stylish modern bedrooms overlook a courtyard and some are duplex. Unwind in the hot tub while the children are busy in the 'Wii' room. Modern menus feature in the four-roomed restaurant.

50 rooms ⊫ – ♦ € 155/255 ♦♦ € 155/255 – 12 suites

The Quay – Southeast : 2.25 km by R 345 off R 346 – 𝒞 (094) 954 5400 – www.thelodgeac.com – Closed 24-25 December and midweek in winter

Michaeleen's Manor

FAMILY · COSY 'The Quiet Man' was filmed in the village over 60 years ago and this house pays homage – with black and white stills on the walls and rooms named after various characters. Homely lounges and brightly decorated bedrooms. Friendly owners.

10 rooms ⊫ – ♦ € 45/55 ♦♦ € 65/75

Quay Rd – Southeast : 1.5 km by R 346 – 𝒞 (094) 954 60 89 – www.quietman-cong.com

REPUBLIC OF IRELAND

XX **Cullen's at the Cottage** 🍴 🏠 AC P

INTERNATIONAL · BRASSERIE Thatched cottage with a terrace and lovely views, located within the grounds of an imposing castle and named in honour of a former maître'd, who was here for 25 years. Relaxed, all-day restaurant serving a modern bistro menu.

Carte € 34/52

Ashford Castle Hotel, – ℰ (094) 954 53 32 – www.ashfordcastle.com – closed November-March

CORK CORCAIGH

Cork – Pop. 119 230 – Regional map n° **22**-B3
▶ Dublin 253 km – Limerick 99 km – Waterford 123 km

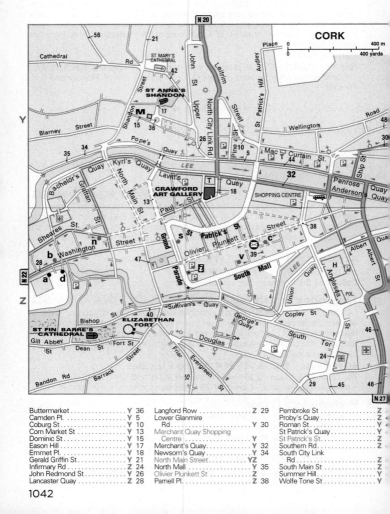

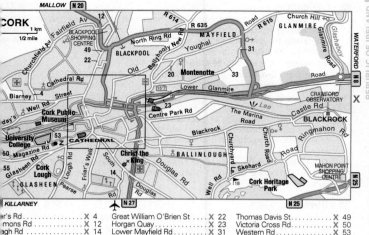

⭐⭐⭐ Hayfield Manor ✿ 🛎 🔲 🕙 ♨ ➗ ⚖ 🤵 🅰🅲 ❄ 🛁 🅿

LUXURY · CLASSIC Luxurious country house with wood-panelled hall, impressive staircase and antique-furnished drawing rooms; the perfect spot for afternoon tea. Plush bedrooms have plenty of extras, including putting machines. Well-equipped residents spa.

88 rooms ⌷ – ♦ € 179/329 ♦♦ € 179/329 – 4 suites

Town plan: X-z – *Perrott Ave, College Rd* – ✆ (021) 484 59 00
– *www.hayfieldmanor.ie*

Orchids • Perrotts – See restaurant listing

⭐⭐ The Kingsley ⓝ ✿ 🔲 🕙 ♨ ➗ ⚖ 🤵 🅰🅲 ❄ 🛁 🅿

BUSINESS · MODERN Contemporary hotel set out of the city centre, on the banks of the River Lee. Stylish bedrooms have a high level of modern facilities. The spa and leisure club is very smart; conference rooms have a more traditional feel. Fairbanks is elegant and formal and has a classic menu; appealing Springboard has a river outlook, a small terrace and serves brasserie-style dishes.

131 rooms – ♦ € 150/165 ♦♦ € 150/165 – 2 suites

Town plan: X-a – *Victoria Cross* – ✆ (021) 480 05 55 – *www.thekingsley.ie*
– *Closed 25 December*

⭐⭐ River Lee ✿ 🔲 ♨ ➗ ⚖ 🤵 🅰🅲 🛁 🚗

BUSINESS · FUNCTIONAL Purpose-built hotel overlooking the river – just 5min walk from the city centre – complete with a whole floor of meeting rooms and a large leisure centre. Uniform bedrooms have a minimalist style and good facilities. Dine in the spacious bar with its terrace or to a weir backdrop in the modern restaurant.

182 rooms – ♦ € 140/240 ♦♦ € 140/240

Town plan: Z-a – *Western Rd.* – ✆ (021) 425 27 00 – *www.doylecollection.com*
– *Closed 23-26 December*

> Your discoveries and comments help us improve the guide.
> Please let us know about your experiences - good or bad!

REPUBLIC OF IRELAND

🏨 Lancaster Lodge

BUSINESS · FUNCTIONAL Purpose-built hotel next to the River Lee and within easy walking distance of the town centre. Spacious, bright bedrooms with bold fabrics and modern artwork; the executive suites have whirlpool baths. A good choice for the business traveller.

48 rooms – 🛏 € 86/146 🛏🛏 € 86/146 – 🍽 €12

Town plan: Z-d – *Lancaster Quay, Western Rd* – *𝒞 (021) 425 11 25*
– www.lancasterlodge.com – Closed 23-28 December

XxX Orchids

MODERN CUISINE · LUXURY Sophisticated formal dining room in a well-appointed country house. Pillars dominate the room, which is laid with crisp white tablecloths. Menus offer refined dishes with some modern twists.

Menu € 69

Town plan: X-z – *Hayfield Manor Hotel, Perrott Ave, College Rd* – *𝒞 (021) 484 59 00 (booking essential)* – *www.hayfieldmanor.ie* – *dinner only* – *Closed Sunday and Monday*

XX Perrotts

MODERN CUISINE · BRASSERIE Conservatory restaurant overlooking the gardens of a luxurious country house. Smart but comfortably furnished with adjoining wood-panelled bar. Menu offers a modern take on brasserie classics.

Carte € 34/59

Town plan: X-z – *Hayfield Manor Hotel, Perrott Ave, College Rd* – *𝒞 (021) 484 59 00* – *www.hayfieldmanor.ie* – *Closed 25 December*

XX Les Gourmandises

FRENCH CLASSIC · ELEGANT Smart, contemporary restaurant which is proudly run by experienced owners – he cooks and she looks after the service. Accomplished dishes have a classic French heart and original Irish twists. The set menu represent good value.

Menu € 33/48

Town plan: Z-v – *17 Cook St* – *𝒞 (021) 425 19 59 (booking essential)*
– www.lesgourmandises.ie – dinner only – Closed Sunday

XX Jacques

REGIONAL · INTIMATE Personally run restaurant with an intimate feel and friendly, helpful service. Honest regional cooking uses good quality local ingredients and has clearly defined flavours. In the evening, they also serve small plates in the wine bar.

Menu € 24 (weekday dinner) – Carte € 35/47

Town plan: Z-c – *23 Oliver Plunket St* – *𝒞 (021) 427 73 87*
– www.jacquesrestaurant.ie – Closed 25 December-3 January, Sunday, Monday dinner and bank holidays

X Cafe Paradiso

VEGETARIAN · INTIMATE They have been serving creative, satisfying vegetarian dishes at this stylish restaurant for over 20 years now – and it's as busy and as popular as ever. Service is bright and friendly and the atmosphere, intimate yet lively. The spacious, modern bedrooms upstairs come in bright, bold colours.

Menu € 40

2 rooms 🍽 – 🛏 € 100/120 🛏🛏 € 120/140

Town plan: Z-b – *16 Lancaster Quay, Western Rd*
– 𝒞 (021) 427 79 39 (booking essential) – www.cafeparadiso.ie
– dinner only and lunch Saturday – Closed 25-28 December, Sunday and bank holidays

Ⅹ Fenn's Quay

TRADITIONAL CUISINE · BISTRO Modest little bistro with whitewashed brick walls, closely set tables and a loyal following. Simple, flavoursome cooking offers light lunches and more substantial dishes at dinner; pop in for morning coffee or afternoon tea.

Menu € 25 (dinner) – Carte € 23/47

Town plan: Z-n – 5 Sheares St – ℰ (021) 427 95 27 – www.fennsquay.net
– Closed 24-27 December, 1 January, Sunday and bank holidays

Ⅹ Farmgate Café

REGIONAL · BISTRO Popular, long-standing eatery above a bustling 200 year old market; turn right for self-service or left for the bistro. Daily menus use produce from the stalls below and are supplemented by the latest catch. Dishes are hearty and homemade.

Menu € 20 – Carte € 19/31

Town plan: Z-s – English Market (1st floor), Princes St – ℰ (021) 427 81 34
– www.farmgate.ie – lunch only – Closed 25-27 December, Sunday and bank holidays

at Cork Airport South: 6.5km by N27 -(X)⊠ Cork

🏨 Cork International

BUSINESS · DESIGN Modern hotel close to the airport terminal; don't be put off by its unassuming exterior. Spacious bedrooms offer good facilities for both modern business travellers and holidaymakers – go for a corner suite with floor to ceiling windows. The informal American-themed brasserie serves an international menu.

145 rooms – ♦ € 79/149 ♦♦ € 79/149 – � €15 – 4 suites
Cork Airport Business Park – ℰ (021) 454 98 00
– www.corkinternationalairporthotel.com – Closed 24-26 December

CORK AIRPORT AERFORT CHORCAI

Cork → See Cork

CORROFIN CORA FINNE

Clare – Pop. 689 – Regional map n° **22**-B1
▶ Dublin 228 km – Gort 24 km – Limerick 51 km

🏠 Fergus View

FAMILY · FUNCTIONAL Charming bay-windowed house – in the family for four generations; the delightful owners offer superb hospitality. Open-fired lounge, cosy breakfast room and country views. Bright, superbly kept bedrooms: smart but tiny bathrooms; no TVs.

5 rooms ⊻ – ♦ € 45/50 ♦♦ € 70/76
Kilnaboy – North : 3.25 km on R 476 – ℰ (065) 683 76 06 – www.fergusview.com
– Closed November-February

CROMANE

Kerry – Pop. 115 – Regional map n° **22**-A2
▶ Dublin 201 km – Tralee 23 km – Cork 73 km – Limerick 78 km

ⅩⅩ Jacks Coastguard

FISH AND SEAFOOD · DESIGN Remote coastguard station; now a bright, glitzy restaurant offering panoramic bay views. Seafood-orientated menus offer well-presented, classic combinations; concise selection at lunch. Smart bar-lounge features live piano at weekends.

Menu € 27/39 – Carte € 27/62

Cromane Lower – ℰ (066) 976 91 02 – www.jackscromane.com – Closed 7 January-9 February, Monday-Wednesday except June-October and Tuesday

CROOKHAVEN AN CRUACHÁN
Cork – Pop. 1 669 – Regional map n° **22**-A3
▶ Dublin 373 km – Bantry 40 km – Cork 120 km

Galley Cove House
FAMILY · HOMELY Detached house just outside the town, affording superb southerly views over the sea towards Fastnet Rock. Conservatory breakfast room and simple, pine-furnished bedrooms with bright colour schemes; all have a sea outlook. Hospitable owners.
4 rooms ☑ – † € 40/50 **††** € 70/90
West : 0.75 km on R 591 – ℰ (028) 35 137 – www.galleycovehouse.com – Closed November-March

CROSSHAVEN
Cork – Pop. 2 093 – Regional map n° **22**-B3
▶ Dublin 170 km – Cork 15 km – Limerick 78 km – Galway 140 km

Cronin's
FISH AND SEAFOOD · PUB In the family since 1970, a classic Irish pub now run by the 3rd generation. Interesting artefacts and boxing memorabilia. Unfussy sea food dishes feature local produce. Limited opening in restaurant, which offers more ambitious fare.
Menu € 19 (dinner) – Carte € 28/42
– ℰ (021) 483 18 29 – www.croninspub.com – Closed 25 December and Good Friday

CROSSMOLINA CROIS MHAOILÍONA
Mayo – Pop. 1 061 – Regional map n° **21**-B2
▶ Dublin 252 km – Ballina 10 km

Enniscoe House
HISTORIC · PERSONALISED Classic Georgian manor, part-dating from 1740 and overlooking Lough Conn; the formal walled garden, heritage museum and tea shop are open to the public. Generously proportioned rooms are filled with an tiques and family portraits. Traditional set menu of home-grown ingredients served in the formal dining room.
6 rooms ☑ – † € 80/120 **††** € 160/240
Castlehill – South : 3.25 km on R 315 – ℰ (096) 31 112 – www.enniscoe.com – Closed November-March

DELGANY
Wicklow – Pop. 5 191 – Regional map n° **22**-D2
▶ Dublin 31 km – Wicklow 21 km – Naas 58 km

Pigeon House Cafe 🆕
BRITISH MODERN · BISTRO This former pub now houses a bakery, a deli and a large restaurant complete with a counter of homemade cakes. Breakfast morphs into coffee, then into lunch and dinner; you can have anything from a bacon sar nie to duck liver parfait.
Carte € 28/42
– ℰ (01) 287 7103 – www.pigeonhouse.ie – Closed 25-25 December and dinner Sunday-Wednesday

DINGLE AN DAINGEAN
Kerry – Pop. 1 965 – Regional map n° **22**-A2
▶ Dublin 347 km – Killarney 82 km – Limerick 153 km

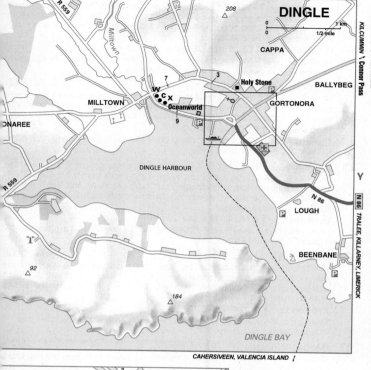

DINGLE

CAPPA

Holy Stone

BALLYBEG

GORTONORA

MILLTOWN

Oceanworld

DINGLE HARBOUR

LOUGH

BEENBANE

DINGLE BAY

CAHERSIVEEN, VALENCIA ISLAND

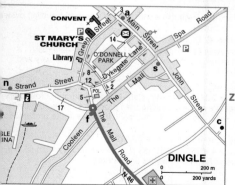

CONVENT

ST MARY'S CHURCH

Library

O'DONNELL PARK

Strand Street

DINGLE

Avondale St	Z 2
Bridge St	Z 5
Goat St	Y, Z 3
Grey's Lane	Z 8
High Road (The)	Y 7
Holy Ground	Z 12
Orchard Lane	Z 14
Tracks (The)	Z 17
Wood (The)	Y 9

⌂ Castlewood House

COUNTRY HOUSE · CLASSIC Spacious house overlooking the bay. Modern bed rooms come with whirlpool baths and extras like robes and chocolates. There' an extensive breakfast buffet and a wide range of cooked options; don't mis the bread and butter pudding.

12 rooms ⌑ – ♦ € 65/125 ♦♦ € 85/195

Town plan: Y-w – The Wood – ℰ (066) 915 27 88 – www.castlewooddingle.com – Closed 6-27 December and 6 January-13 February

⌂ Greenmount House

FAMILY · CLASSIC Well-run hotel in an elevated position above the town, wit views of the hills and harbour. Comfy lounges and spacious, modern bedrooms some have balconies and others, small terraces. Excellent breakfasts with a view

14 rooms ⌑ – ♦ € 60/135 ♦♦ € 80/160

Town plan: Z-c – Gortonora – ℰ (066) 915 14 14 – www.greenmounthouse.ie – Closed 16-27 December

⌂ Heatons

FAMILY · STYLISH Large, family-run house, a short walk from town; a warm wel come guaranteed. Modern bedrooms; most have sea views and Room 8 has balcony. Comprehensive breakfasts include homemade scones, pancakes, omel ettes and Drambuie porridge.

16 rooms ⌑ – ♦ € 55/92 ♦♦ € 84/128

Town plan: Y-c – The Wood – ℰ (066) 915 22 88 – www.heatonsdingle.com – Closed 2 January-1 February

⌂ Coastline

TOWNHOUSE · PERSONALISED This large, peach-painted house overlooks th harbour. Bedrooms are spacious and well-kept and the cosy front lounge is fille with local info. At breakfast, enjoy home-bread bread; choose a window seat t make the most of the view.

7 rooms ⌑ – ♦ € 50/60 ♦♦ € 70/90

Town plan: Y-x – The Wood – ℰ (066) 915 24 94 – www.coastlinedingle.com – Closed December-January

✗✗ Global Village

TRADITIONAL CUISINE · FRIENDLY Homely restaurant with local artwork and relaxed vibe. Wide-ranging menu makes good use of seasonal, organic an home-grown produce; fantastic fresh fish dishes feature. The well-travelled owne has visited 42 different countries!

Menu € 28/50 **s** – Carte € 33/66 **s**

Town plan: Z-a – Upper Main St – ℰ (066) 915 23 25 (booking essential) – www.globalvillagedingle.com – dinner only – Closed January- February and restricted opening in winter

✗✗ Idás ⓝ

MODERN CUISINE · INDIVIDUAL This rustic, slate-faced restaurant is found righ in the heart of town. Creative modern cooking uses produce from the Dingle Per insula. The chef-owner, Kevin, went to art school and it shows in the presentatio of his dishes.

Menu € 29 (weekday dinner) – Carte € 42/49

Town plan: Z-s – John St – ℰ (066) 915 0885 (booking essential) – dinner only – Closed January-February, Tuesday in winter and Monday

✗ Chart House

REGIONAL · RUSTIC This characterful former boathouse sits in a pleasant spo on the quayside. The charming open-plan interior features exposed stone an stained glass, and oil lamps give off an intimate glow. Seasonal, local ingredient feature in rustic, flavoursome dishes and service is friendly and efficient.

Menu € 29 – Carte € 32/45

Town plan: Z-f – The Mall – ℰ (066) 915 22 55 (booking essential) – www.thecharthousedingle.com – dinner only – Closed 2 January-12 February, 22-27 December and Monday

X Out of the Blue

FISH AND SEAFOOD · RUSTIC Simple blue building with a small terrace and views out to the harbour. Rustic interior with nautical artwork. Daily changing menu offers generous portions of the freshest seafood from the day boats. Buzzy atmosphere. Efficient service.

Carte € 37/56

Town plan: Z-n – *Waterside*
- *€ (066) 915 08 11 (booking essential) – www.outoftheblue.ie*
- *dinner only and Sunday lunch*
- *Closed January-mid March*

DONEGAL DÚN NA NGALL
Donegal – Pop. 2 607 – Regional map n° **21**-C1
▶ Dublin 264 km – Londonderry 77 km – Sligo 64 km

Solis Lough Eske Castle

LUXURY · CLASSIC Beautifully restored 17C castle with extensions, surrounded by 43 sculpture-filled acres. Fantastic spa; swimming pool overlooks an enclosed garden. Mix of contemporary and antique-furnished bedrooms, garden suites are worth the extra cost.

96 rooms ⌂ – ♦ € 195/395 ♦♦ € 195/395 – 1 suite
Northeast : 6.5 km by N15
- *€ (074) 972 51 00 – www.solisloughheskecastle.ie*
- *Closed Monday and Tuesday November-March*

Cedars – See restaurant listing

Harvey's Point

FAMILY · CLASSIC A sprawling, family-run hotel in a peaceful loughside setting, with traditional guest areas and huge, very comfortable, country house style bedrooms – all offer a high level of facilities and most have lovely countryside outlooks.

64 rooms ⌂ – ♦ € 150/225 ♦♦ € 198/300
Lough Eske – Northeast : 7.25 km. by N 15
- *€ (074) 972 22 08 – www.harveyspoint.com*
- *Restricted opening in winter*

Harvey's Point – See restaurant listing

Ardeevin

FAMILY · COSY Friendly, brightly painted house set in peaceful gardens and boasting beautiful views over Lough Eske; personally run by the friendly owner. Warm, pleasantly cluttered guest areas are filled with ornaments and curios. Individually designed bedrooms display quality furnishings and thoughtful extras.

4 rooms ⌂ – ♦ € 48/52 ♦♦ € 70/80
Lough Eske, Barnesmore – Northeast : 9 km by N 15 following signs for Lough Eske Drive
- *€ (074) 972 17 90 – www.ardeevin.tripod.com*
- *Closed November - 19 March*

XxX Harvey's Point

MODERN CUISINE · FORMAL A formal, traditional restaurant set within a family-owned country house hotel; its semi-circular windows afford delightful views of the lough. Classic dishes make use of local Donegal produce and are presented in a modern manner.

Menu € 55

Harvey's Point Hotel, Lough Eske – Northeast : 7.25 km. by N 15
- *€ (074) 972 22 08 – www.harveyspoint.com – dinner only*
- *Closed Sunday-Tuesday November-April*

✕✕ Cedars

      🛜 ⅙ 𝔸𝕂 ⇔ 🅿

TRADITIONAL CUISINE · INTIMATE Stylish, modern restaurant in a 17C castle close to the lough, with romantic booths to the rear and a slate terrace boasting views over the lawns and woodland. Small menu with international influences, but Donegal produce to the fore.

Menu € 55
– Carte € 41/64
Solis Lough Eske Castle Hotel, Northeast : 6.5 km by N15
– 𝒞 (074) 972 51 00 – www.solisloughheskecastle.com
– *dinner only and Sunday lunch*
– *Closed Monday and Tuesday November-March*

DONNYBROOK DOMHNACH BROC – Dublin → See Dublin

DOOGORT DUMHA GOIRT – Mayo → See Achill Island

DOOLIN DÚLAINM

Clare – Regional map n° **22**-B1
▶ Dublin 275 km – Galway 69 km – Limerick 80 km

✕✕ Cullinan's

      ⇔ 🛜 🅿

CLASSIC CUISINE · FAMILY Run by a keen husband and wife team; an orange building in the middle of the Burren, with two walls of full length windows making the most of the view. Classical, comforting cooking uses Irish produce and portions are generous. Comfy, pine-furnished bedrooms; some overlook the River Aille.

Menu € 30 (early dinner)
– Carte € 35/46
10 rooms ⌂ – ∳ € 50/85 ∳∳ € 75/120
– 𝒞 (065) 707 41 83 (booking essential) – www.cullinansdoolin.com
– *dinner only – Closed November-March, Sunday dinner and Wednesday*

DOONBEG

Clare – Pop. 272 – Regional map n° **22**-B2
▶ Dublin 286 km – Inis 45 km – Galway 115 km – Limerick 91 km

🏛🏛 Trump International Golf Links and H. Doonbeg

      🏵 ⅗

LUXURY · DESIGN Smart resort complex   ⮜ 🛜 🖼 🌐 🛖 🗓 ⅙ 𝔸𝕂 🏵 🅿
now owned by Donald Trump. Stylish, sumptuous bedrooms and suites are spread about the grounds: some are duplex and feature fully fitted kitchens; all have spacious marble bathrooms and are extremely comfortable. Ocean View offers fine dining with a pleasant outlook over the sea; Trump's brasserie, in the golf clubhouse, serves a traditional menu.

75 rooms – ∳ € 175/200 ∳∳ € 175/245 – ⌂ €22
Northeast : 9 km on N 67
– 𝒞 (065) 905 56 00 – www.trumphotelcollection.com

🄳 Morrissey's

      ⇔ 🏠 ⅙

FISH AND SEAFOOD · PUB Smartly refurbished pub in a small coastal village; it terrace overlooking the river and the castle ruins. The menu may be simple bu cooking is careful and shows respect for ingredients – locally caught fish an shellfish feature heavily. Bedrooms are modern and they have bikes and even kayak for hire.

Carte € 24/43
5 rooms ⌂ – ∳ € 40/50 ∳∳ € 80/90
– 𝒞 (065) 905 53 04 – www.morrisseysdoonbeg.com
– *dinner only*
– *Closed January, February and Monday*

DROGHEDA DROICHEAD ÁTHA

Louth – Pop. 30 393 – Regional map n° **21**-D3

▶ Dublin 46 km – Dundalk 35 km

The D

BUSINESS · STYLISH Smart, modern hotel, in an office and shopping complex on the south bank of the river. Spacious, open-plan guest areas are minimalist in style, with colourful furniture. Decently sized, slightly stark bedrooms; those overlooking the river are the most popular. Informal restaurant; characterful Irish pub.

104 rooms ☷ – ♦ € 129/299 ♦♦ € 139/309

Scotch Hall, Marsh Rd. – ℰ (041) 987 77 00 – www.thedhotel.com – Closed Christmas Day

Scholars Townhouse

TOWNHOUSE · CLASSIC 19C former priest's house: now a well-run, privately owned hotel with smart wood panelling and ornate coving featuring throughout. Appealing bar and cosy lounge; comfortable, well-kept bedrooms. Dine on classically based dishes under an impressive mural of the Battle of Boyne.

16 rooms ☷ – ♦ € 65/120 ♦♦ € 75/150

King St – by West St and Lawrence St turning left at Lawrence's Gate – ℰ (041) 983 54 10 – www.scholarshotel.com – Closed 25-26 December

X Eastern Seaboard Bar & Grill

INTERNATIONAL · BISTRO A lively industrial style bistro; its name a reference to its location within Ireland and also a nod to the USA, which influences the menus. Share several small plates or customise a hearty main course with your choice of sides.

Carte € 19/44

1 Bryanstown Centre, Dublin Rd – Southeast : 2.5 km. by N 1 taking first right after railway bridge – ℰ (041) 980 25 70 – www.easternseaboard.ie – Closed Good Friday and 25 December

X The Kitchen

WORLD CUISINE · BISTRO Glass-fronted riverfront eatery. By day, a café serving homemade cakes, pastries, salads and sandwiches; by night, a more interesting, mainly Eastern Mediterranean menu is served, with influences from North Africa and the Middle East.

Menu € 25/50 – Carte € 29/46

2 South Quay – ℰ (041) 983 4630 – www.kitchenrestaurant.ie – Closed 1 January, 31 August-7 September, 25-27 December and Monday-Tuesday

DROMAHAIR

Leitrim – Regional map n° **21**-D2

▶ Dublin 196 km – Leitrim 23 km – Sligo 12 km

X Luna 🅝

INTERNATIONAL · FRIENDLY A delightful little cottage on the main road of a sleepy village; the loughside drive over from Sligo is beautiful. It might have a neighbourhood feel but the food has global overtones, from the South of France and Tuscany to Asia.

Carte € 29/40

Main St – ℰ (071) 916 47 28 – dinner only – Closed November to March except December, Sunday and Monday

GOOD TIPS!

The Celtic Tiger is back, with a purr if not yet a roar, and the capital's food scene is most definitely showing signs of hotting up. A resurgence in informal dining has seen restaurants like the loft-style Drury Buildings and grocer's shop conversion Delahunt become popular – and these sit happily alongside the city's growing collection of Michelin stars.

DUBLIN BAILE ÁTHA CLIATH

Dublin – Pop. 527 612 – Regional map n° **22**-D1
▶ Belfast 166 km – Cork 248 km – Londonderry 235 km

Hotels

Shelbourne

GRAND LUXURY · CLASSIC Famed hotel dating from 1824, overlooking an attractive green; this is where the 1922 Irish Constitution was signed. Elegant guest areas and classical architecture; it even has a tiny museum. The bar and lounge are THE places to go for drinks and afternoon tea. Chic spa and characterful, luxurious bedrooms.

265 rooms ☲ – ♦ € 190/750 ♦♦ € 190/750 – 12 suites
Town plan: 6JZ-c – *27 St Stephen's Grn.* ⊠ *D2* – ℰ *(01) 663 45 00*
– *www.theshelbourne.ie*
Saddle Room – See restaurant listing

Merrion

TOWNHOUSE · CLASSIC A classic Georgian façade conceals this luxury hotel; it opulent drawing rooms filled with antique furniture and fine artwork. Enjoy 'a afternoon tea' with a view of the formal parterre garden. Stylish bedrooms hav an understated, classic feel and smart marble bathrooms. Compact spa with im pressive pool. Accessible menu in the restaurant and barrel-ceilinged bar.

142 rooms – ♦ € 495/635 ♦♦ € 515/655 – ☲ €29 – 10 suites
Town plan: 6KZ-e – *Upper Merrion St* ⊠ *D2* – ℰ *(01) 603 06 00*
– *www.merrionhotel.com*

The Westbury

BUSINESS · CONTEMPORARY Well-run hotel with a stylish bar, a comfy lounge (popular for afternoon tea) and state-of-the-art conference facilities; modern artwork features throughout and service is excellent. Well-equipped, elegant bedrooms come in browns and creams. Dine in the formal Irish restaurant or the Parisian-style brasserie.

205 rooms – ♦ € 190/535 ♦♦ € 190/535 – � €25 – 8 suites
Town plan: 6JY-x – Grafton St ✉ D2 – ✆ (01) 679 1122
– www.doylecollection.com/westbury

Westin

LUXURY · STYLISH Built in 1860 as a bank; now a smart hotel set over 6 period buildings, with comfy lounges and impressive conference rooms (the old banking hall features ornate plasterwork and chandeliers). Contemporary bedrooms have subtle Celtic touches and media hubs. Atmospheric 'Mint' sits within the old vaults.

163 rooms – ♦ € 150/600 ♦♦ € 150/600 – ☱ €22 – 13 suites
Town plan: 6JY-n – Westmoreland St ✉ D2 – ✆ (01) 645 10 00
– www.thewestindublin.com

Marker

BUSINESS · DESIGN Smart business hotel overlooking the canal basin, with extensive meeting facilities and a well-equipped spa and fitness centre. The striking angular lobby houses a stylish bar and a chic brasserie serving modern Irish cooking. Crisp, contemporary bedrooms have a minimalist style; some overlook the square.

187 rooms – ♦ € 199/425 ♦♦ € 199/425 – ☱ €25 – 3 suites
Town plan: 2CS-s – Grand Canal Sq. ✉ D2 – ✆ (01) 687 51 00
– www.themarkerhoteldublin.com – Closed 25-26 December

Fitzwilliam

BUSINESS · MODERN Stylish, modern hotel set around an impressive roof garden. Contemporary bedrooms display striking bold colours and good facilities; most overlook the roof garden and the best have views over St Stephen's Green. The bright first floor brasserie offers original Mediterranean-influenced menus.

140 rooms – ♦ € 169/500 ♦♦ € 169/500 – ☱ €22 – 3 suites
Town plan: 6JZ-d – St Stephen's Grn ✉ D2 – ✆ (01) 478 70 00
– www.fitzwilliamhotel.com
Thornton's – See restaurant listing

Brooks

BUSINESS · STYLISH Smart townhouse with a cosy basement lounge, good meeting facilities –including a screening room – and a stylish bar with a collection of over 150 whiskies. Bedrooms vary from traditional 'Classics' to modern 'Executives' with thoughtful extras. Good quality Irish ingredients feature in the restaurant.

98 rooms ☱ – ♦ € 140/280 ♦♦ € 140/280 – 1 suite
Town plan: 6JY-r – Drury St ✉ D2 – ✆ (01) 670 40 00 – www.brookshotel.ie

Morrison

BUSINESS · DESIGN Modern, centrally located hotel on the banks of the Liffey, opposite Temple Bar. Bright bedrooms with an Irish phrase on the wall, chic white furniture and either pink or blue cube lights and cushions; smart bathrooms. Appealing bar and a stylish restaurant specialising in steaks from the Josper grill.

145 rooms – ♦ € 140/400 ♦♦ € 140/400 – ☱ €15 – 4 suites
Town plan: 5HY-x – Ormond Quay ✉ D1 – ✆ (01) 887 24 00
– www.morrisonhotel.ie

DUBLIN

Clarence

LUXURY · DESIGN Stop for a drink in the famous domed cocktail bar of this old Customs House on the banks of the Liffey. Open fires and wood panelling feature throughout. Understated bedrooms combine Arts and Crafts styling with modern facilities.

51 rooms – ♦ € 109/259 ♦♦ € 109/259 – ☑ €19 – 5 suites

Town plan: 5HY-a – *6-8 Wellington Quay* ✉ *D2* – ✆ *(01) 407 08 00* – *www.theclarence.ie*

Cleaver East – See restaurant listing

Spencer ⓝ

BUSINESS · MODERN Modern hotel by the Convention Centre – its basement leisure facility is a highlight. Sleek, minimalist bedrooms come in muted tones, with floor to ceiling windows and 'rainforest' showers; some have balconies overlooking the river. Enjoy European dishes in the lounge or Asian fusion dishes in the brasserie.

166 rooms – ♦ € 125/175 ♦♦ € 140/190

Town plan: 2BS-s – *Excise Walk, IFSC* ✉ *D1* – ✆ *(01) 433 8800* – *www.thespencerhotel.com* – *Closed 24-27 December*

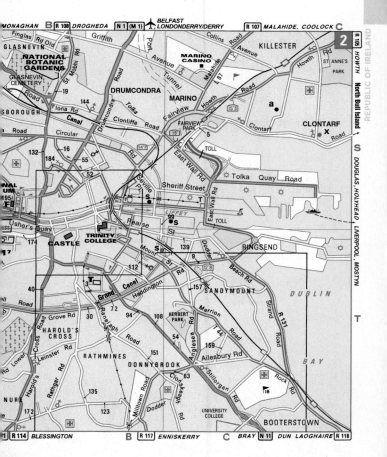

🏠 Ashling

🔆 🖃 ᴄ ⌘ ♨ 🅿

BUSINESS · FUNCTIONAL Corporate hotel close to the tram and rail links and run by a cheery team. Bedrooms are a mix of classic and contemporary; some overlook the river or Guinness Brewery. The bar-lounge serves all day; the restaurant offers carvery lunches and an evening à la carte; and there are over 100 items at breakfast.

225 rooms – 🛏 € 89/199 🛏🛏 € 97/259 – ⌷ €13 – 1 suite

Town plan: 2BS-a – *Parkgate St.* ✉ *D8* – ℰ *(01) 677 2324* – *www.ashlinghotel.ie* – *Closed 24-26 December*

🏠 The Dean 🆕

🔆 🖃 ᴄ 🆎 ♨ 🧖

TOWNHOUSE · STYLISH A cool, informal, urban boutique. Stylish bedrooms include compact rooms named 'Mod Pods'; suites with record players, amps and guitars; and a penthouse with table football, a poker table and a bar! The moody lobby serves an all-day menu and loft-style Sophie's offers Mediterranean dishes and rooftop views.

52 rooms – 🛏 € 109/230 🛏🛏 € 119/260 – ⌷ €15 – 3 suites

Town plan: 6JZ-n – *33 Harcourt St* ✉ *D2* – ℰ *(01) 607 8110* – *www.thedean.ie*

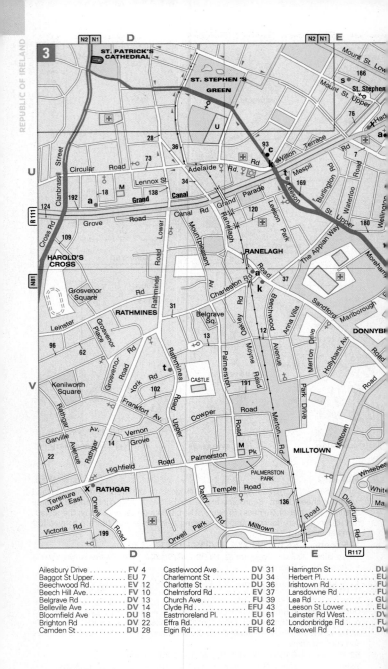

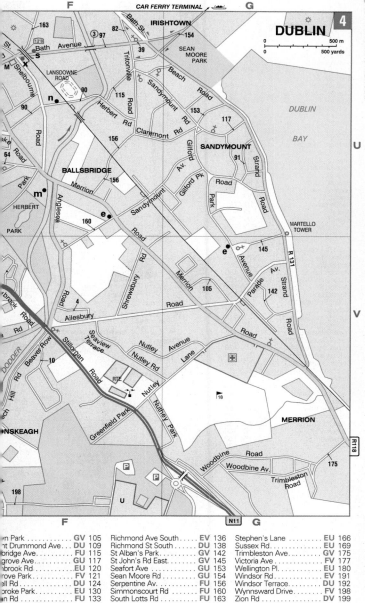

DUBLIN

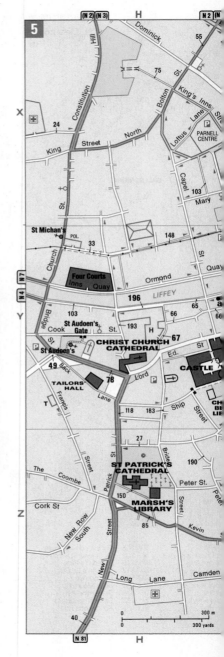

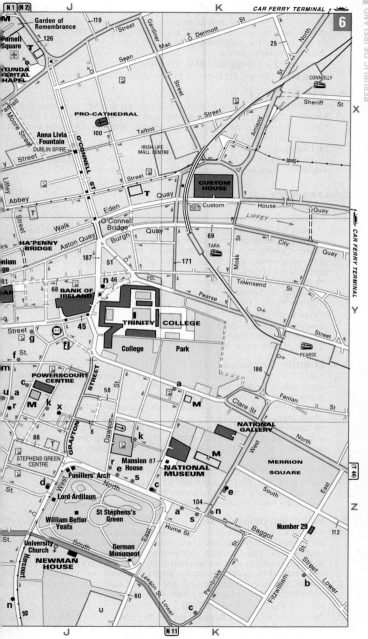

N 1 N 2

J

K

CAR FERRY TERMINAL

6

M

Garden of
Remembrance

—119

Street

Gardiner

St

Mac

Dermott

25

North

St

CONNOLLY

Parnell
Square

126

T

Sean

Street

Street

X

TUNDA
SPITAL
HAPEL

Moore Street

PRO-CATHEDRAL

100

Talbot

Street

Street

Sheriff

St

Anna Livia
Fountain

O'CONNELL ST

DUBLIN SPIRE

DUBLIN SPIRE

IRISH LIFE
MALL CENTRE

Amiens

Street

P

Street

Street

P

T

Quay

CUSTOM
HOUSE

Abbey

T

Eden

15.7

Custom

House

Quay

Walk

O'Connell
Bridge

Quay

LIFFEY

CAR FERRY TERMINAL

Street

HA'PENNY
BRIDGE

Aston Quay

Burgh

Quay

69

City

Quay

Y

nium
ge

81

187

51

171

TARA

Moss

St

Townsend

St

n 46

POL

Pearse

68 BANK OF
IRELAND

45

TRINITY COLLEGE

i

Pearse

St

q.

Street

g

College

Park

PEARSE

f

St.

186

m

POWERSCOURT
CENTRE

a

M

Clare St

Fenian

St

u

a

r

M

c

k

x

GRAFTON

STREET

St.

58

8

Dawson

a

P

M

NATIONAL
GALLERY

North

88

T

k

West

MERRION
SQUARE

East

T 41

STEPHENS GREEN
CENTRE

P

Mansion
House

87

e

NATIONAL
MUSEUM

M

Z

P

Fusiliers' Arch

s

c

e

South

St.

d

North

104

a

n

Lord Ardilaun

St Stephens's
Green

West

East

s

Baggot

Number 29

112

William Butler
Yeats

Hume St.

St.

University
Church

South

German
Monument

Leeson St. Lower

Pembroke

Fitzwilliam

St

Street Lower

b

NEWMAN
HOUSE

Harcourt

n

St.

60

U

c

J

N 11

K

⌂ Number 31

TOWNHOUSE · DESIGN Unusual and very individual property – once home to architect Sam Stephenson. It's classically styled around the 1960s, with a striking sunken lounge; the most modern bedrooms are found in the Georgian house across the terraced garden.

21 rooms ⌂ – † € 135/240 †† € 175/240

Town plan: 3EU-c – *31 Leeson Cl.* ⊠ *D2* – *℘ (01) 676 50 11* – *www.number31.ie*

⌂ Kellys

TOWNHOUSE · MINIMALIST Shabby-chic hotel set among trendy boutiques and bars, in a bustling area. Stripped paint and white emulsioned walls hung with funky artwork; airy, open-plan lounge and bar; spacious, minimalist bedrooms. Breakfast in the restaurant below.

16 rooms ⌂ – † € 74/254 †† € 79/259

Town plan: 6JY-b – *First Floor, 36 South Great George's St* ⊠ *D2* – *℘ (01) 648 0010* – *www.kellysdublin.com* – *Closed 24-26 December*

Restaurants

❈❈❈ Patrick Guilbaud (Guillaume Lebrun) ❀ ⏣ ⟨⟩

❀❀ FRENCH MODERN · ELEGANT A truly sumptuous restaurant in an elegant Georgian house; the eponymous owner has run it for over 30 years. Accomplished, original cooking uses luxurious ingredients and mixes classical French cooking with modern techniques. Dishes are well-crafted and visually stunning with a superb balance of textures and flavours.

→ Red king crab and cucumber maki, lemon croquant, Bombay Sapphire, mint and vanilla oil. Spiced Wicklow lamb, cauliflower two ways, glazed shiitake and crisp sweetbread. Iced caramélia and coffee croquant with Baileys ice cream.

Menu € 50/130

Town plan: 6KZ-e – *21 Upper Merrion St* ⊠ *D2* – *℘ (01) 676 41 92 (booking essential)* – *www.restaurantpatrickguilbaud.ie* – *Closed 25-31 December, 25 March, Sunday, Monday and bank holidays*

❈❈ Chapter One (Ross Lewis) ⏣ ⟨⟩ ⟨⟩

❀ MODERN CUISINE · FORMAL Stylish basement restaurant under the Writers Museum, with a modern bar and several smart dining rooms hung with specially commissioned art. Various set and tasting menus offer flavoursome, classically based dishes prepared using modern techniques; the kitchen table has its own special menu. Service is slick.

→ Japanese pearl tapioca with Gabriel cheese, mushrooms and truffle. Turbot with salt baked celeriac, fried cabbage, Morteau sausage and razor clams. Rose petal and lime jelly with poached rhubarb, white chocolate ganache and yoghurt mousse.

Menu € 38/95 **s**

Town plan: 6JX-r – *The Dublin Writers Museum, 18-19 Parnell Sq* ⊠ *D1* – *℘ (01) 873 22 66 (booking essential)* – *www.chapteronerestaurant.com* – *Closed 2 weeks August, 2 weeks Christmas, Sunday, Monday and bank holidays*

❈❈ L'Ecrivain (Derry Clarke) ⏢ ⏣ ⏱ ⟨⟩

❀ MODERN CUISINE · FRIENDLY A well-regarded and busy restaurant with a glitzy bar, a whiskey-themed private dining room and an attractive terrace. The refined, balanced menu has a classical foundation whilst also displaying touches of modernity; the ingredients used are superlative. Service is structured yet has personality.

→ Scallops with cauliflower, capers, brown butter and vanilla. Suckling pig with celeriac, langoustine, apple, walnut and celery. Caramelised milk chocolate with dark chocolate and tonka bean cream, white chocolate sorbet.

Menu € 45/75 – Carte € 67/78

Town plan: 6KZ-b – *109a Lower Baggot St* ⊠ *D2* – *℘ (01) 661 19 19 (booking essential)* – *www.lecrivain.com* – *dinner only and lunch Thursday-Friday* – *Closed Sunday and bank holidays*

REPUBLIC OF IRELAND

XXX **Greenhouse** (Mickael Viljanen)

❁ **MODERN CUISINE · ELEGANT** Stylish restaurant with studded chairs, turquoise banquettes and smooth service. A plethora of menus include 3, 5 or 7 course midweek dinners and a 5 course 'Surprise' on Friday and Saturday evening. Accomplished, classically based cooking has stimulating flavour combinations and subtle modern overtones.

➔ Crab and scallop lasagne, cucumber and buttermilk. Roast rump-cap of beef with winter vegetables and Alsace bacon cream. Passion fruit soufflé with white chocolate sauce.

Menu € 32 (weekday lunch)/60

Town plan: 6JZ-r – *Dawson St* ✉ *D2*
- ✆ *(01) 676 7015*
- *www.thegreenhouserestaurant.ie*
- *Closed 2 weeks July, 2 weeks Christmas, Sunday and Monday*

XXX **Thornton's**

MODERN CUISINE · FORMAL Elegant first floor restaurant overlooking St Stephen's Green. Eye-catching photo montages taken by the chef hang on the walls. Choose from a concise à la carte or a 5 course tasting menu; modern cooking uses classic combinations.

Menu € 45/75

Town plan: 6JZ-d – *Fitzwilliam Hotel, 128 St Stephen's Grn.* ✉ *D2*
- ✆ *(01) 478 70 08*
- *www.thorntonsrestaurant.com*
- *dinner only and lunch Friday-Saturday*
- *Closed 24 December-2 January, Sunday and Monday*

XXX **Forty One**

MODERN CUISINE · ELEGANT Intimate, richly furnished restaurant on the first floor of an attractive, creeper-clad townhouse, in a corner of St Stephen's Green. Accomplished, classical cooking features luxurious Irish ingredients and personal, modern touches.

Menu € 35 (weekday lunch)/75 – Carte € 60/78

Town plan: 6KZ-x – *41 St. Stephen's Grn.* ✉ *D2*
- ✆ *(01) 662 00 00 (booking advisable)*
- *www.restaurantfortyone.ie*
- *Closed Good Friday, 2-17 August, 25-30 December, Sunday and Monday*

XXX **One Pico**

FRENCH CLASSIC · ELEGANT Stylish, modern restaurant tucked away on a back street; a well-regarded place that's a regular haunt for MPs. Muted colour scheme, mirrors and comfy banquettes; classic French cooking offers plenty of flavour.

Menu € 29/45 – Carte € 50/64

Town plan: 6JZ-k – *5-6 Molesworth Pl* ✉ *D2*
- ✆ *(01) 676 03 00*
- *www.onepico.com*
- *Closed bank holidays*

Prices quoted after the symbol ✝ refer to the lowest rate for a single room in low season, followed by the highest rate in high season. The same principle applies to the symbol ✝✝ for a double room.

REPUBLIC OF IRELAND

XX Pearl Brasserie

FRENCH CLASSIC · BRASSERIE Formal basement restaurant with a small bar, lounge and two surprisingly airy dining rooms; sit in a stylish booth in one of the old coal bunkers. Intriguing modern dishes have a classical base and Mediterranean and Asian influences.

Menu € 25 (lunch and early dinner) – Carte € 33/60

Town plan: 6KZ-n – *20 Merrion St Upper* ⊠ *D2*
- *𝒞 (01) 661 35 72 – www.pearl-brasserie.com*
- *Closed 25 December and Sunday*

XX Amuse

MODERN CUISINE · FRIENDLY Modern, understated décor provides the perfect backdrop for the intricate, innovative cooking. Dishes showcase Asian ingredients – including kombu and yuzu; which are artfully arranged according to their flavours and textures.

Menu € 24 (weekday lunch)/65

Town plan: 6JZ-r – *22 Dawson St* ⊠ *D2*
- *𝒞 (01) 639 4889 (booking advisable) – www.amuse.ie*
- *Closed 2 weeks Christmas-New Year, last week July, first week August, Sunday and Monday*

XX Pichet

FRENCH CLASSIC · FASHIONABLE You can't miss the blue canopies and enamel signs of this buzzy brasserie; bold blue chairs and an enclosed terrace with checkerboard floor make it equally striking inside, too. Modern Mediterranean dishes arrive neatly presented, and a good selection of wines are available by the glass and 'pichet'.

Menu € 25 (lunch and early dinner) – Carte € 32/56

Town plan: 6JY-g – *14-15 Trinity St* ⊠ *D2*
- *𝒞 (01) 677 10 60 (booking essential) – www.pichetrestaurant.ie*
- *Closed 25-26 December*

XX Hot Stove

INTERNATIONAL · ELEGANT A popular pre-theatre spot, in the basement of a Georgian house; it takes its name from the range in one of the immaculate, elegant dining rooms. Flavoursome cooking showcases seasonal Irish produce carefully prepared dishes.

Menu € 20 (lunch) – Carte dinner € 35/58

Town plan: 6JX-a – *38 Parnell Sq West* ⊠ *D1*
- *𝒞 (01) 874 7778 – www.thehotstove.ie*
- *Closed 25 December- 9 January, Sunday and Monday*

XX Saddle Room

MEATS · ELEGANT Renowned restaurant with a history as long as that of the hotel in which it stands. The warm, inviting room features intimate gold booths and a crustacea counter. The menu offers classic dishes and grills; West Cork beef is a speciality.

Menu € 25 – Carte € 35/85

Town plan: 6JZ-c – *Shelbourne Hotel, 27 St Stephen's Grn.* ⊠ *D2*
- *𝒞 (01) 663 45 00 – www.shelbournedining.ie*

XX Bang

MODERN CUISINE · INDIVIDUAL Stylish restaurant with an intimate powder blue basement, a bright mezzanine level and a small, elegant room above. There are good value pre-theatre menus, a more elaborate à la carte and tasting menu showcasing top Irish produce.

Menu € 25 – Carte € 38/62

Town plan: 6KZ-a – *11 Merrion Row* ⊠ *D2*
- *𝒞 (01) 400 42 29 – www.bangrestaurant.com*
- *dinner only and lunch Wednesday-Friday*

XX Fade St. Social-Restaurant 🍷 ⅓ 🕙 🛇 ⇔

MODERN CUISINE · BRASSERIE Have cocktails on the terrace then head for the big, modern brasserie with its raised open kitchen. Dishes use Irish ingredients but have a Mediterranean feel; they specialise in sharing dishes and large cuts of meat such as chateaubriand.

Menu € 30/50 – Carte € 34/53

Town plan: 6JY-u – *4-6 Fade St* ✉ *D2* – *ℰ (01) 604 0066* – *www.fadestsocial.com* – *Closed 25-26 December, Good Friday and lunch Saturday and Sunday*

XX Cliff Townhouse ⇦ 🍷 🕙 ⇔

FISH AND SEAFOOD · BRASSERIE Impressive Georgian townhouse overlooking the green. Large dining room with blue leather seating and a marble-topped oyster counter. Seafood-orientated menus offer plenty of choice, from fish and chips to seafood platters or market specials. Bedrooms display contemporary colour schemes and good comforts.

Menu € 28 (weekdays) – Carte € 34/72

9 rooms ☒ – ♦ € 150/200 ♦♦ € 170/210

Town plan: 6JZ-s – *22 St Stephen's Grn* ✉ *D2* – *ℰ (01) 638 39 39 (booking advisable)* – *www.theclifftownhouse.com* – *Closed 17 March, 25 March, 25-29 December and 1 January*

XX Brasserie Le Pont 🕝 ⅓ 🅰🅲

FRENCH · BRASSERIE Set in the basement of a Georgian townhouse; enjoy lunch at the marble-topped counter or out on the terrace – or nab the intimate booth for more privacy. Cooking has a classic Gallic base but is presented in a light, modern manner.

Menu € 29/48 – Carte € 35/61

Town plan: 3EU-k – *25 Fitzwilliam Pl* ✉ *D2* – *ℰ (01) 669 4600 (bookings advisable at dinner)* – *www.brasserielepont.ie* – *Closed 25-30 December, Saturday lunch, Sunday and Monday*

XX Dax 🅰🅲

FRENCH · INDIVIDUAL Smart, masculine restaurant in the cellar of a Georgian townhouse near Fitzwilliam Square. Tried-and-tested French dishes use top Irish produce and flavours are clearly defined. The Surprise Menu best showcases the kitchen's talent.

Menu € 25 (weekday lunch) – Carte € 46/61

Town plan: 6KZ-c – *23 Pembroke St Upper* ✉ *D2* – *ℰ (01) 676 14 94 (booking essential)* – *www.dax.ie* – *Closed 10 days Christmas, Saturday lunch, Sunday and Monday*

XX Dobbin's 🕝 ⅓ 🅰🅲 ⇔

TRADITIONAL CUISINE · INDIVIDUAL Hidden away in a back alley. A small bar leads through to a long, narrow room with cosy leather booths, which opens into a spacious conservatory with a terrace. Good value lunch and early evening menus; cooking is in the classical vein.

Menu € 25/40 – Carte € 39/54

Town plan: 3EU-s – *15 Stephen's Ln* ✉ *D2* – *(via Stephen's Pl off Lower Mount St)* – *ℰ (01) 661 95 36 (booking essential)* – *www.dobbins.ie* – *Closed 24 December-2 January, Saturday lunch, Sunday dinner, Mondays except December and bank holidays*

XX Peploe's ⅓ 🅰🅲

MEDITERRANEAN · COSY Atmospheric cellar restaurant – formerly a bank vault – named after the artist. Comfy room with a warm, clubby feel and a large mural depicting the owner. The well-drilled team present Mediterranean dishes and an old world wine list.

Menu € 26 (lunch and early dinner) – Carte € 41/65

Town plan: 6JZ-e – *16 St Stephen's Grn.* ✉ *D2* – *ℰ (01) 676 31 44 (booking essential)* – *www.peploes.com* – *Closed 25-26 December, Good Friday and lunch bank holidays*

✗ Delahunt   🕭 ✿

BRITISH MODERN · BISTRO A former Victorian grocer's shop, mentioned in James Joyce's 'Ulysses'. The old counter is now a bar and the clerk's snug is a glass-enclosed private dining room. Lunch offer two choices per course and dinner, four. Precisely executed, flavoursome dishes are modern takes of time-honoured recipes.

Carte € 33/43

Town plan: 6JZ-p – *39 Camden Street Lower* ✉ *D2* – *𝒞 (01) 598 48 80 (booking essential)* – *www.delahunt.ie* – *dinner only and lunch Thursday-Saturday – Closed 15 August-1 September, Sunday and Monday*

✗ Pig's Ear   ✿

MODERN CUISINE · BISTRO Well-established restaurant in a Georgian town house overlooking Trinity College. Floors one and two are bustling bistro-style areas filled with mirrors and porcine-themed memorabilia; floor three is a private room with a Scandinavian feel. Good value menus list hearty dishes with a modern edge.

Menu € 22 (lunch) – Carte € 33/50

Town plan: 6KY-a – *4 Nassau St* ✉ *D2* – *𝒞 (01) 670 38 65 (booking essential)* – *www.thepigsear.ie* – *Closed first week January, Sunday and bank holidays*

✗ Etto

MEDITERRANEAN · RUSTIC The name of this rustic restaurant means 'little' and it is totally apt! Blackboards announce the daily wines and the lunchtime 'soup and sandwich' special. Flavoursome dishes rely on good ingredients and have Italian influences; the chef understands natural flavours and follows the 'less is more' approach.

Menu € 28 (weekday lunch) – Carte € 29/43

Town plan: 6KZ-s – *18 Merrion Row* ✉ *D2* – *𝒞 (01) 678 8872 (booking essential)* – *www.etto.ie* – *Closed Sunday and bank holidays*

✗ Osteria Lucio   🏠 & 🅰️🅲

ITALIAN · INTIMATE Smart restaurant under the railway arches, run by two experienced chefs. Robust, rustic dishes showcase local produce, alongside ingredients imported from Italy; sit by the bar to watch pizzas being cooked in the oak-burning stove.

Menu € 20 (dinner) – Carte € 24/41

Town plan: 2BT-s – *The Malting Tower, Clanwilliam Terr* ✉ *D2* – *𝒞 (01) 662 419.* – *www.osterialucio.com* – *Closed Christmas and bank holiday Mondays*

✗ Drury Buildings   🍸 🏠 📺 ✿

ITALIAN · TRENDY A hip, laid-back 'New York loft': its impressive terrace has a retractable roof and reclaimed furniture features in the stylish cocktail bar which offers cicchetti and sharing boards. The airy restaurant serves rustic Italian dishes.

Menu € 24/52 – Carte € 29/59

Town plan: 6JY-a – *52-55 Drury St* ✉ *D2* – *𝒞 (01) 960 2095* – *www.drurybuildings.com* – *Closed Good Friday*

✗ Fade St. Social-Gastro Bar   🍸 🏠 & 🍽️

INTERNATIONAL · FASHIONABLE Buzzy restaurant with an almost frenzied feel. It's all about a diverse range of original, interesting small plates, from a bacon and cabbage burger to a lobster hot dog. Eat at the kitchen counter or on leather cushioned 'saddle' benches.

Menu € 30 (early dinner) – Carte € 19/40

Town plan: 6JY-u – *4-6 Fade St* ✉ *D2* – *𝒞 (01) 604 0066 (booking essential)* – *www.fadestreetsocial.com* – *dinner only and lunch Saturday-Sunday – Closed 25-26 December and Good Friday*

X **La Maison**   🍴 AC

FRENCH CLASSIC · BISTRO Sweet little French bistro with tables on the pavement and original posters advertising French products. The experienced, Breton-born chef-owner offers carefully prepared, seasonal Gallic classics, brought to the table by a personable team.

Menu € 26 (weekday dinner) – Carte € 22/47

Town plan: 6JY-c – *15 Castlemarket* ✉ *D2* – ✆ *(01) 672 7258*
– www.lamaisonrestaurant.ie – Closed 25-27 December and 1-2 January

X **SÖDER+KO** 🆕   🍸 AC 🎜

ASIAN · MUSICAL A vast, vibrant bar-cum-bistro in a former nightclub, with numerous rooms and even a chill-out lounge. Skilfully prepared Asian small plates are a mix of the modern and the classic; they are appealing, satisfying and good value.

Menu € 14/25 – Carte € 17/22

Town plan: 6JY-s – *64 South Great George's St* ✉ *D2* – ✆ *(01) 478 1590*
(booking essential) – www.soderandko.ie – Closed bank holidays

X **Rustic Stone**   🍴 ⌂ AC 🎜

MODERN CUISINE · FASHIONABLE Split-level restaurant offering something a little different. Good quality ingredients are cooked simply to retain their natural flavours and menus focus on healthy and special dietary options; some meats and fish arrive on a sizzling stone.

Menu € 30/50 – Carte € 27/51

Town plan: 6JY-m – *17 South Great George's St* ✉ *D2* – ✆ *(01) 707 9596*
– www.rusticstone.ie – Closed 25-26 December and 1 January

X **Fallon & Byrne**   ⌂ AC

FRENCH CLASSIC · BISTRO A former telephone exchange: now a bustling New York style food emporium with a basement wine shop and bar and a first floor Parisian brasserie, where you sit among antique mirrors and dine from a menu of seasonal bistro classics.

Menu € 25/40 – Carte € 31/57

Town plan: 6JY-f – *11-17 Exchequer St* ✉ *D2* – ✆ *(01) 472 10 00*
– www.fallonandbyrne.com – Closed 25-26 December, 1 January and Good Friday

X **l'Gueuleton**   🍴 ⌂

FRENCH CLASSIC · BISTRO Rustic restaurant with beamed ceilings, Gallic furnishings, a shabby-chic bistro feel and a large pavement terrace. Flavoursome cooking features good value, French country classics which rely on local, seasonal produce. Service is friendly.

Carte € 20/48

Town plan: 6JY-d – *1 Fade St* ✉ *D2* – ✆ *(01) 675 37 08 – www.lgueuleton.com*
– Closed 25-27 December, 1 January and Good Friday

X **Cleaver East**   ⌂ AC ⌁

MODERN CUISINE · BRASSERIE Once the Clarence hotel's ballroom; now an industrial-style restaurant with old railway sleepers hanging from the ceiling and meat cleavers on the walls. Unfussy modern dishes have a Mediterranean edge; steaks are a speciality.

Menu € 22 (lunch and early dinner) – Carte dinner € 33/49

Town plan: 5HY-a – *Clarence Hotel, 6-8 East Essex St* ✉ *D2* – ✆ *(01) 531 3500*
– www.cleavereast.ie – Closed Monday-Tuesday lunch

X **Camden Kitchen**

CLASSIC CUISINE · BISTRO Simple, modern, neighbourhood bistro set over two floors; watch the owner cooking in the open kitchen. Tasty dishes use good quality Irish ingredients prepared in classic combinations. Relaxed, friendly service from a young team.

Menu € 20 (lunch)/32 – Carte € 30/46

Town plan: 6JZ-x – *3a Camden Mkt, Grantham St* ✉ *D8* – ✆ *(01) 476 01 25*
– www.camdenkitchen.ie – Closed 24-26 December, Sunday and Monday

Ⓧ **Saba** 🏆 & Ⓐ

THAI · FASHIONABLE Trendy, buzzy Thai restaurant and cocktail bar. Simple
stylish rooms with refectory tables, banquettes and amusing photos. Fresh, vi
sual, authentic cooking from an all-Thai team, with a few Vietnamese dishes and
some fusion cooking too.

Menu € 14 (weekday lunch)/30 – Carte € 24/47
Town plan: 6JY-k – *26-28 Clarendon St* ✉ *D2* – *𝒞 (01) 679 2000*
– www.sabadublin.com – Closed Good Friday and 25-26 December

at Ballsbridge

🏛🏛🏛 **InterContinental Dublin** ☆ 🛌 🖂 ⊛ ♨ 🕭 ♿ & Ⓐ ❄ 🎱 🚗

LUXURY · CLASSIC Imposing hotel bordering the RDS Arena. Elegant gues
areas, state-of-the-art meeting rooms and impressive ballrooms boast ornate dé
cor, antique furnishings and Irish artwork. Spacious, classical bedrooms have mar
ble bathrooms and plenty of extras. A wide-ranging menu is served in the bright
airy restaurant.

197 rooms ☲ – ♦ € 200/435 ♦♦ € 220/425 – 40 suites
Town plan: 4FU-e – *Simmonscourt Rd.* ✉ *D4* – *𝒞 (01) 665 4000*
– www.intercontinental.com/dublin

🏛🏛 **Dylan** ☆ & Ⓐ ❄ 🎱

TOWNHOUSE · STYLISH Red-brick Victorian nurses home with a sympatheticall
styled extension and a funky, boutique interior. Tasteful, individually decorate
bedrooms offer a host of extras; those in the original building are the most spa
cious. The stylish restaurant offers a menu of modern Mediterranean dishes and
comes complete with a zinc-topped bar and a smartly furnished terrace.

44 rooms – ♦ € 239/395 ♦♦ € 239/395 – ☲ €25
Town plan: 3EU-a – *Eastmoreland Pl* ✉ *D4* – *𝒞 (01) 660 30 00 – www.dylan.ie*
– Closed 24-26 December

🏛🏛 **Herbert Park** ☆ 🕭 ⊡ Ⓐ ❄ 🎱 🚗

BUSINESS · MODERN Striking modern building with a stark white, open plan
marble-floored lobby displaying eye-catching art. Comfortable bedroom
with plenty of natural light; choose an executive room for more luxury. Chi
terrace lounge and bar. The Pavilion restaurant serves classic dishes and ha
park views.

153 rooms – ♦ € 125/400 ♦♦ € 125/600 – ☲ €22 – 2 suites
Town plan: 4FU- m – ✉ *D4* – *𝒞 (01) 667 2200 – www.herbertparkhotel.ie*

🏛 **Schoolhouse** ☆ 🛌 🛏 ⊡ Ⓐ ❄ Ⓟ

HISTORIC · PERSONALISED Dating back to 1861 and formerly the St Stephen'
Parochial School. Spacious, well-kept bedrooms – most in the extension – boas
William Morris designed fabrics and locally built Mackintosh-style furniture; som
have half-tester beds. Busy bar with vaulted ceiling; formal restaurant serve
classic dishes.

31 rooms ☲ – ♦ € 109/299 ♦♦ € 119/309
Town plan: 3EU-e – *2-8 Northumberland Rd* ✉ *D4* – *𝒞 (01) 667 5014*
– www.schoolhousehotel.com – Closed 23-26 December

🏛 **Ariel House** 🛌 ❄ Ⓟ

TOWNHOUSE · CLASSIC Close to the Aviva Stadium and a DART station; a per
sonally run Victorian townhouse with comfy, traditional guest areas and antiqu
furnishings. Warmly decorated bedrooms have modern facilities and smart bath
rooms; some feature four-posters.

37 rooms ☲ – ♦ € 79/290 ♦♦ € 79/290
Town plan: 4FU-n – *50-54 Lansdowne Rd* ✉ *D4* – *𝒞 (01) 668 5512*
– www.ariel-house.net – Closed 22-28 December

🏠 Pembroke Townhouse

TOWNHOUSE · CLASSIC Friendly, traditionally styled hotel set in 3 Georgian houses. Small lounge with honesty bar and pantry. Sunny breakfast room offering homemade bread, cakes and biscuits. Variously sized, neutrally hued bedrooms; go for a duplex room.

48 rooms – 🛏 € 99/250 🛏🛏 € 99/250 – ☕ €15

Town plan: 4FU-d – *88 Pembroke Rd* ⊠ *D4*
– *𝒞 (01) 66 00 277 – www.pembroketownhouse.ie*
– *Closed 2 weeks Christmas-New Year*

🏠 Aberdeen Lodge

TOWNHOUSE · CLASSIC Two Edwardian townhouses knocked through into a hotel; in a smart suburban street, minutes from the sea and a DART Station. Comfy lounge, warm, homely atmosphere and classically furnished, well-equipped bedrooms – some with garden views.

16 rooms ☕ – 🛏 € 90/109 🛏🛏 € 129/169

Town plan: 4GV-e – *53-55 Park Ave.* ⊠ *D4*
– *𝒞 (01) 283 8155 – www.aberdeen-lodge.com*

✕✕ Asador

MEATS · BRASSERIE Themed around the chargrill (or 'asador'); watch the chefs in the open-plan kitchen. Fresh, tasty cooking has South American and Spanish influences. On your own? Try the counter. In a group? Go for one of the curvaceous booths.

Menu € 22 (early dinner) – Carte € 29/55

Town plan: 3EU-x – *1 Victoria House, Haddington Rd* ⊠ *D4*
– *𝒞 (01) 254 5353 (booking advisable) – www.asador.ie*
– *Closed Monday*

🍴 Old Spot 🆕

TRADITIONAL CUISINE · PUB The appealing bar has a stencilled maple-wood floor and a great selection of snacks and bottled craft beers. There's also a relaxed, characterful restaurant filled with vintage posters, which serves pub classics with a modern edge.

Menu € 30/40 – Carte € 32/50

Town plan: 4FU-s – *14 Bath Ave* ⊠ *D4*
– *𝒞 (01) 660 5599 – www.theoldspot.ie*
– *Closed 25-26 December and 1 January*

🍴 Chop House

MEATS · PUB Imposing pub close to the stadium, with a small side terrace, a dark bar and a bright, airy conservatory. The relaxed lunchtime menu is followed by more ambitious dishes in the evening, when the kitchen really comes into its own.

Menu € 32/45 – Carte € 30/55

Town plan: 4FU-x – *2 Shelbourne Rd* ⊠ *D4*
– *𝒞 (01) 660 23 90 – www.thechophouse.ie*
– *Closed Saturday lunch*

at Donnybrook

✕✕ Mulberry Garden

MODERN CUISINE · INDIVIDUAL Delightful restaurant hidden away in the city suburbs; its interesting L-shaped dining room set around a small courtyard terrace. Choice of two dishes per course on the weekly menu; original modern cooking relies on tasty local produce.

Menu € 49/65

Town plan: 4FV-a – *Mulberry Ln* ⊠ *D4* – *off Donnybrook Rd*
– *𝒞 (01) 269 3300 (booking essential) – www.mulberrygarden.ie*
– *dinner only and Sunday lunch in summer – Closed Sunday-Wednesday*

at Ranelagh

XX Kinara Kitchen 🍸 & 🗚 🛈

PAKISTANI · EXOTIC This smart restaurant has become a destination not just fo
its cooking but for its cocktails too. The friendly, professional team serve a menu o
homely, well-spiced Pakistani classics, including a selection from the tandoor oven
Menu € 17/22 (weekdays) – Carte € 30/52
Town plan: 3EV-a – *17 Ranelagh Village* ⊠ *D6* – *☏ (01) 406 0066*
– www.kinarakitchen.ie – Closed 25-26 December and Good Friday

X Forest Avenue &

MODERN CUISINE · NEIGHBOURHOOD This rustic neighbourhood restaurant i
named after a street in Queens and has a fitting 'NY' vibe, with its jam jar an
antler light fittings and stags' heads lining the walls. Top ingredients feature i
well-crafted modern dishes.
Menu € 27 (weekday lunch)/49
Town plan: 3EU-t – *8 Sussex Terr.* ⊠ *D4* – *☏ (01) 667 8337 (booking essential)*
– www.forestavenuerestaurant.ie – Closed last 2 weeks August,
25 December-10 January, Easter, Monday and Tuesday

X Brioche & 🏶

MODERN CUISINE · BISTRO As the name suggests, it's all about France at thi
lovely bistro in this buzzy, village-like district. Attractive modern French-inspire
small plates use top Irish ingredients; three should suffice, followed by chees
or dessert.
Menu € 23/49 – Carte € 36/55
Town plan: 3EV-x – *51 Elmwood Ave Lower* ⊠ *D6* – *☏ (01) 497 91 63*
– www.brioche.ie – Closed 25-27 December, 1 January, Sunday, Monday and lunc
Tuesday-Wednesday

at Rathmines

XX Zen & 🗚

CHINESE · ELEGANT Long-standing family-run restaurant, unusually set in an ol
church hall. At the centre of the elegant interior is a huge sun embellished wit
gold leaf. Imaginative Chinese cooking centres around Cantonese and spicy Sich
uan cuisine.
Menu € 24 – Carte € 23/34
Town plan: 3DV-t – *89 Upper Rathmines Rd* ⊠ *D6* – *☏ (01) 497 94 28*
– www.zenrestaurant.ie – dinner only and Friday lunch – Closed 25-27 December

at Dublin Airport North: 10.5 km by N 1 – Plan: BS – and M 1 – ⊠ Dublin

🏨 Radisson Blu H. Dublin Airport ⓝ 🏠 🛜 🖭 & 🗚 🎇 🐾 🅿

CHAIN HOTEL · MODERN Modern commercial hotel with well-equipped confer
ence rooms and good-sized bedrooms. They offer 'Grab and Run' breakfasts an
run a 24hr shuttle service to both terminals; and have arrival/departure screen
and a check-in kiosk in the lobby. The informal brasserie serves a wide-rangin
international menu.
229 rooms � – 🛉 € 115/320 🛉🛉 € 160/320 – 2 suites
– ☏ (01) 844 6000 – www.radissonblu.ie/hotel-dublinairport

🏨 Bewleys 🏠 🎜 🖭 & 🐾 🕋

BUSINESS · FUNCTIONAL Eight-floor hotel offering a free courtesy bus to an
from the airport, coupled with holiday parking; they also have good conferenc
facilities. Bedrooms are spacious and up-to-date. The comfy lobby bar an
lounge offers all-day dining; the brasserie serves buffet lunches and a wide-rang
ing evening menu.
469 rooms – 🛉 € 99/399 🛉🛉 € 99/399 – ⊠ €13
Baskin Ln – East : 4 km on N 32 – ☏ (01) 871 1000 – www.bewleyshotels.com

at Blackrock Southeast : 7.5 km by R 118 – Plan: CT

X **canteen @ the market** ⓝ

MODERN CUISINE · SIMPLE Its market location may be unusual but this modest corner unit is well worth a visit. The fortnightly set menu is written up on a roll of brown paper on the wall. Creative modern dishes are full of flavour and use top Irish produce.

Menu € 23/48 – set menu only

Blackrock Market, Main St – ℰ(085) 183 6700 (booking essential)
– dinner only and lunch Saturday and Sunday
– Closed 2 weeks August, 1 week January and Monday-Wednesday

at Clontarf Northeast: 5.5 km by R 105 – ✉ Dublin

🏠 **Clontarf Castle** 🛜 🕼 🗄 🕭 🕅 🛇 🕰 🅿

BUSINESS · HISTORIC A historic castle dating back to 1172, with sympathetic Victorian extensions; well-located in a quiet residential area close to the city. Contemporary bedrooms are decorated with bold, warm colours and many have four-poster beds. The restaurant offers local meats and seafood in a medieval ambience.

111 rooms ⌇ – ♦ € 129/249 ♦♦ € 149/269
Town plan: 2CS-a – *Castle Ave.* ✉ *D3* – ℰ*(01) 833 2321* – *www.clontarfcastle.ie*

X **Pigeon House** ⓝ 🛜 🕭

🟤 MODERN CUISINE · NEIGHBOURHOOD Slickly run neighbourhood bistro that's open for breakfast, lunch and dinner. It's just off the coast road in an up-and-coming area and has a lovely front terrace and a lively feel. Cooking is modern and assured. The bar counter is laden with freshly baked goodies and dishes are full of flavour.

Menu € 25 (dinner) – Carte € 28/42

Town plan: 2CS-x – *11b Vernon Ave* ✉ *D3*
– ℰ(01) 805 75 67 – www.pigeonhouse.ie
– Closed 25-26 December

at Dundrum South : 7.5 km by R 117 – Plan: BT – ✉ Dublin

XX **Ananda** 🛜 🕭 🕅 🕼

INDIAN · EXOTIC Its name means 'bliss' and it's a welcome escape from the bustle of the shopping centre. The stylish interior encompasses a smart cocktail bar, attractive fretwork and vibrant art. Accomplished Indian cooking is modern and original.

Menu € 19/50 – Carte € 31/60

Sandyford Rd, Dundrum town centre ✉ *D14*
– ℰ(01) 296 0099 – www.anandarestaurant.ie
– dinner only and lunch Friday-Sunday
– Closed 25-26 December

at Sandyford South : 10 km by R 117 – Plan: BT – off R 825 – ✉ Dublin

🏠 **Beacon** 🛜 🗄 🕭 🛇 🕰 🕭

BUSINESS · DESIGN Ultra-stylish hotel; its stunning entrance lobby has mirrored walls and a day bed. Stark white bedrooms come with Philippe Starck chairs and luxurious glass-walled bathrooms. After a conference in a low-key meeting room head for the modish Crystal bar. Funky, relaxed My Thai serves authentic Asian dishes.

88 rooms ⌇ – ♦ € 100/130 ♦♦ € 108/150 – 1 suite
Beacon Court, Sandyford Business Region ✉ *D18*
– ℰ(01) 643 7064 – www.thebeacon.com
– Closed 24-26 December

XX **China Sichuan** 🛱 �& 🕮

CHINESE · FASHIONABLE A smart modern interior is well-matched by creativ
menus, where Irish produce features in tasty Cantonese classics and some Sich
uan specialities. It was established in 1979 and is now run by the third generatio
of the family.

Menu € 20 (weekday lunch) – Carte € 27/58

The Forum, Ballymoss Rd. ⊠ *D18 –* ℰ *(01) 293 5100 – www.china-sichuan.ie*
– Closed 25-31 December, Good Friday, lunch Saturday and bank holidays

at Foxrock Southeast : 13 km by N 11 – Plan: CT – ⊠ Dublin

XX **Bistro One**

TRADITIONAL CUISINE · NEIGHBOURHOOD Long-standing neighbourhood bis
tro above a parade of shops; run by a father-daughter team and a real hit wit
the locals. Good value daily menus list a range of Irish and Italian dishes. The
produce their own Tuscan olive oil.

Menu € 29 (weekdays) – Carte € 29/50

3 Brighton Rd ⊠ *D18 –* ℰ *(01) 289 7711 (booking essential) – www.bistro-one.ie*
– Closed 25 December-3 January, Sunday and Monday

at Rathgar South : 3.75 km by N 81

X **Bijou** 🛱 �& 🕮 ✿

BRITISH MODERN · BRASSERIE Friendly restaurant with dining spread over tw
levels and a clubby heated terrace complete with a gas fire. Local ingredient
feature in classically based dishes with modern touches. The experienced owner
also run the nearby deli.

Menu € 20/35 – Carte € 29/42

Town plan: 3DV-x *– 46 Highfield Rd* ⊠ *D6 –* ℰ *(01) 496 1518*
– www.bijourathgar.ie – Closed 25-26 December

DUBLIN AIRPORT AERFORT BHAILE ÁTHA CLIATH

– Fingal ➜ See Dublin

DUNBOYNE DÚN BÚINNE

Meath – Pop. 6 959 – Regional map n° **21**-D3

▶ Dublin 17 km – Drogheda 45 km – Newbridge 54 km

🏚 **Dunboyne Castle** 🕏 🛏 🕸 🛋 🛜 🖾 ⅙ 🕮 🌿 🏊 🅿

BUSINESS · MODERN Vast extensions surround this original Georgian house. Th
large spa has 18 treatment rooms and uses organic Irish seaweed products. Spa
cious bedrooms boast good mod cons – some have balconies looking out ove
20 acres of well-maintained grounds. The Ivy offers modern Irish dishes in a for
mal atmosphere.

145 rooms � – 🛉 € 99/230 🛉🛉 € 99/340 – 4 suites
– ℰ *(01) 801 35 00 – www.dunboynecastlehotel.com*

DUNCANNON DÚN CANANN

Wexford – Pop. 328 – Regional map n° **22**-D2

▶ Dublin 167 km – New Ross 26 km – Waterford 48 km

XX **Aldridge Lodge** ✿ 🛏 🅿

🕸 BRITISH MODERN · FRIENDLY New-build house run by cheery owners. The con
stantly evolving menu offers tasty homemade bread and veg from the kitche
garden. The focus is on good value fish and shellfish – the owner's father is a lo
cal fisherman – with some Asian and fusion influences. Simply furnished bed
rooms come with hot water bottles and home-baked cookies.

Menu € 30/40 **s**

3 rooms ⊆ – 🛉 € 45 🛉🛉 € 90

South : 2 km on Hook Head rd – ℰ *(051) 389 116 (booking essential)*
– www.aldridgelodge.com – dinner only and Sunday lunch – closed Monday and
Tuesday – Closed 3 weeks January and 24-25 December

DUNDALK DÚN DEALGAN
outh – Pop. 31 149 – Regional map n° **21**-D2
◧ Dublin 82 km – Drogheda 35 km

🏨 **Crowne Plaza** ☆ ⇗ 🛏 🏋 ⊡ & 🅰 🎇 🕍 🅿

BUSINESS · MODERN Modern, 14-storey hotel tower block, close to the business park, with a stylish ground floor bar/lounge and good conference facilities. Uniform bedrooms boast a high level of facilities and countryside views; ask for one higher up. 13th floor restaurant offers a seasonal brasserie menu and a 360° vista.

129 rooms ⌂ – 🕴 € 99/169 🕴🕴 € 109/179 – 1 suite
Green Park – South : 2.75 km by R 132
– ℰ (042) 939 49 00 – www.cpdundalk.ie
– Closed 24-25 December

🏠 **Rosemount** 🛏 🎇 🅿

🏡 FAMILY · COSY An attractive dormer bungalow fronted by a delightful flower-filled garden. The welcoming owners serve tea and cake on arrival and a freshly cooked breakfast the next morning. The lounge is warmly decorated and the individually styled, spotlessly kept bedrooms feature fine fabrics and modern facilities.

10 rooms ⌂ – 🕴 € 40/50 🕴🕴 € 70
Dublin Rd – South : 2.5 km on R 132
– ℰ (042) 933 58 78 – www.rosemountireland.com
– Closed 22-27 December

t **Jenkinstown** Northeast: 9 km by N52 on R173

🍺 **Fitzpatricks** 🛏 ☂ 🅿

TRADITIONAL CUISINE · PUB A hugely characterful pub on the coast road, at the foot of the mountains, with beautiful flower displays and a wealth of memorabilia. Extensive menus list hearty, flavoursome dishes; specialities include local steaks and seafood.

Menu € 11 (weekday lunch)/35 – Carte € 28/56
Rockmarshall – Southeast : 1 km
– ℰ (042) 937 61 93 – www.fitzpatricks-restaurant.com
– Closed Good Friday and 25-26 December

DUNDRUM DÚN DROMA – Dún Laoghaire-Rathdown → See Dublin

DUNFANAGHY DÚN FIONNACHAIDH
onegal – ✉ Letterkenny – Pop. 312 – Regional map n° **21**-C1
◧ Dublin 277 km – Donegal 87 km – Londonderry 69 km

XX **Mill** ⇔ ⇗ 🛏 🅰 🅿

TRADITIONAL CUISINE · FRIENDLY Converted flax mill on the waterside, with lovely garden edged by reeds and great view of Mount Muckish. Homely inner with conservatory lounge and knick-knacks on display throughout. Antique-furnished dining room has a classical Georgian feel. Traditional menus showcase seasonal ingredients and fish features highly. Cosy, welcoming bedrooms come in individual designs.

Menu € 43

6 rooms ⌂ – 🕴 € 60 🕴🕴 € 96
Southwest : 0.75 km on N 56
– ℰ (074) 913 69 85 – www.themillrestaurant.com
– dinner only
– Restricted opening January-May, Monday and Tuesday except July and August

DUNGARVAN DÚN GARBHÁN

Waterford – Pop. 7 991 – Regional map n° **22**-C3
▶ Dublin 190 km – Cork 71 km – Waterford 48 km

XX **Tannery**

MODERN CUISINE · FRIENDLY Characterful 19C stone-built tannery, close to th
harbour; they also run the renowned cookery school here. Have small plates a
the counter or head upstairs to the bright restaurant. Attractively presented, clas
sically based dishes use good seasonal ingredients. Stylish bedrooms come wit
DIY breakfasts.

Menu € 30 – Carte € 34/50

14 rooms �㏕ – † € 60/70 †† € 95/110

*10 Quay St – via Parnell St – ℰ (058) 45 420 – www.tannery.ie – dinner only and
lunch Friday and Sunday – Closed last 2 weeks January, 25-26 December, Monda
and Good Friday*

DUNKINEELY DÚN CIONNAOLA

Donegal – Pop. 375 – Regional map n° **21**-C1
▶ Dublin 156 km – Lifford 42 km – Sligo 53 km – Ballybofey 28 km

XX **Castle Murray House**

FISH AND SEAFOOD · FRIENDLY Established restaurant in a delightful coasta
location, offering great castle, sea and sunset views. Start in the snug bar wit
its seafaring memorabilia then move to the spacious dining room, large con
servatory or flagstoned terrace. The classical menu features mussels and oy
sters from the bay. Stylish bedrooms have gilt mirrors, plush fabrics and ver
comfy beds.

Menu € 49

10 rooms �㏕ – † € 90/105 †† € 120/150

*St John's Point – Southwest : 1.5 km by N 56 on St John's Point rd
– ℰ (074) 973 70 22 – www.castlemurray.com
– dinner only and Sunday lunch light lunch in summer
– Closed January-mid February, 24-26 December, and Monday-Tuesday except
July-August*

DUN LAOGHAIRE DÚN LAOGHAIRE

Dún Laoghaire-Rathdown – Pop. 23 857 – Regional map n° **22**-D1
▶ Dublin 12 km – Belfast 176 km – Cork 265 km – Lisburn 164 km

XX **Rasam**

INDIAN · EXOTIC The scent of rose petals greets you as you head up to th
plush lounge and contemporary restaurant. Fresh, authentic Indian dishes com
in original combinations and are cooked from scratch; they even dry roast an
blend their own spices.

Menu € 24 (weekday dinner) – Carte € 31/53

Town plan: -e – *18-19 Glasthule Rd, 1st Floor (above Eagle House pub)
– ℰ (01) 230 0600 – www.rasam.ie – dinner only
– Closed 25-26 December and Good Friday*

X **Fallon & Byrne** ⓝ

MODERN CUISINE · BRASSERIE A former Victorian shelter in the People's Par
offering views over a floodlit fountain towards the sea. Original cast iron pilla
lead through to a contemporary room. All-day menus offer cakes and Mediterra
nean-style bistro dishes.

Carte € 24/53

Town plan: -x – *People's Park – ℰ (01) 230 3300 – www.fallonandbyrne.com
– Closed 25-26 December, 1 January and dinner Good Friday and 24 December*

DUN LAOGHAIRE

Cumberland St	2
Dunleary Hill.	4
George St.	
Longford Pl.	5
Marine Rd	7
Monkstown Ave	8
Monkstown Rd	9
Mount Town Upper . . .	10
Mulgrave St	
Pakenham Rd	13
Patrick St	

✗ Cavistons ⓐⓒ

FISH AND SEAFOOD · BISTRO A landmark restaurant in the town. Guests come here for the fresh, carefully cooked fish and shellfish – go for the scallops or lobster when they're in season. In 2016 they are moving to larger premises, two doors down (number 56).

Menu € 19 – Carte € 30/49

Town plan: -a – *58-59 Glasthule Rd – ℰ (01) 280 9245 (booking essential) – www.cavistons.com – lunch only and dinner Thursday-Saturday – Closed Sunday and Monday*

DUNLAVIN DÚN LUÁIN

Wicklow – Pop. 830 – Regional map n° **22**-D2
◪ Dublin 50 km – Kilkenny 71 km – Wexford 98 km

⌂ Rathsallagh House ✿ ⌘ ≼ ⌂ ⌗ ▣ ✂ ⚒ 🅿

COUNTRY HOUSE · PERSONALISED Collection of converted 18C stables and farm buildings in a peaceful, rural location. Extensive grounds include a golf course and a working farm to the rear. Characterful, open-fired lounges and cottagey bar; spacious country house bedrooms with good facilities. Large formal restaurant serves classic dishes.

29 rooms ☟ – ♦ € 135/175 ♦♦ € 150/190 – 1 suite
Southwest : 3.25 km on Grangecon rd – ℰ (045) 403 112 – www.rathsallagh.com – Closed mid week November-March

DURRUS DÚRAS
Cork – Pop. 334 – Regional map n° **22**-A3
▶ Dublin 338 km – Cork 90 km – Killarney 85 km

🏠 Gallán Mór ⓝ   🕭 ⪦ 🛏 ♿ ⚄ 🅿

RURAL · STYLISH Proudly run guesthouse named after the 3,500 year old standing stone in its garden; set in a lovely rural location overlooking Dunmanus Bay and Mizen Head. Bedrooms have warm fabrics, good facilities and handmade wooden beds. The delightful owners welcome you with homemade cake beside the wood-burning stove.

4 rooms – 🛉 € 65/90 🛉🛉 € 100/130
Kealties – West : 5.5 km. on Ahakista rd
– ℰ (027) 62 732 – www.gallanmor.com
– Restricted opening November-February. Minimum 2 nights stay May-August

✕✕ Blairscove House   🖘 🕭 ⪦ 🛏 🅿

MODERN CUISINE · ELEGANT Charming 18C barn and hayloft, just a stone's throw from the sea, with fantastic panoramic views, pretty gardens, a courtyard and a lily pond. Stylish bar and stone-walled, candlelit dining room. Starters and desserts are in buffet format, while the seasonal main courses are cooked on a wood-fired chargrill. Luxurious, modern bedrooms are dotted about the place.

Menu € 46/58 **s**
4 rooms ⌸ – 🛉 € 105/160 🛉🛉 € 150/260
Southwest : 1.5 km on R 591
– ℰ (027) 61 127 (booking essential) – www.blairscove.ie – dinner only
– Closed November-17 March, Sunday and Monday

ENNISCORTHY INIS CÓRTHAIDH
Wexford – Pop. 2 842 – Regional map n° **22**-D2
▶ Dublin 122 km – Kilkenny 74 km – Waterford 54 km – Wexford 24 km

🏨 Monart   🕭 🛏 📺 ☎ 🐾 ╚ ⚄ ♿ ⚄ 🅿

SPA HOTEL · STYLISH Comprehensively equipped destination spa in 100 acres of beautifully landscaped grounds; a haven of peace and tranquility. The Georgian house with its contemporary glass extension houses spacious, stylish bedrooms with a terrace or balcony. The Restaurant serves light, modern dishes; the minimalistic Garden Lounge offers global dishes in a more informal environment.

68 rooms ⌸ – 🛉 € 140/595 🛉🛉 € 198/895 – 2 suites
The Still – Northwest : 3 km by N 11 (Dublin rd)
– ℰ (053) 923 8999 – www.monart.ie
– Closed 18-27 December

🏠 Ballinkeele House   🕭 ⪦ 🛏 ⚄ 🅿

HISTORIC · CLASSIC Impressive Georgian house in 300 acres; family-run with traditional Irish hospitality. Grand, antique-filled sitting rooms. Bedrooms vary from cosy twins to luxurious doubles with four-posters. Four course, communal dinners feature produce from the garden. Homemade breads and fruit compote for breakfast.

6 rooms ⌸ – 🛉 € 95/115 🛉🛉 € 150/190
Ballymurn – Southeast : 10 km by R 744 and Vinegar Hill rd on Curracloe rd
– ℰ (053) 913 81 05 – www.ballinkeele.ie
– Restricted opening December-January

ENNISKERRY ÁTH AN SCEIRE
Wicklow – Pop. 1 811 – Regional map n° **22**-D1
▶ Dublin 24 km – Belfast 204 km – Cork 273 km – Lisburn 192 km

🏨 Powerscourt

GRAND LUXURY · CLASSIC Impressive curved building overlooking Sugar Loaf Mountain, featuring stylish guest areas, luxurious bedrooms, state-of-the-art conference facilities and a superb spa; outdoor activities include archery and falconry. Sika offers modern, formal dining, while the plush lounge-bar serves a concise menu of classics. McGills is a traditional Irish pub with a menu to match.

200 rooms – 👤 € 155/230 👥 € 170/245 – 93 suites – 👥 € 260/600
*Powerscourt Estate – West : 1.5 km by Powerscourt rd – 𝒞 (01) 274 88 88
– www.powerscourthotel.com*

🏨 Ferndale

FAMILY · HOMELY Homely guesthouse filled with family artefacts; located in the centre of the village, close to Powerscourt House and Gardens. The simple bedrooms are fairly priced. The splendid 1 acre garden has lots of seating and a large water feature.

4 rooms ⊋ – 👤 € 80 👥 € 80
– 𝒞 (01) 286 35 18 – www.ferndalehouse.com – Closed 24-25, 31 December and 1 January

FANORE

Clare – Regional map n° **22**-B1
📍 Dublin 253 km – Inis 51 km – Galway 65 km – Limerick 92 km

🍴 Vasco

MODERN CUISINE · SIMPLE Remotely set restaurant opposite the seashore, with a minimalist interior and a glass-screened terrace. The keen owners collect the latest produce on their drive in; the daily menu ranges from sandwiches and cake to soup and light dishes.

Carte € 25/36
Craggagh – West : 1 km on R 477 – 𝒞 (065) 707 60 20 – www.vasco.ie – Closed October-Mid March, Monday and Wednesday dinner

FENNOR

Waterford – Regional map n° **22**-C2
📍 Dublin 115 km – Waterford 12 km – Cork 75 km – Limerick 89 km

🍴 Copper Hen

TRADITIONAL CUISINE · RUSTIC A simple, likeable little restaurant located above a pub, with rustic décor and a brightly coloured fireplace; set on the coast road from Tramore to Dungarvan. Keenly priced menus offer fresh, hearty, unfussy classics and service is enthusiastic and efficient. The owners raise their own pigs.

Menu € 25
Mother McHugh's Pub – 𝒞 (051) 330 300 – www.thecopperhen.ie – dinner only and Sunday lunch – Closed 1 week January,1 week September, 25-26 December, Monday-Tuesday and Sunday dinner

FETHARD FIODH ARD

South Tipperary – Pop. 1 541 – Regional map n° **22**-C2
📍 Dublin 161 km – Cashel 16 km – Clonmel 13 km

🏨 Mobarnane House

HISTORIC · CLASSIC Lovingly restored house with a Georgian façade; set in 15 acres of grounds complete with a small lake and walks. Classically styled interior with period furnishings; the best bedrooms also have small sitting rooms. Formal set dinners are served around a large mahogany table in the beautiful dining room.

3 rooms ⊋ – 👤 € 105/125 👥 € 150/190
*North : 8 km. by Cashel rd on Ballinure rd – 𝒞 (052) 613 19 62
– www.mobarnanehouse.com – Closed November-February*

FOTA ISLAND OILEÁN FHÓTA

Cork – Regional map n° **22**-B3

▶ Dublin 263 km – Cork 17 km – Limerick 118 km – Waterford 110 km

🏚🏚 **Fota Island** ☆ 🕸 🔚 🖼 🔲 🌐 🄵 🔁 ⅄ ⋇⋇ 🄰 ⅍ ⅍ 🄿

LUXURY · DESIGN A resort hotel set within Ireland's only wildlife park. Extensiv▮ business and leisure facilities include a golf course and a state-of-the-art spa Bedrooms are spacious and well-appointed, and most have island views. The styl▮ ish restaurant offers modern takes on classical dishes.

131 rooms ☲ – 🛉 € 150/204 🛉🛉 € 175/290

– ℰ (021) 488 37 00 – www.fotaisland.ie – Closed 25 December

FOXROCK CARRAIG AN TSIONNAIGH

Dún Laoghaire-Rathdown ➜ See Dublin

FURBOGH/FURBO NA FORBACHA

Galway – Pop. 1 236 – Regional map n° **21**-A3

▶ Dublin 219 km – Belfast 333 km – Cork 209 km – Lisburn 321 km

🏚🏚 **Connemara Coast** ☆ ⋞ 🔚 🔲 𝄞 🄵 ⅍ ⅄ ⋇⋇ ⅍ 🄰 🄿

TRADITIONAL · CONTEMPORARY Over the years this has been transforme▮ from a small house into an extensive hotel. Colonial-style lobby; smart bedroom▮ feature locally made furniture and offer superb views over the bay and The Bur▮ ren. Dine in the bar or restaurant looking down the gardens to the water's edg▮ the latter is adults only.

141 rooms ☲ – 🛉 € 95/175 🛉🛉 € 120/450 – 3 suites

– ℰ (091) 592 108 – www.connemaracoast.ie – Closed 15-27 December

© The Irish Image Colle /Design Pics RM/age fotostock

GOOD TIPS!

When you think Galway, you think music. An effervescent spirit and a non-conformist attitude helped to put music at the heart of the city. A need to do their own thing is also adopted by the city's restaurants which are an eclectic bunch, from the ground-breaking Loam to rustic tapas bar, Cava Bodega, and vibrant Thai restaurant, Lime.

GALWAY GAILLIMH

alway – Pop. 75 529 – Regional map n° **21**-B3

 Dublin 217 km – Limerick 103 km – Sligo 145 km

Hotels

Radisson Blu H. & Spa

BUSINESS · MODERN Corporate hotel overlooking a lough, with a striking atrium, vast meeting facilities and a spa with a thermal suite and salt cave. Spacious, modern bedrooms; 5th floor rooms have balconies and share a business lounge. Marina's offers international dishes, with a 'Food Market Buffet' at lunch; Raw serves sushi and raw meats.

261 rooms ☑ – ♦ € 110/400 ♦♦ € 120/400 – 2 suites

Town plan: D-a – *Lough Atalia Rd* – ☎ *(091) 538 300* – *www.radissonhotelgalway.com*

Raw – See restaurant listing

G

LUXURY · STYLISH Boutique hotel featuring boldly coloured walls hung with flamboyant mirrors designed by Irish milliner Philip Treacy. Bright, spacious bedrooms have a more calming feel. The spa has a thermal suite and a relaxation room overlooking a walled bamboo garden. The colourful restaurant serves modern Irish dishes.

101 rooms ☑ – ♦ € 140/250 ♦♦ € 140/250 – 2 suites

Town plan: D-g – *Wellpark, Dublin Rd* – ☎ *(091) 865 200* – *www.theghotel.ie*
– *Closed 23-26 December*

Clayton

BUSINESS · MODERN Stylish hotel on the edge of the city, close to the famous racecourse. Modern guest areas and smart white bedrooms with sleek dark furnishings; go for a spacious 4th floor executive with a country or city view. The bar doubles as a lunchtime carvery and the restaurant offers a simple, traditional menu.

195 rooms ☑ – ♦ € 79/350 ♦♦ € 89/350

Ballybrit – East : 4 km on N 6 – ☎ *(091) 721 900* – *www.claytonhotelgalway.ie*
– *Closed 20-27 December*

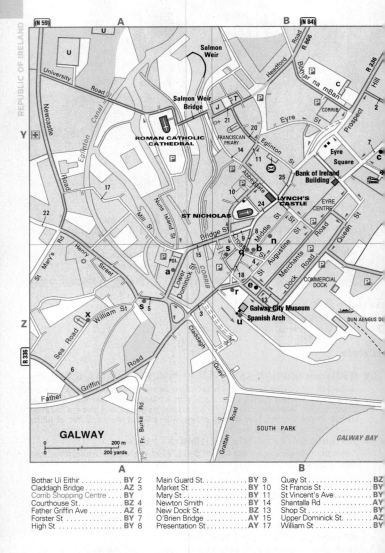

GALWAY

Scale:
0 — 200 m
0 — 200 yards

🏨 Ardilaun   ✿ 🛏 📺 🛎 ㎙ 🚲 ♿ 🚗 🅿

TRADITIONAL · CLASSIC Enlarged Georgian house with extensive leisure facil
ties, surrounded by 5 acres of colourful gardens. It's been family owned and ru
since 1962 and has a homely, traditional style. Bedrooms are spacious; ask for
newer room. Smart bar and restaurant with a sheltered terrace and classic sea
food-based menus.

123 rooms 🖵 – 🛏 € 79/300 🛏🛏 € 79/300 – 4 suites

Town plan: C-a – *Taylor's Hill* – 𝒞 *(091) 521 433* – *www.theardilaunhotel.ie*
– *Closed 23-26 December*

The MICHELIN Guide

A collection to savour!

Belgïe • Belgique & Luxembourg
Deutschland
España & Portugal
France
Great Britain & Ireland
Italia
Nederland • Netherlands
Suisse • Schweiz • Svizzera
Main Cities of Europe

Also: _____

Chicago
Hong Kong · Macau
Kyoto · Osaka
London
New York City
Nordic Cities
Paris
Rio de Janeiro & São Paulo
San Francisco
Tokyo

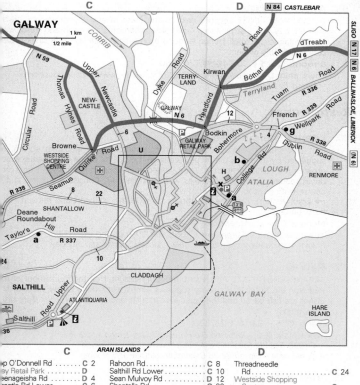

N 84 CASTLEBAR

GALWAY

1 km
1/2 mile

Park House   ☆ 🗗 ⚗ 🚗 ⚗ P

TRADITIONAL · CLASSIC Popular grey-stone hotel in city centre. Marble reception and comfy seating areas. Boss Doyle's Bar is busy and spacious. Dark wood bedrooms with rich, soft fabrics. Strong international flavours define restaurant menus.

84 rooms ⚞ – ♦ € 95/350 ♦♦ € 105/350

Town plan: BY-c – *Forster St, Eyre Sq*
– 𝒞 *(091) 564 924 – www.parkhousehotel.ie*
– *Closed 24-26 December*

House   ☆ 🏠 🗗 ⚗ �AC ⚗

TOWNHOUSE · STYLISH Unassuming hotel with a surprisingly luxurious interior. Smart bedrooms are decorated with eye-catching Italian fabrics and feature quality linens. Service is professional yet friendly. Spacious guest areas include a laid-back lounge, and a bar and dining room serving modern day classics, coffee and cocktails.

40 rooms ⚞ – ♦ € 89/350 ♦♦ € 89/350 – 1 suite

Town plan: BZ-e – *Lower Merchants Rd*
– 𝒞 *(091) 538 900 – www.thehousehotel.ie*
– *Closed 25-26 December*

Ardawn House

TRADITIONAL · COSY Located next to the stadium and the greyhound track with the city just a stroll away. Good-sized bedrooms are clean and fresh, with modern fabrics. A small lounge leads to a breakfast room laid with silver-plated cutlery. Friendly owners.

8 rooms ☲ – ♥ € 50/140 ♥♥ € 70/160

Town plan: D-b – *College Rd.* – ℰ *(091) 568 833* – *www.ardawnhouse.com*
– *Closed 15-27 December*

Restaurants

✕✕ Loam ⓝ (Enda McEvoy)   ఉ 🔢 🕅

❀ MODERN CUISINE · MINIMALIST A large basement with industrial styling; as suggested by its name, the focus here is on the quality of the ingredients, which grow in the fertile local loam. The talented chef understands his craft and produces modern, understated dishes with pure flavours. Concise à la carte and 6 course tasting menu.

➜ Crab, yoghurt, cabbage and radish. Lamb, turnip, saltwort and ramson. Rhubarb, buttermilk.

Menu € 60 – Carte approx. € 49

Town plan: D-x – *Fairgreen* – ℰ *(091) 569 727 (booking essential)*
– *www.loamgalway.com* – *dinner only* – *Closed Sunday and Monday*

✕✕ Raw ⓝ   ఉ 🔢 🅿

JAPANESE · INTIMATE An elegant, modern restaurant on the fourth floor of the Radisson Blu Hotel. As its name suggests, almost everything is raw; most of the dishes are fish-based and they specialise in sushi and sashimi to order. Very tasty 'tuna tataki'.

Menu € 35 – Carte € 23/33

Town plan: D-a – *Radisson Blu Hotel and Spa, Lough Atalia Rd*
– ℰ *(091) 538 212 (booking essential)* – *www.sushiinthesky.ie*
– *dinner only* – *Closed 24-26 December, Sunday and Monday*

✕✕ Vina Mara   🔢 🕅

MODERN CUISINE · BISTRO Bistro-style restaurant in the heart of the city, with a rich Mediterranean colour scheme. Modern Irish cooking has a fresh style, clearly defined flavours and relies on quality local ingredients; vegetarians are also well catered for.

Menu € 24 – Carte € 26/41

Town plan: BY-n – *19 Middle St*
– ℰ *(091) 561 610* – *www.infonamara.com*
– *Closed 25-27 December and Sunday*

✕✕ Seafood Bar @ Kirwan's   🍴 🔢

FISH AND SEAFOOD · BRASSERIE Well-regarded, long-standing restaurant with a large terrace, in an old medieval lane. Lively brasserie atmosphere, with dining on two levels. Modern menus have a classical base; most dishes consist of tasty seafood – go for the specials.

Carte € 30/52

Town plan: BZ-s – *Kirwan's Ln* – ℰ *(091) 568 266* – *www.kirwanslane.com*
– *Closed 25-28 December and Sunday dinner in winter*

Don't expect guesthouses 🏠 to provide the same level of service as a hotel. They are often characterised by a warm welcome and décor which reflects the owner's personality.

✗ Aniar

CREATIVE · INDIVIDUAL Intimate restaurant with a cool, Scandic feel; its name means 'From the West'. Large blackboards list the 'produce of the month' – wild and forage ingredients play a key role. The menu is confirmed at 6pm, when the last of the day's ingredients arrive; interesting modern dishes feature contrasting textures.

➜ Fermented barley, clams and ramson. Monkfish with seaweed and kale. Parsnip, malt and chicory.

Menu € 35/65

Town plan: AZ-a – *53 Lower Dominick St*
– ℰ (091) 535 947 (booking essential) – www.aniarrestaurant.ie – dinner only
– Closed 25-26 December, Sunday and Monday

✗ Oscar's Seafood Bistro

FISH AND SEAFOOD · INTIMATE Very welcoming bistro in a bohemian part of the city. The intimate interior is striking red with fabrics on the ceiling and richly upholstered banquettes. Choose something from the daily blackboard menu, which lists the catch of the day.

Menu € 19 (weekday dinner) – Carte € 25/45

Town plan: AZ-s – *Dominick St*
– ℰ (091) 582 180 – www.oscarsbistro.ie – dinner only
– Closed 1-16 January and Sunday except bank holidays

✗ Latin Quarter

REGIONAL · WINE BAR The menu at this bright, two-floored restaurant alters as the day goes on. Lunch centres around one course – including a soup, a salad and maybe a pie of the day; while dinner is more substantial. Cooking is honest and flavoursome.

Menu € 24 (weekday dinner) – Carte € 26/40

Town plan: BZ-q – *1 High St – ℰ (091) 530 000 – www.thelatinquarter.ie*
– Closed 24-25 December

✗ Cava Bodega

SPANISH · TAPAS BAR This split-level tapas bar – with its reclaimed wood tables – has a rustic, neighbourhood feel; sit downstairs to watch the chefs in the open kitchen. It's all about sharing: choose around 3 dishes each and a Spanish beer or wine.

Carte € 22/30

Town plan: BZ-b – *1 Middle St – ℰ (091) 539 884 – www.cavarestaurant.ie*
– dinner only and lunch Saturday and Sunday
– Closed 25-26 December

✗ Kai

CLASSIC CUISINE · NEIGHBOURHOOD Lovely, laid-back restaurant with a gloriously cluttered interior and old scrubbed floorboards on the walls. Morning cakes morph into fresh, simple lunches, then afternoon tea and tasty dinners. Produce is organic, free range and traceable.

Carte € 34/47

Town plan: AZ-x – *22 Sea Rd – ℰ (091) 526 003 – www.kaicaferestaurant.com*
– Closed Sunday-Monday in winter and bank holidays

✗ Ard Bia at Nimmos

MEDITERRANEAN · COSY Buzzy, bohemian restaurant where tables occupy every nook and cranny. They sell homemade cakes, bread and artisan products. Menus blend Irish, Mediterranean and Middle Eastern influences; the provenance of the ingredients takes precedence.

Carte € 30/43

Town plan: BZ-u – *Spanish Arch – ℰ (091) 561 114 (booking essential at dinner)*
– www.ardbia.com – Closed 25-26 December

X **Lime** N ⌂

THAI · **EXOTIC** A large, lively eatery run by a well-known local restaurateur
Bright, bold colours feature alongside Asian prints; the lovely terrace overlooks
the quayside. Authentic Thai and Malaysian dishes are colourful and full of flavour
Menu € 30 (dinner) – Carte € 27/36
Town plan: BZ-r – Spanish Arch – *𝒞 (091) 534 935* – www.limegalway.com
– Closed Christmas

GARRYKENNEDY

North Tipperary – Regional map n° **22**-C2
▶ Dublin 176 km – Killaloe 14 km – Youghal 2 km

🏠 **Larkins** 🔄 ⌂ P

TRADITIONAL CUISINE · **PUB** Thatched pub in a charming loughside location
The traditional interior boasts old flag and timber floors, original fireplaces and
plays host to folk music and Irish dancers. Choose from the unfussy bar menu o
more ambitious à la carte.
Menu € 21/38 – Carte € 27/40
– *𝒞 (067) 23 232* – www.larkins.ie – Closed 25 December, Good Friday,
Monday-Tuesday and Wednesday-Friday lunch November-April

GARRYVOE GARRAÍ UÍ BHUAIGH

Cork – ✉ Castlemartyr – Pop. 560 – Regional map n° **22**-C3
▶ Dublin 259 km – Cork 37 km – Waterford 100 km

🏨 **Garryvoe** 🔄 ≤ 🔲 🎿 🛁 🔲 🔄 🏖 🚺 P

FAMILY · **MODERN** Modernised hotel with a well-equipped fitness centre, over
looking Ballycotton Bay. The contemporary interior features plenty of natura
wood and slate. Bedrooms are spacious and comfortable; most boast balconie
and sea views. Formal Samphire offers a modern menu of Irish produce. The re
laxed Lighthouse Bistro serves simple pub classics.
82 rooms ☷ – ♦ € 69/96 ♦♦ € 100/160 – 1 suite
– *𝒞 (021) 464 67 18* – www.garryvoehotel.com – Closed 25 December

GLASLOUGH GLASLOCH

Monaghan – ✉ Monaghan – Regional map n° **37**-D2
▶ Dublin 133 km – Monaghan 11 km – Belfast 91 km – Lisburn 79 km

🏨 **Castle Leslie** 🍷 ≤ 🔄 🔄 🔲 🏖 🚺 P

CASTLE · **HISTORIC** Impressive castle set in 1,000 acres of parkland: home to th
4th generation of the Leslie family. Ornate, comfortable, antique-furnished gues
areas and traditional, country house style bedrooms. Dine in Snaffles restauran
in the grounds.
20 rooms ☷ – ♦ € 150/350 ♦♦ € 150/360
Castle Leslie Estate – *𝒞 (047) 88 100* – www.castleleslie.com – Closed
24-27 December

🏨 **Lodge at Castle Leslie Estate** 🍷 🍷 🔄 🔄 🍴 🌐 🔲 🔄 🏖 🚺 P

HISTORIC · **STYLISH** An extended hunting lodge to the main castle, with con
trastingly stylish bedrooms. Unwind in the Victorian treatment room or charming
open-fired bar – or hire an estate horse from the excellent equestrian centre an
explore the 1,000 acre grounds. The mezzanine restaurant offers modern Medi
terranean fare.
29 rooms ☷ – ♦ € 170/260 ♦♦ € 190/280 – 1 suite
– *𝒞 (047) 88 100* – www.castleleslie.com

GLASSON – Westmeath → See Athlone

GOLEEN AN GÓILÍN
Cork – Regional map n° **22**-A3
▶ Dublin 230 km – Cork 74 km – Killarney 67 km

🏠 Heron's Cove

🌳 🦢 ≼ 🅿️

TRADITIONAL · PERSONALISED Long-standing guesthouse hidden away in a pretty location, with views over a tiny harbour. Bedrooms are tidy and pleasantly furnished: all overlook the waterfront and most have a balcony – if you're lucky you might see herons at the water's edge. The busy restaurant offers seasonal menus of local produce.

5 rooms 🍽️ – 🛏️ € 60/80 🛏️🛏️ € 80/100

The Harbour – ℰ (028) 35 225 – www.heronscove.com – Closed Christmas

GOREY GUAIRE
Wexford – Pop. 3 463 – Regional map n° **22**-D2
▶ Dublin 93 km – Waterford 88 km – Wexford 61 km

🏡 Marlfield House

COUNTRY HOUSE · ELEGANT Attractive Regency house surrounded by large informal gardens and woodland. Various stylish, classical lounges and drawing rooms with warm décor, heavy fabrics and antiques. Well-appointed bedrooms in period styles, with a good level of facilities and pleasant views over the grounds. Smart dining room and orangery offer refined, traditional dishes with a modern touch.

18 rooms 🍽️ – 🛏️ € 85/125 🛏️🛏️ € 210/670

*Courtown Rd – Southeast : 1.5 km on R 742 – ℰ (053) 942 11 24
– www.marlfieldhouse.com – Closed 3 January-February*

GRAIGUENAMANAGH GRÁIG NA MANACH
Kilkenny – Pop. 1 543 – Regional map n° **22**-D2
▶ Dublin 125 km – Kilkenny 34 km – Waterford 42 km – Wexford 26 km

🏠 Waterside

🌳 ≼ 🍽️

TRADITIONAL · FUNCTIONAL This granite corn store stands at the foot of Brandon Hill and the Blackstairs Mountains and overlooks the River Barrow; hire one of their bikes to best explore the area. Homely bedrooms feature exposed beams and slate and have pleasant river views. The concise menu offers traditional Irish dishes.

10 rooms 🍽️ – 🛏️ € 49/65 🛏️🛏️ € 78/98

The Quay – ℰ (059) 972 42 46 – www.watersideguesthouse.com – Closed November-February

GREYSTONES NA CLOCHA LIATHA
Wicklow – Pop. 10 173 – Regional map n° **22**-D1
▶ Dublin 32 km – Wicklow 22 km – Rathmines 31 km – Dundalk 128 km

XX Chakra by Jaipur

INDIAN · EXOTIC Smart, spacious Indian restaurant with warm exotic hues and carved wooden statues, unusually set in a suburban shopping centre. Three themed set menus and an à la carte: accomplished, modern dishes feature original spicing and flavours.

Menu € 23 – Carte € 32/48

Meridian Point Centre (1st floor), Church Rd – ℰ (01) 201 7222 – www.jaipur.ie – dinner only and Sunday lunch – Closed 25 December

GWEEDORE GAOTH DOBHAIR
Donegal – Regional map n° **21**-C1
▶ Dublin 278 km – Donegal 72 km – Letterkenny 43 km – Sligo 135 km

🏨 Gweedore Court ✿ ⪕ ⬎ 🖾 🕮 🛖 🖼 🖳 🕭 ⚿ 🏋 🅿

BUSINESS · MODERN Privately owned, whitewashed hotel in a rural location with spacious, comfortable lounges and a well-equipped leisure club. Bedrooms to the front have views over the River Clady to the forests and mountains; feature rooms boast four-posters. Traditional dining room with a menu to match.

63 rooms ☐ – ♦ € 69/89 ♦♦ € 99/150

On N 56 – ℰ (074) 953 29 00 – www.gweedorecourthotel.ie – Closed Christmas and January

HORSE AND JOCKEY AN MARCACH
North Tipperary – Regional map n° **22**-C2
▶ Dublin 146 km – Cashel 14 km – Thurles 9 km

🏨 Horse and Jockey ✿ 🖾 🕮 🛖 🖼 🖳 🕭 ⚿ 🏋 🅿

BUSINESS · MODERN Extended former pub with a horseracing theme; in an area surrounded by racehorse trainers' stables and racecourses. Spacious, modern bedrooms, a superb spa and stylish, state-of-the-art meeting rooms. The coffee shop sells homemade cakes and the characterful bar and restaurant serve unfussy Irish dishes.

67 rooms ☐ – ♦ € 80/100 ♦♦ € 90/130 – 1 suite

– ℰ (0504) 44 192 – www.horseandjockeyhotel.com – Closed 24-26 December

HOWTH BINN ÉADAIR
Fingal – ✉ Dublin – Pop. 8 186 – Regional map n° **22**-D1
▶ Dublin 22 km – Swords 17 km – Belfast 172 km – Cork 276 km

✗✗ Aqua ⪕ 🆎

FISH AND SEAFOOD · DESIGN Smart restaurant at the end of the busy West Pier, with superb views over the Sound to Lambay Island. It has a cosy bar lounge with exposed brick and a wood-burning stove, and a seafood menu which keeps things pleasingly traditional.

Menu € 29 (lunch) – Carte € 34/65

1 West Pier – ℰ (01) 832 0690 – www.aqua.ie – Closed Good Friday, 25-26 December, and Monday in winter

✗✗ King Sitric ⇆ ⪕ 🆎

FISH AND SEAFOOD · CLASSIC A long-standing eatery in a former harbourmaster's house, overlooking the water. Dine in the laid-back ground floor café or the formal first floor restaurant. Seafood is the order of the day, with lobster a speciality. Bedrooms are named after lighthouses; those on the first floor have the best views.

Menu € 37 – Carte € 35/70

8 rooms ☐ – ♦ € 110/145 ♦♦ € 150/205

East Pier – ℰ (01) 832 5235 – www.kingsitric.ie – dinner only and Sunday lunch – closed dinner Sunday, Monday, Tuesday and bank holidays – Closed 25-26 December

INISHMAAN INIS MEÁIN – Galway ➜ See Aran Islands

INISHMORE ÁRAINN – Galway ➜ See Aran Islands

JENKINSTOWN BAILE SHEINICÍN – Louth ➜ See Dundalk

KANTURK CEANN TOIRC
Cork – Pop. 2 263 – Regional map n° **22**-B2
▶ Dublin 259 km – Cork 53 km – Killarney 50 km – Limerick 71 km

🏠 Glenlohane

🏠 🕭 < 🛏 🕓 🅿

HISTORIC · CLASSIC A Georgian country house set in 260 acres – it has been in the family for over 250 years. Traditional interior hung with portraits and paintings. Colour-themed bedrooms; 'Blue' has an antique four-poster and bathtub. Cosy library and drawing room. Open-fired dining room for home-cooked communal dinners.

3 rooms ⬚ – 🛉 € 90/100 🛉🛉 € 180/200

Southeast : 4 km. by R 576 (Mallow rd) and R 580 on L1043 – ☎ *(029) 50 014*
– www.glenlohane.com

KENMARE NEIDÍN

erry – Pop. 2 175 – Regional map n° **22**-A3
🢒 Dublin 338 km – Cork 93 km – Killarney 32 km

🏠 Park

🏠 🕭 < 🛏 🕤 🖼 🖾 SPA ⚗ 🏋 ※ 🖥 ᬐ 🕓 🅿

GRAND LUXURY · CLASSIC Grand country house dating from 1897, with superb views over the bay and hills. Elegant interior with a cosy cocktail lounge and a charming drawing room. Tastefully furnished bedrooms have smart marble bathrooms. The spa adds a modern touch. Informal meals in Terrace. Candlelit dining in the restaurant.

46 rooms ⬚ – 🛉 € 135/245 🛉🛉 € 190/410

Town plan: BY-k – – ☎ *(064) 664 12 00 – www.parkkenmare.com – Closed 6 January-5 March and 27 November-23 December*

Park *– See restaurant listing*

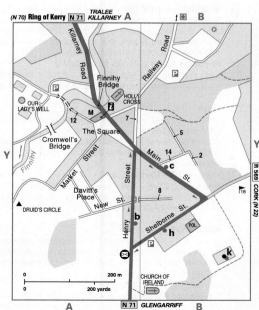

🏚️ Sheen Falls Lodge 🏠 🐾 ⪡ 🛏️ 🔌 🗁 🏶 ♨️ ✖️ 🖥️ ᵭ 🌿 ⛳ 🅿️

LUXURY · CLASSIC A modern hotel in an idyllic spot, where the waterfalls drop away into the bay. Welcoming, wood-fired lobby; spacious, comfortable guest areas and a lovely indoor pool; the well-appointed, good-sized bedrooms over look the falls. The split-level, formal restaurant serves classic dishes with a mod ern touch.

66 rooms ☺ – ♦ € 170/680 ♦♦ € 170/680 – 9 suites
Southeast : 2 km. by N 71 – 𝒞 (064) 664 16 00 – www.sheenfallslodge.ie
– Closed January

🏠 Brook Lane 🏠 🖥️ ᵭ 🌿 ⛳ 🅿️

BUSINESS · MODERN Stylish, personally run hotel close to the town centre. Contemporary bedrooms offer a good level of comfort and range from 'Superior' to 'Luxury'; the latter boasting impressive fabric headboards and designer touches. Informal bar and restaurant offer classic Irish and seafood dishes; regu lar live music.

21 rooms ☺ – ♦ € 75/110 ♦♦ € 100/180
Gortamullen – North : 1.5 km. by N 71 on N 70 – 𝒞 (064) 664 20 77
– www.brooklanehotel.com – Closed 23-27 December

🏠 Sallyport House ⪡ 🛏️ 🌿 🅿️ ⤢

FAMILY · CLASSIC Unassuming 1930s house; its charming interior packed with antiques and Irish art. Pleasant lounge with local information. Breakfast is served from the characterful sideboard and features pancakes, stewed fruits and smoked salmon. Traditionally furnished bedrooms are immaculately kept and boast water views.

5 rooms ☺ – ♦ € 75/85 ♦♦ € 115/120
South : 0.5 km. on N 71 – 𝒞 (064) 664 20 66 – www.sallyporthouse.com – Closed November-March

🏠 Shelburne Lodge 🛏️ ✖️ 🌿 🅿️

TOWNHOUSE · CLASSIC Charming, wisteria-clad farmhouse with sweeping lawns, box hedges and a herb garden. Welcoming owners and an inviting open fire. Home-baked breads and local meats at breakfast. Bedrooms mix antiques with modern colours; simple bathrooms.

10 rooms ☺ – ♦ € 75/95 ♦♦ € 110/160
East : 0.75 km. on R 569 (Cork Rd) – 𝒞 (064) 664 10 13
– www.shelburnelodge.com – Closed November- mid April

XxX Park ⪡ 🛏️ ᵭ 🅿️

CLASSIC CUISINE · ELEGANT Elegant, candlelit dining room in a luxurious hotel with good views over the grounds and a comforting style. Silver candelabra, cloches and gueridon trolleys feature; start with canapés in the lounge. Classically based dishes have a modern touch, with local ingredients to the fore. Highly pro fessional team.

Menu € 70 – Carte € 38/58
Town plan: BY-k – *Park Hotel, – 𝒞 (064) 664 12 00 (booking advisable)*
– www.parkkenmare.com – dinner only – Closed 6 January-5 March and 27 November-23 December

XX Mulcahys

MODERN CUISINE · INTIMATE A welcoming restaurant with a smart bar/lounge for pre and post-dinner drinks. Seasonal ingredients are prepared with care and a modern touch. Combinations are well-judged and some sushi and Asian dishes feature.

Menu € 35/45 – Carte € 29/55
Town plan: BY-c – *Main St – 𝒞 (064) 664 23 83 – dinner only – Closed 24-26 December, Tuesday, and Monday and Wednesday October-April*

XX **Lime Tree**

CLASSIC CUISINE · RUSTIC A 19C property that's taken on many guises over the years. The characterful, rustic interior features exposed stone walls, an open fire and even its own art gallery. Flavoursome, classically based dishes utilise quality local ingredients.

Menu € 45 – Carte € 33/50

Town plan: BY-h – *Shelbourne St.*
– *𝒞 (064) 664 12 25 – www.limetreerestaurant.com – dinner only*
– *Closed January-mid March*

X **Boathouse Bistro**

FISH AND SEAFOOD · BRASSERIE Converted boathouse in the grounds of Dromquinna Manor; set on the waterside and overlooking the peninsula and the mountains. It has a nautical, New England style and a laid-back vibe. Menus are simple, appealing and focus on seafood.

Carte € 30/50

Dromquinna – West : 4.75 km by N 71 on N 70
– *𝒞 (064) 664 2889 (booking advisable) – www.dromquinnamanor.com*
– *Closed December- February, midweek March & November and Monday-Wednesday in April & October*

X **Packie's**

TRADITIONAL CUISINE · RUSTIC Popular little restaurant in the town centre, with two rustic, bistro-style rooms, exposed stone walls, tiled floors and an interesting collection of modern Irish art. Cooking is honest, fresh and seasonal; the seafood specials are a hit.

Carte € 25/53

Town plan: AY-b – *Henry St*
– *𝒞 (064) 664 15 08 (booking essential) – dinner only*
– *Closed mid January-mid February, Monday in winter and Sunday*

KILBRITTAIN CILL BRIOTÁIN

Cork – Pop. 196 – Regional map n° **22**-B3
Dublin 289 km – Cork 38 km – Killarney 96 km

🏡 **Glen Country House**

FAMILY · CLASSIC Victorian house set in 300 acres; the same family have farmed the land for over 350 years and are now in their 10th generation! Comfy open-fired lounge and breakfast room with antique furniture; smart bedrooms have distant sea views.

4 rooms ⌂ – † € 75/100 †† € 130/200

Southwest : 4 km. turning left at crossroads and bearing right at fork
– *𝒞 (023) 884 98 62 – www.glencountryhouse.com*
– *Closed mid October-April*

KILCOLGAN CILL CHOLGÁIN

Galway – ⊠ Oranmore – Regional map n° **21**-B3
Dublin 208 km – Belfast 322 km – Cork 179 km – Lisburn 310 km

🍴 **Moran's Oyster Cottage**

FISH AND SEAFOOD · COSY Attractive whitewashed pub with a thatched roof, hidden away in a tiny hamlet – a very popular place in summer. It's all about straightforward cooking and good hospitality. Dishes are largely seafood based and oysters are the speciality.

Carte € 28/50

The Weir – Northwest : 2 km. by N 18
– *𝒞 (091) 796 113 – www.moransoystercottage.com*
– *Closed Good Friday and 24-26 December*

KILCULLEN

Kildare – Pop. 3 473 – Regional map n° **22**-D1
▶ Dublin 48 km – Naas 12 km – Rathmines 50 km – Navan 88 km

🍴 Fallon's   🛋 🅰🅺 🅿

BRITISH TRADITIONAL · FASHIONABLE A 'proper' bar with a long wooden counter and a flagged floor; albeit one with a boutique colour scheme! The experienced chef offers a wide range of dishes, from pie of the day to grilled salmon followed by tasty homemade puddings.
Carte € 25/45
Main St - 𝒞 (045) 481 260 - www.fallonb.ie - Closed 25 December, Good Friday and Monday

KILDARE

Kildare – Pop. 8 142 – Regional map n° **22**-D1
▶ Dublin 54 km – Portlaoise 37 km – Naas 21 km

🍴 Harte's Ⓝ

CLASSIC CUISINE · RUSTIC Have a local artisan beer in the snug open-fired bar or dine in the small restaurant with large mirrors and exposed brick walls. Kick things off with a gin tasting board, then move on to tasty, well-prepared dishes with modern twists.
Menu € 22 (weekdays) – Carte € 24/43
Market Sq - 𝒞 (045) 533 557 - www.hartesbar.ie - Closed Monday except lunch March-December

KILKENNY CILL CHAINNIGH

Kilkenny – Pop. 24 423 – Regional map n° **22**-C2
▶ Dublin 114 km – Cork 138 km – Killarney 185 km – Limerick 111 km

🏨 Kilkenny   ☆ 🛏 🖥 🌀 ⅃₆ 🖃 ᚕ ⌘ ⚶ 🅿

BUSINESS · DESIGN Unassuming modern property just outside the city centre with contrastingly stylish, contemporary interior. Well-equipped leisure centre and smart function rooms. Funky colour schemes feature throughout. Bright bedrooms have a slightly kitsch style. Mediterranean-influenced menus in pink-hued restaurant.
138 rooms ⌚ – ♦ € 75/195 ♦♦ € 85/300
College Rd - Southwest : 1.25 km at junction with N 76 - 𝒞 (056) 776 20 00 - www.hotelkilkenny.ie

🏨 Pembroke   ☆ 🖃 ⅃ 🅰🅺 ⚶ 🕍 🅿

BUSINESS · CONTEMPORARY A usefully located business hotel with a stylish contemporary look. Spacious, comfortable bedrooms; those at the back are a little quieter and offer views of the castle. Well-equipped business centre. Light lunches in the bar; traditional dinners in the modern restaurant with its appealing courtyard terrace.
74 rooms ⌚ – ♦ € 79/220 ♦♦ € 89/250
Patrick St - 𝒞 (056) 778 35 00 - www.pembrokekilkenny.com - Closed 24-25 December

🏠 Butler House   🛏 ⚶ 🕍 🅿

TOWNHOUSE · ELEGANT Beautifully restored Georgian house with some fine original features, a delightful formal garden and views of Kilkenny castle. Large, comfortable, up-to-date bedrooms. Breakfast is served in the adjacent Design Museum.
13 rooms ⌚ – ♦ € 60/180 ♦♦ € 89/250
15-16 Patrick St. - 𝒞 (056) 776 57 07 - www.butler.ie - Closed 23-29 December

REPUBLIC OF IRELAND

Rosquil House 🛏 & ⅏ 🅿

FAMILY · PERSONALISED Modern, purpose-built guesthouse on the main road out of the city. Leather-furnished lounge filled with books and local information; spacious, comfortable bedrooms and a smart, linen-laid breakfast room. Extensive buffet breakfasts with a cooked daily special; omelettes feature. Experienced, welcoming owners.

7 rooms ⌂ – ♦ € 45/80 ♦♦ € 80/100
Castlecomer Rd – Northwest : 1 km
– ℰ (056) 772 14 19 – www.rosquilhouse.com
– Closed 4-22 January and 23-27 December

XxX Ristorante Rinuccini [AC]

ITALIAN · CLASSIC Set in the basement of a townhouse and named after the 17C papal nuncio, this family-owned restaurant is well-known locally. Classic Italian cuisine with homemade ravioli a speciality. Some tables have views through to the wine cellar.

Menu € 23 (dinner) – Carte € 30/50
1 The Parade – ℰ (056) 776 15 75 – www.rinuccini.com
– Closed 26-27 December

XX Campagne (Garrett Byrne) & [AC] ⅋

❀ **BRITISH MODERN · FASHIONABLE** Stylish, relaxed restaurant with vibrant, contemporary art and smart booths, hidden close to the railway arches, away from the city centre. Modern cooking has a classic base, and familiar combinations are delivered with an assured touch. Popular early bird menu. Well-run, with friendly, efficient service.

→ Ox tongue and cheek with sauce gribiche, pickled salsify and horseradish cream. Rack of suckling pig, trotter and black pudding, tarbais beans, wild garlic and turnip. Crème caramel with Sauternes, Armagnac prunes and almond tuille.

Menu € 32 (lunch and early dinner) **s** – Carte € 41/55 **s**
5 The Arches, Gashouse Ln. – ℰ (056) 777 28 58 (booking advisable)
– www.campagne.ie – dinner only and lunch Friday-Sunday
– Closed 2 weeks January, 1 week July, Sunday dinner and Monday

XX Zuni ⇔ 🛖 🗔 & 🖳 🅿

BRITISH MODERN · BRASSERIE Small wood-furnished café-bar opening out into a chic, light, modern restaurant with mirrored walls, leather panels and a heated terrace. Eclectic modern menus of Irish produce; desserts are a high point. Comfortable black and white bedrooms continue the smart, contemporary theme.

Menu € 29 (dinner) – Carte € 33/46
13 rooms ⌂ – ♦ € 70/100 ♦♦ € 85/130
26 Patrick St – ℰ (056) 772 39 99 – www.zuni.ie
– Closed 25-26 December

X Foodworks & [AC]

TRADITIONAL CUISINE · FRIENDLY A former bank in the town centre: a high-ceilinged, airy space with a bright, fresh look which matches the style of the cooking. Unfussy dishes use quality local produce, including pork and vegetables from the experienced chef-owner's farm.

Menu € 23/28 – Carte € 21/42
7 Parliament St – ℰ (056) 777 76 96 – www.foodworks.ie
– Closed 25-26 December and Sunday

ILLALOE CILL DALUA

are – Pop. 1 292 – Regional map n° **22**-B2
Dublin 175 km – Ennis 51 km – Limerick 21 km – Tullamore 93 km

XX **Cherry Tree** ⪡ 🏠 ⛧ ⌂ **P**

CLASSIC CUISINE · INTIMATE Modern restaurant with interesting local art hung on brightly coloured walls, and views across Lough Derg. Choose from an array of classical menus; dishes are well-balanced, seasonal and nicely presented. Service is cheery and welcoming.

Menu € 26/35 – Carte € 30/44

Lakeside, Ballina – follow signs for Lakeside Hotel – 𝒞 (061) 375 688
– www.cherrytreerestaurant.ie – dinner only – Closed first week January, Good Friday, 25-26 December, Sunday dinner and Monday

KILLARNEY CILL AIRNE

Kerry – Pop. 12 740 – Regional map n° **22**-A2
▶ Dublin 304 km – Cork 87 km – Limerick 111 km – Waterford 180 km

Plans pages 1090, 1091

🏛🏛 **Europe** ⪡ 🏖 ⪡ 🛏 🖐 ⌥ 🗖 📶 🏊 ♨ ⛧ 🎾 🖥 ⛧ 🏖 🛁 **P**

GRAND LUXURY · MODERN A vast hotel in a superb location, boasting views over Lough Leane and Macgillycuddy's Reeks. Opulent guest areas, impressive events facilities and a sublime three-level spa. Bedrooms are lavishly appointed; some overlook the water.

187 rooms ⌷ – ♦ € 210/290 ♦♦ € 230/310 – 6 suites
Fossa – West : 4.75 km. by Port Rd on N 72 – 𝒞 (064) 667 13 00
– www.theeurope.com – Closed 11 December-4 February

Panorama • Brasserie – See restaurant listing

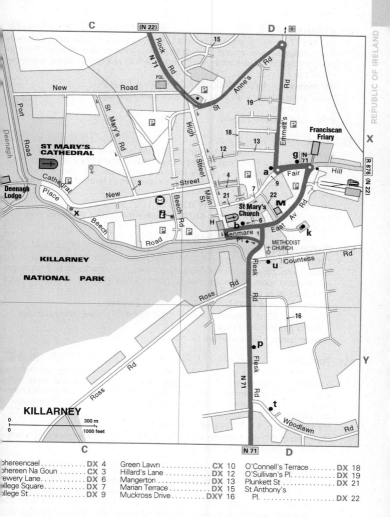

KILLARNEY

KILLARNEY NATIONAL PARK

🏨🏨 **Aghadoe Heights H. and Spa**   ♠ ♨ ≼ 📶 📺 ⊞ 🌀 🏋 🍴 ⬆ 🅰🆓
                                                                    ♨ 🅿
LUXURY · DESIGN Striking, glass-fronted hotel looking out over
lakes, mountains and countryside. Modern interior with an impressive spa and a
stylish cocktail bar complete with an evening pianist. Bedrooms are spacious;
many have balconies or terraces.

74 rooms 🍽 – 🛏 € 120/140   🛏🛏 € 170/440 – 2 suites
Northwest : 4.5 km. by N 22 off L 2109 – ☎ *(064) 663 17 66
– www.aghadoeheights.com – Weekends only November-April*

Lake Room – See restaurant listing

> Good food at moderate prices? Look for the Bib Gourmand ⊛.

Killarney Park

LUXURY · CLASSIC A smart, comfortable hotel run by a well-versed team. Bedrooms range in style, mixing modern furnishings with original features. Plush library and lavish drawing room; light lunches are served in the clubby, wood-panelled bar.

69 rooms ⌂ – ♦ € 230/400 ♦♦ € 250/425 – 2 suites

Town plan: DX-k – – ℰ (064) 663 55 55 – www.killarneyparkhotel.ie – Closed 24-27 December

Park – See restaurant listing

Ross

LUXURY · DESIGN Striking, modern hotel in the centre of town, overlooking the famous 'Killarney Horse and Carriage Tours' HQ. Contemporary bar-lounge with multi-level design. Stylish, boldly coloured bedrooms are comfy and well-equipped. Vibrant basement restaurant features curved timbers, intimate lighting and global menu.

29 rooms ⌂ – ♦ € 160/220 ♦♦ € 160/220

Town plan: DX-b – – ℰ (064) 663 18 55 – www.theross.ie – Weekends only November-March

Cahernane House

COUNTRY HOUSE · HISTORIC Fine Victorian house built in 1877, set in a peaceful location and affording westerly mountain views. Characterful open-fired library and drawing room with stags' heads, portraits and antiques. Bedrooms range from classical to contemporary.

38 rooms ⌂ – ♦ € 110/160 ♦♦ € 150/320 – 2 suites

Town plan: AZ-d – Muckross Rd – ℰ (064) 663 18 95 – www.cahernane.com – Closed December-February

Herbert Room – See restaurant listing

Randles

LUXURY · CLASSIC A gabled and extended, family-run former rectory boasting a marble-floored reception and an antique-furnished lounge with deep sofas and a coal fire. Comfortable bedrooms offer good facilities; those in the original house have more character. The spacious restaurant serves a traditional menu of local produce.

75 rooms ⌂ – ♦ € 79/199 ♦♦ € 99/299

Town plan: DY-p – Muckross Rd – ℰ (064) 663 53 33 – www.randlescourt.com – Closed 3 January-10 February

Killarney Royal

TOWNHOUSE · CLASSIC A traditional, town centre hotel which is family-owned and run; locals enjoy lunch in the bar, while residents have afternoon tea in the comfortable lounge with its original Victorian ceiling. Bedrooms are a good size and all feature a putting machine. Traditional menus are served in the spacious restaurant.

32 rooms ⌂ – ♦ € 79/349 ♦♦ € 89/389

Town plan: DX-g – College St – ℰ (064) 663 1853 – www.killarneyroyal.ie – Closed Christmas, Easter and restricted opening in winter

Fairview

TOWNHOUSE · STYLISH Stylish townhouse in the centre of town, with a cosy leather-furnished lounge and spacious, contemporary bedrooms with marble-tiled bathrooms. The Penthouse has a 4-poster, a whirlpool bath for two and mountain views from the balcony.

29 rooms ⌂ – ♦ € 55/195 ♦♦ € 70/250

Town plan: DX-a – College St. – ℰ (064) 663 41 64 – www.killarneyfairview.com – Closed 24-25 December

⌂ Earls Court House

FAMILY · CLASSIC A well-run hotel close to the town centre. Afternoon tea is served on arrival in the antique-furnished lounges. Spacious bedrooms boast good facilities: some feature half-tester or four-poster beds; some have balconies and mountain views.

30 rooms ☲ – † € 70/120 †† € 95/150

Town plan: DY-t – Woodlawn Rd. – ✆ (064) 663 40 09
– www.killarney-earlscourt.ie – Closed November-February

⌂ Kathleens Country House

TRADITIONAL · CLASSIC Personally run by a charming hostess: this is Irish hospitality at its best! Comfortable, well-kept and good value hotel, with spacious, pine-furnished bedrooms, an open-fired lounge and a cosy first floor library.

17 rooms ☲ – † € 70/100 †† € 100/140

Madams Height, Tralee Rd. – North : 3.75 km on N 22 – ✆ (064) 663 28 10
– www.kathleens.net – Closed October-April

⌂ Killarney Lodge

FAMILY · PERSONALISED Well-located on the edge of the town centre. Spacious, immaculately kept, well-furnished bedrooms; No. 12 boasts lovely mountain views. Bright and airy breakfast room where homemade bread and scones feature. Afternoon tea on arrival.

16 rooms ☲ – † € 60/100 †† € 100/140

Town plan: DX-u – Countess Rd. – ✆ (064) 663 64 99 – www.killarneylodge.net
– Closed 26 October-9 March

XxxX Panorama

MODERN CUISINE · LUXURY Large, formal restaurant with a contemporary style, set in a luxurious hotel. Panoramic windows afford superb views across the lough towards the mountains. Creative modern menus follow the seasons and use the very best of Irish produce.

Carte € 50/80

Europe Hotel, Fossa – West : 4.75 km. by Port Rd on N 72 – ✆ (064) 667 13 00
– www.theeurope.com – Closed 11 December-4 February and Sunday

XxX Lake Room

REGIONAL · DESIGN Smart restaurant in a contemporary hotel; its two different levels making the most of the panoramic water and mountain view. Classical dishes showcase local produce and are executed with a modern touch; there's the odd French influence too.

Menu € 65 – Carte € 38/75

Aghadoe Heights H and Spa, Aghadoe – Northwest : 4.5 km. by N 22 off L 2109
– ✆ (064) 663 17 66 – www.aghadoeheights.com – dinner only – Weekends only November-April

XxX Park

TRADITIONAL CUISINE · CLASSIC An elegant hotel restaurant boasting chandeliers, ornate cornicing and smartly laid tables. Classic menus with some modern combinations; Irish meats are a feature and the tasting menu a highlight. Nightly pianist in summer.

Carte € 39/55 – bar lunch

Town plan: DX-k – Killarney Park Hotel, – ✆ (064) 663 55 55
– www.killarneyparkhotel.ie – Closed 23-27 December

XX Herbert Room

TRADITIONAL CUISINE · TRADITIONAL Set in a fine Victorian house; start with a drink in the atmospheric cellar bar then head for the traditional, two-roomed restaurant with its large fireplace and mountain views. Well-judged, classically based dishes display modern touches.

Menu € 39

Town plan: AZ-d – Cahernane House Hotel, Muckross Rd – ✆ (064) 663 18 95
(booking advisable) – www.cahernane.com – dinner only – Closed
December-February and Sunday-Monday except in summer

XX Brasserie ≤ 🛋 🍴 ⅃ 🗛 🅿

INTERNATIONAL · BRASSERIE Set in a sumptuous lakeside hotel; a modern take
on a classical brasserie, with lough and mountain views – head for the terrace in
warmer weather. The accessible all-day menu ranges from soup and salads to
steaks cooked on the open grill.

Carte € 36/70 **s**

Europe Hotel, Fossa – West : 4.75 km. by Port Rd on N 72 – ℰ (064) 667 13 00
(bookings not accepted) – www.theeurope.com – Closed 11 December-4 February

XX West End House ⓝ ⬦

MODERN CUISINE · NEIGHBOURHOOD A stylish and contemporary restaurant
offering bright, friendly service. Classically based dishes with modern touches
are not only pleasing to look at but full of flavour too. The set price early evening
menu is especially good value.

Menu € 35 (weekdays)/40 – Carte € 38/53

Town plan: CX-x – *58 New St, Cathedral Pl – ℰ (064) 663 22 71*
– www.westendhouse.com – dinner only – Closed Monday and Tuesday

at Beaufort West: 9.75 km by N72 off Glencar rd – ✉ Killarney

🏚 The Dunloe ⬦ ⅋ ≤ 🛋 🔄 🗔 🏖 ✕ 🖼 ⅃ 🅿

LUXURY · CLASSIC This continental-style hotel is set in 65 acres and has superb
views of the Gap of Dunloe and Macgillycuddy's Reeks. Bedrooms have a subtle
modern edge and most have a balcony with a view; the suites feature steam
rooms. It boasts several lounges and bars, an all-day restaurant and a formal dining room.

102 rooms ☑ – † € 180/550 †† € 200/575 – 2 suites
Southeast : 2.5 km on Dunloe Golf Course rd – ℰ (064) 664 41 11
– www.thedunloe.com – Closed mid October-mid April

KILLORGLIN CILL ORGLAN

Kerry – Pop. 2 082 – Regional map n° **22**-A2
▶ Dublin 333 km – Killarney 19 km – Tralee 26 km

X Giovannelli

ITALIAN · RUSTIC A sweet little restaurant, hidden away in the town centre
with a traditional osteria-style interior and an on-view kitchen. The concise
daily changing blackboard menu offers authentic Italian dishes which are unfussy, fresh and full of flavour, with homemade pasta and herbs from the
owners' garden.

Carte € 29/44

Lower Bridge St – ℰ (087) 123 13 53 (booking essential) – dinner only – Closed
Monday

X Sol y Sombra 🍴 ⅃ 🍷 ⬦

SPANISH · TAPAS BAR Spanish restaurant in an imposing 19C former church
with a cavernous interior, stained glass windows and church pews. Fresh, vibrant
cooking: go for the raciones, designed for sharing – 3 per person will suffice. Live
music is a feature.

Menu € 19/40 – Carte € 25/39

Old Church of Ireland, Lower Bridge St – ℰ (066) 976 23 47 – www.solysombra.ie
– dinner only and Sunday lunch – Closed 9 January-9 February and Tuesday
dinner in winter, Sunday and Monday

KINLOUGH CIONN LOCHA

Leitrim – Pop. 1 018 – Regional map n° **21**-C2
▶ Dublin 220 km – Ballyshannon 11 km – Sligo 34 km

✕ Courthouse

ITALIAN · BISTRO Boldly painted former courthouse with a pretty stained glass entrance. The Sardinian chef-owner creates extensive seasonal menus of honest, authentic Italian dishes; local seafood and some imported produce feature. The atmosphere is informal and the service, friendly. Simply styled bedrooms offer good value.

Carte € 23/46

4 rooms � – ♦ € 37/45 ♦♦ € 70/80

Main St – ℰ (071) 984 23 91 (booking essential) – www.thecourthouserest.com – dinner only and Sunday lunch – Closed Monday-Wednesday in winter and Tuesday

KINSALE CIONNE TSÁILE

Cork – Pop. 2 198 – Regional map n° **22**-B3

▶ Dublin 276 km – Waterford 92 km – Cork 25 km

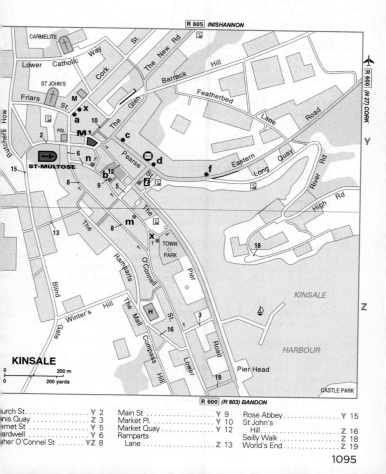

R 605 *INISHANNON*

CARMELITE

Lower   Catholic   Way   St.   Cork   The New Rd   P

ST JOHN'S   Barrack   Hill

Friars   St.   The Glen   Featherbed

Butchers How   **x**   a   10   The   Lane   Road

P   POL.   **M**1   c   Pearse   R 600 (N 27) CORK   Y

2   6   n   d   Eastern   Long Quay   River Rd

ST-MULTOSE   b 12   f

15   8   9   5.   High Rd

13   8   m   P

Ramparts   O'Connell   St   TOWN PARK   Pier   18   Z

Blind   Winter's   Hill   H   KINSALE

Gate   The Mall   Compass Hill   St.   3   16   Road   Lower

KINSALE   HARBOUR

0 ——— 200 m
0 ——— 200 yards   19   Pier Head   CASTLE PARK

R 600 (R 603) *BANDON*

Perryville House

TOWNHOUSE · CLASSIC Luxuriously appointed house in the heart of town, overlooking the harbour and named after the family that built it in 1820. Bedrooms are tastefully styled – the top rooms have feature beds, chic bathrooms and harbour views. It also boasts two antique-furnished drawing rooms, a smart boutique and a tea shop.

22 rooms � – ♦ € 160/300 ♦♦ € 160/300
Town plan: Y-f – *Long Quay* – 𝒞 *(021) 477 27 31* – *www.perryvillehouse.com*
– *Closed November-15 April*

Blue Haven

TOWNHOUSE · STYLISH A small but well-established hotel right in the heart of town; its cosy, vibrant interior features some interesting artwork. Comfortable bedrooms are named after vineyards and have a subtle contemporary edge. The modern wine bar serves tapas dishes, while the all-day bistro serves a global menu; the latter, set in the old fish market, resembles an upturned boat hull.

17 rooms ☑ – ♦ € 55/99 ♦♦ € 70/160
Town plan: Y-c – *3-4 Pearse St* – 𝒞 *(021) 477 22 09*
– *www.bluehavenkinsale.com* – *Closed 25 December*

Old Bank Town House

TOWNHOUSE · CLASSIC Substantial Georgian house in the heart of town. A food store and café, where breakfast is served, occupy the ground floor; above them is a cosy, classically furnished lounge. Bedrooms are traditional – No.17 has great harbour views.

17 rooms ☑ – ♦ € 59/100 ♦♦ € 70/160
Town plan: Y-d – *10-11 Pearse St.* – 𝒞 *(021) 477 40 75*
– *www.oldbankhousekinsale.com* – *Closed 25 December*

Old Presbytery

TOWNHOUSE · CLASSIC 18C building which once housed priests from the nearby church – a few ecclesiastical pieces remain. Bedrooms feature Irish pine furniture and either brass or cast iron beds; Room 6 has a roof terrace. Breakfasts are comprehensive.

9 rooms ☑ – ♦ € 60/100 ♦♦ € 90/130
Town plan: Y-a – *43 Cork St.* – 𝒞 *(021) 477 20 27*
– *www.oldpres.com* – *Closed mid November-mid February*

Desmond House

TOWNHOUSE · CLASSIC Built by a Spanish merchant in 1780 and once belonging to the church – it still displays a tiny altar on the landing. Homemade bread features in the attractive, parquet-floored breakfast room. Traditional bedrooms boast jacuzzis.

4 rooms ☑ – ♦ € 50/70 ♦♦ € 100/140
Town plan: Y-x – *42 Cork St.* – 𝒞 *(021) 477 35 35*
– *www.desmondhousekinsale.com* – *Closed November-January*

XX Finns' Table

REGIONAL · FRIENDLY Behind the bright orange woodwork lie two attractive rooms – one with colourful banquettes, the other in powder blue with wine box panelling. Meat is from the chef's family farm and everything from bread to ice cream is homemade.

Menu € 33 (early dinner) – Carte € 35/58
Town plan: Y-b – *6 Main St* – 𝒞 *(021) 470 9636*
– *www.finnstable.com*
– *dinner only – Closed November, Christmas, Sunday-Thursday January-mid March and Tuesday-Wednesday*

XX Max's

FISH AND SEAFOOD · INTIMATE Two-roomed restaurant on a quaint main street, with a simple yet smart rustic style; a spot well-known by the locals! The unfussy, classically based seafood menu offers good choice, try the tasty 'Fresh Catches'. Efficient, engaging team.

Menu € 25 – Carte € 33/49

Town plan: Z-m – *48 Main St.* – ℰ *(021) 477 24 43 (booking advisable) – www.maxs.ie – dinner only – Closed December, Sunday and Thursday except June-September and bank holidays. Restrictred opening January-February*

X Fishy Fishy

FISH AND SEAFOOD · DESIGN Friendly, informal restaurant that's something of a local institution: dine in the spacious restaurant amongst 'fishy' memorabilia or alfresco on the small terrace. Concise, all-day menus offer well-prepared seafood dishes and interesting specials. The owner often collects the fish himself.

Carte € 29/46 s

Town plan: Z-x – *Pier Rd* – ℰ *(021) 470 04 15 – www.fishyfishy.ie – Closed 24-26 December*

X Bastion 🄽

MEDITERRANEAN · FRIENDLY Simple little wine-bar-cum-bistro run by a keen young couple. Cooking has Mediterranean influences; go for the small plates – three plus dessert should suffice. Dishes are tasty, carefully prepared and often have a playful element. The bar serves prosecco on tap, as well as prosecco cocktails.

Menu € 32 – Carte € 30/40

Town plan: Y-n – *Market St* – ℰ *(021) 470 96 96 (booking advisable) – dinner only and Sunday lunch – Closed last 2 weeks January, first two weeks February, Monday and Tuesday*

🏠 Toddies at The Bulman

FISH AND SEAFOOD · PUB Rustic pub with maritime décor and excellent bay views; look out for the Moby Dick mural and the carved Bulman Buoy. Lunch is in the bar and offers simple pub classics and more ambitious blackboard specials; dinner is in the more formal restaurant and presents carefully prepared, globally influenced dishes.

Carte € 32/53

Summercove – East : 2 km by R 600 and Charles Fort rd. – ℰ *(021) 477 21 31 – www.thebulman.ie – Closed 25 December, Good Friday and Monday dinner*

at Barrells Cross Southwest: 5.75 km on R600 -(Z)⊠ Kinsale

🏡 Rivermount House

FAMILY · PERSONALISED Spacious, purpose-built dormer bungalow overlooking the countryside and the river, yet not far from town. It has a distinctive modern style throughout, with attractive embossed wallpapers and quality furnishings. Bold, well-appointed bedrooms display high attention to detail and have immaculate bathrooms.

6 rooms 🖙 – ♥ € 55/85 ♥♥ € 85/100

North : 0.75 km on L 7302 – ℰ *(021) 477 80 33 – www.rivermount.com – Closed 14 November-9 March*

KNOCK AN CNOC

Mayo – Pop. 811 – Regional map n° **21**-B2

◪ Dublin 212 – Galway 74 – Westport 51

*Hotels see : **Cong** SW : 58 km by N 17, R 331 R 334 and R 345*

LAHINCH AN LEACHT

Clare – Pop. 642 – Regional map n° **22**-B1

◪ Dublin 260 km – Galway 79 km – Limerick 66 km

🏨 **Vaughan Lodge**   ⇪ 🛏 🗗 ⚐ ℘ 🅿

BUSINESS · MODERN Stylish roadside hotel with a bright, modern interior, a leather-furnished lounge and a great selection of malts behind the bar. The smart, spacious bedrooms come in eye-catching colour schemes and offer good facilities. There are many golf courses nearby. The dining room serves a menu of modern classics.

22 rooms ☟ – ♦ € 115/155 ♦♦ € 140/240

Ennistymon Rd – ℰ (065) 708 11 11 – www.vaughanlodge.ie – Closed November-March

🏨 **Moy House**   ⇪ 🐾 ⇐ 🛏 ℘ 🅿

TRADITIONAL · STYLISH 18C Italianate clifftop villa, overlooking the bay and run by a friendly, attentive team. Homely guest areas include a small library and an open-fired drawing room with an honesty bar; antiques, oil paintings and heavy fabrics feature throughout. Individually designed, classical bedrooms boast good extras and most have views. Formal dining is from a 5 course set menu.

9 rooms ☟ – ♦ € 150/240 ♦♦ € 165/380

Southwest : 3 km on N 67 – ℰ (065) 708 28 00 – www.moyhouse.com – Closed November-March

LEENANE AN LÍONÁN

Galway – ✉ Clifden – Regional map n° **21**-A3

▶ Dublin 278 km – Ballina 90 km – Galway 66 km

🏨 **Delphi Lodge**   ⇪ 🐾 ⇐ 🛏 ⚐ ℘ 🅿

COUNTRY HOUSE · HOMELY A former shooting lodge of the Marquis of Sligo, in a lovely loughside spot on a 1,000 acre estate. Bright, simple bedrooms with smart bathrooms. 'Special Experience' days, free bike hire and a large walkers' drying room. Communal dining from a set menu; guests are encouraged to mingle in the drawing room.

13 rooms ☟ – ♦ € 140/195 ♦♦ € 230/320

Northwest : 13.25 km by N 59 on Louisburgh rd – ℰ (095) 42 222 – www.delphilodge.ie – Closed November-February

LEIGHLINBRIDGE LEITHGHLINN AN DROICHID

Carlow – Pop. 828 – Regional map n° **22**-D2

▶ Dublin 63 km – Carlow 8 km – Kilkenny 16 km – Athy 22 km

🏨 **Lord Bagenal**   ⇪ 🗗 ⚑ 🎬 ℘ 🎿 🅿

BUSINESS · MODERN Striking hotel on the banks of the River Barrow. It was originally just a tiny coaching inn – be sure to head to the characterful original bar for a comforting, classical dish and a pint of Guinness in front of the peat fire. Vast modern extensions house the rest of the guest areas and the modern bedrooms.

39 rooms ☟ – ♦ € 65/100 ♦♦ € 90/150

Main St – ℰ (059) 977 40 00 – www.lordbagenal.com – Closed 25-26 December

LETTERFRACK LEITIR FRAIC

Galway – Regional map n° **21**-A3

▶ Dublin 304 km – Ballina 111 km – Galway 91 km

🏨 **Rosleague Manor**   ⇪ 🐾 ⇐ 🛏 ℘ 🅿

TRADITIONAL · CLASSIC Creeper-clad country house in mature grounds, boasting excellent bay and mountain views. Large, classically styled bedrooms. Cosy, antique-filled drawing rooms with open fires; wicker-furnished conservatory for afternoon tea and evening drinks. The formal dining room overlooks the garden.

21 rooms ☟ – ♦ € 95/155 ♦♦ € 140/230

West : 2.5 km. on N 59 – ℰ (095) 41 101 – www.rosleague.com – Closed mid November-mid March

LETTERKENNY LEITIR CEANAINN

Donegal – Pop. 15 387 – Regional map n° **21**-C1
▶ Dublin 241 km – Londonderry 34 km – Sligo 116 km

🏚 Radisson Blu   ⚗ 🗖 🛝 🕰 🖲 🕭 🖾 🕊 🅿

BUSINESS · MODERN Purpose-built hotel with a good leisure club, set on a shopping and retail park close to the city centre; its reception displays photos of the stars who have stayed here. Modern bedrooms are uniformly styled. The spacious bar serves light meals and the popular brasserie offers international dishes.

114 rooms ☐ – † € 84/180 †† € 99/219
Paddy Harte Rd – ℰ (074) 919 44 44
– www.radissonblu.ie/hotel-letterkenny

✗✗ Browns on the Green ⓝ   ≼ 🖾 🅿

MODERN CUISINE · FRIENDLY Situated on the first floor of a golf club but with views of the mountains rather than the course. A cosy lounge leads into the intimate modern dining room. Refined dishes are modern interpretations of tried-and-tested classics.

Menu € 11 (lunch) – Carte € 28/46
Letterkenny Golf Club, Barnhill – Northeast : 5.75 km by R 245
– ℰ (074) 912 4771 (booking advisable) – www.brownsrestaurant.com
– Closed 25-26 December, 1 January, Good Friday, Monday and Tuesday

LIMERICK LUIMNEACH

Limerick – Pop. 57 106 – Regional map n° **22**-B2
▶ Dublin 195 km – Cork 99 km – Galway 102 km – Waterford 127 km

🏚 Savoy   ⚗ 🕰 🖲 🕭 🖾 🕊 🅿

BUSINESS · FUNCTIONAL Corporate hotel named after the theatre that previously stood on the site. Spacious guest areas and a chic bar; good-sized, comfortable bedrooms with smart, modern bathrooms. Those on floors 7 and 8 have balconies and share an executive lounge. Brasserie dishes in the dark and atmospheric Hamptons Grill.

94 rooms – † € 99/350 †† € 99/350 – ☐ €14
Town plan: Z-e – *Henry St – ℰ (061) 448 700*
– www.savoylimerick.com
– Closed 25 December

🏚 Limerick Strand   ⚗ ≼ 🗖 🛝 🕰 🖲 🕭 🖾 🕊 🚗

BUSINESS · MODERN Commercial hotel with extensive, state-of-the-art function and leisure facilities. Modern bedrooms are uniformly styled and come with good amenities; go for an executive, which has a balcony. The terraced bar overlooks the River Shannon.

184 rooms – † € 99/250 †† € 99/300 – ☐ €15 – 13 suites
Town plan: Y-z – *Ennis Rd – ℰ (061) 421 800*
– www.limerickstrandhotel.ie
The River – See restaurant listing

🏚 Absolute   ⚗ 🕰 🖲 🕭 🖾 🕊 🚗

BUSINESS · FUNCTIONAL Set on the edge of the city and designed in the style of an old mill to reflect the area's industrial heritage. Inside it is contrastingly stylish, with well-thought-out bedrooms, modern meeting rooms, treatment rooms and a hair salon. The restaurant serves a traditional menu and overlooks the river.

99 rooms – † € 75/259 †† € 75/259 – ☐ €11
Town plan: Y-a – *Sir Harry's Mall – ℰ (061) 463 600*
– www.absolutehotel.com

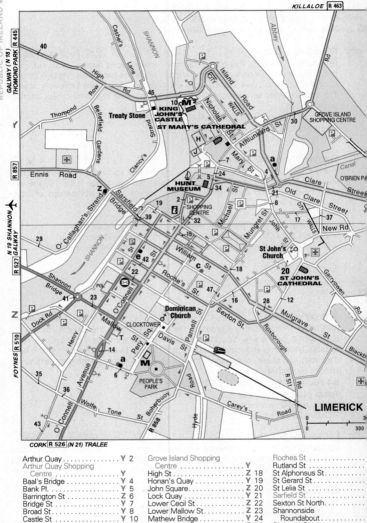

REPUBLIC OF IRELAND

KILLALOE R 463

GALWAY (N 18)
THOMOND PARK R 445

R 857

R 19 SHANNON
GALWAY

R 527 GALWAY

FOYNES R 510

CORK R 526 (N 21) TRALEE

LIMERICK

Treaty Stone

KING JOHN'S CASTLE
ST MARY'S CATHEDRAL

GROVE ISLAND SHOPPING CENTRE

O'BRIEN PA

HUNT MUSEUM

SHOPPING CENTRE

Old Clare Street

New Rd

St John's Church

ST JOHN'S CATHEDRAL

Dominican Church

CLOCKTOWER

PEOPLE'S PARK

300

🏠 No1. Pery Square ✿ 🖰 & 🖿 ⅋ 🅿

TOWNHOUSE · STYLISH A charming hotel in the Georgian Quarter, with a stylish reception and a classically proportioned drawing room overlooking the gardens. Luxurious, classically styled 'Period' bedrooms and more contemporary 'Club' rooms. Superb spa.

20 rooms 🖭 – 🛉 € 99/195 🛉🛉 € 120/225 – 1 suite

Town plan: Z-a – Pery Sq – ℰ (061) 402 402 – www.oneperysquare.com
– Closed 25-26 December

Sash – See restaurant listing

XX The River & 🖿

TRADITIONAL CUISINE · INTIMATE Stylish, modern hotel restaurant with smartly laid tables and river views. The experienced chef name-checks local producers on the menu; dishes are traditional and provide plenty of choice. There's also a good value early bird selection.

Menu € 20 (weekdays) – Carte € 31/42

Town plan: Y-z – Limerick Strand Hotel, Ennis Rd – ℰ (061) 421 800
– www.limerickstrandhotel.ie – dinner only and Sunday lunch

X Cornstore 🍽 🖀 & 🖿 ↔

TRADITIONAL CUISINE · WINE BAR Head past the bar and up to the larger, more comfortable first floor restaurant to enjoy carefully prepared, traditional cooking. Dry aged Irish steaks form the core of the menu; seafood also plays a part – and a cocktail is a must!

Menu € 25 (weekday dinner)/35 – Carte € 28/50

Town plan: Z-c – 19 Thomas St – ℰ (061) 609 000 – www.cornstore.com

X Sash N & 🖿

TRADITIONAL CUISINE · BISTRO A relaxed modern bistro on the first floor of a hotel in the Georgian quarter; its name comes from the type of window often found in houses of this era. Contemporary styling, with a feature wall of pictures and mirrors. Wide-ranging menus.

Menu € 29 (lunch and early dinner) – Carte € 25/48

Town plan: Z-a – No.1 Pery Square Hotel, Pery Sq – ℰ (061) 402 402
– www.oneperysquare.com – Closed Monday

LISCANNOR LIOS CEANNÚIR
Clare – Pop. 129 – Regional map n° **22**-B1
🔃 Dublin 272 km – Ennistimmon 9 km – Limerick 72 km

🍴 Vaughan's Anchor Inn ↔ 🖀 🖿 🅿

FISH AND SEAFOOD · PUB Family-run pub in a picturesque fishing village; the pleasantly cluttered bar comes complete with a small grocery shop. Dishes are a step above your normal pub fare and local seafood plays a big role; the seafood platter is a real hit. Smart bedrooms feature bright local art and colourful throws.

Carte € 24/52

7 rooms 🖭 – 🛉 € 60/90 🛉🛉 € 60/90

Main St – ℰ (065) 708 15 48 – www.vaughans.ie – Closed 25 December

LISDOONVARNA LIOS DÚIN BHEARNA
Clare – Pop. 739 – Regional map n° **22**-B1
🔃 Dublin 268 km – Galway 63 km – Limerick 75 km

🏠 Sheedy's Country House ✿ 🖨 & ⅋ 🅿

FAMILY · CLASSIC Mustard-yellow house in the village centre, with a kitchen garden in front. Relax in the comfy library, the Lloyd Loom furnished sun lounge or the traditional bar. Spacious, well-kept bedrooms feature flowery fabrics and have good facilities. A classical menu is offered in the dining room; service is exacting.

11 rooms 🖭 – 🛉 € 85/120 🛉🛉 € 100/170

– ℰ (065) 707 40 26 – www.sheedys.com – Closed October-March

🏠 Wild Honey Inn ⇔ 🍴

CLASSIC CUISINE · INN Three-storey building at the end of a short terrace, located close to the limestone landscape of The Burren and the Cliffs of Moher. Menus stick with the classics and champion local produce, particularly seafood. Flavours are bold and presentation is modern. Bedrooms are simply furnished; two open onto the walled courtyard. Have breakfast overlooking the garden.

Carte € 32/49

14 rooms ☲ – 🛏 € 55/65 🛏🛏 € 95/110

South : 0.5 km on Ennistimon rd – ℰ (065) 707 43 00 (bookings not accepted) – www.wildhoneyinn.com – Closed January-February, 24-26 December and restricted opening November-December and March-April, Monday and Tuesday

LISTOWEL LIOS TUATHAIL

Kerry – Pop. 4 205 – Regional map n° **22**-B2
▶ Dublin 270 km – Killarney 54 km – Limerick 75 km – Tralee 27 km

🍴 Allo's Bistro ⇔ ⇧

TRADITIONAL CUISINE · COSY Former pub dating back to 1873; now a simple well-run and characterful restaurant. Series of homely rooms and friendly, efficient service. Wide-ranging menus rely on regional produce, with theme nights on Thursdays and an adventurous gourmet menu Fri and Sat evenings. Individual antique-furnished bedrooms.

Menu € 20/45 – Carte € 25/42

3 rooms – 🛏 € 70/100 🛏🛏 € 70/100

41-43 Church St – ℰ (068) 22 880 (booking essential) – www.allosbarbistro-townhouse.com – Closed Sunday and Monday except bank holidays

LONGFORD AN LONGFORT

Longford – Pop. 8 002 – Regional map n° **21**-C3
▶ Dublin 124 km – Drogheda 120 km – Galway 112 km – Limerick 175 km

🏠 Viewmount House ✿ 🌳 🍴 ⅖ 🌿 🅿

COUNTRY HOUSE · CLASSIC Set in 4 acres of mature grounds, a welcoming Georgian house with a charming period feel – original features include an ornate vaulted ceiling in the breakfast room. Bedrooms are traditionally styled, furnished with antiques and have good modern facilities; opt for a duplex room. The breakfasts are delicious.

12 rooms ☲ – 🛏 € 75/85 🛏🛏 € 140/150

Dublin Rd – Southeast : 1.5 km by R 393 – ℰ (043) 334 19 19 – www.viewmounthouse.com – Closed 30 October-10 November

VM – See restaurant listing

🍴🍴🍴 VM 🍴 ⅖ 🅿

MODERN CUISINE · TRADITIONAL Formal hotel restaurant in the old stables of Georgian house. The smart, rustic dining room has stone-faced walls and overlooks a Japanese garden. Cooking is interesting, modern and original, and or chard and garden produce features.

Menu € 60

Viewmount House Hotel, Dublin Rd – Southeast : 1.5 km by R 393 – ℰ (043) 334 19 19 – www.viewmounthouse.com – dinner only and Sunday lunch – Closed 30 October-10 November

MALAHIDE MULLACH ÍDE

Fingal – Pop. 15 846 – Regional map n° **22**-D1
▶ Dublin 19 km – Cork 274 km – Galway 224 km – Waterford 185 km

✗✗ Jaipur   AC

INDIAN · ELEGANT Friendly basement restaurant in a Georgian terrace. The origins of the tasty, contemporary Indian dishes are noted on the menu. The fish curry – sea bass with nigella seeds, lemon leaf, onion and coconut sauce – is a speciality.

Menu € 20 – Carte € 31/44

5 St James's Terr. – ℰ (01) 845 5455 – www.jaipur.ie – dinner only and Sunday lunch – Closed 25 December

✗✗ Bon Appetit   🍷 AC 📋 ⇄

MODERN CUISINE · BRASSERIE Smart Georgian terraced house near the harbour. The intimate, dimly lit bar offers cocktails and tapas; below is a modern brasserie with a lively atmosphere. Modern dishes have a classical French base; the steaks are a highlight.

Menu € 28 – Carte € 33/49

9 St. James's Terr. – ℰ (01) 845 0314 – www.bonappetit.ie – dinner only and lunch Friday-Sunday – Closed 25-26 December and Monday

MALLOW MALA

Cork – Pop. 8 578 – Regional map n° **22**-B2

▶ Dublin 240 km – Cork 34 km – Killarney 64 km – Limerick 66 km

🏰 Longueville House   🌳 🐾 ⇐ 🚘 🍸 ✦ 🐴 P

HISTORIC · CLASSIC Part-Georgian manor house built in William and Mary style, with pleasant views over Dromaneen Castle. Lovely stone-tiled hall, superb flying staircase and stunning drawing room. Well-appointed bedrooms boast antique furniture. Grand restaurant; traditional menus use produce from the kitchen garden and estate.

20 rooms 🖃 – 🛉 € 85/95 🛉🛉 € 179/229

West : 5.5 km by N 72 – ℰ (022) 47 156 – www.longuevillehouse.ie – Closed 24-27 December, Monday-Tuesday and restricted opening in winter

MIDLETON MAINISTIR NA CORANN

Cork – Pop. 3 733 – Regional map n° **22**-C3

▶ Dublin 259 km – Cork 19 km – Waterford 98 km

✗ Farmgate Restaurant & Country Store   🍴 ⇄

REGIONAL · SIMPLE A friendly food store with a bakery, a rustic two-roomed restaurant and a courtyard terrace. Lunch might mean soup, a sandwich or a tart; dinner features regional fish and meats – the chargrilled steaks are popular. Cakes served all day.

Carte € 28/51

Coolbawn – ℰ (021) 463 27 71 (bookings advisable at dinner) – www.farmgate.ie – Closed 24 December-3 January, Sunday and Monday

✗ Sage   ₤ AC

REGIONAL · BISTRO Local produce is the focus at this homely restaurant, with most of the ingredients coming from within a 12 mile radius. Cooking has a classical base and showcases prime seafood and top quality meats – including some lesser-known cuts.

Menu € 23 (weekdays)/44 – Carte € 34/51

The Courtyard, 8 Main St – ℰ (021) 463 96 82 – www.sagerestaurant.ie – Closed 25-27 December, Good Friday and Monday

MOHILL MAOTHAIL

Leitrim – Pop. 928 – Regional map n° **21**-C2

▶ Dublin 98 km – Carrick-on-Shannon 11 km – Cavan 41 km – Castlerea 44 km

🏚 Lough Rynn Castle ✿ 🐾 🚐 & 🄰🄲 🛇 🕹 🅿

LUXURY · HISTORIC 18C country house with superb gardens and peaceful grounds; popular for weddings. Numerous lounges and a baronial hall with original parquet flooring and an impressive fireplace. Large, well-appointed bedrooms – those in the main house are the most characterful. Formal dining room; ambitious French cuisine.

43 rooms ☑ – 🛉 € 89/175 🛉🛉 € 99/199
Southeast : 4 km by R 201 off Drumlish rd – ℰ (071) 963 27 00
– www.loughrynn.ie

🏠 Lough Rynn Country House 🐾 ← 🚐 🅿 🛏

FAMILY · HOMELY Purpose-built stone house in a peaceful country setting, boasting lovely views over Lough Rynn – three of the homely bedrooms share the view and one has a small balcony. There's a comfy lounge and a cottagey breakfast room, and the delightful owner welcomes guests with home-baked scones or muffins.

4 rooms ☑ – 🛉 € 50 🛉🛉 € 100
Southeast : 3.5 km. by R 201 off Drumlish rd – ℰ (087) 922 82 36
– www.loughrynnbandb.ie

MULLINGAR AN MUILEANN GCEARR
Westmeath – Pop. 9 414 – Regional map n° **21**-C3
▶ Dublin 79 km – Cork 242 km – Galway 146 km – Waterford 177 km

🏚 Mullingar Park ✿ 🖥 🦩 🕰 🖻 & 🛇 🕹 🅿

BUSINESS · MODERN Large, contemporary hotel close to a business park and the main road to Dublin – a popular conference venue. Well-equipped, modern bedrooms in a uniform style. Comprehensive leisure facilities. Horseshoe bar-lounge and spacious formal dining room offering classical Irish cooking.

95 rooms ☑ – 🛉 € 99/150 🛉🛉 € 130/180
Dublin Rd – East : 2.5 km on Dublin Rd off N 4 (junction 15) – ℰ (044) 933 7500
– www.mullingarparkhotel.com – Closed 25-26 December

🏠 Marlinstown Court 🚐 🛇 🅿

TRADITIONAL · COSY Clean, tidy guesthouse close to the N4; a very homely personal option for staying away. The light, airy lounge opens into a pleasant pine-furnished breakfast room overlooking the garden. Bedrooms are simply and brightly decorated.

5 rooms ☑ – 🛉 € 40/50 🛉🛉 € 70/80
Dublin Rd – East : 2.5 km on Dublin Rd off N 4 (junction 15) – ℰ (044) 934 00 53
– www.marlinstowncourt.com – Closed 23-27 December

MULRANNY AN MHALA RAITHNÍ
Mayo – Regional map n° **21**-A2
▶ Dublin 270 km – Castlebar 35 km – Westport 29 km

🏚 Mulranny Park ✿ ← 🚐 🖥 🦩 🕰 🖻 & 🛬 🛇 🕹 🅿

HOLIDAY HOTEL · MODERN 1897 railway hotel with stunning views of Clew Bay and Achill Island, and its own causeway to the beach. Modern, slightly minimalist bedrooms; the two-bedroomed suites are ideal for families. Impressive leisure and conference facilities. All-day snacks in the bar; modern menu in the restaurant. Charming team.

61 rooms ☑ – 🛉 € 45/105 🛉🛉 € 90/210 – 20 suites
On N 59 – ℰ (098) 36 000 – www.mulrannyparkhotel.ie – Closed 3-31 January and 24-26 December

MURRISK
Mayo – Pop. 235 – Regional map n° **21**-A2
▶ Dublin 260 km – Castlebar 25 km – Galway 95 km

Tavern

TRADITIONAL CUISINE · PUB Vibrant pink pub with designer colours, leather banquettes and quirky basket lampshades. Wide-ranging dishes display a touch of refinement; the meats and seafood are local and the daily cheesecake is a must. Staff are smart and attentive.

Carte € 23/46

– *𝒞 (098) 64 060 – www.tavernmurrisk.com – Closed Good Friday and 25 December*

NAAS AN NÁS

Kildare – Pop. 20 713 – Regional map n° **22**-D1
▷ Dublin 30 km – Kilkenny 83 km – Tullamore 85 km

Killashee House H. & Villa Spa

BUSINESS · CLASSIC Impressive part-1860s hunting lodge, surrounded by vast grounds and boasting spacious, traditionally styled guest areas, good event facilities and a superb leisure club and spa. Country house style bedrooms - those in the main building are the most characterful. Turners offers elegant fine dining overlooking the garden. Family-friendly brasserie menu in informal Jack's.

141 rooms ☑ – † € 90/130 †† € 130/280 – 12 suites

*Kilcullen Rd – South : 3 km on R 448 – 𝒞 (045) 879 277
– www.killasheehouse.com – Closed 25-26 December*

Vie de Châteaux

FRENCH CLASSIC · BISTRO A smart modern bistro with a great terrace overlooking the old harbour. The keenly priced menu of carefully cooked, fully flavoured Gallic dishes will evoke memories of holidays in France; save room for 'Les Mini Desserts'.

Menu € 24 (early dinner) – Carte € 33/52

*The Harbour – 𝒞 (045) 888 478 (booking essential) – www.viedechateaux.ie
– Closed 24 December-2 January, lunch Monday, Tuesday and Saturday and bank holidays*

at Two Mile House Southwest: 6.5 km by R448

Brown Bear

BRITISH MODERN · BRASSERIE Smart restaurant in a small village, boasting a pubby locals bar and leather-furnished dining room with a subtle brasserie feel. Decide between two menus: a two-choice set selection or a complex, ambitious à la carte with a Gallic twist.

Menu € 20 – Carte € 33/46

– 𝒞 (045) 883 561 – www.thebrownbear.ie – dinner only and lunch Saturday-Sunday – Closed Monday, Tuesday and 24-27 December

NAVAN AN UAIMH

Meath – Pop. 28 158 – Regional map n° **21**-D3
▷ Dublin 48 km – Drogheda 26 km – Dundalk 51 km

Ma Dwyers

BUSINESS · FUNCTIONAL Surprisingly spacious detached house on the main road into town. Simple, brightly painted interior with a comfy lounge and large breakfast room. Good value bedrooms in an up-to-date, uniform style; bathrooms are shower only.

24 rooms ☑ – † € 40 †† € 65

Dublin Rd – South : 1.25 km on R 147 – 𝒞 (046) 907 79 92 – www.madwyers.com

NEW QUAY BEALACLUGGA

Clare – Regional map n° **22**-B1
▷ Dublin 240 km – Ennis 55 km – Galway 46 km

🏠 Mount Vernon   ⇧ ⬡ ⬅ 🛏 ⑨ 🅿

COUNTRY HOUSE · PERSONALISED Charming whitewashed house with a pretty walled garden, set close to the beach and affording lovely views. Antiques and eclectic curios fill the guest areas; spacious bedrooms have their own personalities – two open onto a terrace. Simply cooked dinners rely on fresh, local produce. Warm, welcoming owners.

5 rooms ⥥ – 🛏 € 90/120 🛏🛏 € 180/230

Flaggy Shore – North : 0.75 km on coast rd – 𝒞 (065) 707 8126
– www.mountvernon.ie – Closed November-March

🍴 Linnane's Lobster Bar   ⬅ 🛋 ⬡ 🆒 🅿

FISH AND SEAFOOD · PUB Simple but likeable place, with peat fires and full-length windows which open onto a terrace. They specialise in fresh, tasty fish and shellfish; watch the local boats unload their catch – some of which is brought straight to the kitchen.

Carte € 22/53

New Quay Pier – 𝒞 (065) 707 8120 – www.linnanesbar.com – Closed Good Friday, 25 December and Monday-Thursday October-Easter

NEWMARKET-ON-FERGUS CORA CHAITLÍN
Clare – Pop. 1 773 – Regional map n° **22**-B2
▶ Dublin 219 km – Ennis 13 km – Limerick 24 km

🏨 Inn at Dromoland ⓝ   ⇧ 🛏 🖥 🐾 ⑨ 🖻 ⬡ ♨ 🅿

FAMILY · FUNCTIONAL Spacious modern sister to Dromoland Castle, featuring plenty of meeting rooms and stylish bedrooms. When it comes to leisure, there's a children's games room, a smart pool and gym, tennis courts and a large pitch and putt course. The formal restaurant offers a traditional menu of local ingredients while the pub offers old favourites and bottled artisan beers.

150 rooms – 🛏 € 100/140 🛏🛏 € 140/180

Northwest : 3 km on R 458 – 𝒞 (061) 368 161 – www.theinnatdromoland.ie

NEWPORT BAILE UÍ FHIACHÁIN
Mayo – Pop. 616 – Regional map n° **21**-A2
▶ Dublin 264 km – Ballina 59 km – Galway 96 km

🏠 Newport House   ⬡ ⇧ ⬡ 🛏 🔸 🅿

HISTORIC · CLASSIC Delightful creeper-clad mansion with lovely gardens and river views; they also own Lough Beltra, nearby. Large drawing room with family portraits; traditional, antique-filled bedrooms. The grand staircase is topped by a domed cupola. Dinner is a highlight, with salmon a speciality and a notable wine list.

14 rooms ⥥ – 🛏 € 135/180 🛏🛏 € 280/310

– 𝒞 (098) 41 222 – www.newporthouse.ie – Closed November-18 March

OUGHTERARD UACHTAR ARD
Galway – Pop. 1 333 – Regional map n° **21**-A3
▶ Dublin 232 km – Cork 223 km – Galway 25 km – Waterford 253 km

🏠 Currarevagh House   ⇧ ⬡ ⬅ 🛏 🔸 ⑨ 🅿

TRADITIONAL · CLASSIC Classically furnished Victorian manor house, in 180 acres bordering Lough Corrib. Run by the same family for over 100 years; it has a very 'lived-in' feel and offers a real 'country house' experience. Have afternoon tea by the fire or take a picnic out on the boat. Set dinners of unfussy, flavoursome dishes.

12 rooms ⥥ – 🛏 € 70/95 🛏🛏 € 140/180

Northwest : 6.5 km on Glann rd – 𝒞 (091) 552 312 – www.currarevagh.com
– Closed November-February

🏠 Ross Lake House

TRADITIONAL · CLASSIC Personally run Georgian country house with attractive gardens, set in a wooded estate. Traditionally styled bedrooms; Strefens suite and Killaguile are the best. Begin the evening in the cocktail bar before dining by candlelight at smartly set, cloth-clad tables.

13 rooms ⌧ – 🛏 € 102/110 🛏🛏 € 150/160 – 2 suites

Rosscahill – Southeast : 7.25 km by N 59 – ℰ (091) 550 109
– www.rosslakehotel.com – Closed November-mid March

🏠 Railway Lodge

LUXURY · STYLISH Stylish house in a remote farm setting, with views across the countryside and a beautifully kept, elegantly furnished interior. Bedrooms come with stripped pine furnishings and have a keen eye for detail. The charming owner offers good local recommendations. Homemade bread and scones; tea served on arrival.

4 rooms ⌧ – 🛏 € 50/70 🛏🛏 € 100/110

West : 0.75 km by Costello rd taking first right onto unmarked road – ℰ (091) 552 945 – www.railwaylodge.net

🏠 Waterfall Lodge

TRADITIONAL · CLASSIC Heavily restored Victorian house run by an infectiously enthusiastic owner. A fishing river runs through the garden – look out for jumping salmon! Sympathetically styled bedrooms with rug-covered floors and modern bathrooms; some have four-posters. Pancakes, French toast and smoked salmon at breakfast.

6 rooms ⌧ – 🛏 € 50 🛏🛏 € 80

West : 0.75 km on N 59 – ℰ (091) 552 168 – www.waterfalllodge.net

PORTMAGEE AN CALADH

Kerry – Pop. 109 – Regional map n° **22**-A2
▶ Dublin 365 km – Killarney 72 km – Tralee 82 km

🏠 Moorings

TRADITIONAL · COSY Cosy, personally run hotel overlooking the harbour and bridge, and made up a series of little cottages. First floor lounge offers great views, as do some of the pleasant bedrooms; 4 and 6 boast jacuzzis. Characterful bar with music nights. Nautically themed restaurant with seafood straight from local boats.

17 rooms ⌧ – 🛏 € 60/100 🛏🛏 € 90/140

– ℰ (066) 947 71 08 – www.moorings.ie – Closed 25 December

PORTLAOISE PORT LAOISE

Laois – Pop. 20 145 – Regional map n° **22**-C2
▶ Dublin 88 km – Carlow 40 km – Waterford 101 km

🏠 Ivyleigh House

TOWNHOUSE · CLASSIC Traditional listed Georgian property in the city centre, run by a welcoming owner. Comfy lounge and communal dining area, with antiques and ornaments displayed throughout. Good-sized bedrooms are decorated in a period style. Homemade breads, preserves, muesli and a Cashel blue cheese-cake special at breakfast.

6 rooms ⌧ – 🛏 € 55/85 🛏🛏 € 90/160

Bank Pl, Church St – ℰ (057) 862 20 81 – www.ivyleigh.com – Closed 24-26 December

PORTMARNOCK PORT MEARNÓG

Fingal – Pop. 9 285 – Regional map n° **22**-D1
▶ Dublin 16 km – Belfast 165 km – Cork 271 km – Galway 221 km

🏨 Portmarnock H. and Golf Links ❀ ≼ 🏦 🖼 🛏 ⛱ 🌡 ⅋ 🏊 ♨ 🅿

BUSINESS · CONTEMPORARY Much-extended 19C house with its own champion-ship links golf course, previously owned by the Jameson family of whiskey fame. Bedrooms are well-maintained and classically styled; those in the newer wing are larger and more contemporary; ask for a sea view. The smart brasserie serves traditional menus.

138 rooms ⌛ – ♦ € 99/215 ♦♦ € 115/230 – 3 suites
Strand Rd – ℰ (01) 846 0611 – www.portmarnock.com – Closed 24-27 December

RAMELTON RÁTH MEALTAIN
Donegal – Pop. 1 212 – Regional map n° **21**-C1
▶ Dublin 248 km – Donegal 59 km – Londonerry 43 km – Sligo 122 km

🏠 Moorfield Lodge ≼ 🏦 ⅋ 🅿

FAMILY · CONTEMPORARY Striking, modern house run by a welcoming owner. Bright, stylish bedrooms with underfloor heating, floor to ceiling windows and Egyptian cotton sheets. Room 1 has its own terrace, a double jacuzzi bath and a TV built into the bathroom tiles. Communal breakfasts are served around an an-tique table.

3 rooms ⌛ – ♦ € 130/180 ♦♦ € 130/180
Aughnagaddy Glebe, Moorfield – South : 3.25 km on R 245 – ℰ (074) 989 4043 – www.moorfieldlodge.com – April-October

🏠 Ardeen ⧖ 🏦 ❌ ⅋ 🅿

TRADITIONAL · CLASSIC A Victorian house on the edge of the village, with peaceful gardens and a river nearby. Welcoming owner and homely, personally styled interior. Open-fired lounge with local info; communal breakfasts. Simple, well-kept bedrooms without TVs.

5 rooms ⌛ – ♦ € 45 ♦♦ € 90
bear left at the fork in the village centre and left at T-junction – ℰ (074) 915 12 43 – www.ardeenhouse.com – Closed October-Easter

RANELAGH – Dublin ➜ See Dublin

RATHGAR – Dublin ➜ See Dublin

RATHMINES RÁTH MAONAIS – Dublin ➜ See Dublin

RATHMULLAN RÁTH MAOLÁIN
Donegal – ✉ Letterkenny – Pop. 518 – Regional map n° **21**-C1
▶ Dublin 265 km – Londonderry 58 km – Sligo 140 km

🏨 Rathmullan House ❀ ⧖ ≼ 🏦 🔄 🖼 ❌ & 🏊 🅿

TRADITIONAL · CLASSIC Family-run, part-19C house set next to Lough Swilly. Bedrooms in the original house have a fitting country house style; those in the extension are more modern and come with balconies or private terraces over-looking the gardens.

34 rooms ⌛ – ♦ € 80/125 ♦♦ € 160/250
North : 0.5 mi on R 247 – ℰ (074) 915 81 88 – www.rathmullanhouse.com – Closed 4 January-13 February and restricted opening in winter
Cook & Gardener – See restaurant listing

✕✕ Cook & Gardener 🅝 ≼ 🏦 🅿

CLASSIC CUISINE · FORMAL Formal hotel restaurant comprising several inter-connecting rooms. Daily menus list the best of what's in season, including pro-duce from the house's original walled kitchen garden. Classic cooking is pre-sented in a modern manner.

Carte € 36/57
Rathmullan House Hotel, North : 0.5 mi on R 247 – ℰ (074) 915 81 88 – www.rathmullanhouse.com – Closed 4 January-13 February and restricted opening in winter

RATHNEW

Wicklow – ✉ Wicklow – Pop. 2 964 – Regional map n° **22**-D2

▶ Dublin 45 km – Gorey 44 km – Wexford 97 km

🏠 Tinakilly House

HISTORIC · CLASSIC A substantial Victorian house in extensive grounds which stretch to the seashore: built for Captain Robert Halpin. Original features include an impressive staircase. Spacious, classically furnished bedrooms; some have four-posters.

52 rooms ☑ – 🛉 € 89/140 🛉🛉 € 90/170 – 1 suite

On R 750 – ℰ (0404) 69 274 – www.tinakilly.ie – Closed 24-26 December

Brunel – See restaurant listing

🏠 Hunter's

COUNTRY HOUSE · COSY Late 17C former coaching inn run by the 5th generation of the same family. Traditionally styled throughout with homely lounges displaying flowery fabrics and drapes. Neat, country house style bedrooms boast sleigh beds and antique furnishings. Formal dining room offers menu of traditionally based dishes.

16 rooms ☑ – 🛉 € 65/95 🛉🛉 € 130/190

Newrath Bridge – North : 1.25 km by Dublin rd on R 761 – ℰ (0404) 40 106 – www.hunters.ie – Closed 24-26 December

XX Brunel

BRITISH TRADITIONAL · ELEGANT Spacious, elegant restaurant in a hotel extension, overlooking the gardens: named after the builder of the Great Eastern ship on which Captain Halpin sailed. Flavoursome, traditional dishes use the best Wicklow ingredients.

Menu € 26 – Carte € 40/55

Tinakilly House Hotel, On R 750 – ℰ (0404) 69 274 – www.tinakilly.ie – dinner only and Sunday lunch – Closed 24-26 December

RIVERSTOWN BAILE IDIR DHÁ ABHAINN

Sligo – Pop. 374 – Regional map n° **21**-B2

▶ Dublin 189 km – Cork 309 km – Lisburn 193 km – Craigavon 170 km

🏠 Coopershill

TRADITIONAL · CLASSIC Magnificent Georgian house run by the 7th generation of the same family; set on a working farm within a 500 acre estate. Spacious guest areas showcase original furnishings – now antiques – and family portraits adorn the walls. Warm, country house style bedrooms. Formal dining amongst polished silverware.

8 rooms ☑ – 🛉 € 134/157 🛉🛉 € 198/244

– ℰ (071) 916 51 08 – www.coopershill.com – Closed November-March

ROSCOMMON ROS COMÁIN

Roscommon – Pop. 5 693 – Regional map n° **21**-B3

▶ Dublin 151 km – Galway 92 km – Limerick 151 km

🏠 Abbey

FAMILY · CLASSIC Part-18C family-run manor house with a castellated façade; overlooking the ruins of a 13C abbey. The most characterful bedrooms are in the original house – some boast feature beds and roll-top baths. The function and leisure facilities are good. Dine in the large bar, the carvery or the formal restaurant.

50 rooms ☑ – 🛉 € 70/160 🛉🛉 € 100/240

Galway Rd – On N 63 – ℰ (090) 662 62 40 – www.abbeyhotel.ie – Closed 24-26 December

ROSSLARE ROS LÁIR

Wexford – Pop. 1 547 – Regional map n° **22**-D2

▶ Dublin 167 km – Waterford 80 km – Wexford 19 km

🏠 Kelly's Resort

FAMILY · PERSONALISED It started life in 1895 as a beachfront 'refreshment house'; now it's a sprawling leisure-orientated hotel run by the 4th generation of the Kelly family. Various lounges, large bar and sizeable spa. Well-appointed bedrooms; the newer rooms being the largest. Formal Beaches offers an exceptional wine list.

118 rooms �))) – ♦ € 88/180 ♦♦ € 176/360
– ☎ (053) 913 21 14 – www.kellys.ie – Closed December-Mid February
La Marine – See restaurant listing

✗ La Marine

BRITISH TRADITIONAL · BISTRO A bistro-style restaurant within a beachfront hotel, with an open-kitchen and a glass-fronted wine cellar. A zinc-topped bar from France takes centre stage, while the menu offers tasty brasserie classics, including plenty of fish dishes.

Menu € 26 (early dinner) – Carte € 29/43
Kelly's Resort Hotel, – ☎ (053) 913 21 14 – www.kellys.ie – Closed December-Mid February

ROSSLARE HARBOUR CALAFORT ROS LÁIR
Wexford – Pop. 1 123 – Regional map n° **22**-D2
▶ Dublin 169 km – Waterford 82 km – Wexford 21 km

🏠 Archways

VILLA · HOMELY Spanish villa style bungalow, conveniently located for Rosslare harbour. Contemporary bedrooms feature coffee machines and smart bathrooms, with colour schemes themed around a single piece of art from a local artist. Daily changing set three course dinners use the best of seasonal, local produce.

6 rooms �))) – ♦ € 55/65 ♦♦ € 65/95
Rosslare Rd, Tagoat – West : 6.25 km on N 25 – ☎ (053) 915 81 11
– www.thearchways.ie – Closed 20-27 December and 31 December-3 January

ROUNDSTONE CLOCH NA RÓN
Galway – Pop. 245 – Regional map n° **21**-A3
▶ Dublin 293 km – Galway 76 km – Ennis 144 km

🍴 O'Dowds

FISH AND SEAFOOD · COSY Busy pub in pretty harbourside town; popular with tourists and locals alike. Owned by the O'Dowd family for over 100 years, it specialises in fresh, simply cooked fish and shellfish. Sit in the cosy, fire-lit bar or wood-panelled restaurant.

Menu € 20 (dinner) – Carte € 18/42
– ☎ (095) 35 809 (booking advisable) – www.odowdsseafoodbar.com – Closed 25 December

ROUNDWOOD
Wicklow – Pop. 833 – Regional map n° **22**-D2
▶ Dublin 25 km – Wicklow 12 km – Belfast 137 km – Limerick 144 km

🍴 Byrne & Woods

BRITISH TRADITIONAL · COSY Arguably the second highest pub in Ireland, set up in the Wicklow Mountains. 'Byrne' is a cosy bar with a wood-burning stove; dimly lit 'Woods' has leather and dark wood furnishings and a clubby feel. Cooking is fresh and straightforward.

Carte € 24/42
Main St – ☎ (01) 281 70 78 – www.byrneandwoods.com – Closed 25-26 December

SANDYFORD ÁTH AN GHAINIMH

Dún Laoghaire-Rathdown ➔ See Dublin

SHANAGARRY AN SEANGHARRAÍ

Cork – ⊠ Midleton – Pop. 414 – Regional map n° **22**-C3
🔼 Dublin 262 km – Cork 40 km – Waterford 103 km

🏠 **Ballymaloe House**   ⭐ 🦢 ≾ 🛋 ᗺ ⅀ ₺ 🕸 🖼 🅿

FAMILY · CLASSIC With its pre-18C origins, this is the very essence of a country manor house. Family-run for 3 generations, it boasts numerous traditionally styled guest areas, comfortable, classical bedrooms and a famed cookery school. The 5 course daily menu offers local, seasonal produce.

29 rooms ⊊ – 🛏 € 130/150 🛏🛏 € 200/300

Northwest : 3 km on R 629
- ☎ *(021) 465 25 31 – www.ballymaloe.ie*
- *Closed January and 24-26 December*

SKIBBEREEN

Cork – Pop. 2 568 – Regional map n° **22**-B3
🔼 Dublin 338 km – Cork 85 km – Killarney 104 km

🏠 **Liss Ard** Ⓝ   ⭐ 🦢 ≾ 🛋 🖼 🅿

HISTORIC · PERSONALISED With 150 acres of grounds – including with a lake – this 200 year old manor house, stables and lodge create an idyllic rural retreat. Inside they're surprisingly modern with sleek furnishings and a minimalist Swiss/German style. Staff are friendly and daily menus are led by the availability of local produce.

25 rooms – 🛏 € 145/295 🛏🛏 € 145/295

Liss Ard Estate, Castletownsend Rd – Southeast : 2.5 km on R 596
- ☎ *(028) 40 000 – www.lissardestate.com*
- *Restricted opening January-February*

SLANE

Meath – Pop. 1 349 – Regional map n° **21**-B3
🔼 Dublin 34 km – Navan 8 km – Craigavon 69 km

🏠 **Tankardstown**   ⭐ 🦢 🛋 🕸 🅿

LUXURY · STYLISH A fine Georgian manor house with a lavish interior, set up a sweeping tree-lined drive. Bedrooms in the main house are furnished with antiques; those in the courtyard are more modern and come with kitchens. Have afternoon tea in the cottage, wood-fired pizzas in Cellar or contemporary dishes in Brabazon.

13 rooms ⊊ – 🛏 € 100/200 🛏🛏 € 200/400 – 6 suites

Northwest : 6 km by N 51 off R 163
- ☎ *(041) 982 46 21 – www.tankardstown.ie*
- *Closed 10-30 January and 25-27 December*

Brabazon – See restaurant listing

🏠 **Conyngham Arms**   ⭐ 🛋 🕸 🖼 🅿

FAMILY · PERSONALISED 17C coaching inn on the main street of a small but busy town. It has a laid-back feel, an appealing shabby-chic style and a lovely hidden garden. Some of the bedrooms have feature beds and all come with coffee machines and freshly baked biscuits from their nearby bakery. Dine in the bar, with its open kitchen.

15 rooms ⊊ – 🛏 € 65/99 🛏🛏 € 89/160

- ☎ *(041) 988 4444 – www.conynghamarms.ie*
- *Closed 25-26 December*

XX **Brabazon** 🛋 ℙ

MODERN CUISINE · RUSTIC Relaxed, rustic restaurant in the former piggery of a delightful manor house. Sit at a painted wooden table by the fire or out on the terrace overlooking the landscaped courtyard. Contemporary cooking uses top quality ingredients.

Menu € 35/70 – Carte € 44/60

Tankardstown Hotel, Northwest : 6 km by N 51 off R 163
– *𝒞 (041) 982 46 21 – www.tankardstown.ie*
– *dinner only and Sunday lunch*
– *Closed 10-30 January, 25-27 December and Monday-Tuesday*

SLIGO SLIGEACH

Sligo – Pop. 17 568 – Regional map n° **21**-B2
◪ Dublin 214 km – Belfast 203 km – Dundalk 170 km – Londonderry 138 km

🏠 **Tree Tops** 🖼 ℙ

TRADITIONAL · PERSONALISED An unassuming whitewashed house in a residential area, with immaculately kept bedrooms, a cosy lounge and a smart buffet breakfast room overlooking the garden. The chatty, welcoming owners have an interesting Irish art collection.

3 rooms � – ♦ € 70/74 ♦♦ € 70/74

Cleveragh Rd – South : 1.25 km by Dublin rd
– *𝒞 (071) 916 23 01 – www.sligobandb.com*
– *Closed Christmas-New Year*

XX **Montmartre** 🄰🄲

FRENCH CLASSIC · BISTRO Smart, modern restaurant in the shadow of the cathedral, with a tiled exterior and wooden blinds. The French chefs prepare classic Gallic menus which follow the seasons. The all-French wine list features interesting, lesser-known wines.

Menu € 24/37 – Carte € 26/48

Market Yard
– *𝒞 (071) 916 99 01 – www.montmartrerestaurant.ie*
– *dinner only*
– *Closed 11 January-4 February, Sunday and Monday*

🄽 **Hargadons** 🛋 🄰🄲

TRADITIONAL CUISINE · RUSTIC Hugely characterful pub with sloping floors, narrow passageways, dimly lit anterooms and a lovely "Ladies' Room" complete with its own serving hatch. Cooking is warming and satisfying, offering the likes of Irish stew or bacon and cabbage.

Carte € 21/31

4-5 O'Connell St
– *𝒞 (071) 915 3709 (bookings not accepted)*
– *www.hargadons.com – Closed Sunday*

at Strandhill West: 7 km on R292

🏠 **Strandhill Lodge & Suites** ⟨ ▣ ⅙ 🖼 ℙ

TOWNHOUSE · MODERN Modern property with a comfy lounge and a small breakfast room. Standard bedrooms look inland; go for one with a patio or a balcony overlooking the rooftops to the Atlantic. The suites have small kitchens and are ideal for longer stays.

22 rooms ⊒ – ♦ € 59/109 ♦♦ € 79/149 – 4 suites
Top Hill – 𝒞 (071) 912 21 22 – www.strandhilllodgeandsuites.ie

SPANISH POINT RINN NA SPÁINNEACH

Clare – ✉ Milltown Malbay – Regional map n° **22**-B2
◪ Dublin 275 km – Galway 104 km – Limerick 83 km

✗✗ **Red Cliff Lodge** ⇐ ≼ ⍟ ⌂ ⏚ ⓥ 🅿

MODERN CUISINE · INTIMATE Thatched cottage in a superb spot on the headland; later extensions have created a U-shaped arrangement around a cobbled courtyard. The décor is bright and eye-catching, the tables are elegantly set and modern classics are served with flair. Smart, spacious bedrooms have kitchenettes and coffee machines.

Menu € 35 (weekdays) – Carte € 33/49

6 rooms – ♥ € 100/120 ♥♥ € 120/150

– ℰ (065) 708 57 56 – www.redclifflodge.ie – dinner only and Sunday lunch
– Closed October-Easter and Monday

STEPASIDE

Dún Laoghaire-Rathdown – Regional map n° **22**-D1

▶ Dublin 10 km – Dún Laoghaire 7 km – Belfast 121 km – Cork 164 km

✗✗ **Box Tree** ᪵ 🅰 ⇔

BRITISH TRADITIONAL · BISTRO Modern eatery beneath a small new-build apartment block. The attractive restaurant serves unfussy, good value classical dishes; to the other side of the bar is the Wild Boar pub, which offers a similar but slightly lighter menu.

Menu € 20 (weekday lunch)/25 – Carte € 38/53

Enniskerry Rd ⊠ D18 – ℰ (01) 205 20 25 – www.theboxtree.ie
– Closed 25-26 December and Good Friday

STRAFFAN TEACH SRAFÁIN

Kildare – Pop. 635 – Regional map n° **22**-D1

▶ Dublin 29 km – Belfast 192 km – Cork 238 km – Lisburn 180 km

🏨🏨 **K Club** 🏡 🐎 ⍟ 🍴 🄻 🖵 ⊕ 🛁 𝄞 ✗ 🖵 ᪵ 𝄞 🏊 🅿

GRAND LUXURY · CLASSIC A golf resort with two championship courses, an extensive spa and beautiful formal gardens stretching down to the Liffey. The fine 19C house has elegant antique-filled guestrooms and luxurious bedrooms. Elegant Byerley Turk serves a 6 course tasting menu; grand River Room offers refined classics; Legends has a brasserie menu; and K Thai serves Thai and Malaysian fare.

134 rooms – ♥ € 179/399 ♥♥ € 179/399 – ☑ €29 – 9 suites

– ℰ (01) 601 72 00 – www.kclub.ie

🏨 **Barberstown Castle** 🏡 ≼ ⍟ 🖵 ᪵ 𝄞 🏊 🅿

COUNTRY HOUSE · HISTORIC Set within 20 acres of grounds; a 13C castle with whitewashed Georgian and Victorian extensions – a popular venue for weddings. Large, luxurious country house bedrooms feature good facilities; many have four-poster beds and garden outlooks. Dine on traditional dishes in the informal, conservatory style bistro or from French menus in the Georgian house and stone keep.

55 rooms ☑ – ♥ € 125/200 ♥♥ € 140/280

North : 0.75 km – ℰ (01) 628 81 57 – www.barberstowncastle.ie – Closed
January-February and 24-26 December

STRANDHILL – Sligo ➜ See Sligo

TERMONBARRY

Roscommon – Pop. 366 – Regional map n° **21**-C3

▶ Dublin 130 km – Galway 137 km – Roscommon 35 km – Sligo 100 km

🏨 **Keenan's** 🏡 🏠 𝄞 🅿

INN · COSY A modern extension to a characterful village pub, which is run by the 5th generation of the same family. There's a cosy lounge and breakfast room. Bedrooms are stylish with compact bathrooms; some have balconies overlooking the Shannon. The restaurant offers classic menus, while the bar serves pub favourites.

12 rooms ☑ – ♥ € 95/120 ♥♥ € 110/140

– ℰ (043) 332 60 52 – www.keenans.ie – Closed 25-26 December

THOMASTOWN BAILE MHIC ANDÁIN

Kilkenny – Pop. 2 273 – Regional map n° **22**-C2

▶ Dublin 124 km – Kilkenny 17 km – Waterford 48 km – Wexford 61 km

🏚 Mount Juliet

HISTORIC · CLASSIC Georgian gem situated in 1,500 acres, with a Jack Nicklaus designed golf course, a spa, an equestrian centre and even a stud farm. Bedrooms range from traditional in the main house to two-roomed garden lodges and smaller but equally comfy rooms in the former hunting stables. Grand restaurant; simple French dishes in the brasserie and light lunches in the clubhouse bar.

58 rooms 🖭 – † € 99/189 †† € 179/289 – 13 suites

Southwest : 5.5 km by N 9 on R 4286 – 𝒞 (056) 777 3000 – www.mountjuliet.ie
❀ **Lady Helen** – See restaurant listing

🏠 Abbey House

TRADITIONAL · COSY Attractive whitewashed Victorian house with a neat, lawned garden and a friendly, hospitable owner; set opposite the ruins of Jerpoint Abbey. Traditionally styled lounge with plenty of local info. Simple bedrooms with antique furniture.

6 rooms 🖭 – † € 50/80 †† € 80/110

Jerpoint Abbey – Southwest : 2 km on N 9 – 𝒞 (056) 772 41 66
– www.abbeyhousejerpoint.com – Closed 20-30 December

XxX Lady Helen

❀ **MODERN CUISINE · FORMAL** Classical hotel restaurant consisting of two grand rooms with beautiful stuccowork, overlooking the River Nore. Accomplished cooking uses ingredients from the estate, the county and the nearest coast. Original, modern dishes are well-prepared, attractively presented and feature some stimulating combinations.

➜ Veal sweetbreads with artichoke, truffle, onion and parmesan. Suckling pig with octopus, cabbage and shiitake mushrooms. Tonka & caramel soufflé with banana ice cream and chocolate crémeux.

Menu € 65/99

Mount Juliet Hotel, Southwest : 5.5 km by N 9 on R 4286 – 𝒞 (056) 777 3000 (booking essential) – www.mountjuliet.ie – dinner only – Closed Sunday and Tuesday

TOORMORE AN TUAR MÓR

Cork – ✉ Goleen – Pop. 207 – Regional map n° **22**-A3

▶ Dublin 355 km – Cork 109 km – Killarney 104 km

🏠 Fortview House

FAMILY · PERSONALISED Well-kept guesthouse on a 120 acre dairy farm, run by a very bubbly owner. It has a rustic, country feel courtesy of its stone walls, timbered ceilings, coir carpets and aged pine furniture. Breakfast is an event, with home-baked scones and bread, eggs from their hens and other local products all featuring.

3 rooms 🖭 – † € 50 †† € 100

Gurtyowen – Northeast : 2.5 km on R 591 (Durrus rd) – 𝒞 (028) 35 324
– www.fortviewhousegoleen.com – Closed October-April

TOWER – Cork ➜ See Blarney

TRALEE TRÁ LÍ

Kerry – Pop. 20 814 – Regional map n° **22**-A2

▶ Dublin 297 km – Killarney 32 km – Limerick 103 km

🏨 **Grand**

TOWNHOUSE · CLASSIC Opened in 1928 and located right in the heart of this bustling town. Small first floor lounge and comfy, contemporary bedrooms; those to the rear are quietest. Traditional bar, once the post office, is a popular spot, offering hearty all-day dishes. Global menu and Irish specialities in classical dining room.

49 rooms ⊊ – 🛉 € 60/90 🛉🛉 € 80/200

Denny St – 𝒞 (066) 712 14 99 – www.grandhoteltralee.com – Closed 25 December

🏨 **Brook Manor Lodge**

COUNTRY HOUSE · PERSONALISED Spacious detached house with views to the Slieve Mish Mountains; good for those who like golf, hiking or fishing. Traditionally styled lounge and airy conservatory breakfast room. Immaculately kept bedrooms; those at the back have the view.

8 rooms ⊊ – 🛉 € 75/90 🛉🛉 € 85/135

Fenit Rd, Spa – Northwest : 3.5 km by R 551 on R 558 – 𝒞 (066) 712 04 06 – www.brookmanorlodge.com – Closed November-March

TRAMORE TRÁ MHÓR

Waterford – Pop. 9 722 – Regional map n° **22**-C2

▶ Dublin 177 km – Belfast 345 km – Cork 123 km – Lisburn 333 km

🏨 **Glenorney**

TRADITIONAL · CLASSIC Smart cream house with pretty gardens, set on the hillside, overlooking the bay. A homely lounge leads through to a dark wood furnished breakfast room where they serve pancakes, French toast and homemade preserves. Simply furnished bedrooms are well-kept; the book-filled sun lounge is a good place to relax.

6 rooms ⊊ – 🛉 € 60/80 🛉🛉 € 80/90

Newtown – Southwest : 1.5 km by R 675 – 𝒞 (051) 381 056 – www.glenorney.com – Closed December-February

TRIM BAILE ÁTHA TROIM

Meath – Pop. 1 441 – Regional map n° **21**-D3

▶ Dublin 43 km – Drogheda 42 km – Tullamore 69 km

🏨 **Trim Castle**

FAMILY · FUNCTIONAL Modern family-run hotel opposite the castle, complete with a café, a homeware shop and a delightful roof terrace with a great outlook. Good-sized bedrooms come in contemporary hues – those to the front share the view. Dine in the bar or opt for classic European dishes in the stylish first floor restaurant.

68 rooms ⊊ – 🛉 € 65/155 🛉🛉 € 65/175

Castle St – 𝒞 (046) 948 30 00 – www.trimcastlehotel.com – Closed 25 December

🏨 **Highfield House**

TOWNHOUSE · STYLISH Substantial 18C stone house close to the river and the oldest Norman castle in Europe. Well-appointed lounge and breakfast room, boldly coloured bedrooms and a delightful terraced courtyard. Comprehensive breakfasts; scones on arrival.

10 rooms ⊊ – 🛉 € 55 🛉🛉 € 86

Maudlins Rd. – 𝒞 (046) 943 63 86 – www.highfieldguesthouse.com – Closed 21 December-2 January

TULLAMORE TULACH MHÓR

Offaly – Pop. 11 346 – Regional map n° **22**-C1

▶ Dublin 104 km – Kilkenny 83 km – Limerick 129 km

✗ Blue Apron

CLASSIC CUISINE · BISTRO Friendly, engaging service sets the tone at this intimate restaurant, which is run by an enthusiastic husband and wife team. All-encompassing menus offer generous, flavoursome dishes that are prepared with care and understanding.

Menu € 27 (weekdays) – Carte € 26/55

Harbour St – ℰ (057) 936 0106 – www.theblueapronrestaurant.ie – dinner only and Sunday lunch – Closed 2 weeks February, 2 weeks August, 24-27 December, Monday-Tuesday and Sunday dinner

TWO MILE HOUSE → See Naas

VIRGINIA

Cavan – Pop. 2 282 – Regional map n° **21**-C3

▶ Dublin 89 km – Monaghan 76 km – Belfast 153 km – Craigavon 99 km

✗✗ St Kyrans

CLASSIC CUISINE · DESIGN This rurally set restaurant may look plain from the outside but it's a different story on the inside. The smart linen-laid restaurant offers breathtaking views over Lough Ramor and the menu lists classic dishes with an Irish heart and hints of modernity. Five of the modern bedrooms have water views.

Menu € 25 (weekday dinner) – Carte € 31/49

8 rooms 🖵 – ♦ € 60/80 ♦♦ € 100/120

Dublin Rd – South : 2.25 km. on N 3 – ℰ (049) 854 70 87 – www.stkyrans.com – Closed 5-29 January, 24-27 December, Monday and Tuesday

WATERFORD PORT LÁIRGE

Waterford – Pop. 46 732 – Regional map n° **22**-C2

▶ Dublin 154 km – Cork 117 km – Limerick 124 km

🏨 Waterford Castle H. and Golf Resort

CASTLE · HISTORIC An attractive part-15C castle, set on a charming 320 acre private island in the river. The carved stone and wood-panelled hall displays old tapestries and antiques. Elegant, classical bedrooms have characterful period bathrooms.

19 rooms 🖵 – ♦ € 89/149 ♦♦ € 138/258 – 5 suites

The Island, Ballinakill – East : 4 km by R 683, Ballinakill Rd and private ferry – ℰ (051) 878 203 – www.waterfordcastleresort.com – Closed 24-26 December and weekends only 1 January-12 February

The Munster Room – See restaurant listing

🏨 Fitzwilton

BUSINESS · FUNCTIONAL Close to the Guinness brewery and the main bridge, with a modern glass façade and a chic bar. Bedrooms are spacious, good value and come with everything you might need, including an iron and ironing board; those at the back are the quietest. The restaurant offers international dishes made from Irish produce.

90 rooms 🖵 – ♦ € 65/170 ♦♦ € 78/240 – 1 suite

Town plan: Y-b – Bridge St – ℰ (051) 846 900 – www.fitzwiltonhotel.ie – Closed 23-28 December

🏡 Foxmount Country House

TRADITIONAL · CLASSIC Striking Georgian mansion in a delightful 150 acre farm setting; it's immaculately kept, with classical styling and charming hosts. Bedrooms are named after flowers: Honeysuckle and Bluebell are two of the best. Good communal breakfasts.

4 rooms 🖵 – ♦ € 50 ♦♦ € 100

Passage East Rd – Southeast : 7.25 km by R 683, off Cheekpoint rd – ℰ (051) 874 308 – www.foxmountcountryhouse.com – Closed mid October-mid March

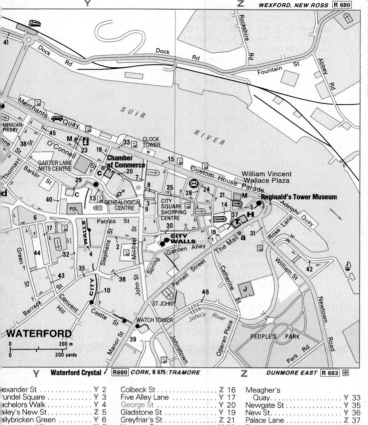

WATERFORD

0   200 m
0   200 yards

XxX The Munster Room

CLASSIC CUISINE · INTIMATE Beautiful oak wood panelled dining room in a castle hotel, boasting an ornate ceiling and a delightful hand-carved fireplace. Dine on boldly flavoured classic dishes to live piano accompaniment. The menu name-checks local producers.

Menu € 35 – bar lunch Monday-Saturday

Waterford Castle Hotel and Golf Resort, The Island, Ballinakill – East : 4 km by R 683, Ballinakill Rd and private ferry
- ℰ (051) 878 203 (bookings essential for non-residents)
- www.waterfordcastleresort.com
- *Closed 24-26 December and restricted opening 3 January-12 February*

XX La Palma on The Mall   ♿ AK ⚄ ⇔

ITALIAN · FAMILY This established, split-level restaurant is set next to the Waterford Crystal factory and has a cosy lounge and boldly papered dining rooms. Classic Italian menus feature superb antipasti, delicious ravioli and tasty homemade gelato.

Menu € 24 (weekdays)/35 – Carte € 27/53

Town plan: Z-a – *20 The Mall* – ℰ *(051) 879 823 (booking essential)* – *www.lapalma.ie* – *dinner only* – *Closed 25-26 December, 1 January, 17 and 25 March and Sunday*

XX La Bohème   ⚄ ⇔

FRENCH CLASSIC · INTIMATE Characterful candlelit restaurant in the vaulted cellar of a Georgian house. The French chefs offer an array of classic Gallic dishes and daily market specials. For something lighter, try a sharing platter in the stone-floored bar.

Menu € 24 (early dinner)/35 – Carte € 33/50

Town plan: Y-c – *2 George's St* – ℰ *(051) 875 645 (booking essential)* – *www.labohemerestaurant.ie* – *dinner only* – *Closed 25-27 December, Sunday except bank holidays and Monday*

X Dennison's 🆕   ♿ AK 1⊙

TRADITIONAL CUISINE · BISTRO This spacious restaurant is located in a former cinema and comes with a big bar and a pleasant contemporary style. Unfussy, traditional dishes and salads are followed by a good value seasonal menu and a modern à la carte at dinner.

Menu € 25 (dinner) – Carte € 25/62

Town plan: Y-d – *The Forum, The Glen* – ℰ *(051) 871 122* – *www.dennisons.ie* – *Closed Monday*

WESTPORT CATHAIR NA MART

Mayo – Pop. 5 543 – Regional map n° **21**-A2

▶ Dublin 262 km – Galway 80 km – Sligo 104 km

🏨 Knockranny House H. & Spa   🍸 ≤ 🛏 🖼 📶 ⚛ 🐾 🛗 💆 ♿ 🍽 🧖 🅿

FAMILY · PERSONALISED Modern hotel in an elevated position overlooking the town, mountains and bay, and furnished in contemporary yet classical style. Large, smart bedrooms offer excellent comforts; some have marble bathrooms or four-poster beds. Superb spa.

97 rooms ⌒ – ♦ € 90/135 ♦♦ € 65/100 – 10 suites

Castlebar Rd, Knockranny – *East : 1.25 km on N 5* – ℰ *(098) 28 600* – *www.knockrannyhousehotel.ie* – *Closed 24-26 December*

La Fougère – See restaurant listing

🏨 Ardmore Country House   ≤ 🛏 🍽 🅿

FAMILY · PERSONALISED Brightly painted hotel looking out over pretty gardens towards Clew Bay. Spacious, very well-kept bedrooms with good quality furnishings; some have sleigh beds or jacuzzi baths. Relax in the cosy lounge or piano bar. Classical set menu features plenty of local seafood. Service is personal yet professional.

13 rooms ⌒ – ♦ € 90/160 ♦♦ € 90/160

The Quay – *West : 2.5 km on R 335* – ℰ *(098) 25 994* – *www.ardmorecountryhouse.com* – *Closed November-mid March*

🏨 Augusta Lodge   🛏 🍽 🅿

TRADITIONAL · COSY Family run guesthouse with a small pitch and putt course on the front lawn and golfing memorabilia covering every surface inside. Simple, brightly coloured bedrooms have a homely feel. The welcoming owner has good local knowledge.

9 rooms ⌒ – ♦ € 45/80 ♦♦ € 60/100

Golf Links Rd – *North : 0.75 km by N 59* – ℰ *(098) 28 900* – *www.augustalodge.ie* – *Closed 23-27 December*

XxX La Fougère

CLASSIC CUISINE · FORMAL Spacious hotel restaurant with a large bar, several different seating areas and huge windows offering views to Croagh Patrick Mountain. The three menus feature fresh, local produce, including langoustines from the bay below. Formal service.

Menu € 52/72

Knockranny House Hotel & Spa, Castlebar Rd, Knockranny – East : 1.25 km on N 5 – ☏ (098) 28 600 (booking advisable) – www.knockrannyhousehotel.ie – dinner only – Closed 24-26 December

X An Port Mór ⇔

CLASSIC CUISINE · COSY Tucked away down a small alleyway and named after the chef's home village. Compact interior with shabby-chic, Mediterranean-style décor. Classically based menu showcases local produce in elaborate dishes; seafood specials on the blackboard.

Menu € 23 (weekday lunch) – Carte € 25/47

Brewery Pl, Bridge St – ☏ (098) 26 730 – www.anportmor.com – dinner only – Closed Monday and 24-26 December

⏏ Sheebeen 🏠 P

TRADITIONAL CUISINE · PUB Pretty thatched pub with lovely bay and Croagh Patrick views. Hearty, unfussy dishes feature shellfish and lobsters from the bay, and lamb and beef from the fields nearby. Sit outside, in the rustic bar or in the first floor dining room.

Carte € 23/41

Rosbeg – West : 3 km on R 335 – ☏ (098) 26 528 – www.croninssheebeen.com – Closed Good Friday, 25 December and lunch weekdays November-mid March

WEXFORD LOCH GARMAN

Wexford – Pop. 19 913 – Regional map n° **22**-D2
▶ Dublin 141 km – Kilkenny 79 km – Waterford 61 km

🏨 Whites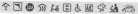

BUSINESS · STYLISH Striking angular hotel built around a paved central courtyard; its spacious lobby decorated with local art. Tranquility spa, coffee shop and library bar. Modern, minimalistic bedrooms; executives are larger with water views. Internationally influenced menu of traditional dishes in the contemporary restaurant.

157 rooms ⊆ – ❙ € 75/150 ❙❙ € 99/249 – 5 suites
Town plan: Y-a – *Abbey St – ☏ (053) 912 23 11 – www.whitesofwexford.ie – Closed 24-27 December*

🏨 Ferrycarrig

HOLIDAY HOTEL · FUNCTIONAL Sitting pretty on the banks of the Slaney estuary and popular with families is this purpose built hotel with a busy leisure centre. The comfortable bedrooms have superb views and superior rooms have balconies. Waterside bar serves an all-day menu. Spacious Reeds offers traditional fare; ask for a window seat.

102 rooms ⊆ – ❙ € 85/105 ❙❙ € 120/160 – 4 suites
Town plan: V-a – *Ferrycarrig – Northwest : 4.25 km on N 11 – ☏ (053) 912 09 99 – www.ferrycarrighotel.ie*

🏠 Rathaspeck Manor ⅏ 🏠 P ✻ P

HISTORIC · PERSONALISED Georgian house with its own 18 hole golf course. Comfortable first floor drawing room. Large, luxurious, individually furnished bedrooms with impressive bathrooms featuring underfloor heating; Father Albert's Room is the most comfortable.

4 rooms ⊆ – ❙ € 110/200 ❙❙ € 110/200
Town plan: X-k – *Rathaspeck – Southwest : 6.5 km by R 730 off Murntown rd – ☏ (053) 914 16 72 – www.rathaspeckmanor.ie – Closed November-February*

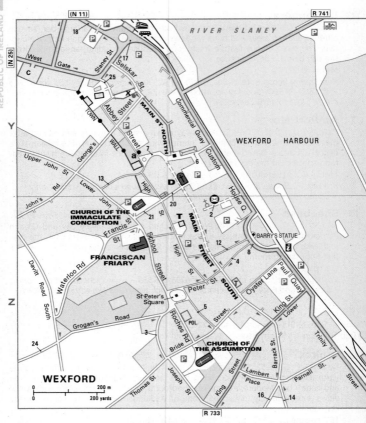

WEXFORD

Killiane Castle

COUNTRY HOUSE · HOMELY A 17C house and 12C castle on a family-owned dairy farm. Individually decorated, antique-furnished bedrooms look out over the surrounding farmland. Breakfast includes pork from their own pigs, home-laid eggs and homemade bread and yoghurt.

8 rooms ☲ – † € 70/80 †† € 100/140

Drinagh – South : 5.5 km by R 730 off N 25 – 𝒞 (053) 915 88 85
– www.killianecastle.com – Closed mid December-mid February

Take note of the classification: you should not expect the same level of service in a ✗ or 🏠 as in a ✗✗✗✗ or 🏠🏠🏠.

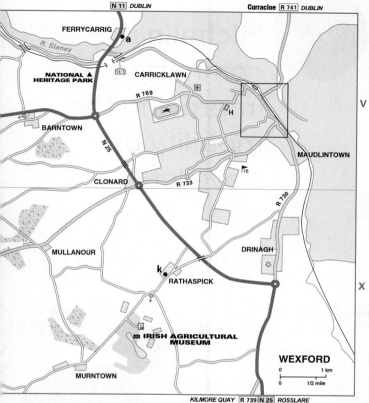

FERRYCARRIG

a

R. Slaney

NATIONAL ▲
HERITAGE PARK

14'1

CARRICKLAWN

R 769

H

V

BARNTOWN

N 25

MAUDLINTOWN

CLONARD   R 733

18

R 730

MULLANOUR

DRINAGH

X

k

RATHASPICK

P IRISH AGRICULTURAL
MUSEUM

WEXFORD

0   1 km
0   1/2 mile

MURNTOWN

KILMORE QUAY R 739 N 25 *ROSSLARE*

✗ Greenacres   🏠 🍴 & AC ⇔

BRITISH TRADITIONAL · BISTRO Set over 3 floors, with a bistro, deli, wine store, bakery and art gallery. Wide-ranging menu of classic dishes, with daily fish specials. Amazing choice of wine from around the world, with some sensational vintages in the private salon.

Menu € 30 (dinner) – Carte € 30/50

Town plan: Y-x – *Selskar* – ℰ *(053) 91 22 975* – *www.greenacres.ie* – *Closed 25-26 December and Good Friday*

YOUGHAL EOCHAILL

Cork – Pop. 6 990 – Regional map n° **22**-C3

▶ Dublin 235 km – Cork 48 km – Waterford 75 km

✗✗ Aherne's   ⇔ ⇔ P

FISH AND SEAFOOD · FRIENDLY Traditional seafood restaurant dating from 1910, keenly run by the 2nd and 3rd generations of the same family. Lunch in one of the bars; dinner in the restaurant. Fish and shellfish from local boats; hot buttered lobster a speciality. Antique-furnished bedrooms, some with balconies; comfy, open-fired lounge.

Menu € 25 (dinner) – Carte € 34/64 – bar lunch

12 rooms ⌂ – ♦ € 75/120 ♦♦ € 100/190

163 North Main St – ℰ *(024) 92 424* – *www.ahernes.com* – *Closed 23-27 December*

Michelin is committed to improving the mobility of travellers

ON EVERY ROAD AND BY EVERY MEANS

Since the company came into being – over a century ago – Michelin has had a single objective: to offer people a better way forward. A technological challenge first, to create increasingly efficient tyres, but also an ongoing commitment to travellers, to help them travel in the best way. This is why Michelin is developing a whole collection of products and services: from maps, atlases, travel guides and auto accessories, to mobile apps, route planners and oneline assistance: Michelin is doing everything it can to make travelling more pleasurable!

→ Michelin Apps

Because the notions of comfort and security are essential, both for you and for us, Michelin has created a package of six free mobile applications. A comprehensive collection to make driving a pleasure!

→ **Michelin MyCar** • To get the best from your tyres; services and information for carefree travel preparation.

→ **Michelin Navigation** • A new approach to navigation: traffic in real time with a new connected guidance feature.

→ **ViaMichelin** • Calculates routes and map data: a must for travelling in the most efficient way.

→ **Michelin Restaurants** • Because driving should be enjoyable: find a wide choice of restaurants, in France and Germany, including the MICHELIN Guide's complete listings.

→ **Michelin Hotels** • To book hotel rooms at the best rates, all over the world!

→ **Michelin Voyage** • 85 countries and 30 000 tourist sites selected by the Michelin Green Guide. Plus a tool for creating your own travel book.

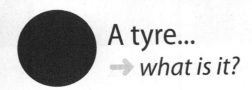

A tyre...
→ what is it?

Round, black, supple yet solid, the tyre is to the wheel what the shoe is to the foot. But what is it made of? First and foremost, rubber, but also various textile and/or metallic materials... and then it's filled with air! It is the skilful assembly of all these components that ensures tyres have the qualities they should: grip to the road, shock absorption, in two words: 'comfort' and 'safety'.

1 TREAD
The tread ensures the tyre performs correctly, by dispersing water, providing grip and increasing longevity.

2 CROWN PLIES
This reinforced double or triple belt combines vertical suppleness with transversal rigidity, enabling the tyre to remain flat to the road.

3 SIDEWALLS
These link all the component parts and provide symmetry. They enable the tyre to absorb shock, thus giving a smooth ride.

4 BEADS
The bead wires ensure that the tyre is fixed securely to the wheel to ensure safety.

5 INNER LINER
The inner liner creates an airtight seal between the wheel rim and the tyre.

Michelin
→ *innovation in movement*

Created and patented by Michelin in 1946, the belted radial-ply tyre revolutionised the world of tyres. But Michelin did not stop there: over the years other new and original solutions came out, confirming Michelin's position as a leader in research and innovation.

→ *the right pressure!*

One of Michelin's priorities is safer mobility. In short, innovating for a better way forward. This is the challenge for researchers, who are working to perfect tyres capable of shorter braking distances and offering the best possible traction to the road. And so, to support motorists, Michelin organises road safety awareness campaigns all over the world: «Fill up with air» initiatives remind everyone that the right tyre pressure is a crucial factor in safety and fuel economy.

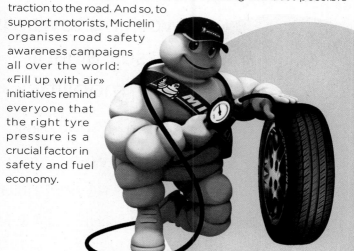

The Michelin strategy:
→ *multi-performance tyres*

Michelin is synonymous with safety, fuel saving and the capacity to cover thousands of miles. A MICHELIN tyre is the embodiment of all these things – thanks to our engineers, who work with the very latest technology.

Their challenge: to equip every tyre – whatever the vehicle (car, truck, tractor, bulldozer, plane, motorbike, bicycle or train!) – with the best possible combination of qualities, for optimal overall performance.

Slowing down wear, reducing energy expenditure (and therefore CO_2 emissions), improving safety through enhanced road handling and braking: there are so many qualities in just one tyre – that's Michelin Total Performance.

MICHELIN
Total Performance

Every day, **Michelin** is working towards sustainable mobility

OVER TIME,
WHILE
RESPECTING
THE PLANET

Sustainable mobility
→ *is clean mobility... and mobility for everyone*

Sustainable mobility means enabling people to get around in a way that is cleaner, safer, more economical and more accessible to everyone, wherever they might live. Every day, Michelin's 113 000 employees worldwide are innovating:

• by creating tyres and services that meet society's new needs,

• by raising young people's awareness of road safety,

• by inventing new transport solutions that consume less energy and emit less CO_2.

→ *Michelin Challenge Bibendum*

Sustainable mobility means allowing the transport of goods and people to continue, while promoting responsible economic, social and societal development. Faced with the increasing scarcity of raw materials and global warming, Michelin is standing up for the environment and public health. Michelin regularly organises 'Michelin Challenge Bibendum', the only event in the world which focuses on sustainable road travel.

MICHELIN CHALLENGE BIBENDUM

INDEX OF TOWNS

1144

TOWN PLAN KEY

Sights

Place of interest

Interesting place of worship

Roads

Motorway
Numbered junctions: complete, limited

Dual carriageway with motorway characteristics

Main traffic artery

A 2   Primary route (GB) and National route (IRL)

One-way street • Unsuitable for traffic or street subject to restrictions

Pedestrian street • Tramway

Piccadilly P P   Shopping street • Car park • Park and Ride

Gateway • Street passing under arch • Tunnel

Low headroom (16'6" max.) on major through routes

Station and railway

Funicular • Cable-car

Lever bridge • Car ferry

London

BRENT WEMBLEY   Borough • Area

Borough boundary

Congestion Zone • Charge applies
Monday-Friday 07.00-18.00

Nearest Underground station to the hotel or restaurant

Various signs

	Tourist Information Centre
	Church/Place of worship • Mosque • Synagogue
	Communications tower or mast • Ruins
	Garden, park, wood • Cemetery
	Stadium • Racecourse • Golf course
	Golf course (with restrictions for visitors) • Skating rink
	Outdoor or indoor swimming pool
	View • Panorama
	Monument • Fountain • Hospital • Covered market
	Pleasure boat harbour • Lighthouse
	Airport • Underground station • Coach station
	Ferry services: passengers and cars
	Main post office
	Public buildings located by letter:
C H J	County Council Offices • Town Hall • Law Courts
M T U	Museum • Theatre • University, College
POL.	Police (in large towns police headquarters)

Great Britain: Based on the Ordnance Survey of Great Britain with the permission of the Controller of
Her Majesty's Stationery's Office © Crown Copyright 100000247
Northern Ireland: Ordnance Survey Ireland Permit No. 8948
Ordnance Survey of Northern Ireland 9015
© Ordnance Survey Ireland/Government of Ireland
This is Crown Copyright and is reproduced with the permission of Land & Property Services under
delegated authority from the Controller of Her Majesty's Stationery Office, © Crown copyright and
database right 2014 PMLPA No 100507.

POPULATION - Source:
ONS / Office for National Statistics (www.statistics.gov.uk) [census 2011]
CSO / Central Statistics Office (www.cso.ie) [census 2011]

Michelin Travel Partner

Société par actions simplifiées au capital de 11 288 880 €
27 Cours de l'Ile Seguin - 92100 Boulogne Billancourt (France)
R.C.S. Nanterre 433 677 721

© **Michelin, Propriétaires-Éditeurs**
Dépôt légal September 2015
Printed in Italy - August 2015
Printed on paper from sustainably managed forests

Typesetting: JOUVE, Saran (France)
Printing - Binding: Lego Print (Lavis)